HAMILTON II
(1789–1804)

HAMILTON II
(1789-1804)

Robert Hendrickson

MASON / CHARTER   NEW YORK 1976

Library of Congress Cataloging in Publication Data

Hendrickson, Robert A 1923–
Hamilton.

Bibliography: p.
Includes index.
CONTENTS: 1. 1757–1789.
1. Hamilton, Alexander, 1757–1804.
E302.6H2H44   973.4'092'4 [B]   75–45436
ISBN 0–88405–139–0   *Ap 15 77*

For
Alex and Rob

CONTENTS

LIST OF ILLUSTRATIONS

ix

Credit public and private is of the greatest consequence . . . the invigorating principle . . . Credit is an *intire thing*. Every part of it has the nicest sympathy with every other part. Wound one limb and the whole Tree shrinks and decays.
—Final Report on the Public Credit, January 16, 1795

In the twilight, in the evening, in the black and dark night:
There met him a woman with the attire of an harlot,
And subtil of heart.
So she caught him, and kissed him,
And with an impudent face said unto him,
Come, let us take our fill of love until the morning:
Let us solace ourselves with loves.
For the goodman is not at home,
He is gone a long journey:
He hath taken a bag of money with him,
And will come home at the day appointed.
With her much fair speech she caused him to yield,
With the flattering of her lips she forced him.
He goeth after her straightaway,
As an ox goeth to the slaughter,
Or as a fool to the correction of the stocks;
Till a dart strike through his liver;
As a bird hasteth to the snare,
And knoweth not that it is for his life.

—Proverbs 7:9–23.

1

SUSPICION
IS EVER EAGLE-EYED

I HAVE EXPERIENCED ALL THE BITTERNESS OF SOUL, ON YOUR
ACCOUNT, WHICH A WARM ATTACHMENT CAN INSPIRE.
—*To William Duer, March 14, 1792*

On November 5, 1789, at about five o'clock in the afternoon, Alexander Hamilton stood in the twilight on the ramparts of the Battery at the southern tip of Manhattan Island and watched the vessel carrying Angelica Church, the sister of his wife, Elizabeth, back to England and her husband, John Barker Church, from the late summer and early fall visit she had made to New York without him.

There on the Battery beside Hamilton stood his eldest son, Philip, age seven, and his friend Baron Friedrich von Steuben, the gruff old war hero who had been the Hamilton family's more or less permanent houseguest ever since the end of the Revolution. Hamilton wrote Angelica three days later, "with aching hearts and anxious eyes we saw your vessel, in full sail, swiftly bearing our loved friend from our embraces. Imagine what we felt. We gazed, we sighed, *we wept;* and casting 'many a lingering longing look behind' returned home to give scope to our sorrows, and mingle without restraint our tears and our regrets. . . ." The line Hamilton quoted from his favorite Latin poet's *Aeneid* was the best way he knew to tell her that *"some* of us are and must continue inconsolable for your absence."

Her New York stay in the separate lodgings he had rented for her had been full of "precious and never to be forgotten scenes." But writing her now, he dared not go further than this one passing glance back on them:

> But let me check, My dear Sister, these effusions of regretful friendship. Why should I alloy the Happiness that courts you in the bosom of your family by images that must wound your sensibility. It shall not be.

Hamilton was a man whose impulse it always was to speak his heart openly, but here he forbore to do so: "However difficult, or little natural it is to me to suppress what the fulness of my heart would utter, the sacrifice shall be made to your ease and satisfaction."

Looking back at the three of them standing there on the Battery from her ship as she sailed out of sight, Angelica felt her heart overflowing with the same sense of inconsolable loss as Hamilton's. She responded to his Vergil in her own unique quicksilver French:

> Me voilà mon très cher bien en mer et le pauvre coeur bien effligé de vous avoir quitté. . . . Remember this also my dearest Brother and let neither politics or ambition drive your Angelica from your affections . . . adieu my dear Brother, may God bless and protect you, prays your ever affectionate Angelica ever ever yours . . . Adieu my dear Hamilton, you said I was as dear to you as a sister keep your word, and let me have the consolation to believe that you will never forget the promise of friendship you have vowed. . . . A thousand embraces to my dear Betsey, she will not have so bad a night as the last, *but poor Angelica* adieu mine plus cher.

Even after her long wintry sea passage, Angelica's ardor for Hamilton lost none of its edge. Two months later she was writing him, "I sometimes think you have now forgot me and that having seen me is like a dream which you can scarcely believe. Adieu I will not write this idea of being lost in the tumult of business does not enliven my spirits—*adieu soyez heureux au-dessus de tout le monde.*"

If autumn in New York is sometimes shadowed by tears, it is more often quickened by bright blue skies, cool sea breezes, and the sight and sound of New Yorkers briskly buckling down to a tumult of business after a summer season of fevers, amours, and longueurs. The fall season of 1789 promised to be the most exciting one in New York's history. It was the first year of operation of the new constitutional union. And New York was the first capital of the Union's government.

Thoughtful men in America and elsewhere who had made a study of the history of human attempts at free self-government through the ages found the record to be a sorry one of one failure after another. Yet with foreknowledge projected from such discouraging backward glances, practical men of affairs were now setting out, self-consciously but matter-of-factly, to make the new union of the 13 former British colonies on the eastern seaboard of North America the first successful and lasting example of its kind that history had ever known. Though they were by and large practical men, not often given to rousing rhetoric, they had emerged from the process of composing their Constitution and securing its adoption by the states with an intense conviction that they were lighting a beacon of hope for oppressed mankind everywhere for all time.[1] Many of them were surprisingly unreticent about saying so, and they took a quiet pride in the enterprise.

The personification of the enterprise at its capital was 32-year-old Alexander Hamilton, a hometown boy who had arrived as a penniless immigrant 16 years earlier and made good. It was he who was perceived by his family, friends, clients, and fellow townsmen alike as the young man who had been the brave and resolute right hand of George Washington, their aging Fabius Cunctator. His generalship of the successful Revolution had won them the freedom to experiment with the new enterprise.[2] But who could forget that it was Hamilton who, with sword upraised, had personally led the night bayonet charge on the last redoubt at Yorktown to win the Revolution's greatest victory? At Annapolis in 1786 it was he who had taken the lead in framing the call for the Constitutional Convention. And at Philadelphia the following year it was he who had championed the most far-reaching reforms in the discredited old Articles of Confederation.

Although the Constitution that had emerged did not give the Union all the strength Hamilton had sought to bring to it and did not provide for the elimination of slavery as his friend Gouverneur Morris had urged with his support, still there was good reason to hope there remained in it strength enough, after all the inevitable compromises, for it to make possible its own self-preservation and permit the doing someday of all those important things that 1787 had left undone.

Had not Hamilton himself, despite his disappointment with the weak aspects of the document, been the leader of the fight for its ratification throughout all the states? Moreover, as the floor leader of New York City's pro-Constitution delegation at the Poughkeepsie ratifying convention, where his supporters had at first seemed hopelessly outnumbered by Governor George Clinton's anti-Constitution majority, had he not almost miraculously turned a 41–18 majority against it into a 31–28 majority for ratification? Most knowledgeable men were aware by now that Hamilton, the Publius who had written most of *The Federalist Papers,* knew and could explain the workings of the complex document better than anyone else. And had not Hamilton, almost single-handedly, as a member of the expiring Continental Congress, facing a majority who wanted to move the Union's capital southward, done more than anyone else to make certain that when the new government got under way his own hometown would be its first capital?

The most serious weakness of the old Articles of Confederation—the one that had proved fatal—was its economic debility—its total dependence on, and powerlessness to enforce tax levies and other economic measures against, the sovereign states. During the summer just past, much of the time of the new House and Senate that convened in separate chambers in Federal Hall, the remodeled and renamed old City Hall building at the corner of Broad and Wall Streets, just a block from Hamilton's town house at 57 Wall, had been taken up with the subject of the vast powers over the economic system of the Union that were to be exercised by the man who would be head of the Department of the Treasury. Knowledgeable New Yorkers knew that Hamilton was the man whom President Washington was most likely to appoint to the post; so the harshest and most hectic debates across the long, hot summer had all really been debates about Hamilton in power.

Even when they were at the presidential residence in Cherry Street and not at home in Mount Vernon, George Washington and his Martha seemed as remote as ever, more the same old revered symbol of, or substitute for, monarchical authority than an active new republican executive presence. Squat, rotund Vice-president John Adams seemed to be only a stiff, choleric, splenetic, humorless Yankee. To the supple, elegant, wry, and witty New Yorkers of the Hamiltons' circle, Adams's discomfiture at the insignificance of his walk-on role was comically highlighted by the sword and scabbard he liked to sport and pose in. With most New Yorkers, Adams was never at home, which did not matter much because he was usually off with Abigail in Quincy anyhow.

Thomas Jefferson remained sequestered out of touch with the common man in his château at Monticello and would not arrive to take up his duties as secretary of state for months to come. Stout old Henry Knox, the secretary of war, and his incredibly stouter wife seemed no more than a typical, tippling old army couple and not to be sought out socially by New Yorkers except when his official position as a department head made their mammoth ubiety unavoidable.

Yet after Hamilton's appointment as secretary of the treasury had become official on September 11, 1789, there was no sense of a power vacuum or lack of energy in the executive branch of the government. The conduct of the Union's military affairs and foreign affairs, like its Congress, its presidency and its judiciary, all needed funds for day-to-day operations; and Hamilton was the man to whom all looked for funding. It is not surprising that with a firm belief in the implied powers in the Constitution and few precedents except his own from *The Federalist Papers* to constrict his sphere, Hamilton as secretary of the treasury could spread his influence into all branches and offices of the new government. Little in his experience of life to date at 32 had taught any sense of limits to his inward perception that no limits existed to the number of possibilities and opportunities that would open up to application of the steady pressure of his ideas, energy, and push.

As secretary of the treasury, Washington's former chief aide immediately became the functional equivalent of prime minister of the new government, partly on the strength of the trust his chief reposed in him, partly by default of rivals, partly by superior knowledge of how the system was supposed to work, and partly by seizing the opportunity. In one important way, his power in the tripartite constitutional system exceeded that of a parliamentary prime minister in that he was not subject to overthrow by the legislative branch.

His commanding presence in any company was more often noted than the fact that his appearance made him look to some even younger than his 32 years. He was only about five feet seven inches in height and quite thin. His eyes were a bluish violet that could turn steely gray in anger. His complexion was exceedingly fair with a rosiness in his cheeks that gave it an almost feminine aspect. But he carried himself with remarkable erectness and dignity; and in the portrait of him painted by Robert Edge Pine about 1786, the noted colorist catches the deep-set eyes, the thick arching brows, the strong and slightly Roman nose, firmly set mouth, long jawbone, and high forehead and reddish brown hair turned back and powdered white, of a mature man who could be any age from 30 to as much as 60 or more. In the repose of his pose for Pine, his face has a rather severe and thoughtful expression, but many a friend remarked on how, when he was engaged in social conversation, his face could quickly take on a warm and genial glow. He was a man whose portrait would be painted often, and many portraits of him would be painted from portraits—John Trumbull did 17. From all of them it appears that Hamilton's was an uncommonly handsome face, one well formed to fit the still surprisingly young man who was already perceived by many of his peers as the greatest political success story of the age.

No American's rise except Washington's, and possibly Benjamin Franklin's, could come close to matching his. In all history and literature, as far as the public was aware, there were only a few comparable successes—Julius Caesar, Shakespeare's Othello, the Joseph of Genesis, Alexander of Macedon, and a handful of Plutarch's avatars—that equaled his to date. What the public did not know or had heard only vague rumors about was how much further down the ladder the rise of the penniless, illegitimate orphan boy who had arrived on the continent at 16 from St. Croix without knowing a soul in New York had begun than any of these others.

Most of the sentient public of 1789 were self-made men themselves or the children of self-made men. Had they known Hamilton's whole story, many would have agreed with justifiable pride in New York's adopted hometown boy that the speed and height of his escalade to the summit of a significant political society were without precedent in the history of the world. As Washington and Adams, who were a generation and more older, served out their terms betimes, it appeared, in 1789 at least, that no one would remain on the national scene as a more logical successor to them in the highest office than an Alexander Hamilton ten or 15 years older.

By comparison with the writings of most other men of remarkable attainments, Hamilton's own writings, as well as statements about him by others who knew him well, contain relatively few examples of self-references to his own accomplishments or references to himself that even enemies could describe as manifesting vanity. The few that have been recorded were made by him only toward the end—as he saw his earlier promise unfulfilled. To his friends, and he had a great many passionately devoted friends—Fisher Ames did not believe "that he left any worthy man his foe who had ever been his friend"—Hamilton was open, frank, and unguarded in his personal style of expression. Some of his closest friends and greatest admirers like Gouverneur Morris would wag their heads and call him too frank and indiscreet. But no statements by Hamilton himself from 1789 or the years immediately following, while his career was soaring near its zenith, have been reported that tell how he inwardly felt about his own singular experience. Except perhaps two passages from the eulogium he had delivered in memory of General Nathanael Greene on July 4, 1789. He had spoken it from the lectern in St. Paul's Chapel to the assembled members of the Society of the Cincinnati, the president's lady (President Washington being indisposed), Vice-president John Adams and his Abigail, and the members of the Senate and the House of Representatives, all in all one of the most distinguished audiences ever assembled in New York to listen to one man's rhetoric. What Hamilton admired most about General Greene's rise were some of the most striking features of his own:

> Nathanael Greene descended from reputable parents, but not placed by birth in that elevated rank, which under a monarchy is the only sure road to those employments, that give activity and scope to abilities, must in all probability have contented himself with the humble lot of a private citizen . . . scarcely conscious of the resources of his own mind, had not the violated rights of his country called him to act a part on a more splendid and ample theater.

Hamilton's works are full of theatrical figures of speech; the Publius who wrote *The Federalist* was an actor who knew that life was played out on a stage. There was no limit to the amplitude that the "resources of his own mind" and his own energy and will could bring to any role he played.

Hamilton's admiration for Greene, who had recommended him to Washington to be his aide, has the unmistakable ring of a projection of a self-perception that is as admiring as it is well earned:

> The vigor of his genius corresponding with the importance of the prize to be contended for overcame the natural moderation of his temper [Hamilton proclaimed].
>
> Though not hurried on by enthusiasm, but animated by an enlightened sense of the value of free government, he cheerfully resolved to stake his fortune, his hopes, his life and his honour upon an enterprise the danger of which he knew the whole magnitude in a cause which was worthy of the toils and of the blood of heroes.

Hamilton's best friends like Robert Troup dehorted him against taking the Treasury post. The summer's fierce congressional debates about the scope of the Treasury Department and the bitter charges and accusations that had beset the efforts of his friends Robert Morris and William Duer to manage the Confederation's fiscal affairs at the old Board of Treasury before him should also have forewarned Hamilton that no Treasury Department head could remain immune from calumny or, what was worse, preserve his own integrity in the office. But in accepting the Treasury, Hamilton cheerfully, indeed eagerly, brushed such warnings aside and resolved, like Greene, to stake his fortune, his hopes, his life and his honor on the cause of free government, a cause worthy of the toils and blood of heroes. Although he may have thought such imagery well suited to a Nathanael Greene commanding a theater in a revolutionary war, he probably would have been the first to laugh out loud at the overblown pretentiousness of anyone's applying it to his own acceptance of a position in civil government, at least at the beginning.[3]

Such modesty would lead him, unlike General Greene, to make the mistake of misjudging the magnitude of the danger of the enterprise for a man with a weakness for openhearted indiscretion among friends.

Out of gratitude for the liberating generalship bepraised by Hamilton in his eulogium, the state of South Carolina at the end of the war had granted Greene, who had made his home in New York, lands and a homestead to induce him to settle there. Greene and his wife, the former Catherine Littlefield, whose family came from Rhode Island, accepted the grant and moved south. Hamilton was sorry to see such close and dear friends leave the city, and he missed them.

Way back in October of 1783,[4] after seeing Catherine Greene and the general on one of their return visits to New York, Hamilton had written to Greene with thoughts of an absent mistress on his mind, more or less as usual: "I have been afraid, and have not yet banished my apprehensions, that your new mistress would detach you from your old." Hamilton added, "I could not very much blame your inconstancy when I consider how much South Carolina has done to attach you to her. Yet now you have revisited the ruddy and health teeming countenance of our Northern lass, you may prefer it to the pale-faced charms of the one you have left behind." Hamilton knew that the "Northern lass" would "have a powerful advocate" in Catherine, "one that will have a powerful influence with you."

Greene having died, leaving Catherine, his widow, in financial distress, and their friend Hamilton having delivered such a moving eulogium to his memory, nothing would seem more natural, after Hamilton had been secretary of the treasury for some months, than for Catherine Greene to turn her "powerful influence" on him. "Surely it is not a crime" to seek a favor, she wrote him on May 30, 1790.

By her disclaimer she showed that she sensed that it probably should have been a crime if it was not. "Surely it is not wrong," she added, "to solicit a favor of one, who is as eminent for the goodness of his heart, as he is celebrated for his abilities."

She wanted a job as a collector of customs for her "beloved and only brother," William Littlefield, who had been a captain in the Second Rhode Island Regiment. In addition, for herself, she would like some especially sensitive inside information that she or her agents could quickly turn to a speculative profit: "Permit me also to ask if there are any funds in France to pay the interest of The National Debt."

She was rather ashamed to be asking such things, she confessed. "Why do I palputate [*sic*] —why blush and condemn myself?" But she asked them anyway. Because of his old affection for her, she was sure there could be no harm in his telling her, she said. "I am justified by my reason," she adds, "and prompted by my affection to commit it. Could you know my feelings I am sure you would pardon me. I will suppose you do and therefore proceed."

If Hamilton was too discreet to give her the inside information she wanted by letter, she would let him tell it to her in person, in confidence: "Will you permit me to beg the favor of an hour's conversation with you some time betwixt this and Wednesday? God bless you my dear friend and believe me most sincerely and affectionately yours."

She had already enlisted the aid of New York lawyer Royal Flint and one Peter W. J. L. Glaubeck, who went by the bogus title of Baron de Glaubeck, as her agents to obtain funds for her from the Treasury. Their three names appear as the last entry on a long list of additional Treasury moneys appropriated on March 1, 1790 "to make good some deficiencies in the former appropriation by Congress—and for other purposes." The three of them obtained the substantial sum of 3,029 livres. In time, this payment would become one basis for public charges and years of congressional investigation that were typical of a great many brought against Hamilton for the rest of his life to the general effect that he had abused his post at the Treasury to enrich himself and old friends and cronies—and ladies not his wife who held high place in his warm affections.

As soon as it was known that he would become secretary of the treasury, all sorts of applications for favors poured in—not just from old affections like Catherine Greene, but from old soldiers, acquaintances, and practically anyone with whom he had ever had contact. The College of New Jersey at Princeton had turned down Hamilton's application for early admission and a speeded-up course of study, but this did not shame President John Witherspoon out of writing Hamilton that he had heard that the collector of customs at Philadelphia was "in such a state of health as to leave little hope of recovery." "In case of a vacancy," when the unfortunate man died, Witherspoon would cheerfully recommend a patriot friend of his, John Bayard, to replace him.

Jonathan Lawrence, Jr., the son of another friend, wrote that "distress, penury and want stare me in the face with all their horrors and no prospect of employ. Hire me."

Hamilton's old wartime comrade in arms Henry Lee wrote from Virginia on November 16, 1789, that "from your situation you must be able to form with some certainty an opinion concerning the domestic debt." He had three questions: (1) "Will it speedily rise," (2) "Will the interest accruing command specie or anything nearly as valuable," and (3) "What will become of the indents already issued?"

These were the three big questions that every speculator, businessman, and financier in the country was asking everyone he knew. If he were a friend, crony, or acquaintance of Hamilton, he was probably asking Hamilton, too. But few dared or thought they knew Hamilton well enough to commit the obvious impropriety of writing him a letter to ask the answers to the riddles, like Catherine Greene and Lee.

Lee said, "These queries are asked for my private information," as if that would make supplying it all right, instead of worse. He admitted that "perhaps they may be improper," as if it would not be obvious that they were. Perhaps rolling his eyes heavenward, Lee piously asserted, "I do not think so, or I would not propound them," but "of this, you will decide, and act accordingly. Nothing can induce me to be instrumental in submitting my friend to an impropriety."

To Lee's pious cant, most reasonably sophisticated recipients' angry reaction would be, "Nothing, indeed, except greed; nothing except the hope of making a speculative profit by the improper use of inside information."

Hamilton's reaction was softer than might have been expected. On December 1, 1789, he replied to Lee, "I am sure you are sincere when you say, you would not subject me to an impropriety. Nor do I know that there would be any in my answering your queries."

Hamilton followed this surprisingly weak answer with a passage that is often cited to illustrate his high personal standards of propriety in the conduct of public office: "You remember the saying with regard to Caesar's wife. I think the spirit of it applicable to every man concerned in the administration of the finances of a country. With respect to the conduct of such men, *suspicion* is ever eagle-eyed. And the most innocent things may be misinterpreted." He added, "Be assured of the affection and friendship of your A. Hamilton."

But Hamilton's striking words about the standards of Caesar's wife do not erase the disturbing ambiguity of the two sentences that precede them. Hamilton was polite, but he could not have been "sure" Lee was sincere when he professed that he would not subject a friend in high place to an impropriety. He should have known that there would be impropriety in answering Lee's queries with anything but silence or possibly the words *no comment*.

Hamilton was, of course, giving Lee a soft answer to avoid embarrassing a friend, comrade-in-arms, and old crony. The disturbing thing is that Hamilton probably really believed what he wrote. Being a friend, *because he was a friend* or at least a crony, Hamilton seemed to believe that he would not make improper speculative use of inside information Hamilton might give him. In Lee's place, Hamilton would not have done so. Therefore, there would be nothing improper in Hamilton's giving it to him. The information was merely conversational. Hamilton's own motives were pure. If this premise of Hamilton's were correct, it was easy enough for him to take the next and fatal step and add, not simply out of politeness, "Nor do I know there would be any [impropriety] in my answering your queries."

All his life Hamilton seemed to put public good ahead of his own private financial welfare. His closest friends like James McHenry and Robert Troup were constantly urging him to pay more attention to his own personal financial security. He ignored them. There is no direct evidence that he made an improper personal profit out of any of the innumerable opportunities he had to do so in the course of all his Treasury Department operations. That he was forced to borrow small sums from friends from time to time; that he never seemed to have funds available beyond what could be reasonably accounted for by government salary, legal fees, and occasional help from Betsy's family; and that his estate was insolvent when he died are the most convincing evidence of his personal financial probity. Tempting opportunities for improper self-enrichment pressed in on him from every side. It was not so much that he governed his personal financial affairs by a rigid set of rules to enforce self-probity; it was more that his overriding concern for the public good simply crowded out thoughts of feathering his own nest. He was content with his comfortable financial subsistence. He showed little or no drive to enrich himself past that level. He made a mistake in projecting this highly unusual, if not quixotic, personal attitude of his on others. Most old cronies did not share his genuine regard for the public good and disregard for personal enrichment.

Hamilton was a supreme realist when it came to appreciating the greed and depravity of mankind in general in the mass and in mobs. But his intense attachments to individual people, old friends and cronies, blinded him to the fact that they, too, often acted from venal, speculative, and peculative motives that seemed to be missing from his own makeup. In this projection of his own nature on his cronies, Hamilton saw a reversed image of many of them. The reality was that in such cronies, as in most of mankind, private enrichment took priority over the public good.

Perhaps the most striking instance of this blind spot of Hamilton was his appointment, a day or two after his own appointment was confirmed on September 11, of William Duer to be his assistant secretary of the treasury. Here was the classic folly, straight out of La Rochefoucauld or Aesop, of appointing the sly fox to guard the hen house.

Duer had served as secretary of the old Board of Treasury. The wretched malfeasances of that board should have served as instant disqualification. Instead, his service on it recommended him to Hamilton on grounds of experience that Hamilton himself lacked. Eight years older than Hamilton, of English origin, he had come to America, like Hamilton, from the West Indies. George and Martha Washington had been guests at Duer's marriage to Catharine Alexander Stirling. She was the daughter of General William Alexander, an American who went by the name of Lord Stirling, claiming to be an earl on the strength or color of a cloudy title to some Nova Scotia land grants. In 1776, Lord Stirling had been brigade commander of Hamilton's New York Provincial Artillery Company, and in 1778, at Valley Forge, he had attested Hamilton's oath of allegiance to America. Duer's wife, called Lady Kitty like her mother, Catharine Livingston Stirling, was a cousin and childhood friend of Hamilton's own wife, Betsy. Duer had introduced John Barker Church to his Angelica.

At the time of his appointment by Hamilton, Duer was probably the most notorious speculator in New York. He had gotten an early start by entering upon large-scale contracts to supply meat to the Revolutionary army which became more famous for being ill-fed than well fought. True, Duer had published three essays in support of the Constitution under the name of Philo-Publius, but Hamilton had not deemed them quite worthy of being incorporated in *The Federalist*, thereby denying Duer a better sort of fame than would fall to his name as Hamilton's assistant secretary. Duer had been a law client of Hamilton; but a still more particular disqualification was that at the time of appointing him, Hamilton held Duer's unpaid promissory demand note for two thousand specie dollars—that is, it was payable immediately to Hamilton in gold.

Knowing of some of the ties that bound Hamilton and the Duers to each other from before the time of Hamilton's arrival in America, Andrew Craigie, a Boston merchant and financier, could write as early as May 23, 1789, a date when Hamilton's own appointment to the Treasury was still only a matter of rumor and speculation, that "D[uer] probably will be secretary to Hamilton." On July 11, with debate raging in Congress, Craigie began to doubt his earlier assurance, confiding to a Dutch banking firm that "altho' Duer will not be in that Department he will no Doubt be well provided for & have great Influence which will be of importance, if secured, to your views."

Craigie made no bones about his own interest in such appointments. In May 1788 he had written, "The public Debt affords the best field in the world for speculation—but it is a field in which strangers may easily be lost. I know no way of making safe speculations but by being associated with people who from their official situation know all the present & can aid future arrangements either for or against the funds."

Craigie probably did not know the men Hamilton appointed to lesser Treasury posts as well as he knew Duer, but, except for Oliver Wolcott, Jr., their backgrounds gave no indication that they would be less congenial cronies than Duer. Nicholas Eveleigh of South Carolina, the comptroller; Samuel Meredith of Pennsylvania, the treasurer; and Oliver Wolcott, Jr., of Connecticut, the auditor —all had been comrades-in-arms in the Revolution, and Eveleigh and Meredith had served in the Continental Congress. Like Duer and Hamilton himself, they were well-known men of the world. Like Hamilton, they were public-spirited amateurs in the art of governmental administration. Some, like Duer, were the kind of men whose experience of the world had taught them to be tolerant of a little nest feathering by men of good will in the private sector as long as their operations did not arouse the public by unseemly or notorious examples of cupidity.

Like Duer, some of the others appeared to men like Craigie to be the kind of "people who from their Official situation know all the present" and "can aid future arrangements either for or against the funds. . . ."

Craigie and Duer, as well as another notorious speculator, Daniel Parker, were American members of a French-American syndicate to purchase and speculate in the American public debt. They had already made some speculative killings of the kind that induce successful gamblers to plunge on until they die broke. For example, on June 24, 1788, Duer had bought public securities with a par or redemption value of $10,000 for $1,851 and sold them within two months for $2,500. The French investors in Duer's and Craigie's syndicate were represented by another old wartime friend of Duer and Hamilton, Jean Pierre Brissot de Warville. He wrote Duer gleefully from Paris to congratulate him on his appointment and to introduce to him Theophile Cazenove of Amsterdam, who "is to settle himself in America, & I believe to make some speculations in your funds. I am sure, knowing your obliging temper you'll give him good informations about his speculations: & I'll be much obliged to you to do it." Duer would oblige.

Two days after Hamilton's own appointment had become official and after sending congratulations to his other appointees, Hamilton sent Assistant Secretary Duer to Philadelphia on his first official mission, to Thomas Willing, president of the Bank of North America, to obtain a loan of $50,000. Duer was given broad authority to settle all details. Indeed, Hamilton gave Duer more authority than seemed absolutely necessary for the particular assignment. To Willing, he added with curious superfluity that "whatever arrangements he may concert with your bank shall be strictly observed on my part." There is no evidence that the side arrangements included Willing's arranging a loan to Duer so that he could pay off in full his $2,000 specie note to Hamilton, which was now due. Many a banker would have welcomed such a golden opportunity to be helpful.

In a less easygoing age, the following concluding remark that Hamilton added to Bank President Willing, going beyond gentlemanly politeness to a Henry Lee, would have earned Hamilton instant self-destruction as a public official: "Permit me to add, sir, that in the conduct of the business of my Department it will always give me pleasure to promote the interest of the institution over which you preside." Such a genial assurance from the new secretary of the treasury would be mighty helpful smoothing Duer's way at the bank with whatever accommodations he might seek. These might even go beyond help in paying off a specie debt to the secretary of the treasury himself. In any event, the possibilities opened up for Duer by his new position as number two man in the Treasury would have brought a smile to the lips of any fox, and he may have been already wiping away figurative feathers as he made his jaunty way back home from Philadelphia to New York.

Nothing could have been more confused and chaotic than the state of American public finance that fall of 1789. Congressmen sought answers to the same questions Henry Lee and Catherine Greene had asked Hamilton, for whatever use they might make of them. Being congressmen, they had the right to demand them publicly. They did so by congressional resolutions of September 21, which were duly recorded by the clerk, John Beckley, and compared for accuracy by William Duer. Mindful that "an adequate provision for the support of the public credit" was "a matter of high importance to the national honor and prosperity," the House "directed" the secretary to "prepare a plan for that purpose, and to report the same to this house at its next meeting." It was due to reconvene on the first Monday in January 1790.

As he took up the almost innumerable administrative duties of his office,

Hamilton also began formulating his monumental first *Report Relative to a Provision for the Support of Public Credit,* to be submitted to the House in little more than three months. He began by collecting a formidable mass of fact and opinion from many sources.

On October 10, 1789, Hamilton wrote William Bingham of Philadelphia that "there is a species of information highly requisite for the government in adjusting the policies of its treaties and laws respecting navigation for obtaining which with proper accuracy and detail no regular plan has ever yet been perused in this country."

Hamilton's assertion that a "regular plan" in the economic sphere was a "highly requisite" matter echoed the words he had used at the Annapolis Convention of 1786 to underline the exigent need for the political constitution that had resulted from the Philadelphia convention. He saw more clearly than any other man in the country that by it a potentially strong political order had been superimposed on an economic order that remained weak and chaotic. But reform of the political order had created the political structure and some of the political machinery that could be made use of to create a strong economic order by wise legislation, energy in its administration, and effective enforcement. To Hamilton, a sound economic order was of even more importance than the political order created by the Constitution because the political order had its foundations in the economic and rested on it.[5]

He enclosed a list of searching questions, requesting Bingham to send him "any thoughts that may occur to you concerning the finances and debts of the United States. It is my earnest wish to obtain all the light I can on these subjects in order that I may be the better able to discharge the trust reposed in me."

Hamilton sent out similar inquiries to collectors of customs like Jacob Wray at Hampton, Johnathan Fitch at New Haven, William Lindsay at Norfolk and Portsmouth, Virginia, John Rice at Boston, Otho H. Williams at Baltimore, Stephen Hussey at Nantucket, Sharp Delany at Philadelphia, and many others. He also sought ideas from William Constable, his rich New York merchant client; John Witherspoon, the president of Princeton; Stephen Higginson of Boston; James McHenry; Richard Harison; Oliver Wolcott, Jr.; and Tench Coxe, a prominent Philadelphia businessman who would soon follow Duer as an assistant secretary of the treasury and give Hamilton almost as much grief.

Hamilton sought political expertise by a similar letter of inquiry to James Madison of Virginia. "May I ask of your friendship," he wrote Madison on October 12, 1789, "to put on paper and send me your thoughts on such subjects as may have occurred to you for an addition to our revenue; and also as to any modifications of the public debt, which could be made consistent with good faith —the interest of the public and of the creditors." He added, "The Question is very much what further taxes will be *least* unpopular."

While waiting for answers, he busied himself tightening up administration in his department. With import duties the chief source of federal revenue, his first duty was to maintain the flow of collections. Regulations should not be too harsh, or they would be mocked by departures that had long been indulged. He informed himself of state and local requirements and urged collectors to suggest all improvements that could be made in federal rules. He issued warnings against traders' tricks he knew from his own experience as Cruger's clerk on St. Croix. He admonished one collector, who reported a failure to pay bonds punctually, that "my instructions on this point must be strictly executed. Should any bonds which are now due remain unpaid you will place them in the hands of the Attorney of the District."[6]

Hamilton was always specific; collectors should not let themselves be fooled.[7] "Should any vessel come within your district from another which has not her name painted upon the fixed work of her stern, which is nailed or screwed to her, it will . . . be advisable to demand from her foreign tonnage and if disputed . . . let it be persisted into a judicial determination." He notified collectors of "my desire that the Notes of [the Banks of North America and of New York], payable either on demand or at no longer period than Fifty-days . . . should be received in payment of duties . . . equivalent to Gold and Silver." Accepting paper money on an equal basis with gold and silver would ease remittances from the states without drawing away their gold and silver specie.

Drafts on collectors to pay the salaries of members of Congress should be received in payment of duties or in exchange for specie. Hamilton sent each collector "the signatures of the president and cashier of the Banks of North America and New York; together with a . . . description of those notes; which will enable you to guard against . . . Counterfeits. . . ." He carefully explained that "the mode in which the Bank-notes are to be transmitted" was that each note was to be divided into two equal parts, from top to bottom, one part containing the name of the president and the sum, the other the name of the cashier and the sum, adding, "Your own name in your own hand-writing is to be written on the back of each half, together with the number and sum of the note." When sending the notes to the treasurer, the collectors were to send "one half of each note by one post, and the other half by the next, accompanied in both cases with a list of the notes." In addition, a collector should also obtain a receipt from the postmaster. If such a transmission would not be safe, nothing would.

Hamilton's directions reduced arbitrary and discretionary authority to the minimum. Should a discount be allowed for prompt payment where a bond was given for securing the duties? No. When American goods had been exported but were brought back for want of a market or other cause, were they liable to the same duties as foreign goods of the same kind? Yes. Congress had failed to consider this contingency, but the law contained no exemption; duties must be collected until Congress saw fit to provide legislative relief. Must vessels pay tonnage at each entry? Yes, on opinion of counsel. Were duties demandable after August 1, 1789, the date the federal law went into effect, but before the customhouses were organized? Yes. Though collectors might still be operating under state law and vessels might be obliged to pay double duties, the federal tax must be demanded under an action for debt. "But in the manner of advancing . . . the claim, I . . . recommend all the moderation which is compatible with the end."

Hamilton authorized collectors "to employ Boats for the Security of the

Revenue against contraband." These were the beginnings of the United States Coast Guard as one of the many long arms of the Treasury Department. In approving two such vessels, and no more, to be based at New London, Hamilton was glad to know that they "would not be disagreeable to your merchants; as I feel a strong conviction that a certain number of cruising vessels will be found equally beneficial to the fair trader and to the revenue."

He focused minute attention on all details of outfitting the Coast Guard vessels. "A complete Vessel capable of keeping this Coast in the Winter season may be fitted for One Thousand Dollars," he wrote. Local construction was desirable, and base cost was not to be exceeded by more than 10 percent. There should be no costly "add-ons"; so "all requisite masts, spars, sails, cables, cordage, anchors, a Boat & c," must be included in the estimate. Contracts should specify Number One sailcloth made by a certain Boston factory in a piece warranted to contain 39 yards, three-quarters of an inch wider than the British, which sold at $11. He wanted to know how much of it would be needed for each vessel so that he could order all at a quantity discount.[8] He enumerated the items in a sailor's rations, not forgetting that "the article of rum may be as sparingly supplied as possible"; he thought half a gill per man per day would be enough.

From his experiences as Continental receiver of taxes for New York, Hamilton knew well that there was no better way to win unpopularity than to enforce collections of taxes, but of Hamilton it can be said with more conviction than of any other public figure of the time, including Washington, that he did not bend a policy he believed to be right to public criticism. In fact, he seemed intentionally to defy it when to do so seemed to him to invigorate the public credit.

Tax evasion and tax avoidance had always been popular and patriotic sports for rebellious British colonials. "To . . . overreach a revenue officer was highly meritorious in this Country. The Hero . . . had the most cordial winks . . . from men of eminence," he noted. Discriminatory state imposts met with similar contempt, "so that we daily see many articles retailed at a less price than the sum of the duty on them . . . it will . . . take a length of time to lead the public mind into a just train of thinking on the subject." Throwing tea into the sea to protest taxation without representation had created easy heroes. Not surprisingly, winning the right to representation had not made the heroes of the exercise much more eager to pay their taxes.

Hamilton knew that "unless an Eagle eyed comptroller" made constant checks, "one half of your customs House officers will turn rascals within a year." He cracked down hard by constant writing, checking, and nagging. Customs Officer William Heth on the James River testified that Hamilton's hectoring was more than he could stand: "The incessant application I was obliged to pay to the duties of my office for the past 2-½ years," he complained, "injured me more, than all the fatigue . . . which I experienced thro' the late war."

John Marshall of Virginia, who would compose his own judicial opinions with the same intense personal application that Hamilton brought to the administration of the Treasury and the writing of his great reports, commented that "to talents equally splendid and useful," Hamilton "united a patient industry, not always the companion of genius, which fitted him, in a peculiar manner, for subduing the difficulties to be encountered by the man . . . placed at the head of the American finances."⁹

Hamilton carried out international economic diplomacy like a secretary of state. He wrote his old comrade-in-arms the Marquis de Lafayette on October 6, 1789, that, as part of the subject of foreign and domestic debt, "the debt due to France will be among the first objects" of Congress's and his own attention. It was necessary to set the stage for a proper congressional response, although he was discreet enough to add, "I am not in a situation to address anything officially to your administration." He was indiscreet enough to go on to say that he planned to offer "a speedy payment of the *arrears of interest* now due, and effectual provision for the punctual payment of future interest as it arises." As quid pro quo, France must suspend its demands for repayment of the principal of the debt for a few years.

Hamilton was seeking to arrange matters behind the scenes so that France would receive full credit for her magnanimity to America, notwithstanding the charges of anti-French bias with which his enemies always assailed him. He scorned to score points with political adversaries for having driven a hard bargain with France. He proposed to Lafayette that if this would "meet the approbation of your government, it would be best on every account that the offer should come unsolicited as a fresh mark of good will."

Replies to Hamilton's letters of inquiry trickled in as the three-month deadline for his first "Report on Public Credit" to Congress approached. The second most important of these was the long thoughtful letter from William Bingham of November 25, which contained much that Hamilton would refine and include in the final version of the report.¹⁰ Bingham, a founder and director of the Bank of North America, a frequent associate in investment ventures of Robert Morris and William Constable, was reputedly the wealthiest man in the United States, his fortune being based on successful privateering operations and wartime speculations in the West Indies and elsewhere. He and his beautiful wife, the former Anne Willing, daughter of the bank president, had often entertained the Hamiltons at their Philadelphia mansion when he and Hamilton had been fellow members of the Continental Congress.

Citing recent British experience at a time of similar financial distress, Bingham reminded Hamilton that "when Mr. Pitt came into administration [as first treasury lord and Chancellor of the Exchequer in 1783] he saw the deranged state of the National affairs and the necessity of restoring public credit." By raising taxes, he had obtained a considerable surplus. He had established a sinking fund, providing a trust under the control of commissioners for the purpose of accumulating funds to be invariably applied to the gradual extinction of the national debt. Bingham noted that "this stroke of finance operated like a charm." The result was that as soon as the resources of Great Britain were discovered to be so far beyond the actual demands for interest as to admit of paying off a portion of the principal of the debt, "public credit revived, and all the train of advantages that result from it, accompanied it." Then "money flowed into the country and every channel of industry was supplied."[11] Hamilton in submitting his report would be assuming the role as well as many of the policies of Pitt.[12] "Taxes, when used for this stimulating purpose, do not impoverish the society by diminishing the common mass of property," Bingham went on. They only "interrupt the circulation to the extent of the sum drawn from the people, combined with the time that elapses, before it returns to the common mass."

Obviously, Bingham went on, to propose taxes is "an arduous and invidious task as it is impossible to select those, that are free from solid & manifest objection, considering the various interests of the different states." But a zeal for the national credit will impel a nation to raise taxes, to create a gradual diminution of the national debt, and hold out hope of future relaxation of taxes to "place the country in a situation to support that rank of power & grandeur, which she is entitled to enjoy."

James Madison of Virginia had stood with Hamilton at Philadelphia for a strong constitution. He had served as Hamilton's associate in writing *The Federalist*. He had been his full partner in the crucial interrelated battles for ratification in Virginia and New York. The pair had stood shoulder to shoulder at the Annapolis Convention and as members of the Confederation Congress back in 1783, where they had faced up to similar intractable questions of public finance. Now Madison was the floor leader of the House of Representatives and chief spokesman for the most populous and influential state. The most important reply to Hamilton's request letters was Madison's, not for the economic ideas it contained, but as a political document, with fatefully negative implications for the future. To Hamilton, Madison's statements themselves contained no surprises, but his letter's evasive and distant tone, so uncharacteristic of his friend's style, came as a shock.

Madison's letter to Hamilton of November 19 called for taxes on home distilleries, an increase in duties on imported liquor, a national land tax (before the states should start to levy a real estate tax) and a stamp tax on federal court proceedings. As for what to do about the public debt, Madison was equivocal, but not specifically opposed to anything in Hamilton's program. It was "a subject on which I ought perhaps to be silent having not enough revolved it to form any precise ideas," he said. Madison approved settling the foreign part of the debt "on the most satisfactory footing," perhaps at a reduced rate of interest. This would mean a settlement less favorable to France than the generous terms Hamilton had proposed privately to Lafayette.

The domestic part of the debt was more controversial, Madison felt. It "is well known to be viewed in different lights by different classes of people. It might be a soothing circumstance to those least favorably disposed, if by some operation the debt could be lessened by purchases made on public account." But there was no question in Madison's mind that it was "very desirable that the provision to be made should be such as will put the debt in a manifest course of extinguishment."

The debt must be kept small, and what there was must be paid off quickly, he felt, for reasons peculiar to the situation of the United States. Even heavier taxes would be "more acceptable than lighter" taxes if they would accomplish this. Why? Because as soon as a definite provision was made for paying off past and future interest, as soon as "the permanent views of the government" are ascertained, a very bad thing would happen. The debt would "slide into the hands of foreigners," Madison feared. "As they have more money than the Americans, and less productive ways of laying it out, they can and will pretty generally buy out the Americans." Madison admitted that he might be mistaking "local for general sentiments" on this, but was sending them to Hamilton anyway because of "unwillingness to disobey your commands."[13]

There was not a word in Madison's letter calling for a discrimination between first and subsequent holders of public debt or opposing federal assumption of state debts, the two most critical issues in Hamilton's program. Madison had spoken out forcefully in favor of nondiscrimination between holders and federal assumption when he was in Congress with Hamilton as far back as 1783. There was nothing in Madison's letter to suggest to Hamilton now that his old collaborator had abandoned his former views and adopted opposite ones except that Madison's protestations seeking excuses for delay and complaining of unprecise ideas, of inaccurate and local views, of obedience to Hamilton's command, and so on, to his recent collaborator on *The Federalist* were so uncharacteristic of Madison as to appear contrived and disingenuous. Nothing in his letter hinted at the precise, knowing, detailed, deadly opposition to Hamilton's program that Madison would lead in Congress less than three months later.

Public suspense, as well as speculation, mounted as the date for submission of Hamilton's report to Congress approached. Joseph Barrell asked Samuel B. Webb for a market tip: "You know I have a considerable Sum in indents, and as you are intimate with Mr. Hamilton, the man to whom we look for the resurrection of the Public Credit, I wish you would find out how his Ideas [are] upon that matter, and whether he purposes to do anything about them in his plan, which no doubt he will lay before the Congress at their next session; and if anything, what. I can then judge whether I had best dispose of them at the present price, or purchase more."

In the face of all the speculators' suspense, Hamilton wrote his friend Thomas FitzSimmons on November 27 that he feared inviting public discussion of his report in advance: "I have several times had an inclination to feeling the public pulse about the debt; but this has given way to the reflection, that bringing on a discussion might be as likely to fix prejudice as to produce good." He was satisfied to trust the people's representatives when the time came for all information to be made public: "It may be safest to trust to the effect of the legislative sanction to good measures. . . ."

Here it is useful to reflect on what is meant by *speculation* and to what extent it differs from *investment* as something that is right or wrong, or good, bad, or indifferent.

Speculation in the public debt of the United States or any other country neither was nor is something new, nor is it wrong in itself. It occurs every day in multiples of millions of dollars. The debts, or promises to pay, issued by the

Continental Congress and the several states during and after the Revolution had depreciated greatly in value. Many of the original holders—some poor, some wealthy—had sold them at discounts. Others, as late as June 1788, when final ratification of the Constitution was still in doubt, had been able to buy up large quantities sometimes at discounts of over 80 percent of face value. From this point, of course, it might either become worthless—or increase in value. Sellers, buyers, and holders naturally desired an intimate view of the minds and intentions of the men in official posts whose actions would affect the ultimate value of their paper. Like the final ratification of the Constitution, the appointment of Hamilton as secretary of the treasury might be expected to raise, not depress, the value of their holdings. Anyone could make such a judgment with or without inside information.

Hamilton and Federal Republicans generally drew much political support from merchants, bankers and businessmen, small tradesmen, landowners like the Schuylers, and mechanics and small farmers as well. In selling and buying public debt certificates at a discount, such people were acting from several motives, most of which were pure enough: to avoid loss, to invest savings, to make a profit if they rose. To show faith in their country or to demonstrate confidence in Hamilton as its chief fiscal officer were of minor concern to most.

All were taking risks of loss, "speculator" and "investor" alike. In writing by people not familiar with the operation of the capital market system, the words *speculator* and *investor* are often used as epithetical shorthand to denote no more than that the person being described is considered, respectively, "bad" (speculator) or "good" (investor). Willingness and ability to take risks of loss in hopes of profit are the essence of the free enterprise capitalist system. The functional distinction between the pejorative word *speculation* and praiseworthy *investment* is a fuzzy one, the latter generally being thought to involve a less rapid turnover of money. Yet no so-called investor objects to a quick profit.

The point is that speculation and speculators are not evil per se. They are useful and important for maintaining liquid markets. Impropriety or illegality arises from either "speculation," or "investment," whichever it is called, based on inside information wrongly given or received by or from officials or others who have a duty to deal fairly with all members of the public and treat them alike. The morals of the free marketplace do not condemn private use of information once it has become publicly available, even if not all potential investors have bestirred themselves to pay attention to it. What is right and what is wrong are easy enough to understand in practice, although easier to sense and exemplify than to define.

Back on October 2, 1789, William Constable had written Robert Morris that it was more or less common knowledge that Duer in his first two months in the Treasury had been "working with John Hopkins at buying up the soldiers' pay. . . . He may not only incur censure but be turned out."

Duer's ouster would destroy his usefulness to Morris and Constable, but Constable knew that what he was doing was wrong.

Noah Webster, the journalist and dictionarian, was able to deduce from "the outdoor talk of Col. Duer, the Vice-Secretary," that the debt would be funded and a national bank established. So Webster, whose journal often tartly scolded public officials, including Hamilton, for peccadilloes, quickly wrote to a friend to tell him what Duer had said and to advise him that "this will be the time for your speculations."

Because Webster was a scholar and a journalist, his ability to sense that what he was doing was wrong lacked the acuteness of that of a businessman like Constable as a result of Webster's inexperience or naïveté or merely greater greed, he being poorer. Such a lack is typical of many moralists, including journalists. It permits them to chastise with special fury on scanty evidence politicians and businessmen whose moral sensibilities may be more acute, if not higher than their own. Hamilton was destined to be an early victim of this high journalistic ethos.

The year and the decade turned. The mind through which so many abstruse, tortuous, complex ideas, figures, and tabulations were flowing into the first of Hamilton's great public reports was lonely and apprehensive when he wrote Angelica Church on January 7, 1790, misdating it 1789, in the jumble of all the numbers on his mind aching with thoughts of her:

> Tomorrow I open the budget and you may imagine that today I am very busy and not a little anxious. I could not however let the Packet sail without giving you a proof, that no degree of occupation can make me forget you.
>
> We hope to hear shortly that you are safe arrived and that everything is to your wish . . . that your sons promise all to be great men, and your daughters to be like yourself.

On January 4, Hamilton had advised the House of Representatives that, pursuant to its resolution of September 21, 1789, he had prepared his plan for support of the public credit, which he was ready to deliver in person. He suggested January 14 for the date. This seemingly innocuous proposal touched off a hot debate. Elbridge Gerry of Massachusetts was on his feet immediately with an amendment to the motion: "That it [the report] should be made in writing."

But Hamilton's political and personal ally Elias Boudinot rose to protest. The secretary should be allowed to make his report in person. "It is a justifiable surmise," he maintained, "that gentlemen will not be able clearly to comprehend so intricate a subject without oral illustration."

During the previous summer's debates on the establishment of Hamilton's department, Congress had decided that officers of the executive departments should not appear in person to present their reports: Congress was fearful of being too much swayed by the eloquence of a secretary like Hamilton. The House overwhelmingly voted down a threatening personal appearance by him.

In avoiding the establishment of one precedent, the House established the opposite one. After Hamilton was thus rebuffed, the principle became established that no cabinet member should appear before Congress personally to explain and defend his proposals (although there would, of course, be much testifying before committees). The interaction between cabinet ministers and Parliament, an important feature of British government, has never become a part of the American. The American cabinet evolved as an adjunct of a powerful presidency not responsive or beholden directly to Congress.

By its rebuff to Hamilton, Congress thus brought about a thing it feared more than its own weakness before Hamiltonian eloquence—an increase in the power of the executive at its own expense. Hamilton thereafter laid his reports before Congress in the form of a series of massive written documents, of which the first, "The Report on Public Credit," as it came to be called, dated January 9, 1790, was submitted without his oral commentary on January 14. It and his subsequent reports are major documents and building blocks of the structure of American government.

"The Report on Public Credit," with proposed implementary legislation, statistical tables, and so on, runs to more than 120 pages in the Hamilton Papers. Parts of the report are tortuous and all but impossible to follow, so "intricate and so complicated it appears to require some time and attention to understand," complained Joseph Jones of Virginia, who added that "at first view I think it well calculated to keep us all in the dark excepting those . . . who thrive on speculation."

Governmental finance "presents to the imagination a deep, dark and dreary chaos," as Fisher Ames had said during the debates creating Hamilton's office, and even Hamilton never claimed he could make lively reading of it. But because so much of Hamilton's, and America's significant history flows out of this report, a reader will be well rewarded for the pain of concentration on its five main points as set forth in the following paragraphs. Three of them would arouse a storm of opposition led by James Madison.

First, the national debt should be "funded," more or less for the reasons and in the manner that William Bingham had recommended, drawing, for example, on the success of William Pitt in Great Britain; that is, a permanent fund of money should be collected and put in trust for paying off the whole national debt.

The debt existed in various different forms, and it was the differences in the various forms that caused most trouble. The foreign debt of $11,700,000 included $1,600,000 of defaulted interest. The $42,000,000 domestic debt included overdue interest of $13,000,000. The great bulk of the domestic debt consisted of 6 percent certificates that had been issued to settle back pay owed to soldiers and on farmers' and contractors' claims for wartime services and supplies. Other debt certificates outstanding represented wartime loans by citizens and Continental currency redeemed after the 40 to 1 devaluation of 1780. Hamilton placed a value of only $2,000,000 on almost $80,000,000 worth of old Continental currency still outstanding, and it was later redeemed at 100 for 1.

Hamilton proposed that the various existing forms of the debt (but not Continental currency)—loan office certificates, army certificates, and all the rest of such government IOUs—should be consolidated into an orderly series of new interest-bearing government securities. The sinking fund would be drawn from "the net product of the post office" and be a sum not exceeding a million dollars, to be applied by the trustees of the sinking fund "to the discharge of the existing public debt, either by purchase" of government obligations in the market, "or by payments on account of the principal, as shall appear to them most advisable . . . ; to continue so vested, until the whole of the debt shall be discharged."

This would serve the triple purpose of reducing the debt, bolstering the market price of the remaining outstanding debt, and increasing public confidence in the system. Hamilton suggested that the trustees be the vice-president (John Adams), the chief justice (John Jay), the secretary of the treasury, and the attorney general (Edmund Randolph). The cardinal point of the whole system was that Hamilton "ardently wishes to see it incorporated, as a fundamental maxim, in the system of public credit of the United States, that the creation of debt should always be accompanied with the means of extinguishment."

Second, he dealt with the claims of the various classes of public creditors. There was no real dispute about the foreign debt, mostly to the governments of France and Holland, or to private bankers in those countries. It "ought to be provided for according to the precise terms of the contracts relating to it," subject only to extensions of payment of principal, which might be wangled by backstage negotiations like those Hamilton had suggested to Lafayette. Precise public compliance with terms would avoid even the suggestion that the United States was attempting to renege on promises to pay when due.

Third was the question of "discrimination." As to the domestic debt or "that which has been contracted at home," Hamilton was putting it mildly when he observed, "It is to be regretted that there is no such unanimity of sentiment" about domestic "discrimination" as there was with respect to the foreign debt. "It involves this question," Hamilton explained, "whether a discrimination ought to be made between original holders of the public securities, and present possessors by purchase." The practical problem was that the original evidences of debt had been given during the Revolution and afterward to soldiers as pay and to merchants for supplies because the struggling Confederation had no hard money with which to pay them. But many of the poorer holders, especially the soldiers, had been compelled to sell them off for cash money, at discounts, in order to continue the business of living.

Speculators with ready capital like Andrew Craigie and William Duer and their agents had been able to buy up such debt certificates from old soldiers at discounts that ranged as low as 12 cents on the dollar. Was it fair now to pay off present speculative holders in full while the poor old soldiers, the deserving first holders, who had sold for what they could get, would receive nothing more? Or should some discrimination be made by somehow making present holders share their profits with the first holders? Hamilton said that those who favored discrimination "are for making a full provision" for paying the original holders at face value, whereas the subsequent holders should receive no more than what they had paid and the interest.

Hamilton's answer was troubled, but firm: "After the most mature reflection on the force of this argument," Hamilton rejected it. The doctrine is "equally unjust and impolitic; as highly injurious, even to the original holders of public securities; as ruinous to public credit." Furthermore, "it is inconsistent with justice because in the first place it is a breach of contract; in violation of the rights of a fair purchaser." As a member of the Committee on Style, which had seen Article VI inserted in the Constitution at the last moment, he knew well that it required that "all Debts contracted and Engagements entered into, before the adoption of this Constitution, shall be valid against the United States under this Constitution as under the Confederation." Failure to pay debts contracted had been the most conspicuous cause of the failure of the old government. He admitted the hard case of the needy sellers, but declared that their complaint, if any, was against the government itself and not against "the persons who relieved their necessities, by giving them the current price of their property." Their hard cases, like most hard cases, would make bad general law.

The practical problem of handling discrimination seemed insoluble. Most certificates had passed through several hands, and each passage had been at a different price. How could any Treasury unravel the tangled skein of many transactions and restore each holder in the series to his original position? Would not such a precedent also in effect establish the rule that government securities were not freely and validly assignable? If so, what would happen to the national credit? What about original holders who had hastened to sell, not because of financial needs, but because of a lack of faith in the new American state? Should they be rewarded for their lack of faith, and those who had purchased from them be penalized for their faith?

"The difficulties," Hamilton averred, "would be found immense, insurmountable . . . absurd . . . inequitable" and would "disgust even the proposers of the measure."

Fourth was the "assumption" of state debts. States, as well as the national government, had issued their own paper to cover wartime obligations. He estimated the total at $25,000,000. It would be wrong, he reasoned, to distinguish between local and national defense. After more "mature reflection," he had come to a "full conviction, that an assumption of the debts of the particular states by the union, and a like provision for them as for those of union, will be a measure of sound policy and substantial justice." The national government would substitute its own obligation to creditors of the states for the states' separate obligations. Such "assumption," like "discrimination," would rouse up a political uproar.

The fifth point dealt with the practical means of consolidating all the old debt into a single national debt, embodied in a new issue of government securities, and raising the money to cover interest service charges for carrying the debts to be assumed. "The debt should," he recommended, "with the consent of the creditors, be remoulded into such a shape as will bring the expenditures of the nation to a level with its income." Creditors would be entitled to prompt payment of current interest, but the government would not be required to redeem the principal of the old domestic debt at any set time. Hamilton outlined a plan by which existing public creditors could exchange their obligations for various forms of new bonds, public lands, or annuities. This adopted some of the ideas Madison's letter had suggested. Hamilton estimated government expenses, interest, and other annual obligations that would have to be covered down to the last penny: $2,839,163.09. This was to be raised by existing duties and also by increasing duties on imports that were luxuries, particularly liquor. "The consumption of ardent spirits particularly, no doubt very much on account of their cheapness," he said, "is carried to an extreme, which is truly to be regretted, as well in regard to the health and morals, as to the economy of the community."

The whole point of the report was in its title, he concluded: public credit. It was a delicate, precious thing, like private credit. It could be maintained only "by good faith," by a punctual performance of contracts. States, like individuals, who observe their engagements are respected and trusted, whereas the reverse is the fate of those who pursue the opposite course.

He made a further point, which can be understood by reasonably apt students, but still is not well understood by the public at large and was not really grasped by Jefferson and Madison.

The true question, according to Hamilton, was not whether the new government should refuse to pay any part of the debt, nor whether it could, by devious methods, pay a part instead of the whole. The real question was how to fund, recast, and deal with the debt for the future in such a fashion that all creditors would gain confidence in the sanctity of government debt and henceforth consider it as a valuable asset, as credit, not debt.

Hamilton declared that "it is a well known fact, that, in countries in which the national debt is properly funded, and an object of established confidence, it answers most of the purposes of money." When public credit is thus created, gold and silver, specie money, is no longer necessary in quantity. As William Bingham had pointed out, gold and silver can then be taken "imperceptibly" out of circulation, and paper substituted. Hamilton agreed with him that "it costs the country a vast sum of productive labor" to produce the necessary quantity of these inert metals. There simply was not enough of them to serve as money. But with public credit once established, transfers of public debt would be equivalent to payments in specie, and cumbersome specie itself could be removed from circulation.[14] After two centuries, the United States Treasury is still urging this very point on a world still crawling with goldbugs mistrustful of paper money issued by governments that fail to follow Hamiltonian policies.

Hamilton's critics, omitting his contextual qualifications that the debt be no larger than the sum to be set aside for payment of interest, funding, and "extinguishment," have always belabored him for allegedly exalting the virtues of a permanent national debt of unlimited amount, without means of repayment, by quoting his words to the effect that "a national debt is a national blessing." What he actually wrote meant the opposite. It was that "the proper funding of the present debt will render it a national blessing." He wished "to see it incorporated as a fundamental maxim in the system of public credit of the United States, that the creation of debt should always be accompanied with the means of extinguishment." This he regarded as the "true secret for rendering public credit immortal."

This first of Hamilton's great public reports, taken together with his major and minor reports that followed it, and his drafts of implementing legislation intended to carry out their recommendations constituted the seven-point legislative program of President George Washington's first administration. The seven points were (1) the restoration of public credit, (2) a sound system of taxation, (3) a national bank, (4) a sound currency, (5) the promotion of commerce, (6) a liberal immigration policy, and (7) the encouragement of manufactures.

In the almost two centuries since, no newly emerging or developing nation's government has ever placed such intense though politically painful emphasis on establishing public credit at its beginnings or succeeded so well in establishing such a large and enduring fund of it.

In a paper entitled "Defence of the Funding System," Hamilton would later write, "The effect of energy and system is to vulgar and feeble minds a kind of magic which they do not comprehend." The program that Hamilton had begun to introduce to Congress, report by great report, as Washington's new administration got under way, was more comprehensive and far-reaching than any new president's administration has ever launched since.

Hamilton's seven points would bring social, economic, and political gains of more depth, breadth, and meaning to "the people" than any amount of prating, preening, and posing as their personal champion would ever do.

To Catherine Greene's single question, Hamilton had now given a public answer, "Yes"; and to Henry Lee's three, "Yes," "Yes," and "Yes." Public debts would be paid, but only if the administration's program passed Congress.

Assistant Secretary of the Treasury William Duer was in large measure responsible for turning what in the long view of history would turn out to be one of Hamilton's greatest public achievements into the beginnings of personal and private disaster for both men. It has to be assumed that Duer had privately, and earlier, been giving the same kinds of answers to his partners in speculation as Hamilton had held back from Catherine Greene and Henry Lee. Details of Hamilton's report were particularly important to guide speculators on such points as whether their stake should be channeled into foreign debt, which appeared safest, or national government debt or state debts, which appeared less so, and when.

To successful speculators, timing is everything; and after Hamilton's "Report on Public Credit" became public, it would be too late to make maximum profits.[15] On December 23, two weeks before it was due, William Constable, the money man, and William Duer, the inside information man, who knew that federal assumption of state debts would be a part of Hamilton's program, signed a contract "to enter into a speculation in the funds generally . . . to purchase on time as many continental securities as can be obtained, the money arising therefrom to be immediately invested in the debts of North and South Carolina, to the extent of sixteen thousand specie dollars." The Carolina debt was widely scattered among many smallholders, and Duer had already had agents in the field there for months, operating under cover of the vague story that they were interested in "purchasing rights to lands." In fact, they were locating holders and buying up their debt claims at discounts. The residue would be used to buy up "indents of interest or such other paper as may be determined on." The Duer-Constable account for such speculations, leveraged and pyramided by further borrowing against what they had bought through Dutch bankers, would turn over rapidly and eventually reach a level of over $170,000.

Here is an example of the way it worked, not much different from speculative schemes in the headlines and courts today. One million dollars of Carolina debt could be purchased at two shillings per pound, or $100,000. Only $20,000 would actually be needed by Duer's field agents to pay for them, because as the $100,000 worth of Carolina certificates were acquired, they could be pledged to secure the balance of an $80,000 loan.

On their side of the water, the Dutch bankers could issue 5 percent notes in small denominations to thousands of Dutch public "investors," secured by the Carolina certificates held at 80 percent of the $1,000,000 par.

After deducting the full cost of the $100,000 collateral, the remaining $700,-000 would be invested by the Duer-Constable syndicate in British bonds at 4 percent. The first year the Duer-Constable group would owe $50,000 interest in Holland, receive $28,000 of interest in England on the British bonds, and sell $22,000 of the British bonds to cover the deficit. In the fourteenth year, the interest payable in Holland would still be $50,000 and the interest received in England only $13,367 because $36,633 of English capital would have to be sold.

But by then the passage of Hamilton's "assumption," "nondiscrimination," and funding programs would have brought the Carolina certificates up to face value, or par, at which amount they could be sold to pay off the Amsterdam "actions" and still leave the Duer-Constable syndicate holding $297,558 in British bonds, all earned out of their original capital investment of only $20,000.

Although Constable's papers do not show that this precise plan was put into effect, a list of his foreign obligations on August 16, 1790, included debts of $840,000 to the Dutch banking house of Peter Stadnitski and Son, $2,156,479.32 to Gerrit Nutches and others, $700,000 to Etienne Lespinasse and others, and a grand total owing abroad of $5,447,042.27.

Thus it is not surprising that only four days after Hamilton's "Report on Public Credit" was placed before Congress, Senator William Maclay fumed to his journal that "an extraordinary rise of certificates has been remarked for some time past. This could not be accounted for, neither in Philadelphia nor elsewhere." But the report from the Treasury now explained it all. Hamilton had recommended indiscriminate funding, and "in the style of a British minister, has sent down his bill. 'Tis said a committee of speculators in certificates could not have formed it more for their advantage."

Thomas Willing, besides being president of the Bank of North America to whom Hamilton had sent Duer on his first mission, was a business partner of Robert Morris. According to Maclay, Willing openly avowed that he had seen Hamilton's report in manuscript before it had been laid before Congress. Morris,

Maclay's fellow senator from Pennsylvania, was also in on the speculations, as was Pennsylvania Representative Thomas FitzSimmons; and Maclay was certain that both had been tipped off by Hamilton or someone working under him in the Treasury.

Although there is no evidence that Hamilton speculated in purchase and sale of the public debt for his own account, he acted as agent for John Barker Church, absent with Angelica in England, in negotiations with Thomas Willing for purchase and sale of public debt. On February 24, 1790, Willing wrote to Hamilton: "I have had this day the honor of your's inclosing your power of substitution on behalf of Mr. Church. At present the sale of stock, & indeed every other Money transaction is nearly at a stand . . . respecting the sale of what remains of Mr. Church's shares, I shall do whatever may be in my power to dispose of them whenever I receive the Certificates & your Orders to make the sale."

Hamilton's father-in-law, Philip Schuyler, too, was active in the market, though not in as great volume as Church. In 1791 the New York loan office registered securities on Schuyler's account totaling $67,509.53.

So persistent were the charges against the whole Schuyler family that long afterward Hamilton's son, James A. Hamilton, found it necessary to state flatly that Hamilton had requested Schuyler to keep Schuyler's son, Van Rensselaer, from speculating in the public securities to avoid suspicious inferences. Van Rensselaer had complained, but complied, and stayed out of the roaring bull market.

When the House voted to delay taking up Hamilton's report, Maclay thought it was deliberate so as to give some members time to buy up securities themselves in remote parts of the Carolinas and elsewhere before news of the report reached the original holders. A man coming up from North Carolina told Maclay that he had "passed two expresses with very large sums of money on their way to North Carolina for purposes of speculating in certificates." Maclay also heard that Congressman Jeremiah Wadsworth of Connecticut had sent two small, fast vessels to the South on a similar errand. "I really fear that members of Congress are deeper in this business than any others," Maclay concluded mournfully. "Nobody doubts but all the commotion originated from the Treasury; the fault is laid on Duer but respondeat superior [*sic*]." He added, with grim fatality, "The business of yesterday will, I think, in all probability, damn the character of Hamilton as a minister forever."

Madison, too, noted that "the avidity for stock" had raised the price from a few shillings in the pound, to eight or ten even before the report was laid before Congress. As late as January 24, he said, "emissaries are still exploring the interior & distant parts of the Union in order to take advantage of the ignorance of holders."

Excluded from the debates in the House, shocked by Madison's opposition to his report on the question of discrimination, Hamilton was seen by Maclay as he walked through the galleries of Federal Hall outside the session, trying to rally wavering congressmen. On February 1, Maclay acidly observed that "Mr. Hamilton is very uneasy, as far as I can learn, about his funding system. He was here early to wait on the Speaker, and I believe spent most of his time in running from place to place among the members."

But with prices of debt obligations already being bid upward above ten cents on the dollar and with angry opposition building up to the report in Congress, the Duer-Constable plan of December to buy certificates cheap and sell them high began to look more like a bubble. Assistant Secretary Duer had it in his power to disallow or deny payment to present debt holders. Such refusal would tend to damp down value to the holder, who might then sell out at the old discount to one of Duer's agents.

It takes one to know one. Thomas FitzSimmons, a speculator himself, lacking the position of ultimate control over the value of certificates that Duer enjoyed as assistant secretary, launched a congressional investigation. Duer, he reported, had "carried his speculations to such extent, as to prevent any Claimant scarcely getting an account passed against the United States."

FitzSimmons told Hamilton that Duer must be dismissed or the committee would be obliged to issue a damning report. There is no evidence that Duer's resignation was volunteered by Duer or demanded by Hamilton until after FitzSimmons and his congressional committee forced Hamilton's hand.

Conspicuous by its absence from Hamilton's letter to his departing assistant William Duer is any thanks for, or even reference to, any useful services he was supposed to have performed for the public during his six months in public office:

> [New York, April 4–7, 1790]
> While I truly regret, my dear friend, that the necessity of your situation compels you to relinquish a station in which public and personal considerations combine to induce me to wish your continuance, I cannot but be sensible of the force of the motives by which you are determined. . . . I confess, too, that *upon reflection* I cannot help thinking you have decided rightly.
> I count with confidence on your future friendship, as you may on mine.
> Adieu—God bless you, and give you the success for which you will always have the warmest wishes of
> Your affectionate, A. Hamilton

Even before Duer's appointment, his own partner William Constable had told Robert Morris that "Duer talks a good deal of going to Europe next fall, at any rate he will not continue in office longer than that period." Constable summed up Duer thus: "making schemes every hour and abandoning them simultaneously . . . I have always known him better at maring [sic] a plot than furthering any project."

It cannot be gainsaid that Hamilton's appointment of Duer and toleration of him in office for more than six months was an inexcusable blunder. Loyalty to a warm friendship of long standing made it a flagrant example of cronyism as well, but no excuse. Washington, for example, would never have let himself be the victim of any such warmhearted mistake.

Hamilton had not yet begun to feel the force of all the blows that would rain upon him as a result of his friendship for Duer, but his loyalty never flagged, and he never reproached him. During the next two years Duer plunged into ever-deepening speculations. In August 1790, one of his Carolina agents quit in disgust at finding the Hillsboro region full of other speculators who "bid upon each other with a spirit of mischief." Duer gambled in bank stock and in the Scioto Land Company, and by March 8, 1792, his outstanding notes and other obligations came to $456,183.37 by his own reckoning, with a thousand of them overdue, at a time when the speculative orgy had collapsed in a sudden, sharp financial panic. On March 12, 1792, Oliver Wolcott, Jr., comptroller of the Treasury, announced that the Treasury Department intended to bring suit against Duer to recover a $200,000 deficiency in his accounts with the United States, unresolved from the period of his stewardship of the old Board of Treasury.

The same day, in desperation, Duer wrote Hamilton that "if a suit should be brought on the part of the public, under my present direst circumstances, my ruin is complete." He swore: "I pledge my honor" that "my public transactions are not blended with my private affairs. Every farthing will be immediately accounted for." He pleaded with Hamilton, "For heaven's sake, use for once your influence to defer this."

Duer's use of the two little words *for once,* a resentful *for once,* wrung out of him spontaneously in a letter beseeching help, is perhaps the best evidence that exists to exonerate Hamilton from complicity in Duer's egregious abuses of his friends' and the public's trust.

Hamilton replied to Duer on March 14 that he was "affected beyond measure" by his letter. But it was "too late to have any effect" upon Wolcott's lawsuit, which he had instructed Wolcott to institute the day before receiving it.

Duer's collapse, brought on in great part by Hamilton's refusal to depart from the standards of Caesar's wife by ordering Wolcott to halt his lawsuit, had financial repercussions throughout the entire country. Surveying the wreckage, Hamilton asked William Seton, cashier of the Bank of New York, in alarm on March 25, 1792, in the course of frantic efforts to allay panic, support the funds by discreet government purchases, and "relieve the distressed," "Does Duer's failure affect the solidity of the government?"

The same day Hamilton had written Seton, March 25, 1792, Madison wrote Edmund Pendleton: "The gambling system which has been pushed to such an excess is beginning to exhibit its explosions. Duer of New York, the prince of the tribe of speculators, has just become a victim to his enterprises, and involves an unknown number to an unknown amount in his fate." Some said his operations extended to "several millions of dollars." He was kept afloat only by "usurious loans from three to six percent per month." According to Madison, "every description and graduation of person, from the church to the stews, are among the dupes of his dexterity and the partners of his distress."

Hamilton's letter of March 14 to his friend had counseled Duer to "act with *fortitude* and *honor.* If you cannot reasonably hope for a favorable extrication do not plunge deeper. Have courage to make a full stop."

He showed delicate consideration for Duer's feelings: "God bless you and take care of your family. I will not now pain you with any wise remarks, though if you recover from the present stroke, I shall take great liberties with you. Assure yourself in good and bad fortune of my sincere friendship and affection."

After all the grief that Duer had cost him during the two years since the submission of his first "Report on Public Credit," such kindnesses did not flow glibly from Hamilton's pen. Only by one graceful sentence did Hamilton for a revealing moment lay bare the suffering that loyalty to his friendship for Duer had cost him: "I have experienced all the bitterness of soul, on your account, which a warm attachment can inspire."

Duer was thrown into debtors' prison. Its thick walls sheltered him from a possible quick death penalty by violence at the hands of mobs of his bilked creditors, who rioted outside.

The seven years that Duer was spared before dying in prison in 1799 gave him time to see unfolding many other reasons for Hamilton's bitterness of soul on his account, besides his warm attachment for his friend.

2

A DEAL BY CANDLELIGHT
AT THOMAS JEFFERSON'S

A STRANGER TO THE GROUND . . . AS YET UNAWARE OF THE OBJECT,
I TOOK NO CONCERN IN [THE PROSPECT OF ASSUMPTION] . . . TO
THIS I WAS MOST INNOCENTLY AND IGNORANTLY MADE TO HOLD
THE CANDLE.

—Thomas Jefferson to his Anas, *1815?*

During his first year in office, Hamilton was often engaged on three and four major political battlefronts at the same time. Events on each tended to overlap, entwine, and interreact simultaneously with all the others. The first public combat zone was the internal administration of his own Treasury Department. There Oliver Wolcott, Jr., was proving to be a strong right arm, whereas William Duer was proving to be something less. Second was the formulation of the administration's legislative program, as exemplified by the "Report on Public Credit," and the political strategy necessary for pushing it through Congress. Third was Hamilton's role in the executive government through the leading part he was playing in creating policy as a member of Washington's cabinet. Fourth was his part in helping plan and carry out foreign policy, particularly foreign economic policy, at a level of detail and consistency that seemed to him to be beyond the characteristic style of Secretary of State Thomas Jefferson.

A fifth concern was not public; it was intensely private. It was not a battlefield; it was more of a haven for skirmishers, but Hamilton probably suffered more anguish in this arena than in the other four put together. Preoccupation with public battles could not distract his mind from Angelica Church for long. By February 4, 1790, she had already received three recent letters from him, including the one of January 7, when he was "busy and not a little anxious" about opening the budget "tomorrow." But even at such a time "no degree of occupation can make me forget you."

As unexpected opposition to his first report arose, his mounting anxiety seemed to wireless to her across the ocean. It caused her to have an anxiety attack of her own as she responded to his:

> London february the 4, 1790
> You are happy my dear friend to find consolation in words and thoughts. I cannot be so easily satisfied. I regret America, I regret the separation from my friends and I lament the loss of your society. I am so unreasonable as to prefer our charming family parties to all the gaieties of London. I cannot now relish the gay world, an irresistible apathy has taken possession of my mind, and banished those innocent sallies of a lively Imagination that once afforded pleasure to myself and friends—but do not let me pain your affectionate heart, all will be well and perhaps I may return to America.

Her dread of having offended her father the summer before by taking separate lodgings at Hamilton's expense had been patched up, but not forgotten:

> My fathers letters have relieved me from the *dread* of having offended him. He speaks of you with so much pride and satisfaction, that if I did not [love] you as he does, I should be a little Jealous of his attachment.

She would make Hamilton's anxieties her own now, ridiculous as she might seem to herself for pretending to be amused by the dreary subject of public finance.

> I shall send by the first ships every well written book that I can procure on the subject of finance. I cannot help being diverted at the avidity I express to whatever relates to this subject. It is a new source of amusement or rather of *interest*.

To prove it, she would send him a copy of Adam Smith's *The Wealth of Nations*.

But with all this said and done, Oh, how her heart still ached for her amiable absent friend.

Adieu my dear Brother, remember me affectionately to Eliza. I have this moment received her letter, and have received three from you. I accept this attention on your part, as *I ought,* and if in return I cannot give you any agreeable information, I can at least give you the History of my Mind, which is at present very much occupied by a very great, and very amiable personage. Adieu my dear *friend.*

On the first of Hamilton's public battlefields, reverses within his own department brought on largely by William Duer, seriously weakened his position on the second, the political struggle to push his legislation for support of public credit through Congress. When the House finally began debate on his report on January 28, the surge of speculation had alienated many of the members Hamilton counted on to support his plan of no discrimination as between original holders and later speculative transferees. One of these waverers, James Jackson of Georgia, opened the long-awaited debate to crowded galleries, rising to address the House. He had formerly agreed with Hamilton's views, he avowed,

but circumstances have occurred, to make me almost a convert to the other. A spirit of havoc, speculation, and ruin, has arisen, and been cherished by people who had an access to the information the report contained.

His angry passion rose:

Three vessels, sir, have sailed within a fortnight from this port, freighted for speculation; they are intended to purchase up the State and other securities in the hands of the uninformed, though honest citizens of North Carolina, South Carolina and Georgia. My soul rises indignant at the avaricious and immoral turpitude which so vile a conduct displays.

Shocked but knowing members of the public in the galleries followed the hard stare that Jackson focused on his fellow representative Jeremiah Wadsworth there in his seat before him. Two of the ships had been Wadsworth's. Jackson's mind was "almost made up in favor of some discrimination," he cried, "by reason of the speculation, which has been carried on." On the subject of the "assumption" of the state debts, he wanted to hear first from the states themselves before he committed himself. Therefore, he proposed a long adjournment.

Both Hamilton's early opponents and later converts to the opposition favored a lengthy adjournment. This would give the still absent North Carolina delegation time to appear with more votes for the opposition. Hamilton's supporters demanded an early vote. Elias Boudinot of New Jersey attempted to defend the speculators. He would be sorry, he said, "if, on this occasion, the House should decide, that speculations in the funds are violations of either the moral or political law." Yet he was compelled to admit "that the spirit of speculation had now risen to an alarming height." The only way to put a stop to it, he counseled, "is to give the public funds a degree of stability as soon as possible."

The opposition moved to adjourn until the beginning of March; Hamilton's supporters mustered enough strength to limit the delay to a week. The House resumed consideration of the report on February 8 as a committee of the whole, with Jackson of Georgia again taking the lead in the debate. All agreed that the foreign debt must be properly provided for and approved funding for it. But Jackson feared the evil effects of a permanent funded debt. He would rather impose heavy direct taxes immediately or use the proceeds of sale of public lands to pay off the principal as fast as possible. This amplified a vague hint that Madison had put forward in his letter of November 19 to Hamilton.

As for the domestic debt, Samuel Livermore of New Hampshire argued that it was "not incurred for efficient money lent, but for depreciated paper, or services done at exorbitant rates," or for goods or provisions charged for at more than their real worth. Why should not present holders be paid at only the current market value, high enough in all conscience, rather than at face value?

Now it was time for Hamilton's supporters. Boudinot of New Jersey and Fisher Ames of Massachusetts rose in turn. They cited the sacredness of contract, appealed to legal principles, and made passing references to "honor, justice and policy." "Shall it be said that this Government," demanded Ames, "evidently established for the purpose of securing property, that in its first act, it divested its citizens of seventy millions of money, which is justly due to the individuals who have contracted with Government!"

Ames's high-pitched argument failed to mention the old Continental bills, which Hamilton's report had not proposed to redeem at face value. Almost everyone still assumed that they were "not worth a Continental."

So Livermore slyly asked whether Ames would be willing to pay off the holders of the old Continentals at face value. They had been "issued with as much confidence, and were received with as firm reliance on the public faith, as any species of securities whatever." Logically, this was unanswerable; for everyone knew, as Livermore pointed out, that there simply would not be money enough to redeem these now all but worthless bills at par. For the moment, at least, the Hamiltonians sat silent, stunned by the force of this argument.

James Madison had not yet declared himself openly. His earlier letter to Hamilton had seemed to approve, or at least not oppose, Hamilton's plans. So far he had given no hint of opposition, but now he sat silent when his help was desperately needed.

The day before Madison was to deliver his principal speech on the issue of discrimination, he received an anonymous letter, signed *Foreigner*, but probably written by William Duer, who had been the secretary of the old Board of Treasury. The letter of *Foreigner* told how in that capacity Duer had once given reassurance to Dutch bankers that there would be no discrimination "under the seal of his office to confirm the facts," thus permitting the Dutch bankers to sell "actions" at or near par to the Dutch investing public. *Foreigner* warned Madison that favoring discrimination now would shatter European faith in American fiscal integrity.

To his colleagues in the House, including the Hamiltonians, Madison's views would carry great weight and authority. He had helped draft the Constitution and explain what it meant by his contributions to *The Federalist.* His learning was considered profound; his logic, severe. On the floor, at least, he was the leader of the powerful bloc from Virginia and was known to have Washington's ear. He was also close to Thomas Jefferson, the tall, broad-browed, brooding omnipresence to whom most of the Virginians looked for counsel, the man who would soon accept the proffered post of secretary of state.

Hamilton had thought to cement Madison's support by including in his report some statements Madison had made during debates in Congress in 1783, when both had been colleagues there. Madison had then opposed discrimination between first holders of government paper, and later holders in due course by transfer. No wonder all eyes in the House focused intently on Madison when he finally rose to speak on February 11.

Fisher Ames described Madison as he addressed the House: "He speaks low, his person is little and ordinary. He speaks decently, as to manner, and no more. His language is very pure, perspicacious, and to the point. Pardon me, if I add, that I think him a little too much of a book politician, and too timid in his politics." Yet Ames had to grant that in a House from which Hamilton, Jefferson, and Adams, among others, were absent on duty in the executive branch, "He is our first man."

Madison spoke in his dry, small voice both to the excited members on the floor and the crowd up in the galleries behind. He admitted that the domestic debt was valid. But to whom was the government indebted? He divided domestic creditors into four classes: (1) original creditors who still held their securities, (2) original creditors who had alienated them, (3) present holders of alienated securities, and (4) intermediate holders who had bought and sold and were no longer in possession. As to the first class, there was no dispute. They must be paid in full. As to the last class, they could be dismissed, for "their pretensions, if they have any, will lead us into a labyrinth, for which it is impossible to find a clue." With these two out of the way, he concentrated on the second and third groups as presenting the main subject for debate. The second group, he felt, had never really been paid. They had been compelled by hard necessity to sell at a fraction of face value. For them, human sympathy reinforced justice. The third group—the present holders by alienation—also had valid claims, it was true. He presented the arguments in their behalf fully and fairly. But it would be paying double to pay both what good faith in the first instance, and legality in the second, demanded. It was equally unfair to reject wholly either group. Therefore, he suggested a compromise and so formally moved as follows: "let it [the compromise] be a liberal one," he said, "in favor of the present holders, let them have the highest price which has prevailed in the market; and let the residue belong to the original sufferers."

But the recent speculators would be deprived of their hoped for profit: the difference between what they had paid when they bought at a discount and par, or face value.[1]

Madison's compromise proposal angered partisans on both sides. The Hamiltonians accused Madison of having suddenly switched his stand after misleading their leader into believing he would back the report. In the Senate, Senator William Maclay was as critical of Madison as he had been of Hamilton. Madison's scheme was even more dangerous than Hamilton's, he thought, for it would require as heavy or heavier taxes to fund it.

What was even worse to a self-anointed champion of "the people" like Maclay was Madison's vote-catching appeal to "the people" by his moving but specious plea in favor of "the little people" who were the original holders. It takes one to know one. Though he was in basic agreement with Madison on the issue, he was angry at him for appropriating his own Populist, vote-getting techniques.

Expecting Madison's motion to be defeated, Senator Maclay besought his colleague in the lower house to accept amendments. He would pass them along to him through the medium of Jefferson's protégé, Chief Clerk of the House John Beckley, because "if he is led," said Maclay of Madison, "it must be without letting him know; in other words, he must not see the string." But Maclay's arguments succeeded no better with Madison than had Hamilton's or Duer's as *Foreigner*. They only rigidified him in pride of his newly adopted opinion. As Maclay acutely observed, "It hurt his *littleness.*" Madison seemed "absorbed in his own ideas. His pride seems of that kind which repels all communication." Fortunately for Hamilton and his report, as Maclay grumbled, "the obstinacy of this man has ruined the opposition."

Arguments largely based on professed sympathy for poor old veterans and scorn for rich speculators raged. Poor old soldiers had allegedly accepted two shillings sixpence for twenty shilling notes from the likes of Duer's agents in the Carolinas. It was now said that they should have held on. And leave their children to starve on a dunghill? Livermore ironically cited scripture for the subject of the sanctity of contract: "Esau sold his birthright for a mess of pottage, and heaven and earth confirmed the sale."

A sometimes impoverished veteran himself, Hamilton was not unmindful of poor old soldiers and their widows, many of whom had undoubtedly sold their certificates to speculators for a pittance. He characteristically whittled down the theoretical magnitude and Populist political exploitation of their plight by reducing it to a dollar figure. He wrote Washington on May 28, 1790, that "the whole of the property in question of this meritorious class of men is less than fifty thousand dollars which, when distributed among those principally to be benefitted . . . does not exceed twenty-five dollars per man. . . . Courts of justice are competent to give relief to them [if] the fact of fraud or imposition or undue advantage can be substantiated." If they were too poor to hire a lawyer to bring their suit, Hamilton suggested that they be given government legal aid by an attorney or agent who would press their rights by a legal class action.

As he wrote Washington, the basic reasons for nondiscrimination against present holders were clear: "If partial inconveniences and hardships occasion legislative interferences in private contracts, the intercessions of business become uncertain, the security of property is lessened, the confidence in government destroyed or weakened."

He continued with all the authority the leading Federalist could command: "The Constitution of the United States interdicts the states individually from passing any law impairing the obligation of contracts . . ." But it did not prohibit the national government from doing so. Therefore, "the *example* of the National government in a matter of this kind may be expected to have far more influence than the precepts of the Constitution."

The test of strength on Madison's motion came on February 22; his plan was defeated by the decisive vote of 13 to 36. Hamilton's supporters now pressed for swift action. In rapid succession they passed Thomas FitzSimmons's original motion to appropriate permanent funds for the payment of interest on, and gradual reduction of, the public foreign debt and also a motion to fund the accrued interest. That first part of Hamilton's plan, the one that called for nondiscrimination, funding, and assumption of national debts, as distinguished from state debts, had passed all tests and won.

But the most intractable issue of all still remained: federal assumption of state debts.

Why should the states oppose instead of favoring a plan that would relieve them of a heavy burden of debt? Seven years earlier during debates in Congress in February 1783, Hamilton had strenuously urged assumption on a basis similar to that which he now urged, and Madison had favored it then too. Hamilton had never swerved; his position now was the same he had taken for years; everyone knew where he stood. But for Madison, these were other times, and though the issue was the same, the politics of the issue were different now. The nub of the question was well outlined in a report by the Grand Committee on the National Debt issued back in April of 1784, written in Thomas Jefferson's handwriting: All states complained of inequitable quotas, of having to carry burdens rightly belonging to other states, because "almost every state thinks itself in advance" on its quotas to the United States. Thomas Jefferson had been intimately involved with the issue of assumption for years and understood it well in all its arcane refinements.

Hamilton argued that if the national government took over the states' war debts, these local centers of separatism would have a continuing interest in the success of the Union that had agreed to pay them off. The states' creditors would support the federal government out of similar gratitude. The obvious need to fund the debts thus assumed would also give the Union its most powerful argument for a uniform and universal system of taxation.

The states viewed the matter from various points of self-interest. The New England states, especially Massachusetts, with the heaviest war debts of all, warmly embraced the theory of assumption. Massachusetts' zeal to tax herself heavily had brought on Shays' Rebellion. On the other hand, states like Georgia, whose war effort had not involved large borrowings, were opposed, fearing that national taxes on their citizens to pay off the heavier debts of other states like Massachusetts would be unfair to them. But Massachusetts felt it deserved more help, having contributed more to the war effort than Georgia. States that had already paid portions of their war debts in varying degrees feared that they would not receive due credit from the national government. Madison again listened in silence as the debate on assumption rumbled on. Much of it was predictably preprogrammed, dictated to each representative by the status of his home state's debt. Among Southerners it was also a matter of bitter comment that local holders of much state debt had already sold out at large discounts to Northern speculators. Assumption would thus mean taxing poor Southerners to pay off rich Northerners.

The case of Jefferson's and Madison's state, Virginia, was more complex than most. In 1783 Virginia's $5,000,000 war debt was larger than her pro rata share of the taxes required to pay all state debts. But since then, by 1790, Virginia had paid $2,000,000 more of her war debt. Unadjusted assumption, as Hamilton had originally proposed, would now call for Virginia to pay more than her share of taxes, in effect paying the debt twice or at least more than once. Jefferson had earlier noted the inequity of assumption unadjusted to take such payments into account. Injustice would be compounded now that speculators were plunging heavily into debt themselves to buy out smallholders of state debts and put them into foreign hands, as part of pyramiding schemes like those of Duer and Constable. Before the debate ended, amendments offered by Madison and others and accepted by Hamilton amended the legislation to minimize this sort of inequity, but Virginia and most of the Southern states remained opposed.

Many Southern champions of states' rights were put in a difficult logical position if they opposed assumption, because by insisting on state sovereignty, they would be forfeiting state solvency. Aedanus Burke of South Carolina, one of the few Southerners on Hamilton's side, frankly confessed that his state would end in bankruptcy if assumption did not pass, "for she was no more able to grapple with her enormous debt, than a boy of twelve years of age is able to grapple with a giant." Ames and Sedgwick of Massachusetts and Sherman and Wadsworth of Connecticut also orated for Hamilton on similar general grounds.

Opponents were more specific. Alexander White of Virginia moved to compel Hamilton to submit a further report to show the exact amounts to be applied to payment of state debts if the bill should pass. Jackson of Georgia now was firmly opposed to assumption "not only in its original form, but in every possible modification it might assume." He paid ironical tribute to Hamilton's abilities when he cried, "I trust we shall not run ourselves enormously in debt, and mortgage ourselves and our children, to give scope to the abilities of any Minister on earth."

House votes were closer all the time. On White's motion calling for a further report from Hamilton, there was a tie, 25 to 25. The Speaker of the House, Frederick A. C. Muhlenberg, broke the tie by voting for White's motion, thus laying a new draft of work on the scope of the minister's abilities. Meanwhile,

Maclay in the Senate, where, unlike the House, the debates were secret, was recording in his journal that Hamilton was causing constituents to put heavy pressure on their congressmen to push assumption through—on clergy, government officials, "the Order of the Cincinnati—and God knows who else!" Maclay heard that a certain representative had been offered a thousand guineas for his vote, but thought this unlikely. He thought the man might have been purchased for "a tenth part of the sum."

With forces so evenly balanced, opponents suddenly moved to discharge the House from consideration of the bill. Hamilton's supporters rose in protest. Carroll of Maryland explained that this was not a final discharge, merely a halt until Hamilton could report back the information called for by White's motion. Hamilton's forces still controlled enough votes to defeat Carroll's motion to discharge the House, 20 to 28. Hamilton rushed in his report the following day. It proposed some additional duties to cover the interest on the state debts when and if assumption should be carried.

There were a few time-outs for debates on other subjects, including one on bills having to do with the subject of slavery, while absent supporters of assumption looked after private affairs. Jonathan Trumbull reported to the absent Jeremiah Wadsworth that "the whole of the past Week has been wasted with the Quakers & the Negroes. The So. Carolina & Georgia members have taken up the matter with as much warmth & zeal as though the very existence of their States depended on the decision . . . in the meantime all discussion on the Secretarys Report is at a stand—& will remain so till you & Clymer & FitzSimmons return."

Attention to their own speculations may have been keeping some of Hamilton's own strongest supporters like the absentees named by Jonathan Trumbull away from the debates in Federal Hall. More votes switched as more reports of speculators buying up more debt reached congressmen's ears.

On March 29, with absent members back, debate resumed. On April 1, Wadsworth confessed, "I almost begin to despair of the assumption of the State debts, and with that I shall despair of the National Government." The brand-new constitutional union was threatening to founder on the same kinds of fiscal shoals that had sunk the old Confederation. Now, suddenly, at the moment when friends of assumption needed every vote they could muster in the House, fiery Aedanus Burke of South Carolina switched from vigorous support to irate opposition. Someone—it could easily have been one of Madison's Virginia men like John Beckley, the clerk of the House, or Alexander White—had called Burke's attention to a passage contained in Hamilton's "Eulogium" for General Nathanael Greene, delivered the previous fourth of July, which seemed to cast a slur on the honor of all South Carolinians. As the example of Hamilton's late friend John Laurens had taught him well, no sense of personal honor was more sensitive than a South Carolinian's, except possibly that of Hamilton himself.

Burke cried out from the floor of the House to the galleries that Hamilton had called South Carolina's "Militia . . . the mere mimicry of soldiers [*sic*] . . . " As a friend described it, on Thursday last, "Mr. Burke Head over Heels brought in the Assertion that it was false, and called to the Gallery . . . that Col. Hamilton was a Liar."

Two exalted senses of honor were suddenly locked onto a collision course.

Burke "was called to order, stopped, and sat down," as Otto H. Williams wrote to Philip Thomas on April 8, but "after some time he rose, and told the speaker he was perfectly cool—*never more so in his life."* He went on: "supposing Colonel Hamilton in the Gallery which was filled with ladies, he faced about and said aloud: 'I throw the lie in Colonel Hamilton's face!' " "He was silenced," Williams concluded, but "What will be the consequences I do not know, Mr. Hamilton's situation is critical."

As another fearful correspondent wrote, "He is a man of spirit."

On the face of it, there seemed no way for Hamilton to preserve his honor except by challenging Aedanus Burke to a duel. But winning the duel would mean losing his vote.

In his "Eulogium" to Greene, Hamilton had indeed said approximately what Burke claimed he had said: that the Carolinians, before Greene had taken over leadership and restored their courage, were but "small fugitive bodies of volunteer militia, the mimicry of soldiership!" Taxing Southern old soldiers to pay off Northern speculators at face value was bad enough. Nothing could be calculated to inflame North-South antagonisms further than the suggestion that a Northern general was required to make South Carolinian soldiers shape up. Beckley or whichever of Madison's other supporters had dredged Hamilton's slur out of the boneyard of forgotten eulogia to inflame Aedanus Burke, could not have brought to Madison and Southern opposition to assumption generally more inspired last-minute reinforcement. Making a former supporter of Hamilton like Burke switch was really worth two votes, not one.

Maclay called dueling a custom of aristocratic decadence. Now, he wrote, "many people concerned in the business may really make the fools fight." Hamilton and Burke each named three friends to review the correspondence, and these included Elbridge Gerry, Rufus King, and James Jackson. Their solution was simple; there was no difference at all between the two gentlemen; each had misunderstood the other. Hamilton should write again to Burke, explicitly disavowing any reflections on the honor of South Carolina, and Burke should write an apology to Hamilton for calling him a liar from the floor of the House. Even when somebody called him a liar in the most public possible place, Hamilton well knew how to finesse a duel with honor intact when he had more important challenges to meet. On April 12 assumption finally came to a vote in the House and lost by 29 to 31. Hamilton was short of a tie by Burke's switched vote. Killing him in a duel, he would still have lost, but only by one.

It was a stunning blow. Theodore Sedgwick of Massachusetts rose to deliver a post mortem. Massachusetts, he warned, would not submit tamely! "We have demanded justice; we have implored the compassion of the Representatives of the People of America, to relieve us from the pressure of intolerable burthens; burthens incurred in support of your freedom and independence. Our demands and entreaties have both been ineffectual."

The chairman called Sedgwick out of order. According to Senator Maclay, who had walked over from the Senate chamber to watch the momentous vote in the House, "Some confusion ensued; Sedgwick took his hat and went out. When he returned, his visage, to me, bore the visible marks of weeping." Maclay here is etching unforgettably in acid sketches men he believes have lost much more than a vote on a bill—they are speculators who have bought up the debt at discounts and now are hit hard in the purse: "Fitz Simons reddened like scarlet; his eyes were brimful. Clymer's color, always pale, now verged to a deadly white; his lips quivered, and his nether jaw shook with convulsive motions. . . . Ames's aspect was truly Hippocratic—a total change of face and features; he sat torpid, as if his faculties had been benumbed. Gerry delivered himself of a declaration that the delegates of Massachusetts would proceed no further, but send to their State for instructions. Wadsworth hid his grief under the rim of a round hat. Boudinot's wrinkles rose in ridges and the angles of his mouth were depressed and assumed a curve resembling a horse's shoe."

Maclay goes on to depict the drama as the tableau of despair comes back to life: "Thomas Fitz Simons was one of the first to recover recollection, and he endeavored to rally the discomfited and disheartened heroes. He hoped the good sense of the House would still predominate and lead them to reconsider the vote which had been now taken; and he doubted not but what it would yet be adopted under proper modifications. The Secretary's group pricked up their ears." In the case of some at least—like his colleague Robert Morris in the Senate and Wadsworth and FitzSimmons in the House—the prospect of further successful "Speculation wiped the tear from either eye."

Maclay's journal gives a gleeful glimpse of good prospects for defeating assumption in the Senate as well. On April 8, he wrote:

> I never observed so drooping an aspect, so turbid and forlorn an appearance as overspread the partisans of the Secretary in our House this forenoon . . . Ellsworth and Izard in particular walked almost all the morning back and forward. Strong and Patterson seemed moved, but not so much agitated, King looked like a boy that had been whipped, and General Schuyler's hair stood on end as if the Indians had fired at him.

For experienced speculators who like to stick as closely as possible to riskless investments being long or short in a market that could turn on an insult extracted by a touchy South Carolinian from a forgotten eulogium unsurprisingly begot a certain mournfulness.

Madison wrote to James Monroe on April 17 that the "eastern members intimate danger to the union from a refusal to assume." A threat of secession? But, he added, with surprisingly little concern for preservation of the union, "we shall risk their prophetic menaces."

By April 14, two days after the debacle in the House, Hamilton had rallied his supporters. One after another, they rose to make motions designed to reintroduce the defeated portions of the bill in the guise of amendments. By April 22, Madison, in a long speech, had noted "the uncommon perseverance with which the advocates for an assumption adhere to their object." Now for the first time he introduced the question of its constitutionality. On April 26—to give Hamilton time for working out other means to reverse their defeat—FitzSimmons suddenly moved to discharge the House from further consideration of the assumption measure. Caught by surprise, the opposition thought this signaled Hamilton's surrender. They agreed to the motion and fell into his trap. Summer wore on, and the Federalists kept pushing their efforts to bring assumption back to life by way of amendments that restored it transplant by transplant. Somehow the subject gradually became inextricably tangled up with the logically unrelated question of where to put the permanent national capital.

Perhaps, in the end, assumption and funding could have been pushed through by the process of further clarification and amendment without any deal on the location of the national capital, or perhaps the capital would have ended up on the Potomac in any event, but the famous bargain and its aftermath make it impossible, as well as unnecessary, to answer either question by itself. In the expiring Confederation Congress of 1788, Hamilton had done more than any other man to keep New York from losing the capital for the time being. He was well rehearsed in all the arguments for the placement of the capital, which were simple enough, as simple as a glance at a map. Southerners demanded, nay, insisted, that the capital rightfully belonged nearer the South. New Englanders demanded that it be placed at least equidistant between the two sections of the country. Pennsylvanians pointed as usual to Philadelphia.

An important law applicable to human affairs is that nothing endures like the provisional. But a realist like Hamilton knew that even such a powerful law of nature could not keep the national capital in New York forever, on a temporary basis, convenient for him as it would be. But on the competing claims of particular cities elsewhere, no agreement could be reached, and New York thus remained the capital provisionally.

Most of the votes against assumption came from the southward. Virginians wanted the capital for their state more than Hamilton did for his. But his efforts of 1788 had given him a brightly colored poker chip to push before Southerners' eyes to win the larger issue he was pushing for the nation. He would lose New York the capital, but exact a price.

The Senate remained closely divided. But in it there was no stubborn, prideful presence of a Madison to hold out against him. Opinion there offered Hamilton's invisible hand better prospects for a favorable vote. On May 31 the House voted to hold the next session of Congress in Philadelphia. Ames suspected that Madison had made a secret bargain with the Pennsylvanians to gain votes from them against assumption as a quid pro quo for letting the capital go to Philadelphia at least temporarily, pending its later displacement southward to the Potomac.

But on June 10 backers of assumption in the House won over three Marylanders to join a 31 to 28 vote in favor of Congress's going to Baltimore instead of to Philadelphia. This might mean that Baltimore would become the permanent, as well as the temporary, capital, leaving Philadelphia with no tenure as capital at all. "A very surprising result," as Madison remarked in a letter to his father. The following Monday, William Maclay, a leader of the opposition bloc in the Senate, paid a call on Hamilton's new assistant secretary of the treasury, the well-known Pennsylvanian, Philadelphia's Cincinnatian and merchant, Tench Coxe, who had replaced William Duer in that sensitive office. Coxe proposed that Pennsylvania might have the permanent capital "on the Susquehanna," that is, a place west of Philadelphia, near Harrisburg perhaps, which was supposed to be near the center of population of the country, if Pennsylvanians would vote for assumption.

That night Maclay wrote in his journal, "I constrained my indignation at this proposal with much difficulty" because "Hamilton, the principal in this business, was not sincere." Later that same mid-June Monday morning, Maclay learned that Tench Coxe and William Jackson, President Washington's personal secretary, had made the same proposal to Pennsylvania Congressmen Clymer and FitzSimmons and Senator Robert Morris only a few hours after Hamilton's assumptionists had won the surprising vote in the House to make Baltimore the permanent capital.

Robert Morris told Maclay that he did not trust Coxe and Jackson. But he wrote a note to Hamilton saying "that I would be walking early in the morning on the Battery, and if Colonel Hamilton had anything to propose to him [Morris] he might meet him there, as if by accident." Morris duly went there next morning "and found him *on the sod before me.*" As they strolled by the ramparts and gun ports of the old fort that Hamilton knew so well, he told Morris that "he wanted one vote in the Senate and five in the House" for assumption. He "would agree to place the permanent residence of Congress at Germantown or the Falls of Delaware," both quite near Philadelphia, if "Morris would procure him these votes." As Hamilton had shrewdly foreseen, Morris and the Pennsylvanians would continue to hold out for placing the temporary capital at Philadelphia, not off in the woods at a distance to the westward.

Morris and FitzSimmons worked over Senator Read of Delaware, and he produced the one additional vote in the Senate that Hamilton needed. Next day Hamilton sent Morris a note that Morris took to mean that Hamilton now had the votes he needed to keep Congress in New York and carry assumption as well, although an opposite meaning could also be read into the secretary's ambiguous note. Hamilton privately realized that though he now could be sure of the Senate, the vote in the House would be so close that he would somehow have to win some votes from Virginia and Maryland, as well as from Pennsylvania. Winning Virginia meant winning the acquiescence of Madison, its leader, from his recent switch to implacable opposition. Hamilton knew that the place he had once held as mentor to Madison, as when Madison had supported him in Congress and dutifully expanded the outlines he had suggested for the numbers of *The Federalist* assigned to him, had now been taken over by his fellow Virginian Thomas Jefferson.

Although Jefferson had finally accepted his appointment as secretary of state on February 14, Hamilton had seen little of him at cabinet meetings since then. Jefferson had been attending to the marriage of his daughter Martha to Thomas Mann Randolph in February, and then he was detained in Virginia during the first three weeks of March. Then he had been disabled by one of his migraine headaches for all of May, and this lasted on into early June. He appeared to have an open, but not vacant mind on the much vexed subject of assumption. He seemed to be full of vague general feelings of good will. Jefferson had even written helpfully to George Mason, one of Madison's Virginia die-hards in opposition to assumption on June 13 to soften him up: "The question of assumption will be brought on again . . . perhaps its opponents would be wiser to be less confident of their success, and to compromise by agreeing to assume the state debts." The plan would have to be fair to states that, like Virginia, had made some repayments. Jefferson was well aware of all the complexities involved in such adjustments. But "in general," Jefferson generalized, "I think it necessary to give as well as take in a government like ours."

According to Jefferson, he met Hamilton completely by chance one mid-June day on the street in front of the McComb house, where George Washington now lived, on lower Broadway near the Battery. It was only a day or two after Hamilton had walked and talked "on the sod" there with Robert Morris to secure another Senate vote for assumption.

As Jefferson described the meeting three years later, the usually immaculate, spruce, and elegant secretary of the treasury must have been wearing one of his Publius' poverty masks, if Jefferson's account is to be believed. On the occasion of their meeting outside the door of the president's house, according to Jefferson, Hamilton's look was "sombre, haggard & dejected beyond description, even his dress uncouth & neglected, he asked to speak with me, we stood in the street near the door, he opened the subject of the assumption of the state debts, the necessity of it in the general fiscal arrangement & its indispensable necessity towards a preservation of the union." If Hamilton did not have enough influence to put through assumption, he said, "he . . . was determined to resign." However, before he gave up, he would remind Jefferson that "the Administration & its success was a common concern, and . . . we should make common cause in supporting one another." Jefferson agreed: "I thought the first step towards some conciliation of views would be to bring Mr. Madison & Colonel Hamilton to a friendly discussion of the subject. I immediately wrote to each to . . . dine with me the next day. . . ."

The next evening at Jefferson's newly remodeled establishment on Maiden Lane, the three statesmen sat down by candlelight to a dinner cooked to a gourmet's taste, perhaps by the host's imported French maître d'hôtel or by Sally Hemings's brother, Jim Hemings. He had been well trained to cook *à la française* at Jefferson's establishment in Paris. The newly imported French wines and brandies and liqueurs passed round by soft-footed slaves were undoubtedly of the very best vintages. Their master had recently returned with a whole shipload from France, and back at Monticello he was becoming an earnest dabbler in the art of viticulture.

As the host later described the evening, he had apparently known of the breach between the two former friends who were his guests. He gave them no opportunity to close it by preliminary amenities or social small talk. With no civilities he plunged them into the subject.

As the host described the conversation a year later,

> They came, I opened the subject to them, acknowledged that my situation had not permitted me to understand it sufficiently, but encouraged them to consider the thing together. They did so, it ended in Mr. Madison's acquiescence in a proposition that the question should be again brought before the House . . . that tho' he would not vote for it, nor entirely withdraw his opposition, yet he should . . . leave it to its fate. It was observed, I forget by which of them, that as the pill would be a bitter one to the Southern states, something should be done to soothe them, that the removal of the seat of government to the Potomac was a just measure.[2]

Rerembering that same evening a quarter century later, Jefferson would put into his own mouth an uncharacteristic, more Hamiltonian argument than he had remembered making 24 years closer to the event: he had arranged the deal to help preserve the Union. Other interesting new facts were also embroidered into his rerememberance.

He was not attempting to pass on the propriety of assumption in and of itself, Jefferson claimed. He had exhorted Madison, as Hamilton had, that for "preservation of the union . . . the vote of rejection should be rescinded, to effect which, some members should change their votes." It was necessary to give the Southern members "an anodyne," Jefferson said, a soothing pill to calm "the ferment" excited by assumption.

Jefferson thought that "Giving [the seat of government] to Philadelphia for ten years, and to Georgetown permanently afterwards . . . might, as an anodyne, calm . . . the ferment which might be excited by the other measure alone."

This "anodyne" turned out to be much the same pill that Hamilton had previously offered to Pennsylvania, except that now the capital was to be placed permanently in Virginia at Georgetown. Jefferson did not say so, but it is logical to believe that Hamilton at the dinner proposed the ten-year "pill" for Pennsylvania. Her votes were essential now to carry the question. In any event, it was finally agreed that the capital would be placed for ten years in Philadelphia and, after that, transferred permanently to Georgetown. "So," continued Jefferson, "two of the Potomac members [Alexander] White and [Richard Bland] Lee (but White with a revulsion of stomach almost convulsive) agreed to change their votes [on assumption] & Hamilton undertook to carry the other point."

Knowing well Madison's stubborn pride and the "littleness" that Maclay had noted in him, Hamilton no doubt was more than content to let his newfound friend from Virginia carry the burden of exhortation for his program to Madison across the breach in their former friendship, which Madison's switch of allegiance had caused.[3]

For Hamilton, the subdued and elegant atmosphere of Jefferson's New York town house, his well-trained slaves, the talk of these two schoolmasterish intellectuals, one a tall widower, the other a small bachelor, must have provided an evening out in town of striking contrast to the typical hectic evenings at his own cramped household. Fifty-seven Wall Street was full of the clamors of three boys and two girls under eight, Betsy's struggles with their cantankerous hired girl Gussie, Baron von Steuben's gruff guffaws, and whatever miscellaneous Treasury business might have happened to overflow into his household from the office he kept next door.

As he listened in the quiet candlelight, Hamilton may have recalled John Randolph of Roanoke or another Virginia wit's having said of Madison that he was always fated to be some great man's mistress. In any event, if Madison was being led by his new mentor in the dim candlelight, he would never see the puppet string or the one who, in fact, was tweaking it.

Hamilton's natural eloquence must have found it difficult, as Jefferson spoke softly at the dinner, to suppress the desire to unleash now on Madison all the arguments his own exclusion from speaking on the floor of Congress which he had silently rehearsed for so long. But if Jefferson flagged, Hamilton may have remembered from Madison's letter of November 19 to him Madison's fear that American public debt might slide into foreign hands. It was a string for Hamilton to tweak a little. Yes, Duer and Constable and their ilk might buy up debts from smallholders in the Carolinas at large discounts and pledge these to Dutch bankers abroad at near face value. Unfortunately, on the security of this American state debt, pledged abroad, the Dutch bankers would issue debt certificates to smallholders there, *based on the face value of the Carolina state debts.*

Because all agreed that foreign-held national debt would be honored according to its terms and because that assurance itself would give value to such debt abroad, to say now that state debt would not be honored at face value in the same way would create a hopelessly misleading situation abroad. To tell the Dutch smallholders who had bought for face value American state securities that they were now to be paid off only at a much lower market value would have a devastating effect on American public credit abroad. In so voting, Congress would make a mockery of assurances already given and further impair American public credit abroad.

It would not be surprising if on that particular June evening poor Madison hardly got a word in edgewise.[4]

But it was Jefferson who pulled the laboring oar for Hamilton where it drew most water. After working over both George Mason and James Madison, he next went to work on Senator James Monroe, another hostile Virginian. He wrote Monroe June 20, a few days after his dinner by candlelight for Madison and Hamilton, that "unless they can be reconciled by some . . . compromise . . . our credit will burst and vanish, and the states separate to take care everyone of itself." On July 11 Jefferson wrote to Monroe again: "This measure will secure to us the credit we now hold at Amsterdam . . . Our business is to have great credit and use it little. Whatever enables us to go to war secures our peace

. . . it is essential to let both Spain and England see that we are in a condition for war . . . our object is to feed and theirs to fight."[5]

Hamilton himself could not have put the case for assumption more forcefully or belligerently than the new secretary of state.

There was no way Monroe, a lifelong bender to the moods of his mentor, Jefferson, could mistake his master's carefully formulated opinion for uninformed naïveté. Jefferson insisted to Monroe that "I see the necessity of yielding for this time to the cries of the creditors in certain parts of the union for the sake of union, and to save us from the greatest of all calamities, the total extinction of our credit in Europe." Jefferson had caught and passed on to Monroe the drift of Hamilton's clinching argument to Madison.

On July 1 the Senate voted 14 to 12 to open the next session of Congress in Philadelphia, to remain there for ten years, and then move the permanent capital to the Potomac, somewhere near Georgetown. The House adopted the same proposal July 9 by the close vote of 32 to 29, with Pennsylvanians, Virginians, and North Carolinians in the majority, and the members north of Pennsylvania and some South Carolinians in the minority. At this point, the Southerners had won. Assumption was still dead, and they had an agreement to bring the capital to Philadelphia and then the Potomac after ten years. But the smug complacency of the opposition, thinking they had won, was their undoing.

All through July more votes on the two issues in the House and Senate interlocked and interreacted with Byzantine complexity. Suddenly, surprisingly, assumption passed the Senate on July 21 by the same 14-to-12 vote—as an amendment to a House passed bill that had scuttled it.

In the House, Gerry of Massachusetts urged that accommodation was imperative. He would "swallow a political porcupine," to save the scheme. Most Northern members did not much care much where to southward the capital went. Previously so forceful in argument, Madison now fell strangely mute. Just before the final vote, he wrote Monroe, "I shall wish it to be considered as an unavoidable evil, and *possibly* not the worst side of the dilemma." Perfunctorily, he voted against assumption, but he did not speak against it from the floor. Noting his curiously limp opposition, the House reversed its earlier vote against assumption, revived it 32 to 29, and then accepted the Senate bill 34 to 28. After more wrangling to iron out differences between Senate and House versions of the bill, it passed both houses on July 29, 1790. The whole funding measure, of which assumption was a major part, became law on August 4. Thanks to a deal by candlelight at Thomas Jefferson's, Hamilton had hatched a famous victory out of an oft defeated bill.

"And so," Jefferson concluded his reremembrance of the event 25 years later, "the assumption was passed." Hamilton, said Jefferson, had "effected his side of the engagement" and produced the votes to ratify the changes in the location of the capital to Philadelphia for ten years and then to the Potomac.

Jefferson's further point was that when "the assumption was passed," there were "20 millions of stock divided among favored states, and thrown in as pabulum to the stockjobbing herd."

With the indispensable yielding of Madison and Monroe, Jefferson had made possible Hamilton's victory. At first Jefferson seemed to be Hamilton's willing, even enthusiastic coadjutor, casually dragging Madison and Monroe along behind him like glum puppets.

Madison's double switch on assumption, from longtime support to adamant opposition and back to mute acquiescence, did nothing to restore him to Hamilton's friendship. Two years later, writing to his friend Edward Carrington on May 26, 1792, Hamilton still recalled with pain that when he had taken office, he had counted on the "similarity of thinking" and "personal goodwill" and "support of Mr. Madison." It was a still a "matter of surprise" that Madison had switched over to opposition. The surprise was all the greater because before the House debate had commenced, said Hamilton, "I had a conversation with him," and told him how I thought he felt and my grounds for thinking he agreed with my report. "He did not deny them," Hamilton said.

Madison's only justification for his switch had been that "the very considerable alienation of the debt" between the time of this conversation with Hamilton and his switch had "changed the state of the question." In fact, Madison's conscience was so full of shame for it that he found it necessary to write out a memorandum on a scrap of paper and attach it to his private notes. He referred to himself in the third person: "This explains the apparent change in Mr. Madison's opinion from his previous one opposed to discrimination. At that time the debts were due to the original holders."

In his 1792 letter to Carrington, Hamilton added that "the change of opinion he had avowed on the point of discrimination diminished my respect for the force of Mr. Madison's mind and the soundness of his judgment." Speculations in the debt had gone on for months and years; so well it might.

Yet to Carrington, Hamilton generously added that "my previous impressions of the fairness of Mr. Madison's character and my reliance on his good will towards me disposed me to believe that his suggestions were sincere."

Watching the articulate Madison sit glumly mute while the measures he had so eloquently opposed prior to the night of the deal by candlelight at Thomas Jefferson's all passed would weaken Hamilton's disposition to believe that Madison's suggestions had been sincere.

Hamilton had not, of course, known Jefferson or studied his moods anything like as long as he had known Madison's. So it did not come with quite the same sense of personal loss and shock when he learned that Jefferson too had now switched sides to join the opposition. About a year after the famous deal, Jefferson told Washington that he had been tricked by Hamilton. "I was duped into it by the Secretary of the Treasury and made a tool for forwarding his schemes, not then sufficiently understood by me; and of all the errors of my political life, this has occasioned me the deepest regret," he said.

For one of the acknowledged intellectual giants of American history to have confessed serving as Hamilton's "dupe" and "tool" tends to exalt Hamilton to a position of mastery that he hardly deserves credit for. The evidence is clear that Jefferson was a knowledgeable and active persuader of Mason, Madison, and Monroe to switch from earlier opposition to favor assumption. He simply decided after the fact that it would serve his political purposes better to claim he had made a mistake in being misled by Hamilton.

He also seems to have wished to mislead Washington about his own role, and rewrite history. Years later, long after his first disagreement with Hamilton had hardened into enmity, writing as an old man will, with his enemy long dead, to polish up a rough spot in his earlier life for posterity, Jefferson claimed that he was "but a stranger to the ground, a stranger to the actors on it . . . and as yet unaware of [the] object. I took no concern in it . . . [the prospect of assumption] was on the carpet at the moment of my arrival; and to this I was most innocently and ignorantly made to hold the candle."

The passage quoted above about the famous deal by candlelight is from Jefferson's *Anas*. According to the dictionary, *ana* is a suffix denoting items of bibliography, anecdotes, or literary gossip, as in *Jeffersoniana*, for example. In the singular, it is also "a recollection, originally of the memorable sayings of a person, later of items of information relative to a subject of curious interest." Jefferson himself described his *Anas* as "memorandums, on loose scraps of paper, taken out of my pocket in the moment, and laid by to be copied at fair leisure, which, however, they hardly ever were." He had "these scraps . . . ragged, rubbed and scribbled as they were," bound together, he claimed, without giving the binder "the opportunity of seeing a single paper." How this alleged miracle of bookbindery was performed he does not disclose. Beginning when he was about 72, Jefferson goes on: "after the lapse of twenty-five years, or more, I have given to the whole a calm revisal, when the passions of time are passed away, and the reasons of the transactions act alone on the judgment." In a "calm revisal" from the remoteness of a Monticello a quarter of a century later, facts are just as easily twisted, forgotten, or changed to fictions.

Much modern historical scholarship has been directed toward proving that no deal was made that night at Thomas Jefferson's or that moving the capital to the Potomac was not the quid pro quo for Madison's and Monroe's acquiescence in assumption or that if a deal was made, that dinner at Thomas Jefferson's had nothing to do with it. The fact that a year later and 25 years later Jefferson still took personal blame upon himself and sought so unconvincingly to explain away his role makes such exercises an interesting challenge to scholarly ingenuity. After all, Jefferson arranged the dinner and was there.

Jefferson's severest critics have rarely charged him with being foolish, forgetful, or untruthful enough to have confessed so painfully to a crime that his ardent apologists claim he had no hand in.

If Madison had held out against Jefferson's urgings at the dinner and successfully opposed assumption to the end, he, not Jefferson, might have been hailed by posterity as the Father of American Democracy. Madison never admitted that his switches from early support to active opposition to silent acquiescence had anything to do with Jefferson's influence or a deal at Jefferson's dinner. When he was an old man, Madison did offer as a reason for the breach between Jefferson and himself, on the one side, and Hamilton and Washington,

on the other, that Hamilton had made plain "his purpose and endeavor to administration the Government into a thing totally different from that which he and
I both knew perfectly well had been understood and intended by the Convention
who framed it, and by the People adopting it."

This statement is from a letter from Nicholas P. Trist to Martin Van Buren
of May 31, 1857, but it does nothing to explain Madison's support of, opposition
to, and acquiescence in Hamilton's report, all within the space of less than a year.
As for Hamilton, there is no record of his ever saying anything afterward at any
time about making a deal by candlelight at Thomas Jefferson's. He had won
assumption and let the Potomac have the permanent capital it was bound to have
anyway.

Hamilton's "Report on Public Credit" and the passage of his program with
Jefferson's and Madison's help and acquiescence constitute a watershed in
American history. It marks the end of an era of American bankruptcy and
repudiation of debt and the beginning of a long era during which the public credit
of the United States would be sounder than that of any other nation. At the same
time, the debates on discrimination and assumption opened a wide gulf in opinion
between Hamiltonian nationalists on one side and the proponents of states'
rights, now championed by Madison, on the other. The cleavage led shortly to
the formation of the Federal Republican or Federalist and the Anti-Federalist
or Democratic Republican parties.

Men like Senator Maclay, who rightly suspected a double bargain involving
both Robert Morris and Jefferson, were outraged. Jefferson decided he had made
a mistake. But he was too hard on himself when he shouldered the blame for
having been instrumental in making possible the killings of the speculators.
Many speculators were taken by surprise and suffered losses. Andrew Craigie
of Boston wrote mournfully that he had not made the profit he should have made
if he had known what he would later know. He had purchased a large amount
of the South Carolina debt at under three shillings, eight pence per pound, "but
was unfortunate enough a few days before the compromise took place & when
the Assumption was thought by the knowing ones to be lost to part with it at
4/. in the pound. . . . Mr. Cazenove, a Dutch Agent, I afterwards found was the
fortunate purchaser & of large Sums besides on the same day."

Was assumption really a windfall to the speculators? Was it a heartless
repudiation of the nation's obligations to its old soldiers, their widows, and their
children, who had helped save it? In his 1791 paper, "Vindication of the Funding
System, No. 2," Hamilton ruefully commented that "it is a curious phenomenon
in political history (not easy to be paralleled), that a measure which has elevated
the credit of the country from a state of absolute prostration to a state of exalted
preeminence, should bring upon the authors of it reprobation and censure." It
took two to "speculate."

A speculator, investor, or saver, who had bought public debt at the time
when Hamilton was appointed secretary of the treasury, knowing his public
record of support for assumption and Madison's as well, and who still held when
Madison switched to opposition on the issue, would have had many anxious

moments if he had then sold. Like Craigie, he would have lost money. But if he had held on till final passage of assumption, he would have made money. Who could have told him that Madison, the self-proclaimed foe of speculators, by his second switch under Jefferson's prodding, had made some of the speculators' profits, as well as lost profits, possible? Certainly not anything he could have heard from Hamilton, William Duer, Tench Coxe, or Andrew Craigie. The general public's confidence in Hamilton and his abilities that had caused the debt to rise in value had been public knowledge, not inside information, from the very beginning.

As Hamilton explained to Washington on August 18, 1792, when Madison and "other distinguished characters of the South started in opposition to the assumption: the inhabitants of the Southern states sustained a considerable loss," because "the high opinion entertained of them made it be taken for granted in that quarter that the opposition would be successful . . . certificate holders were eager to part with them at their current prices, calculating on a loss to the purchasers from their future fall." Madison's switch had caused losses to many Southerners.

Yet sellers were spared a loss later: "A great part of the debt has been purchased by Northern and Southern citizens at higher prices—beyond the true value. In the late delirium of speculation large sums were purchased at twenty-five per cent above par and upward."

Most important of all, much of the speculation occurred after Hamilton had publicly promulgated the assumption plan in his report to the House. "After that," he pointed out, "purchasers and sellers were upon equal ground . . . If purchasers speculated upon the sellers, in many instances the sellers speculated upon the purchasers. Each made his calculation of chances . . . It has turned out generally that the buyer had the best of the bargain, but the seller got the value of his commodity according to his estimate of it, and probably in a great number of instances more."

Passage of assumption provoked immediate repercussions in Virginia. Patrick Henry introduced a fiery resolution to the legislature denouncing it as "repugnant to the Constitution of the United States, as it goes to the exercise of a power not expressly granted to the general government." Madison and Jefferson did nothing to oppose Henry's resolutions. John Marshall and other Federalist followers of Hamilton fought them and lost. They passed by a large majority.

An even more intransigent Protest and Remonstrance from Virginia followed. This declared that all powers not expressly given in the Constitution were reserved to the states and that assumption was an effort "to erect and concentrate and perpetuate a large monied interest in opposition to the landed interests." This would prostrate "agriculture at the feet of commerce" or result in a "change in the present form of Federal Government, fatal to the existence of American liberty."

Here was rebellious action that posed a new threat to Hamilton's precious Union and Constitution. He sent copies of the resolutions to John Jay on November 13, 1790, with a grim note: "This is the first symptom of a spirit which must either be killed, or it will kill the Constitution of the United States. I send the resolutions to you, that it may be considered what ought to be done." Hamilton's own "sudden and indigested thought," as he put it, was that the "collective weight of the different parts of the Government [ought] to be employed in exploding the principles they contain."

Hamilton's old intimate and mentor of more than 15 years replied on November 28 from Boston like the smooth statesman that he was. Hamilton should not treat the resolutions as more important than they were. The pieces then being published in the press by the Hartford wits could do justice to the subject better by making light of it. "The assumption will do its own work—it will justify itself and not want advocates," Jay wisely counseled. Out of long friendship, Jay added a few wise words that were good advice for any government for any time, as well as for Hamilton personally:

> The National Govt has only to do what is right and if possible be silent. If compelled to speake, it should be in few words strongly that evince Temper Dignity and Self Respect.

Jay's long view was right—for the short run. The Virginia resolutions had no immediate effect. But as Hamilton, the farseeing prophet of future America, had foreseen in his "sudden and indigested thought," their long-range consequences proved to be devastating. Jefferson's and Madison's great state was saying that an important national law passed by Congress was unconstitutional. Here was the inception of the doctrine of "strict construction" of the Constitution, which Jefferson and Madison were to wield with telling effect in future debates. Here was the first respectable precedent for nullification and for secession. In an angry flash of foresight, Hamilton had rightly identified to Jay the "spirit which must either be killed or will kill the Constitution of the United States."

Jay's reply to his mortal friend was also right. The task of binding up the wounds to which this defection of mighty Virginia led would have to wait another 70 years for another great American, who also favored freeing the slaves, but, above all else, preserving the Union.

3

FOREIGN AFFAIRS

WE THINK IN ENGLISH.
—*In a conversation reported by George Beckwith,
October 1789*

In the summer of 1789, Hamilton's friends were urging him to run for the United States Senate or to indicate his willingness to accept appointment as chief justice of the United States or to accept a draft to run against George Clinton for governor of New York State. All these flattering proposals he "steadily rejected in the most explicit manner." He had a more important job in mind.

Some said that in the United States "a good financier is as rare as a phoenix." So when both James Madison and Robert Morris suggested Hamilton to Washington for secretary of the treasury—Morris said he was "damned sharp" —Washington had sent his name along to the Senate. He was quickly confirmed. "In undertaking the task," Hamilton said in October, "I hazarded much, but I thought it an occasion that called upon me to hazard." Hamilton's had been the first appointment to Washington's cabinet. The second, that of General Henry Knox to be secretary of war, took effect the day after Hamilton's.

From then on, Washington referred appointments of other men to Hamilton and John Jay for review. On September 25, Washington wrote to ask Hamilton's and Jay's advice on a list of 35 names scheduled for further appointments. "Who," he asked, would be "more eligible for the Post Office" than Colonel Samuel Osgood? The list for consideration included the names of Jonathan

Dayton, Robert R. Livingston, William North, Lewis Pintard, Arthur Lee, James Duane, and other prominent men. Washington enclosed another list to show Hamilton exactly "how the appointments stand to this time." So that Hamilton would know how all appointments balanced out, Washington added, "and, that you may have the matter *fully* before you, I shall add that, it is my *present* intention to nominate Mr. Jefferson for Secretary of State and Mr. Edmund Randolph as Attorney General; though their acceptance is problematical, especially the latter." Hamilton let pass this one opening to offer a demurral to their appointments.

After some characteristic wavering, Edmund Randolph on September 26 accepted the office of attorney general, then only a part-time job. Thomas Jefferson, the American minister to France, had planned a temporary sojourn at home before returning to his Paris post, but was held up at Cowes by contrary winds and was unable to sail for America until near the end of October 1789. He was at sea when his friends in Europe heard that Washington would offer him the secretaryship of state. Jonathan Trumbull's news from America of September 27 mentioned Senate confirmation of Hamilton as secretary of the treasury and Jay as chief justice, but added that "no Secretary for foreign affairs is nominated." The same day, however, John Barker Church in London read John Rutledge a letter from Hamilton of September 28, telling of the appointments of Jay, Osgood, and Wilson. Hamilton had added, "Mr. Jefferson will have offered him the foreign department."

Chief Justice John Jay temporarily assumed the additional duties of secretary of state while waiting for some litigation to work its way up the trial and appellate court ladder to give the highest court something to do. By the time Jefferson was officially installed in his office on March 22, 1790, Hamilton had already been in office more than six months. In Jefferson's absence, Hamilton had been actively dealing with a range of foreign as well as domestic affairs. Various personal matters and a monthlong migraine headache during May 1790 kept Jefferson from taking up official duties in earnest until shortly before the mid-June candlelight dinner he arranged for Madison and Hamilton at his new house on Maiden Lane. His long absence gave a little color to his later claim of being an uninformed "stranger to the ground" when he forced Madison to let Hamilton's assumption bill pass the House.

Washington was proud of the way his first cabinet looked, at least on paper. He wrote to Lafayette that "by having Mr. Jefferson as the Head of the Department of State, Mr. Jay of the Judiciary, Hamilton of the Treasury, and Knox of that of War, I feel myself supported by able co-adjutors." He added that they "harmonize extremely well together." But that was before Jefferson had attended very many meetings at which Hamilton was also present. The cabinet had looked better on paper than it did when Washington, after more than a year as president, finally got it all together at his house.

Washington spoke of his cabinet as his "family," just as he had spoken of his wartime aides. Hamilton, the first member to join it, seemed to be returning to a family he had left after only a temporary absence. Neither then nor now did

Washington draw sharp lines of distinction between functions of one aide or his department and another. For example, when faced with preparing his December 1790 message to Congress, Washington asked Hamilton to "revolve in [your] mind such matters as may be proper for me to lay before congress not only in your own department, but such others of a general nature, as may happen to occur to you."

To Hamilton, "most of the important measures of every government are connected with the treasury," as he would write Edward Carrington May 26, 1792. This, of course, included foreign economic policy, particularly because Jay's early stewardship of the Department of State had been "more nominal than real." Hamilton had always thought and acted internationally and continentally. During his boyhood under four different colonial flags on Nevis, St. Kitts, and St. Croix and possibly on St. Eustatius too, the West Indies had "figured grandly in the world's affairs." As Washington's wartime aide, he had dealt in comradely friendship on many missions with leading British, French, German, and Polish officers, diplomats and travelers. As a 20-year-old, he had warned Robert R. Livingston in June 1777 of the complex maneuverings and intrigues of European power politics. Writing to Duane in 1780, he had urged that Congress appoint a full-time secretary for foreign affairs. He had served with Madison and Richard Peters in 1783 on the congressional committee to study and report on whether the Treaty of Paris with Britain ending the Revolution should be ratified; he and Madison had offered plans to get the British out of the posts they had hung onto after the war on the northwest frontier. After first opposing Madison's plan, Hamilton had ended by supporting it. In 1784 he had formed a warm friendship with the soldier of fortune Francisco de Miranda, the "flaming son of liberty" and Venezuelan apostle of Spanish American independence. He introduced Miranda to his friends and helped him lay plans for breaking the power of European monarchs in the remaining colonial areas of the New World. He had even helped Miranda devise a system of government for such Latin American lands as he might liberate. At the 1788 term of Congress, Hamilton had been chairman of the committee that had demanded "a clear and absolute right" to free navigation of the Mississippi. With von Steuben a more or less permanent houseguest boarding at home with his family, Hamilton never lacked a fund of German and Polish vernacular jokes, and von Steuben anecdotes were always good for a laugh.

Within a week after Washington's inauguration, the States General had met at Versailles. By July 1789 the French revolution had exploded, blowing the lid off a whole new set of hazards for America. Six of the northwest frontier posts Britain still held were on the Canadian borders of New York State. Britain seemed to intend to hang on to all of them permanently. From these posts Britain reaped large profits from the fur trade and kept the Indian tribes in thrall as a constant threat to American settlers moving west. Spain controlled the Floridas and New Orleans and maintained a strong influence in the Southwest through Indians, explorers, and missionaries. America's Treaty of Paris with France remained officially in effect, but moribund. Debts due to France, Spain, and the

Netherlands remained unpaid. The British Parliament had adopted restrictive trade measures to keep American merchants and commerce out of the West Indies by requiring goods to be transported in British ships, shipment from or through designated ports, and other crippling measures. France, though a nominal ally, granted only limited trading privileges there. She claimed the right, under Article XXXII of the Treaty of 1778, to "regulate" all American West Indies trade. In *The Federalist*, Nos. 24 and 25, Hamilton had warned that "The territories of Britain, Spain and the Indian nations . . . encircle our union from Maine to Georgia."

Partly because of the American alliance with France, a coldly aloof Britain had refused to send an officially accredited minister to the United States. Now Hamilton advised Washington to open regular diplomatic channels with Britain to improve commercial relations. He recommended his friend Gouverneur Morris, then in France on private business—some said Morris was arranging financing for his own and others' speculations in American public debt—to Washington as an emissary to sound out the British on an exchange of ministers and to find out whether Britain would be interested in a treaty of commerce. Washington consulted John Jay, who approved Hamilton's suggestion. Madison opposed it, preferring, as he told Washington, to wait until Jefferson returned to take charge of foreign affairs. Washington followed Hamilton's and Jay's advice and gave instructions to Morris to act as an unofficial emissary. The British responded warmly, but seemed interested only in a treaty of commerce, not an exchange of ministers or in the matter of evacuating the forts on the northwestern frontiers.

As Washington moved Morris like a knight in chess from Paris to London to act as unofficial American emissary to Britain, Sir Guy Carleton, the first Baron Dorchester, and also British governor general of Quebec, moved George Beckwith like a pawn from Canada to New York as unofficial British emissary to the United States. Beckwith was one diplomatic degree more unofficial than Morris. Hamilton explained to Washington on July 15, 1790, that he had put down Beckwith by telling him that "Morris' credentials though not formal proceed from the proper source. Yours are neither formal nor authoritative." The point was that Beckwith reported back only to Carleton in Canada, not directly to the British Foreign Office. Carleton forwarded Beckwith's reports to William Wyndham Grenville, later Baron Grenville. The distinction was more significant as a point of diplomatic protocol than as a practical matter because Grenville was William Pitt's secretary of state for Home affairs and after June 1791 for foreign affairs. There was little room to doubt that despite the fiction that Beckwith was an unofficial unofficial emissary, functionally he was Morris's counterpart: an official unofficial emissary.

During the Revolution, Beckwith had been in the British army secret service. There he had used the alias of G[eorge] B[eckwith] Ring. It was derived from the fact that when communicating with Benedict Arnold concerning treason plans, Beckwith had used one ring and Arnold another to authenticate secret messages that passed between them through the lines. When in London, Beckwith was a gossipy confidant of Angelica Church.

From there on April 25, 1788, Angelica had written her sister Elizabeth, with high hopes of returning soon to New York, "How many happy evenings have I already past! from dwelling on my future happiness!"—happiness that awaited her on her visit to New York the following summer without her husband. Angelica went on to say that "Colonel Beckwith tells me that our dear Hamilton writes too much, takes no exercise, and grows too fat. I hate both the word and the thing." But nothing that Beckwith could cattily whisper in her ear could disenthrall her from Hamilton's spell. She went on:

> I desire you will take care of his health and his good looks. Why I shall find him on my return a dull heavy fellow! He will be as unable to flirt as Robert Morris; pray, Betsy, make him walk, ride and be amused. You will see by some of Church's letters, which have caused me to shed the most delicious tears of joy, that it will not be long before we return to America. Embrace dear Hamilton for me, it is impossible to know him, and not to wish him health and pleasure. I am so proud of his merit and abilities, that even you, Eliza, might *envy my feelings.*

Angelica's summer and autumn with Hamilton in New York the next year and the rush of her tears and his at their parting showed Angelica that her fears that her "petit fripon," Hamilton, had become a "dull heavy fellow" were foolish. It also showed her that George Beckwith, however amusing his whispers might be in her ear, was a vivid but not always reliable reporter on Hamilton. Just before Angelica had sailed home, George Beckwith reported back to Carleton a conversation he had had with Hamilton in New York in October 1789 that was more candid, open, and pointed, if not indiscreet, than diplomatic exchanges are supposed to be.

To protect Hamilton's confidentiality, Beckwith substituted the secret code number "7," or "seventh" for Hamilton's name, just as he used "2" or "second" in his despatches to denote Philip Schuyler. According to Beckwith, Hamilton had said, "we have lately established a government upon principles, that in my opinion render it safe for any nation to enter into treaties with us, either commercial or political, which has not hitherto been the case; I have always preferred a connexion with you, to that of any other country, *We think in English,* and have a similarity of prejudices and of predilections."

No doubt what Hamilton was saying was intended for diplomatic impact, but it was probably revealing of Hamilton's own convictions as well, as in ". . . we are a young and growing empire, with much enterprize and vigour, but undoubtedly are, and must be for years, rather an agricultural than a manufacturing people."

His comments about France, to her chief rival's unaccredited minister, were careful, not unfriendly to France, and realistic. For the United States, Britain was by far the more important trading partner. As he said, "I am free to say that although France has been indulgent to us, in certain points, yet, what she can furnish is by no means so essential or so suited to us as your productions, nor do our raw materials suit her so well as they do you."

Hamilton wished to "form a commercial treaty with you to every extent to which you may think it for your interest to go" because it would lead to expansion of peaceful trade. No one would know better than Hamilton that "it would be better for Great Britain to grant us admission into her [West Indian] islands . . . than by a rigid adherence to your present plan to produce a system of warfare in commercial matters." Such warfare, Hamilton observed prophetically, was "encouraged by France in this country . . . to promote coldness and animosity" between the United States and Britain. This Hamilton "viewed with much regret" as "being directly opposed to that system, which upon mature reflexion, I have thought it most eligible for us to pursue."

Although Hamilton was no doubt making self-serving statements in the interest of American foreign policy in these conversations with Beckwith, nothing in them betrays hostility to France. It would have pleased Beckwith no end to report back to Carleton much more of such hostility on Hamilton's part.

Beckwith's reportage did include some vivid personal comments by "number 7" that might better have been reserved for Angelica's ear than Lord Dorchester's eyes. They have caused Hamilton's reputation for diplomatic discretion no end of grief. Critics without apparently much personal experience of how one public man makes another open up and say more about large matters than he really intends to say have fretted about the typically frank, but relatively harmless, sort of personal comments about Madison, for example, that Hamilton let drop to another man of the world just as the congressional battle over discrimination, assumption, and funding was about to break. During the previous House session, Beckwith had noticed that Madison manifested a severe anti-British bias in pressing for discriminatory trade legislation. Hamilton was a fellow sufferer from Madison's tergiversations too. He told Beckwith he was surprised that "the only opposition to General Washington" came from Madison's side. "The truth is," Hamilton added, "that although the gentleman [Madison] is a clever man, he is very little acquainted with the world. That he is uncorrupted and incorruptible I have not a doubt; he has the same end in view that I have, and so have those gentlemen who act with him, but their mode of attaining it is very different."

There was wide public criticism in America of Gouverneur Morris for being seen in London associating too frequently with Charles James Fox, leader of the opposition to William Pitt's government, and with the French Ambassador to Britain, Chevalier Anne-César de la Luzerne.

In another private conversation with Beckwith Hamilton went along with the unofficial British minister's criticism of Morris's hobnobbing in London so publicly with leading public symbols of opposition to his government's policies. After all, Morris had been despatched to curry favor there, not criticism.

Gouverneur Morris and Hamilton would always be the closest of friends. Morris would deliver the "Eulogium" over Hamilton's corpse at his funeral. Each was secure enough in his own self-esteem and had enough wit and respect for the other's judgment to recognize ruefully that whatever the other might say of him might with equal justice have been said by himself about himself.

Beckwith reported that in conversations in late September 1790 Hamilton had said, "I do not question this gentleman's [Morris's] sincerity in following up those objects committed to his charge, but to deal frankly with you, I have some doubts of his prudence. This is the point on which he is deficient, for in other respects he is a man of great genius, liable however to be occasionally influenced by his fancy, which sometimes outruns his discretion."

Morris's opinion of Hamilton was the same as Hamilton's of him: indiscretion was his friend's most serious flaw. Morris would confide to his diary that dealing with it was the most difficult aspect of composing a eulogium for his late friend after the duel. However, Julian Boyd, the leading Thomas Jefferson scholar, in his book *Number 7*, took it upon himself to snort that Hamilton's comment was "a libel on an honorable public servant." But a characterization so largely true is not a libel except in the loosest sense, and being called a "public servant" would have given the elegant Gouverneur a good guffaw with his alleged traducer at the pomposity of his self-appointed champion's defense.

Instead of using statesmanlike restraint, Beckwith turned Hamilton's disarming personal confidences into vivid reportage. Hamilton laundered all gossipy doubts of Morris "prudence" from the report of the same conversation with Beckwith that he made to Washington on September 30, 1790. Hamilton tried to explain away his old friend's imprudence by telling their chief of Morris's earlier close friendships with Luzerne and Fox and their "similarity of dispositions and characters." Morris and Fox were "both brilliant men, men of wit and genius; both fond of the pleasures of society." Hamilton had assured both Beckwith and Washington that "it is impossible that there can be anything wrong." These were all Hamilton's kind of men, projecting their favorite vices, and virtues, on each other. An unofficial minister in London could not be expected to shun the pleasures of the society of other old friends or cronies who also happened to be the same kind of men or at least men much more like each other than any of them were men like a Madison or a Jefferson.

Catharine Church, the third child and eldest daughter of Angelica and John, named for Angelica's and Elizabeth Hamilton's mother, came to be called Lady Kitty as she was growing up, just like her cousins Catharine Duer and Catharine Livingston. It was Angelica's Lady Kitty and her younger sister, Elizabeth, who were on Hamilton's mind when Angelica's "affectionate friend and brother" wrote her January 7, 1790 (anxious about "opening the budget") and fondly wishing all Angelica's sons "to be great men, and your daughters like yourself."

When Angelica had brought her Lady Kitty to Paris in December 1787, they and their escort, the painter John Trumbull, were both warmly welcomed to town by the American minister to France, Thomas Jefferson, and into "our charming coterie in Paris," as he liked to describe it. Jefferson's headquarters at the Hôtel de Langeac was a great Paris house built for one of the mistresses of Louis XV by the same architect who would later design the Arc de Triomphe. Discreetly fenced off from the curious crowds that moved along the Champs Elysées, Thomas Jefferson reigned serenely over a court of philosophers and attractive women like a prince of the *ancien regime*. He dressed in high fashion and powdered his hair. A maître d'hôtel managed his establishment. The epicurean viands he served at table there led Patrick Henry later to upbraid him for abjuring his native victuals. They caused another American to say that he wished Jefferson's French politics were as good as his French food.

Although Jefferson sometimes scolded his countrymen about the dangers of "female intrigue," his coterie that Angelica and her little Lady Kitty joined there already included the 27-year-old Maria Hadfield Cosway, with her pretty head of golden curls, and the delicate, cozily domestic Madame de Corny, at whose house in the Rue Chausée d'Antin, not far from the Opéra, Angelica and Kitty lodged.

Angelica installed Lady Kitty in the boarding school at the Abbaye de Panthemont, where she quickly became a friend of Jefferson's daughter Polly. Madame de Corny, who had no children, vied with the rich widower Jefferson in doing kindnesses for both girls. Both Madame de Corny and Jefferson, no doubt, often solemnly discussed their schooling with Angelica over teacups at the Hôtel de Langeac.

After Madame de Corny had gone off to visit Angelica and John Church at their manor house, Down Place, near Windsor on the Thames, Jefferson wrote Angelica to accuse her of having "bitten" Madame de Corny, made her country-mad, and afflicted her with an awful Anglomania. This was the same all-purpose charge that the American minister to France would level at many people over the years, particularly Hamilton. Jefferson usually considered it an extremely serious accusation. But with Angelica, the sage of Monticello intended it to pass muster for light badinage. When Angelica returned to England with John Trumbull after her two-month visit, she carelessly left behind in Paris a trunk, which Jefferson was obliged to send after her. During their visit to Paris, Trumbull had painted the likenesses of some of the French officers into his heroic panoramic painting *Surrender of Lord Cornwallis* at Yorktown, which also prominently featured Hamilton. He had also painted the likeness of his host, Jefferson, from life for the original of his panoramic *Declaration of Independence*. Trumbull painted Jefferson, showing him with unpowdered hair and ruddy face, a likeness younger and more vigorous than in Mather Brown's, less the courtier, and probably a better likeness. When the artist and Angelica brought a copy back to London with them, Maria Cosway liked it so well that she asked Jefferson for another copy for herself. "It is a person who hates you that requests this favor," she coyly wrote Jefferson. Perhaps she was jealous of Angelica because neither Trumbull nor Angelica had brought a painting or a letter back with them from Jefferson to her. So Trumbull dashed off two more replicas of his little painting —one for Maria and the other for Angelica. At this point, Maria was calling Angelica her "dearest sister," but Angelica was calling Maria merely "sister." Maria's copy seemed to be a better likeness of Jefferson than Angelica's, and she told Angelica so. Angelica snapped back that she had a better likeness in her memory anyway and did not mind. Jefferson wrote to Angelica, "The memorial of me which you have from Trumbull is the most worthless part of me." He added, "Could he paint my friendship to you, it would be something out of the common line."[1]

It seemed that no man or woman could fail to be smitten with Angelica.

"You are capable of feeling the value of this lovely woman," Maria Cosway, visiting Angelica, nervously wrote Jefferson, fearing that she was all too right and letting her sometime consort know her suspicions and warning him off. Jefferson did seem to go almost as far overboard as Hamilton would in telling Angelica of his grief at one of her departures. Jefferson also thought of Angelica when he rode in the Bois de Boulogne, he said. And when he traveled up the Rhine earlier that year in the spring, he had had Angelica and Maria with him, one on each hand, at least in his perfervid imagination. In his letters to Angelica during the months after her visit to Paris, he chattered on about her Lady Kitty and his Polly coming for Sunday dinner with him and about the adventures of Monsieur and Madame de Corny in quest of a country house. But Angelica really had no wish to trouble his nice little lady friend who was staying with her by encouraging Jefferson's randy thoughts to stray towards herself. So she tactfully gave the 44-year-old widower a polite but firm push back to reality, back up on to the pedestal of avuncular sage, where he seemed to be most at home. Writing him from Down Place, where she and Maria were enjoying the quiet of the country, Angelica coolly said that they often wished Mr. Jefferson were there, "supposing that he would be indulgent to the exertions of two little women to please him, who are extremely vain of the pleasure of being permitted to write him, and very happy to have some share of his favorable opinion."

Conscious, perhaps, that the eyes of such lovely ladies tended to glaze when over the teacups he launched into disquisitions against Anglophilia, Jefferson wrote to Angelica, who was sending Adam Smith's *The Wealth of Nations* along to Hamilton about the same time, that "the tender breasts of ladies were not formed for political convulsions." What Jefferson liked about Angelica and Maria was that they were so feminine. To him, they were not at all the "complex, intricate and enigmatical beings" that the 20-year-old Hamilton had told Kitty Livingston he thought all women were.

Jefferson wrote Angelica that "the French ladies miscalculate much their own happiness when they wander from the field of their influence into that of politics." He thought the beautiful glass that Madame de Corny had sent him as a present was a better symbol of his and her relationship than was the copy of the memoir of Calonne that he had previously sent to her.

Beyond the stout grillwork and sharp points of the iron palings that fenced off the well-funded little coterie ensconced within the Hôtel de Langeac from ordinary people outside on the Champs Elysées, trouble was brewing in France during the years from 1784 to 1789 that Jefferson was there.

When the carriages of the rich rolling by choked them with dust or spattered them with mud, the poor growled and grimaced and sometimes dared to spit at them. But the Bastille still stood. At Versailles, ladies and gentlemen played as shepherds and shepherdesses at pastorals. Some came to think of America as an Arcadia for all—many on the basis of Jefferson's interesting conversations and his much admired *Notes on Virginia*. He deplored the extravagances of the French court and the degraded condition of the poor, many of whom were trying to emigrate to America. He talked politics to many American visitors like Anne Willing Bingham, the wife of William Bingham, Hamilton's friend, adviser, and confidant. Many called Anne—out of Angelica Church's hearing, no doubt—the most beautiful and glamorous of all the remarkable women that revolutionary America had produced.

Jefferson assured Anne earnestly that the simple domestic pleasures of America were much to be preferred to the superficial society of Europe. He tended not to worry much about rumbles of distant revolutions that troubled other honest souls, especially capitalists, closer to the upheavals. When Daniel Shays had taken up arms in western Massachusetts in 1787 to halt the dispossession of farmers by creditors in the courts, the well-to-do were appalled. Abigail Adams told Jefferson that "ignorant, wrestless desperadoes, without conscience or principals [sic] had led a deluded multitude to follow their standard, under pretense of grievances which have no existence but in their imaginations." Jefferson, undisturbed, wrote James Madison calmly that "a little rebellion now and then is a good thing." To Abigail Adams's son-in-law, William Stephens Smith, Jefferson made the dramatic declaration that "the tree of liberty must be refreshed from time to time with the blood of patriots and tyrants. It is its natural manure." The poor patriots' blood was spilled 3,000 miles from Paris.

Poor Daniel Shays had fallen into such poverty that he had been forced to sell the sword that the Marquis de Lafayette had presented to him in recognition of his valiant services in the Revolution. But the revolutionary views Lafayette espoused in conversations with Jefferson's coterie at the Hôtel de Langeac often seemed too radical for the host. One could carry a good thing too far by bringing "a little rebellion now and then" a little too close for comfort.

Three months before he was to leave France, the "beautiful revolution," as Jefferson called it, had begun with the storming of the Bastille. When he sailed from France that golden autumn in 1789, he thought he was going only for a short holiday to inspect his vast estates and slave holdings, to try to untangle his confused personal finances, and put off paying his debts a little longer, before returning to rejoin his charming coterie in Paris. To Jefferson, as to most citizens of the United States of his day, his state, Virginia, not America, was "my country," to which he was going home. He sailed from Le Havre on the *Clermont*, a vessel of 230 tons, which he had chartered to transport his party alone, sparing them any personal contact with ordinary people not of his own little coterie. He was bringing home only part of his possessions, but they added up to a whole shipload. The rest, which would follow next year, made such a large cargo that a revolutionary mob insisted upon inspecting it, taking one small part of Jefferson's French things for the belongings of a fleeing French aristocrat. This first shipload contained statuary, paintings, cases of wine, boxes of books, muskets for the War Department, and presents for President Washington, John Jay, and the dying Benjamin Franklin. On his way to the sailing, Jefferson made an impulsive purchase of a Normandy shepherd bitch, which was pregnant with puppies.

Besides his two daughters, 17-year-old Martha, called Patsy, and 11-year-old Maria, called Polly, Jefferson's party included two slaves, Sally Hemings, a pretty 16-year-old octoroon, who had come to France with Polly as her attendant two years before, and Sally's brother, Jim, who had now been well schooled in the arts of cordon bleu French cuisine. As the great Virginian's biographer Dumas Malone wrote, the diplomat came home to America with "slaves, bitch and baggage." Tenaciously held slave tradition has it that beauteous young yellow-skinned Sally was pregnant, too, by her owner. The shape Sally was in was reason enough for the man of the people to shun them and travel with her by his own private ship instead of public transportation that would be segregated and full of gossips.

At Monticello, on its high Albemarle hilltop surrounded by gullied, eroded, and heavily mortgaged fields, in the great house with its graceful dome, quaint cupolas, 35 rooms, hidden stairways, and many ingenious gadgets for the convenience of its owner, Jefferson would always be happy. There, as one perceptive historian observed, he was in a "château high above contact with man." It had been designed by his architect after Jefferson's own sketches. Unfortunately, when Jefferson's wife, Martha (Wayles) Skelton, who had borne him six children in ten years, had died at 33 in 1782, its twisting staircase proved too narrow for her corpse to be gotten down it; so it had to be lowered on ropes out of an upstairs window.

Jefferson's daughter Martha reported that her father came home two days before Christmas, 1789, to a tumultuous greeting from all his slaves. Although they had not seen him for five years, they were ecstatically happy in their bondage (which he sometimes said he deplored), to have back the absentee owner who had been living so happily off them in Paris during his absence. The homecoming scene became a part of enduring Southern slave plantation legend. Martha told how his Negroes had showed their happiness by unhitching the horses from the shafts of his carriage and replacing the animals with themselves to pull it like a chariot up the steep road to his château. After carrying him into the vestibule and setting him on his feet, the happy blacks, laughing and weeping with joy, kissed the hands and feet of the master and even the ground beneath them. Jefferson would throw his weight behind expansion of slavery and bequeath to the South the image of Hamilton's antislavery views as a Federalist mask for economic exploitation. Samuel Johnson looked contemptuously across the Atlantic and asked, "How is it that we hear the loudest yelps for liberty among the drivers of Negroes?"

The vast lands he had inherited from his dead wife had been added by Jefferson to those he had inherited from his father, but debts and mortgage obligations to Dutch and British creditors went with them and grew larger and more pressing under inattentive absentee management. At home he fitfully busied himself, trying to arrange extensions and moratoriums to avoid having to meet payments on debts he had owed for years. Even with about 10,000 acres and almost 200 slaves, hard money and public credit were scarcer than lands or blacks in Virginia.

British creditors brought constant pressing demands for payment against many large Southern land and slave owners like Jefferson, who were delinquent in debt repayment. National policies that weakened British influence in the country would weaken pro tanto the ability of Britishers or of Americans who were alleged to be former loyalists to collect debts that had been owing to them for years.

As he left Monticello on the long journey to New York City to take office as secretary of state, Jefferson was already sketching plans for redecorating his newly acquired house in Maiden Lane to serve as a suitable setting for candle-light dinners. Though it would be an inconsiderable establishment by comparison with his mansion in Paris or his château at Monticello, he would remodel it for his few months' stay in the city even though it would cost him more than a year's rent to do so.

Senator William Maclay, the doughty democrat from backcountry Pennsylvania, wrote in his diary that Jefferson "had been long enough abroad to catch the tone of European folly." In Philadelphia, where Jefferson stopped off on his way north to his new establishment, the rich Quakeress Deborah Logan reported that he wore "a suit of silk, ruffles, and an elegant topaz ring." Others noted admiringly that the returned diplomat gentleman farmer was "conspicuous in red waistcoat and red breeches, the fashion of Versailles."

When he finally arrived in New York, Jefferson was warmly welcomed by friends like John and Abigail Adams. Two weeks later, Abigail, in a letter to her sister, wrote that Jefferson added much to the society of the capital. One fanciful reminiscer described him as a Parisian fashion plate at an elaborate dinner party given by the Adamses in their great house at Richmond Hill. He soon became the center of another charming coterie in New York.

But he wrote later in his *Anas* of his "wonder and mortification" at the talk at the tables. The conversation, he said, was much about politics: "A preference of kingly over republican government was evidently the favorite sentiment." He disapproved of it.

"An apostate I could not be," he recalled, "nor yet a hypocrite." Despite his dandified dress, he later wrote: "I found myself for the most part, the advocate of the republican side of the question, unless among the guests there chanced to be some member of that party from the legislative houses."

When Jefferson arrived, he would find his department boasted only two clerks: Henry Remsen, Jr., in charge of the foreign office, and Roger Alden, in charge of the home office, both commended to him by John Jay. Alden soon resigned, leaving Remsen the sole clerk, until he too resigned in 1792 to be succeeded by George Taylor. Jefferson's whole staff was five men, including one part-time translator, and he did little to increase its size.

Hamilton, by contrast, had by far the largest departmental staff with 39 on the payroll in his central office at the end of 1789 and 70 by the end of the following year. The field service of the Treasury, under the collectors at the ports, grew by leaps and bounds. Nevertheless, as Jefferson understood the situation, Hamilton's department, supposed to deal only with the single object of revenue, was much more limited and less important than his own, which, as he saw it, was the one "embracing nearly all the objects of administration."

The total annual budget of Jefferson's department, including his own salary of $3,500 (he himself used no dollar sign), was about $8,000. His "staff" did little but copying, and he would try to do many important things that could be done himself or else pass them over to Hamilton or someone else for action.

The department heads were expected to speak in President Washington's name and act only with his approval, in much the same way his wartime aides had done. Usually, each cabinet officer would make up a packet of important correspondence, with drafts of his own proposed reply letters, and send it to the president for review. Washington was orderly, industrious, and exacting, though not dictatorial, and would return these promptly, generally signifying his approval by saying nothing. Sometimes he made comments or queries, and sometimes he would hold letters back until he could have a conference with the writer. At first, he would confer with his aides singly, sometimes asking for written opinions from each of them on the same matter and making the final decision himself only after seeing all opinions. As a result, the policies of his administration were not typically group decisions nor the result of group conferences or of what later came to be called cabinet meetings, but Washington's own decisions, based on his own review of one or another "option" suggested by one or another aide. Lines of responsibility were as clear as they had been in the army. As Jefferson put it, he "formed a central point for the different branches" and "preserved a unity of object and action among them" through his own person. He was not the captain of a team; he was the general of a command to which the departmental heads reported like staff officers.

The status of Hamilton as secretary of the treasury was somewhat different from that of his three colleagues, Jefferson, Knox, and Randolph, because he was expected to be much closer to Congress than they were. Unlike the enabling legislation creating the other departments, the act creating the Treasury provided that he give reports—the key word—to the legislative branch on its request. He was required to digest and prepare plans respecting the revenue and the support of the public credit and report them to Congress periodically, as he had the "First Report on Public Credit." Congress even prescribed the internal structure of his department. Another former military man might have resented these legislative intrusions on his independence as an executive officer, but Hamilton accepted them as a challenge and quickly turned the burden of his special access to the legislature into an element of power.

Washington continued to rely heavily on Hamilton and entrust him with important missions just as he had during the war. The president's own military experience surpassed that of his secretary of war. Dealings with representatives of Britain and France had been a large part of his experience as supreme commander at a time when Jefferson had absented himself in Virginia. But most fiscal and economic matters Washington had always left to Hamilton or others. He well knew the importance of foreign economic aid: it had made it possible for him to lose most of the battles but still win the Revolution. So Washington tended to let Hamilton operate the Treasury under a much looser rein than he gave to his secretary of war or his secretary of state, and the dynamic young secretary of the treasury abhorred a power vacuum. Although it was necessary for Hamilton to gain Washington's approval of the legislative proposals of his program, under the procedure followed in the early months of Washington's administration, at least, it was not necessary for him to win his cabinet colleagues, Knox, Jefferson, or Randolph, to them. Maintenance of the "unity of object and action" of his administration depended on the president alone.

On May 9, Washington was taken with a bad cold. The next day it turned into pneumonia. Two of his three attending physicians gave up hope of saving his life. William Maclay went to call and reported that tears were in every eye. Jefferson who had been laid up almost all the same month with a headache wrote to William Short in London that public alarm had passed all conception and that it proved how much depended on one man's life. Concerned perhaps about Jefferson's health too, Maclay wrote that the secretary had a rambling, vacant look and spoke unceasingly in a loose and rambling way. In foreign affairs he was obviously a poor substitute for Washington, who, it was said, had the look of an uncrowned king.

Washington rallied and soon was able to ride out again in his six-horse carriage, and some said that he looked better than ever. But because he was surrounded by four servants and two gentlemen fore and aft, it was not easy for the curious public to get a good look at him. Washington himself remarked that he had undergone more and more severe illnesses since he had been president than in the 30 previous years together. This was the second severe attack he had had, and he believed that a third would put him to sleep with his fathers. His physicians advised him to take more exercise and apply himself less to business, but, as he wrote Lafayette, he could not escape the conviction that he had to accomplish what he had undertaken to the best of his abilities, come what might.

Washington was fervently hoping that Congress would recess before the summer was over and that he could then get back to Mount Vernon for a long rest when he had made the remark to Lafayette that "I feel myself supported by able coadjutors, who harmonize extremely well together." It was not long after the deal by candlelight at Thomas Jefferson's that these words took on an ironic ring.

When Washington and Jefferson had recovered from their illnesses, Washington took to consulting more often with his department heads. After an important conversation with George Beckwith on July 8, 1790, Hamilton reported to Washington the alarming intelligence that Beckwith's travel plans had been changed because of "the prospect of a war between Great Britain and Spain." Also, the British cabinet "entertained a disposition not only towards a friendly intercourse but towards an alliance with the United States." Beckwith had presumed that it would be in the interest of the United States "to take part with Great Britain rather than with Spain." The background of this new threat of war was that on May 6, Lord Grenville, Pitt's Home Secretary, had written Lord Dorchester, Beckwith's immediate superior, that Spain's seizure of three British ships in Nootka Sound off the western coast of Vancouver Island constituted a hostile act that might lead to war between the two. Grenville feared that such a war would provide the United States a pretext for seizing the posts on the northwest frontier that the British had hung on to since the Revolution.

Washington now requested Jefferson, Hamilton, Jay, Adams, and Knox "to revolve this matter in their minds that they may be better prepared to give me their opinions thereon in the course of two or three days." Passing on Washington's report of these circumstances to John Jay, Hamilton stressed that *"they press."* Jay was to come to the capital to confer about them—even though his father-in-law, Governor William Livingston, was ill and soon to die—because Washington had expressed a "strong wish" that he do so. After talking with Hamilton and Jay, but not Jefferson, Washington directed Hamilton to continue his conversations with Beckwith "very civilly." Hamilton was to make use of the British agent who was making use of him: he was "to intimate, delicately," that Beckwith's remarks carried no official weight and that his references to an alliance were too vague to indicate what the British cabinet really thought. "In a word," Washington explained, Hamilton was to "extract as much as he could from Major Beckwith and report to me, without committing by any assurances whatever, the Government of the United States, leaving it entirely free to pursue, unreproached, such a line of conduct in the dispute as her interest (and honour) shall dictate."

Proceeding to extract all he could, Hamilton kept on with his conversations with Beckwith. In the course of a conversation the following day, July 15, Beckwith reported to his government that Hamilton had told him that any negotiations toward a treaty must originate with the secretary of state, Thomas Jefferson. However, Beckwith should keep Hamilton advised of progress behind the scenes because "our present secretary of state is I am persuaded a gentleman of honor, and jealously desirous of promoting those objects, which the nature of his duty calls for." But "from some opinions which he has given" against the British government "and possible predilections elsewhere" Hamilton feared "there may be difficulties which may possibly frustrate the whole, and which might be readily explained away." If any such difficulties arose with Jefferson, Beckwith should let Hamilton know so that he could make sure they were "clearly understood and candidly examined." Hamilton extracted from Beckwith the intelligence that the British were actively preparing to go to war with Spain and were drawing up plans for a naval attack on New Orleans, for an overland attack against Mexico, and even an expedition "to seize the heart of North America for herself and erect the remainder of America into a client state."

Washington, alarmed by the threat of "so formidable and enterprising a people as the British on both our flanks and rear, with their navy in front," asked Hamilton on August 27 what the government's response should be in case Lord Dorchester "should apply for permission to march troops through the territory of said states from Detroit to the Mississippi." Second, "What notice ought to be taken of the measure, if it should be undertaken without leave, which is the most probable proceeding of the two?" Washington asked Jay, Jefferson, and Knox for their answers to the same questions.

Jefferson's opinion was offhandedly but shrewdly elliptical, covering only a few of the several possibilities. Hamilton took more time, and his reply of September 15, 1790, covered more possibilities. Jefferson preferred to "avoid giving any answer" to Dorchester, should he make the request. "They will proceed notwithstanding," Jefferson went on, "but to do this under our silence, will admit of palliation, and produce apologies, from military necessity; and will leave us free to pass it over without dishonor, or to make it a handle of quarrel hereafter, if we should have use for it as such." Jefferson shrank from coming to a decision on such a difficult question. "If we are obliged to give an answer," he continued, "I think the occasion not such as should induce us to hazard that answer which might commit us to the war at so early a stage of it; and therefore that the passage should be permitted."

This was a step back from the instructions Jefferson had given to the American chargé d'affaires at Madrid, William Carmichael, on August 2 to demand that Spain immediately open the Mississippi to American navigation. He told William Short, United States minister in Paris to advise France that the United States would be hostile to Spain "if she does not yield our right to the common use of the Mississippi." He instructed Gouverneur Morris in London to tell the British government that the United States would remain neutral provided the British would abide by the Treaty of Paris—that is, surrender the northwest posts—and stay away from the Spanish possessions north of the Gulf of Mexico.

These were surprisingly undiplomatic, veiled threats of war against the world's three strongest powers, but were made without at the same time having prepared American public opinion for war or even making any military preparedness efforts. Notwithstanding the provocative threat he ordered Carmichael to deliver to Spain, Jefferson told him privately that it was "not our interest to cross the Mississippi for ages, and will never be our interest to remain united with those who do." It added up to hasty but undiplomatic, quixotic, blustery, and dangerous, backing and filling on the part of the secretary of state. Hamilton by contrast made his reply to Washington the occasion for a careful review of all American foreign policy. It reads as if he, not Jefferson, were the secretary of state. Hamilton thought Washington should call a special session of Congress to make preparations for war, if it should come, and in the meanwhile open negotiations to determine what concessions could be obtained by an agreement that the United States would remain neutral in the impending war. The United States had "much to dread from war; much to expect from peace."

Economic considerations were important. The nation should cultivate "commercial . . . intercourse with all the world in the broadest basis of reciprocal privilege." Its "true policy," therefore, was to "cultivate neutrality." Any "permanent interest" or "particular connection" with any foreign power should be avoided. Hamilton believed that the United States must eventually annex the Northwest into its territory and take possession of the Mississippi Valley, its outlet at New Orleans, and the Floridas as well.

As for the passage of British troops, because it would be by water "and almost wholly through an uninhabited part of the country, if it were unaccompanied with any violence to our citizens or posts, it would seem sufficient to be content with remonstrating against it, but with a tone that would not commit us to the necessity of going to war." But if they should force the American post on the Wabash River by arms, "there seems to be no alternative but to go to war with them, unwelcome as it may be." It was a long and masterful paper. It examined one by one all the options open to Washington with detail and precision.

France failed to come to Spain's support. Spain gave in to Britain's demands. The Nootka Sound crisis died down as suddenly as it had blown up. But it had provided Washington with a set of examination papers by which he could rate the performances of the three men he looked on as his ministers for foreign affairs, Jay, Hamilton, and Jefferson. On the strength, depth, and thoroughness of his analysis, though not for its brevity, Hamilton had to be placed at the head of the class.

It was late summer and vacation time. American officials were too busy scattering to their homes and plantations to concentrate on getting organized for a really first-class war. On September 15, still in New York City, Hamilton wrote Betsy, who was in Saratoga with the children, a rather perfunctory but typical letter of a summer bachelor to his absent wife. "I am the only one of the Administration now here . . ." he wrote her. "You do not hope in vain my love that I am tired of living alone." But "it might be very awkward for me to be absent also." He is sad that he cannot join her, but for some as yet unrevealed reason he seems oddly uneager for her to hurry back down to rejoin him: "Your health may be benefitted by your continuance where you are somewhat longer."

Angelica Church had earlier written him with an intuitive touch of reproach for his epistolary neglect of her: "Many thanks my dear brother for having written to his friend at a moment when he had the affairs of America on his mind." Did feminine intuition whisper to her that a lesser affair was also on his mind? She was "extremely anxious for your success," but "I sometimes think you have now forgot me and that having seen me is like a dream which you can scarcely believe. Adieu I will not write this idea of being lost in the tumult of business and ambition does not enliven my spirits—*Adieu soyez heureux audessus de tout le monde.*"

Hamilton replied—eight months later—lamely and tamely on September 2, "I cannot let the packet go my dear friend without dropping you a line to prove to you that you are always of more consequence than the great affairs which you have so often represented as the rival of all my friendships."

There was simply no letup at the Treasury. As Thomas Jefferson prepared to leave for Monticello for two months or more, he asked Hamilton at the Treasury on August 28 to make him out a blank check to cover all the expenses he might have on his trip, "which I am absolutely unable to calculate before hand." Jefferson said he would be responsible "for the due application of the money for which an account shall be rendered, on my return." He ordered Hamilton to take care of one other thing: "The collections of the Acts of Congress are to be sent to the members" by post "and ought to be franked; but I shall not be present to perform that duty." Would Hamilton please take care of it? And would he also kindly frank any other official state papers that might have to be sent out in his absence?

Hamilton would oblige. Neither he nor foreign affairs would much miss the secretary for foreign affairs while he was gone.

4

A PROSPECTUS FOR THE SUM—AND U.S.A., INC.

EVERY NEW SCENE WHICH IS OPENED TO THE BUSY NATURE OF
MAN TO ROUSE AND EXERT HIMSELF, IS THE ADDITION OF A NEW
ENERGY TO THE GENERAL STOCK OF EFFORT.
—*"Report on Manufactures," December 5, 1791*

From Hamilton's point of view, the new law of July 16, 1790, which provided that "prior to the first Monday in December next, all offices attached to the seat of the government of the United States, shall be moved to Philadelphia," was merely a personal inconvenience to be cheerfully endured for the sake of the mid-June deal by candlelight at Thomas Jefferson's that had clinched the passage of assumption, the cornerstone of Hamilton's program to establish public credit for America. On August 5, Hamilton asked his old friend Colonel Walter Stewart to find him a new house in his least favorite town. "My next wish," he wrote, "would be to have a house as near my destined office as possible. A cool situation & exposure will of course be a very material point to a New Yorker. The house must have at least six rooms. Good dining and drawing rooms are material articles. I like elbow room in a yard. As to the rent the lower the better consistently with the acquisition of a proper house." He had asked James Wilson to be on the lookout for a house, too; so when Stewart found one, he should let

Wilson know, "For *two houses* would be more than I shall *probably* have occasion for."

Three weeks later he wrote Stewart that he had engaged a house for an office at the corner of Chestnut and Third Streets and asked Stewart to find a residence as close as possible to this. When he finally found one close enough —at the corner of Walnut and Third in the so-called "court end of town"—Betsy and the four children moved down to join him with no more than the usual misgivings any New Yorkers might experience moving to Philadelphia. After a while, the Hamiltons would move to a house further away from his office, outside the city and close to Robert Morris's estate, where they would remain for most of the next five years.

Writing from London, Angelica moved with them in spirit, but with unhappy foreboding. She wrote Betsy that "my inclinations lead me to prefer New York," but "If you remain at Philadelphia, I must be there." With characteristically expressive rush of elision and sly setoff, of endearments with commas, she added, "My affections where you reside, but not altogether for my love to you Eliza, my dear, Hamilton has his share in this determination."

Soon after reaching Philadelphia, Abigail Adams wrote her daughter, "If New York wanted any revenge for the removal, the citizens might be glutted if they could come here, where every article has been almost doubled in price, and where it is not possible for Congress and the appendages to be half as well accommodated for a long time."

Hamilton helped out Washington's secretary Tobias Lear by sending down his old New York barber, John Wood, with a letter of introduction on October 29, 1790. Wood "shaved and dressed me in New York" and was "sober and punctual and has done my business to my satisfaction. He desires to have the honor of dealing with the heads and chins of some of your family."

Other officials took up residence in the greater city, with its population of more than 60,000, with a similar lack of enthusiasm. Oliver Wolcott, Jr., wrote his father, complaining that "the manners of the people are more reserved than in New York." After having seen "many of their principal men," he had "seen nothing to tempt [him] to idolatry." After a closer acquaintance, he still had no "self-humiliating sensations." According to the blunter comments of Jeremiah Smith, "The Philadelphians are from the highest to the lowest, from the parson in his black gown to the fille de joie or girl of pleasure, a set of beggars. You cannot turn around without paying a dollar."

The principal streets of the period were Front, Second, Third, and Fourth. Beyond Sixth there were few habitations. Along Arch and Chestnut Streets west of Tenth, the land was thickly dotted with frog ponds, and practically all of business and fashion was to be found east of Fourth Street. The houses were attractive, mostly of brick, often with a shop on the street floor. Many were architecturally pretentious, suggesting comfort and solidity if not opulence.

An English tourist observed that with the exception of Broad and High Streets the thoroughfares were not more than 50 feet wide. They reminded him of "many of the smaller streets of London except that the foot pavement on either side is of brick instead of stone." The streets were paved with pebbles in the middle, a gutter made of brick or wood, and lined with strong posts and trees, which protected the sidewalks. At frequent intervals town pumps offered refreshment to the thirsty. In the night, according to Brissot de Warville, they served as accommodating hanging-posts for inebriates staggering home from the popular taverns. In summer, many of the ordinary houses would offer to the view a garden filled with old-fashioned flowers—lilacs, roses, pinks, and tulips, morning glories and snowballs, and gourd vines climbing up over spacious, open porches. But around the grounds of the largest mansions walls shut off the view from the common folk, who could only catch whiffs of the fragrance of the hidden gardens when a breeze wafted it up and out over the parapets.

The governmental centers were close together. Congress Hall was at Sixth and Chestnut Streets next to the State House, now Independence Hall. There a visitor who found his way into the gallery and looked down upon the House chamber, 100 by 60 feet, with semicircular rows of seats facing the Speaker's rostrum—"a kind of pulpit near the center"—could see an Ames busy at his circular writing desk, a Madison on his feet, or a Sedgwick in conference with a lobbyist. The precincts of the Senate were on the floor above, but their sessions were closed to public view. John Beckley, the clerk of the House, and the other clerks had offices near it on the upper floor at the top of the stairs, just off the hall leading to the Senate chamber.

Jefferson's office was a two-story brick building at Third and Chestnut, which had been taken over for the purposes of the State Department. Next door, Hamilton's Treasury office was the old Pemberton mansion with a well-cultivated garden in the rear. A short distance away was George Washington's residence in the Robert Morris town house. Washington lived there as the paying guest of Morris, who was praised by many for his sacrifice in giving up his home. But one sour New Yorker doubted that Morris's "giving up a house of moderate dimensions for 700 pounds a year can be deemed a great sacrifice . . . when . . . the President was accommodated in this city [New York] with a much more elegant house at 400 pounds per annum."

If properly presented, the visitor to the presidential residence might be received by Washington with a rather cold, stately bow and be offered a cup of tea with Mrs. Washington. If the invitation were for a dinner, it was sure to be a bountiful one. Senator Maclay, who was a frequent guest, described one menu in detail. The soup was followed by roasted and boiled fish; then came fowls and a variety of meats. For dessert there were pies, puddings, and ice creams; then a variety of fruits and nuts. The important business of eating was transacted with solemnity, scarcely a word being said until the tablecloth had been removed. Then the host would drum on the table with a spoon and arise and drink a toast to every person round the table. The other men would then offer their own responding toasts as their turns came round. Those whose social or political status did not gain them an invitation to the Washingtons might, with patience, see the great man as he drove forth in his ornately decorated coach or, sometimes, as he walked with his secretaries, Tobias Lear and William Jackson, one on either side, hats cocked forward on their heads, the aides a little to the rear of the president. On their little walks he did not stoop to converse with his secretaries.

Private houses opened their doors to members of Congress. Their owners turned them into rooming houses and made the same kind of hospitable sacrifice as Robert Morris had by taking them in as high-paying guests. Francis the Frenchman, on Fourth Street, rented a room to Vice-president Adams, who frequently had his meals served upstairs in his rooms. The head of the table downstairs was reserved for him; and when he did come down, all ceremonial forms were scrupulously observed. Fisher Ames moved out of the Indian Queen, which had gone downhill since the days when so many delegates had lodged there during the Constitutional Convention. He found lodgings "at the house of Mrs. Sage," where he finally began "to feel settled and at home." The boarding-houses had their famous romances, too. One day Senator Aaron Burr took James Madison to pay a call upon the winsome daughter of his own landlady, and history was made for the dry, little bachelor in Dolley Todd's candlelit parlor.

Hamilton, like many a successful lawyer, had saved little from the income of his law practice. He was generous to a fault and too busy with national finances to give much thought to his family budget. The move from New York was costly, and prices were much higher in Philadelphia, but, as a prominent member of Washington's cabinet, Hamilton was the last man to try to live below the standards expected of his station. While he worked on his "Further Report on the Public Credit" and his "Report on a National Bank" and his "Report on the Mint" and his "Report on Manufactures" and continually made arrangements for new foreign loans of as much as $14,000,000 and more, he was often in debt to his friends for small sums of money.

Betsy paid some bills out of her own money or contrived to postpone them and stretched the family income miraculously and acquired some public credit of her own for efficient household management. Intimate friends like James McHenry knew how much she was helping out her husband. He wrote Hamilton on January 3, 1791, "Pray present me to Mrs. Hamilton. I have learned from a friend of yours that she has as much merit as your treasurer as you have as treasurer of the wealth of the United States."

On December 13, 1790, Hamilton laid before the House of Representatives two more of his great reports. One was his report on the "further provision" necessary for establishing public credit, and the other, which had been promised in the first report he had submitted back in January, was the "Report on a National Bank." *Report* is not a word that adequately encompasses Hamilton's great reports. It has overtones and undertones of children's essays in school or else of murky, voluminous word products of modern "think tanks" and foundations, which shovel in all facts and opinions and balance all pros and cons to produce an innocuous, praiseworthy conclusion. By its Treasury Department enabling legislation, after much debate, Congress had purposefully used the word *report,* for what the secretary should present to it, in place of another word such as *recommendation,* which had broader, more dynamic, more forceful connotations. But Hamilton characteristically saw in the word *report* implied powers that Congress had failed to see. His separate "reports" turned out to be the separate building blocks of one great legislative program for the nation that the Washington administration through Hamilton was laying before Congress block by block. As Hamilton presented it, each piece came complete with sheaves of historic, philosophical, and economic background material; avalanches of statistics; precipitates of domestic and international implications; projections as to future operation; and estimates of political impact. Drafts of proposed implementing legislation were appended. They were so complete that congressional debates on the proposed legislation were often reduced merely to such matters as reasserting with greater or lesser emphasis the same points that Hamilton's report had covered, weighed, and made positive judgments about. The material in the reports thus preempted much of the opposition's factual and logical ground for opposition and reduced it to more or less emotional, partisan, personal, petty, or predictable Pavlovian political responses.

The first of the two reports of December 13, 1790, was a proposal for paying the interest on the state debts that the Union had now assumed. Such interest would begin to accrue after 1791, and the amount necessary to pay it, Hamilton calculated, would be $826,624.73. His means of raising it? A further tax on foreign and domestic distilled whiskey.[1]

Of greater importance was the second of the two: his "Report on a National Bank." Its importance was as much for what it did not say as for what it said, as much for what it represented as for what it recommended. Its opening sentence announced that "a national bank is an institution of primary importance to the prosperous administration of the finances, and would be of the greatest utility in the operations connected with the support of public credit."

Hamilton had, accordingly, devised a plan for one upon a scale that would entitle it to public confidence and "render it equal to the exigencies of the public." *Exigencies,* like *energy,* was one of Hamilton's favorite words. It always signified that he considered the subject to be discussed one of supreme economic importance. Of the three existing banks, the Bank of North America in Philadelphia, the Bank of New York, and the Bank of Massachusetts in Boston, only the first had ever had a direct relation to the government. But the new state charter imposed on it by Pennsylvania was now so "materially variant from the original one" and "so narrows the foundation of the institution, as to render it an incompetent basis for the extensive purposes of a national bank."

Hamilton's politically unacknowledgeable model was the Bank of England. The similarities included partial limitation of liability of shareholders, prohibitions against trade in commodities, prohibition of financial aid to the state without legislative approval, and strict limits on any branch banks. In order "to attach full confidence to an institution of this nature, it appears to be an essential ingredient in its structure that it shall be under a *private* not a *public* Direction, under the guidance of *individual interest,* not of public policy; which would be supposed to be . . . liable to being too much influenced by public necessity." He added vividly that "public necessity" would "most probably be a canker, that would continually corrode the vitals of the credit of the bank."

By contrast, the bank would prosper under "the keen steady, and, as it were magnetic sense, of their own interest, as proprietors, in the Directors of a bank, pointing invariably to its true pole, the prosperity of the institution." This is "the only security, that can always be relied upon, for a careful and prudent administration."

Back in 1779, as a youth of 22, Hamilton had written a famous letter to Robert Morris, advocating a national bank; and, during the 11 years since, he had never let the subject drop. In letter after letter, in address after address, in private conversation and in public debate, to Continental Congress, Confederation Congress, and now Union Congress, he had insisted that a bank underwritten by, but only partially controlled by, the national government was the fundamental basis for a successful system of public finance.

Now that he was secretary of the treasury, his was an idea whose time and office had come. Pressing forward on the momentum of his just-won battle for assumption, using his first "Report on the Public Credit" as a springboard, he put forth his "Second Report on the Further Provision Necessary for Establishing Public Credit," now known as the "Report on a National Bank," which was a plan somewhat narrower in conception than his earlier plans. It provided that the government might acquire one-fifth of the shares and could name five out of the 25 directors. It was, therefore, a bank more clearly under private control than in his earlier proposals, really a private bank with semipublic functions, just as the Bank of England was.[2]

The organizational details, not important now, included a capital stock of $10,000,000 divided into 25,000 shares, of which the United States might subscribe to 5,000, the balance being open to private subscription; shares were payable one-fourth in gold or silver, and three-fourths in the 6 percent public debt.

The bank was to have the power to issue notes, limited only by the provision that the total of its debts could not exceed its deposits by more than $10,000,000. These notes were to be payable on demand and would be legal tender for all obligations to the United States. Loans were limited to a 6 percent interest rate. The government would have the right to borrow the $2,000,000 it had paid into the bank and repay the loan in ten annual installments. The sole economic interest of the government in the bank was to consist of its share in the profits, its borrowings, and the receipt of reports as to its condition and resources. In all other respects, the bank would be a private venture.[3]

Its charter was to run for 20 years; it was to be a unique monopoly during its existence. Branch banks might be established, but only for convenience of discount and deposit. With its large capital, the national bank would, in effect, be able to create money on the basis of public debt. The fact that three-fourths of the capital could be paid in certificates of the public debt, instead of gold or silver, would greatly increase the available supply of money. He explained it thus: "The chief object of this is to enable the creation of a capital sufficiently large to be the basis of an extensive circulation, and an adequate security for it. . . ." This would reduce dependence on gold and silver, for ". . . to collect such a sum in this country, in gold and silver, into one depository, may, without hesitation, be pronounced impractical."

Hamilton further explained: "This part of the fund will always be ready to come in aid of the specie. It will more and more command a ready sale; and can therefore be expeditiously be turned into coin if an exigency of the bank should at any time require it."[4] Hamilton shrewdly omitted from his report any discussion of the inflationary effects of the bank's power to create new money based on public debt, without specie backing. He knew that this had been an important issue in the debates over the rechartering of the Bank of North America that had helped to destroy its usefulness as a national bank.

The economic purposes of the bank were sound. It was an important institution; in many ways it was the forerunner of the national central bank, the Federal Reserve System. Its insulation from governmental politics, the "canker" that would "corrode the vitals" of the money, was an idea that the experience of recent years suggests was not only far ahead of its time, but timeless. Important as they were, the economic consequences of the bank were less remarkable than the political consequences of Hamilton's report and the legislation he introduced to carry it out.

In the political sense, the most important thing in the report was the legal point that the great constitutional lawyer had left out of it: It made no mention of the question of whether Congress had the power under the Constitution to charter a national bank. Yet this point, too, had been a much vexed one in the debates over the rechartering of the Bank of North America. In the inscrutable way that great events unfold, Hamilton's "Report on the National Bank," which nowhere mentioned constitutional powers, would become the vehicle by which Hamilton set Washington's administration firmly on the side of broad, not strict, construction of the Constitution. This is the construction that finds in it implied powers, powers that are inherent in government though not expressly stated, the existence of which had been left in doubt by the record of the Convention of 1787.

Hamilton's dryly detailed plan turned out to be even more controversial and explosive than assumption had been. Out of it grew the unending debate on the theory and capabilities of the Constitution of the United States that has continued to the present day, with only a little loss of original heat. Out of it grew the great decisions of Chief Justice John Marshall and the doctrine of "implied powers," without which the Constitution as a living instrument of government would probably soon have become unworkable. With it, the aged instrument has continued strong and flexible through all the changing stresses of 200 years.

The immediate impact of the report on the public was also prodigious, but in a different way. Fisher Ames sent a copy of it to a friend, with the comment: "The late surprising rise of public stock is supposed to be owing in part to this report, because it affords an opportunity to subscribe three fourths paper and one fourth silver into the bank stock." Sir John Temple, British minister in Philadelphia in charge of British financial interests, advised his government that "some of the Public Securities of these States have risen 16, & 17/ the pound! and are still rising! The Dutch have been great Purchasers into these funds, and if nothing should happen to alter present appearances, they will have made great proffit indeed by their purchases, two & three for one!" Just as the speculative excitement produced by funding and assumption were wearing off, Hamilton's proposal for a national bank gave the worldwide markets in the public securities of the United States another upward boost.

Senator Maclay read the report, considered it "an aristocratic engine," doubted its constitutionality, yet feared the bank would pass. It vexed him to despair. He was grieved that Washington seemed oblivious to all the trickery his Treasury secretary was up to. "Would to God this same General Washington were in heaven! We would not then have him brought forward as the constant cover to every unconstitutional and irrepublican act."

As Maclay had feared, the Senate acted first and passed the bank bill. Maclay's amendment to give the government the right to subscribe on equal terms with individuals failed. Robert Morris reported that Philip Schuyler had told him that Hamilton insisted that there should be no amendments to the bill. Maclay scoffed, "Schuyler is the supple-jack of his son-in-law Hamilton."

The House was the arena where the battle over the report on the bank reached its climax, but its members were slow to pick up another of Hamilton's bristly porcupines. Finally, after three leisurely readings, on February 1, 1791, Jackson of Georgia opened debate. By now a determined foe of every Hamilton measure, he charged that the plan was "calculated to benefit a small part of the United States, the mercantile interest only; the farmers, the yeomanry, will derive no advantage from it." Then he struck at the fundamental weakness. "This bank," he cried, "is unconstitutional! We have no power to grant a charter to any private corporation!" With a triumphant smile, he quoted passages from *The Federalist Papers*—written by Hamilton, Madison, and Jay—to prove his point.

This set the stage once more for the entrance of the first man of the House, James Madison. When he rose to speak on a subject like *The Federalist* or the meaning of the Constitution, no one on the floor could gainsay him; off the floor there was no one but Hamilton.

Madison's speech in opposition from the floor had been the climax of the drama of assumption. His quietude during and after the candlelight dinner at Thomas Jefferson's had been the second, if glum silence can properly be called a climax. Now to a third climax of the drama of Hamilton's great reports, he rose: To speak against the bank.[5]

He well recollected, he said, "that a power to grant charters of incorporation had been proposed in the General Convention and rejected." His constitutional argument was careful, dispassionate, legalistic, powerful, and basically quite simple: you must adhere strictly to the letter of the document. It did not specifically permit incorporation of a bank. The simplistic symmetry of Madison's argument was unanswerable, if there were no such thing as an implied power. Madison's argument became the basis of all future arguments for "strict con-

struction." In his later opinion to Washington on the bank, Jefferson took over
Madison's arguments almost word for word.

Fisher Ames replied the following day. The ablest of Hamilton's supporters
in the House, he did not attempt to meet Madison on his own ground. Instead,
he invoked Hamilton's ground—the doctrine of "implied powers." "If Congress
may not make laws conformably to the powers plainly implied, though not
expressed in the frame of government," he asserted, "it is rather late in the day
to adopt it as a principle of conduct. A great part of our two years' labor is lost,
and worse than lost to the public, for we have scarcely made a law in which we
have not exercised our discretion with regard to the true intent of the Constitution." Of what use was the power to borrow, as expressly provided for in the
Constitution, if its most efficient instrument, a bank, were not implied in that
power?[6]

These two powerful statements of the issue drew a significant demarcation
line between the political philosophies of the two great emerging parties—
Federalist and Republican—but not the only such line. Another significant line
—a geographical line—seemed to divide the continent laterally on such issues.
William Giles of Virginia was specific—and filled with foreboding: "I have observed with regret a radical difference of opinion between gentlemen from the
Eastern and Southern States, upon great Governmental questions, and have
been led to conclude, that the operation of that cause alone might cast ominous
conjecture on the promised success of this much valued Government."

By this time, no simple solution of the issue at a candlelight dinner of the
three men at Thomas Jefferson's was possible. The relationships of the three
men had changed, primarily because of Jefferson's bitterness at allegedly having
been tricked by Hamilton into holding a candle to poor Madison at the first. But
none was necessary. By February 8, 1791, the opponents of the bank had played
out all possible variations on their one-note argument for strict construction. It
was, indeed, an argument not easy to elaborate much beyond the simple two-
word phrase. Hamilton's bill passed by an overwhelming margin of 39 to 20.[7]

Less than a week after submitting his two monumental reports, the "further provision" for public credit and "Report on the Bank," to Congress, Hamilton demonstrated that mastery of grand continental plans had not blunted the
seemingly manic intensity he could focus on the tiniest details of Treasury
departmental administration. Into one of the frequent Treasury Department
circulars, with which he constantly harried the collectors at the ports into more
efficient collections, he wrote five pages of instructions on how to determine
duties on distilled liquors by the use of Dycas's hydrometer.

"It may serve to aid the officers to be informed," he informed them, "that
the first of the classes of the proof mentioned in the law corresponds with Gin,
the second with St. Croix rum, the third with Antigua rum, the fourth with
Jamaica spirits, the fifth with the usual strength of high wines, & the sixth or
last with what is called *Alcohol.*"

He gave detailed directions for operation of the gadget and followed them
with specific example:

Suppose the degree of the Temperature found by the Thermometer to be 40. Place then 40, the corresponding graduation on the left of the Slider in coincidence with the stem of the *flower de liece,* . . . Look for the last number on the Slider, and directly above it on the Scale you find the number 10 which denotes the liquor is ten cent above proof. etc.

I am, sir, your obedient servant,

Alexander Hamilton

P.S. You will also receive herewith a Tin Cylinder which you will find useful for containing the liquor to be proved.

Although both houses of Congress had passed the bank bill, the loud cries that it was unconstitutional troubled Washington, and he declined to sign it. He asked Randolph, the attorney general, for his opinion. Randolph declared it unconstitutional. He next asked Jefferson, his secretary of state. On February 15, Jefferson also returned a written opinion, which repeated Madison's "strict construction" argument: the bank was unconstitutional.

As Jefferson elaborated, the proposed incorporation of a bank did not come within any of the delegated powers, either enumerated or nonenumerated: "To take a single step beyond the boundaries thus especially drawn around the powers of Congress, is to take possession of a boundless field of power, no longer susceptible of any definition." He dismissed as quibbling the argument that the "necessary and proper" clause ("to make all laws necessary and proper," and so on) justified the bank. The enumerated powers, he said, "can all be carried into execution without a bank. A bank therefore is not necessary, and consequently not authorized by this phrase." It is easy to imagine that Southern speculators who had bought up public debt, hoping it would rise further with passage of the bill listening in panic as word spread among insiders that their powerful leaders Madison, Randolph, and Jefferson were telling their fellow Virginian Washington to veto the bill, and unloading. With the opinions of three self-proclaimed men of the people opposing the vote of the people's branch of the government in hand, Washington turned to Hamilton. The opinion he would receive from the constitutional lawyer who was the author of the report on the question of its constitutionality would not be one likely to take him by surprise.

It was up to Hamilton as a minority of one to overcome the majority of three formidable Virginians, Madison, Randolph, and Jefferson, in their attempt to persuade a fourth to go along with them. A solid majority against him was an exigency that often summoned up Hamilton's best energies.

Washington sent Randolph's and Jefferson's opinions to Hamilton with a letter dated February 16, in which he wrote, "I now require yours on the validity and propriety of the [Act] . . . that you may know the points on which the Secretary of State and the Attorney-General dispute the constitutionality of the act, and that I may be fully possessed of the arguments *for* and *against* the measure before I express any opinion of my own, I give you an opportunity of examining & answering the objections . . . I require the return of them when your own sentiments are handed to me (which I wish may be as soon as convenient); and further, that no copies of them be taken. . . ."

The stern tone and admonition to secrecy of Washington's letter must have reminded Hamilton of the seriousness of his own position. There could be no doubt of what his conclusion would be. But preservation of his preeminent place in Washington's councils depended on the force of his rebuttal to Madison's, Randolph's and Jefferson's arguments. No secretary of the treasury who was also a lawyer could expect to keep his reputation if his bills stirred up the speculators, roiled both houses of Congress, outraged Washington's fellow Virginians, and were, or were widely believed to be, unconstitutional to boot.

Hamilton's opinion to Washington of February 23, 1791, is one of the major state papers of American history. His argument was not narrowly limited to the question of banks or corporations generally, but went to the fundamental meaning of the constitution itself. He struck at the jugular of the opposition's argument in terms that Washington and the people could easily follow. Narrow, legalistic "principles of construction like those espoused by the Secretary of State and the Attorney General would be fatal to the just and indispensable authority of the United States," he wrote.

Furthermore, Jefferson's and Randolph's objections "are founded on a general denial of the authority of the United States to erect corporations."

They were wrong, Hamilton said, because

> This *general principle* is *inherent* in the very *definition of government*, and *essential* to every step of the progress to be made by that of the United States; namely—That every power vested in a government is in its nature *sovereign*, and includes, by *force* of the *term*, a right to employ all the *means* requisite and fairly *applicable* to the attainment of the *ends* of such power; and which are not precluded by restrictions and exceptions specified in the Constitution; or not immoral, or not contrary to the essential ends of political society.

He insisted "that there are *implied*, as well as *express* powers, and that the former are as effectually delegated as the latter."

Therefore, it followed, "that as a power of erecting a corporation may as well be *implied* as any other thing; it may as well be employed as an *instrument* or *mean* of carrying into execution any of the specified powers. . . ."

Incorporation, Hamilton argued, was only a means to an end. If the end were a "necessary and proper" object of the government created by the Constitution, incorporation of a bank would be "necessary and proper." Jefferson had misread the word *necessary*. Jefferson maintained "that no means are to be considered as *necessary*, than those without which the grant of power would be nugatory."

But, as Hamilton saw it, "neither the grammatical, nor popular sense of the term requires that construction." Ordinary people's understanding should prevail over Jefferson's narrow technicality: "*Necessary* often means no more than needful, requisite, incidental, useful, or conducive to."

Hamilton recognized that "it is a common mode of expression to say, that it is *necessary* for a government or person to do this or that thing, when nothing more is intended or understood, than that the interests of the government or person require, or will be promoted by, the doing of this or that thing." This is the true meaning, he said, "in which it is used in the constitution. The whole turn of the clause containing it [so] indicates. It was the intent of the convention, by that clause to give a liberal latitude to the exercise of the specified powers."

Therefore, because the bank bill did not abridge a preexisting right of any state or individual, a strong presumption existed in favor of its constitutionality.

Hamilton rested his case.

With remarkable promptness, Hamilton sent his monumental "Opinion on the Constitutionality of an Act to Establish a Bank" (70 pages in the Hamilton Papers) to Washington within a week of his request. It quickly plugged the large hole he seemed to have purposely left in his original report. His offhand reference to it in his transmittal letter of February 23 seemed to share an inside joke with Washington: Hamilton "presents his respects to the President and sends him the opinion required which occupied him the greatest part of last night."

Washington was not noted for his ability to weigh all such abstruse arguments and calculations set down in longhand and issue quick decisions. Yet he signed the bank bill, and it became law on February 25, 1791, two days after he had received Hamilton's overnight opinion. Only if Washington had been fully familiar with and convinced of the rightness of Hamilton's opinion long before he asked for it in writing would this time sequence of these events be otherwise than unbelievable.

On Hamilton's opinion are based all later arguments and opinions upholding the Constitution as a flexible instrument of modern government. When in 1819 Chief Justice Marshall affirmed the constitutionality of the bank in the case of *McCullough vs. Maryland,* Hamilton's opinion on the Bank was the foundation of the Supreme Court's reasoning. On Hamilton's doctrine of implied powers, which has prevailed most of the time since, over Madison's and Jefferson's doctrine of strict construction rests the case for calling Hamilton, not Madison or anyone else, the father of the living Constitution.

If one tin cylinder "useful for containing the liquor to be proved" had not yet been sent on to a collector, Hamilton in his office at the Pemberton house may have filled it "with what is called *alcohol,*" placed "the gradation on the left of the Slider in coincidence with the stem of the *flower de liece,*" lifted it high with a smile, and downed the whole cup in one gulp.

The success of yet another segment of Hamilton's system infuriated Jefferson. He later claimed that Hamilton had bought off the opposition by giving them speculator's profits: "While our Government was still in its most infant state," he fumed, "it enabled Hamilton so to strengthen himself by corrupt services to many that he could afterwards carry his bank scheme, and every measure proposed in defiance of all opposition."

Hamilton, undaunted, swiftly pressed his winning streak. When his "further provision" for an increase of import duties and internal excise taxes came before Congress, there was little trouble about the import duties, but internal excise taxes touched off another one of the violent debates that were becoming the usual reaction to Hamilton's reports. The unwillingness of people to pay taxes "even very moderate in their amount" engaged Hamilton's ready sympathy. It was a disarming theme running through all of his writings on the subject, but such words did not disarm Congress. In general, and predictably, the popular branch of government was loath to levy any type of internal taxes. The states maintained that such taxes were in their sole province. Besides, the farmers and artisans of the representatives' constituencies felt that they bore on themselves with unequal hardship.

The particular tax that Hamilton pressed, a tax on whiskey, aroused extreme opposition at the fringes of the country. The settlers on the western frontiers could market their grain in the East for cash only in the form of easily transportable liquor. Four years later the same opposition would explode into armed rebellion. Even so, Congress, under the lash of Hamilton's dynamic party, laid duties on domestic spirits of 9 to 25 cents a gallon, among other taxes, and passed his proposed "further provision" for funding of state debts into the Act of March 3, 1791.

The Pennsylvania frontiersmen, like those of North Carolina and Western Virginia, were hard hit by these measures. Their spokesman, Senator Maclay, grew more discouraged and bitter, but more vocal than ever before. Of the Excise Bill he wrote: "War and bloodshed are the most likely consequences of all this. Congress may go home. Mr. Hamilton is all-powerful, and fails in nothing he attempts."

Hamilton pressed on with his newly won power. In response to an order of the House to him of April 15, 1790, he laid before Congress his "Report on the Establishment of a Mint," of January 28, 1791, which runs to 145 pages, including editorial apparatus, in the Hamilton Papers. A mint was not just molding machines and printing presses and plates for churning out money, he pointed out. Its operations, like a national bank's, extended into the furthest recesses of national money management. As Hamilton explained it, a mint involved "considerations intricate, nice and important," and he added, "A plan for an establishment of this nature must not only contemplate the principles of a coinage of the United States, but must extend to the coins of all other countries which shall have been introduced into them. All the revenues of the country; the general state of debtor and creditor; all the relations and consequences of *price;* the essential interests of trade and industry; the value of all property, the whole income both of the state and of individuals are liable to be sensibly influenced, beneficially or otherwise, by the judicious or injudicious regulation of this interesting object."

Those who pejorate Hamilton as a "conservative" ignore his unmatched record of incessant calls for reform. The "question naturally arises," he noted, "whether it may not be most advisable to leave things, in this respect, in the state in which they are. Why, since they have so long proceeded in a train, which has caused no general sensation of inconvenience, should alterations be attempted, the precise effect of which cannot be calculated?" He had a quick answer. He knew, if his opposition could not see, "the immense disorder, which actually reigns in so delicate and important a concern" as national monetary policy. And so, "The still greater disorder, which is every moment possible, calls loudly for a reform."

The dollar had depreciated in value. This depreciated the value of property dependent on past contracts. Fluctuations in value of foreign money under regulation of foreign sovereigns affected domestic values. Moreover, "Unequal values were allowed in different parts of the Union to coins of the same intrinsic worth, and counterfeits, defective species of them, embarrass the circulation of some of the states." At the time, the pound was the money of account in all the states; there were also many standard coins, including the dollar, but it had never had a fixed value in terms of gold or the pound or any other certain standard. Gold specie had greater stability as a standard of value than silver.

But after weighing all arguments for either gold or silver as the monetary reserve unit, Hamilton decided in favor of both, with silver and gold as legal tender at a ratio of 15 to 1. Despite "the prejudices of mankind," there was no intrinsic, or inherent difference between the two metals, except that gold's greater scarcity as a commodity tended to make it more stable in value. Bank circulation as an expandable *auxiliary* to, but not as a complete substitute for the two precious metals was what was most important. Use of both gold and silver as a reserve was necessary, he wrote, because "to annul the use of either of the metals as money, is to abridge the quantity of circulating medium, and is liable to all the objections which arise from a comparison of the benefits of a full, with the evils of a scanty circulation."

He deplored persons who acted from "a fanciful predilection to Gold" and pointed out the error of thinking that gold or silver coins in circulation "are to be considered as bullion, or in other words, as a raw material." What happened was that "the adoption of them, as money, has caused them to become the fabric." That is, as coins, regardless of the metal content, they have "a sanction and efficacy equivalent to the stamp of the sovereign." He was troubled by the twin problems of inflation and deflation: "There is scarcely any point, in the economy of national affairs of greater moment, than the preservation of the intrinsic value of the money unit. On this the security and steady value of property depend."

He discussed the effects of favorable and adverse trade balances on the money of the country and also the effects caused by adjustments of exchange rates and transfers of gold from one country to another to balance out imbalances between nations. The situation of France, as an example of a self-sufficient country able to surmount easily any mistakes in her government's economic management, called forth singular admiration, when compared to the situation of Britain:

> There is perhaps no part of Europe, which has so little need of other countries, as France. Comprehending a variety of soils and climates, an

immense population, its agriculture in a state of mature improvement, it possesses within its own bosom most, if not all the productions of the earth, which any of its most favored neighbors can boast. The variety, abundance and excellence of its wines constitute a peculiar advantage in its favor. Arts and manufactures are there also in a very advanced state—some of them in higher perfection than elsewhere.

But a Hamilton would not be deluded into thinking, like Jefferson and his followers, that France sought strong ties to the United States for reasons that went much deeper than the immediate and fluctuating interests of her own internal power politics.

Hamilton specified a series of coinages, including their weights, sizes, alloy composition, and nomenclature, classified according to a decimal system. It included a copper piece, a cent (to be one-hundredth part of a dollar), a half-cent piece, a silver piece to be one-tenth of a dollar, a silver dollar, and gold dollar pieces and also a ten-dollar gold piece to be known as an eagle "not a very expressive or apt appellation for the largest gold piece, but nothing better occurs." He called for setting up a mint at Philadelphia and gave a table of organization for the personnel and also methods for periodically spot-checking the assay of the alloy composition of the coinage.

Hamilton's program rolled on. The plan embodied in his "Report on the Mint" was favorably received and became law in the Mint Act of April 2, 1792.

William Maclay's reaction was predictable: "The resolution on the Mint was foully smuggled through." Privately, Hamilton had much sympathy with Maclay's concerns and his remote constituents. Hamilton's and Maclay's argument was really over means. His reform measures relegated Maclay, Madison, and others to the do-nothing position of seeking to block the positive programs of Hamilton, the progressive reformer.

Obviously, if Hamilton had introduced the various programs set forth in his separate reports in one omnibus report, political opposition to one or another of their features would have been able to unite to kill the whole. Later, after most of them had passed, Hamilton would give greater emphasis to the interrelationships among the various basic aspects of all. Each of his separate and politically discrete reports basically had to do with an aspect of national and central bank management of national economic policy. It was not until the emergency that would arise out of the so-called Quasi War with France of the years 1797 to 1800 that Hamilton would find it politically safe to sketch out his unified view of national central bank economic policy. In a letter to his protégé and successor as secretary of the treasury, Oliver Wolcott, Jr., he would write on August 22, 1798:

> No one knows better than yourself how difficult and oppressive is the collection even of taxes, if there be a defective circulation. This is our case in the interior parts of the country.

Individual capitalists, and consequently the facility of direct loans, are not very extensive in the United States. The banks can only go a certain length, and must not be forced. Yet government will stand in need of large anticipations.

I have come to a conclusion that our Treasury ought to raise up a circulation of its own. I mean by the issuing of Treasury-notes payable, some on demand, others at different periods, . . .

This [is] necessary to keep the circulation full and to facilitate the anticipations which government will certainly need.

Still another subject on which the House had requested Hamilton to report to it, back on January 15, 1790, was a plan for the encouragement of manufactures that would make the United States independent of other nations, particularly in the matter of military supplies. From the earliest years of the Confederation, Hamilton had taken a strong stand in favor of enlarging the powers of the federal government to regulate trade. This had been the immediate reason for the calling of the Annapolis Convention and for its call, in turn, for the Constitutional Convention of the following year. Hamilton favored a broad interpretation of the commerce clause of the Constitution. He did not agree with those more rigid disciples of Adam Smith who felt that trade should not be subject to federal regulation: Although he believed in free markets as a general rule, he also believed that there must be "a common directing power" in the government.

As far back as April 18, 1782, in No. 5 of *The Continentalist*, Hamilton had written:

There are some who maintain that trade will regulate itself, and is not to be benefited by the encouragements or restraints of government. Such persons will imagine that there is no need of a common directing power. This is one of those wild speculative paradoxes, which have grown into credit among us, contrary to the uniform practice and sense of the most enlightened nations.

Commerce, like other things, has its fixed principles, according to which it must be regulated. If these are understood and observed, it will be promoted by the attention of government; if unknown, or violated, it will be injured—but it is the same with every other part of administration.

He called attention to a nice, typically Hamiltonian distinction between governmental regulation of trade, which was desirable, and regulation of prices, which was not. "The contrary opinion, which has grown into a degree of vogue among us, has originated in the injudicious attempts made at different times to effect a REGULATION of PRICES. It became a cant phrase among the opposers of these attempts [to regulate prices] that TRADE MUST REGULATE IT-SELF." He held that the cant phrase must be closely analyzed: ". . . it had its fundamental laws, agreeable to which its general operations must be directed, and any violent attempts in opposition to these commonly miscarry." Limited to this sense, the maxim was reasonable, ". . . but it has since been extended to militate against all interference by the sovereign; an extreme as little reconcilable with experience or common sense as the practice it was first framed to discredit. . . ." He would put the same thought more concisely in the "Report on Manufactures," following Vattel: Moderate commercial restrictions do not constitute violations of natural law. Of all Hamilton's great state papers, his "Report on the Subject of Manufactures," would be by far his most original, best informed, farsighted, far-reaching, and generally remarkable. It would have been just short of two years in preparation by the time he finally laid it before Congress on December 5, 1791. One reason it took him so long was the thoroughness with which he sought out the factual background material that he poured into it. In his own bold, angular hand he wrote letters seeking facts and opinions to people all over the United States and all over the world. He read, filed, and digested replies that came back from such distant parts as Canton, China; from London, Liverpool, and Glasgow; from France, Connecticut, and Massachusetts. The great realist sought to learn for himself what the reality of ordinary people's workaday lives was really like all over the world. The handwritten correspondence he carried on in his "spare" time all through 1790 and 1791, while he was officially engaged in setting in place the other parts of his great economic structure, fills almost two closely printed 500-page volumes of the Hamilton Papers.

A poor, anonymous "Hosier" in Glasgow sent him samples of cotton woven in England with a pathetic letter explaining the impossibility of his emigrating to the United States to work in a factory there:

> It would be an Act of Humanity to the poor Hosiers in Britain—
> If Congress or private Societys would grant a Bounty upon all Hosiers
> imported from this Country. You'll get plenty by that Means—other
> ways No Man in that Branch will be able to Come Over to America—
> As it is utterly impossible for the Poor Stocking Weavers to raise as
> much as pay his freight & none dare indent him—for their is a penalty
> of £700 & 12 Months imprisonment, for every such Act. This Country
> is quiet overstocked with Hosiers—& of Course their Wages very low
> —were 1000 or 2000 to be imported into America their would be plenty
> left in this Country; while it would serve America, it would only raise
> the Wages of those left in Britain to a proper Levell, with the price of
> Provisions. And you will by this receive the Blessing of the Poor in
> Britain & of every—Hosier.

Here was one of the "poor in Britain" appealing to Hamilton or his government to help him out of a real life situation where Adam Smith's "invisible hand" had failed him. In the real world of the poor, it was not adjusting supply to demand through the workings of the free market, as Professor Smith's abstractly beautiful theorem had claimed it would if markets were free enough.

From China, Thomas Randall sent Hamilton a long and detailed report on trade between the United States and Canton. A circular letter of June 22, 1791, from Hamilton to his collectors of revenue requested them to gather information concerning manufactures in their localities, and responses flooded in from John Chester in Connecticut, Nathaniel Hazard in New York, John Dexter in Rhode Island, Edward Carrington in Virginia, and others and from private friends and merchants everywhere.

George Cabot gathered data in Massachusetts, and Joseph Dana said that he was getting still other merchant and manufacturer friends of his to forward more information, for, as he put it, "we have full confidence, that the ultimate object is to befriend the manufacturers of our country, and not to take advantage of them." The mosaic of responses to Hamilton's inquiries presents a vivid, unforgettable picture of the way working people lived in the United States and around the real world in 1790 and 1791. Often quaintly worded and badly misspelled, they revealed in America a new, industrially backward country groping out of an agrarian economy toward an industrial revolution. The United States had remained a largely agrarian country with but a few, small industrial and manufacturing enterprises because, as the replies from his correspondents told Hamilton over and over again, "We have no capital. We have limited knowledge of business practices. We have no skilled workmen. We cannot compete with English goods." As Cabot put it, "Our artisans have been learning their trades at our expense." With such costs added in, how could they compete? Bounties and import duties were needed to protect struggling manufactories. American entrepreneurs agreed with the poor Glasgow hosier that the Congress of the United States "alone are Competent to this Business—the separate States having neither Authority or Funds for the purpose."

Hamilton knew businessmen well enough to know that most of them he was hearing from greatly exaggerated their own difficulties—no doubt partly for self-serving purposes. As the responses to his inquiries poured in and he put all the facts together, he came to understand better than any other man in the country what the real problems were and how to surmount them. They led him to the conclusion that a new manufacturing enterprise set up on a larger scale than anyone had ever dreamed was possible in America would have a better chance of success than anything previously attempted or envisioned.

Unlike a typical bureaucrat, he did not stop with putting his thought into another report to be filed and forgotten. He put them into practice in real life by fostering the founding of the largest and most ambitious industrial corporation ever conceived in the United States up to that time. With William Duer, out of the Treasury now and back in private life, Hamilton formulated elaborate plans over the summer of 1791 for the Society for Establishing Useful Manufactures. It was to be capitalized at one million dollars—more than the total assets of all the joint stock companies then in existence in the United States. Hamilton and Philip Schuyler selected the site: beside the Great Falls of the Passaic River, which Hamilton had first seen with Washington as they were moving north with the army after the Battle of Monmouth and had picnicked there one July day in 1778 on the craggy rocks beside the misty gorge. The factories and mills at the site would be powered by a 77-foot-high roaring wall of water, the highest waterfall Hamilton had ever seen. Indeed, it was the second highest waterfall in the eastern part of the continent.

The prospectus Hamilton wrote and began circulating in August 1791 boldly challenged the fears of which his businessmen correspondents had complained: "What is to hinder the profitable prosecution of manufactures in this Country, when it is notorious, that . . . provisions and various raw materials are even cheaper here than in the Country from which our principal supplies come?"

His answer: "The dearness of capital and the want of capital are the two great objections to the success of manufactures in the United States."

What could be done to eliminate these objections?

"Improvements in the construction and application of machines" to decrease manual labour, employment of women and children as "auxiliary to undertakings of this nature; bringing in immigrants from countries where labor is cheap," and bringing men like the Glasgow hosier to the United States would all contribute to overcoming these objections.

To remedy the lack of capital, the Society for Establishing Useful Manufactures would make a public offering of its stock. "To effect the desired association an incorporation of the adventures must be contemplated as a means necessary to their security." That is, the SUM must be carried on by the investors in corporate form, so that their personal liability as owners would be limited to loss of the money they had invested; otherwise, no one would dare to invest.

According to its prospectus, the SUM expected to manufacture paper, sail cloth, stockings, blankets, carpets, shoes, and cotton and linen goods. It would even operate a brewery. It was a free-form conglomerate with a memorable acronym for a name—the SUM. It would be located in its own industrial park in the exurbs of New York City. It lacked little more than Harvard Business School graduates in its executive suite and the word *synergy* in its lexicon—and SEC-mandated reservations in its prospectus—to be indistinguishable from a present-day paradigm of the genus conglomerate.

The optimistic projections of future profits in its prospectus would not have passed muster; indeed they would have earned stern reproof under a modern SEC. Hamilton's prospectus, like its millions of descendants, made the strongest permissible appeal to the profit motive of potential investors. It hinted that "the pecuniary aid even of Government, though not to be counted upon ought not wholly to be despaired of."

Within a fairly short time the initial $100,000 was subscribed; by the beginning of October more than $250,000 had been invested or promised. The subscribers met on August 9, 1791, in New Brunswick and authorized Hamilton to take the necessary legal steps to procure a charter and seek artisans skilled in cotton manufacture. As the prospectus had stated, New Jersey "is thickly populated, —provisions there are abundant and cheap. The state having scarcely any external commerce and no wastelands to be peopled can feel the impulse of no supposed interest hostile to the advancement of manufactures."

The legislature was amenable to the influence of Hamilton's friends like the Boudinots, Jonathan Dayton, and others who were also the promoters and among the directors. It did no harm to rename the site Paterson, after the governor, William Paterson.

The corporate charter drafted by the secretary of the treasury—one of his several dubious extracurricular activities of 1791—was comprehensive and peculiar. Subscriptions from state and national governments, as well as individuals, were welcome. All subscribers would have the right to investigate the proceedings of the society. It would enjoy exemption from all taxation of its goods and chattels forever and of its land and buildings for ten years, much as corporations in developing areas like Puerto Rico, for example, do today. Artificers and workers in its employ would be exempt from personal taxes and all military duty, except in case of actual invasion. It would have the right to build canals and roads, to operate lotteries, to charge tolls, and to exercise the power of eminent domain. The society's board of 13 directors and a "governor" would govern throughout an area of 36 square miles, to be called "the Corporation of the Town of Paterson," in much the same way Disney World now operates its fiefdom in the state of Florida.

Hamilton and others lobbied in the New Jersey legislature to "elucidate anything that may appear obtuse" in these remarkable provisions. They succeeded in persuading the lawmakers to charter the Society for Establishing Useful Manufactures on November 22, 1791. But it was a second ill-starred beginning for Hamilton that he did nothing to prevent his former assistant in the Treasury, William Duer, from being chosen governor.[8] Nehemiah Hubbard of Connecticut was offered the position of superintendent-general. Major Pierre Charles L'Enfant, the French engineer who in 1791 was also drawing the plans for the great Columbian federal city at Washington, drew an architect's typically overambitious set of magnificent plans for an entire industrial park of factories surrounding the Great Falls and in the township of Paterson. Land was purchased; machinery ordered. As the prospectus said, early prospects, at least, were glowing.

Hamilton personally interviewed and hired workmen and superintendents, among them William Hall and Thomas Marshall, who had learned cotton spinning under Richard Arkwright in England. Putting the prayer of the Glasgow "Hosier" to practical use and gently jogging the invisible hand of Adam Smith, Hamilton suggested sending a Mr. Most to Europe to engage and bring back more workmen with him. In doing this, the secretary of the treasury was suggesting something that the Glasgow hosier had told him was a criminal act under the laws of England: the procurement of skilled workers for export from that country. But American patriotism prevailed. Besides, the conflicts rule is that one country, typically, does not enforce such penal laws of another. The SUM appropriated $20,000 for luring skilled hands to America, specifying in their minutes "that the whole Business of procuring such Hands be committed to the direction and management of the Governor of this Society, subject to the advice of the Secretary of the Treasury."

Owners of large plantations worked by cheap slave labor, mostly in the southerly states, who used their free time for politics, gained political strength by also claiming to represent, under the agrarian banner, free men who worked their own small farms by their own labor. Thomas Jefferson, James Madison, and John Taylor of Virginia were exemplars of such large owners. They objected to any government patronage of manufacturing industry that would transfer its natural current "from a more to a less beneficial channel." To leave industry to private, unaided interests, they said, is "the soundest as well as the simplest policy." Agricultural labor would not be lured away from the farms and would remain cheap.

Hamilton began his "Report on Manufactures" by anticipating their opposition. "The expediency of encouraging manufactures in the United States," Hamilton began, "which was not long since deemed very questionable, appears at this time to be pretty generally admitted." Yet there were still many who argued that "agriculture is the most beneficial and productive object of human industry" and that capital and labor should be employed in converting the existing wilderness into farms so as thus to "contribute to the population, strength, and real riches of the country."

Hamilton agreed at the outset that agriculture was primary and fundamental to the well-being of a nation. But it was not the exclusive source of its well-being. He reasoned that agriculture's real interest was advanced, not injured, by encouraging manufactures. They, too, were a source of wealth to a nation. He pleaded for division of labor and for diversification of the resources of the country. The greater the number of industrial hands, the greater the number of mouths to consume the surplus that agriculture produced from the land. He pointed out that "women and children are rendered more useful, and the latter more early useful, by manufacturing establishments, than they would otherwise be." For example, in the cotton manufactories of England "four sevenths, nearly, are women and children, of whom the greatest proportion are children, and many of them of a tender age." He did not swerve in his argument to stress the grim social consequences of child labor that were obvious to a later age.

Other nations exported manufactured goods to America, but set up import barriers against American goods. Only by becoming independent and competitive could America force free, unimpeded, and equal exchange. European nations aided their manufactures by bounties and tariffs; in order to attract capital into home industries, the United States should do the same.

He denied that protection gave "a monopoly of advantages to particular classes, at the expense of the rest of the community" or that his plan would favor the North and middle states, as against the South. "The internal competition which takes place soon does away with every thing like monopoly, and by degrees reduces the price of the article to the minimum of a reasonable profit on the capital employed," he argued. The interests of the North and South were interrelated; the "aggregate prosperity of manufactures and the aggregate prosperity of agriculture are intimately connected."

He specified how government could aid manufactures: by protective duties, which had the added merit of producing revenue; prohibition of rival imports or prohibitive duties on them; prohibition of export of raw materials peculiar to this country; pecuniary bounties—upon which Hamilton was particularly insistent; exemption from import duties of raw materials essential to home manufactures; drawbacks and rebates; encouragement of inventions and bringing them in to the country from abroad; governmental inspection of manufactured commodities to prevent frauds, cheats, and inferior quality from being imposed on the consumer; and facilitation of cash remittances from one part of the country to another.[9] He urged the building of a national highway system and a national system of canals for swift, economical, and nondiscriminatory transport of goods from one region to another.

Hamilton did not stop at this point, as many a political man would have done, for a round of polite applause for a range of fine-sounding general ideas. With him such generalities were only the prelude to specific recommendations for specific actions, each of which would rouse cries of anguish from one or another powerful sector of special interest.

The "Report on Manufactures" called attention to the private SUM, saying that "it may be announced that a society is forming, with a capital which is expected to be extended to at least half a million dollars, on behalf of which measures are already in train for prosecuting, on a large scale, the making and printing of cotton goods."

Thomas Jefferson recoiled in horror from Hamilton's vision of the future. The sound of whirring looms, the clang of machinery stitching shoes faster than the human hand could follow—these were anathema to him and everything dear to him. Assembling workers in congested factories would draw them to cities away from farms and plantations and transform them into robots, in messy, disorderly, inhuman crowds. To him, people who were industrial workers seemed vicious, morally reprehensible, and enemies to the liberties of free government. In his *Notes on Virginia,* he wrote: "I consider the class of artificers as the panders of vice, and the instruments by which the liberties of a country are generally overturned." He added, "The mobs of great cities add just so much to the support of pure government, as sores do to the strength of the human body."

Hamilton valued agriculture in a more practical way than Jefferson. He would write into a speech of Washington's to Congress of December 7, 1796, that "agriculture, considered with reference either to individual or national welfare, is the best basis of the prosperity of every other object of labor and industry." Accordingly, through Washington, it was he who proposed the establishment and funding of the Board of Agriculture, which later, of course, became a cabinet department, a vast bureaucratic empire, although a nightmare for an Adam Smithian economist. With Hamilton, agriculture was not the sole activity with which the little people must be kept contented.

Hamilton's "Report on Manufactures," despite its title, acknowledged that agriculture fostered "a state most favorable to the freedom and independence of the human mind," but its main thrust was that the interdependence of agriculture and manufacturing, of farmer and artificer, would benefit both. He understood Jefferson's point at its deepest political level and disagreed with it:

It ought readily be conceded that the cultivation of the earth, as the primary and most certain source of national supply, as the immediate and chief source of subsistence to a man, as the principal source of those materials which constitute the nutriment of other kinds of labor, as including a state most favorable to the freedom and independence of the human mind—one, perhaps, most conducive to the multiplication of the human species, has intrinsically a strong claim to preeminence over every other kind of industry.

But, that it has a title to any thing like an exclusive predilection, in any country, ought to be admitted with great caution; that it is even more productive than every other branch of industry, requires more evidence than has yet been given in support of the position. That its real interests, precious and important as they truly are, will be advanced, rather than injured, by the due encouragement of manufactures, may, it is believed, be satisfactorily demonstrated.

Hamilton patiently explained, as if to a backward child:

If, instead of a farmer and artificer, there were a farmer only, he would be under the necessity of devoting a part of his labor to the fabrication of clothing and other articles, which he would procure of the artificer, in the case of there being such a person; and of course he would be able to devote less labor to the cultivation of his farm, and would draw from it a proportionately less product. The whole quantity of production, in this state of things, in provisions, raw materials, and manufactures, would certainly not exceed in value the amount of what would be produced in provisions and raw materials only, if there were an artificer as well as a farmer.[10]

Again—if there were both an artificer and a farmer, the latter would be left at liberty to pursue exclusively the cultivation of his farm. A greater quantity of provisions and raw materials would, of course, be produced, equal, at least, as has been already observed, to the whole amount of the provisions, raw materials, and manufactures, which would exist on a contrary supposition. The artificer, at the same time, would be going on in the production of manufactured commodities, to an amount sufficient, not only to repay the farmer, in those commodities, for the provisions and materials which were procured from him, but to furnish the artificer himself with a supply of similar commodities for his own use. Thus, then, there would be two quantities or values in existence, instead of one; and the revenue and consumption would be double, in one case, what it would be in the other.[11]

"Hence it results," concluded Hamilton, "that the labor of the artificer is as positively productive as that of the farmer, and as positively augments the revenue of the society."

Jefferson and the Jeffersonians insisted that they were unconvinced.

Hamilton went on to enumerate seven elementary points of national economics. These held that "manufacturing establishments not only occasion a positive augmentation of the Produce and Revenue of the Society, but that they contribute essentially to rendering them greater than they could possibly be without such establishments." These points are:

1. The division of labor.
2. An extension of the use of machinery.
3. Additional employment to classes of the community not ordinarily engaged in the business.
4. The promoting of emigration from foreign countries.
5. The furnishing of greater scope for the diversity of talents and dispositions that discriminate men from each other.
6. Affording a more ample and various field for enterprise or "the spirit of enterprise."
7. The creating of and securing for all "a more certain demand for the surplus produce of the soil."

These points were not so elementary that they do not still erupt occasionally in emotion-laden contemporary headlines. For example, when workers strike and sabotage new cars on assembly lines because they feel that their jobs are boring and uncongenial, it means that their employers have ignored Hamilton's point 5: "that minds of the strongest and most active powers for their proper objects, fall below mediocrity, and labor without effect, if confined to uncongenial pursuits."

Hamilton's remedy?

The results of human exertion may be immensely increased by diversifying its objects. When all the different kinds of industry obtain in a community, each individual can find his proper element, and can call into activity the whole vigor of his nature. And the community is benefited by the services of its respective members, in the manner in which each can serve it with most effect.

Hamilton had not missed the oft-noted aptitude that Americans of his day at least had for working with mechanical things. "If," he added tellingly, "there is, in the genius of the people of this country, a peculiar aptitude for mechanic improvements," the propagation of manufactures "would operate as a forcible reason for giving opportunities to the exercise of that species of talent."

But more important even than increase of material production was the enhancement of human capabilities. Here is one of Hamilton's greatest and most characteristic themes: "To cherish and stimulate the activity of the human mind, by multiplying the objects of enterprise, is not among the least considerable of the expedients by which the wealth of a nation may be promoted. Even things in themselves not positively advantageous sometimes become so, by their tendency to provoke exertion." Here Hamilton couples two of the watchwords of his life, *energy* and *effort*, in the same clause: "Every new scene which is opened to the busy nature of man to rouse and exert itself, is the addition of a new energy to the general stock of effort."

A great nation was more than farmers and merchants, too: "The spirit of enterprise, useful and prolific as it is, must necessarily be contracted or expanded, in proportion to the simplicity or variety of the occupations to be found in a society. It must be less in a nation of mere cultivators, than in a nation of cultivators and merchants; less in a nation of cultivators and merchants, than in a nation of cultivators, artificers, and merchants."

Hamilton's point 7, the "creating" and "securing" for all "a more certain demand for the surplus" was so far ahead of its time that it was not until the 1960s that the originality of it received wide recognition when it surfaced as a principal theme discovered by John Kenneth Galbraith's best seller, *The Affluent Society.*

As Hamilton put it, "the multiplication of manufactories not only furnishes a market for those articles which have been accustomed to be produced in abundance in a country, but it likewise creates a demand for such as were either unknown or produced in inconsiderable quantities. The bowels as well as the surface of the earth are ransacked for articles which were before neglected. Animals, plants, and minerals acquire a utility and a value which were before unexplored."

Hamilton recognized a problem common to all underdeveloped countries: foreign demand for their products is casual and occasional, not certain or constant. Natural causes render external demand for the surplus of agricultural nations a precarious reliance, what with differences of weather and soils in different years. Even plentiful harvests, if they occur at the same time in other countries, may occasion a glut that proves economically disastrous. The subject of world commodity cartels and agreements is high on statesmens' agendas in the late twentieth century.

The only substitute for precarious reliance on foreign demand, said Hamilton, is "an extensive domestic market." In the nature of things, it would be far more to be relied upon:

> The exertions of the husbandman will be steady or fluctuating, vigorous or feeble, in proportion to the steadiness or fluctuation, adequateness or inadequateness, of the markets on which he must depend for the vent of the surplus produced by his labor.
>
> To secure such a market there is no other expedient than to promote manufacturing establishments. Manufacturers, who constitute the most numerous class, after the cultivators of land, are for that reason the principal consumers of the surplus of their labor.[12]

Thomas Jefferson really should not worry about agricultural workers being drawn off the land, for the outcome might indeed help, not harm, men like him, Hamilton explained:

> If the effect of manufactories should be to detach a portion of the hands which would otherwise be engaged in tillage, and a smaller quantity of lands to be under cultivation; by their tendency to procure a more certain demand for the surplus produce of the soil they would, at the same time, cause the lands which were in cultivation to be better improved and more productive. The condition of each individual farmer would be meliorated, and the total mass of agricultural production would probably be increased.

Hamilton even foretold a little of what would come to be called by such names as *The Greening of America.* After a time, an immigrant brought in to be an artificer might return to the land: "Many, whom manufacturing views would induce to emigrate, would, afterwards, yield to the temptations which the particular situation of this country holds out to agricultural pursuits." But there was no blinking away the problem that there would not be enough jobs on the farm or in handcrafts to support all former artificers who might wish to return to the simple life on the farm and there eke out a living: "While agriculture would, in other respects, derive many signal and unmingled advantages from the growth of manufactures, it is a problem whether it would gain or lose, as to the article of the number of persons employed in carrying it on."

Hamilton's "Report on Manufactures" was an eagle-eyed vision of *The Affluent Society* within *The New Industrial State*, strikingly modern in basic concept and essentials, lacking only the overlay of such developments as advertising, blue jeans, hard rock, acid, and grass. It contained the seed of modern America. But it was too far ahead of its time to receive serious consideration from Congress. Jefferson and *The Greening of America* beat back Hamilton's last great political effort of 1791.

The House pigeonholed his report and did not take it up again. The proposals it contained were so wide-ranging and far ahead of their time that it comes as no surprise that nothing came of his appended drafts of legislative recommendations. But his report remained a source of ready reference and a mother lode of ideas for all who came after him who would urge government programs to aid and encourage American industry, agricultural technology, transportation, manufactures, mining, interstate highways, canals, and capital formation. It gave eloquent expression to the idea of economics that came to be known as "the harmony of interests" principle: that government-supported industry would strengthen rather than weaken agriculture, make more jobs for workers, attract immigrants, and open up new opportunities for enterprise and investment.

On behalf of their contrary dream, which was victorious in the short run, Jefferson and the Southern politicians who followed his lead continued to battle gallantly against Hamilton's vision, until Lincoln's Union confirmed the industrial reality by winning the war between the Northern and Southern states—at an immediate cost of something like half a million lives.

"A man is indeed a city," wrote William Carlos Williams of *Paterson*, "and for the poet there are no ideas but in things." The grayish yellow, polluted spume that rises from the mud and thickets where the Great Falls of the Passaic "comes pouring in above the city and crashes from the edge of the gorge," seasonally vociferous, is "associated with many of the ideas upon which our fiscal colonial policy shaped us through Alexander Hamilton." He and it "interested me profoundly," says Williams in his epic poem of industrial America, "and what has resulted therefrom."

> Oh married man!
> He is the city of cheap hotels and private
> entrances . . . of taxis at the door, the car
> standing in the rain hour after hour by
> the roadhouse entrance . . .
> You knew the Falls and read Greek fluently
> It did not stop the bullet that killed you
> You wanted to organize the country so that
> We should all stick together and make a little money.

In the late twentieth century, the South has come round to Hamilton's vision with a vengeance that falls on the ghosts of both the great antagonists. Old established manufactories like the textile mills that once rose proudly in the SUM's industrial park moved away to brand-new state subsidized sites, cheap labor, and cheap government-generated power in once (but no longer) rural areas of the new industrial states of the southern sun belt. All over northeastern America, as at Paterson, stand abandoned red brick mills with no future but a forlorn oblivion crumbling into brick dust behind bronze Historical Preservation Society plaques in polluted spume like that below the Falls where Hamilton and Washington had once picnicked beside a rainbow sparkling in white mist as they journeyed north with their victorious army after the Battle of Monmouth.

5

JEFFERSON, MADISON, BECKLEY, AND BURR HUNT DOWN THE HESSIAN FLY

WE ARE GOING HEADLONG INTO THE BITTEREST OPPOSITION TO
THE GENL. GOVERNMENT—I PITY YOU— *DELENDA EST CARTHAGO*
IS THE MAXIM APPLIED TO YOUR ADMINISTRATION.
　　　　　—from Robert Troup, January 19, 1791

THERE WAS A PASSIONATE COURTSHIP BETWEEN THE CHANCELLOR
[ROBERT R. LIVINGSTON] BURR, JEFFERSON AND MADISON
WHEN THE TWO LATTER WERE IN TOWN. *DELENDA EST
CARTHAGO* IS THE MAXIM ADOPTED WITH RESPECT TO YOU. . . .
　　　　　—from Robert Troup, June 15, 1791

As Jefferson and Hamilton began to know each other better at cabinet
meetings, they liked each other less. They were men quite unlike each other, not
each other's kind of man at all. Before becoming members of Washington's
cabinet, neither would have known much about the other except by report,
although Hamilton would have known more about Jefferson than Jefferson
would have known about him. About Jefferson there was so much that could be

told that one lost sight of how much remained obscure. Born August 13, 1743, at Shadwell, Albemarle County, in western Virginia to parents who were married to each other—Peter and Jane Randolph Jefferson—he was 14 years older than Hamilton. In 1776 the 33-year-old Jefferson had been helping draft the Declaration of Independence while the 19-year-old Hamilton had been training his New York Provincial Company of Artillery how to manhandle, load, and aim their cannons in preparation for imminent amphibious invasion of New York City by the British expeditionary force mobilizing out in the harbor.

Jefferson had been wartime governor of Virginia until his panicky flight into hiding from Richmond before Cornwallis's advance. This occurred shortly before Hamilton would lead the American assault on the last Yorktown redoubt and help arrange for Cornwallis's surrender there. The contrasting sequence of events of 1781 may have been behind the curiously pointed but otherwise uncharacteristically irrelevant passage that Hamilton had inserted in his "Eulogium" to General Nathanael Greene of July 4, 1789. Hamilton had commiserated with poor "Virginia debilitated by the dissipation of its revenues and forces in domestic projects incumbered by a numerous body of slaves bound by all the laws of *injured* humanity to hate their masters—deficient in order and vigour in its administration." In his text, above the reference to the Virginians' slaves, Hamilton had underscored the word *injured*, and written in above it the word *degraded*.

Abroad in Paris as American minister to France during the hectic years from 1784 through 1789, which had seen Hamilton through the Annapolis Convention, the Constitutional Convention, *The Federalist Papers*, and the state ratifying conventions, Jefferson's busy Virginia friends like Madison, with whom he kept in touch by correspondence, would probably have had scant occasion to mention Hamilton's name. Hamilton's powerful support of a strong and auspicious central government during this period would come through to Jefferson as little more than an echo of the same views Madison had espoused in those years before Jefferson's return.

In those years, the political faction that held Hamiltonian views had less influence in New York's politics than in Virginia's. But now in cabinet meetings the man who in 1776 stood for the idea of throwing off strong government rule sat opposite the man who in 1787 stood for the idea that enduring freedom and liberty were possible only under a strong, popularly elected national government. But unlike Hamilton in 1790 and 1791, Jefferson was pressing no comprehensive and specific legislative program to further such general views.

Jefferson himself recognized the change that had taken place in the country while he had been away. On January 8, 1789, he had written an Englishman, Dr. Richard Price, that "I did not at first believe that eleven states out of thirteen would have consented to a plan consolidating themselves so much into one. A change in their dispositions, which had taken place since I left them, had rendered this consolidation necessary, that is to say, had called for a federal government which could walk upon its own legs, without leaning for support on state legislatures." But it was not easy to understand where Jefferson really stood.

He had written Francis Hopkinson on March 13, 1789, that "I am not of the party of the federalists. But I am much farther from the party of the anti federalists." Nor was he yet "a trimmer between parties," he said. But if he were neither a Federalist nor an Anti-Federalist nor "a trimmer between," his assertions all canceled each other out. On specific hard questions of public finance like those raised by Hamilton's program of nondiscrimination, assumption, funding, the national bank, and an increase in the public debt, with provisions for paying it off by increased taxes and repurchases for the sinking fund, Jefferson took a firm stand, at least after his candlelight dinner had helped make it all possible: he was against it in principle. As he struggled ineptly with his own private burden of old private debts, Jefferson explained to Madison that no present generation had any right to incur debt that would bind future generations. He had written Madison on September 6, 1789, that "the earth belongs to the living." To Jefferson, this meant something deep to do with economics, something more complicated than a truism.

After making elaborate mathematical calculations on the life expectancy of living persons, he had come to the astounding, if weird, conclusion that "every constitution, then, and every law, naturally expires at the end of 19 years. If it be enforced longer, it is an act of force and not of right." If this meant that all debts presently incurred could be repudiated after 19 years, it would, of course, mean imminent destruction of the public credit that Hamilton's program was enacted to create. On the other hand, it would greatly relieve Jefferson from his private debt obligations.

Jefferson was bound to be upset by Hamilton's view that a public debt, if properly funded by a proper provision for scheduled repayment at the time it is incurred through repurchases by a sinking fund, could be a public blessing. Jefferson had written Madison that "no nation can make a declaration against long contracted debts so disinterestedly as we, since we do not owe a shilling which may not be paid with ease, principal and interest, within the time of our own lives." When the assumption bill had suffered defeat on one of the early votes in the House, Oliver Wolcott, Jr., shocked at Madison's sudden switch to opposition, had written his father in Connecticut a comment that applied with equal force to Jefferson's quaint ideas on economics. On April 12, 1790, Wolcott wrote, "The southern states seemed unprepared for the operation of systematic measures." He added that "very many respectable characters entertain political opinions which would be with us thought very whimsical."

It was a vote on a proposed amendment to the assumption bill that had led to the very first direct clash in the cabinet between Hamilton and Jefferson. A man named James Reynolds from New York and others had been moving about in rural areas of Virginia and North Carolina, buying up rights to collect arrearages of pay the Treasury owed to old soldiers. As it turned out, this man was the same James Reynolds Hamilton had known at least three years earlier, in 1787. That August, Reynolds had called Hamilton's attention to scare stories in the press to the effect that, behind the closed doors of secret sessions of the Constitutional Convention, plans were afoot to install Frederick, the bishop of

Osnaburg, son of King George III, as the monarch of America. The story had been leaked out of Philadelphia the very day after Hamilton's five-hour speech of June 18 to the convention, the day before the crucial vote upholding the Virginia plan for a stronger union. Details of the story lent it a spurious plausibility that convinced Hamilton that someone hostile to him—someone like John Beckley—had leaked details from the convention's proceedings to a hostile journalist. Outraged, Hamilton angrily launched an investigation. He made inquiry of Jeremiah Wadsworth, who knew Reynolds, but whether he ever found out for certain the source of the leak so devastating to his future reputation is not known. Nothing that happened later would dispel a strong suspicion that John Beckley was the fabricator of the canard with which James Reynolds had come to him.

In March and April of 1790, Gustavus B. Wallace, a former officer of a Virginia regiment and member of the state legislature—an unimpeachable reporter—sent James Madison two angry eyewitness accounts describing how James Reynolds carried on his fraudulent operations. They provided Madison with vivid proof not only of his thesis that Hamilton's policy of nondiscrimination permitted crooked speculators to prey on poor widows and old soldiers, but also that Hamilton's Treasury was directly involved in the frauds. According to Wallace, either Reynolds or his partner in the temporary capital, William J. Vredenbergh, of 40 Dock Street, New York City, had obtained lists of the names of the old soldiers and widows and the amounts owing to them. Where had they obtained these lists? From a clerk in Hamilton's Treasury Department.

This was shocking enough, but "What makes the speculation worse," Wallace explained to Madison, is that Reynolds would show the soldier a list "with a smaller sum than is actually due him." Then he "gets a power of attorney for the whole that is due him without mentioning the sum." This was, of course, out-and-out fraud and a very different thing from mere speculative purchases of soldiers' claims. For example, Wallace added, "There are soldiers that have £24 due them and some less but in his list [there] appears to be none over six dollars and this he buys for 1/6 or 2/." Wallace had seen Reynolds's lists. Madison passed this information on to Jefferson, as well as to the governor of Virginia, Beverley Randolph, for prosecution in the law courts.

While Madison had been ill during the early debates on assumption, Theodorick Bland of Virginia sought to prevent such crude frauds by introducing resolutions into Congress on May 21, 1790, that would require payment of the arrearages to the old soldiers in person. If payment were to be made to someone else who had acquired his claim by assignment and purchase, the purchaser would have to produce a power of attorney that expressly stated the full amount of the claim and was witnessed by two justices of the peace. This would mean that claims that had been bought up before the resolutions were adopted could not be collected afterwards unless reauthenticated in the prescribed manner.

Oliver Ellsworth of Connecticut, Rufus King, and others of Hamilton's supporters moved for a compromise amendment that would validate powers of attorney that had been drawn up previously, though not in accord with the required form, provided that no evidence of forgery or fraud, such as Reynolds's, had been adduced within a specified limitation period. There was a tie vote on these compromise amendments. Vice-president John Adams broke the tie by voting against them. This tie-breaking vote probably marked the first clash on a public issue between John Adams and Hamilton. It would open a gulf between these two men whose consequences would be as far-reaching as the gulf the vote opened between Hamilton and Jefferson.

Bland's resolutions directed Hamilton as secretary of the treasury to have transmitted to the state governors, for publication, complete lists of the amounts due each officer and soldier, as Gustavus B. Wallace's letter to Madison had suggested. Having received in many instances a good specie value for their claims, although less than face value, the veterans were now free to collect the whole again from the Treasury, if no one else did so, thus recovering more than once on the same claim. Reynolds and Vredenbergh, as well as other less dishonest speculators who had paid hard money, if less than face value, for the assigned claims that these resolutions would invalidate, were outraged. Because the Senate vote had been so close, Hamilton thought that Washington, by making known his disapproval, might change Adams's or some other senator's vote and defeat the resolutions on a new vote. By his letter of May 29, 1790, Hamilton had urged Washington to make his objections known. The total of all such claims involved only about $50,000 he estimated. Retrospective invalidation of claims that had already been sold would involve incalculably greater damage to all public credit.

Hamilton was "sensible, that an inflexible adherence to the principles contended for must often have an air of rigor," but it was better that "partial evils should be submitted to, than that principles should be violated," particularly, "in the infancy of our present government." Those who had actually been defrauded by the likes of Reynolds could sue and recover in the courts. But few could afford the legal fees.

Hamilton was sensitive to the plight of individual claimants who "would probably not be in a condition to seek that relief [from fraud] from their own resources" and to "the defenceless situation of the parties." Therefore, he offered a legal aid plan by which an attorney or agent would institute a class action on behalf of all of the original holders against allegedly fraudulent assignees: "The attorney general should be directed either to prosecute or defend for the original claimants, as should appear to him most likely to insure justice."

Washington asked Jefferson for his opinion on the Bland resolutions. Jefferson disagreed with Hamilton. Jefferson contended that as a matter of local law in Virginia the original assignments were void in any event. The Bland resolutions would only tend to confirm this. Congress, as Jefferson wrote to Washington on June 3, should prefer to pay the assignor rather than the assignee in any event. This would put the burden of proof on the latter and give "the advantage to the party who has suffered wrong rather than to him who has committed it." This assumed, ipso facto, that all who had paid good money for claims were as guilty of fraud as Reynolds had been. Every "speculator" was presumed to be guilty of fraud. *Speculator* and *monocrat* were two of Jefferson's favorite words to impute automatic guilt by association. Washington accepted Jefferson's advice; at least, there is no evidence that he took any action to follow Hamilton's urging to seek to change the congressional resolutions. On a matter of Treasury Department policy at the heart of the area of Hamilton's presumed expertness, Jefferson had won the first of many a round that would be contested between them.

This first clash of opinion in the cabinet was confined to narrow legal grounds. There were good arguments on both sides. Jefferson was merely recommending that Washington follow the course of least resistance by going along with the congressional resolutions. Nothing in Jefferson's opinion created differences with Hamilton so deep that they would stand in the way of his arranging the candlelight dinner for him with Madison later the same month of June to help him crush Madison's opposition to the assumption-residence trade-off. Jefferson had not been much perturbed by the cries of old soldiers when he had written his friend Edmund Randolph, the attorney general, that "in the present instances, I see the necessity of yielding to the cries of creditors in certain parts of the Union; for the sake of union, and to save us from the greatest of all calamities, the total extinction of our credit in Europe."

Even as 1791 began, Hamilton and Jefferson still had a fairly effective, practical working relationship. Louis G. Otto, the French chargé d'affaires, had complained to Jefferson that the tonnage tax on French shipping was a violation of Article V of the Franco-American treaty of commerce of 1778. Jefferson wrote Hamilton on January 1, 1791, that "I think it is essential to cook up some favour which may ensure the continuance of the good dispositions they have towards us." They buy staple products from us, and we take hard money from them, which we "pour into the coffers of their enemies" in Britain. "I would thank you sincerely to suggest any thing better than what I had thought of."

Hamilton obliged. He had a better idea than to "cook up" a unilateral trade concession to France. He opposed foreign giveaways and handouts for purposes of general "good dispositions," as distinguished from specific reciprocal concessions. Hamilton saw no reason now to "cook up" a favor to France.

On January 11 he wrote back, "Though there be a collateral consideration, there is a want of reciprocity in the thing itself." Jefferson's scheme would "place French vessels upon an equal footing with our own, *in our ports*, while our vessels in the *ports of France* may be subject to all the duties which are there laid on the mass of foreign Vessels." Besides, Hamilton reminded Jefferson, the funds from the tonnage tax had, in effect, been mortgaged by his funding plan to pay off the public debt. Therefore, said Hamilton, "the same act which should destroy this source of revenue should provide an equivalent. This I consider as a rule which ought to be sacred, as it affects the public Credit." No unilateral trade concessions were granted to France. Hamilton had won the second round.

Hamilton wrote to Jefferson again on January 13, still rejecting ex parte trade concessions in exchange for vague "good dispositions." He offered Jefferson a still better idea: "endeavor, by a new treaty of commerce with France, to extend reciprocal advantages, and fix them on a permanent basis. This would be more solid, and less likely to beget discontents elsewhere." In foreign affairs, Hamilton believed in avoiding exceptions and preferences that "might lead to commercial warfare with any power" less favored by such preferences than some other. This would give "a free course to trade," and be "cultivating good humor with all the world." Jefferson did not follow through on Hamilton's idea on improving relations with France; so their efforts in this round must be rated a draw.

A month later Washington would be secretly showing Jefferson's and Randolph's opinions holding a national bank to be unconstitutional to Hamilton, brusquely rejecting their opinions and adopting Hamilton's. Score an important round for Hamilton.

The private dispute Jefferson had provoked by urging Hamilton to "cook up some favour" to ensure the "good dispositions" of France paled into insignificance by comparison with the public controversy Jefferson was cooking up by another letter that would become much more famous or, to Federalists, notorious. Broadly speaking, though, it would win Jefferson a large round of popular applause. The introductory blurb that the American secretary of state wrote to the printer of Thomas Paine's *The Rights of Man* would inject the French Revolution into the mainstream of American politics for many years to come. It would also serve to inject Jefferson's name into public consciousness as the leader of the political party that opposed strong governmental institutions like those exemplified by Britain and Hamilton and those that had been destroyed by the French Revolution.

In England, Edmund Burke, in opposition to English praise of the French Revolution, had published his essay, *Reflections on the Revolution in France*, in 1790. Soon thereafter Thomas Paine had answered Burke in England with his pamphlet, *The Rights of Man*. This linked the French Revolution to the American, praised both, and attacked the British constitution. In England, Paine was charged with treason and fled to France. John Beckley, the clerk of the House and a close friend and cohort of Madison and Jefferson and a mortal enemy of Hamilton because Hamilton had been instrumental in preventing his election as clerk of the Constitutional Convention, had handled all arrangements for having *The Rights of Man* reprinted in America by the printer John (or Jonathan) Bayard Smith. Beckley, of course, was not a publisher himself nor a patron of the arts nor a man of means who could finance a substantial printing bill, nor was he a man who took any political action independently. All his activities served the political interests of his masters Madison and Jefferson. As their creature, he often served as their *agent provocateur*, cover, and informer as well. The story Jefferson and Madison later gave out was that before giving *The Rights of Man* to Smith, the printer, for publication, Beckley had loaned it to Madison. Madison had passed it on to Jefferson with the request that, after reading it, he give it to Smith. When Jefferson passed the book on to Smith, he accompanied it by the following transmittal letter:

Th. Jefferson presents his compliments to Mr. Jonathan B. Smith
... he is extremely pleased to find that it will be reprinted here, and that
something is at length to be publicly said against the political heresies
which have sprung up amongst us. He has no doubt our citizens will
rally a second time round the standard of *Common Sense.* He begs
leave to engage three or four copies of the republication.

Smith published Jefferson's letter of endorsement in the preface to the
Philadelphia edition as a blurb. He introduced it with a fulsome political advertisement for Jefferson: Jefferson's views, he averred, reflected honor on the
secretary of state by "directing the mind to a contemplation of that Republican
firmness and Democratic simplicity which endear their possessor to every friend
of *The Rights of Man.*"

The genius of the secretary of state's endorsement of Paine's indirect attack
on the British constitution by fulsome praise of the French and American Revo-
lutions was that it would hit not one, but three high flying Federalist birds with
one semiofficial stone. Hamilton was the lowest of the three. John Adams, as
Jefferson conceded, was the one who suffered most. Adams's *Discourses on
Davila* had been appearing in the Philadelphia newspapers for many months.
Referring to them, Jefferson, writing to Washington on May 8, 1791, attacked
Adams's "apostasy" from republicanism "to hereditary monarchy and nobility."
At the same time, Jefferson called Adams "my friend," for whom he professed
"a cordial esteem." To Washington himself, *The Rights of Man* and Jefferson's
blurb were a glancing blow at his own strong government, but he held his temper
and remained above the fray.

Jefferson's blurb was republished in newspapers all over the country. Washington was aghast at the offense his own secretary of state's end or sement of
the fugitive from British justice would give to the most threatening world power
on the frontiers. Jefferson told Washington that publication of his blurb was only
"the indiscretion of a printer," that "committed me with my friend, Mr. Adams."
He was, he said, "an utter stranger to J. B. Smith, both by sight and character."
But he would not, however, withdraw, repudiate, or remove his endorsement of
Paine's *The Rights of Man.*

In private he affirmed that he was appalled at the situation in Britain and
at the "rottenness" of Edmund Burke's mind. To a distinguished Englishman,
Sir John Sinclair, Jefferson's reaction to the flight and recapture of the French
king was that "it would be unfortunate" to defeat "so beautiful a revolution."
Jefferson added to Washington, "I certainly never made a secret of my being
anti-monarchial, and anti-aristocratical, but I am sincerely mortified to be thus
brought forward on the public stage, where to remain, to advance, or to retire,
will be equally against my love of silence and quiet, and my abhorrence of
dispute."

As a public speaker, Jefferson seemed to mumble. He was so soft-spoken
that he could hardly be heard across a room. He asserted often that he never
wrote anything for the press. It was unintentional, he said, and it was to his

embarrassment, he averred, that his name and blurb on the flyleaf of *The Rights of Man* would now be advertised by reprints and discussions of it in newspapers everywhere throughout the land. More angers exploded as spring came on. Adams's son John Quincy Adams assailed Jefferson in the press over the signature of *Publicola*. Attacks on Jefferson and Madison spread throughout the country, but only in the Federalist press. George Beckwith, the unofficial British minister, remonstrated in pained surprise to Tobias Lear, Washington's secretary, at publication of treasonable sentiments against the British government by a fugitive from its justice carrying the secretary of state's personal endorsement.

Jefferson rather smugly noted that Hamilton and Major Beckwith were "open-mouthed" against him. Protests like Hamilton's on grounds of damage to national interests were drowned out by the roar of domestic political approval from republican papers. Jefferson, the aristocratic patrician, was suddenly acclaimed as the leader of all those who wanted no aristocratical ideas in the government of their country. Wherever copies of Paine's best seller carried his enthusiastic self-advertisement, the domestic political stock of the secretary for foreign affairs soared high.

Not very surprisingly, Senators Rufus King and Philip Schuyler of New York were indispensable pillars of support for Hamilton's national economic program in the closely divided Senate. In national politics, by and large, the New England representatives usually backed him; an equally strong majority in the South usually opposed him. Most of the swing votes were in the two great middle states of New York and Pennsylvania. The voting was a very close thing, as it had been on Bland's resolutions. Nor could it be said that in New York Hamilton's political base was ever really secure.

The perennial governor, George Clinton, had been bitterly anti-Hamilton since the days of the Constitutional Convention.

The Livingston clan of Livingston Manor on the Hudson had supported the Constitution, backed Hamilton's early policies, and earned the right to expect reciprocity of consideration when Hamilton became a power on the national stage. They had once been Hamilton's most powerful supporters. But Livingstons were passed over when Hamilton made his intimate friend Rufus King a senator instead of one of them, and Robert R. Livingston lost out to Hamilton's even closer friend John Jay as chief justice of the Supreme Court. Livingstons were also passed over for local appointments even after Schuyler had defeated Duane, a Livingston in-law, to win the other Senate seat. After his narrow victory for reelection, Clinton had sought to divide his opposition by appointing moderate Federalist Aaron Burr as his attorney general.

Trying to explain the Byzantine New York State politics of the time, a thing essentially unexplicable, in one sentence, James Parton, in his life of Aaron Burr said, "The Clintons had the power, the Livingstons had the numbers, and the Schuylers had Hamilton."

Schuyler, to whom by lot the short Senate term had fallen, was up for election again in January of 1791. With Federalists safely in control of the state legislature, which elected the senators, Schuyler's reelection seemed to be as certain as anything in New York politics could ever be.

But the Livingstons of Livingston Manor were a touchy old family, unused to slights from even a Washington, a Jay, or a Schuyler, not to speak of a young upstart with a bar sinister from the West Indies. Here was a chance to humble Hamilton and restore their own to power by cutting down Schuyler. Aaron Burr was a moderate, not closely identified either with Clinton and extreme Anti-Federalism or with Hamilton and Schuyler. He had served with dignity and avoided disgrace as the state's attorney general. Burr let it become known that if the Livingstons would support him to upset Schuyler in the race for Schuyler's seat, Governor Clinton would appoint Robert R. Livingston's brother-in-law, Morgan Lewis, to succeed Burr as attorney general. Clinton did nothing to discourage such talk. He relished the idea of giving a comeuppance to Hamilton and Schuyler no less than did the Livingstons and Burr.

James Kent in the New York assembly thought "things look auspicious for Burr. It will be in some measure a question of northern and southern interests [within N.Y. State]." Kent thought Hamilton would be a liability to his father-in-law: "The objection of Schuyler's being related to the Secretary has weight." Schuyler was a crusty patrician, and Kent added that some objected to the "unprepossessing austerity of [his] manner."

Burr told Sedgwick that "there was uncommon animosity and eagerness in the opposition" to Schuyler. A Federalist friend warned Hamilton that "strange unions have been brought about by our artful persevering Chieftain [Governor Clinton]."

James Livingston of Montgomery, only an obscure distant relation of the colonial lords of Livingston Manor, was artfully selected by Schuyler's supporters to place his name in nomination in the state assembly, but this failed to paper over the family's breach with the Livingstons who counted. John Smith of Orange County moved as an amendment that the name of Burr be inserted in place of Schuyler's. James Livingston's motion lost, 32 to 27; and Smith's nomination of Burr then carried, 32 to 27. Cornelius J. Bogert, a Federalist of New York City, moved to strike the name of Burr and substitute Egbert Benson's, but this was rejected by a larger vote, 35 to 24. Most of the votes for Burr, who was from the city, came from upstate, whereas most of Schuyler's, who was from Albany, came from New York City and Westchester. The state senate concurred, 14 to 4. Schuyler had been unceremoniously ousted from his seemingly secure seat in the United States Senate by Aaron Burr, owing to a combination of the Livingstons, Clinton, and Burr and upstate opposition to Hamilton and his dynamic but controversial federal programs.

Aaron Burr must have had Hamilton in his eye when he gloated, with mock restraint, "I have reason to believe that my election will be unpleasing to several Persons now in Philada."

Fresh from the shock of the upset, Hamilton's oldest friend, Robert Troup, wrote him, on January 19, 1791, "About an hour ago the election of Senator was brought in the assembly. Burr succeeded by a decided majority . . ." Troup was also one of Aaron Burr's old and intimate friends, so he was in a position to know many more confidences than he could honorably disclose to his other old friend, Hamilton.

"The twistings, combinations and maneuvers to accomplish this are incredible," wrote Troup, adding, "We are going headlong into the bitterest opposition to the Genl. Government—I pity you Most sincerely—for I know that you have not a wish but what is combined with the solid honor & interests of America."

Troup feared that there was no limit or proportion, short of complete annihilation, to the lengths to which the opposition's hatred of Hamilton and his system would go. They aimed to destroy both, said Troup: "*Delenda est Carthago* is the maxim applied to your administration." Troup, of course, remained an unwavering ally: "My advice to you is to continue as you have done . . . The time will come when your enemies will blush they are in opposition to you."

Nothing could have galled Hamilton more than the realization that his own successes in Philadelphia and the instrumentality of his archrival, New York City Lawyer Aaron Burr, had heaped humiliation on the proud father whom his adoring Elizabeth and his adoring Angelica and he himself all adored with powerfully reciprocal fervor.

Making an effort to put a mild face on the degrading upset he had helped cause her father, Hamilton wrote Angelica on January 31 that "our republican ideas stand much in the way of accumulating offices in one family." He would try to use all his influence in Philadelphia to get Schuyler a ministerial appointment abroad, although by now the secretary of state was bound to block the way. This would be the least of the things he would try to do for her, Hamilton promised, because "there is no proof of my affection which I would not willingly give you."

Wistfully, he added, "I look forward to a period, not *very* distant, when the establishment of order in our Finances will enable me to execute a favorite wish. I must endeavor to see Europe one day; and you may imagine how happy I shall be to meet you, and Mr. Church there."

By his small but significant comma setting her name off from her husband's, which her eyes alone would know how to read, he punctuated his love for her alone. He closed: "God bless you, A.H."

William Duer, whose collapse and imprisonment was still a year in the future, had acted as the floor leader in Schuyler's defeat. He characteristically assigned the blame for the debacle to everyone, including Hamilton, except himself.

The election of Burr, Duer wrote Hamilton on January 19, 1791, "is the fruit of the Chancelor's [*sic*] Coalition with the Governor." Duer had wanted the voting postponed to give time to rally support, but had been "unfortunately overruled" [*sic*] by Hamilton's friends in the House. He was sure "that the measures which were taken to bring over several who had United with the Anti-federalists would have proved successful."

Duer's own private business ventures were in such disarray that only wildly successful future speculations could bail him out. Despite his implied reproaches, he still professed ardent loyalty to Hamilton and even more to the future success of Hamilton's economic program; his outrage at Burr's upset of Schuyler was beyond words: "I can not Express how much I feel on the present Occasion! To see the Fabrick you have been rearing, for Ensuring the Happiness of Millions, undermined by the most profligate Part of the Community, and its most faithful Servants treated with the blackest Ingratitude, . . . The greatness of the Evil, requires however the Exertion of all our Fortitude. God knows, that my own private Concerns require all that I can Summon." Duer implied that Hamilton had been "undermined" and betrayed by everyone but himself: "Rest assured however, that whatever Defections you may Experience, in others, that in me you will Ever find that warm, and Unabated Friendship, which you have a Right to Claim. Point out what is to be done, to rally a broken Party, and trust to my Exertions to carry your Views into Execution."

With friends like Duer, Hamilton hardly needed enemies. Later in January, James Tillary, another of Hamilton's loyal supporters in New York City, assessed the somber political situation less emotionally, but in a way that showed Hamilton even more menacing danger than even Troup's and Duer's warnings:

> A coalition of Interests from different principles produced his [Burr's] Election—He is avowedly your Enemy, & stands pledged to his party for a reign of Vindictive declamation against your Measures. The Chancellor [R. R. Livingston] hates, & would destroy you—Nay so incautious was he at a public Masonic Dinner last St. John's Day that he declared himself to me without any Stipulation of Secrecy, that he was not only opposed to your Funding System, but that R. Morris & several other well informed Influential Characters, viewed it as a system of public injustice. . . . We want a Head, to repress & keep down the machinations of our restless Demagogue [Clinton], but alas where is he to be found?

Badly as a leader was needed, Tillary had no use for Duer: "Duer never can prop the *good old cause* here. He is unfit as a leader & unpopular as a man." Furthermore, Duer was in unwitting cahoots with crooks, Tillary said. "He is duped by some characters without ever suspecting it."

As the New York State attorney general, Aaron Burr had been ex officio member of the Board of Land Commissions, which early in 1791 had sold 5,-542,173 acres of state lands at eight pence apiece, the price of a loaf of bread, to a group of speculators led by Alexander McComb, who had been a client of Burr, as well as of Hamilton. It was unknown at the time that the attorney general was a silent partner of McComb and the other speculators and owned a significant financial share in the transaction. When news of the bargain leaked out into public print, there were loud cries of protest, but Burr's participation as the silent partner had remained a secret. Federalist papers accused Governor Clinton of collusion with McComb, and the assembly weighed a resolution to indict the commissioners for fraud.

Newly elected United States Senator Burr calmly cleared himself of the scandal by pointing to the minutes of the board, which showed that he had been "absent on official duty" on the date of the land sales. Although important business of this kind could hardly have been consummated at a single sitting or without knowledge of all five members of the commission, this transparent alibi sufficed to exonerate Burr. If profitable fraud in sales of public lands were to escape prosecution, it was always a great help to have as one of the silent partners who would profit from its success the state's attorney general.

Burr now suddenly came up with the funds to acquire from Trinity Church the unexpired portion of the 99-year lease on Richmond Hill, the proudest estate in New York. It was the establishment that John and Abigail Adams had occupied when they first moved to New York to embark upon vice-presidential duties with the highest possible aristocratic tone. Its splendor of white columns stood above gardened lawns sloping down to the Hudson. Here Senator Burr and his Theodosia would entertain at sumptuous banquets. A story that later went the rounds was that after dinner guests and host would sometimes retire to the veranda for a contest at marksmanship. Harry, one of the household slaves, would toss up apples from a distance. He was quoted as saying, "De Colonel would hit 'em almos' ebery time, but d'oder gentlemen couldn't hit 'em no whar."

At no estate in New York would wealthy plantation owners from Virginia like Thomas Jefferson and James Madison who would come to visit the senator that summer feel more at home than with Aaron and Theodosia Burr at Richmond Hill. It was the nearest thing a self-made New York City man could find to a Montpelier or a Monticello.

Although Schuyler's humiliation did not cause him to evince any resentment toward his favorite son-in-law for whatever his role in it had been, Hamilton's own conscience would not exonerate him of a heavy portion of the blame. All through 1791, for a year and more, he repeatedly urged Schuyler to take some kind of reprisal against Burr. On January 29, 1792, Schuyler finally had to caution Hamilton, "As no good can possibly result from evincing any resentment to Mr. Burr for the part he took last winter, I have on every occasion behaved towards him as if he had never been the principal in the business."

Troup had closed the ominous and mysterious letter he had written to Hamilton half an hour after the news of the voting:

> I shall withdraw from politics for the present. I am disgusted to my heart.
>
> God bless you.

For Hamilton, time passing could not erase the anguish or permit him, like Troup, to resign his exposed office before it was too late.

While the capital was still in New York, Jefferson had begun to smolder with resentment at, among other things, what he considered to be the one-sided treatment of news about governmental doings in the local press. The *United States Gazette*, which John Fenno started in New York in 1789, purported to be a semiofficial newspaper, devoted almost entirely to governmental affairs. The

34-year-old secretary of the treasury had, of course, been the most active and visible member of the government that had been launched in his hometown, and Fenno's *United States Gazette* had come to seem to Jefferson as if it were Hamilton's own personal house organ, even if it were not. When the seat of government moved to Philadelphia, Fenno and his newspaper followed. To Jefferson, their seemingly pro-Hamilton and progovernment bias seemed to continue unchanged.

The newspapers were the dominant communications medium used by all the adversaries of the day. Public interest in the doings of the demigods who now held unsceptered sway in the newly invented executive branch of the constitutional government was high. Newspapers keeping it that way kept up their own circulations. As is true of most newspapers today, at least half and usually more of their space was taken up by advertisements and public announcements. Most of the rest was news or features of entertainment value, which enticed readers into purchasing the heavy freight of advertising—reports of murders, ship sinkings, scandals, obituaries, and social events. The newspapers of the 1790s also carried some baggage of opinion and editorializing, which could usually be pulled out at the last minute by editors to make room for important advertising or more exciting stories. Much of the political material had a sharpness and depth that bespeak a higher regard on the part of editors like Fenno for the intelligence and reasoning powers of their readers (as distinguished from appeals to their presumed visceral, or animal, responses) than editors of modern newspapers usually demonstrate toward present-day readers.

Unlike many modern newspapers those of the 1790s did not preen themselves on "objectivity" in political reporting. Nor did they run self-serving statements issued by party officials with whom they agreed as news items as if they were matters of observable fact like fires. Instead, they ran them as polemical broadsides by anonymous partisans who used assumed names. Often the names had a classical resonance that reinforced the subject matter.

The pointed or colorful or extravagant or barbed or witty style of many of these polemics lent them an entertainment value that seems absent from all but a few of their modern counterparts. Such polemics did not fail to draw counterfire.

Jefferson called Fenno's *United States Gazette* "a paper of pure Toryism, disseminating the doctrines of monarchy, aristocracy and the exclusion of the influence of the people." Hamilton's cash books show that he made a loan of $100 to Fenno on October 19, 1790, and another loan of $100 on January 8, 1791. It seems likely that Fenno needed help from Hamilton and others to cover extra expenses made necessary by the move from New York to Philadelphia, over and above the regular payments he was receiving from the Treasury Department itself and the Senate for printing official government notices. Hamilton was too poor a man to forgive IOU's, or let them go for long unpaid. The freedom of the press guaranteed by the Bill of Rights' First Amendment has always been a splendid freedom—but one that can be fully enjoyed only by those at a relatively high economic level, the level that seems to be assumed in the panegyrics to the

First Amendment generally carried as lead stories by the press.

None of this was lost on a champion of the Bill of Rights like Jefferson, but he tended to be secretive when he operated on the exalted level of freedom of the press. Although Philip Freneau had had no previous experience as a translator or in running a newspaper, he was a Princeton man like Madison and Burr. He had done some writing for Francis Childs's *Daily Advertiser* in New York, but he was best known as a poet of republican persuasions. On February 28, 1791, Jefferson wrote to him in New York offering him the post of translating clerk in the State Department. The State Department job paid only $250 a year, but, as the secretary pointed out, its limited duties would "not interfere with any other calling" its occupant might choose. "Another calling" would be the use of Freneau's sharp, satirical pen in anti-Hamilton journalism.

This was not a lavish offer of political subsidy with the government's money, as was later charged. Some of Jefferson's later gifts and loans to amenable journalists were small by Jefferson's lavish standards, but large by the standards of most newspapermen or of anything that Hamilton could afford even to lend them. Freneau turned down this first of Jefferson's offers. The secretary of state tried to persuade the equally Republican Benjamin Franklin Bache to make a national paper out of his *Philadelphia General Advertiser,* which would later become famous as the *Aurora.* Bache shared many of Jefferson's opinions, but not his idea of keeping a newspaper on the payroll of the State Department.

Jefferson turned back to Freneau and sought Madison's help in changing Freneau's mind. From New York, Madison wrote Jefferson on May 1 that he thought he might have brought Freneau around. But when there was no follow-up from Freneau, Jefferson wrote Madison unhappily on May 9 that Freneau must have turned them down once more: "your favor of the 1st came to hand on the 3rd. Mr. Freneau has not followed it: I suppose therefore he has changed his mind back again, for which I am really sorry." On May 15, Jefferson sent a copy of Fenno's *United States Gazette* to Thomas Mann Randolph, expostulating that it was a "paper of pure Toryism," and adding, "we have been trying to get another weekly or half weekly paper set up excluding advertisements, so that it might go through the states, & furnish a whig vehicle of intelligence. We hoped at one time to have persuaded Freneau to set up here, but failed."

Jefferson himself would go to New York and make another bid to Freneau. As Jefferson wrote Madison July 21, 1791, in addition to the $250 State Department salary, he would give Freneau and his paper "perusal of all my letters of foreign intelligence." He would subsidize him with "the publication of all proclamations and other public notices within my department and the printing of the laws." Freneau finally changed his mind, came to Philadelphia, and started his own newspaper called the *National Gazette.* It began publishing on October 31 with a series of attacks on Hamilton and his policies. Soon it became recognized as the official news organ of Jefferson and Madison.

When Hamilton later angrily charged that Jefferson was using a government job in the State Department to subsidize a newspaper that continuously attacked the government, Jefferson replied that Freneau had first applied to him for a job long before, in New York, but that there had been no vacancy then. Jefferson alleged that only after the government had moved to Philadelphia and Freneau applied again, had the vacancy arisen.

Washington took Freneau's attacks as attacks on himself and asked Jefferson for an explanation. Jefferson's answer of September 9, 1792, has the ring of that of a witness unprepared for the questions of a skeptical congressional investigating committee. Jefferson could not recollect at what point in time he learned of Freneau's running the *National Gazette*, but there were good reasons related to foreign policy for the State Department's hiring him anyway. "I cannot recollect," he testified, "whether it was at the same time, or afterwards, that I was told he had thought of setting up a newspaper there." Jefferson was saying, in effect, that though he could not remember, he also had a cover story, too. "But whether then, or afterwards, I considered it as a circumstance of some value, as it might enable me to do, what I had long wished to have done, that is, to have the material parts of the Leyden gazette brought under your eye & that of the public, in order to possess yourself and them of a juster view of the affairs of Europe. . . ."

The rationalist son of the enlightenment called upon heaven as witness. He told the man who could not tell a lie that he had not attempted "any kind of influence" to get Freneau to Philadelphia. Washington would not know of all the contrary facts that lay behind Jefferson's stammering denial. A prosecuting attorney in Washington's place who did would have paused before putting the final question of the series intended to discredit the witness. He would then introduce as an exhibit Jefferson's May 15, 1791, letter to Thomas Mann Randolph, pause again, and allow the witness to read the exhibit. He would then ask him what he had meant by writing, "We have been trying to get another *weekly* or *half weekly* paper set up . . . so that it might go through the states; & furnish a whig vehicle of intelligence. We hoped at one time to have persuaded Freneau to set up here, but failed."

Besides having Thomas Paine's best seller *The Rights of Man* to carry Jefferson's advertisement for himself to all parts of the country and Freneau on his payroll to help the *National Gazette* to carry favorable publicity as current news, Jefferson would obviously find it useful to have his own man inside Hamilton's Treasury Department. So the day after Nicholas Eveleigh, the comptroller, died on April 16, 1791, Jefferson sent Washington an application for the vacancy from Tench Coxe, then the assistant secretary. All Washington had to do was to sign the blank commission form Jefferson sent on with it to ratify Coxe's appointment. Jefferson did not bother to consult Hamilton, or Madison either, for that matter. He told Coxe he hoped his application would be successful. Hamilton, on the other hand, recommended Oliver Wolcott, Jr., the auditor, about whom he had previously spoken to Washington, for the comptroller's office. Hamilton told Washington that other candidates would be brought to the president's attention by "weighty advocates." When reports of Jefferson's meddlesome interference with personnel promotions in Hamilton's department began to circulate, Madison minimized them. Jefferson covered his own role, at least to Madison, on July 27, by accusing Hamilton of giving out the Tench Coxe story in garbled form: Hamilton had improperly revealed confidential inside secrets of governmental administration. There is no record of Hamilton's having discussed the matter with anyone but Washington, who approved Hamilton's recommendation of Wolcott and discarded Jefferson's blank form.

As Hamilton's great reports came before Congress in majestic progression and their recommendations bit by bit became law over Madison's opposition, Jefferson's rising feelings of frustration and anger at the seemingly irresistible advance of the Hamilton program tended to prick his interest in Aaron Burr. The newly elected senator from New York, who had upset Hamilton's father-in-law and weakened, pro tanto, Hamilton's hegemony in the Senate, was the only man in the country who had so far shown himself able to interpose a check to the surge of success that the secretary of the treasury was riding in the spring of 1791.

Jefferson's warm curiosity about an alliance with Burr was further heightened by an unsolicited letter he received shortly after Burr's election from Henrietta Maria Colden. She was a beautiful widow who lived in New York, knew Elizabeth and Alexander Hamilton, and was a frequent guest of the Burrs at Richmond Hill. The more or less usual rumors that both Burr and Hamilton had enjoyed affairs with Henrietta Colden did nothing to dispel Jefferson's curiosity. Madison, much to the chagrin of some of his friends to the southward, was lingering in New York from April through August, and the prim little man was known to have taken a warm interest in this peacock lady, too. Dr. Samuel Latham Mitchell wrote in 1802 that Madison "was fascinated by the celebrated Mrs. Colden, of our city, she who was so noted for her masculine understanding and activity as well as for feminine graces and accomplishments." Henrietta was even said by some to have "inspired in Jefferson a momentary flash." By reputation arising largely from the shaky assumption that her politics were inseparable from those of her late departed husband, Cadwallader Colden, Henrietta was reputed to be a Federalist. Hence it was especially remarkable that she should now write to Jefferson to call his attention to the man who had suddenly risen from local political obscurity into the strongest possible position to do Federalists harm:

> The attention of the good folks of this city was lately engrossed by the choice of a new Senator to Congress. The gentleman brought in by Governor Clinton's party, 'Not to oppose, but to keep a sharp look out on the measures of the Government' is a man of too considerable abilities, for the side he has taken. If he moves on antifederal ground, he may do *harm*.

Some specialists have suggested that Hamilton inspired Henrietta to write her letter to Jefferson; in view of the tensions that were building between him and Jefferson and Madison at the time and of Hamilton's deep chagrin at Schuyler's upset, it is more likely that Hamilton was the last man in the country to have wished anyone to write such a letter to Jefferson. By the same token nothing would have served Burr's interests better at the moment as an enticing way to break the political ice with Jefferson.

The press of departmental and legislative business that kept the secretary of the treasury engaged at the capital did not detain the secretary of state from junketing afar. On May 17, Jefferson set out from Philadelphia on a trip of 920 miles that would keep him out of touch with his office for more than a month. It was elaborately given out that the junket was for scientific purposes, including the collection of data on the Hessian fly. Jefferson's itinerary included New York City, where Aaron Burr and Freneau could be found; the Hudson River valley, where Governor George Clinton and Chancellor Robert R. Livingston could be found; and Lake George, Lake Champlain, Bennington (Vermont), Pittsfield (Massachusetts), the Connecticut River valley, and Long Island, where, among other things, the Hessian fly could probably be found, if not indeed in Philadelphia or Monticello. From there he would proceed to Flushing, Brooklyn, and back again to New York City. Arriving in New York, Jefferson stayed at Mrs. Ellsworth's boarding house, where Madison and Freneau were lodged awaiting him. He joined in Madison's urgings to Freneau to come to Philadelphia. John Beckley, too, was in New York. While the two middle-aged politicians from the South would proceed on their junket up the Hudson, Beckley would split off and proceed by way of the New England coast to Boston.

Hamilton's confidant George Beckwith wrote home that he thought Jefferson's and Madison's trip was designed to promote anti-British policies. Beckwith had tried to counter their purposes by making a more or less parallel trip of his own. Sir John Temple, the British consul at New York, reported his suspicions about Jefferson's, Madison's, and Beckley's trips and their true purposes.

"I am sorry to inform your Grace," he told the duke of Leeds, "that the Secretary of State's Party and Politicks gains ground here, and I fear will have influence enough to cause acts and resolves which may be unfriendly to Great Britain, to be passed early in the next session of Congress. The Secretary of State, together with Mr. Madison . . . are now . . . gone to the Eastern States, there to proselyte as far as they are able to a commercial war with Great Britain."

In Boston John Beckley found that John Adams was still enraged at Jefferson for reading his *Discourses* and misrepresenting them. "And overwhelming me with floods and whirlwinds of tempestuous abuse, unexampled in the history of this country," Adams snorted. Beckley's report that sentiment around Boston was pro-Jefferson and anti-Adams in the debate aroused by Jefferson's advertisement pleased his mentor. Beckley also reported that the *Publicola* pamphlet was thought to be the work of John Quincy Adams using materials furnished by his father.

Years later Jefferson denied that he had conferred with Burr on this trip or that he had ever met Burr at any time before or during this trip. Reclusive as Jefferson was, he and Burr had both been among the most prominent of New

York City's 30,000 or so citizens (of whom only about 13,000 were freeholders) during the year the government had been in the city.

"I had never seen Colonel Burr," Jefferson wrote to his *Anas* years later, "until he came [to Philadelphia] . . . as a member of the Senate." Furthermore, from the first, Jefferson claimed to have distrusted the man Hamilton's followers alleged he had journeyed so far to seek to enlist as his political ally. Jefferson added to his *Anas* that Burr's "conduct very soon inspired me with distrust. I habitually cautioned Madison against trusting him too much."

To claim that he had not "seen" Burr in New York is not to say that all necessary communications with Burr could not have passed discreetly back and forth between them through Jefferson's usual agents Madison and Beckley. What was Jefferson trying to hide by the unlikely claim that while he had been in New York on a scientific expedition, he had not seen the brightest new rising political star of the anti-Hamilton party?

Hamilton's son and biographer, John C. Hamilton, had no doubt that Jefferson was untruthful. He wrote that "after frequent interviews with Chancellor Livingston and Burr," Jefferson and Madison "made a visit to Clinton under the pretext of a botanical excursion to Albany, thence extended their journey to Vermont; and, having sown a few tares in Connecticut, returned to the seat of government." John Quincy Adams similarly attributed to Jefferson a "double dealing" character. Charles Francis Adams, grandson of John Adams and the editor of his collected works agreed with Hamilton's and Adams's sons:

"More ardent in his imagination than his affections, he did not always speak exactly as he felt towards either friends or enemies," Adams wrote; "as a consequence, he had left hanging over part of his public life a vapor of duplicity, or, to say the least, of indirection, the presence of which is generally felt more than it is seen."

A contemporary report received by Hamilton after Jefferson's and Madison's junket ended ridiculed them because "they scouted silently through the country, shunning the gentry, communing with and pitying Shaysites." But this odd junket was no joke to friends who knew and loved Hamilton best and were in a position to know the threat to him it posed. To them it was Hamilton, not the Hessian fly, who was now to be hunted down.

Writing to Hamilton from New York again on June 15, 1791, Troup repeated with still more ominous anxiety the same words of warning he had sent in January when Burr had ambushed Schuyler to win his seat: "There was every appearance of a passionate courtship between the Chancellor [Robert R. Livingston], Burr, Jefferson and Madison when the two latter were in town. *Delenda est Carthago* is the maxim adopted with respect to you . . . if they succeed they will tumble the fabric of the government in ruins to the ground." To the quarry selected for the coming implacable manhunt, Troup gamely tried to provide some cheer: "I cannot say I have the slightest uneasiness." But it was the tone of a man whistling in the eye of a whirlwind: "You are too well seated in the hearts of the citizens of the Northern and Middle States to be hunted down by them."

In February, as one of the three vice-presidents of the American Philosophical Society, Jefferson had passed the name of Alexander Hamilton for admission to this select group. It had been established "for promoting useful knowledge . . . advancing the Interest of the Society by associating to themselves Men of distinguished Eminence, and of conferring Marks of their Esteem upon Persons of literary Merit . . . Rights of Fellowship, with all Liberties and Privileges thereunto belonging."

While protests and applause continued to mount in the country that spring over Jefferson's endorsement of *The Rights Of Man,* he had called a committee meeting of the society and seriously charged it with the task of hunting down information about the Hessian fly. Whatever else Hamilton and Adams and their circles might say about Jefferson, none would deny him credit for skill and success as a political operator, a game of which duplicity is sometimes the name. The choice of the Hessian fly for the name of the quarry of their foray into New York had about it a touch of political genius. *Hessian* carried connotations of British monarchs and monarchists, foreign invaders and cruel atrocities. The fly seemed to be a foreign threat to the wheat, barley, rye, and straw crops of all good and usually anti-Federalist small agrarians. To hunt down an enemy like the Hessian fly would never lose a shrewd political operator a single vote. It would win applause from all who had a grievance against insect pests, British monarchs, or overseas creditors. It was as safe a subject for fearless political attack as the rattlesnake. Only a member of the American Philosophical Society of a more scientific bent than Jefferson would quibble that the Hessian fly might more properly be called the gall midge, or that other cecidomyiids without such politically suggestive popular names were of as much or more interest to science.

From his and Madison's "passionate courtship" of Burr while ostensibly hunting down the Hessian fly, Jefferson brought back to his daughter Maria some notes he had scribbled on birchbark while sailing on Lake George. He had also shot three squirrels and, indeed, killed two rattlesnakes "of a sutty dark color and obscurely chequered." But for the scientific purposes of the American Philosophical Society's committee, Jefferson's notes on the Hessian fly were undecipherable and useless. No matter. No more perfect code name than Operation Hessian Fly could have been conceived as a cover, and a cry to the pack as well, for a hunting down of a Hamilton to a kill. *Delenda est Paterson!*

6

SOMETHING . . .
TO DISSOLVE THE CHARM

THOUGH I WAS NOT COMPLETELY THE DUPE OF THE ILLUSION—YET
I WAS MADE TO DOUBT OF THE REAL STATE OF THINGS
—The Reynolds Pamphlet, *August 25, 1797*

Shortly after Thomas Jefferson returned from his northward junket to his house at Eighth and Market in Philadelphia, Hamilton received a surprise visit at his own house from a rather well-connected woman who had also just recently journeyed down from New York, or so she said.

The best source of information about the first of her many visits to Hamilton's house in Philadelphia is the account Hamilton wrote for the American public and published in the newspapers in August of 1797 after having succeeded in keeping it a secret from all but a widening circle of insiders for more than six years. The autograph draft of this account is in the Hamilton papers in the Library of Congress. The draft is reproduced in the Hamilton Papers along with the final printed version. The differences between the draft and the printed version are slight but significant and tell a small story of their own. What follows is based on the draft. Notes from time to time are added to point out how Hamilton revised the story for the later printed version. It is well to keep in mind that this account is one written by a man of 40 who is looking back on an illicit love affair that he had begun when he was 34, or earlier, and telling the newspaper reading public how it all began.

> Some time in the summer of the year 1791, a woman called at my house in the city of Philadelphia, and asked to speak with me in private. She was shown into the parlour where I went to her.

In the printed version Hamilton changed the second sentence to read, "I attended her into a room apart from the family." The first version implies that Betsy and the children were away at the time (would a strange woman otherwise pay a call there without a prior invitation from Betsy?) and that Hamilton and Maria Reynolds were there alone, except for the servant who showed her into the parlor. By contrast, the later version changes the story to affirm that Hamilton and Maria Reynolds were not alone in the house and that "the family"—Betsy and the children—were at home at the time, but "apart." Both versions confirm that Maria Reynolds was not a social friend or acquaintance of his and Betsy's; otherwise, Betsy would not have remained apart during Maria's unannounced call. Hamilton's family being at home, instead of away at Albany for the summer, seems to fix the time of Maria Reynolds's first visit to their home at an earlier date in 1791 than would have been the case if it had occurred when the family was away, unless her first visit to him had been a year or years earlier. Hamilton's draft continues:

> With a seeming air of distress she informed me that she was a daughter of a Mr. Lewis, sister to a Mrs. G. Livingston of the State of New York, and wife to a Mr. Reynolds, whose father was in the Commissary or Quarter Master Department during the war with Great Britain—that her husband who for a long time had treated her very cruelly, had lately left her to live with another woman, and so destitute that though desirous of returning to her friends, she had not the means —that knowing I was a citizen of the same state of New York, she had taken the liberty to address herself to my humanity for relief.

His first draft goes on: "There was something odd in the application and the story yet there was a [genuineness] simplicity and modesty in the manner of relating it which gave an impression of its truth."

The words *something odd*—an admission that her mysterious visit instantly aroused his suspicions—are omitted from the later printed version.

More or less as usual, the secretary of the treasury was short of ready cash. With customary gallantry, he made amends for being short by his response to the pleas of the attractive New Yorker who allegedly lacked coach fare home:

> I replied, that her situation was an interesting one and that I was disposed to afford her as much aid as might be [necessary] sufficient to convey her to her friends, but that at the instant it was not convenient

to me (which was truly the case) . . . I would send or bring it to her in
the course of the day.

Perhaps, if it were true that his family had not yet gone north, his own house
did not seem quite the right place for making such a payment.

"She gave me the street and the number of the house where she lodged,"
continued Hamilton.

Although Hamilton's telegraphic account of their meeting does not include
the Reynoldses Philadelphia address, the later account of Richard Folwell, who
had also known the Reynoldses over a number of years, supplies it. It was not
a humble rooming house. Folwell wrote that they "lived in stile in a large house
in Vine Street next to the corner of Fifth." Folwell had gone there to visit them,
he said, "to see if possible how people supported grandeur, without apparently
friends, money, or industry." She was not an itinerant visitor from New York
at all; they lived in a Philadelphia town house.

One way to support such grandeur would be money from men like Hamilton
or preferably men much richer. But it would be surprising if seeing the "stile"
and "grandeur" of her "large house in Vine Street" did not strengthen Hamilton's original suspicions that her sad tale of being a transient, impoverished New
Yorker longing to be home from Philadelphia was a pack of lies—if he had ever
believed it in the first place.

Hamilton continued, "In the evening I put a thirty dollar bill in my pocket
and went to the house. I inquired for Mrs. Reynolds and was shewn up stairs,
at the head of which she met me and conducted me into a bedroom."

At this dramatic high point in his draft occurs an extraordinary, indeed,
ludicrous slip of his pen. He first wrote, "I took the bill out of my pocket and
delivered it to him." Then he struck out the pronoun *him* and rewrote *her*. In
the printed version he rewrote the whole sentence to change the word *delivered*
to say that he "gave" it to her. This changed the earlier thought that he was
"delivering" a previously agreed upon quid pro quo, as he might to a pimp, who
would be collecting for her, into the later assertion that he was "giving" spon-
taneous charity to a poor woman in distress, without thought of quid pro quo
of any kind. Thereafter, "some conversation ensued which made it quickly apparent that other than pecuniary consolation would not be unacceptable." He added
that "it required a harder heart than mine to refuse it to a pretty woman in
distress." Then he struck out the words *pretty woman* and made her a "beauty"
instead. In the printed version he struck out the whole sentence.

Peter A. Grotjean, a Philadelphia merchant, who a few years later became
a friend of one Mrs. Maria Clement, a widow whom he discovered to be the
former Maria Reynolds, described her as a person of intelligence, sensibility, and
gentleness of manner. Aaron Burr is known to have found her agreeable; and
she, him. Nathan Schachner, in his *Alexander Hamilton*, describes her as a
"bold, florid, handsome woman" with "coarsely handsome features." Hamilton's
old friend Jeremiah Wadsworth and others of their circle knew her and also
found her attractive. Hamilton said she had a highly emotional temperament and

was much given to weeping. All accounts agree that she must have been a woman whose generous exudations of sex appeal would have instantly shown any visitor like Richard Folwell the means by which she contrived to support "grandeur, without apparently friends, money or industry."

After these first two meetings, Hamilton went on to say that "I had frequent meetings with her—most of them at my own house. Mrs. Hamilton being absent on a visit to her father with her children." He added starkly that "the intercourse with Mrs. Reynolds, in the meantime continued." It would continue for at least the next year and a half. He explained that "her conduct made it very difficult to disentangle myself."

Nothing in Hamilton's account tells of anything personal to her or to himself or any flaw in their relationship that would have been a reason for his breaking off their affair when he did, except Hamilton's concern for what her husband might do. If it had ever been true that her husband, James Reynolds, had "treated her very cruelly and left her to live with another woman," as she had at first told Hamilton to arouse his sympathy, Reynolds was not long returning so as to become again a troublesome figure on the domestic scene.

"Various reflections (among these the knowledge I had acquired of Reynolds' speculating character and pursuits and certain symptoms of contrivance and plot between her husband and her) induced me to wish to drop it," Hamilton explained in the draft. But in the printed version Hamilton removed the pointed references to Reynolds's "speculating" character and softened his own word *knowledge* of the "plot" between them to mere vague "suspicion" of "some concert" between them.

Because he was writing six years after these events, it may have slipped Hamilton's mind that a written record existed that showed that he had had some acquaintance with Reynolds in New York at least four years earlier—ever since Reynolds had brought him the false and damaging reports originating from Philadelphia that seemed to impute to him advocating that the bishop of Osnaburg, the son of King George III, be installed as the monarch of America. Originally from Connecticut and a former member of Jeremiah Wadsworth's Commissary Department, Reynolds's name had needed no introduction to a prominent New York businessman like Jeremiah Wadsworth when Hamilton had mentioned it in a letter to him. Wadsworth was John Barker Church's former partner, a representative from Connecticut, and always a staunch friend and supporter of Hamilton. James Madison, too, had heard all about Reynolds, of course. The letters Madison had received in the spring of 1790 from Gustavus B. Wallace describing Reynolds's frauds on poor old Virginia and North Carolina soldiers made possible by the use of lists obtained by Reynolds and his New York partner William J. Vredenbergh, of 40 Dock Street, from a clerk in Hamilton's Treasury Department had helped to shock Madison into switching to the strongest kind of opposition to Hamilton's economic program. Hamilton probably did not know what Madison knew about Reynolds. Reynolds's frauds had also helped shock Jefferson into the unwavering support of Bland's resolutions that had led to his first, but not last, clash in the cabinet with Hamilton.

Some of Madison's friends had reproached him for lingering too long in New York after Jefferson returned southward the summer of 1791, suspecting him of overfondness for Henrietta Maria Colden. Jefferson might have reproached him too, but he did not. One thing that could have waylaid Madison other than Henrietta was the task of obtaining evidence of Reynolds's and Vredenbergh's ties to whoever the clerk in the Treasury Department was who had leaked out the lists of old soldiers' names and amounts in the days before the Treasury Department had moved south. Circumstantial evidence of ties between Reynolds and Wadsworth and of ties linking Reynolds to William Duer, the former assistant secretary of the treasury, was strong. With inside help from John Beckley, the clerk of the House, and from Tench Coxe, inside the Treasury but unhappily unpromoted, solid evidence that might implicate Hamilton as well as Duer might be hunted down by Madison at 40 Dock Street, at the Duers, at Mrs. Colden's, at the Burrs at Richmond Hill, and at many other places he might explore in the former capital.

Describing his intercourse with Maria Reynolds as it continued through the busy, hot Philadelphia summer of 1791, Hamilton's first draft coldly describes Maria as doing no more than "play acting" the "appearances of a violent attachment." She seemed merely to simulate "extreme distress at the idea of an interruption of the connection"—as a good, experienced, professional prostitute should when servicing a philandering man of the world. But his printed version transmutes this earlier, worldlier reading into the idea that she felt a believable, lustful, yet romantic passion for him that was genuine. In either case, she performed with "an infinite art, aided by the more genuine effects of an ardent temperament and a quick sensibility." So much so that "though I was not completely the dupe of the illusion—yet I was made to doubt of the real state of things." He made himself seem genuinely uncertain. "My vanity perhaps admitting too easily the *possibility* of a [sincere] real fondness on the part of Mrs. Reynolds, I adopted the plan of a gradual discontinuance rather than a sudden cessation of the intercourse as likely to occasion least pain."

In most men's lives, if no real affection is felt in such an affair, a sudden breaking off is the customary and, once the first shock of coitus interruptus is past, the less painful method of ending it. Hamilton's announced plan of "gradual discontinuance" proved its own absurdity; their affair would continue for at least a year and a half. The abrupt and terrifying manner by which it would finally be broken off was nowhere within the ken of any such unlikely plan of "gradual discontinuance." While the plan supposedly remained on the agenda, currents of intense passion—or at least, on her part, the convincing semblance of it—flowed between the two of them.

There can be few cat's cradles of emotion and suspicion more tangled and complex than the one in which Hamilton found himself trapped that summer of 1791. His very first impression of it was that his affair with Maria Reynolds had grown out of some sort of a plot. Why had she come to his house unannounced? Why had she thrust herself on him with the flimsiest of hard luck stories when the last shred of believability would vanish the same day when he saw her luxurious lodgings and found her quickly willing to accept "other than pecuniary consolation" from him. But why should she seek money from him? There were many richer men in Philadelphia than he. She seemed to need his money less, really than he needed hers. Richer Philadelphia gentlemen had more leisure time than he did to devote to caressing her and fewer preoccupations to distract them. At his and her mature ages, only leisurely cultivation of the art of making love to her whole body and soul would excite in her a real fondness for him, as he would know. *"Lentement, lentement,"* as the French sometimes say in bed.

Only a man of great leisure and charm could quickly capture a woman of Maria's beauty and experience who could normally be expected to feel nothing more than a quickly passing flash of excitement for a harried, married, exposed, underpaid, and overworked public official like Hamilton. On his part, Hamilton had been a realist about women, like most else, at least since 20, when he had found Kitty Livingston, like most women, an enigmatical being through whose head thoughts yet coursed not much differently than through his own. Realism had warned him and made him suspicious that Maria Reynolds was acting out a role in a plot. But what plot? Whose plot? Why should Reynolds, as Maria had first alleged, have left her to live with another woman and then quickly rejoined Maria in a "plot and contrivance between them"? Did their distracting, joint "plot and contrivance" blot out for Hamilton the subplot that was the main plot that had sent the two of them to his Philadelphia home to hunt him out in the first place?

This writer's opinion is that Hamilton's first impression was correct. Maria was playacting when she paid her first call on him in Philadelphia. Realism should then have told him that it was not the modest price of coach fare back to New York that she wanted nor even the price he could afford to pay for a night's pleasure, but that she was part of a far more sinister plot. But the fact that their affair had seemed to begin in a tawdry way was no reason why it might not suddenly have tumefied into a love affair with strong bonds of passion, suffering, and pleasure on both sides. Everything that is known about Maria Reynolds reveals her as a woman as passionate, indiscreet, and compelling to the opposite sex as Hamilton was a man.

Badger baiting was a game much better known to sports-minded eighteenth-century gentlemen than to those of the twentieth century. It was the cruel sport of setting on dogs to draw out a badger from its hole. By humorous association it also meant to be overextended, to overdraw one's bank account, as in the expression "he had overdrawn his badger." To badger also, of course, meant "to subject (one who cannot escape from it) to persistent worry or persecution." Then it was the strongest possible term for irritating, persecuting, and injuring a man in every way. It lacked most of the gentler modern shades of meaning merely to pester or to tease.

A badger game was the kind of game whose rules men who were gentlemen born like Jefferson, Madison, and Burr would know in their bones from boyhood. A gentleman self-made in later life like Hamilton might well grow up with a blind spot to the fun of it or to its uses. In any event, as his and Maria's intercourse continued and their commitment to each other became more passionate and intense, Hamilton clearly suffered from a serious blind spot about what really was happening to him. Later on, his earlier suppressed suspicions would burn the blind spot away. His printed version of the affair would hide both his own blind spot and his early and late suspicions of the sinister real plot that lay behind the conventional cuckolded husband blackmail plot, of which he told the public all—or almost all.

Aaron Burr was a humorous eighteenth-century gentleman who had enjoyed innumerable extramarital affairs. Few schemes could have seemed to him more innocuous, yet full of humor and other hopeful possibilities, than setting up Hamilton in a badger game by the use of a beautiful New Yorker like Maria Reynolds. She was a woman of good family and excellent connections. In Philadelphia she would provide amorous pleasure for the displaced summer bachelor there who was too overworked, and financially overextended to woo and keep satisfied any such desirable mistress without some outside help. And on the frequent nights when the press of business would detain the secretary of the treasury at his office, Maria Reynolds could also provide the newly elected senator some New York style consolation for the absence of his own Theodosia in New York when he would take his seat in Philadelphia for the new Senate session beginning in October.

Reynolds had already proved himself adept at shady schemes and frauds, and Beckley, Madison, and Jefferson would not mind his adding yet another to his criminal record—at Hamilton's expense. Hamilton and Wadsworth had seemingly known him and relied on his reports. All Burr would have had to do was write one letter of recommendation to Maria and one to Hamilton, warmly commending each displaced and lonely New Yorker to the other. He might have gained much credit and thanks from both, at least at the beginning. In any event, her call provided its own cover. There is no direct evidence that Burr, after the meetings in New York reported by Troup while Jefferson, Madison, and Beckley were there, used the Reynoldses as his long-bodied, short-legged badger dogs to hound Hamilton from home and family, make him overdraw his accounts, and harry him at last to a kill. Some may find in the circumstantial evidence and psychological inferences suggested above some things that are rather persuasive.

After the first weeks or a month or two of the first fine, careless rapture of an affair between an extremely overworked married man and a beautiful, desirable, and passionate mistress, it is surprising if she does not insist that he leave his wife or give her a great deal more money or spend less time at the office or all three. Not even the second of these alternatives was very far open to Hamilton. He was always badly badgered at his bank. Other circumstantial and psychological evidence that their affair was instigated by outside help from Burr or Beckley was that Maria Reynolds continued to serve Hamilton lovingly as mistress longer than is usual in such affairs without very much more from Hamilton than his occasional harried, preoccupied, nervous presence. On June 15, 1791, Hamilton was forced to ask his friend Robert Troup for $200. Troup, who had just warned Hamilton that he was now about to be hunted down, told him he could take his time repaying.

Congress bucked most problems of revenue and provision for the domestic and foreign debt over to the secretary of the treasury for answers, although many congressmen feared that they might be abdicating their proper role by leaving such matters so completely to an appointed department head. All money measures were supposed to be the exclusive responsibility of the House. However, the nature of money measures is such that they usually cannot be carpentered satisfactorily in a deliberative democratic assembly. To be effective, they must usually spring without too much advance publicity from one superior mind. Congress had passed a stopgap import duty and found the little work it had done very time-consuming, arduous, hit-or-miss, and ineffective. Hamilton politely admonished Congress to desist until a coherent policy could be reported.

On June 20, 1791, William Seton, cashier of the Bank of New York, reported that New York's $60,000 quota for subscriptions to the stock of Hamilton's newly approved Bank of the United States had been oversubscribed by $20,000 within half an hour after the legal opening. If Hamilton wished to increase the limit by another $60,000, "it would be immediately filled up." From Philadelphia, from Baltimore, and from Boston, reports poured in of the rush of moneyed men to buy in on the ground floor of his new bank. Initial success outraced Hamilton's most optimistic projections. By a single discreet word to Seton or another friend or relative as his nominee, Hamilton could at any time have been well on his way to becoming a rich man by riskless speculations in government or bank securities.

Henry Lee, en route from Philadelphia to Virginia, painted a vivid picture of the speculative excitement. "My whole route," he told Madison, "presented to me one continued scene of stock gambling; agriculture, commerce & even the fair sex relinquished, to make way for unremitted exertion in this favourite pursuit."

Hamilton's problem was the reverse of Lee's. Instead of relinquishing the fair sex for "stock gambling," he had relinquished stock gambling for "unremitted exertion" in the other "favourite pursuit." But it was against nature and foolish for Hamilton to delude himself into thinking that money and sex could remain for long unlinked.

Fearing that he might be accused of making a personal profit from his own small holdings of government bonds while the Treasury was engaged in supporting the market, he ordered William Seton to sell them for him, though at the time the price was considerably below par. All he owned was a mere $800 in the three-percents. Seton chided him for such "extreme delicacy" in the face of the current low prices and held off selling, in spite of Hamilton's repeated requests, until they had risen to 30 percent over par. Seton then proudly reported to him, "behold it has since risen four or five p Cent more very unexpectedly." In spite of the accession to Hamilton's bank account from this sale, all that remained of his bank balance on August 30 was $175.31. Hamilton wrote to another friend asking for a loan of $20 "for a few days," and the friend kindly sent him back $50.

Madison complained to Jefferson in July 1791 that

> The subscriptions [to the bank] are consequently a mere scramble for so much public plunder, which will be engrossed by those already loaded with the spoils of individuals. . . . Of all the shameful circumstances it is among the greatest to see the members of the legislature who were most active in pushing this job openly grasping its emoluments. . . . Nothing new is talked of here. In fact, stock-jobbing drowns every other subject.

Bank stock sold at $400 a share, but the funded debt and state and federal government notes, bonds, and securities of various maturities were selling in denominations as small as 13 shillings or so. Traditionally, sophisticated American investors had always placed much of their capital abroad. Now if the "moneyed men" were buying shares of America in denominations as small as 13 shillings, at least some of the buyers must be smallholders and yeomen and small farmers becoming confident enough to put their savings behind Hamilton's system. As in all good bull markets, both "investors" and "speculators" as well had to be drawn into the arena to make the market as broad and liquid as it was. Prices went up and down. It fluctuated, as markets will. Some sold their holdings of bank stock to buy and sell government bonds. Some did the reverse. Most observers, including Jefferson, interpreted the popular enthusiasm for the securities investments created by Hamilton's program as a public vote of confidence for him. It was confidence that Hamilton wanted for the new government, not himself. The people's confidence in it seemed more important to him than their huzzahs. He had always stressed that to supplement patriotic zeal and bring the people of far-flung states into support of the new, distant national government, it would be a good idea for it to let them in on the ground floor of a piece of the national debt.

Jefferson was looking at peoples' investments in naïve economic, but calculatingly political, terms when he complained to his protégé of many years, Senator James Monroe, on July 10, 1791, that

> the bank filled and overflowed in the moment it was opened. Instead of 20 thousand shares, 24 thousand were offered, & a great many unpresented who had not suspected that so much haste was necessary. Thus it is that we shall be paying 13 per cent, per ann. for 8 millions of paper money instead of having that circulation of gold & silver for nothing.

Anti-Hamilton local politics gave comfort to Jefferson because "very few subscribers have offered from Virginia or N. Carolina, which gives uneasiness to H[amilton]."

For local political reasons and to add to Hamilton's other reasons for private "uneasiness" amid public acclaim, Jefferson was publicly talking down local Virginia and North Carolina markets in U.S. government-backed securities. In a world where there has never been such a thing as a perfect long-term investment, the next best thing for most people, especially for the middle class and the poor, beginning with Hamilton's 1790 program to establish public credit and lasting to approximately the present time, has been obligations backed by the U.S. government.

Privately, Jefferson, too, was bullish on America in general and on shares of Hamilton's Bank of the United States in particular. He quietly advised his friend William Short to buy some, and Short included bank shares among his many active speculations in securities for his own personal account. Short had been secretary of the embassy at Paris when Jefferson was minister there, had stayed on when Jefferson came home, and now was chargé d'affaires in Paris. Short was knowledgeable, active, and prompt and knew the ground. Hamilton accepted him as a legacy from Jefferson and used him as his principal financial agent abroad. As is the case with most agents, Short's actions had the disadvantages of rigidity and uncertainty as to the scope of his authority. Hamilton left much to Short's "judgment, circumspection and delicacy," but only Hamilton himself, on the ground, could have been as flexible as the circumstances really required.

Hamilton took great pains to write Short long letters full of strict and detailed instructions, but the capital was a month or more removed by correspondence from fast-moving political, military, and economic events in a Europe still stunned by the French Revolution. Hamilton simply could not know and react promptly to all that was going on. Of necessity, much of importance had to be left to Short's discretion.

An act of Congress of August 12 had authorized borrowing at a rate of interest of 5 percent, but foreign bankers always added extra charges for such items as brokerage, ½ percent; sealed notary signature, advertising, paper for bonds, another ½ percent; premiums, commissions, and so forth, all of which added an additional 4 or 4½ percent in extras. Hamilton realistically interpreted the law's reference to a rate of 5 percent as exclusive of the customary "extras." He warned Short against obtaining a low rate of interest at the cost of higher extras. "A higher rate of interest upon a sum actually received, is preferable to a lower rate upon a nominal sum" with large extras, he explained. The bright prospect was that "as our resources become more unfolded and better understood," we would be able later on to refinance the loans at still lower interest rates. Therefore, with the right to repay before maturity reserved, paying a higher interest rate, but lower extra charges at the beginning would be the soundest policy over the longer term, at least if one shared Hamilton's confidence in the country.

When Hamilton became secretary of the treasury, the British were burdened with huge debts. Disputes over noncompliance with the treaty of 1783, which had ended the war, still poisoned Anglo-American relations. France was in revolutionary turmoil, and the United States was already a substantial debtor to her. Spain was short of money. By a process of elimination, Dutch bankers and the Amsterdam money market became the principal source of foreign loans. The most important of several American banking relationships there was with the firm of Willink, van Staphorst, and Hubbard.

When Short switched from this traditional Amsterdam firm of lenders and opened a loan at Antwerp at 4½ percent interest at a time when twice the amount could have been obtained at Amsterdam at 4 percent, the Amsterdam lenders were annoyed. They complained to Hamilton that Short had sold bonds to the Brabanters "at our very noses" that otherwise would have been sold through Amsterdam. Hamilton reproved Short for neglecting the advantage of a long-standing relationship while at the same time paying a higher rate of interest. In the banker's words: "Whenever a debtor borrows . . . here, there, and wherever he can find lenders, it argues . . . that either the wants are immensely great, or the means of satisfying them very confined." A poor public credit rating for the borrower would be the result. Acting through Short, Hamilton obtained agreement from France to forgo installments of principal on the United States debts to France for five or six years, provided all interest was punctually paid.

Jefferson regularly passed along to Hamilton without analysis foreign financial proposals that came to him as secretary of state, requesting Hamilton to write the replies. Hamilton had no choice but to analyze and deal with all such foreign economic policy matters through his own department. On April 15, 1791, he warned Jefferson against a French banker's scheme to pledge the debt the United States owed to France to bankers in Amsterdam to borrow money from them to pay off France. He explained to Jefferson as simply as possible the dangers in this scheme. The speculators would obtain, on the credit of the United States, hard Dutch currency at the usual exchange rate, use it to buy up French currency at its depreciated exchange rate, and pocket the difference. Hamilton explained patiently the point that Jefferson seemed to have overlooked: "France would receive from them as much *as she is entitled to receive from us,* but we should be obliged to pay [the speculators] *much more than we are obliged to pay France.*"

The summer of 1791 brought just such an opportunity to prepay the debt to France with large savings in rates of exchange, then upwards of 20 percent in favor of Holland. Hamilton instructed Short to proceed with borrowing "to an extent sufficient to discharge the entire debt to France," thereby earning for the United States the kind of profit that would have gone to the speculators if Jefferson had continued to overlook the kind of dealing that Hamilton was trying to help him understand.

In giving instructions to Short, Hamilton enjoined respect and care not to hurt the pride of the French government; he worked out for Short desirable mechanics of making transfers. The question arose not only of how, but whom to pay in France. The Amsterdam bankers complained that the problem was "to ascertain who is . . . the Sovereign of France at this moment?" Hoggner, Grand & Co. at Paris had refused to give a general receipt; if the American payments were held by them at the order of the king, the revolutionary "administration of affairs" might be angered. By Short's direction the remittance was made to the order of Commissaries of the National Treasury of France. As a bloody revolution unwinds, no banker can be sure of whom he should pay in order to obtain a valid receipt.

Hamilton asked Jefferson to help him engage the French artist and assayer Jean Pierre Droz to set up a coin stamper for the mint, as Washington had directed, and Jefferson had agreed to do so. But Jefferson's limp efforts to enlist Droz were unsuccessful, and he set up his coinage machinery for England instead.

When the American bankers in Amsterdam, Willink, van Staphorst, and Hubbard, decided to launch a loan of three million florins for the United States before the necessary authority was given by act of Congress, Hamilton warned against proceeding. But the loan money was urgently needed to help the United States meet momentary repayment demands from France, Spain, and Holland; so Hamilton accepted the loan and interpreted broadly his executive authority under different acts of Congress as permitting the borrowing to be allocated to one or the other, or partly to both of the two acts granting authority. Hamilton's eagle-eyed vision for "implied powers" in doing so outraged some in Congress. He would soon be pilloried there for merging the purposes of the two authorization laws without specific, express written authority from President Washington or Congress itself.

Hamilton also sent Short plenty of good general arguments why lenders should give the United States the best terms, or "prime rate," of interest: the smallness of the national debt compared to developing resources and also the facts that the government was conducted economically, that it was receiving immigrants from troubled Europe, and that it expected to remain at peace while other countries continued to accumulate heavy debt to wage foreign wars like those that had recently been declared by revolutionary France on Austria and Russia.

Hamilton knew that money and public credit are not respecters of national boundaries but only respecters of sound economic management. Funding, assumption of state debts, nondiscrimination, the sinking fund, the national bank, and new taxes were stern measures and usually politically unpopular at home. But such measures would bring high credit standing abroad to a new nation; failure to enact such measures would prevent it from enjoying a high credit standing. Foreign credit was necessary to permit it to purchase manufactured goods, to pay interest on borrowings, and to carry on foreign trade.

As a result of Hamilton's handling of American foreign economic policy and the success of Hamilton's legislative program in reviving the domestic economy, the securities of the new country gradually earned the highest credit ratings in all world securities markets. The interest rate and extra financing charges that the new country had to pay bankers fell below the rates that bankers demanded of Russia, Austria, and most other foreign countries. American public credit at home and abroad came to rank with the best in the world.

Learning that Washington had returned home to Mount Vernon after a tour of the South while Jefferson, Madison, and Beckley had toured in New York and eastward while Hamilton alone remained at the capital, he wrote Washington on June 19, 1791.

> There is nothing which can be said to be new here worth com-
> municating, except generally that all my accounts from *Europe*, both
> private and official, concur in proving that the impressions now enter-
> tained of our government and its affairs (I may say) *throughout* that
> quarter of the Globe are of a nature the most flattering and pleasing.
> Warmest wishes for your health and happiness.

Things were beginning to look a little too rosy. Henry Lee's and Jefferson's and Madison's July warnings that "stock jobbing drowns every other subject," including, for some, at least, "the fair sex," could not be laughed off. The most notorious of all the speculators about whom Jefferson, Madison, and their friends were complaining so bitterly was as usual, Hamilton's old friend, former assistant secretary of the treasury and cosponsor of the Society for Establishing Useful Manufactures, William Duer.

Hamilton wrote Duer a pointed warning on August 17:

> The conversation here was, Bank Script is getting so high as to become
> a bubble in one breath—in another "tis a South sea dream," in a third
> "There is a combination of knowing ones in New York to raise it as high
> as possible by fictitious purchases in order to take in the credulous and
> ignorant"—in another "Duer, [William] Constable and some others are
> mounting the balloon as fast as possible—If it don't soon burst, thou-
> sands will rue it" etc. etc.

Hamilton politely assured his friend that he could not harbor "the most distant thought" that Duer could "wander from the path either of public good or private integrity"; nonetheless, "I had serious fears for you—for your *purse* and for your *reputation*. My friendship for you and my concern for the public cause were both alarmed." Duer "would certainly have had a large portion of the blame" if "extensive mischief had ensued."

Hamilton's inside tip that "stocks are all too high" raced around the financial districts. He was forced to defend himself for speaking out to his friend Senator Rufus King. When he had "perceived the extreme to which Bank Script and with it other stock was tending," he explained, "I thought it advisable to speak out, for a bubble connected with my operations is of all the enemies I have to fear, in my judgment, the most formidable . . . To counteract delusions, appears to me to be the only secure foundation on which to stand." He had, therefore, thought it "expedient to risk something to dissolve the charm." It was a figure of speech gracefully turned for a mistress's bedroom, but as a finance minister's public defense of official jawboning of the securities markets, it had a starkly naked nuance.

The place where his revealing metaphor seemed more properly at home was in trying to explain away Angelica Church's suspicion that his old passion for her had gone suddenly slack—after Maria Reynolds had come to call. Angelica seems to have sensed—more than a year earlier than Hamilton would ever admit that Maria had paid her first visit to him—that Maria or someone like her—"something to dissolve the charm"—had one day come along. That was when, as Hamilton was nervously preparing to introduce his budget, Angelica seemed to be suffering an anxiety attack at the thought of her Hamilton's becoming as preoccupied with the tumult of business as her husband, Church, was. She had written forlornly "that having seen me is a dream which you can scarcely believe. This idea of being lost in the tumult of business and ambition does not enliven my spirits."

Still, as recently as January of 1791, Hamilton's longing for Angelica had been a matter of first person singular intensity: "There is no proof of my affection that I would not willingly give you." But by October 2, Maria's advent had diffused it to a noncommittal double entendre that brought his wife prominently into the foreground. Betsy consents "that I should love you as well as herself and this you are too reasonable to expect."

By November, Hamilton had receded to "kindly" feelings toward Angelica. He was lumping himself with Betsy under first person plural pronouns and coupling their joint "affection" to a stiff, dry, lawyerish verb: "We have been so long without a line from you. Does your affection for us abate?"

It was necessary now for him to insist to her that nothing had changed because, of course, everything had changed. Under the spell of Maria Reynolds, all his singular hunger for her had been sated or blotted out: "I think as kindly as ever of my Dear Sister in Law and Betsy has lately given me stronger proof than she ever did before of her attachment to you."

Naturally, Betsy's attachment for Angelica could hardly help growing stronger as Angelica ceased to be her rival for her husband.

While Maria Reynolds continued her visits to their house in Philadelphia that summer, Hamilton wrote Betsy in Albany on August 9 not urging her to return and willing to sacrifice her presence for her health. His own health was good, he said. "I cannot be happy without you. Yet I must not advise you to urge your return. The confirmation of your health is so essential to our happiness that I am willing to make as long a sacrifice as the season and your patience will permit."

Hamilton was shocked to learn from one of her letters of "the indisposition of my darling James," their three-year-old son. Engrossed as he was in the future of industrial America that he was now describing as he drafted his monumental "Report on Manufactures," he had written Betsy on August 2, 1791, full of practical home remedies:

Remember the flannel next his skin, and If he should not be better when this reaches, try the bark-waistcoat. Remember also the benefit he received from Barley water with a dash of brandy. Be very attentive to his diet . . . Not much fruit of any kind. Be sure that he drinks no water which has not been first boiled in some iron vessel. I hope he will have had some rhubarb or antimonial wine. Paregoric at night in moderation will do him good & a little bark will not do him harm.

    Take good care of my lamb;

He awaited "with all the patience I can the time for your return." "But," he added, perhaps hearing Maria's exigent knock on the door, "you must not precipitate it."

James was recovering, but now Betsy's health was suffering from anxiety attacks. For her, he prescribed bark, vitriol, cold baths, and more exercise:

    You will easily imagine how much pleasure it gives me to learn that my Dear James was better: but then My Betsy, your health had suffered by your anxiety and you were not so well as when you left me! . . . For Heaven's sake, do not yield too much to the little adverse circumstances that must attend us in this pilgrimage. Exert your fortitude. Keep up your spirits. Never forget for a moment the delight you will give me by returning to my bosom in good health. Dear Betsy—beloved Betsy —Take care of yourself—Be attentive to yourself—Use every mean that promises you benefit.

    You say you have not forgotten your bark & Vitriol. But have you *constantly* remembered it? Have you used the other remedy also?

    I have a wish that you would try the Cold bath, beginning by degrees. Take the air too as much as possible and *gentle* exercise.

    I am myself in good health & only want you with me, & in health also, to be as happy as it is reasonable to wish to be.

Still, she should not hurry back.

I charge you (unless you are so anxious as to injure you, or unless you find your health declining more) not to precipitate your return. I cannot help hoping that your native air if taken long enough will be of service to you.

    Adieu My angel. Assure yourself always of my tenderest affection & unceasing prayers.

She wrote him late in August that she most certainly would be coming back about the first of September. Still, he replied that his "extreme anxiety" for her health would "reconcile me to you staying longer." In any event, she must not arrive by surprise in Philadelphia. She "must inform me beforehand when you set out" for home. He closed his letter of August 21 to her with

Think of me—dream of me—and Love me my Betsey as I do you. Yours for ever.

                                        A. Hamilton

In a remarkably suggestive piece urging neutrality that Hamilton would write for Fenno's *Gazette of the United States* in March or April of 1793, just after his affair with Maria Reynolds had broken off, he personified three nations, Britain, France, and America, as a man, his wife, and the man's mistress. The point he was trying to make about neutrality got lost as these three stock characters from commedia dell'arte spring into vivid life out of the jumble of the passions of his plot:

> A . . . virtuous Citizen . . . [he wrote] will regard his own country as a wife, to whom he is bound to be exclusively faithful and affection- ate, and he will watch with a jealous attention every propensity of his heart to wander towards a foreign country, which he will regard as a mistress that may pervert his fidelity, and mar his happiness.

Far off the subject of neutrality into something obviously more intense and personal, Hamilton added,

> There are persons among us who appear to have a passion for a foreign mistress; as violent as it is irregular; and who, in the paroxysms of their love, seem perhaps without being themselves sensible of it, too ready to sacrifice the real welfare of the . . . family, to their partiality for the object of their tenderness.

The real-life foreign mistress who had for so many years "perverted" Hamilton's fidelity to his wife was nonetheless a member of her family; so Angelica had not really perverted his fidelity, at least by Hamilton's close, if twisted, reasoning. But now the violent and "irregular" passion he had projected on his sister-in-law had reprojected back with the same intense focus and scarcely a flicker of interruption on the domestic mistress who had pushed the foreign one out of its beam and into limbo. In paroxysms of love for the new mistress, who now came so often to his home, Hamilton had been "all too ready to sacrifice the welfare" of his family to the object of his tenderness. He seemed hardly "sensible" at the time of what he was doing to them or to himself.

Betsy and the children finally returned from Albany, and it was not long before she was pregnant again. On November 26 she and Hamilton took their precious firstborn son, Philip, almost ten, to Trenton and entered him in the boarding school there run by William Frazer, rector of St. Michael's Episcopal Church. In December, Hamilton replied to a letter of Philip from boarding school, congratulating him on a good report card: "Your master informs me that you recited a lesson the first day you began, very much to his satisfaction." Betsy would be sending on to him some odds and ends that Philip needed, as well as two books, a volume of Ovid and John Mairs's *An Introduction to Latin Syntax . . .* , to which is subjoined an *Epitome of Ancient History.*

Hamilton had promised to send for Philip the following Saturday to come home for the weekend, but the Christmas break was so near that Hamilton felt it would be better to put off the trip till the holidays. However, if Philip really wanted to be picked up for the weekend, Hamilton would do as he had promised: "A promise must never be broken; and I will never make you one, which I will not fulfill as far as I am able."

A marriage vow to Betsy was a promise that he fulfilled, but only "as far as I am able." He lacked the ability to fulfill it without exceptions for Angelica and Maria Reynolds.

Such exceptions did not mean that, when they were out of the way, Hamilton's affection for his wife and family would not flow on again with as much or more intensity and depth as before, except that, in the case of Angelica, love might become less exigent with age, and more familial, but would always remain. In 1793 he had passed off the consequences to "a virtuous citizen" of perverted, irregular, and violent passions in extramarital "paroxysms of love" as no more than a thing that "may . . . mar his happiness." But by 1797 and four years of living with the secret, Hamilton's love for his family and his sense of honor had branded on his heart a grimmer perception of what he had done to them and to himself. It was unforgettable, unforgivable, and shattering. "I can never cease to forgive myself," he would write in his public confession of that summer, "for the pang which it may inflict in a bosom eminently entitled to all my gratitude, fidelity, and love."

7

MORE FREQUENT
INTERCOURSE WAS PRESSED
UPON ME

HE WILL WRITE MRS. HAMILTON . . . COME HERE SOON DO NOT
SEND OR LEAVE ANYTHING IN HIS POWER.
—*from Maria Reynolds, December 15, 1791*

By the time of Thomas Jefferson's return from hunting down the Hessian
fly, most of the expensive alterations he had ordered for his Philadelphia mansion at 274 High Street, commonly called Market, on the south side west of
Eighth, had been carried out. Upwards of 80 packing cases had arrived from
France and a good many more from Monticello, and the lavishly furnished
establishment gleamed with a new coat of paint. Earlier, hearing that George
Beckwith, the unofficial British agent who was such a close confidant of Hamilton and Angelica Church, was lodged at Mrs. Mary House's boarding house, at
Fifth and Market, where Madison was also staying, Jefferson had invited Madison to escape such politically odious company by taking bed and plate at home
with him. "It will be a relief from a solitude of which I have too much," Jefferson
complained. "Let me, I beseech you, have a favorable answer." But Madison had
stayed on at Mrs. House's. In fact, he was able to improve his time there by

passing one or two useful confidences back and forth through Beckwith, as Hamilton had been doing.

Jefferson's chariot, a four-wheeled carriage with back seats and a coach box, and his two-wheeled sulky had also arrived from France, but even so, his large stable had room left over. He offered this to recently elected Senator James Monroe, his near neighbor from Albemarle County and his principal liaison man and floor leader in the Senate, to use for the stabling of his horses. Jefferson's old maître d'hôtel from the Hôtel de Langeac in Paris, Adrien Petit, and a large shipment of wines from Bordeaux and Champagne were also duly installed to provide the same kind of elegant appointments for candlelight dinners that had proved so useful at his former Maiden Lane establishment in New York.

Abigail and John Adams's new Philadelphia house, Bush Hill, compared unfavorably with the more regal vice-presidential residence they had in New York. Abigail wrote her daughter (also Abigail), the wife of Colonel William S. Smith, "The grand and sublime I left at Richmond Hill; the Schuylkill is no more like the Hudson than I to Hercules."

When the new political Hercules from New York, Senator Aaron Burr, who had brought down General Philip Schuyler with a crash, arrived in Philadelphia in October, he would miss Richmond Hill too. He took lodgings in a boarding house at 130 South Second Street, from which he wrote back to Theodosia in New York, "I am at length settled in winter quarters" with "many invitations to dine etc. All of which I have declined, and have not eaten a meal except at my own quarters." This was a reassuring fib for home consumption of a terminally ill wife who remained in seclusion. Their lavish parties at Richmond Hill were now a thing of the past.

Of that Philadelphia winter of 1791 and 1792, when the government finally unfurled itself into full swing there, Rufus W. Griswold, in *The Republican Court; or, American Society in the Days of Washington*, wrote, "You have never seen anything like the frenzy which has seized upon the inhabitants here. They have been half mad ever since this city became the seat of government."

Hamilton's friend and assistant at the Treasury, Oliver Wolcott, Jr., who had won youthful literary fame as one of the Hartford wits, sent reassurance like Aaron Burr's back to his own wife. "We have Eves in plenty, of all nations, tongues, and colors," he wrote her the following summer from Gray's Gardens, where he had taken refuge from the yellow fever, "but do not be jealous—I have not seen one yet whom I have thought pretty."

At the center around whom all social orbits wheeled were the world's most revered hero and his comfortable wife, Martha. One of her most intimate friends from as far back as wartime days at Morristown and Newburgh was Hamilton's devout and steadfast wife, Betsy. Next to the Washingtons at the center of the social nebulae were Hamilton's good friends Mr. and Mrs. William Bingham. Bingham, still reputedly the richest man in the United States, had made a great fortune during the Revolution as a government purchasing agent in the West Indies, where Hamilton had grown up. He had furnished Hamilton with many of the ideas for public finance, assumption, funding, and the National Bank that were now emerging as the law of the land from Hamilton's great reports. Bingham's wife, the former Anne Willing, whom he had married when she was 16, was the daughter of Thomas Willing, Robert Morris's senior partner and president of the Bank of North America. She was one of the greatest belles in American history. After their marriage, when the Binghams had spent some five years traveling abroad, she had sparkled at courts like those of Louis XVI, George III, and Thomas Jefferson at the Hôtel de Langeac.

It was only a short walk from Hamilton's office or house to the demimonde of the Reynolds's "large house in Vine Street next to the corner of Fifth" or from there to the Binghams' still larger and more opulent mansion on Third Street. The Binghams' was modeled after the London residence of the duke of Manchester, "the dimensions of the original being somewhat enlarged in the copy," according to Griswold's report. It was set in a garden of rose shrubs and flower beds surrounded by lemon and citron trees, and only the branches of the oaks and a row of Lombardy poplars could be seen above the wall that enclosed the mansion from stares of curious plebeians passing in the street.

A fascinating, new political star in town like Aaron Burr would receive as many invitations to dine at the Binghams' as an older friend of theirs like Hamilton. What went on at the balls and levees given by the mistresses of Philadelphia's great houses like Anne Bingham or at private meetings in the hall of the Indian Queen often had more to do with the most important and secret matters of governmental policy being formulated than the daily routine in the government offices and the floor debates in Congress Hall. The social life of the great houses provided a setting in which charismatic newcomers like Hamilton and Burr would be much in demand and at their best.

The grandson of Jonathan Edwards, son of a president of Princeton College, and as precociously keen-minded as Hamilton, Aaron Burr had graduated from Princeton at 16. When the Revolution broke out, he had gone off with Benedict Arnold to seize Quebec and returned with a citation for valor and a reputation for heroic insubordination. He had served briefly on Washington's staff in New York City and as an aide to General Putnam until, in 1777, he was appointed lieutenant colonel of Malcolm's Regiment, the youngest officer in the army to hold so high a rank. His aggressiveness won applause and citations, but four times in his military career Burr had disobeyed the orders of his superiors— Arnold's at Quebec, Washington's at Manhattan, and General Israel Putnam's in Orange County, to go chasing after Governor Tryon. The fourth time, at Monmouth, had led to calamity and well-earned self-reproach by Burr for the loss of many lives and the risk to which he had put the rest of the army. For all practical purposes, Burr had dropped out of the war after Monmouth. He wrote to Washington, with whom he shared a mutual lack of regard, in September of 1778:

> I have consulted several physicians; they all assure me that a few month's retirement and attention to my health are the only possible means to restore it . . . a delicacy, perhaps censurable, might otherwise

hurry me unnecessarily into service to the prejudice of my health and without advantage to the public.

Washington replied, "You, in my opinion, carry your ideas of delicacy too far."

This crushing reply kept Burr nominally in the army on meaningless duties for a short while longer. But in March of 1779, Burr dropped out again, this time for good, without mentioning to Washington the name or loyalist connections of the lady on whom he had finally focused his heretofore notoriously random affections. She seemed to be the real reason for his military disaffections, although, to Washington, Burr continued to plead reasons of health: "The reasons I did myself the honour to mention to your excellency in a letter of September last still exist and determine me to resign my rank and command in the army." This time Washington curtly accepted his resignation.

The lady's name was no secret to Burr's friends. William Paterson wrote him: "I congratulate you on your return to civil life, for which (I cannot forbear the thought) we must thank a certain lady not far from Paramus."

On leaving the army, Burr had gone to Albany, like Hamilton, to study for quick admission to the New York bar as a veteran of the service. Hamilton's friend Alexander McDougall gave Burr letters of introduction to the Schuylers, and Burr and Hamilton probably often studied side by side in the quiet of the Schuyler library at The Pastures. Since disobeying orders at the Battle of Monmouth and leading his men into a British trap there, instead of protecting the army's left flank as he had been ordered to do, Aaron Burr had been steeping himself in melancholia not unlike a young Werther, but one more worldly.

While he crammed for his bar exams, he suffered from a headache, and when he recovered, he wrote Theodosia Prevost, "I took the fine Indian cure . . . made a light breakfast of tea, stretched myself on a blanket before the fire, fasted till evening, then tea again." He missed her desperately: "I thought through the whole day that if you could sit by me and stroke my head with your little hand, all would be well."

Their relations by correspondence ranged beyond health and gallantry. "Write me facts and ideas," he demanded, "and don't torment me with compliments or yourself with sentiments." He was going to try to pull himself together.

In his thought processes, less linear and intense than Hamilton's, more speculative and diversified, Burr's mind would lead him into worlds of print further beyond the classics, law, and political economy than Hamilton's usually probed. Burr filled his mind with the iconoclasms of Voltaire, Rousseau, and Lord Chesterfield. He would coin worldly mottoes of success and submit them to Theodosia by letter for her approval.

"The maxim of a man whom neither of us esteem very highly is excellent on this occasion," he wrote, "—'*Suaviter in modo, fortiter in re.*' See, my dear Theodosia, what you bring upon yourself by having piddled in Latin. The maxim, however, will bear sheets of comment and weeks of reflection."

He added another, *"Les grandes âmes se soucient peu des petits moraux."*
These two would be his psalm of life, and he would live to be "suave in manner,
strong in deed" and to believe that "great souls have small use for petty bour-
geois morality."

Burr's mother, Esther Burr herself, could not have replied to him with
warnings more maternal than those Theodosia shot back:

> Such lessons from so able a pen are dangerous to a young mind and
> ought never to be read till the judgment and the heart are established
> in virtue . . . Les faiblesses de l'humanité is an easy apology; or rather
> a license to practise intemperance . . . Virtue, like religion, degenerates
> to nothing because it is convenient to neglect her precepts. You have,
> undoubtedly, a mind superior to the contagion.

Theodosia's husband, a British officer, had conveniently died in 1779, about
the time Burr was quitting the army for good. Her home, The Hermitage, near
Paramus, became a center of entertainment for the American officers who
manned the outposts around occupied New York City. Major James Monroe,
Jefferson's protégé, and Lieutenant Colonel Alexander Hamilton also sometimes
dined there, as did General Washington, whose private secretary wrote:

> At Mrs. Prevost's . . . we talked—and walked—and danced and gal-
> lanted away the leisure hours of four days and would have [continued]
> till now had not the General given orders for our departure.

A thoughtful, mature widow ten years older than Burr, Theodosia did not
on the face of her seem to be the lodestone to draw an amorous young spark like
Burr from the pursuit of glory and glamour. The names of Jacatacqua, Catherine, Margaret, Betsy, Hannah, Pamela—these and the many "Miss ——s" are
the fair names (and blanks) that spill out of Aaron Burr's amorous correspondence. "His intrigues were without number," his friend and official biographer,
Matthew L. Davis, wrote, and "his conduct most licentious."

At no other period of his life is it probable that a man like Burr would have
looked twice at a woman like Theodosia. His friends could not understand Burr's
clinging affection for her and her protective devotion to him. At first, they
thought his attentions focused on her younger and much prettier sister, Catherine de Visme, and Theodosia took note of their gossip: "Our being the subject
of much inquiry, conjecture, and calumny is no more than we ought to expect
. . ." She did not mind, for "your esteem more than compensated me for the worst
they could say."

At the Schuylers' house, Burr's old jauntiness returned. "Attune your organs to the genuine ha ha!" he crowed to his and Hamilton's old friend Robert
Troup, who had also been studying law with both of them in Albany. " 'Tis to
me the music of the spheres; the sovereign specific that shall disgrace the
physician's art, and baffle the virulence of malady." Burr promised Theodosia

that he would study assiduously and settle down and earn a fortune if she would marry him. She would not hear of his forgetting this promise or of any sparking in Albany with the Schuyler sisters or frivolous reading or any other nonsense of his "genuine ha ha." He needed her to coax his weakness into strength, to deny his dependence on her, and to prod his pride. She wrote him:

> When I am sensible I can make you and myself happy, I will readily join you. . . . But till I am confident of this I cannot think of our union. . . . I wish you to study for your own sake; to insure yourself respect and independence. . . . I shall never look forward with confidence till your pride extends to that.

Burr replied to Theodosia that she was the first woman to prove to him that a woman could have a soul, as well as an instinct for coquetry. But Burr saved letters written to him by dozens of other females too. "They were cast into one common receptacle," according to Davis, "the profligate and corrupt, by the side of the thoughtless and betrayed victim. All were held as trophies of victory—all esteemed alike valuable."

"Why," Burr once asked Theodosia, "is man alone . . . discontented, anxious, sacrificing the present, never enjoying, always hoping?"

Admitted to the bar, married, and moved to New York City, Burr would be cocounsel with, or opposed to, Hamilton in many causes, but he had many enthusiasms besides the law. There were politics and land speculations; dabblings in fireside science; and the reading of innumerable works of fiction, philosophy, and economics. Burr became a patron of the arts, gave many banquets, attended many others, and found time enough left over to be the companion and tutor of his wife, Theodosia; stepfather to her five children; and devoted father to their only child, Theodosia, and an adopted daughter Theodosia's age. He would also eventually sire at least three children out of wedlock and still remain in the good graces of an uncountable covey of mistresses. Burr and Maria Reynolds remained close friends for years.

Matthew Davis wrote of Burr, as Hamilton would learn, "The sacred bonds of friendship were unhesitatingly violated when they operated as barriers to the indulgence of his passions." By March 19, 1792, Robert Troup told Hamilton he had discovered a secret "with regard to Burr's election . . . which I cannot communicate till I see you. I have reason to suspect we have both been abused." But Troup was afraid to entrust Burr's guilty secret to the post. Newly seated as senator from New York, Burr took no partisan position toward Hamilton's pending economic measures. He was willing to consider them on their merits, he told a correspondent. He had not yet had a chance "to read with proper attention the proposed establishment. I am therefore wholly incompetent to give an opinion of its merit. . . . It certainly deserves deliberate consideration—a Charter granted cannot be revoked. This appears to me to be one of those cases in which Delay can be productive of no Evil." His suave habitual manner made him many quick, casual friendships, few deep ones, dislike from Hamilton's and Washington's direction, and eventually the enmity of Jefferson. But few political opponents could lay a partisan hand on Senator Burr, who usually on all issues hovered somewhere near the middle.

Having won election to the Senate by upsetting the strongly Federalist and Hamiltonian Schuyler, Burr was now letting it be known that he might be available to run with moderate Federalist backing against Clinton for governor of New York in the election to be held in June 1792. Because Burr would draw support from moderate and disaffected Clintonians as well as Federalists, he would make a strong candidate. Isaac Ledyard would soon write Hamilton on February 1, 1792, that "to oppose Mr. B. with success, your friends will be necessitated to promote the interest of the Old Incumbent," Clinton. There was no one Hamilton would less rather support than Clinton, except Burr. Hamilton urged Federalists to support Robert Yates as a lesser evil than either, even though as a fellow delegate of Hamilton to the 1787 Constitutional Convention, Yates had strongly supported Clinton and opposed the Constitution. Now chief justice of the New York Court of Appeals, Yates seemed receptive to a Federalist bid to oppose Clinton, but was reluctant to run for various reasons, one being that he feared that he could not afford to. For lieutenant governor, Hamilton and Philip Schuyler were pushing Stephen Van Rensselaer, husband of Margarita Schuyler, Betsy's and Angelica's younger sister, and patroon of the Van Rensselaer estates.

As Burr's candidacy for governor threatened to wrest control of Hamilton's own party from his grasp, Burr continued to profess to friends of Hamilton like Isaac Ledyard "an entire confidence in the wisdom and integrity of [Hamilton's] designs & a real personal friendship." As Ledyard wrote Hamilton, Burr "does not seem to suppose you doubt of his real personal friendship" or "ever will unless it may arise from meddling interveners." Objectionable to Hamilton as Yates might be, Hamilton would urge all of his Federalist followers to support him, being less objectionable than either Clinton or Burr. He posed no threat to Hamilton's control of the party, which controlled the national government.

That early winter of 1791, Anne and William Bingham were seeing less of Hamilton at the Mansion House; and Maria Reynolds, more of him at Fifth and Vine. Hamilton's and Maria's affair was becoming more exigent. But suddenly Maria's husband, James, demanded a reconciliation with her. At this, Maria "pretended to ask my advice," Hamilton recalled. He "advised her to the accommodation; which she shortly afterwards told me had taken place." Notwithstanding the reconciliation, "Mrs. Reynolds, on the other hand, employed every effort to keep up my attention and visits. Her pen was freely employed, and her letters were filled with those tender and pathetic effusions which would have been natural to a woman truly fond and neglected. . . . The variety of shapes which this woman could assume was endless."

Hamilton's and Maria's bedroom conversations rambled over many matters. She "informed me that her husband had been engaged in some speculation in claims upon the Treasury and she believed could give me information respecting the conduct of [some] persons in the department which would be useful to me.

I desired an interview with him and he came to me accordingly."

The passage quoted above from the draft of Hamilton's public statement implies that he asked Maria to have her husband come see him; in the printed version, Hamilton creates the impression that he sent for Reynolds in a peremptory and prosecutorial manner: "I sent for Reynolds who came to me accordingly."

At their interview, Reynolds "confessed that he had obtained a list of claims from a person in my department which he had made use of in his speculations. I invited him, by the expectation of my friendship and good offices, to disclose the person."

As Hamilton tells the story, at the time of this interview, Reynolds had no knowledge of Hamilton's ongoing intercourse with his wife. Thus there was no reason then for Reynolds to be suspicious of Hamilton's "friendship and good offices."

Hamilton quizzed Reynolds: "After some affectation of scruple, he pretended to yield, and ascribed the infidelity to Mr. Duer, from whom he said he had obtained the list in New York, while he [Duer] was in the department." So, Hamilton goes on, "as Mr. Duer had resigned his office some time before the seat of government was removed to Philadelphia, this discovery, if it had been true, was not very important."

Hamilton here is saying, rather shockingly, that as far as the public was concerned, the leak of secret lists from the Treasury only a year earlier was hardly more serious than a third-rate burglary. Only the lapse of six years and overwhelmingly self-serving sentiment can account for such a misjudgment. But talking to Reynolds, Hamilton pretended that he thought Reynolds's information about the leak was more important than he really believed it to be. Hamilton explained, "Yet it was the interest of my passions to appear to set value upon it, and to continue the expectation of friendship and good offices."

At this point in Hamilton's 1797 account of events that supposedly occurred in the summer, fall, and winter of 1791, Hamilton threw in mention of an apparently innocuous circumstantial fact that probably dates from March or April of 1790, not the fall of 1791:

> Mr. Reynolds told me he was going to Virginia, and on his return would point out something in which I could serve him. I do not know but he said something about employment in a public office.

In 1797, Hamilton still would not know of Gustavus B. Wallace's letters to Madison that placed Reynolds in Virginia with leaked lists in his hands and frauds on old soldiers on his mind in March and April of 1790, not 1791. By 1791, Bland's resolutions had made the kinds of frauds and profits that were possible for Reynolds in 1790 all but impossible in late 1791. It seems far more likely than not that Hamilton in 1797 was slipping back in recollection to a conversation he had had with Maria or James Reynolds early in 1790 in New York. This was more than a year and a half earlier than the first of their meetings to which he was confessing in his public statement: the interview late in 1791 in Philadelphia.

When and where did Hamilton first meet James and Maria Reynolds? When did his affair with her really begin? Circumstantial evidence places their first meeting well before her 1791 summer visitation to his house the time Hamilton suggests. But nowhere in his public statement did Hamilton explicitly assert that the beauteous New Yorker's summer visit to him immediately after Jefferson's and Madison's "passionate courtship" of Aaron Burr in New York was the first meeting he had ever had with her or her husband. Robert Troup had reiterated to him Cato's warning that they intended to destroy him utterly: *Delenda est Carthago.* Hamilton knew that he was the victim of some kind of a plot, but he seemed or pretended not to grasp the shape and depth of the real plot hidden beneath the surface conventions of a wronged husband's scheme to blackmail Hamilton for seducing his wife.

Perhaps in Philadelphia in 1791, Hamilton at first thought he was only resuming an old affair begun several years earlier in New York with a mistress who had conveniently turned up in the new capital like many another camp follower. The coincidence would have made it easier for him to delude himself into misbelieving that he was entrapped only by the small, conventional blackmail plot. In any event, when Reynolds returned from a trip, whether it was in early 1790 to Virginia or late 1791, he applied to Hamilton for a job in the same Treasury whose leaked secret lists he had been using so successfully for his frauds in Virginia. By 1797, Hamilton realized that he should have rejected Reynolds's request emphatically, but that is not what he said he did in 1791.

"The knowledge I had acquired of him was decisive against such a request," Hamilton wrote decisively. But his answer to Reynolds fell well short of being "decisive": "I parried it by telling him, what was true, that there was no vacancy in my immediate office, and that the appointment of clerks in the other branches of the department was left to the chiefs of the respective branches."

Nowhere did Hamilton flatly state that Reynolds did not receive an appointment as a clerk in another branch of the department from the chief of the branch. Hamilton limited his rejection of Reynolds's employment to his own immediate office, while seeming to suggest to Reynolds that an appointment elsewhere in the Treasury would not be out of the question by action of the chief of the branch (who, of course, would report to Hamilton).

Even so, Reynolds became angry. He complained that Hamilton "had promised him *employment* and had *disappointed* him." Hamilton confessed that his replies to Reynolds had been equivocal: "The situation with the wife would naturally incline me to conciliate this man. It is possible I may have used vague expressions which raised expectation; but the more I learned of the person, the more inadmissible his employment in a public office became. . . ."

Hamilton argued that this equivocal refusal proved that he could not have had a connection with Reynolds in speculations because, if he had, he would not have "hazarded his resentment by a persevering refusal."

The odd thing is that Treasury Department records show that a clerk named Reynolds, who, like James Reynolds, hailed from Connecticut, was hired in the register's office of the Treasury Department in January of 1791 or perhaps earlier. The records indicate that the first name used for the Reynolds who was actually hired was Simeon. Another odd thing was that about the time Hamilton, according to his 1797 public account, turned James down for employment in the Treasury, Simeon was discharged from the register's office in unexplained circumstances. Did Hamilton so far attempt to mollify James that he arranged indirectly through the head of a separate branch, the register, for the short engagement of James's kinsman Simeon? Or was "Simeon" really only a cover name for James himself?

Hamilton's affair with Maria grew more exigent in other ways than James's demands for employment in the Treasury. At Anne and William Bingham's Mansion House, the approach of Christmas brought with it the glittering crescendo of the social season, but less was seen of Hamilton. Swept aside by "paroxisms of love," Hamilton's earlier plan for a "gradual discontinuance" with Maria failed. Her sexual appetite for him became insatiable. A more intimate kind of party became his habit.

"A more frequent intercourse continued to be pressed upon me on the pretext of its being essential to the party," he wrote. "The appearances of a violent attachment were played of and of a genuine extreme distress at the idea of an interruption of the connection . . ."

The only way for him to end the affair would be for him to break it off abruptly. "My suspicions of some [foul p] sinister contrivance at the same time increasing," he wrote, "I resolved to put an end to the affair and to see Mrs. Reynolds no more." He would stride out of her trap once and for all. He would celebrate his liberation at the Binghams. Such a public occasion of glittering good cheer would also be useful for probing inquiries and thrusts in diplomacy, economics, and politics. A carefully dropped word there could change the course of the history of relations with France or Britain or the state of New York with a minimum of risk.

It was only a short walk from the demimonde of Maria Reynolds's house at Fifth and Vine to the beau monde of the Binghams' Mansion House at Third and Chestnut. The name of no guest arriving at the Bingham mansion would be more proudly shouted by the liveried flunkies to each other across the sidewalk, relayed up the staircase and into the salons, than that of Secretary of the Treasury Alexander Hamilton. The Binghams' house provided not only social leadership, but also the perfect setting for the compactly built reddish-haired financial genius of the government. Having laid his monumental "Report on Manufactures" before Congress on December 5, 1791, he was now at the ascendancy of his fame, the kind of fame that meant the most to men like William Bingham.

Although conversations among men high in American government and their ladies at levees like the Binghams' in 1791 may have done as much or more to influence governmental policy than floor debates in Congress or cabinet meetings, no documentary record of specific conversations at a specific levee that qualifies as historically acceptable evidence exists. But there is no doubt that the atmosphere and setting from which historic events emerge tend to shape their character. Therefore, it seems as useful to recreate the scene of a levee at the Binghams in composite form as it would be to reproduce a congressional debate or cabinet meeting. What follows is a nonhistoric event, a levee like one that the Binghams might have given in mid-December 1791, based on anecdotal accounts of such levees like those in Rufus W. Griswold's *The Republican Court*, Claude Bowers's *Jefferson and Hamilton*, and similar accounts of social life in the federal period.

With Hamilton sometimes, but not always, would be his wife, Elizabeth, an appealing type of woman, popular with other women, especially with Martha Washington. Elizabeth's delicate face was set off by her "fine eyes which are very dark, and hold the life and energy" of her restrained countenance. She was gentle and retiring, but in small groups she was gay and full of humour. She often would be missing from such parties or leave early because with her, in these years, life seemed to be one pregnancy, accouchement, childbirth, and weaning after another. Her healthy pregnancies were occasionally interrupted by a miscarriage.

Home from her European travels, Anne Bingham had introduced to America the custom of having servants announce each arriving guest, calling his name as he entered the door and shouting his name and full honorific title, if any, ahead of him into the ballroom to the expectant guests. Such imported extravagances were really about the only fault anyone, even other women with sharp tongues, could find with Anne Bingham. Abigail Adams considered her "taken altogether . . . the finest woman I ever saw. The intelligence of her countenance, or rather, I ought to say, its animation, the elegance of her form, and the affability of her manners convert you to admiration; and one had only to lament too much dissipation and frivolity of amusement, which have weaned her from her native country, and given her a passion and thirst after all the luxuries of Europe." Such glowing descriptions of contemporaries like Abigail Adams are confirmed by an unfinished portrait of Anne Bingham by Gilbert Stuart. Hers was the sort of patrician beauty that through centuries still shimmers from old canvas. Above medium height and well-formed, she had sprightliness, dignity, elegance, and distinction in her carriage. She sparkled with wit, bubbled with vivacity, and had the knack of convincing the most hopeless yokel, introduced into her drawing room by nothing more than high political rank, that she found his personality peculiarly appealing. Daring at the card table, graceful in the dance, witty in conversation, adept with all devices of Congreve dialogue, fond of all the dissipations prescribed by fashion, and tactful in the seating of her guests at table, she well earned the scepter she waved so authoritatively over all of Philadelphia society. If Martha Washington had to be acknowledged as the queen mother, Anne Bingham reigned as the crown princess of her Republican court.

An English visitor to Philadelphia described the Binghams' residence as "a magnificent house and garden in the best English style, with elegant and even superb furniture." The chairs in the drawing room were from Seddon's in London and of the latest fashion: each chair's back was in the form of a lyre, adorned with festoons of crimson and yellow silk. The curtains of the room were a festoon of the same. The carpet was one of Moore's most expensive patterns. "The room was papered in the French taste after the style of the Vatican at Rome."

François René de Chateaubriand, later famous as a Napoleonic statesman, was amazed at the "elegance of dress" and the "profusion of luxury" of all the rich Philadelphians' wives and daughters. However, another political Frenchman, the duc de La Rochefoucauld-Liancourt, complained that "the English influence prevails in the first circles and prevails with great intolerance." An English visitor happily confirmed this by remarking smugly that "nothing could make them happier than that an order of nobility should be established."

Anne Bingham's grand, imported custom of having doormen and footmen regally relay the name and title of each arriving guest into the ballroom caused much discomfiture to Senator James Monroe as he awkwardly entered. It made him so nervous that he got his arm caught in the sleeve of his coat as he tried to take it off.

"Senator Monroe," called the doorman.

"Coming," cried the senator.

No one came.

"Senator Monroe," echoed a footman down the hall.

"Coming," he cried, in nervous fury. "As soon as I can get my greatcoat off." He swore a string of oaths as he continued to wrestle frantically with the lining of his sleeve.

"Senator Monroe."

Still no one.

But at such a spectacle, no flicker of amusement would cross Anne Bingham's beautiful face to add a wince to the newly elected senator's gauche embarrassment. Anne Bingham ignored the advice Thomas Jefferson had given her when she was in Paris for presentation at the court of Louis XVI. The American minister had told her how much happier she would be in the domestic pleasures of America than in the sophisticated society of Europe. But once home, she spent her money, wit, and vivacity at Mansion House, duplicating his elegant Paris salon as nearly as possible and, indeed, enlarging a little upon the original.

Hamilton seemed born for the court over which she reigned. Having made his own way in life from the bottom, he felt no need to playact the part of a man of the people. Now feeling himself the social equal of any man or woman at any level of society, and they of him, he had no need to pretend to be anything other than he was. Being no Puritan and no self-anointed democrat herself, Anne found the spruce, handsome secretary politically and personally congenial. When she pursed her pretty lips in wicked oaths, it was said that she swore as daintily as the duchess of Devonshire. If she relished anecdotes too spicy for the official puritanic tone set by George and Martha, it was because she was doing her beautiful best to dispel their austere chill. Hamilton was only too glad to help her.

Within the few square blocks of the government quarter of federal Philadelphia, the recent comings and goings of the most conspicuous figure in the government at the large house at Fifth and Vine would hardly remain un-remarked in Anne's repartee. Others at her levees would profess to be shocked by her earthy vocabulary and taste for risqué jibes, but Hamilton would respond in kind to her wit and join her laughter. No guest appeared to be so much the confident, gallant, sophisticated man of the world as he. It would be to Anne's husband, William Bingham, not to a closer friend like Robert Troup, that Hamil-ton would later entrust his entire file of documentary evidence of the Reynolds affair for safekeeping.

"Monsieur Jean Baptiste de Ternant, minister plenipotentiary of King Louis XVI of France!"

As the footmen's voices unfurled the titles of nobility like a plume, all eyes would turn to the new French minister, who had arrived in August 1791. The king had been deposed, and Ternant was only a holdover from the deposed king's regime, but the old titles introduced a touch of glory to Philadelphia; besides, no one knew what the new republican regime's man was supposed to be called. Ternant was still the minister plenipotentiary from the most dynamic and dan-gerous nation in the world. He suffered from no gaucherie slipping his arm out of his sleeve, nor had his hostess any need to hide a smile at his clumsiness. Monroe's new political rank might force her to invite him despite his lack of charm and social grace. The minister from France was no such embarrassment.

Philadelphia hostesses would have showered Jean Baptiste de Ternant with invitations even if he had had no credentials. He had been officially, though informally, received by Washington and Jefferson when he arrived before they left Philadelphia for Virginia. No empty-headed nobleman, Ternant, now a little past 50, had served as an officer in the American Revolution. Lafayette wrote, "He in a great measure belongs to both countries." Washington and Hamilton remembered him well and agreed with the marquis. Ternant believed that his warm reception augured well. Although Thomas Jefferson avoided informal personal contact with him, the secretary of state was reclusive with many peo-ple. He maintained strict proprieties in his official intercourse with Ternant at all times.

On August 12, 1791, shortly after Ternant's arrival, Hamilton had described him to George Beckwith as "a man of easy, pleasing manners, and very fit for the objects of his appointment." Beckwith and Britain could expect no special favors from Hamilton through Ternant because, Hamilton said, "foreign affairs are totally in the Department of the Secretary of State . . . therefore I am a stranger to any special views."

Seeing his old comrade-in-arms, Hamilton would have no aversion to infor-mal personal contact and whatever unguarded disclosures such contact might bring. He moved across the room to give Ternant a warm greeting through groups of beautiful women who seemed to glide in circles beneath tall head-dresses, their bosoms swelling out of deeply slashed décolletages, drawn down by tightly laced corsets into tiny waists above huge, bouffant skirts. He could be seen gracefully bowing with a smile to one, lightly flirtatious with another, clasping the white-gloved fingers of a third warmly in both his hands. He would leave them behind for brief conversations with notable friends like Henry Knox and Robert Morris and Oliver Wolcott, Jr. Then he would turn back to the beckoning ladies before his longer absence should come to seem to them an implied affront to their exquisite beauty.

Before Ternant arrived in America, Jefferson had protested against the action of the French Assembly in imposing heavier charges on tobacco carried in American ships than in French ships. Commercial relations between the two countries continued to worsen while Jefferson took his summer's ease at Monticello. Hamilton suggested to Ternant when he came that all disputed questions might be settled in the new treaty of commerce that he himself strongly favored. Hamilton also sought to draw Ternant out to make him reveal what his instructions from his own government were, much as he had drawn out Beckwith earlier on the subject of his authority, but Ternant did not reveal them. He dryly observed that a scrupulous observance of the existing treaty by the United States was a necessary preliminary to the negotiation of any new one.

Jefferson's already smoldering anger at Hamilton and his policies burned more corrosively as the realization reached him of Hamilton's searching and intimate conversations with both Beckwith and Ternant about matters that Jefferson felt should be his alone to discuss with them, but only if he saw fit to do so. Ternant professed indifference he did not feel to the arrival in Philadelphia of a new minister from Britain. Hamilton told Ternant that the United States would regard the full admission of American shipping to the British West Indies as a necessary condition of any new treaty of commerce with Britain. Hamilton expected to receive a new British proposal for a treaty of alliance and commerce, but, he predicted to Ternant, the United States would reject it. He assured Ternant of his own strong attachment to France. Ternant and Hamilton remained great personal friends, and both expected to continue their informal interviews in the future. Hamilton was certain that Washington desired him to continue them, too.

Ternant was right in fearing that the arrival of the new British minister altered the political and diplomatic, as well as the social, situation. While doubt might linger that the minister from deposed King Louis XVI could be properly accredited to Philadelphia, if not to Anne Bingham's, there could be no like doubts about the status of George Hammond. He was the officially accredited minister, whom local government and society alike had been breathlessly awaiting as the replacement for the vexatiously unofficial George Beckwith. As the young British lion stepped down from his carriage, Anne Bingham's footmen made the sills and rafters ring for the newest and most important member of the resident diplomatic corps: "The minister plenipotentiary of His Majesty King George III, George Hammond." Such style and title would recall for some the excitements of the now unmentionable winter of British occupation 13 years earlier.

After he bowed deeply to Anne Bingham and lifted the back of her hand gently to his lips, bestowing a kiss upon it, and paid his respects to her husband, among the first of the others he would greet would be Secretary of the Treasury

Hamilton. If Jefferson had made one of his rare appearances at such a party, it is likely that he would have turned on his heel and walked away in disgust. He insisted on none but official contacts with foreign diplomats. Hammond would report to his chief, Lord Grenville, in the Foreign Office in London, that he preferred to have most of his communications with Hamilton and to have no relations with Jefferson that were not absolutely necessary. After reaching Philadelphia in October 1791, George Hammond, the first British minister plenipotentiary to the United States, then only 28 years old, would remain in residence until 1795. He had called on Jefferson the week after his arrival, only to be given word that the secretary of state was out.

Hammond had been out when Jefferson tried to return his call. Jefferson insisted that the British must take the first step in establishing full diplomatic relations; Hammond was biding his time until he had proof that an American minister would be appointed to his own country. Hammond finally learned from Jefferson that the mission to England had been offered to an unnamed gentleman —afterwards revealed as Thomas Pinckney of South Carolina. After this diplomatic minuet, Hammond was formally presented to the president by the secretary of state on November 11.

Ternant made no ceremonial visits except to officials with whom it was his duty to deal and complained because the young Britisher visited with everybody, especially the senators, even before being officially received. Hammond had been specifically instructed to make a point of cultivating influential people like Hamilton. Whether or not he had called on the secretary of the treasury immediately upon arrival, Hammond's first long and confidential conversation with Hamilton fully confirmed his previous judgment of the secretary of the treasury's "just and liberal way of thinking." Hammond never had any doubt that Hamilton still belonged to the American "party of the English interest."

Jefferson, playing the part of wary diplomat, sparred with the bright young Britisher. The issues between the two countries that could now be the subject of negotiation fell into two groups: those connected with the alleged failure on both sides to carry the treaty of peace into effect and those relating to commerce. Jefferson, like Hamilton, wanted to get the British out of the posts on the northwest frontier before talking about commerce and to apply all possible pressure on the British at all times through every official and private diplomatic channel to get them out. But Hamilton also wanted to maintain close personal contact and regularize and normalize commercial relations with France through the kind of personal diplomacy with Ternant that Jefferson avoided. These differences brought Jefferson and Hamilton into further ongoing collisions.

On official visits to Washington and Jefferson, Ternant found them disappointingly uncommunicative about official matters. Following heated discussion in Congress about a navigation act with France like the one with Great Britain, Ternant was also disappointed when the president's message to Congress contained no reference to the report on commerce that Jefferson had been instructed to prepare. Ternant attributed Jefferson's delay in submitting his report to pending negotiations with Hammond. Hamilton had discussed these freely with

Ternant, but Ternant continued to be suspicious of the real purpose behind Jefferson's delay. The secretary of state's official reserve was extreme, Ternant said, though he had not given up hope of seeing in Jefferson more signs of confidence in himself and more attachment to France in the future.

Jefferson did assure Ternant, with Hamilton's concurrence and using his phraseology, that the United States would not take advantage of France by paying debts to France in depreciated French assignats. A year later, when Jefferson was away on one of his vacations at Monticello and a delegation arrived from the French colony of Saint Domingue, seeking help in putting down the Negro insurrection on that island, Ternant appealed to Hamilton and Knox. Hamilton promptly made money and arms available to help the French put down the insurrection. Washington ratified their actions and assured Ternant that the United States would give every aid to their good friends and allies the French to help them quell this alarming revolt.

The gaiety and warmth of the setting of the levees and balls at the William Binghams and other great Philadelphia houses helped keep such important diplomatic moves and countermoves friendly, constructive, and useful, without the risks attendant upon formal moves through official channels. They created the usual countervailing risks of misunderstandings and misquotations, although to sophisticated diplomats, even purposeful misunderstandings have always had important diplomatic uses. The same could hardly be said of the suspicious, fretful peevishness and ire with which the absent Jefferson regarded Hamilton's friendly, informal, private conversations with Beckwith, Ternant, and Hammond.

Some said that George Washington, standing alone, had the look of an uncrowned king. But standing tall beside short, squat, comfortable Martha as half of a faintly comic pair dispelled the illusion that they could qualify as an unsceptered royal couple. The accolade for the most regal-looking couple at the Binghams' would belong to those dazzling ornaments of American society and diplomacy, Chief Justice John Jay and his wife, Sarah Livingston Jay. Abigail Adams's daughter—and, no doubt, many another of the ladies at the Binghams' —would be impressed with Jay's "benevolence stamped in every feature." He stood tall, if slightly stooped; his coal-black, deep-set eyes were the most striking feature of his pallid countenance. He wore his hair a little down over his forehead, tied behind, and moderately powdered; he was always kindly, gracious, and courtly in society and sternly uncompromising in matters of honor. He looked with abhorrence on the excesses of the French Revolution and once wrote a friend, "That portion of the people who individually mean well never was, nor until the millennium will be, considerable."

Seeing the chief justice of the United States here at the Binghams' with so few cases yet on his docket would remind Hamilton that his old friend and colleague would make a splendid candidate for governor of New York—infinitely preferable to Yates, Burr, or Clinton. Hamilton's memories of Sarah Livingston Jay, Lady Kitty Livingston's younger sister, went all the way back to his own first winter on the continent in 1773. Gouverneur Morris had noticed Sally, as she was then, a belle of 17 with little time to waste on their 16-year-old boarder, Hamilton, raw and fresh from the West Indies, probably seeing snow for the first time in his life.

Morris wrote her 22-year-old sister, "What do you think, Kitty? I have adopted Sally for my daughter. Never was a little creature so admired. As to her heart when in the midst of her admirers it singeth with joy. The rosy fingers of pleasure paint her cheeks." There were "gentle Strephons who hang about her, bending forward . . . rolling [their eyes] sighing most piteously . . . another sitting sidelong on her chair with melancholic and despondent phiz prolongated unto the seventh button of his waistcoat . . . another his elbows fastened to his short ribs . . . in the midst of all this sits Miss with seeming unconsciousness of the whole. . . ."

Now at Anne and William Binghams', standing beside the tall, permanent Strephon she had chosen, she was a statuesque and beauteous 35. Many another slightly aging Strephon like Hamilton and Hammond and Ternant still swarmed admiringly about her, "bending forward" and exchanging compliments. To Hamilton, the image of Sarah Livingston as the unself-conscious 17-year-old belle with whose family he had spent that first winter in America would not blind him to the fact that the handsome, stout 35-year-old Sarah Jay seemed easily able to dominate her John. Indeed, she might be as happy to move back to New York from Philadelphia with him as governor and herself as first lady as Hamilton would. He lingered in conversation with the Jays longer than he did with any other couple.

When Hamilton finally moved on past John and Sally Jay and back to his hostess, Anne, he whispered something into her delicate ear that caused her beauty to light up with a smile. It may have been something about their always witty friend who was now in Paris, Gouverneur Morris. He was always good for an admiring laugh among friends of their circle. Adelaide, or as she preferred, Adèle de Flauhaut, the novelist, Morris's witty French mistress, kept a Paris salon of her own that was frequented by more artists and writers than could be found at Anne Bingham's. Adèle's other faithful lover was Charles Maurice de Talleyrand-Perigord. Her and Talleyrand's child, little Charles, lived with her, Morris, and Talleyrand and added warmth to their *ménage à trois*. Perhaps Hamilton had repeated to Anne, Gouverneur's amusing description of his Adèle as "a pleasing woman . . . not a sworn enemy to intrigue." Such an admiring characterization bore much retelling, especially when whispers were also going the rounds about Hamilton's own intriguing involvements with the likes of Angelica Church and Maria Reynolds.

Jefferson, as he told his *Anas* later, was ill at ease in circles like that of the Binghams. All the aristocratic talk and monarchical decadence and corruption like that which he saw on display there would come to dominate American life, he feared. Jefferson chided his hostess for her admiration of sophisticated, liberated Frenchwomen like Adèle de Flauhaut, whose manners unfortunately seemed to be Anne's ideal.

One reason for Jefferson's uneasiness with Anne's easy ways may have been the stories going the rounds that for some years before, beginning in 1768, Jefferson had made a number of attempts to seduce Elizabeth Walker, the wife of his best friend from college days, John Walker. Walker had been foolish enough to complain of the matter to several people. More or less as a consequence, poor Walker had just been dumped from his safe seat in the Senate by Jefferson's hatchet man, Monroe, as unceremoniously as Burr had ousted Schuyler from his. Years later, in 1805, Jefferson would tell his presidential secretary, William Burwell, that Hamilton "had once threatened him with a public disclosure" of his affair with Elizabeth Walker. At the same time, Jefferson pretended to minimize the threat by saying that his affair "had been long known." In Hamilton's history there is no other record of this threat to calumniate Jefferson. At Anne Bingham's, any such gossipy, usually bantering indiscretions were supposed to be privileged as they are in all the best houses. But Jefferson had a way of jotting down as *Anas* all manner of such scraps, many of them third and fourth hand hearsay, relayed or invented by the likes of his creature John Beckley. Things that might have been said as a joke in society, delivered with a smile and a twinkle to denote a meaning intended as the ironic opposite of the literal meaning of the words, when relayed literally from Beckley to the absent Jefferson and jotted down for posterity, would cause Jefferson to brood and smolder and dream of other reprisals.

Having been a guest of Jefferson and his little coterie at the Hôtel de Langeac and observed the place the beautiful Sally Hemings occupied in it as something more than a slave, Anne Bingham could hardly be expected to deny her wit a scintillating sally about his concubine. She had not hesitated to give a spirited, smiling rebuke to the self-anointed sage.

"Do you not admire clever women like Adèle de Flauhaut and the Marchioness de Brehan?" Anne had asked. "Or Madame de Corny?" whom he had known so well and written of so warmly. Did not such women, Anne would pertly ask him, "possess the happy art of making us pleased with ourselves?" Still another reason why she admired French women so much, she said, was that they could "please both the fop and the philosopher."

Mindful of the place Madame de Pompadour and Madame du Barry had won in recent French history, as well as the role of Madame de Brehan and Adèle de Flauhaut herself, Anne Bingham would press her rebuke. Such French mistresses, she said, despite the appearance of frivolousness in them, which so displeased the sage who was content with merely owning his, could even "interfere with the politics of the country and often give a decided turn to the fate of empires." Could no American mistresses do as well?

Ten days after laying before Congress his dream of modern industrial America, "The Report on Manufactures," a few days after resolving to make an abrupt break with Maria Reynolds and secretly celebrating it publicly at the Binghams' pre-Christmas ball, Hamilton was to receive a nightmarish letter. Ever since he had vowed to break off with Maria Reynolds, Hamilton said, she had "persisted in persecuting me with letters filled with the strongest professions of tenderness and [distress] grief—to which I made no reply." But now her husband had either "discovered the connection" or "my resolution to end it having now become unequivocal, the time was arrived for a [demon] the catastrophe of the plot."

On arriving home from the Binghams' ball or perhaps a day or two after, Maria Reynolds's letter was at his house awaiting him. It was as follows:

COL. HAMILTON,

    Dear Sir:—I have not time to tell you the cause of my present troubles only that Mr. has rote you this morning and I know not wether you have got the letter or not and he has swore that If you do not answer It or If he dose not se or hear from you to day he will write Mrs. Hamilton he has just Gone out and I am a Lone I think you had better come here one moment that you May know the Cause then you will the better know how to act Oh my God I feel more for you than myself and wish I had never been born to give you so mutch unhappiness do not rite to him no not a Line but come here soon do not send or leav any thing in his power

MARIA

Looking up from reading the letter trembling there in his hand, with thoughts of Maria's misery, Mrs. Hamilton's also, perhaps Angelica's too, flashing past his mind's eye, Hamilton could hardly have been blamed if he had indulged himself in an atavistic outburst of Caribbean Creole patois: *"Tous songes sont mensonges!"*

Unlike the "Report on Manufactures," there was no way Maria's letter could be ignored, tabled, or pigeonholed. James Reynolds had gone into the kind of dangerous angry action that was always to be feared from a cuckold. Hamilton must now come to her at once; he must leave nothing in James's power. But James followed up by issuing him a separate summons to come to him. An invitation to more frequent intercourse at Anne Bingham's instead would have pleased him more.

8

HIS POWER
TO HANG COLONEL HAMILTON

ALL THIS NATURALLY GAVE SOME UNEASINESS.
                    —The Reynolds Pamphlet, *August 25, 1797*

James Reynolds was now claiming, after all these months, that he had just
found out that his angel of a wife had betrayed him with Hamilton. He followed
up Maria's letter of December 15 with his own.

SIR:
    I am very sorry to find out that I have been so cruelly treated by a
person that I took to be my best friend instead of that my greatest
Enimy. You have deprived me of everything thats near and dear to me, I
discovered whenever I came into the house. There I found Mrs. Reynolds
weeping I ask'd her the Cause of being so unhappy. She always told me
that she had bin Reding, and she could not help Crying when she Red any
thing that was Afecting. But seing her Repeatedly in that Setevation
gave me some suspicion to think that was not the Cause, as fortain would
have it. before matters was carred to two great a length.

Now suspicious,

> I discovered a letter directed to you which I copied of . . . without being discovered by her . . . the evening after I see [her] give a letter to a Black man in the Market Street. which I followed him to your door . . . I broached the matter to her and Red the Copy to her which she fell upon her knees and asked forgiveness and discovered every thing to me Respecting the matter.

She had confessed to Reynolds how "she called on you for the lone of some money. which you toald her you would call on her the Next Evening. which accordingly you did. and there Sir you took the advantage a poor Broken harted woman."
Now she had fallen in love with Hamilton and cared for no one but him. Reynolds continued:

> Instead of being a friend, you have acted the part of the most Cruelist man in existence, you have made a whole family miserable. She ses there is no other man that she Care for in this world. now Sir you have bin the Cause of Cooling her affections for me. She was a woman. I should as soon sespect an angiel from heven. and one where all my happiness was depending. and I would Sacrefise almost my life to make her Happy.

Reynolds demanded satisfaction for alienation of her affections:

> it shant be onely one family thats miserable. for I am Robbed of all happiness in this world I am determined to leve her. and take my daughter with me that Shant see her poor mother Lot. . . . call and see me. for there is no person that Knowes any thing as yet. put it to your own case and Reflect one moment. that you should know shush a thing of your wife. would not you have satisfaction yes. and so will I before one day passes me more.
>
> I am yours
JAMES REYNOLDS

"On answer to this," Hamilton explained coolly, "I sent him a note, or message, desiring him to call upon me at my office, which I think he did the same day." This letter of Hamilton has not been found. They met. Hamilton's confession went on:

> He in substance repeated the topics contained in his letter, and that he was resolved to have satisfaction. I replied that he knew best what evidence he had of the alleged connection between me and his wife, that I neither admitted nor denied it; that if he knew of any injury I had done him, entitling him to satisfaction, it lay with him to name it.

Reynolds was evasive. According to Hamilton:

> He concluded with the same vague claim of satisfaction, but without specifying the kind which would content him. I resolved to gratify him. But willing to manage his delicacy, if he had any, I reminded him that I had, at our first interview, made him a promise of service, that I was disposed to do it as far as might be proper, and in my power, and requested him to consider in what manner I could do it, and to write to me. He withdrew with a promise of compliance.

Oddly enough Reynolds does not seem to have demanded that Hamilton break off the affair with Maria, nor did Hamilton offer to do so. Reynolds replied by a long, inconclusive letter asking Hamilton to meet him at the Sign of the George, a public tavern, on Tuesday morning at eight o'clock.

"On receipt of this letter," Hamilton said, "I called upon Reynolds." But before going to that rendezvous, Hamilton said he wrote a mysterious letter to an unnamed correspondent, describing his strong suspicion that he was the victim of a plot. He may have intended the addressee to be Oliver Wolcott, Jr., his assistant secretary of the treasury, or he may never have sent it, or, as some would charge, he may have written it in 1797 as a self-serving explanation and backdated it to the time of his eight o'clock rendezvous with Reynolds at the Sign of the George in 1791.

Hamilton wrote, "I am at this moment going to a rendezvous which I suspect may involve a most serious plot against me." It was risky to meet Reynolds in such a public place, but he would go anyway. "Various reasons, and among others a desire to ascertain the truth induce me to hazard the consequence," Hamilton added. The last sentence is the one that suggests that the letter was addressed to a public that was wider than Wolcott alone:

> As any disastrous event might interest my fame; I drop you this line, that from my impressions may be inferred the truth of the matter.
> Yrs. sincerely,   A. Hamilton

Hamilton dated this mysterious letter "Sunday, December 17th, 1791," but Sunday that year was in fact the eighteenth, making the following Tuesday the twentieth. At the turn of a year, Hamilton had once or twice earlier persisted in giving the new year the number of the old, but he almost never wrote the wrong date for a day of the week anywhere else in his correspondence. In either case, the rendezvous to which he actually went was not "at this moment," but two or three days later.

At their rendezvous at the Sign of the George, Hamilton recalled being peremptory:

> Assuming a decisive tone, [I] told him that I was tired of his indecision, and insisted upon his declaring to me explicitly what it was he aimed at. He again promised to explain by letter.

Hamilton went on, "On the 19th, I received the promised letter."

PHILADELPHIA, 19th December, 1791.

SIR.

I have this preposial to make to you. give me the Sum of thousand dollars and I will leve the town and take my daughter with me and go where my Friend Shant here from me and leve her to Yourself to do for her as you thing proper . . .

yours
JAMES REYNOLDS

MR. ALEXR. HAMILTON.

The secretary of the treasury was, as usual, short of personal funds. He did not have $1,000 to his name; so he had to pay the heart balm, or hush money, in two separate installments, one of $600 and the other of $400. Hamilton wrote that "I determined to give it to him and did so in two payments, as per receipts." His receipts from Reynolds are dated the twenty-second of December and the third of January. Later denying that these documents were evidence of his collaboration with Reynolds in illegal speculations, Hamilton ruefully wrote, "It is a little remarkable that an avaricious speculating Secretary of the Treasury should have been so straitened for money as to be obliged to satisfy an engagement of this sort by two different payments!"

The businesslike secretary of the treasury kept the signed receipts from Reynolds for years.

Hamilton's fresh resolve to end the affair lasted for about two weeks. It was Reynolds, not Maria, who asked Hamilton to come back again. In Hamilton's words: "On the 17th of January, I received the letter by which Reynolds writes me to renew my visits to his wife. He had before requested that I would see her no more."

Here is Reynolds's ludicrous explanation for his quick switch: "She would onely wish to see you as a friend."

PHILADELPHIA 17th January, 1792

SIR

I suppose you will be surprised in my writing to you . . . its Mrs. R. wish to See you. and for My own happiness and hers. I have not the Least Objections to your Calling. as a friend to Boath of us. and must rely intirely on your and her honnor . . . I am pritty well Convinsed, She would onely wish to See you as a friend. and sence I am Reconciled to live with her, I would wish to do every thing for her happiness and my own.

Here was a new way to squeeze some more money out of poor Hamilton. Pointing to this letter six years later, Hamilton asked the rhetorical question that remains a crucial one about the whole episode: "Is the preexistence of a speculating connection reconcilable with this mode of expression?"

The "mode of expression," the twists and turns, the hesitations and reversals of the correspondence display comedic and dramatic invention that range far beyond anything known about James Reynolds's literary talents or Hamilton's. The journalist James Thomson Callender and Professor Julian Boyd, the noted Jefferson scholar, and others have charged that Hamilton forged the letters from James and Maria Reynolds to him to provide documentary buttressing for his denial to a congressional committee investigating his alleged connection with Reynolds in speculation. In making this charge, they credit Hamilton with summoning up a novelistic richness of literary invention for this singular series of compositions found nowhere else in his voluminous writings. Yet the pointless hesitation and the indecisiveness of Reynolds's Sign of the George letter, for example, seem as inconsistent with the direct, linear, forward thrust of Hamilton's usual style as they are consistent with Reynolds's acting upon advice from someone behind the scenes like Aaron Burr about what to do next. In its crude way, Reynolds's December 15 letter stated a good legal cause of action for a lawsuit for alienation of affections.

This writer's conclusion is that the mode of expression that the Reynoldses used in their letters and the strange tergiversations of the underlying plot cannot be reconciled with the theory that Hamilton forged the whole series of documents and invented the story of the affair as a cover for speculating connections with Reynolds. Only a master dramatist of black comedy with the genius of, say, a Marlowe or life itself, could have contrived a plot so odd, grimly comic, and horrible for its victim.

To accept the conclusion that the main events of the Reynolds affair actually occurred and were not entirely fabricated by Hamilton is not to say that, in contriving them, nature was not assisted a little by the "genuine ha! ha!" of Aaron Burr. A nudge or shove or touch or wink from him or an occasional contribution of expense money to Maria and James Reynolds when Hamilton was short might add embroidery and curlicues to the basic plot line that nature herself would not have invented unaided. To credit Burr with such contributions is not to say that when Hamilton described the affair in his defense to the congressional committee in the closed session of 1792 and in his public defense of 1797, he did not further embroider it with some self-serving plot twists of his own. In long retrospect, these self-serving embellishments of his would become the darkest stain that the affair would leave on the honor of his name.

Hamilton did not at once accept Reynolds's astonishing invitation to resume seeing Maria as a platonic friend. Nor was a platonic friendship exactly what Maria had in mind.

"If I recollect rightly, I did not immediately accept the invitation," Hamilton said, "nor till after I had received several very importunate letters from Mrs. Reynolds."

As for Maria, she would never ask to see him again. Or else she would commit suicide if he refused to see her again:

> Monday Night, Eight C., L
>
> SIR,
>   . . . Yes Sir Rest assurred I will never ask you to Call on me again I have kept my Bed those two dayes and now rise from My pillow wich your Neglect has filled with the shorpest thorns . . . [My] heart is ready Burst with Greef I can neither eat or sleep I have Been on the point of doing the moast horrid acts at I shudder to think where I might been what will become of me . . .

She did not want to see him, but she insisted on seeing him.

> . . . all the wish I have is to se you once more that I may my doubts Cleared up for God sake be not so voed of all humanity as to deni me this Last request Call some time this night I no its late but any time between this and twelve A Clock I shall be up if you wont Come to send me a line oh my head I can rite no more do something to Ease My heart Or Els I no not what I shall do for so I cannot live Commit this to the care of my maid be not offended I beg.

Two days later she was still suffering pangs of his withdrawal from her service:

> Wednesday Morning ten of Clock
>
> DEAR SIR
>   . . . I shal be misarable till I se you and if my dear freend has the Least Esteeme for the unhappy Maria whos greateest fault is Loveing him he will come as soon as he shall get this and till that time My breast will be the seate of pain and woe
>
>   adieu
>
> Col. Hamilton.
> P.S. If you cannot come thie Evening to stay just come for only one moment as I shal be Lone Mr. is going to sup with a friend from New York.

Few things would seem more difficult for the kind of writer Hamilton was to invent than the unqualified passion of her effusions or the absurdity of her quick self-contradictions. She was still at it a week later.

Monday Morning.

My dear Col Hamilton on my kneese Let me Intreatee you to reade my Letter . . . you need not be the least affraid let me not die with fear have pity on me my freend for I deserve it . . . My heart Is ready to burst and my tears wich once could flow with Ease are now denied me Could I only weep I would thank heaven and bless the hand that _____

Her letter breaks off at the point where tears that can no longer flow are about to burst her heart.

Hamilton resumed the affair.

The boom in business and the securities markets that Hamilton's program had ushered in was appreciated by the powerful New York business community. So was the shrewd "fine tuning" of the market he had been doing to prevent the boom of 1791 from turning into a bust. On August 13, 1791, the New York *Daily Advertiser* had issued a public warning: "It has risen like a rocket. Like a rocket it will burst with a crack and down drops the rocket stick. What goes up must come down—so take care of your pate, brother Jonathan."

Hamilton had promptly responded on August 15 and 16 by transferring $150,000 from the sinking fund to William Seton, treasurer of the Bank of New York, to purchase public debt in the public market, covering the transfer with a confidential letter advising Seton that "a principal object with me is to keep the stock from falling too low in case the embarrassments of the dealers should lead to sacrifices. . . . If there are any gentlemen who support the funds and others who depress them, I shall be pleased that your purchases may aid the former —this in great confidence."

Hearing that William Duer was lofting the values of his securities by fictitious purchases and sales—wash sales in modern market jargon—Hamilton on August 17 had sent a friendly warning to Duer to stay out of the market. Seton promptly used substantial portions of the sinking fund money to purchase $52,-685 of securities from Duer, of all people, thus keeping Duer temporarily afloat and the market on an uptick. Hamilton's apparent intervention in the market on behalf of his friend became one of the most damaging charges later leveled against him. His defenders, of course, could reply that such intervention was made at Seton's, not Hamilton's, discretion and that the resultant increase in the money supply helped stave off a general panic that without it might have been more serious and come sooner.

Criticism from all sides did not keep Hamilton from throwing further cash from the sinking fund into the market. On September 7 he sent Seton $50,000 more with a note that "I wish I could have gone farther, but my hands are tied by the want of a majority of the Trustees being present. . . . You may, however, make it known that the Treasurer is purchasing here."

Before Seton could spread the good news or commence his purchases, the secret had leaked out, probably from the messenger who had carried the letter of authority. On September 12, Seton wrote to Hamilton, "The bearer of the letter I apprehend knew or conjectured the contents, as it flew over the town like wildfire that I had orders to purchase. Therefore, before I got to the coffee-house, at noon, every one was prepared, and no one would offer to supply at less than the former price." He reported that the scrip, which had been down to 110, was now up to 135 and 145, adding philosophically that "they are now getting into the proper hands."

Hamilton's intervention not only kept the market steady, but was largely responsible for a resumption of the rise. By October, bank stock of a par value of $400 had risen to $500, and most other stocks were higher too, and by the end of January they were moving higher still.

The Bank of the United States had opened branches in New York and elsewhere, and its New York branch competed with the Bank of New York not only in normal business of discounts, but also as a depository for government funds. When Seton wrote to complain of this competition, Hamilton replied on November 25 that the branches had been established without consulting him and against his judgment. "Ultimately it will be incumbent on me to place the public funds in the keeping of the branch," he acknowledged, "but it may be depended upon that I shall precipitate nothing, but shall so conduct the transfer as not to embarrass or distress your institution." He was, after all, a founder of the Bank of New York.[1]

It was very clear to New York bankers and businessmen like Seton and Duer that they had an understanding friend at Washington's court in Philadelphia. A group of them, including Roger Alden; Brockholst Livingston; Gulian Verplanck, the president of the Bank of New York; and Joshua Waddington, who had been Hamilton's client in the famous case of *Rutgers v. Waddington*, raised a subscription to commission John Trumbull to execute a portrait of Hamilton, to be hung in a place of honor in a public building in New York City. The subscribers particularly requested that the portrait "exhibit such part of your political life as may be most agreeable to yourself." Just then the most serious part of Hamilton's life was the least agreeable and the last that he would want to exhibit to public view. Hamilton at first declined, replying on January 15 that his portrait ought to appear "unconnected with any incident of my political life," but the project went forward.

Upon unveiling, the full-length portrait showed a Hamilton standing erect in fuller flesh than would appear in later portrayals, after suffering from further near fatal Philadelphia fevers of various kinds. Not by a drooping eyelash does his ruddy facade in 1792 at the height of his career betray a flicker of worry about the secret payments he was making to James Reynolds in small installments to keep him quiet. The Trumbull portrait now hangs in the Assembly Room of the New York State Chamber of Commerce building in New York City. Hamilton stands confidently beside his writing desk with the arch of a classical temple looming in the background. The inturned fingers of his right hand rest gracefully on the top page of what appears to be an important state paper awaiting immediate attention after the necessary interruption to strike a confident pose for the benefit of Trumbull and all his grateful friends now riding the boom in the market.

Amid the general prosperity for which Hamilton's New York friends gave him much credit some gaps remained. Philip Freneau, whom Jefferson had brought to Philadelphia from New York by putting him on the State Department payroll, ridiculed false Hamiltonian prosperity in a satirical verse published in his pro-Jefferson paper, *The National Gazette:*

> And, Sir, 'tis true
> (Twixt me and you)
> That some have grown prodigious fat,
> And some prodigious lean.

The art critic of the Philadelphia *Advertiser* also snickered at Hamilton's portrait by saying that John Trumbull had finally finished and unveiled "the best work that ever came from his pencil." Hamilton's sophisticated adulators could hardly read "pencil" as high praise. Hamilton himself might manage a thin smile with sophisticated intimates like Anne Bingham, but not be particularly amused.

Besides, the whole "superstructure of credit" that Hamilton had jawboned safely through 1791 collapsed at the end of February 1792. William Duer had mismanaged his official accounts as assistant secretary of the treasury, after four years of mismanaging the accounts of the old Board of Treasury, to such an extent that in 1792, his successor, Oliver Wolcott, Jr., remained unable to straighten them out. In one transaction Duer had taken official Treasury warrants and pledged them as security for his own private loans. On his failure to pay the loans, the warrants had been offered for sale and purchased by one Andrew G. Fraunces, an employee of the Treasury, who sought to collect on them. On other occasions, Fraunces had been a coadjutor of Duer inside the Treasury, if not, indeed of James Reynolds as well. The Philadelphia loan office duly honored Duer's warrants on presentation and returned them to the Treasury for payment, but there Hamilton discovered Duer's fraud and refused to clear the payments. Hamilton made no public mention of the transaction and accepted Duer's assurances that he would make good the loss, but Duer failed to pay, and the default of the former assistant secretary remained an open item.[2]

The private manipulations of Duer and his partners, Alexander McComb and Royal Flint, became matters of public notoriety. On March 12, 1792, Oliver Wolcott, Jr., wrote to Richard Harison, the United States attorney in New York, demanding that Duer settle his accounts as secretary of the old Board of Treasury or give security for a shortage of $200,000. In the event of noncompliance, Harison was to commence suit for the money. Rumors that Duer and McComb were on the verge of bankruptcy caused securities markets to fall sharply. Hamilton had sought to prevent too high a rise in 1791; now he had to support the market to prevent a crash. Duer had written Hamilton on March 12, demanding that he hold off Wolcott's suit, else "my ruin is complete," but Hamilton refused to interfere. By the nineteenth, Troup was telling Hamilton of Duer, "this poor man is in a state of almost complete insanity; and his situation is a source of inexpressible grief to all his friends." But nothing could be done. "Duer's notes unpaid amounted to about half a million dollars and Duer has not a farthing of money or a particle of stock to pay them with." There were "widows, orphans, merchants and mechanics" all unpaid. Troup warned that Duer's total bankruptcy would bring Hamilton's funding system into "odium."

Wolcott followed up the prosecution. On March 21 he wrote Harison that "no person can be less disposed than I am to increase [Duer's] misfortunes, yet when I consider the nature of his engagements to the public, the repeated assurances which I have personally recd. And the embarrassments which I am expecting, in consequence of his failing to perform his promises I feel no inclination to neglect my duty & sacrifice my character on his account."[3]

On March 25, Hamilton sent $50,000 to William Seton at the Bank of New York, with instruction to support the six-percents at par if they should sink below that figure. Seton was not to declare specifically on whose account he was buying, because formal authority to buy for the sinking fund was lacking—"the thing is not formally arranged and this is Sunday," Hamilton wrote. Besides, there was an advantage in acting without formal authority from the trustees because "it will very probably be conjectured that you appear for the public." Hamilton also passed along the good news from abroad that William Short had just effected a loan of three million florins at 4 percent. "This may be announced," Hamilton felt, but "as in the present moment of suspicion some minds may be disposed to consider the thing as a mere expedient to support the stocks, I pledge my honor for its exact truth."[4]

Freneau's *National Gazette* picked this moment of crisis in public confidence and threats of odium for Hamilton's funding system to declare war on the Treasury. On April 2, James Madison, writing as *Brutus*, assailed men who "pampered the spirit of speculation." *Brutus* was no more alarmed than was Hamilton himself, who wrote Philip Livingston the same day, " 'Tis time there should be a line of Separation between honest Men & knaves, between respectable Stockholders and dealers in the funds, and mere unprincipled Gamblers. Public infamy must restrain what the laws cannot."[5] Probably one reason for Hamilton's harsh language to Philip Livingston was that a number of Livingstons "were actively speculating on the 'bear' side of the market and were due to *deliver* most of the New York bank stock Duer was to *receive* in *May.*" In other words, Livingston bears were making money pushing down stocks in the market in a way that would bankrupt bulls like Duer.

At a meeting of the closely divided commissioners of the sinking fund on April 3, Jefferson argued that the prices at which it was buying were all unrealistically high and would favor the speculators. Hamilton knew or sensed that more bankruptcies of his friends were on the way. He suggested to William Seton On April 4 that he hold off purchases for a while, till things got worse, even if some of his own friends should go bankrupt. "You may apply another $50,000 to purchases at such time as you judge it can be rendered most useful," Hamilton advised. But it might be best to "wait the happening of the crisis which I fear is inevitable . . . a pretty extensive explosion is to take place . . . then it may be more important than now to enter the market in force."[6]

Hamilton was right. Alexander McComb's failure on April 12 fueled more fears and panic. "This misfortune has a long tail to it," Hamilton wrote Seton and sent on $100,000. Seton went into the market with it and explained to Hamilton on April 16, 1792, that "the applications were so numerous & so vastly beyond my expectations, I found it necessary to declare I could take but very small sums from each . . . Everyone pressed forward & were so eager, that I could only take down names." I averaged the whole "that no one would be left without some relief—so that the investment of the $100,000 goes to upwards of 80 persons."

Seton complimented Hamilton on his astute market strategy: "Your orders for purchase were well timed." But he added that such "great and universal distress prevails" that "it would be utterly impossible to make purchases equal to the relief." As an experienced Wall Streeter, Seton knew that what goes down must also go up; every well has a bottom. "It cannot now be worse," he reflected, "when the public mind calms down a little . . . the spirit of Industry, instead of Gambling will revive, and the Stocks will come to their proper and real value."

Before they did, however, news of Duer's failure spread, and other creditors pressed him. He had taken usury on loans to "Widows Orphans Butchers & Carriers" at rates ranging from 2 to 4 percent a month. Their life savings were down the drain. He also lost large sums that the SUM had entrusted to his keeping and left its books of account rigged and indecipherable. One of Duer's and Hamilton's associates in the SUM, John Dewhurst, fled his New York creditors and declared bankruptcy in Philadelphia. Duer was clapped into jail. His angriest creditors howled for hauling him out and lynching him. Many, recalling his position at the Treasury, implicated Hamilton in Duer's fall. James Watson wrote Jeremiah Wadsworth on April 3, 1792, "I observe with extreme anxiety the State of many minds respecting the Government—And particularly the bitter use which the Secretary's enemies make of his attachment to Colo Duer."[7]

Hamilton struggled to stave off the bankruptcy of the SUM, writing a careful letter to its board of directors on April 14. "Among the disastrous incidents of the present juncture," he told them, "I have not been least affected by the temporary derangement of the affairs of your Society." He sketched a businesslike salvage operation, suggesting that "the Society confine themselves at first to the cotton branch. The printing business to commence as early as possible." Unprofitable subsidiaries should be spun off. "Means should be taken to procure in Europe a *few essential* workmen." If the directors desired, he would arrange a loan. Through William Seton he managed to arrange a $10,000 loan at interest of only 5 percent—a prime rate that was as favorable as the United States itself could obtain from the bank.[8]

When Nehemiah Hubbard, the superintendent general, resigned his splendid title in disgust, Hamilton asked him to reconsider. "This institution has presented itself to my mind of such real public importance," he wrote Hubbard on May 3, 1792, "that I feel myself much interested in its success." Peter Colt, treasurer of the state of Connecticut and owner of the only cloth-making factory in the country was engaged in Hubbard's place. He set up a cotton spinning mill for the SUM known as the Bull Mill because the looms were operated by costly oxen power—hence the name—instead of free hydraulic power. The mill race to bring water from behind the waterfall over the mill wheels had not been completed to provide falling waterpower.

Until Duer's collapse and the panic of 1792, it had seemed that Hamilton's services as financial consultant might just save the sick company. But then the SUM subscribers refused to pay up their stock subscriptions. Dissension arose among directors and shareholders. Hamilton's political enemies, of course, charged him with corruption, ambition, fraud, and misconduct for being involved in this private, quasi-public sibling of his "Report on Manufactures."

New mills were actually constructed, limited operations commenced, and in 1794 the "cradle of American industry" finally finished its first waterpowered mill, the SUM mill, and began the manufacture of cotton, yarn, and candlewicks and printed calico. In the next few years it continued to suffer reverses from strikes, financial panics, scandals, shortages of skilled labor, and bankruptcy. The vast original plan never materialized. By 1796 everyone involved was sick of the venture. The plant was put up for sale, and a plan of dissolution was proposed, but even this failed. The SUM sold its goods, leased its buildings, buried its hopes, and continued as a mere landholder and lessor, possessed of the unique privileges Hamilton had written into its original charter. Not until recent years under the general corporation laws of New Jersey, Delaware, New York, and other states, have business corporations, even the most insignificant paper corporations, been granted authority to exercise powers as broad as those that Hamilton, the corporation lawyer, had conceived almost two centuries earlier for the SUM, which made little use of them all. After the Hamiltonian Tariff of 1816, prosperity gradually arrived. In Paterson's prime in the 1830s, the SUM plants brought Paterson many cotton and silk mills, and Paterson became the "silk city of the world." It also boasted four machine shops, two bleaching mills, and the factory that produced Samuel Colt's famous revolver.

Such success was much too late to provide solace or return on investment to Hamilton and his friends. They lost all they had ever invested in the SUM when the Treasury Department's suit sent Duer to prison.

By June 10, 1792 Fisher Ames was able to write Hamilton from Boston that "all goes well in the state. The people really prosper, and, what is more, they know it, and give credit to the general government for the change they have witnessed." Seton likewise was able to report that all was well between the Bank of New York and the New York branch of the Bank of the United States, thanks to Hamilton: "With respect to ourselves & the Branch we go in perfect Harmony, & there does not appear any disposition on their part to do otherwise." If, however, "should any Circumstances occur that argues hostilities, I shall address myself freely to you."

Later on, Seton thanked Hamilton for ordering the collector of New York to deposit his receipts in the Bank of New York, for, as he put it in confidence, he felt that the branch was trying to drain him of specie: "If I find they persist in the draining us, I must implore the aid of your all powerfull hand to convince them we are not destitute of aid in the hour of need." With and without Hamilton's "all powerfull hand," unlike the SUM, the Bank of New York weathered the storm and continued to flourish to the present day.

The letters of Maria and James Reynolds went on and on through 1792, repeating with incredible variations the same basic cycle of her professions of love for Hamilton and James's sullen, but complaisant, cuckoldry, to a total of 22 by Hamilton's numbering, the last being dated August 30, 1792. In it, James, still professing outrage, is still demanding small sums of hush money from Hamilton.

Hamilton had written some notes replying to one or the other of the Reynoldses, and these became the most damaging part of the case the prosecution would bring against him. One said merely, "To-morrow what is requested will be done. 'T will hardly be possible to-day." Hamilton explained that this was an answer to a note of Reynolds asking for a loan "to-day," "A scarcity of cash, which was not very uncommon," said Hamilton, had "modelled the reply."

The star witness for the congressional committee that later constructed the case against Hamilton would be Jacob Clingman, a prepossessing young man who had collaborated with James Reynolds in at least one scheme that made fraudulent use of lists wrongfully leaked from the Treasury Department. Clingman had seen Hamilton at the Reynoldses' house on several occasions, had joined in conversations with him there, and would replace him as one of Maria's lovers. A letter from Reynolds of June 1792 had solicited "a *loan* of three hundred dollars towards a subscription to the *Lancaster Turnpike.*" Here seemed to be a prima facie evidence of Hamilton's speculation in securities through the agency of Reynolds. Clingman testified that Reynolds had told him that Hamilton refused the $300 loan by the following note:

> It is utterly out of my power, I assure you 'pon my honor, to comply with your request. Your note is returned.

In rebuttal, Hamilton pointed out that his letter "demonstrates, that here was no concern in speculation on my part—that the money is asked as a *favor* and as *loan,* to be reimbursed simply and without profit in *less than a fortnight.* My answer shows that even the loan was refused."

Clingman had obtained Hamilton's original note from Reynolds and kept it in his possession. Clingman went on to say that Reynolds boasted to him that if he wanted money, Hamilton was "obliged to let him have it," because "he had it in his power to hang Col. Hamilton." Clingman said he had occasionally lent money to Reynolds himself and did not worry about repayment because Reynolds claimed "that he could always get it from Col. Hamilton to repay it." On one occasion, Clingman lent Reynolds $200, which Reynolds promised to repay him "through the means of Col. Hamilton." One day Clingman went with Reynolds and saw him go in to Hamilton's house, and after Reynolds came out, he paid Clingman $100. This, Reynolds said, was part of the sum he had got from Hamilton. When Reynolds paid Clingman the balance a few days later, he again told Clingman that it came from Colonel Hamilton "after his return from Jersey, having made a visit to the manufacturing society there."

Hamilton admitted making these two payments of $100, explaining that Reynolds had demanded the money from him for "furnishing a small boarding-house, which Reynolds and his wife were, or pretended to be, about to set up."

One of Hamilton's other notes to Reynolds said merely, "My dear sir, I expected to have heard the day after I had the pleasure of seeing you." To Hamilton, "this fragment, if truly a part of a letter to Reynolds, denotes nothing more than a disposition to be civil to a man whom, as I said before, it was the interest of my passions to conciliate. But I verily believe it was no part of a letter to him, because I do not believe that I ever addressed him in such a style."

More likely, Hamilton thought, Reynolds had stolen from his office a letter he had started to write to someone else and then thrown away. Reynolds had procured it "by means of which I am ignorant, or it may have been the beginning of an intended letter, torn off, thrown into the chimney in my office, which was a common practice, and there, or after it had been swept out, picked up by Reynolds, *or some coadjutor of his."*

But if "some coadjutor" of Reynolds were still employed in the Treasury Department at the time he wrote these notes, then Hamilton had slipped into a self-damaging admission. He went on to admit that *"there appears to have been more than one clerk in the department somehow connected with him."* Apparently, there was more than one "coadjutor" of Reynolds still in the department. One of these suspected coadjutors may have been the "Simeon" Reynolds of Connecticut, who was a clerk in the register's office, or Andrew Fraunces. Writing his public account in 1797, Hamilton failed to follow up or explain this cold trail of other coadjutors. Instead, he turned to the task of discrediting the last of the fragments of correspondence in his own hand with which his accusers confronted him.

The final fragment was, "The person Mr. Reynolds inquired for on Friday waited for him all evening at his house, from a little after seven. Mr. R. may see him at any time to-day or to-morrow, between the hours of two and three."

Hamilton explained this away too with surprising subtlety: "Mrs. Reynolds more than once communicated to me that Reynolds would occasionally relapse into discontent at his situation, would treat her very ill, hint at the assassination of me, and more openly threaten, by way of revenge, to inform Mrs. Hamilton." Hamilton expressed his reaction to this in a laughable—or majestic—understatement: "All this naturally gave some uneasiness."

For once, Hamilton admits to being confused. Was it "artifice or reality"? "In the workings of human inconsistency it was very possible that the same man might be corrupt enough to compound for his wife's chastity, and yet have sensibility enough to be restless in the situation and to hate the cause of it."

The series of notes between the Reynoldses and himself explained the entire matter of his payments to Reynolds, Hamilton avowed. He was the victim of someone's plot against him. In sum, "The endeavor . . . to induce me to render my visits to Mrs. Reynolds more public, and the great care with which my little notes were preserved, justify the belief that at a period before it was attempted, the idea of implicating me in some accusation, with a view to the advantage of the accusers, was entertained. Hence the motive to pick up and preserve any fragment which might favor the idea of friendly or confidential correspondence."

Hamilton's denial of speculating connection with Reynolds is further buttressed by his habitual avoidance of conflicts between personal interest and discharge of public duty. The only securities Hamilton owned at the time, apart from a qualifying share in the SUM, were five and one-half shares of the Ohio Company, which held land grants in the Western Territory. He now found himself obliged in his official capacity to determine whether some of these grants were valid. He declined to do so. Instead, he obtained the opinion of the attorney general on the question and then referred it to the accounting office of the Treasury. He explained apologetically to Washington on May 9, 1792, that his all-powerful hand had been unable to handle so small a matter because he had applied the standards of a Caesar's wife to his official conduct to avoid even the appearance of impropriety:

> It is with regret that I find myself required by Law to discharge
> an official duty in a case in which I happen to be interested as a party,
> and which is capable of being regulated by different constructions.

"Thus circumstanced," he concluded, "I have conceived it proper to repose myself on the judgment of others . . . [and] have governed myself by the determination of those Officers."

A dangerous feature of owning an all-powerful hand is that the eye that should govern it is tricked out of seeing how many kinds of things are "capable of being regulated by different constructions."

9

A TISSUE OF MACHINATIONS

I WILL NOT SUFFER MY RETIREMENT TO BE CLOUDED BY THE SLAN-
DERS OF A MAN WHOSE HISTORY, FROM THE MOMENT AT WHICH
HISTORY CAN STOOP TO NOTICE HIM, IS A TISSUE OF MACHINA-
TIONS AGAINST THE LIBERTY OF THE COUNTRY WHICH HAS NOT
ONLY RECEIVED HIM AND GIVEN HIM BREAD, BUT HEAPED ITS
HONORS ON HIS HEAD.
—*Jefferson to Washington, September 9, 1792*

The Senate met daily at noon, a time when an early riser like Burr had
already been abroad for six or seven hours, but Burr absented himself often
from the floor, particularly on days when controversial questions were up for a
vote. To keep himself occupied in Philadelphia and avoid too much commitment
to tiresome controversies in which a stand on either side would cost popularity,
Burr undertook to write a book. "Of all races of animals," he wryly remarked,
"authors are the vainest." But several times in his life he had started out to
become one. His project beginning in December of 1791 was a history of the
American Revolution.

"I am much in want of my maps ..." he wrote Theodosia in New York. "Send
them all carefully put up in a box ... Ask Major P[revost] for the survey he gave
me of the St. Lawrence, of different parts of Canada and other provinces."

Thomas Jefferson made a point of putting a man like Burr, who could deliver
a stunning election defeat to a Hamilton candidate, early in his debt whether or

not he liked him as a friend. Perhaps he was reciprocating to Burr for the favor
that had brought Maria Reynolds to Philadelphia early that summer. He furnished Burr with an office in the State Department.

Every morning at five, Burr walked to his new office and breakfasted over
his work. A servant fueled the fire, a copyist took notes, and, in due season, said
Burr, "I [had] got together . . . letters, documents, memoranda, all carefully
labelled, tied up and put into many tin boxes."

But when Burr surveyed his research, he confessed that "these documents
. . . detailed things which would falsify many matters now supposed to be
gratifying national facts." With a vigorous prose style, a hardy iconoclasm, a
mind steeped in bookish lore, and much inside information, he was on his way
to becoming America's first debunking historian. His failure to complete the job
occasions as much regret as Hamilton's failure to write the history of the same
subject in heroic vein as Hugh Knox had enjoined him to do.

Some of Burr's personal characteristics mirrored Jefferson's as if seen in a
fun house mirror. He was a dilettante and patron rather than an expert himself
in the arts. He read every conceivable form of print and learned to quote from
eight foreign languages. Unlike Jefferson, he shunned "the mechanical labor of
writing which I hate." He frequented the opera and concert halls and had "great
sensibility to music, but no science."

He loved his Richmond Hill mansion as Jefferson loved his Monticello. For
it, he constructed a steam furnace, and he also designed a special chariot to
combine speed and comfort of travel. Both men affirmed official liking for President Washington without receiving much reciprocal show of fondness from
Washington's quarter.

When Washington heard of Burr's labors at the State Department in 1793,
he ordered its archives closed to him. Burr appealed to Jefferson, but Jefferson
backed away, washing his hands of Burr's project. Burr's debunking history was
never finished, and his notes were lost. Burr's only recorded comment was
characteristic of a man whom no one could pin down: "It is perhaps politically
well."[1] By the time Burr's tenure in Jefferson's office was cut short, he had more
than earned his keep there by helping inflict a second stunning electoral setback
to a Hamilton candidate for the second year in a row.

By early 1792 Burr's political star had risen so high in midsky that he stood
a good chance of winning the nomination to run for governor of New York as
the candidate of either the Federalist party or the Anti-Federalist party. He was
personally on good terms with a majority of the lesser Federalist leaders and
with many of the major leaders as well. A founder of Tammany Hall, Burr
received much well-organized support from artisans, mechanics, and laborers in
New York City. Large holders upstate like the Livingstons and many a small
farmer were also favorably disposed toward him, as much because he seemed
to be an antidote to Hamilton and Schuyler as for any other reason. Even Robert
Yates, Hamilton's and Schuyler's early choice to oppose George Clinton for the
governorship seemed favorably disposed toward Burr. Yates at first was
tempted, but then finally declined to become the Federalist candidate. Twice

before, Chief Justice John Jay had also refused to run for elective office; so Hamilton and Schuyler must have been remarkably persuasive with him or with Sarah, his wife, or with both of them to obtain Jay's consent to make the race now. Even so, Jay stipulated that he would not campaign actively and would not "make any efforts to obtain suffrages." He would stand entirely on his reputation for ability and integrity.

A mass meeting of Federalists on February 9, 1792, followed Hamilton's lead and nominated Jay for governor and Stephen Van Rensselaer for lieutenant governor. Judge Yates was persuaded to appear and back the ticket. Hamilton thought he had put down the threat from Burr.

Now among the Anti-Federalists, or Republicans, as they were beginning to call themselves, a movement sprang up to replace the five-term governor Clinton with Senator Burr, who, they felt, had a better chance of defeating the formidable Chief Justice Jay. After producing the maximum show of support from both sides, Burr announced that he was not a candidate, and Clinton rammed through his own renomination. The remarkable fact that Senator Burr might have won the nomination of either party was not lost on any astute political leader in the country.

The election was closely contested, and Hamilton's policies, rather than the merits of two already well-known candidates, became the central issue. James Tillary wrote pessimistically to Hamilton that "the Bank Mania rages violently in this City, & it is made an engine to help the Governor's re-election." The panic brought on by Duer's collapse hurt Hamilton here, as in every quarter.

Chief Justice Jay could not actively campaign without violating judicial ethics even if he had wanted to. Hamilton, knowing that he and his policies could only cost his own candidates wavering votes from voters in the middle of the political spectrum, avowed that he, too, "scrupulously refrained from interference in elections." The nationwide newspaper war between Hamilton and Jefferson had begun. Even the politics of the French Revolution came to be an issue in the New York State election.

After the close of voting on April 13, a majority of the canvassers, all Clinton supporters, reported that Clinton had been elected by a majority of less than 150 votes. By New York law the ballot boxes were supposed to be delivered to the secretary of state by the sheriff of each county. But in three counties, Otsego, Clinton, and Tioga, as the result of accidental combinations of the sheriff's illness and carelessness, minor officials and sheriffs' deputies had handled the boxes instead. No seals had been broken; no fraud proved; no votes disputed; but the majority of the canvassers ruled that none of the votes from these three counties could be counted. All the ballots from them were then burned. A minority of the canvassers found that if the ballots from these three counties had been counted, Jay would have won the election.

Jay's supporters estimated that his majority in Otsego County alone would have been 500 votes. Philip Schuyler wrote Hamilton on May 9 that if the votes for Jay were fairly canvassed, Jay would prevail, "but I apprehend foul play in the returning officers at least." Omitting all the votes from the three counties, the canvassers reported that Clinton had won by 8,440 to 8,332, a margin of 108 votes. The canvassers, a joint committee of the senate and assembly, divided along predictable party lines, seven for Clinton to four for Jay. But no one disputed the fact that if the ballots from the three counties had not been disqualified, Jay would have won.

The outcome was so controversial that the canvassers invited the two senators from New York, Rufus King and Aaron Burr, to furnish them with legal opinions on the result. An opinion that the votes from the three counties could be counted would mean Jay's election. Robert Troup and a group of leading members of the New York bar joined Rufus King in giving it as their legal opinions that the majority of the canvassers were wrong in throwing out the three counties' ballots. Jay had indeed been elected.

After considerable delay, Burr took the opposite side, chose the more expedient of two evils, and in a long and legalistic explanation backed Clinton, whom a Republican-dominated board of electors forthwith pronounced to be the new governor. Burr's friend Robert Troup said:

> The quibbles of chicanery he made are characteristic of the man
> . . . and will damn his reputation as a lawyer. . . . We all consider Burr's
> opinion as such a shameful prostitution of his talents, and so decisive
> a proof of the real infamy of his character, that we are determined to
> rip him up.

Josiah Ogden Hoffman, a young friend of Hamilton and Troup, angrily observed that "the ingenuity of Col. Burr was not in vain. He acted a principal part in the drama, or rather, remained behind the scenes, *slyly* instructing each man in his part . . . whether he was urged by a resentment to a more fortunate rival, or by motives yet more base and mercenary, God only knows. . . . I pity the man"

With this crucial assist from Aaron Burr, to whom he had given his first boost up the political ladder, George Clinton seized the governor's chair for a sixth term.[2]

The more fiery Federalists urged calling a convention to override the decision. There was even loose talk of forcible resistance. When Jay returned to New York City, he was honored with toasts and cannon salutes. Rufus King, ever firm for law, described taking Egbert Benson with him in his carriage to meet Jay: "The concourse was immense. . . . The shout was for 'Jay & Liberty.'" Such receptions and addresses, King acknowledged to Hamilton, "together with Mr. Jays answers leave no . . . doubt that the question will be brought to a decision. . . ." But an appeal to the people would be imprudent, he thought. Jay for once seemed fighting mad. He "deems the occasion such as will justify the step should it be found that the powers of government are insufficient to afford a Remedy." Should Clinton cling to the governor's seat in the face of the hostile majority "and the sword be drawn, he must go to the wall." To King, the situation in New York foreshadowed the even worse situation that might arise if there should be

a disputed election for the presidency itself. This "is a dreadful alternative
. . . if this case will justify a recurrence to first principles [violent ouster], what
are we to expect from the disputes, which might . . . arise in the succession of
the Presidency? and how are we to place confidence in the security of our
Government?" The "dreadful alternative" of which King had had a premonition
in 1792 became a threat in the national election of 1800, and Burr was again one
of the principals. Even usually staunch supporters of Clinton like Chancellor
Robert R. Livingston disapproved the outcome in New York. He wrote to Edward Livingston on June 19, "I confess I could have wished that all the votes
might be counted whatever might have been the event."

While the uproar over the uncounted ballots raged, Hamilton set his face
firmly against extralegal action by his friends. Hamilton advised King on July
25, 1792: "I do not feel it right or expedient to attempt to reverse the decision
by any means not known to the Constitution or laws. The precedent may suit us
to-day; but to-morrow we may see its abuse."

And to his wife Sarah's excited and perhaps ambitiously hopeful reports of
the rioting in New York in his support, Jay, calmer now, replied that "a few years
more will put us all in the dust; and it will then be of more importance to me to
have governed *myself* than to have governed the *State.*"

No Founding Father's tombstone boasts a nobler epitaph.

The consequences of Jay's defeat cast long shadows over Hamilton. With
Jay as their candidate, Hamilton and his supposedly unpopular party and policies
had won a majority of the people's votes against Clinton and his self-proclaimed
party of the people. With his old friend John Jay, who had run at Hamilton's
urging, instead of his perennial foe, George Clinton, secure in the governor's
chair for the new term, Hamilton's New York political base would for once have
been secure behind him. As the successful state leader, Hamilton would have
been in full control of his national party's reins for the national elections of 1792
and after.

If only Otsego County's ballots had not been handled by a deputy sheriff,
if only they had not been burned, if only Burr's opinion had coincided with Rufus
King's, thus assuring Jay's election, it is not difficult to project a logical series
of events that would have thrust Hamilton's name to the fore as a candidate for
vice-president among the many Federalists who, like Washington himself, were
more and more unhappy with Vice-President Adams. As Washington's vice-
president in 1792, Hamilton would have stepped into the direct line of succession
to the presidency whenever Washington should decide to retire. Only Burr's
opinion had blocked the way to that smooth *cursus honorum.*

Having squeaked by with Burr's aid, Clinton immediately reached for
higher office. By June he was the leading candidate among Anti-Federalists to
succeed Adams as vice-president in the Federal election to be held in the fall.
Hamilton thought his close call had damaged Clinton's chances when he wrote
to John Adams cheerfully on June 25, "M. Clinton is to be your competitor in the
next election. The issue of his late election will not help his cause. Alas! Alas!"
Jefferson saw Clinton's failure to decline to accept his disputed victory as hurting

the Anti-Federalist party's chances. He would have liked to repudiate him. Jefferson said, "I really apprehend that the cause of republicanism will suffer and its votaries be thrown into schism by embarking it in support of this man, and for what? to draw over the anti-federalists who are not numerous enough to be worth drawing over."

To an instinct for the political jugular, Jefferson joined a deadly ability to hit two targets with one well-aimed missile. Not long after Jefferson's return the previous summer from his and Madison's "passionate courtship" of Aaron Burr, George Clinton, Robert R. Livingston, and Philip Freneau in New York, where they concerted all their plans to erase Hamilton, a series of public letters signed *Publicola* had appeared in the newspapers. Jefferson angrily denounced Vice-President John Adams for their authorship. It did not unduly trouble Jefferson that the true author was Adams's son, John Quincy Adams. John Adams was guilty by association, being the author's father. Hamilton tried to soothe the secretary of state, but only supplied Jefferson with an additional target of opportunity in himself.

On August 13, 1791, Jefferson jotted down the following notes on some private remarks that Hamilton had made intending to dampen down Jefferson's ire at Adams and heal the rift between two prominent members of the cabinet:

> A. H. condemning Mr. A's writing . . . as having a tendency to weaken the present govmt declared in substance as follows:
>
> 'I own it is my own opinion tho' I do not publish it in Dan and Bersheba, that the present govnmt is not that which will answer the ends of society, by giving stability & protection to its rights, and that it will probably be found expedient to go into the British form. However, since we have undertaken the experiment, I am for giving it a fair course, whatever my expectns. The success indeed so far, is greater than I had expected . . . & therefore at present success seems more possible than it had done heretofore.'

Hamilton was merely saying in a sympathetic way that nothing, not even the Constitution, was perfect and that anybody, including Adams, could find things in it to criticize, but Jefferson professed to find in Hamilton's soothing assurances sinister signs of dangerous monarchical tendencies. In defense of Adams, Hamilton had gone on to say that "there are still other and other stages of improvement . . . that a mind must be really depraved which would not prefer the equality of political rights which is the foundation of pure republicanism if it can be obtained consistently with order." Hamilton had added that "whoever by his writings disturbs the present order of things, is really blameable, however pure his intentions may be, and he was sure Mr. Adams' were pure." Hamilton was agreeing with Jefferson, but Hamilton also was trying to say that Adams had done nothing reprehensible—his motives were pure.

Later, Jefferson claimed he heard Hamilton say "that this constitution was a shilly shally thing of mere milk & water, which could not last, & was only good as a step to something better." And referring to Jay and Hamilton, Jefferson wrote on July 28, 1791, to William Short, claiming that "both are dangerous. They pant after union with England as the power which is to support their projects, and are most determined Anti-gallicans. It is prognosticated that our republic is to end with the President's life. But I believe they will find themselves all head and no body."

Jefferson's *Anas* are filled with such reflections on Hamilton and his colleagues, recorded to bolster up his false charge that Hamilton was a "monocrat," or "monarchist," a too close friend of Britain, and anything but a firm supporter of the Constitution he had helped to write.

Hamilton had hailed George Hammond's appointment as a sign that "the British Cabinet wish to be thought disposed to enter into amicable & liberal arrangements with us." He had written Benjamin Goodhue on June 30, 1791, that "if some liberal arrangement with Great Britain should ensue it will have a prodigious effect upon the Conduct of some other parts of Europe. Tis however most wise for us to depend as little as possible upon European Caprice & to exert ourselves to the utmost to unfold and improve every domestic resource." To Hamilton, the practical interests of America came first in all matters of foreign policy and diplomacy. This led him to favor improving relationships with all countries, including Britain, with whom America had by far the most important commercial ties.

During the Revolution, of course, Great Britain had been the enemy and France the ally, but in the decade since there had been vast change. The French Revolution, so different from the American, had spilled over in French threats to the rest of Europe and seemed to threaten the New World as well. Hamilton at first was favorably disposed toward the French Revolution, but, as the convulsion widened and turned more violent and rabbles gave way to tyrants, with bloodbaths at each transfer of power, it had revealed itself as a social, religious, and economic, as well as a political, upheaval. It aroused his liberal, religious, and conservative instincts and enhanced his admiration for ordered stability under law on the British pattern. Jefferson, on the other hand, was a passionate admirer of the French slogan of *Liberté, Égalité, Fraternité*, regardless of the facts, or at least he professed to be. He seemed obsessed with a hatred for Britain, his fellow countrymen who did not share it, and all he dubbed as "monarchists" and "monocrats." These were the most pejorative epithets that Jefferson could find for political adversaries. These words were supposed to mean that the accused advocated a monarchy along British lines. But in his use of the term, Jefferson imputed to monocrats all the worst excesses of the old royal regime in France. Jefferson seemed blind to the virtues of limited constitutional republican monarchy in the form that closer students of world affairs saw emerging in Britain. His criticisms applied with more force to the form of strong, presidential, executive government emerging in America under Washington than to Britain.

At the Constitutional Convention, in *The Federalist Papers*, and in many letters and state papers, Hamilton made penetrating analyses of the British experience with monarchy to extract such useful lessons as it might offer America on the subject of an executive with sufficient but limited powers. Hamilton always insisted that monarchy was not right for America. But it served Jefferson's political purposes to ignore the truth of the matter and to belabor Hamilton instead as chief examplar of the hated monarchist tribe.

In his contributions to *The Federalist Papers*, James Madison, like Hamilton, had argued eloquently for a strong executive and against divisive political factions. Now Jefferson and Madison were speaking and writing of a "republican interest" and a "republican party," posing as the only protectors of American liberties against an allegedly subversive "monarchical party." No such party existed. But by their shrewd exploitation of and interchangeable use of scare words like *monarchical* and *monocrat*, Jefferson and Madison rallied to their faction many whose grievances were against any strong executive government like Washington's, as administered most conspicuously by Hamilton.

Theirs was a familiar form of political hyperbole. The words *monarchist*, *monarchical*, and *monocrat* had strong emotional connotations of loyalty to Britain and disloyalty to America. There is always a significant group of voters to be won over by candidates who are not above imputing treason to opponents by pejorative emotional epithets, without proof, in the face of evidence to the contrary. False charges of treason to the government were also in vogue in France. Accused fell under the accusers' guillotine as successive waves of accusers accused their way to power.

Hamilton usually met such false charges in typical advocate's fashion at a somewhat higher level than his accusers by charging his opponents with the intention of destroying what he called "good government." Reasonable men could, of course, differ about what constituted "good government," but in a way that they could not differ about false charges of treason. It added to Hamilton's annoyance that the presence within the government of the harshest critics of the government itself, not merely its policies but its very form, lent authority to charges that imputed disloyalty to its highest officials. Hamilton did not stoop to the use of words that falsely imputed or implied secret disloyalty or treason to his opponents.

To Jefferson's basic charge that the Hamiltonians were a monarchical party that sought the destruction of the federal form and all state governments, Hamilton replied, "To this there is no other Answer than a flat denial, except this: that the project, from its absurdity, refutes itself."

He reinforced refutation with classical instance: "It has aptly been observed, that Cato was the Tory, Caesar the Whig of his day. The former frequently resisted, the latter always flattered, the follies of the people. Yet the former perished with the republic—the latter destroyed it. . . ."

He went on, "No popular government was ever without its Catilines and its Caesars—these are its true enemies. . . ." Hamilton acidly held up Jefferson's hysterical charges to ridicule:

> It is curious to observe the anticipations of the different parties. One
> side appears to believe that there is a serious plot to overturn the State
> governments, and substitute a monarchy to the present republican

system. The other side firmly believes that there is a serious plot to overturn the general government, and elevate the separate power of the States upon its ruins. Both sides may be equally wrong, and their mutual jealousies may be naturally causes of the appearances which mutually disturb them and sharpen them against each other.

He did not seek the destruction of state governments: "As to State governments, the prevailing bias of my judgment is that if they can be circumscribed within bounds, consistent with the preservation of the national government, they will prove useful and salutary." The states were a threat to "preservation of the national government," but easy as it would have been to ignore the problem, he could not forbear to call attention to his premonition of civil war: "As to any combination to prostrate the State governments, I disavow and deny it."

In his extraordinary private confession to his old army friend Edward Carrington by his letter of May 26, 1792, Hamilton delivered a moving, rather touching affirmation of personal innocence of the charge of being a monarchist: "As to my own political creed, I give it to you with the utmost sincerity. I am affectionately attached to the republican theory." His commitment was broad, deep, and specific: "I desire above all things to see the equality of political rights, exclusive of all hereditary distinction, firmly established by a practical demonstration of its being consistent with the order and happiness of society."

He was not naïve enough to believe that perfection in a state of republican grace was at hand in the summer of 1792:

> I said that I was affectionately attached to the republican theory. This is the real language of my heart, which I open to you in the sincerity of friendship; and I add that I have strong hopes of the success of that theory; but, in candor, I ought also to add that I am far from being without doubts. I consider its success as yet a problem. It is yet to be determined by experience whether it be consistent with that stability and order in government which are essential to public strength and private security and happiness.
>
> On the whole, the only enemy which Republicanism has to fear in this country is in the spirit of faction and anarchy. . . .

Perhaps drawing a lesson from Jefferson's ability to hit more birds than one with a single broadside, Hamilton, retorting to Jefferson and Madison, also hit a "man on horseback" who was Senator Aaron Burr to the life.

The "man on horseback" who had upset Schuyler and reelected Clinton over Jay was one of "those, then, who resist a confirmation of public order." They "are the true artificers of monarchy." "This is [not] the intention of the generality of them," like Jefferson and Madison, Hamilton acknowledged. But he could "lay the finger upon some of their party who may justly be suspected." To Hamilton, Burr was such a man: "unprincipled in private life, desperate in his fortune, bold in his temper, possessed of considerable talents, having the advantage of military habits, despotic in his ordinary demeanor, known to have scoffed in private at the principles of liberty." He had recently been seen "to mount the hobby-horse of popularity, to join in the cry of danger to liberty, to take every opportunity of embarrassing the general government and bringing it under suspicion, to flatter and fall in with all the nonsense of the zealots of the day." His object "is to throw things into confusion, that he may 'ride the whirlwind and direct the storm.'" There was not a man among those who "entertain theories less Republican" than Jefferson or Madison "who would not regard as both criminal and visionary any attempt to subvert the republican system of the country."

That Madison did not mean to do so "I also verily believe; and I rather believe the same of Jefferson, but I read him upon the whole thus 'A man of profound ambition and violent passions.'"

But to say that Jefferson was a man of "profound ambition" and "violent passions" was not the worst thing Hamilton could say of him. A nonzealot like Burr who would fall in with all the "nonsense of the zealots of the day" was still worse.

After King George's minister George Hammond had finally presented his credentials to the secretary of state on November 11, 1791, Jefferson in a stiff and formalistic manner presented Hammond with a list of alleged violations of the peace treaty, listing as principal grievances the continued British retention of the posts on the frontiers, the disputed U.S.-Canada boundary in the area of the St. Croix River, and the British carrying off of American slaves at the end of the war without payment to their owners. During the war thousands of slaves in Virginia and other states had fled to the British, including 22 of Jefferson's. Cornwallis had "carried off" another 30. Of those who fled from Jefferson, 12 had died, and only six had returned to their old master after the war.

On their side, the British saw as grievances the continuing harassment of American loyalists and the laws that many states had passed that prevented British merchants and creditors from collecting prewar debts owing to them, debts like some of those Jefferson owed. As for the freed slaves, Hammond's reasoning was that the peace treaty did not apply to slaves like Jefferson's who had escaped from their masters to freedom by joining the British army. These had "acquired indefeasible rights of personal liberty, of which the British government was not competent to deprive them, by reducing them again to a state of slavery, and to the domination of their ancient masters." The treaty required reparations to the slave masters only for slaves that remained "actual property" of their owners at the end of the war. As to slaves "taken" by Cornwallis, there was a question of fact for arbitration. Those that had died would not count. Hammond reported to his superior, Lord Grenville, that in friendly private conversations with Hammond early in January 1792, Hamilton "with respect to the negroes" had "seemed partly to acquiesce in my reasoning upon this point."

With healthy slaves selling for perhaps a hundred pounds apiece or more, any yielding on the slave point would mean a substantial loss of cash money to a large slave owner like Jefferson. But Hamilton had pointedly told Hammond that "this matter did not strike him as an object of such importance as it had appeared to other members of this government." Hamilton added that "the surrender of the posts was the only one which could produce any lengthy or difficult investigation."

A point on which a large slave owner like Jefferson would more violently disagree with Hamilton, who favored manumission, can hardly be imagined. Hamilton not only threatened his political ambitions, but also threatened to cost him money.

As Gertrude Atherton put it acidly in *The Conqueror,* her fictional biography of Hamilton, "Jefferson was like a volcano with bowels of fire and a crater which spilled over in the night. He smouldered and rumbled, a natural timidity preventing the splendor of fireworks. But he was deadly."

Both evolutionary Britain and revolutionary France had rushed their ministers to America to gain advantages for themselves and create an atmosphere of hostility each against the other. Hammond from Britain and Ternant from France both gravitated toward Hamilton and found Jefferson distant, reclusive, and difficult.

But Hamilton was by no means Hammond's only confidant. Senators leaked him tidbits of confidential information—but Jefferson pretended to believe the worst about Hamilton. When the Senate held a secret session to ratify ministerial appointments to Great Britain and France, Hammond sent the results along to Grenville. "In the whole course of this discussion," he reported blandly on January 9, 1792, "I have been regularly informed of the proceedings of the Senate, and have received every mark of personal and unreserved confidence."

Jefferson fumed to Washington about Hamilton's secret diplomacy with Hammond and Ternant, but Washington thought useful information was obtained and transmitted through Hamilton's unofficial private talks. He refused to cancel his instructions to Hamilton to continue them.

On February 28, 1792, during the course of a quarrel over whether the State or the Treasury Department had jurisdiction over the Post Office, Jefferson was provoked to an outburst to Washington that "the department of treasury possessed already such an influence as to swallow up the whole Executive power, and that even future Presidents (not supported by the weight of character which himself possessed) would not be able to make head against this department." Jefferson spoke of resigning in protest. Washington asked him not to, on the ground that it would only sharpen the discontents against the government, whose best interest ought to be paramount.

Jefferson retorted to Washington that "there was only a single source of these discontents," and that was the Treasury. Hamilton's [system] was pernicious, he exclaimed. It was poisoning the government and the country, he raged. The legislative branch was no better than the executive, he charged; indeed it was worse, because members of Congress had feathered their own nests by enacting most of Hamilton's system. Hamilton was guilty of communicating secret governmental views to Hammond behind his back. To this troublesome eruption, Washington patiently interposed soothing words. Jefferson consented to continue in office.

What Washington told Hamilton of Jefferson's outburst is not known, but Hamilton serenely continued to carry on his intimate talks with Hammond and Ternant. During the war Hamilton had conducted innumerable secret negotiations with British representatives for Washington about all sorts of sensitive matters—prisoner exchanges, surrender terms, and the like, without giving the game away by an error that might be laid to indiscretion, and in all of these diplomatic conversations he had had Washington's full approval, backing, and trust.

Hamilton did not limit his usefulness in foreign affairs to questions involving France and Britain. At Jefferson's request, he had occasion to correct some misstatements Jefferson had made in instructions given to William Carmichael and William Short on March 1–4, 1792, for dealing with Spain. Jefferson accepted eight out of ten of Hamilton's corrections before submitting the document to Washington for his approval.

Another source of Jefferson's resentment was the success Hamilton's economic program was enjoying in Congress. The special relationship by which Congress called directly on the secretary of the treasury for reports permitted Hamilton, unlike other department heads, to introduce legislation and act almost independently of Washington. At Jefferson's behest, Madison introduced a resolution in Congress whereby it would request the president to direct the secretary of the treasury to provide it with information concerning the mode of raising supplies for troops on the Western frontiers. This would create a precedent for putting the president between Hamilton and Congress. Like the other department heads, he would then be forced to deal only through Washington. To Hamilton and his followers, Madison's motion was a call by Hamilton's enemies for a vote of no confidence in him. Madison had even enlisted support from some of Hamilton's habitual followers from motives of their "vanity, self-importance," and so on. "My overthrow was anticipated as certain," Hamilton told Edward Carrington on May 26. "Mr. Madison, laying aside his wonted caution, boldly led his troops, as he imagined, to certain victory. He was disappointed." Madison's and Jefferson's resolution failed, but by only four votes.

Hard-won public victories, like the private agonies Hamilton was suffering to keep the Reynold's affair secret, had a high personal cost. To his old Virginia friend Carrington, whom he had first known in 1780 when they had served with Arthur St. Clair as American commissioners for prisoner exchanges, Hamilton unburdened himself of a rare flash of inward self-revelation and anguish. When Madison had aimed Jefferson's resolution at him, both of them "well knew that if he had prevailed a certain consequence was my resignation; that I would not be fool enough to make pecuniary sacrifices and endure a life of extreme drudgery, without opportunity to do material good or to acquire reputation." Only the margin of four votes in the House had spared Hamilton the shame of resignation under fire.

Still in the same personal and confiding mood with Carrington, Hamilton reflected ruefully on the widening and deepening hostility between himself and the two Virginians. In Madison now he saw:

a more uniform & persevering opposition than I had been able to resolve
into a sincere difference of opinion. Mr. Madison and I, whose politics
had formerly so much the same point of departure . . . now diverge
widely in our opinions of the measures which are proper to be pursued.
The opinion I once entertained of the candour and simplicity and fairness of Mr. Madisons character has, I acknowledge, given way to a
decided opinion that it is one of a peculiarly artificial and complicated
kind . . .

Jefferson was the reason behind Madison's switch:

Mr. Jefferson manifests his dislike of the funding system generally, calling in question the expediency of funding a debt at all.

"In various conversations with foreigners as well as citizens," Jefferson
"has thrown censure of my principles of government and on my measures of
administration. He has predicted that the people would not long tolerate my
proceedings & that I should not long maintain my ground."
Concerning the bank, Jefferson had delivered his opinion against constitutionality "in a stile and manner which I felt as partaking of asperity and ill
humour towards me. As one of the trustees of the sinking fund, I have experienced in almost every leading question opposition from him." Still worse,
Jefferson spread abroad suspicious tales of Hamilton's private life:

Some of those, whom he immediately and notoriously moves, have
even whispered suspicions of the rectitude of my motives and conduct.

Indeed, Hamilton felt that "when any turn of things in the community has
threatened either odium or embarrassment to me," Jefferson "has not been able
to suppress the satisfaction which it gave him. . . ."
Hamilton suggested that Madison's switch had been accounted for not
merely by a high regard for Jefferson, but because he was "seduced" by the
"expectation of popularity" and "advantage to Virginia."
To Hamilton, the conclusion was inescapable "that Mr. Madison cooperating
with Mr. Jefferson is at the head of a faction decidedly hostile to me and my
administration." To Hamilton it came naturally enough to refer to "my administration" in frank speaking. Jefferson and Madison were "actuated by views in
my judgment subversive of the principles of good government and dangerous
to the union, peace and happiness of the country." Indeed, if left to their own
course, Hamilton thought, "there would be in less than six months open war
between the U. States and Great Britain."
A principal reason for this danger was that Madison's and Jefferson's "womanish attachment to France and womanish resentment against Great Britain"
would "draw us into the closest embrace of France" and "involve us in all the
consequences of her politics."
Why such a seemingly unaccountable course of action? As Hamilton saw it,

> Tis evident beyond a question, from every movement, that Mr.
> Jefferson aims with ardent desire at the Presidential Chair . . . My
> influence, therefore, with the community becomes a thing, on ambitions
> & personal grounds, to be resisted & destroyed.

By May of 1792, Jefferson had finally prepared a harsh and devastating reply to the list of British grievances that Hammond had submitted to him on March 5. Jefferson stretched his argument beyond his evidence, but seemed to think his piecemeal evidence refuted every British argument. He submitted the letter to Madison, Edmund Randolph, and Hamilton for review. Hamilton replied that it went too far, supplying Jefferson with detailed reasons why. For one thing, Jefferson's reply made basic assumptions about American right and British wrong in the dispute. Hamilton pointed out that "the rule in constructing treaties" should be "to suppose both parties in the right, for want of a *common judge.*" Jefferson had tried to vindicate completely all American repudiations of debts to British creditors, ignoring the treaty provision that seemed to protect such creditors. Hamilton advised him that *"Extenuation* rather than *Vindication* would seem to be the desirable course." Jefferson accepted some of Hamilton's revisions, but insisted on full vindication of all American actions, including repudiation of debts. Ten years later, in April 1802, Hamilton would write that Jefferson's handling of these negotiations with the British seemed designed "to widen, not to heal, the breach between the two countries."

George Hammond's reaction to the final version of Jefferson's letter was consistent with the existence of such a design and Hamilton's apprehensions. Hammond dispatched Jefferson's letter to his chief, Lord Grenville, accompanied by shocked comments on its "great quantity of irrelevant matter," the "positive denial of many facts," its "unjustifiable insinuations" as to the conduct of His Majesty's ministers subsequent to the peace, "and the general acrimonious stile and manner" of "this extraordinary performance."

In private, Hamilton sought to pour oil on troubled international waters. "After lamenting the intemperate violence of his colleague," reported Hammond to Grenville on June 8, 1792, "Mr. Hamilton assured me that this letter was very far from meeting his approbation, or from containing a faithful exposition of the sentiments of this Government." Hamilton loyally absolved his chief from Jefferson's breach of diplomatic good manners by telling Hammond that Washington had not been aware of Hamilton's reservations, having just returned from Virginia, and "had relied upon Mr. Jefferson's assurance, that it was comfortable to the opinions of the other members of the executive government" when he knew it had not been conformable to Hamilton's.

Jefferson continued to smolder at the fact that Hammond remained in such close and regular communication with Hamilton, but avoided Jefferson himself, and Senator Philemon Dickinson of New Jersey, who was friendly to Jefferson, asked Hammond why. He reported that Hammond commented that "the Secretary of the Treasury is more a man of the world than Jefferson and I like his manners better, and can speak more freely to him. Jefferson is in the Virginia interest and that of the French. And it is his fault that we are at a distance. He prefers writing to conversing and thus it is that we are apart."

Hamilton's unofficial diplomatic relations, first with Major Beckwith and later with George Hammond, had their counterpart in Jefferson's contacts, through his instrument and go-between, John Beckley, with the British consul in Philadelphia, Sir John Temple. Julian Boyd, the editor of the Jefferson Papers, describes Temple as "vain, garrulous, indiscreet and lavish with exclamation points." He was also rich and, like Jefferson, resentful of the informal contacts between other agents of his own government, Beckwith and Hammond, with Hamilton. Jefferson described His Majesty's consul as a "strong Republican" on the basis of secondhand reports he received from Beckley. By way of Beckley, Jefferson received and duly recorded in his *Anas* an amazing report about Hamilton taken from a letter supposedly received by Temple from the highest levels of the British government.

It was, Jefferson wrote, "of the following purport: that the government was well apprised of the predominancy of the British interest in the United States; that they considered Colonel Hamilton, Mr. King and Mr. W. [William Loughton] Smith of South Carolina, as the main supports of that interest; that particularly they considered Colonel Hamilton, and not Mr. Hammond, as the effective minister here; that if the anti-Federal interest [that was his term], at the head of which they considered Jefferson to be, should prevail, these gentlemen *had secured* an asylum to themselves in England." So, Jefferson wrote—no longer quoting his creature Beckley quoting the local consul—Hamilton, King, and Smith knew they could continue unworried their machinations to change the government because "if they should be overset and choose to withdraw," they could count on such protection and pension as Benedict Arnold had received from Britain. Sometime after he had first written this down, not even Jefferson could allow such a vicious libel to stand. In the margin beside what he had first written, at some later time, he added a note: "Impossible as to Hamilton; he was far above that." Jefferson made no such marginal exceptions for the names of Senator Rufus King or Congressman William Loughton Smith of South Carolina, one of Hamilton's supporters in the House who occasionally belabored Jefferson in the press with broadsides over the name of *SCOURGE*.

Philip Freneau was a kept journalist, although Hamilton and his friends, at first, were content to call him nothing worse than a poetaster. The first number of his *National Gazette* had appeared on October 31, 1791, the week after the opening of Congress, shortly after Jefferson and Madison had moved him from New York to Philadelphia, and Jefferson had put him on the State Department payroll under the cover story that he was a translator. Many historians have marked the date of Freneau's first issue as the beginning of party opposition to Washington's administration or, as Hamilton sometimes put it, "my administration."

By 1792, Freneau's *National Gazette* was ranging far beyond double-edged needling like the *Advertizer*'s criticism of Hamilton's portrait by Trumbull. The secretary of the treasury was a conspicuous target of opportunity, and guilt by association tarred anyone ever connected with him. William Duer was blamed for originating the president's monarchical levees, but a deeper sin was being the "councillor . . . of the S— of the T—." The Society for Establishing Useful Manufactures was fraudulent and worse because it furthered Hamilton's ambition to encourage industry instead of small farmers.

Aside from foreign news, mainly translations from Dutch and French papers, and reports of debates in Congress, Freneau filled his columns mostly with jibes at Federalists. These often came in the form of reprints from other papers and letters to the editor, some fabricated. Phrases and words like "monarchical party," "monied aristocracy," and "monocrats" appeared so regularly they might have been kept in standing type. Hamilton's funding system came in for regular drubbings that echoed Jefferson's woolly wrongheadedness: "An irredeemable debt . . . is hereditary monarchy in another shape. It creates an influence in the executive part of the government, which will soon render it an overmatch for the legislative. It is the worst species of *King's evil.*"

Fenno's *Gazette of the United States* had always been an independent newspaper, although, like most newspapers, it received certain payments from government departments for space bought for the publication of official notices. It published a wider and better balanced spectrum of political material than Freneau.

On July 25, 1792, a letter from someone to Fenno's *Gazette* signed *Q* scolded Fenno for reprinting so often "the anti-federal sentiments with which the *National Gazette* is stuffed." *Q* commented that if Fenno were being paid for advertising the opposition, it was understandable, but that if Fenno were printing material from kept journalists as the other side's views, he would injure the reputation of his own paper.

Q's letter was followed by an inquiry of Hamilton over the anonymous initials *T. L.* He queried:

> The editor of the *National Gazette* receives a salary from government.
>
> Quaere.—Whether this salary is paid him for translations or for publications, the design of which is to vilify those to whom the voice of the people has committed the administration of our public affairs. . . . In common life it is thought ungrateful for a man to bite the hand that puts bread in his mouth; but if the man is hired to do it, the case is altered.

T. L. was saying that it was wrong for Freneau to attack the government, but that if Jefferson had hired him for that express purpose, the case was altered, because in that event Jefferson was responsible to answer for it. Three days later an anonymous Hamilton supporter writing over the name of *Detector* followed up *T. L.* by charging that Freneau's *National Gazette* "is only the tool of a faction, . . . the prostituted vehicle of party spleen and opposition to the . . . principles of order, virtue and religion."

"No man," *Detector* said, "who loves the government, or is a friend to the public tranquility, but must reprobate it as an incendiary and pernicious publication. . . ." The object of Freneau's paper was "to villify and depreciate the government of the United States, to . . . traduce the administration of it" (except for the Department of State).

Was not the editor in pay of a department of the very government he opposed?

One of Hamilton's greatest weaknesses as a politician was in not allowing supporters like Fenno and Q to do battle for him or else ignore attacks; Jefferson's ability to get others to do hatchet jobs for him while professing complete innocence was one of his greatest strengths.

Freneau obtained and published an affidavit sworn to before Mayor Matthew Clarkson, saying that he was "at no time urged, advised or influenced [by Jefferson to set up his paper in Philadelphia] but that it was his own voluntary act. . . ." Jefferson's and Madison's private correspondence, of course, shows this affidavit to be false.

Behind the scenes, Jefferson on May 23 had submitted to Washington 21 objections to Hamilton's funding system, which Washington passed on to Hamilton for reply on July 29, accompanied by a reassuring and sympathetic note saying that "known friends to the government agree that the country is prosperous and happy" but some were "alarmed at that system of policy, and those interpretations of the Constitution" which have taken place in Congress.

Hamilton replied with a long document entitled "Objections and Answers Respecting the Administration of the Government," transmitting it to Washington with a short personal note dated August 18. Hamilton's answers by and large repeated all his old rebuttals to all the old charges that had been made for years, threw in some counterthrusts at his opponents for good measure, and gave Washington, like Carrington, a disavowal of any monarchical designs and a further glimpse of troubled inward feelings. Hamilton admitted that "I have not fortitude enough always to bear with calmness, calumnies, which necessarily include me, as a principal Agent in the measures censured . . . expressions of indignation sometimes escape me, in spite of every effort to suppress them. I rely on your goodness for the proper allowances."

The necessity for a lengthy self-defense to Washington behind the scenes no doubt produced some of the irritation that erupted publicly from Hamilton in the columns of Fenno's *Gazette*. Three public letters, signed *An American*, attacked not only Freneau and the circumstances of his employment, but Jefferson, his employer, as well. Certain letters of Jefferson showed that he had opposed the Constitution in the beginning and had since opposed every important act of the government of which he pretended to be a part. Jefferson had imported the art of political intrigue learned amid the intrigues of a European court. "If he disapproves of the government itself, and thinks it deserving of his opposition, can he reconcile it to his own personal dignity, and the principles of probity, to hold an office under it, and employ the means of official influence in that opposition?" Hamilton asked. Hamilton condemned as transiently expedient, not durably right, Jefferson's 1789 recommendation that the American debt to

France be assumed by private individuals in Holland, with American approval, so that if there should be an American default, the loss would fall upon small private holders in Holland, instead of the French court, whose good will was more important to Jefferson than the losses of small holders.

A defender of Jefferson, who was probably one or another of Edmund Randolph, Madison, or James Monroe, rushed into print under the name of *Aristides* to answer and counter attack Hamilton. *Aristides* charged that the accusations against Jefferson were "founded in the basest calumny and falsehood." Jefferson should not be reproached for offending against the public credit unless the particular facts were given, which would show the opposite of what Hamilton alleged. As *Amicus*, Hamilton answered, speaking of himself in the third person. How could it be asserted that he had opposed the Constitution as too republican when, in fact, he was the only delegate from New York who had signed it?

Heavy verbal artillery on both sides volleyed and thundered: Monroe and Madison weighed in with a series on the *Vindication of Thomas Jefferson*. Hamilton was a man of many parts: *Catullus, Amicus, Metellus, Civis,* and *A Plain Honest Man.* Jefferson remained on the sidelines, shrinking, as always, from public polemics, and let Madison, Randolph, and Monroe as *Aristides* and Freneau as *Mercator* and others hurl shafts of polemical thunder and lightning for him.

Hamilton, as *Catullus*, in a peculiarly Roman mode, probably thinking of Jefferson's concubine Sally Hemings or his seduction of his friend's wife, wrote that the true character of Jefferson would only be revealed "when the visor of Stoicism is plucked from the brow of the epicurean; when the plain garb of Quaker simplicity is stripped from the concealed voluptuary; when Caesar coyly refusing the proferred diadem, is seen to be Caesar rejecting the trappings by grasping the substance of imperial domination. . . ." William Loughton Smith of South Carolina, Hamilton's staunchest ally in the House, echoed him as *SCOURGE.* Jefferson's pretences had "long ago excited the derision of many, who know that under the assumed cloak of humility lurks the most ambitious spirit, the most overweaning pride and hauteur . . . the *externals* of pure democracy afford but a flimsy veil to the *internal* evidences of aristocratic splendor, sensuality and epicureanism."

Smith's needling polemical style matched Hamilton's, but, unlike Hamilton, he was not above recalling Jefferson's headlong flight before Tarleton's raiders, deserting his post as governor of Virginia, and his pseudo scientific observations that proved the inferiority of blacks:

> Had an inquisitive mind sought for evidence of his Abilities as a Statesman, he would have been referred . . . to certain theoretical principles fit only for Utopia: As a Warrior, to his Exploits at *Monticello;* as a Philosopher, to his discovery of the inferiority of Blacks to Whites, because they are more unsavory and secrete more by the kidnies; as a Mathematician, to his whirligig Chair.

George Washington's own political leanings were strongly Federalist and Hamiltonian, and when Freneau and others attacked Hamilton's measures, which constituted almost the whole legislative program of his executive government, he keenly felt that he himself was under siege. But he was appalled at the public eruption of the private differences that smoldered between members of his cabinet. He had long been aware of them, but he had hoped to keep them private, perhaps even reconcile them. With all the weight of his character, office, and history, he tried to bring about a truce. He sent cautiously phrased appeals to both antagonists. To Hamilton he wrote on August 26:

> Differences in political opinions are as unavoidable, as, to a certain point, they may perhaps be necessary; but it is exceedingly to be regretted, that subjects cannot be discussed with temper on the one hand, or decisions submitted to without having the motives, which led to them, improperly implicated on the other; and this regret borders on chagrin, when we find that men of abilities, zealous patriots, having the same general objects in view, and the same upright intentions to prosecute them, will not exercise more charity in deciding on the opinions and actions of one another.[3]

Hamilton replied on September 9 with due respect and a frank admission of responsibility for some of the milder counterattacks on Jefferson. But he declared that he could not recede "for the present." He went into the history of the quarrel and hinted at willingness to resign for the good of the administration, if Jefferson would resign too. Against Jefferson he offered no personal adjectival animadversions. "I pledge my honor to you, sir," he added, "that if you shall hereafter form a plan to reunite the members of your administration upon some steady principle of cooperation, I will faithfully concur in executing it during my continuance in office; and I will not directly or indirectly say or do anything that shall endanger a feud." The feud between the two men flourished; nothing would "endanger" its continued existence. Perhaps Hamilton in agitation had really meant to write *engender*. On September 11, 1792, three days after Hamilton's letter to Washington, Hamilton as *Civis* retorted to Jefferson's spokesman, *Mercator,* that it would be happy for the country and "honorable for human nature" if the *"test of experience"* for his measures "were permitted to be fairly made." But his enemies dared not make such a test. They "misrepresent," they "inflame the public mind," and they "disturb the operations of government." They were about to "precipitate the laudable work of destroying what has been done" by combining all their forces in a desperate effort "by means of the ensuing election."

Jefferson answered Washington on September 9, 1792, with a defense of all his actions, starting off with the old complaint that he had been duped into support of assumption "by the Secretary of Treasury and made a tool for forwarding his schemes, not then sufficiently understood by me." From that low ground he went on to attack all of Hamilton's measures, singling out especially the "Report on Manufactures" as a scheme for corrupting members of Congress so as to have a "corps under the command of the Secretary of Treasury for the purpose of subverting step by step the principles of the constitution. . . ." He complained of Hamilton's interference in his department by discussions of foreign affairs with ministers from abroad. He criticized the attacks on him in Fenno's *Gazette*. He attempted to defend his hiring of Freneau by the incredible statement that he "could not recollect" having urged him to come to Philadelphia. As one member of the Virginia elite to another, he closed with a slash at his young arriviste rival's cloudy pedigree. It bespoke unplumbed depths of snobbish malevolence: "I will not suffer my retirement to be clouded by the slanders of a man whose history, from the moment at which history can stoop to notice him, is a tissue of machinations against the liberty of the country which has not only received him and given him bread, but heaped its honors on his head."

For the record, at least, both men had indicated willingness to resign, but each seemed to fear the loss of his own place unless the other lost place, too. Washington induced both to remain. It was one way to keep a watchful eye and checkrein on both, either of whom would be dangerous in opposition. But their feuding sorely tried his temper.

The split was real; the line was drawn. Though for awhile the president and the two great antagonists might try to screen it from the public by pseudonyms and surrogates, a continental rift ran between Hamilton's and Jefferson's followers that would divide them and their successors down to the present day. John Fiske observed that:

> All American history has since run along the lines marked out by the antagonism of Jefferson and Hamilton. Our history is sometimes charged with a lack of picturesqueness because it does not deal with the belted knight and the moated grange, but to one who considers the moral impact of events, it is hard to see how anything can be more picturesque than the spectacle of these two giant antagonists contending for political measures which were so profoundly to affect the lives of millions of human beings yet unborn.

William S. Gilbert, paraphrasing his Private Willis in *Iolanthe*, might have said that every little boy and gal born alive as an American was either a little Jeffersonian, or else a little Hamiltonian. Through history the two persuasions would exchange labels from time to time. "New Deals," claiming Jefferson as their political mentor, would call for greater centralization of power in the national government, whereas "New Federalists," proudly claiming Hamilton as a forebear, would call for returning governmental powers to the states.

By 1792 Americans were beginning to discover the deep political, economic, and social fissure that Hamilton and other Federalists had tried to hide from them, but which have divided them ever since. Washington did his best to stand above the partisan fray, insisting that the two avatars of these profound tendencies toward polarization remain in office under him, bottled up there safely like two poisonous spiders in his cabinet.

But out in the country, finding themselves on one or the other slope of their continental divide, but still within close range of the opposing lines, Federalists and Anti-Federalists, the latter now often calling themselves Republicans, formed up as skirmishers and laid down an intensifying cross fire of anonymous squibs, cheap shots, slung mud, blind libels, and polemical broadsides. 1792—the first big quadrennial state and federal election year—was at hand, setting a familiar pattern for all to follow.

10

THE UNMAKING
OF THE VICE-PRESIDENT—1792

THIS IS A CHARGE OF SO SERIOUS A NATURE THAT IT IS INCUMBENT
ON COLO. HAMILTON TO CLEAR IT UP.
                  —*George Washington to David Stuart, September 9,*
                  1792

The prospect of another four years as president filled the 60-year-old Washington with gloom. His health was poor, and his hearing was failing. His factious cabinet seemed about to explode. He was weary of mediating the endless disputes between Hamilton, usually backed by Knox on the one side, and Jefferson, usually seconded by Randolph, on the other. The prospect of slippered ease in retirement at Mount Vernon to bask in the honors heaped upon him by grateful countrymen beckoned invitingly.

Although he approved the dynamic legislative programs Hamilton was pushing through Congress in his name, Washington could not delude himself into failing to realize that Hamilton to a significant extent was also serving as a lightning rod to draw off on himself mounting Republican criticism of his administration. Much of the polemical abuse of their broadsides was more applicable to Washington than to Hamilton. Long service with Washington had taught Hamilton never to act without authority from above except in the most exigent of circumstances. Who really was a monocrat if not Washington? When he left Philadelphia for Mount Vernon in mid-July 1792, Washington was still undecided on a second term.

In private conversations, Hamilton had urged him to run again. He followed his urgings up by a letter of July 30, 1792, in which his tone to his chief went beyond mere urging. Its tone was as proprietary as his casual references elsewhere to "my administration": "The impression is uniform—that your declining would be deplored as the greatest evil, that could befall the country at the present juncture, and as critically hazardous to your own reputation." There was "evident necessity" for Washington's continuance because "the affairs of the national government are not firmly established." Furthermore, "its enemies, generally speaking, are as inveterate as ever. If you quit,"—who but Hamilton would dare accuse Washington of being a quitter?—"much is to be dreaded . . . on patriotic and prudential considerations, the clear path to be pursued by you will be again to obey the voice of your country."

This was as close to a direct order as anyone ever issued to the father of his country. Washington obeyed. He agreed to run again for president. There would be no question of a rival candidate for the first office.

But the question of the making or unmaking of the vice-president in 1792 remained a rift that divided the cabinet. John Adams, the incumbent, was, of course, the Federalists' likeliest candidate. Although Hamilton had reservations about the peppery, crusty, old patriot from Massachusetts, he realized that the vigorous Republican opposition springing to life in every state meant that all Federalist energies must be directed toward returning the incumbent to office.

The Republicans recognized that Washington, from the consistent backing he gave to Hamilton's system, his legislative program, and his opinions and from the whole general tenor of his policies, far from being above party, as he sought to appear, was really a Hamiltonian Federalist at heart. Jefferson, the Republican leader, posing as an outsider inside the cabinet and as an insider outside the cabinet, knew this better than anyone else. But he was not disposed to squander growing Republican strength in direct attacks on the aging national hero who would not be in his way forever. Republicans would concentrate on unseating Adams, a less conspicuous and more vulnerable target. If they should lose, it would matter little in either the short or long run. For Jefferson's own presidential ambitions, if Jefferson himself could not displace Adams, it would probably be better for Adams to remain in office than for a younger Republican or Federalist to replace him and thus threaten Jefferson's own place in the line of succession behind him.[1]

The first to announce for Adams's place was the perennial candidate, Governor George Clinton of New York, who had just squeaked through the disputed election over Jay to a sixth term. Hamilton, replying to an earlier letter from Adams, wrote him on August 16, "You forgot that Mr. Clinton could feast on what would starve another . . . I hope the starvation policy will not long continue fashionable."

But by September 9, Hamilton was no longer confidently joking. He was becoming alarmed at Adams's overconfident absence from Philadelphia and his apparent inattention to the threat to him and the Federalists posed by Clinton's candidacy. He warned, "I learnt with pain that you may not probably be here till late in the session . . . it best suits the firmness and elevation of your character to meet all events, whether auspicious or otherwise, on the ground where station & duty call you."

To the same tone of respectful command with which Hamilton had bidden Washington to obey his duty, Hamilton added a touch of asperity in his summons to Adams to bestir himself to meet the threat to Federal interests: "One would not give the ill disposed the triumph of supposing that an anticipation of want of success had kept you from your post." Adams must not dawdle getting from Quincy to Philadelphia. Adams was not to doubt that he had Hamilton's full backing: "You observe, My Dr. Sir, I speak without *ménagement.* You will ascribe it to my confidence and esteem . . . But it is the universal wish of your friends you should be as soon as possible at Philadelphia."

News of a second, more formidable opposition candidate than Clinton soon darkened Hamilton's impatience with Adams to anger. On September 17, Rufus King wrote Hamilton the news that Aaron Burr's hat was also in the ring and that he stood a good chance of winning. "If the enemies of government are secret and united, we shall lose Mr. Adams. Burr is industrious in his canvass, and his object is well understood by our Antis. Mr. Edwards is to make interest for him in Connecticut, and Mr. Dallas . . . informs us that Mr. Burr will be supported as Vice-President in Pennsylvania. Should Jefferson and his friends unite in the project, the votes of Mr. A. may be so reduced, that though more numerous than those of any other person, he may decline the office." Adams's failure to respond quickly to what Hamilton saw as a serious threat probably reinforced Hamilton's impression of Adams as too sluggish, unreliable, and quixotic to be a satisfactory political ally.

Clinton was an old, stubborn, well-known, but self-limiting quantity; but Burr was another matter. He was young—only a year older than Hamilton— brilliant, able, vigorous, and with a good war record, at least in his public image. Hamilton wrote back to King on September 23, "Though I had had a previous intimation of the possibility of such an event; yet the intelligence contained in your letter of the 17th surprised me. Even now I am to be convinced that the movement is anything more than a diversion in favor of Mr. Clinton. Yet on my part it will not be neglected. . . . A good use will be made of it in this state."

Hamilton's "good" partisan use of King's news consisted of a series of letters to friends around the country in which he attacked Burr not merely as a politician, but as a private man. He attacked his probity, his honor, his honesty, and his personal life, calling him by names that would certainly have brought on a challenge to a duel, had they come to Burr's notice, although some 12 years before the event. Mr. Clinton, Hamilton wrote to one correspondent, was "a man of property, and in private life, as far as I know, of probity," but "Mr. Burr's integrity as an individual is not unimpeached. As a public man, he is one of the worst sort—a friend to nothing but as it suits his interest and ambition. Determined to climb to the highest honors of the State, and as much higher as circumstances may permit; he cares for nothing about the means of effecting his purpose. . . . In a word, if we have an embryo-Caesar in the United States, 'tis Burr." To another he wrote that Burr "is unprincipled, both as a public and a private man. . . . Embarrassed, as I understand, in his circumstances, with an extravagant family, bold, enterprising, and intriguing, I am mistaken if it be not his object to play a game of confusion." He concluded, "I feel it to be a religious duty to oppose his career." Burr, charged Hamilton, was determined "to make his way to be the head of the popular party, and to climb *per fas aut nefas* to the highest honors of the State, and as much higher as circumstances may permit." To all of this Hamilton added, "I pledge my character for discernment, that it is incumbent upon every good man to resist the present design."

Hamilton knew many things about Burr—some also known to many other people, some to only a few insiders—that could account for such dislike and mistrust on Hamilton's part: Burr's military intrigues and insubordination, his role in Schuyler's upset and Jay's defeat, his scandalous financial involvements, his many paramours and mistresses, perhaps also his shady tactics as a lawyer. Yet there were almost as many reasons for Hamilton to dislike and mistrust other political rivals, including Jefferson. Burr professed friendship for Hamilton; Jefferson and others were openly his opponents and enemies. Yet toward none of the latter did Hamilton's language convey the same apprehensive enmity as the language he used about Burr. At a more broadly political level than the smoldering personal malevolence and contempt of the language Jefferson used about Hamilton, the language Hamilton used about Burr is more like Jefferson's on Hamilton than it is like Hamilton's on Jefferson. Hamilton's on Burr is addressed to both public and private concerns. It carries undertones of danger and even fear, but none of contempt. Hamilton must have known despicable things about Burr that almost no one else knew. What could conjure up in Hamilton toward Burr but toward no one else "a religious duty to oppose his career?"

To other men of affairs who were only formally religious, Hamilton's apparent emotional overreaction in these letters would be largely counterproductive of the political effect they were intended to induce. They are uncharacteristic of the usual urbane, matter-of-fact epistolary style Hamilton used when writing political allies who were not intimate friends. They are difficult to account for except by speculating that Hamilton had whispers, perhaps from Maria or James Reynolds, that Burr had contrived or abetted the plot in which he was now so deeply entangled.

Hamilton knew that he would be a "fool to make pecuniary sacrifices and endure a life of extreme drudgery, without opportunity to do material good or acquire reputation." The money Reynolds was extracting from him, the extreme emotional and physical anxieties the affair was costing him, and the possibility of its public exposure at any time constantly threatened to make of him just such a fool. Resignation from office could not save him. If Burr were indeed the trigger of the plot—there is no direct evidence that he was—Burr and the Reynoldses now held hostage all the things in life that mattered most to Hamilton. If so, it is easy to understand the shockingly apocalyptic tone of Hamilton's statements about Burr that is so difficult to account for in any other way.

On September 23, Hamilton passed along to Washington extracts from Rufus King's letter of September 17, which had expressed fears of losing Adams to Burr. Hamilton added that "Mr. Burr was here [in Philadelphia] about ten days since and everybody wondered what was meant by it . . . I forbear any further comment on the event—But I thought it of enough importance to apprise you early of it." Knowing that Washington's opinion of Burr came as close to matching his own as that of any other public man in the country, Hamilton needed to say no more.

Unfortunately, at just this critical moment, another heavy strain on Hamilton's time, temper, and proprietary place at the helm of Washington's administration entangled him in a vicious dispute with Congressman John F. Mercer of Maryland. It had begun in September and would be protracted into the following year. It might at any time explode into a duel or public disgrace. A report had come to Washington's ears that Mercer was charging that Hamilton had tried to bribe him with money for his vote in support of assumption. On October 21, Washington wrote his friend Dr. David Stuart for confirmation. "This is a charge of so serious a nature," Washington wrote, "that it is incumbent on Colo. Hamilton to clear it up—or for the President of the U. States to take notice of it. For this reason, before I communicate the matter to Colo. Hamilton, I beg to be informed whether I precisely understood the information."

Stuart reported to Washington that he had been told that at a dinner party "Colo. Mercer had said, that Mr. Hambleton [*sic*], the Secretary had offered him, Money if he would Vote for the Assumption." William Bayly, Stuart's informant, "asked Colo. Mercer if he had said so, he Answered Yes, by God he had."

What were the circumstances of this shocking charge that Hamilton was buying votes?

It seemed that during the war Mercer had paid 45 guineas for a horse, which not three hours later "was killed under him by the enemy in the action of Green Spring." Mercer made claim for reimbursement of the 45 guineas, but the controller in Hamilton's Treasury office had refused to pay it because it was not for "personal services." War damage claims of former soldiers against the government had been barred by the statute of limitations, the controller said.

"But Congress suspended the bar for two years," Mercer angrily replied.

"Only for personal services," the controller insisted, "not dead horses."

In fury, Mercer cried out that his claim would not have been refused by "any other man on the Continent."

As he stamped down the stairs of Hamilton's office, Mercer met Hamilton coming up and told him angrily what had happened.

Hamilton tried to head Mercer off with some ill-timed jocularity: "Colo. Hamilton remarked in a jocular manner that the limitation on payment had been removed only with respect to personal services, and not dead horses." Hamilton added that "unless he, Colo. Mercer, could prove that he and his Horse were one person, it could not pass."

Mercer did not think this was funny. He kept arguing about it with Hamilton, there on the stairway. Finally, "Hamilton replied that to cut the matter short he had only to vote for the assumption & he would pay the account out of his own pocket."

It was an unwise joke to make with an unsatisfied claimant, particularly one whose person was so intimately identified with a horse's posterior. Bayly reported that one of the dinner guests said that Colonel Mercer had at first told the story "in a jocular way." Bayly later asked Mercer "if he thought Mr. Hambleton was Serious or Jesting?"

Mercer replied truculently, "that he had a Right to take it either way." Bayly insisted on a straightforward answer. Mercer than admitted that "he could not have taken Hamilton in earnest, or he must have knocked him down if he was able."

By demonstrating Hamilton's perhaps overstrict enforcement of the mandate of Congress against a worthy old soldier, the discrediting of Mercer's shocking charge served to reinforce Washington's confidence in his secretary of the treasury's probity. It would also reinforce both his and Hamilton's realization that with politicians, attempts at humor usually tend to backfire.

Hamilton's impassioned epistolary campaign against Burr had less to do with the outcome of the election than other agencies that were at work against Burr for entirely different reasons.

Down in Virginia a protégé of Jefferson with ambitions of his own also had misgivings about Burr's sudden ascendancy. James Monroe had deprived Burr by one year of the honor of being the youngest member of the Senate. Monroe wrote Madison on September 18, "My opinion is briefly this that if Mr. Burr was in every respect inexceptionable it would be impossible to have him elected." The trouble, said the youngest senator, was that Burr was too young. "He is too young, if not in point of age, yet upon the public theatre, to admit the possibility of a union in his favor." Like everyone else, Monroe was also dubious about where Burr stood when it came to political principles. Madison, who had ambitions like Monroe's, shared his doubts about the reliability of Burr's politics.

To head off Burr's candidacy, Monroe suggested that he be given soothing assurances of esteem and confidence and that opposition to his nomination be placed "solely on his youth and late arrival on the national scene." Adams was 64; Clinton, 53; Jefferson, 49; Madison, 42; Burr, 36; and Monroe, 35. Time would take care of Adams and Clinton as competitors of the Virginia junto for the presidency; but if Burr were allowed into the direct line of presidential succession, such a formidable adversary would block Old Dominion ambition for years to come. They would stick with Clinton as a better-known candidate "warmly supported by sundry influential characters."

Jefferson had also been mentioned as a vice-presidential possibility, but with Washington as the unanimous choice for president, two Virginians on the ticket would be one too many for electors from the other 12 states to swallow. Jefferson, who loved to tinker with mechanisms, years later confided to his *Anas* that he considered Burr "as a crooked gun, or other perverted machine, whose aim or shot you could never be sure of." Such a gun would be useful enough—at short range—to hit a Hamilton, but for little else. It might have been a coincidence, although more likely it was a cover, that Jefferson's very close, newly converted Republican friend, Dr. Benjamin Rush, chose just this time of feverish political excitement to put into the record a direct call for aid to Aaron Burr—by Jefferson's usual instrument for intrigue, John Beckley.

"This letter will be handed to you by Mr. Beckley," Dr. Rush wrote to Burr from Philadelphia on September 24, 1792. "He possesses a fund of information about men and things. The Republican ferment continues to work in our state; and the time, I think, is approaching very fast when we shall universally reprobate the maxim of sacrificing public justice and national gratitude to the interested ideas of stockjobbers and brokers, whether in or out of the legislature of the United States."

Dr. Rush enjoined Burr warmly: "Your friends everywhere look to you to take an active part in removing the monarchical rubbish of our government. It is time to speak out, or we are undone."

Jefferson could hardly have found a better man by whom to introduce Beckley to Aaron Burr than Dr. Rush. Theodosia Burr's failing health was increasingly on Burr's mind. In New York she had the attention of Dr. Samuel Bard, whom Washington had consulted as his physician there, but when in Philadelphia, Burr constantly got second opinions from Dr. Rush.

At no time in the history of the country so far had the unpolluted air been more redolent with talk of political deals. The Senate chamber and the office of the clerk of the House were both on the second floor of Congress Hall in Philadelphia. After one ascended the stairs from ground level it was necessary for a senator or anyone else to walk down a narrow hall past the door of the clerk's office to reach the Senate chamber. Innumerable details of legislative matters required constant communication between the clerk and each senator. Nothing seems less likely than that after he had spent a year in Philadelphia as a senator, an elaborate letter of introduction from Dr. Rush to Burr would have been necessary to introduce the clerk of the House to him, except for purposes of cover. Few gaps are more regrettable in the history of the period than the lack of a transcript of the ensuing conversation between Beckley and Burr concerting the "active part" Burr would take "in removing the monarchical rubbish of our government."

The secretary of state was in the habit of jotting down gossip that John Beckley brought him. It was said that the clerk of the House had the biggest ears in the early Republic, and his mouth was never long away from Jefferson's ear. Albert Gallatin would later describe Beckley as belonging to the "hotheaded faction of the Republicans." Beckley could write, speak, organize, and strike a blow that hurt. Both henchman and bookman, he would later be installed by Jefferson as the first librarian of Congress.

No one would be as strategically placed as the clerk of the House to keep his big ears open, hear much, and report what he heard. When he came to New York, he stayed, as Madison did, at Mrs. Ellsworth's boarding house.

Jefferson, Madison, and Monroe were near neighbors in Virginia and met often during the long holidays. All disapproved of all Hamilton's measures and everyone in the new government, from Washington down, Jefferson only excepted. Even Edmund Randolph was not close to them. Although he had opposed the Constitution and refused to sign it, he had taken office under it as attorney general. His being a Virginian was enough to make him a natural ally of Jefferson without need of a deeper unifying principle. He would be unreliable as a protégé.

Madison served as Jefferson's antiadministration leader in the House; Monroe, in the Senate, while Jefferson acted as generalissimo from his command post in the cabinet. Jefferson shunned open conflicts and by nature feared them, preferring to work by subtlety and indirection through letters to supporters, private meetings, and the like. He did not fight Hamilton's measures openly himself, but worked against them through his disciples, chiefly from Virginia, but with some allies also in Pennsylvania and New York. For them he posed as philosopher guide and sage above the fray.

As secretary of state, Jefferson tended to fret that he was not the chief minister of the government, and hardly in foreign affairs, in anything but name. His *Anas* for this period reflect a diarist who is bored with his work, self-conscious, avid for gossip disparaging others,[2] and puffed up with egotism. Many more pages record trivia and carping than important affairs of state. Whenever he was in Philadelphia, he sighed to quit it as soon as possible for Monticello.

Hamilton by contrast, kept no secret diary. He was too busy organizing and conducting his department; researching, writing, and pushing through Congress the many parts of his program for the economic security of the United States; and actively carrying on private affairs. He did not take time to collect and record in private forgettable personal slights to himself, imagined injustices, smoldering resentments, or pressures on his psyche.

Among other things, sales of public lands were in Hamilton's department, and, until he relinquished it, so was the Post Office. The policies and programs that made the Treasury felt in every quarter of the domestic scene reached far beyond formal lines of cabinet organization. The policies of the Treasury, not foreign relations, touched off the longest, most heated debates in Congress.[3]

Hamilton also helped out in all other departments and with the running of the presidency as well, partly because these things impinged upon the Treasury and partly because of his eager competence and concern for success of the national experiment. Henry Knox, Hamilton's old comrade-in-arms at the War Department usually backed him up in cabinet disputes; Jefferson complained about his doing so.

Edmund Randolph, as attorney general, vacillated, first one way and then the other. This prompted Hamilton, also a lawyer, of course, to preempt the attorney general's function to a degree. When William Bradford took over as attorney general, his personal congeniality with Hamilton gave Hamilton a sense of continuing hegemony there.

One of Hamilton's most persistent congressional critics at this period, William Findley of western Pennsylvania, later said of Hamilton that he was "intrusted with the most influential portion of the administration" and that "circumstances have . . . combined in exalting the power and extending the influence of the present Secretary of the Treasury" until "it is not surprising that he has acted the most conspicuous part in the administration, not only of the fiscal, but other important governmental transactions." Newspaper reviews of his services at the time of his death recognized the relative place he held in Washington's first cabinet: "He was the vital principle of the first administration under the Constitution; and for the establishment of that Constitution we were more indebted to him than to any other man." Dr. John M. Mason, in a discerning sketch of Hamilton, said that "although the Treasury was his particular province, his genius pervaded the whole administration, and in those critical events which crowded each other, had a peculiar influence upon its measures."

On September 27, 1792, Jefferson left Monticello for Philadelphia and stopped on the way at Mount Vernon for a long morning's conversation with Washington only a day or two after Washington had received King's and Hamilton's warnings about Burr's presidential candidacy. Each Virginian as usual expatiated on his preference for his plantation to public office. Washington spoke of his concern about the differences between Jefferson and Hamilton. He dismissed as nonsense Jefferson's fears of a monarchy. There were not, he scoffed, "ten men in the United States whose opinions were worth anything, who entertained such a thought." No, Jefferson argued, there were many more than he imagined, mentioning specifically the names of Hamilton and Schuyler. Weary old Washington ended the dispute with "another exhortation" that Jefferson not decide too positively on early retirement. Jefferson returned the compliment. By the time Jefferson reached Philadelphia on October 5, the backstage maneuvering was reaching a feverish pitch. A new political party was being organized in a tangible way by the process of selecting its first candidate for national office and putting off another by a deal promising future support.

Many important Republicans—who did not look upon Burr as a threat to their own ambitions—pressed his candidacy over Clinton's now. On October 11, Madison and Monroe received letters by special messenger from Melancton Smith and Marinus Willett in New York and also from John Nicholson in Philadelphia, urging that Burr be substituted for Clinton as the republican candidate for vice-president. Smith and Willett had brought Burr into politics as a Sons of Liberty candidate in 1788 and remained political powers in New York. Nicholson was a partner of Robert Morris and a power in Pennsylvania politics. As holder of 125 shares of the Pennsylvania Population Company, Burr was a coventurer with Nicholson in a speculative enterprise that had acquired 7,000 lots on the Potomac, where the new capital was about to be built. They planned to import thousands of refugees from Saint Domingue to clear, populate, and build on them—and vote—a synergistic speculation to gladden the heart and enhance the power of any stockjobbing senator.

The power struggle between Clinton and Burr was resolved at a key Republican caucus held in Philadelphia the night of October 16 that no one later mentioned except John Beckley, who reported to Madison about it the following day: "A meeting which was had last evening between Melancthon Smith on the part of the republican interest of N.Y. (specially deputed) and on the principal movers of the same interest here (Pennsylvania), to conclude *finally and definitely* as to the choice of a V.P.—the result of which was, unanimously, to exert every endeavor for Mr. Clinton, and to drop all thought of Mr. Burr." Beckley added that Colonel Burr had assured him "that he would cheerfully support the measure of removing Mr. A[dams] & lend every aid in his power to C[linton]'s election."

Obviously, Beckley had helped arrange a deal with Burr whereby Burr would release his powerful New York and Pennsylvania support to join in support of Clinton. Burr was in a position to extract a high political price for such a deal. After the presidential election of 1796, Burr claimed that his price had been the promise of support by the Virginians in 1796 and that the Virginians had reneged on the deal. Burr stood by his side of the deal in 1792. Washington was unanimously reelected on December 5. Adams was reelected, but rebuked with only 77 votes out of a possible 132. The Republican alliance between New York and Virginia held firm, contributing its full share of 50 votes to Clinton. Jefferson got four votes, and Burr received only one, from a friend in South Carolina.

In view of the Federalists' preelection alarm over Burr's candidacy and the powerful support he had received from moneyed Republicans of New York and Pennsylvania, the total defection of Northern votes from his candidacy in the final tally made the reality of the deal behind it embarrassingly obvious. Hamilton did not credit his own impassioned private epistolary attacks on Burr with more than a minor part in such a remarkable result.

By some letters he had written suggesting that Adams be rebuked for monarchical views by the withholding of some votes from him, but not enough to defeat him, Jefferson kept his own political flanks well covered.

John Beckley was in his element in smoke-filled rooms full of political intrigue out of which came such curious results.

With the immediate threat from Burr put down, Hamilton remained the powerful Mr. Federalist. John Beckley knew that nothing would make his masters happier than rooting out some publishable scandal about the fountainhead of all "monarchical rubbish." *Delenda est Carthago* remained their purpose with respect to Hamilton. Beckley wrote Madison that William Heth, a disgruntled collector of customs on the James River who knew Hamilton, had told him that Hamilton considered Madison to be "his *personal & political* enemy." Writing Madison again on October 17, 1792, Beckley curried favor by crying down Hamilton's feat in linking the states together in a strong union under the Constitution by his programs in a way that unwittingly paid tribute to Hamilton as only an enemy could. With more precision and eloquence than any Federal eulogist had yet brought to Hamilton's achievement, Beckley wrote, "It would be wise to 'be watchful,'" because "there is no inferior degree of sagacity in the combinations of this *extraordinary* man. With a comprehensive eye, a subtle and contriving mind, and a soul devoted to his object, all his measures are promptly and aptly designed, and like the links of a chain, dependent on each other, acquire additional strength by their union & concert."

Beckley thought he had finally come up with a lead that would undermine, if not destroy, the secretary of the treasury. One Jacob Clingman, a man who worked for the Speaker of the House, Frederick A. C. Muhlenberg, with whom Beckley as clerk of the House also worked closely, had told Beckley that a Treasury clerk named Andrew G. Fraunces, a marplot with a well-known love of money and drink, had told him of being the confidential go-between in speculations by which Hamilton, in a deal with the now bankrupt jailbird William Duer, had made $30,000.

Fraunces had also been the go-between when Duer sought to realize cash for Treasury warrants he had wrongly pledged to cover his private debts, but Hamilton had refused to let the Treasury pay for them. With Duer's fraud frustrated, Fraunces lost the promised fee. Beckley tracked this promising lead as far as Fraunces's failure to negotiate the warrants that Hamilton had stopped and hit a dead end. Worse than a dead end, the lead had led only to further proof of the probity of the secretary of the treasury. Beckley would have to find a better lead for his general and generalissimo. The next lead he got from Clingman would strike pay dirt.

Meanwhile, Beckley dug up and brought to Jefferson another tidbit about Hamilton that to Jefferson was damning enough to record in his *Anas.* On November 19, 1792, "Beckley brings me the pamphlet written by Hamilton, before the war, in answer to Common Sense. It is entitled 'Plain Truth.' "

To Jefferson, Hamilton's differences with Tom Paine meant he was guilty of less than wholehearted support of the Revolution. Only malevolent hostility would grasp at such a farfetched imputation in the face of Hamilton's known pamphlets like *The Farmer Refuted,* defending the patriot cause, his defense of Rivington, his war record, and the fact that Beckley's preferred tidbit was more than 15 years stale.

Hamilton's private feelings toward Jefferson remained on the political level. He wrote his old friend General Charles Cotesworth Pinckney on October 10 that Jefferson was a "Gentleman whom I once very much esteemed, but who does not permit me to retain that sentiment for him . . . a man of sublimated and paradoxical imagination—entertaining & propagating notions inconsistent with dignified and orderly Government."

For Adams, too, Hamilton felt personal, private respect: "Whatever objections may be made against some of his theoretic opinions he is a firm honest independent politician." To no one's real surprise, except possibly Rufus King's, the humiliation of having so many votes withheld did not cause John Adams to refuse to serve again as vice-president. Instead of being downcast at his own amazingly small total of a single vote, Aaron Burr, when he returned for the new term, exuded all the serene confidence of a man who held a large political due bill still uncashed—as well as an unsuspected trump card yet unplayed.

By correspondence, Burr kept up the instruction of his ten-year-old daughter, Theodosia, correcting her misspelling of *laudanum* and urging her to learn the difference between *infusion* and *decoction*. All such things were vital to her mortally ill mother.

One sentence in a letter to him from young Theodosia ran: "Ma begs you will omit the thoughts of leaving Congress." Burr corrected her. *Omit* was wrongly used in the sentence. "You mean *'abandon, relinquish,* or *abjure* the thoughts.' "

It was obvious, despite his protestations, that the rising young senator was not about to "relinquish, abandon or abjure" his place in Philadelphia to stay in New York with them. They had been right in saying what they meant in the first place, and he should *omit* such pious humbug from intimate correspondence with those who understood him better than he seemed to understand himself.

Three unexpected rays of epistolary sunshine arrived as breaks in the clouds of bad news that shadowed Hamilton's private and public life that autumn of 1792 in Philadelphia. On September 10 his old friend Henry Lee, after gloomily praying "would to God you had never been the patron of the [funding system] I augur ill of its effect on your self personally," reminded Hamilton that Hamilton had already paid him ten guineas he owed him for a horse of "which perhaps you may have forgot." That was a welcome reduction of a personal debt.

The second was an honorary degree of Doctor of Laws from Harvard College. It also awarded honorary degrees at the same time to two other popular revolutionaries, John Hancock and Samuel Adams.

Hamilton wrote a grateful letter of thanks and acknowledgment to President Joseph Willard on September 6. It reads a little like a cry of grateful thanks for succor from a lonely defender of a beleaguered outpost about to be overwhelmed by the Catonians: "Amidst the many painful circumstances, that surround a station like mine—this flattering mark of the esteem of a body so respectable—the overseers of the ancient and justly celebrated institution, over which you preside—is a source both of satisfaction and consolation." He added, "If my past endeavours have been, in any degree, useful to the community, my future cannot but be rendered more zealous, by the approbation of the wise and good."[4]

In August the Jacobins had seized control of the French government, suspended King Louis XVI, and imprisoned the royal family. On September 21 the national convention of the people had abolished all monarchs and royalty. As one of its first pieces of business on October 10, 1792, the people's national assembly of the French Republic bestowed on Hamilton the title of honorary citizen of France. A new French revolutionary law authorized this new honor to be granted to friends of humanity and society who, like Hamilton, had served the cause of liberty and fought the battles of the people against the despotism of kings.

Hamilton's accolade came in the post addressed to him as "M. Jean Hamilton." Here was proof positive for Jefferson that the French revolutionists, his own ultimate authority on all that was politically sacrosanct, felt that Hamilton was not a monarchist and was, indeed, a foe of monarchs and kings—at least if Jefferson had any sense of humor at all about the absurdity of his oft-repeated charge.

Hamilton might well have thought it a good joke to send Jefferson a copy.

Other revolutionary friends of the common man that the French people found to be worthy of honor were Joseph Priestley, Thomas Paine, Jeremy Bentham, William Wilberforce, N. Pestalozzi, Thaddeus Kosciuszko, George Washington, and "N. Maddisson [*sic*]."

The serious-minded revolutionists of *l'an quatrième de la Liberté* had lost none of the Gallic verve that brought a touch of *la gloire* to all such kudos.

The citation recited that Hamilton had consecrated his arms and waking hours to defend the cause of the people against the despotism of kings, to banish prejudice from the earth, and to push back the limitations on human attainments and had done three more fulsome paragraphs full of other right-minded revolutionary things. Now officially certified, along with Washington and Madison, by the godless revolutionists as one of only three American champions of the rights of man, Hamilton jokingly jotted on the back of the elaborate certificate, underscoring the word *Christian*, "Letter from Government of French Republic transmitting me a Diploma of citizenship mistaking the *Christian* name."

On second thought, ruefully remembering Colonel Mercer and how attempted jocularity with politicians often backfires, Hamilton would discard the idea of any such joke. An attempt to josh Jefferson out of his favorite libel by showing him such a testimonial from the people's revolution would probably jar his malevolent ire more than his sense of irony.

Why had the revolutionary experts on the rights of man granted Hamilton, Madison, and Thomas Paine the cachet of listings in their new social register while denying it to the former master of the palatial Hôtel de Langeac? From Jefferson's life style during his years among them sequestered behind the iron palings did they suspect in him the monarchical yearnings that he so persistently projected on his enemies? Among Jefferson's many jottings of trivia concerning Hamilton, and Madison too, appears no entry taking note of this singular honor to them that had been denied him.

11

HOW MANY COVER-UPS?

WE LEFT HIM UNDER AN IMPRESSION OUR SUSPICIONS WERE
REMOVED.
—*Senator James Monroe, Sunday, December 16,
1792*

On Monday, December 17, 1792, Jefferson jotted down the following note
about a number of his prominent countrymen. It was anything but trivia as far
as Hamilton was concerned or as far as the history of the United States is
concerned:

> Dec. 17. The affair of Reynolds and his wife.—Clingman Muhlen's
> clerk, testifies to F. A. Muhl. Monroe Venable.—also Wolcott at [and?]
> Wadsworth. Known to J[ames] M[adison]. E[dmund] R[andolph]. [John]
> Beckley and [Bernard] Webb.
> *Reynolds was speculating agent on the speculations of Govt.*
> *arrearages. He was furnished by Duer with a list of the claims of*
> *arrearages due to the Virga. and Carola. lines and brought them up,*
> *against which the Resolutions of Congress of June 4, 1790. were*
> *levelled. Hamilton advised the President to give his negative to those*
> *resolutions.* [1]

Later, the paragraph italicized above was scored out by Jefferson in his
jotting, and the name of Hamilton was heavily obliterated.

The prosecution's case against Hamilton for wrongdoing in Treasury Department operations could hardly have been more succinctly stated. It was based on Jefferson's attribution of dishonest motives to Hamilton for his opposition to Bland's resolutions. This had led to the very first clash between him and Hamilton in Washington's cabinet.

Hamilton had kept the secret scandal of his affair with Mrs. Reynolds suppressed for more than a year and a half at a cost in blackmail payments to James Reynolds of every cent that he could afford. The nonmonetary cost to his family, honor, health, psyche, and opportunity to serve his country with public credit could not be measured. Everything he had lived for was now held hostage, not just by Burr and the Reynoldses, but by all his principal political enemies, everybody but the public.

When John Beckley had gone back to ask Jacob Clingman for a better lead than the dud that led to Andrew G. Fraunces and the story of Duer's warrants, he had picked up a new one that led him straight to Hamilton. The secretary of the treasury's substantial payments to James Reynolds transmuted his commonplace visitations to a harlot from the small change of gossip hardly mentionable by gentlemen and newspapers into an affair of state worthy of public attention.

As both comptroller and auditor, Oliver Wolcott, Jr., was, for all practical purposes, Hamilton's first assistant and alter ego as secretary of the treasury. The pressures that caused Jacob Clingman to become the chief witness against Hamilton to three leading Congressmen were created by the zeal with which Wolcott brought prosecutions against three men alleged to have perpetrated frauds upon the Treasury. From the time he had become comptroller, Wolcott concerned himself with the kind of intermingling of public and private business that had brought about the dismissal of his predecessor and friend, William Duer. Once when another friend of Wolcott had sent him a power of attorney authorizing him to deal in government securities for him, Wolcott returned it with a blunt statement that it would be highly improper for him to accept any such agencies from friends or be "concerned in any private business relating to the Treasury." He was alert in detecting forgeries, counterfeits, and fraudulent claims. He had insisted on prosecuting Duer to recover the $200,000 shortage in Duer's accounts as secretary of the old Board of Treasury, and this had led directly to Duer's crash and imprisonment for debt—and to widespread financial panic. Wolcott's insistence on such prosecutions demonstrated his own rigorous concept of public office as a public trust.

Wolcott was becoming particularly concerned about frauds being practiced in obtaining letters of administration of the estates of deceased persons to whom the government owed money. These seemed to be growing so great that Wolcott felt it necessary to make "a strenuous attempt . . . to discover the authors and bring them to punishment." On November 16, 1792, he initiated suit in the Philadelphia mayor's court against three of the most notorious offenders: James Reynolds, Jacob Clingman, and John Delabar.

Reynolds and Clingman were charged with suborning, or persuading, Delabar to commit perjury to defraud the government of more than $400. Clingman was released on bail the same day he was arrested, but both Reynolds and

Delabar were flung into the Philadelphia jail and kept there. Reynolds immediately "threatened to make disclosures injurious to the character of some head of a department." Hamilton angrily instructed Wolcott to "take no step toward a liberation of Reynolds, while such a report existed and remained unexplained."

The way the fraudulent scheme worked was that Reynolds would somehow obtain from the Treasury Department a list of the names and amounts the government owed to living individuals. He or Clingman would find someone like Delabar, who would falsely swear to the register, or probate clerk, that the living individual was dead and that Clingman was the dead man's next of kin or assignee of the next of kin. Clingman would collect the money, pay part of it to Delabar for his false swearing and another part to Reynolds for the use of his list, and pocket the balance.

Wolcott's suit alleged that Reynolds, Clingman, and Delabar had obtained letters of administration in this manner on the estate of one Ephraim Goodanough, who was very much alive. Wolcott set the trial date for the third Monday in December, December 17, 1792, the same date Thomas Jefferson would jot down his private note on the Reynolds affair.

Maria Reynolds later told Richard Folwell in her own inimitable way how Clingman and Reynolds had bungled the fraud, been caught, and been brought to justice. Like crooks in a farce, after safely pocketing the money collected from the government, they had turned the administration bond over to the real heir to permit him to commit a second fraud by collecting from the bondsman a second time. The real heir got cold feet and turned them in for fraud. As Maria described it, they *"incautiously* and *imprudently* having given the Heir-Apparent an indemnifying Bond, when the Soldier came to life, the Administrator delivered the indemnifying Bond up to the real Heir, [and] was detected." To Maria, the moral was that if the crooks had a chance to collect twice for the same fraud, it was amateurish to collect only once but get caught for such unprofessionalism. The hilarious moment when "the soldier came to life," as Maria told the tale, may convey a little of the flavor of the raffish charm by which she entrapped Hamilton.

Just as Maria finished telling Richard Folwell the sad tale, Jacob Clingman had walked into the parlor, and Maria introduced him to Folwell. As Folwell recalled, "She referred to [Clingman] for a more correct Narrative." But he seemed so ashamed of himself that "his Conversation seemed to me as if he wished to darken instead of throwing Light on this Information."

Then Clingman asked Maria "what Luck she had in her applications for Reynolds's Liberation" from jail. According to Folwell, Maria replied that she had "called on the Governor, Mr. Mifflin, and that he felt for her." He had "referred her to Mr. Dallas and that he felt also." She had then "called on Mr. Hamilton, and several other Gentlemen; and that they had all felt."

With so much feeling going on, tactile humor is felt in Maria's telling. With the coincidence of so many gentlemenly feelings for Maria, it seemed no coincidence to Folwell that "In a few Days after Reynolds was liberated." Folwell owlishly explained that this was "possibly in consequence of the Coincidence of Sympathy these Gentlemen had in Feeling."

With this brief glimpse into the domestic goings-on at the James Reynoldses, Folwell closed his account with the line "Here the curtain dropt from my view."

The same kinds of Treasury lists that showed names and addresses of old soldiers and other citizens and amounts due them from the Treasury would be just as useful for obtaining fake letters of administration on their estates if they happened to be dead or, indeed, alive as for buying up the amounts owing to them. Numerous different lists of this kind giving names and sums owing to citizens were compiled from time to time in the ordinary course of Treasury Department business. Such a list a year or two old would be much in need of updating, but might still be of some use. There are all sorts of ways to bamboozle someone entitled to money, and having a list is a great help, although not necessarily a crime in itself.

Jacob Clingman later testified that when Wolcott had first ordered his and Reynolds's arrest, Clingman had urged Reynolds to seek Hamilton's aid, that Reynolds had done so, and that Hamilton had advised Reynolds to "keep out of the way, a few days, and the matter would be settled."

After being taken into custody, Reynolds appealed by letter to Hamilton, who refused to assist him. Reynolds also applied to Andrew G. Fraunces, the clerk and ubiquitous marplot who had replied to Reynolds that Hamilton had threatened him with discharge if he made a move to help Reynolds out of his scrape.

Clingman then urged Maria Reynolds to appeal to Hamilton, and she told him she had already done so. Besides, she said, she had even received some more money from Hamilton after her husband's imprisonment. Clingman testified that she also told him that Hamilton had advised her to go see Wolcott, but not to mention Hamilton's name. She had done so, but had nevertheless disclosed Hamilton's name—thereby, she said, surprising Wolcott. Wolcott had promised her he would consult Hamilton.

Wolcott must have been more than surprised by what he heard from Maria Reynolds; he must have been appalled at what he had done. Upon charges that he had brought, a public trial of Reynolds and Clingman now was set down for the third Monday in December. If defense counsel for Reynolds should call Reynolds or Maria or Clingman to the stand and question them about Hamilton's payments to Reynolds or Maria, for example, his prosecution could backfire on Hamilton himself. Hamilton would be called as a witness; no claim of executive privilege would protect him.

Newspapers enjoy a limited privilege to report testimony given at a trial, even if false, without fear of libel suits. Anti-Hamilton papers like Freneau's *National Gazette* would have a field day telling the sordid tale of Hamilton's affair in the convincing form of a deadpan report of the trial. Without a trial to report, no newspaper would dare print a word about the scandal. It would remain a secret kept from the general public by the strict laws of libel.

Clingman had demanded from Mrs. Reynolds any letters she had from Hamilton because "he might probably use them to obtain her husband's liberty." She told him Hamilton had asked her to burn all letters that were signed and in his hand, and she had done so. But Clingman pressed her for some scrap of written evidence. She searched about and found and gave Clingman "two or three" unsigned notes, which she identified as being from Hamilton. Wolcott, told about these notes, knew that such written evidence tending to corroborate Clingman's story made Hamilton's situation still worse. A clever trial lawyer like Aaron Burr, for example, would, of course, rivet every eye and thought upon these little notes and scraps in Hamilton's hand. To allow the scheduled public trial to go forward would simply be unthinkable.

These notes from Hamilton to Reynolds were the most damning part of the case. In private to gentlemen, Hamilton could explain them away, but the last thing in the world he or any other public man would want to have to do was try to explain them away in public at a trial. The meaning of Reynolds's threat that he had it in his power to hang Colonel Hamilton would spring to the front of Wolcott's mind. When asked, Hamilton would furnish Wolcott the same explanation given in chapters 7 and 8 for his scraps to the Reynoldses and the long series of letters from the Reynoldses to him. Hamilton had better have his story well rehearsed.

When they came to Hamilton's note that said merely, "My dear sir, I expected to have heard the day after I had the pleasure of seeing you," and Hamilton told Wolcott his suspicion that Reynolds had forged, fabricated, or stolen the note and had a collaborator in the department, Wolcott would be aghast all over again.

Another clerk in the department connected with Reynolds leaking him letters and lists? This would be an indiscreet slip of Hamilton's tongue likely to hang him. Why had not such another "coadjutor" of Reynolds been rooted out of the department? It was just as well for Wolcott to go over the whole defense story carefully with Hamilton at once. Even so, the fateful slip about Reynolds's "coadjutor" slipped into the story Hamilton wrote out for the public in 1797.

The notes between the Reynoldses and himself explained the entire matter, Hamilton avowed. It was, in sum, "the endeavor . . . to induce me to render my visits to Mrs. Reynolds more public." Their disclosure of his notes to them proved this, he claimed. They had kept them with "the idea of implicating me in some accusation."

Hamilton's explanation conflicted sharply with Clingman's testimony. Far from saving all the many letters Hamilton had written her, Maria had burned all of them but these few fragments. Far from preserving them and thrusting them upon Clingman to corroborate a preconceived plot to blackmail Hamilton, she believed she had burned them all. She had only found these fragments for Clingman when he demanded that she scour the house for them. This was the kind of contradiction that could not stand exposure to public airing at a trial.

With the trial date only about three weeks away, Clingman decided to tell all to his employer, Frederick A. C. Muhlenberg, a former clergyman; a moderate Federalist; a man generally respected for his honesty, impartiality, and good judgment. As Speaker of the House, Muhlenberg was also Clerk John Beckley's immediate superior. Now Clingman's story would be getting an airing in the highest political circles without any extra nudges from Beckley or Burr. Although Muhlenberg was acquainted with Reynolds, and Clingman had appealed to him both "on behalf of himself and Reynolds," Muhlenberg agreed to help only Clingman. He rather pointedly avoided involvement with Reynolds, saying "not being particularly acquainted with Reynolds [I] in a great measure declined so far as respected him." Muhlenberg did take one small measure in behalf of Reynolds that had great significance: he "waited on Col. Hamilton" to discuss the matter "in company with Col. Burr." Guessing their mission, when Burr's presence in his waiting room was announced, Hamilton must have been horrified, but not necessarily surprised.

This statement of Muhlenberg, dated December 13, 1792, marks Burr's first recorded appearance in the Reynolds case, whatever may have been his unrecorded role earlier. Muhlenberg does not say who requested Burr to accompany him—whether Muhlenberg or Clingman or Reynolds, or whether Burr invited himself. Nor does Muhlenberg say why Burr accompanied him or in what capacity; Muhlenberg's statement is elliptically casual and matter-of-fact and says nothing more of Burr's role. Muhlenberg makes it clear that his own good offices extended only to Clingman, "who had hitherto sustained a good character." As to Reynolds, Muhlenberg said he had information that confirmed his decision that "I could not undertake to recommend Reynolds; as I verily believed him to be a rascal."

What lay behind Burr's little noticed appearance? The most obvious explanation is that Reynolds, who had several criminal charges and convictions already on his record—Clingman did not—immediately upon being arrested by Wolcott, retained Burr as his counsel for legal advice. Reynolds would know Burr from New York and that he was in Philadelphia as Reynolds's senator, was reputed to be the wiliest lawyer at the bar for delicate causes, enjoyed beautiful women like Maria, and, while affably professing friendship for Hamilton, did not yet seem to be in the prosecution's camp. There was no way for Muhlenberg to make it clearer that his intercession was limited to Clingman than to bring Burr with him as counsel for Reynolds. If Burr were acting as Reynolds's counsel, that would be the only situation in which his appearance on this curious occasion would not require more extended explanation by Muhlenberg, Burr, or Hamilton.

When the Speaker of the House and the senator from New York paid their call at Hamilton's Treasury Department office toward the end of November, the effect on him was profound: "A powerful influence foreign to me was exerted to procure indulgence to them—that of Mr. Muhlenberg and Colonel Burr." Hamilton was at pains to emphasize the force of their influence by denying that Reynolds had also enlisted Jeremiah Wadsworth, to whom Reynolds had needed no introduction by Hamilton in 1787, to exercise his. Wadsworth's influence, Hamilton said, had been "certainly put in motion by the entreaty of Mrs. Reynolds." Muhlenberg commended Clingman to Hamilton for the good character he had had, at least until falling in with Reynolds. The record is silent as to what

Burr said to Hamilton about Reynolds—or whether the senator's cold eye betrayed even a glint of amusement. *Les grandes âmes se soucient peu des petits moraux.* Hamilton, so far as is known, committed himself no further to them than to signify willingness to do all that might be done for the defendants with propriety. He suggested that they take the matter up with Wolcott, the man who had initiated the prosecutions.

Whether Hamilton revealed anything to Burr or Muhlenberg about his payments of blackmail to the Reynoldses is not known. It would be surprising if Clingman and Reynolds had failed to tell their representatives all, to alert them to telltale clues in Hamilton's responses. Hamilton would say as little as possible to them and volunteer nothing. For Hamilton, it must have been among the tensest of a lifetime of tense confrontations with Burr. It is easy to speculate that something despicable that passed at this meeting or that related to it was the secret cause of the implacable enmity between them. Each would continue in public to profess friendship for the other.

Muhlenberg next called on Wolcott, telling him, "I verilly believe [Reynolds] to be a rascal," but Wolcott would disclose no more than Hamilton except to say that, as he had also told Maria Reynolds, he would discuss the matter with Hamilton. At a second meeting, Wolcott stipulated with Muhlenberg that (1) if "a certain List of Money due to individuals which Reynolds and Clingman were said to have in their Possession" should be delivered up and (2) if Clingman should name the person in the public offices from whom it was obtained, his request for release "might perhaps be granted with greater Propriety." Plugging the leak, recovering the leaked information, and discovering the source of the leak had been the larger purpose behind Wolcott's prosecution. The jailing of two or three clumsy small-time crooks had been his means to accomplish this, but not an end in itself. The list and the name of the faithless insider were the two key pieces of evidence.

Clingman testified that Reynolds "had books containing the amount of cash due the Virginia Line, at his own house at New York, with liberty to copy, [that] were obtained through Mr. Duer." But Duer had left the Treasury in 1790 before the move to Philadelphia. Lists obtained through Duer would by now be more than two and a half years old, dangerously out-of-date for purposes of fraud, made so partly by the notarization requirements and other formalities imposed by way of Bland's resolutions.

Wolcott thought Reynolds and Clingman were lying in placing all guilt on Duer, a gentleman who would hardly stoop to small-scale skulduggery. Wolcott insisted that ". . . nothing occurred at any time to my knowledge, which could give colour to a suspicion, that Mr. Duer was in any manner directly or indirectly concerned with or privy to the transaction"—the fake heir claim—for which Clingman and Reynolds had been arrested. Wolcott strongly suspected that Duer's name was only a red herring or a cover for someone who was still on the Treasury payroll—as Hamilton's slip had suggested. Did Hamilton already know what Wolcott now only suspected—that Reynolds's coadjutor was still employed at the Treasury?

Muhlenberg passed the word back to Clingman that Wolcott was making no promises, but that he would regard his case in a much more favorable light if he would give up the list and also the real name of the person from whom he had obtained it.

Maria Reynolds passed on to Clingman a slightly different method of obtaining his release that she had heard from Hamilton. Clingman "should write a letter to Mr. Wolcott, and a duplicate of the same to himself, promising to give up the list and refund the money." The significant difference between Hamilton's stipulation and Wolcott's was that Wolcott had demanded to know the name of the man who was the leak, whereas Hamilton did not demand the name. If Hamilton already knew the guilty man's name, it would, of course, be unnecessary for Clingman to tell him.

Clingman agreed to the bargain. He would repay the money, give up the lists, and "disclose the name of the person *in the utmost confidence.*" He hoped that this would cause Wolcott to drop the prosecution. Clingman's plea bargain made no mention of Reynolds, but it was understood that Clingman also spoke for his accomplice, who was still in jail. Muhlenberg was informed that Clingman had agreed to the deal, that the actions against both men would be dropped, and that Reynolds would be released. This ended Muhlenberg's role as sponsor for his clerk, but not his curiosity about Hamilton's true role.

Wolcott, on his part, informed the attorney general of Pennsylvania that an important discovery had been made, and a plea bargain had been struck "by which it could be rendered useful to the public in preventing future frauds." The Commonwealth dismissed the prosecutions. Wolcott explained why he had agreed to the deal to free both men and drop the case:

> The infidelity was committed by a clerk in the office of the Register —Mr. Duer resigned his office in March, 1790 . . . the clerk who furnished the lists was first employed in Philadelphia in January 1791. The Accounts from which the lists were taken, were all settled at the Treasury subsequent to the time last mentioned; on the discovery . . . the Clerk was dismissed, and has not since been employed in the public offices. The name of the Clerk . . . has not been publicly mentioned for a reason which appears in Clingman's letter but if the disclosure is found necessary to the vindication of an innocent character, it shall be made.

The only reason "which appears in Clingman's letter" is that Clingman insisted he had disclosed the name of the clerk to Wolcott "in the utmost confidence." What did Clingman care about such secrecy? How could he impose such a secrecy requirement on his prosecutors? Why would not Wolcott and Hamilton gain great public credit for rigor and make a useful example by announcing publicly that a vigilant Treasury Department had stumbled upon corruption within its ranks, and rooted it out? Why all the secrecy?

Treasury Department records indicate that on Monday, December 17, 1792, the date scheduled for the trial, the date Jefferson jotted down his note, the employment of one "Simeon" Reynolds, as a clerk in the register's office of the Treasury Department ceased. He had first been employed in January 1791. Hamilton's affair with Maria Reynolds had commenced a little later that same year, according to Hamilton. The first appearance of the name Simeon Reynolds on Treasury rolls is on March 31, 1791, at a quarterly salary of $125, his last on December 17, 1792. James Reynolds had sought a job in the Treasury, and Hamilton had half promised him one. If Jefferson could hire a Freneau in his department, could not Hamilton hire whom he wished in his?

Specialists speculate that Simeon Reynolds might have been the son of Gamaliel Reynolds of Norwich, Connecticut; James Reynolds hailed from upstate Connecticut, too.

This remarkable series of interlocking coincidences of names, places, and dates raises a cloud of questions that history does not answer. Was Simeon Reynolds a close kin of James, a friend, a coconspirator, or no connection whatever—or the same James Reynolds listed under a different Christian name for payroll purposes? Did Hamilton hire Simeon in compliance with a blackmail demand of James? Was Simeon really the clerk who leaked the lists or only a handy cover scapegoat for someone else? Did Hamilton know the names of James's coadjutors still within the Treasury?

Hamilton fully agreed with Wolcott in placing all guilt on the unidentified clerk and justifying the dismissal of the prosecutions on the ground that a greater public interest was being served by the plea bargain. "It was certainly of more consequence to the public," Hamilton declared, "to detect and expel from the bosom of the Treasury Department an unfaithful clerk to prevent future extensive mischief, than to disgrace and punish two worthless individuals." He appealed to men of candor to draw proofs of his own innocence and delicacy "from the reflection that, under circumstances so peculiar, the culprits were compelled to give a real and substantial equivalent for the relief which they obtained from a department, over which I presided."

Far from trying to cover up a scandal or a fraud in his department, Hamilton was claiming all possible credit, short of revealing the name of Simeon Reynolds, for prosecuting the ostensible offenders. When his prosecution had brought him to the "leak" in his own department, he had fired the guilty man. But the name of "Simeon" Reynolds, the clerk upon whom both Wolcott and Hamilton finally placed all the blame, was concealed from all their contemporaries. Duer's name was the guilty name that Jefferson jotted down. James Thomson Callender, who analyzed the evidence more searchingly than any other investigator of the time, suspected that the real culprit was Andrew G. Fraunces. This was a plausible surmise because Fraunces was a clerk in the Treasury, at the Board of Treasury before that, and close to Duer. Clingman testified that Reynolds had sought help from Fraunces, that Hamilton had told Fraunces to stay out of it, or he would have to leave the department. Fraunces did, in fact, soon leave the department, shortly afterward, spouting bitter imprecations against Hamilton.

Chains of circumstantial evidence can be constructed to support, flimsily, any number of hypotheses that point to Hamilton's implication in, or innocence of, the frauds perpetrated on the Treasury by the likes of James Reynolds through the use of leaked lists. The law recognizes that innocence is usually one of the most difficult of all hypotheses to prove to a naturally suspicious world. It rightly places the burden of proof of guilt on the prosecution. On this basis and, more important, on the basis of ultimately trusting Hamilton's probity in the face of much temptation, most of which would be inadmissible evidence in court, this writer acquits Hamilton of wrongdoing. But not of a cover-up.

Why was the public made to believe that only Duer was the guilty man— the name Jefferson jotted down—instead of "Simeon" Reynolds? Why did Hamilton and Wolcott keep Simeon Reynolds's name so secret, under the cover of Duer's, risking censure for a slow cleanup of a stale scandal instead of inviting applause for the prompt rooting out of newly uncovered corruption?

The answer begins with another question. Could Hamilton possibly hope to escape being pilloried in Freneau's press for guilt by association if, on the same day that he was discharging one Reynolds from the Treasury in disgrace for leaking the lists, he was allowing the other Reynolds, who had admitted to making fraudulent but profitable use of them, to walk out of jail scot free? What alert journalist could resist the temptation to banner a sensational scandal by blurring the nice distinction between Simeon, and James? To Hamilton and Wolcott, this much of a relatively innocent cover-up would have been justified as a political necessity. It was also a small kindness that would serve to spare a small-time loser like Simeon the consequences of confusion with the rascally James and his long criminal record.

All of which shows (for Hamilton, at least) the vital importance of not being named Reynolds.

During the weeks Clingman had been soliciting Muhlenberg's help, he had hinted that "Reynolds had it in his power very materially to injure the Secretary of the Treasury and . . . knew several very improper Transactions of his." Muhlenberg paid little attention until Clingman quoted Reynolds as saying he could hang the secretary of the treasury, that Hamilton was deeply concerned in speculation, and that Hamilton had frequently advanced money to him. This echoed other sinister rumors Muhlenberg had been hearing about the leader of his party. When Clingman showed Muhlenberg Hamilton's scraps of notes, Muhlenberg felt it his duty to consult others in Congress, especially because Reynolds was about to be released from jail.

On Wednesday, December 12, a week after Clingman had agreed to Wolcott's stipulations, Muhlenberg spoke to Senator James Monroe and Representative Abraham B. Venable, both from Virginia; showed them Hamilton's notes to Reynolds; told them what Clingman had said; and intimated that Reynolds could tell them a great deal more.

Zeal for the public weal and zest for scandal were the meat of the bare knuckle politics of 1792. Jefferson had written Washington angrily on Septem-

ber 9, charging that Hamilton's system "was calculated to undermine and demol-
ish the republic." To corrupt and manipulate the legislative branch, Hamilton
had been guilty of "dealing out Treasury-secrets among his friends in what time
and measure" he pleased. The president had shown deep concern when John F.
Mercer had brought similar charges against Hamilton arising out of a jest.
Clingman's lead now seemed to inculpate seriously the author of the system
their leader hated. Monroe and Venable hastened to visit Reynolds in the Walnut
Street jail the same day they heard from Muhlenberg. They did not identify
themselves to him by name, but only as members of Congress, and said they had
been told that Reynolds was from Richmond (their cover story) and was accused
of committing frauds on their constituents. Madison must have heard Clingman's story from Burr or someone else, remembered Reynolds's name from
Gustavus B. Wallace's letters to him in 1790, and coached the congressmen in
their oblique approach. Being told that Reynolds was not a Virginian, they
questioned him about "the other particulars" of which Clingman had spoken.
Reynolds could indeed reveal "the misconduct . . . of a Person high in Office."
But he would not do so until after his release, which he had been assured would
take place that evening. Reynolds's visitors had no doubt that he meant Hamilton: he had said that Wolcott was in the same department and under him.
Boasting that the high official was in his power, Reynolds declared, at the same
time, that the official had initiated the prosecution to oppress and drive him away,
had found a merchant to offer bail so as to decoy him into custody, had promised
to give him employment without having done so, and yet now was pressing
Wolcott to have him released. Reynolds was probably acting on advice of counsel, Burr, in not telling all he knew for fear he would not be discharged. He
promised to tell them the whole story next morning at ten o'clock.

But the congressional committee would never see or hear from him again.
Overnight he would disappear from history except (according to Clingman's
testimony) for two clandestine, early morning meetings next day on the thirteenth and again on the fifteenth with Hamilton.

After leaving Reynolds's jail cell the evening of the twelfth, Monroe left
Venable and picked up Muhlenberg and walked up Fifth Street to the Reynoldses' house, where they found Maria alone. At first, she refused to talk. They
showed her the notes "from Secretary Hamilton Esqr." that she had turned over
to Clingman, told her that Clingman had talked, and soon she began to talk, too.
The unsigned notes were indeed from Hamilton. She had indeed destroyed other
notes and letters from Hamilton, adding that when James had gone, at Hamilton's request, she had "burned a considerable number of letters from him to her
husband . . . touching business between them, to prevent their being made
public." She said Reynolds "could tell something, that would make some of the
Heads of departments tremble." She told them that Hamilton had advised her
to go stay with friends, that he had offered to assist her, and—again confirming
Clingman's report—that Hamilton had urged her husband to "leave the parts,
not to be seen here again . . . in which case, he would give something clever."
This offer, wide-eyed Maria told the congressmen, "did not proceed from friend-

ship to him, but on account of his threat." She also revealed that their congressional colleague Jeremiah Wadsworth had already been active to obtain Reynolds's release, at first at her request and then, she thought, with the knowledge and prompting of Hamilton.

This much merely corroborated Clingman's story. But now came a new disclosure. The visit of the congressmen to Reynolds's jail cell earlier that day had not gone unnoticed. Learning of it or perhaps at Hamilton's urging, Wadsworth had come to Maria before the congressmen arrived to ask her what they had been seeing Reynolds about. Wadsworth had told her that "Mr. Hamilton had enemies who would try to prove some speculations on him, but . . . he would be found immaculate." To this, so Maria told Muhlenberg and Monroe, she had replied "she rather doubted it."

She then showed them two more notes, one from Hamilton dated December 6, two days after Clingman's agreement to the plea bargain, and one from Wadsworth written the eleventh, the day before their visit to her, "both expressing a desire to relieve her." This was how the congressmen carefully described the purport of these apparent new offers to pay her hush money. But she denied any "recent" communications with Mr. Hamilton, "or that she had received any money from him lately."

Although their suspicions were strengthened, the two congressmen had obtained no conclusive new evidence. They set down an account of their interview immediately afterward and the next day signed the clerk's fair copy of it. Leaving Maria Reynolds's house that night, they looked forward in eager suspense to meeting her husband following his release at ten o'clock next morning, to hear the whole complex story, of which so far they seemed only to have scratched the surface.

But at the appointed hour next morning at the jail, Monroe and Venable were told that Reynolds "had absconded or concealed himself." The mysterious disappearance of the key witness tended to confirm their darkest suspicions of a cover-up by Hamilton.

Having been accompanied only by Venable at one interview and only by Muhlenberg at the other, only Monroe now held all the strands of the story within his grasp. Only he knew where all gaps and conflicts lay. From now on, Jefferson's protégé took over the leading role in the congressional investigation. "I should have considered myself as highly criminal, advised as I was of your conduct," he would write Hamilton July 21, 1797, "had I not united in the inquiry into it: for what offence can be more reprehensible in an officer charged with the finances of his country, than to be engaged in speculation? And what other officer who had reason to suspect this could justify himself for failing to examine into the truth of this charge?"

Monroe proceeded with as much circumspection as could be expected with such a weight of political animus pressing him on. The senator and the two representatives would now confront Hamilton with their evidence. After hearing his defense and giving him prior notice of what they proposed to do, they would lay the whole matter directly before the president. They drafted a letter to

Washington, dated the fourteenth, the day after Reynolds's mysterious disappearance. The letter transmitted to Washington "some documents respecting the conduct of Colo. Hamilton, in the Office of Secretary of the Treasury," to wit, Muhlenberg's statement of his role in behalf of Clingman, Monroe's and Venable's account of their interview with Reynolds in jail, Monroe's and Muhlenberg's interview with Maria Reynolds the night of the twelfth, and a separate affidavit from Clingman that they would obtain from him the next day. They would permit Hamilton either to exculpate himself or force his resignation or force him to make an investigation into official misconduct at the Treasury without a public scandal until further evidence was in.

Their letter to Washington indicates that they gave credence to Clingman's and Maria's accusations against Hamilton. Monroe wrote out the letter for all three to sign. "We think proper, however, to observe," they wrote Washington, "that we do not consider ourselves as prosecutors, but only as communicating, for his information, to the Chief Magistrate, intelligence, it highly imports him to know."

The next day, on the thirteenth of December, Jacob Clingman testified to the congressmen with convincing particularity about Hamilton's long intimacy with Maria and James Reynolds. Of more immediate interest was his account of what had happened the night before after Monroe and Muhlenberg had left Maria's house and what had happened early that morning just before Reynolds was last seen. Neither Hamilton's nor any other testimony in the record contradicts Clingman on the following particulars, although Hamilton and others would draw sharply conflicting inferences as to the meaning of the facts. Hamilton would aver generally that Clingman's and the Reynoldses' statements concerning his participation in speculations were untrue and not worthy of belief.

Clingman had first met James Reynolds in September 1791 and soon became intimate with him. He had met Hamilton at the Reynoldses' house in January 1792 and often thereafter. On one occasion, Hamilton gave Mrs. Reynolds a paper, which Hamilton said he "was ordered to give Mr. Reynolds."

"Ordered" to give?

"Who," Clingman asked Maria, could "order" the secretary of the treasury of the United States to "give" something to Reynolds. She replied "he did not want to be known," having seen someone else with her. "This happened in the night" Clingman said. Reynolds had told Clingman "in confidence that if Duer had held up three days longer, he should have made fifteen hundred pounds, by the assistance of Col. Hamilton . . . that Col. Hamilton had made thirty thousand dollars by speculation; that Col. Hamilton supplied him with money to speculate . . ." and that "Col. Hamilton said, he knew Reynolds and his father; that his father was a good whig in the late war; that was all he could say."

Clingman went on to testify that, after Reynolds had been arrested and thrown in jail, Maria had gone to see Jeremiah Wadsworth because Reynolds's father had served under him in the commissary department. He had agreed to give her his assistance, saying " 'now you have made me your friend, you must apply to no person else.' " Clingman himself had seen Wadsworth at Maria's on Sunday, December 9. Wadsworth had promised to do what he could for both

Clingman and Reynolds's family, but his name must not be mentioned. Clingman "should not speak to him if he should meet him in the street" and if his name were mentioned, he would do nothing. On Wednesday the twelfth, when Wadsworth had called on Maria again, Clingman saw him leave her the note that she had shown to Monroe and Muhlenberg. Delivering it, Wadsworth had assured her that "he had seen every body and done every thing."

That same Wednesday evening of Wadsworth's and the congressmen's visit, at about eight or nine o'clock, Reynolds had been discharged from jail. At about midnight he had "sent a letter to Col. Hamilton by a girl; Reynolds followed the girl," and Clingman followed Reynolds through the dark, cobbled streets down to Hamilton's house near Treasury Row. Clingman saw the girl go into Hamilton's and then joined Reynolds. They "walked back and forward in the street" for a while in front of Hamilton's until the girl emerged with a message from Hamilton. It told Reynolds "that he need not go out of town that night," but should "call on him early in the morning." Clingman must have risen early after a late night because he testified that "in the morning between seven and eight o'clock" in the wintry dawn of the thirteenth he had seen "Reynolds go to Hamilton's house and go in." He had not seen him since, Clingman testified on the thirteenth and supposed he had left the state. At no time afterward would Hamilton deny Clingman's testimony that he had received a letter from Reynolds the night of the twelfth and another visit from him early the next morning.

The confrontation between the congressmen and Hamilton was set for December 15. During the interval between Thursday the thirteenth and Saturday the fifteenth, Clingman brought the congressmen important new evidence. Reynolds, he reported, had secretly returned home Thursday night, bringing Clingman a letter written earlier that day. At his house, in front of Clingman, Reynolds tore out part of the letter, threw the fragment into the fireplace, and handed the mutilated remnant to him. What was left of the note seemed to accuse the secretary of the treasury—more serious than a cover-up—with obstruction of justice and subornation of perjury, among other crimes. It read:

> My dear Mr. Clingman . . . I am convinced [. . .] to have satisfaction from HIM at all events, and you onely I trust too. I will see you this evening. He has offered to furnish me and Mrs. Reynolds with money to carry us off. If I will go, he will see that Mrs. Reynolds has money to follow me, and as for Mr. Francis, he says he will make him swear back what he has said, and will turn him out of office. This is all I can say till I see you.—I am, dear Clingman, believe me, forever your sincere friend, James Reynolds.

Clingman turned this new scrap of evidence over to the congressmen. The torn-off portion must have puzzled them—Hamilton's name perhaps? It seemed to corroborate Clingman's previous testimony that Hamilton had wanted to get Reynolds and his wife out of the way and to explain Reynolds's sudden disappearance.

Clingman had still more important evidence, supported by another document. This was a note from the comptroller of the Treasury, which read: "Mr. Wolcott will be glad to see Mr. Clingman tomorrow, at half after nine o'clock. Thursday." At the appointed time, but on Friday the fourteenth instead of Thursday, Clingman reported, he had been grilled by Wolcott in the presence of Hamilton. He "was strictly examined by both respecting the Persons who were inquiring into the Matter and their Object." Clingman had not told who they were. He said that Wolcott "should not consider himself bound" by the plea bargain, unless Clingman disclosed to Wolcott and Hamilton the congressmen's names. But Clingman professed not to know the identity of Monroe and Venable, hard as this story might be for Wolcott to swallow from an employee of Muhlenberg. Hamilton had even "desired him to go into the Gallery where he would see them and enquire their names of the Bystanders."

Clingman further reported that, under intense pressure, he claimed, he had admitted giving Hamilton's scraps of notes to the congressmen. Hamilton had angrily told him "he had done very wrong." He had also told Hamilton about Reynolds's letter of the thirteenth. Of Reynolds's statement that Hamilton would cause Fraunces to "swear what he had said," Hamilton said he had meant only that "he would make Fraunces unsay any Falsity he had declared." Hamilton had added that Reynolds was "a villain or rascal and he supposed would swear to any Thing." In this interrogation, Hamilton had admitted, according to Clingman, that "he had had some Transaction with Reynolds, which he had before mentioned . . . to Mr. Wolcott, and need not go into Detail with Wolcott present." Clingman now recalled that Reynolds had said to him that "when he was about to set out to Virginia, on his last trip to buy up cash-claims of the Virginia line, he told Mr. Hamilton that [John] Hopkins [commissioner of loans for Virginia] would not pay upon these powers of attorney . . . to which he [Mr. Hamilton] replied, he would write Hopkins on the subject."

To elicit statements like these from Clingman so damaging to Hamilton, the congressmen must have been cross-examining Clingman sharply, well-prepared for the interrogation. Gustavus B. Wallace's 1790 letters to Madison about Reynolds's and Vredenbergh's buying up the Virginia soldiers' claims must have served as one basis for their questioning. It was a cold trail and a rather misleading one because it seemed to end at the name of Duer. From Hamilton's point of view it was fortunate that it did, because at least it led the congressional investigators away from the secret name of Simeon Reynolds, whose employment at the Treasury would not be terminated until the following Monday. Clingman's new evidence would lay the foundation for new questions, with which the congressmen would surprise Hamilton at two confrontations the next day, the first in the late morning, the second that night.

Very early that same Saturday morning, as Clingman testified later the same day to Monroe, Muhlenberg, and Venable (in a statement recorded by John Beckley's assistant, Bernard Webb), Reynolds had come back to see Hamilton one last time. At this meeting, Hamilton had been "extremely agitated, walking backward and forward, striking, alternately, his forehead and his thigh; observing to him, that he had enemies at work, but was willing to meet them, on fair ground, and requested him not to stay long, lest it might be noticed." Reynolds had left Hamilton at sunrise. Hamilton later would admit that he had met Reynolds on the thirteenth, but never admitted to the meeting at sunrise on the fifteenth (to which he was allegedly shadowed secretly by Clingman).

From his and Wolcott's intense grilling of Clingman in Wolcott's office of the day before, Hamilton was painfully aware that his scraps of notes, partly written in a disguised hand—the most damaging evidence against him—were in the hands of the congressional committee and might be revealed to Washington or the public at any moment. Both Maria and Clingman had said that the last two meetings between Hamilton and Reynolds had been for the purpose of concocting an explanation.

Still another broadside written by Hamilton as *Catullus*, No. VI in the series in the press war raging with Jefferson and his allies, was scheduled to appear in Fenno's *Gazette of the United States* that same Saturday, the fifteenth. Hamilton missed his deadline. A note in that day's issue stated that it "was not received in season! for this day's Gazette, but shall appear in the next." But *Catullus* (Vivamus, mea Lesbia, atque amemus, rumoresque senum severiorum.) would miss the next deadline, too.

Here follows Hamilton's account in his own words of his two Saturday confrontations with the three congressmen:

> On the morning of the 15th of December, 1792, the above-mentioned gentlemen [Monroe, Muhlenberg, and Venable] presented themselves at my office. Mr. Muhlenberg was then speaker. He introduced the subject by observing to me that they had discovered a very improper connection between me and a Mr. Reynolds.

Hamilton was outraged: "Extremely hurt by this mode of introduction, I arrested the progress of the disclosure by giving way to very strong expressions of indignation."

His accusers backed off a little from their opening charge:

> The gentlemen explained, telling me in substance that I had misapprehended them; that they did not take the fact for established; that, unsought by them, information had been given them of an improper pecuniary connection between Mr. Reynolds and myself. They had thought it their duty to pursue it, and had become possessed of some documents of a suspicious complexion.

Hamilton held his temper; there was worse still to come: "They had contemplated laying the matter before the President, but before they did this they thought it right to apprise me of the affair and to afford an opportunity of explanation." Hamilton notes wryly that "they added that they were 'influenced solely by a sense of public duty and by no motive of personal ill-will.' "

They next proceeded to lay before him the six incriminating scraps in his own disguised handwriting. Too hastily, perhaps, but goaded on by fury, "without a moment's hesitation I acknowledged [them] to be mine."

Hamilton went on, saying that he had told them, "The affair [is] now put upon a different footing—I always [stand] ready to meet fair inquiry with frank communication—it happens, in the present instance, to be in my power by written documents to remove all doubts as to the real nature of the business, and fully to convince that nothing of the kind imputed to me [does] in fact exist."

Hamilton and his accusers then adjourned, agreeing to meet at his house that same evening for the fuller explanation he had promised them. They left.

"I immediately after saw Mr. Wolcott," Hamilton went on, "and for the first time informed him of the affair and of the interview just had." If, as this artfully worded statement of Hamilton seems intended to imply, Wolcott was not aware of "the affair" nor of the congressmen's knowledge of it till that morning, it conflicts with Clingman's account of the grilling he had given given the day before in Wolcott's office. Only if the reference of the word *affair* in Hamilton's statement is limited to Hamilton's admission to Wolcott of his sexual liaison with Maria, can it be read as not in conflict with Clingman's.

Hamilton turned all the letters from the Reynoldses he had kept over to Wolcott and asked him to be at his home that night for the second confrontation.

That night at Hamilton's, as Wolcott would later certify, the interrogation was begun by Monroe. He read out Hamilton's notes and "a Narrative of conversations which had been held with the said Reynolds and Clingman." He stated fully "the grounds upon which the suspicions rested."

Hamilton took a deep breath and "entered into an explanation." As Hamilton recalled, "I stated in explanation, the circumstances of my affair with Mrs. Reynolds and the consequence of it." In corroboration, he produced the letters that Maria and James Reynolds had written to him, giving the explanatory commentary for each that begins in chapter 6 of this book, "Something . . . to Dissolve the Charm."

"I insisted on going through the whole," Hamilton said, "and did so." His interrogators soon wearied of the painful exercise. "One or more of the gentlemen," according to Hamilton, "were struck with so much conviction, before I had gotten through the communication, that they delicately urged me to discontinue it as unnecessary."

Wolcott said that Mr. Venable "requested Mr. Hamilton to desist from exhibiting further proofs." Hamilton thought Muhlenberg had felt the same way. Wolcott said the explanation and the "written documents, which were read, fully evinced, that there was nothing in the transactions to which Reynolds and Clingman had referred, which had any connection with, or relation to speculations in the Funds, claims upon the United States, or any public or official transactions or duties whatever. This was rendered . . . completely evident . . . As however an explanation had been desired by the Gentlemen before named, Mr. Hamilton insisted upon being allowed to read such documents as he possessed, for the purpose of obviating every shadow of doubt respecting the propriety of his Official conduct."

Hamilton at no point during the confrontation or afterward "entreated a suspension of the communication to the President, or from the beginning to the end of the inquiry asked any favor or indulgence whatever." He always denied "that [he] discovered any symptom different from that of a proud consciousness of innocence."

Wolcott, of course, was satisfied with the extraordinary explanation, and so, it seemed at first, were Monroe, Muhlenberg, and Venable. Wolcott wrote that "after Mr. Hamilton's explanation terminated Messrs. Monroe, Muhlenberg and Venable, severally acknowledged their entire satisfaction, that the affair had no relation to official duties, and that it ought not to affect or impair confidence in Mr. Hamilton's character;—at the same time, they expressed their regrets at the trouble which the explanation had occasioned."

As Hamilton put it,

> The result was a full and unequivocal acknowledgement on the part of the three gentlemen of perfect satisfaction with the explanation, and expressions of regret at the trouble and embarrassment which had been occasioned to me. Mr. Muhlenberg and Mr. Venable, in particular, manifested a degree of sensibility on the occasion. Mr. Monroe was more cold but entirely explicit.

As gentlemen, they were even a little apologetic about their role in such an embarrassing matter. Hamilton said, "One of the gentlemen, I think, expressed a hope that I also was satisfied with their conduct in conducting the inquiry. I answered that they knew I had been hurt at the opening of the affair; that, this excepted, I was satisfied with their conduct, and considered myself as having been treated with candor or with fairness and liberality."

Walking home from Hamilton's, Mr. Venable repeated the same thought to Wolcott:

> During a conversation in the streets of Philadelphia immediately after retiring from Mr. Hamilton's house Mr. Venable repeated to me, that the explanation was entirely satisfactory, and expressed his concern, that he had been a party to whom it had been made. Though in the course of the conversation Mr. Venable expressed his discontent with public measures which had been recommended by Mr. Hamilton, yet he manifested a high respect for his Talents, and confidence in the integrity of his character.

Neither Hamilton's nor Wolcott's accounts of these famous confrontations were contemporaneous with them. They were written in July 1797, four and a half years after the night of December 15, 1792. The day after the confrontations, Monroe set down what was later represented to be the only contemporaneous account on Bernard Webb's [the clerk's] copy of Clingman's statement of December 13. Monroe's account more or less agreed with Hamilton's, up to a point:

[Sunday] 16th [December 1792]. Last night we waited on Colo. H. when he informed us of a particular connection with Mrs. R. the period of its commencement and circumstances attending it—his visiting her at Inscheps [Inskeep was the proprietor of The George, an inn at the southwest corner of Second and Mulberry—later Arch—streets]

The reference to Inskeep's is puzzling because the Reynoldses letters say that their meetings occurred at her or Hamilton's house. James Thomson Callender thought this was a significant discrepancy because Inskeep's The George "was never a house of that sort."

Monroe went on to say that Hamilton had confirmed Clingman's testimony about receiving Reynolds's note on the night of the twelfth; that he had met with him the next morning, the thirteenth; and that he had never seen him before he came to Philadelphia. Apparently no questions were asked or answers given about Hamilton's last secret meeting with Reynolds at dawn that very day. Monroe further noted that Hamilton had told the congressmen that the prosecution against Reynolds and Clingman had been dismissed because Reynolds had surrendered the leaked list and that the culprit "had it not in his power now to injure the department, intimating he meant Mr. Duer." The name of Simeon Reynolds never came up.

Hamilton went on to tell of

the frequent supplies of money to her and her husband and on that account—his duress by them from the fear of a disclosure and his anxiety to be relieved from it and them. To support this he shewed a great number of Letters from Reynolds and herself, commencing early in 1791.—He acknowledged all the letters in a disguised hand, in our possession, to be his [these latter were the six brief notes or fragments].

Monroe's statement concluded with a sentence of sinister ambiguity: "We left him under the impression our suspicions were removed."

An expert wordsmith like Hamilton could read into a maddening ambiguity like this one of Monroe his total belief or disbelief in his innocence of a speculating connection with Reynolds. It also left the door open for Monroe later to change his mind about Hamilton's innocence without going back on his word or much imputation of earlier duplicity.

Monroe concluded that Hamilton "acknowledged our conduct toward him had been fair and liberal—he could not complain of it. We took back all the papers even his own notes, nor did he ask their destruction."

A day or two after the confrontation, Hamilton wrote letters to each of the three congressmen, requesting copies of the notes of his that they had shown him, the mutilated letter from Reynolds to Clingman, and the Clingman statement they had shown him at the confrontation. He also requested that the originals "be detained from the parties of whom they were had, to put it out of their power to repeat the abuse of them in situations which may deprive me of the advantage of explanation." This seemed fair and reasonable to Monroe, Muhlenberg, and Venable at the time, judging from their eagerness to comply.

Muhlenberg replied December 18, 1792, that Monroe "has all the papers . . . in his possession" and that "your very reasonable request will be speedily complied with."

Monroe sent back copies of all the papers on December 20, just as Hamilton had asked, writing,

> SIR:
>
> I have the honor to enclose you copies of the papers requested in yours a few days past. That of the notes you will retain; the others you will be pleased, after transcribing, to return to me.
>
> With due respect, I have the honor to be,
> Your very humble servant,
> Jas. Monroe.

In a postscript, Monroe, like Muhlenberg, seemed to go out of his way to reassure Hamilton that all suspicions were at rest and that the secret would be kept:

> Everything you desire in the letter above mentioned shall be most strictly complied with.
> The Hon. ALEXANDER HAMILTON, Esq.,
> Philadelphia.

Nothing in this warned Hamilton of the change that would soon come in Monroe's contemporaneous assessment of Hamilton's role. So, to Hamilton's vast relief, the matter seemed to rest. Simeon Reynolds was gone from the Treasury, his surname still a secret and Duer blamed for an old scandal. James Reynolds was well out of the way in hiding, and the story of Hamilton's affair was blocked from press and public by the word of gentlemen of honor.

So it seemed, but Hamilton failed to reckon with men on the fringes not bound by the same code as gentlemen of honor. No such code forbade men like Clingman; Beckley; and his clerk, Bernard Webb, from keeping the affair very much alive in their private whispers or Jefferson from jotting down his note about it.

Word of the nature of Hamilton's defense would quickly spread among members of Congress of both parties, including friends of Hamilton like Rufus King and Theodore Sedgwick. Monroe would, of course, give Jefferson a firsthand account of all details.

Two weeks after the confrontation, January 3, 1793, Clingman called on Monroe, who now had custody of all the papers, and informed him "that he had been apprized of Mr. Hamilton's vindication by Mr. Wolcott a day or two" after the confrontation. Clingman, the peripatetic witness, said "that he communicated the same to Mrs. Reynolds, who appeared much shocked at it and wept immoderately." Maria denied that she had had any affair with Hamilton at all: "It had been a fabrication of Colo. Hamilton." Reynolds had joined in it, she said. He had told her so, and he had given Hamilton receipts for money and written letters "so as to give the countenance to the pretence." Clingman insisted to Monroe that Maria "was innocent and that the defense was an imposition." Monroe recorded this new testimony of the star witness in his own hand below his earlier account of the December 15 confrontation.

If this new tale of Clingman and Maria could now be believed, Hamilton's defense was nothing but a tissue of lies. One point, at least in Clingman's new tale, seemed to be a lie that cast doubt on the credibility of all the rest.

Oliver Wolcott's probity, sense of official decorum, and loyalty to Hamilton were beyond question. A talebearer like Clingman, whom Wolcott had just prosecuted for fraud and released on a plea bargain, was the last man in the world, or next to last, to whom Wolcott would have spoken "at this point in time" on any subject, let alone a subject as sensitive as the nature of Hamilton's defense. Clingman could, of course, easily have learned its nature from his fellow clerk, Beckley, or Bernard Webb. Whoever suggested that he give the name of Wolcott was creating a false trail leading away from the true source, but it was a self-discrediting cover.

Besides, Clingman's and Maria's new claim that Maria had never had an affair with Hamilton at all conflicted sharply with their earlier stories, which no one doubted confirmed that she and Hamilton had indeed had an affair. It also conflicted with Hamilton's defense, which all who heard it had believed.

There was a better reason for Clingman and Maria to tell new tales. One was that, James Reynolds having vanished, Maria soon became Clingman's "wife." Hamilton would remember sadly, years later, that Maria could assume an endless variety of shapes and guises.

The later statement of Maria's old friend and family confessor, Richard Folwell, was also helpful to Hamilton. In 1795 or 1796, he recalled, Maria "wrote me a Letter to call on her at a very reputable and genteel Lodging House in Arch Street, No.—. When he called at her lodgings," she "apprized him of her marriage with Mr. Clingman." She told him that she now lived in East Nottingham, Cecil County, Maryland, and had "lived there happily with Mr. Clingman, at the House of a Distant Relation of mine." The reason she had now sent for the faithful Folwell was that one careless day "she had mentioned knowing of our Family in Philadelphia." This had been a terrible gaffe on her part. A cousin of Folwell had exclaimed in a state of shock that "she must be the same Person who had left with her an infamous Character by the name of Mrs. Reynolds." What Maria now wanted Folwell to do was "clear up her Character." The ever faithful Folwell fussed and fumed at this challenging assignment. "I expostulated on the Inconsistency of this," he said. He told her "that as it was bad before she had certainly increased it." He was censorious because she was now living in Maryland with Jacob Clingman, while her husband, James Reynolds, was still alive and well and living in New York. How could he clear up her character "in that situation"? Folwell had a point there, Maria conceded. But it was not a serious problem. "She said she had a Divorce." Folwell was relieved. But there was a catch, Maria explained. Folwell was unrelieved. There was "only one Fault she had incurred in her Change,—that she got married to Clingman one half hour before she obtained the divorce."

New loves had not lost Maria one whit of her raffish charm.

What lawyer would make a mistake like that?

The lawyer who had arranged Maria's late divorce from James Reynolds, she said, had been their old family counselor, Aaron Burr. "Les grandes âmes," etc.

In high dudgeon, Richard Folwell stalked out of Maria's genteel lodgings in Arch Street. When she appealed to him soon again, Folwell mislaid her invitation. "Since then," he said, "I have heard nothing from her," except "Only that she wrote me a very pathetic Letter—" again "begging as she was to return, that I would clear up her Character. This I have mislaid—." Though it had been mislaid, Folwell said, he would not forget her. Hamilton would have remembered how he felt. What she had written him, Folwell said, "would move anyone almost to serve her, that was not fully acquainted with her character, confirmed by actual observation."

Reynolds and Clingman, Folwell and Wadsworth and Hamilton, and Aaron Burr. She could indeed move almost anyone to serve her. The story of the Reynolds affair would remain buried in Jefferson's jottings and Hamilton's and Monroe's files, at least for a while. Whenever the story was retold, insiders would wag their heads in sympathy with Hamilton or rub their hands with glee at a further example of his folly and indiscretion. No one in on the secret would forget it. Hints about it would appear from time to time in the press, but the general public remained unaware of it until the whole story broke wide open in the summer of 1797 with the publication of Hamilton's own account of it in his *Reynolds Pamphlet*. In it he would serve up the same defense he had told to the three congressmen and Wolcott the night of December 15, 1792, garnished with angry political attacks on his accusers. As exhibits to his pamphlet would be the correspondence between himself and the Reynoldses; the statements of Clingman and Wolcott; and some, but not all, of the other documents upon which the foregoing narrative is based. Knowledge of the affair would color the way Hamilton's friends and enemies would think about him for the rest of his life and forever afterward. To a man whose ambition and sense of public credit were as high as Hamilton's, its cost to his self-esteem, psyche, id, ego, superego, and mental and physical health would be incalculable. The worst of it was that although it remained a secret from the public *at large*, his self-knowledge that all the insiders who counted knew about it could only fester and swell inside him like a cancer on his heart. There was no way to absolve himself further, either publicly, to the insiders, or to himself. Meanwhile, through the crevice left by the sinister ambiguity of Monroe's parting words, his enemies would thrust shafts of doubt that would take root and grow until they would darken Hamilton's name, honor, reputation, and all his works through history with their shadow and stain. They will probably never be removed. As 1793 began, for a while, at least, Monroe's private assessment that "we left him under an impression our suspicions were removed" was all he had. Indeed, it was as much as, or more than, any man who had told such a strange story on himself had a right to expect from his auditors. It rested entirely on his own credibility. Acceptance or rejection of that depended, for many, on the political party to which he happened to belong. Republicans were certain now that they could ultimately checkmate their archenemy and erase him when they chose—Delenda est Carthago. They now moved the combat zone from the interiors of offices and bedrooms known only to insiders out before the public on the floor of Congress Hall. It is rather surprising that the end game took as long to play out as it did.

12

IMPEACHMENT

SHOULD YOUR PROSECUTORS NOT COME FORWARD AT THE NEXT
SESSION WITH AN IMPEACHMENT . . . YOU SHOULD EXPLICITLY
CALL FOR ONE . . . RESIGN . . . AND YOU FAIL IRRETRIEVABLY.
—*from Edward Carrington, July 2, 1793*

AS YOU HAVE WRITTEN—THE THROAT OF YOUR POLITICAL REPUTA-
TION IS TO BE CUT, IN *WHISPERS.*
—*from William Willcocks, September 5, 1793*

The first letter Hamilton would write to any close friend after the night of
December 15, 1792, is the letter of a man close to the breaking point. On December 18 he wrote John Jay, "ashamed" that earlier letters from Jay had gone so
long unanswered as a result of his own "delinquencies." "Tis not the load of
official business that alone engrosses me," he confessed, "though this would be
enough to occupy any man. Tis not the extra attentions I am obliged to pay to
the course of legislative mannoevres that alone add to my burthen and perplexity." No, he groaned, "tis the malicious intrigues to stab me in the dark, against
which I am too often obliged to guard myself, that distract and harass me to a
point, which rendering my situation scarcely tolerable interferes with objects to
which friendship and inclination would prompt me."

After this impassioned cry of anguish, Hamilton dealt with the business
matters Jay's earlier letters had raised. He then reverted to his obsession with

his enemies. Adams's reelection was a source of some satisfaction; Clinton's election would have been a source of "mortification and pain." Hamilton would willingly "relinquish my share of the command, to the Anti-foederalists if I thought they were to be trusted—but I have so many proofs to the contrary as to make me dread the experience of their preponderancy."[1]

On the face of it, Hamilton was writing about the retention in office of an incumbent vice-president of his own party, a subject on which reasonable men could differ, but hardly one about which they got very excited, let alone discussed in apocalyptic accents of "dread," "malicious intrigues to stab me in the dark," and "mortification and pain." Hamilton's words connoting this extreme, even unbalanced reaction to, and obsession with, his enemies contrasted sharply with the judiciousness and moderation of his own political comments of earlier years. It is true that by dint of the force of his prose, even then his panegyrics in support of moderation and orderly procedures sometimes sounded little short of hysterical.

The same note of obsession with enemies and overreaction to them crept into the series of polemical attacks on Jefferson and all his followers and works that Hamilton had been writing for the press that summer and fall under such names as *T.L.*, *Metellus*, and *Catullus*. *Catullus* No. VI, which had been scheduled to appear in Fenno's *Gazette* on December 15, but had missed the deadline, also missed the next deadline for the issue of December 19, before finally appearing on December 22. It elaborated in argumentative form mostly the same sort of animadversions toward Jefferson, Madison, and their followers that were so conspicuous in Hamilton's long letter to Edward Carrington of May 26, 1792.[2]

The authors of the *Vindication of Thomas Jefferson*, probably Monroe and Edmund Randolph, using some material furnished by Madison, had charged that Hamilton's broadsides were "in gratification of private revenge," a "pernicious example of gross violation . . . of . . . a public trust, and a glaring outrage."

Such charges, though nothing new, gave good reason or excuse for harsh reply in kind.[3] But good reason for Hamilton to remain silent and leave them unanswered obviously now outweighed them. Instead, with a sort of weary desperation, saying little that was new, but in dour phrases that seemed to approach the borders of hysteria, Hamilton hit back in *Catullus* No. VI. The old charges against him were "hypocritical rant" and "pathetic wailings." Their authors were "political pharisees" of "hollow and ostentatious pretensions." If *Catullus'* judgment had not been seriously skewed by the pressures of the night of December 15, he would have known that, instead of firing off such argumentative blanks, it was far wiser for him to withhold such stuff from many future deadlines of Fenno's *Gazette*, if not indefinitely.

In his reply of December 29, Jay reached out to Hamilton with compassionate understanding. It went so far beyond his usual reserved style that it is obvious that he had heard the whispers that explained the terrible personal anxieties behind Hamilton's "dread" of "intrigues to stab me in the dark."

Jay wrote:

The thorns they strew in your way, will (if you please) hereafter blos-
som and furnish garlands to decorate your administration. Resolve not
to be driven from your station . . . Your difficulties from *persons* and
parties will by time be carried out of sight, unless you prevent it.

Some humorous and otherwise encouraging observations written to him by
Gouverneur Morris from Paris on December 24 would also help buck up Hamilton's spirits before a new storm broke. Morris attributed recent French military
victories largely to luck, favoring weather, and shrewd selection of inept opposition. "In spite of blustering," wrote Morris, the French "will do much to avoid
a war with Britain *if the people will let them* but the populace of Paris influence
in a great degree the public councils." Street mobocracy ruled. Morris predicted
more massacres like those of September 2–7, 1792. There was real comfort for
Hamilton in Morris's complaint that Jefferson, whom he guardedly called Scipio
in correspondence with Hamilton (whom he called Paulus), was trying to place
all blame on his shoulders for America's difficulties in relations with France. "I
hate little things as much as you do and more I cannot say," Morris said. "Keep
me clear of little people . . . Do not put me to the Draught with a horse who looks
behind him and tries to get his neck out of the collar."

By December 29, Hamilton had recovered enough of his usual sangfroid to
write his dear old friend Susanna Livingston to help her find some of her mislaid
Treasury Certificates. But beneath his gallant good humor lurked a rare hint of
jocular self-reproach for what he had done to his wife. For the first time in ages
he remembered her in a letter to someone outside the family.

"Of all delinquencies, those towards the Ladies I think the most inexcusable," he told Susanna. He held himself "bound by all the laws of chivalry to make
the most ample reparations in any mode you shall prescribe." Flirtatious gallantry was not yet beyond him: "You will of course recollect that I am a married
man!"

For all the compassion Jay's letter had expressed, incidental observations
in it would fan the fears of any man obsessed by "dread" that his enemies would
stop at nothing to stab him in the dark. Jay told Hamilton he suspected that
Hamilton's letter "had been opened. The wafer looked very much like it. Such
letters should be sealed with wax, impressed with your seal." Jay predicted
grimly, "Your situation is unpleasant; your enemies will endeavour to render it
still more so."

Jay was right. On December 31, Congress demanded from Hamilton lists of
all Treasury Department employees and their salaries, as well as lists of all
employees of the other departments. Simeon Reynolds's name was absent from
the Treasury's list, but Andrew G. Fraunces's was still there.[4]

Of much more seriousness was another set of resolutions that Thomas
Jefferson was drafting. Anything but mere jottings, these would amount to a bill
of impeachment against Hamilton as a public man. They minced no words. They
charged Hamilton with specific violation of two acts of Congress, dated August
4 and 12, 1790, respectively, in applying portions of appropriated funds to pur-

poses not authorized by law. They charged him with deliberately deviating from the president's instructions in handling the transfer of money raised by loans in Europe to the United States and with failing to provide Congress with official information of his actions in connection with these funds. They charged him with mishandling the sinking fund and disregard of the public interest in negotiating a loan with the Bank of the United States at 5 percent interest at a time when ample public funds were lying idle there and in other banks. They further charged him with being "guilty of an indecorum to this House" by attempting to judge of its motives in requesting information from him on these and kindred matters and with withholding essential information in complying with their request.[5]

These on their face were specific charges of wrongdoing in office. The concluding counts in Jefferson's indictment went further. One discredited Hamilton with Washington by charging "that the Secretary . . . has violated the instructions of the President . . . for the benefit of speculators and to increase the profits of [the bank]." The last demanded Hamilton's discharge from office in disgrace: "That the Secretary of the Treasury has been guilty of maladministration of the duties of his office, and should, in the opinion of Congress, be removed from his office by the President of the United States."

The word *impeachment* did not appear in Jefferson's statement of the charges, but no one would know better than Hamilton that impeachment was what the effect of the resolutions was and that impeachment was what Jefferson intended: Hamilton in *The Federalist,* No. 65, had defined impeachment for all constitutional time as "those offences which proceed from the misconduct of public men, or, in other words, from the abuse or violation of some public trust." They may, Hamilton explained, "with peculiar propriety be denominated POLIT-ICAL, as they relate chiefly to injuries done immediately to the society itself." Impeachment proceedings would "agitate the passions of the whole community" and "divide it into parties more or less friendly or inimical to the accused," Hamilton explained. They would also connect "with the preexisting factions, and will enlist all their animosities, partialities, influence and interest on one side or on the other." In such cases, as Hamilton had foreseen, "there will always be the greatest danger that the decision will be regulated more by the comparative strength of parties, than by the real demonstrations of innocence or guilt."

Jefferson's resolutions were drawn to make Hamilton the first victim of his own uncanny foresight of five years earlier. Hamilton would be saved or fall, not so much by any real demonstration of innocence or guilt, but on the basis of opinions and suspicions nowhere in the formal record, by the comparative strength of the factions that stood for and against him in Congress.[6] If there were one thing he had fought against more than any other man as "the greatest danger" to government, it was the spirit of faction, or parties. His own party now was all that stood between him and public disgrace.

The season of peace on earth and good will toward men of 1792–1793 had been further darkened for Hamilton when the Republicans in the House began laying the groundwork for Jefferson's resolutions by introducing other resolutions on December 24 and 27, calling on Hamilton for detailed information on government loans, in particular the two loans that Congress had authorized August 4 and 12, 1790. One of these was a $12 million borrowing, with the proceeds to be used to pay interest and amortize principal of the *foreign* debt; the other was a $2 million borrowing, with the proceeds to be used to purchase and retire *domestic* debt. The money had been duly borrowed in Amsterdam and Antwerp, but for a variety of reasons that had seemed sufficient to Hamilton at the time, the $12 million and $2 million had not been used separately to retire foreign and domestic debt, respectively. Instead, as Hamilton had advised Washington on August 26, 1790, he had used two-thirds of the $12 million and one-third of the $2 million to make a payment on the debt to France, which France was urging, plus a payment of a half year's interest on the debt to Holland plus arrears of interest on the debt to Spain. This would still leave "a sum of consequence to the operation . . . towards the reduction of our Debt and supporting our funds in conformity to the intention" of the $2 million loan to pay off domestic debt.

Hamilton quickly responded to Congress with his "Report on Foreign Loans" of January 3, 1793. It reproduced many pages of complex ledger entries showing the details of all receipts and disbursements of the proceeds of these loans. An explanatory remark referred to "reasons of weight, respecting the interests and credit of the United States" for one loan taken without previous authority. Such reasons included relative rates of interest and exchange between dollars, florins, livres, guilders, and francs at various times and places. Few subjects are worse-suited to be topics of freewheeling congressional debate or defense.[7]

This time Hamilton's enemies did not leave him with an impression their suspicions were removed. The House made clear it was not satisfied. But his prompt responses to House demands tended to deflate his enemies' hopes that enough would be found to back up wide-ranging, general charges of impeachable offenses, at least without further explorations. On January 23, William Branch Giles, a Virginia friend of Jefferson who often served as his spokesman in the House, introduced five resolutions that in form were a demand for a bill of particulars: they did not specifically charge wrongful conduct, but they demanded particulars on which later charges in the form of impeachments like those Jefferson was drafting could be based. These five "demand" resolutions called on Hamilton for copies of specific written authority for his use of the proceeds of the two loans; lists of the persons to whom payments had been made in France, Holland, and Spain; statements of transactions between the Treasury and the Bank of the United States and its branches; statements of balances in the sinking fund; and all unapplied balances. Similar resolutions were introduced into the Senate.

The timing was significant. Congress was scheduled to adjourn at the beginning of March and would not reconvene until late in the fall. In the short space of little more than a month left before adjournment, it seemed impossible that any human being could compile the voluminous and incredibly complicated data that Giles's resolutions called on Hamilton to produce. During the long months of adjournment, suspicions generated by the unanswered questions would fester throughout the country. Later on, even if all Hamilton's books should turn out to be in perfect order, Giles and his partisans could make political capital of Hamilton's failure to submit his report earlier, before adjournment. All manner of dark suspicions could be conjured up out of nothing more than alleged delay.

Giles introduced these "demand" resolutions with a long argumentative speech criticizing Hamilton's just submitted "Report on Foreign Loans" of January 3, 1793. The official papers, Giles said, "instead of elucidating, seem rather to obscure the inquiry." Giles's resolutions were immediately adopted by both House and Senate, laying another backbreaking load of work on the secretary.

Grinding away day and night with his Treasury staff, Hamilton assembled figures, ran off sums, reproduced ledgers, arranged explanations, and appended footnotes. His reports contain thousands of entries. In effect, they were financial accountings for the life of an entire nation prepared in the space of less than a month. Between February 4 and 19, he delivered to Congress the following reports in compliance with the House and Senate resolutions, and a mere listing of their shortened names serves to suggest how wearisome a work it was: "Report on the Balance of all Unapplied Revenues," a "Report Exhibiting the Amount of All Public Funds, and What Remains," three separate reports on foreign loans, a "Report on Revenue Appropriations and Expenditures," another on the "State of the Treasury at the Commencement of Each Quarter" in 1791 and 1792," and still another on the "State of the Stock Market and Stock Prices" in the same two years.[8]

> With his submission, Hamilton humbly inquired of his tormentors: Is it not truly matter of regret that so formal an explanation, on such a point, should have been made requisite? Could no personal inquiry, of either of the officers concerned, have superseded the necessity of publicly calling the attention of the House of Representatives to an appearance, in truth, so little significant?

All but ready to drop from exhaustion, Hamilton failed to resist an opportunity to overreact by adding a further thrust at his persecutors. His rhetorical question implied criticism of a Congress extremely touchy about its prerogatives and sensitive about its inability to detect an error in the mass of figures he had unloaded on it. "Was it seriously supposable," he asked, "that there could be any real difficulty in explaining that appearance, when the very disclosure of it proceeded from a voluntary act of the head of this Department?"

By such a challenge he had dramatically raised the stakes; one or the other, Congress or the secretary, now had to be guilty before the bar of public opinion. A test of strength loomed. Giles and his Virginia allies could find nothing specifically wrong with his numbers themselves. It was probably too much to expect that Hamilton would have allowed any unexplainable items to appear in any of the reports he furnished to them. Of course, Hamilton from the first had admitted deviating from the express congressional authority granted for the August 4 and 12, 1790, loans, as well as some other seemingly minor matters, such as whether the payments to help out the French in Saint Domingue could properly be credited to payment of the French debt.

The stage was set. On February 27, 1792, Giles introduced Jefferson's "charge" resolutions against Hamilton. These dealt almost entirely with the specifics of his manner of handling the debt. Giles omitted from Jefferson's draft only the passages that charged Hamilton with benefiting speculators and demanded separation of the treasurer's office from the Treasury and the impeachment article that charged Hamilton with "maladministration" and demanded his removal from office. Evidence of such studied malevolence would embarrass its author out on the floor. But even without these paragraphs, if the other charges should be sustained, they would leave only impeachment or resignation under fire as the next logical steps for Hamilton. Here was another confrontation that threatened Hamilton's public credit, political honor, and public life. It was not one he could explain away in private, among gentlemen. The public's suspicions, too, had become aroused.

On February 28, the day after Giles introduced his "charge" resolutions, he moved to have them considered by the House sitting as a committee of the whole. With adjournment now only a few days away, this would achieve the kind of delay through the summer that Giles had earlier failed to obtain. Hamilton's supporters objected. "Why delay?" demanded Hamilton's friend, William Loughton Smith of South Carolina. Let us proceed at once to a consideration of these charges: "The question was, had the Secretary violated a law? If so, let it be shown; every member was competent to decide so plain a question."

Hamiltonians failed to prevent commitment to the committee of the whole, but their protests against delay were so vigorous and their attitude so determined that they forced immediate consideration of Giles's resolutions on the very day Congress had earlier scheduled for adjournment. On March 1, Giles led off the great debate with an all-out attack. He called on Congress to help the president get rid of the guilty secretary. Robert Barnwell, a Southern Federalist scoffed. He had heard no complaint from the president. Why did the House need to rush to his aid unasked?

Smith, although regretting that the charges against Hamilton had been brought on at the tag end of the session, was happy, nevertheless, that "the vague charges of mismanagement, with which the public had long been alarmed, were at length cast into a shape susceptible to investigation and decision." He then proceeded to analyze the criticisms of the secretary implicit in Giles's resolutions, compared the specific facts and figures that the secretary had so promptly supplied with the vague, argumentative charges of misconduct, showed that the secretary's handling had been proper, stripped away all factual basis for the charges, and left of them only a husk of personal animus empty of a kernel of evidence.

Smith's analysis of the chapter and verse of all of Hamilton's voluminous reports in the context of Giles's charges was so penetrating and showed such minute familiarity with every detail of Hamilton's intricate financial operations there that there can be no doubt that Hamilton himself prepared the speech that Smith so eloquently delivered for him. When Smith sat down, it was obvious that Giles's resolutions could never pass.

What all Jefferson's hot air boiled down to, as Barnwell had put it, was not "the foul stain of peculation," but the possibly "illegal exercise of discretion, and a want of politeness in the Secretary."

Giles rose to attempt a rebuttal to Smith, but, as though realizing that it was all over, quit abruptly halfway through. Madison delivered a cautious, moderate, legalistic speech intended to show that Hamilton had violated the law. Boudinot and Ames defended Hamilton. The House moved into a night session. Hamiltonians blocked all efforts to adjourn with the question unresolved. The hour grew late. Candles guttered and smoked. The opposition tired. The chairman called the question. One after another, Giles's resolutions went down to overwhelming defeat. In the end, only five die-hard Republicans, including Giles and Madison, voted for all six. Giles's best effort was 15 to 33 on the fifth resolution. On the others, the vote ranged from 12 to 40, to 7 to 34. Congress adjourned.

Hamilton had won not merely vindication, but, by means of his risky, over-reactive challenge to Congress, he had constructed a smashing personal victory; out of a thicket of political nettles self-sown by his challenge to his enemies, he had luckily snatched a victor's laurels. It turned out that Giles's arguments in the debate had been based on a memorandum written by Madison, analyzing in detail Hamilton's report of January 3, with special reference to the suspicion "that the funds raised in Europe & which ought to have been applied to the paiment of our debts there, in order to stop interest, have been drawn over to this country & lodged in the bank [of the United States], to extend the speculations and increase the profits of that institution."

Jefferson sought to minimize Giles's and Madison's crushing defeat. Writing to his son-in-law, Thomas Mann Randolph, on March 3, 1793, Jefferson explained it away by accusing the House of being one-third "bank directors and stock jobbers," who "would be voting on the case of their chief," and another third persons "blindly devoted to that party" or "persons not comprehending the papers" or "too indulgent to pass a vote of censure." The "people's" self-appointed champion wrote substantially the same criticism of the people's branch into his *Anas* on March 2. Not long after, on March 23, he made up a list of what he called "paper men" in Congress, a kind of "enemies list," saying that he got it from his creature, John Beckley. Writing to Washington early in the month, he had referred to the men named on his enemies list as "a corrupt squadron of voters in Congress at the command of the Treasury." Jefferson's extreme views and scorn of the people's House may have come about because, as Jefferson wrote to his diary on February 7, 1793, he kept himself aloof from "all cabal and correspondence on the subject of the government" and saw and spoke with as few people as he could.

Hamilton often publicly aired fears of mob opinion and mob action, as exemplified by the Paris massacres Gouverneur Morris had described, and of the shiftiness, unsteadiness, and unreliability of the opinions of the populace in the mass. But, unlike Jefferson, he did not make up enemies lists or express sulfurous scorn for the intelligence, strength, and integrity of his peers in Congress or the wisdom of the electorate that had sent them there. This was not particularly surprising when they had just rejected Jefferson's attempt to impeach him.

A week after Hamilton's vindication by the House, a set of resolutions similar to those of Giles were introduced in the Senate, castigating Hamilton and his alleged "fiscal corps," the same men Jefferson named on his enemies list. They charged, among other things, that Hamilton had made members of Congress subservient to him by securing them appointments as bank directors, so that when his official conduct was questioned, they would find him "immaculate, angelic, and partaking perhaps of something still more divine." Indeed, of the 35 representatives finding Hamilton blameless, it appeared that 21 were stockholders in the funds, and three of them were bank directors. Hamilton's reports, it was charged, assumed "a complexity and obscurity which rendered them almost impenetrable." His Bank of the United States was "capable . . . of polluting every operation of the government," and if the form of Giles's resolution had been for approbation of Hamilton rather than censure, Hamilton would have been discredited. In that event, those in doubt would not have given him affirmative votes. But these resolutions, too, withered in the face of Hamilton's massive reports and died with the adjournment of Congress. Hamilton's swift responses to his enemies' demands and his rapid vindication by supporters like Smith before adjournment would lead his enemies all during the summer recess to charge that his vindication had been rushed through too swiftly. It could not possibly be complete.[9]

In preparing for renewed attacks or else to slam the door on them, Hamilton that same March asked Jefferson for a statement of particulars of what he knew about the cabinet discussions of 1790 on the question of allocating the two European loans either to retirement of foreign debts or to payment of domestic debts. Jefferson gave a loftily offhand and distant reply on March 27. It gave no inkling that he had instigated the impeachment charges himself. He wrote, "having no occasion afterwards to pay attention to it, it went out of my mind altogether, till the late enquiries brought it forward again." Having suddenly looked into the matter anew, Jefferson went on, he now remembered that the president's instructions had given no sanction to what Hamilton had done. Jefferson closed by saying, "I did not take it up then as a Volunteer, nor should now have taken the trouble of recurring to it, but at your request; as it is one in which I am not particularly concerned, which I never had either the time or inclination to investigate, & on which my opinion is of no importance."

Jefferson sent copies of this untruthful letter to Attorney General Edmund Randolph and to Madison, referring to Hamilton's request. Jefferson appended a sly, smug wink to Madison that "I presume however he will not find my letter to answer his purpose." Jefferson asked them for their opinions of his letter to be sure they had read it carefully. This would make them remember his bald claim that he had had nothing whatever to do with writing the resolutions he had

written for Giles. Their deferential written replies would confirm his story, be
their testimony to corroborate it, and confirm them in their agreement with his
statement of what Washington had said. Jefferson's overreaching hand in his
minions' abortive attempt to impeach their enemy would be covered up and all
but invisible.

At Hamilton's request, his friend Edward Carrington saw to it that his
vindication was prominently reported in the Philadelphia newspapers of March
1793. But Carrington cautioned Hamilton that many of those who had supported
him might weaken. They "were carried away by the storm" and "are much
ashamed of their conduct." Nor was Jefferson's Virginia junto yet inclined to let
him rest.[10] Nor had they forgotten the night of December 15, 1792. Somewhere
in all the massive reports he had submitted, he must have inadvertently allowed
to slip in an entry that would corroborate the charges of a speculating involvement with James Reynolds or Andrew G. Fraunces or William Duer or someone
else. John Beckley, for one, had heard a story from Jacob Clingman that Hamilton had paid Fraunces a bribe to give him back some papers that would implicate
Hamilton in a scandal with Duer. Beckley urged Clingman to obtain corroboration. William Willcocks wrote Hamilton in August 1793 that "your enemies are
at work upon one Francis. . . . They give out that he is to make some affidavits
criminating you in the highest degree, as to some money matters. As you have
written—the throat of your political reputation is to be cut, *in whispers.*"

Congress might take a recess, but not Hamilton's enemies. To follow their
off-season throat-cutting campaign, one must pick up some bypassed strands of
the story. Nathanael Greene's widow, Catherine Greene, had importuned Hamilton May 30, 1790, for a favor as "a friend whom she loves and admires"; writing
from Mulberry Grove, Georgia, January 26, 1791, she importuned him for another—would "my dear good friend" "Lose no time in bringing my affair before
Congress." She importuned him a third time—June 26, 1792, as his "sincerely
affectionate" friend to help her out by paying off Baron de Glaubeck's certificate
obtained for her through Royal Flint and Thomas Bazen at face value. Hamilton
made mighty efforts to fulfill all such demands from his old patron's widow as
a special favor, without doing anything that might be considered illegal, at least
by the easygoing standards of the day.

To provide supplies for his beleaguered Southern army, Greene had given
a personal guarantee to the Charleston firm of Hunter, Banks and Company, his
commissary suppliers; and when they defaulted, he became bound to pay their
creditors "upwards of thirty thousand pounds sterling." Hamilton had prepared
Catherine Greene's petition to Congress for reimbursement, with exhibits from
A to *Z*, consisting of letters and statements from Edward Carrington, Nathaniel
Pendleton, Anthony Wayne, Charles Cotesworth Pinckney, William Washington, Clement Biddle, and others, which runs to 62 pages in volume X of the
Hamilton Papers. Greene's and Hamilton's opponents in Congress charged that
Greene had in reality been a secret silent partner in the Hunter, Banks firm, and
stood to profiteer on commissary supplies; besides, he had failed to give timely

and proper notice to the Treasury of his claim for reimbursement on his guarantee. Hamilton concluded that the first charge, was false; but on the second, that the failure to give notice was a valid technical obstacle to allowing the claim. He added that "motives of national gratitude" for Greene's "very signal and very important services . . . must serve to give a keener sting to the regret, which ought ever to attend the necessity of a strict adherence to maxims of public policy." He mournfully apologized to Catherine Greene on March 8, 1791: "I love you too well not to be very candid with you. I am afraid my report will not promote your interest," Yet "it is impossible that I can have stronger motives than I have to view the matter in conformity with your interests." Eventually, most of Greene's claim would be approved by Congress.

On the Baron de Glaubeck claim Hamilton had better news for her, but at the same time he had given his enemies an opening, which they were quick to exploit. De Glaubeck, a foreign officer during the Revolution—some said an imposter—had obtained Greene's guarantee of his debt of more than 5,000 livres tournois, then defaulted, leaving Greene to make good the debt and then try to recover from de Glaubeck. De Glaubeck had back pay of $701.33 plus interest coming to him as an army captain. Hamilton used a Treasury clerk, Andrew G. Fraunces, to arrange an assignment of de Glaubeck's Treasury certificate (or warrant, an order directing a bank or other agency to pay the sum) for this back pay, first to one Thomas Bazen at a deep discount (for $273) and then a reassignment to Royal Flint and Catherine Greene, who eventually was able to collect the face value, plus interest, totaling $909.59, less attorney fees to Flint, and so on. Hamilton paid Fraunces $50 for helping to arrange the deal. The interposition of Thomas Bazen as a "straw man" in the chain of assignments was probably necessary to make it possible for Catherine Greene and her attorney of record, Flint, to collect the full sum due, instead of having to share it pro rata with others of de Glaubeck's creditors. The success of this somewhat dubious exploitation of the "holder-in-due-course" doctrine, which did not cause loss to the Treasury, only to de Glaubeck's other creditors, would supply Jefferson with at least the basis for a charge of "unclean hands" with which to discredit Hamilton. This would be strengthened by the helping hand Hamilton was widely known to extend to all old friends come upon hard times, like Catherine Greene and William Duer.

Fraunces, the son of Samuel Fraunces, erstwhile proprietor of Fraunces Tavern in New York, had worked for the old Confederation Board of Treasury when Duer was its secretary several years before Hamilton had become secretary of the treasury; Hamilton had kept him on as a clerk until March 1793; then he had ousted him. Fraunces returned to New York to open an office, proclaiming himself a real estate agent, stock broker, and notary public, expert in pressing claims against the Treasury for money. Somehow or other Fraunces obtained from Duer or someone else two warrants for payment in specie—numbers 236 for $3,500 and 1155 for $2,000—and began to demand that Hamilton agree to have the Treasury pay them at face value—as the de Glaubeck warrants for army pay had been paid off to Catherine Greene. This was despite the fact that

Fraunces's warrants had probably been stolen from Treasury files by Duer or Fraunces, had been presented and dishonored before, and were marked "cancelled" on their face in red ink, in accordance with usual Treasury practice in such matters.

"In whispers" would aptly characterize Jefferson's indistinct manner of speaking, or mumbling, in private when plotting with John Beckley to cut the throat of Hamilton's political reputation. As is customary in such matters at the highest political levels of command, no direct orders would be given, but John Beckley would understand them perfectly and carry them out. On June 12, 1793, after such a conversation with Beckley, Jefferson jotted down in his *Anas* another note that presaged almost as much grief for Hamilton as Jefferson's Reynolds jottings of five and a half months earlier:

> Beckley tells me that Klingham has been with him today, and relates to him the following fact [*sic*]. A certificate of the old Congress had been offered at the Treasury and refused payment, and so endorsed in red ink as usual. This certificate came to the hands of Francis (the quondam clerk of the treasury, who, on account of his being dipped in the infamous case of the Baron Glaubeck, Hamilton had been obliged to dismiss, to save appearances, but with assurances of all future services, and he accordingly got him established in New York). Francis wrote to Hamilton that such a ticket was offered him, but he could not buy it unless he would inform and give him his certificate it was good . . .

Jefferson went on to note down that "Hamilton wrote him a most friendly letter" [which was true] and that Fraunces "bought the paper, came on here, got it recognized, whereby he made twenty five hundred dollars," [all of which was false]. Did Beckley know this for a "fact"? No, but Beckley had it from his favorite talebearer, Jacob Clingman, who "saw both the letter and the certificate."

Beckley pushed the plot along for Jefferson by starting a letter on June 22, which he did not finish until July 2, to an unnamed addressee in New York who was probably Governor George Clinton. Beckley told him that Fraunces (who needed no introduction) had told Clingman that "he could, if he pleased, hang Hamilton" (an all too familiar threat) and that Fraunces was "privy" to Hamilton's whole connection with Duer and his agent for supplying him with money. Beckley also reported that Clingman had told him that "Mrs. Reynolds has obtained a divorce from her husband, in consequence of his [*sic*] intrigue with Hamilton to her prejudice, and that Colonel Burr obtained it for her; she is thoroughly disposed to attest all she knows of the connection between Hamilton and Reynolds." Clingman had been sent for by Hamilton and was about to be grilled by him so that Clinton (or whoever the unnamed addressee might be) should use Clingman as an *"instrumentality"* but not tell or show him anything that might be compromising if Hamilton should worm it out of him; he should communicate only "thro' our common friend, Melancton Smith," a New York merchant and Anti-Federalist known to be one of Clinton's henchmen.

Hamilton would have liked nothing better than to worm out of Clingman the lead that would link him to Jefferson, the master puppeteer in the loft moving all his persecutors. So when Clingman went to Hamilton, according to Beckley, Hamilton "used every artifice to make a friend of him, and asked many leading questions." On June 25, Hamilton cross-examined Clingman, his persecution's chief tale bearer, as follows (this is Clingman's report of it to Beckley):

H: Are you a friend of Mr. A. G. Fraunces of New York?
C: I know him.
H: Did you ever board at his house?
C: I never did.
H: Do you not frequently dine and sup with him?
C: Only once, at a stranger's house.
H: Do you not frequently visit Fraunces' office?
C: I have been there several times.
H: Do you not visit Mr. Beckley sometimes?
C: I know Mr. Beckley, I have seen him at Mr. Muhlenberg's
H: [In disgust] Mr. Clingman, you do not put that confidence and trust in me that you ought. Every answer you give is as secretive as the grave.

Clingman did not record his reply, which was probably smugly defiant silence.

H: Does not Beckley visit often at Mr. Muhlenberg's house? Who else visits there?

From Clingman, only silence. Hamilton gave up.

To "counterwork Hamilton" in "speculations and connection with Duer," Beckley set forth a plan of nine numbered points, which included obtaining from Fraunces the power of attorney for Glaubeck's pay with the correction in Hamilton's writing, obtaining Thomas Bazen's deposition concerning his part in the Glaubeck payment, Fraunces's first letter to Hamilton, Hamilton's friendly reply, copies of the two warrants, and receipts of Duer's. Clinton (or whoever) was also to find out more about the divorce Burr had obtained for Mrs. Reynolds and all she knew about Hamilton and also obtain an affidavit from her and all other evidence he could find of Hamilton's speculating in public funds and collaborating with Duer. Clinton and others whose hands and strings remained invisible duly carried out much of this program.

After politely, but rashly, indicating he might approve payment to Fraunces, Hamilton's Treasury refused to honor the two warrants. Fraunces then made threatening demands on Hamilton and also on George Washington and Attorney

General Edmund Randolph, who referred his demands back to Hamilton for explanation and reply. Hamilton's friends in New York watched in alarm as the threat to him grew; newspapers aired the dispute several times during September, October, and November of 1793. Willcocks wrote Hamilton on August 25 that "your enemies are at work upon Mr. Francis . . . he is to make affidavits, criminating you in the highest degree, as to some money matters etc." and again on September 5 that "the idea was, that Mr. Francis can substantiate some official criminality against you, of a very serious nature. And yet no one pretends to any *precision.*" Robert Affleck, a New York city merchant friend of Hamilton, also wrote him in alarm on September 7 that a "lawyer from Philadelphia"— probably Beckley or possibly John M. Taylor, a close associate of Beckley—had been with Fraunces and had sought to make Thomas Bazen sign a 23-page affidavit implicating Hamilton in frauds. Bazen had refused as he could neither read nor write. Affleck's purpose in writing Hamilton was "to put you on your guard . . . to thwart the efforts of *Malice, envy* and *treachery,* which . . . are combined against uncommon abilities and worth." On August 25, Fraunces had published a long pamphlet attacking Hamilton, including copies of his correspondence with Hamilton and Washington; and on December 18 he submitted his pamphlet to Frederick A. C. Muhlenberg, speaker of the House, by now a familiar figure in "get-Hamilton" intrigues, thus launching yet another Congressional investigation that would drag on through 1794 until December 1795 before the case was finally closed. After investigation, Congress eventually dismissed all charges against Hamilton and commended him for the vigilance with which he detected frauds and frame-ups like the one Fraunces and his puppet masters were trying to pin on him.

But obviously, fending off all such attempts to cut the throat of his political reputation in whispers took an incalculable physical and psychic toll on Hamilton that comes through the lines of his poignant plea to Catherine Greene for evidence from her to exonerate himself for trying to do her a favor:

> It is not an uncommon thing for you women to bring us poor men into scrapes. It seems you have brought me into one . . . it is an affair of delicacy . . . it is not in one way only that I am the object of unprincipled persecution—but I console myself with these lines of the poet—
> > He needs must have of optics keen
> > Who sees what is not to be seen—

The lines fit Jefferson well. Hamilton added, "with this belief that in spite of Calumny the friends I love and esteem will continue to love and esteem me."

Hamilton analyzed the persecution: "Fraunces, partly, I believe from its having been made *worth his while* by some political enemies of mine, endeavours to have it believed that this transaction was a speculation in which I was engaged; and in proof of it professes to have a draft of a power of attorney corrected by some interlineations in my handwriting."

Closing the exchanges with Fraunces in exasperation, Hamilton wrote him on October 1: "contemptible as you are, what answer could I give to your last letter?" He enclosed a copy of an advertisement to be published in the *Daily Advertiser* assuring the public that "Fraunces has been regularly and repeatedly called upon, to declare the grounds of [his charges]; that he has repeatedly evaded the inquiry; that he possesses no facts of the nature pretended; and that he is a despicable calumniator."

Personal pressures, exigencies of departmental business, relations with France and Britain, and threats of American involvement in war pressed in on Hamilton more heavily than ever.[11] Control of events more and more seemed to be slipping from his grasp, though his eloquent efforts to engage popular support for his political views continued unabated in a series of broadsides over the names of *Americanus, Pacificus,* and *No Jacobin.* He may have heard it whispered that Monroe had now placed his original set of the Reynolds documents in the hands of a "respectable character in Virginia," his friend Thomas Jefferson.

On June 21, Hamilton wrote Washington that "considerations relative both to the public interest and my own delicacy, have brought me, after mature reflection, to a resolution to resign the office I hold, towards the close of the ensuing session of Congress." He was postpoining "the final act" till then because "propositions necessary to the full development of my original plan" and "of consequence to my reputation" still remained to be submitted to Congress. Secondly, "I am desirous of giving an opportunity" while still in office for the "revival and more deliberate prosecution of the inquiry into my conduct, which was instituted during the last session." His overly keen defensiveness about his reputation would not permit him to avoid making a dangerous situation worse by letting bad enough alone.[12]

His friend Edward Carrington relentlessly abetted him in his folly. He goaded him on, writing on July 2, 1793, that "should your persecutors not come forward at the next session with an impeachment . . . you should explicitly call for one—it would ensure at once their destruction." Carrington thought the eyes of the new members would be opened to the falsity of the Republican complaints. Perhaps down there in Virginia, Carrington had not yet heard whispers of the covered up scandal. "Stand fast, and you cannot fail," he exhorted. "Resign, under the pressure of the present opposition and you fail irretrievably."

Hamilton's series *No Jacobin,* in which he attacks France and neutrality, ends abruptly with No. IX on August 28. Hamilton's passion, drive, and energy had overcommitted his physical strength. His body crumpled under the stressful incursions made upon it by his public, private, and secret lives and by the plaguey Philadelphia summer. The plague, a form of yellow fever, raged in Philadelphia that summer. Hamilton and his Betsy both contracted it, although she caught a less severe case than his. It fastened on him in its most virulent form. Few who showed his symptoms survived, and for a time his life was despaired of. The epidemic lasted from mid-August till late November. More than 4,000 died of it. Loads of the dead were carted away out of the city every day. Explaining to his legislature that the plague was a vile, imported, foreign thing, Governor Mifflin of Pennsylvania described the "complicated scene of terror, wretchedness and mortality" that caused "total derangement of public and private business." It was "not immediately engendered by any noxious quality of our soil, or climate, but was brought hither from a foreign port."

Not knowing what else to do, the Hamiltons attempted to flee the fevers by moving to a house two miles outside the city. When Washington heard that Hamilton was coming down with the plague, he wrote him a kind note on September 6, 1793, expressing "extreme concern" that he might be "in the first stages of the prevailing fever." He hoped Hamilton was mistaken about the symptoms and that he and Betsy would be able to dine with him at three o'clock that day.

The usual method of treatment was the one prescribed by Dr. Benjamin Rush: purging and bleeding the victims. There being no notion that the disease was carried by mosquitoes, every supposed preventive of contagion was used, such as the burning of brimstone and sniffing of vinegar-soaked sponges. As a result of this, ". . . many valued themselves highly on the skill with which they got to windward of every person whom they met."

But Dr. Edward Stevens, Hamilton's boyhood friend from St. Croix who was now a practicing physician in Philadelphia, disagreed with Dr. Rush. He thought Dr. Rush's therapy was the worst possible one for the disease. The Rushites reciprocated by insisting that Stevens was all wrong. Called in to treat Hamilton, Dr. Neddy Stevens ordered cold baths in constant succession and dosage with infusions of tanbark tea. A host of attendants was required to fill the baths, carry the gasping man in and out, and attend him in accordance with Dr. Stevens's orders. The five Hamilton children, the youngest now only a year old, were sent off to a neighbor's house and not even allowed to see their mother, except in the distance through the window. Later on, the children were sent still farther away to the Schuylers.

That both father and mother recovered was considered a miracle of science due to Dr. Stevens's treatment. On September 13, 1793, the *Federal Gazette* announced the recovery of the secretary and his lady. The servant girl who had nursed Mrs. Hamilton also was on the mend. "This is a strong confirmation," its writer went on, "of goodness of the plan, pursued by Dr. Stevens, and ought to recommend it to the serious consideration of our Medical Gentlemen. In such a case, the pride of theory, ought to give way to the fact and experience." A friend from nearby Burlington joined "with all ranks in the general joy . . . upon hearing of your safe recovery." Benjamin Walker wrote, "for God sake or rather for our sakes take care to avoid a relapse." Washington's secretary Tobias Lear, congratulating Hamilton on his recovery, had found in New England "unfeigned sorrow . . . on a report of your death and . . . marks of joy . . . when the report was known to be unfounded."

Congratulations on survival poured in to the Hamiltons from all directions. But the good news riled Jefferson's bile.

As Jefferson saw it, Hamilton could do nothing right, not even get well. He wrote Madison: "Hamilton is ill of the fever as is said. He had two physicians out at his house the night before last, his family think him in danger, & he puts himself so by his excessive alarm." Of the hero of the last redoubt at Yorktown, the deserter of Richmond added, "He had been miserable several days before from a firm persuasion he should catch it, a man as timid as he is on the water, as timid on horseback, as timid in sickness, would be a phaenomenon if the courage of which he has the reputation in military matters were genuine."[13]

Still much enfeebled, the convalescent quit the pestilent city and, with Betsy, drove by slow stages to the Schuylers' in Albany for a rest cure. But the mayor of Albany took alarm when he learned that Philadelphia plague victims would be bringing foreign contagion to town and placed them all under a quarantine. He wrote Schuyler that "fears of the Citizens are up beyond conception from the Idea that the carriages and baggage . . . and servants may contain infection, and possibly spread that disorder." Before entering the city, the Hamilton family must stop at an inn at Greenbush, three miles out of town, and be examined by a group of physicians at Schuyler's expense. Even if pronounced free of contagion, they must burn their clothing, put on new clothing provided by the city, and come on with no baggage or servants in an open chair.

Ostracized from the family seat after the long, hot journey on top of everything else, Hamilton angrily, if foolishly, put the matter in terms of legal rights. Schuyler must assure the mayor that he would "accede to everything that is reasonable," but that "the rights of citizenship cannot be violated, and that he does not consider his stay here as a matter of grace or favor." Schuyler smoothed over Hamilton's nervous derangement and gave the mayor positive assurances that physicians had certified there was no danger and that the Hamiltons would not contaminate the town. Thanks to Schuyler, one tense confrontation was finessed.

During Hamilton's absence, his friend Oliver Wolcott, Jr., the comptroller, took over his duties in Philadelphia, until he, too, departed the "infectious air, sickness and Death" at Philadelphia to take refuge at the "Falls of Schuylkill." Safely out of town, Wolcott ordered the Treasury offices thoroughly cleaned and fumigated with brimstone. When Hamilton and Betsy returned late in October, they too remained outside of town at Robert Morris's house, The Hills, on the Schuylkill. On November 5, the mayor was still issuing warnings against coming back into the city just yet, "as the distemper is still lurking in several parts."

His lifelong history of illness, his recent brush with death, and his life saved by his boyhood friend made Hamilton think of himself as an authority on medical matters. When an epidemic of the plague struck New York two years later, Hamilton remembered Dr. Stevens's treatment and prescribed it to Wolcott: "The fever in this Town . . . is sufficiently mortal. Bleeding is found fatal. Most of our physicians purge . . . I fear more than does good." Wolcott should pass this voucher for his prescription to Dr. Stevens. This would remind him that though doctors might disagree, Hamilton knew that Stevens's way was right and that Benjamin Rush's was wrong. Hamilton's opinion should stand as that of the court of last resort on the medical question.

Now back in Philadelphia after a good rest with family and Schuyler in-laws at Albany and Schuylerville, Hamilton felt fully recovered, but perhaps stronger and feistier than he should have. On December 16 he wrote a formal letter to the House of Representatives, requesting "that a new inquiry may without delay be instituted in some mode, the most effectual for an accurate and thorough investigation; and I will add, that the more comprehensive it is, the more agreeable will it be for me."

He was reopening the whole cancerous subject that might otherwise have remained in remission, by himself calling for a new investigation of himself. To Hermione in *A Winter's Tale*, honor was "a derivative from me to mine." Therefore, "If powers divine behold our human actions, as they do," her innocence would "make false accusation blush," without need of a public proof of it. To Hamilton, unlike Hermione, inner knowledge or even divine knowledge of his innocence was not enough, assuming he possessed it. His reputation and his honor had to be shown to the public. It had to be "devised and play'd to spectators." Public credit was his watchword. Hamilton recklessly ignored Shakespeare's warning against asking too much. "This is more than history can pattern."

Perhaps Hamilton's request was not so much the rash example of his heroic inability to let sleeping dogs lie as it seemed on its face. Washington, having heard the whispers, may have been forcing his hand behind the scenes. In September, replying to complaints about Hamilton's policies from Edward Pendleton of Virginia, Washington had said that doubtless Hamilton would seek a further inquiry into his conduct at the coming session. Washington added that he devoutly wished all charges to be "probed to the bottom, be the result what it will."

In any event, Hamilton was now blundering into the tactical mistake against which the earlier charges of his enemies, as well as the counsel of his friend Edward Carrington, should have warned him. If the form of the question presented were an affirmative finding of Hamilton's innocence, all those whom Jefferson had called undecided, stupid, lazy, or ignorant in voting against Hamilton's censure or impeachment would be ranged against him. Who could affirmatively vote that, in all the complex mass of material on his operations before Congress, there was not some telltale clue to his lost innocence? Who could really know, pro or con? Honor or dishonor all came down to the form in which the issue was presented.

If anything, Hamilton's near brush with death had whetted the desire of the Virginia junto to carry out Jefferson's orders now to "cut him to pieces." Giles had led the onslaught before—and failed. Their leader, Jefferson, offered his resignation from the cabinet on the last day of 1793, about the time Hamilton's test case would be before Congress. After some delay, a committee appointed to inquire into the Treasury Department focused on the hoary—and already much-investigated—issue of Hamilton's management of the two foreign loans of August 4 and 12, 1790. The inquiry bogged down almost at once and dragged on through all of 1794, producing little light and much heat. The committee demanded that Hamilton turn over every communication that he had ever made to Washington; Hamilton created one of the earliest precedents for the doctrine of executive privilege by retorting that he would yield only those he judged to be pertinent to the specific issue. The committee wished to know "by what authority any portion of the moneys borrowed abroad have been drawn to the United States?" He replied that he had received a general commission from the president and specific sanctions for each disposition, "always bottomed upon the representation of the Secretary, and always expressly or tacitly qualified with this *condition*—that whatever was to be done, was to be agreeable to the Laws." The committee failed to force Hamilton into retirement, and Jefferson informed Washington on February 7 that he wanted to stay on in office for awhile longer.

On March 28, 1794, Madison wrote to Jefferson: "The enquiry into the Treasury is going on, tho' not very rapidly. I understand that it begins to pinch where we most expected—the authority for drawing the money from Europe into the Bank. He endeavored to parry the difficulty by contesting the right of the Committee to call for the authority. This failing he talks of constructive written authority from the P. but relies on parol authority, which I think it impossible the P. can support him in."

Hamilton wrote Washington, asking him for a stronger written endorsement of what he had done and reminding Washington that "the sanctions were [*sic*] verbal whenever the President was at the seat of Government. In a case of absence they were in writing." Washington endorsed a "certificate" for Hamilton in the form of a letter dated April 8, 1794, written on Hamilton's official report on the 1790 borrowings. It was broad enough, but not one word broader than necessary, to give Hamilton what he needed for vindication in the inquiry:

> Sir,
>
> I cannot charge my memory with all the particulars, which have passed between us, relative to the disposition of the money borrowed. Your letters, however, and my answer, which you refer to in the foregoing statement, and lately reminded me of, speak for themselves, and stand in no need of explanation.
>
> As to verbal communications, I am satisfied, that many were made by you to me on this subject; and from my general recollection of the course of proceedings, I do not doubt, that it was substantially as you have stated it in the annexed paper, that I have approved of the measures, which you, from time to time, proposed to me for disposing of the Loans, upon the condition, that what was to be done by you, should be agreeable to the Laws.
>
> Go. Washington
>
> United States
> April 8, 1794

Hamilton replied to Washington the same day in great distress. Washington's letter was not a sufficient endorsement. Hamilton feared his enemies would read into it an approval withheld. Enemies were too much on his mind to let him see that his chief had saved him by the surest way there was to be saved.

"Under all that has happened Sir, I cannot help entertaining and frankly expressing to you my apprehension, that false and insidious men, whom you may one day understand, taking advantage of the want of recollection, which is natural, where the mind is habitually occupied with a variety of important objects, have found means by artful suggestions to infuse doubts and distrusts very injurious to me," Hamilton wrote.

The pain of apprehension skewed his judgment: "Those who are disposed to construe everything to my disadvantage will affirm That the Declaration of the President has entirely waived the main point and does not even manifest an opinion that the Representation of the Secretary of the Treasury is well founded."

Here is sad evidence of preoccupation with enemies blunting Hamilton's wonted ability to make accurate judgments of the effect of political actions. Washington's laconic ratification of all of Hamilton's official acts was worth more to defend him with Congress than a peck of predictable, praiseful opinion, but Hamilton failed to see it that way.

His desperate, inward, personal need was not so much to be "rescued" from indesinent investigation by Congress—he could ride that out—but to obtain some signal from Washington that whispers of scandal had not cut away the only base on which Hamilton had erected "my administration." Hamilton concluded that to what his enemies said "would be added, that the reserve of the President is a proof that he does not think that representation true [that is, Hamilton's defense]—else his justice would have led him to rescue the officer concerned even from suspicion on the point."

After he had observed Hamilton resolve innumerable hard questions over 15 years of service, Washington's life conclusion was that Hamilton's judgment was "intuitively great." Here it was wrong, and Washington's was right. Washington, having heard the whispers, could easily make and act on the correct judgment of Hamilton's situation, yet also sympathetically understand the pressures warping Hamilton's judgment into error. A lawyer who takes his own case has a fool for a client.

Hamilton was right to be apprehensive of the use his enemies would make of Washington's certificate, but wrong in his fear of the end result. On April 14, 1794, Madison wrote sycophantically to Jefferson: "The letter from the P. is inexpressibly mortifying to his [H's] friends, and marks his situation to be precisely what you always described it to be."

Few forms of political activity promise more titillation to the public, political payoffs in popularity at minimum risk to investigators, and torture to the investigatee than a congressional investigation of suspicious doings in high places. As in an impeachment proceeding, but not in a court trial, the investigators have no responsibility to resolve ultimate questions of the truth or falsity of even the wildest charges. Of all the congressional investigations in American history, the Virginia junto's two-year investigation of Hamilton's Treasury Department operations proved to be one of the most resounding flops. The sacrosanct president's stiff and formal but unimpeachable and unarguable blanket endorsement of all of Hamilton's operations served the secretary as a better security blanket than any manifestation of opinion. The investigation stumbled on, but spiritlessly.

The very length and persistence of the inquiry became in itself for his enemies evidence of Hamilton's guilt; for his friends, of his innocence. But it was he who had demanded reopening of the inquiry; so the time tilt sloped against him. Had he not done so, its failure to strike pay dirt would have been evidence of his innocence, at least to the wide public who reach political conclusions on emotional, not legally admissible evidence.

The congressional committee's report of April 1794 approved Hamilton's Treasury administration. It found he had not used official influence with the banks to secure private favors. It concluded that "no moneys of the United States, whether before or after they have passed to the credit of the Treasurer, have ever been, directly or indirectly, used for, or applied to any purposes, but those of the Government, except so far as all moneys deposited in a bank are concerned in the general operations thereof." The committee's report was unanimous.

When Hamilton finally resigned as secretary of the treasury in 1795, a local New York Republican, ironically named Fairly, spread the rumor that Hamilton had done so because, as Schuyler indignantly reported him saying, "the affairs of your department were so deranged, that it was not possible for you to extricate It from the confusion In which it was Involved." To his prodigal son-in-law who had strayed to Maria, but returned to Betsy, Schuyler supplied the warm vote of confidence Hamilton had cried out to Washington to give him, but never received. Schuyler snorted that "the propagator of such a calumny was a liar and a villain." Such an emotional snort of support from Washington, happy as it would have let the inner Hamilton feel for a little while, would have left the slaughterhouse door ajar far enough to let in his Jeffersonian enemies to "cut him to pieces."

Whether an impeachment proceeding or a congressional investigation succeeds or fails, either way it remains an impeachment. There is nothing to end it like a jury's verdict of "not guilty." It compounded Hamilton's anxieties so that all the pressures on him had driven out of his mind what *The Federalist* had once known better: "The decision will be regulated more by the comparative strength of the parties, than by the real demonstrations of innocence or guilt."

13

NEUTRALITY

MY HEALTH WHICH HAD SUFFERED A SEVERE SHOCK BY AN ATTACK
OF THE MALIGNANT DISEASE LATELY PREVALENT HERE IS NOW
ALMOST COMPLETELY RESTORED. THE LAST VESTIGE OF IT HAS
BEEN A NERVOUS DERANGEMENT; BUT THIS HAS NEARLY YIELDED
TO REGIMEN, A CERTAIN DEGREE OF EXERCISE AND A RESOLUTION
TO OVERCOME IT.

—To Angelica Church, December 27, 1793

Jonathan Ogden, farmer, of Morristown, New Jersey, wrote Hamilton on
March 18, 1793, that "people universally here" were so pleased by the defeat of
Giles's "malitious" [*sic*] impeachment resolutions that "they put you in danger
of the curse denounced against him who every one speaks well of."

From New York, Dr. John Bard reported on March 4 that at a large gathering at Judge James Duane's even the man whom Hamilton had once looked upon
as chief cabalist against him and Washington, General Horatio Gates, had applied to him "the beautiful epitaph" that Alexander Pope, Hamilton's favorite
eighteenth-century poet had written:

> Statesman yet friend to Truth, of Soul Sincere
> In action faithful, and in Honour Clear!
> Who broke no promise, served no private end,
> Who gained no title, and who lost no friend,

> Ennobled by himself, by all approved
> Praisd, wept, and Honoured, by the muse he lov'd.

Such exhilarating praise from such sources left Hamilton unbemused. Writing on April 5 to his old friend James McHenry—"My dear Mac"—in Baltimore to explain why an appointment Mac had recommended had been turned down, he noted confidentially, with irony, that "you know I have no occasion to make enemies."

Hamilton's letter closed with a large question: "What say your folks as to peace or war in respect of the U States?"

No issue would give rise to fiercer battles in the war going on inside Washington's cabinet than the subject of American neutrality. Questions of handling the proceeds of foreign loans were compounded with questions of recognition of foreign governments, particularly revolutionary foreign governments like those in France—and Saint-Domingue—and compounded the departmental war between Jefferson and Hamilton. The French Revolution had changed from a movement for a limited monarchy to one for a republic. Amid the massacres of September 1792, it deposed and imprisoned King Louis XVI, who, when Hamilton was at Valley Forge, had been woebegone America's most "powerful friend among the princes of the earth." Now Hamilton had suspended American payments on the French debt. It mattered little to Hamilton that shortly after suspending the king, the Revolutionary National Assembly had named Hamilton —and Washington and Madison, but not Jefferson—honorary citizens of the revolutionary republic.

In November 1792, Ternant, the French minister, had requested payments to help the French keep down a threatening slave uprising in Saint-Domingue (the French name for the colony later known as Haiti on the Caribbean island known as Hispaniola or Santo Domingo), suggesting that such American payments might be credited against the debt to France. On November 19, Hamilton had warned Washington against further payments because of the revolutionary situation in France:

> If a restoration of the King should take place, I am of opinion that no payment which might be made in the interval would be deemed regular or obligatory. A payment to the newly constituted power, which would subject it to be used in support of the change, would doubtless be rejected.

When it came to questions that engaged his attention to the general interests of the "U States" without directly involving his own department or his honor, as he saw it, Hamilton's judgment remained as acute as ever. If we look back over the conflicting claims made for the leaders of the period, it seems fair to say (there will be argument) that no man's activities were more single-mindedly directed toward the objective of keeping America out of wars with Britain,

France, or Spain with less selfish concern for domestic political consequences to his career than Hamilton's.

No doubt, Hamilton's activities in foreign affairs were more effective because his own personal reputation was not immediately involved in that sector. No doubt, Jefferson's were less so because his was. In foreign affairs, circumstances and character made it easier for Hamilton to act selflessly and impossible for Jefferson to do so. It also seems fair to say rather surprisingly of a man who was not the president or the secretary of state—that when it came to formulating policy and devising actions, contacts, statements, and documents for carrying out the policy of American neutrality, no man did more in his time than Hamilton to keep America out of the great powers' wars.

The practical effect of Hamilton's suspension of payments on the French debt on events in France was minimal, but it was significant for the French masters of Saint-Domingue. For Jefferson, as a matter of domestic politics, it symbolized Hamilton's practical support of two causes that he resisted: the freeing of black slaves from colonial masters in Saint-Domingue and the possible restoration of a limited monarchy in France. But a further danger of affirming American support of the French revolutionary government by such a payment was that France was on the point of declaring war, in the name of the rights of the people, on a number of other European countries.

On March 7, 1793, when only rumors of war were abroad, George Hammond wrote home that Hamilton "has assured me that *he* shall exert his influence to defeat the success of any proposition on the part of France, which, tempting as it might appear, might ultimately render it necessary for this government to depart from the observance of as strict a neutrality as is compatible with its present engagements, and which is so essential to its real interests." Hammond took note that the new nation was being established according to Hamilton's system and that the chief architect might one day succeed to its presidency. He attributed Hamilton's stand to "the knowledge that any event which might endanger the *external* tranquility of the United States, would be as fatal to the systems he has formed for the benefit of his country as to his present personal reputation and to his future projects of ambition."

On April 2, under the heading, *"Most Secret* and *Confidential,"* Hammond was able, on Hamilton's word, to assure his government that the United States would not permit its treaties with France to involve it "in any difficulties or disputes with other powers." All Hamilton's policies were directed toward the "continuance of peace." Hammond would continue to cultivate Mr. Hamilton, he added pointedly to his chief.

On April 5, the same day Hamilton had asked McHenry for his views on "peace or war," he wrote Washington of reports that "War had been declared by France against England, Russia and Holland . . . There seems to be no room for Doubt of the Existence of War." He added by postscript that "English Papers in Town by way of St. Vincents mention that on the 8th of February the late Queen of France was also put to Death after a Trial and Condemnation."

Communications were slow and unreliable in the late eighteenth century.

Hamilton's report of the queen's death was premature. Although the revolutionary government of France had cut off the head of America's friend Louis XVI on January 21, 1793, it would not lop off Marie Antoinette's until October 16. The revolutionary government had indeed declared war on Britain and Holland on February 1, but not on Russia. This word from Hamilton was probably the first that George Washington received of these calamitous foreign affairs.

News of new war between the two greatest European powers created a sensation in America. Washington, vacationing at Mount Vernon at the time, cut short his stay and rushed to Philadelphia, reaching the capital on April 17. The next day he submitted a series of 13 questions to the members of his cabinet "with a view to forming a general plan of conduct for the executive" in this grave emergency.

When Jefferson received Washington's questions, he saw in them Hamilton's hand, which was becoming an obsession with him. "It was palpable from the style," he confided to his *Anas,* and from "their ingenious tissue & suite that they were not the President's, that they were raised upon a prepared chain of argument, in short that the language was Hamilton's and the doubts his alone." Edmund Randolph, the attorney general, had confirmed his suspicions, he declared.

Through 15 years of working together in war and peace, Washington and Hamilton had by now each discovered in the other a remarkable consanguinity of thought and style. From the point of view of national interest, what difference did it make that Hamilton had drafted Washington's questions, as he had, if Washington had sent them out as his own? For Jefferson to write later, for posterity, after Washington and Hamilton were dead, that the questions were "not the President's," but Hamilton's "alone," was rewriting history. Taken literally, this accusation was in snide effect making Hamilton a forger and Washington a dupe. It adds nothing to Jefferson's reputation for good judgment or truthfulness.

The questions Washington had posed to his department heads ranged across all American involvement with the war. Should the United States issue a proclamation of neutrality? Should the United States consider the old treaties with France that had created the alliance during the American Revolution to be still in effect, or ought they to be renounced or suspended? Did they require America to join France and declare war on Britain? Ought the United States receive the new minister from the French revolutionary government, Edmond Genêt, now on his way, absolutely or with qualifications or refuse to receive him at all?

War between the two great European powers and Holland too placed the United States in grave peril. The great powers had territorial interests throughout the world and on the American frontiers that impinged on American territorial and commercial interests of every kind. Two such antagonists in such a war would care little about niceties of private international law respecting neutrals. The interests of a weak America could be ground up and crushed between them.

As Jefferson saw it, there was no occasion for "doubts" to be raised: According to the treaties, the United States and France were bound to each other as allies. Hamilton, of course, was prepared to answer the president's questions before they arrived. On April 9 he had set forth his views on the subject to John Jay in language almost parallel to the answers he would return to Washington's questions. He followed up his letter to Jay with a request that Jay draft a proclamation of neutrality along the lines he suggested for Washington's review and signature. Two days later Jay obliged with a hasty draft of ideas for such a proclamation. Hamilton forwarded this useful material to Washington. Jefferson did nothing. No secretary of state could fail to smolder and fume with rage, or at least sulk, if the secretary of the treasury has preempted the making of policy on the most important foreign policy issue to confront his administration.

According to the treaties with France, the United States was, in effect, the ally of France in any war with England in which England was the aggressor. By the treaty, the United States had also extended protection and favored status to French possessions in the West Indies. Answering Washington's 13 questions, Hamilton and Jefferson split to the maximum extent that it was possible to do for two men who were in basic agreement over policy. Both agreed with the view Washington had already laid down from Hamilton's draft: neutrality was the best policy. Neither would disagree with Washington or wished to drag the weak, unarmed United States into a war. But on details of neutrality and the complex questions in its train, there was no agreement and wide divergence. It was partly a question of which way the government's officially neutral stance would tilt.

After early favoring the French Revolution, Hamilton had come to see faction and anarchy in its brutal excesses. Jefferson had said, in unguarded moments, that no revolution worthy of the name could be made without breaking some eggs, which seemed to include chopping the queen's head off. Hamilton had alluded to the British system as a good model for government of a free people. Attracted by the French revolutionary slogan of Liberty, Equality, and Fraternity, Jefferson feared the Industrial Revolution in Britain and the growing industrial and merchant classes there as threats to the physiocratic society of small farmers and artisans that he saw as the ideal—as long as a place high above it remained for rich large land and slaveholders like himself. In France, Hamilton saw faction and anarchy in the people's cutting off the executive's head, whereas in Britain, Jefferson saw in the people's failing to follow the French example a monarch holding a people in bondage.

The cabinet met at Washington's house in Philadelphia on April 18 to give their opinions on "a general plan of conduct for the Executive." Hamilton argued for an immediate proclamation of neutrality. Jefferson opposed. Let us act neutrally without expressly saying so, he recommended. "It would be better to hold back the declaration of neutrality," he suggested, "as a thing worth something to the powers at war, that they would bid for it, & we might reasonably ask a price, the *broadest privileges* of neutral nations." He also argued that the president had no inherent or implied power under the Constitution to issue such a proclamation without the consent of Congress. To this, Hamilton retorted that Congress was not in session and that Washington had ample authority under the implied constitutional powers of the executive to act, at least until Congress convened.

Differences were resolved only after much argument. Hamilton's minutes of the meeting next day show that "it was determined by all that a proclamation shall issue." On this point Hamilton won. Action was not delayed by technicalities. His minutes do not say whether or not the word *neutrality* should appear in the proclamation. On April 22, Washington published the famous proclamation, which Edmund Randolph, the attorney general, had drafted for him. It was not, in so many words, a proclamation of neutrality. The fact was proclaimed, but the word itself was avoided. It expressed a determination on the part of the United States to "adopt and pursue a conduct friendly and impartial toward the belligerent powers" and "to exhort and warn the citizens of the United States carefully to avoid all acts and proceedings whatsoever, which may in any manner tend to contravene such disposition."

This saved the good points Jefferson had made. At Hamilton's prodding, the thing was done, and for the record. Jefferson's reservations preserved the subtleties of his approach. The joint result is a good example of how both men, working against each other together in Washington's cabinet, could bring about a result better for the nation than either would have arrived at by himself. It is a good illustration of the advantages of a committee system, but, above all, of Washington's genius as president for coping patiently with two contentious rivals yoked together and making the most of the peculiar contributions of each for the good of the nation. The end result was more of a leaning away from entanglement in the treaties with France than a noticeable tilt toward Britain.

A yet more subtle question was what to do about "Citizen" Edmond Charles Genêt, the new envoy now on his way from France to replace Ternant, the holdover minister from Louis XVI. Any French envoy would hold due bills against the United States. But acknowledging them now would contradict the terms of the neutrality proclamation and tie the country more closely to France in the war that she had just declared against England. But to refuse to receive Citizen Genêt at all would not be "conduct friendly and impartial" toward a belligerent that the proclamation required of the country.

"The King has been decapitated," Hamilton had written Jay on April 9. If the European powers ranged against France should appoint a regent who, in turn, should appoint an ambassador to the United States, "Should we in such case receive both?" Receiving Genêt and not the regent's appointee would not be "perfectly neutral." We ought to receive Genêt, Hamilton said, but "with qualification—declaring that we receive the person as the representative of the Government *in fact* of the French nation," whichever it might turn out to be, "reserving to ourselves a right to consider the applicability of the Treaties to the *actual situation of the parties.*" Hamilton's point here was as subtle as Jefferson's earlier one. At the moment, it was uncertain which government of France was the *established* one: if the revolutionary government were not, then its demand for enforcement of the existing treaties need not be recognized. Moreover, the United States had no obligation to support France—she was the aggressor in a war she had declared; the American obligation was only to help defend her against aggression by others. Hamilton acknowledged the validity of the treaties themselves: "I doubt whether we could *bona fide* dispute the ultimate obligation of the treaties."

All this was too subtle for Jefferson. He opposed Hamilton's approach. He held that it was the French people with whom the treaty had been made, regardless of the form supported by their governmental representatives, whether monarchy or republic. Besides, France as a republic was much more legitimately entitled to demand its treaty rights than the monarch had been, he claimed, ignoring the plain fact that it was the monarch who had made the treaty.

No, not all. On the contrary, Hamilton argued. To abandon Louis XVI now might be regarded by "mankind as not consistent with a decent regard to the relations which subsisted between them and Louis XVI." But the crux of the matter was that, in dealing with foreign governments, practical outcomes, not slogans or sentiments or old attachments, were what counted most.

"A struggle for liberty is in itself respectable and glorious," Hamilton told Washington May 2. "When conducted with magnanimity it ought to command the admiration of every friend of human nature. But if sullied by crimes and extravagancies, it loses its respectability." It would be judged by historical hindsight, and the glorious end would not justify criminal means: "Though success may rescue it from infamy, it cannot in the opinion of the sober part of mankind attach to it much positive merit or praise." So "the pending revolution of France has sustained some serious blemishes. There is too much ground to anticipate that a sentence uncommonly severe will be pronounced upon it, if it fails."

Jefferson's notes of their ferocious argument in the cabinet meeting show contemptuous scorn for Hamilton's ingenious legal argument that would keep the United States out of too close entanglement with the French revolutionists while still honoring the existence of the treaty. Secretary of War Henry Knox was as contemptible as Hamilton. Jefferson failed to grasp or else misrepresented Hamilton's subtle approach: "Knox subscribed at once to Mr. H's opn that we ought to declare the treaty void, acknowledging at the same time, like a fool as he is, that he knew nothing about it." Jefferson sneered to Monroe that "Hamilton is panic struck if we refuse our breach to every kick which Gr Brit. may chuse to give it. He is for proclaiming at once the most abject principles, such as would invite & merit habitual insults. And indeed every inch of ground must be fought in our councils to desperation in order to hold up the face of even a sneaking neutrality, for our votes are generally 2½ against 1½." Hamilton and Knox were two, Jefferson 1, and the vacillating Randolph usually Mr. One-half —one-half. Jefferson had recently turned down a personal financial accommodation requested by Randolph, which Hamilton had then extended to him.

Hamilton's minutes of the same April 19 cabinet meeting show that it was finally agreed by all present that Genêt should be received. On the subordinate question of just how he should be received, Hamilton noted: "The Attorney General Randolph and Secretary of State are of opinion he should be received absolutely & without qualifications." As for the secretaries of the treasury and war, Hamilton recorded only a "?" and added, "This & the subsequent questions are postponed to another day."

Adjourning on this deadlock in disagreement, Hamilton drew up instructions for Washington on the exact procedure for receiving Genêt "with qualification" and explained why he thought "qualification" was necessary. But Washington followed Jefferson's advice to receive Genêt without any qualifications. The practical difference was hardly perceptible. All awaited the arrival of the new French minister with strong emotions, strongly counterpoised along partisan lines.

In the beginning, in 1789, most people in the United States had been elated by the outbreak of the French Revolution. In 1790, George Washington had written Catherine Macauley Graham of his joy in seeing that "the American Revolution had been productive of happy consequences on both sides of the Atlantic." He recognized that the French Revolution was "of such magnitude and of so momentous a nature that we hardly yet dare to form a conjecture about it." He had not believed that it was directed against Louis XVI, of whom he still spoke as "our great and beloved Friend and Ally." Jefferson in his *Anas* recalled that he had been the first to tell the president "the news of the King's flight and capture," adding that "I never saw him so dejected by any event in my life." It is difficult to believe that anyone who knew Washington at all well could have written such a sentence truthfully.

Hamilton, too, had been pleased by the early news from France. To him, a nation's "struggle for liberty" was "respectable and glorious." In his youth he had described the French as a people oppressed and justified in revolution. When the outbreak came, he rejoiced to see the French throw off their condition of "slavery" and claim "freedom." He had advised Jefferson that French commerce would probably expand rapidly under the new "free government."

As minister to France from 1785 to 1789, Jefferson had been a "privileged observer" of the outbreak and remained unswervingly committee to it. When it was called to his attention in 1792 that it had brought violent death to a great many innocent people, he compared such victims to innocent civilians who are killed on the fringes of a battle. With "the liberty of the whole earth . . . depending on the issue of the contest," he asked, "was ever such a prize won with so little innocent blood?" He added that he would rather see "half the earth disabled" than to see the French Revolution fail, for "were there but an Adam and Eve left in every country, and left free, it would be better than it is now."

Hamilton's early approval of the French Revolution slowly turned to misgivings, anxiety, and apprehension. In October of 1789 he had written to Lafayette, confessing both "pleasure and apprehension." He feared "disagreements" among the French leaders, the "vehement character" of the French people, the "interested refractoriness" of the nobles, and the "reveries" of French "philosophic politicians, who appear in the moment to have great influence, and who, being mere speculatists, may aim at more refinement than suits either human nature or the composition of your nation." He foresaw that it would prove easier to "bring on" the people than to keep them "within proper bounds." He was at the point of mailing this letter when he received the startling news of the French legislation of August 4, 1789, by which the nobility had abandoned many of their ancient privileges. He had added, in a postscript to the same letter to Lafayette, that the nobles' "patriotic and magnanimous policy" promised "good both to them and their country" and lessened some of his own "apprehensions." But in 1790 the issuance of the all but worthless assignats by the National Assembly for money seemed to illustrate new "weakness, folly and turbulence" and revived his fears. In May 1793 he wrote an unknown correspondent, "Would to heaven that the comparison" of the French Revolution with the American "were just. Would to heaven that we could discern in the mirror of French affairs, the same humanity, the same decorum, the same gravity, the same order, the same dignity, the same solemnity, which distinguished the course of the American Revolution." Instead, all Hamilton could now see was Marot and Robespierre, "bloody scenes . . . assassins . . . the monarch brought precipitately to the block without proof of guilt. . . . atheism . . . fanaticism . . . rapacity . . . passion, tumult and violence . . . where reason and cool deliberation ought to preside."

Gouverneur Morris was in France when the revolution began and returned there from England to serve as American minister from 1792 to 1794. The realism and pessimism of his letters to Hamilton had much to do with forming the opinions of the event held by his old and trusted friends Washington and Hamilton. France, Morris wrote, "was as near to anarchy as society can approach without dissolution." To him the failure of the Constitution of 1791, which had survived less than a year after taking two years to formulate, was "a natural accident to a thing which was all sail and no ballast." The French government wanted to keep peace with Great Britain, but Morris was afraid that in their agitation "the people" would not allow it. The "best picture" he could convey of the French populace was that of "cattle before a thunderstorm."

Like Gouverneur Morris, John Adams was fearful of tides of sentiment for the French Revolution now running high in America. On February 3, 1793, he ended a letter to Abigail, saying, "Our countrymen are about to abandon the good old grave solid manners of Englishmen, their ancestors, and adopt all the aping levity and frivolity of the French."

When the British had set up their Nootka Sound base on Vancouver Island, thereby extending British territorial encroachment to a new area of potential American westward expansion, and Spanish resistance to the British had collapsed, Hamilton was dismayed that revolutionary France had failed to stand by her treaty with her old ally Spain. Concerned then with maintaining a balance of power to protect American interests, he said that France was the "only weight" that could be "thrown into the scale" against Britain, "capable of producing an equilibrium." But he did not expect to see "much order or vigor in the affairs of France for a considerable period to come." Its "transition from slavery to liberty" might prove to be a "spring of great exertions," but, unfortunately, "the ebullitions of enthusiasm must ever be a precarious reliance."

Making a new effort "to cement the friendship and interests of the two nations," the French National Assembly had conveyed a warm expression of appreciation to America on the death of Benjamin Franklin on April 17, 1790. Hamilton had drafted Washington's reply to the National Assembly, which included some pointed homilies on the principles of good, steady government. A "virtuous policy" and "the true principles of liberty" were related to laws and "public order." Louis XVI was still "the friend of the people over whom he reigns."

For more than a year before August of 1792, when Louis XVI had been deposed and royalty "abolished," Hamilton, with Washington's approval, had been making payments at Ternant's request to help the French keep down the unrest in the colony of Saint-Domingue. Ternant had praised Hamilton as a friend of France for the liberal manner in which he had responded to the emergency. Hamilton recognized that the French National Assembly had come to power in a constitutional manner, and it had been recognized by the king. It was the dethroning of Louis XVI that now cast in doubt the legitimacy of the current French government.

Gouverneur Morris had tried to help the king escape from France and failed. He would objurgate the beheadings of the king and queen. If a king were a traitor, Hamilton did not dispute the right of his people to take his life, but to him Louis's execution was only a mob's act of political expediency, and so was the beheading of Marie Antoinette. Hamilton agreed when Morris wrote wryly that Louis's only "crime" was in "not suffering his throat to be cut which was certainly a nefarious Plot against the People and a manifest Violation of the Bill of Rights."

Surprisingly contrary winds or else a design to make his first landfall in politically friendly Republican territory brought Citizen Genêt to the United States at Charleston, South Carolina. One apprehensive Federalist in North Carolina described him to Hamilton: "He has a good person, fine ruddy complection . . . and seems always in a bustle, more like a busy man than a man of business." He had held posts at a half dozen courts in Europe.

To John Adams, as he wrote Abigail on December 19, 1793, Genêt was "a youth totally destitute of all experience in popular government, popular assemblies, or conventions of any kind: very little accustomed to reflect upon his own or his fellow creatures' hearts; wholly ignorant of the law of nature and nations, the civil law, and even of the dispatches of ancient ambassadors with which his nation and language abound. . . ." He had "a declamatory style, a flitting, fluttering imagination, an ardor in his temper, and a civil deportment."

Like Robespierre, Saint-Just, and others of the Jacobins of the Mountain who had sent him, Genêt was egotistic, brash, full of self-importance, and convinced that his mission was to reexport revolution to the populace of the United States. With a tendency to ignore the constitutional government to which he had been accredited and to act as if only "the people" counted, he was the worst possible sort of minister that the revolutionists could have sent to cement official relations with France's old ally.

Genêt's enthusiastic reception at Charleston only helped inflate his innate vainglory. As Hamilton later put it in his broadside *No Jacobin,* "The best penmen among the patriots were at work composing congratulatory addresses." Because they were unaccustomed to producing French glottal *r* sounds, "their choicest orators were gargling their throats to pronounce them."

Genêt's instructions from the Executive Council reminded him that "military preparations in Great Britain become every day more and more serious . . . we ought to excite . . . the zeal of the Americans . . . if we fail they will sooner or later fall under the rod of Great Britain . . . the American government will finally . . . make a common cause with us . . ." Not only did Genêt have trade privileges to confer, France would also send an armada of 45 ships of the line to emancipate South America, with Francisco Miranda as generalissimo. America could repay her war debt to France by providing supplies and armaments for the invasion of the Spanish colonies. This did not set well with Spain, which responded by threatening war on America. In hasty alarm, Jefferson wrote Monroe June 28, ". . . Spain is so evidently *picking a quarrel* with us that we see a war absolutely inevitable with her. We are making a last effort to avoid it, but our cabinet is without any division in their expectations of the result."

Instead of proceeding straightway to Philadelphia to present his credentials to Washington, Genêt lingered in the South to bask in adulation and arrange for the recruitment and outfitting of privateers to prey on British shipping. He distributed military commissions to American adventurers to serve in French incursions against Florida and Louisiana. He gave letters of marque or authority (he came with 300 of them) to American privateers "who may fit out and try their chance against the English, Dutch, Russians, Prussians and Austrians." The French consul condemned and sold the first prize ship brought in. All of this was illegal by the rules of international law. But as the Federalist pamphleteer *The Porcupine* (William Cobbett) observed, the enthralled Republicans of the Carolinas "had cut the strings of their culottes, and the Citizen pulled them down about their heels."

Gouverneur Morris had originally been accredited to the king. To the Republicans of America, Genêt was as popular as Morris was unpopular with Republicans in France. At his own elegant Paris table, in the presence of company and, of course, the servants, Morris had "cursed the French ministers as a set of damned rascals" and "said the King would be replaced on his throne." Jefferson often complained to Washington about the cares and duties of office and of his wish to retire. Washington, with his customary punctilio and finesse, sought to return the compliment Republican France had paid him by sending Genêt to America and offered to send Jefferson back to France to replace Morris there. But Jefferson declined to be traded for Genêt and remained at home.

Through the Southern towns Genêt traveled slowly northward through tableau after tableau of triumph. At each, the Republicans of the populace welcomed him in vast throngs, full of cheers for France and anathemas for Britain. Federalists watched his stately, triumphal progress with mounting alarm. The more alarmist saw in Genêt the imminent onset of the wildest excesses of the Reign of Terror. One who had observed portents in Virginia wrote

Hamilton that only he could now save the people from "the man that we are all afraid of." He added, "The best men in this country rely chiefly upon your talents and disposition to avoid the rocks which lie upon the right hand, and upon the left, ready to dash our young government to pieces upon the least unskilful pilotage."

With a keen sense of affronted dignity, Washington awaited Genêt's dawdling advent in Philadelphia.

Jefferson, by contrast, seemed thrilled at the approach of this live apostle of liberty, who spoke directly from "the people" to "the people," not to their governments. He described with obvious relish the enthusiasm of the "yeomanry" of the city at the sight of a French frigate victoriously bringing into port a beaten and captured British prize, portentously named the *Grange*, which had been seized inside American territorial waters. Randolph and Hamilton agreed that this violated international law; the cabinet, including Jefferson, concurred; Genêt eventually had to give orders to yield the prize.

When Genêt finally arrived at the capital May 17, 1793, five and a half weeks after landing in Charleston, he wrote home to his minister, "Mon voyage a été une succession de fêtes civiques, non interrompues et mon entrée à Philadelphia un triomphe pour la liberté. Les vrais Americains sont au comble de la joie."

True Americans not exactly bowled over by Genêt's brand of the politics of joy included Washington and Hamilton. Washington received Genêt with frigid politeness, which Genêt ascribed to jealousy. He wrote home, "Old man Washington is jealous of my success, and of the enthusiasm with which the whole town flocks to my house."

British Minister George Hammond strongly protested Genêt's commissioning of the many privateers that preyed on British shipping, as well as seizures of ships like the *Grange*. By the law of nations, they were clearly unneutral acts. Hamilton agreed and reported to Washington on May 15 that "the British minister plenipotentiary demands a restitution of these prizes." Hamilton gave Washington his opinion that the demand ought to be complied with, as a matter of international law; the seizures "make us an instrument of hostilities against Great Britain." For France to equip, man, and commission vessels of war within the United States to prey on British ships was "an injury and an affront of a very serious kind" under the law of nations.

Immediately after presenting his credentials, Genêt demanded advances on payments of the debt to France. Washington refused, but, as Jefferson advised, with more tact in the manner of doing so than Hamilton had suggested to be shown to Genêt. Emboldened, Genêt refused to permit payments to American creditors for aid given by them earlier to the French in Saint-Domingue under the agreement made earlier with Ternant. Hammond reported that an angry Hamilton had told him that "Mr. Genêt's conduct was a direct violation of a formal compact, originally entered into with Ternant." Hamilton retorted to Genêt that the American government would have to apply the next installments due on the French debt to paying these American creditors whose claims Genêt had disavowed.

Genêt's privateers continued to seize and send British ships into American ports. Two new privateers were being armed in Baltimore, and Hammond renewed British protests. Washington disregarded Hamilton's advice that the British prizes be returned, as Hammond demanded, and only partly followed Jefferson's. He took a middle course: no privateers could be fitted out or supplied in American ports, but captured prizes could remain. The cabinet would merely "consider whether any practicable arrangement can be adopted to prevent the augmentation of the privateer force." This response to Hammond's remonstrance was much too feeble for Hamilton. Genêt simply ignored the feeble protest and went on arming privateers in American ports.

With few of his recommendations on how best to protect neutrality by dealings with Genêt being followed by Washington and with Jefferson's efforts to impeach him having closed with the defeat of Giles's resolutions, Hamilton decided the time had come for his resignation. He had submitted it June 21, to take effect "toward the close of the ensuing session of the Congress." Riding high the previous September, he had warned Washington that the "public good" would soon "require *substitutes* for the differing members of your administration," not suggesting that it was he himself who would be the first to be erased. He had added that "on my part there will be a most cheerful acquiescence in such a result." Since the night of December 15, the tides of politics and cabinet war had been running against him. His continued presence in the cabinet would only weaken the Union and the system he had done so much to build. It appeared that Jefferson had succeeded in forcing him out of office and outlasting him in power. But the secretary of state's word of reassurance to Hammond that he would "prevent the augmentation" of the privateer force, feeble as it was, would soon leave Jefferson open to charges of duplicity.

The *Little Sarah*, an English merchant vessel, had been captured sailing out of Philadelphia by a French frigate, *L'Ambuscade*, and brought back to port as a prize of war in May. Hamilton and Knox warned Jefferson pointedly in July of reports coming to them that the *Little Sarah*, renamed the *Petit Démocrate*, was being secretly outfitted as a French privateer with 14 iron cannons, six swivels, and a crew of 120 to prey on British shipping. No kind of privateer would be more deceptive and effective to prey on the British than a former British merchant vessel like the *Petit Démocrate*.

Governor Thomas Mifflin of Pennsylvania and Charles Biddle told Hamilton that some of her new guns had even been paid for by Republican citizens of Philadelphia and that some of her crew were United States citizens. Governor Mifflin sent the secretary of the Commonwealth, Alexander J. Dallas, to Genêt's house at midnight on July 6 to ask him to hold up departure of the new privateer.

"With great passion," Genêt "absolutely refused" to give any assurance, complained bitterly of his treatment by the authorities, and "declared that he would appeal from the President to the people." Any attempt to seize the *Petit Démocrate* would be resisted with force.

Governor Mifflin at once called up 100 infantry and 20 artillerymen with their cannon and gave orders that no pilot take the vessel out. Dallas told Jefferson of Genêt's flat and absolute refusal to cancel the orders for sailing.

Jefferson hurried to Genêt's house Sunday morning, July 7, to request him to hold it back, at least until Washington, then at Mount Vernon, returned to Philadelphia. Genêt again refused. According to Jefferson, he merely indicated that the ship would not be ready to sail "for some time," but that she would drop down the river just a little way in order to continue her outfitting and preparations.

As Jefferson described his meeting with Genêt, whenever he tried obtain Genêt's commitment to fix the departure to the president's return, Genêt "gave the same answer, that she would not be ready for some time, but with the look and gesture, which showed he meant I should understand she would not be gone before that time." Jefferson failed to insist that Genêt direct the vessel not to sail; he failed to carry out the cabinet's policy expressed in the reassurance given to Hammond. Nothing would have been easier for Genêt than to overbear a mild remonstrance by a politically sympathetic Jefferson and take Jefferson's inaction upon being overborne as an assent. Jefferson told Mifflin and Dallas that "though the vessel was to fall somewhere down the river, she would not sail." Mifflin countermanded the orders to arrest the privateer he had given his militia.

At the cabinet meeting on July 8, the day after Jefferson's meeting with Genêt, with Washington and Randolph absent, Jefferson reported the conversation "between the Secretary of State and the Minister Plenipotentiary of France." Hamilton noted that Jefferson "infers with confidence that she will not sail until the President will have an opportunity of considering and determining the case."

Defending Genêt, Jefferson added that Genêt had declared that the additional guns were French property. But Mifflin, to whom Hamilton had talked the night before, had told him that at least two had been purchased by citizens of Philadelphia. Hamilton, with Knox concurring, would not be put off and insisted on a firm stand. They demanded that a battery of guns at once be placed in position on Mud Island, below Philadelphia, to fire on the ship if she should attempt to sneak out to sea. Jefferson strongly disagreed. He insisted that nothing be done to detain the vessel until Washington's return three days later. Dallas, the secretary of the Commonwealth of Pennsylvania, had reported that Genêt had told him *"that he would appeal from the President of the United States to the people."* Hamilton, supported by Knox, argued that Genêt's conduct must be interpreted as part of *"a regular plan to force the United States into the war."* Furthermore, Hamilton said, there was evidence of "a *regular system to endeavour to control the government itself, by creating, if possible, a schism between it and the people,* by enlisting them on the side of France."

Hamilton composed a 13-point written opinion to Washington giving the reasons for his stand. Jefferson forwarded Hamilton's and his own opinions to Washington for review. By the time Washington returned, the cabinet was in an uproar. Factions in the country at large reflected the division in the cabinet. Washington sent a request to Genêt to detain the privateer in port until the legal questions involved could be referred to "persons learned in the laws," which Jefferson transmitted July 12.[1]

Jefferson's dilatory and feeble execution of Washington's instructions had given Genêt all the time *Petit Démocrate* needed. She hauled anchor, hoisted sail, and escaped unscathed to the open sea. She would soon seize at least four British vessels as prizes. Many belabored Genêt for what seemed to be insolent flaunting of American neutrality. Yet nowhere in anything Jefferson said to him could be found anything directing Genêt not to do as had been done. Indeed, Genêt had only done what he had consistently announced to all, including Jefferson, that he intended to do.

When the justices of the United States Supreme Court assembled in Philadelphia July 18, they had before them 29 questions, the first 22 drafted by Hamilton, the last seven by Jefferson and others, all agreed to, concerning the legal problems raised by privateering and related matters under the Proclamation of Neutrality. It was a very deliberate way of trying to deal with ultimate questions like war or peace. What made it still more deliberate was that the justices, who were then in Philadelphia, refused to begin to consider the questions "without the advice and participation of our absent Bretheren." While the country waited on the judges, war fevers rose.[2]

Years later, John Adams recalled the frightening scenes of the summer of 1793, when "ten thousand people in the streets of Philadelphia, day after day, threatened to drag Washington out of his house, and effect a revolution in the government, or compel it to declare war . . . against England." Benjamin Franklin Bache, editor of the Republican Philadelphia *Aurora*, attacked Washington as a modern day Cosimo di' Medici; Freneau compared Washington to the tyrant Sulla and imperial Caesar. John Adams winced under the lash, too, writing Abigail in early 1794, "I have held the office of Libelee General long enough." Adams was convinced that only the yellow fever epidemic of 1793, which had carried off some of the leaders of the mob and driven others out of the capital, "saved the United States from a fatal revolution."

In New York anti-Hamiltonian leaders—James Nicholson, Melancton Smith, Brockholst Livingston and others—held a meeting in The Fields to show their support for Genêt. A Federalist reported to Hamilton that these leaders "will not be stopped by Trifles; they already affirm that the cause of France is the cause of America." Rufus King added that a recent, warlike French decree had caused marine insurance rates to be quadrupled. Robert Troup, Nicholas Cruger, John Jay, King, and others rallied a larger counterdemonstration in New York to show support of Washington's neutrality policy.

Under the pseudonym *Pacificus*, Hamilton had been defending the Proclamation of Neutrality against attacks of the Republicans in the press. His first paper of the series appeared on June 29, 1793, in Fenno's *Gazette of the United States;* and the seventh and last, on July 20. Republican attacks on Federalists like Hamilton had focused on the existing treaties with France. Under them the United States was an ally of France and bound in good faith and gratitude to come to her aid in the war now raging in Europe. But, as Hamilton pointed out, the treaties called for a defensive alliance only, and France had declared offensive war. The United States had no duty to go behind that declaration, he argued, to determine who had been first to injure whom. "Self-preservation is the first duty of a nation," he declared. "Good faith does not require that the United States should put in jeopardy their essential interests, perhaps their very existence, in one of the most unequal contests in which a nation could be engaged, to secure to France—what? Her West India islands and other less important possessions in America?"

Pacificus ridiculed the argument that gratitude for French aid during the Revolution required repayment by aid to her now. "The rule of morality in this respect is not precisely the same between nations as between individuals," he declared. France had aided the United States then not from motives of altruism, but to seek revenge for former defeats at the hands of England. The revolutionary government that now sought to bring America into war "are not ashamed to brand Louis the XVI as a tyrant, Lafayette as a traitor." Such things "ought to teach us not to over-rate *foreign friendships*—to be on our guard against *foreign attachments.*" Here was a muffled echo of his "paroxisms of love" for a "foreign mistress" and the awful consequences that could ensue. They were "hollow and delusive" and "make us the dupes of foreign influence." This "is truly the *Grecian* HORSE to a Republic." It is most dangerous "when it comes under the patronage of our passions, under the auspices of national prejudice and partiality."

Hamilton's *Pacificus* broadsides, white-hot from week to week, roused Jefferson's hot ire. Never effective in direct debate, he called on Madison to respond to mighty *Pacificus*. "Nobody answers him," he wrote urgently to Madison, "& his doctrines will therefore be taken for confessed. For God's sake, my dear Sir, take up your pen, select the most striking heresies and cut him to pieces in the face of the public. There is nobody else who can & will enter the lists with him."

With Jefferson bravely egging Madison on to fight and to "cut him to pieces" and pointing the way to the battle, Madison cringed. He thought "silence better than open denunciation and crimination." He expressed indignation over *Pacificus,* but begged off entering the lists. He replied dryly to Jefferson, "I will feel my own pulse and if nothing appears, may possibly try to supply the omission."

With no one else to carry Jefferson's spear, Madison finally took up his pen under the mask of *Helvidius.* He found the task "the most grating one I have ever experienced . . . One thing that particularly vexes me is that I foreknow from the prolixity & pertinacity of the writer Hamilton, that the business will not be terminated by a single fire, and of course that I must return to the charge in order to prevent a triumph without a victory." As *Helvidius,* Madison branded *Pacificus'* arguments superficial, but there was little fire or conviction in his rebuttal. Genêt's antics had cut much ground from under his pleas for sympathy and gratitude toward France.

At a cabinet meeting on August 1, Hamilton moved to notify France that Genêt must be recalled. Knox added that in the meantime he should be considered suspended from his functions. Jefferson proposed that the matter and

Genêt's abusive correspondence be communicated to France "with friendly observations." Jefferson noted that Washington remained silent while his cabinet heads debated.

Even Jefferson was becoming disenchanted with Genêt, whom he described as "Hotheaded, all imagination, no judgment, passionate, disrespectful and even indecent towards the President." He eventually came to believe, he said, that Genêt's appointment had been "calamitous" and that he would "sink the Republican interest if they do not abandon him."

Hamilton was for disclosing to the public all the Genêt papers—the secret diplomatic record that lay behind the *Petit Démocrate* incident and other events by which the backers of France had succeeded in bringing the public's emotions up to a pitch of excitement that would support a war with Britain. Jefferson insisted that the Genêt papers be kept secret from the people. No wonder tempers were short at the cabinet meeting of August 1.

Hamilton led off with a statement about Genêt's flouting of the law of nations and of French law as well. Too, Genêt had just been elected president of an American democratic political society, the Friends of Liberty and Equality. There was his outrageous declaration that he would appeal from the president to the people.

On August 2, according to Jefferson's notes, the cabinet "met again, Hamilton spoke again ¾ of an hour." Jefferson opposed publishing the Genêt papers and trusting the people, but the president, like Hamilton, was "manifestly inclined to the appeal of the people." At this point, Knox called Washington's attention to a recent broadside, "The Funeral Dirge of George Washington and James Wilson, King and Judge," attributed to Philip Freneau. It described the death by the guillotine and the funeral of the president and of Associate Justice of the Supreme Court James Wilson. Freneau's name was a flash point with Washington; back on May 23, Jefferson had jotted down in his *Anas* that Washington "was evidently sore and warm" because he wanted Jefferson to "interpose in some way with Freneau" by removing him from the State Department payroll. "But I will not do it," Jefferson said. "His paper has saved our constitution, which was galloping fast into monarchy." Now, again, at this August meeting, according to Jefferson's notes, "The President was much inflamed, got into one of those passions when he cannot command himself, ran on much on the personal abuse which had been bestowed on him, defied any man on earth to produce one single act of his since he had been in the govmt which was not done on the purest motives, that he had never repented but once the having slipped the moment of resigning his office, and that was every moment since, that *by god* he had rather be in his grave than in his present situation."

Washington's outburst lost nothing in Jefferson's retelling. He raged on "that he had rather be on his farm than to be made *emperor of the world* and yet that they were charging him with wanting to be a king." He railed at the newspaperman that Jefferson kept on the payroll as a State Department employee: "That that *rascal Freneau* sent him 3 of his papers every day, as if he thought he would become the distributor of his papers, that he could see in this nothing but an impudent design to insult him." In his long note of the outburst, Jefferson scornfully added, "He ended in this high tone." There was a pause. There was "some difficulty in resuming our question—it was however after a little while presented again, & he said there seemed to be no necessity for deciding it now." Hamilton's notes of cabinet meetings discreetly omit all mention of his old comrade and friend's Aetnaen eruptions.

The Supreme Court justices refused to ease matters for Washington and his irreparably cleft cabinet. They refused to give a ruling on the 29 questions on neutrality that Hamilton and Jefferson had submitted to them. Instead, they established an important new constitutional doctrine by holding that the court would refuse all requests to issue advisory opinions.

On August 8, John Jay sent Washington a letter explaining that "the Lines of Separation drawn by the Constitution between the three Departments of government—their being in certain Respects checks on each other—and our being Judges of a Court in the last Resort"—are reasons "against the Propriety of our extrajudicially deciding the questions alluded to; especially as the Power given by the Constitution to the President of calling on the Heads of Departments for opinions, seems to have been purposely as well as expressly limited to the *executive* Departments."

This established the doctrine that the court does not give advisory opinions, only opinions in justiciable controversies. It firmly underscored the constitutional doctrines of separation of powers, checks and balances, and the independence of the executive branch. It followed the letter and spirit of Federalist doctrines laid down by Hamilton in *The Federalist*. Without a specific case before it to decide, as far as the Supreme Court was concerned, all questions of neutrality were moot. In practical effect, Jay's opinion greatly strengthened the power of the executive department.

Hamilton outlined his cabinet charges against Genêt in two memoranda, and Jefferson was forced to draft the letter demanding Genêt's recall. When the cabinet reviewed Jefferson's lengthy draft on August 20, Hamilton had an objection to a passage in it saying that it would be a shame if, through Genêt's tactics, America were drawn into war with France, as that would be "liberty warring on herself." Hamilton argued that this should be stricken because the United States should not affirm that the cause of France was ipso facto the cause of liberty. Hamilton said "that he had at first been with them with all his heart, but that he had long since left them." Jefferson reported that "Knox according to custom jumped plump into all his [Hamilton's] opinions." Jefferson argued that his allusion to French liberty would be an antidote to charges that America "in some of its parts was tainted with a hankering after monarchy." That was no way to win arguments with Hamilton and Washington. Hamilton won. The offending clause was deleted.

Hamilton reacted as sternly to British threats to American neutrality as he did to Genêt's efforts to bring the United States into war on the side of France. It was not until August that word was received in Philadelphia of a British directive of June 8 ordering naval commanders to seize all ships carrying provisions to France or French-occupied ports or ports under British blockade. George Hammond reported Hamilton's angry remonstrances on August 21. "Hamilton regarded it as a very harsh and unprecedented measure" against American exports, commerce, and navigation. The government would make a representation against it through Thomas Pinckney, its minister in London. Hammond had "defended it, as well as I was able, on the ground of expediency," but Hamilton remained unyielding. Hammond concluded: "I however perceived that he was not convinced by my reasoning."[3]

A letter from Angelica Church, the only "foreign attachment" toward which Hamilton would always be unneutral, written by her on August 15 would reach him with a stab of ironic rebuke as he was about to die of the plague and all the other onslaughts of that awful Philadelphia summer:

Are you too happy to think of us? Ah *petit Fripon* you do not believe it: no I am not too happy, can I be so on this side of the Atlantic? Ask your heart and read my answer there.

My silence is caused by despair; for do not years, days and moments pass and still find me separated from those I love!

There was no cure for her anguish either.

"Can a mind engaged by Glory taste of peace and ease?" She must have heard of his plans of resigning. "When will you come and receive the tears of joy and affection?"

Genêt was recalled in disgrace. Jefferson was widely criticized for having supported him. Genêt turned on Jefferson and charged him with having led him on to his downfall. Jefferson submitted his own resignation, to take effect on December 31, 1793. Hamilton stayed on.

Six months after Jefferson's letter demanding Genêt's recall, Genêt still lingered in the United States. When his successor, Jean Antoine Fauchet, arrived, he demanded that Genêt be arrested and sent back to be tried by the new set of Jacobins now in power. Guilty verdicts were keeping the guillotine busy, and the United States declined to ship the former minister plenipotentiary back home for one last ride in the tumbrels in the name of *Liberté, Egalité,* and *Fraternité.* Citizen Genêt became an American citizen; certified his Republicanism by marrying Cornelia Clinton, the daughter of Governor George Clinton; and bought a 325-acre farm near Jamaica, Long Island, with her dowry and his savings, which he named "Cornelia's Farm." He wrote to Cornelia on February 24, 1794, that his sole desire now was to settle in a country where virtue was honored and liberty respected and where a man who obeyed the law had nothing to fear from despots, aristocrats, or ambitious men.

Genêt attributed his own downfall to the "deception" he said had been practiced on him by Thomas Jefferson. He may well have believed he had had Jefferson's tacit approval for the sailing orders he issued to the *Petit Démocrate.* After Genêt's death, his son published a memoir claiming that Jefferson had played a double role, pretending to Genêt that he favored France, while secretly working all the time for an alliance with England.

As 1793 ended, confusion beset Hamilton's enemies. Neutrality tilting away from the French treaties had won. Genêt was in disgrace and blaming Jefferson for duplicity. Jefferson had cried out to Madison to cut *Pacificus* to pieces, but *Helvidius* had only reluctantly and feebly gone through the motions of doing so. Jefferson's impeachment resolutions had been discredited and backfired on their supporters. The follow-up congressional investigation that Hamilton had insisted upon to clear himself (of what he failed to realize was an ineradicable stain) was about to vote to clear him of misconduct in the Treasury. And Jefferson had resigned under a Genêt cloud.

There is no record of frank comments by Hamilton on Jefferson's resignation, but there is little doubt that he would have agreed with every word of John Adams on the subject:

"Jefferson's want of candor, his obstinate prejudices both of aversion and attachment; his real partiality in spite of all his pretensions, and his low notions about many things have so nearly reconciled me to it that I will not weep. . . . Instead of being the ardent pursuer of science that some think him, he is indolent and his soul is poisoned with ambition. . . . He has talents I know, and integrity I believe; but his mind is now poisoned with passion, prejudice, and faction." By his retirement, Adams wrote to his son John Quincy, on January 3, 1794, Jefferson "thinks by this step to get a reputation of an humble, modest, meek man, wholly without ambition or vanity. He may even have deceived himself into this belief . . . Ambition is wonderfully adroit in concealing itself from its owner, I had almost said from itself. . . . But if a prospect opens, the world will see and he will feel that he is as ambitious as Oliver Cromwell though no soldier . . . Numa was called from the forest to be King of Rome. And if Jefferson, after the death or resignation of the President, should be summoned from the familiar society of Egeria, to govern the country forty years in peace, so be it. . . . I am not sorry for his desertion on the whole, because . . . his temper [is] embittered against the constitution as I think."

An affectionate letter from Angelica came to revive for Hamilton something of the old charm that his affair with Maria had dissolved. Surveying the year just past from the pinnacle of these successes, Hamilton had little reason to feel the same "dread" of his enemies that he had expressed only the year before to Jay three days after his confrontation with their "malicious intrigues to stab me in the dark."

Unfortunately, the pinnacle of success and power Hamilton now occupied only a year later, far from lifting his spirits, left them in still greater obsessive dread of his enemies. Hamilton's mental processes confused their political opposition to "his" administration with a conspiracy he saw as a personal threat. He described it in an unpublished fragment of a manuscript found among his papers entitled "On The Rise of a War Party." It was more and more apparent to Hamilton that his enemies "watch to defame and if possible to convulse the government." He wrote: "No important measure can escape their malevolent vigilance . . . they endeavour to seduce the public . . . in paroxysms of their frenzy; they tear aside the veil of their own hypocrisy . . ." They are "incorrigible adversaries of national order." Virtuous men were made "the dupes of perpetual and implacable conspiracy against the general weal."

In such a mood, no score of triumphs over real enemies in the objective world was able to cancel out for Hamilton even a single such nightmarish subjective delusion. He must have written the fragment while suffering from a nervous disorder and, after recovering his senses sufficiently to see the touch of madness in what he had written, put it aside. By December 27 he was well enough to write Angelica a letter to be delivered by his friend James Marshall, the brother of John Marshall, to tell her that his health had "suffered a severe shock by an attack of the malignant disease lately prevalent here," but was now "almost" completely restored. "The last vestige of it has been a nervous derangement; but this has nearly yielded to Regimen, a certain degree of exercise and a resolution to overcome it." Writing her, he was enjoying, for a while at least, a period of remission from morbid "dread" of "malicious intrigues to stab me in the dark." Not recommended by alienists for total dependence as a permanent cure for a "nervous derangement" is what was probably most important in Hamilton's "almost" complete restoration: "a resolution to overcome it."

14

SENDING JOHN JAY
ON HIS WAY

ALAS MY BELOVED JOHNNY—WHAT SHALL I HEAR OF YOU! THE
QUESTION MAKES MY HEART SINK. ADIEU.
　　　　　—*To Elizabeth Hamilton, July 31, 1794*

"In this sublunary scene, I am just where I do not wish to be," Hamilton groaned to Angelica Church. "How long dear sister are the best friends to be separated?" he asked, after confiding to her the secret of his nervous derangement. "I know how I could be much happier," he sighed. "I will break the spell. Nothing can prevent it at the opening of the spring, but the existence or the certainty of a war."

Nicholas Cruger's brash, irrepressible bookkeeper, whose earliest letter to friend Neddy Stevens had cockily crowed, "I wish there was a war," had grown up to be a statesman saddled with too many responsibilities. To the nation's treasurer, a war would now be "an event which I most sincerely deprecate but which reciprocal perverseness, in a degree, endangers." Worst of all, a war just now would keep him from the early spring rendezvous with Angelica in London that he was promising her and planning to fit into his political future.

Nearly, but not quite recovered, he told her that in his makeup "a certain elasticity of constitution and temper reacts with a degree of vigour at least proportioned to the pressure." To one who loved him as well as Angelica, this was glum reassurance indeed. It made her still glummer that he found it necessary also to add, as if still in doubt, "I hope it will be so still."

The day before writing Angelica in this "sublunary" mode on December 27, 1793, Hamilton had written an even more alarming letter about his own and Betsy's health to Philip Schuyler. It has not been found, but it so badly worried Schuyler that on January 5, 1794, he wrote back to Hamilton that "I fear much from the incessant application which you are under the necessity to give to the business of your department." Schuyler had earlier been averse to Hamilton's resignation, but now had changed his mind. "The danger which your health is exposed to" reconciled him to it.

Schuyler would also be troubled by, but take sympathetic note of, another onset of Hamilton's terrible obsession with enemies: "The chagrin you experience from the weakness or wickedness of those you have to contend with."

Like the kindly, old Dutch patroon father-in-law he was, Schuyler extended sympathy the best way he knew how to a sick and troubled political man by restating in his own upstate vernacular Edmund Burke's conservative credo: "I hope the real friends to liberty and good order will not suffer themselves to be entraped by the wily arts of those who wish for confusion that they may fish in troubled waters, and yet I have much apprehension as the honest and well meaning are seldom very seldom sufficiently on their guards." Though this came too late to put Hamilton on guard against Maria Reynolds, much sympathy was in order for a 37-year-old son-in-law with a "nervous derangement" but nothing with which to cure it but a "regimen," "exercise," and "a resolution to overcome it." Knowledge of effective "regimens" and therapeutic "exercise" was primitive, indeed practically nonexistent, among the alienists of the day.

As a one-woman cultural exchange program during 1793 and 1794, Angelica Church would be sending on to America with letters of introduction to Alexander and Betsy Hamilton all sorts of distinguished French refugees from the turmoil and terror in Paris, including the statesman Charles Maurice de Talleyrand-Périgord, and the jurist Bon-Albert Briois, the Chevalier de Beaumetz, as well as the British scientist and philosopher Joseph Priestley, who, like Hamilton, had been made an honorary citizen of revolutionary France. Priestley sought refuge in America more from the terror of poverty than politics. He was part owner of a real estate development group that owned something like 300,000 acres on the Susquehanna River about 150 miles west of Philadelphia "where they project a considerable settlement."

Angelica recommended that all such friends of hers who had fled "anarchy and cruelty" in their own countries see the "image of your domestic happiness and virtues for all that they have suffered in the cause of moderate liberty." Having followed up her introductions, Talleyrand and Beaumetz would "write in raptures to all their friends of your kindness, and Colonel Hamilton's abilities and manners," as she told Betsy on July 30, 1794. "I receive innumerable compliments on his and your account—dear Alexander the amiable." When Hamilton's children had been with the Schuylers while the plague was raging, and during Hamilton's nervous derangement afterward, her grandfather had loved to call the Hamiltons' eldest daughter "My Angelica," which was what Hamilton loved to call Schuyler's eldest daughter, too.

His clashes in the cabinet with Jefferson over the French treaty did nothing to keep Hamilton from writing his own Angelica in November that he "was very glad to learn, my dear daughter, that you were going to begin the study of the French language." Public battling to keep America from becoming "entraped" by "wily arts" in the French treaty in no way affected Hamilton's love of French friends, French culture, and the French language.

More fluent in French than any other American governmental leader, he spoke the language with an Antillean lilt that rang quaintly but not unattractively in ears bred to the accents of Paris and Touraine. When visiting grandparents for extended periods, Hamilton solemnly reminded his daughter, "we hope you will in every respect behave in such a manner as will secure to you the good-will and regard of all those with whom you are . . . If you displease any of them, be always ready to make a frank apology. But the best way is to act with so much politeness, good manners, and circumspection, as never to have occasion to make any apology." She should be conspicuous by being inconspicuous.

Avoiding "entrapment" with France in toils of the French treaty and the blandishments of Genêt was but the first and easiest part of preserving American neutrality. The more difficult part was avoiding war with Britain over issues that had little to do with the French treaty or even with the war that France had declared on Britain now raging around the globe. Dangerous issues that festered included the fortified British posts on the Anglo-American frontier, British influence over the Indians and the fur trade, British interference with American commerce, and British impressment of American seamen.

The Constitution had given body to American nationality. But as Samuel Flagg Bemis sums up the matter on the first page of his authoritative treatise, *Jay's Treaty*, "The administrative genius of Alexander Hamilton endowed the body with life and kept it functioning. Without commerce life would have been impossible, because the revenue which vitalized the nation came from the imposts." Some of the revenue came from interior excises, like the tax on whiskey, which would soon plunge Hamilton into trying to put down an insurrection, but, as Bemis notes, "Most of the commerce in those years was with Great Britain. Therefore the life of the new nation depended on the tranquility of Anglo-American relations."

Seven of the eight British fortified positions were on the American side of the frontier. They served as the "military guaranty of civilized nations" over the immense domain claimed but not settled by America that stretched into the heart of the continent all the way to the Lake of the Woods in northern Minnesota at the headwaters of the Mississippi River. Roaming this vast expanse were French habitants and priests; Canadian fur traders; British soldiers; and warlike Indian tribes, allied with the British and increasingly dependent on the lucrative fur trade. Unfortunately, there were few American settlers to bolster and ratify America's far-ranging claims.

Article II of the peace treaty of 1783 ending the Revolution had provided for the evacuation of American soil by British troops with "all convenient speed." But soon after, as the strategic importance of the posts for the protection of Canada, for the increasingly profitable fur trade, and for the profitable trade with the Indians became more obvious to Britain, "there was a settled policy to refuse delivery of the posts, notwithstanding the terms of the treaty." The fur trade at the time was the most profitable single industry in America, producing about £ 200,000 revenue annually.

To protect this rich trade, British and Canadian authorities naturally backed the Indian tribes against the occasional American military expeditions and attempts to establish permanent settlements in the Mohawk and Ohio River valleys. These expeditions often erupted in bloody frontier warfare and massacres. When various separate American states passed jingoistic laws putting obstacles in the way of collection of British debts guaranteed by the peace treaty and took to harassing former loyalists and Tories, it gave the British all the justification they needed for refusing to comply with the treaty obligations on their side to evacuate the posts. They would continue to hold them firmly until finally forced out when Jay's Treaty became effective in 1796.

As Hamilton was acutely aware, all but two of the British forts were in the upper reaches of New York State or on its Canadian border. Those at Oswego, Oswegatchie, Niagara, and Fort Erie controlled all navigation down the St. Lawrence River, Lake Ontario, and the eastern end of Lake Erie. To the west, Detroit and Michilimackinac, at the north end of the Michigan peninsula, controlled all waterborne commerce moving toward upper New York State from Lakes Michigan, Superior, and Huron. Dutchman's Point and Pointe-au-Fer secured the northern outlet of Lake Champlain and the old military corridor from Montreal to Albany. From these posts, small British garrisons not only held sway over the increasingly profitable commerce of the interior of the continent, but also attracted dangerous and divisive commercial and political affiliations of all inhabitants, including new American settlers. Hamilton had acknowledged the kind of geopolitical reality involved when he helped Vermont become a separate state in 1791, independent of New York, in order to prevent its falling under the eagerly proferred umbrella of British Canada.

Only a dozen years had passed since Indians supported by British raiders had terrorized the Schuyler house in Albany, nearly causing Hamilton's Betsy, pregnant with their firstborn son, Philip, to miscarry him. Burgoyne's men had burned Schuyler's farmhouse at Old Saratoga to the ground. Hamilton's state had suffered more than any other—more than a third of all the battles and raids and skirmishes of the Revolution—and for more than seven years during the whole war the British had occupied and ravaged his hometown. Many thousands of Hamilton's fellow citizens had died of scurvy and plagues and other unnatural causes in British prisons there, and in the dank, sinister holds of the prison ships in New York harbor. It is not surprising that British presence in these frontier posts troubled Hamilton more than other members of the cabinet. To some of them, it might seem'of more importance to avoid having to pay old prewar debts owing to British creditors or to obtain reparations from the British for slaves lost to freedom.

Until Jay's Treaty went into operation in 1796, no commercial treaty existed between the United States and Great Britain. This left all commerce legally subject only to the vagaries of the municipal law of each country, including British wartime orders-in-council, which were directed primarily toward protecting British interests in the war France had declared on Britain. To Britain, foreign commerce, then as always, was a matter of life or death; and for Britain, America was the single most important and profitable trading partner. To the United States, trade with Britain was even more vital than it was to Britain. It constituted more than 75 percent of all foreign commerce of the United States; over 50 percent of American trade was carried in British ships. British navigation, trade, and commercial laws were intended to protect British manufacturers and commerce and preserve British national sea power and freedom of the seas; nothing in them was for the benefit of any foreign nation, certainly not the former colonies with which Britain had fought such a long, bitter, costly, and losing war.

No American understood such economic, political, and emotional realities better than Hamilton. None forged national policies more carefully designed and calculated to take them into account. Hamilton's domestic political opponents of the period—those whom he characterized in his black moods as his "enemies" —seemed to him to speak often from smug, but naïve domestic isolation unschooled by contact with realities of worldwide power politics.

After it became known that Genêt had turned against Jefferson, Hamilton's old friend Robert Troup wrote Rufus King on January 1, 1794: "What a pleasant thing it is to see Jefferson, Randolph and Genêt by the ears. All has ended well." But nothing significant had ended for Hamilton except the immediate threat of Jefferson's impeachment resolutions to Hamilton's guidance of national policy. War between Britain and revolutionary France would continue to convulse Europe and all colonial lands and commerce-carrying seas across the world. No American commerce was safe from seizure at sea, no matter what flag the ship carrying it might fly. Divided at home against themselves, Americans seemed to be stumbling heedlessly toward war with Great Britain.

France was no threat for the moment, but to meet affronts from Britain required armed external power, especially a naval force, and the nation did not have one. Embattled in mortal struggle for its own survival, Britain had no sympathy with neutral rights claimed by former colonies. By a series of orders-in-council, the British had forbidden all American trade with the French West Indies. They seized hundreds of American ships and cargoes that disobeyed those orders. Jefferson, as secretary of state, had protested these apparent breaches of American neutrality, but the British claimed legal justification, pointing to the United States' guarantee of the French West Indies contained in Article II of the 1778 treaty of alliance between the United States and France. By British reasoning, the United States was not a neutral. Therefore, American vessels and cargoes were not entitled to the immunities of neutrals. A principal reason Hamilton had labored so diligently to avoid re-recognition of the French treaty was to cut the ground from under just such later, after the fact British justifications for refusing to grant American commerce the same immunities granted to true neutrals.

For domestic consumption, as *Pacificus III*, published in the *Gazette of the United States* on July 6, 1793, Hamilton had denounced the American commitment to the French West Indies and explained that the United States should not be bound by it: "Our guarantee does not respect France herself. It does not relate to her own immediate defence or preservation. It relates merely to the defence & Preservation of her American colonies; objects of which (though of considerable importance) she might be deprived and yet remain a great and powerful and a happy nation."

Pacificus warned domestic readers that "we are wholly destitute of naval force. France, with all the great maritime Powers united against her, is unable to supply this deficiency." He scouted the frontiers and flanks and found the United States dangerously vulnerable:

> With the possessions of Great Britain and Spain on both Flanks, the numerous Indian Tribes, under the influence and direction of those Powers, along our whole Interior frontier, with a long extended sea coast—with no maritime force of our own, and with the maritime force of all Europe against us, with no fortifications whatever and with a population not exceeding four Millions—it is impossible to imagine a more unequal contest, than that in which we should be involved in the case supposed; a contest from which, we are dissuaded by the most cogent motives of self preservation, as well as of Interest.

America's denunciation of the guarantee would not be a breach of the laws of nations, said *Pacificus*. "We may learn from Vattel" that "if a State which has promised succours finds itself unable to furnish them, its very inability is its exemption; and if the furnishing the succours would expose it to an evident danger this also is a lawful dispensation."

Keeping open informal channels of communication with British ministers George Beckwith and later George Hammond made it possible for Hamilton to explain away official American actions that on their face seemed hostile toward Britain in terms of American domestic politics or personalities in ways that made them seem less hostile. He also received valuable, unofficial feedback on British reaction to American actions. Although these conversations sometimes tended to undercut official stances on each side that were intended as bluff or bluster, they also made possible timely transmission of the real, often secret views of each side toward the other. The early warning lightning rod and shock absorber effect of Hamilton's secret diplomacy tended to minimize the greatest risk—that one side or the other would leap into hasty or misguided action or fail to take action, owing to a misreading of the other's bluff for true intentions or true intentions for bluff. As the weaker and more vulnerable party to the arrangement, with no military or naval strength to repel demands or back up bluffs, the advantages to the United States outweighed the disadvantages.

American protests against British seizures and other discriminations against American commerce like Hamilton's August 1793 protest to Hammond of the order-in-council of June 8 seemed to do no good. The seizures continued. Tench Coxe, Hamilton's assistant at the Treasury, helped Jefferson prepare a long report on foreign interferences with American trade by supplying him with statistics, reasoning, and suggestions that Jefferson incorporated in his report. On December 19, 1793, two weeks before finally resigning from office, Jefferson submitted this report to Congress, emphasizing that British depredations against American commerce were much more extensive than French depredations. Jefferson held that any British reprisals that might be brought on by American discrimination were as "nothing when weighted against the loss of wealth and loss of force, which will follow our perseverance in the plan of indiscrimination."

This was a strongly pro-French tilt. Any secretary of state was foolish to say that British reprisals would, in effect, be "nothing."

On January 3, 1794, Madison followed up Jefferson's report by reintroducing in the House his resolutions of 1791, which called for retaliation against Britain by a levy of additional duties on all imports and shipping coming from countries, like Britain, with whom the United States had no commercial treaty. Madison also called for extra tonnage duties on British vessels trading between the West Indies and the United States, trade from which American ships were excluded by the British Navigation Acts.[1]

News of unprecedented new seizures of American ships by the British in the Caribbean under a new and harsher order-in-council of November 6, 1793, gave impetus to Madison's resolutions. Even neutral ships plying routes to the French colonies would be seized; it did not matter now whether the French treaty was operative or not. Hamilton joined other angry Federalists in denouncing the British order-in-council, calling it "atrocious." In March 1794 a rumor swept the Senate that the duke of York had been captured by the French and carried in a cage to Paris and that the British fleet had surrendered to the French. This greatly cheered the French faction. A British fleet sailed into the Caribbean and swept up more than 250 American ships as prizes, half of which were condemned in British Admiralty Courts. Francophiles in the United States demanded immediate war on Britain on the side of France. On March 8 Hamilton sent Washington a well-considered plan for "vigourous though prudent" measures to meet the new British threat. "We ought to be in a respectable military posture, because war may come upon us, whether we choose it or not," he said. The increasing severity of the British orders in council tended in a warlike direction. France's declaration of war and the French treaty would provide Britain all the pretext necessary for new outrages. "To be in a position to defend ourselves and annoy any who may attack us will be the best method of securing our peace," Hamilton advised. Then "there will be much less temptation to attack us and much more hesitation to provoke us."

Furthermore, Hamilton counseled, "the Legislature ought to vest the President . . . with a power to lay an embargo partial or general and to arrest the exportation of commodities partially or generally." An embargo would be painful to American commercial interests, particularly Hamilton's staunch friends and supporters in New York and Boston, but it would also be somewhat painful to a Britain at war. Modest as its effect on Britain might be compared with its momentous adverse effects at home, an embargo was the only really effective weapon in the whole American arsenal for waging big power politics. To Hamilton it also deserved consideration "whether the Executive ought to take measures to form some concert of the neutral powers, who also suffered from British seizures under the new order in council, for common defense."

Hamilton's measures were carefully defensive, but Madison's resolutions were offensively hostile. Such official actions would provide new grounds for a British declaration of war or still more devastating orders-in-council just short of a declaration of war.

But Republicans pressed for immediate adoption of Madison's resolutions. Hamilton's followers maneuvered for delay and sought to allay the popular frenzy. Hamilton's friend William Loughton Smith of South Carolina rose in the House to oppose Madison's resolutions with a powerful speech, whose arguments soon became famous.[1] They were the same ones Hamilton had used in his *Pacificus* and *Americanus* papers of January and February 1794, urging neutrality. Madison's resolutions, he charged, were "a covert design to embark the United States in the war" on the side of France.[2]

In the course of House debates that rumbled on until May, Uriah Tracy of Connecticut made the sage comment that Madison's resolutions went too far and not far enough. For commercial purposes they were too costly for America, and for political purposes they were too little to hurt Britain significantly.[3] Republicans knew that Hamilton had written William Loughton Smith's speech for him to deliver. Jefferson, from retirement at Monticello, wrote Madison: "I am at no loss to ascribe Smith's speech to its true father. Every tittle of it is Hamilton's except the introduction. . . . The very turn of the arguments is the same, and others will see as well as myself that the style is Hamilton's. The sophistry is too fine, too ingenious, even to have been comprehended by Smith, much less devised by him." Jefferson's "Scourge" Smith, according to Jefferson, was literally Hamilton's puppet. Jefferson's letter reproached the House for letting itself be overborne by proxy by a member of the executive department. The lash of Jefferson's scorn was not lost on Madison.

Congress was full of hot headed proposals: 80,000 militia in readiness to march, a Continental Army to be raised, Coast Artillerists to be emplaced at the ports. Jonathan Dayton urged sequestration of all debts due from Americans to British citizens.

It was perfectly clear to John Adams that the seemingly unaccountable frenzy of Francophiles in America was based on their desire to avoid paying British debts. To him, this was the "real object of all the wild projects and mad motions which have been made during the whole session," he wrote Abigail, adding with a sneer, "Oh, Liberty! Oh, my country! Oh, debt and oh, sirs! These debtors are the persons who are continually declaiming against the corruption of Congress. Impudence! they front in brass." Abigail knew exactly what he was railing about. She replied on May 10, 1794, "If the Southern States force us into a war I hope their Negroes will fight our battles and pay these real and haughty aristocrats all the service due to them from the real and true Republicans."

Following Hamilton's advice, Washington declared a 30-day embargo on all vessels bound for British ports. Congress ratified it on March 26. Britain's limited war against America was escalating. The American embargo was extended another 30 days to May 25.

Hamilton left George Hammond in no doubt of the seriousness with which he and the country at large regarded escalating British seizures of American vessels. On April 14 and 15, 1794, Hammond wrote back to Lord Grenville that Hamilton, who had hitherto been "uniformly the most moderate of the American Ministers," now reflected the dangerous popular ferment and anger against Britain.

To Hamilton, Hammond put the best face he could on British seizures by saying, in effect, that in war neutrals ought to expect a few inconveniences. But Hamilton "did not receive these explanations with the cordiality I expected." Instead, he staged a private diplomatic blowup: "Mr. Hamilton interrupted me with some degree of heat." Not only did he enter into a "pretty copious recital of the injuries which the commerce of their country had suffered from British cruizers," he suggested that British outrages might soon have domestic political repercussions in Britain.

According to Hammond, Mr. Hamilton remarked "that however the government and people of Great Britain might be united against France, he doubted not that when the wrongs which the American Commerce had suffered were known in Great Britain, a very powerful party might be raised in that nation" in favor of the United States. Here was a thrust or threat of an appeal by Hamilton to the British people over the heads of the British government. The threat would not be lost on any minister of an elected government, any more than Genêt's had been lost on Washington.

The same day of this explosive conference with Hammond, Hamilton wrote Washington to suggest cooling the tension by sending a special envoy to Britain, while at the same time preparing defenses for war. The envoy "should be a person, who will have the confidence of those who think peace still within our reach." The idea of appointing such an envoy was not a new one with Hamilton. More than a month earlier, on March 10, a coterie of influential Federalists had met in the rooms of Rufus King, senior senator from New York, to see what they could do to rescue the country from the disastrous war that they feared was coming. They were the best minds of Hamilton's party: King, George Cabot and Caleb Strong of Massachusetts, and Oliver Ellsworth of Connecticut. All agreed that Ellsworth should go to the president, propose that the country be put speedily in a state of defense, and, more important, that a special envoy be dispatched to England to adjust all matters of dispute.

Ellsworth was also instructed to tell Washington that "unless a person possessing Talents of the first order, enjoying the Confidence of the friends of

Peace, and of the Government, and whose character was unexceptionable in England was selected, it would be fruitless to make such an appointment." Who was such a man? Colonel Hamilton was such a man, they all agreed. Hamilton was not present at the meeting, but he would not be displeased with the name of the man his friends had unanimously come up with. Apart from all the reasons his friends could urge on Washington better than he could himself, he longed to see Angelica and find himself an honorable way out of the day-to-day calumnies and pressures of the Treasury. There was a world of difference between a resignation under fire and the public credit that would accrue to a resignation to accept a mission to save the peace.

Ellsworth reported back on March 12 that the president had been "at first reserved," but finally much impressed. However, he was doubtful that Hamilton would be a proper envoy, because although Washington was sure of him, he "did not possess the general confidence of the country." The same group approached Robert Morris, and he promised to do all he could do to push Hamilton's appointment forward. The country still drifted closer to war with England, and Republicans, at least as Federalists saw it, continued to press policies that seemed designed to bring it still closer.

Washington sent for Robert Morris on April 8. By this time, Washington himself was convinced of the necessity of sending an envoy. The only question was, who? Washington had thought of John Adams, Hamilton, Jay, or Jefferson as possibilities. Morris objected to either Adams or Jefferson and expressed a decided preference for Hamilton. Four days later, when Jay arrived in Philadelphia to hold circuit court, he met with King, who informed him of what his group had done. They had picked either Hamilton or him for the post, though acknowledging that they would prefer Hamilton because of his cabinet experience and knowledge of commerce. Jay agreed "in the propriety of Hamilton's appointment."

Meanwhile, the news leaked out that the name of an envoy was being considered and that Hamilton would very likely be given the mission. Federalists were delighted. "Who but Hamilton would perfectly satisfy all our wishes?" demanded Fisher Ames. "He is *ipse agmen*." Republicans were as far from being thrilled as Angelica Church and Ames would be thrilled with the thought of Hamilton in London. Monroe wrote a hasty hatchet man's protest to Washington that "I should deem such a measure not only injurious to the publick interest, but," he added menacingly, "also especially so to your own." That last he said he would gladly explain to Washington in private. It would be all he needed to say about the confrontations of December 15, 1792, even though his triumvirate had not released the charging letter he had prepared for it to send on to Washington.

Furious at the impropriety of a senator's advance interference in an executive appointment of this kind, Washington referred Monroe's letter to Edmund Randolph; who waffled. Randolph said, "It is that he has considered and made up his mind, as to the kind of interference, which a senator ought to make in a nomination beforehand: that upon this idea, the President will be ready to afford an interview at a given time."

With Hamilton still apparently at the top of his list for the appointment, Washington wrote Monroe on April 9, "If you are possessed of any facts or information, which would disqualify Col. Hamilton for the mission to which you refer, . . . you would be so obliging as to communicate them to me in writing." Washington had no intention of setting Hamilton's name aside upon the senator's presumptuous remonstrance, he said. "No one (if the measure should be adopted) is yet absolutely decided on in my mind; but as much will depend, among other things, upon the abilities of the person sent—and his knowledge of the affairs of this Country—and as I *alone* am responsible for a proper nomination, it certainly behooves me to name such an one as in my judgement combines the requisites for a mission so peculiarly interesting to the peace & happiness of this country."

Jefferson joined the anti-Hamilton campaign with snide vigor: He wrote Monroe: ". . . I learn by your letters & mr Madison; that a special mission to England is meditated, & H. the missionary . . . besides the object of placing the aristocracy of this country under the patronage of that government," Jefferson suspected that it "has in view that of withdrawing H. from the disgrace & the public execrations which sooner or later must fall on the man who partly by creating fictitious debt, partly by volunteering in the payment of the debts of others, . . . has alienated for ever all our ordinary & easy resources, & will oblige us hereafter to extraordinary ones for every little contingency out of the common line." Hamilton had also, Jefferson said, "brought the P. forward with manifestations that the business of the treasury had got beyond the limits of his comprehension."

Randolph, who had been appointed secretary of state after Jefferson's resignation, discussed with the new French minister, Jean Antoine Fauchet, with whom he was becoming intimate, possible ways to kill Hamilton's appointment. Madison also worked to scuttle it.

By April 14, Hamilton could see that desperately as he had hoped for the appointment, it would be difficult for Washington, divisive for the country, and probably a political impossibility. The country at the moment needed all the unity Washington and Hamilton could find for it. He advised Washington "with decision" to "drop me from the consideration and fix upon another." He knew of Washington's "byass" in his favor, but he was also "well aware of all the collateral obstacles which exist." Such "collateral obstacles" included, of course, what his enemies knew or suspected about the night of December 15 and the nervous derangement of the following year. "Of the persons whom you would deem free from any constitutional objections," Hamilton went on, "Mr. Jay is the only man in whose qualifications for success there would be a thorough confidence . . . I think the business would have the best chance possible in his hands."

The Federalist caucus this time, including Hamilton, went to Jay and urged him to accept as "the only man in whom we could confide." He agreed, and on April 16 Washington sent on his name to the Senate. Madison exulted that Hamilton, whom he had feared more than any one else, had been finally "laid aside, & Jay named in his place." But Jay's appointment was almost as bitterly opposed as Hamilton's would have been. Monroe and Aaron Burr led Republicans opposition to him on grounds of his being pro-British.

On April 18, the Senate approved Jay by a bare party-line, two-thirds vote of 18 to 8. If nothing else, Jay's mission won the country a few months' more respite from war. Francophiles were furious. "You cannot imagine what horror some persons are in, lest peace should continue," John Adams wrote Abigail in December 1794, but also ruefully letting slip the threat to his own preeminence. Jay's mission, he said, "will recommend him to the choice of the people for President as soon as a vacancy shall happen."

Three days later, Hamilton, Ellsworth, King, and Cabot sat down with Jay and gave him some instructions to follow in carrying out his new mission. Twelve years older than Hamilton, John Jay seemed to have a character so fine and qualifications so perfect for every high office that everyone marveled at his lack of personal influence. But no one could have had better qualifications for the mission Hamilton had created for himself than Hamilton himself. Active early as a patriot in the colonies, in the first and second Continental Congresses Jay had drawn up important appeals to the people of Great Britain, Canada, Jamaica, and Ireland, as well as the resolutions that authorized the New York delegation to sign the Declaration of Independence. He chaired the committee that drafted the New York State constitution, served as first chief justice of the state, returned to the Continental Congress, and became its president. Sent to Spain in 1789 to seek an alliance similar to the French treaty—to guarantee Florida to Spain in case of Britain's defeat and to reserve to the United States free navigation of the Mississippi—he was still negotiating firmly when Cornwallis surrendered at Yorktown. Commissioned in 1781 along with Franklin, John Adams, Jefferson, and Henry Laurens to negotiate the peace treaty with Great Britain, Jay, for reasons that proved to be well founded, suspected French good faith, and persuaded his fellow negotiators to treat independently with Great Britain for a treaty more favorable to the United States than Congress had dared to expect, so good it had been a rude shock to the courts of France and Spain. On his return to New York in July of 1784, he was awarded the freedom of the city. A delegate to the Continental Congress, he later resigned his seat to become secretary for foreign affairs under the Articles of Confederation. As *Publius*, he had written numbers two, three, four, five, and 64 of *The Federalist*, dealing primarily with foreign affairs. Under the new Constitution, he would serve as first chief justice from September 1789 to June 1795. In the most famous case to come before him, *Chisholm v. Georgia*, it was his opinion for the court that permitted a citizen of another state to sue the state of Georgia. Georgia had no "sovereign immunity," he held, because in the United States sovereignty rested not in the states, but in the people alone.

His wide experience in diplomacy, stern rectitude, unchallenged probity, and status as chief justice, which he retained, clothed his mission to Britain with the greatest possible prestige, authority, and significance. At Washington's request on April 23, Hamilton submitted a set of instructions for Jay's mission that were specific, concise, and precise. Little scope was left to Jay's "discretion." He should obtain: (1) indemnification for depredations on American commerce according to a rule to be settled by resort to the law of nations, (2) future guarantees of freedom from seizure of all cargoes except articles that were specifically contraband of war, and (3) prompt compliance by the British with the terms of the peace treaty of 1783 for indemnity for the slaves who had been carried away and surrender of the frontier forts still held, in return for which the United States would pay damages for obstructions the states had put in the way of the recovery of British debts, not exceeding a total to be specified in the treaty.

These points looked to settling all past differences that had arisen under the old treaty of peace. But there were many points of dispute, particularly in the seizure of ships and cargoes in West Indies trade that could in no way be resolved in the context of merely sorting out problems arising under the old treaty. The presence in the West Indies of island colonies of France, Britain, Holland, Spain, and Denmark and fortified bases like those at English Harbour on Antigua, Brimstone Hill on St. Kitts, and Fort-de-France on Martinique, as well as significant black independence movements like those in Saint-Domingue, made commercial regulations complex even in peacetime. Now the rich Antilles bristled with battle fleets, privateers, revolutionaries, and pirates. Therefore, to Hamilton, a commercial treaty "on the basis of the *statu quo* for a short term (say five Years)" might "be advisable as an expedient for preserving peace between the two countries."

In such a treaty, for a limited practical purpose and term, the United States would receive certain trading privileges with the West Indies, England, and Ireland. In return, the United States would offer a most-favored-nation clause on imports from England. Hamilton allowed room for modification of these demands, but he laid down two inflexible rules: (1) no treaty was to be entered into that would affect unfavorably the existing treaty with France, and (2) American ships must be granted unrestricted entry into the West Indies.

Hamilton's instructions were limited to the main points of dispute, concrete and specific. By contrast, Secretary of State Edmund Randolph's instructions to Jay were more than five times as long and a hodgepodge of detailed exhortations left entirely within Jay's "discretion." Jay was to present expressions of "general irritation" with "vexations, spoliations," and so on. In content, they were nothing but a grab bag of complaints to be "strenuously pressed."

Randolph's instructions seemed purposefully written more to exacerbate the breach with Britain than to heal it. They contained inept, rather silly, and to Britain, potentially offensive exhortations to Jay that, for example, while in London, he should sound out the local ministers of Russia, Denmark, and Sweden about an alliance with their countries, as if they could act usefully in such a delicate matter. At the same time, he should ask Britain, as well as Russia, Sweden, and Denmark, to intercede for American captive seamen with the dey of Algiers. Such distractions gave little evidence that Randolph was in any way acquainted with usual diplomatic procedure in such matters.

It would have been impossible for any diplomat to comply with such a farrago. No matter what the outcome of the negotiations might be, each topic head of Randolph's grab bag would suggest a sector of attack on Jay for any critic whose hindsight was unconnected to his foresight. Randolph, like Hamilton, also gave suggestions for a commercial treaty, listing more objects, but not indicating minimum terms. He did not expect that Jay would effect any treaty "with so great a latitude of advantages."

Hamilton had shrewdly calculated in advance the relative bargaining power of the two countries. He sent Jay his insights along with a copy of his suggested instructions on May 6: "This country in a commercial sense is more important to G Britain than any other." American imports "are certainly precious . . . perhaps essential to the ordinary subsistence of her islands . . . as a consumer we stand unrivalled. We now consume of a million to a million and a half sterling more in value than any other foreign country." Furthermore, whereas consumption by other countries was stationary, "that of this country is increasing and for a long long series of years will increase rapidly."

Hamilton's economic forecast would remain pretty good for more than a century and a half. Hamilton called Jay's attention to the point that the opinion prevailed that a treaty of commerce ought not to be concluded without further instructions. But Hamilton urged him to "push the British Ministry in this respect to a result that the extent of their views may be ascertained."

For better or worse, judging by the result, Jay followed Hamilton's instructions. The younger man was his political ally, and Jay often, but not always, sought Hamilton's advice. It is ridiculous to believe the charges made later and throughout American history that Jay was no match for his British counterparts in firmness and shrewdness negotiating what later came to be called, often pejoratively, Jay's Treaty. Probably no man in the United States at the time could have negotiated a better treaty in the circumstances except Hamilton himself.

Sending Jay on his way to the mission for which he had urged him on Washington in place of himself, Hamilton suddenly, indeed, rather surprisingly, surveyed the world scene from a new pinnacle of power in "my" administration. With Jefferson out of office, Hamilton now dominated the much weaker Randolph, who usually opposed him at first, but often would yield in the end. William Bradford, the new attorney general, was a congenial friend. Knox in the War Department was always his faithful follower. Washington listened with profound respect to Hamilton's advice and usually followed its broad thrust if sometimes differing in detail. Hammond, the British minister, treated almost wholly with Hamilton, exhibiting an insulting disregard for the nominal secretary of state. The French minister, Fauchet, was only a little less confiding. Federalist leaders were devoted followers. Hamilton's unpopularity with Republicans was the natural tribute that reverses they frequently suffered at his hands would pay to the successes of the elder statesman of the ruling party, still only 37 years old. Washington had stiffly discountenanced James Monroe's attempts to whisper firsthand reports of secret scandal into his ear. The select committee of the House had unanimously cleared him of all impeachable offenses.

To insure the success of Jay's mission and all it meant toward securing the removal of the British from the frontiers and his commercial system from the vicissitudes of foreign war, Hamilton would have to remain in office instead of going through with his resignation, now that he had been cleared by the House. On May 27, reminding Washington of his plan of a year earlier to resign, Hamilton noted that recent events "render the prospect of a continuation of our peace in a considerable degree precarious." He was "reluctantly obliged to defer the offer of the resignation."

Hamilton still feared that whispers that might have come to Washington's ear or Washington's concern about his fever or nervous derangement undercut his support. Washington's impersonal confirmation of Hamilton's authority in dealing with the two foreign loans, but withholding a strong personal endorsement still rankled.

The inner Hamilton still pleaded for some such endorsement: "If any circumstances should have taken place" since his resignation announcement, he wrote Washington, "or should otherwise exist which serve to render my continuance in office in any degree inconvenient or ineligible . . . I should yield to them."

Hamilton felt that even a "momentary stay" in office by him was opposed by "the strongest personal and family reasons and could only be produced by a sense of duty or Reputation." Washington responded that he was pleased to have the secretary remain "until the clouds over our affairs, which have come on so fast of late, shall be dispersed." It had taken a year and a half, but Hamilton had finally extracted from Washington this one line of affirmation he had to have to "leave him with the impression his suspicions had been removed."

Hamilton had opposed the passage in Randolph's final instructions to Jay that he sound out the ministers of Denmark, Sweden, and Russia with a view to joining the United States in an Alliance. He had written Randolph on July 8 that "Denmark and Sweden are too weak and too remote to render a cooperation useful; and the entanglement of a treaty with them might be found very inconvenient." Such "entanglement" foreshadowed a famous passage he would write into Washington's *Farewell Address*.

Professor Bemis claims that Jay and Hamilton failed to understand the depth of British fears of such an unwieldy, but offensive alliance. Jay submitted a draft of a proposed treaty to Lord Grenville that contained, for the record at least, many of the maximum demands suggested by Randolph's instructions, but Grenville rejected its terms. Nonetheless, Jay wrote privately to Hamilton that "appearances continue to be singularly favourable, but appearances merit only a certain degree of circumspect reliance . . . I will endeavour to accommodate rather than dispute; and if this plan should fail, decent and firm representations must conclude the business of my mission." He had just dined with Lord Grenville as the only foreigner present, and next Monday he was to dine with the lord chancellor, the first Baron Loughborough; on Friday he was dining with Prime Minister William Pitt himself.

Jay told Hamilton that these "favorable appearances" should best "remain unmentioned for the present and they make no part of my communications to Mr. Randolph or others." His old friend Hamilton would understand his businesslike reasons: "They may be misinterpreted, tho' not by you."

Of a visit Jay and his handsome and formidable wife, Sarah had with Angelica and John Church, Jay wrote that "we are much indebted to their civilities and friendly attentions." Hamilton's lonely heart must have skipped a beat or two as he thought of Angelica, reading between Jay's prosy lines that were as personal as Jay ever managed to be: "She looks as well as when you saw her, and thinks as much about America and her friends in it as ever. She is certainly an amiable, agreeable woman. Remember me to Mrs. Hamilton."

Of armed neutrality proposals and treaties involving Sweden, Denmark, and Russia, Hamilton told Hammond in private, "with great seriousness and with every demonstration of sincerity . . . that in the present conjuncture it was the settled policy of this government in every contingency, even in that of an open contest with Great Britain, to avoid entangling itself with European connexions." Such alliances, as the troublesome one with France demonstrated, might "commit it in a common cause with allies, from whom in the moment of danger it would derive no succour."

This was consistent with what Hamilton had always said on the subject of treaties, publicly in pamphlets, and particularly in relation to the French treaty. It was also consistent with American policy as officially proclaimed. No doubt, confirmation of it now was welcome to Hammond, but it was not classified information. Hamilton's opponents and Jeffersonian historians, commenting on Hamilton's conversations with Hammond about the proposed treaty with Denmark and the like while Jay was negotiating in London, have described Hamilton as "standing behind Jay . . . holding a mirror, however unconsciously, which reflected the American negotiator's cards to the enlightenment of the suave and smiling Grenville."

Given all the uncertainties of the time, including the unreliability of transatlantic communications, it may indeed have been a mistake for Hamilton to have talked at all with Hammond while Jay was negotiating in London. In Hamilton's defense it may be said that the card of Jay he is supposed to have given away was a ludicrously weak one, face up in full view of all players, and anyway Jay had been given no Senate authority to play it. Whether Jay had or had not been given authority, it was obvious to any astute observer of the American political scene like Grenville or Hammond without a word from Hamilton that the 18 to 8 Federalist majority in the Senate that had ratified Jay's mission would strike down any such farfetched entangling alliance if the objections Hamilton had voiced to Washington meant anything to other Federalists at all.

What Hamilton was doing for Jay was ostentatiously throwing a weak card, at minimal cost to any significant American interest, but avoiding admission of real American weakness by preventing Jay from leading from such weakness. At the same time, Hamilton was establishing invincible credibility with Hammond and Grenville at considerable domestic political risk to himself to win the big hand: getting the British out of the forts on the frontiers with no credible American military strength to fight them out. Whatever else came of his mission, if Jay could succeed in this, it would have saved America many regiments, warships, casualties, and millions of dollars.

On November 19, 1794, after five months of intense give-and-take, Jay signed a treaty, which won the two points his instructions had indicated as minimum terms, but not much more. Britain committed itself to evacuate the forts still held by June 1, 1796. The Mississippi would be "entirely open to both parties." Britain yielded permission for vessels of 70 tons or less to enter the West Indies, with the counterproviso that American vessels were to be prohibited from exportation of molasses, sugar, coffee, cocoa, and cotton, the assumption being that those would have originated in the West Indies. British vessels were to be allowed unlimited trade between the islands and the United States. The United States agreed to pay for British vessels seized by Genêt's privateersmen. The United States would pay private debts of Americans to British subjects in cases where payment had been prevented by legal obstructions interposed by the states after the Revolution.

Britain was to pay for all American ships seized "under color" of right. Commissioners were to be appointed to establish the boundary line between Maine and New Brunswick and in the upper Mississippi Valley and Lake of the Woods areas. Jay had dutifully demanded indemnity for slaves lost, by Southerners mostly, during the Revolution. Jay, like Hamilton, had pressed Americans to free their slaves and probably did not press the British, who had freed them, very hard for payment to American slave owners whose slaves had probably not resisted much being "carried away." Far from perfect, the treaty nonetheless helped to protect and enhance the free status of former slaves. It also went far to safeguard the small farmers, fur traders and trappers, artisans and settlers, pioneers and new frontiersmen who had sought to make new lives by moving west near the New York, Ohio, Michigan, Minnesota, and Mississippi frontiers. It tended to ease the threats to such people posed by the British, the Indians, the French, and Spain.

It did less for merchants, shipping interests, and traders, but its wide-ranging commercial provisions did provide some security within delineated limits of risk for them. Surprising provisions opening up to Americans trade with the British East Indies would in years to come offer unexpected but inspiriting rewards to clipper ships and risk-taking enterprise. The treaty did nothing for former slave owners whose chattels had fled to freedom.

It boldly advanced the interests of most of the people of America, at the cost of some money claims by the wealthy. It provided an accurate reflection of Hamilton's basic political concerns for the poor, the enterprising, and the unprotected and his unconcern for the interests of slave owners. It also assured the Federalists some peace without dishonor in their time for Hamilton's system to revive public credit and prove itself.

A few days after signing it, Jay wrote to Hamilton, "My task is done; whether *finis coronat opus*, the president, senate and public will decide . . . If the treaty fails, I despair of another." What Hamilton's emotions may have been as he read its confidential text is unknown. For the benefit of the public, he put upon it the best political face he knew how. As in the battle for ratification of the Constitution, his basic argument was "better than nothing." Jay's Treaty finally liquidated the Revolutionary War a dozen years after the close of hostilities. Gaining possession of the military posts on the frontiers and fixing the disputed western boundaries opened the way to westward territorial expansion and the new frontier. Some of the differences that had divided the people were subdued, though others were heightened. The way was cleared for a period of economic and political consolidation of nationhood.

Jay's Treaty would govern American foreign policy far into the future until the eras of World Wars I and II. By the time Jefferson and his Republican party came to power in 1801, their earlier radical policies had become sufficiently tempered so that in important respects, notably in the purchase of the Louisiana territory, they perpetuated Hamilton's and Jay's westward-looking domestic and foreign policies. Jay's Treaty was peculiarly Hamilton's brain child. He had proposed it to Washington as a practical measure to avert war with Britain and preserve the chief source of American public revenue, import duties. He helped to choose Jay and draw up Jay's instructions. At every stage he was President Washington's principal adviser concerning it.

With Jay off negotiating in London and Betsy pregnant again, she was off to Albany with the two youngest boys, James Alexander, age six, and ailing John Church, two. Hamilton remained in Philadelphia to look after the three oldest, Philip, now 12; Angelica, ten; and Alexander, eight. After seeing Betsy as far as New York City and then returning to Philadelphia, he wrote her on July 31,

"The precious little ones we left behind are well."

"I shall expect with infinite anxiety a letter from you and heaven grant that it may bring me good tidings of the health of yourself and the dear children with you." He sent them off with a dual purpose valediction that would serve for both his Johnnies: "Alas my beloved Johnny—what shall I hear of you! The question makes my heart sink. Adieu."

Among other health problems that John Jay's treaty would soon add to Hamilton's lengthening list was an insurrection of the interior and a bloody bruise on the temple caused by being stoned by a Wall Street mob.

15

THE WHISKEY INSURRECTION

YOU MUST NOT TAKE MY BEING HERE FOR PROOF THAT I CONTINUE
A QUIXOT.
   —*To Angelica Church, from 205 miles westward of
   Philadelphia, October 23, 1794*

The illness of Hamilton's "beloved Johnny," Betsy's indisposition during a difficult pregnancy before leaving for Albany, and perhaps also some other unmentioned afflictions of his own had caused Hamilton to miss some recent cabinet meetings. The family's troubles brought a warm and solicitous letter from George Washington, expressing his sorrow and wishing "you to carry [Johnny] into the country for a few days" for exercise and a change of air.

School was out. It was vacation time. Betsy, Johnny, and James Alexander were off at Old Saratoga. Congress adjourned and scattered to the far reaches of the country. Chief Justice John Jay was negotiating in London, President Washington sojourned at Mount Vernon, Vice-president John Adams relaxed at Quincy, Secretary of State Edmund Randolph took his ease at Carter Hall in Virginia, Secretary of War Henry Knox packed up to leave for Boston and a tour of his property interests in Maine, and Thomas Jefferson was retired at Monticello. All that remained of the government of the United States at the capital were the office staffs and Secretary of the Treasury Hamilton. But even with no one but Hamilton in town, no sense of slack was felt in the reins of the government. Hamilton was sending daughter Angelica and son Alexander out to the country to stay with Mary Morris, the wife of Robert Morris, who had asked for them. So had Susan Bradford, wife of his friend William Bradford, the new attorney general. There they would be beyond the immediate reach of the usual summer plague. With no one left at home in town but his eldest and favorite son, Philip, Hamilton could look forward to a quiet, restful August, free at last of the clandestine visits and harrowing blackmail threats of the summers of 1791 and 1792 and of the fevers and nervous derangement of 1793. But bright prospects of a summer of domestic tranquillity were never more falsely beguiling.

Within a few days came news of insurrection in the four western counties of Pennsylvania and adjacent parts of western Virginia. They had erupted into the most dangerous threat yet to the unfolding progress of "his" administration. Back of the uprising he would see the hand of his enemies.[1]

At a meeting held July 23, 1794, at the Mingo Creek Meeting House in Washington County, Pennsylvania, "consisting generally of the most respectable people of that County," it had been proposed that the people of the area work together and stand by each other until the excise tax law was repealed and an act of oblivion passed. But this lawful proposal, which envisaged working through the established structure of the constitutional government, had been voted down at the meeting. Instead, the Mingo Creek Meeting House Convention had proposed an extra legal rump caucus. The four western counties of Pennsylvania and the neighboring counties of Virginia were summoned "to assemble by delegates in a Convention to be holden on the fourteenth of [August] in Mingo Creek at Parkinson's Ferry." The summons to the mid-August convention, like Hamilton's call from Annapolis that had summoned the Framers to Philadelphia, was not limited in its objects to dealing with specific grievances against the tax on whiskey or commerce and trade. It was broader, more defiant, and threatening. It proposed to "take into consideration the situation of the Western Counties and adopt such measures as should appear suited to the exigency." The rebels had appropriated one of Hamilton's own favorite words—*exigency*—to rouse up a broad-based rebellion against all established federal authority.

A reliable reporter, Colonel Francis Mentges, of the Pennsylvania militia, who had just returned from the rebellious areas, gave Hamilton a firsthand account of the situation, and Hamilton took down his testimony in a sworn statement. Mentges testified that "it is entirely impracticable to execute the laws aforesaid by means of civil process and judiciary proceeding." There were civil disorder, defiance of national laws, and implied threats of disunion and secession on the frontiers where the borders shaded off into the conflicting and often encroaching claims of Britain, Spain, and the Indian tribes. Jay in London was doing his utmost to remove the British from the frontier forts and all that their stand on American soil meant in terms of divisive threats to the nation. To Hamilton only open war could have seemed a more serious threat or come at a worse time than what came to be called, in a misleadingly derisory phrase, the Whiskey Insurrection.

The force of the rebellion fell directly upon the revenue collectors of his department who had local responsibility for collecting the excise tax. Mentges reported that on July 17 armed men had "made repeated attacks upon the house of General John Neville, Inspector of the Revenue, for and on account of his holding and exercising the said office and to oblige him to relinquish the same." The United States marshal for the district, David Lenox, who had tried to serve process to collect the tax on whiskey and stills, had been seized by the mob. Isaac Craig described the attack in a letter to Henry Knox of July 18, 1794, written the day after 700 armed men had assembled and attacked Neville's house, with only Neville and Major Kirkpatrick and ten soldiers defending it. "During the attack General Neville seeing it impossible, to defend the House, against such numbers, took an opportunity of escaping and concealing himself in a thicket. Major Kirkpatrick continued to defend the house, till one of his men was Killed and four wounded having killed two and wounded several of the Insurgents."

General Neville, emerging from the thicket where he had hidden, rallied David Lenox, Isaac Craig, and two others. They led an attack to try to break through the besieging armed mob to bring ammunition to Major Kirkpatrick and raise the siege, but their rescue attempt failed. They were seized, made prisoners, disarmed, and confined. The brave Major Kirkpatrick surrendered. According to Craig, "The enemy set fire to the house, which is consumed to ashes with all the property it contained, not a single article saved."

The enemy seized Lenox, Neville, and the other law enforcement officials and carried them several miles to their secret rendezvous. They "treated Major Lenox with the utmost indignity, and all of us with insult in the night, I was happy enough to make my escape, and to find General Nevill & to Escort him to my House, where he now is. . . ." According to Mentges, Lenox and Neville later "descended the Ohio in a boat to avoid personal violence or the being compelled by force to enter into engagements or do acts contrary to the duties of their respective offices." Craig called the insurrectionists "the enemy." It was as much a matter for the attention of the secretary of war as for the Treasury.

At mass meetings Republican orators churned up the passions of whiskey producers and consumers alike. Liberty poles—reminiscent of the Revolution and of the world war between Britain and France raging around the globe— appeared on courthouse lawns and meetinghouse squares, flying flags with such inscriptions as: "An equal tax, and no excise" and "United we stand, divided we fall." Some bore the significant device of the Union as a writhing snake cut up into separate sections, which ranged in number from two to 13. Mass meetings broke out into riots. Rioting spread south into western Virginia and South Carolina. Other United States marshals and revenue collectors were terrorized and forced to flee for their lives. The United States mails were intercepted, seized, and trashed.

News of these disorders were anything but disheartening to British Minister George Hammond, who cheerfully reported them to his chief, Lord Grenville, on August 3: "The avowed pretext for these discontents is a dislike of the excise law, but the real origin of them is unquestionably a rooted aversion to the federal constitution, and to all the measures emanating from it." Hammond was briskly optimistic. The outlook was dark for the former colonies, he said, "in this emergency which is certainly the most serious and alarming that has yet arisen, since the establishment of the constitution." He made it clear that the British Foreign Office should not be misled by anything John Jay might say into thinking that he was negotiating his treaty from strength.

Unrest on the frontiers provoked by the excise tax on whiskey and failures by federal officers to collect it and enforce the tax laws had a long history, one that Hamilton knew as well as anyone else in the government. Such violence was painfully reminiscent of the scattered outbreaks of violence in the colonies during the years before the Boston Tea Party.

The Whiskey Insurrection came to be so called because the specific grievance that had given rise to the general defiance of all federal law was the federal government's excise tax on whiskey. The tax had originally been imposed by Congress at Hamilton's urging in order to help fund—pay for—Hamilton's hard-won program for federal assumption of state debts. General discontents had a way of coming to a focus in violent protests against excise taxes.[2] That the immediate provocation for general defiance of established government was the tax on whiskey was no more reason to make light of the matter than the fact that a tax on tea could be said to be the immediate provocation of the Revolution. The British might have had more success putting it down if they had thought to label it lightly the "tea rebellion." The parallels in the two situations probably hit Hamilton harder in his present unhealthy mood than the differences.

There was no mistaking the early signs of rebellion. Like the intoxicating personality of Citizen Genêt, whiskey was a stimulus to high Republican spirits. Their orators did little to discourage attacks on Treasury officials, on the courts, and the U.S. mails. For frontiersmen on the western fringes—western Pennsylvania, Virginia, and North and South Carolina—whiskey was, of course, a common article of consumption. But what was not consumed was also the best available medium of exchange, better than money. The ranges of the Alleghenies were a formidable barrier to easy traffic with the seaboard. It cost too much to transport grain over the mountains, but grain distilled into whiskey found a ready market in the East. It brought western distillers cash with which to purchase manufactured goods from the East. To the farmer-distillers of the western frontiers, the tax on whiskey—payable in hard earned cash—seemed an intolerable burden. Eastern plantation owners like Jefferson grew their own grapes from slave-tended vines or drank mostly vintages imported from abroad, on which they paid import duties. It cost them nothing extra to proffer political sympathy to the rebels in the West, won them great political credit, and served their main purpose of discrediting the secretary of the treasury.

Furthermore, the states had always claimed internal revenue for themselves. Fear of federal encroachment on their tax base had been one of the most effective arguments state supremacists had raised against the Constitution. For Hamilton, the very existence of the tax on whiskey was proof positive that the national government had the right and power to impose internal taxes within a state. As though Hamilton had deliberately sought to force the issue, the tax on whiskey was the most hated of all possible taxes that could have been imposed on those who had to pay it.

Hamilton's pressure for the tax to cover the huge national debt incurred by assumption had forced Congress reluctantly by the act of March 3, 1791, to tax domestic spirits on a sliding scale ranging from nine to 25 cents a gallon. This had stirred up wrath in the West then. Mass meetings were held. Congress was deluged by petitions and memorials. Even then, mobs had chased away tax collectors who had to flee empty-handed for their lives. Tax rates were reduced. Very little money trickled in.

Now, on August 5, 1794, Hamilton reminded Washington of these threats of violence and mass meetings in opposition to the tax of three years earlier. Then, too, the rebellion had not been limited to specific taxpayer complaints. Then meetings at Red Stone Old Fort and elsewhere in Washington County had declared that every federal officer who attempted to carry out the law "should be considered as inimical to the interests of the country." They had proclaimed that every citizen should treat federal officers "with contempt, and absolutely refuse all kind of communication . . . and withhold from them all aid, support or comfort."

Rebellious rumblings from the West like these in 1791 had prevented federal officers from collecting the taxes. In 1794, Hamilton reminded Washington of one 1791 incident when "a party of men armed and disguised waylaid" an unfortunate tax collector at Pigeon Creek and "seized, tarred and feathered him, cut off his hair," and stole his horse, "obliging him to travel on foot a considerable distance in that mortifying and painful situation." When charges against the armed men came to court and the men were ordered to be brought to justice, the deputy sent to serve process on them was also stripped, tarred, and feathered. No process was served. The rebels had successfully defied the process of the federal courts.

Collections of import duties under the Tariff Act of 1790 were not sufficient to fund the state debts assumed by Hamilton's program. There was not much objection to import duties, but internal taxation of whiskey by the federal government was something else. No wonder Hamilton and his system were controversial; the wonder is that they were politically possible at all. The tax on whiskey fell directly on a not very numerous group of self-sufficient frontiersmen; it hardly touched the rich landed gentry. In terms of higher costs of whiskey, it probably fell hardest on small farmers, merchants, and artificers, the people among whom Hamilton found most of his support. Hamilton would also pick up some scattered approval from all who deplored strong drink on moral grounds. But frontiersmen found no solace in the self-administered tax shelter that remained available to them by simply imbibing their own distillations instead of selling them. Human resentment of a tax never rises to quite as high a level as the human happiness that arises from avoidance of the tax by use of a tax shelter.

In 1792 Congress had turned to the executive branch and asked for its recommendations on what to do. While James Reynolds's blackmailing letters were raining on him thick and fast, Hamilton had taken the political onus off Congress by submitting to it on March 6, 1792, his long "Report on the Difficulties in the Execution of the Act Laying Duties on Distilled Spirits." In it he noted that four main objections to the excise taxes had been made: their "supposed tendency" (1) "to contravene the principles of liberty," (2) "to injure morals," (3) "to oppress by heavy and excessive penalties" and (4) "to injure industry and to interfere with the business of distilling."

Hamilton's report discussed all such objections with minute particularity. He disposed of one principal objection in two sentences that exposed its speciousness: "The argument, that they are obliged to convert their grain into spirits" to transport it to distant markets, "does not prove the point alleged. The duty on all they send to those markets will be paid by the purchasers. They will still pay only upon their own consumption." As a general rule, he observed, "duties on articles of consumption are paid by consumers."

The right to levy internal taxes was as essential to any government, he argued, as the generally conceded right to levy taxes on foreign imports. There was nothing in the one that restricted the liberty of a country to levy the other. The national government must have an adequate income. The purchaser of domestic products should pay his share just as the purchaser of foreign articles was required to do. Small farmer and frontiersman and merchant and Eastern landowner, all alike should shoulder the burden of taxes.

Hamilton was sympathetic to complaints of imperfect justice in any tax structure, but firmly realistic on the subject of equality of bearing tax burdens. As to equality, "It may safely be affirmed to be impracticable to devise a tax which shall operate with exact equality upon every part of the community. Local and other circumstances will inevitably create disparities more or less great."

In his report, Hamilton had proposed a number of amendments to improve the law, including an increase in the compensation of collectors. It passed Congress and became law on May 8, 1792. But the success of another of his important reports with Congress did not end his problems in the western counties. A reading of Hamilton's report, particularly his constructive suggestions for ameliorating grievances, tends to confirm his judgment that objections to the tax on whiskey were largely a cover or focal point for general rebellion against all federal authority.

On July 30, 1792, while urging Washington to stand once again for the presidency, Hamilton had called his attention to the fact that "nonexecution of the law in certain scenes begins to produce discontent in neighboring ones, in which a perfect acquiescence had taken place." This was a natural and obvious result of failure to enforce the law vigorously and "implies a danger of a serious nature." On August 5, 1792, Washington had agreed that if opposition in western counties continued and peaceable procedures proved ineffectual, "the public interest and my duty will make it necessary to enforce the laws . . . however disagreeable this would be to me, it must nevertheless take place."

Hamilton replied to Washington on August 10 that "it affords me much satisfaction to observe that your mind has anticipated the decision to enforce the law, in case a refractory spirit should continue to render the ordinary & more desirable means ineffectual. My most deliberate reflections have led me to conclude, that the time for acting with decision is at hand. . . ."

Just at this time, mounting demands of James Reynolds for larger blackmail payments, of Maria for more frequent intercourse and longer visits as their affair approached its climax and breaking off, and of George Washington for Hamilton's response to the indictment contained in Jefferson's "Twenty-one Objections Respecting the Administration of the Government," left Hamilton with little patience to spare for Western rebels.

On September 1, Hamilton sent Washington a full report of the Western insurgency and spoke of the "persevering and violent opposition to the law" that "seems to call for vigorous & decisive measures." He had already taken some. He had ordered a survey and report made of the rebellious districts; he had asked the attorney general for an opinion whether indictable offenses had been committed and whether legal redress was possible in the courts. To Washington, he added that "it is indispensable, if competent evidence can be obtained, to exert the full force of the law against the offenders." After all, peaceful steps had proved ineffective and "if the processes of the courts are resisted," but only then, it would be necessary "to employ those means which in the last resort are put in the power of the executive." "If this is not done," Hamilton added, "the spirit of disobedience will naturally extend, and the authority of the government will be prostrated." It is important to note that Hamilton was specifically urging resort to prosecutions in the courts, not military action, when he added, "Moderation enough has been shewn; 'tis time to assume a different tone."

The old surveyor was in full agreement with his secretary of the treasury. "Forbearance," he wrote Hamilton on September 7, "under a hope that the inhabitants of that Survey would recover from the delirium & folly into which they are plunged, seems to have had no other effect than to increase the disorder." He gave Hamilton express authority to institute court proceedings if the opinion received from the attorney general should warrant it. Hamilton drafted a proclamation for Washington to issue, warning the public against interfering with the collectors and proclaiming that "the laws will be strictly enforced against the offenders."

Attorney General Edmund Randolph and Secretary of War Henry Knox had agreed with him that the proclamation should issue and with most of its provisions. Nothing in Hamilton's recommendation or the proclamation as issued went beyond an exhortation to the people to comply with the laws. There was no threat to go beyond prosecutions in the courts for violators or to call out military force for the enforcement of the laws. The draft was sent off to Monticello for Secretary of State Jefferson to sign. He did so. It was returned to the capital and was published there on September 25, 1792. For two years past it had served to damp down the Western rebels.

But now in 1794, Western defiance of the excise tax had erupted anew. Losses of import duties owing to French and British seizures of American ships and cargoes were cutting off the government's most important source of revenue. If America were ever going to be able to muster regular troops and a naval force and build harbor fortifications to assume even the most limited posture of credible defense against British and French depredations, secure internal tax revenue was more desperately needed than ever.

Hamilton patiently listened to complaints and made administrative changes.

He had been urged to raise the duty on capacity of stills higher so that distillers would want to keep accurate accounts and pay at lower rates by volume instead of capacity, but some poor Western distillers were too illiterate to keep the necessary records. For them he left the rate as it was. He rejected more severe measures to collect the tax from itinerant distillers, who would otherwise evade it. The noisy objections of the Westerners obscured the fact that Eastern distillers were subject to and peaceably paid the same tax.

Levi Lincoln of Worcester, Massachusetts, even offered praise of the excise, claiming that it was "much approved of . . . will be very popular," and Melancton Smith, who had once fought Hamilton so effectively against ratification of the Constitution now made light of the threat to states' rights and of those who claimed that the excise "will subvert the rights of free citizens of America." To the charge that the Pennsylvania excise was subversive of liberty, Fenno observed that it "has . . . lasted so long, that most of the people [objecting] were born in slavery." Hamilton pointed out that distillers in other parts of the country had paid more than a million dollars in tax, which the Western counties had completely evaded. Hamilton had already told Washington of his wish to resign office, but he felt he could not honorably do so while one-sixtieth of the country was able to defy successfully all the rest of the nation as well as his own Treasury Department.

Now in the western counties it was the responsible local officials, not just poor moonshiners or a disorderly rabble, who were summoning up a new independence movement against the five-year-old constitutional union under the cover of local objections to a tax that was part of the funding system, the keystone of Hamilton's entire fiscal system. Hamilton condemned those who defied national authority and collection of national revenue as Shaysites. Here was the kind of internal defiance that the Constitution had to put down or be put down by, or it would wither into impotence as the Articles of Confederation had done.

This long, troubled history of defiance of federal law in the western counties and the long history of Hamilton's patience and moderation in devising measures to cope with it meant that there was a deep base under George Washington's ire when he called upon Edmund Randolph in August 1794 to advise him without delay of "all the means vested in the President for suppressing the progress of the mischief."

Why not simply call out the regular army to put down the rebellion? Hamilton knew this was impossible both as a practical and as a political matter. When it had ventured north from the protection of its base at Fort Washington (Cincinnati) into Indian country under General Josiah Harmar in 1790, the U.S. Army —what little there was of it—had suffered a bloody defeat at Fort Jefferson before skulking back to safety; in 1791 a reorganized army under Arthur St. Clair had been all but wiped out by the Miami Indians when it dared approach their villages on the Maumee River in present northeastern Indiana. Now, in the summer of 1794, after three years of further reorganizing, under General Anthony Wayne, the army had just moved out on yet another armed—but apprehensive—sortie into Indian country. In the vast Northwest Territory it claimed, the United States had never yet established an effective presence or control to protect settlers and establish the national government's authority. The British and their Indian allies still held sway throughout most of it from their forts at Detroit and Michilimackinac, on the Maumee, and from similar garrisons elsewhere. No help was to be expected from the little army.

On August 2, 1794, Washington called Randolph, Hamilton, Henry Knox, William Bradford, and the leading officials of Pennsylvania—Thomas Mifflin, the governor; Thomas McKean, the chief justice; Jared Ingersoll, the attorney general; and Alexander J. Dallas, the secretary of the Commonwealth—to an emergency conference on the insurrection.

The minutes of the "conference concerning the Insurrection in Western Pennsylvania" from the Pennsylvania archives show Washington's angry determination to act with force, even without the army, with Hamilton's full support. Washington declared to all present that "the circumstances . . . were such as to strike at the root of all law & order; that he was clearly of opinion that the most spirited & firm measures were necessary to rescue the State as well as the general government from the impending danger, for if such proceedings were tolerated there was an end to our Constitution & laws." He called attention to, and demanded that Randolph read aloud, the letters from General Neville describing the two days of attacks on his house, the deposition of Francis Mentges, and the deposition of the postrider whose U.S. mail had been intercepted and stolen.

Washington vowed "to go every length that the Constitution and Laws would permit, but no further." He called for cooperation of the Pennsylvania state government and enquired whether the governor could not adopt some preliminary measures under the state laws, "as the measures of the General Government would be slow, and depended on the certificate of Judge Wilson."

Here Washington was referring to the fact that Randolph had referred Washington's earlier demand to be informed of the legal basis for federal action to Justice James Wilson of the Supreme Court for his opinion, but this had not yet been handed down. At the August 2 conference, Randolph turned to Secretary of the Commonwealth Dallas and asked whether the governor had the power to call out the militia on such occasions. Dallas was a staunch Republican, but he wavered only a little. He thought some military measures might be taken: "independent of the law referred to, or any other special law, the executive Magistrate was charged with the care of seeing the laws faithfully executed."

When Washington said he intended to proceed against the rioters in Allegheny County, the chief justice of Pennsylvania, Thomas McKean, emphatically disagreed. It was McKean's "positive opinion, that the judiciary power was equal to the task of quelling and punishing the riots, and that the employment of a military force, at this period, would be as bad as anything that the Rioters had done—equally unconstitutional and illegal."

Now came Hamilton's turn to speak. No one was surprised at his ultimate opinion, but the force of his reasoning, the weight of his citation of authority, and his familiarity with the long history of the problem brought so forcefully to bear on the issue must have impressed all doubters, including Chief Justice McKean, with its reach and power.

He began "by argument upon the general necessity of maintaining the Government in its regular authority," noting a number of other recent examples of serious local opposition to the Constitution and laws of the United States and citing the "Judiciary, excise, Mississippi navigation, erecting a new State, etc., etc." By opposition to "the Judiciary," Hamilton was referring to John Jay's decision in *Chisholm v. Georgia*, in which he struck down Georgia legislation declaring that the state would not be bound by the decision of the Supreme Court. By opposition to the "excise," Hamilton was, of course, referring to his own five-year history of coping with opposition to the tax on distilled spirits in the western counties. By "Mississippi navigation," Hamilton meant the objections of citizens of Kentucky, embodied in the secessionist-leaning Kentucky Resolutions of May 24, 1794, to the government's negotiations with Spain for free navigation of the Mississippi River. And by "erecting a new State," Hamilton meant the efforts of Major General Elijah Clark and his followers to erect a new state on Georgia lands in defiance of action by the United States, which had reserved the same lands for the Creek Indians.

Finding in these striking recent examples of defiance of federal authority a trend toward national disunity, disintegration, and separatism only seven years after the Union had been forged at the cost of heroic effort, Hamilton insisted that an immediate show of military force would be proper. It would not be enough if the rioting were merely quieted down. That would not be enough to restore the country to the state in which it had been only a few weeks earlier. Previously, defiance of the laws of the United States had not been expressed in the same formal, explicit manner as in the Mingo Creek resolutions. They had flung down the gage. The Government must show it could maintain itself. The exertion must be made not only to quell the rioters, but to protect the officers of the Union in executing their offices, to compel obedience to the laws, and to show George Hammond and John Jay in London that the Union was not about to dissolve.

The Pennsylvanians at the meeting disagreed with Hamilton's argument. Dallas stated that Judge Addison, the presiding judge of the County Court of the Western District of Pennsylvania, had declared it as his opinion that the business should be left to the courts, the rioters prosecuted and punished there, and the matter peaceably terminated. A resort to military force would unite both the peaceable as well as the riotous opponents of the excise in resistance.

Hamilton retorted sharply that "Judge Addison was among those who had most promoted the opposition in an insidious manner." He added that "it would lead to a disagreeable animadversion to point out the particulars of the Judge's conduct; but that they were stated at large in a report to the President, which the President said was the case." The report of the meeting abruptly ends, "Here the minutes of the conference suddenly terminate"—probably with all conferees stalking away in hot anger.

Hamilton sent a formal opinion to Washington that amplified the argument he had made at the conference on the insurrection. He called for immediate and vigorous measures. The states where the disturbances were centered had failed to quell the insurrection locally. Let the national government act. Issue a call for 12,000 militia, 9,000 foot, and 3,000 horse. They should rendezvous in Pennsylvania and Virginia on September 10. Hamilton, not alone, but joined by the other cabinet members, advised Washington to invoke a federal statute under which the president was empowered to call up the militia if he were "notified" by a member of the Supreme Court that military force was needed to enforce federal law or suppress disorder. Three days later, Hamilton followed this up with another and even more urgent report and drafted a new proclamation for the president to issue, calling on the insurgents to disperse.

On August 4, 1794, pursuant to the federal statute, Justice James Wilson of the Supreme Court submitted his opinion to the president that, in the counties of Washington and Allegheny, "laws of the United States are opposed, and the Execution thereof obstructed by Combinations too powerful to be suppressed by the Ordinary Course of judicial proceedings, or by the Powers vested in the Marshal of that District." Now judicial opinion conferred the highest legal sanction on the action Washington had proposed and Hamilton seconded. Without awaiting further action by Pennsylvania, action bound to be politically distasteful for local elected officials, the federal government had all the authority it needed to step in.

On August 7, Washington issued a stern proclamation following Hamilton's outline calling out the state's militia under federal colors. It warned "all persons, being insurgents . . . on or before the 1st day of September next, to disperse and retire peaceably to their respective abodes. And I do moreover warn all persons whomsoever, against aiding, abetting, or comforting the perpetrators of the aforesaid treasonable acts. . . ."

5,000 insurgents rose in defiance of Washington's proclamation and staged a riotous demonstration on Braddock's Field near Pittsburgh. Hugh Brackenridge wrote Tench Coxe on August 8, 1794, that "the United States cannot effect the operation of the law in this country. It is universally odious in the neighboring parts of all the neighboring states, and the militia under the law in the hands of the President cannot be called out to reduce an opposition. . . ." Brackenridge added that "the first measure . . . will be the Organization of a New Government" comprehending the western counties. To Hamilton's assistant at the Treasury, he sent the further threat that "should an attempt be made to suppress these people, I am afraid the question will not be, whether you will march to Pittsburgh, but whether they will march to Philadelphia?"

Hugh Brackenridge was the most prominent of all rebel leaders in the area. A member of the state assembly in 1786–1787; a founder of Pittsburgh's first newspaper, its first academy, and its first bookstore; and a lawyer and playwright as well, his warning to Tench Coxe could not be dismissed by Hamilton and Washington as but the perfervid product of a literary man's imagination.[3]

Secretary of War Henry Knox chose August 8, the day after Washington's proclamation summoning up the militia and the beginning of the rioting on Braddock's Field, to ask permission for a leave of absence as secretary of war to go up to Maine for a look at real estate interests there. Otherwise, Knox said, he was faced with "permanent pecuniary ruin or something very like it." Responsibility for administration of the War Department, as well as the Treasury, would have to be turned over to Hamilton, at least until Knox's return to Philadelphia.

The opposition commented that this was just as well; Hamilton was now doing openly what he had been doing secretly for a long time behind the stout figurehead of Henry Knox: administering the War Department. Hamilton's critics who tax him with overplaying his military role in the crisis ignore the fact that it was not Hamilton's militaristic aggressiveness, but Knox's real estate speculations in Maine that fobbed off the War Department's duties on Hamilton at the climax of the crisis.

From the War Department on August 12 word came to Hamilton that the mob of insurgents on Braddock's Field had continued to run riot and demonstrate there, swelling in numbers, for an entire week. They were threatening to assault Fort Fayette at Pittsburgh, seize Colonel Thomas Butler and his garrison there, and burn the whole fort down.

The house burnings, seizures, woundings, and killings of federal officers reliably reported by Neville, Mentges, and others, egged on by local newspapermen and community leaders like Hugh Brackenridge; formal actions like the Mingo Creek resolutions to form a new government; and threats to Fort Fayette, the last remaining outpost of federal authority in the area, meant that at least one-sixtieth of the nation had accomplished a de facto secession from the Constitutional union. Contemporary academics who are inclined to ridicule Washington's and Hamilton's resort to military measures, after three years of patience and under judicial authority, as overreaction might consider what the response of a contemporary American president to formal and warlike secession on such a scale might be. It would probably include (without judicial authority) calling out the FBI, the CIA, the National Guard, the regular army and air force, and armed helicopter gunships laying down barrages of tear gas, merely as a starter, to deafening popular applause, without a peep of criticism from a single college president.

On the same August 12 that Hamilton received such alarming news from the West, more alarming news came in from the North. From Albany, Eliza had written that their beloved Johnny was still ailing. Pregnant Eliza's own health remained in a precarious state. Johnny had lost strength and "was not so well as he had been."

"Would to heaven I were with you but alas 'tis impossible," Hamilton wrote Betsy. "My fervent prayers are not wanting that God will support you and rescue our loved child." Since late 1792 the religious bent that had marked Hamilton's earlier years had begun to be more evident again.

Besides prayers, he also had practical advice to offer in lieu of his presence: "I am somewhat afraid of the relaxing effect of the laudanum. I think well of the lime water but I count most on exercise and nourishment." His concern is not for beloved Johnny alone. "Alas my Betsey how much I wish you with me," but she is better off out of feverish plaguey Philadelphia. "I really hope more from the climate you are in than from this . . . Receive my most tender and affectionate wishes for you both. They are all I can now offer." At the close, with an impulsive flourish that takes force from its contrast with the usual stylistic regularity of even his most intimate correspondence, he adds, "hard, hard situation."

And by a postscript he adds, "I can advise you nothing better than to pursue the Doctor's advice."

Suffering rare second thoughts about his own earlier expert advice and the doctor's, he wrote her a second letter the same day full of more prescriptions. "My heart cannot cease to ache till I hear some more favorable account from you," he began. "If my darling child is better when this reaches you persevere in the plan which has made him so. If he is worse—abandon the laudanum and try the cold bath." But not at once. "Abandon the laudanum by degrees giving it overnight but not in the morning—then leaving it off altogether." As for the cold baths, let the water stand in the kitchen overnight, and then "let the child be dipped in it head foremost wrapping up his head well and taking him immediately out, put in flannel & rubbed dry with towels. Immediately upon his being taken out let him have two teaspoonsfull of brandy mixed with just enough water to prevent its taking away his breath."

Hamilton continues:

> Observe well his lips. If a glow succeeds, continue the bath. If a chill takes place forbear it. If a glow . . . the quantity of brandy may be lessened.
> Try the bark at the same time in tincture about midday. . . .
> When you exercise him, if he can bear it, give him eight or ten miles at a time.
> May heaven direct and bless the means which shall be used. My love to all the family.

Because of, or in spite of, such a rugged regimen, two-year-old John Church Hamilton survived to become his anxious, loving father's adoring first biographer.

Henry Knox issued orders to the governors of New Jersey, Pennsylvania, Maryland, and Virginia to call out 12,950 militiamen and promptly set off for the Maine woods, dumping the War Department in Hamilton's lap. Writing Lord Grenville again on August 16, George Hammond had more good news, even better than two weeks earlier. Hammond thought that the government's force of 15,000 "will be found inferior to that of the insurgents." In fact, he added, "the present general situation of this country is . . . extremely critical." The silver cloud that Hammond saw had a black lining for John Jay in London. He had just written Hamilton in cautious terms that he considered the "scale as capable of turning either way." He strongly advised "not to relax in military preparation."

Hamilton continued to do everything possible to avoid having to make combat use of the militia in the field. He sent three federal commissioners west to negotiate with the insurgents, but they reported back that they saw little hope for success of their mission and planned to return to the capital. Hamilton, Washington, and Randolph pressed them to stay and continue their efforts.

Pennsylvania authorities remained temporizing and difficult. Governor Mifflin had already fallen into the habits of heavy drinking, which would totally disable him in later years, and the whiskey rebellion crisis made them worse. Hamilton's real opposition was Mifflin's alter ego, Secretary of the Commonwealth Dallas, just as he had been in the argument at the president's conference on the insurrection.

Dallas was a prominent Republican and a leader in the Philadelphia Democratic Society, which Genêt had inspired and which had fostered similar organizations elsewhere. Two of these societies figured prominently in the western disturbances at Pittsburgh and Mingo Creek. Dallas, called to place the state at the service of national power, found excuses to temporize. The governor's mandate to employ the militia was only constructive, Dallas argued, for the law that gave him power had been repealed. He must wait to call the legislature into emergency session. Judge Alexander Addison had declared that judicial processes had not been fully exhausted.

Hamilton, writing for Edmund Randolph, answered Dallas's doubts and evasions with the same arguments he had used before.

In all of these exchanges seeking local backing for exercise of national authority, Hamilton was meticulous, patient, and moderate. No doubt, he was mindful of his own experiences of a decade earlier when, as a member of Congress, threatened by mutinous revolutionary troops, he had sought but been unable to enlist protection from Pennsylvania militia and had found it necessary to adjourn Congress to Princeton for safety. On August 24 the proclamation for mobilizing the militia was formally issued. At the same time Hamilton was doing his best with his pen to keep people in the rest of the country in sympathy with his policy. Under the pseudonym of Tully in four essays issued between August 23 through September 2, 1794, addressed "To the People of the United States," he put the arguments for federal intervention directly in the form of questions: "Shall the majority govern or be governed? Shall the nation rule or be ruled? Shall the general will prevail, or the will of a faction? Shall there be government or no government?"

Writing Rufus King on September 17, Hamilton reported that "all the militia are going forward as fast as they can be got forward. Virginia all below mountains is *zealous*. Jersey is also zealous—so are the Eastern shore of Maryland and the town of Baltimore." But west of Fredericktown there is "a very insurgent spirit and some insurrection." Governor Mifflin, who at first had "showed some untoward symptoms appears now to be exerting himself in earnest." When one of the rebels at Parkinson's Ferry had loudly denounced the government and all its works, Hugh Brackenridge had told him to be patient, explaining, "Let us bull bait the excise law for the present, and, in due time, we will knock down everything else."

With pressures on him building in intensity, Hamilton fell into his now habitual summer illness, and it aroused Washington's concern. Pressure lifted a little when Hamilton received word that Johnny and Betsy were getting better and would soon be home. He wrote her on August 21 that her last to him "gave me inexpressible pleasure." His prescriptions had worked. "My precious boy was fast recovering." He would pick up his dear ones at Elisha Boudinot's.

But mobilizing the militia to march westward was his immediate duty. He wrote out the orders to Henry Lee, governor of Virginia and field commander, on August 25: "The President anticipates, that it will be as painful to you to execute, as it is to him to direct, measures of coertion against fellow citizens however misled." He trusted that he "might count ever" on his old friend Lee's "zealous personal service towards suppressing an example fatal in its tendency to every thing that is dear and valuable in political society."

The commissioners hung on in the western counties and tried to treat with the insurgents. As mobilization of militia proceeded, in Fayette County, a center of terrorism, under the guiding hand of Albert Gallatin, some committees hastily drafted a set of resolutions, which exhorted followers to employ only peaceful means when agitating for repeal of the tax and not to resist in anywise the military expedition set in motion against them. From the War Department on September 10, Hamilton, his health recovering, reassured the governors that their militia would no longer be in much danger of actual combat: "Although the restoration of order had gained powerful advocates and supporters; yet . . . there is a violent and numerous party which does not permit to count upon a submission to the laws without the intervention of force. . . . The final resolution has been taken by the president . . . to put the force which had been provisionally called for in motion." Nearly, but not fully recovered now in health, an autumn outing across Pennsylvania might be a welcome change from Philadelphia for Hamilton. Circumstances in Philadelphia prevented him from striking back at enemies he could not touch or only imagined; out west were palpable enemies against whom he could strike punishing blows.

He wrote Washington on September 19 for permission to accompany the troops:

> It is advisable for me, on public grounds, considering the connection between the immediate ostensible cause of the insurrection in the western country and my department, to go out upon the expedition against the insurgents. In a government like ours it cannot but have a good effect for the person who is understood to be the adviser or proposer of a measure, which involves danger to his fellow-citizens, to partake in that danger; while not to do it might have a bad effect. I therefore request your permission for the purpose.

It was a permission Washington could hardly refuse to grant or wish to refuse. Although not a real consolation for his aborted hope for the mission to London, field service in the west was an honorable respite from the fevers of Philadelphia. Hamilton's spirits lifted. To his friend Rufus King, he wrote on September 22: "It will give you pleasure to learn that there is every prospect of our being able to apply this effectually—& of the issue being favourable to the authority of the laws." For the only time in this administration, the Secretary of War overruled the secretary of the treasury: "It will occasion a large bill of costs, but what is that compared with the object."

By September 28, Hamilton was writing last instructions for procurement of supplies to meet the militia on their march and directing that future correspondence be with his deputy, Tench Coxe. To the Bank of New York, Oliver Wolcott, Jr., wrote in Hamilton's name for an emergency loan to cover expenses of the punitive force. On September 29, Hamilton dashed off a last letter to his two sons Philip and Alexander, now after vacation back at school under William Fraser, rector of St. Michael's Church at Trenton. Like the rest of the family, his dear Alexander had been unwell, too, "but thank God he was better." Hamilton went on, "I expect to set out tomorrow for Carlisle. . . . There will be no fighting and of course no danger. It will only be an agreeable ride which will I hope do me good." He did not miss a dramatic occasion for paternal exhortation: "I give you both my best love & blessings as does your Mama. It will give me great pleasure when I come back to know that you have not neglected your studies and have been good boys during the vacation."

When Hamilton and the president arrived at Carlisle on October 4, they shared in a gala reception given by the Philadelphia house and the governors of Pennsylvania and New Jersey. Hamilton here was occupied with every sort of expedition business. At camp he found 3,000 citizen soldiers as remarkable for the variety of their fortunes as for the uniformity of their loyalty. He wrote to Mifflin for Washington, expressing the president's deep regret that two militia men had lost their lives in accidents. The army should guard against them in future. He was strict with looters. He insisted that those who came out to enforce the laws had a duty not to offend against them.

The show of federal force worked peaceable wonders.

With Gallatin's resolutions calling for nonviolent solutions in hand and with the commissioners still at work and the disturbances quiescent, the question arose whether earlier plans for marching on into the western counties should be put into effect at all. Hamilton's opponents were ridiculing him for having called up an unnecessarily large force.

William Findley and David Reddick had posted across the mountains from a much chastened meeting at Parkinson's Ferry on October 2 to plead with Hamilton that the region would now support the laws and required no troops to compel obedience. Hamilton demanded more assurances that distillers along the Monongahela would comply with the law and that offices of inspection could be opened. One witness now to sudden compliance was Judge Alexander Addison, whom Hamilton had described two months before as "among those who had most promoted the opposition in an insidious manner." Treating these delegates with respect but firmness, the president refused to call off the march.

Findley felt he was expressing the common view when he said that Hamilton "gave the supreme direction to the measures that were pursued" in suppressing the disturbances. Much of his "paramount influence" was in seeing to efficient supply arrangements and the comfort of the men. Hamilton's critics were sure that the secretary went beyond his proper function in accusing and arresting suspects. At any rate, "while the President was with the different wings of the army, the secretary accompanied him, and appeared to act as his official secretary."

Hamilton swung south with the president from Carlisle to Williamsport and Cumberland, Maryland, to inspect the southern wing of the army and from there back to the northern wing at Bedford, Pennsylvania. From Bedford the president retired to Philadelphia to report to Congress, leaving the army to the command of Governor Henry Lee of Virginia and under Hamilton's civil supervision giving orders in Washington's name. As the militia marched on west to Pittsburgh and Washington beyond for four weeks through rugged, mountainous country, Hamilton kept Washington informed of all developments. They pitched camp at tiny settlements in the valleys or at places designated simply by the name of the nearest resident—Berlin, Jones's Mill, Cherry's Mill, Roshaven Township. The force was more than competent to put down any opposition it might meet; so Washington ordered ill-equipped units coming up to join it to turn back. Hamilton's orders were to deal with all public letters for Washington and pass the strictly military ones on to the commanding general.

Personal observation while on the march confirmed Hamilton's earlier impression of the seriousness of the dissidence. He recommended that Congress authorize the raising of 500 infantry and 100 horse "to be stationed in the disaffected country. Without this, the expense incurred will be essentially fruitless." The ringleaders, the best objects of exemplary punishment, would doubtless flee. Very well, he reported. "They ought to be compelled by outlawry to abandon their property, homes, and the United States. This business must not be skinned over. The political putrefaction of Pennsylvania is greater than I had any idea of. Without rigor everywhere, our tranquillity is likely to be of very short duration, and the next storm will be infinitely worse than the present one."

Alexander Dallas came along on the expedition as paymaster for the Pennsylvania militia, and with each westward mile he swallowed his political pride and, like Hamilton, put more blame on the insurgents. "Nothing but fear and coercion . . . will ensure their submission," he declared. Though he considered that Gallatin, Findley, and Smilie, so recently his allies, would flee and escape the law, Dallas believed they were "inconceivably obnoxious as the original perpetrators of the doctrines which have eventually produced these violences." The conversion of early critics like Mifflin and Dallas to Hamilton's view of the rebellion by direct observation in the field is the best answer to all who continued to charge from afar that Hamilton had unnecessarily improved the occasion to aggrandize the national government.

Still in the field with the army, Hamilton was full of concern for his family on October 20, when he wrote Elizabeth that he was "very sorry that some of my sweet angels have been again sick. You do not mention my precious John. ... Have patience my love & think of me constantly as I do of you with the utmost tenderness. Kisses & blessings to you and my children."

Three days later, in a letter he datelined "Bedford, Pennsylvania, 205 miles westward of Philadelphia," he unburdened himself jokingly to Angelica Church of self-conscious concern that his westward foray made him look quixotic in the eyes of those who loved him, as well as his critics. In intimate moments, when at his best, Hamilton was never too sure he was right or afraid to reveal self-doubts to those he loved most and whose love meant most to him:

> I am thus far my dear Angelica on my way to attack and subdue the wicked insurgents of the West. But you are not to promise yourself that I have any trophies to lay at your feet. A large army has cooled the courage of these madmen & the only question seems now to be how to guard against the return of the phrenzy.

Hamilton knew as well as anyone that the easy, conventional wisdom of most political men would be to laugh off such an insurgency as a mere unpleasantness, avoid doing anything about it, and remain popular. He adds to Angelica, "You must not take my being here for proof that I continue a quixot."

Hamilton was not a man living an unself-examined life. He went on, "In popular governments 'tis useful that those who propose measures should partake in whatever dangers they may involve. 'Twas very important there should be no mistake in the management of the affair—and I *might* contribute to prevent one." He seemed to hold himself responsible as a national steward for the well-being of all the inmates of America and of foreign visitors as well: "I wish to have every thing well settled for Mr. Church and you, that when you come, you may tread on safe ground. Assure him that the insurrection will do us a great deal of good and add to the solidity of every thing in this country. Say the same to Mr. Jay to whom I have not time to write & to Mr. Pinkney." He closed saying, "God bless You dear sister & make you as happy as I wish you. Love to Mr. Church."

Hamilton owed John Jay a reply to the cheerful letter Jay had written him September 17, saying, "There is something very pleasant in the reflection that while war and discord and oppression triumph in so many parts of Europe, their domination does not extend to our country. I sometimes flatter myself that Providence in compassion to the affected in these countries, will continue to leave America in a proper state to be an asylum to them."

From "205 miles westward of Philadelphia," Hamilton thought it might be just as well to remind his special envoy in London that to keep peace in the asylum more than the compassion of providence was sometimes necessary. From time to time even in America it was necessary for men of goodwill to leave their comfortable homes and take risks in the field to preserve the peace that Jay remembered as so idyllic from a distance.

One whispered word of this from beautiful Angelica into the ear of Envoy Extraordinary John Jay and to Minister Plenipotentiary Thomas Pinckney would be a way to make more unforgettable to them the real meaning of Hamilton's apparent quixotry than any self-serving prose of his he could possibly put in a letter.

Jay's smug reflection had prefaced a letter of his introducing Hamilton to François Alexandre Fréderic, duc de La Rochefoucauld-Liancourt, a French social reformer who had founded a school of arts and crafts, which became known in 1788 as *École des Infants de la Patrie*. Rochefoucauld-Liancourt had become president of the Estates General in 1789, but when the royal palace was captured on August 10, 1792, he had fled first to England and then to America. Jay had written Hamilton that "his rank and character are known to you." The fate of Rochefoucauld-Liancourt had touched Angelica's warm heart too, for she had written her "brother" on September 19 that he had "loved liberty with good sense and moderation; and he meant so well towards his country as to introduce into France a better system of agriculture and to soften the situation of the lower class of the people there." Like Jay, she saw America from afar as the ultimate asylum for the great free spirits of the world, including refugees from lawless killers mouthing slogans like *Liberté, Égalité,* and *Fraternité.* In the case of the duc de La Rochefoucauld-Liancourt, "Virtue, has not found its reward," she wrote, "for in the many scenes of distress that has afflicted his unfortunate country, he like many more good men, has been obliged to leave his possessions and seek an asylum in this country." From England, "He goes to America, and goes here without a friend, unless my dear Brother, who is always so good, will extend . . . his care—." To Hamilton from Angelica not one word more was needed. But if one should be, she had added, "besides many good qualities, this gentleman is the friend of the Marquis de LaFayette."

Hamilton firmly believed that the men who had been responsible for violence and defiance of the Union in the western country and who had not come in under his offer of amnesty should be brought to law. For this purpose, Richard Peters, the district judge, and William Rawle, the district attorney, accompanied the army. Exemplary prosecutions were the most important, but, ipso facto, the most unpopular part of Hamilton's mission. The visible opposition having melted away before the advancing troops, the arrest of individuals in a now quiet district was easily represented as harsh and vindictive. Some of the principal offenders escaped. The most bellicose of the rebels, David Bradford, who had been the self-styled general at Braddock's Field, fled to Louisiana. Gallatin had played an early part in urging that the excise be brought into contempt, but he was judged by the attorney general of the United States not to have committed an indictable offense. Hugh Brackenridge, the most conspicuous leader of the rebellion, was early described by Hamilton as "the worst of all scoundrels." But he had cooperated with the commissioners and so purchased immunity. Other insurgent leaders, among the more sophisticated, would claim that although pretending to sympathize with the insurgents and attending their meetings, they had really been using their influence to prevent violence. Brackenridge, when interrogated by Hamilton, likened himself to Richard II speaking before the mob of 100,000 people assembled on Blackheath, trying to keep it from becoming lawless. When "the young prince addressed them," he said, and he "put himself at their head, and said, What do you want, gentlemen? I will lead you on." John Hamilton, the colonel of a regiment of militia in the Mingo Creek settlement and sheriff of Washington County, claimed that he had tried to dissuade David Bradford from the demonstrations at Braddock's Field, but that when this effort failed, went there at the head of his troops, resolved to prevent outrages. Such men won favor both ways—they had encouraged the insurgents and, later on, would stand well with the government. The smaller fry, who would be caught, would be objects of sympathy for their ignorance and poverty. Rigorous punishment of them would be criticized because there had been no more bloodshed since Hamilton's show of force.

No such reflections could dissuade Hamilton from making the most of the demonstration. As soon as General Morgan, with the light troops, crossed into Washington County, which held "the most disaffected scenes," he supervised preparations for the military to seize suspects and deliver them for disposition by the judiciary. In some cases, time did not allow "for preliminary investigations to apprehend the guilty upon process." Some arrests were justified on the dubious theory that any man may arrest a suspected traitor. Four days later, "the measures for apprehending persons and seizing stills" were to be carried into effect. Hamilton wrote Washington: "I hope there will be found characters fit for examples, and who can be made so." Sheriff John Hamilton had surrendered himself, though it was not certain how much could be proved against him.

Alexander Hamilton declared that all possible means were being used to obtain evidence and that "accomplices will be turned against the others." Hamilton personally questioned many suspects. Findley charged that the secretary used threats to browbeat some suspects and witnesses, but such stories were all secondhand. Brackenridge thought his own examination by Hamilton had been fair, but said that while he as a lawyer and literary man could protect his own rights, he thought Hamilton's tactics might put the ignorant and fearful at a disadvantage. There was no direct evidence of Hamilton's having used any browbeating tactics beyond skillful cross-examination.

Hamilton had been busy with rounding up suspected insurgents when he wrote to the president from Washington, November 15, 1794, that 20 men were in confinement there, mentioning a half-dozen "most conspicuous . . . for character or crime." Two days later, when he arrived at Pittsburgh with the judiciary, the list of prisoners had increased to 150. General Lee had been informed from Marietta that John Holcroft, "Tom the Tinker," a man who had threatened with violence all distillers who complied with the excise had been seized fleeing down the river.

In the meantime, President Washington, though he had departed the scene, was still as zealous as Hamilton for catching as many as possible of the rascals who had been responsible for so much trouble and expense. He wrote Hamilton from Wright's Ferry on the Susquehanna, "I hope you will be enabled by Hook or by Crook, to send B____[radford] and H____[usbands] together with a certain

Mr Guthrie, to Philadelphia for their winter Quarters." Five days later, he noted with satisfaction that Husbands and others were safely locked up in custody there. The two men were eventually found guilty of treason, after which Washington quietly pardoned them.

While examining prisoners and witnesses, Hamilton was also setting up more effective tax collection machinery for the future. He instructed the supervisors of revenue that an office of inspection was to be opened in each county even where none had been before. Where there had been offices and legitimate reasons for delinquencies, Hamilton made practical compromises that forgave some of the back taxes that were due. Much as he would like to have found a prominent scapegoat in Hugh Brackenridge, Hamilton would change his mind after a careful examination into all the facts showed him that his earlier impression had been wrong. Brackenridge had neglected to sign the oath of submission to the excise laws before the time limit for amnesty expired. He told what it was like to be quizzed by a hostile Hamilton. Examining him on November 18, Hamilton, he said, had "that countenance, which a man will have, when he sees a person, with regard to whom his humanity and sense of justice struggles;—he would have him saved, but is afraid he must be hanged;—was willing to treat me with civility, but was embarrassed with a sense, that, in a short time, I must probably stand in the predicament of a culprit, and be in irons." Hamilton began by asking some general questions. Brackenridge told him that they seemed to be getting on slowly and offered to give Hamilton a narrative of his role in the uprising. Hamilton agreed, took up his pen, and copied down Brackenridge's story. When Brackenridge had finished, Hamilton laid down his pen and said sternly, "Mr. Brackenridge, I observe one leading trait in your account, a disposition to excuse the principal actors . . . before we go further, I must be candid and inform you of the delicate situation which you stand; *you are not within the amnesty; you have not signed upon the day* . . . it will depend upon your candour what your fate will be."

The examination went on all that morning, all afternoon, and into the evening before Hamilton felt an attack of illness, saying, "my breast begins to ache, we will stop tonight; we will resume it tomorrow morning at 9 o'clock." Brackenridge said, "I was struck with his last expression. I was at a loss to know whether his breast ached for my sake, or from the writing; but disposed to construe everything unfavorable, I supposed it was for my sake, and that he saw I must be arrested."

Hamilton's examination of Brackenridge resumed next morning, and after some time, Brackenridge noticed, "his countenance began to brighten." Soon it was over. "Mr. Brackenridge," said he, "yesterday I had uneasy feelings, I was concerned for you as a man of many talents; my impressions were unfavorable; you may have observed it, I now think it my duty to inform you, that not a single one remains. . . . Your conduct has been horribly misrepresented, owing to misconceptions. . . . You are in no personal danger. You will not be troubled, even by a simple inquisition by the judge; what may be due to yourself by the public is another question."

Hamilton had asked General Lee to map out homeward routes for the troops, so that their provisions and pay could be deposited to await them at Pittsburgh. He also felt, "I would add . . . that it would scarcely appear advisable to leave any considerable number of Artillery in so disaffected a Country." Hamilton would hardly still have been worrying about leaving cannon in the insurgent country if he had considered the expedition only a show of force and nothing more. On November 19, the same day he completed his examination of Brackenridge, Hamilton notified President Washington by a hasty line from Pittsburgh that the army was in motion homeward and that he would himself set out for home in five minutes.[4]

Edward Carrington of Virginia, who had been in the expedition, later wrote to Hamilton, "Our returned troops pretty generally agree, that a less force than was called forth could have been opposed, and that a small army could have effected nothing but the establishment of a civil war." Recent years have retaught the lesson of the national agony that can arise from launching a military force against a civil insurrection if the force is not seen to be sufficiently overwhelming. To escalate the progovernment force inconspicuously insures escalation of the insurrection. It is the show that makes a success of the force.

Hamilton, thought to have ordered all the arrests, feared assassination attempts on his return journey through the wild rugged rebel country.[5] The secretary of the treasury, acting secretary of war, and ad hoc, de facto attorney general was therefore escorted by a protective guard cordon of six armed horsemen for a hundred miles through the hostile mountains and forests all the way from Pittsburgh to safe arrival back at Bedford. There awaited him news, transmitted at the president's express request, of a death in the family.

Henry Knox's letter of November 24 reported that Mrs. Hamilton "has had, or been in danger of miscarriage, which has much alarmed her." Doctor Kuhn and Hamilton's boyhood friend Edward Stevens had been in close attendance and "assure that she is in no danger to her." But "she is extremely desirous of your presence to tranquilize her." She had been in danger of a miscarriage. She had now suffered one. Her own life had been in danger. They would not have another child for three more years. In Hamilton's absence, Eliza's father, Philip Schuyler, had done his best to console her. He assured her on December 2 that her husband would return safely and in health "and as usual triumph over his ungenerous enemies."

On December 1, 1794, immediately upon return from the field, Hamilton wrote to George Washington:

> I have the honor to inform you that I have fixed upon the last of January next as the day for resignation of my office of Secretary of the Treasury. I make the communication now, that there may be time to mature such an arrangement as shall appear to you proper to meet the vacancy when it occurs.
>
> With perfect respect & the truest attachment I have the honor to be Sir Your very obedient servant.

On December 8 he wrote Angelica Church, "My dear Eliza has been lately very ill. Thank God, she is now quite recovered, except that she continued somewhat weak. My absence on a certain expedition was the cause [with the army to suppress the Whisky Insurrection in Pennsylvania]. You will see, notwithstanding your disparagement of me, I am still of consequence to her."

It was coldly quixotic, to say the least, to take comfort in the pain of a sister's miscarriage—or feebly explain away a deeply felt hidden guilt concerning her.

Not to be numbered among triumphs over ungenerous enemies were illness and mortality within his family, caused by himself. In the circumstances, the misguided, skewed, indeed cockeyed callousness of this attempt at humor would suggest to her that he was suffering a recurrence of the nervous derangement of the previous winter. Here was the best possible reason for an irreversible resignation from too many pressures of too many offices for reasons of health that were unmentionable because they were mental.

16

PUBLIC CREDIT

OUR FINANCES ARE IN A MOST FLOURISHING CONDITION. HAVING
CONTRIBUTED TO PLACE THOSE OF THE NATION ON A GOOD FOOT-
ING, I GO TO TAKE A LITTLE CARE OF MY OWN WHICH NEED MY
CARE NOT A LITTLE.

—*To Angelica Church, December 8, 1794*

Hamilton returned home from his "agreeable ride" through the "disaffected country" looking forward to release at last from the pressures of not one too many cabinet offices but two. He had successfully demonstrated to the western insurgents that they could not get away with defying federal tax collectors or the process of federal courts or seceding from the Union. By now Eliza was recovering from her miscarriage. He was in a lighthearted mood on December 8, 1794, when he wrote Angelica Church:

You say I am a politician, and good for nothing. What will you say when you learn that after January next, I shall cease to be a politician at all? So is the fact. I have formally and definitely announced my intention to resign at that period, and have ordered a house to be taken for me at New York.

If there were any danger that in flood tide of success and power of two high offices Hamilton would once more postpone his decision to resign, a letter he received from James McHenry, the old comrade-in-arms who had written the "Epithalamium" for his and Betsy's wedding night, would help him hold to his resolve. McHenry wrote from Baltimore:

> I have built houses, I have cultivated fields, I have planned gardens, I have planted trees, I have written little essays, I have made poetry once a year to please my wife, at times got children and at times thought myself happy. Why cannot you do the same, for after all if a man is only to acquire fame or distinctions by continued privations and abuse I would decline to prefer a life of privacy and little pleasures.

After the miscarriage of her sixth pregnancy while he remained with the militia command in western Pennsylvania, Elizabeth desperately needed some tender care. "Little" Philip, now 13, and the four other children stairstepping down to John Church, two and a half and just beginning to mend, commanded his attention to parental office and financial preparation for many expensive educations. Without the more or less continuous but surreptitious aid of Philip Schuyler, the Hamiltons would have been in even more serious financial straits than they were. But it is probable that few of Hamilton's contemporaries realized that when he quit his Treasury post, he was a poor man. From his elegant air and comfortable style of living and Schuyler connections, most of his acquaintances would have assumed that by now he was at least well-to-do, if not rich. It suited his enemies to say he was wealthy to support their imputations of corrupt financial dealings with William Duer, James Reynolds, A. G. Fraunces, and others during his tenure as secretary of the treasury.

Not only was Hamilton poor, but he was also continually involved in money difficulties. He regularly overdrew his account and from time to time was forced to borrow petty sums of as little as $50 from friends. Ruefully, he told Tobias Lear and Major William Jackson, both of Washington's secretarial family: "I am not worth exceeding five hundred dollars in the world; my slender fortune and the best years of my life have been devoted to the service of my adopted country; a rising family hath its claims."

He found a small house at 56 Pine Street, which served for about a year as both living quarters and office. From there he and the family moved from one address to another, winding up at 24 Broadway, where they remained until 1802, when they finally moved to The Grange on Harlem Heights. As he resumed his law practice he was compelled to borrow some money from his old friend and college classmate, Robert Troup, who had never quit the law to hold public office. Troup sympathized with Hamilton and his politics and would help him out by bringing him into cases as cocounsel with him now and all during the rest of his life.

Troup also tried to bring him into a land speculation in Ontario County on which he was embarking with English and Dutch capitalists to buy several million acres. He hoped Hamilton and John Jay, too, would serve them secretly in an advisory capacity. "Why should you object to making a little money in a way that cannot be reproachful?" Troup asked. He confided to Hamilton a homely truth about the economics of much of ordinary law practice. "Be assured that the hard-earned profits of the law will wear you out and leave a net residue at the end of ten years that will not maintain a family with decent economy . . ." But Hamilton was determined to guard his reputation in private life as carefully as he had in the Treasury—especially because of his near fatal entanglement with the Reynoldses. He rejected Troup's offer, writing him April 13, 1795, that "I am now in no situation that restrains me." However, "I think there is at present a great crisis in the affairs of [man]kind which may in its consequences involve this country. . . . The game to be played may be a most important one." Private people could get into the kind of dubious private deal Troup had invited him in on, but out of office, Hamilton continued to see himself as a public exemplar—unlike his enemies. With sad sarcasm, Hamilton noted that such deals were "very harmless in the *Saints,* who may never fatten themselves on the opportunities or if you please the spoils of the office" and "profit by every good thing that is going . . . [without] hazarding their popularity."

Hamilton had learned the hard way he was not one of those lucky saints like Burr who could get away with anything: "Those who are not of the *regenerating* tribe may not do the most unexceptionable things without its being thundered in their ears—without being denounced as speculators, peculators British agents etc. etc." Still, as Hamilton saw it, "There must be some *public fools*" like himself "who sacrifice private to public interest at the certainty of ingratitude and obloquy."

Troup thought Hamilton had delayed too long looking to his financial future. "I sincerely hope . . . that you may by some fortunate & unexpected event acquire the means of perfect independence in spite of all your efforts to be poor," he replied to him. But Hamilton insisted, "My *vanity* whispers I ought to be one of those fools and ought to keep myself in a situation the best calculated to render service."

Troup answered, "I have often said that your friends would be obliged to bury you at their own expense." His grisly prophecy turned out to be grimly true.

Though he was still only 37, the time was overdue for Hamilton to retire. $3,500 a year as secretary of the treasury had obliged him to exhaust "almost the whole of the small fortune he had acquired" before taking office. The duc de La Rochefoucauld-Liancourt had arrived with Angelica's letter of September 19 to him. "I pay him the attentions due to his misfortunes and merits," Hamilton wrote her, but he was still financially embarrassed. "I wish I was a Croesus, I might then afford solid consolations to these children of adversity, and how delightful it would be to do so. *But now,* sympathy, kind words, and *occasionally a dinner, are all I can contribute.*"

Despite his being out of office, Angelica should not fear for the country:

Don't let Mr. Church be alarmed at my retreat—all is well with the public. Our insurrection is most happily terminated. Government has gained by it reputation and strength, and our finances are in a most flourishing condition. *Having contributed to place those of the nation on a good footing, I go to take a little care of my own; which need my care not a little.*

Contrary to the idyllic picture of the country he jocularly sketched for Angelica's and John's benefit, all was far from well with the public. As the Republicans, at least, saw it, the insurrection had been brutally repressed. Congress was in an uproar. The opposition press, led by Benjamin Franklin Bache's *Aurora*, stormed with public criticism. Fenno's *Gazette of the United States* had suspended publication and no longer functioned to publish Hamilton's rebuttal. It had failed the year before owing mainly to subscribers and advertisers who failed to pay debts they owed it. Alarmed at the *Gazette*'s demise, Hamilton had written Rufus King back on November 11, 1793, that "we must lose his services or he will be the victim of his honest public spirit."

At that time, Fenno had called on Hamilton for help, apologized for the "intrusion," and wished that his "health may be firmly reestablished" after the "nervous derangement." Fenno's leanings toward Hamilton and the administration had sharpened their enemies' glee at the demise of Fenno's paper. But the efforts of Hamilton and Rufus King and others to raise a subscription to help Fenno's paper survive failed. However, suppression of the insurrection had done much good for the country, Washington believed, and as the new year of 1795 arrived, Hamilton found a more authoritative spokesman than Fenno for his view of it.

The proclamation Hamilton drafted for Washington to issue January 1, 1795, called attention to "the great degree of internal tranquility we have enjoyed." Such tranquillity had recently been confirmed "by the suppression of an insurrection which so wantonly threatened it." Washington went on to "bow down before the majesty of the Almighty" and to set Thursday, February 19, "as a day of public Thanksgiving and prayer."

Washington, in Hamilton's words, would call for a day of grateful thanks for "the reasonable check which had been given to a spirit of disorder." The "kind author" of America's blessings was beseeched "to preserve us from the wantonness of prosperity." (Washington softened the hard word *wantonness* of Hamilton's draft to *arrogance*, but changed little else.) This would "render this country more and more a secure and propitious asylum for the unfortunate of other countries." Hamilton's view of what his enemies liked to dismiss as the "Whiskey Rebellion" thus became the specific occasion for Washington's first proclamation of the unique American holiday, Thanksgiving Day.

From the army's rendezvous at Carlisle two months earlier, President Washington had also commissioned from Hamilton a draft of the message he would present to the new session of Congress. The bustle of camp would not permit Washington to do more than edit paragraphs supplied to him, but he wanted to emphasize one topic: reproof of "these self created societies" which threatened to "destroy the government of this Country." Angry disapproval of the Republican-Democratic societies like the one at Mingo Creek, whose members had stirred up the insurrection, had been a major theme with Washington for the past year. Washington took much of his text from the report on the rebellion that Hamilton had prepared for him. Leaders of these societies would "destroy all confidence in the Administration, by arraigning all its acts . . ." The parent society had been founded by Genêt in Philadelphia "for the express purpose of dissension." The western insurrection was the "first *ripe fruit* of the Democratic Societies."

Political parties by now had already taken form, and the issue of the insurrection was firming up ranks on both sides. The president's declaration of "public odium" upon the Democratic societies in his message to Congress begat swift rebuttal from Republicans. Some congressmen declared that Washington was mistaken on the facts. Hamilton's report was the only paper before it, they said, "that brings any evidence on the subject." Their argument ran that the seeds of insurrection were planted, not by the societies, but by Hamilton's excise tax law, which had been adopted long before the societies were established.

Thomas Scott, the representative in Congress from Washington County, at the very epicenter of the insurrection, rose to his feet at the same moment as Fisher Ames to put such misconceptions to rest. The quick-witted gentleman from Massachusetts instantly yielded the floor. Scott's knowledge of local conditions in western Pennsylvania would outweigh the most eloquent rhetoric. Scott "knew that . . . self-centered societies in that part of the country . . . had inflamed the insurrection; some of the leaders of those societies had likewise been the leaders of the riots." Scott avowed that he could not, with all his personal knowledge, give "a more candid and accurate account" of the rebellion "than the President and Hamilton had given." The deluded people of the western region were "objects of real pity. They were . . . grossly ignorant, and they had been persuaded by . . . utmost diligence . . . that the American Government was . . . the very worst in the world . . . when people had got their length in absurdity, it was not difficult to make them fight against such a Government."

Tired of Republican cant about "the people," the hackneyed, automatic, knee jerk response that served them in lieu of logical argument, Uriah Tracy of Connecticut shied a simile at McDowell of North Carolina that echoed through later speeches. ". . . if the President had not spoken of the matter," Tracy said, he "should have been willing to let it alone, because whenever a subject of that kind was touched . . . certain gentlemen . . . shook their backs, like a sore-backed horse, and cried out 'the Liberties of the People.' " McDowell sprang up to retort "that he believed his back to have been rubbed harder in the last war, than that of" his critic.

Hearing that in the turn of the debate "self created" societies were being excused from blame, Hamilton hastened to the house of Thomas FitzSimmons "to state some facts." True, "opposition to the excise laws began from causes foreign to Democratic Societies," Hamilton conceded, "but it is well ascertained . . . that the insurrection immediately is to be essentially attributed to one" of them, the Mingo Creek Society. Members of it had commanded the attacks on Neville's house. Hamilton should not be named as the source of this information, but FitzSimmons should make use of it in floor debate.

Votes on significant phrases of the president's message were evenly divided, and the result turned on the votes of only one or two members. In the end, to the surprise of the Federalists, it was John Nicholas of Virginia who came forward with the compromise that upheld the president's statement on the insurrection. Avoiding a pointed verbal chastising of democratic clubs everywhere, it left standing his reproofs to those in the western counties.

In the Senate a committee under Rufus King's chairmanship charged the societies with being "founded in political error, calculated if not intended to disorganize the government." To rebut him, Aaron Burr and Senator James Jackson of Georgia, whom Albert Gallatin had once called a "pugnacious animal," rose and spoke in their turn. Federalists held a two-to-one majority in the Senate and beat the Republicans back. Madison's and Jefferson's private correspondence of this period is full of chagrin at the military and political credit Hamilton had won, first by crushing the insurrection in the field and then by defeating all political efforts to discredit the suppression in Congress. Madison relayed scare stories to the effect that returning militia would favor a standing army to enforce the laws. Jefferson minimized the misdeeds of the democratic societies and assailed the Federalists as "the faction of monocrats" for denouncing them. He added "It is wonderful indeed, that the President should have permitted himself to be the organ of such an attack on the freedom of discussion, the freedom of writing, printing and publishing . . ." To Jefferson, as to Hugh Brackenridge, the "infernal" excise would yet be "the instrument of dismembering the Union."

Fisher Ames took up the defense when Thomas Scott subsided. "The private history" was "that the faction in the House fomented the discontents without; that the clubs are everywhere the echoes of the faction in Congress." James Madison was an honorary member of one of the societies, and the Speaker, Frederick A. C. Muhlenberg, was a member of one, too, although he had taken pains in casting his vote to disclaim their influence.

Of the president's address, largely drafted by Hamilton, which had touched off the long congressional debate, Pamphleteer James Thomson Callender would later write, "To hear the Representatives . . . disputing for three weeks upon the wording of the answer to a speech of his own composition, must have been . . . soothing to the self importance of the secretary."

As the date of his resignation approached, the attention of everyone in Congress, as well as of the public at large, remained riveted on Hamilton for important reasons other than the debate over Washington's denunciation of the insurrection. His friend Edward Carrington wrote Hamilton, "Your notification to the House of Representatives is a necessary caveat against future slander, for had you remained till the last day of the session, and then resigned without such a precaution, a retreat from inquiry would have been charged against you."

Accordingly, on December 1, 1794, the same day he had submitted his resignation to be effective January 31, Hamilton requested of Speaker of the House Muhlenberg that the unfinished business of the investigation of his stewardship of the Treasury be wound up. Ever since his confrontation with Hamilton on the night of December 15, 1792, Muhlenberg, a former moderate Federalist, had been moving leftward along the political spectrum toward joining the Republicans. He had voted with the members of the House who had criticized Washington's observations on the insurrection. Hamilton wrote Muhlenberg that "I make this communication in order that an opportunity may be given, previous to [resignation], to reinstitute any further proceeding which may be contemplated, if any there be, in consequence of the inquiry during the last session into the state of this department." None were reinstituted.

Still another controversy raged around Hamilton's resignation. His opponents refused to take the reasons he gave for resigning at face value. Philip Schuyler wrote him on January 5 that some were saying that he was resigning because of "a wish to be Governor of this state." Others charged that he was resigning because "the affairs of your department were so deranged, that it was not possible for you to extricate it from the confusion in which it was involved." Schuyler had denounced Fairly, the man who issued the last calumny, as "a liar and a villain."

Hamilton's last days in office were some of his most significant. On November 19, 1794, George Washington in his sixth annual message to Congress had called for "a definitive plan for the redemption of the public debt," and two days later the House had appointed a committee to report such a plan, naming as its committee chairman Hamilton's friend and spokesman William Loughton Smith of South Carolina. The Smith committee struggled with the problem for a while and proposed some statutory amendments to existing law, but, finally, as previous Congresses had done, it turned to Hamilton to supply it with well-organized and definitive answers to many large questions. Hamilton obliged. If it were true that his department was involved in confusion, Hamilton would allow Congress to share it with him through the medium of his last great and unaccountably neglected public report, his "Report on a Plan for the Further Support of Public Credit," often called his Final (or Second) Report on the Public Credit. The tactics and timing of Hamilton's submission of this valedictory report on January 16 were as masterful as its text. The disgruntlement it caused Madison and Jefferson is an index of its significance. "Hamilton has made a long and arrogant valedictory Rept," Madison wrote Jefferson. "It is not yet printed, & I have not read it. It is said to contain a number of improper things. He got it in by informing the Speaker he had one ready . . . for the House whenever they shd please to receive it. Berdinot [Boudinot] the ready agent of all sycophantic jobs, had a motion cut & dry, just at the moment of the adjournment . . . which passed without opposition & almost without notice."

Hamilton's Final Report on the Public Credit," which runs to 103 pages in the Hamilton Papers, is divided into three separate, but related sections. The first is a history of the fiscal system of the United States during his almost five-and-a-half-year term as secretary of the treasury, the second sets forth ten "propositions, which appear necessary . . . to complete our system," and the third is a wide-ranging essay on the nature and meaning of public credit. The report is followed by a series of statistical tables designed to illustrate, illuminate, and document the points he makes.

"Credit public and private is of the greatest consequence to every country . . . it might be emphatically called the invigorating principle . . . No well informed man can cast a retrospective eye over the progress of the United States, from their infancy to the present period, without being convinced that they owe, in a great degree, to the fostering influence of credit, their present mature growth."

"Credit," Hamilton insisted, "is among the principal engines of useful enterprise and internal improvement. As a substitute for capital it is little less useful than gold or silver, in agriculture, in commerce, in the manufacturing and mechanic arts . . ."

Hamilton's enemies had always charged that he wished to impose an everlasting debt structure upon the country, but the major emphasis in the report is on plans for extinguishing the debt. Citing the statement in Washington's sixth annual message to Congress that "progressive accumulation of debt must ultimately endanger all governments," Hamilton warned that "a tendency to it is perhaps the NATURAL DISEASE of all governments . . . There is a general propensity in those who administer the affairs of a government, founded in the constitution of man, to shift off the burden from the present to a future day; a propensity which may be expected to be strong in proportion as the form of a state is popular . . ." To Hamilton, it was a common "spectacle to see the same men clamoring for occasions of expense . . . declaiming against a public debt, and for the reduction of it as an *abstract thesis;* yet vehement against every plan of taxation which is proposed to discharge old debts, or to avoid new by defraying the expenses of exigencies as they emerge . . ."

Hamilton laid down as two fundamental principles for all public debt that (1) there be established at the time of contracting it, a sinking fund or retirement fund, a fund both for the repayment of the principal and the interest on it within a determinate period, and (2) that it be made a part of the contract that the fund so established "shall be inviolably applied to the object."

Hamilton gave ten propositions for completion of the fiscal system he had established, which would, if followed, provide for every obligation, deferred and accruing, to be met out of revenue sources existing at the time of creation of the debt and without resort to new sources of revenue at later times. Tables appended to his report gave the figures down to the last penny. As of December 31, 1794, domestic debt of the United States was $64,825,538.70; foreign debt owed to France, 14,000,000 livres ($3 million); and foreign loans owed at Amsterdam and Antwerp (the guilder at 40 cents), $12,387,000. By Hamilton's proposals for management of the sinking fund, the whole of the existing debt, foreign and domestic, funded and unfunded, would be redeemed in 30 years or by the year 1826. The government was currently operating in the black. Current expenditure was $5,481,843.84, and the excess of revenues beyond expenditures was $1,070,456.90.

Hamilton warned Congress that without the kind of national self-discipline he had urged, "the public debt swells till its magnitude becomes enormous, and the burthens of the people gradually increase, till their weight becomes intolerable. Of such a state of things, great disorders in the whole political economy, convulsions and revolutions of government, are a natural offspring." He cast imprecations on any who would divert the sinking fund, in whatever emergencies, to uses other than its original objects. He declared again that his purpose was to create public credit, not to accumulate debt; the two things were antithetical.

He rejected the proposal that the government was at liberty to tax its own bonds or to seize and sequester them in time of war. He protested, with logic and moral conviction, that to do either in any form would be to violate its commitment to the lender. "The true definition of public debt," he observed, "is a property subsisting in the faith of the Government. Its essence is promise." Once it contracts a debt, the government loses legislative power to change its terms and becomes, like an individual, a "moral agent" obligated to faithful compliance with them. No compulsory modification not provided for in the instrument was allowable. This was "a principle . . . most sacred." Even war should not impair the claim of an enemy who was also a creditor. Any partial and temporary gain obtained from wronging a few creditors must produce vastly larger losses to the nation because "credit is an *intire thing*. Every part of it has the nicest sympathy with every other part; wound one limb, and the whole tree shrinks and decays. The security of each creditor is inseparable from the security of all creditors . . ." He concluded by saying, "Twill be the truest policy in the United States to give all possible energy to public credit."

Hamilton's valedictory report unified, orchestrated, and dramatized the piecemeal resolutions of William Loughton Smith's committee with an almost poetic, Shakespearean intensity. It was spare language for a prospectus for U.S. government bonds that yet blazed with emotion never since found in such a document. The Smith committee saw the debt as a problem; Hamilton approached it as a challenge. He offered a variety of solutions that added up to a comprehensive fiscal and monetary policy for the United States that would keep its public credit high for the years, decades, and centuries to come.

Often before, Smith had been the Treasury's spokesman and champion in the House. Smith now complimented the president for promoting prosperity through keeping the country at peace and paid tribute to the retiring secretary, whose "assiduous labors had given energy and system to the complex machinery of an extensive and intricate Department." A large committee of the House had recently (after investigation) borne testimony to his "fidelity and services." Smith's resolutions went beyond providing for paying interest only; they looked to the complete redemption of all public debt. The Treasury supplied Smith with statistics and arguments to support his motions to continue temporary taxes, sell western lands, and devote the surplus to the retirement of the principal.

By resolute taxation and a well-nourished sinking fund, the Federalists would redeem and extinguish all debt and thus refute the charge of the Jeffersonians that they proposed to perpetuate public debt as their instrument of party and personal power. With biting sarcasm, Fisher Ames denounced the charges of Southern aristocrats that "represent the Eastern members as the patrons of a system of paper influence, of Treasury corruption, of certificate nobility." He branded as false their projections that Federalists have "succeeded to pervert and stretch the Constitution, to organize . . . systems of concealed aristocracy." It was not true "that they deem the Debt, as it promotes these vile purposes, a blessing," or that "to oblige one another [They] will not part with it, lest . . . popular principles . . . should prevail over . . . corrupt connexions. . . ."

Crucial features of the bill embodying Hamilton's plan were fought in the House by William Giles, McDowell, Smith of Maryland, Hillhouse, and many more and in the Senate by Aaron Burr and others. Theodore Sedgwick stood beside Smith of South Carolina in the lower chamber, and King led Hamilton's backers in the upper. Opponents suffered under a double disability. Having charged that the hateful debt was the darling of the Federalists, how could the Republicans criticize virtue now that it was to be put in the way of complete discharge? Hamilton's foes made a flank attack by objecting to continuance of excises (as one means of payment) and called for direct taxes instead. Direct taxes meant national land taxes, as Madison had suggested, but agricultural interests—and Hamilton—considered these a far greater evil than excises.

Smith's bills embodying Hamilton's last great report passed both houses of Congress, carrying with them all of his objects except one; it omitted a proposal of Hamilton for paying off "non subscribers" and certain other holders of U.S. loan office certificates of obligation. Nonsubscribers were persons who held debt certificates issued under the Confederation who had failed to exchange them for new debt certificates of the new government, some because they had applied too late, others because they believed the exchange terms offered were too low. Their numbers and claims were small in comparison with all classes of security holders affected, but Hamilton was intensely concerned that the government treat all smallholders fairly as a matter of sacred principle, regardless of the unimportance of the sums involved.

Despite the success of his overall program, he was grieved and angry. Some weeks out of the Treasury and away from the Philadelphia scene, he entreated Sedgwick and King to retrieve the country's honor by keeping faith with all creditors, including poor nonsubscribers. He wrote Sedgwick on February 18 that he was "tortured" by the discrimination. On February 21 he wrote King, "The unnecessary capricious & abominable assassination of the national honor by the rejection of the propositions respecting the unsubscribed debt . . . haunts me every step I take, and afflicts me more than I can express." At the moment of one of his greatest triumphs, he seemed to be suffering another anxiety attack, when he asked his friend King, in a mixture of violence and pathos, this curious question: "Am I, then, more of an American than those who drew their first breath on American ground? Or what is it that thus torments me at a circumstance so calmly viewed by almost everybody else? Am I a fool—a romantic Quixote—or is there a constitutional defect in the American mind?" He called on King: "I conjure you, my friend, make a vigorous stand for the honor of your country! Rouse all the energies of your mind, and measure swords in the Senate with the great slayer of public faith—the hackneyed veteran in the violation of public engagements. Prevent him if possible from triumphing a second time over the prostrate credit and injured interests of his country. Unmask his false and horrid hypothesis."

Who was this man who was the "hackneyed veteran in the violation of public engagements"? Who had led the fight against his report in the Senate? The inimical *"man of subtleties"* Hamilton was describing was Aaron Burr. Hamilton had never forgotten how Burr had won his Senate seat by a sneak upset victory over Philip Schuyler and that Burr had cast the deciding vote on the disputed ballots that lost Hamilton's candidate John Jay the disputed New York gubernatorial election of 1792. He now implored King to "root out the distempered and noisome *weed* which is attempted to be planted in our political garden —to choke and wither in its infancy the fair plant of public credit."

Fisher Ames had fought hard on the floor of the House for the Treasury's bill and was well satisfied with the overall outcome. True, he said, Hamilton had retired "full of the horrors" on account of the refusal of Congress to cover the unsubscribed debt. But the bill as a whole was a famous victory for the Federalists and Hamilton and was anything but the defeat he considered it to be. The shape of the bill, Ames exulted to Gore, "pins fast the funding system, converts the poison of faction into food for federalism; it puts out of the reach of future mobocrats" control of the funds. "It is therefore the finale, the crown of federal measures." Although the crown was a little tarnished by refusal to embrace the small unsubscribed debt, "prudence prevented many of us, who think as formerly, from pressing the right principle, which would have been in vain."

In this blaze of public credit, Hamilton resigned office full of praise and honor from his friends—and "horrors" mostly of his own imagining. The small threat to his own ideal concept of public credit linked with the name and person of Aaron Burr tended to bring on him strange symptoms of nervous derangement.

Hamilton's last days in office were no less vexed and hectic than the rest of his term had been. He fought out arguments with Tench Coxe and Jonathan Dayton over collection of the carriage tax in Kentucky and Virginia. He issued orders to collectors on such subjects as gauging wines and paying duty ad valorem and advances for the support of New Jersey militia, arming of cruisers in American ports for the service of France, payments on the foreign loans, and buying copper for use by the mint and for coppering vessels. He reported to Congress on all goods on which duties of 7½ and 10 percent were paid in 1793 and also on the quantities of coffee, cocoa, and coal imported in that year. He issued a report on erecting a lighthouse at Watch Hill, Rhode Island and a last long "Report on the Improvement and Better Management of the Revenue of the United States," which he turned in to Speaker Muhlenberg on January 31, 1795, his last day in office.

The Monday after his resignation became effective, Hamilton received one of the supreme testimonials of American history:

Dear Sir,

    After so long an experience of your public services, I am naturally led, at the moment of your departure from office—which it has always been my wish to prevent—to review them.

"In every relation," George Washington wrote, "which you have borne to me, I have found that my confidence in your talents, exertions, and integrity, has been well placed. I the more freely render this testimony of my approbation, because I speak from opportunities of information which cannot deceive me, and which furnish satisfactory proof of your title to public regard.

"My most earnest wishes for your happiness will attend you in your retirement, and you may assure yourself of the sincere esteem regard and friendship of

"Dear Sir Your Affectionate Go: Washington"

On February 2 Hamilton gratefully acknowledged Washington's thank-you note by saying, "As often as I may recall the vexations I have endured, your approbation will be a great and precious consolation."

He guarded the deep bond linking the two of them beneath a surface reserve and dignity of expression that were no less intense for matching Washington's own. "I entreat you to be persuaded," Hamilton wrote "(not the less for my having been sparing in professions) that I shall never cease to render a just tribute to those eminent and excellent qualities which have been already productive of so many blessings to your country—that you will always have my fervent wishes for your public and personal felicity . . ."

Only one thing could have better served than Washington's letter to raise Hamilton's spirits out of the "horrors" he had expressed to Fisher Ames and Rufus King. It was Angelica Church's letter to Elizabeth of December 11, which his wife would receive about the time of his leaving office. "Do you believe there is hope of your going to New York to sit for life! . . . I confess I should not like to settle at Philadelphia (much more expensive . . . than in cities of the same size in England)." If the Hamiltons came back to New York, Angelica would rush there to join them, without waiting for her husband: "If my brother resigns there will be no reason for my not going immediately to New York and be under his and your care till Mr. Church can leave this country."

Hamilton had not seen her since that late afternoon in November of 1789 just after first assuming the office he was now resigning, when he had stood on the Battery with Baron von Steuben and his little Philip and watched her ship sail down toward the Narrows and wept, remembering the earlier weeks of that summer when she had lived with him there in his loving care. Perhaps in Vergilian melancholy he would murmur again *forsan et haec meminisse iuvabit.* On March 6, 1795, he wrote her from Albany, where he was sojourning with Eliza and the children, "here at your fathers house who is himself at New York attending the Legislature, we remain till June, when I become stationary at New York . . . My dear sister, I tell you without regret . . . that I am poorer than when I went into office. I allot myself full five or six years of more work than will be pleasant though much less than I have had for the last five years . . . You know how much we all love you. Tis impossible you can be so well loved where you are."

George Hammond, the British minister, was almost as unhappy about Hamilton's resignation as Angelica was thrilled. He commented to his home government that "Hamilton's resignation, deprives me of the advantages I derived, from the confidential and friendly intercourse, that I have uniformly had with him," when he was "the most influential member of this administration." He supposed that Oliver Wolcott, Jr., the comptroller, would succeed Hamilton. Wolcott, Hammond thought, was "a very candid and worthy man, and has been much in Hamilton's confidence. He is also said to possess very considerable talents. Yet . . . it is not probable that he will ever be able to acquire the influence which his predecessor possessed."

As Hammond had predicted, on Hamilton's recommendation, Washington elevated Oliver Wolcott, Jr., to succeed him as treasury secretary. Wolcott proved to be as friendly to Hammond as his mentor had been. Five months later, Wolcott was furnishing Hammond with useful confidential news of the Senate's rejection of Article XII of Jay's Treaty.

Another thing that helped to lift Hamilton's spirits out of "horrors" at Congress's repudiation of nonsubscribers—and Burr's brightening prospects of election as New York's next governor—was that on February 23 the Chamber of Commerce of New York City gave him testimony of their esteem at a dinner in his honor attended by more than 200 gentlemen, "the rooms not being large enough to accomodate more." The *Daily Advertiser* reported that both "great dignity" and "great conviviality" marked the entertainment. The company found "peculiar satisfaction" in "demonstrating their respect for a man who . . . HAS DESERVED WELL OF HIS COUNTRY." On March 16, Richard Varick, the mayor, and the aldermen and commonalty of New York City resolved that "as a testimony of the high sense they entertain of the public services of Alexander Hamilton . . . he be presented with the freedom of the City."

After 1792, Hamilton's policies at the Treasury had given Populist-leaning New York State Republicans the kind of issues they needed to build a strong, statewide party in opposition to him. British raids on neutral shipping gave George Clinton's men a rallying cry in a city that depended on seaborne trade, and Clinton had welcomed Edmond Genêt into his family as a son-in-law. Republican uproar over Hamilton's firm suppression of the Whiskey Insurrection helped Republicans win a majority of New York's congressional delegation in the elections of 1794. So when George Clinton announced that he would not run for governor again in 1795, members of both parties began looking to Aaron Burr as a possible successor. His chances seemed bright. But if John Jay, although now absent in London, should return to the United States with a treaty that removed the British from the posts on New York's frontiers and settled some of the rights and wrongs of British seizures of ships at sea, the Federalists might be able to snatch the "peace and prosperity" issue away from the Republicans, run John Jay for governor, and win the state for themselves.

One David Campbell wrote Hamilton offering his support and that of his friends to elect Hamilton governor. Suspicion of a tactic of Burr may have led Hamilton to scribble on the back of Campbell's letter: "This letter was probably written with some ill design—I keep it without answer as a clue to future events." Philip Schuyler placed a notice in Noah Webster's paper of Hamilton's "firm determination to serve in no public office whatever." Hamilton and Schuyler warned that public opinion should not be confused by talk of Hamilton as a candidate for governor. That would divide votes between himself and his friend John Jay and serve only the fell purposes of Aaron Burr.

Hamilton's friends hoped, and his enemies feared, that his withdrawal from the Treasury left him available for a call to run for higher office even than the governorship of New York. Through the years so far, Hamilton's affair with Maria Reynolds had been kept a secret from the public at large, although at all times after the night of December 15, 1792, his reputation had been held hostage to the gossip of prominent insiders. His enemies' suppressed and publicly unmentionable knowledge of the affair had certainly contributed to the extraordinary malice and heat behind the attacks made on Hamilton and his programs in Congress for other ostensible reasons during the years since 1792.

John Beckley kept as busy as ever digging up new shards of Hamilton scandal and sending them to Madison for his and Jefferson's and Monroe's delectation and files. On May 25, 1795, Beckley wrote Madison that "about six or eight weeks ago, whilst Hamilton was in N. York Commodore James Nicholson in conversation with the friend of Hamilton's [Josiah Ogden Hoffman] stated that he had authentic information . . . that Hamilton had vested 100,000 sterling in the British funds, whilst he was Secretary of the Treasury, which sum was still held by a Banking house in London, to his use and interest." Hamilton ignored the charge. To his enemies, his failure to come forward to refute it tended to lend it substance.[1]

Back in 1788, Commodore Nicholson had been commander of the symbolic model ship *Alexander Hamilton*, which had served as the centerpiece of the parade celebrating New York's ratification of the Constitution. Now he was one of the chiefs of Hamilton's enemies. Nicholson told Beckley that "if Hamilton's name is brought up as a candidate for any public office, he will instantly publish the circumstance."

The dealings Hamilton had carried on over the years for his brother-in-law and principal client, John Barker Church, had a remarkable scope and dimension, from which a John Beckley could easily root out other shards of suspicion of scandal for his mentors' jottings. Church had large funds to invest and kept a shrewd speculative eye on America. Hamilton had served as his agent most of the time he had been secretary of the treasury and diligently attended to Church's private affairs. He appointed William Seton of the Bank of New York as his subagent, with instructions to purchase or sell the funded debt and United States bank shares for Church as the occasion might require. Somewhat similar to the use of a "blind trust" by politicians in contemporary times, this served to insulate Hamilton from charges that he himself was making improper use of inside information obtained in his official capacity, but this was a refinement easily left unmentioned by a Beckley. In 1793, Church's transactions involved substantial sums and unusual circumstances, for Church's orders to purchase national bank shares, relayed through Hamilton, were not backed up by cash. In alarm, Seton had written to Hamilton: "I think you will not blame me for making this further observation; Mr. Church's circumstances and responsibility I am totally ignorant of, £10,000 [sterling] is a very large sum to run the risk of even a 20 p Cent [damages?] upon. Now my dear Sir for you or under your absolute guarantee of course I would commit myself for any sum." Even a banker like Seton seemed under the illusion that Hamilton himself was affluent enough to make good Church's debts: "I must confess to you sincerely that unless I had you to look to, I should deem my self unjustifiable to my family to enter into this negotiation."

Hamilton or Church furnished Seton the necessary assurances, and Seton commenced purchasing the shares at attractive prices until, by the end of March 1794, he had on Church's account investments valued at £7,856.16 sterling. At this time the price began to fall, and Hamilton instructed Seton to discontinue further purchases until the market was stabilized. By May the bottom had been reached. Seton went into the market again for Church, bought more than £10,000, and was able to report to Hamilton that their mutual client was well satisfied with his operations. To retrieve his private credit by going back to private law practice meant serving profitable but often embarrassingly un-meritorious causes, or riding out excruciating conflicts of interest.

From abroad Church also lent out money, through Hamilton, as his attorney in fact, at substantial rates of interest. One of the borrowers was no less a personage than Robert Morris, whose reputation as the Financier of the Revolution and one of the richest men in the country kept Hamilton and Church from realizing until too late that he had overextended himself and was secretly bank-rupt. The sum he owed to Church was large; and Morris, to stave off a final crash like Duer's and debtors' prison, asked repeatedly for extensions, which Hamilton granted.

Finally, Church demanded that Hamilton insist upon immediate payment by Robert Morris. Instead, Morris offered a mortgage on 50,000 acres of land near Pittsburgh as security. Hamilton was also rendering legal services to his erst-while friend Morris, who had been his sponsor for appointment to the Treasury office. Their dealings continued until by 1797, another terrible year of pressure and nervous derangement for Hamilton, Morris owed legal fees to Hamilton of $12,088.33 and still had not been able to pay back Church. Under the pressure of Church's lash, Hamilton pressed Morris to pay up both accounts. Morris was so desperate he now asked Hamilton to represent him as his own lawyer against Church. "I would fain hope that he does not wish to take advantage of my necessities and obtain my property at less than its worth," he complained to Hamilton.

When Hamilton, still under pressure from Church, finally issued an attach-ment against Morris's property, Morris complained: "Your agency in it astonishes me, if it is for the balance of the money you lent me, I shall deem myself more unfortunate than ever before." Hamilton explained to Morris that he was not suing on his own account for his fee, but on behalf of Church only. Morris accepted the explanation and promised repayment as soon as possible. But Morris never recovered. His magnificent home outside of Philadelphia was seized by his creditors, and in 1798 the man who had managed the economy of the revolutionary states through the most perilous period of their history was thrown into the debtors' prison at the corner of Prince Street (now Locust and Sixth). Only after Gouverneur Morris, who had once been Robert Morris's junior partner, returned from Europe in 1799, was a plan worked out to set up a trust in the name of his wife, Mary, and settle the most pressing debts so that he could be released from jail. In this, Hamilton's services as counsel were instrumental in helping arrange his ultimate deliverance from debtors' prison.

The tension and pressure of his lawyer-client relationship with a brother-in-law like John Barker Church were a curious complement to the ties of affection that bound Hamilton to Angelica. Once when he wrote of the possibility that he might make "a short excursion to Europe," Angelica was suddenly thrilled. Months passed, the prospect faded, and she told her sister Eliza despairingly: "You and my dear Hamilton will never cross the Atlantic, I shall never leave this Island and as to meeting in heaven—there will be no pleasure in that."

Rarely did she mention her successful businessman husband; always it was Hamilton, his career, his prospects, her pride in his fame and achievements, her despair at his absence. To her sister she wrote recklessly of her "Amiable"—"by my Amiable you know I mean your husband, for I love him very much and if you were as generous as the old Romans, you would lend him to me for a little while, but do not be jealous, my dear Eliza, since I am more solicitous to promote his laudable ambition, than any person in the world, and there is no summit of true glory which I do not desire he may attain; provided always that he pleases to give me a little chit-chat, and sometimes to say, I wish our dear Angelica was here."

Having cast an unforgettable spell on American ministers in Europe like John Adams and Thomas Jefferson, Angelica Church had the same effect on Europeans heading for America. She passed on to the hospitality of the Hamiltons the duc de La Rochefoucauld-Liancourt, Talleyrand, Beaumetz, Chastellux, Moreau de Saint-Méry, and many others. They found in Hamilton a charming host full of sympathy for all they had suffered at the hands of the terror they had fled. His elegant manners; lively, warm, confiding personal style, and political point of view were something few had expected to find in what many still thought of as the raw American wilderness. Arriving in Philadelphia while Hamilton was still secretary of the treasury, Saint-Méry was amazed by the Spartan simplicity of the office of a man whose power seemed to be that of a prime minister. But he thought of Hamilton's West Indies French, while fluent, as "very incorrect." Rochefoucauld-Liancourt thought Hamilton "one of the most interesting men in America," uniting dignity and feeling and much force and decision with delightful manners and great sweetness. In short, he found him "infinitely agreeable."

Charles Maurice de Talleyrand-Périgord, that subtle fox who outlived the greatest lions of Europe, symbolized in his own slight frame the old European diplomacy. In America in 1794 he wished to meet the men who had succeeded in creating what had so far failed in France, a workable, liberal constitutional republic. He saw Hamilton as his own American counterpart and had little contact with Republicans like Jefferson, who professed such fervent admiration for the terrifying French regime that had driven him into exile.

During the two winters that Talleyrand was compelled to spend in Philadelphia and New York until recall to France, to rise to new heights under Napoleon's Directory, the Empire, and the Bourbon Restoration, Hamilton and Talleyrand became close friends. Hamilton considered Talleyrand "the greatest of modern statesmen, because he had so well known when it was necessary both to suffer wrong to be done and to do it."

Hamilton's "Final Report on the Public Credit" followed many of Talleyrand's ideas about the meaning of public credit. They carried a useful cargo of meaning for an individual's credit as well. Private credit, like public, was "a faculty to borrow at pleasure considerable sums on moderate terms, the art of distributing over a succession of years the extraordinary efforts found indispensable in one, a means of accelerating the prompt employment of the abilities of [a nation] and even of disposing of a part of the overplus of others." For his part, Talleyrand later was quoted as saying: "I consider Napoleon, Pitt and Hamilton as the three greatest men of our age, and if I had to choose between the three, I would unhesitatingly give the first place to Hamilton. He has divined Europe."

Talleyrand, projecting on others an obsession for which he himself was notorious, observed rather scornfully that in America money was worshiped with a devotion "very often coarsely expressed." Late one evening during his stay in New York, Talleyrand passed Hamilton's law offices on his way to a social engagement. Through the window he saw the spare figure of his friend bent over his desk, quill in hand, writing out a long legal document by yellow candlelight. When he arrived at the party, said to have been a glittering levee, bright with beautiful women in shimmering crinolines, brilliant conversation, and Mozartean divertimenti rippling through the salons, Talleyrand exclaimed, "I have just come from viewing a man who made the fortune of his country, but who is working all night in order to support his family." Talleyrand was not the man to understand such a scene. In France, Talleyrand and men like him became richer, not poorer, while holding high public office. Of Hamilton's having to resign office to support his family, Talleyrand joked to a lady that he "found this a very strange reason, and one that was perhaps a bit silly." The wounding edge of Talleyrand's jibes at his friend's expense at least served to cut the ground from under the tales endlessly circulated by enemies that Hamilton had enriched himself by speculations and peculations in public office.

When Talleyrand sought to be officially received by the president, it was probably Hamilton who handed Lord Lansdowne's letter of recommendation to Washington. Jefferson, as secretary of state, strongly opposed Washington's receiving him, and Washington followed Jefferson's advice. For a long time in Paris, Talleyrand and Gouverneur Morris had shared the favors of Adèle de

Flauhaut, who presided as joint mistress over their *ménage à trois*. The résumé that Morris sent on about Talleyrand, the Bishop d'Autun, a bishop of the Catholic Church, had probably not helped open doors for him at Martha Washington's. Morris had said, "With respect to morals, none of them [Talleyrand, Narbonne, and Choiseul] is exemplary. The Bishop [Talleyrand] is particularly blamed on that score. Not so much for adultery, because that was common enough among the clergy of high rank, but for the variety and publicity of his amours, for gambling, and above all for stock jobbing during the Ministry of M. de Calonne . . ." Talleyrand was a past master of the uses in diplomacy of nonrecognition and snub. For denying him the public credit of an official reception after Hamilton's introduction, he would pay back Washington, Jefferson, and the United States, in kind with interest three years later by means of the nocuous affair of XY and Z and maybe W.

John Jay had finally returned to New York from his mission to London on May 28, 1795, while the votes in his race against Robert Yates for governor of New York were still being canvassed. On June 5 the chief justice of the United States was officially proclaimed the winner over Yates, the chief justice of New York. Jay resigned his chief-justiceship on June 29 and took over from George Clinton, who was retiring undefeated after five terms. William Bradford of Pennsylvania, a friend and admirer of Hamilton, who had replaced Edmund Randolph as attorney general, needed Hamilton's advice when he wrote him on July 2, 1795. "Your squabbles in New York have taken our Chief Justice from us," he noted; "ought you not to find us another?" In Bradford's mind and probably also in Washington's, Hamilton would be the ideal choice. They wanted him, but it was not a draft. Bradford added, "I am afraid that department, as it related neither to War, finances nor negotiations, has no charms for you: and yet when one considers how immensely important it is, where [the justices] have the power of paralyzing the measures of the government by declaring a law unconstitutional, it is not to be trusted to men who are to be scared by popular clamor . . . I wish to heaven you would permit me to name you: If not, what think you of Mr. Randolph?" Bradford's comments on the immense importance of the highest court's powers of judicial review and judicial supremacy were as startlingly prescient as the name of his candidate. It would be eight years before John Marshall's opinion in *Marbury vs. Madison* ratified much of the reasoning of Hamilton's brief in the case of *Rutgers vs. Waddington* of 1784, and *The Federalist Papers* he had written in 1787 and 1788 concerning the powers of the Supreme Court.

No lawyer who was also a devoted friend of Hamilton could have made him a more persuasive argument for accepting the appointment. Who else but Hamilton would be more likely to interpret the Constitution in a way that would give reach and power to public credit, to the Federal government, and to the court itself? When would such interpretations be more necessary than in the immediate future? Appointment to the chief-justiceship of the United States Supreme Court for one of the most critical periods of American history was Hamilton's now for the asking.

The chief-justiceship was loftily above the political arena. It was far removed from the cross fire of partisan politics, where Hamilton, as Federalist party leader, remained the prime target of opportunity for Republican enemies like John Beckley, James Nicholson, Madison, Jefferson, Burr, and all their congressional and journalistic myrmidons. Its light, early case load and regular hours and terms would free Hamilton from the economic pressures of working late into the night to support his family and the political pressures of the attacks by his enemies that would bring on worse nervous derangements than any he had yet suffered.

Bradford would settle for a lesser commitment from Hamilton. If Hamilton insisted on renouncing all offices except his law office, would the champion of enforcing federal excises in the remotest western counties permit Bradford to retain him as special counsel to the attorney general in a pending case in which the government was seeking to uphold the validity of the carriage tax law? This was a vital case, necessary in order to secure Supreme Court confirmation of the national government's right to levy excise taxes. If Hamilton would not serve the Supreme Court full time back of the bench as chief justice, then at least he could serve before it as an advocate. By way of a final salute, Bradford added, "I hear that you have renounced everything but your profession—that you will not even pick up money when it lies at your feet, unless it comes in the form of a fee!" He knew his friend well. He concluded, "But it is vain to kick against the pricks. You were made for a Statesman & politics will never be out of your head." Left unsaid was deep sympathy for what must have been Hamilton's most compelling reason for declining the chief-justiceship: the hope that he could earn more money in private law practice to make up for the deprivations his family had suffered and the funds Schuyler had helped supply while he had busied himself creating the public credit of the nation.

Of all the sad things a sympathetic follower of Hamilton's career may say of it with perfect hindsight, one of the saddest is that he could have been the second chief justice of the United States Supreme Court beginning on or about July 2, 1795, but turned down the offer. If he had only taken this road not taken and wrapped himself in the nonpartisan armor and dignity of the chief justice's robes at 38, he would have been shielded from all the skeans and skeins of scandal with which Beckley and Callender and their masters soon would assail him. He would have escaped the eye of the political storm over Jay's Treaty that was about to break around his head. His innate style and sense of the dignity and propriety the role demanded would probably have restrained him from nervous and violent overreaction to enemies real and imagined that would mark and mar the rest of his life. Positioned above the political fray for three or four decades to come—longevity in this Valhalla of the law is real, not legendary— he would have brought to the fleshing out of a supreme Constitution for the Union a tone of strength and power to match or even surpass the achievement of his great friend and admirer John Marshall. He would have remained ready, waiting, and supremely eligible to accept a call to the presidency at any time it might come during the next decades and more and pass the robes of chief justice on to Marshall when it came. But Hamilton felt too much the need to make some money quickly in the private practice of law and restore his private credit to the level of the public credit he had left the nation as his legacy on leaving office. Yet no conceivable sum of lucrative fees ground out of a private law practice would compensate him for the loss of psychic dividends foregone with this last proffered office of public credit. He turned down Washington's and Bradford's offer of the chief-justiceship. He consented, however, to act as special counsel in the carriage tax case. Seven weeks later, on August 23, William Bradford died, and the other offer would never come his way again.

17

AN INSOLVENT COLOSSUS
IS STONED
BY A WALL STREET MOB

BUT WHAT CAN I DIRECT WHO AM (I FEAR) INSOLVENT?
—*To Robert Troup, named executor of Hamilton's
last will and testament, July 25, 1795*

HAMILTON IS REALLY A COLOSSUS TO THE ANTI-REPUBLICAN
PARTY—WITHOUT NUMBERS, HE IS AN HOST WITHIN HIMSELF.
—*Jefferson to Madison, September 21, 1795*

John Jay and Lord Grenville had signed Jay's Treaty in London on November 19, 1794, but the first copy of it did not reach Philadelphia until March 7, 1795. For the next two months George Washington and Secretary of State Edmund Randolph kept its contents secret before they submitted it to the special session of the Senate that convened on June 8, printed in 31 copies, one for each of 30 senators and one for Secretary of State Randolph, all "under an injunction of secrecy." All the while, public suspicions smoldered. By June 26, Hamilton in New York heard that the Senate had approved the treaty. He wrote Oliver Wolcott, Jr., that "decorum requires" that the French minister be told of it "to satisfy him that there is nothing in it inimical to his country." France must be treated as fairly and evenhandedly as possible because "it is well to guard our peace on all sides as far as shall consist with dignity." He disapproved of the secrecy: "All further mystery at present is unnecessary & ought to be waived for the satisfaction of the public mind." He was for full and prompt disclosure to the public: "I do not think any samples of diplomatic decorum of weight enough to stand in the way." Indeed, such secrecy was political folly: "The non publication of the treaty is working as I expected, giving much scope to misrepresentation & misapprehension."

The most objectionable provision was Article XII. It was one of the commercial provisions, limited as to time, which granted America only restricted trading privileges in the West Indies. Hamilton foresaw that the Senate would not approve it, and on June 11 he suggested a shrewd device to Rufus King that might yet save the worthwhile parts of the treaty. "No time is fixed for the ratification," he pointed out. The United States should ratify the treaty as a whole, but declare that they take Article XII as being intended by Britain as a "privilege." Then the United States should declare that they forbear to exercise the "privilege" until a more acceptable modification is agreed on between the American minister and the British court. Final ratifications of the treaty would not be exchanged unless this qualification were accepted.

In the still secret Senate debates, Aaron Burr moved on June 22 to reject Jay's Treaty *in toto* and renegotiate it. Senator Henry Tazewell of Virginia moved on June 24 to vote it down on various grounds, one being that it "hath not secured satisfaction from the British government, for the removal of negroes, in violation of the treaty of 1783." The treaty also asserted "a power in the President and Senate, to control and even annihilate the constitutional right of the Congress . . . over their commercial intercourse with foreign nations." Complaints about noncompensation for slaves were to be expected from Virginians, but Tazewell also seemed to be raising the new constitutional point that the House of Representatives, as well as the Senate, must pass implementing laws before the treaty could take effect.

But on June 24 the Senate approved the treaty, except for Article XII, by a vote of 20 to 10, a bare two-thirds Federalist majority, with not a single vote to spare. On Article XII it followed Hamilton's advice, suspending its effectiveness until the British should modify it. After rescinding the president's injunction of secrecy, but enjoining themselves "not to authorize or allow any copy of said communication," the Senate adjourned on the twenty-sixth. Several senators explained to Hamilton that the reason they had still not authorized publication of the text was because "they thought it the affair of the President to do as he thought fit."

Washington and Randolph agreed that the full text of the treaty should be published in *The Philadelphia Gazette* on July 1, perhaps because that was the earliest date that Randolph could get back his only copy of the British treaty from the new French minister, Pierre Auguste Adet, to whom he had lent it. But as is customary with secret Senate deliberations, a copy was leaked to the press earlier. On June 29 an abstract of the treaty was published in Benjamin Franklin Bache's Philadelphia *Aurora*. The whole intensely curious nation pounced on it with cries of outrage.

Thomas Jefferson sounded off with characteristic extravagance, telling Madison in private that it was the boldest "party stroke ever struck." He imputed sedition to its supporters, calling it "an attempt to undermine the government." He wrote Edward Rutledge that it was "a treaty of alliance between England and the Anglomen of this country against the legislature and people of the United States." He wrote Mann Page that "a rogue of a pilot" had run the ship of state "into an enemy's port." He was still fulminating behind the scenes the following year when he wrote on March 27, 1796, that Washington was "the only honest man who has assented to" the treaty. He charged that through intrigue "a faction" had "entered into a conspiracy with the enemies of their country to chain down the legislature at the feet of both." Still later, after Washington had finally signed the treaty, Jefferson lamented to his friend and neighbor Philip Mazzei that Washington had been duped: "Men who were Samsons in the field and Solomons in the council . . . have had their head shorn by the harlot England." It was characteristic of Jefferson to attack the person and character of political opponents in terms of sleeping with harlots instead of arguing out his differences with their views on the issues. It was also characteristic of him that he would later deny that his allusion to a Samson "shorn by the harlot England" had meant Washington. Madison duly pleased Jefferson by joining him in his simplistic attacks, but rather perfunctorily, saying vaguely that Jay's Treaty "granted everything to Great Britain for nothing in return" and also that it would make it impossible to get a good commercial treaty with "any other nation." It irked Madison that merchants and people in the carrying trade generally favored the treaty, despite his assertion that it appeared "to assassinate the interest" of such people. Senator William Maclay of Pennsylvania even chimed in by wishing that Washington were dead, so that he would not "be brought forward as the constant cover to every unconstitutional and irrepublican act."

Other Southern slave owners like John Rutledge and General Charles Cotesworth Pinckney of South Carolina, who were normally Federalist supporters, also opposed the treaty, although Rutledge later, upon sober reflection, let it be known that he regretted having spoken intemperately against it. At first, even in Boston the "merchants and steady men" joined the emotional opposition, although Massachusetts later swung round to support the treaty. At a public meeting in Faneuil Hall, not a single voice was raised in its favor. In Philadelphia on July 3 a sullen mob turned out in response to handbills that urged attacks on a British vessel at Goldbury's Wharf in the harbor. The following night, only calling out the cavalry had prevented another mob from burning John Jay in effigy in front of Washington's house on Market Street. They burned the sober, upright envoy in the image of a straw man in the suburb of Kensington instead. The ten senators who had voted against ratification were toasted by Republicans for having "refused to sign the death warrant of American liberty." Glasses were raised to "a perpertual Harvest to America—but clipped wings, lame legs, the pip and an empty crop to all Jays." Three weeks later, still another mob demonstrated angrily in Philadelphia in front of the residences of the British minister, the British consul, and the Mansion House of Anne and William Bingham, setting fire to copies of the treaty.

Opponents sneered that Jay had resigned from the Supreme Court to serve as governor of New York, just in time to escape being impeached. Washington nominated John Rutledge of South Carolina to succeed him, but Rutledge had been the bitterest foe of Jay's Treaty in his home state, and when the South Carolina legislature, under his leadership, indicted the treaty for its lack of compensation to slave owners for slaves carried off by the British, Adams had called the vote "the meanest which has ever been passed; not one of the mobs have been so sordid as to put the whole treaty upon the single point of pay for the Negroes . . ." The Federalist Senate rejected Rutledge, but the unpopularity of the treaty bearing Jay's name removed him as a future rival to Adams for the presidency—and also as a Federalist counterweight to Jefferson. In the end the uproar strengthened only Jefferson, who had, as usual, absquatulated from the public fray.

Oliver Wolcott, Jr., noted to Hamilton that the British could hardly help thinking the worst of America, with "the country rising in a flame; their minister's house insulted by a mob; their flag dragged through the streets." He wished that Hamilton or Rufus King or Jay himself could come to Philadelphia to give him counsel in the crisis.

Washington knew that Jay's Treaty left much to be desired, but he was appalled by the violence of attacks like Jefferson's, Madison's, and Maclay's and their incitement of mobs to demonstrations. He complained to Hamilton that it was like "a paroxysm of the fever," a cry "like that against a mad dog," with "everyone, in a manner . . . engaged in running it down."

Washington had not yet signed it. Before doing so, like Wolcott, he pleaded for Hamilton's counsel: "Aid me, I pray you, with your sentiments." Sending Hamilton a copy of the treaty on July 3, Washington sought his opinion as a "dispassionate" man who had "knowledge of the subject, and abilities to judge of it." Hamilton, he said, had "given as much attention to" the entire subject "as most men," and "your late employment under the general government afforded you more opportunities of deriving Knowledge therein, than most of them who had not studied and practiced it scientifically, upon a large and comprehensive scale." He also asked Hamilton whether, if one assumed that Britain should agree to suspension of Article XII, as the Senate directed, it was necessary to have the treaty again ratified by the Senate.

Hamilton's reply of July 9–11, running to 43 pages in print, is characteristically scholarly, penetrating, and moderate in criticism and advocacy of the treaty in his best "better than nothing" vein.

As Hamilton explained, during the Revolution many slaves had gained freedom from their owners by joining the British army or by escaping during British occupation of their owners' plantations to one of the few states like Pennsylvania where the gradual abolition of slavery had been instituted by law. In other cases, the British had taken the slaves away from their owners.

The Treaty of Paris ending the war provided that restitution should be made to the former owners in the latter cases. But the question of whether the British —or the slaves' own human desire for freedom—had resulted in the loss to the owners was a vexed one in many cases. When the slave owners returned, they had demanded compensation in money from the British for loss of their cattle, slaves, and other chattels. Back in 1784, when Virginia had opened its courts to permit British nationals to sue to collect pre-Revolutionary War debts owing to them from large plantation owners like Thomas Jefferson, it was made a condition of suit that the British first pay compensation for loss of slaves. But under English common law, as laid down by Sir William Blackstone, following the law of nations generally, Hamilton explained, once a slave became free, he "becomes a free man" for all purposes forever afterward. Once the original contract of servitude between slave and master was broken, the relation of slave and master could not be resumed, "that Right being now Extinct, which the victor by war obtained over his slave, natural liberty returns." Jay's Treaty omitted compensation to slave owners and breeders like Jefferson for slaves the British had permitted to become free. The British were being asked to pay compensation for slaves for which they had received no equivalent value, only nonmonetary credit for humaneness in freeing them.

Advising a Virginia slave owner like Washington, Hamilton dealt judiciously, but humanely with the issue. Britain's action in "seducing away our negroes" during the war was infamous, he allowed, but, "having done it, it would be still more infamous to surrender them to their masters." Though in the interpretation of treaties, "the restoration *of property* is a favoured thing yet the surrender of persons *to slavery* is an odious thing speaking in the language of the laws of nations." Nothing, neither Hamilton's concern for his Virginia friend's delicate position as a slave owner nor his usual insistence on respect for the rights of private property, the sanctity of contracts, and the obligations of the enemy to pay reparations nor the political expediency from the Federalist point of view of avoiding offense to such staunch Southern Federalists as John Rutledge and Charles Cotesworth Pinckney, could cause Hamilton to compromise his hatred of slavery on economic, political, moral, and humane grounds by softening his stand. Later in his *Camillus* series, No. III, he put it still more strongly at still greater personal risk to himself, saying, "The abandonment of negroes, who had been induced to quit their masters on the strength of official proclamations promising them liberty, to fall again under the yoke of their masters and into slavery is as *odious* and *immoral* a thing as can be conceived . . . odious, as it imposes an act of perfidy on one of the contracting parties . . . odious as it tends to bring back to servitude men once made free. The general interests of humanity conspire to repel this construction."

The question of which nation had first broken the treaty of peace was a vexed one. Hamilton concluded that American obstructions to payment of private British creditors had occurred even prior to British taking of the Negroes.

He heartily endorsed the promise not to sequester British property in American funds. Any taking of these would be disreputable to public credit.

Other objections to the treaty had more merit, he thought. It failed to deal with the impressment of American seamen by the British navy. A disarmed border between Canada and the United States had been one of Hamilton's cherished goals throughout his career, ever since he had urged, as a member of the Continenetal Congress in 1783, that a provision for it be included in the peace treaty, but Lord Grenville had rejected this because Hamilton's plan interfered with his own scheme of erecting a "neutral" Indian barrier state south of the boundary. Jay's Treaty did provide that the British posts were to be evacutated by June 1, 1796, after which Indians living on either side of the border would be free to cross it to carry on normal trade without payment of fees or duties. This was objectionable to Hamilton because it involved a delay of evacuation by more than a year. But under the treaty, "citizens of both the United States and Canada would have access to inland waterways of both parties." Other points to which objection might be made by others were the provisions that American citizens would not join the French army or navy and that, to keep faith in public credit, private debts would not be confiscated, even in the event of war. The treaty declared it "unjust and impolitic" that such debts be "destroyed or impaired . . . on account of national differences and discontents." The commercial articles of the treaty, which were to be binding for only 12 years, included guarantees against future tariff and tonnage discrimination and opened East Indies and West Indies trade to American vessels. But the West Indies were only partially opened—to American vessels of not more than 70 tons burden. To make doubly sure that American bottoms would not preempt all the carrying trade between the islands and Britain, a specific prohibition was added against exportation of "molasses, sugar, coffee, cocoa, or cotton" in American vessels even from the United States, the assumption being that these items would have originated in the West Indies. This restriction was the notorious Article XII, on which Republican cries against the treaty came to focus. But this had already been rejected by the Senate before ratification. Hamilton told Washington he considered this article "exceptionable," "unprecedented," and "wrong." Hamilton had always thought Article XII was inadmissible because it forbade the United States to reexport commodities that were products of the British West Indies, but which also might be products of other places as well, including in the case of cotton, the United States. Hamilton was glad, "though at the risk of the treaty, that the Senate has not accepted it." Hamilton gave Jay credit for his reasoning in accepting the article—that gaining even limited access to the British West Indian islands while Britain and France were at war was all-important—but Hamilton thought this was insufficient to warrant that limitation on American trade with other customers even for a limited period. By contrast, the article giving American ships admission to the ports of India was a clear gain, for which Britain had obtained no quid pro quo.

The worst article in the treaty after Article XII was XVIII. Jay's Treaty embodied the old rule of 1756 sanctioned by international law that an enemy's goods might be taken from a neutral's vessel. Under the "Armed Neutrality" doctrine, Americans had contended that "neutral ships made neutral goods" or "free ships made free goods." Many Americans had hoped to win that new rule because it would protect American ships carrying noncontraband goods to France. Opponents cried that Jay had given sanction to Britain's order-in-council of June, permitting the seizure of provisions as contraband if they had been paid for. This would cut off food shipments to France. Hamilton thought it not so seriously defective because it had been found impossible to agree on all possible circumstances warranting seizures of goods, and Britain and France were at war. Jay had gone along to keep negotiations going. Britain might abuse this clause, and France complain of it, but Hamilton did not think it alone was ground for rejecting the entire treaty.

The treaty expressly provided that it could not be repugnant to prior American commitments to France. True, it would stop Americans from permitting France to sell her prizes in American ports, but this was not a treaty commitment to Britain. It simply eliminated an unneutral concession to France, which should have been done away with in any event.

In general, Jay's Treaty finally clinched the peace with Britain and promised America immunity from "the dreadful war that is ruining Europe." America's prime need was for peace. War now would seriously check growth; if we could escape war for ten or a dozen years, we might match the great powers' strength with strength of our own. By the treaty we must compensate Britain for debts, but this was a small price to pay for substantial long-term benefits. The commercial articles, all temporary, would matter little one way or the other in the long run. We preserved our faith with other powers, particularly France, made no improper concessions, and gained "rather more" than we gave. It was better than nothing, Hamilton counseled, and should be signed by Washington. Hamilton's advice to Washington served as the Federalist brief for political defense of the treaty.

Jefferson later wrote that Hamilton, when discussing the treaty with Talleyrand, called it an "execrable" one and said that Jay was "an old woman for making it." Such typically open but indiscreet comments in private conversation were not inconsistent with Hamilton's advice to Washington. It was far from perfect, and it was "execrable" because Hamilton could have negotiated better terms, but Jay's Treaty was still better than no treaty. Having weighed the question carefully and reached his conclusion upon a preponderance of evidence that tipped the balance slightly in its favor, Hamilton set to work to make it a reality as if none of its defects had ever crossed his mind. He soon became famous, or infamous, as the chief sponsor of Jay's Treaty. This earned him a place beside Jay as the chief target of public and private Republican abuse, from the highest on his hilltop to the mad dogs in the street—mobs attacking and burning straw Jays in effigy.

Fisher Ames, a supporter of the treaty, wrote Thomas Dwight that a measure that had secured "peace abroad" had kindled "war at home." Oliver Wolcott, Jr., wrote Hamilton on July 28 that "attempts are made to stir up a flame

& convulse the country." He suspected that the uproar was being orchestrated by the unseen hand of a master puppet master: "Though the actors hitherto are known to be a factious set of men & their followers generally a contemptible mob, yet from the systematical manner in which they have proceeded and some curious facts which have recently come to my knowledge, I cannot but suspect *foul play*, by persons not generally suspected."

Hamilton, too, suspected, as he told Wolcott, "that our Jacobins meditate serious mischief to certain individuals," including himself. The New York militia was not to be relied on for protection. The regular soldiers in the fort had just received marching orders, and he wanted Wolcott to ask the secretary of war to countermand them, so that regular troops would be on hand in case of a New York emergency of mob violence. Wolcott assured Hamilton that the troops would remain in New York, as he wished, in case of trouble, which came.

The plague broke out in New York that summer. Heat waves came on early. Hamilton's family fled north to the Schuylers', and Talleyrand and others journeyed north to pay visits to them there. Hamilton, who by now had a lengthening medical history of serious illnesses and derangements each summer, stayed behind to perform what he saw as his duty.

Handbills and notices in newspapers, carefully timed and coordinated with similar ones in Philadelphia and Boston, summoned the citizens of New York City to meet at city hall at high noon on Saturday July 18, 1795, "to deliberate upon the proper mode of communicating to the President their disapprobation of the English Treaty." They urged New Yorkers to follow the recent unanimous action taken at the similar meeting held in Boston's Faneuil Hall. None should be deceived by reports circulated by friends of "coalition" with England that the president had already ratified the treaty; this was a false report designed to discourage enemies of the treaty into thinking further opposition was useless. In New York the name of Faneuil Hall was a code word symbolizing revolution.

Hamilton had written Robert Troup on April 13, "The game to be played may be a most important one. It may be for nothing less than true liberty, property, order, religion and of course *heads*. I will try, Troup, to guard yours and mine." In this, he would be only half successful.

The tactics of treaty opponents in Boston had been skillfully contrived, he pointed out: "It was published one day, and the next a town meeting was convened to condemn it, without ever being read; without any serious discussion, sentence was pronounced upon it." The same tactic was about to succeed in New York unless someone did something to block it.

To forestall the devastating threat of a seemingly unanimous mass public condemnation of the treaty like that contrived at Faneuil Hall, Hamilton and Rufus King hastily called a meeting of merchants and other supporters at the Tontine Coffee House for the Friday night before the Saturday meeting. James Watson served as the chairman. Impassioned speeches by Hamilton and King drawn from the texts of a series of pamphlets called "The Defence" by *Camillus*, which they were just then composing to publish beginning the following week, warmed the ardor of their supporters. They cried down the "spirit of precipitation" and "intemperance" that would prevent the "most considerate citizens from attending the meeting." If good citizens took their ease or fled to estates in the countryside for the July weekend, those who would attend would be "under the guidance of a set of men, who, with two or three exceptions, have been the uniform opposers of government."

Hamilton and King objected particularly that the Saturday meeting had been called not "to consider or discuss the merits of the treaty," but "to induce the citizens to surrender their reason to the empire of their passions" by inflammatory calls for its "disapprobation" without having read it.

As they said farewells to each other outside the Tontine that night, Hamilton and his friends were undertaking a task of seemingly Sisyphean deoppilation: to lift mass public opposition to the treaty into reasoned support for it. Hamilton was accustomed to staying up nights, working Wall Street lawyers' hours, writing copy, and reading proof by candlelight to meet the usual early morning deadlines of Wall Street financial district job printers on the eve of a weekend. Saturday morning the city was filled with a new set of handbills signed by James Watson, containing Hamilton's and King's condemnation of the tactics of the opposition. Their handbill declared that the treaty was not *quite* as bad as represented by its opponents and challenged opponents to debate it on its merits. They pressed fair-minded citizens to be critical of the arguments of its opponents. In a good, but not perfect, cause, the demand for a fair hearing is a better tactic than a head-on argument for the cause itself.

As a result of the handbills issued by both sides, a crowd of 5,000 to 6,000 people—some said 7,000—had collected by high noon Saturday in front of City Hall, filling up Broad Street for a block to the southward and west in Wall Street almost to Trinity Church at the corner of the Broad Way. Leaders of the opposition to the treaty standing on the steps of City Hall were preparing to call their followers to order as the bells in the Trinity church belfry tolled twelve. Suddenly, out of the surging mass of people jamming Broad Street a few dozen yards south of the Wall Street corner strode Hamilton and two or three followers. He leaped up on the stoop of an old Dutch frame building, just south of the famous buttonwood tree where the New York Stock Exchange was founded and its neoclassic facade now stands. His friends Josiah Ogden Hoffman, Senator Rufus King, and Richard Harison quickly closed ranks around him up on the stoop. He began to speak to the crowd in low-keyed words of intense ardor. Thousands of heads and eyes that had been focused on the opposition leaders whispering on the steps of City Hall swung round to stare at Hamilton and his supporters. He had hardly got beyond an innocuous disclaimer of having called the meeting himself, when hoots and calls from down in the crowd interrupted him. "Let us have a chairman," they yelled. Opponents called the crowd's attention back to their leaders on the steps of City Hall. When order was restored, Col. William S. Smith, Vice-president John Adams's son-in-law, was nominated chairman of the meeting. He climbed up onto the balcony where his father-in-law had first taken his oath of office as vice-president.

Peter R. Livingston then began to address the chairman, but from the stoop on the west side of Broad Street, where he stood, Hamilton resumed speaking again and interrupted him. Some voices from the crowd called out for order or perhaps even for a "point of order, Mr. Chairman, point of order!" The question? Who should be allowed to speak first, Livingston or Hamilton? It was a vote on a parliamentary point, not critical to the substantive issue, but it would give some reading of the relative strength of the two factions all mixed up together in the crowd without risk to either of losing the vital vote itself. Chairman Smith put the question to the crowd, and a large noisy majority shouted Hamilton down. Motion carried in favor of Peter Livingston!

Livingston cried that the purpose of the meeting, as the announcements proclaimed, was the same as the meeting in Boston, to call on the president not to sign the treaty. But as he spoke, more shouts and catcalls rose on all sides to levels that drowned his words. Livingston angrily accused the friends of the treaty of disrupting the meeting, of trying to prevent discussion, and of staving off a vote on the provisions of the treaty itself. He moved "that those who disapproved of the treaty should go to the right, and those who approved of it to the left." This would send the part of the disorderly crowd that supported Hamilton over to the front of the stoop where he was standing and leave the treaty's enemies clustered around the steps of City Hall or filling up Wall Street backed up all the way to Trinity. Pushing, shoving, shouting, confused, and hemmed in as it was by the buildings lining the streets, the crowd kept growing more noisy, rancorous, and disorderly and turning into a mob. Believing that the die-hard enemies of the treaty had moved away, Hamilton resumed speaking above the hubbub, passionately urging upon his listeners temperate discussion before they jumped to, or voted on, misguided conclusions. Very little of what he said could be heard "on account of hissings, coughings and hootings, which entirely prevented his proceeding." Conflicting pressures and self-generated excitement soon transformed the crowd into a mob, and some of its members began to turn to other modes of expression than words. They picked up stones and rocks and sticks, and some took aim and flung them toward the stoop where Hamilton stood.

John Jay's brother-in-law, another Livingston, Brockholst Livingston, took his turn trying to cry Hamilton down. He shouted that the treaty had been published for two weeks, that the people had already made up their minds about it, that the street was an improper place for discussion because the speakers could not be heard, that it was impossible to find a building large enough to hold the whole crowd, and that the purpose of the meeting would be defeated by procrastination. Word of ratification might arrive at any moment! If anyone had not already made up his mind against the treaty and would retire to Trinity Church, he would send someone there to discuss it with him, article by article, in opposition to Mr. Hamilton. Hamilton again tried to make himself heard. Opponents of the treaty found it impossible to silence him or draw off the friends of the treaty from the opposition. Hamilton had stood up to New York mobs before to defend the King's College gates and to preserve the freedom of Rivington's press to publish opposition views. Unable to organize a unanimous vote of disapprobation, about 500 of the enemies of the treaty finally drew off themselves, marched three blocks down to the Battery, formed themselves in a circle, and "there BURNT *the treaty,* opposite the government house."

While the most militant members of the mob were off on this mindless mission, Hamilton introduced a resolution written by Rufus King and handed it up to Chairman Smith, who attempted to read it above the tumult. With the treaty burners off in the distance, the crowd quieted down a little and listened out of respect for the chairman and the resolutions' authors. Hamilton's and King's resolution "declared it unnecessary to give an opinion on the treaty" and reposed full confidence in the president.

But when the opponents in the crowd who had stayed to listen grasped the import of the resolution, according to the account contained in the following Monday's *Argus,* a Republican newspaper, it "roared, as with one voice: *We'll hear no more of it, tear it up, etc."* A volley of rocks and stones punctuated the interval of quiet as the mob's most violent members returned in triumphant exaltation from the treaty-burning ceremony. Like the "mad dogs" Washington had called them, they were now panting, yowling, and slavering for new targets of violent opportunity.

Shouts from the mob called for a vote on the question of appointing a committee of 15 to draft resolutions *"expressive of their disapprobation of the treaty,"* though there had not as yet been any discussion of the merits. Probably at about this time, one of the stones the mob had been shying toward the stoop struck Hamilton on the forehead. Seeing that he and his supporters could never carry any question against the angry passions of this mob or even get a hearing from them, Hamilton called out the question of approving his and Rufus King's resolution. His supporters, at least those standing within his hearing, loudly called *aye!* As if celebrating an overwhelmingly victorious vote on his and King's resolution, Hamilton then loudly called out to those who were "friends of order" to follow him. They separated themselves from the truculent, dangerous mob that filled the streets and moved away. Wiping the blood streaming from the stone bruise on his temple out of his eyes, Hamilton, according to his son John Church Hamilton, made a graceful bow to the mob and announced, "If you use such knock down arguments I must retire."

According to one eyewitness, Hamilton's retreat from the mob was less graceful than Hamilton's beloved son Johnny, too young at only three to have been an eyewitness to anything but the bloody wound, had reported. Grant Thorburn, a young Scotsman got himself hoisted up into the branches of the stock exchange's famous buttonwood tree. He later wrote that Hamilton's eloquence had "inflamed their plebeian souls." So "they cut short his speech, forced him from the stoop, and dragged him through the gutter." Thorburn was appalled: "Said I to myself, and this is all the thanks you have got for fighting along side of Washington for the . . . freedom of speech."

With Hamilton gone, the question of appointment of the committee of 15 to draft the resolutions and report back on the following Monday was moved and seconded. But on the voice vote, Chairman Smith could not determine whether

the majority was louder for than against it, any more than he could be certain
which way the vote had gone on Hamilton's resolutions. Many in the crowd, in
holiday high spirits or high jinks, as crowds will, had yelled out approval or
disapproval of both. To Adams's son-in-law, it seemed likely that the loudest
shouters had the least idea of the issues all the uproar was about.

In Monday morning's Republican newspaper, "a citizen voiced alarm because friends of the treaty might yet be victorious" in recording New York in
its favor, if only as a rebuke to the mob violence of the Saturday before. Here
was an enemy's testimonial to the impressive turnout of popular support for the
treaty Hamilton and King and their friends of Friday night's meeting at the
Tontine had mustered. "A citizen" summoned opponents to a second meeting:
"be not tramped on by *tories*, or those who, under the *mask* of federalism, are
tories at heart; suffer them not to brow beat you," But this time they should stop
short of throwing stones at them and gaining them sympathetic support by
violence against their speaker's person.

With another tumultuous fight in prospect, Monday's crowd was even larger
than Saturday's. Those hostile to the treaty clearly controlled the meeting. They
permitted no discussion of it before Brockholst Livingston read the hostile resolutions, which were rubber-stamped paragraph by paragraph and dispatched to
the president. Filling four newspaper columns, they damned the treaty roundly.
It was injurious to agriculture, manufactures, and commerce of the United
States, "derogating from their national honour, and dangerous to their welfare,
peace and prosperity." According to the *Argus*, all present had unanimously
approved.

Hamilton and the other leading Federalists made no appearance at the
Monday meeting. Next day at a full meeting of the Chamber of Commerce, the
entire treaty was read and discussed. Then a vote was taken. A majority passed
a set of resolutions reading like King's of the Saturday before, which expressed
qualified approval. They deplored the passion that misled the popular mind and
commended the treaty in general and in important particulars. Nevertheless, the
Monday's mass meeting added New York to other ports—Boston, Philadelphia,
Baltimore, and Charleston—admonishing the president to reject the treaty.

Before the terms of the treaty became known, New York Federalists had
easily elected John Jay governor. Now the treaty bearing his name had been
shouted down. Fresh from triumphs at the national capital, Hamilton's latest
cause had lost in New York City. Two days after this setback, on July 22, while
Hamilton was still nursing the stone bruise on his forehead, there began to
appear in Greenleaf's *Argus* or *New Daily Advertiser* the first of a series of
papers of his authorship entitled "The Defence" of the treaty and signed *Camillus*, which would continue to appear for the next five and a half months and
eventually total 38 numbers in all.

The series is known to history as the *Camillus* papers. It is believed that
of the 38, Hamilton wrote 28 himself and outlined, provided material for, and
edited most of the remaining ten, which are attributed to Rufus King. Before
the series ended on January 9, 1796, with Number XXXVIII, Hamilton had

defended the treaty generally, provided a detailed analysis and defense of each of its articles, argued its constitutionality, and sought to refute the arguments brought against it by Republican pamphleteers like Brockholst Livingston.

The first numbers cited the malignant hostility of his enemies—the leaders of the mob that had stoned him—for reasons having nothing to do with the treaty: "There will always exist among us men irreconcilable to our present national constitution . . . such men will watch with Lynx's eyes, will display a hostile and malignant zeal . . . for opportunities of discrediting the government. . . ." To such men, men like Aaron Burr, for example, the advantages and weaknesses of the treaty itself were unimportant; it was important to them only as a handy tool to use for personal aggrandizement: "Every country, at all times, is cursed by the existence of men, who, activated by an irregular ambition, scruple nothing which they imagine will contribute to their own advancement . . . In monarchies, supple courtiers; in republics, fawning or turbulent demagogues, worshipping still the idol power wherever placed, whether in the hands of a prince, or of the people." Such men trafficked in "weaknesses, vices, frailties or prejudices . . . more on the passions than on the reason of their fellow citizens."

On a higher level, Hamilton argued that, imperfect as the treaty might be, it was a means of staving off a war that might end in disaster. "If we can avoid a war for ten or twelve years more," he argued, "we shall then have acquired a maturity, which will make it no more than a common calamity, and will authorize us, in our national discussions, to take a higher and more imposing tone."

He played down its weak points and hammered on the strong. The impressment of seamen was a complex issue, not easily remediable. He exalted the clause calling for compensation to British creditors as recognizing "the sacred obligation of a just debt." By England's agreement to hand over the frontier forts, we had gained an immeasurable advantage. "The statesman must be an educator," Secretary of State Henry Kissinger observes. "He must bridge the gap between a people's experience and his vision, between a nation's tradition and its future."

Forcing the British out of the western posts would clear the way for peaceful expansion of the American empire across the entire continent to the westward. Not incidentally, Marcus Furius Camillus was a Roman soldier and statesman of patrician descent, the censor in 403 B.C., who was honored with the title of second founder of Rome. Professor Mommsen summed up his place in history by calling him the man who "first opened up to his fellow countrymen the brilliant and perilous career of foreign conquest."

The *Camillus* papers were Hamilton's most masterful and effective essays in molding public opinion. While arguing for a particular action, the papers range wide, amounting to a survey of the political and economic situation of the Western world of the time. They are distinguished by an incisive style, richness of citation, and logical narrative flow. Without Hamilton and *Camillus*, popular clamor would probably have never allowed Jay's Treaty to go into effect.

After reading "The Defence, No.1," Washington wrote Hamilton on July 29,

1795, with unusual warmth: "To judge of this work from the first number, which I have seen, I augur well of the performance; & I shall expect to see the subject handled in a clear, distinct and satisfactory manner."

The president urged Hamilton to disseminate the papers widely to counter the "poison" spreading in all directions from the opposition. He ended with the striking observation that "the difference of conduct between friends and foes of order & good government, is in nothing more striking than that the latter are always working like bees to distil their poison; whilst the former, depending oftentimes *too much* and *too long* upon the sense and good disposition of the people to work conviction, neglect the means of effecting it." Here is another of Washington's striking restatements of a conservative's creed.

Jefferson's angry reaction to the *Camillus* series produced the strongest personal testimonial to Hamilton that has ever been written. Here was Jefferson's master plan to discredit the Federalists on a burning national issue about to be thwarted by Hamilton, but he seemed to stand alone in the van of the Federalists. From his retreat in Monticello on September 21, Jefferson wrote in alarm to Madison, his usual confidant in desperate situations, "Hamilton is really a colossus to the anti-republican party. Without numbers, he is an host within himself."

Jefferson railed on, "They have got themselves into a defile, where they might be finished; but too much security on the republican part will give time to his talents, & indefatigableness to extricate them." He did not mind driving his protégés on by a shrewd mix of insult and compliment: "We have had only middling performances to oppose him. In truth, when he comes forward, there is nobody but yourself who can meet him. . . . For God's sake take up your pen, and give a fundamental reply to Camillus." Madison had little heart for the exercise and failed to respond to Jefferson's carrot and lash.

Beyond calling the treaty "execrable" in private correspondence and pressing poor Madison to take on Hamilton again in public, the former secretary of state and former minister to France did not deign to try to arm the antitreaty populace with weapons of reasoned argument for use in execration of the treaty or help them with the mantle of the majestic authority his name would have provided. He preferred to remain withdrawn from the people, nursing his ambitions in his mountaintop château in careful, silent seclusion.

In the group of Hamilton's Federalist friends who had bravely mounted the stoop on Broad Street with him to face the mob and defend the treaty was Josiah Ogden Hoffman, a young lawyer about ten years Hamilton's junior. It was his name John Beckley had passed along to Madison and Jefferson for their files as Hamilton's friend to whom Commodore James Nicholson had made the charge that Hamilton had vested £100,000 sterling in British funds in London while secretary of the treasury. Very likely, Nicholson or someone else had shouted these charges at Hoffman during Saturday's hubbub in the street, perhaps just after Hamilton, followed by his friends, had shoved his way out or been dragged away, blood trickling down his forehead. The quarrel at first seemed to lie between Nicholson and Hoffman standing in the street defending Hamilton against the shouted charges. Then Hamilton had stepped in to take his own part, trying to calm both men down. Commodore Nicholson later admitted that Hamilton's first words were intended to apply equally to himself and Hoffman. But, according to Hamilton, "Mr Nicholson replied very harshly . . . that he [Hamilton] was not the man to prevent his quarrelling [,] called him an Abettor of Tories and used some other harsh expressions." According to Beckley, Nicholson also charged that in the Constitutional Convention, Hamilton had sought a government of kings, lords, and commons. Hamilton had told Nicholson that the city street was not a fit place for yet another fierce altercation. Nicholson retorted that Hamilton feared to pursue the affair because on a former occasion Hamilton had backed off from challenge to a duel.

Hoffman was forgotten. Furious at Nicholson's slur on his honor, Hamilton cried out that "no man can affirm that with truth!" Hamilton added, "I pledge myself to convince Mr. Nicholson of his mistake." Hamilton had been scraped raw by the hostility of the crowd in Wall Street, made to bleed by the stone striking his forehead, and aroused to thrust himself into mortal peril by the street fight with Nicholson that Saturday afternoon. His mental balance, always hypersensitive to pressures from enemies, was near a breaking point. He and Hoffman roamed the hot New York City streets, seeming to seek out new enemies everywhere to be confronted. At the door of Edward Livingston's house, Hoffman engaged Peter Livingston in another fierce argument that turned personal. Rufus King and Peter's brother, Edward, interposed, telling them that personal disputes should be settled somewhere else. As Edward Livingston wrote his mother two days later, Hamilton then thrust himself forward belligerently, almost like a mad dog, saying, "If these two are going to fight, I will fight the whole opposition party one by one." Edward Livingston moved toward him to try to calm him. Hamilton threw up his arms and repeated, "I am ready to fight your whole detestable faction one by one." Another brother, Maturin Livingston, arrived just then and said very coolly that he accepted Hamilton's challenge and would meet him in half an hour anywhere Hamilton pleased.

Hamilton replied that he had one such affair on his schedule already, with Nicholson. When that was settled, he would get back to Maturin Livingston. To their mother, Edward Livingston confided of Hamilton, "you may judge how much he must be mortified at his loss of influence [to] descend to language that would have become a street bully."

But as Hamilton saw it, perhaps still wiping blood from the concussion from his brow, Nicholson had clearly given him "a violent offense without provocation." The following Monday, July 20, the day the mass meeting of treaty opponents reassembled, Hamilton sent his friend Colonel Nicholas Fish to Nicholson with a challenge written out in Fish's hand:

> Sir [:] The unprovoked rudeness and insult which I experienced from you on Saturday leaves me no option but that of meeting with you, the object of which you will readily understand. I propose to you for the

purpose Paulus Hook as the place and Monday next eleven o'clock as the time. I should not fix so remote a day but that I am charged with trusts for other persons which will previously require attention on my part.

It was a vital part of the code duello, as well as to avoid being arrested for violating penal laws against dueling, to keep the intended meeting absolutely secret and outside of New York. Until the day, both principals must appear normal in their most intimate relations while giving attention to transfers of trusts for other persons for whom the duelist might feel responsible.

Commodore Nicholson answered briskly. He declined the invitation of Mr. "Hambleton"; the "peremptory tenor" of the challenge precluded his "discussion of the merits of the controversy." Nicholson added that Fish's call had alarmed Nicholson's family. He feared interference from them.

Hamilton's wounds had healed a little. If Nicholson could explain his remark "on a certain very delicate point," Hamilton would not decline "an explanation if you see in the original transaction room for it." He hoped the Commodore could quiet the alarm of his family. More exchanges sped back and forth between the two men during the next few days.

Late the afternoon of July 21 the Nicholsons received a visit from a lady "of our (evidently mutual) Acquaintance," who tried to speak to Mrs. Nicholson alone in the garden. The commodore guessed her errand, interrupted her intended confidences, and ushered her home. He was left with "no doubt . . . she came to Alarm my family of what was likely to take place." He told Hamilton of the mysterious vist in a predawn note penned at half-past five of Wednesday morning.

Who was that mysterious lady? Mrs. Rufus King? Elizabeth Hamilton? Mrs. Josiah Ogden Hoffman? Most likely the last, who must have felt compunction that Hamilton's defense of her husband in his quarrel with Nicholson had drawn Hamilton into mortal danger. One woman at least was not willing to see two able men make fools of themselves if she could prevent it in the only way open to a lady.

Even though he knew as well as any man how to avoid a duel without sacrificing honor, he had not done so by July 25, the Saturday after being stoned by the Wall Street mob. Ominous exchanges with Nicholson were still passing back and forth as Hamilton made out his will. He wrote instructions to his old friend Robert Troup, whom he named as executor. There would be nothing left over for legatees: "I might have dispensed with the ceremony of making a will as to what I may myself leave, had I not wished that my little property may be applied . . . readily and . . . fairly . . . to the benefit of my few creditors. For after a life of labor I leave my family to the benevolence of others, if my course shall happen to be terminated here." He had quit the Treasury a poor man—"I hope what I leave may prove equal to my debts." His list of debts added up to about $30,000.

He wanted to give a preference to only one creditor, Nicholas Fish, one of his seconds in the impending duel with Nicholson. The amount was small, but Hamilton wished "to secure him in this mere act of friendship from the possibility of loss . . ." He was pained not to be able to make a preference for drafts drawn by his father, James Hamilton, for $700 "lest they should return upon him and increase his distress," But these were a "voluntary engagement," and he "doubted the justice" of putting them ahead of other commitments. His brother-in-law, John B. Church, was by much his largest creditor. Hamilton hoped that Church would accept any net loss from settlement of the estate. Uncharacteristically apologetic, Hamilton wrote that "I regret that his affairs as well as my own have suffered by my devotion to the public service . . . they will not have been as profitable to him as they ought to have been & as they would have been if I could have paid more attention." There were special instructions for certain mysterious bundles he would leave marked *AA*, *AB*, and *D*. He felt he had been overpaid by retainers from some of his clients, "large fees for which the parties could not have had equivalents," at least if he died just then before finishing their cases. He named them, but added poignantly, "It would be just if there were means that they should be repaid." Unfortunately, there was no way because "what can I direct who am (I fear) insolvent?"

No mention was made of any £ 100,000 allegedly secreted in a London bank. The more than $1,100 of blackmail money he had paid to James Reynolds could hardly have been far out of mind as he wrote these painful self-reproaches for the fact of his own insolvency.

By way of postscript to this last testament before the impending duel, Hamilton pointed to one last mysterious bundle that was in the leather trunk:

In my leather trunk where the bundles above mentioned are is also a bundle inscribed thus—J R *To be forwarded to Oliver Wolcott Junr. Esq*
I entreat that this may be early done by a careful hand.

Wolcott, of course, as well as the host of Hamilton's enemies—Beckley; his assistant, Bernard Webb; Madison; Monroe; Jefferson; and Burr would easily identify the initials *J R* on this last little bundle of "interesting papers" as standing for the name of James Reynolds. Troup, like John Jay and other close friends, could also probably guess the secret by now, but from prior knowledge only Wolcott would be certain to know the contents of this last pathetic bundle.

Following Hamilton's entreaty to "careful hands," the last sentence of his testament reads: "This trunk contains all my interesting papers." Below this sentence, at some later date, five more words were written, probably after he was dead, in the firm regular script of Elizabeth Hamilton: "To be retained by myself."

In the continuing exchanges with Commodore Nicholson through their seconds, Hamilton denied he had prompted the unnamed lady to call on Nicholson's family. He sent back a reply by Nicholson's second, De Witt Clinton, the fiery young nephew of Governor George Clinton. Hamilton wrote, "Measures it is true toward an accommodation have been subsequently in train but I have had no other agency in the affair than that of meeting them . . . in a liberal & Gentleman-like manner."

Nicholson's answer, written a few minutes after receiving Hamilton's note, expostulated against the suggestion that it was he who had commenced the peace move. The real origin of the truce plan is revealed in a brief note of Wednesday, July 22, dated six o'clock in the morning from Udny Hay, a new second for Nicholson, to Fish, requesting "an interview with him as soon as possible, Mr. Clinton being Absent." Young De Witt Clinton, who would normally have acted for Commodore Nicholson, was now being bypassed by Hay.

By the end of the week, after more exchanges, Rufus King joined Hamilton's seconds; and Brockholst Livingston, Nicholson's; and all joined good office to ease the way to an understanding between the principals. Nicholson signed a written statement denying having said that Hamilton "had declined a former interview." He regretted the pain his insult had caused.

The significance of this episode is that it shows that Hamilton knew as well as any man the etiquette of the dueling code and the graceful means available for settling such an affair without dishonor to either party, if he should be disposed to settle, without bloodshed. The timely intervention of friends as seconds could usually manage things so as to avoid a final confrontation if the principal wished them to do so. When such an episode reached the exchange of bullets, it did so because a principal insisted on no other way out.

By the end of August, Hamilton's early *Camillus* papers had helped convince Washington that the treaty should be signed and ratified.[1] Earlier, Washington had understood that his attorney general, William Bradford, his secretary of state, Randolph, and the majority of the Senate were all of the opinion that if the British accepted the American revision of Article XII, the treaty need not go before the Senate a second time for its advice and consent. The president had been disturbed to learn that Hamilton was of the contrary opinion and had told his cabinet and attorney general to change their opinion to agree with Hamilton's.

Washington wrote Hamilton in his own hand, marked "Private," on July 14, "I have told Mr. Randolph that your sentiments do not agree with those which I received from the officers of the government and have asked him to revise them." In the end, the treaty was not resubmitted to the Senate. Washington's reliance on Hamilton's advice had become so habitual and unthinking that he had insisted Randolph follow it, even when it was wrong.

By the end of August, the president's mind was made up. He told Hamilton he would ratify the treaty. But, as Hamilton advised, his first instructions to the American agent in London were to withhold final exchange of ratifications, while urging that the British order-in-council of April 1795 preventing neutrals from carrying provisions to France be rescinded. But Washington's later instructions called for exchanging ratifications forthwith, and ratifications were finally exchanged in London. The president proclaimed the treaty in effect and laid it before the House of Representatives on March 1, 1796. In the administration's view, the treaty was now in full force and effect. The role of the House was merely to vote the funds necessary to implement the treaty in various ways.

But the Republicans in the House did not see themselves confined to any such mere rubber stamp role. They were for the most part unreconciled to the treaty and to the constitutional principle that a treaty was the supreme law of the land.

Hamilton's secret instructions to Jay for the treaty negotiations had called for Jay to "insert a formal *stipulation*" in the treaty agreeing to pay for British vessels seized by American privateersmen that had been commissioned by Citizen Genêt. With remarkable political foresight, Hamilton had carefully instructed Jay to insert this provision in the text of the treaty itself instead of leaving it to implementing laws, so that "the Senate only will have to concur. If provision is to be made by law, *both Houses* must concur. The difference is easily seen." There would be trouble in the House.

The British order-in-council of April 1795 for seizure of all neutral vessels carrying provisions to France had inflamed its anger. Voting down this provision would be a splendid opportunity to embarrass Washington, Hamilton, the administration they governed, nullify the treaty, and strike a Republican blow for France.

Edward Livingston of New York now moved that the president furnish the House with Hamilton's secret instructions to Jay and other pertinent information concerning the treaty. After debate, the motion carried by a comfortable Republican majority of 62 to 37. Madison seemed to have more than enough votes to nullify important provisions of the treaty when the final vote came.

Hamilton had forewarned Washington how to respond to such a resolution on March 7, and the president was forearmed: "If the motion succeeds, it ought not to be complied with. In a matter of such a nature the production of the papers cannot fail to start a new and unpleasant game—it will be fatal to the negotiating power of the Government."

Hamilton then gave Washington the language he thought the president ought to use in denying the House demand. The right of the House to demand "communications respecting a negotiation with a foreign power cannot be admitted without danger. A Discretion in the Executive Department how far and where to comply in such cases is essential to the due conduct of foreign negotiations and is essential to preserve the limits between the Legislative and Executive Departments." The executive "cannot therefore without forming a very dangerous precedent comply." The narrower principle at stake was that the power to make and ratify a treaty was vested exclusively in the president and Senate, with the House having no part in the process. Washington followed Hamilton's advice and his text and refused the House demand. This advice of Hamilton created the earliest precedent for the broad doctrine that later came to be known as "executive privilege."

The Republicans were not yet finished with Hamilton, Washington, and Jay's Treaty. James Madison drafted a set of resolutions declaring that the House had the right to pass on portions of treaties involving matters that were its constitutional responsibility—such as voting appropriations—and that the president must make available all information that concerned the House's functions. William Blount introduced them for Madison on April 15. Hamilton wrote out for Rufus King a plan for meeting this new flank attack on the treaty that reads like an order of battle: "To me our true plan appears to be the following: The President ought immediately after the House has taken the ground of refusal to send them a solemn protest." The Senate should "express strongly their approbation of this principle, assure him of their firm support and advise him to proceed in the execution of the Treaty."

Merchants should "meet in the cities . . . second the president and Senate . . . address their fellow citizens to cooperate . . ." Petitions "should be handed throughout the United States . . ." The Senate should "hold fast and consent to no adjournment till the expiration of the term of service of the present House . . ." The president should confidentially communicate to the British his adherence to the treaty. "I prefer that measures should begin with a protest of the President."

A constitutional crisis was at hand, said Hamilton. "A most important crisis ensues. Great evils may result, unless good men play their card well and with promptitude and decision . . . In all this business celerity, decision and an imposing attitude are indispensable. The Glory of the president, the safety of the constitution, the greatest interests depend upon it."

But no matter how important it might be to beat down the House's opposition to Jay's Treaty, the great end did not justify illegal or improper means. It would not be "eligible" for Federalists in the House to trade off execution of the Spanish and Algerine treaties, also pending, as a quid pro quo for Republican approval of Jay's Treaty: "The misconduct of the other party cannot justify in us an imitation of their principles. . . . Let us be *right*, because to do right is intrinsically proper, and I verily believe it is the best means of securing final success. Let our adversaries have the whole glory of sacrificing the interests of the nation." Hamilton's ultimate faith in the wisdom of the people—properly informed, not as mobs—is characteristic: "we must seize and carry along with us the public opinion . . . in the confidence that . . . the virtue and good sense of the people, constitutionally exerted, . . . may still be the instrument of preserving the Constitution, the peace, and the honor of the nation."

The House continued to insist that it was within its constitutional rights in refusing to enact the laws necessary to carry this or any treaty into effect. Madison argued for this view in a long speech on April 7. But the eagle eye of the now ailing dean of Federalists in the House, Fisher Ames of Massachusetts, caught a nuance: Madison had seemed to draw back at the edge of the abyss when arguing the issue. In a voice now quavering a little, Ames crowed, "conscience made him a coward. He flinched from an explicit and bold creed of anarchy." It would be the unraveling of his majority. Working closely with

Rufus King and Philip Schuyler, Hamilton wrote and circulated petitions supporting the treaty at another mass meeting, in The Fields in New York City on
April 22 and in other counties as well, throughout New York and other states.
By April 24 he had sent off a petition by express and reported to King that "it
had more than 3,200 signers which is within 300 of the highest poll we ever had
in this city *on both sides*, at the most controverted election." Schuyler had
similar success in registering the people's support for the treaty at Albany. The
great debate came to a climax on April 28, when Fisher Ames made a last famous
appeal. He began by speaking of his own frail health. He closed by saying that
ill as he was, his country would perish first if Jay's Treaty were not upheld.
Between exordium and peroration, his mental vigor and emotional force belied
his physical weakness. His speech was Hamilton's *Camillus* compressed, but
his advanced age, failing health, and the dramatic circumstances added to it an
eloquence that none but he could have supplied. He ridiculed Anti-Federalists,
as pretended champions of the people against a tyrannical government. They
seemed more like a little group of wilful men. The speech of the greatest of
Federalist orators "was attended to with a silence and interest never before
known, and made an impression," according to John Adams, "that terrified the
hardiest" of the Antis and "will never be forgotten."

Ames recalled the struggle for independence and nationhood and found it
now imperiled by the implacable stubbornness of the little band of willful Jeffersonians. By refusing to accept the treaty and thus procure the British evacuation
of the frontier posts, the House would "light the savage fires . . . bind the victims
. . . The darkness of midnight will glitter with the blaze of your dwellings. You
are a father—the blood of your sons shall fatten your cornfield; you are a mother
—the war whoop shall wake the sleep of the cradle."

"My God! how great he is," murmured Supreme Court Justice James Iredell
of North Carolina, a good Federalist, to Adams.

"He is delightful," Adams replied.

"Gracious God!" exclaimed Iredell. "How great he has been!"

Adams: "He has been noble."

Iredell: "Bless my stars, I never heard anything so great since I was born."

Adams: "It is divine."

Ames found in the Constitution no such powers as Madison claimed for the
House and stressed the rightness of the treaty and the constitutional duty of the
House to vote the government the funds to carry it out. Venable moved that the
Committee of the Whole should rise. Two days later, April 30, 1796, a motion to
make the necessary appropriations narrowly carried, 51 to 48. Passions still ran
so high that after casting a deciding vote in favor of the treaty, Frederick A. C.
Muhlenberg, Speaker of the House, was stabbed by a fanatical Republican—who
was also his brother-in-law.

It is hardly overstating Hamilton's role to conclude that his instructions to
Jay, to Washington, to Rufus King, to Ames and others; his tactical foresight;
his personal advocacy; his *Camillus* papers; his substantive arguments in favor
of the treaty; his invention of the doctrine of executive privilege; and his half

year long spent in reasoned appeals to all the people in its behalf had made the difference between winning over the three votes by which it—and some essential constitutional precedents—were saved.

In the closing paragraphs of his magisterial work, *Jay's Treaty*, Professor Samuel Flagg Bemis observes that "the political and economic foundations of the American nation had been laid by the hands of genius, but those foundations in 1794 were by no means unshakeable. The power of the Federal Government to hold the union together under the Constitution depended on the financial system which Hamilton had created . . . national credit which energized the government depended almost wholly on imports, which a war or even commercial hostility with Great Britain would have destroyed. . . . This danger is what Alexander Hamilton realized with the clear eye of the *realpolitiker.*" The treaty gave the United States time to develop in population and resources and in a consciousness of nationality that made resistance to Britain possible in 1812 that would have been impossible in 1794. As Hamilton had written Washington in 1794, disruption of commerce with Britain would "bring the Treasury to an absolute stoppage of payment—an event which would *cut up credit by the roots.*" The last words of Bemis's treatise are the following:

> The terms of [Jay's] treaty were the result of the powerful influence of Alexander Hamilton to whom in the last analysis any praise or blame for the instrument must be given. . . . More aptly the Treaty might be called Hamilton's Treaty.

As he ruefully fingered the scar of his stone bruise and reflected on his insolvent estate, the farseeing *realpolitiker* would not disclaim some responsibility.

18

HELPING WASHINGTON OUT

AID ME I PRAY YOU . . .
> —*From George Washington, October 29, 1795*

WE ARE LABORING HARD TO ESTABLISH IN THIS COUNTRY PRINCI-
PLES MORE AND MORE *NATIONAL* AND FREE FROM ALL
FOREIGN INGREDIENTS, SO THAT WE MAY BE NEITHER *GREEKS*
NOR *TROJANS,* BUT TRULY AMERICANS.
> —*To Rufus King, December 16, 1796*

Since long before the Indians had massacred General Arthur St. Clair's expedition 90 miles north of Fort Washington, the present day Cincinnati, back on November 4, 1791, Hamilton had labored to improve relations between the American states and the national government with the settlers and the Indian tribes on the frontiers. Over the years, Washington had broadly delegated to him the duty of drafting instructions to commissioners like General William Hull for conducting negotiations looking to peaceful settlement of territorial and trading disputes.

The British and the Canadian Indian Department, as a matter of policy, had long sought to make use of the forts still occupied on the northern and western frontiers as bases for their project of creating an Indian buffer state lying between the United States and Canada. Hamilton always resisted British and Canadian pretensions to control the Indians. His position was that all Indians within American territory were "in some sort the subjects of the United States." To him the most important gain won by Jay's Treaty would be the end of British exploitation of the Indians as pawns to interfere with American control over the American Northwest Territory.

Clinging to hopes that Hamilton's opponents in the House might nullify Jay's Treaty and keep the possibility of their Indian buffer state alive, the British delayed evacuating the posts until the last possible moment—several weeks after the date stipulated in the treaty, June 1, 1796, before they finally gave up and withdrew. News of Jay's Treaty, coupled with Hamilton's and Jay's earlier efforts to settle differences with the Indians by mediation, had made possible the Treaty of Greenville, signed with the western tribes on August 3, 1795, by which the Indians ceded to the United States most of the present state of Ohio, leaving the Indians a broad strip of land along the shore of Lake Erie between the Maumee and the Cuyahoga Rivers. The Treaty of Greenville was the precursor and model for many other territorial cessions by the Indians during the next 15 years by means of which Indian title to most of the old Northwest Territory was extinguished and the frontier opened for peaceful settlement of the areas of the present states of Indiana, Illinois, Michigan, Wisconsin, and Minnesota.

In recognition of all that Hamilton had done to foster peaceful settlements with the Indian tribes, Chief Good Peter and other Oneida and Mohawk tribal chiefs joined the Reverend Samuel Kirkland, an Indian missionary, on a visit to Hamilton at his office in Philadelphia on January 8, 1793, to request him to continue his aid and become a trustee of Hamilton Oneida Academy, the forerunner of Hamilton College, at Clinton, New York. Hamilton "cheerfully consented." On August 15, 1795, he joined the other trustees of the college in binding himself to be liable as mortgagee on two parcels of land for the college to the extent of $700, a sum he probably did not have free and clear to his name at the time, notwithstanding his large stock of public credit. But when 1796 came around, the fact that Hamilton's obligations, as usual, exceeded his assets did not keep him from lending another $50 to an old friend and crony who was probably as bad a credit risk as anyone who could be found in the country: William Duer. He was still languishing in the New York debtors' prison.

With Hamilton out of Philadelphia, it became clearer than ever from the correspondence that passed between him and Washington that Washington realized how badly he missed Hamilton's advice and counsel in what Washington saw as a crisis of implacable opposition to his government, manipulated and led by Jefferson and Madison, respectively.

In the summer of 1795, just after the popular uproar over Jay's Treaty had reached a crescendo with the stoning of Hamilton in Wall Street, Washington wrote Hamilton on July 29 from Mount Vernon, "after a hot and disagreeable ride," complimenting him on the "clear, direct and satisfactory" defence of Jay's Treaty his *Camillus* series was providing to the people. The writings against the treaty, Washington complained, "are pregnant of the most abominable misrepresentations . . . which are very industriously circulated." Only the day before, Secretary of the Treasury Oliver Wolcott, Jr., had written Hamilton of the "curious facts" that had recently come to his knowledge that led him to "suspect *foul play*, by persons not generally suspected." He added, "Everything is conducted in a mysterious and strange manner by a certain character here." Two days later, Wolcott wrote Hamilton again, still more alarmed, in need of more advice and counsel from Hamilton, and his physical presence at the seat of government as well: "I dare not *write* & hardly dare *think* of what I *know* & believe respecting a certain character; whose situation gives him a decided influence." The "certain character" to whom Wolcott referred was none other than that uncertain character, Secretary of State Edmund Randolph.

Wolcott felt keenly that grave danger of provoking Britain into war would arise from "the Treaty clogged with one condition by the senate, with another by the President—no answer given in a precise form, after forty days, no minister in that country to take up negotiations proposed by ourselves, the country rising into a flame, their ministers house insulted by a mob—their flag dragged through the streets as in Charleston & burnt before the doors of their consul— Can they believe that we desire peace?" Wolcott would take counsel with two of his Philadelphia colleagues, Timothy Pickering of Massachusetts, the new secretary of war and Attorney General William Bradford. They, unlike that "certain character," were "firm and honest men." Wolcott and his two honest friends would, if possible, "to use a French phrase *save our country.*" But it would be well, Wolcott concluded, if Hamilton or Rufus King or John Jay "could be here some time next week—provided too much speculation would not be excited."

If in this highly charged political atmosphere Randolph, the highest ranking and senior member of Washington's cabinet, were to be confronted with proof of treasonous solicitation of a bribe from France, publicly disgraced, and drummed out of office, Washington and Wolcott would need all the advice, counsel, and backing they could muster from among their own friends at the critical moment. Wolcott, Pickering, and Bradford sent off a summons to Washington, calling him back from Mount Vernon. They arranged to have Randolph urge him to return, too, without Randolph's suspecting why he was being asked to do so. During the next few weeks, from New York, Hamilton wrote out a lengthy essay, "Defense of the Funding System," turned out and published new papers of the *Camillus* series every few days, and furnished advice and counsel to Wolcott, Bradford, George Washington, and Pickering—and to Randolph, too —concerning many different matters relating to the treaty.

Hamilton would recall that only the year before Randolph had privately besought him to help procure a personal loan through Abijah Hammond of New York, and Hamilton had obliged. Randolph's money came through just before Hamilton had left to show force to the western insurrection, and he had sent Hamilton warm thanks for his "disinterested kindness in helping arrange it." For public consumption, however, Randolph mouthed Jefferson's lines about Hamilton and criticized him as leader of the faction that would make Washington a monarch and then, somehow, also enslave America to England.

On August 16, 1795, Randolph sent Hamilton a letter addressed to John Jay for Hamilton to review and then transmit, Randolph noting that his own and Hamilton's views on the handling of the ratification of the treaty had not been far apart. Hamilton did not comply with Wolcott's request to come to Philadelphia to be present at the moment of Randolph's disgrace, which took place on August 19, only three days after he had written Hamilton.

That morning Randolph was on his way to the president's house for a cabinet meeting at the usual hour of nine when he was notified by messenger to delay his visit. On arrival a short while later, he found that Wolcott and Pickering had already been in consultation with the president. Without preface, in a towering rage, Washington thrust under Randolph's eyes a copy of a dispatch that the French minister, Jean Antoine Joseph Fauchet, had sent to his home government on October 31, 1794, designated "Dispatch no. 10." According to the translation, Fauchet in Dispatch no. 10 had declared that Randolph vowed that he was committed to the French cause. Randolph wanted money from France, which, he said, would be used to pay for evidence that Hamilton's suppression of the Whiskey Insurrection had been stirred up by British agents in order to discredit the democratic societies and American supporters of France generally. The British had intercepted the secret French dispatch on March 28, 1795, and in the last week of July, George Hammond, the British minister, had passed it on to Wolcott who had, in turn, alerted Hamilton, Washington, and Pickering.

According to Fauchet, Randolph had privately confided that the western insurrection threatened civil war and required all of the government's 15,000 troops to put it down. Randolph had added that the democratic societies were the American Jacobins and were getting stronger all the time, just as Washington and Hamilton had charged. This official word from Randolph by way of Fauchet to his home government in Paris would make it every bit as happy as similar secret forecasts of imminent dissolution of the nation had made Hammond's government in London.

As Fauchet had put it, "To confine the present crisis to the simple question of the excise is to reduce it far below its true scale; it is indubitably connected with a general explosion for some time . . . prepared".

As Fauchet understood it from Randolph, since the autumn of 1794, Federalist fortunes had been declining; there was a Democratic majority in Congress; popular democratic societies were springing up everywhere, there was continued harassment of American commerce by Britain and wide disenchantment with Jay's "ridiculous negotiations lingering at London." Hamilton had artfully covered up Federalist weakness by denouncing "an atrocious attack on the constitution . . ." when the real issue was "the destruction of the triumph of the treasurer's plans." Hamilton had found in "the very stroke which threatened his system . . . the opportunity of humbling the adverse party. . . ." But this was only a tactical success that would prove temporary.

As Wolcott wrote Hamilton on November 16, at the confrontation in Washington's parlor, Randolph denied having received money from Fauchet or having made any proposition to him asking for money except on one occasion—

as the trembling Randolph blurted out to Washington, Pickering, and Wolcott. That was the summer before, Randolph stammered, in August of 1794. Fauchet had drawn him out by telling him a story of a meeting held in New York by a "British faction"—Hammond, Joseph de Jaudenes, the Spanish commissioner to the United States, and others—who were "conspiring to destroy Fauchet, Randolph and Governor Clinton."

To Wolcott, this sounded like an absurd fabrication. He challenged Randolph. "What do you mean, destroy you and Fauchet and Governor Clinton?"

Randolph replied, "Our influence and popularity were to be destroyed." Yet Clinton had always proved to be indestructible, and British attacks on Fauchet would build him up while cutting Randolph down. Wolcott wrote Hamilton, "This foolish story could make no impression, and though Mr. Randolph promised to reduce it to writing he omitted to do so."

Wolcott pressed Randolph, "What do you mean, destroy you and Governor Clinton?" Randolph replied lamely, "I asked Fauchet whether proof could be got of his conspiracy."

Wolcott, and Pickering, too, thought Randolph was concocting this rambling cock-and-bull story under the pressures of the confrontation and the stony stares of the three implacable Federalists.

Wolcott pressed him: "What happened then?"

"I told Fauchet," Randolph replied, "that as you have the resources of the French government at command you can obtain the proof."

Thus the secretary of state had defended himself to Washington, Wolcott, and Pickering by the narrow quibble that he had not asked the French minister to give him money. Instead, he had merely told Fauchet to use his own government's money to pay French spies. Wolcott warned Hamilton that "attempts will be made to represent you as concerned in it." Your involvement is in every page. Wolcott was shocked: "What must have been the footing of these men when they could familiarly talk about subversion of the Government and inviting the French to aid the insurrection with money?" Writing to John Marshall in 1806 about that August morning's confrontation with the secretary of state charged with receiving a bribe from France, Wolcott would add that Randolph "after a short hesitation . . . proceeded to look over [Dispatch no. 10] with great attention." When he reached the passage in which Fauchet referred to his solicitation of the bribe, "Randolph's conduct was very remarkable. He expressed no strong emotion, no resentment against Fauchet. He declared that he could not certainly tell what was intended by such remarks."

Protesting weakly under fire only that he "never made an improper communication to Mr. Fauchet," Randolph resigned as secretary of state the same day.

Randolph posted off to Newport, saying he would seek explanation from Fauchet that would exonerate him, but Fauchet sailed off for home. At length Randolph obtained, through Fauchet's successor, Pierre Auguste Adet, a certificate and some missing documents, which seemed to clear him of criminal conduct and intent. But they confirmed Wolcott's conclusion that he had been on too intimate and confiding a footing with Fauchet and had even claimed to hold ascendancy over the president.

Hamilton never made known his own personal knowledge of the former secretary of state's desperate need for money in 1794 or how he had helped him obtain money from Abijah Hammond in a way that would at least not dishonor his office or country. Instead, Hamilton insisted to Wolcott on October 30 that no slanted or mistranslated version of Fauchet's Dispatch no. 10 ought to be published. Poor Randolph's behavior should not be made to seem worse than it was for partisan Federalist purposes. No one had suffered more from false charges than he: "I am very anxious that Fauchet's whole letter should appear just as it is—strange whispers are in circulation . . . foreign to truth . . . implicating honest men with rascals."

Washington exploded all over again when he read the pamphlet that Randolph published on December 18, 1795, *A Vindication of Mr. Randolph's Resignation.* On December 22, Washington wrote Hamilton, now almost a year out of office, for advice. He was resentful of Randolph's "long promised vindication, or rather accusation" and asked what notice should be taken of it. He went on to say:

> You are fully acquainted with my sentiments relative to the rival & warring powers of F. & E. and have heard as strong sentiments from me with respect to both as ever he did. His declaration that he was always opposed to [Jay's] negotiation is as impudent and insolent an assertion as it is false . . . but if you have seen his performance, I shall leave you to judge of it, without any comment of mine.
> With much sincerity and truth
> I am always and affectionately. Yours
> Go: Washington.

Hamilton replied promptly on December 24. He could not fail to note Randolph's wild tergiversations on whether he had or had not favored Jay's Treaty:

> I have read with care Mr. Randolph's pamphlet. It does not surprise me. I consider it as amounting to a confession of guilt and I am persuaded this will be the universal opinion. It appears to me that by you no notice can or ought to be taken of the publication. It contains its own antidote.[1]

Hamilton saw the Randolph episode as an event that would help turn the tide of public opinion against the strong antitreaty majority that Madison had mustered in the House as 1796 wore on. Madison just now was demanding disclosure of Hamilton's and the executive's secret instructions to John Jay. "I greatly miscalculate if a strong and general current does not now set in favor of the government on the question of the Treaty," Hamilton wrote.

Jefferson came to much the same conclusion as Hamilton about what his fellow Virginian and erstwhile follower Randolph had done. His usefulness ended, Jefferson washed his hands of poor Randolph in a memorable characterization.

He wrote to Madison that Randolph "has generally given his principles to the one party, & his practice to the other; the oyster to one, the shell to the other. Unfortunately the shell was generally the lot of his friends the French and republicans, & the oyster of their antagonists."[2]

Without Hamilton at the capital to help dispose of such crises briskly one by one as they arose, a whole rack of them piled up for Washington, Wolcott, and Pickering in Philadelphia. They had to be posted up to Hamilton in New York for his consideration, review, advice, and counsel. The pace of the government seemed to slow to accommodate the time it took for exchanges of correspondence between New York and Philadelphia, as well as the time that Hamilton could spare from churning out issue after issue of "The Defence" of Jay's Treaty and handling cases for private clients. These earned him the fees to make up for the low salary that had forced him to leave the government—and made it possible for him to continue to render *pro bono* services to Washington's government in a role that seemed more exigent now than when he had been on its payroll.

"Give me the points on which our new negotiator [John Quincy Adams] is to dwell when we come into the field of negotiation again, agreeably to the recommendation of the Senate," Washington demanded of Hamilton on August 31. "What do you conceive *ought* to be brought forward and *insisted* upon on this occasion?"

Washington added, "Although you are not in the administration—a thing I sincerely regret—I must nevertheless (knowing how intimately acquainted you are with all the concerns of this country) request you to note down proper subjects for communication to Congress." In a rare touch of confiding humor, he added that it will be "the source of much declamation & will, I have no doubt, produce a hot session." Hamilton complied.

Attorney General William Bradford's death and Randolph's disgrace created two vacancies in the cabinet, but no one seemed to want to join an administration that now seemed to be under siege by smear of Madison and Jefferson and their followers. "What am I to do for a Secretary of State?" Washington asked Hamilton on October 29. Four men, William Paterson of New Jersey, Thomas Johnson of Maryland, General Charles Cotesworth Pinckney of South Carolina, and Patrick Henry of Virginia, all had turned him down. Would Hamilton see if Rufus King would accept, or, if not, what did he think of the qualifications of Senator Richard Potts of Maryland? "I will decide on nothing until I hear from you—pressing as the case is," Washington added. John Marshall had turned down the attorney generalship, and Hamilton's close friend and confidant Edward Carrington had refused to take over the war Department in the event Washington should decide to switch Pickering, the secretary of war who was now also acting secretary of state, to head the State Department. Washington passed on his thoughts on a number of other possibilities for Hamilton's consideration, but what with "the nonacceptance of some; the known dereliction of those who are most fit; the exceptionable drawbacks from others; and a wish (if it were practicable) to make a geographical distribution of the *great* officers of the administration, I find the selection of proper characters an arduous duty."

Washington also implored Hamilton for help in writing his seventh annual message to Congress both as to "the proper subjects for my communications to Congress . . . and the manner of treating them." This would include the prickly subject of Jay's Treaty, the proper manner of dealing with the actions of the House and Senate concerning it, the pending negotiations with Spain being handled by Thomas Pinckney, the problems of treaty negotiations with Algiers and Tunis, the problems of treaties with the Indian tribes on the frontiers, the statement concerning the military establishment, and what to say about domestic fiscal matters and foreign loans. All were problems for which Washington pleaded for Hamilton's help: "Aid me I pray you with your sentiments on these points." If there were any other problems about which he had forgotten to ask Hamilton for advice, Hamilton should also aid him with "such others as may have occurred to you."

Still other vexing questions backed up on the national agenda. George Washington Motier Lafayette, the son of the Marquis de Lafayette, Washington's favorite of all his wartime aides, had arrived in New York with his tutor, Felix Frestal, on October 1, and the Hamiltons had given them temporary hospitality in their already overcrowded household. Strong appeals to receive the lad officially showered in on Washington from Frestal, from George Cabot, and from Henry Knox. The boy was "a lovely young man of excellent morals and conduct." The boy and his tutor had arrived incognito in New York, expecting that the childless president would receive them warmly acting a surrogate grandfather's part.

The problem was that the marquis, his father, was now being held in prison in Austria under orders of the French Directory, and Washington had no wish to give offense to the official French government. Washington hesitated. He saw himself about to be cut by one or the other of "two edges, neither of which can be avoided without falling on the other. On one side, I may be charged with countenancing those who have been denounced as the enemies of France; on the other, with not countenancing the son of a man who is dear to America."

Washington's first impulse was to have the young man and his tutor "proceed to him without delay . . . to take them at once into my family . . . unless some powerful reasons can be announced to the contrary." What did Hamilton think?

Another problem was that after Hamilton had turned down Bradford's offer of appointment to be chief justice of the Supreme Court, Washington had nominated John Rutledge, but he now seemed to be suffering from physical and mental instability and decline. Wolcott had to know what should be done about the nomination—withdraw it? Leave him dangle? Or what? Pickering wanted Hamilton to review a list of more than 22 names of possibilities for secretary of war, select the ones to whom the secretaryship should be tendered, and advise him.

John Beckley, writing as "A Calm Observer," published "a virulent attack" on Washington in the [Philadelphia] *Aurora or General Advertiser.* It accused him of having overdrawn his annual salary of $25,000 year after year, by $5,150 in the fiscal year 1791, $4,150 in fiscal 1792, $5,150 in 1793, and so on. John Beckley was an accountant, as well as a clerk. With the allegation that *"at the time of payment,* there was not an existing appropriation to authorize the same," buttressed by a bewildering smokescreen of figures, he transformed a bookkeeping technicality into a smear charge that made Washington sound like an embezzler with the secretary of the treasury as his accomplice to anyone who did not understand figures.

Wolcott pleaded: could Hamilton frame some reply to these charges? Wolcott also wanted Hamilton's opinion of Tench Coxe, still in the Treasury, who was now writing attacks on Jay's Treaty under the pseudonym of *Juricola.* There were still other appeals for advice to his "judgment intuitively great."

Hamilton doggedly dealt with them all. As for appointments to the vacant cabinet posts, he had asked Rufus King to take over State and been turned down. He canvassed the field to Washington on November 5 with obsession with enemies and corrosive wit:

> Circumstances of the moment conspire with the disgust which a virtuous and independent mind feels at placing itself *in but* to the foul and venomous shafts of calumny which are continually shot by an odious confederation against virtue . . . for a secretary of State . . . [William Loughton] Smith, [Congressman from South Carolina] though not of full size is very respectable and . . . has more real talent than the last incumbent of the office . . . He is popular with no description of men from a certain *hardness* of character and more than most other men is considered as tinctured with prejudices toward the British . . . Mr. [James] Innes I fear is too absolutely lazy for Secretary of State. The objection would weigh less as to Attorney General. Judge Nathaniel Pendleton writes well, is of respectable abilities and a gentlemanlike smooth man . . . But I fear he has been somewhat tainted by the prejudices of Mr. Jefferson and Mr. Madison and I have afflicting suspicions concerning these men . . .

Having reviewed all the possibilities, Hamilton gave the following hard-headed advice:

> A first rate character is not attainable. A second rate must be taken with good dispositions and barely decent qualifications . . . Tis a sad omen for the government.

Of course, there was his old crony and former aide of Washington, James McHenry of Maryland. "I mean the doctor," he reminded Washington. "You know he would give no strength to the administration but he would not disgrace the office—his views are good—perhaps his health, etc. would prevent his accepting."

Among many others who might not turn down attorney general (where absolute laziness was no real objection) was Charles Lee, a former Treasury Department collector of revenue of Alexandria, Virginia.

After shifting Pickering from the War Department to secretary of state, Washington obediently to Hamilton's advice appointed Charles Lee attorney general on November 19, 1795, and James McHenry secretary of war on January 24, 1796.

For good measure, Washington also appointed Hamilton's friend and mentor Elias Boudinot as director of the Mint.

As for Rutledge's imminent appointment as chief justice, the subject was a perplexing one, as Hamilton wrote Senator Rufus King December 14:

> If it be really true—that he is sottish or that his mind is otherwise deranged or that he has exposed himself by improper conduct in pecuniary transactions, the byass of my judgement would be negative.

This decision was more important than many others to Hamilton because "it is now, and in certain probable events will be still more, of infinite consequences that our judiciary should be well composed." There should be "careful inquiry of persons of character who may have had an opportunity of knowing" more about Rutledge. Hamilton's perplexity was quickly dispelled in the best way he could have hoped for. King wrote Hamilton on December 16, "Rutledge was negatived yesterday by the Senate."

To refute Beckley's smear that Washington had embezzled from the Treasury, Hamilton obtained from Wolcott and reviewed voluminous Treasury records—journals, ledgers, receipts, and so on. He organized them into a detailed pamphlet, which he published as "An Explanation," and proved that Beckley's smear was false. As for Tench Coxe's criticisms, he counseled Wolcott on August 5, 1795, that he could safely ignore them: "That man is too cunning to be wise. I have been so much in the habit of seeing him mistaken that I hold his opinion cheap."

Hamilton's fondest wish would have been to send the beautiful son of his and John Laurens's dear old comrade-in-arms and intimate Lafayette straight along to the president without ado. The boy himself was suffering keen disappointment, which was sharpened when he received a letter from his mother that enclosed a copy of her warm entreaty to the president. But Madison still seemed to control enough votes in the House to cripple Jay's Treaty. Hamilton, therefore, doubted "whether at the actual crisis it should be prudent to give publicity" to Washington's "protection of young Lafayette." He feared that "the factions might use it as a weapon to represent you as a favorer of the anti-revolutionists of France; and . . . it would be inexpedient to furnish at this moment any aliment to their slanders."

The political context suddenly changed in a way that vindicated Hamilton's astuteness in delaying Washington's embrace. On March 4, 1796, Edward Livingston introduced a resolution in the House to appoint a committee to inquire whether Lafayette's son was in the United States and what might be done for his support. All who cared to inform themselves knew that the young Lafayette was indeed in the United States, either staying with the Hamiltons, or tucked away under Hamilton's protective custody at Ramapo, New York. This was another Republican tactic to cut up Washington on one or the other edges of the dilemma.

The man who more than any other symbolized France's aid to the American Revolution now languished in prison, kept there by the present French government. Hamilton's and Washington's patronage of Lafayette's son, who had escaped its clutches, symbolized to them, at least, their support for the France that had stood for revolutionary freedom, not the France of the pro-French Republicans in America that was now carrying on war and warlike imperial aggression and repression under General Napoleon Bonaparte. Now Hamilton saw that the Republicans had overplayed their hand by seeking to make a formal political issue of Hamilton's and Washington's protection for young Lafayette. Hamilton happily sent him and his tutor off to Philadelphia on April 9, where Washington had "a room prepared for him." "It gives me great pleasure," Hamilton wrote Washington. "I share by anticipation the satisfaction which the meeting will afford to all the parties . . . Mr. Frestal who accompanies him . . . more and more convinces me that he is entirely worthy of the charge reposed in him and every way entitled to esteem."

The carriage tax had been enacted on June 5, 1794, as one of the key measures of Hamilton's program for the creation of public credit. It was a crude form of graduated income tax because it was borne by the well-to-do, who bought carriages, and not by the less well-to-do, who did not. The carriage tax case was the first to come before the Supreme Court in which it would pass upon the constitutionality of an act of Congress.

Just as he was now denying the supremacy of treaties from the House floor, Madison was claiming that the carriage tax was unconstitutional because it was a "direct" tax. A "direct" tax properly would have to be apportioned state by state, according to state populations. This the federal carriage tax did not do.

Following Madison's lead, some well-to-do Virginians refused to pay the tax. Political ambitions and a desire to please Jefferson tended to mislead the Father of the Constitution into expedient misunderstanding of his only progeny. One well-to-do Virginia carriage owner, Daniel Hylton, brought suit. The judges of the circuit court divided evenly. Hylton's attorney, John Taylor, "advised the defendant to make no further argument and to let the Supreme Court do as they please. . . ." By agreement with the attorney general, Hylton confessed judgment for tax evasion, creating the foundation for a writ of error to test constitutionality of the tax. Charles Lee, the new attorney general who had replaced William Bradford, joined Hamilton to argue the government's case for the carriage tax in the Supreme Court on February 24, 1796. Against them for the plaintiff were Alexander Campbell, attorney of the Virginia District, and Jared Ingersoll, attorney general of Pennsylvania.

Hamilton's argument to the Court, with a distinguished audience in attendance, filled three hours. He found no reliable distinction, legal or economic, between a "direct" and an "indirect" tax. The distinction was historical and traditional, not logical. It was "matter of regret that terms so . . . vague in so important a point are to be found in the Constitution." Was it an indirect tax when ultimately borne by a person different from the person who paid in the first instance? No. An import duty was the likeliest example; sometimes it could be shifted; sometimes not. One who imported for his own use paid the tax both first and last. The same tax could not be both indirect and direct. Nor would it do to say that an indirect tax is one paid unconsciously, for any reflecting man sees that the tax is included in the selling price. The physiocrats and Locke would say that the only "direct" taxes were land taxes, but it seemed reasonable to include also in this category taxes on buildings, poll taxes, and taxes on personal property.

If a carriage tax were considered a "direct" tax, one to be levied only according to state-by-state representation, absurd consequences would follow. A state with a large population might have relatively few carriages; one with a small population, many. If a tax on carriages were direct, then a tax on ships according to tonnage was direct also. But no one claimed taxes on ships should be apportioned state by state.

It was enough if the tax were uniform like other duties, imposts, and excises under the Constitution. Because the Constitution had, for better or worse, made a distinction between taxes (direct and to be apportioned state by state according to population) and excises (indirect, to be uniform throughout the nation), it was "fair to seek the meaning of terms in the statutory language of that country from which our jurisprudence is derived." In British statutes a carriage tax was held to be an excise and, therefore, an indirect, not a direct tax.

Then, as he often did, Hamilton enlarged his frame of reference to sound a national theme that went far beyond the narrow issue of the case: "No construction ought to prevail . . . to defeat the . . . necessary authority of the government . . . a duty on carriages . . . is as much within the authority of the government as a duty on lands or buildings."[3]

Chief Justice Oliver Ellsworth, who had just been sworn in after Rutledge's rejection by the Senate, and Justice Cushing, who had been ill during the argument, took no part in the decision. Justice William Paterson, writing for the majority, joined by Samuel Chase and Iredell, held with Hamilton that the carriage tax was a circuitous means "of reaching the revenue of individuals, who generally live according to their income." It was not a direct tax. It was properly an excise tax and, therefore, constitutional so long as it was uniform. It did not need to be proportioned to the populations of the several states. All agreed with Hamilton that the framers of the Constitution intended that Congress should have power "over every species of taxable property, except exports."

Hamilton's was the seminal Supreme Court tax case. Since then, most federal levies have been covered by its broad rule. Few any longer doubt the principle that the authority of Congress under the Constitution to levy taxes is sovereign, though many, might wish with Madison that such were not the case.

Hamilton's meticulous account book records on May 10, 1796, receipt from the "United States for attendance in Philadelphia [and] for a fortnight's work in arguing the question of the Constitutionality of the Carriage Tax" the fee of $500.

The sovereign power of Congress to levy nationwide taxes for support of the federal government was the cornerstone on which Hamilton's fiscal system rested. The Supreme Court's adoption of his winning argument in the carriage tax case cemented this power into the plan for a strong, spacious national Constitution Hamilton was continuing to build over Madison's and Jefferson's efforts to cripple and stunt it.

Writing Hamilton from London on March 4, Gouverneur Morris summed up the angry reactions he had heard from France to presidential and senatorial ratification of Jay's Treaty. "The governments here are highly displeased with ours," wrote Morris. "A fleet is to be sent to our shore with a new minister . . . The government are to declare that our Treaty with them is annulled." Morris rather relished the thought that this would put James Monroe, the enthusiastically pro-French American minister to France who had been dispatched as Gouverneur Morris's replacement there in 1974, "in a cruel dilemma. He is already much displeased and a war will probably be the consequence. The British will be glad of this."

Morris had sent a similar warning to Washington, who, as usual, asked Hamilton to send him his advice on what to do, after discussing the matter with Jay. Hamilton replied calmly to Washington that he should not worry himself over much with speculation about what French reactions would be until he should learn exactly what the Directory currently ruling in France actually did. If the Directory should demand that the United States renounce Jay's Treaty, "the answer will naturally be that this . . . [is] too humiliating and injurious to us . . . a thing impossible . . . the sacrifice of our honor by an act of perfidy which would destroy the value of our friendship to any nation." Besides, Hamilton added, "The executive is not competent to it—it being the province of Congress by a declaration of war or otherwise in proper cases to annul the operation of treaties." If France should demand that the United States fulfill a term of the old treaty by guaranteeing the West Indies colonies against the British, Washington should answer that the decision belongs to Congress, who "will be convened to deliberate upon it." Hamilton hoped that by then Congress would have adjourned. "For to gain time is everything," he felt.

Senator Rufus King, who had been helping Hamilton defend Jay's Treaty as ten thirty-eighths of *Camillus*, confided to Hamilton that he was "not a little tired" of his senatorial burdens. Thomas Pinckney was resigning as minister to England. Hamilton advised Washington that he should name his friend King to the post. King was "a remarkably well informed man—a man of address—a man of fortune and economy—a man of unimpeached probity where he is best known —a firm friend to the government—a supporter of the measures of the president —a man who has strong pretensions to confidence and trust." Washington hastened to appoint him.

In June the American ship *Mount Vernon,* just out of Philadelphia, perhaps within coastal waters, was seized by the French privateer *Flying Fish.* Outraged American demands brought out the news that the Directory on July 2, 1796, had ordered French privateers to stop and seize the cargoes of all neutral vessels bound to English ports. James Monroe, the American minister in Paris, had failed to send back news of the order, then excused himself by minimizing its significance, and finally raised doubts about whether it had been issued at all. As 1796 wore on, reports of new French attacks on American merchant vessels began to come in thick and fast. Far from protesting such outrages, Monroe in Paris continued to minimize them and to exude warm and friendly support for the Directory. A troubled Washington, of course, asked Hamilton to discuss with Governor Jay what to do and report some answers back to him. It was a difficulty as well as an advantage that by July 5, when Hamilton replied, the Senate was no longer in session. In Hamilton's and Jay's opinion, Senate concurrence would indeed be necessary for the appointment of an envoy extraordinary to France. Although at least in periods of derangement Hamilton would tend to see Monroe as his archenemy, now "there are weighty reasons against removing Monroe," Hamilton responded to Washington. "But we think those for it preponderate." A new man "ought at the same time to be a friend to the government and understood to be *not unfriendly* to the French Revolution." General Charles Cotesworth Pinckney "is the only man we can think of who fully satisfies the idea." An even weightier matter loomed. Washington's second term was drawing to a close, and he was determined not to seek a third. Hamilton's counsel was the political wisdom of the best second term presidents: "It is not to be regretted that the declaration of your intention should be suspended as long as possible . . . you should *really hold the thing undecided to the last moment."* Washington, of course, appointed Charles Cotesworth Pinckney as envoy extraordinary to Paris and held off announcing his irrevocable decision to leave office, at least until after he had released the *Farewell Address* that Hamilton had been helping him to compose since May.

One of the greatest joys in prospect for Hamilton when his impending resignation would remove from his shoulders all the cares of the government's problems—or so he thought—was symbolized by the search he was making for a New York house for John and Angelica Church to live in when they returned to America. But concerns for the public's political welfare no longer served as a viable excuse for a lawyer in private practice who dared to allow his attention to wander a moment from the immediate concerns of private clients.

By February 19, 1796, Angelica Church had received some letters from Hamilton, "but no plan of the lot, and no description of the house. How can I bring out the furniture when I do not know the number of rooms my house contains," she wrote him reproachfully.

To the petulant annoyance characteristic of a slightly neglected client with time on her hands, Angelica joined her own special barb. It was almost as if she were suffering an anxiety attack brought on by fear of a rejection by a lover. Nothing could have brought more anguish to Hamilton, nor have been calculated to do so:

"I am sensible how much trouble I give you," she went on, "but . . . it proceeded from a persuasion that I was asking from one who promised me his love and attention if I returned to America . . . for what do I exchange ease and taste, by going to the new world, where politics excludes all society and agreeable intercourse, where all that is not given to fame seems to be regretted and forgotten . . . what an agreeable amiable fellow, has Jay's LITTLE treaty turned into a defender of what he never would himself have designed to submit to. Viola mon sentiment, changes le si vous veules."

Letting all other concerns slide, Hamilton arranged to pay $4,250 for the house and four lots on the east side of Broadway, near Robinson Street north of Marketfield, and finally sent off to Angelica some sketches of the house and lot. He sought forgiveness, pleading with her June 25, "How do you manage to charm all that see you? Naughty tales are told to you of us, we hear nothing but of your kindness, amiableness, agreeableness etc."

But there was no mistaking that a welt remained from the lash of her February anxiety: "Why will you be so lavish of these qualities upon those who forget them in six weeks and withhold them from us who retain all the impressions you make, indelibly?" Hamilton and Eliza were "strangely agitated between fear and hope, anxiously wishing for your return . . . we feast on your letters . . . The only rivalship we have is in our attachment to you and we each contend for preeminence in this particular. To whom will you give the apple?"

The persecutions he was suffering also at the hands of enemies had not abated. "Jacobins have made a violent effort against me," he told her, "but a complete victory has been gained to their utter confusion." He closed: "Yours as much as you desire. A. H."

When Hamilton had been in Philadelphia in February to help Charles Lee argue for the constitutionality of the carriage tax, Washington had asked him to *"re-dress* a certain paper" that he had prepared sometime before. On May 10, Hamilton reminded Washington that "it is important that a thing of this kind should be done with great care and much at leisure touched and retouched." Washington should send it to him "as soon as you have given it the *body* you mean it to have." On May 15, Washington sent Hamilton the "certain paper" intended for "re-dress." It turned out to be nothing less than the first draft of his *Farewell Address.*

On May 15 the "certain paper" consisted of two separate papers, the first being a rough draft written by James Madison following conversations with Washington in May of 1792, headed "Substance of a Conversation with the President." The second was a paper written by Washington very recently, intended to explain the "considerable changes" that had "taken place both at home and abroad" since 1792 during Washington's second term.

On May 12, three days before sending these two papers to Hamilton for his help, Washington had invited Madison to a private dinner. Before the public, Madison was now the leader for Jefferson behind the scenes of the opposition to all of Washington's policies. The subject of the "considerable changes" in their relationship since 1792 was, no doubt, a principal topic of their conversation.

When the dinner was over, Washington lost no time in taking Madison off work on the "certain paper."

Washington struck out all references to Madison and Jefferson and expunged Madison's name from the first page of Madison's draft. Learning of intentions Washington had wished to keep secret and elaborately ascribing the source to Hamilton, no doubt falsely, Madison's and Jefferson's protégé John Beckley, who constantly talked with them, sarcastically revealed that a friend had "extracted" from Hamilton in the early summer of 1796 the information "that the president [Washington] does not mean to resign, but merely to decline a reelection, and that to make known his intention, he designs about the month of August to publish an address to the people. We may presume whose pen will indite it, and what . . . principles it will . . . propagate; happily however the control of events is less within the power than the wish of the American Catiline . . ." Beckley announced that Washington's valedictory would be a partisan paper that would anticipate Federalist success in the national election, "which taking a contrary issue . . . may wholly frustrate a well schemed object."

Washington wished to preserve for the 1796 address a quotation from Madison's 1792 draft "as an evidence that it was much against my inclination that I continued in office then." This was necessary, Washington confided to Hamilton, to show "that I could have *no* view in extending the powers of the executive beyond the limits prescribed by the constitution." It would also blunt the charges that his retirement was forced by "fallen popularity" and "despair of being reelected." Because Madison and Jefferson were "now stronger and foremost in opposition to the government," his quotation of Madison's own words against such charges "will cause it more readily to be believed."[4]

Washington would like to see expunged not only Madison's name, but also Madison's statement that Washington's departure from office (after only four years) would "accord with the Republican spirit of our constitution, and the ideas of liberty and safety entertained by the people." Washington also disliked some purple passages of Madison, which seemed to claim too much credit, such as a reference to his government as one which "must approach as near to perfection as any human work can aspire, and nearer than any which the annals of mankind have recorded." Washington insisted on "discarding egotism" and avoiding personalities and pointed allusion to particular measures and to "expressions which could not fail to draw upon me attacks which I should not find it agreeable to repel."

When Washington and Hamilton had talked it over in February, they had considered two alternative ways to proceed, either by Hamilton's revising the earlier drafts or by preparing an entirely new address. All these observations of his, Washington said in his letter forwarding the earlier drafts to Hamilton, are confined "to *my draft* of the valedictory address. If you form one anew it will, of course, assume such a shape as you may be disposed to give it, predicated upon the sentiments contained in the enclosed paper."

He was sending Hamilton his only copy of the earlier draft; so "even if you should think it best to throw the *whole* into a different form," Hamilton should send back Washington's old version together with the new, "with such amendments and corrections, as to render it as perfect as the formation is susceptible of."

Recognizing Hamilton's mastery of a style appropriate to such an address that was superior to that of the two earlier scriveners, Washington felt that the old paper should be "curtailed, if too verbose; and relieved of all tautolgy, not necessary to enforce the ideas in the original or quoted part. My wish is, that the whole may appear in a plain style; and be handed to the public in an honest, unaffected, simple garb."

Hamilton was still working on his draft on June 26, and Washington was "a little tenacious of the draught I furnished you with to be modified and corrected . . . let me hear from you as soon as convenient." He regretted "exceedingly" that "I did not publish my valedictory address the day after the adjournment of Congress" two months earlier because then it would have rendered "my retreat less difficult and embarrassing." Having missed the best time, Washington could not decide now: "Let me ask your opinion of the next best time"—some time prior to the presidential elections of October 1796, perhaps? Hamilton obliged on July 5: "The proper period for your declaration seems to be *two months* before the time for the meeting of the electors. This will be sufficient."

He also reassured Washington that "I do not think it is in the power of party to throw any slur upon the lateness of your declaration." He would be sending back shortly both his own newly written farewell address and the corrected version of Washington's earlier draft "so that you may have both before you for a choice in full time and for alteration if necessary."

On July 30, Hamilton sent along his own completely rewritten "Draft of Washington's Farewell Address," and on August 10 he returned Washington's draft with his own corrections entitled "Draft on the Plan of Incorporating." Hamilton much preferred his own completely rewritten draft to Washington's. His own he had "endeavoured to make as perfect as my time and engagements would permit . . . *importantly* and *lastingly* useful, and avoiding all just cause of present exception, to embrace such reflections and sentiments as will wear well, progress in approbation with time and redound to future reputation."

As for Washington's own draft, he said frankly, "There seems to be a certain ackwardness in the thing." And it was not necessary to quote from Madison's 1792 draft because "it seems to imply that there is a doubt whether the assurance without the evidence would be believed." "Nonetheless," Hamilton added, "when you have both before you you can better judge." Washington did, and his judgment was that Hamilton was right. He had given Hamilton's draft "several serious attentive readings, and prefer it greatly to the other." Hamilton's, he thought, was "more copious on material points, more dignified, with less egotism less exposed to criticism, better calculated to meet the eye of discerning readers." It comprehended most, if not all, of what was contained in the earlier draft, "is better expressed," and "goes as far as it might with respect to any personal mention of myself."

He sent it back to Hamilton on August 25 for minor revisions in accordance with some marginal notes he made in pencil, but to be used only if Hamilton wished to accept such revisions. Any further revisions Hamilton made now should be "clearly interlined" so that the printer would make no mistake setting it in type. There would be no further reading or change by Washington.

Washington also wanted the New Yorker to tell him what paper in Philadelphia he should send it to, what kind of a note of instruction he should send with it, and whether his own private secretary should deliver it. He needed Hamilton's help for every detail of the timing and manner of issuance of the most important document of his career, as well as for the composition of its text. "Let me ask you to sketch such a note as you may judge applicable to the occasion" of sending it to the printer, he humbly asked.

On September 1, Washington wrote Hamilton again with an afterthought. There was a point that Hamilton had omitted: "Education *generally* as one of the surest means of enlightenment." It was a favorite idea of Washington: "The establishment of a university . . . at the seat of the general government . . . where those who were disposed to run a political course . . . might not only be instructed in the theory and principles . . . but the practical part also."

Washington had thought deeply about political matters, and here was an idea he had pushed in his very first address to Congress as president. Indeed, it went all the way back to thoughts he had cherished since Revolutionary War memories associated with his and Hamilton's collaboration on other momentous papers. Assembled together in such a national university of practical politics from different parts of the country, young people, Washington believed, "would by degrees discover that there was not that cause for those jealousies and prejudices which one part of the union had imbibed against another part . . ." "A century in the ordinary intercourse," Washington's own experience had taught him, "would not have accomplished what the seven years association in arms did."

Hamilton would need less convincing of this than any other man Washington knew. Hamilton agreed with Washington that "a general suggestion respecting education will very fitly come into the address." He wrote it in. On the other hand, he added, "The specific idea of the university is one of those which I think will be most properly reserved for your speech at the opening of the session of Congress to follow." He later wrote into the draft he was writing for Washington's eighth annual message to Congress to be delivered on December 7, proposals for the creation of both a national university and a military academy.

When Hamilton sent back his final corrected version of Washington's *Farewell Address* on September 5, he noted that there were several other things that would "come much better" in his speech to Congress "than in a general address to the people." Besides, they "would swell the address too much." He told Washington the name of the Philadelphia paper to which to send the *Farewell Address:* Dunlap's and Claypoole's *American Daily Advertiser.* Washington should send it there by his secretary, Tobais Lear. Hamilton reminded him that someone "on the spot ought to be charged with a careful examination of the proof sheet." Suffering pangs of conscience, Hamilton had one profound regret.

"Had I health enough," he apologized. "it was my intention to have written it over, in which case I could both have improved and abridged." But he had not been able to do so. Washington would know and remember well from the earliest days of their collaboration at Valley Forge, when Hamilton had almost died returning from the mission to Horatio Gates, through all the terrible summers in the plague-infested capital, the physical sicknesses and nervous derangements from which the first of all his aides suffered. He would know and understand why Hamilton had been unable to do the best job it was possible for him to do on one of the most important missions of both their lives. There was a note of suffering, resignation, and despair in Hamilton's uncharacteristic effort to make excuse for himself: "I seem now to have regularly a period of ill health every summer."

On September 15, Washington submitted his *Farewell Address* to the cabinet for its approval. His secretary, Tobias Lear, asked David Claypoole to come to see Washington. At the interview they fixed on Monday, September 19, as the date for first publication. Lear brought the copy to Claypoole on Friday, and Claypoole brought back a proof and then a corrected proof to Washington, who made only a few corrections in punctuation. All followed the instructions Hamilton had sent. The *Farewell Address* was also printed on the same day in Fenno's *Gazette of the United States,* which after its period of insolvency was now back in print.

The exact authorship of the *Farewell Address* was disputed for more than a century. Hamilton's family insisted that Hamilton had been responsible for both content and phrasing. Madison's champions claimed the largest credit for him on grounds of priority. John Jay, in 1811, recalled that Hamilton had consulted him on this, as on so much else, and had gone over it with him "paragraph by paragraph, until the whole met with our mutual approbation." Washington's admirers tended to deny all such claims as a reflection on the hero. Comparison of the various drafts makes clear that although most of the general ideas were Washington's, the organization, elaboration, and phrasing of the text were Hamilton's.

As years and decades and a century and more rolled on, the words and phrases of the *Farewell Address* took on the authority of an American credo. The *Farewell Address* was and will always be one of the greatest documents of American history.

After Hamilton and Washington were both dead, Nathaniel Pendleton, one of Hamilton's executors, turned over all of Hamilton's papers relating to composition of *The Farewell Address* to Rufus King "to prevent their falling into the hands" of Hamilton's family because of Elizabeth Hamilton's "endeavour to show that General Hamilton, not General Washington, was the author and writer of the Farewell Address." After a suit in chancery court, the Hamilton family finally obtained the papers in 1826. In 1840, when Elizabeth Hamilton was 83 years old and still as passionately devoted to her husband, who had been dead for 36 years, as she had been when they were married 60 years before, she made the statement for posterity that "in the year 1796 General Hamilton suggested to him the idea of delivering a farewell address to the people on his withdrawal from public life, with which idea General Washington was well pleased." The address was written by Hamilton "principally at such times as his office was seldom frequented by his clients and visitors, and during the absence of his students to avoid interruptions." As Elizabeth fondly recalled, "He was in the habit of calling me to sit with him, that he might read to me as he wrote, in order, as he said, to discover how it sounded upon the ear." He was not thinking of illnesses when he remarked to her, "My dear Eliza you must be to me what Molière's old nurse was to him."

"The whole or nearly all the 'Address' was read to me by him as he wrote it," Elizabeth Hamilton reminisced, "and a greater part if not all was written by him in my presence." Washington approved of it all, she remembered, "with the exception of four or five lines, which if I mistake not was on the subject of public schools, which was stricken out . . . Mr. Hamilton made the desired alteration, and it was afterward delivered and published in that form." She added, "The whole circumstances are at this moment, so perfectly in my remembrance, that I can call to mind his bringing General Washington's letter to me, which returned the 'Address' and remarking on the only alteration which he had requested to be made."

The *Farewell Address*, in its final form, spoke to both future and past. In 1792, Madison had interposed no objection to the president's retirement, was pleased with the prospects that would be opened up by the event, and his biases were evident in his verbal revisions of Washington's early draft. What Washington had put with simple sincerity, Madison had made indirect, cautious, and apologetic to the point of false modesty. The most important tasks of Washington's first term had been the establishment of the new government on the sound basis created by Hamilton's fiscal system. That done, in Washington's second term, foreign policy had dominated the scene. The worldwide war between Britain and her allies and France and hers pressed in close upon America. The colonies of the warring powers encircled the new nation on the North American continent.

To Washington, Jay's Treaty was one of the most important events in the short history of the Republic. Washington viewed the attempts of the House to thwart foreign policy by means of its power over the purse as a violation of the Constitution, which had confided the treaty-making power to the president and the Senate alone. To him, such interference by the House in foreign affairs brought the entire Constitution "to the brink of a precipice."

The debates in the House over Jay's Treaty in March and April of 1796 had shown Washington the virulence of partisan divisions in the field of foreign policy, but the result had not been entirely negative. The outcome represented approval of his foreign policy and clarified the constitutional issues involved in its conduct. If his first administration had established the foundation for internal organization of the Republic for the long future, Washington could rightly believe that his second had similarly laid down a strong foundation for management of its foreign affairs for the long future.

Only the year before Hamilton began work on the *Farewell Address*, he had written, under the name *Horatius*, a defense of Jay's Treaty, which contained a warning against entanglement "in all the contests, broils and wars of Europe," words similar to those he used in the *Farewell Address*. Other formulations that the *Farewell Address* and the *Horatius* papers have in common can also be found as far back as Hamilton's Memorandum of September 15, 1790, the first written presentation of his opinions on foreign affairs as a member of Washington's cabinet. Other ancestors of the *Farewell Address* among Hamilton's writings include the *Federalist*, number 6, in which he wrote that "there have been . . . almost as many popular as royal wars." Europe possessed a special political system; the corollary was that America, too, should have a political system of her own. The *Federalist*, number 11, argued that the United States ought "to aim at an ascendant in the system of American affairs . . ."

Hamilton had shared Washington's background as a self-made man, long years of service to the nation in peace and war, and the same national political principles. He was a practiced writer, animated by his own goodwill, putting down words that would be attributed to Washington. No one knew Washington's style better—particularly his crushingly direct quality: it expressed the man in words that were forthright, downright, balanced, and blunt. He was drawing on great advocacies long familiar to him from the battles of the Revolution, the Constitution, *The Federalist Papers*, and his great reports. He had turned them over in his mind and pared and refined them until he was able to express them with precision and eloquence that would sound and read as if ready-made to be graven in granite on a monument.

The *Farewell Address* was also a report on the testing of the Constitution during the first seven years of its life, based on experience, that drew from them guidelines as projections of that past into the long future. For its two writers and many of its first readers, the *Farewell Address* was electrically charged with muted references to the burning controversies of the politics of 1796. The growing pains of government, the antagonisms of parties, sectional interests, tax burdens, overseas affinities, and the menaces and blandishments of warring foreign powers were the lava of which the *Address* was compounded. But, veiled by the dignity of the style, the immediate controversies faded from the memories of later generations, leaving only the proverb, not the parable.

Washington began matter-of-factly enough by noting that with "the period for a new election of a citizen to administer the executive government" not very distant, he had formed a resolution "to decline being considered among the number of those out of whom a choice is to be made." He thus set a precedent for no more than two presidential terms. The unwisdom of defying this precept having been proved for most by the single exception, it is now embedded in the Twenty-second Amendment to the Constitution. He thanked his fellow citizens for the honors they had conferred upon him and then said, "here perhaps I ought to stop." But he did not. Instead, he would offer some "sentiments" as "the disinterested advice of a parting friend." Hamilton, who would never, like Gouverneur Morris, familiarly slap Washington on the back or expect to see

Washington's demeanor with even his closest friends evince anything but dignified reserve, here now helped Washington put a friendly arm with warmth and familiarity around the shoulders of all of his fellow citizens—figuratively speaking: "In offering to you my countrymen! These counsels of an old affectionate friend—I may flatter myself that they may produce some partial benefits, some occasional good."

Washington's and Hamilton's "sentiments" on the nation's future course admonished "that unity of government which constitutes you one people claims your vigilant care and guardianship." Ever vigilant against the machinations of enemies, Hamilton warned, "The batteries of internal and external enemies will be most constantly and actively however covertly and insidiously leveled" against the unity of "your political fortress. . . . you should watch for its preservation with zealous solicitude."

"The great rule of conduct for us in regard to foreign nations," he counseled, "ought to be to have as little political connection with them as possible. . . . It is our true policy to steer clear of permanent alliances with any portion of the foreign world" and "trust to temporary alliances for extraordinary emergencies. . . . Inveterate antipathies against particular Nations, and passionate attachments for others, should be excluded," in favor of "amicable feelings towards all."

"We should," he went on, "observe good faith and justice towards all nations; cultivate peace and harmony with all. Religion and Morality enjoin this conduct; and can it be, that good policy does not enjoin it?" But he warned, "Europe has a set of primary interests, which to us have none, or a very remote relation . . . Hence therefore, it must be unwise in us to implicate ourselves, by artificial ties in the ordinary vicissitudes of her politics, or the ordinary combinations and collisions of her friendships or enmities. Our detached and distant situation invites us to pursue a different course . . . we may choose peace or war as our interest guided by justice shall dictate."

"Why," he asked, "should we forego the advantages of so felicitous a situation? Why quit our own ground to stand upon foreign ground? Why by interweaving our destiny with any part of Europe should we entangle our prosperity and peace in the nets of European ambition, rivalship, interest or caprice?"

Hamilton abhorred such things as the complacency with which a modern government devalues currencies by fiat or liquidates obligations through inflation. In governmental management of the economy, integrity of public credit was his abiding rule. No modification of debt, however immediately beneficial in a legislator's view, should be executed without consent of the creditors. Under Hamilton's fiscal system, he charged, "Cherish public credit as a means of strength and security. As one method of preserving it, use it as little as possible. Avoid occasions of expense by cultivating peace. Avoid the accumulation of debt [,] . . . not ungenerously throwing upon posterity the burthen which we ought to bear ourselves. Recollect that towards the payment of debts there must be revenue, that to have revenue there must be taxes . . . which are . . . more or less inconvenient and unpleasant."

In time, his every paragraph seemed to call the attention of the nation and the world to America as a supreme example of the harmony and freedom that were possible under law for "a people always guided by an exalted justice and benevolence." In the *Farewell Address*, Hamilton was groping toward a definitive statement of the grand theme of his own life work, but not yet quite expressing it in its perfect form: "The name of American must always gratify and exalt just pride of patriotism . . . you have slight shades of difference [but] the same religion, manners, habits and political institutions and principles . . . By your union you achieved them, by your union you will most effectually maintain them." He did not complete the formulation of the thought until four months later that same year, in the closing sentence of the letter he wrote to Rufus King in London on December 16, 1796: "We are laboring hard to establish in this country principles more and more *national* and free from all *foreign ingredients*, so that we may be neither 'Greeks' nor 'Trojans' but truly Americans."

The address was republished everywhere throughout the United States to great acclaim. As it first appeared, it began with the simple salutation "To the People of the United States" and closed with the signature "G. Washington, United States, September 17, 1796." Only later reprintings carried the caption "The Farewell Address."

There were also the inevitable derisory yawns and yawps. James McHenry reported to Washington that "the enemies of the government . . . discovered a silence and uneasiness, that marked chagreen and alarm, at the impression it was calculated to make on the public mind."

Forty-four years later, Elizabeth Hamilton still remembered one fine day in New York City when "shortly after the publication of the address, my husband and myself were walking in Broadway." An old soldier accosted the two of them and familiarly begged Hamilton, a former comrade-in-arms, to buy a reprint copy of General Washington's *Farewell Address* that he was peddling. Hamilton smilingly did so. Then he turned to Betsy and said, "That man does not know he has asked me to purchase my own work."

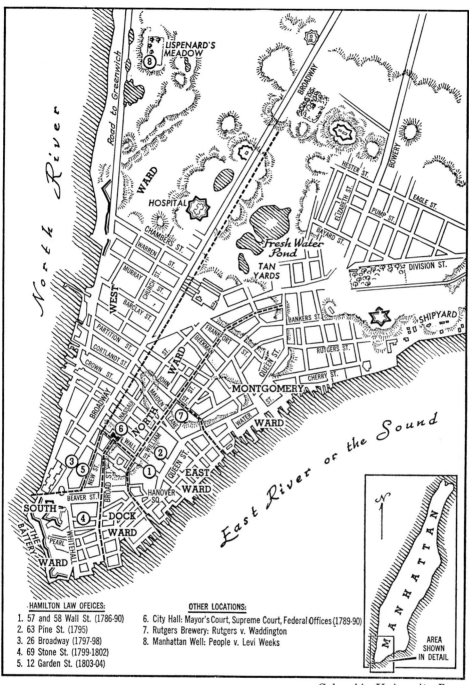

New York City in Hamilton's time

Washington (right) poses with his first cabinet: Secretary of War Henry Knox (seated); Secretary of State Thomas Jefferson; Attorney General Edmund Randolph (back to artist); Secretary of the Treasury Alexander Hamilton. T. Phillibrown's 1857 engraving after Alonzo Chappel's painting.

(Right) Hamilton considered Thomas Jefferson (here in Rembrandt Peale's 1800 portrait) "tinctured with fanaticism, crafty, not scrupulous nor very mindful of the truth, and a contemptible hypocrite" but infinitely preferable to Aaron Burr.

Although Col. William and Lady Catherine (Kitty) Duer (below) were among Hamilton's closest friends, Duer's appointment as assistant to Hamilton in the Treasury caused many problems and much sorrow for Hamilton.

White House Collection

Culver Pictures

The Tontine (left) and Merchant's (right) coffee houses on Wall Street, not far from Hamilton's office, were always redolent with heady draughts of political gossip and scandal.

REPORT

OF THE *Abr Baldwin*

SECRETARY of the TREASURY

TO THE

HOUSE of REPRESENTATIVES,

RELATIVE TO A PROVISION

FOR THE

S U P P O R T

OF THE

PUBLIC CREDIT

OF THE

UNITED STATES,

IN CONFORMITY TO A RESOLUTION OF THE TWENTY-FIRST DAY OF
SEPTEMBER, 1789.

———

PRESENTED TO THE HOUSE ON THURSDAY THE 14th DAY OF JANUARY, 1790.

PUBLISHED BY ORDER OF THE HOUSE OF REPRESENTATIVES.

N E W - Y O R K :
PRINTED BY FRANCIS CHILDS AND JOHN SWAINE.
M,DCC,XC.

Library of Congress, Manuscript Division

The title page of Hamilton's first report on the public credit for Congress, 1789. Five years later he presented his final report in which he wrote, "credit, public and private, is of the greatest importance . . . the invigorating principle . . . . Credit is an entire thing. Wound one limb and the whole tree shrinks and decays."

A view of Congress Hall (with cupola) in Philadelphia c. 1790 and the State House (now Independence Hall) where both the Declaration of Independence and the Constitution were written.

A rooftop view of Philadelphia in 1790 showing from left to right the Episcopal Academy, Congress Hall, the State House, the Philosophical Hall, and the Philadelphia Library.

Jefferson, as Secretary of State and Hamilton, as Secretary of the Treasury, occupied the twinned office buildings (left) at the corner of Third and Chestnut Streets, Philadelphia.

Independence National Historical Park

Charles Willson Peale painted his 1791 portrait of the
34-year-old Hamilton at the peak of his public career.

Hamilton, hazarding a secret rendezvous with his blackmailer, James Reynolds, wrote this misdated letter to an unnamed friend "as any disastrous event might interest my fame."

Hamilton's letter to Congressmen Monroe, Muhlenberg, and Venable asking for the return of all documents pertaining to the Reynolds affair. His accusers complied with Hamilton's wishes but not until copies were made. Sometime later the story was leaked to the newspapers.

Courtesy of The New-York Historical Society

Within the space of six months, James Madison, shown in Asher B. Durand's portrait, switched from nationalist and friend to Hamilton, to opposition and implacable hostility, under the influence of his new-found aegis, Thomas Jefferson.

By John Trumbull: Yale University Art Gallery, gift of Nicholas Roosevelt

Oliver Wolcott, Jr., Hamilton's trusted assistant in the Treasury, was privy to Hamilton's darkest secrets and cover-ups.

Anne Willing Bingham, seen in this engraving from the portrait by Gilbert Stuart, chose to entertain lavishly in the French style and earned the reputation of hostessing the most brilliant of all the Philadelphia balls.

Culver Pictures

William Bingham, a wealthy Philadelphia merchant and director of the Bank of North America, was a source for much information for Hamilton's reports.

Culver Pictures

Charles Maurice de Talleyrand-Perigord admired Hamilton but laughed at him for becoming poor in public office rather than rich as he had become as French Foreign Minister.

Without Elizabeth Hamilton's permission, Talleyrand took this Chartres miniature of Hamilton from the Hamilton home during a visit but returned it to Elizabeth as a token of his affection after her husband's death.

Edmond Charles "Citizen" Genêt, minister from revolutionary France to "excite the zeal of Americans," thrilled (and fooled) Jefferson but infuriated Washington and Hamilton by commissioning privateers and appealing over their government's head directly to "the people."

New York Public Library, Picture Collection

Dr. James McHenry had few qualifications to serve as Secretary of War for both Washington and Adams, yet for Hamilton he was useful as an informant inside Adams' cabinet.

New York Public Library,
Manuscripts and Archives Division,
Emmet Collection #9293

New York Public Library, Picture Collection

To Elizabeth and Alexander Hamilton, no man could be a gentleman of honor who, like James Monroe, would leave him "with an impression his suspicions were removed" but later act as if they had not been.

Aaron Burr painted by Gilbert Stuart in 1794.

In this engraving from Alonzo Chappel's painting, Sally Jay has the look of an uncrowned queen entirely equal to ruling her husband John, the incorruptible ruler of himself.

New York Public Library, Picture Collection

John Jay, seen in the portrait by Joseph Wright, served as first chief justice of the United States. When defeated for the office of Governor of New York by Aaron Burr by a few disputed votes against him, Jay replied, "A few more years will put us all in the dust; and it will then be of more importance to me to have governed *myself* than to have governed the *State*."

Courtesy of The New-York Historical Society

Broad Street and old Federal Hall, the nation's first capitol in 1789 and 1790, as it looked in 1795 when Hamilton was stoned in the street by the Wall Street mob protesting Jay's Treaty.

In this Federalist cartoon of 1793, Washington is seen in the Federal chariot leading troops against the French "cannibals" (left). Albert Gallatin, Citizen Genêt, and Thomas Jefferson try to halt the chariot's progress (right).

In the summer of 1794, 5,000 insurgents rioting on Braddock's Field near Pittsburgh attacked and killed some Federal revenue agents and threatened to march on Philadelphia. Hamilton organized and accompanied the Federal troops to put down the Whiskey Rebellion.

Our First Century *by R. M. Devens, (1878)*

Hamilton often suspected that perceptive friends like Angelica Church and Gouverneur Morris saw him as a Quixote. Here is his copy of Cervantes' classic.

Columbia University Libraries, Hamilton Collection

John Adams, as President, painted by William Winstanley, was often said to be "absolutely out of his senses" by enemies as well as his friends.

Adams National Historical Park

The Republican Court *by Rufus W. Griswold, 1859*

Abigail Adams, no admirer of Hamilton, feared "That man would become a second Bonaparte if he was possessed of equal power."

Charles Cotesworth Pinckney,
"the first gentleman of America," was a man who valued
Hamilton's friendship.

From a miniature by J. G. Malone

Timothy Pickering, shown here
in an engraving from a drawing by J. B. Longacre after a
painting by Gilbert Stuart,
served as both Secretary of
War and State, but pleaded
with Hamilton to "play his
cards for him" during the
Quasi War crisis.

Library of Congress

OBSERVATIONS

ON

CERTAIN DOCUMENTS

CONTAINED IN NO. V & VI OF

"THE HISTORY OF THE UNITED STATES
FOR THE YEAR 1796,"

IN WHICH THE

CHARGE OF SPECULATION

AGAINST

ALEXANDER HAMILTON,

LATE SECRETARY OF THE TREASURY,

IS FULLY REFUTED.

WRITTEN BY HIMSELF.

PHILADELPHIA:

PRINTED FOR JOHN FENNO, BY JOHN BIOREN.
1797.

Yale University Library

Accompanying Hamilton's published confession concerning the Maria Reynolds affair (title page seen here) were two oval portraits taken from stock engravings by an English publisher, labelled "The Subtle Seducer" and "The American Financier."

Hamilton's commission as Inspector and Major General was signed reluctantly by John Adams.

P. T. Weaver's portrait of Hamilton in the uniform of Inspector General was considered by him to be his best likeness. He gave the portrait to his childhood friend in St. Croix, Edward Stevens.

Toussaint L'Ouverture led a successful slave revolt against the
French colonial masters of Haiti and was encouraged by Hamilton, who supplied him through Edward Stevens with a practical
plan of government for a newly emerging black nation.

To Henry Lee, "Light Horse Harry," Hamilton confided out of a manic defense, "I feel that I stand upon ground which, sooner or later, will ensure me a triumph over all my enemies . . . the country is too young and vigorous to be quacked out of its political health."

Dr. Benjamin Rush, father of American psychiatry, attended Philip Hamilton at the time of his death. To Dr. Rush, Hamilton wrote that the death of his son had been beyond comparison the "most afflicting" event of his life.

Independence National Historical Park

Gouverneur Morris was a close friend and mentor in the world of finance.

New York Public Library, Picture Collection

At the Constitutional Convention, Hamilton had "revolutionized the mind" of his close friend Rufus King, later Senator from New York and minister to England.

·Pictorial Field-Book of the War of 1812
by Benson J. Lossing (1868)

Journal of American History *(1908)*

Hamilton's brother-in-law and client, John Barker Church, shocked New Yorkers by playing cards all night while Hamilton squired Angelica Church all over town.

Senator Harrison Gray Otis' racy letters home to his Bostonian wife, Sally, contained scandalous details of Angelica Church's amorous flirtation with Hamilton.

New York Public Library, Picture Collection

Elizabeth Hamilton remembered Washington's sitting for this magnificent Gilbert Stuart portrait of which he made a cherished present to the Hamiltons.

A pastoral view of Georgetown (left) and the Washington waterfront on the Potomac in 1801.

New York Public Library

Library of Congress

John Adams, the first President to live in the White House, seen here in 1799 prayed, "I Pray Heaven To Bestow The Best of Blessings on This House And All that shall hereafter Inhabit it May none but Honest and Wise Men overrule under This Roof."

On Harlem Heights in Upper Manhattan, where in 1776 he had fought British troops, Hamilton built his "sweet project," the Grange in 1800.

On Hamilton's bookplate the "Esq" identifies him as a New York lawyer, of Grange and the Advocate.

"His countenance is strongly stamped with grief" over his eldest son Philip's death in a duel, said Robert Troup of his old King's College roommate near the end of Hamilton's life when he sat for this portrait by Ezra Ames.

Columbia University Libraries, Hamilton Collection

Union College, Schaffer Library

On the ledge at Weehawken, Hamilton faces Burr while Nathaniel Pendleton, Hamilton's second, asks, "Will you have the hair spring set?"

The Hamilton monument on the site of the duel at Weehawken.

19

AN OUT-OF-TOWN, UNDERCOVER PRIME MINISTER

IT WOULD BE REPUGNATE TO THE FIRST PRINCIPLES OF OUR GOV-
ERNMENT TO EXCLUDE MEN FROM PUBLIC TRUSTS BECAUSE THEIR
TALENTS AND VIRTUES HOWEVER CONSPICUOUS ARE UNACCOM-
PANIED BY WEALTH.
—*Hamilton's Draft of Washington's Eighth Annual
Address to Congress, November 10, 1796*

By way of reciprocating Angelica Church for sending him with her glowing
letters of introduction the stream of refugees from the terror, the Directory, and
other bouleversements of the French Revolution, Hamilton packed off Senator
Rufus King on August 20, 1796, as his handpicked minister plenipotentiary to
Great Britain with a glowing letter of introduction to her. Hamilton's letter
forewarned Angelica that "you must not think less well of him for not being a
Jacobin." Unlike his friend John Jay, King would not "give me the trouble of
defending any Treaty of his making." Now, "to be sure of everybody's approbation he is instructed to do nothing but after a previous consultation with you."
There would be no more entangling alliances, except with Angelica. Would that

"have no charm for your____?" he asked her. Then he filled in the flirtatious—or salacious—blank he had left: "But I had forgotten. You have none."

King had a fat wife, the former Mary Alsop, a fully fleshed out figure of a woman. She looked not at all like the slender Angelica as he would always remember her from the very first time he had seen her years earlier at the army's winter encampment at Morristown, (or was it at The Pastures in Albany almost 20 years ago on his mission to Gates?). Angelica would always pride herself on possessing the smallest waist in any company of elegant women, and her firmly boned and tightly laced corsets cinched her slenderer still. Hamilton envisioned her now only a little plumper with age and, after at least four pregnancies, still tightly laced into the exigent fineness of line that for her would be *de rigueur* in the glittering salons of the London of the *fin de siècle*.

On some occasion of the past that she would well remember without more than his passing reference to it, Hamilton had spoken an old proverb to Angelica to compliment her on her unexceptionable figure. Now when he repeated it, joking with her about Mary Alsop King, there was no need of his spelling it all out again for her: "She has not the proverb in her favor *'the nearer the bone,* etc.' "

For Hamilton there would probably never be any sweeter flesh than Angelica's. His unfinished phrase was all that either of them need murmur to the other to summon up a memory more precious than a succulent piece of meat. With no Maria Reynolds in his private life now to occupy the urge he always seemed to feel for someone on whom to focus his passion accessory to his wife, his old yen for Angelica rearoused itself in his mind. For Mary Alsop King's defense, however, the gentleman in him could muster up nothing kinder than a tired sigh, "But I dare say she is sweet enough."

Thomas Pinckney, Rufus King's predecessor in London from 1792 to 1796, had also doubled as envoy extraordinary to Spain in 1794 and 1795 and, while there, successfully negotiated the Treaty of San Lorenzo el Real. By this important treaty fixing the boundaries of Florida and Louisiana, Spain had relinquished all other claims east of the Mississippi, and the United States had secured freedom of navigation of the river all the way down the delta. Thomas Pinckney was now returning home to become Hamilton's handpicked favorite to join John Adams on the Federalist presidential ticket for the election of 1796. As King had written Hamilton on May 2, "to his former stock of popularity" Pinckney "will now add the good will of those who have been peculiarly gratified with the Spanish Treaty . . . will he not receive as great, perhaps greater southern and western support as any other man?"

Hamilton wholeheartedly agreed with King about Thomas Pinckney. Like his beloved, long dead, but never-to-be-forgotten, wartime friend John Laurens, Pinckney was a South Carolinian who had served with distinction during the Revolution until being badly wounded at the Battle of Camden and captured by the British. He had presided over the South Carolina constitutional ratifying convention and served as governor of the state. Soon Hamilton would be dispatching his elder brother, Charles Cotesworth Pinckney, another fellow Cincinnatian, as his handpicked successor to the discredited James Monroe, to be minister plenipotentiary to France. James Monroe's ambiguous behavior at and after the confrontations of the morning and night of December 15, 1792, and in Paris since, were never to be forgotten or forgiven. Nothing seemed more important to Hamilton now than a trustworthy Pinckney in Paris. Monroe? He would handcull him home. Patrick Henry, a former anti-Federalist, had, like Pinckney, been scouted by Rufus King and Hamilton as a possible presidential candidate, but Hamilton wrote King on May 4, "I rather wish to be rid of P.H. that we may take up" Thomas Pinckney, who "ought to be our man . . . it is an idea of which I am fond in various lights."

What were these "various" mysterious lights?

Hamilton, in Washington's *Farewell Address,* had vowed to the people "that Heaven may continue to you the choicest tokens of the beneficence merited by national piety and morality—that your union and brotherly affection may be perpetual—that the free constitution, which is the work of your own hands may be sacredly maintained—that in fine the happiness of the people of these states under the auspices of liberty [will] acquire them the glorious satisfaction of recommending it to the affection the praise—and the adoption of every nation which is yet a stranger to it."

In less exalted, more immediately practical terms, this to Hamilton meant keeping Jefferson from winning the presidential election of 1796 and, if possible, denying him the vice-presidency as well. If Washington's farewell meant that Jefferson would be his successor, Hamilton saw his whole coherent system of government being plunged into chaos. It is "all-important to our country," Hamilton wrote, that Washington's "successor shall be a safe man. But it is far less important who of many men that may be named shall be the person, than that it shall not be Jefferson. . . . All personal and partial considerations must be discarded, and every thing must give way to the great object of excluding Jefferson."

Few good Federalists could contemplate Thomas Jefferson without a similar shudder. Remote in his cupolated château on its mount, served by platoons of slaves, he was thought of by most as one of the largest and richest property owners of America, yet a man who repudiated, on philosophic grounds, repayment of debts he owed and debts in general. To them his liberal protestations seemed merely a self-serving touching up of a self-created self-image as a Francophile, a Jacobin, a Deist, a physiocrat, a leveler and a random radical — a random tandem radical! To most of the small handful of Federalists rich enough to qualify for membership in the propertied elite into which Jefferson had been born he was a traitor to his class.

Back in 1793, John Adams was quite pleased to have been invited to join the American Philosophical Society; and when Jefferson came to escort him to his first meeting, they must have exchanged some political—and private—views. Adams came away from the meeting with little doubt that greed—or conventional Adam Smithian economic interest—was the seed of Jefferson's revolutionary zeal: "I wish somebody would pay his debt of seven thousand pounds to Britain and the debts of all his countrymen [Virginians]" he had written Abigail privately on February 3, 1793, "and then I believe his passions would subside, his reason return, and the whole man and his whole state become good friends of the Union and its government." But no Federal gentleman, at least, would tell the plebs such a secret about a fellow member of his philosophy club.

Even though Vice-president John Adams, now 60 years old, had been a prominent figure on the national scene for more than two decades, he remained something of an enigma, even, or especially, to those who knew him best. In his well-known political work "A Defence of the Constitution of . . . America," Adams had argued that in every society there is a constant conflict between rich and poor, each trying to despoil the other, and that the task of statesmanship is to set bounds and limits to the struggle. Adams had a strong, sometimes violent temper, a thin skin, a highly developed sense of his own importance, and an impulsiveness that many considered dangerous in a man a heartbeat away from the highest office. They agreed with Benjamin Franklin's remark that "Adams was an honest man, often a wise one, but sometimes wholly out of his senses." Enemies called him squeamish, cold, and unsocial. So did friends. One of them remarked that, unlike a Hamilton, for example, "He can't dance, drink, game, flatter, promise, dress, swear with gentlemen, and small talk and flirt with the ladies." Hamilton would, of course, privately agree with Adams's friend's appraisal.

To men who did not know both men well, to men who knew them only by report, Hamilton and Aaron Burr seemed to have more in common than any other pair of great antagonists of their time. But to those who knew Hamilton and John Adams well—in their rather humble backgrounds, frequent illnesses, paroxysms of obsession with enemies, formidable wives, and firm Federalist convictions forged in wide experience of the world and the creation of the nation —no two of the Founding Fathers were on a fundamental level more alike, except perhaps Hamilton and Washington. Such close affinities with Hamilton— Burr's on a superficial level, Adams's on a profound level—prepared Burr and Adams better by nature than any other two men of Hamilton's acquaintance to rank second to none but Jefferson as the deadliest of the extraordinary circle of enemies that Hamilton would summon up to test the meaning of his life and all his works.

If Adams himself did not quite share his own party's general abhorrence of Jefferson, this was due, in part, to his suspicion that many Federalists—including Hamilton—would have much preferred to see Thomas Pinckney—or Hamilton—elevated to the presidency in place of himself. But among most Federalists, Adams was generally acceptable as the candidate for president, as was Thomas Pinckney for the vice-presidency. However, Hamilton and others feared that New England might withhold some of its votes from Pinckney to ensure more votes for Adams than for Pinckney, whereas Southerners, out of sectional pride, might vote for Pinckney and Jefferson. This would mean that Jefferson might receive more votes than either one of the Federalists. The constitutional electoral system, by which the electors cast two votes, one for president and one for vice-president, without designating which man for which office, did not work at all well in the context of an unforeseen two-party system. This defect in the draftsmanship of the demigods—including Hamilton—would produce frantic intrigues and strange and fateful consequences for Hamilton in 1796 and 1800.

Fisher Ames said that Washington's *Farewell Address* was "a signal, like dropping a hat, for the party racers to start." Among the charges leveled against Adams was the old canard, published in the *Aurora* that it was he who had drafted the proposal Hamilton submitted to the Constitutional Convention advocating a government consisting of a king, lords, and Commons. In his *Defence* and *Discourses on Davila*, Adams had shown "an *active unfriendliness* to the *essential* and *cardinal* principles" of all American constitutions, state and federal. It was to his discredit with others that he disapproved of the funding and banking systems and was an enemy of Hamilton's whole fiscal policy. But now Federalist prospects seemed to be improving. Washington's *Farewell Address* had made "a deep impression upon the mind of the public." It "has so raised his reputation for wisdom, ability and patriotism that his enemies" were silenced. Republicans, with John Beckley acting as campaign manager, began spreading reports that Federalist strength in the coming election would be divided among Adams, Pinckney, Hamilton, and Jay. The way for Republicans to win would thus be by concentrating all votes for either president or vice-president on Jefferson. As their vice-presidential candidate, a man from a middle state who would draw no presidential or vice-presidential votes away from Jefferson, the Republicans shrewdly selected Aaron Burr.

From the Federalist point of view, the difficulty was that Adams was weak in the South, and Pinckney was weak in the North. Jonathan Dayton of New Jersey thought Adams's chances of election were dim. Pennsylvania would vote unanimously against Adams, and so would South Carolina, which would vote for Pinckney. The rest of the South would cast its votes for Jefferson and Burr. Whereas Massachusetts and New Jersey would throw all their first place votes to Adams, what about the second? If they scattered them, as planned, might not then Jefferson win the first place? He suggested to Theodore Sedgwick of Massachusetts that there was only one way to keep Jefferson from winning the presidency by picking up both first and second place votes all over the map. What did Sedgwick think about having the Federalists support Burr?

Although no true Federalist would consider crossing over to vote for Jefferson, by no means all of them felt the same antipathy toward Burr. In policy he always stood somewhere near the middle of the political spectrum, he was personally on good terms with many staunch Federalists, and his suave, genial, yet aristocratic, bearing and his ready wit made him *persona grata* to many men who looked on Jefferson as the reclusive horned beast of anarchy. Already at odds with Federalist leaders in his own state, Dayton launched an undercover campaign to win over Federalist votes for Burr. Without waiting for Sedgwick's reply, Dayton wrote him again, this time boldly urging what he had merely hinted at before: "Every moment's reflection serves only to impress me more with the importance of our fixing upon some plan of cooperation to defeat the designs of Mr. J[efferson]'s friends. If Mr A[dams] cannot succeed, is it not desirable to have at the helm a man who is personally known to, as well as esteemed & respected by us both? I assure you that I think it possible for you & me with a little aid to effect this." Burr was his man. The fact that a Federalist like Dayton was urging Burr upon his Federalist friends for vice-president instead of Pinckney or even Jay was a bitter blow to Hamilton.

Sedgwick did not rise to Dayton's bait and remained loyal to Hamilton's leadership. He felt that Adams would get some votes in Pennsylvania and that South Carolina would not desert him. Pinckney must be dealt with honestly by giving him every possible Federalist vote, even if it meant his election over Adams. "Respecting Mr. Burr," said Sedgwick to Hamilton, "no man better than yourself knows the estimation in which I hold him. But in my conscience I do not believe that every vote in Massachusetts would give him the least chance of an election to either of the offices." Sedgwick volunteered a prophecy of how Jefferson and Beckley would deal with Burr that proved prophetic. "They court the aid of his character & talents," he declared, but they "have not the smallest confidence in his hearty union to their cause. Indeed it is my firm belief that their views and his are not only distinct but opposite." He reminded Dayton of the occasion when Monroe had been chosen over Burr for the ministry to France "by the insidious machinations of that party." They had backed Monroe against Burr then, not because he was superior, or even equal, in talents and integrity, but because "they knew the one would & the other would not condescend to act as their tool. They doubtless respect Burr's talents, but they dread his independence of *them.*" Therefore, Sedgwick was certain that the Republicans would deliberately withhold votes from Burr to prevent any possibility of his election to either office over Jefferson. Dayton's scheme would not work.

Sedgwick secretly sent copies of this exchange of correspondence with Dayton to Hamilton with the warning: "I need not say that this information must be kept secret, for however proper it may be, and I esteem it highly so, Dayton would doubtless deem it a breach of confidence." On the back of Sedgwick's letter, Hamilton wrote, "concerning Dayton's intrigue for Burr."

This effort of Dayton and others to wrest control of his own Federalist party away from him by obtaining Federalist votes for Burr would strike Hamilton as a more serious grievance than almost anything Jefferson might have done. When a party leader loses a hard-fought election to a powerful opponent riding a strong popular tide, he has only lost a battle, not a war, as long as he remains the leader to fight the next election, perhaps to ride a new tide running back his way. Only the party leader who loses control of his own party is finished for good and all. Dayton joined Burr as a man whom Hamilton would afterward regard with deep distrust. With powerful friends in both parties now, Aaron Burr was a threat to him who might, unless halted, wrest control of the Federalists from Hamilton's hands and go on to gain the "highest honors." This was a future Hamilton was ready to oppose with every weapon at his command.

From the other side of the political lines, John Beckley was also busily sowing tares in Hamilton's path. He was certain that if there were no schism in Virginia, Jefferson and Burr would be chosen. He falsely put it about that Hamilton had "admitted . . . there may be a state of things in which it would be desirable that Mr. J should be elected without opposition. . . ." This was because the Southern states would never consent to the United States declaring war on France. If France declared war on America (which some Federalists believed was inevitable), "Mr. J's influence could alone preserve the Union, and produce a favorable termination of the breach. . . ." Beckley, here pretending to give Hamilton credit for putting national welfare in a war crisis ahead of personal and party success by yielding the presidency to Jefferson, was charging Hamilton with an intrigue to win the presidency for himself or at least for a pliable surrogate like Thomas Pinckney. Beckley trotted out Hamilton's name as a stalking horse that would be of maximum horrific aspect to Republicans. Beckley explained that though "Hamilton himself industriously propagates that Adams and Pinckney are [the Federalists'] choice," this was only a cover-up for himself. Hamilton's real plan was this: "Quere: May not Strong & Cabot design to become electors, and if a suitable election prevail thro' Massachusetts, to suddenly nominate & by their influence carry Hamilton in that State? Rh. Island, Vermont, Connecticut, New York, New Jersey, & Maryland, would all probably follow . . . unanimously. Some late indications seem to warrant the suspicion." Therefore, every Republican effort must be made to preserve all Virginia votes solid for both Republican candidates to keep out Hamilton.[1]

Jefferson went along with Beckley's strategy, writing Madison on January 22, 1797, that "He [John Adams] is perhaps the only sure barrier against Hamilton's getting in." The threat of Hamilton, just turning 40, was not limited to the election of 1796, but would loom in future elections as well. On the Federalist side, John Adams found no difficulty in going along with Beckley's and Jefferson's theory that Hamilton was leading a conspiracy to slip himself into the presidency by scuttling Adams.

Years after Hamilton's death, Adams approved William Cobbett's appraisal that "all Parties affected to regret that loss of Washington, but none were truly Sorry." The fact was, said Adams, that "one party acquiesced in the resignation of Washington because they believed it a step towards the introduction of Mr. Jefferson, and the other because they thought it an Advance toward the election of Mr. Hamilton who was their ultimate Object." This led to a characteristic self-pitying reflection from Adams, "As both parties despaired of obtaining their favorite, Adams was brought in by a miserable majority of one or two votes, with the deliberate intention to sacrifice him at the next election. His administration was therefore never supported by either party, but vilified and libelled by both."

None of the objective evidence lends credibility to Beckley's and Jefferson's and Adams's charges that Hamilton was seeking to intrigue his way into the presidency, and the weight of it indicates that such charges were false. Hamilton's role was that of the professional party leader. He and Jay formally withdrew their own names from consideration as candidates so that no votes would be wasted on them. Hamilton's letter to his close friend Jeremiah Wadsworth on

December 1 is typical of the forthright exhortations he was sending to other Federalist leaders. He had been "appraised of the machination to cheat us into Mr. Burr," but that would not succeed. "My chief fear is that the attachment of our Eastern friends to Mr. Adams may prevent their voting for *Pinckney* likewise & that some irregularity or accident may deprive us of Adams and let in Jefferson." For example, Vermont's votes, all for Adams, might be disqualified by an irregularity in the choosing of the electors there. In Georgia, too, there had been rumors of irregularities. "Tis therefore a plain policy to support Mr. Pinckney equally with Mr. Adams."

Hamilton exhorted Stephen Higginson in Massachusetts to hold that state's electors in line for both men. Higginson passed on Hamilton's advice and was glad to report back that "a majority of them were at first inclined to throw away their votes from M. Pinckney, lest he should rise above Adams, but your information as to Vermont, with some observations made to them, showing the dangers of so doing, decided all but three, who were determined, upon interested and personal motives, to waste theirs."

What probably counted more than all the intrigues and polemics on both sides were the grass roots organizing efforts that John Beckley made for Jefferson throughout the nation, especially in the swing state of Pennsylvania. He distributed thousands of sample ballots bearing the names of the Republican electors, as well as reams of handbills, pamphlets, and broadsides. His was the first organized presidential political campaign in the modern sense.

When all the votes were in, the official tally was Adams, 71; Jefferson, 68; Pinckney, 59; and Burr, 30, with the rest of the electoral votes thrown away among George Clinton and others. Vermont's questioned ballots were allowed to be counted and gave Adams his winning edge of three.

It was about what Hamilton realistically had expected. It could have been much worse, he was not dissatisfied with the result. His calm acquiescence in it betrays no suggestion of disappointment that an intrigue he had planned had failed. But ominous for the future union of the nation was the sectional distribution of the votes: not a single vote for Jefferson came from any state north and east of the Delaware River. Northern Federalists had thrown away their votes rather than vote for Pinckney; Southern Republicans had thrown away theirs rather than vote for Burr.

With Adams president, Jefferson vice-president, and Burr running well behind Pinckney, Hamilton wrote King on February 15, 1797, "our Jacobins say they are well pleased and that the *Lion* & the *Lamb* are to lie down together." The election of Washington's vice-president to the presidency to succeed him had just created the strongest possible precedent for the "Jacobins' " vice-presidential lion to move up the same way in due course. As for the Federalists, "Mr. Adams *personal* friends talk a little in the same way." Hamilton even had some kind words for Jefferson: "Mr. Jefferson is not half so ill a man as we have been accustomed to think him." He and Adams had made the usual pronouncements that "there is to be a united and vigorous administration," but "skeptics like me quietly look forward to the event—willing to hope but not prepared to believe."

It gave Hamilton some grim satisfaction that Jefferson's Virginians and other Southern Republicans had held back so many votes from Burr. He wrote King, "The event will not a little mortify Burr. Virginia has given him only one vote."

Hamilton's live-and-let-live attitude toward Jefferson and Adams contrasted sharply with theirs toward him. Jefferson wrote a letter to Adams eagerly looking ahead to 1800, but pretending no personal interest in what might happen then. He elaborately disclaimed disappointment at not having won the top post —and sowed some Beckley style tares: "Indeed it is possible that you may be cheated of your succession by a trick worthy the subtlety of your arch-friend of New York, who has been able to make of your real friends tools to defeat their & your just wishes. Most probably he will be disappointed as to you; & my inclinations place me out of his reach."

Jefferson sent this revealing letter to Madison for review and then forwarding to Adams. An embarrassed Madison wrote back that he was holding it up, dryly remarking that Adams was aware of Jefferson's warm feelings toward him and adding, "it deserves to be considered whether the idea of bettering it is not outweighed by the possibility of changing it for the worse. . . . There is perhaps a general air on the letter which betrays the difficulty of your situation in writing it." Madison reassured Jefferson that Adams was already aware of Hamilton's alleged machinations: "There may be danger of his suspecting in mementos on that subject, a wish to make his resentment an instrument for avenging that of others."

After all Hamilton's urgings to Federalists north and south to vote for Adams and the fact that he had won, the "resentment" they were trying to teach Adams to feel toward him seemed unfair, but it was real, and Adams made it manifest to all. Even before the election, Higginson had warned Hamilton that Adams and his friends "will swear that the union of Pinckney with him was a trick to prevent his election . . . he will never forgive . . . he may be hurried by his temper to break with everyone who preferred the public to him." After the votes were in and Adams's victory assured, Higginson wrote again on January 12 that instead of being satisfied with his being elected, Adams and his partisans are "alarmed at the danger he was in of failing."

They placed Hamilton and Jay "at the head of this junto, as they call it" who were intriguing to exclude "Mr. A. from the chair." Believing this, "Adams may be cool & distant" toward men like Hamilton "whom he ought to be intimate with & consult upon important occasions." Adams would "adopt a line of conduct toward his former friends" that will divide and weaken the Federalist interest." He urged Hamilton to "think of some mode of preventing the inconveniences which I fear to result from Mr. Adams feelings." Here Higginson was accurately apprehending new disasters that the mistrust sown between the two men would bring. It would in the end, among other things, destroy the political fortunes of Hamilton, Adams, and the Federalist party; keep Adams from a second term; insure the succession of Madison and Monroe after Jefferson's presidency; and threaten the secession of the New England states, New York, and New Jersey from the constitutional union.

At first, Adams himself seemed to make light of the stories that Hamilton and Jay had intrigued to slip Pinckney into the presidency ahead of him. Whether or not these stories were true, he wrote Abigail, "they shall make no impression on my friendship for those characters. I believe that their motives were what they [conceived] for public good." But Abigail was incensed. On December 31, 1796, she reminded John how she had often warned him against Hamilton as a man "ambitious as Julius Caesar, a subtle intriguer." She added, "His thirst for fame is insatiable. I have ever kept my eye upon him." She had hoped that Jefferson would win out over Pinckney for vice-president. Her "friendship for that gentleman has lived through his faults and errors—to which I have not been blind." By January 9, Adams had come round to Abigail's view of Hamilton's role. Hamilton was "a proud spirited, conceited, aspiring mortal, always pretending to morality, with as debauched morals as old Franklin," who was "more his model than anyone I know." Hamilton was also "as great an hypocrite as any in the U.S., his intrigues in the election I despise. That he has 'talents' I admit, but I dread none of them. I shall take no notice of his puppyhood but retain the same opinion of him I always had and maintain the same conduct towards him that I always did—that is, to keep him at a distance." Abigail assured her husband of how right he was: "Beware of that spare Cassius, has always occurred to me when I have seen that cock sparrow," she wrote. "Oh, I have read his heart in his wicked eyes many a time. The very devil is in them. They are lasciviousness itself . . . Pray burn this letter. Dead men tell no tales."

The congressional election of December 13–15, 1796, in his home New York City constituency kept the Federalist party leader busier than the making of that year's president. The Republican candidate was the incumbent Edward Livingston, whose pointedly hostile resolutions had demanded executive disclosure to Congress of Hamilton's secret instructions to John Jay and pitilessly spotlighted Hamilton's custody and care of Lafayette's son. It was Livingston who, after Hamilton had been stoned in Wall Street, had described him to his mother as roaming the streets of New York like a mad dog, swearing like a "street bully."

The Federalists nominated John Watson, a merchant who had served as speaker of the assembly in 1794 and was now a member of the state senate. Hamilton managed his party's campaign for Watson and wrote handbills and broadsides as its leading campaigner. The *Argus* reported on December 15 that "Mr. Hamilton does not confine his attention to any ward in particular. He patrols the whole city and strains every nerve in favor of the yankee candidate, ne quid res publica detrimento capiat." Writing for Noah Webster's *Minerva & Mercantile Evening Advertiser* as a "Federal Republican," Hamilton compared the two candidates, calling Livingston's resolution demanding disclosure of his instructions to Jay "a flagrant inroad upon the constitution of his country."

A member of the great family of the colonial lords of Livingston Manor, Edward Livingston was a scion of inherited wealth; Watson, a self-made man. Hamilton felt the distinction keenly while he tried to repair his own precarious economic position by the private practice of law, at least to the extent that his concern for the politics of his city, state, and nation—a nonpaying client on seemingly permanent retainer—left him time and energy to do so. "If Mr. Livingston has some outside showy talents," Hamilton wrote, "they are more than counterbalanced by the good sense, discretion, knowledge of business and commerce, maturity of years and experience of Mr. Watson." Hamilton had no use for what later New Yorkers would come to call "limousine liberals." Watson was "a man of republican principles, *manners* and *habits.*" Voters could "judge for themselves how this description" would apply to Watson's aristocratic young rival. As for Mr. Livingston, *"his democracy if genuine, is at least more at ease in a coach."* He, too, was a random tandem radical.

But such talk has rarely kept rich aristocrats who profess to be men of the people from winning New York elections. Watson's campaign lagged so badly that two days before the election, some Federalists met at A. Moore's in Chatham Street and sought to replace him with Hamilton. They resolved that Hamilton as a man of "literary abilities" is "better calculated to represent this city and county in Congress than James Watson at this alarming crisis." Hamilton was not nominated, and Livingston was reelected by a margin of 550 votes in a total of 4,174.

To Hamilton, the problem of how any self-made man could afford to serve a republic in high office was one of painfully acute, personal perplexity. Watson had been charged with making money by being a speculator. Was this on its face less honorable than inheriting it like Livingston? The only answer "Federal Republican" could give was by way of confession and avoidance, not rebuttal. "Every merchant is a *speculator* by the nature of his calling. Is he therefore a bad man?" In his November draft of Washington's Eighth Annual Address to Congress, Hamilton had also analyzed the problem of keeping in public office honest men who were poor. His words read as if wrung from the heart of his own bitter experience with calumnies of illicit speculation.

The compensation of high public offices must be raised, he warned. "The expense of the most frugal plan of living in our great cities" was prohibitive to men without private means. "It would be repugnate to the first principles of our government to exclude men from public trusts because their talents & virtues however conspicuous are unaccompanied by wealth. . . . The compensations which our government allows ought to be revised and materially increased. . . . The character & success of Republican government appear absolutely to depend on this policy. . . . If their own private wealth is to supply in candidates for public office the deficiency of public liberality then the sphere of those who can be candidates is much narrowed." "Those who have talents and are too virtuous to abuse their stations cannot accept public offices . . . if they have talents without virtue they may indeed accept offices to make a dishonest & improper use of them."

Hamilton tactfully did not cite the vast wealth his good friend Talleyrand, the bishop of Autun, had already accumulated in ostensibly low salaried offices of public trust in France.

"The tendency is to transfer the management of public affairs to wealthy but incapable hands or to hands which if capable are as destitute of integrity as of wealth." The general lesson about men and governments to be drawn was that "no plan of governing is well founded which does not regard man as a compound of selfish and virtuous passions. To expect him to be wholly guided by the latter would be as great an error as to suppose him wholly destitute of them." For proof of such conclusions, Hamilton needed only to look deep within himself.

It pained Hamilton that the only way he could afford to continue to render his indispensable services to the nation as its out-of-town prime minister was by keeping out of public office and in his private one. As many a president of middling talent has shown by wide travels or low golf handicaps—or less innocent diversions—running the country is hardly a full-time job, unlike the private practice of law, which even for men of the quickest talent, like Hamilton, is more than a full-time job. Hamilton would now try to do both jobs at once.

Also picked up in Hamilton's draft of Washington's Eighth Annual Address to Congress was Washington's plan for a national university. Here and elsewhere, Hamilton laid the basis for his claim to being the ancestor of the Departments of Commerce and Agriculture; the regular army, navy, and marines; and the service academies. It was important to establish a Board of Agriculture with adequate funding to remedy the problems "of soil impoverished by an unskillful tillage," he argued. This "yields but a scanty reward for the labor bestowed upon it, and leaves its possessors under strong temptation to abandon it and emigrate to distant regions more fertile not yet exhausted by an unskillful use." The same Board of Agriculture or a companion board might also "embrace the encouragement of the mechanic and manufacturing arts with an eye to the introduction from abroad of useful machinery." Hamilton called for the creation of a military academy because "however pacific its general policy," every government ought to preserve "a solid fund of military information always ready for national emergencies." Furthermore, "creation of a modern navy" was necessary because "an active external commerce demands a naval power to protect it . . . the most equitable and sincere neutrality is not sufficient to exempt a state from the depredations of other nations at war with each other." Besides a permanent navy there should be stockpiling of strategic materials. It would be prudent to "lay up magazines of ship timber and to build and equip annually one or more ships of force—so that a future war of Europe, if we escape the present storm may not find our commerce in the defenceless situation in which the present found it."

As Hamilton and Washington had said in the closing paragraphs of the *Farewell Address*, their Neutrality Proclamation of April 22, 1793, had "continually governed me uninfluenced and unawed by the attempts of any of the warring powers or their agents or partisans to deter or divert from it."

Efforts to help the nation "escape the present storm" that beset it during the last months of Washington's tenure in 1796 and the early months of Adams's in 1797 were demanding more of Hamilton's thought, time, and "literary abilities" than all his other activities in New York City politics and private law practice combined. As news of Jay's Treaty had become known in France, Secretary of State Timothy Pickering had sent James Monroe a set of official explanations intended to appease or counteract French discomfiture. Monroe failed to press these upon the French. On the contrary, he gave them to understand that, like his fellow influential Republicans Jefferson and Madison, he himself had little sympathy with Jay's Treaty. All that had then kept the Directory from declaring war against the United States was the realization that doing so would drive America still closer into the outstretched arms of Britain. The Directory went no farther than declaring that the Treaty of Paris with France of 1778 had been breached by America. Adams's son John Quincy Adams, American minister at The Hague, heard that the Directory had been told by Monroe that Jay had been taking bribes in London and that the House of Representatives had also been bribed to give its final three-vote margin of funding approval to the treaty. Most of the French anger over Jay's Treaty did not "proceed from themselves" according to John Quincy Adams, but was "inspired by Americans at Paris" like Monroe. "The greatest enemies of America in France," he said, "are Americans themselves."

For his part, Monroe, who was sharing lodgings in Paris with Thomas Paine, blamed Hamilton for the "evil" treaty that his secretary of state had charged him to defend. Monroe complained to Madison on September 1, 1796, that Pickering had written him like "an overseer on the farm to one of his gang." Pickering's explanation "corresponds so much" with Hamilton's *Camillus* that Monroe suspected both "were written by the same hand," that is, Hamilton's. Monroe shed some crocodile tears: "Poor Washington. Into what hands has he fallen."

Oliver Wolcott, Jr., for whom the confrontation with Senator Monroe and the two congressmen the night of December 15, 1792, would be almost as unforgettable as it was for Hamilton, thought that Monroe ought to be recalled to "stop the channels by which foreign poison is introduced into the country." Hamilton, too, sought Monroe's recall, writing to Secretary of War McHenry that he should "be superseded with a kind letter to him" because "we must not quarrel with France for *pins* and *needles.*" McHenry should bring this to the attention of the president or the secretary of state "even at the expense of being a little officious." After Hamilton had repeated the suggestion to Washington in June, saying that the United States should "have some faithful organ near the French government to explain their real views," Washington agreed. He followed Hamilton's recommendation that Charles Cotesworth Pinckney be appointed to replace Monroe.

By May of 1796, Washington was incensed by the rumors that France would declare war and launch an invasion. "We will not be dictated to by . . . any nation under heaven," he thundered. Through the storm over Jay's Treaty Hamilton continued to counsel conciliation and moderation toward France. But French raids of all kinds on American seaborne commerce had been increasing. In a report to President Adams on French depredations of June 21, 1797, Timothy Pickering pointed out that as a result of the Directory's decree of July 2, 1796, the seas of the West Indies "swarm with privateers and gun boats called forth by the latitude allowed to depredations" by French agents at Guadaloupe and Saint-Domingue. Pickering's report contained a list of 316 American vessels illegally seized by the French.

There were older, more deep-seated grounds for suspicion and antagonism toward France as well. The aggressive Directory was in the process of trying to wrest the Floridas and the Louisiana territory from Spain with the idea of setting up a "Western Republic" there. This area would be a far more menacing neighbor as a dominion of dynamic, aggressive Napoleonic France than as a decaying colony of feeble, depleted old Spain. In the succession of French ministers to the United States, Genêt had been outrageous, whereas Fauchet, although less obtrusively persistent, was privately more troublesome, as Randolph, Talleyrand, and Washington had all learned in various ways. And Fauchet's successor, Pierre Auguste Adet, was even more outspoken than either of his predecessors in circulating propaganda for France throughout America.

Adet wrote Pickering on November 15, calling Jay's Treaty "equivalent to a Treaty of Alliance with Great Britain." He complained about Pickering's slow responses to his complaints. He accused Jay and Washington of duplicitous secrecy in negotiating it. He denounced the feeble American resistance to British impressment of seamen whom they claimed as British subjects from American ships. Adet's critical comments were published and summarized in many American newspapers as the election campaign of 1796 grew most intense. Washington, Pickering, and Wolcott all sought Hamilton's advice and counsel on how to deal with Adet's outrages, although by the time they did so, Pickering had already sent Adet sharp reproofs. It was not clear whether Adet had been acting as he had on orders of the Directory or whether, as the Federalist pamphleteer William Cobbett hinted, John Beckley had arranged the publication for Adet at a meeting at Beckley's house.

After consulting Jay, Hamilton advised Washington on November 4 that whether Adet had acted with or without authority, "he committed a disrespect towards our government which ought not to pass unnoticed. The manner of noticing it ought to be *negative* . . . that is, by the *personal conduct* of the President towards the minister."

Adet should be received by Washington "with a *dignified reserve,* holding an *exact medium* between an *offensive coldness* and *cordiality.*" Hamilton added that "the point is a nice one to be hit, but no one will know better how to do it than the President." Few, if any, were on such intimate terms with him as to take note of the famous presidential reserve by even so mild a joke at his expense as this.

Overt insult to Adet was to be avoided. Indeed, Hamilton was "afraid of Mr. Pickering's *warmth*" toward Adet. He disapproved the caustic tone of Pickering's reproof. It was too "epigrammatical and *sharp.*" The proper "card now to be played is perhaps the most delicate that has occurred in our administration." Hamilton's use here of the first person plural form—"our" administration —writing confidentially from New York, retains the old prime ministerial ring. "Nations, like individuals, sometimes get into squabbles from the manner more than the matter," he reminded the chief of state. Furthermore, it was "all-important . . . if possible to avoid rupture with France, and if that cannot be, to evince to the people that there has been an unequivocal disposition to avoid it." All discussions should be *"calm"* and *"smooth,"* in the "language of moderation, and, as long as it can be done, of friendship . . ."

He and Washington both knew they were dealing with a cabinet now of men of the second rank. He recognized his friend Pickering's limitations as a secretary of state: "Mr. Pickering, who is a very worthy man, has nevertheless something warm and angular in his temper, and will require much a vigilant, moderating eye."

Such tact was of no avail. On November 15, making a careful distinction between Hamilton and Washington's government on the one hand and the American "people" on the other, for which France still professed the warmest friendship, Adet claimed that the government had betrayed its words, declared himself suspended from duty, and commenced to work actively for Beckley and Jefferson in the presidential election campaign.

Washington protested to Hamilton on January 12 against Adet's barefaced appeal to popular emotion over the head of the elected government. It was "outrageous beyond conception." John Adams fumed at Adet's "most opprobrious and contumelious language". Federalist citizens of Philadelphia, fearful of war with France, would switch their votes to Jefferson's party because they believed that "the election of Mr. Jefferson was necessary to prevent a rupture with France."

Once again the time had come for someone of "literary abilities" to give an answer to France that would help the public understand, appreciate, and support the Federalist government's policy. On December 8 in *The Minerva* appeared a long piece written by Hamilton, entitled "The Answer," signed *Americanus*.

Americanus pointed out that Adet had had the effrontery to publish his indictment of the American government in American newspapers. Here was a foreigner meddling in domestic affairs. Adet's purpose, Hamilton declared, was to persuade the timid, in the approaching election, to vote out the president and vice-president, whom he traduced. He cited French officials' pronouncements about neutrals' rights, then contradicted them by citing their own contrary laws on the same points. He quoted obscure authorities on international law and French practice. Recondite beyond the comprehension of much of the public, "The Answer" was an expert brief aimed at members of the new Congress, who had just assembled, and served as an unofficial white paper defending "our" administration's policy in relations with France.

Redoubtable old Fisher Ames, believing that the country stood on the verge of anarchy and ruin, was delighted with Hamilton's "Answer" and "Warnings." He felt that Congress, an aggregation mostly of fools, needed a strong leader like Hamilton in it to point the way. "We expect, confidently, that the House of Representatives will *act* out of its proper character," he told Hamilton wryly, "for if it should act according to it, we are lost. Our government will be, in fact, a mere democracy, which has never been tolerable nor long tolerated."

Had there not been a series of suspicious fires breaking out in various sections of New York City? Were these not incendiary attempts of Jacobins to burn down the city and initiate the first stage of a French-style revolution?

Friends of Hamilton who thought like Fisher Ames but whose health was stronger armed themselves and patrolled the city each night, dividing themselves into bands of 20 each, one to a ward. Hamilton did not share such hysterical fears, but took his turn marching with the rest. In one of these nightly watches, he turned his ankle and pulled a tendon. Lamed and hobbling, he was compelled to keep to his house for some weeks and leave the freedom of the city to other and sounder limbs.

Extreme Federalists began to call for immediate war with "that monster, France," but, by so doing, they parted company with Hamilton. The reasons that had made him send Jay to Britain to seek peaceful means to settle the dispute with Britain now held good in the present conflict with France. Earlier, Hamilton had closed "The Answer" on a note of moderate, disinterested patriotism that almost, but not quite, echoed the organ tones of the *Farewell Address:*

"Our government," he summed up, "has acted with firmness, consistency, and moderation, in repelling the unjust pretensions of the belligerent powers. . . . Into whatsoever hands the administration . . . may now come, they are called on by . . . wise policy, and the voice of their country, to pursue the same general line of conduct . . . without yielding to the violence of party on either side."

As 1797 began, the *Americanus* who had written "The Answer" contracted his pen name slightly to an *American* to write a new, more partisan series of six broadsides dealing with the French imbroglio entitled "The Warning." Numbers I through VI appeared on January 27, February 7, 21, and 27 and March 13 and 17, of 1797. Between "The Answer" in December and No. VI of "The Warning" late in March, Hamilton's tone waxed ever more ominously shrill and provocative, suggesting the kind of pressures that on earlier occasions had signaled illness and nervous derangement.

Gratitude for France's aid during the Revolution should not permit France now to impinge on the freedom won then by means of it. The principal purpose of her aid then was to enfeeble a hated and powerful rival: "He must be a fool, who can be credulous enough to believe, that a despotic court aided a popular revolution, from regard to liberty or friendship to . . . principles. . . ." Her bargain had brought France trade advantages here and a guarantee from the United States of her West Indies possessions in every future defensive war. The machinations of France, through her envoys like Adet, now sought to keep the American government feeble and distracted, perpetually in quarrels with Britain, and the dupe of French designs. French aggression was more iniquitous than anything hitherto suffered at the hands of the British. "The man who, after this mass of evidence," Hamilton wrote, working up to the sort of hysterical climax that was becoming all too typical of his style when he dealt with enemies, "shall be the apologist of France, and the calumniator of his own government, is not an American. The choice for him lies between being deemed a fool, a madman or a traitor." Writing Pickering on March 22, Hamilton called for "a day of humiliation and prayer . . . it will be politically useful to impress our nation that there is a serious state of things—to strengthen religious ideas in a contest . . . against atheism, conquest and anarchy . . . the war may call on us to defend our firesides and our altars."

Adams had no friends among the leaders of the Federalist party who gave personal fealty to him in the same way so many gave close personal fealty to Hamilton: Fisher Ames, Theodore Sedgwick, Stephen Higginson, John Jay, Rufus King, Thomas and Charles Cotesworth Pinckney, William Loughton Smith, Uriah Tracy, Timothy Pickering, Oliver Wolcott, Jr., James McHenry—and their brooding omnipresence emeritus, George Washington himself. Lacking such support for himself, Adams after his election sought to draw it toward him by retaining Washington's cabinet and chief diplomatic appointees without change, all of whom had been handpicked for Washington by Hamilton. Adams seemed to be entirely ignorant of the strength and depth of their fealty toward their selector, leader, and master.

As vice-president, Adams had spent the long months when Congress was not in session at home with Abigail in Quincy far from day-to-day touch with the men who ran the government in Philadelphia. Few expected that election to the presidency would much change his ingrained habits. So as Washington looked toward retirement at Mount Vernon and Adams made his way to Philadelphia for his inauguration on March 4, 1797, the power of the lawyer in private practice up in New York to control the executive government through its department heads in Philadelphia and diplomatic representatives abroad did not diminish, but markedly increased. Three years more would pass before a thunderstruck and furious Adams would comprehend the full reach of the control Hamilton had exercised over his presidency's government.

Before leaving office, Washington had asked Hamilton for his advice on sending a special envoy to France, as Jay had been sent to London in 1794 during a similar crisis with Britain over depredations against American shipping. Washington was worried lest a special emissary offend his and Hamilton's new ministerial appointee, General Charles Cotesworth Pinckney, who had only just sailed for France in December. On January 25, Hamilton replied that he favored a special mission to France "under some shape or other." To France, "Pinckney will be considered as a mere substitute in ordinary course to Monroe." An extraordinary mission, in addition, "will in some degree soothe her pride." Besides if the mission should include a Republican and fail, "the influence on party" would be favorable. "And it will to be to France a bridge over which she may more easily retreat." The best form would be three persons, called *"Commissioners* plenipotentiary and extraordinary." Two of the three should be Madison and Pinckney, and the third should be George Cabot of Massachusetts, "the Nestor of the Federalists," to give geographical balance, but with any two empowered to act. Even two—Madison and Pinckney—without the third would be satisfactory, but "unless Mr. Madison will go there is scarcely another character that will afford advantages."

But Washington took leave of office without appointing the new commission. Hamilton soon realized that Adams would be in a better position to carry out Hamilton's policy than Washington would have been in any event. On February 26, Hamilton wrote his and Adams's good friend Theodore Sedgwick that a change of president "may give a change to the passion, and may also give a bridge to retreat over. . . . a great advantage for a new president . . . the most ought to be made of it." He added, "It is much our interest to preserve peace, if we can with honor, and if we cannot it will be very important to prove that no endeavour to do it has been omitted." Sedgwick had Adams's ear; so Hamilton told him, too, that the commission should consist of Madison, Pinckney, and Cabot. Adams at first rejected Hamilton's advice. On the day before his inauguration, Adams asked Vice-President Jefferson to be his special emissary to France. Jefferson refused. Then Adams suggested Madison, Pinckney, and his friend Elbridge Gerry, a lukewarm Federalist with Republican leanings. Jefferson said he would use his good offices to see if Madison would accept. Adams's inaugural speech warned against foreign meddling in domestic politics: by such interference it would be foreign nations "who govern us, and not we, the people, who govern ourselves." He also expressed "personal esteem for the French nation," but promised to seek reparation for injuries to American commerce. Federalists like Ames thought his speech was weak, whereas Republicans praised Adams as a "friend of France, of peace an admirer of Republicanism, the enemy of party." Next day at his first cabinet meeting, Adams proposed a three-man commission with Madison as a member. Wolcott opposed Madison and offered his resignation. Adams refused to accept it. Adams found that most others of his fellow Federalists agreed with Wolcott in opposition to Madison. Then Jefferson reported back that Madison would not agree to serve in any event. After being led into this humiliating cul-de-sac, Adams ceased to consult Jefferson on the policies of his administration.

Timothy Pickering soon sent Hamilton word that the Directory had not only refused to receive Pinckney, a man whom many considered "the first gentleman of America," but had driven him out of Paris like a despised, undesirable alien or common felon. According to Pickering, Charles Delacroix, the French foreign minister, had "condescended" to tell Pinckney that *"his future stay should compel him to give information to the police!!!"*

The Directory had also passed a harsh new edict on March 2 that allowed French warships to bring all neutral vessels carrying any British goods into French ports. The French would treat Americans on enemy ships as pirates and would seize as prizes all American ships not carrying a full list of crew and passengers. Such a list was a *"rôle d'équipage,"* which American ships usually did not bother to carry. By this edict, the Directory had, in effect, launched a limited maritime war against the United States in complete violation of the commercial treaty of 1778.

To orthodox Federalists like Fisher Ames, but not to Hamilton, such a declaration justified a reciprocal American declaration of war. Extreme Federalists like William Loughton Smith, chairman of the Ways and Means Committee and for long Hamilton's spokesman in the House; Uriah Tracy; and others seemed eager for such a declaration of war against France and angry at what they saw as the hesitant, weak-kneed peace policy of Hamilton and Adams.

On March 7, 1796, Adams wrote Abigail in profound alarm about talk of disunion, "I sometimes think I am laboring in vain and spending my life for nought, in a fruitless endeavor to pursue a union that, being detested on both sides, cannot long last." The root of the trouble was "the pride of aristocracy" in the Southerners which thwarted every measure and man who did not serve their interests.

Uriah Tracy, in a violent letter to Hamilton of April 6, 1797, advocated dismemberment of the North from the South should the latter, through its representatives, "add to this their opinion by a public vote, that the Governement has injured France." He feared that the South, "increasing by frequent importations of foreign scoundrels as well as by those of home manufacture," would swallow up the North, "& the name & real character of an American soon be known only as a thing of tradition." Rather than let this happen, Tracy would demand a separation of the Union into two separate sections; in fact, if it should ever come to a choice, he would prefer to be a colony of Great Britain again than of France.

But the idea of prominent Federalists advocating secession of the Northern states from the federal Union was abhorrent to Hamilton. He fired off a sharp note to Smith: "It is unpleasant to me to know that I have for some time differed materially from many of my friends on public subjects . . . We seem now to feel and reason as the *Jacobins* did when Great Britain insulted and injured us, though certainly we have at least as much need of a temperate conduct now as we had then. I only say, God grant that the public interest may not be sacrificed at the shrine of irritation and mistaken pride."

In the mounting crisis, Adams turned to Pickering, Wolcott, and McHenry and asked them a series of questions. What preparations should we make for war? Should the government commission new frigates? Commission more privateers? Or try new negotiations? On March 25, 1797, he summoned Congress to a special session to convene on May 15. Some high Federalists like Fisher Ames said war should be avoided, but not, however, at the cost of honor, whatever that might mean. Jefferson and Republicans generally put it about that all of the Federalists were taking "the high ground of war."

Hamilton and his friends in Adams's cabinet exchanged many letters discussing the crisis. Pickering, Wolcott, and McHenry opposed the mission to France, but Hamilton still favored it because it would meet the Republicans "on their own ground and shut their mouths." Hamilton warned Wolcott "that a suspicion begins to *dawn* among the friends of government, that the *actual* administration is not much averse to war with France." By "actual" administration, he meant his three old friends who headed the Departments of State, Treasury, and War, not the figurehead Adams. "How very important to obviate this!" he insisted to them. Furthermore, they must agree to putting a prominent Republican like Madison or Jefferson on the commission. Hamilton told McHenry, "No *mortal*" must see "his letter or know its contents."

All three department heads dutifully swallowed their own opinions and adopted Hamilton's. They duly advised Adams as Hamilton had told them to do. He should send the commission, but at the same time arm merchant ships and create a naval force. As Wolcott meekly confessed to Hamilton on March 31, 1797: "You know that I am accustomed to respect your opinions; and I am not so ignorant of the extent of your influence upon the friends of government, as not to be sensible, that if you are known to favor the sending of a commission, so the thing must and will be."

Thereafter, President John Adams's cabinet sought and followed Hamilton's advice on the most important issues that would come before it during the rest of the century. Adams remained largely unaware of Hamilton's role until the explosion near the very end. Out of office and ostensibly a busy New York lawyer immersed in private affairs, Hamilton remained, in fact, the guiding spirit, the hidden prime minister, of Adams's administration down in Philadelphia. Although Adams himself never called on Hamilton for suggestions or advice—nor did Hamilton attempt to proffer any to him directly by word of mouth or letter—Adams's official family turned to him on every significant occasion for aid, comfort, revealed Federalist truth, as well as specific language in which to clothe answers to questions Adams would ask. Adams's discovery of the curious truth at last would produce the paroxysms of pigheadedness on all sides that wrecked the Federalists, assured loss of the election of 1800 to Jefferson, the demise of the party, and mortal enmity between the two men. The peculiar paradox of it all was that no important Federalist was more closely in agreement than Hamilton with Adams's basic policy of practical steps to preserve neutrality and peace. Through his department heads, Hamilton was spoonfeeding Adams the arguments that persuaded him of its rightness.

French depredations on American shipping were causing havoc with American commerce. Marine insurance rates rose higher with the addition of war risk riders. Adams turned to his department heads. What should he say in his special message to Congress? What should be his reaction to Pinckney's humiliation? What instructions should he give to emissaries? What should they demand of France? What defensive forces would be needed to protect the country from invasion? What would be the cost?

As before, Pickering, Wolcott, and McHenry severally passed Adams's questions back to Hamilton for answers. Hamilton was occupied in Albany with "court avocations" and the serious illness of his father-in-law, Philip Schuyler. But his dear old friend "Mac" McHenry needed Hamilton's "answer at length" because "you have all at your finger tips." Hamilton must not tell anyone of Mac's request or his reply. Hamilton turned back to his main avocation and replied promptly to McHenry with detailed advice covering virtually all aspects of governmental relations with France.

The United States had little to gain and much to lose from war with France, he warned. Indeed, they might be "left alone to contend with the Conquerors of Europe." Even a "considerable degree of humiliation may, without *ignominy* be encountered to avoid the possibility of much greater and train of incalculable evils." In this context, the word *honor* could be spoken at an unusually low level of intensity. Like a patient Dutch uncle counseling a problem child given to ranting, petulance, and pique, Hamilton warned that Adams's tone should be "cautious, solemn, grave, and perfectly derobed of all asperity or insult" McHenry simply recopied Hamilton's letter in his own hand, added a few paragraphs, and handed it to Adams as his own program.

Wolcott's reply to Adams also incorporated Hamilton's advice, and Pickering laced Hamilton's advice to him into a 25-page report otherwise his own. Taken together, their three reports to President Adams provided a many-sided yet amazingly unified and cogent platform for policy toward France—not really so amazing because most of it flowed from Hamilton's pen. Adams was quite pleased by the cabinet's advice. He wove whole conciliatory sentences and phrases, combined with a verbally defiant attitude, all derived from Hamilton, into his own speech to Congress. "As to going to war with France lightly," he wrote, "I know of nobody who is willing for it—but she has gone to war with us lightly. She is at war with us but we are not at war with her." In Congress, most Federalists now reacted with pleased surprise to Adams's more defiant tone imported from Hamilton unbeknownst to their speaker. Republicans, on the other hand, now were shocked and alarmed at Adams's warlike pose that screened placating deeds. Public passions rose, and the popularity of the Federalist stance with it.

At this time, it was still the custom for each house of Congress to give a ceremonial reply to the president's message. Congress's reply, as well as the government's preparedness program, embroiled Congress in debates of ever-mounting acrimony until it would finally adjourn July 8. On June 5, William Loughton Smith introduced, and Congress approved, ten resolutions that ostensibly embodied the president's program and were, in fact, Hamilton's, including appointment of the three commissioners. Adams called his cabinet together and proposed to appoint Pinckney, John Marshall of Virginia, and Elbridge Gerry of Massachusetts. The cabinet, departing from Hamilton's wishes, but reflecting most Federalist opinions, objected to Gerry and demanded a more reliable Federalist in his place. They refused to accept "a piebald commission." Adams yielded and substituted the name of Francis Dana of Massachusetts for Gerry's, and the Senate confirmed the three nominations. Dana then withdrew. Without consulting his cabinet again, Adams appointed Gerry to Dana's place. This suspicious sequence of events outraged the cabinet and most good Federalists—not so much the action itself, but Adams's quirky, secretive manner of doing it. Republicans were full of glee. Jefferson wrote Gerry that his appointment and confirmation brought "infinite joy to me."

In July the plague came on in Philadelphia. Congress adjourned without declaring war. Adams and his family left the capital for Quincy. John Marshall sailed for France from Philadelphia on July 20, and Gerry departed from Boston three days later, carrying with them toward Paris Hamilton's and Adams's fondest hopes for averting war. As Hamilton had calmly told Wolcott on June 6, "I like very well the course of Executive conduct in regard to the controversy with France."

Contributing greatly to Hamilton's serene mood in giving generous credit to Adams's policy, aside from the fact that it happened to be his own, was a momentous event that had occurred in Hamilton's private life two weeks earlier.

For eight years past he had been repining for Angelica Church to return from London. He had obtained for her and her family as a permanent residence the governor's former private mansion house just off Broadway in Partition Street. "Our impatience increases as the prospect becomes more promising," he had written her a whole year earlier. But "expectations must be converted into realities," he added. "Life is too short to warrant procrastination on of [*sic*] the most favorite and precious objects." He had written both words—*on* and *of*— for his "precious objects." Perhaps this was in the secret code they sometimes playfully used with each other; perhaps it was only a mistake. He added a heartfelt "we are anxiously wishing for your return." But by September his hopes had been dashed again: "Our apprehensions are realized and your coming is deferred . . . life is too short to lose a winter in the passage from hope to enjoyment . . . do really come in the spring . . . prithee do not let winter freeze the inclination . . . one cannot always live on hope. Tis thin diet at best." Thin indeed.

Winter had brought to her the frightening reports of arsonists' fires set in New York City. Then Hamilton had marched out on patrol and injured his leg. She implored him in January, in a contemporary way, to tell her that in moving to New York City, she and her four children would be safe "from terrors of fevers and negro plots . . . the cause of your fires."

She was not at all impressed with Rufus and Mary Alsop King, whom he had sent to her with his warmest kind of introduction. Yet she could not keep herself from re-arousing in him the old prurient desire for herself, as she delicately put both the Kings down: "Mon très cher monsieur, my eyes have recovered all their former lustre, and have been ineffectually employed in searching for the grace and elegance of your friend, nor have I yet been able to discover that ease and je ne sais quoi by which Sterne observes *the gentleman* may be so readily ascertained. . . . As to his capacity for bargain making that I cannot deny. I really do believe that he took his *Carasposa* weight and measure."

Neither had Angelica forgotten Hamilton's taking of her own sweet flesh nearer the bone in some intimate intercourse of long ago, murmuring the old proverb he had not needed to complete when he had written her a whole long year before. She closed her letter to him: "It was not so in the days of chivalry, nor when you were young."

Now, after all the years of repining and living on a thin diet of hope and growing older, winter had passed, and spring had come again, and with it from London on May 22 aboard Captain Dupleix's well-named ship, the *Fair American*, Angelica Church had at last come home to stay. But little more than a month would be left them before onslaughts of enemies and his preoccupation with honor—and a sore throat—would destroy all his joy at having her back.

20

THE THREADBARE LAWYER'S OLD AFFAIR LAID BARE

[THOSE WHO] HAVE LONG KNOWN YOU AS OUR EMINENT AND ABLE
STATESMAN . . . WILL BE HIGHLY GRATIFIED BY SEEING YOU EXHIB-
ITED IN THE NOVEL CHARACTER OF A LOVER.
—*From James Thomson Callender, July 10, 1797*

As he waited for Angelica and John Church to arrive from London, another source of domestic pleasure for Hamilton was how well his eldest son, Philip, was doing at Columbia. Philip rehearsed a speech he was to give in class as his father listened. Philip came to "the best and most animated" sentence of it, which was this one: "Americans, you have fought the battles of mankind; you have rekindled that sacred fire of freedom which is now—etc." His father applauded warmly, even for the "etc."

But just like his father before him, Philip ran into a friendly disagreement with the college president over patriotic fervor that was too intense. When Philip delivered the speech in class, William Samuel Johnson, the president of the college, had liked his delivery well enough, but not the text. As Philip explained to his father, President Johnson had "blotted out" this sentence, the most Hamiltonian one in the whole exercise. His bad mark from President Johnson was a scholarly forewarning of the fatality to which Philip's too perfervid patriotic zeal would lead him.

In the same letter, written from college to his father in Albany on April 21, 1797, Philip politely asked his papa, please to thank his grandpapa and name-sake, Philip Schuyler, for a gift of shares in the Tontine Tavern—and also for

> all the good advice his letter contains—which I am very sensible of its being extremely necessary for me to pay particular attention to in order to be a good man.
>   I remain your most affectionate son.

In Albany, where he was busy in court with the trial of one of his most notable cases, *Le Guen v. Gouverneur and Kemble,* Hamilton had found grand-papa Schuyler ailing. Still, both men were in spirits a good deal more cheerful than they might otherwise have been. The New York legislature had just ree-lected Schuyler out of the state senate back into the United States Senate to succeed Aaron Burr, whose term there had expired on March 3. Schuyler's reelection had finally turned the tables on their old enemy Burr. It helped to blot out the humiliation he and his son-in-law had suffered six years earlier when Burr had ousted Schuyler from the same seat. Elizabeth and her sister Margarita Van Rensselaer would also be pleased. And to welcome Angelica home with the good news would dispel the shadow of blame Hamilton had always sensed that she placed on him for having been a root cause of her father's chagrin, without being able to prevent it.

The brother of Hamilton's own father,—a father whom he had not seen for more than 30 years—was now the laird of the Grange at Ayrshire, Scotland, William Hamilton. The laird had a son, Robert W. Hamilton, not very much older than Philip, who now besought the aid of his self-made cousin for advancement in life. Robert W. Hamilton of the Grange wished to become an officer in the new American navy Hamilton was so busily working to expand. Hamilton replied to his uncle William Hamilton on May 2 that "it will give me the greatest pleasure to receive your son Robert in New York and still more to be of use to him." As good as his word, Hamilton eventually wangled from President Adams an ap-pointment for his cousin Robert W. Hamilton to be a lieutenant aboard the new warship, the *U.S.S. Constitution.*

Uncle William had written Hamilton an "extremely gratifying" account of all his Hamilton relations living in Scotland. Hamilton replied in a letter whose twelve paragraphs constitute a thumbnail autobiography of Hamilton at his, and every man's, milestone age of 40. Hamilton's letter to the uncle he had never seen is precious for containing some of the only extant statements he ever made privately about himself, why he had done what he did, and how he had become the man he was.

Unlike John Adams, Thomas Jefferson, and other American demigods, Hamilton kept no diaries full of special pleading for the plaudits of posterity. So his letter to William Hamilton, like his *Reynolds Pamphlet* of the same year, are unique examples of Hamiltonian self-revelation.

He had, he told his Uncle William, "engaged in some interesting operations" at the siege of Yorktown. He had then settled in New York "in a very lucrative" law practice. But "the derangement of our public affairs . . . drew me again reluctantly into public life." Having taken part in the framing of the Constitution, "I conceived myself to be under an obligation to lend my aid towards putting the machine in some regular motion." As secretary of the treasury, "I met with many intrinsic difficulties, and many artificial ones, proceeding from passions, not very worthy, common to human nature."

He had succeeded in his object of "establishing public credit and introducing order into the finances." However, Hamilton went on sadly to his uncle, "public office in this country has few attractions." There is "inconsiderable emolument"; there is "pecuniary sacrifice"; there is "jealousy of power and the spirit of faction." These "diminish a virtuous man's power of doing good." In fact, "the prospect was even bad for gratifying in future the love of Fame, if that passion was to be the spring of action." This suggests that at only 40 Hamilton had already given up the idea of pressing on in future to try to reach the assured fame of the American presidency.

Neither Jefferson, Burr, Adams, Monroe, Madison, or John Beckley would have believed Hamilton capable of etching a self-portrait in such muted halftones. Had they believed him, what followed would have had to be overkill or self-destruction.

Having resigned himself now to private life, Hamilton went on to his uncle, "It is impossible to be happier than I am in a wife. I have five children, four sons and a daughter, the eldest a son somewhat past fifteen, who all promise well, as far as their years permit and yield me much satisfaction . . ."

Hamilton had "strongly pressed the Old Gentleman" his father, William's brother, now living on the island of St. Vincent in the West Indies, "to come to reside with me . . . to afford him every enjoyment . . . but he has declined . . . on the advice of physicians that the change of climate would be fatal to him." Hamilton would, of course, continue sending him all the money he could spare as his father needed it for support from time to time. On the whole, then, Hamilton felt, "my situation is extremely comfortable and leaves me nothing to wish but a continuance of health. With this blessing . . . other prospects . . . will render the eve of life easy and agreeable."

In this forecast of his future, by far the most personal of any Hamilton had made so far in life, he could not have been more hideously wrong. The plagues, passions, fevers, follies, and nervous derangements of the following months would render for him "the eve of life" unblessed, unhealthy, uncomfortable, disagreeable, anxious, bizarre, mad or half mad, tragic, and short.

Unlike Angelica Church's New York homecoming, James Monroe's arrival in Philadelphia from France at the height of the war crisis on June 27 brought no joy to Hamilton. Republicans, of course, hailed Monroe's return as if he were some bringer of glad tidings of great joy in the nick of time. What lent more zest than anything else to their joy in Monroe's advent was the series of humiliating setbacks Republicans had been suffering at the hands of Hamilton's surrogates in the still pending session of Congress that Adams had called to push forward Hamilton's peace program as his own. It was still in session grinding down to the next recess. Summer came on, bringing the fever season to the capital and partisan political temperatures to a tired boil.

Typical of factional rancors was the case of William Blount, a former British soldier and Indian agent and also a Republican senator from Tennessee, whom Federalists gleefully implicated in a British plot backed by Robert Liston, the British minister. Blount was charged with being the leader of a proposed filibustering attack against the Spaniards in Florida and Louisiana. This would be a violation of Thomas Pinckney's treaty with Spain. John Adams sent Attorney General Charles Lee for prosecution an intercepted letter from Blount that clinched the case against him. The Federalist-dominated Senate found Blount guilty of a high misdemeanor and expelled him from the world's most exclusive club. The closely divided House then took up his case amid talk of impeachment. Wagging their fingers at Blount, Federalist orators charged that he was not the only Republican who was tainted with treason. Jeffersonians seized on the scandal as British interference in American affairs as bad as anything done by Genêt, Fauchet, or Adet.

Jefferson's protégé Tom Paine had written a letter to Washington, his former friend and benefactor, that said, "And, as to you, sir, treacherous in private friendship (or so you have been to me, and that in the day of danger) and a hypocrite in public life, the world will be puzzled to decide whether you are an apostate or imposter, whether you have abandoned good principles, or whether you ever had any." Bache's Republican *Aurora* published Paine's letter, piously professing pained outrage at its insult to Washington, thereby making sure, Beckley style, that no one could possibly miss it. Federalists called Vice-president Jefferson and the journalists on his payroll Washington's chief traducers.

During the uproar over Jay's Treaty a year earlier, Jefferson had written his friend and neighbor Philip Mazzei that there were apostates "who were Samsons in the field & Solomons in the council, but who have had their heads shorn by the harlot England." Here was Jefferson, even worse than Paine, calling Washington a pitiful, helpless giant. Years later, Jefferson claimed rather sheepishly that he had been referring only to the Society of the Cincinnati, not to Washington who, it happened, was its lifetime president. Two months before writing this snide critique to Mazzei, Jefferson had been at pains to assure Washington that any person who tried to sow tares between the two of them was a "miserable tergivisator." Federalists disbelieved Jefferson and rumbled ominously in Congress and committees that the vice-president should be impeached along with Blount.

The holder of the second highest office in the land, having fallen only three votes shy on his first try for the first, would not have had to be a man as thin-skinned as Thomas Jefferson to cast about for ways to strike back at these would-be impeachers. On second try, after Jefferson had finally become president, he would confide to his secretary, William A. Burwell, that Hamilton had long known about the affair between Jefferson and Betsey Moore Walker, the

wife of one of Jefferson's oldest friends, and that "about the time he was attacked for his connection with Mrs. Reynolds," Hamilton "had threatened him
—with a public disclosure." Now, however, it seemed safer for the Federalists
to strike at Jefferson through his chief aide, informer, traducer of Hamilton,
organizer of the Republican party of Pennsylvania, campaign manager, and
chief clerk of the House, John Beckley.

On the first day of the session called by John Adams to convene on May 15,
Federalists, led by Hamilton's spokesman William Loughton Smith, had
managed to beat back Beckley's bid for reelection as clerk by a vote of 41 to 40,
with 25 congressmen absent or not voting. Smith had shrewdly taken advantage
of a political fact that Jefferson had let slip to Genêt; more Federalists, mostly
from city constituencies, were able to be present at the beginning of a session
than Republicans, more of whom came from farm districts. Jefferson had written
indignantly to Madison that "besides the loss of the ablest clerk in the U.S. &
the outrage committed on the absent members . . . it excited a fear that the
Republican interest has lost by the new changes." Jefferson seemed to take for
granted his party's vested right to a clerk wholly beholden to it. Bache's *Aurora*
denounced the Federalists' ouster of John Beckley as "a specimen of party
rancour."

Ordinarily, the return home of a discredited diplomat is passed over as
quietly as possible. But just now as Republicans seemed to be sinking under a
sea of troubles, Monroe's arrival in Philadelphia served as the occasion for a
triumphal banquet at Oeller's Hotel on Chestnut Street. As one Federalist writer
described it, Monsieur Vice-president Jefferson, Monsieur Governor Thomas
McKean of Pennsylvania, and some 50 other messieurs who were members of
Congress (he called them all *monsieur*) whooped it up in a fine French frenzy
of oo-la-las. The Federalist observer, far from being carried away by the politics
of joy, or rather *joie*, wrote, "Here you saw an american [*sic*] disorganizer &
there a blundering wild Irishman . . . in one corner a banished Genevan & in
another a french [*sic*] spye."

In Hamiltonian hindsight, it is easy to see that he would have been much
safer leaving both men undisturbed in their old posts. Beckley's ouster and
Monroe's recall struck partisan sparks that touched off a powder train of events
that would explode in Hamilton's face, causing him to react in anger against his
enemies in a way that would eventually destroy him as a significant figure in the
American politics of his lifetime.

To Federalists like Hamilton and Smith, John Beckley was nothing but a
political hatchet man in the service of Jefferson, Madison, and Monroe. His
ouster by Hamilton's men, reminiscent of his earlier defeat by them for the office
of secretary of the Constitutional Convention a decade earlier, left Beckley a
jobless, impecunious, angry man with a growing family to feed.

Beckley became the partner in poverty of another man whom William
Loughton Smith had also helped to remove from a congressional livelihood, the
Anti-Federalist journalist James Thomson Callender. Callender had formerly
been employed by the *Philadelphia Gazette* to report congressional news at a

salary of $4,000 a year. Callender had dared to dub Smith, chairman of the powerful House Ways and Means Committee, the "British agent," adding that "Dr. Smith was far more rancorous than the other gentlemen collectively." Thomas Jefferson, on the other hand, had called Callender "a man of genius suffering under persecution." In January 1794 a rancorous Smith and Federalist allies had set to work to put an end to the outrages committed by this pertinacious "genius" of Jefferson's.

Callender's book, *The Prospect Before Us*, had described the British Parliament as "a phalanx of mercenaries"; the English constitution was but "a conspiracy of the rich against the poor." Having been indicted in England in 1793 for sedition and radical views for items like these appearing in the Edinburgh *Bee*, Callender had fled to the United States with his wife and four young children. Full credit to Jefferson for his helpful patronage had been given by Callender in his advertisement for the second American edition of *The Prospect Before Us* in November 1794. A pro-Jefferson study of Jefferson's relations with Callender published in 1896 would begin, "Of all the foreigners who were connected with journalism in the United States at the beginning of the century, James Thomson Callender was easily first in the worst qualities of mind and character." Others merely called him "a hack writer." He had studied medicine, was an expert shorthand reporter, and had once been, he wrote, "one of the happiest of human beings." On the evidence of his writings, he was a well-educated man with a gift for caustic phrasemaking that was the equal of Beckley's.

Upon being fired from the *Philadelphia Gazette* through Smith's efforts, Callender appealed to James Madison to find him a new job as a schoolmaster in Virginia. He was still looking for a job when in June of 1797, according to Jefferson's notebooks, the vice-president paid a personal call upon him at the shop of Snowden & McCorkle, a newly established firm of job printers. There Jefferson paid $15.14 for 15 copies of a series of pamphlets of Callender's authorship that the printers were about to publish under the collective title of *The History of the United States for 1796*. The series was quickly forgotten for what it said about the United States or about 1796, but it will never be forgotten for what it said about Hamilton. It revealed to the public for the first time Hamilton's affair with Maria Reynolds in 1791 and 1792, which had remained covered up ever since. Carefully, characteristically, Jefferson later wrote that it was "probably not till 1798" that he first "saw" James Thomson Callender.

Sometime after December 17, 1792, two days after James Monroe, Muhlenberg, and Venable had confronted Hamilton and Wolcott the night of December 15, and Thomas Jefferson had carefully made the following entry in his Anas:

> The affair of Reynolds and his wife—Clingham Muhlenb's clerk, testifies to F. A. Muhl Monroe Venable—also Wolcott at [and ?] Wadsworth. Known to J[ames] M[adison], E[dmund] R[andolph], [John] Beckley and [Bernard] Webb.
>
> *Hamilton advised the President to give his negative to those resolutions.*

Jefferson had scored out the second paragraph and heavily obliterated Hamilton's name. But Jefferson's informer, John Beckley, had no reason to be as discreet for posterity as his monitor. Quite the contrary. During the nearly five years since Jefferson had made his note, a widening circle of insiders had come to know the secret. And Hamilton knew they knew.

Way back on May 6, 1793, Hamilton's old, war hero friend Henry Lee had written him from Richmond, Virginia, "was I with you I would talk an hour with doors bolted & windows shut, as my heart is much afflicted by some whispers which I have heard." On October 23, 1795, Bache's *Aurora*, a leading Anti-Federalist paper, had twitted Oliver Wolcott, Jr., about "a certain enquiry of a very suspicious aspect, respecting real mal-conduct on the part of his friend, patron and predecessor in office in the month of December 1792." *Aurora* had asked, "Why has the subject been so long and carefully smothered up?"

When Federalists turned toward the election of 1800 and beyond and the question of who might become their presidential candidate after John Adams, they naturally thought of their elder statesman Hamilton. Thus built up reciprocal pressure on Anti-Federalists to expose Hamilton's secret affair to the public's gaze. If all else failed, the news of it would serve to puncture Hamilton's swelling pretensions to the highest executive power.

During the presidential campaign of 1796, Noah Webster's *Minerva* had suggested that "Mr. Hamilton would be an advisable candidate" for president. On seeing such a significant Hamilton-for-president trial balloon go up, "someone" in Philadelphia told "someone" in New York to tell Hamilton to tell Noah Webster that if the *Minerva* in future should dare "print a single paragraph" boosting Hamilton for president, all the Reynolds papers "were instantly to be laid before the world." Federalists had no doubt that John Beckley was the "someone" in Philadelphia who had contrived the threat. Beckley's friend and coadjutor Callender later sneered that "the message was delivered to Mr. Hamilton" with the result that "the *Minerva* became silent." Callender implied that only this threat, not Hamilton's self-abnegating concern to advance the 1796 Federalist ticket of Adams and Pinckney, was what had forced Hamilton to withdraw his own name from consideration for the presidency in 1796.

Later, Hamilton and Noah Webster severally branded Callender's insinuation that they had yielded to threats of blackmail to muzzle the press as "totally false." But no sort of rebuttal could erase the stain of such a devastating charge.

The more partisan animosities over relations with France became embittered, the more certain it became that someone would unleash Beckley and Callender to expose the scandal about Hamilton that had been "smothered up" since 1792. Libel laws were much harsher then than now. Neither would have dared to act by himself to make such a sensitive secret public. Both needed the protection and patronage of principals higher up.

On June 24, three days before Monroe's arrival in Philadelphia, Hamilton's loyal old friend Senator Theodore Sedgwick of Massachusetts wrote Rufus King in London that Beckley's ouster from the clerkship was "resented not only by himself but the whole party [Republicans]. They were rendered furious by it."

Trouble was coming. For revenge, "Beckley has been writing a pamphlet mentioned in the enclosed advertisement. The authentic papers there mentioned are those of which you perfectly know the history, formerly in the possession of Messrs. Monroe, Muhlenberg and Venable. This conduct is mean, base and infamous."

The very day before Monroe landed in Philadelphia under his own cloud of controversy, rightly suspecting Hamilton of a major role in his recall, Callender published issue Number V of his *History of the United States for 1796*, containing "some singular and authentic papers relative to Mr. Alexander Hamilton." Federalists at once traced the source to John Beckley. Even Abraham Venable, a Virginia Republican, admitted that Beckley, the man who had copied all the papers, "had been present during the whole investigation, both before and after my being called on." But Callender coyly denied that Beckley had "written a single sentence of it."

Callender's scandalous chronicle began with a pietistic preface. His *History*, he said, was only a response to scurrilous Federalist journalism like Hamilton's *Camillus* papers. Noah Webster's Connecticut was not the true center of Republicanism, Callender went on, because that honor belonged to the Old Dominion of his mentor, admirer, and charter subscriber, Thomas Jefferson, which was Virginia. The first four numbers of Callender's *History*, Numbers I through IV, replying to Hamilton's writings as *Camillus* and *Phocion*, had taken him to task on such public issues as Hamiltonian finance, Jay's Treaty, and relations with France and England, but were relatively free of personal attacks. Number V, issued June 26, now took the offensive.

Callender's purpose, he declared, was only to reply in kind to the calumnies Federalists had heaped upon poor James Monroe as minister to France. Hamilton's affair with Mrs. James Reynolds had been known for a long time to many members of Congress. "If any republican character had been the hero of the story," Callender whined, "it would have been echoed from one end of the continent to the other." It was greatly to Monroe's credit, Callender toadied, that he had "observed profound silence . . . Attacks on Mr. Monroe have been frequently repeated from the stockholding presses. They are cowardly because he is absent. They are unjust, because he displayed, on an occasion that will be mentioned immediately, the greatest lenity to Mr. Alexander Hamilton, the prime mover of the Federal Party."

There seemed no obvious reason why Callender should ladle out fulsome praise for Jefferson, except to give Jefferson his money's worth. Jefferson, he wrote, had nobly kept silent about Hamilton's scandal. Jefferson's *Notes on Virginia* were historically important because in them Jefferson "unites the sweetness of Zenophon with the force of Polybius, information without parade, and eloquence without effort." He was a happy contrast to Hamilton's disgraceful antics. With Jefferson's presence gone out of Washington's cabinet, Callender felt, the government had sagged. By contrast to rich Jefferson, Hamilton, far from being the colossus of the anti-Republican party, was but "a threadbare lawyer, forgetting to earn daily subsistence for his family, that he may write 200 newspaper columns for nothing." Beckley's and Callender's public animadversions toward Hamilton closely tracked the private animadversions toward Hamilton that Jefferson had been writing in letters to Madison for a long time.

Unless Jefferson had ghostwritten Callender's preface for him, it was a stroke of genius for an unemployed hack journalist like Callender to have hit upon the epithet "threadbare lawyer" to describe Hamilton. For years the former secretary of the treasury had been charged in the press with vast, lucrative, illicit speculations and with being the crony of capitalists like William Bingham, Robert and Gouverneur Morris, John Barker Church, William Constable, and Theophile Cazenove. He was a founder of the SUM and the Bank of New York and the son-in-law of Patroon Philip Schuyler. He dressed with elegance and seemed to have plenty of money. How could a Callender have probed deeply enough beneath the surface of his public image to come up with the word *threadbare?* Who but a man with inherited wealth of his own and his late wife's and an incisive style like Thomas Jefferson could have perceived that behind his colossal facade, Hamilton was living high in hand-to-mouth, but cash-short style. It was a secret Hamilton knew about himself. But only a rich patrician with the peculiar but pointed perceptions of a Thomas Jefferson would be able see him as he saw himself. A threadbare journalist like Callender, even if he were the genius Jefferson had said he was, would hardly see a Hamilton as being almost as threadbare as himself, unaided by the insight of a man like Jefferson.

Callender's series was subsequently published as a book of eight chapters, *The History of the United States for 1796; Including a Variety of Interesting Particulars Relative to the Federal Government Previous to that Period,* but the way Callender first issued it section by section proved to be a trap for Hamilton. On July 3, Oliver Wolcott, Jr., from Philadelphia sent Hamilton a copy of Pamphlet No. V, warning him that "the subject is but partially represented." Callender's design, he said, was to establish that Hamilton "was concerned in speculations in the public funds." Wolcott added that Venable "speaks of the publication as false and dishonorable." Wolcott had "good reason," probably firsthand from Venable, "to believe that Beckley is the real author, though it is attributed to Callender." It was certainly false "that Duer had any hand in the transaction." Wolcott had the Treasury lists in his own hands, he said. Simeon Reynolds, the faithless clerk who had leaked the lists had been dismissed, and "his name has hitherto been concealed"—for the obvious reason that his surname, of all possible surnames in the world, was also Reynolds. The working of the human mind is such that it rejects in disbelief the possibility that two people allegedly involved in the same conspiracy with the same surname are not ipso facto coconspirators. Twice Wolcott cautioned Hamilton to "write nothing at least for the present . . . the faction is organized . . . public business is at a stand, and a crisis is approaching."

Most men of the world in their right minds would have followed Wolcott's advice and written nothing. But for years July for Hamilton had been a month of fevers, plagues, a stoning, and the onset of nervous derangements. So it was now.

Callender's "partial" account in Pamphlet No. V, enclosed to him by Wolcott, included only the four documents that Monroe, Muhlenberg, and Venable had been prepared to transmit to Washington with their accusatory letter the night of December 15, 1792: (1) Muhlenberg's account of his first visit to Hamilton to intercede for Jacob Clingman in the company of Aaron Burr representing James Reynolds, (2) Monroe's and Venable's statement of the charges that Reynolds and Clingman had made against Hamilton, (3) Monroe's and Muhlenberg's account of their interview with Mrs. Reynolds, during which she had given them the six notes Hamilton had written, and (4) part of Clingman's statement to them of December 13, but not his later statements.

Like a shrewd prosecutor, Callender had held back from No. V later statements of Clingman's to Monroe that Hamilton still knew nothing about. So the first angry rebuttals that he would fire off would contradict, or fail to explain away, the later statements of the witnesses held back to impeach the first outraged, ill-thought-out testimony Hamilton would blurt out. His first hot, impetuous denials would inadvertently confirm or fill in gaps of worse revelations Callender still had up his sleeve.

Beckley's and Callender's tactics were masterfully "organized," as Wolcott had forewarned Hamilton they would be. The greatest Wall Street lawyer of the day took the bait. On July 5, 1797, Hamilton wrote Senator Monroe and the two congressmen, astonished at their breach of confidence and demanding that each reconfirm the affirmation of Hamilton's innocence with which he had departed the unforgettable confrontation of four and a half years before:

> I shall rely upon your delicacy that the manner of doing it, will be such as one Gentleman has a right to expect from another—especially as you must be sensible that the present appearance of the papers is contrary to the course which was understood between us to be proper and includes a dishonourable infidelity somewhere.

With his letter, Hamilton enclosed what he alleged to be a copy of a memorandum of the "substance of your declaration made by me the morning after our interview."

The memorandum, which seemed suspiciously more apposite to 1797 than to 1792, read as follows:

> Memorandum of Substance of Declaration of Messrs. Monroe, Muhlenberg, and Venable concerning the Affair of J. Reynolds.
>
> That they regretted the trouble and uneasiness which they had occasioned to me in consequence of the representations made to them, that they were perfectly satisfied with the explanation I had given, and that there was nothing in the transaction which ought to affect my character as a public officer or lessen the public confidence in my integrity.

Hamilton demanded that each send him "a declaration equivalent to that which was made at the time," a contradiction of Callender's comments, and "the favor of expedition in your reply."

A man of the world, even a rash one, ought to have cooled down enough by this time to let the matter end with these requests for private reassurance. But not Hamilton. The following day, July 6, he fired off a public reply to Callender for publication in Fenno's *Gazette of the United States.* By the very particularity of its denials, it for the first time publicly admitted the truth of the general substance of Callender's charges. Hamilton admitted that the four documents Callender published appeared to be authentic. But he went on to charge that the three congressmen's inquiry of 1792 had been politically motivated. Through their intercession, two of "the most profligate of men" had sought escape from prison "by the favour of party spirit," he wrote. Two of the three congressmen were his "known political opponents." But to the public, learning of it for the first time, the statements he offered as proof of his innocence would be seen as an admission of theretofore uncorroborated charges. "A full explanation took place between them and myself . . . in which by written documents I convinced them of the falsehood of the accusation," Hamilton said. "They declared themselves perfectly satisfied with the explanation and expressed their regret at the necessity which had been occasioned to me of making it."

Hamilton added a rash promise "to place the subject more precisely before the public," thus publicly burning behind him any bridge of silence that a sensible man's discretion might have left open for retreat.

Publication of No. VI of Callender's *History,* following publication of Hamilton's hasty retort in Fenno's *Gazette* on July 12, transmuted Callender's No. V from nothing more than a one-sided, one-day, scurrilous wonder to a credible public paper that could no longer be brushed aside, even by Hamilton's partisans, as partisan poppycock. With the public's tongues wagging and heads shaking, Callender released pamphlet No. VI on July 4 or 5 with disclosures of juicy new details. Callender also gave a separate direct reply to what Hamilton had just published in Fenno's *Gazette.* Callender's reply was all the more devasting because, instead of being a wordy, adjectival, polemical broadside like Hamilton's, it took the form of an understated dialogue that cut the heart out of the credibility of Hamilton's denial in Fenno's *Gazette,* sentence by sentence, line by line, and phrase by phrase.

Hamilton had harshly said "the papers" were "the contrivance" of Clingman and Reynolds "to obtain *their* liberation from imprisonment, for a serious crime, by the FAVOUR OF PARTY spirit."

Not so, said Callender; Clingman had not been in jail during any of the time in question (he was out on bail). And Reynolds had been released by December 15—being last seen that day with Hamilton before vanishing. Reynolds had no part in "the contrivance" of the papers. Far from being motivated by party spirit, Muhlenberg and Venable had received no information until *after* Reynolds had been released from jail. Reynolds had refused to talk at all until after his release: "He was afraid of speaking to them." On their face, the documents in Callender's

Numbers V and VI tended to refute Hamilton's publication in Fenno's *Gazette* and corroborated Callender. Lamely, Hamilton was forced to admit that his memory had been at fault in what he had first written to Fenno, thus badly damaging the credibility of all his defenses to come.

Callender's reply scoffed that the "written documents" by which Hamilton claimed he had "convinced them of the falsehood of the accusation" were nothing but "a series of letters pretended to be written relative to your alleged connection to Mrs. Reynolds . . . they did not believe a single word." Callender derided him: "They must have found it hard to help laughing in each other's faces" "at your penitential tale of your depravity at The George. A more ridiculous scene cannot be conceived," Callender taunted him. When "you place the matter more precisely before the public," as you promised, your friend Wolcott and the others who "have long known you as an eminent and able statesman . . . will be highly gratified by seeing you exhibited in the novel character of a lover."

Mockingly, Callender goaded Hamilton to reprint "the whole original papers on which the suspicion is grounded . . . no extract . . . or general reference to them can be satisfactory." Little did Callender dream that the onset of nervous derangement under his onslaught would drive Hamilton to such an extremity of folly. But seeking a cure for the sickness, he gulped down Callender's poisonous prescription.

The most important of the new documents never before seen by Hamilton now published in Number VI of Callender's *History* was Monroe's memorandum, dated December 16, 1792, written the day after the confrontation, that concluded with the fatefully ambiguous phrase "we left him under an impression our suspicions were removed." This could hardly have been more equivocal on the essential point. It would leave any percipient reader with at least a gnawing doubt that although they had placated Hamilton with the "impression," Monroe's, Muhlenberg's, and Venable's suspicions were far from entirely removed.

A second new revelation of Callender's Number VI was Monroe's memorandum of the conversation he had had with Jacob Clingman on January 2, 1793, two weeks after the confrontation, a date Hamilton had always thought until now was one when the matter had already been "smothered up" for more than a fortnight. According to Monroe's memorandum, Clingman said then that he had heard from Oliver Wolcott, Jr.—of all people—that the three congressmen, in an interview, had vindicated Hamilton of any guilt in his public capacity. Clingman "further observed to me," Monroe had written, "that he communicated the same to Mrs. Reynolds, who appeared much shocked at it, and wept immoderately." Clingman added that Maria Reynolds denied that she had ever had an affair with Hamilton "and declared, that it had been a fabrication of Colonel Hamilton, and that her husband had joined in it."

Yet if it were true that Aaron Burr had obtained a New York divorce for James and Maria on adultery grounds—the only grounds—less than six months after the confrontation, Hamilton would have had to be the unnamed corespondent; or if not, her alleged affairs with other men concurrently with her intense involvements with Hamilton, Clingman, and James—not to mention James Wadsworth—imply such reckless, randy promiscuity that it further discredits her testimony on this point and confirms Hamilton's.

According to Clingman and Maria, James Reynolds had written out the receipts and fabricated the letters at Hamilton's behest so as to give countenance to Hamilton's defense. Maria added that Reynolds had been "with colonel Hamilton, the day after he left the jail, when we supposed he was in Jersey." Clingman also said he believed Maria when she said she was entirely innocent of having had intercourse with Hamilton. What gentleman could contradict Clingman without compromising his own honor as a gentleman by compromising hers?

The thing that made this alleged statement of Clingman to Monroe of January 2 so damaging to Hamilton was that, as far as the public could tell, neither Clingman nor Maria would have had any way of knowing the nature of the defense Hamilton had pleaded to the "three gentlemen" the night of December 15. Therefore, it would appear that the tale that Clingman was telling to Monroe coincided with the truth. It would not occur to the public at large that Monroe (or Beckley or Callender or Aaron Burr) had told them. Besides, why would Clingman be telling Monroe something Monroe had already known, and why would Monroe be ostentatiously listening and jotting it down? But to anyone who knew Oliver Wolcott, Jr., Monroe's recording of Clingman's tale that it was Wolcott who was the leak would be unbelievable on its face. A discreet, experienced public servant like Oliver Wolcott, Jr., who was also Hamilton's closest associate in the Treasury, personal friend, and confidant, as well as the official who had instituted the original prosecutions against Clingman and Reynolds, was the last (or next to the last after Hamilton) man in the world to have let the secret of Hamilton's defense slip out to a couple of ex-prosecutees. To Hamilton, anyone who, like Monroe, could have given enough credence to such a charge as to jot it down, let alone allow it to be published without further checking—could be no gentleman.

In the meantime, Muhlenberg and Venable, by similar letters written from Philadelphia on July 10, both reassured Hamilton that they had kept no copies of the papers, that they had given them all to Monroe, and that they did not know how they had come to be published. They were shocked that they had been. They had both been "perfectly satisfied with Hamilton's explanation." They had not sought to mislead Hamilton: the impression with which they left him coincided with their own true beliefs. Muhlenberg, a fellow Federalist, added some friendly counsel that Hamilton continued to ignore: "were I to undertake to contradict the many absurdities & falsehoods which I see published on a variety of subjects . . . it would require more time than I am willing to sacrifice."

On July 10, Hamilton demanded an interview with Monroe as soon as possible. Monroe happened to be visiting in New York in the process of collecting information to vindicate himself from charges like Hamilton's that had led to his recall from France by Pickering under a cloud. He agreed to meet Hamilton Tuesday morning, July 11, at the house of Thomas Knox, a merchant, at 46 Wall Street, with whom Monroe was lodging. Monroe, himself a lawyer, brought with

him another lawyer, David Gelston, a veteran Republican politician, the surrogate of New York County, the holder of an office awash with dispensable patronage, which only the sliest and shrewdest of lawyers ever comes to hold. Hamilton
brought with him his brother-in-law, bluff businessman John Barker Church,
only recently arrived from London. The outcome provides yet another illustration of an old saw Hamilton would never learn: that the lawyer who handles his
own case has a fool for a client.

Gelston afterward wrote out a memorandum of the meeting on which the
following account is based. Unfortunately, no transcript was made for Hamilton's side to compare with what Monroe's own lawyer wrote down to serve his
client.

On entering the room, according to Gelston, Hamilton "appeared very much
agitated." He announced that "the cause or motives of this meeting, I presume,
are pretty well understood."

Then, Gelston said, "he went into a detail of circumstances" about the
Philadelphia confrontation of December 15, 1792. "At considerable length."

"What's all that mean?" asked Monroe. "If you wish me to tell you anything
relating to the business all this history is unnecessary. Get to the point."

"I shall come to the point directly," Hamilton snapped back.

Here Gelston notes that "some warmth appeared in both gentlemen."

They calmed down for a moment. Then "some explanation took place."
Monroe explained that "it was merely accidental my knowing anything about the
business at first . . . I was told that one Reynolds *from Virginia* was in Gaol."
Monroe did not say who had told him—whether it had been fellow Senator Aaron
Burr, who had visited Reynolds in jail earlier, or someone else. Monroe may have
been told vaguely that the man had been in trouble in Virginia, not that he was
from Virginia.

In any event, "I called merely to aid a man that might be in distress,"
Monroe went on, "But I found it was a Reynolds from New York."

After the Philadelphia confrontation with Hamilton, Monroe said, "I sealed
up my copies of all the papers and sent or delivered them to my friend in
Virginia." He added, "I had no intention of publishing them."

Oddly enough, according to Gelston, upon this interesting revelation, no one
found it necessary or had the curiosity or dared, to ask the name of Monroe's
"friend in Virginia." Probably it was because none was in any doubt that Monroe's "friend in Virginia" was Thomas Jefferson. If anyone present in the room
did, in fact, say out loud the name of the powerful leader of Gelston's party,
Gelston was too shrewd a politician to leave it stand undeleted from his transcription.

"How then did these papers come to be published?" Hamilton demanded to
know.

"Upon my honor," Monroe vowed, avoiding a direct answer to Hamilton's
question, "I knew nothing of their publication until I arrived in Philadelphia from
Europe. In fact," Monroe added, "I was sorry to find they were published." It
seemed obvious that he knew how, but refused to tell Hamilton.

"I've written to you," Hamilton said evenly, his anger rising, "and Muhlenberg and Venable too, to find out how the papers came to be published. You haven't replied."

"Calm down," said Monroe.

But Hamilton grew still more agitated. "My own character and the peace and reputation of my family are deeply involved," he cried.

"If you'll be quiet for a moment," Monroe interrupted, "and be a little temperate, I'll tell you candidly why I haven't answered."

"Why?"

"I didn't receive your letter until ten o'clock at night and I had planned to leave for New York the next morning and did. Even so, I went to Venable's lodgings late that night, to look for him, but it was impossible for the three of us to get together then."

Hamilton and John Church stared at Monroe in disbelief. Venable's letter to Hamilton of July 9 had made no mention of any such extraordinary late night visit by Monroe.

Church angrily pulled out of his pocket and brandished in Monroe's face copies of the two offending pamphlets, Numbers V and VI of Callender's *History*.

Monroe went on, "Since all three of us were present then and all three signed the certificate then, I thought we should all meet and return a joint answer now. I still mean to do this on my return to Philadelphia." Monroe still artfully dodged answering the real question.

"Number V contains the statement signed by all three," Hamilton agreed. "But number VI contains statements signed by you alone."

"If you wish me to give the story of the facts and circumstances as they appear to me, individually," Monroe let go, "I'll do it on my return to Philadelphia."

"Do so," Hamilton snapped back.

"As I said before," Monroe began again, "I still believe that the packet of papers that I had still remain sealed up with my friend in Virginia."

"What you say is totally false!" Hamilton shouted. The words Hamilton had shouted at Monroe may well have been, "You're a liar." But Gelston would, no doubt, have transcribed it "your representation is totally false," as, in fact, he did.

To these words, Gelston added, by way of a discreet escape hatch from hard words muted by euphemism, "(as nearly as I recollect the expression)."

Next, according to Gelston, "the gentlemen both instantly rose, Monroe rising first."

Monroe: "Do you say I represented falsely?" You are a scoundrel."

Hamilton: "I will meet you like a gentlemen."

Monroe: "I am ready. Get your pistols!"

Both: "We shall not or it will not be settled any other way."

Gelston and Church jumped to their feet "at the same moment. We put ourselves between them," Gelston wrote.

Church: "Gentlemen, gentlemen, gentlemen, be moderate."

After a few moments, Gelston went on, "we all sat down and the two gentlemen, Colo. M. and Colo. H soon got moderate."

Gelston noted "very clearly" that "Colo. H appeared extremely agitated & Colo. M. appeared soon to get quite cool."

Monroe then "repeated his entire ignorance of the publication and his surprise to find it published." Furthermore, he told Hamilton, if he would not be so "warm and intemperate" he "would explain everything he knew of the business."

But Hamilton, too agitated, and Church, no lawyer, let this sudden door opening for meaningful cross-examination of Monroe slip by.

For Monroe, Gelston quickly stepped in and slammed the door shut. Gelston "addressed myself to Colo. H.," saying he had a "proposition." Would Hamilton like to hear it?

"By all means," said Hamilton, taking the bait, distracted from the opening Monroe had left.

"As Colo. M. has satisfied you" on the question of the leaked publication and "as the other part was a transaction of the three gentlemen," Gelston proposed, "would it not be much the best way to let the whole affair rest until Colo. M. returned to Philadelphia." Then he could get together with the other two on a joint answer "as Colo. M. had proposed."

Hamilton and Church had pried nothing out of Monroe in the confrontation they themselves had demanded, and Monroe, by Gelston's quick thinking, had seemingly gained their acquiescence in Gelston's smooth confirmation of Monroe's total ignorance of the source of the leak.

"I observed a silence," wrote Gelston. Then "Colo H. made some answer in a word or two which I understood as not disapproving" the Gelston proposition. "But what Hamilton had actually responded," Gelston said, "I cannot recollect with precision." With Hamilton seemingly about to repudiate his formulation, Gelston quickly turned to Church, saying, "Perhaps my proposition would have been made with more propriety to you than to Colo. H." Church now took the lure, too.

Church asked Monroe when he would be going back to Philadelphia. Monroe said Friday (three days later) at the latest. Like the brusque businessman he was and weary of so much lawyers' technical twaddle about an unprofitable old affair and anxious to close, Church said briskly that he and Hamilton "would go on Saturday and as the business could be finished on Saturday he thought it would be much the best way."

Church rose, and Gelston and Monroe eagerly jumped up, too.

Hamilton seem dissatisfied and unhappy.

Church tried to buck him up some by saying, "there will be an explanation by all three gentlemen."

He disassociated himself with Hamilton's white-hot chagrin at the outcome by adding, "any warmth or unguarded expressions that happened should be buried . . . considered as though it had never happened."

Monroe threw in bluntly, "I shall be governed by Hamilton's conduct." This and probably a hard stare from Church forced Hamilton to swallow his own mortification. "I think any intemperate expressions should be forgotten," he agreed meekly.

As Church hustled Hamilton out the door, Monroe said, "I agree."

Gelston closed his statement with the words "The interview continued about an hour or a little over." Skillful lawyer that he was, in order to insure that there would be no gap that might permit his account to be discredited later he added, "myself being present throughout the whole."

Obviously at odds with his brother-in-law and most important client on how much to make of the matter from this point on, Hamilton rushed off to Philadelphia the next day, Wednesday, instead of waiting till Saturday. Church begged off making the trip at all. For excuse, he said "my Angelica is not very well— she complains that her throat is a little sore." As for Hamilton's Eliza, Church wrote him, "she put into my hand the newspaper" with Callender's letter in it. "It makes not the least impression on her . . . she considers the whole knot of them opposed to you to be scoundrels."

Against similar shafts of Callender's, Abigail Adams would warn her John with shards from *Julius Caesar* like the one she quoted to her sister Mary Cranch on June 3, 1797:

> There is no terror, Jack cuss, in your threats,
> For I am arm'd so strong in honesty
> That they pass by me as the idle wind,
> Which I respect not.

Unfortunately Hamilton had no one who could give such good advice so eloquently to, much less make him take it.

Church told Hamilton tactfully that "from what I observed yesterday," Monroe is "inclined to be very generous." He "is much embarrassed how to get out of the scrape in which he has involved himself . . . from present appearances you will not be long detained at Philadelphia, but be able to return Sunday or Monday."

From his lonely Philadelphia lodgings, Hamilton wrote home to Elizabeth, with the weird lack of proportion that was typical of his periods of nervous derangement. How happy he would be "to return to her embrace and the company of our beloved Angelica. I am very anxious about you both, you for an obvious reason [Elizabeth was eight months along in at least her seventh pregnancy with their sixth child], and for Angelica because . . . Church mentioned she complained of a *sore throat*. Let me charge you and her to be well and happy, for you comprize all my felicity."

Two days later, his "avocation here" still detained him, but he sent his "love to Angelica and Church. I shall return full freighted with it for my dear brunettes."

Hamilton's stay dragged on for almost two weeks as he busied himself with his challenge to Monroe and with writing and documenting the public reply to his enemies that all who befriended him counseled him not to publish. But he seemed hell-bent on digging out more ore for Callender's scandalmongery. During the season of the plague in Hamilton's unluckiest city at a time when he now regularly suffered from summer sicknesses and nervous derangements, he shared the lodgings of his old friend William Loughton Smith, whom he had characterized to Washington as a man "of an uncomfortable temper . . . a certain hardness of character." The unfortunate impact of such an environment would be imprinted plainly on Hamilton's performance. From Philadelphia between mid-July and early August, he fired off a dozen challenging letters to Monroe. Monroe fired back replies in kind that did not much change the stands the two men had aired in the heat of the interview in New York recorded by David Gelston. On July 17, Monroe and Muhlenberg sent Hamilton a joint statement that was all any man in Hamilton's position could have wished—if he had been in his right mind. They explained that Venable was away, but in agreement with them, "that we had no agency in or knowledge of the publication of these papers till they appeared," and that the original papers had been "deposited in the hands of a respectable character in Virginia where they are now." Also, "the impression which we left on your mind . . . was that which rested on our own." Hamilton's explanation of his connection with Reynolds "removed the suspicions we had before entertained of your being connected with him in speculation." To drive home this reassurance, they added that, as gentlemen of honor, "had this not been the case we should certainly not have left that impression on your mind." And had this not been the case, they would not "have desisted from the plan we had contemplated in the inquiry of laying the papers before the President of the United States."

As to Clingman's statement of January 2, taken down over Monroe's signature alone, which Hamilton charged made it appear that Clingman "had revived the suspicions which my explanation had removed," Monroe insisted that "I did not convey or mean to convey any opinion of my own, as to the faith which was due to it, but left it to stand on its own merits reserving to myself the right to judge of it, as of any fact afterwards communicated, according to its import and authenticity."

But in the hardness of mind that attacks of enemies always brought on, this joint statement was not enough for Hamilton. Out of Hamilton's anxiety, Monroe's innocuous, legalistic, basically rather silly reservation extracted from Hamilton the black charge that Monroe now betrayed a disposition toward him that would "merit epithets the severest that I could apply" (on July 20, 1797) and, two days later, as the fever season heated up, that "you are actuated by motives toward me malignant and dishonorable." His mind now seemingly out of touch with any coordinate of objective reality to mark reasonably sane opinion, Hamilton added, "This will be the universal opinion when the publication of the whole affair which I am about to make shall be seen."

Monroe replied July 25, "Why you have adopted this style I know not," but he would not issue Hamilton a challenge to a duel. On the other hand, he would

not shrink from one if "called in a way which always for the illustration of truth,
I wish to avoid, but which I am ever ready to meet."

Hamilton's customary iron sense of the formality appropriate to such affairs
was so far askew by July 28 that he unguardedly, yet disarmingly, let slip in a
letter to Monroe that "the subject is too disgusting to leave me any inclination
to prolong this discussion of it."

Helping him in these harsh and pitiful exchanges as Hamilton's intermediary
was William Jackson, Washington's longtime personal secretary, the same
man Hamilton had helped start on his way to an important footnote in history
by successfully backing him as secretary to the Constitutional Convention, while
at the same time earning for himself unforgiving hatred from John Beckley for
a hand in his defeat for the office.

Jackson's comments would probably reflect Washington's view of the whole
sorry affair as well as his own. He wrote Hamilton on August 7 that though
"injured you may be by his conduct . . . it by no means appears to me that you
are the person injured by the correspondence . . . there is not a word in *his
correspondence* that calls for a direct challenge from you." Moreover, if Monroe
were the kind of man "whose sense of injury is not to be awakened" by being
told that his motives are "malignant and dishonorable," he was not a person
Hamilton should challenge, Jackson suggested. Monroe was not really a gentleman, or he would have responded by a challenge to Hamilton. Or else there was
some secret reason for his failure to respond. I "advise you to decline giving a
direct challenge," Jackson advised, "and await the effect of your publication."

Hamilton's close friends like Jeremiah Wadsworth and James McHenry
continued to implore him to forget about further publications and let the whole
matter drop. Elizabeth gave birth to their sixth child, William Stephen Hamilton,
on August 4. Hamilton apologized for being late in repaying $100 that McHenry
had sent him, as well as a further sum to reimburse "some money paid for me
by Lewis." But he forgot to enclose the check. McHenry's reply had a tactful
P.S.: "There was no money in your letter."

Elizabeth pregnant and lying in with a new baby, Angelica complaining of
a sore throat, and good paying clients neglected to rehash an old affair for the
sake of public honor left Hamilton no money to repay IOUs to friends.

Although Monroe, in his exchanges with Hamilton and William Jackson,
stuck rigidly to the same agonizingly equivocal stance, in private he was meekly
endorsing on his copy of one letter of Hamilton's "no occasion for a reply, as it
may lead on and irritate." Still busy composing his own vindication for his recall,
Monroe sent copies of the whole Hamilton correspondence to Aaron Burr in New
York, saying, "I never meant to give him a challenge." Monroe was ready to
accept one from him—but would not be ready for three months or so. "In case
of accident I should leave Mrs. M. almost friendless in Virginia she being of New
York," Monroe added. Burr should arrange all details for him with Hamilton.
The place for the duel should be "somewhere near the Susquehanna," Monroe
explained fearfully. "He is pushed on by party friends here [like Smith?] who
to get rid of me would be very willing to hazard him." Burr's reaction to the

correspondence was that "I wish it all burnt." Burr added that he himself
believed and that Monroe, Muhlenberg and Venable must also believe that "H
is innocent of the charge of any concern in speculation with Reynolds. You
expressed to me the same idea when we were together." Burr added that "it will
be an act of magnanimity and justice to say so in a joint certificate." To Burr,
the amusing little badger game of a sex scandal that he may have helped his New
York clients, the Reynoldses, set in motion was now threatening too many lives
and wives and children. He duly wrote out a certificate for Monroe's signature,
dated August 16, affirming "that it was not my intention to give any sanction
to" Clingman's statement. This certificate probably never reached Hamilton or,
if it did, came too late.

To leave no doubt about where he and Martha stood amid all the uproar,
George Washington from Mount Vernon on August 21 sent Hamilton and Betsy

> Not for any intrinsic value the thing possesses, but as a token of my
> sincere regard and friendship for you, and as a remembrancer of me
> . . . a wine cooler for four bottles . . . one of four which I imported in
> the early part of my late administration . . . I pray you to present my
> best wishes, in which Mrs. Washington joins me, to Mrs. Hamilton &
> the family; and that you would be persuaded, that with every sentiment
> of the highest regard, I remain your sincere friend, and affectionate
> Hble Servant
>
> Geo. Washington

At just this time of desperately needed reassurance, it would mean much to
Hamilton that with exquisite tact George and Martha's affectionate remem-
brancer did not make special mention of the family's new baby as the particular
reason for the gift.

It would mean almost as much to receive a reply written August 4 from his
uncle, William Hamilton, laird of the Grange, by way of William's son, Hamilton's first cousin and namesake, Alexander Hamilton of the Grange. He was
writing further at his father's request about his younger brother, Robert W.
Hamilton, the sailor whose "open honest & ingenious mind is . . . characteristic
of the best qualities of the British tar." The Scottish Alexander found his own
"trivial circumstances" forming "a very unpleasant contrast with the narrative
you have sent my father." Their famous American cousin's "conduct and character" in a "life spent in rearing an infant state, in forming its constitution &
regulating its polity . . . have acquired him a degree of reputation in which our
family is sensibly interested." If any of Hamilton's sons, like young Philip or
William Stephen, should be destined for the learned professions, the University
of Edinburgh was "justly celebrated for the eminence of its professors." Hamilton's kinsmen would see to it that every attention was paid to his brilliant sons'
admission applications.

Such a heartwarming testimonial probably made it that much easier for

Hamilton to brush aside sympathetic counsel of friends and besetting second thoughts of his own as he strode unswerving into the jaws of his next self-made disaster: the publication on August 25, 1797, of what came to be known as *The Reynolds Pamphlet.*

21

THE REYNOLDS PAMPHLET

I PRESUME THAT BECKLEY PUBLISHED THE PAPERS IN QUESTION.
—*James Monroe to Aaron Burr, December 1, 1797*

Never has a tract containing such violent political partisanship coupled with such intimate personal revelations borne a more innocuous title: *Observations on Certain Documents, Contained in No. V and VI of "The History of the United States for the Year 1796," in which the Charge of Speculation against Alexander Hamilton, late Secretary of the Treasury, is Fully Refuted. Written by himself.* In the Hamilton Papers the printed version of what came to be known as *The Reynolds Pamphlet* runs to 29 pages without exhibits. Fifty-two separate documents are appended as exhibits. These are referred to in, and explained by, the text. The blurb announced that the pamphlet "presents . . . a statement of the base means practiced by the Jacobins . . . to asperse . . . characters of those . . . considered as hostile to their disorganizing schemes. It also contains . . . correspondence . . . proving . . . that the connection between [Hamilton] and Reynolds, was the result of a daring conspiracy on the part of the latter and his associates to extort money."

Hamilton leads off his *Observations* with a tirade against his political enemies. In subject matter and sense it approaches the line that marks off hysteria and incoherence from rationality. All that seems to save it from crossing over the line that marks the edge of madness is the ingrained elegance of Hamilton's habitual style and manner of writing.

He sets out in full-throated cry:

THE spirit of Jacobinism, if not entirely a new spirit, has at least been
clothed with a more gigantic body and armed with more powerful weapons than it ever before possessed . . . it threatens more extensive and
complicated mischiefs to the world than have hitherto flowed from the
three great scourges of mankind, WAR, PESTILENCE and FAMINE
. . . its progress may be marked with calamities of which the dreadful
incidents of the French revolution afford a very faint image. Incessantly
busied in undermining all the props of public security and private happiness, it seems to threaten the political and moral world with a complete
overthrow . . .

It is hard to keep firmly fixed in mind that what Hamilton is raving about
with such eloquence here is a published charge that he had paid a hustler a little
hush money five years or more earlier to keep him quiet about a good thing,
which was true. It seemed to have slipped his mind as he wrote now that he had
been the victim of a badger game, probably Burr's. To treat such ancient trivia
in such extravagant terms only demonstrated the seriousness of Hamilton's loss
of touch with reality and the distortion of his sense of proportion in the most
serious onset yet of his recurrent nervous derangement.

All the gigantic forces he described were targeted in and bearing down upon
him. "A principal engine is calumny . . . men of upright principles shall at all
events be destroyed". Their best efforts for public good are traduced, their
motives misrepresented, their criminality inferred. "Direct falsehoods are invented and propagated with undaunted effrontery and unrelenting perseverance. Lies detected and refuted are revived and repeated . . . profligate men are
encouraged, probably bribed . . . with patronage . . . money to become informers
and accusers . . . corroding whispers wear away the reputations which they could
not directly subvert . . ." There is "a conspiracy of vice against virtue . . . odious
insinuations . . . rancour and venom . . . any little foible or folly traced out
. . . becomes in their hands a two edged sword . . . to wound the public character
and stab the private felicity" of the persecutee. "With such men, nothing is
sacred. Even the peace of an unoffending and amiable wife is a welcome repast
to their insatiate fury against the husband."

He sums up his role as an innocent victim of his and all mankind's enemies:

Relying upon this weakness of human nature, the Jacobin Scandal-
Club, though often defeated, constantly return to the charge. Old
calumnies are served up afresh, and every pretext is seized to add to
the catalogue. The person whom they seek to blacken, by dint of repeated strokes of their brush, becomes a demon in their own eyes,
though he might be pure and bright as an angel but for the daubing of
those wizard painters.

The elegance of his usual mode of self-expression would, of course, not bend
far enough to permit Hamilton simply to say, "I am not a crook." The words in
which the self-made man clothed the same thought were: "no man ever carried

into public life a more unblemished pecuniary reputation . . . a character marked
by an indifference to the acquisition of property rather than an avidity for it."

Going on and on in this frantic mode, he had worked his mad way far into
his pamphlet before getting around to stating the real question at issue, as he
should have done at the beginning:

> The charge against me is a connection with one James Reynolds for
> purposes of improper pecuniary speculation. My real crime is an amo-
> rous connection with his wife for a considerable time, with his privity
> and connivance, if not originally brought on by a combination between
> the husband and wife with the design to extort money from me.

He argued that the 52 documents attached as exhibits to his pamphlet
refuted the charges of the Jacobin scandal club. These exhibits included copies
of all the statements and correspondence of Muhlenberg, Venable, and Monroe,
and all the letters to and from the Reynoldses. The most significant of these
documents and his explanation for them have been quoted or paraphrased in
earlier chapters of this book in the context of the time in 1791 and 1792, when
they first came to be a part of the record of the affair in Hamilton's mind, and
are not repeated here.

Hamilton also included a certificate of a Philadelphia boardinghouse keeper
identifying Mrs. Reynolds's handwriting in her letters and also Noah Webster's
certificate giving the lie to Callender's charge that Hamilton had forced him to
suppress stories sending up trial balloons for his now suddenly forever self-
scuttled prospects for the presidency. He sideswiped Jefferson by quoting two
friendly letters the vice-president had written to the discredited scandalmonger
Andrew G. Fraunces.[1] He decried Monroe's conduct throughout. Hamilton said
that though he was "not permitted to make a public use" of an important
witness's statement by Richard Folwell, "I am permitted to refer any gentleman" who wanted to see it "to the perusal of his letter in the hands of William
Bingham, Esq., who is also so obliging as to permit me to deposit with him for
similar inspection all the original papers which are contained in the appendix to
this narrative." At the conclusion of the appendix to his pamphlet, Hamilton
again referred to "the gentleman" with whom the papers are deposited, referring back to his old friend William Bingham.

Hamilton seemed to think his public confession would cause only a little mild
embarrassment. He betrayed his complete miscalculation of the sensational
impact it would have by tendering only a mild apologia for it:

> I owe perhaps to my friends an apology for condescending to give
> a public explanation. A just pride with reluctance stoops to a formal
> vindication against so despicable a contrivance, and is inclined rather to
> oppose to it the uniform evidence of an upright character.

The only reason he was breaking this wise rule on this occasion was that
"the tale" seemed "to derive a sanction from the names of three men of some

weight and consequence in the society; a circumstance which I trust will excuse me for paying attention to a slander that, without this prop, would defeat itself by intrinsic circumstances of absurdity and malice."

In the above passage, Hamilton touches in a vague way on the symptom of his inner sickness that William Jackson had identified and isolated and warned Hamilton about, almost like a skilled psychiatrist. Hamilton's agonizing sense of injury arose not so much from the words contained in Monroe's "*correspondence,*" as from his "conduct" toward him. By refusing to rise to Hamilton's challenge to a duel as a gentleman should, Monroe seemed to be denying to Hamilton his pretensions to being a fellow gentleman. No sort of put down would inflict a sharper, but less localizable, ineradicable, or unforgivable sting to pierce the heart and soul of a self-made gentleman like Hamilton. No amount of heroic effort in pursuit of public credit could turn a gentleman self-made into a gentleman born like a good old boy Virginian of the Jacobin scandal club. While busy, bustling practical men of the world like Church might not be able to see much difference between Monroe's telling Hamilton that the impression he had intended to leave with him coincided with his own, but refusing to add that Clingman's later testimony had not changed it, the refined insight of a genius like Jefferson would quickly descry the inestimable importance of such an affirmation to a Hamilton.

Hamilton himself could see that his inward need to put his personal public credit ahead of every private consideration would come as no surprise to those, even enemies, who understood him best. In the pamphlet he said, "This confession is not made without a blush. I cannot be the apologist of any vice because the ardor of passion may have made it mine. I can never cease to condemn myself for the pang which it may inflict in a bosom eminently entitled to all my gratitude, fidelity, and love." But public credit was of more importance:

> That bosom will approve, that, even at so great an expense, I should
> effectually wipe away a more serious stain from a name which it
> cherishes with no less elevation than tenderness. The public, too, will,
> I trust, excuse the confession. The necessity of it to my defence against
> a more heinous charge could alone have extorted from me so painful an
> indecorum.

James Thomson Callender took malicious glee in the sweet journalistic revenge he had visited upon King of the Feds who had helped contrive his own and John Beckley's recurrent unemployment. With pride, Callender wrote to Jefferson that Hamilton's *Observations* were "worth all that 50 of the best pens in America could have said against him. My sale has been repaid beyond all hope. In less than five weeks, 700 have gone off, and some commissioners and subscribers are yet unanswered." He was delighted that the Episcopal Bishop of Pennsylvania, William Whyte, the brother-in-law of Robert Morris, had declined at a public function to drink to the health of Hamilton, the self-confessed adulterer.

James Madison on October 20, 1797, piously called Jefferson's attention to Hamilton's "malignant insinuations" against him, adding "The publication is a curious specimen of the ingenious folly of its author. Next to the error of publishing at all is that of forgetting that simplicity and candor are the only dress which prudence would put on innocence." The malignant insinuation against you "is a masterpiece of folly, because its importance is in exact proportion to its venom."

Jefferson would know from any one of Monroe, Madison, Beckley, Webb, Randolph, or Callender that Hamilton knew that he was "The respectable character in Virginia" with whom Monroe had lodged all of the original Reynolds papers. Jefferson, privy to the whole affair since December 17, 1792, at latest, could surmise that Hamilton's glancing references to him in *The Reynolds Pamphlet* meant that Hamilton suspected him of being the hidden prime mover who had set the whole affair in motion a year and a half earlier than the date of his entry. Jefferson's air of distantly amused detachment belied his close, intense involvement with the intimate details of the affair from beginning to end as he disclosed to John Taylor of South Carolina,

> I understand that finding the strait between Scylla and Charybdis too narrow for his steerage, he had preferred running plump on one of them. In truth, it seems to work very hard with him; and his willingness to plead guilty to adultery seems rather to have strengthened than weakened the suspicions that he was in truth guilty of speculations.

Writing Jefferson on September 28, 1797, Callender smirked that "no anticipation can equal the infamy of this piece. It is worth all that fifty of the best pens in America could have said against him, and the most pitiful part is his notice of you." Other Anti-Federalists wallowed waggishly in Hamilton's political wake. *Zanga,* whose style was exactly like John Beckley's, writing in the *Aurora,* took Fenno to task for copyrighting Hamilton's pamphlet: ". . . this precious piece of property of yours is not a vindication of the Ex-Secretary, but . . . of . . . adultery . . ." Hamilton "holds himself out as trotting from one lodging in Philadelphia to another after . . . a prostitute!" His ambition was "to bring a . . . strumpet, to the level of his own personal infamy." Andrew G. Fraunces replied to Hamilton's thrusts at him and Jefferson by a series of questions: Did not Hamilton procure one of Fraunces's letters from Jefferson under false pretenses? "Have not you been the instrument of robbing me . . . of liberty, health, property, wife, and children?" He recalled another of Hamilton's amours: "I speak nothing of the Lady in Market Street" [the Reynoldses lived at Fifth and Vine]—"time will shape that!"

James Cheetham, another popular polemicist, reminded his readers that Hamilton had "rambled for 18 months in this scene of pollution, and squandered . . . above $1,200 to conceal the intrigue from his loving spouse." The *Chronicle* chortled over Mrs. Reynolds's "violent attack" on "the virtue of the immaculate secretary . . . in Mr. Hamilton's own house." He had fallen "as compleat a sacrifice to his passions, as ever an old soldier did to his funding system." Jefferson had at last found a writer worthy to take up the pen against "the colossus of the anti Republican party." The pen was Hamilton's own.

In *The Reynolds Pamphlet*, Hamilton had called Callender the "hireling editor" of Numbers V and VI of the *History*. Callender, of course, fired back. It was nonsense, all nonsense, he charged, to accept Hamilton's story of having had an affair with Maria Reynolds at face value at all. His tale of their affair was nothing but a cover-up for a larger and more heinous scandal that involved embezzling money from the Treasury. He had had no affair with beauteous Maria Reynolds. Callender charged that no originals of the correspondence between Hamilton and Maria and James Reynolds had ever existed or that if they had, they had been forged by Reynolds and Hamilton, just as Maria and Clingman had charged. Callender issued a direct challenge to Hamilton on October 29, 1797:

> As the facts which you . . . bring forward, and the conclusions which you attempt to draw from them do not appear Satisfactory to me, I intend introducing a reply to them in a volume upon your administration that I am now engaged in writing. My object in this letter is, to request that you will give an order to a friend of mine and myself to inspect the papers lodged with Mr. Bingham, that I may judge what credit is due to them. . . . if they appear to be genuine, I shall be as ready to confess my conviction to the public, as I was to declare my former opinion.

Callender pointed out to Hamilton that he had made "a palpable mistake" in writing of "visiting her at Inskeeps" because it "never was a house of that sort." Hamilton would certainly have to publish a second pamphlet to correct such ridiculous mistakes as this.

Hamilton had specified that only "gentlemen" might apply to Bingham to see the papers. Callender was notoriously no gentleman. This was demonstrated, ipso facto, by the fact that he had had the effrontery to apply to see the papers lodged with Bingham. On the back of Callender's letter, Hamilton wrote "Impudent Experiment *NO NOTICE*." He made no further reply. Callender did not give up his investigative digging and reporting. In his *Sketches of the History of America* published early in 1798, he claimed to find many other contradictions in Hamilton's story.

Clingman had married Maria Reynolds, and they were now living in Alexandria; Reynolds was living in New York. Aaron Burr had arranged their divorce.

"If the letters published by Mr. Hamilton in the name of Maria are genuine," Callender argued, "it would be very easy to obtain her attestation of the fact. A justice of the peace . . . could dispatch the business in half an hour. She could be directed to give a sample of her hand; and by comparing this with the letters, it would be ascertained whether or not they really came from her pen. But Camillus dares not meet this test."

Callender also called attention to textual incongruities in the Reynolds letters: "The construction of the periods disagrees with this apparent incapacity of spelling. . . . A few gross blunders are interspersed . . . but, when stript of such a veil, the body of the composition is pure and correct. In the literary world, fabrications of this nature have been frequent." Callender piously added: "He who acknowledged the reality of such epistles, could feel no scruple to forge them. The latter supposition is as favourable as the former to his good name." This comment of Callender's echoes the same doubts concerning the authenticity of the Reynolds letters that Jefferson was confiding to his diary at about the same time.

> Callender then addresses Hamilton directly: The whole collection would not have required above an evening to write. . . . You speak as if it was impossible to invent a few letters. Yet, upon this very business, you wrote a feigned hand. And what is your molehill appendix, altogether, to the gigantic fabrications of Psalmanazar and of Chatterton? Send for the lady, and let us hear what she has to say. . . . Never pretend that you scorn to confront accusers. The world will believe that you dare not.

Of course, Maria and James Reynolds were as easily available to interrogation by a journalist like Callender as they were to Hamilton. Because they would on the face of it be witnesses friendly to Callender—he accepted their latest story—and hostile to Hamilton—he did not credit their story—a greater mystery than why Hamilton failed to question them is why Callender did not.

If a "hireling editor" like Callender were to be believed, Hamilton was not only a defalcating secretary of the treasury, a speculator, a peculator, and an adulterer, he was also a liar and a forger. According to Callender, he was the contriver of a vast cover-up scheme put out under the false guise of coming clean. He was not a seducer and an adulterer; he was a false confessor to nonexistent affairs. He was the traducer of the good reputation of a virtuous woman and a bumptious boaster wearing false hair on his chest.

Present-day Jefferson scholars who have studied these matters closely go farther than Callender. They are certain that Hamilton forged the Reynolds letters. Although the original documents have never been found, they prove that Hamilton was a forger by careful textual examination of the printed documentary evidence. Foremost among these learned scholars is Professor Julian P. Boyd, the editor of the definitive edition of *The Papers of Thomas Jefferson*. In an 80-page appendix to Volume 18 of *The Papers of Thomas Jefferson* entitled "The First Conflict in the Cabinet," Professor Boyd writes (page 680):

> . . . the letters of James Reynolds and his wife as published by Hamilton present a character that is so immediately recognizable as to place their true nature beyond doubt . . . the conclusion is obvious. . . . They exhibit in their texts, in their substantive incongruities, and in their conflict with verifiable evidence overwhelming proofs of their own insufficiency. They are the palpably contrived documents of a brilliant and daring

man who, writing under much stress in the two or three days available
to him in 1792, tried to imitate what he conceived to be the style of less
literate persons. The result was inexpert to the point of naïveté, but its
character is beyond doubt. The purported letters of James and Maria
Reynolds as published in Hamilton's *Observations* cannot be accepted
as genuine.

It is a shocking charge. Professor Boyd's argument runs that Mrs. Reynolds's letters contain good grammatical construction and correct spelling of
longer words like *tortured, happiness, disappointment, anguish, insupporta-
ble, language, affliction, inexorable, consolation, existence, complaining,* and
adieu, but misspellings of easy words of one or two syllables like *se* for *see, rite*
for *write, mutch* for *much, moast* for *most, pilliow* for *pillow,* and so on. This
is suspicious. Also, she misspelled words in ways unusual even for unlettered
persons of the day, such as *kneese* for *knees, youse* or *yuse* for *use, greateest*
for *greatest, gleme* for *gleam, voed* for *void,* and so on, and also misspelled
some words the same way her husband did. This is still more suspicious.

James Reynolds's letters and receipts, beginning with his discovery of the
alleged amour, changing in tone from that of an outraged and threatening
husband to one of an importunate, obsequious, and wheedling extortionist pimp,
misspell simple words, too, *fue* for *few, boath* for *both,* and *shush* for *such,* but
he spells polysyllabic words without error, such as *distraction, imprudent,
disagreeable,* and *calculation.* Also, like Maria, he spells the same word sometimes correctly and sometimes incorrectly, sometimes both ways in the same
letter. Thus Maria could write *deer freend* and also *dear sir,* and James could
write *exspess* as well as *express.* Such peculiarities give away Hamilton as an
inexpert and naïve forger, Boyd argues.

At such confident modern reaffirmations of Callender's view of his guilt,
Hamilton might well smile grimly while spinning in his sepulcher. The polemics
that lead off his *Reynolds Pamphlet* sometimes seem only a little more unbalanced than some of the scholarship of his accusers. Five years were not long
enough for his guilt to be forgotten, nor the better part of two centuries under
his sarcophagus in Trinity Churchyard long enough for his name to escape the
further blackening by "old calumnies served up afresh" by Jefferson's "wizard
painters" and "hireling editors."

Did Hamilton fabricate the Reynolds letters? Did he, with Reynolds's help,
forge them during the day or two between Reynolds's release from jail and the
confrontation with Monroe and the others in his office on the night of December
15? Was his affair with Maria Reynolds not merely one that he did not enjoy for
very long, but one that he never had? Are we dealing with a fine example of the
free press at its best laying bare without fear or favor covered up moral rot and
political corruption? Or at its worst, with hireling editors printing an artful
hatchet job of unsubstantiated innuendoes and insinuations, guilts by association, and character assassination, with no opportunity for rebuttal?

Are we dealing here with the tragedy of *Othello?* Of the dark stranger from a far land become great in his adopted Venice, whose paranoiac mind begins by seizing on and magnifying a small misjudgment no bigger than a lady's handkerchief planted by an enemy professing to be his friend, and ends by bringing him down in made folly? Or is it a French bedroom farce like one of Feydeau's, starring a very married federal demigod caught lying about the wrong bed in the wrong tavern, pursued by a pack of Jacobin scandal club men slamming in and out Inskeep's swinging doors?

Hamilton's defense begins with his own pleading of it in *The Reynolds Pamphlet*, but does not end there. The pamphlet's heavy freight of polemical special pleading directed at the Jacobin scandal club weakens a basically convincing defense. His own exhaustive explanation of the correspondence, of each letter and note passing between himself and the Reynoldses, one by one, need not be repeated here. He refers to the long series of impeachment inquiries brought against him in Congress that had grown out of Jefferson's and Giles's impeachment resolutions. By these, he argued, his enemies "finding no handle for their malice," exonerated him of corruption in office. Like Jefferson, Giles had probably known of the affair from almost the beginning, but Congress's investigation of all Treasury operations failed to turn up any link to it that would open the door to bringing in Reynolds. The charges of Andrew G. Fraunces against him relative to the Baron de Glaubeck's pension and Duer's warrants had also been extensively investigated by Congress and exposed as groundless. Furthermore, Hamilton pleaded, nothing in the evidence "ever specified the objects of the pretended connection in speculation between Reynolds and me." If the sums of $20 or $30 or $50 or a total of $1,100 that he had given Reynolds were all that was involved, "what a scale of speculation is this for the head of a public treasury" charged elsewhere with funding at $40 million a debt that ought to have been funded at $10 million or $15 million to enrich himself and his friends. Yes, Hamilton had written notes to Reynolds in a disguised or feigned hand. But this was so that Reynolds would not be able to use these notes as an "engine of false credit" with third persons. When confronted by his own accusers with these notes, Hamilton had admitted at once they were his.

Callender had snickeringly charged that Hamilton would not have paid hush money to Reynolds because Hamilton "had nothing to lose as to his reputation for chastity concerning which the world had fixed a previous opinion." A foul blow, Hamilton groaned. "No man not indelicately unprincipled with the state of manners of this country, would be willing to have a conjugal infidelity fixed upon him with positive certainty." On the contrary, he was "tender of the happiness" of his "excellent wife" and felt "extreme pain" at the affliction she would endure from the disclosure. "Those best acquainted with the interior of my domestic life will best appreciate the force of such a consideration," he agonized. He "dreaded extremely" a disclosure—and was willing to make large sacrifices to avoid it."

But Hamilton's preoccupation with his political enemies of the Jacobin scandal club, his outrage at the "gentleman" who shrank from rallying to his side to furnish him an unequivocal defense, and his old prurient preoccupation with

Maria Reynolds herself—all converged to weaken his brief for his own defense contained in *The Reynolds Pamphlet*. Reflections on Maria spoiled the impact of his star witness's testimony when he introduced Richard Folwell, a solid and persuasive character witness, who corroborated Hamilton's bizarre tale in important particulars, most of which would be inadmissible as irrelevant in a courtroom.

In *The Reynolds Pamphlet*, Hamilton introduced Folwell's testimony abstractedly by saying, "The variety of shapes which this woman could assume was endless." In a conversation with "a gentleman whom I am not at liberty publicly to name, she made a voluntary confession of her belief and even knowledge, that I was innocent of all that had been laid to my charge by *Reynolds* . . . spoke of me in exalted terms of esteem and respect, declared in the most solemn manner her extreme unhappiness lest I should suppose her accessory to the trouble which had been given me . . . and expressed her fear that the resentment of Mr. Reynolds on a *particular score* might have urged him to improper lengths of revenge." The gentleman was an impartial witness. The statement of Richard Folwell had been deposited with William Bingham, Esquire, and shown to James Monroe.

Richard Folwell was a reputable journalist who in 1797 had published *A Short History of the Yellow Fever*. In 1801 he would issue the authorized Folwell edition of the *Journals of Congress*, and from 1805 to 1813 he would publish a periodical called *The Spirit of the Press*, for which he solicited a subscription from Thomas Jefferson as "the principal Pillar of the public Will" and to which Jefferson subscribed for eight months. Folwell came forward as a volunteer while Hamilton was in Philadelphia collecting the material for his *Reynolds Pamphlet*. He wrote Hamilton's friend Edward Jones on August 12, 1797, that he had read Callender's charges against Hamilton in Nos. V and VI of his *History*, had been shocked and outraged, and wished "to see Right prevail, and Innocence protected." He had personal knowledge "that would render Improbably . . . the Imputations" that Callender had leveled at Hamilton.

According to Folwell, "a few days after Mrs. Reynolds' first appearance in Philadelphia," Folwell's mother was persuaded "to receive her for a few days into our house, as she was a stranger in the city, and had come here to endeavour to reclaim a prodigal husband, who had deserted her and his creditors in New York." Folwell's mother had taken her in because "her innocent countenance appeared to show an innocent heart." Maria soon found her husband. "He had been in gaol and was but just liberated." Maria and James had a meeting, she said, "but could not come to terms of pacification." In Maria Folwell had noted the same emotional fireworks Hamilton had seen. They are on tumultuous display in Maria's letters appended to *The Reynolds Pamphlet*. "Almost at the same minute that she would declare her respect for her husband, cry and feel distressed, they would vanish, and levity succeed, with bitter execrations on her husband." Hamilton, too, had written allusively of "paroxyisms" of love for a foreign mistress. Folwell at first ascribed the "inconsistency and folly" Maria displayed "to a troubled but innocent and harmless mind," until, "in one or other of these Paroxysms, she told me, so infamous was the Perfidy of Reynolds, that he had frequently . . . insisted that she should insinuate herself on certain . . . high and influential Characters . . . endeavour to make assignations with them, and actually prostitute herself to gull Money from them."

After five days of this, Folwell and his mother decided she had to go. "She commanded commiseration," the Folwells thought, but "a character so infamous as her Husband should not enter our House."

So Maria and James Reynolds moved "to a reputable Quaker Lady's at No. —— North Grant Street." There "they lived together; but . . . did not sleep together." Instead, she kept busy at night plying their trade.

"Letters were frequently found in the Entry inviting her Abroad;—and at Night she would fly off . . . to *answer* their Contents."

"Contents" of the letters or contentments of the writers? Both. So different from Hamilton's characteristic style, Folwell's sly, slightly old maidish sense of humor describing the harlot and her procurer plying their trade out of a respectable Quaker lady's house rules out, for many readers at least, the possibility that Hamilton could have fabricated Folwell's testimony. His self-characterization as he also characterized the Reynoldses is too convincing to have been worked up that August in Philadelphia by a frantic, feverish, and deranged Hamilton. The respectable Quaker lady's "house eventually getting too hot for them," Folwell went on, "they made their exit." Before their hasty exit, however, somebody proposed that money be paid to somebody else by a method confusingly described by Folwell as follows:

> She informed me she had proposed pecuniary aid should be rendered by her to her Husband in his Speculations, by her placing Money in a certain Gentleman's Hands, to buy of him whatever public Paper he had to sell, and that she would have that which was purchased given to her,—and, if she could find Confidence in his future Prudence, she would eventually return him what he sold."

Later, Reynolds tried to get Folwell to "adventure with him" in Lancaster turnpike scrip. One of the Reynolds-Hamilton letters had contained a similar reference to Reynolds's investing in Lancaster turnpike scrip. Professor Boyd cites the above quoted passages from Folwell's statement as proof that Hamilton forged Folwell's statement as well as the Reynolds letters because, as he reasons by bootstrap, Folwell's statement ties in so neatly with Hamilton's other forgeries. This writer submits that it ties in more neatly with the disinterested character witness's testimony.

For a reader familiar with Hamilton's usual style of precisely recording—often with a true bookkeeper's mindless zeal—money transactions in his army paybook, his cash books, journals, ledgers, and Treasury Reports—even the expenses he laid out for a private rendezvous with Angelica Church—these passages from Folwell prove the opposite of Professor Boyd's conclusion: it would be an impossibility for a man of such deeply ingrained habits of careful reporting of complex money transactions as Hamilton to describe such simple ones with such confusion.

"Some considerable Time after [if necessary, data can be procured]," Folwell wrote, "they removed and lived in stile [*sic*] in a large House in Vine Street, next to the Corner of Fifth. Here I had an Invitation, and being disposed to see if possible how People supported Grandeur, without apparently Friends, Money or Industry, I accordingly called."

But at the point in time, when Folwell paid his call to see this new-found "grandeur," Reynolds's latest fraudulent scheme had just been found out by Oliver Wolcott, Jr. Fallen again from his sudden grandeur, Reynolds languished in jail. Folwell sympathetically asked Maria, "In jail for what?" Out came her comical tale of Reynolds and Clingman applying for letters of administration on the supposedly deceased soldier's estate—and the solemn moment preceding by a beat the farcical denouement she describes, when "The soldier came to life." After which, Folwell concluded, "the curtain dropt from my view."

Later, after receiving Maria's "very pathetic letter"—Hamilton well knew her pathetic mode—Folwell had mislaid it, but, as he recalled, "it would move almost anyone to serve her."

Checking himself in the nick of time at the edge of an abyss of fond reverie to escape this fatal Circe's circle of servitors, Folwell amended his recollection: not everyone would serve her—only someone who "was not perfectly acquainted with her character, confirmed by actual observation."

Folwell's statement said nothing of knowledge that Maria and Hamilton had enjoyed an affair or that Reynolds had blackmailed Hamilton, but this is not very surprising. Word of such affairs was generally forbidden to pass the lips of a proper gentleman like Folwell. Folwell's corroboration of Hamilton's own account of the Reynoldses' activities and proclivities remains a convincing piece of juridically inadmissible evidence for the defense, which Hamilton, writing his feverish public defense, all but threw away and mostly wasted.

The most important point of all about Folwell's willingness to testify for Hamilton is the fact of his having done so. Such an uninvolved man's willingness to bear witness to a man he did not know confirms better than any friendship-serving words from him could ever have done that he believed in the essential truth of Hamilton's defense and the falsity of Callender's charges. In this he agreed with practically all of the men and women of the time who knew most about the Reynolds affair and all the leading actors in it. Besides Folwell there was his and Hamilton's helpful friend Edward Jones. Wadsworth, Wolcott, McHenry, William Jackson, and George Washington also stood by Hamilton. Muhlenberg and Venable unequivocally believed his story, too. Aaron Burr told Monroe that he must believe him.

Monroe's refusal to provide Hamilton with the same unequivocal public affirmation of his private belief in the truth of Hamilton's story, which his actions affirmed, coupled with Hamilton's deranged reaction to Monroe's cover-up of Beckley as the source of the leak and Monroe's counterreaction to Hamilton's suspicion, deprived Hamilton of the strongest possible character witness to his public defense: James Monroe. Hamilton, not seeing this, was blinded by his obsession with his enemies.

Monroe was not directly responsible for the leak of the papers, but he, of course, had known the source of the leak all along. Hamilton knew Monroe would know. Who then was the source of the leak? And why did Monroe refuse to name him?

In his December 17, 1792, memorandum of the Reynolds affair, Thomas Jefferson had written: "Known to J[ames] M[adison], E[dmund] R[andolph] [John] Beckley and [Bernard] Webb." (The names in brackets were filled in by editors familiar with Jefferson's shorthand code.) Gentlemen with public reputations to be safeguarded by the use of such initials, like the first two men on Jefferson's list and like Monroe, could not afford to be involved in such a leak.

But a party hatchet man like John Beckley and an obscure hack like Bernard Webb had no future personal political hopes at risk—they were creatures available to do as told by principals—lack of scruples would be more or less expected of them in any event. One of the two of them was the leak. There is no documentary evidence that Jefferson told either of them directly in so many words to leak the papers to Callender. But if he did not or did not intend that they make some such use of them, he knew enough about them to jot their two surnames carefully (without guarding them under initials as he did the gentlemen) among the four nonprincipals besides himself who knew the secret.

Monroe's repeated statements that he had deposited the *originals* "in the hands of a respectable character in Virginia" was a meaningless red herring as a denial of knowing the source of the leak, but it shut off further inquiry. The apparently disarming candor of the disclosure successfully served to switch Hamilton's further inquiry at the confrontation in New York off the track that would have led straight to Beckley and Webb.

After the uproar had died down, Monroe rather casually owned up to having known all along the truth he had so evasively kept from Hamilton. As a throwaway postscript to a letter to Aaron Burr dated December 1, 1797, Monroe wrote, "I presume that Beckley published the papers in question. By his clerk [Webb] they were copied for us."

Hamilton had been so rattled at the confrontation the night of December 15, 1792, that he had forgotten to ask for copies of the original documents in his hand for which they had demanded his explanation; the next day he had asked Monroe for copies. Monroe gave the originals to John Beckley, to be copied, and Beckley had given them to Webb. Webb had then "carried a copy to H." At H's, a second confrontation had occurred, which Beckley had told Monroe all about. Hamilton had asked Webb "('as B. says,')," "Is anyone else privy to the affair?"

Webb replied, "Beckley is."

Hamilton: "Tell Beckley I consider him bound not to disclose it."

Webb took this injunction back to Beckley.

Beckley "replied by the same clerk that he considered himself under no injunction whatever." Beckley added that "if Hamilton has anything to say to me it must be in writing."

In his December 1 letter to Burr, Monroe certified, "This from B."

To Burr, Monroe concluded with a resigned shrug and an implied grin, "After our interviews with H. I requested B. to say nothing about it."

By this extraordinary postscript Monroe was admitting to Burr that he had known all along what he had stubbornly refused to admit to Hamilton that he knew. But he had consciously kept the secret hidden from Hamilton all along. Hamilton knew all along he was hiding it.

Monroe failed to copy this devastating postscript of self-revelation on his retained copy of his December 1 letter to Burr.

Thus Monroe seemed to hide from himself for the future, perhaps subconsciously, written reminder of the secret of his duplicity toward Hamilton, which he had expiated a little by confessing in the original to Aaron Burr. Remembering his secondary confrontation with Monroe's agent Beckley in the proxy of Webb, Hamilton would always be just as certain as Monroe that Beckley was, of course, the immediate source of the leak. But for Hamilton to have publicly charged these two, Beckley and Webb, with responsibility—they were not gentlemen and known mainly as creatures of Jefferson—would be leveling a charge against the vice-president for which he had no proof to support firm conviction.

None doubted, though most averred, but not for the record, without naming Jefferson's name, that he was the highly placed "respectable character in Virginia" with whom Monroe's set of the original documents had been lodged. No one dared ask publicly why they should have been lodged there. Only if Hamilton could succeed in goading Monroe into letting slip out the names of Beckley and Webb, would they become fair game to stalk to the lair of their lofty principal. Otherwise, no one, not even *Camillus*, though he might scatter oblique hints and insinuations and even Jefferson's name through his *Reynolds Pamphlet*, would dare to level against Jefferson the direct charge that he, the Republican empire builder, was indecently exposed as the sponsor of the leak. Newspapers and journalists that dared reprint charges against public figures in those days were subject to criminal prosecution under libel laws much harsher than any today, particularly if Jefferson were involved, as Callender and Hamilton's own client Harry Croswell would one day learn the hard way.

But Monroe, at risk of his life and the charge of cravenly avoiding a duel, held back from all but Burr the two nonpublic surnames that Jefferson had written out in his diary.

It was probably awareness of this lack of forthcoming in Monroe's conduct toward him (although no one else knew of it) that caused Hamilton to fail to see that to the public the certificate Monroe had already given him made Monroe by far the best witness Hamilton could possibly have used to bolster the credibility of his defense: A prominent public man who was known to the public as a political enemy of Hamilton.

The threadbare lawyer who pleads his own case has a fool for a client. Hamilton's failure to present a better case in his own defense than he managed to do in *The Reynolds Pamphlet* was a self-inflicted wound. Weaknesses in his lengthy brief opened the door for James Thomson Callender and Professor

Julian P. Boyd and others of their ilk to raise up new charges far more serious than those he had sought to rebut by confessing to an old affair. Now his once bright prospects of being called by the Federalists to stand for the presidency were "smothered up" forever. Sapped was his power as a leader from the moderate center of the Federalist party to keep the northeastern states yoked firmly into the Union by curbing the secessionist tendencies of the High Federalists of New England.

Upon Elizabeth, his children, Angelica, John Barker Church, and uncounted friends, clients, acquaintances, and admirers who loved him passionately, respected him deeply, liked him warmly or admired him fervently, he had inflicted incalculable pain, sorrow, regret, disappointment, and disillusionment. At Hamilton's folly, Talleyrand, back in an office of power under the Directory in Paris, growing richer every day in every way, would sadly wag his head. And when the gross enormity of his miscalculation dawned on him in a period of remission from the derangement that had brought it on, Hamilton would lose an irrecoverable measure of confidence in himself.

Professor Harold C. Syrett, the editor of the *Hamilton Papers*, finds that "most historians" assume that the Reynolds documents are authentic. For what it is worth, this writer agrees with Professor Syrett and the majority of historians. In this writer's view, James Thomson Callender and Professor Julian P. Boyd and their ilk are wrong. Hamilton did not forge or fabricate the Reynolds documents attached as the appendix to the printed version of *The Reynolds Pamphlet*, and the documents, notably the letters from Maria and James Reynolds, are essentially what they purport to be and what Hamilton represented them to be.

The dispute and the mystery will probably never be cleared up to the satisfaction of all until the originals are found, and they probably never will be, for reasons that are part of yet another mystery.

That the printed version of the Reynolds documents differs in minor respects from the originals would not necessarily change this writer's conclusion that the missing basic documents are authentic. Variances in orthography and spelling between the original manuscripts and the printed version may have arisen from inaccurate transcription by Hamilton for the printer or inaccurate typesetting by the printer from Hamilton's copy or faulty proofreading by Fenno or some of all three. Evidence of white lies, self-serving recollections, forgetfulness, haste, and carelessness on Hamilton's part can be nitpicked out of *The Reynolds Pamphlet* and its appendix. For example, Hamilton probably met or had prior acquaintance with James or Maria Reynolds well before the time he says Maria first came to his house in Philadelphia—Hamilton mentioned James Reynolds in his letter to Jeremiah Wadsworth of August 20, 1787. Nevertheless, this writer's opinion remains that Hamilton's account of the affair in *The Reynolds Pamphlet* is essentially truthful.

It is not accurate to assert that Hamilton need not have disclosed his adulterous affair at all, but did so only to distract attention from and cover up illegal financial dealings with Reynolds. Hamilton had quickly admitted to Monroe, Muhlenberg, and Venable that the six notes, receipts, and fragments they confronted him with were written by him, though partly "in a feigned hand." From then on, it became necessary for him, somehow or other, to explain them away. Far from being an irrelevant ruse to throw investigators off the track, the tale of the adulterous affair was relevant, material, and essential to provide an innocent explanation of admittedly genuine documentary evidence that was compromising, if not incriminating, on its face.

To this writer and, it may be, many a reader who has stayed with this account of Hamilton's life, words, and actions this far, the most convincing of all the evidence of the truth of Hamilton's account of the Reynolds affair in *The Reynolds Pamphlet* is evidence that is mostly legally inadmissible. Such evidence includes the fact that Hamilton was a poorer man when he left office as secretary of the treasury than when he came into it; that, in or out of office, he was a man singularly unconcerned with accumulating a personal fortune; and that he was scrupulous in money dealings all his life. Much else has been shown that attests to his conscientious attention and probity, subject to occasional forgetfulness, in all money matters. For him to have knowingly carried on improper pecuniary speculation or engaged in secret monetary transactions of any kind (except to pay hush money to a procurer, as he admitted doing) is inconsistent with all else herein shown of his character.

The other body of evidence that supports the conclusion that *The Reynolds Pamphlet* is essentially true is the documentary evidence he produced during his entire life. The reader of this life story should by now be sensitive to the fact that, for purposes of history, documentary evidence cannot always be relied on for the truth of what it purports to show on its face—it is often self-serving or inaccurately recorded—yet being documentary, it is too easily taken at face value by cloistered scholars without sufficient experience of the world to apply sufficient discount for such defects.

The more one reads the written life evidence—which consists of all Hamilton's output of writing in many different modes—the more convinced one becomes that it would have been impossible for him to have concocted the letters from Maria and James Reynolds to himself. *Publius* could write in many modes —dignified state papers, crisp letters of advice, monumental great reports, proposed statutes, gravely ardent or playful love letters, and stilted imitation pastorals. But the mode of the Reynolds letters was one that on the evidence of all his other writing was beyond his powers of invention. Their mercurial twists, turns, reversals, and wild emotional tergiversations were clown suits of a pair of characters that *Publius* simply did not know how to put on or play in. Hamilton's ingrained characteristic style of writing is a thing as different from the Reynoldses' style as a lusty young harlot is from a busy, married, harried statesman and father of five.

This entire book and *Hamilton I* as well, are offered for identification and into evidence as Exhibit A in Hamilton's defense. Practically every word and action of Hamilton they relate is a piece of cumulative evidence that, whatever other capacities he might have possessed, he lacked the capacity of inventing or fabricating the letters Maria and James Reynolds wrote to him.

Introducing himself to a new audience, a popular leader of the House of Representatives hailing from the Hoosier State would smile and demurely confide, "I'm from Indiana where they always say, 'Never name your son after the Governor—until after the Statute of Limitations has run.'" He would squeeze off a jocund wink waiting for the warm friendly laughter to subside. On the subject of voluntary confessions the winning conventional wisdom of American politics has changed little from Hamilton's time through Representative Charlie Halleck's and to date: Forget it.

Few public figures at any time in any country, even under pressure of imminent threat of involuntary disclosure, have made a clean breast of misdeeds theretofore successfully covered up, by confessing to crimes other than, different from, and more unsavory than those charged, except as part of the charade of copping a plea. Already five years old, the Reynolds affair was a small personal peccadillo largely forgotten until Beckley's disclosures to Callender heated it up again to roil public debate for Jefferson's benefit. Looking back on Hamilton as a public figure in American history from the vantage point of almost two centuries (ignoring for the moment the terrible pressures that the five-year-long cover-up of the affair had on his political, professional, and personal life, his psyche, and his soul) one may affirm that Hamilton's folly in issuing *The Reynolds Pamphlet* was, nevertheless, one of his finest hours as an American public man. In it he set a precedent for full disclosure by a public man that has rarely been followed since. Having done so he stands, in this as in so many other ways, unique in lonely self-tarnished grandeur. Few would argue that no American public man has committed misdeeds more serious than his. To the probity of American public life, followers of Hamilton's lonely and painful precedent are welcome recruits at any time.

22

THE BASTARD BRAT
REESCALADES!
QUASI COMMANDER
OF THE QUASI WAR

[WASHINGTON] COMPELLED ME TO PROMOTE . . . THE MOST REST-
LESS, IMPATIENT, ARTFUL, INDEFATIGABLE, UNPRINCIPLED INTRI-
GUER IN THE UNITED STATES, IF NOT IN THE WORLD, TO BE SECOND
IN COMMAND UNDER HIMSELF.

—John Adams

War? War with France? The very thought of war with the ally of the
Revolution, with the great senior partner in the Treaty of Paris of 1778, first
announced at Valley Forge, was unthinkable. But in relations between nations
it often is a process of no more than a year or two for the impossible to evolve
into the unthinkable, the unthinkable into the unmentionable, the unmentionable
into the debatable, and the debatable into a torrid political issue, until the political issue detonates into an international crisis—or the unthinkable evolves into
official policy. American ratification of Jay's Treaty with Britain had touched off

a powder train that through 1797 and 1798 would lead to an unthinkable crisis in relations between the United States and France. This first of the nation's many undeclared wars came to be known as the Quasi War.

Domestically, it takes two strong factions to fight an undeclared war. One big factional question of 1797 was whether John Beckley's and James Thomson Callender's laying bare of the threadbare lawyer's old affair had destroyed the dovish influence Hamilton might otherwise have had as the out-of-town, under-cover prime minister over the hawkish chief members of Adams's cabinet, Secretaries of State, Treasury, and War Pickering, Wolcott, and McHenry. Did he retain enough influence with the Federalist party members of Congress to check the extreme High Federalists' popular thrust toward secession or else an all-out war with France? Few of his fellow Federalists thought there was any question. Becoming the focal point of Republican smears made Hamilton's influence greater than ever with all true Federalists. The members of Adams's cabinet continued to seek his advice and counsel as much as or more than before. Friends and believers remained friends; enemies, enemies—with basic opinions much the same, but held at a higher pitch of emotion and unreason than before. The nagging question of whether the laying bare of the Reynolds affair in the press had lost or cost him prestige and public credit really loomed largest in the interior of Hamilton's own mind. But the reassurances of his Federalist friends and his own private insistence that the public accept his self-disclosure as proof of the fiscal integrity of his Treasury operations were not enough for him. His peculiar sense of public credit—in personal contexts he thought of it as public honor—required something more. Some sort of trial on the public stage, a public verdict, and a victory were needed to complete the record in the case, to set the seal of public acknowledgment on the fact that the charges of his enemies had been discredited and his own all but incredible explanation accepted whole.

Perhaps, too, such a public vindication would clear the air for Hamilton's friends to urge his name for the presidency again in the elections of 1800, now less than two years away. Before, in 1796, when Noah Webster had published a trial balloon suggesting Hamilton instead of Adams as the Federalist presidential candidate that year, John Beckley had used the threat of laying bare the old affair to force Webster to haul it down: His *"Minerva* immediately became silent." But now that they had published the worst, the scandal would no longer be news.

As disclosure of the scandal was breaking, Hamilton received a letter from his old friend and protégé Rufus King, now American minister in London, written June 27, 1797, that added to the pressures on his mind. It reported the British reaction to John Adams's (and Hamilton's) special message to Congress of May 16, copies of which had just reached London.

"It has arrived at a critical hour," King said ominously, adding, "These are days of wonder. The march already made by France has astonished, and confounded almost every beholder . . . All Italy will be overturned—Venice is no more; Genoa has been completely revolutionized; Portugal sees, but seems unable to escape her fate." Napoleon Bonaparte was installing puppet governments subservient to France all over the Continent. But this was only the first stage of the threat Napoleonic France posed to the world. Neither Britain nor the United States nor the rest of the Western Hemisphere were safe. "She meditates and will attempt projects still more gigantic—which will operate a change in the whole face of Europe, and extend to every other quarter of the Globe," King warned.

In addition to the fact that French cruisers had captured 316 American ships as prizes in 1795, as Secretary of State Pickering had reported in outrage in February, France had laid embargoes on American ships at Bordeaux, seized American goods for public use without paying for them, and condemned American ships and cargoes under laws that violated her commercial treaties with the United States. On Christmas Day of 1796 a French privateer had fired a broadside into the unresisting American ship *Commerce*, wounding four of the crewmen. In March 1797 a French armed brig had captured the *Cincinnatus* out of Baltimore and tortured the American captain with thumb screws to make him say that his cargo was English property so that the French could then confiscate it legally. When he refused to blurt out a false confession, they robbed him and plundered his ship's provisions. Here was more provocation than, for example, the uncertain sighting of a torpedo near a destroyer in Tonkin Gulf.

The French justified their plundering of American commerce as reprisals for America's allegedly abandoning the principle of "free ships, free goods." This doctrine meant that if a ship flew the flag of a neutral country, neither the vessel nor the cargo it carried, as long as it was not contraband such as guns or ammunition, was subject to capture. It would not be molested. The French-American treaty of commerce of 1778 had committed both countries to the doctrine of "free ships, free goods" in their relations with each other. But now, the French claimed, the broad definition of goods that were contraband of war in Jay's Treaty gave the British excuse for seizing many new classes of goods, as well as the ships that carried them. Arguably, the American government had thus violated its obligations to France under the French treaty. France and her colonies in the West Indies desperately needed the imports from the States that the British now were seizing for themselves under color of right. French journalists scored American perfidy: "In vain we have hoped for some time that gratitude or at least self interest, would make of the Federal Republic a loyal ally of France. Now Washington has concluded with our most implacable enemies a treaty wholly inimical to our interests."

Hamilton's enemies charged that the British treaty should have been called Hamilton's Treaty, not Jay's. Hamilton's friends and admirers, many of them merchants and bankers becoming suddenly wealthy with the vast increase in trade with Britain, agreed with his enemies, but admiringly. Republican attacks like this on their leader further cemented their loyalty to him.

At the top of the agenda of the dynamic, imperialistic policy of France under the Directory with Napoleon as its all-victorious general was reconstructing France's lost empire in the New World by regaining Louisiana from the feeble grip of Spain. Hearing rumors that Spain had ceded both Louisiana and the

Floridas to France, Secretary of State Timothy Pickering commented, "The Spaniards will be certainly more safe and quiet neighbors."

The recovery of Louisiana had indeed been a major secret goal of French diplomacy since at least 1795. It added to Secretary of State Pickering's sense of menacing danger that France by recovering Louisiana intended "to renew the ancient plan of her monarch of *circumscribing* and encircling what now constitutes the Atlantic States." John Quincy Adams fanned Pickering's fears by reporting from Berlin on June 26, 1797, of "some project of momentous magnitude carried on for several years past by the French, and of which our government is not well informed."

Britain too eyed control of Louisiana. It had demanded rights there during the 1797 peace negotiations with France, which collapsed in October of that year. The shrewdest and most effective avatar of France's old dream of accomplishing exactly what Pickering and John Quincy Adams feared most in Louisiana was none other than Hamilton's old friend and admirer Charles Maurice de Talleyrand-Périgord. With a cold realism that seemed more Hamiltonian than that of any other statesman in either country, Talleyrand had remarked in a speech to the French National Institute on April 4, 1797, that "in every part of America through which I travelled [during his exile in 1794 and 1795] I have not found a single Englishman who did not feel himself to be an American, not a single Frenchman who did not find himself a stranger." If the French could establish themselves in Louisiana, it would be the best means of putting a checkrein on both the British and the Americans that would keep them apart.

Although Talleyrand considered Hamilton the greatest of all Americans, he did not much like Americans in general. When President Washington refused to receive him, he had written Madame de Staël, "If I have to stay here another year I shall die." The reason he was so contemptuous of Americans in general, Talleyrand said, was because gold was their God. Talleyrand, a bishop of the Roman Catholic Church, but far from observing vows of poverty, had grown rich as France's minister of foreign relations. He supported himself and his famous mistresses, including Adèle de Flauhaut, whom he had shared for a while with American Minister Gouverneur Morris, by demanding and obtaining from people with whom he dealt in his official capacities commissions, loans, tips, presents, gifts, gratuities, emoluments, and bribes. Talleyrand had come to know the Hamiltons and the Philip Schuylers well during his exile in the United States, but despite his lofty opinion of Hamilton's abilities, Talleyrand laughed at his scruples—at the spectacle of the man who had made the fortune of his country becoming poor, instead of rich, in public office—so poor that, after leaving it, he had to labor late into the night in his private law office to support his family. In Paris, in July 1797, less than a week before John Marshall and Elbridge Gerry would set sail to join Charles Cotesworth Pinckney on the peace mission to France that Hamilton had urged on Adams, the Directory restored Talleyrand to official favor by appointing him as its new minister of foreign affairs.

Talleyrand's perception that Americans were materialistic and that gold was their only God squared with that of other observers, including de Tocqueville. But the amusement Talleyrand found in the fact that a holder of high office like Hamilton in a revolutionary, constitutional republic became poor in it, instead of rich, would not be shared by any but a tiny handful of Americans and certainly not by men of the probity of Pinckney and Marshall.

Even as logical and realistic a mind as Talleyrand's, being French, could fail to catch the significance of this perhaps illogical yet characteristic manifestation of American character and stumble over it. Having done so and noting the uproar caused in the United States by his solecism in the XYZ Affair, a Talleyrand would probably dismiss the revulsion eighteenth-century Americans felt at paying bribes to foreign governmental officials as typically American humbug. He would lose no support of his ministers as a result of the contretemps, at least as long as he split the bribe with them.

In France the question of relations with the United States produced a political crisis almost as bitter and divisive as the crisis the issue of relations with France had produced in the United States. It appeared that the French legislature, divided into two chambers, one the Council of Five Hundred and the other the Council of Elders, leaned toward favoring better relations with America; the executive, which was the Directory, consisting of five men elected one each year by the legislature, seemed to pursue a policy of hostility. But both the legislature and Directory were bitterly divided within themselves. As Marshall and Gerry arrived in Paris, the coup d'état of 18 Fructidor, on September 4, 1797, directed by Napoleon Bonaparte, produced a Directory that John Marshall saw as being under the control of directors who had instituted the most hostile measures against the United States. Although the Directory's policy seemed openly warlike, that of its foreign minister, Talleyrand, was quietly opposed to hostility and favored diplomatic gestures instead of war. However, he called himself only "the editor responsible for other people's works." He claimed he gave effect to his own views, if at all, only within the authority conferred on him as its foreign minister by the Directory. Marshall and Pinckney finally reached Paris on September 27, and Gerry joined them there a few days later.

On October 8 they met with Talleyrand for the first time, but only informally, not officially, at his home. From then on, for more than six months, Talleyrand kept the three American commissioners dangling in Paris while Napoleon consolidated his mastery of Europe, and the Directory became more hostile and warlike toward America. In January, with the three Americans still cooling their heels in Paris, the Directory adopted a harsh new decree aimed at American shipping, which would permit French ships to seize all American ships having any English goods of any kind aboard, whether such goods were contraband of war or not. It was insult direct to the already long-suffering commissioners.

The instructions the commissioners had brought with them were to carry out Hamilton's foreign policy of seeking to put an end to all French seizures, not to provoke more rigorous anti-American decrees like the new one just adopted. The instructions did not suggest much quid pro quo to offer France beyond restoring friendly relations. Yet there were a great many things Talleyrand wanted from America, mostly quid pro quo under the table. He and the Directory refused to accord to Marshall, Pinckney, and Gerry any official reception. Instead, while he kept them dangling, he sent them various agents and emissaries, including Pierre Augustin Caron de Beaumarchais, the Revolutionary War head of the secret French lend-lease program and author of *The Marriage of Figaro;* Jean Conrad Hottinguer, a Swiss financier; a Monsieur Bellamy; John Trumbull; James C. Mountflorence; Monsieur Lucien Hauteval; Nicholas Hubbard of the Dutch banking firm with which Hamilton had done business; and even Madame de Villette, the landlady of the pension where Marshall and Gerry lodged, to demand from them bribes of various sorts and loans and what not. The amount of the main bribe Talleyrand's agents demanded was one million two hundred thousand *livres,* or approximately a quarter of a million dollars, "for the purpose of making the customary distribution in diplomatic affairs" to Talleyrand himself, to the directors, and to various other officials, or so the American commissioners were told. In addition, the Americans must make them a "loan" by buying 32 million Dutch florins, paying their face value of $12.8 million, thereby giving France a profit of more than 100 percent because the discounted current market value was only $6 million.

In great indignation, the commissioners refused.

Hottinguer threatened all-out war on America. The commissioners should beware of the "power and violence of France."

The commissioners replied that if war came, the United States would defend itself.

"You do not speak to the point," Hottinguer cried. "It is money, it is expected that you will offer money."

"We have already answered that demand," the commissioners retorted.

"No you have not," Hottinguer insisted. "What is your answer?"

Charles Cotesworth Pinckney told him again with scorn: "It is no, no; not a sixpence."

And back in America, "No, no, not a sixpence!" soon became one of the great political rallying cries for the Federalist faithful.

While President Adams and Congress were waiting anxiously for some news of the mission, alarming news was coming back from Britain that the Bank of England had stopped cash payments; that sailors of the Royal Navy had mutinied; that an alliance between France, Holland, and Spain was bringing together a battle fleet larger than Britain's; and that Napoleon was poised at Boulogne, gathering a force of veterans known as the *Armée d'Angleterre,* ready to launch an invasion across the channel. It appeared that Britain indeed might fall, thereby exposing America's commerce, ships, and frontiers to the full fury of a Napoleon flushed with his greatest victory. On January 24, 1798, Adams asked his department heads to furnish him with their recommendations for dealing with these mounting threats. What should he do if France continued to rebuff the commissioners? Should he declare war? Or an embargo? What if England fell, and with her the protection her command of the seas afforded America against Napoleonic encirclement by control of Louisiana and Florida?

Should the United States seek an alliance with Britain? Would the conflict between the two great powers lead to civil war between their partisans within the United States?

On January 26, 1798, McHenry, as usual, forwarded Adams's inquiries to Hamilton for answer, entreating him "will you assist me or rather your country with such suggestions and opinions as may occur to you . . . I cannot do such justice to the subject as you can." Though heavily engaged in court in Albany, Hamilton replied within two weeks.

The first and most important point that should guide McHenry's thinking, he said, was the views of the American people. "There is a very general and strong aversion to war in the minds of the people of this country," Hamilton noted. "Next there is nothing to be gained by a formal war with France." This would "take all the chances of evil which can accrue from the vengeance of France stimulated by success." Therefore, his conclusion was that the course to be pursued was "a truly vigorous defensive plan, with the countenance of a readiness still to negotiate."

With his usual unusual prescience, Hamilton by one of his January comments anticipated exactly what would happen later in the year. Outraged by the bribe demand, Marshall and Pinckney broke off negotiations with Talleyrand, quarreled with Gerry, and left Paris in April of 1798. Gerry remained there alone as a presence and symbol of nonwarlike American intentions toward France until August. In January, Hamilton had advised McHenry that, even if rebuffed, "if one or more of our commissioners remain in Europe it may be expedient to leave him there (say in Holland) to have the air of still being disposed to meet any opening to accommodation." An embargo against France, he added, "seems now to be out of place and ineligible."

As to England, it is "best in any event to avoid *alliance*. Mutual interest will command as much from her as Treaty." With a treaty "we take all the chances of her fall. Twill be best not to be entangled." For "a truly vigorous defensive plan," Hamilton urged that, in the event of failure of the negotiations, merchant vessels should arm for defense; that the three frigates whose construction had been delayed, the *Constitution*, the *United States*, and the *Constellation*, be completed as quickly as possible; that more be built in the event of open rupture; that a number of smaller sloops of war of 10 to 20 guns each be built or converted; that a regular army of 20,000 men, including 2,000 cavalry, be raised; and that an auxiliary provisional army of 30,000 also be organized.

To support these preparedness measures, all sources of revenue should be seized, and a loan raised. "By taking a *rank* hold from the commencement, we shall the better avoid an accumulation of debt. This object is all important," Hamilton exhorted. With all this, the "hope of accommodation without open rupture ought not to be abandoned while measures of self preservation ought not to be omitted or delayed." All should be done by Adams "with *manly* but *calm* and *sedate* firmness and without strut."

As far as they went, Hamilton's recommendations generally reflected Wolcott's and Pickering's views, as well as those of Attorney General Charles Lee, but Pickering and Lee now went farther than Hamilton. Like other extreme Federalists, but not Hamilton, whose position remained moderate throughout the crisis, both contemplated seizing Louisiana from Spain before France could reacquire it. Pickering wanted to form an alliance with England. Lee recommended recall of the three commissioners and an immediate declaration of war.

McHenry rewrote Hamilton's plan with a few changes in his own hand and sent it on to Adams as his own. As it turned out, Adams's policy in the ensuing crisis closely followed the guidelines Hamilton offered in this letter. Viewed by hindsight, Adams's course hewed closer to Hamilton's policy than to that of any of the more extreme High Federalists like Pickering or Lee except in one respect that to Hamilton was as important as anything else, the matter of style. Instead of carrying out Hamilton's policy steadily, in a manner that was "solemn and manly" and "grave and firm but without invective" and, in two words, "without strut," Adams in his manner, as Hamilton saw it, seemed to oscillate back and forth between extremes of belligerency and pusillanimity. By so doing, as Hamilton saw it, he nullified the useful effects that consistent adherence to either one policy or the other might have produced. His vacillations exacerbated the provocative effects abroad and divisive effects at home that were the dangers inherent in both extremities.

Republican papers like Bache's *Aurora* kept fanning up the smoldering enmity between Hamilton and Adams by charging publicly the same thing Hamilton was so far, at least, saying only privately to insiders like McHenry: that Adams's unstable, vacillating style of leadership would entangle the country in war with France. For his address of May 15, 1797, Bache charged that Adams, foolishly believing he was under no *"extraneous influence"* had been cranked up and "fed upon pepper pot these three weeks past in order to bring his nerves to a proper anti-Gallican tone." It was Hamilton and his lackeys, the cabinet secretaries, who had warmed up their puppet president's "cold Northern constitution" to warlike bellicosity.

When the dispatches describing Talleyrand's bribe demands and other insults to the commissioner finally arrived in Philadelphia on March 4, Adams's first reaction was a lunge toward all-out war. On March 13 he asked his department heads whether he should not recommend "an immediate declaration of war." Should he whip up public enthusiasm for war by making public the whole story of French insults to the commissioners, including the bribe demands and Pinckney's "No, no, not a sixpence"? Disregarding Hamilton's more moderate advice, Adams drafted a war message to Congress denouncing the Directory. In it he demanded from Congress "a state of declared war." He was full of empty "strut."

Mere arming of vessels would not be enough. It would be inefficient and dangerous to American lives, said Adams. "All men will think it more honorable and glorious to the national character when its existence as an independent nation is at stake," Adams wrote, "that hostilities should be avowed in a formal declaration of war."

This demand of Adams for a declaration of war followed the hard, hawkish line of his secretary of state, Timothy Pickering. It ran directly counter to the advice that Hamilton was giving Pickering by his letters of March 17 and 23. He was now pleading almost desperately with both men for "solemn," "temperate," and "firm" demeanor, for an attitude of calm defiance," but no actual declaration of war. Hamilton said, "Tis vain to talk of peace with a power with which we are actually in hostility." Hamilton also repeatedly recommended that Adams seek to unite rather than divide the American people in the crisis by calling for "a day of fasting humiliation and prayer. This will be no less proper in a political than in a religious view. We must oppose to political fanaticism religious zeal." Hamilton more and more was coming to see a common fund of shared religious beliefs as an indispensable concomitant of successful American polity.

Realizing that, if nothing else, the timing of his impulsive insistence on a declaration of war from Congress would endanger the lives of his commissioners who remained in France, Adams rewrote his message, omitted from it his demand for a declaration of war, and called instead for limited hostilities. He recommended that Congress adopt most of the other measures of quasi war that Hamilton had called for. He followed the substantive program Hamilton had advised, but not his steadiness of style.

Pickering called the three commissioners home. Even though Adams, following Hamilton's recommendations, had held back his demand for a declaration of war, Jefferson called his message "insane" or almost so in its truculence. The leading Republican newspaper, Bache's *Aurora* of Philadelphia, charged that Adams had, in effect, declared war on the side of England without consulting Congress and the people. Republicans joined by some of the more extreme Federalists in Congress demanded for opposite reasons that all the deciphered dispatches from the three commissioners be laid before to the House. Some of the shrewder Congressional Republicans like William B. Giles were overheard saying, "You are doing wrong to call for those dispatches. They will injure us." Giles and Gallatin had been so successful in persuading their fellow Republicans that Adams had exaggerated the contents of the dispatches in order to whip up war fever for partisan purposes—when instead he had been withholding them —on Hamilton's advice in order to avoid having their inflammatory contents whip up war fever—that they were now powerless to halt the House's demand for them. Some militant Federalists, unhappy with Hamilton's moderate policy, also demanded the dispatches, knowing that they would serve to whip up war fever, but this did not alert the majority of Republicans to the trap into which they were rushing. But Jefferson called such Federalist support of the demand for the dispatches an intrigue of Hamilton, explaining to a bewildered Madison on April 5, 1798, that Hamilton wished to discredit Adams with the war hawk Federalists and had used Pinckney as his creature to help him out.

On April 3, Adams complied, sending over all the dispatches, but substituting for the names of Hubbard, Beaumarchais, Hottinguer, Bellamy, and Hauteval the letters *W, X, Y,* and *Z.* Congress voted that copies of the dispatches be reprinted and distributed. Wide republication whipped up American public opinion to a frenzy of outrage over the degrading bribe demand rebuffed that came

to be known in infamy as the XYZ Affair. Few forms of self-righteous indignation can match that of a newly emerging republic or supply it with more smug
self-satisfaction than that provided by the demonstration of its moral superiority
to a rich, old, would-be empire when the former's ministers are caught in the
unusual posture of rejecting the latter's bribe demand.

To Hamilton the realist, nothing would appear as greater folly than Adams's
first hasty and ill-considered strut toward a declaration of open war with France,
unless it should be Adams's failure to prepare the minds and opinions of the
people by presidential leadership toward such a war. Yet Adams's policies
seemed to be lurching toward war without foresight or plan or advice other than
his repeated call for advice from aides so inept that Hamilton had to supply them
with all the answers.

"The enlightened friend of America never saw greater occasion of disquie-
tude than at the present juncture," was the way Hamilton began a public broadside entitled "The Stand No. 1," signed *Titus Manlius*, which appeared in the
New York Commercial Advertiser on March 30, 1798. It was the first of a series
of six articles from *Titus Manlius* that would appear as the crisis continued to
deepen that spring. The people's views were what counted, and they had to be
brought around to backing the government if there were to be a war crisis.
Hamilton denounced the current French Directory dominated by Napoleon as
the most "flagitious, despotic and vindictive that ever disgraced the annals of
mankind." It was "marching with hasty and colossal strides to universal empire
in a hideous project wielding with absolute authority the whole physical force
of the most powerful nation on earth." To protect the United States against its
veteran French troops "drenched with blood and slaughter and led by a skillful
and daring chief," Hamilton called for firm support of the "respectable" defensive measures he had earlier recommended to Adams through McHenry, Pickering, and Wolcott. In "The Stand No. II," Hamilton applied Alexander Pope's
definition of "vice" to the revolutionary government of France. It was

> A MONSTER of such horrid mien,
> As to be *hated*, needs but to be *seen*.

The emotional tone of his broadsides was well calculated to bring members of
the public still open to persuasion around to backing the government, but Hamilton's summons to action did not call for anything more than limited hostilities
—quasi war.

Through the series runs an undercurrent of criticism of the style and manner of John Adams's government in dealing with the crisis: "How great is the
cause to lament," *Titus Manlius* grieved, "how afflicting to every heart, alive
to the honour and interest of the country, that distracted and inefficient councils,
a palsied and unconscious state of the public mind afford too little assurance of
measures adequate to the urgency of the evils or dangers."

Taking their cue from Jefferson, Republicans adopted the line that France
and the Directory had not been the humiliators of Marshall, Pinckney, and

Gerry; the villain was Talleyrand alone. Pickering reported to Hamilton that Bache's *Aurora* of April 7 had turned the knife of blame back on Hamilton in this ingenious way: "M. Talleyrand is notoriously anti Republican; he was the intimate friend of Mr. Hamilton, Mr. King and other great federalists." Bache concluded "that it is probably owing to the determined hostility which Talleyrand discovered in them toward France, that the government of that country considers us only objects for plunder." Jefferson detected hopeful signs of open insurrection in Pennsylvania and "inquietude" in New Hampshire and New York. Jefferson saw in Adams's sending Rufus King to make a treaty with Russia and William Smith of Maryland to make a treaty with Turkey a sinister plot to infuriate the Directory into declaring war on the United States. Adams shot back by publishing a series of addresses charging his opponents with placing loyalty to France above loyalty to their own country.

Factious divisions within the country cut deeper. War hysteria rose. Samuel Sewall of Massachusetts introduced into Congress the defense program Hamilton had outlined to McHenry. The Navy Department was created. President Adams set aside the day for fasting and prayer that Hamilton had called for. When the day came, May 9, it brought with it anti-French sermons, riots between pro-French Republican wearers of French tricolor cockades or all red Republican cockades and Federalist wearers of their recently adopted black cockade badge. The black cockade was a rose of black ribbon about four inches in diameter that resembled the cockades worn by soldiers in the American Revolution. Now black cockades were to be worn "as the open and visible sign of Federalism."

From May to August, Adams stomped about the country making demagogic speeches that linked "foreign hostility with domestic treachery." In August he told a Vermont regiment that the Directory was trying to obtain control over the American government. "Rather than this I say with you let us have war!" he cried. He whipped up another crowd shouting, "The finger of destiny writes on the wall the word: war!"

Writing privately to Wolcott on June 5, 1798, Hamilton called all such talk of Adams "indiscreet, intemperate and revolutionary." He explained, "It is not for us to breathe an irregular of violent spirit. There are limits . . . I begin to be apprehensive that he may run into indiscretion . . . some hint must be given . . . we must make no mistakes."

The new Speaker of the House matched Adams in hysteria. Jonathan Dayton announced that the troops Napoleon Bonaparte was massing in Boulogne and other French ports under the name of *Armée d'Angleterre* were not, in fact, poised to invade England, as had been thought. No, they were about to embark for an amphibious assault on the United States itself. Pickering told Robert Goodloe Harper of South Carolina that France was secretly fomenting a slave rebellion in the South and would support it with an invasion from the island colony on the western part of the island of Hispaniola, then called Saint-Domingue.

When John Marshall returned to Philadelphia on June 18, Secretary of State Pickering helped stage a hero's homecoming for him. At the banquet in Marshall's honor that night at Oeller's Hotel, the thirteenth of the 16 toasts was the one that received the loudest applause: "Millions for defense, but not one cent for tribute!" It became another Federalist rallying cry to match Pinckney's "No, no, not a sixpence!"

In June and July, Congress authorized increases in the army, the use of force against the French at sea, an embargo against French ships, and naval operations against the French everywhere on the high seas. Bache's *Aurora* accused Adams and his son John Quincy of profiteering at the expense of the people for having received $80,000 between them during a two-year period and described Adams as "old, querulous, bald, blind, crippled, toothless Adams." Stories like this led Abigail to write her sister and others in the spring of 1798 that "in any other country Bache and all his papers would have been seized. . . . Nothing will have an effect until Congress pass a sedition bill . . . If their lies were not suppressed we shall come to a civil war." Sure enough, Jefferson opposed defensive measures.

Adams and the Federalists rammed through Congress the Naturalization Act, the Alien Friends Act, and the Alien Enemy and Sedition Acts. The Naturalization Act extended the period of residence for an alien before he could become a citizen from five to 14 years. Thirty thousand Frenchmen were reputedly in the United States, and the Alien Friends Act gave Adams the power to deport any of them, as well as anybody else who was deemed to be "dangerous to the peace and safety of the United States." The Alien Enemies Act, which would apply only in the event of declared war or invasion, gave the president power to restrain, arrest, or deport enemy aliens. The Sedition Law was intended as a gag on the hostile press. It prescribed punishment by fine and imprisonment for conspiracies or scandalous statements against the government; it was to expire on the last day of Adams's term of office.

Hamilton deplored these repressive laws. "Let us not be cruel or violent," he counseled Pickering on June 7. On June 29 he wrote Wolcott that the draft of the Sedition Act was "highly exceptionable" and objectionable and "may endanger civil war." It should "not be hurried through. Let us not establish a tyranny. Energy is a very different thing from violence. If we push things to an extreme we shall then give to faction *body* and solidarity." When he complained to Pickering that, at the distance of New York City from the capital, his difficulty was that he "does not see all the cards," Pickering urged him to come to Philadelphia. He should help lead in the crisis. "I wish you were in a situation not only 'to see all the cards' but to play them," he wrote. To a better player like Hamilton, Pickering would "give you my *hand* on the same side *to win the stakes.*"

Throughout the crisis, Hamilton's policy remained one of evenhanded dealing with both Britain and France. "The same measure to both of them," he insisted, "though it should ever furnish the extraordinary spectacle of a nation at war with two nations at war with each other . . . It will evince that we are neither *Greeks* nor *Trojans.*" When Governor John Jay offered Hamilton an appointment to the United States Senate to fill the seat vacated by the appointment of John Sloss Hobart to a federal judgeship, Hamilton declined to join

Pickering in Philadelphia to play the cards from the position of a mere senator. As such he would have less influence than he already had as the undercover Federalist prime minister in New York.

When Congress finally adjourned on June 19, the formal declaration of all-out war that Adams had at first thought called for and Hamilton had feared and opposed, remained unadopted, dead, at least until the next session. Hamilton's program of defensive preparedness, not Adams's push of policy toward war remained the government's policy.

"To have a good army on foot will be the best of all precautions to prevent as well as repel invasion," Hamilton proclaimed as *Titus Manlius* in "The Stand No. VI" on April 19. But who would command such an army? Washington, of course, Hamilton and most others assumed. In a rather peremptory Dutch Uncle fashion on May 19, Hamilton wrote him, telling him he would have to assume command and how best to go about it. Washington should first make a ceremonial circuit through Virginia and North Carolina "which would throw the weight of your character into the scale of government." Then, "in the event of an open rupture the public voice will again call you to command the armies of your country . . . you will be compelled to make the sacrifice." Washington in command again would "give an additional spring to the public mind."

Washington groaned. He replied that though he would have no choice but to return to public life if called, he would do so with "as much reluctance . . . as I should do to the tombs of my ancestors." He flatly refused to go out on the Southern junket. Hamilton replied on June 2, satisfied that at least he would not refuse to serve as commander in an "adequate emergency." As for himself, Hamilton added, "if I am invited *to a station in which the sacrifice I may render is proportioned to the sacrifice I am to make,* I shall be willing to go into the army. If you command," said Hamilton, his own place ought to be "Inspector General with a command in the line."

Here now was dealt a hand to be played for the highest command in the land below Washington's own. In other national games, faithful subalterns like Pickering, McHenry, and Wolcott in Philadelphia could play his cards for him well enough, given feedback time for signals from him in New York. But in the command game now for the highest stake of his life, he would play his own hand. At the end of June, he journeyed to Philadelphia so he could not only "see all the cards" but play them. Shortly before he left New York, he had written to Betsy in Albany that "I continue to enjoy good health and my spirits are as good as they can be in absence of my love." He went on, "But I find as I grow older her presence becomes more necessary to me. In proportion as I discover the worthlessness of other pursuits, the value of my Eliza and of domestic happiness rises in my estimation." Nevertheless, his closing line to her was of other pursuits: "There is every prospect that we shall not put on the French yoke."

Under the urgings of Hamilton and others, Congress finally authorized the president to increase the regular army, in accordance with tables of organization largely laid out by Hamilton, by an "additional army" of 10,000 men and also to call up a "Provisional Army" of 50,000 more, including 12 infantry regiments of

700 men each and six troops of light dragoons, but only when and if full scale war should begin or when the president decided that national security was threatened by invasion. Congress also authorized calling 80,000 militia to active duty if necessary. A formal declaration of war would thus automatically lead to the calling up of an army many times larger than any Washington had commanded at any time during the Revolution.

By July 4, Washington still had not received the word that Adams had appointed him lieutenant general and commander in chief of the new army. He wrote the secretary of war and the president to say that, if called to serve, he demanded a free hand in naming his principal subordinate officers whom he "considered as so many parts of the commander in chief." Adams looked to Washington for advice as to whether to rely on "old generals . . . or appoint a young set?" Washington said selections must be made "without respect to grade." To McHenry, Washington insisted still more emphatically that he must have the choice of his own staff of officers. Some he had in mind, like Hamilton, he thought would not agree to serve under anyone but him. Writing Washington from Philadelphia on July 8, Hamilton was critical of Adams for having announced Washington's appointment publicly and and having it ratified by the Senate all without having received Washington's prior consent to serve.

Another problem to Hamilton was that Adams "has no relative ideas and his prepossessions on military subjects in reference to such a point are of the wrong sort." It was essential that all arrangements be "such as you would approve."

Washington approved.

Secretary of State Pickering urged upon Washington that Hamilton rank second only to him "and Chief in your absence." Hamilton would not and ought not to serve in a lower capacity. All felt unspoken, or spoke of, concern for who might succeed to the supreme command should the aging and infirm Washington be disabled or die. Washington must place Hamilton next to himself because, said Pickering, President Adams was all for giving him a lower place.

Washington agreed that Hamilton's services "ought to be secured at almost any price." Almost. The difficulty was that any French invasion would strike at the southern coast below Maryland. It was the part weakest, most partisan, closest to French possessions, full of sullen, rebellious slaves eager to be armed against their masters. This southern strategy suggested that General Charles Cotesworth Pinckney of South Carolina should be first of the generals. He enjoyed high military and public reputation and influential family connections, was indispensable to Southern resistance, and, being senior in rank to Hamilton from the Revolution, would probably refuse to serve under him now. However, Pinckney was still over in France, and if he would not be returning soon, Hamilton might be preferred.

Intrigues and counterintrigues roiled the Federalist inner circle. President Adams was still posing as if he believed that it was he who had final say in his administration's appointments to commands and offices. An early inkling of his error should have come when he consulted Pickering on the appointments.

"Whom shall we appoint Commander in Chief?" he asked.

"Colonel Hamilton," answered Pickering flatly.

"Oh no! It is not his turn by a great deal," said Adams. "I would sooner appoint Gates or Lincoln or Morgan."

"No," Pickering replied. "General Morgan is now here in Congress, a very sick man, with one foot in the grave." And "as for Gates, he is now an old woman —and Lincoln is always asleep."

After spending five days with Washington at Mount Vernon, McHenry brought back to President Adams word of Washington's acceptance of command as well as a private and confidential letter that would have surprised and gratified Hamilton. Washington expressed "love and esteem" for Knox, but ranked him below both Pinckney and Hamilton. Although Washington's tentative list of general officers put Hamilton first, he was fearful lest Pinckney, if made junior to Hamilton, would refuse to serve. Anyhow, President Adams must "use his pleasure." Washington hoped all three would place national welfare above personal ranking. It was an unfounded hope. When McHenry brought the list in to Adams while he was at breakfast with Abigail on July 17, Adams questioned McHenry sharply. McHenry insisted the order of names was the one Washington had insisted on. Adams wrote out the list for submission to the Senate with the names in Washington's order. To the list, which included a number of other names, Adams added that of his son-in-law, William S. Smith of New York to be a brigadier general and adjutant general. Pickering and McHenry strongly objected to Smith, but Adams stood fast.

Washington told Hamilton that he wanted his former aide as "coadjutor and assistant" (whatever his relative ranking might be), but was frank to point out the obvious problem that if Hamilton were to be made senior major general, he would have to be leapfrogged over the heads of the other senior major generals, Knox and Pinckney, who had far outranked him at the end of the Revolution. Adams completely agreed. He held up issuing the commissions.

In Philadelphia, Pickering loyally reported to Hamilton all he had done to help his promotion along. Hamilton replied to Pickering by letter on July 17 that he was "content to be second to Knox, if *thought indispensable. Pinckney*, if placed over me puts me a grade lower . . . I am willing that the relative ranks may remain open to future settlement . . . I am not satisfied with the principle that every officer of higher rank in the late army is to be above me . . . this will not accord with my own opinions of my own pretensions." Public opinion was of great importance: a rank below the highest would "fall far short of public opinion." Few had made as many sacrifices as he. To few others "would a military appointment be so injurious as to myself—if with this sacrifice, I am to be degraded below my just claim in public opinion—ought I to acquiesce?" He would if he had to accept second, but not third place.

The Senate approved the list of appointees in the order presented, with Hamilton's name listed first. It rejected William S. Smith, and Adams would add that to his score of grievances against Hamilton. Adams went home to Quincy without having signed the generals' commissions. By July 29, Hamilton was becoming increasingly impatient and annoyed with what he saw as further proof of Adams's wavering, indecisiveness, incompetence and, indeed, personal hostility toward himself. He wrote Washington: "With regard to the delicate subject of the relative rank of major generals, it is very natural for me to be a partial judge, and it is not very easy for me to speak upon it." But public opinion drove him to do so: "In a case like this, am I not to take the opinion of others as my guide? It is a fact, there is a flood of evidence that a great majority of leading federal men were of opinion, that in the event of your declining command of the army, it ought to devolve upon me, and that in case of your acceptance, which everybody ardently desired, the place of second in command ought to be mine."

There was another side to it, Hamilton added, that was "of far greater moment" than the relative rank of the general officers. That was "that my friend McHenry, is wholly insufficient for his place, with additional misfortune of not having himself the least suspicion of the fact!"

True as it was—Hamilton had the evidence, in all of McHenry's appeals to him for help—it was a rather shocking thing for Hamilton to say about his loyal, old, admiring friend, McHenry. But by saying so here in his letter to Washington, he was leading from his strongest suit. All acknowledged his abilities as an administrator, if not as a commanding general. He went on, "You perhaps may not be aware of the whole extent of the insufficiency." He knew Washington knew McHenry well—"It is so great as to leave no probability that the business of the War Department can make any tolerable progress in his hands." This was particularly true in view of "the large scale upon which he is now to act."

Obviously, neither Knox nor Pinckney had the administrative skill to plug up such a large insufficiency in a crisis, in which ultimate blame for the results of any insufficiency would inevitably fall on Washington. Coming to Philadelphia, Hamilton now was playing his hand for all it was worth.

"My real friendship for McHenry concurring with my zeal for service predisposed me to aid him in all that he could properly throw upon me . . . the organization of the army . . . the conduct of the recruiting service," Hamilton wrote. But there remained much to do. "The idea had been thus far very partially embraced." Without first place in formal rank and status, Hamilton could not be properly useful. The mere thought of trying to preside himself with credit over such a large new enterprise with no coadjutors but the inept McHenry, an aging limited Knox, and a remote Pinckney must have made the reluctant Washington shudder. It would be all aging chiefs and no young Indians. Hamilton knew the strength of the card he was leading. He zealously kept helping out McHenry. To bring matters to a head, he suggested that Washington summon the major generals to Philadelphia to begin contingency planning for the war. But Knox still insisted on clear rank over Hamilton and Pinckney. Adams, mindful of the political damage his rebuff to Knox would do in his own New England, finally made up his mind to issue the commissions. He made Knox the senior major general.

He thought he saw a clever way out of the impasse with Washington by declaring that the Senate's order of nomination of the major generals meant nothing. What governed was "rank according to antecedent services." This way,

Hamilton, of course, would have no rank above any other major general and no command in the line. Adams was "willing to settle all decisively" by dating the commissions in order of Knox first, Pinckney second, Hamilton third.

Such power was in the president, and he was ready to exercise it. "Any other plan will occasion long delay and confusion," he said. "The five New England states will not patiently submit to the humiliation that has been meditated for them" if Knox were put third. If the question went back to Washington, it would be further vexed. "In spite of all meddling with relative rank of generals," Adams declared firmly and boldly, "I foresee it will come to me at last, after much . . . exasperation of passions and I shall then determine it exactly as I should now—Knox, Pinckney and Hamilton."

Learning from McHenry of Adams's final decision, Hamilton, perhaps recalling that earlier brinkmanship—resignation of his commission in protest had ultimately won him his command at Yorktown—wrote the secretary of war on September 8, "My mind is unalterably made up. I shall certainly not hold the commission on the plan proposed."

Letters crisscrossed; injunctions of senders to burn them lest embarrassment follow went unheeded. Washington learned from McHenry that Adams had reversed Washington's own order of ranking. But to hear it from him officially, Washington addressed an unusually long letter to Adams, reiterating his reasons for placing Hamilton's name first. He all but said he would resign himself if his wishes were disregarded. Once again, he gave Hamilton a striking and discerning testimonial. He pointed out that although Hamilton had never been a general officer, yet "as the principal and most confidential Aid of the Commander in Chief" he could survey the scene of war more broadly than could a division or brigade commander. His civil posts like the Treasury were further entitlements. "By some," said Washington, "he is considered as an ambitious man, and therefore a dangerous one. That he is ambitious I shall readily grant, but it is of that laudable kind which prompts a man to excel in whatever he takes in hand. He is enterprising, quick in his perceptions, and his judgement intuitively great; qualities essential to a military character, . . . his loss will be irreparable."

Events shoved Adams unhappily toward one of the most distasteful reversals of his life.

Washington had written stiffly, "I have addressed you, Sir, with openness and candor, and I hope with respect, requesting to be informed, whether your determination to reverse the order of the three Major-Generals is final . . ." The implication was clear: Washington might resign himself.

To prideful President Adams it must have come as a shock that, like his party in Congress and his principal department heads, his commander in chief was also under the thumb of the upstart outsider in New York. Unlike Adams's descent from an ancient "virtuous and irreproachable race of people," in whom he took great pride, Hamilton, said Adams, was nothing but "a bastard bratt of a Scotch Pedlar."

Cursing Hamilton, Adams caved in to him. He was not the man to stand against Washington and the "Triumvirate"—as he called Pickering, McHenry, and Wolcott. Adams dated all three major generals' commissions the same day, explaining ingenuously to Washington that he had done so "in hopes, similar to yours, that an amicable adjustment, or acquiescence, might take place among the gentlemen themselves. But, if these hopes should be disappointed and controversies should arise, they will, of course, be submitted to you as Commander-in-Chief, and if, after all any one should be so obstinate as to appeal to me from the judgment of the Commander-in-Chief, I was determined to confirm that judgment."

This was either incredibly ingenuous or ingenious; it saved face all around and fudged the question of ultimate responsibility. Washington promptly made Hamilton second to himself in titular command. This meant first in actual command, at least until Congress should formally declare war. He would be the quasi commander of the Quasi War.

Henry Knox, fat and old and sick, struggling under intense personal pressures from creditors to pay debts that "must be paid or General Lincoln and myself must both be committed to goal [sic]," was still not yet ready to fade away. He refused to serve under Hamilton. His plaint to McHenry could be read as another Hamilton testimonial: ". . . Mr. Hamilton's talents have been estimated upon a scale of comparison so transcendent, that all his seniors in rank and years of the late army, have been degraded by his elevation." Knox could not "act under a constant sense of public insult and injury."

Charles Cotesworth Pinckney, known as the greatest gentleman of the age, declared to McHenry, "It was with the greatest pleasure I saw his name at the head of the list of the major-generals, and applauded the discrimination that had placed him there." Pinckney immediately sent Hamilton word that he was gratified to serve under him, adding that he would have also yielded place to Knox, had not the latter insisted so strongly on precedence.

In a personal letter a few months later, Hamilton tried to soothe his former friend Knox by saying he had struggled between attachment for Knox "and the impression of duty," to accept the responsibility for which he had been chosen by others. But Knox remained irreconcilable. He joined Jefferson and Adams in laying yet another slur on Hamilton's origins only a little less venomous than theirs: He told a friend of "the insult offered me . . . The faction [,] the miserable animals who were the cause of it [,] are known to me, and ere long they will be compelled to hide their heads in their original obscurity."

Knox's pain saddened Hamilton. Through McHenry he had earlier urged Knox to accept, letting him reserve the right to claim his superior rank dating from the Revolution. Although Hamilton felt that sentiment in the country justified him in standing fast, rather than embarrass Washington, he was willing to consent to an arrangement that would place Knox first to appease him.

In the end, it turned out to be Pickering, not Hamilton, who had made the surprise play that won his leader the appointment to the first place. "Altho', by the delay of the nominations one day," he wrote Hamilton, "I received your letter expressing your willingness to serve under Knox, yet I concealed it, in order that the arrangement of nominations . . . by Genl Washington . . . which I saw would govern, might leave you . . . in the first place."

McHenry wrote Hamilton on October 5, 1798: "The sun begins to shine." To which Hamilton responded: "I cannot but observe with satisfaction the conclusion of your letter as to the relative rank of the three major-generals."

It was a characteristic use of understatement by Hamilton to express much satisfaction. No brighter beams of sunshine to burn away the miasmic suspicions with which *The Reynolds Pamphlet* had enshrouded his public honor could be imagined than the gleam reflected from the brand-new major general's stars pinned on Hamilton's epaulets by Adams's unwilling hands, forced to put them there by Washington's invisible hand still guided by Hamilton's invisible hand.

By way of clinching his comeback, Hamilton forced Adams to yield on yet another seemingly less important issue. Adams had nominated Aaron Burr, for whom he had high regard, for the rank of brigadier general. Hamilton and his triumvirate reminded Washington that Burr was an "intriguer." Washington vetoed Burr's name, on the ground that Burr was an intriguer.

Hamilton, through the cabinet and Washington, calling Burr an intriguer? Adams all but atomized in choleric bursts of outrage at such procacity.

He was still fulminating years later. "How shall I describe to you my sensations and reflections at the moment?" he spluttered splenetically. Washington "compelled me to promote, over the heads of Lincoln, Gates, Clinton, and Knox and . . . Pinckney, one of his own triumvirate, the most restless, impatient, artful, indefatigable and unprincipled intriguer in the United States, if not in the world, to be second in command under himself."

And now, in Aaron Burr, Hamilton, that "bastard brat," "dreaded an intriguer in a poor brigadier."

All the same, Adams was not allowed to appoint Aaron Burr, the Reynoldses' lawyer, or even his own son-in-law, William S. Smith, to the rank of brigadier. A big winner like Hamilton might have been wiser to let losers like Adams and Burr and Smith win a few little throwaway cards like these.

He had played the cards he held for all they were worth and then some and had a little winner's luck besides to reescalade to quasi command of the quasi war. Having won out, on July 9, the night before leaving Philadelphia for home, he wrote Betsy a letter, as a quasi commander should, in a very commanding tone: "I command you as you love me to take care of yourself, to keep up your spirits, and to remember always that my happiness is inseparable from yours." Like a small boy with a new toy, in the closing line he added that Decatur's capture of a 12-gun French privateer "gives general satisfaction." Oh yes, and "God bless my beloved. A. Hamilton."

23

WITHOUT STRUT?

YOU CAN HARDLY CONCEIVE WHAT A POWERFUL INTEREST IS MADE
FOR HAMILTON . . . THAT MAN WOULD IN MY MIND BECOME A
SECOND BUONAPARTY IF HE WAS POSSESSED OF EQUAL POWER.
—*Abigail Adams to William S. Smith, July 7, 1798*

Nature abhors a vacuum. By nature, Hamilton abhorred a power vacuum. Adams's eight years of on-the-job training for the powerful office of the presidency had been as a powerless, unconsulted, do-nothing vice-president who spent half the year at home up in Quincy, at least four days' journey from the capital, except when the Senate happened to be in fitful session. It seemed to Hamilton that Adams, when he succeeded to the presidency, brought to the first office all the slack habits and "desultoriness" he had learned in the second. It is hardly an exaggeration to say that two such men would drive each other crazy.

To a nature like Hamilton's, a man like Adams was a walking, talking, breathing power vacuum who fitfully spouted fire. As soon as Congress adjourned on July 19, 1798, with the war crisis and the political divisions within the country becoming more and more menacing, John and Abigail Adams set off northward as usual for Quincy. But the warlike line Adams had been taking toward France had for the first time in his life won him a measure of popularity with the people, or at least Federalist people.

Testimonial receptions and dinners at towns along his and Abigail's northward route fed his vanity. He loved it and responded with ripsnorting speeches that whipped up listeners' enthusiasm for a declaration of all-out war. The journey was long, hot, and tiresome, and by the time the Adamses arrived in Quincy, Abigail had fallen seriously ill.

While they remained there during the long dispute over Hamilton's appointment as inspector general, which was not finally resolved until October, Hamilton did not so much usurp or seize power in the capital as simply lay hold on slack reins as Adams idly let them slip through his fingers. Hamilton's subalterns Pickering, McHenry, and Wolcott, secretaries of state, war, and the treasury—and, to a lesser extent, Benjamin Stoddard, secretary of the navy, and Charles Lee, the attorney general—all sought out his views. So did so-called High Federalists in Congress, men influential in their states like George Cabot, Stephen Higginson, Theodore Sedgwick, Fisher Ames, and Philip Schuyler and others. Rufus King, Hamilton's minister in London, kept him informed of developments abroad. Hamilton was the leader of a strong Federalist party in his home city and state and nation, a potential future presidential candidate, and the most visible target for all Republican abuse.

From the abstracted distance of Mount Vernon, Washington told Hamilton pointedly to "Give, without delay, your *full* aid to the Secretary of War." After the long delay over the question of command, Hamilton set to work.

One conventional view of Hamilton, as most recently set forth by Professor Richard H. Kohn in his book *Eagle and Sword: The Beginnings of the Military Establishment in America,* is that Hamilton was the leader of a small group that "embraced militarism completely; the standing army was in their minds the last anchor for Constitution and government, for their values, for political intimidation, for patronage, and to enhance their own personal power." According to Professor Kohn, Hamilton did not fear armies as most others of his countrymen did. "He loved them, lusted for military command, and never spoke out against the standing army in peacetime unless such a statement became politically obligatory. . . . Throughout his career he exploited armies or force for political gain . . . Alexander Hamilton was the personification of American militarism." This, of course, ignores Hamilton's secret inward need after 1797 and the Reynolds disclosures to reescalade somehow back into public credit.

Yet even the harshest critics of Hamilton in this personification, like Professor Kohn, acknowledge that, if a national army were necessary for America (not seeming to agree that it is), Hamilton had more to do with its creation than anyone else.

"Hamilton created the American military establishment," Professor Kohn admits in *Eagle and Sword,* "as its chief spokesman in Congress in 1783 and its chief public defender during the struggle to ratify the Constitution in 1788. From 1792 to 1794, he helped put the War Department on a sound administrative footing." But, Professor Kohn adds cryptically, "No one posed a greater danger to the nation's emerging military tradition." Only if by this Professor Kohn is referring to the possibility that after 1797 Hamilton's reescalade might overtop all bounds of reason (if he is he leaves it unstated), could this writer agree with him that Hamilton posed a danger to the emerging American military tradition. Through 1797, at least, Hamilton contributed more cogent thought and action to the subject of the American military establishment and the emerging American military tradition than anyone else.

As the Revolution dwindled to a close in 1783, the unpaid Continental Army, after some brushes with mutiny to enforce its claims that Hamilton helped forfend, melted back into civilian life and all but disappeared as a standing army, reduced to about 600 rank and file under command of Henry Knox, guarding leftover stores at West Point and Springfield, Massachusetts, and reoccupying New York City as civilian officials reestablished Continental rule. The question of what to do about a civilian army was assigned by Congress in April 1783 to a committee, of which Hamilton was chairman, consisting also of James Madison, James Wilson, Samuel Osgood, and Oliver Ellsworth, "to provide a system for foreign affairs, for Indian affairs, and for military and naval establishments."

Though peace was breaking out, Hamilton agreed with his friend John Jay, a negotiator of the peace treaty with Britain and, after 1784, the Confederation's secretary for foreign affairs, who said: "That nations should make war against nations is less surprising than their living in uninterrupted peace and harmony."

It was easy enough for Jay to talk in this usual Olympian way of his, but the practical matter of the future of the American military establishment had been dumped in Hamilton's lap. He promptly solicited expert views from Washington, under whose authority the views of Inspector General von Steuben, Chief of Artillery Henry Knox, Quartermaster General Timothy Pickering, Secretary at War Benjamin Lincoln, Governor George Clinton of New York, and others were commandeered. Hamilton fashioned them all into a concise but comprehensive "Report on a Military Peace Establishment," which he submitted to Congress on June 18, 1783. Hamilton was the chairman and leading military expert of the congressional committee, with by far the most wartime combat and staff experience. This report for better or worse, is the basis of Hamilton's claim to being father of the American military establishment.

Without dissent, all military experts whose opinion Hamilton obtained recommended the establishment of a national army—despite the existence of the militia, despite the Confederation's slight financial resources, in order to protect the frontiers, to defend settlers and property there against the Indians, and to maintain internal order in extreme situations.

But would not the militia be enough for these functions?

No, von Steuben snorted, recommending a horse guard to protect the government and adding, "Congress and its followers should never be exposed to the Mad proceedings of a Mob." The country also needed the skeleton of a regular army in peacetime to serve as a model for expansion into wartime armies. Hamilton reported, "There are conclusive reasons in favor of federal in preference to state establishments." But the federal military establishment recommended by Hamilton's civilian congressional committee had been less extensive than those recommended by Washington and the other experts. If Hamilton's motive in championing a peacetime military establishment had been to serve his own political aggrandizement, for patronage, or some other such unworthy purpose conventionally ascribed by scholars to him as their chief horrific exemplar of American militarism, would not his recommendations have sought a larger military establishment or one at least as extensive as those of the other military experts, whose purposes, being narrower, are spared similar *ad hominem* attack?

There was not the slightest doubt among the majority at the Constitutional Convention that the new government had to be able to create a standing army and navy. When the "raise armies" clause was considered in August 1787, the convention changed the wording to "raise and support" to make the authority for peacetime national forces unmistakable. Gouverneur Morris, chairman of the Committee of Style, of which Hamilton was a member at the Constitutional Convention, writing to Moss Kent on January 2, 1815, remembered that "those, who, during the Revolutionary storm, had confidential acquaintance with the conduct of affairs"—his friend Hamilton had more than any other member of his committee—"knew well that to rely on militia was to lean on a broken reed."

Hamilton's Numbers 8, 16, and 22 through 29 of *The Federalist* are largely devoted to the same subject. Hamilton characteristically begins with first principles in No. 23: "Whether there ought to be a Federal Government intrusted with the care of the common defence, is a question in the first instance open to discussion; but the moment it is decided in the affirmative, it will follow, that that government ought to be cloathed with all the powers requisite to the execution of its trust . . . if we are in earnest about giving the Union energy and duration, we must abandon the vain project of legislating upon the states in their collective capacities; we must extend the laws of the Federal Government to the individual citizens of America."

Hamilton, the champion of the people's rights, sympathized with their traditional fear of militarism and standing armies. As Hamilton explains in No. 26, such fear arose in England after the Norman Conquest, when "the authority of the Monarch was almost unlimited," and his standing armies encroached on the liberties of the people. But after the "revolution in 1688, which elevated the Prince of Orange to the throne, the kingly prerogative was abolished, and it became an article of the Bill of Rights then framed that the raising or keeping a standing army within the kingdom in time of peace, *unless with consent of Parliament* was against law." The same power of restraint was created for the American people by the constitutional provisions restricting military appropriations to two years, Hamilton pointed out. This obliges Congress "once at least in every two years, to deliberate upon the propriety of keeping a military force on foot; to come to a new resolution on the point; and to declare their sense of the matter, by a formal vote in the face of their constituents. They are not *at liberty* to vest in the executive department permanent funds for the support of an army." To Hamilton, we, the people, through our elected representatives in Congress, remain always supreme. As if by prescript, in reply to the conventional cavils of critics, Hamilton adds dryly in No. 26, "The provision for the support of a military force will always be a favourable topic for declamation."

If we, the people, not the states, are sovereign, Hamilton, argues, as he did at the Constitutional Convention, it becomes necessary to "discard the fallacious scheme of quotas and requisitions [of militia, and so forth] as equally impracticable and unjust." It follows "that the Union ought to be invested with full power to levy troops; to build and equip fleets, and to raise the revenues, which will be required for the formation and support of an army and navy, in the customary and ordinary modes practiced in other governments."

"The fabric of American Empire," he counsels in No. 22, "ought to rest on the solid basis of THE CONSENT OF THE PEOPLE. The streams of national power ought to flow immediately from that pure original fountain of all legitimate authority." In No. 25, he adds that a prohibition against the *"raising* of armies in time of peace . . . would exhibit the most extraordinary spectacle, which the world has yet seen—that of a nation incapacitated by its constitution to prepare for defence, before it was actually invaded. . . . We must receive the blow before we could even prepare to return it. We must expose our property and liberty to the mercy of foreign invaders, and invite them, by our weakness, to seize the naked and defenceless as prey."

Hamilton's military peace establishment was to consist of only four regiments of infantry and one of artillery incorporated in the Corps of Engineers. Each infantry regiment would consist of two battalions, each battalion of four companies, each company of 64 rank and file, to be recruited up to 128 rank and file in time of war. His total force of 2,048 peacetime infantrymen would hardly be an awe-inspiring juggernaut. Yet its mission was to protect thousands of miles of frontiers and interior territories that extended from the farthest reaches of Maine, west beyond Fort Michilimackinac, to Lake of the Woods in Minnesota, down the Mississippi to Louisiana, east to Florida, and up all the continental coastal reaches northward back to Maine. If such a tiny army did not get itself lost in so vast a sector of operations, it would at least have enough room in which to disperse itself to keep it out of mischievous schemes for overthrowing a duly constituted national government—whose personnel outnumbered it. Congress finally approved a plan similar to Hamilton's recommendation in June 1794, and this led to creation of the Legion—the first real American peacetime military establishment.

Hamilton did his best to raise and outfit the Quasi War army from practically nothing in the face of public apathy and partisan hostility. Republicans with few exceptions stood sullenly apart. In his own party, Adams after his humiliation on the generalships, was bitterly hostile to Hamilton. The temper of the people did not favor a standing army. As usual, it was harder to recruit privates than generals for service in an undeclared war in what still appeared to be a time of peace. Hamilton had to conjure up training manuals and recruits both at the same time.

Much of the work was routine, or confined him to petty details that subordinates far down the line could as easily have dispatched, had there been such subordinates. Hamilton had only a single aide, his nephew, Angelica and John Church's son, Captain Philip Church. He took care of copying dispatches and as much of the other office detail work as he could manage. A secretary was later added to the staff, but a large proportion of the reports and other communications, many dealing with trivial matters, are written in Hamilton's own hand. James McHenry, the secretary of war, who had been at least nominally responsible for the prior neglect of preparedness, seemed incapable of managing a preparedness program on any new enlarged scale.

Hamilton gave his old friend a tactful lecture on how to administer a large government department. Depute responsibility to those below, he said. Do not waste your own time dealing with minor matters: "Present to consideration this important rule, that the efficient execution of any extensive branch of military service can only be . . . by confining the principal actors to general arrangement, & by . . . employing competent organs and leaving to them the more minute details."

Hamilton shifted to oblique stimulation. He suggested to Washington that he ask McHenry for an inventory of supplies and munitions and a statement of future needs. "This will give you necessary information, and prompt McHenry to exertion," he explained. Hamilton assured Washington there would be no want of exertion on his own part, but cautioned, "I more and more . . . apprehend that obstacles of a very peculiar kind stand in the way of an efficient and successful management. . . ." He could not explain at present, but in future confidential reports he would substitute code letters for the name of the president and the cabinet members. Criticism of three of his oldest and most loyal friends, and his leading current enemy came more easily when he encoded them as *X, Y* and *Z.*

Washington agreed with Hamilton as to "the unfitness of a certain Gentleman for the office he holds." He was willing to tell McHenry to permit Hamilton to take full charge of matters that would ordinarily belong to the War Department, not to an inspector general. General Gunn wrote Hamilton:

> I am persuaded it can be no part of your plan merely to execute the feeble arrangements of other men. The President has no Talent for War, and McHenry is an infant in detail, and, if I am correct, Genl. Washington is not to take the field, but in the event of the provisional army being called into Service—you are of course not only charged with the command of the army, but, in a great degree, the direction of the War Department . . .

Hamilton forwarded to Wolcott in confidence a copy of the program he had submitted to McHenry earlier for providing and issuing military supplies: "Make the Secretary of War talk to you about it, without letting him know that I have sent it to you. And urge . . . some plan which will effectually organize this important branch. . . ."

Hamilton explained to Wolcott that although it would have suited his professional convenience and his law clientele to remain inactive in the beginning like the other general officers, he nevertheless felt obliged to aid McHenry, who was unable to cope with mobilization by himself. In his recent advice to McHenry, he had "sacrificed . . . delicacy to . . . friendship & public zeal," begging that the secretary apportion duties to others and keep himself free for "a general but vigilant superintendence." Wolcott urged Hamilton to come on at once, "with the expectation of being Secy of War in fact."

Of Hamilton's energetic reemergence as both civilian and military commander of the quasi war, Hamtramck said, "America will see once more these military talents which were confined in their execution to too small a compass . . . now diffuse themselves into every Department. . . ."

McHenry, acknowledging that his own talents were "unequal to great exertions or deep resources," at least by comparison with Hamilton's, was only too happy to follow Hamilton's advice and depute most of the work of his department. He deputed it to Hamilton. He requested him, among many other things, to draft all the bills for the provisional army that were to be submitted to Congress. "Permit me . . . to request," began a typical communication, "that laying aside other business you will occupy yourself on the two military bills only. . . . If possible, let me have the bills by Monday's mail or at furthest Tuesday's." These bills were the basis for the laws passed by Congress expanding the military establishment.

McHenry, still the "principal actor," would confine himself to "general arrangement," employ a "competent organ," and leave to him the more "minute details." Thus by Hamilton's own unexceptionable administrative precept, responsibility for such minute details as the color of artillerymen's buttons, the cockaded corners on hats of recruits, and the medication for boils on drummer boys' necks would devolve on Hamilton, McHenry's supremely competent, but perilously overworked administrative organ.

Hamilton's health was failing during this hectic period and several times slowed his work or confined him to his bed, but throughout the yellow fever epidemic that gripped New York and Philadelphia in 1798, he tried to remain on the job. There is no record that his fevers were specifically nervous derangements or disorders, but it would not be surprising if they were, as they had been during many past summer periods of plagues and heavy pressures.

The most painful thing about all these labors of Hamilton through sickness and health was that he was not billing or getting paid for any of them. He had acquiesced in President Adams's request that the generals receive no pay until called into actual service. In October 1798 he was summoned to Philadelphia for six weeks to confer with the commander in chief and the secretary of war, and by the first of the new year 1799, he had forfeited most of the income from his law practice. What remained was fast melting away. "Were I rich," the inspector general wrote McHenry in desperation, "I should be proud to be silent on such a subject," but he was not. With a wife and six children to support, he would be obliged to reduce his sacrifices to the public unless his army pay, small at best, should immediately commence. McHenry's executive talents were at least equal to acting on the realization that he must act swiftly or he might lose his mentor-deputy, who spared him all big decisions as well as all minute details. His reply, by return mail, fixed Hamilton's pay and emoluments; President Adams directed that he be considered formally on duty from November 1, 1798, at a salary, with allowances for subsistence and forage, of $268.35 a month, less than one fourth of what he had recently been earning as a preeminent Wall Street lawyer.

McHenry wondered whether it might be advisable to withdraw troops from the southern and western frontiers to guard the seaboard. Hamilton thought not, counseling against doing so on December 13. But troop dispositions in the west and south required careful rethinking. Brigadier General James Wilkinson, the commander of the western army, should be directed to return to Philadelphia for conferences on these matters.

A lifelong master of the art of serving more masters than one, Wilkinson during the Revolution had helped foment the Conway cabal against Washington and Hamilton or, depending on how one interpreted his role, expose it. Whatever his real role may have been, he was the most experienced marplot Hamilton could possibly have found. With very few troops in his command, he dispensed a fuzzy brand of diplomacy on the vague western frontiers with Spain, treated with a heterogeneous collection of independent local entrepreneurs of independence there, and played off angry tribes of Indians, who regarded all later comers as hostile interlopers, against the Spaniards, British, French, and American settlers, and each other.

Wilkinson's contacts with the Spanish authorities called for him to act as a diplomat as well as a commander. Hamilton distrusted him, but thought he could make use of his peculiar talents. He ordered Wilkinson's reports sent back open to the secretary of war for reforwarding to him and wrote McHenry's letter informing Wilkinson of this arrangement. There are many corrections in Hamilton's draft of the orders summoning Wilkinson from the Mississippi to the capital for personal conferences. The American situation vis-à-vis foreign powers, Hamilton explained carefully, made such discussions at the seat of government necessary. In deputing military authority in his absence, Wilkinson must warn his subordinates against any act that would inadvertently entangle the United States in war. Opening his official correspondence with the inspector general, Wilkinson replied with obsequious, ironic pomposity of "the high satisfaction I feel, at finding myself under orders of a Gentleman, able to instruct me in all things." Such flattery did not make Hamilton less suspicious of him. It is not known whether Hamilton knew for certain at the time a fact that later historical discoveries confirmed, that Wilkinson, the American commander of the whole vast western area, was also in the pay of Spain.

On January 24, Hamilton told McHenry how the orders dividing up other commands between himself and Pinckney should read. Hamilton would command "all the troops and posts north of Maryland"; and General Pinckney, all to the south. All the separate commands on the Great Lakes, the Miami River, and in Tennessee and supreme command of the western army should also "be placed under the superintendence of the Inspector General."

This meant that General Charles Cotesworth Pinckney, from headquarters at Shepherdstown, Virginia, had command of all troops in Virginia, the Carolinas, Georgia, and Kentucky, whereas Hamilton, based mostly in his office at 26 Broadway and occasionally at the capital in Philadelphia, had command of the far-flung garrisons on the Great Lakes, in the Northwest Territories, on both banks of the Ohio, down the Mississippi, and in all states from Maryland north and eastward to the remotest reaches of Maine. He committed the artillery to his trusted friend from Revolutionary days Major Louis Tousard, with Major Hoops and Captain George Izard as his deputies. Command of the cavalry was entrusted to Brigadier General William Washington and Lieutenant John de-Barth Walbach, who were stationed with General Pinckney at his Shepherds-town headquarters. To complete the final implementation of Jay's Treaty, Hamilton commissioned Major J. J. U. Rivardi, commanding at Niagara, to make a wide-ranging survey of the whole northern region for both defense and trade purposes and to report back to him in person.

Scanning the American frontiers of the new world beyond his far-flung command from his New York and Philadelphia offices as supreme quasi commander of the quasi war for opportunities as well as weak spots, Hamilton's piercing gaze would pause to contemplate the military and political situation in the French colony of Saint-Domingue and the Spanish possessions of Louisiana and the Floridas. At one time, the territory claimed by the French on the western third of the island five years and more earlier (before the 1793 slave revolts had driven out most of the French planters) had been considered one of the richest French possessions in the world. Hamilton knew well that it produced more sugar profits than all the islands of Hamilton's own native British West Indies put together.

Many American vessels being seized by France in the West Indies were brought into the French-held ports of Saint-Domingue as prizes. The colony itself would be a tempting prize for America in the event of open war with France. From as far back as 1791 and 1792, Hamilton had been deeply involved in American relations with the colony. Then he had counseled Washington on how to respond to appeals from France for funds and supplies to aid it in putting down the slave revolts on the island. He had warned Washington that "nothing can be done without risk to the United States" because it was unclear which government, French or insurgent, was of sufficient legitimacy to be entitled to recognition. Therefore, *as little as possible ought to be done"* and "whatever may be done should be cautiously restricted to the single idea of preserving the colony from destruction by famine." This would "avoid the explicit recognition of any regular authority or person." On this basis, for purely humanitarian reasons, "succours ought to be granted."

The principal leader of the slave revolt was François Dominique Toussaint (usually called Toussaint l'Ouverture), the son of an African chieftain who had been sold into Negro slavery. By 1798, Toussaint had driven the British and French out of all but a few parts of the island, subdued a rival group of mulattoes under Benoit Joseph Rigaud, and turned to the United States to ask for recognition and foreign aid. But France had not acknowledged Toussaint's de facto control, and Saint-Domingue officially still remained a French colony.

Secretary of State Pickering and Secretary of the Treasury Wolcott called on Hamilton for advice on how to respond to Toussaint's plea. Adams thought the United States "should make some kind of agreement with the blacks" and open regular trade relations. But internationally, to do so might touch off a reprisal by France or open war. Domestically, to do so would certainly be politically divisive because Southerners like Jefferson were horrified at the idea of giving official recognition to a country of former Negro slaves who had successfully won a bloody revolution for freedom against their white masters. A free Saint Domingue under Toussaint little more than a hundred miles off Florida would stand like a dangerous beacon of freedom or a tree of liberty, always beckoning his own slaves to revolt.

Jefferson thought a slave revolt in Virginia would be even bloodier than Toussaint's because in Virginia whites and blacks were more closely matched in numbers than in Saint-Domingue. Jefferson put his strong objections to aiding Toussaint on the ground that it "is to facilitate the separation of that island from France" and would offend her, even though France had lost most of her military footing on the island to Toussaint.

Hamilton answered Pickering on February 16, 1799, that the law authorized opening relations with Toussaint's black government in Saint Domingue, but that the United States "must not be committed to the independence of St. Domingo—nothing that can rise up in judgment." Toussaint must first formally declare independence. He could be assured verbally by the American consul general that once he had done so, the United States would open trade if American vessels would be protected in his ports. This was the policy the government adopted.

The consul general who was picked to carry out this delicate mission of such intense interest to Hamilton was none other than his oldest boyhood friend, Dr. Edward Stevens of St. Croix. Hamilton and Pickering usually saw to it that men they knew and could trust were installed in the most important diplomatic missions. To Neddy Stevens before his departure, Hamilton furnished a suggested plan of government for Saint-Domingue that would not offend a Toussaint still battling pockets of resistance held by Rigaud and the French. "No regular system of liberty will at present suit Saint Domingue," Hamilton advised. "The government if independent must be military—partaking of the feudal. . . . A hereditary chief would be best but this I fear is impracticable."

Idealism yielded to a realism grounded in early West Indian experience. Unfortunately, it accurately divined the truth of the island's subsequent unhappy history. Not every embattled society of former slaves who throw off the yoke of the colonial oppressor and its Jeffersonian supporters is ipso facto ready for Jeffersonian democracy.

Hamilton's plan called for "a single executive to hold his place for life," his successor to be either the officer next in rank or one chosen by a plurality of commanders of regiments. There would be a supreme court of 12 men chosen for life by the chief military officers, with trial by jury in criminal cases. The most important laws, those for raising revenue and for capital punishment, would be passed by the assembly of military commanders; other laws would be decreed by the executive. The executive would be advised by ministers of finance, war, and foreign affairs. This political blueprint, for better or for worse, resembles that of many of today's newly emerging nations much more than it does Hamilton's American constitutional republic. This cautious advice of Hamilton for helping Toussaint's black revolutionary government against its colonial masters without much trying to reform it while the fighting was still going on, given "for what it was worth" to his intimate old friend Neddy Stevens, was later twisted by Jefferson into the usual charge that Hamilton would help or recognize no free revolutionary government except one that was headed by a king.

Saint-Domingue was more a prize than a menace. The wide open, largely unpopulated, undefended, and almost limitless expanse of the Florida and Louisiana quadrants as Hamilton scanned them on the situation maps in his New York office were both a menace—and a prize—of incalculable size and scope.

In April of 1798, Pickering had asked him "what ought we to do, in respect to Louisiana?" It had been suspected for years that France was on the point of forcing Spain to cede these territories to her or could compel Spain to do so at any time it might suit her plan for world dominion. Hamilton's reply to Pickering had been emphatic and unequivocal: "If Spain would cede *Louisiana* to the United States I would accept it, absolutely if obtainable absolutely, or with an engagement to *restore* if it cannot be obtained absolutely." But by April that dream was over. In "The Stand No. IV," Hamilton was telling the public that "the probability is that before this time" Spain had secretly yielded to France's demand to retrocede Louisiana back to France. "With the acquisition of Louisiana, the foundation will be laid for stripping her of her mines; and perhaps for dismembering the United States," he speculated. He stood ready at all times to give aid to any plan that would make Louisiana and the Floridas part of the United States short of entangling the United States in open war with France by doing so.

As far back as 1784, Hamilton had listened sympathetically in New York as Francisco de Miranda described his own dream of liberating all the Spanish possessions in the New World from the yoke of Spain. Recently Miranda had written Hamilton again, sure that the time was now ripe "for the Execution of those grand and beneficial projects we had in Contemplation, when in our Conversation at New York the love of our Country exalted our minds with . . . Ideas, for the sake of unfortunate Columbia."

Seven years older than Hamilton, Francisco de Miranda was a Venezuelan soldier of fortune fully armed with a quiver of charm, eloquence, and a personality yeasty with the spirit of liberty. A minor Lafayette, he was more romantic, but less effective. He had fought in the American Revolution, fought the Moors with the Spanish army, and been imprisoned once for insubordination and once again for smuggling. He had served in Cuba and helped Spain capture Pensacola. A refugee from his Spanish overlords when he had visited the United States in 1784, he had preserved a list of names of some 30 American officers he considered qualified for an ambitious campaign against Spanish possessions, written out in Hamilton's own hand. The names of Washington, Greene, Knox, Lafayette, von Steuben, and Arthur St. Clair headed the roster, which Hamilton must have written out still earlier and perhaps for another purpose, because it also included two of the brightest and best of Hamilton's friends, Colonels Francis Barber and John Laurens, who were both dead by 1784.

General Knox had copied out the names Hamilton supplied and added budgetary estimates of the expenses of raising, equipping, and supporting an army of 5,000 New Englanders for a year, including infantry, cavalry, and artillery, with all appropriate logistical support. To outfit such a force required funds, and Miranda had sailed off to England to obtain them. The British had given only vague words of encouragement then and no money. Discouraged, off to the Continent, into the French Revolution, promoted to a general, Miranda had become disillusioned with Napoleon as he turned imperial, had been arrested for treason, tried, acquitted, rearrested, and expelled from France. He looked on the American Federalist system as the perfect pattern for popular freedom under government everywhere. He was a visionary plotter and dreamer, a precursor of Martin and Bolivar as a liberator of Spanish America, and he invented his own legend as he went along. He counted Hamilton as the greatest of all American revolutionaries and one of his best friends.

From Paris in 1797, he had written to Hamilton about his latest plans and also attempted to open negotiations with the American minister, James Monroe. On February 7, 1798, he wrote Hamilton yet again—this time from London. He had seen Rufus King there, who seemed to him an excellent man, and he had taken him into his confidence. Would Hamilton be so good as to write King on the following subject? On the back of this letter, at some time after receiving it—how long after is the critical question—Hamilton wrote a cautious, slightly acrid, self-serving comment:

> Several years ago this man was in America much heated with the project of liberating South America from the Spanish Domination. I had frequent conversation with him on the subject, and I presume expressed ideas favourable to the object and perhaps gave an opinion that it was one to which the United States would look with interest—he went then to England upon it—Hence his present letter. I shall not answer because I consider him as an intriguing adventurer.

If Hamilton endorsed this negative endorsement on the back of the letter immediately upon receipt of it, then the events that followed immediately in train are most surprising. It is more likely that Hamilton wrote the endorsement several years later, when it seemed to be the part of wisdom to dissociate his name from Miranda's scheming and dreaming. In 1798, Hamilton, probably responded warmly to Miranda's plan as it unfolded in rather impressive detail.

In June of 1798, Miranda had sent a fellow revolutionist, Pedro José de Caro, on from London carrying dispatches for President Adams and confidential messages for Hamilton. The moment of emancipation approached! Miranda proclaimed, "the establishment of liberty on the whole continent of the New World is . . . entrusted to us by providence." The British were to be drawn in to a suitable form of joint government for all the emancipated country. Miranda pleaded that Hamilton must not refuse aid at this critical moment: "We should like to have you with us for this important object. Your Greek predecessor Solon would have done no less, I am sure!"

If France should indeed reacquire Louisiana from Spain, a unique opportunity to seize it for the United States would be at hand. William Cobbett as *Peter Porcupine*, summed up the strong appeal of Miranda's plan for all High Federalists: "A war with Spain is absolutely necessary to the salvation of this country, if a war with France takes place, or if the Spaniards have ceded Louisiana to France. They must both be driven into the Gulf of Mexico, or we shall never sleep in peace. Besides, a war with Spain would be so convenient!" To seize the gold and silver of Spain's mines "would be the cream of the war."

Hamilton, still tensely waiting out the results of his efforts to escalade over Adams's refusal of his appointment as inspector general, delayed answering until August 22, 1798. Then he sent his reply to Miranda's plea via Rufus King, giving King the option after reading it to deliver it to Miranda or not as circumstances warranted. "With regard to the enterprise in question," Hamilton confided, "I wish it much to be undertaken, but I should be glad that the principal agency to be in the United States," which should furnish the whole land force, of which he expected soon to be named the field commander. Even though Adams had not yet reversed his refusal, Hamilton seemed confident that "the command in this case would . . . naturally fall upon me, and I hope I shall disappoint no favorable anticipation. The independence of the separate territory under a moderate government, with the joint guaranty of the cooperating powers, stipulating equal privileges in commerce, would be the sum of the results to be accomplished."

But American opinion, said Hamilton, though fast rising to the pitch needed to back a declaration of war with France, was nowhere near ready yet for an imperial joint venture with Britain. Hamilton favored Miranda's plan, but would do nothing without proper authority: "The Sentiments I entertain with regard to that object have been long since in your Knowledge. But I could personally have no participation in it unless patronized by the Government of this Country." It was frustrating that Adams had not yet issued his commission: "It was my wish that matters had been ripened for a Cooperation in the Course of this fall on the part of this Country. But this can now scarcely be the Case." If winter should bring progress, "I shall be happy in my official station to be an Instrument of so good a work."

He pointed out that success of the expedition was conditioned on support of a British fleet, an American army, and a government for the liberated territory agreeable to the joint venturers. "To arrange the plan a Competent Authority from Great Britain to some person here is the best Expedient," Hamilton told King. "Your presence here will in this Case be extremely essential." As he sent off his letter to Miranda via King, Hamilton could not have known that the highest levels of the British government now saw Miranda's plan almost exactly as he did and took it seriously.

John Adams in Quincy, preoccupied with Abigail's illness and unused to carrying on presidential work in the summer months, had done nothing about the dispatches received from Miranda. Pickering was left with no instructions to go further toward arranging the joint venture with Britain even though William Pitt and Lord Grenville both confirmed they were interested in pursuing Miranda's plan. They sent Robert Liston, the British minister in Philadelphia, journeying to Quincy in September to pursue with Adams the idea of an American alliance or joint venture with Britain. Liston reported back that on September 27 Adams had finally agreed that it would be in the United States' best interest, as well as Britain's, to join in a temporary alliance against France. That was why it seemed so inexplicable to anyone not familiar with what Hamilton called the "desultoriness" of Adams's mind that two weeks later Adams switched and turned down Miranda's plan.

The missing fact necessary to explain Adams's sudden switch is that it was during the span of those same two weeks that he had humbly but furiously caved in to Washington's insistence, reversed another earlier stand, and signed Hamilton's appointment as inspector general. Meanwhile, King was as eager for the joint offensive as Hamilton was, or rather more so. He quickly passed on Hamilton's letter to Miranda, who answered with mounting excitement that all had progressed as Hamilton wished: ". . . we await only the fiat of your illustrious President to leave like lightening . . . Let us save America from the frightful calamities that, in upsetting a large part of the world, threaten with destruction the parts which are still whole."

Unfortunately for the project, de Caro, the emissary Miranda had sent to Adams, detoured to South America without seeing him to buck up his resolve. There he had postponed a small and partial revolution that was about to break out until the United States and Britain could join him in a large complete one, to "save the whole world which totters on the brink of the abyss." King had prepared the way with the highest officials in Britain for "lightening action" the moment America was ready. What Hamilton had suggested—though Pickering remained unresponsive to King's pleas—had been formally approved by the British government. Venezuela would be the ultimate objective, but along the way Louisiana and Florida would be plucked from Spain to add to the United States.

At the opening of the new year, 1799, King from London was still begging Hamilton for God's sake to attend to the subject of his recent ciphered dispatches to the secretary of state. The time had arrived to push ahead toward Miranda's main objective: "Providence seems to have prepared the way, and . . . pointed out the instruments of its will. Our children will reproach us if we neglect our duty . . ." Once a large force had been mustered by Hamilton for defense against France, it could easily be turned to offensive uses against Spain. It was manifest destiny. It "will be the moment for us to settle . . . the extensive system of the American nation. Who can hinder us? One nation alone has the power; and she will cooperate in the accomplishment in South America of what has so well been done in North."

Hamilton's power was burgeoning in all directions following his appointment as inspector general, and his enthusiasm for ambitious offensives warmed to a degree that almost matched Miranda's and King's. Adams's enthusiasm reciprocally cooled. Gradually it receded toward the moderate policy line that Hamilton had advocated from the beginning of the war crisis: "leaving to France the option of seeking accommodation, or proceeding to open war."

Hamilton duly noted and gave full credit to Adams for his striking switch in backing away from his earlier fire-breathing stance, so that "the latter course prevailed." Hamilton gave him credit for this even while publicly attacking Adams a year and a half later on many other counts for alleged misfeasance in office: "Considering the prosperous state of French affairs" when Adams finally adopted Hamilton's cogent policy, Hamilton granted, "the conduct pursued bore sufficiently the marks of courage and elevation to raise the national character to an exalted height throughout Europe." But notwithstanding all the heady temptations toward aggrandizement that supreme command proffered, at no time did Hamilton suggest that any of his military projects be undertaken without proper authority from the president and Congress and with the backing of a fully informed public.

More than mere mistrust of Hamilton in command at the pinnacle of power had caused Adams's switch from aggressive belligerence of the summer and fall to the conciliatory tone he adopted in his message to the third session of the Fifth Congress assembled on December 8, 1798. Although debate still rumbled on over what might be done about French seizures and spoliations against American shipping, the most virulent manifestations of the summer's "black cockade fever" were already subsiding. The popular passion for a declaration of all-out war against France that had been so strong when the second session adjourned in July had begun to fade at the very time when Hamilton, finally secure in his appointment to quasi supreme command, was most eager to exploit the possibilities that such vast power opened up to his ambition for vindication of his public honor.

A discrete series of events both at home and abroad changed the basic geopolitical facts of the crisis. As Congress was adopting a strong posture of preparedness for war on land and sea and abrogating the French treaties of 1778 and 1788, the Directory under Talleyrand's silken hand repealed many of the obnoxious restrictions on American shipping and lifted the harsh embargo it had proclaimed only a short time before. The British navy under Admiral Horatio Nelson defeated the French fleet at Aboukir Bay. Newly launched American frigates on patrol in the West Indies were winning engagements with French armed raiders and privateers. American commerce and shipping were prospering as a result of more profitable voyages. Marine war risk insurance rates were coming down.

Talleyrand, observing the United States under the guidance of the invisible hand of his old friend Hamilton, the only American statesman he would rate as the equal of Napoleon and Pitt, pursuing a realistic policy of limited maritime hostilities but avoiding a declaration of war, silkily steered the Directory onto a course a few degrees less belligerent. His was almost a mirror image of Hamilton's American policy: Talleyrand would leave to America the option of seeking accommodations or proceeding to open war. Talleyrand also blandly let it be known that the *WXYZ* imbroglio had been caused, not by his government or himself, but by inept and bungling underlings. He suavely also let it be known in the United States through many unofficial channels that France preferred détente to war. He made use of a heterogeneous collection of helpful emissaries —Elbridge Gerry, who had lingered on in France; William Vans Murray, the young American minister at The Hague; Louis André Pichon, a young French foreign office employee; Victor Marie du Pont, the former French consul general at Philadelphia; Constantin François Chasseboeuf Volney, a French scientist whom Jefferson had said was marked for Federalist vengeance; Dr. George Logan of Philadelphia, a private physician friend of Jefferson and self-anointed diplomat who thought private negotiations by a private citizen would be a good idea; the poet Joel Barlow, who more or less thought the same as Logan; and the Polish soldier and patriot Thaddeus Kosciuszko, whom Jefferson had asked to join all the others in the fun of bypassing the secretary of state to help forge a better French connection. Talleyrand also passed the word to Richard Codman, a Boston businessman who just happened to be passing through Paris on business; Fulwar Skipwith, the Virginian who was American minister in Paris; Robert Fulton, the inventor who was in Paris trying to sell a submarine to the Directory; Nathaniel Cutting the American consul at Le Havre; Thomas Paine; and Adams's young sons, John Quincy Adams and Thomas Boylston Adams, who were in Europe on a roving commission to keep their father independently informed on matters of state.

Talleyrand, like Hamilton, understood the uses of influencing public opinion in a free country in support of the interests of an adversary. Talleyrand's policy of making use of all these influential contacts while avoiding the wide open official channel of Secretary of State Pickering and more or less ignoring Commissioners Pinckney and Marshall, strengthened the hands of American Republicans and weakened and angered High Federalists. He thus kept France's potential enemy divided against itself internally while committing the Directory to nothing and risking nothing at home.

After more than three months away at Quincy, Adams returned to the capital in late November and asked his department heads, as in the past, for ideas for a second annual message to Congress. He incorporated most of Wolcott's reply in the message without being aware that Wolcott, more or less as usual, had merely served up more policy recommendations that originated with Hamilton. The substance of these was that a declaration of war remained "inexpedient and ought not to be recommended." This also reflected the views of Pickering, McHenry, and Stoddert, as well as a majority of Federalists in Congress—all but the extreme High Federalist wing of the party who still seemed to favor an early declaration of war.

To one of these, Hamilton suggested a happy compromise that might help avert a party split. When Harrison Gray Otis, chairman of the House Committee on Defense requested "instruction" from him, Hamilton suggested that Congress might pass a law empowering the president *at his discretion* "to declare that a state of war exists between the two countries if negotiations with France should fail." Although the Constitution reserved to Congress the power to declare war, the provision was not intended to deprive the president of full power to lead the country to the brink of war and thus make a declaration inescapable. To Hamilton the Framer, the executive was responsible for leadership of the people and Congress. Congress's formal power to declare war was meant only as a curb on a rash presidential declaration, for which popular opinion was unprepared. If there were to be a war, the president should have the power to unite the country in support of it first. Hamilton's view tended to add responsibility, as well as power, to the office of the president and made it more important that any president be a strong one. Hamilton's proposal prodded Adams into irascible rage. He wrote to Otis of Hamilton: "This man is stark mad, or I am. He knows nothing of the character, the feelings, the opinion and the prejudices of this nation. If Congress should adopt this system, it would produce an instantaneous insurrection of the whole nation from Georgia to New Hampshire." Yet the authority Hamilton besought Congress to confer on the president to preclude his playing politics with the war issue presaged the power that modern presidents have assumed without such authority.

Hamilton had also suggested to Adams through Wolcott that he put something in his message to the effect that, after France's repeated rebuffs of American ministers, "it should be left with France in future to make the first overture." If France should send a minister, "he would be received with due respect to his character and treated with in the frankness of a sincere desire of accommodation."

Adams blew up all over again! This was pussyfooting. "If France should send a minister tomorrow," he swore, "I would order him back the day after."

The three cabinet ministers waited patiently till Adams's pugnacious paroxysm passed. They then counseled him that such a threat would be a foolish and "imprudent idea." They reported his silly outburst back to Hamilton. Not 48 hours later, according to Hamilton, "the mind of Mr. Adams underwent a total revolution." Adams suddenly decided to go far beyond what Hamilton had suggested. He would send a minister if France gave explicit assurances he would be received. This was a "pernicious" reversal, Hamilton and the others felt, because it would deprive France of the opportunity to bargain to get what should be the ultimate outcome: a new American mission to Paris. "Here some salve for her pride was necessary," Hamilton felt. In his message as finally delivered, Adams moved back to the middle ground and more or less echoed Hamilton. He satisfied all but the most extreme High Federalists by proclaiming that "we have uniformly and perseveringly cultivated peace . . . harmony between us and France may be restored at her option." He stressed that "to send another minister without more determinate assurances that he would be received would be an act of humiliation to which the United States ought not submit."

Most Republicans, taking their cue from Jefferson, denounced this seemingly mild stand as uncompromising, provocative, and warlike. Thus reassured, a majority of Federalists seemed reasonably well satisfied with it. President Adams's address had managed to keep his potentially badly split party united behind him. His very success in having done so on December 8 by declining to name a new minister to France except on reasonable assurances from France would lead straight on to his splintering the party by taking the opposite tack less than three months later when he seemed to forget the importance of the fragile party unity he had here succeeded in preserving.

To Rufus King's continual urging that Hamilton get on with the alliance with Britain and get Miranda's plan under way, Hamilton replied in January 1799 with the same suggestion he had used to put off that other hawkish High Federalist Harrison Gray Otis. He hoped Congress at the present session would empower the president, in case differences with France had not been smoothed over by the following August, to declare war on that country. American forces could then be used against France either directly "or indirectly through any of her allies," by which he meant against Spain. This would give time for negotiation or, that failing, "would tend to reconcile our citizens to the last extremity . . ." He would leave the way open for accommodation, but if France attempted to take the Floridas and Louisiana from Spain, the United States should be prepared to fight. These regions were the key to the whole western country. Hamilton had long considered their acquisition "essential to the permanency of the Union . . ."

Hamilton went further. If universal empire were the ambition of France, what could better counteract it "than to detach South America from Spain, which is only the channel through which the riches of Mexico and Peru are conveyed to France?" As Hamilton's vision of an ever-expanding command widened to take in the best part of both continents of the hemisphere, a letter arrived from Christopher Gore written from London on March 4, 1799, at Rufus King's urging. It sent Hamilton for anonymous publication a lengthy manuscript entitled "The Present State of the United States, and the Consequences of not adopting vigorous . . . measures of war against France." It was manifestly the product of Gore's cordial exchanges with King and perhaps Miranda as well. America could look to England, he said, for "hearty cooperation in any . . . liberal Plan for emancipation of all the settlements of North and South America held by the Spaniards." With high emotion, Gore exhorted America to violent vengeance. Hesitant only because he had not yet heard President Adams's views, King was inclined to advise that Hamilton publish Gore's reflections. But Gore's memorandum apparently was too bellicose even for Hamilton's mood when in quasi supreme power in 1799. Found among Hamilton's posthumous papers unpublished, it serves to illustrate the limits beyond which Hamilton's strut of power would not take him.

On February 18, 1799, without prior consultation with the secretary of state or any of his other department heads, without seeking outside advice from other

Federalist leaders, and without any formal assurances from France that his minister would be properly received, Adams impetuously sent the name of William Vans Murray to the Senate, asking for his confirmation as American minister plenipotentiary to the French Republic. Through informal channels, Murray's name had been suggested to Adams by Gerry, whom many Federalists now considered as more or less a traitor to party and country; also by Logan, Barlow and a clutch of other Republicans; and also by Talleyrand!

But not by any regular Federalist or friends of the government, as they often called themselves. Such Federalists were thunderstruck. Here was a suspicious reversal of the hawkish pose of Adams's December 8 message. He had been taken into camp by all of Talleyrand's doves. To Hamilton the "measure was wrong, both as to mode and substance . . . Surely, Mr. Adams might have benefited by the advice of his ministers." Hamilton's further strictures on Adams's "mode" are worth noting: "The greatest genius, hurried away by the rapidity of its own conceptions, will occasionally overlook obstacles which ordinary and more phlegmatic men will discover, and which when presented to his consideration, will be thought by himself to be decisive objections to his plans." These words of Hamilton describe as well as any others his own folly in issuing *The Reynolds Pamphlet* and the worse one he was soon to commit by publishing his infamous attack on John Adams. He added, "When, unhappily, an ordinary man dreams himself to be a Frederick and through vanity refrains from counselling with his constitutional advisers, he is very apt to fall into the hands of miserable intriguers, with whom his self love is more at ease, and who without difficulty slide into his confidence, and by flattery govern him." Here Hamilton's reobsession with "Miserable intriguers" signals a recurrence of another spell of nervous derangement.

Other influential Federalists attacked Adams harshly too: Murray is "feeble, unguarded, credulous, and unimpressive," fumed Senator Theodore Sedgwick. "There is not a sound mind from Maine to Georgia that has not been shocked at it," cried Stephen Higginson, the Boston merchant. "The most embarrassing and ruinous measure," Sedgwick agreed. "Adams was duped by the wiles of French diplomacy, and the folly of Gerry," Higginson snarled. His being led around by the nose by Talleyrand smacked of treason.

Adams was deluged with threatening letters. One warned, *"Assassination shall be your lot,"* signed *"a ruined merchant, alas! with ten children!!!* made beggars by the French."

Pickering told an incredulous Harrison Gray Otis that Adams had not consulted him beforehand. "Why, is the man mad?" Otis exclaimed rhetorically. Otis thus answered the same rhetorical question Adams had asked him about Hamilton in a way Adams had not expected.

Hamilton agreed with Otis. The answer was yes: "The precipitate nomination of Mr. Murray," Hamilton wrote in his attack on Adams a year and a half later, "brought Mr. Adams into an awkward predicament."

A committee of five Federalist senators stalked off to call on Adams. They demanded that he withdraw Murray's appointment.

In high dudgeon, Adams refused. Never, he swore.

The senators would vote against the confirmation of Murray on the ground that he was unqualified, they replied.

In a hot huff, Adams threatened to resign the presidency. Yes, the presidency itself.

And let in Jefferson? They cried.

Hamilton hastily suggested a face-saving way out of the impasse: appoint two trustworthy envoys to accompany Murray.

The Senate caucus urged appointment of George Cabot as one—and Hamilton as the other.

Adams exploded again all over the ceiling. Appoint Hamilton again? Never. Never. Never. "I have upon mature reflection, made up my mind," he said when he came down, grimly trying to appear calm. "I will neither withdraw nor modify my nomination."

The Senators evenly told him they would reject it.

Adams caved in. He agreed to enlarge the commission to three. But he would be damned if Hamilton would be jammed down his throat again. Or Cabot either.

After further bickering, it was agreed that Chief Justice of the United States Oliver Ellsworth and William R. Davie, the Federalist governor of North Carolina, would join Murray as the commissioners.

What with one delay and another, more than a year would go by—and two more revolutions of the regime would roil France—before the three commissioners would sit down in Paris on April 2, 1800, to begin negotiations with their opposite number. He would be the recently reappointed minister of foreign relations of First Consul Napoleon Bonaparte. Who? None other than that suave survivor the bishop d'Autun, Charles Maurice de Talleyrand-Périgord. In French revolutions, *plus ça change plus c'est la même chose.*

However, two things were a little changed from earlier unhappy American ministerial confabulations in Paris, and this represented progress or at least sort of inching ahead. The chief justice and the governor added to the mission at Hamilton's suggestion would keep their young colleague Murray, whom Talleyrand had help handpick, on a shorter leash than Marshall and Pinckney had kept Gerry. And this time Talleyrand, a quick learner from past miscalculations, would not send X or Y or Z or W around to collect for a pretalk bribe. He recognized a diplomatic check when it was delivered to him by his *realpolitiker* opposite number across the water—and it was a costly check for him and those of the consuls with whom he usually split. But Talleyrand would never cease to profess amazement that such a man, while making—and conserving from him and the consuls—the fortune of his country and being vilified for his peculations and his friendship with Talleyrand in the process, could have failed along the way to learn from him how to keep some recompense to secure his own.

24

MANIC DEFENSE

ALL SOVEREIGNTY THEN EXISTING IN THE NATION WAS IN THE
HANDS OF ALEXANDER HAMILTON. I WAS AS PRESIDENT A MERE
CIPHER.

—John Adams to Harrison Gray Otis, 1823

BELIEVE ME, I FEEL NO DESPONDENCY OF ANY SORT. AS TO THE
COUNTRY, IT IS TOO YOUNG AND VIGOROUS TO BE QUACKED OUT
OF ITS POLITICAL HEALTH—AND AS TO MYSELF, I FEEL THAT I
STAND ON GROUND WHICH, SOONER OR LATER, WILL ENSURE
ME A TRIUMPH OVER ALL MY ENEMIES.

—to Henry Lee, March 7, 1800

A constitutional republic like the United States seems constitutionally incapable of waging an undeclared war with the vital élan necessary for signal
success. This did not prevent Hamilton from making the first all-out effort to
prove this melancholy proposition wrong and fail.

While Washington remained inactive at Mount Vernon, more infirm than the
public knew, Hamilton as inspector general took on full responsibility for all
aspects of raising, equipping, and drilling a brand-new American army, as well
as full command of the dispositions of its forces in the field.

He gradually withdrew from his "extensive & lucrative" private practice of
law. He had just won an important lawsuit for Louis Le Guen, who had paid him
the largest single fee he would ever earn. He wound up as much of his office

practice as he could and substituted Robert Troup as counsel for himself in continuing matters. With all the political and private distractions that engaged him, it was not until January 1799 that he turned his full attention to the large duties and small emoluments of the inspector general's office.

First among his problems was recruiting the "Additional Army" of 10,000 men that Congress had authorized by legislation he had helped draft. Over and above that, the further "Provisional Army" of 50,000 more—12 regiments of infantry and six of troops of light dragoons—had to be planned, mostly on paper, because it could not be activated until such time as full-scale war broke out, or President Adams declared that a threat to national security required its mobilization. The 80,000 militia that Congress had authorized could be called to the colors only by further orders of the president.

The first casualty produced by this formidable paper army was its acting commander. "My dearly beloved Eliza," Philip Schuyler wrote in alarm from Albany on February 1, 1799:

> I am deeply affected to learn that my beloved Hamilton is so much indisposed. Too great an application to business and too little bodily exercise have probably been the cause of his disorders. Immersed as he is in business, and his mind constantly employed, he will forget to take that exercise, and those precautions which are indispensable to his restoration. . . . You must order his horse every fair day, that he may ride out . . . draw him as frequently from his closet as possible.

He knew Hamilton was a work addict, but urged her anyway to

> try to prevail on him to quit the busy scene he is in.
>
> Embrace my dear Hamilton and your children for me. All here unite in love to you, to him, and them. God bless you . . . Ever most tenderly and affectionately yours.
>
> > Ph. Schuyler.

When recruiting for the "Additional Army" finally began in the spring of 1799, Washington noted acidly that "none but the riff-raff of the country, and the scape gallows of the large cities would enlist." Naturally, most who would enlist demanded to be commissioned as officers; few were willing to volunteer as privates. There was one seemingly minor matter that Hamilton considered of fundamental importance, and he wrote to McHenry and the commanding officers about it: "The Hats . . . received for our Recruits are not three cornered but round Hats, sans buttons, loops, cockades, or bands, and of . . . base stuff" and workmanship. This was poor economy. "Nothing is more necessary than to stimulate the vanity of soldiers. To this end a good dress is essential"; otherwise, "the soldier is exposed to ridicule and humiliation." The hat "ought to be delivered with its furniture complete." The men could not and should not be expected to procure accessories for themselves.

The uniform of the general officers as described in the draft letter Hamilton wrote for Washington to send to McHenry was "a blue coat with yellow buttons, gold epaulets (each having two silver stars) with lining, caps, cuffs and facings of buff; in winter, buff vest and breeches, in summer a white vest and breeches of nankeen. The coat to be without lapels and embroidered on the cape, cuffs and pockets." For the commander in chief, the plume in the hat "to be a further distinction" would be white; for the inspector general, blue; and for the lesser major generals, the plumes would be black and white, with the black below. All commissioned officers must, of course, wear swords, and all members of the army of every rank must wear a black cockade. There can be no doubt that when turned out in full regalia and ceremonial sword, the inspector general himself set an example to bedazzle every eye of lesser ranks.

A great many men who would have made fine soldiers proudly refused to enlist because they opposed the Quasi War on political grounds. In this they took their cue from the pronouncements of the Republican party leaders Thomas Jefferson and James Madison. They contended that the Quasi War was a "phony" war, a crisis that had been whipped up by the Federalists for political purposes to keep themselves in office and as an excuse to ram through the Alien and Sedition Laws, suppress domestic criticism and dissent, build up the standing army, increase government expenditures, pass a new Stamp Act and a direct tax on land, and put on the payroll a large number of new revenue agents to go out and collect all the new taxes. Indeed, during the four-year period of the Quasi War crisis, the federal budget authorized by Congress almost doubled, from $5.8 million in 1796, to $6 million in 1797; it then jumped to $7.6 million in 1798 and alarmingly in 1799 to $9.3 million. Jefferson told Madison that the authorized budget misleadingly masked the much greater real cost of the enlarged army and navy. He figured that in reality it was $11.5 million for 1799 alone. A Dedham, Massachusetts, Republican warned that the new house taxes and land taxes caused great resentment. Some refused to pay: "Silent indignation hath not yet exploded—tho' hard threatened. I fear civil war may be the result of government measures."

Jefferson saw that a Republican attack on the Alien and Sedition Laws would serve as a powerful political weapon to bring together the fragmented opposition to the entire costly federal war preparedness and tax programs. He shrewdly noted in January 1799 that "the Alien and Sedition acts have already operated as powerful sedatives of the XYZ inflammation." He dramatized the issue for maximum political effect by writing sets of resolutions that he arranged to have introduced into the Kentucky and Virginia legislatures and signed into law as 1799 began. By the Kentucky and Virginia resolutions, as they came to be known, the sovereign commonwealths of Kentucky and Virginia declared that the Federal Alien and Sedition Laws were unconstitutional and void and demanded their repeal. By these laws, the resolutions asserted, the federal government had arrogated to itself illegal power that would drive the states to "revolution and bloodshed." Jefferson's Kentucky and Virginia resolutions struck not only at the legitimacy of the government's defense program just when Hamilton was trying to get it under way, they also created respectable precedents for later movements toward state secession in both New England and the South. They also provided strong constitutional underpinning to the "revolution and bloodshed" of the Civil War and dissolution of the Union, to whose cementing together Hamilton had devoted the greatest efforts of his life.

On their face, the resolutions meant that state laws remained supreme and that Virginia and Kentucky would not enforce federal laws within their borders. This, in turn, raised the vexed question that had plagued Hamilton at the time of the Whiskey Insurrection: would his new "Additional Army" troops from states like Virginia and Kentucky obey their officers or their political leaders, if the military commands of the former conflicted with the political dictates of the latter? Some extreme High Federalists went so far as to charge that Jefferson's resolutions were part of a French plot to detach Kentucky from the Union and annex it to Louisiana—which Talleyrand was now on the point of snatching back from Spain.

A Virginian, writing in Bache's pro-Republican *Aurora,* alleged that McHenry had laid down loyalty tests for officers: he would not accept volunteer companies "composed of disaffected persons who might from improper motives . . . intrude themselves into the army, under the pretence of Patriotic Association. . . ." It was charged that the newly recruited "Additional Army" units were nothing but Federalist "Pretorian Bands" and instruments of "Party Persecution." Every member would be ready at command to "imbrue his hands in the blood of a fellow citizen, a neighbor or a brother, should the president or his Little Mars [Hamilton] think proper. . . ."

McHenry denied that he or Hamilton were responsible for the loyalty oath requirement. All officers' appointments had to be confirmed by the Senate, and the Federalist-dominated Senate insisted on proof of loyalty. Some candidates for commissions had been rejected, McHenry learned, because they were "anti Federal" or "nobody" or because they were "opposed to the Government" or were "of French principles," and so on. But Hamilton deplored the Senate's rejection of Colonel Caleb Gibbs for command of a Massachusetts regiment and demonstrated his antipathy to the idea of imputing general guilt by association, or did he? "Their rule of judging of military qualification is most likely no very accurate one . . . the objection against Antifederalism has been carried so far as to exclude several of the Characters proposed by us. We were very attentive to the importance of appointing friends of the Government . . . but we thought it well to relax the rule in favor of particular merit in a few instances. . . ."

Hamilton recommended his old comrade of revolutionary days, Colonel Louis Tousard, to be inspector of artillery, a critical post, but he had a French name. President Adams demurred. Guilt by association outweighed admitted merit. Hamilton's recommendation would have great weight, said Adams, but "an angel with the name & tongue of a Frenchman would not in a French war have the confidence of this nation." Some months later, John Rutledge, Jr., urged Tousard to apply to Hamilton again for the appointment, adding, ". . . Hamilton's mind is much too great to be susceptible of any of these prejudices which unfortunately exist in the fountain of Power. . . ."

Hamilton took a serious view of the threat to the Union implicit in the Virginia and Kentucky resolves. He advised Senator Theodore Sedgwick to refer the matter to a special committee of the Senate, and he suggested to Sedgwick the text of the recommendation that the committee should report out to the Senate at large. The defiance of Virginia emphasized the importance of a national standing army, he pointed out. In the Whiskey Rebellion, Hamilton had "trembled every moment lest a great part of the Militia should take it into their heads to return home rather than go forward." With a professional army, he would have no hesitation in proceeding to "subdue a refractory and powerful State." In the present crisis, he suggested, let a force "be drawn towards Virginia for which there is an obvious pretext—& then let measures be taken to act upon the laws, & put Virginia to the Test of resistance."

No Jeffersonian precedent that a state could declare its own law supreme over the Union's should be allowed to stand untested by a national force.

No "pretext" was necessary. Once again, it was refractory Pennsylvanians who rose, not Virginians. They still violently objected to paying direct taxes. Once again, charge of the army responsible to see that federal revenue laws were enforced fell to Hamilton; once again, Hamilton saw the crisis as a way to reassert the supremacy of federal law over defiant and rebellious states and localities. Once again, Hamilton's opponents charged him with overreacting and thus creating a crisis where none existed in reality. Once again, the episode was dubbed with the name of a potable liquid that smeared it with faintly comic connotations and allowed many to brush it aside. It was easy to forget all the national symbolism with which such episodes were surcharged for Hamilton.

Instead of being called the Whiskey Insurrection, this one was called the "hot water insurrection"; it was a milder potation than its predecessor. When revenue agents came to assess the new direct tax on houses and land, they would count the windows. Housewives of Germanic origin in Bucks and Northampton Counties of Pennsylvania would pour scalding water out of upstairs windows on the heads of revenue agents standing down below counting to prevent them from doing so. John Fries, 50 years old, father of ten children, gathered a band of more than 50 armed horsemen and galloped from house to house and village to village attacking the unfortunate revenue agents, some, no doubt, still nursing fresh hot water burns. Eighteen demonstrators were arrested and clapped into jail in Bethlehem on March 6, 1799. Next day, John Fries and a band of about 140 rumbustious farmers, some armed with rifles and swords, some wearing tricolor cockades, some drunk, ramped uproariously into town and cowed the federal marshal into releasing all the prisoners. Not a shot was fired.

Word of the incident reached Adams in Philadelphia just as he was preparing to depart for Quincy. On March 12 he issued a stern proclamation denouncing Fries and his roughnecks as rebels who had committed acts of treason by defying the tax laws. Years later, writing to Jefferson in 1813, he would explain that "you certainly never realized the terrorism of Fries's most outrageous riot and rescue." Adams called on bibulous Governor Thomas Mifflin to send in the state militia. Mifflin shoved the call on over to the state legislature, where partisan debate prevented action. Adams was finally reduced to going back to McHenry —and Hamilton—for help from the regular army. He then quickly scuttled off to Quincy. All responsibility was left in Hamilton's hands, and he moved fast. He sent Captain John Henry on his way to the rebellious townships next day with a detachment of 100 from Fort Jay, New York. He sent William Macpherson forward with 240 horsemen and two companies of artillery in support. There was talk that the insurgents were led by officers commissioned by Pennsylvania; so Judge Richard Peters of the United States District Court was sent along to be on hand when arrests were made, to hold prompt hearings, to discharge those wrongly accused, and to commit to prison any who might be found guilty of the treasonous offenses that Adams had publicly charged to Fries and his men. Wolcott spurred Hamilton on by complaining that Governor Mifflin had woozily allowed the insurrection to run on too long and spread too wide. It might, indeed, encourage more formidable rebellions. He added that all at the capital is "languor & indecision," and "we have no Prest here. . . ." Governor Mifflin "is habitually intoxicated every day & most commonly every forenoon." The governor's relaxation due to intoxication had helped inspirit the hot water insurrection.

From experience, Hamilton counseled the secretary of war, "Beware of magnifying a riot into an insurrection by employing in the first instance an inadequate force. 'Tis better to err on the other side. Whenever the Government appears in arms it ought to appear like a *Hercules*, and inspire respect by the display of strength . . . expence is of no moment compared with the advantages of energy." Of course, wise discretion should be used. "I only offer a *principle* and a *caution.*" To prevent bloodshed, a large force should be put under provisional marching orders "as an eventual support of the corps to be employed to awe the disaffected."

Hamilton took his own advice. His troops marched briskly into Bucks County, captured Fries and a few other ringleaders, clapped them into confinement, and marched them off to the capital to stand trial for the treason with which Adams had charged them. After two jury trials in federal court, the second lasting nine days, the jury found Fries guilty of treason as charged. He was sentenced to be hanged. While the trials were pending, Hamilton understood that Adams had made rash and improper comments that might tend to prejudice the jury. According to Hamilton, Adams "more than once imprudently threw out that the accused must found their hopes of escape either in their innocence or in the lenity of the juries; since from him, in case of conviction, they would have nothing to expect." Adams had also said that grants of clemency by Washington after the Whiskey Insurrection was what had helped bring on Fries's. Moreover, "he would take care that there should not be a third, by giving the laws their full course against the convicted offenders."

Adams asked his cabinet if he should pardon the rebels, and they said no. Almost a year later, on May 21, 1800, the day before the date set for Fries's hanging, Adams pardoned the rebels. "It is by temporizings like these," Hamilton railed at the time in the depths of a serious onslaught of nervous crisis, that men at the head of affairs, in time of fermentation and commotion, lose the respect of both friends and foes."

A gap seemed to be widening in Hamilton's mind between the political principles and maxims to which in the past he insisted that he unwaveringly adhered and the actions that he took in the political arena in these hectic times to bend or accommodate these timeless principles to what he now more and more was coming to see as the realities of the political arena. He could do this bending, he continued to insist, without dishonorably compromising his rigid and abiding standards of personal and public honor. His efforts to bridge this widening inner gulf between principles and practical reality were bringing new symptoms of inner tensions, doubts, and frustrations that had rarely been manifested before by one of the great political realists of the age.

He took a characteristically serious view of the new precedents for local defiance of federal measures created by Jefferson's Virginia and Kentucky resolutions and defiance like Fries's, but he was still careful to draw the line between political opposition to the party and policies ruling executive government and disloyalty to the nation. He sought to enlist the aid of a timorous Congress by suggesting to Jonathan Dayton, an independent and moderate New Jersey congressman who was outside the inner circle of Federalists, that "the internal situation of the U States . . . presents many discouraging reflections to the enlightened friend of our Government and Country." He outlined the problems as he saw them and also the solutions.

The mass of voters, particularly in the interior, were basically loyal. They became restive only because neglected. Now, if assisted, the people themselves would restrain the more violent politicians who courted their support. On the other hand, clamorous leaders of several sorts who disregarded Constitution and statutes ought to be put down, for "opposition to the government has acquired more system than formerly, is bolder in the avowal of its designs, less solicitous than it was to discriminate between the Constitution and the Administration, and more open and . . . enterprising in its projects." The efforts of Virginia and Kentucky "to unite the state legislatures in a direct resistance to certain laws of the union can be considered in no other light than as an attempt to change the Government." The Virginians, reorganizing their militia and preparing arsenals, meant to make the "existence of government a question of force."

He offered a winning platform. There should be "establishments which will extend the influence and promote the popularity of the Government." These should include extension of the judiciary system, with more local "conservators or Justices of the Peace" with ministerial functions. "The improvement of the roads would be a measure universally popular." A loan for a million dollars for a "national system" of turnpikes could be readily repaid by tolls and postal revenue. The Constitution should be amended to empower Congress to open interstate canals. These would exploit our abundant resources for internal navigation, facilitate commerce and agriculture, bind distant parts of the Union together, and extend the influence of the federal government. By these proposals Hamilton anticipated by a decade Gallatin's later report on internal improvements and by twice as long the constitutional liberality of John Quincy Adams, which finally overcame the crippling objections of James Monroe to such projects. An officially sponsored society offering premiums for inventions and improvements in agriculture and the mechanic arts would "speak powerfully to the feelings and interests of those classes of men to whom the benefits derived from the Government have been heretofore . . . least manifest." There should also be a provision for keeping the army on its current footing unless universal peace should ensue, in which case every company, except of the artillery, should be reduced to 20 soldiers. A military academy "will be an auxiliary of great importance"; government should establish manufactures of all military articles; the naval force should be increased "proportionately to our resources." Temporary laws for calling out the militia to suppress unlawful combinations and insurrections should be made permanent. He went so far as to offer a Populist proposal that would bring all the people into still closer touch with their state governments: "The subdivision of the great states is indispensable to the security of the General Government and with it of the Union." This should be a "cardinal point in the Federal policy," for, without it, large states like Virginia in favorable situations would be able to machinate against "the common head . . . with decisive effect." Their reduction to smaller size was better suited to the people's management of local affairs. It could be accomplished through an amendment permitting setting up of a new commonwealth on petition of 100,000 persons dwelling within an existing state. But Hamilton remained realistic enough to recognize that dividing up the large states was too audacious a proposal to broach in the present climate of bitter political animus in Congress, in the states, and throughout the country at large.

Few things could have been more frustrating to Hamilton than seeing the symbolism of his strong response to Adams's call for a show of force by the regular army against Fries's insurrection dissolve in Republican ridicule of the whole episode as another repressive overreaction. Hamilton was hardly less mortified when the Republican press gleefully twisted Pickering's suspicions of a secret French plot to foment a slave rebellion in the South into a charge that General Charles Cotesworth Pinckney, while on the peace mission to Paris, had sired an illegitimate mulatto bastard child, whose abandoned mother had pursued the general to Charleston. Gleeful airing in the Republican press of the "Tale of the Tubs" with false bottoms to hide in could not fail to rouse the public's memories of that sex scandal two years earlier in high Federalist places in which that other high Federalist general had been involved. Hamilton wrote Dayton that there should be "laws for restraining and punishing incendiary and seditious practices." The reputations of federal officers, necessary to the discharge of their duties, should be taken under guardianship of the national judiciary and not be left to "the cold and reluctant protection of State courts always temporizing." It was an outrage: "Are laws of this kind passed merely to excite odium and remain a dead letter?" Executive vigor now conspicuous by its absence was called for: "If the President requires to be stimulated those who can approach him ought to do it." But Hamilton no longer was among those who could communicate with the absent president.

It may have been the Republican's airing of the Tub Plot against Hamilton's old friend, fellow commander, and frequent confidant General Pinckney, or it may have been a new attack on Hamilton that had appeared in Greenleaf's *New Daily Advertiser* in Philadelphia on September 20, 1799, or it may have been fear of some other kind of reprisal by others of his busy enemies. In any event, something made Hamilton suddenly "beg" McHenry to get back for him his set of the original Reynolds letters. In his *Reynolds Pamphlet*, Hamilton had written that "all the original papers" contained in his appendix had been deposited with William Bingham, Esq., for "perusal" by "any gentleman." No one but Callender, who was no gentleman, had applied to peruse them, and Callender had been rebuffed. But McHenry's reply to Hamilton on November 18 must have come as an incredible shock:

> I recd two hours ago your letter of the 14th, begging me to call upon and send you certain papers you had lodged with Mr. Bingham. . . . I dispatched my servant with a note to which I have received the following answer enclosed: "I do not remember to have seen the papers alluded to."

By this last stunning sentence, McHenry purported to transcribe the contents of the enclosure, Bingham's letter, when he replied to Hamilton. This spared Hamilton the entire text of Bingham's letter. The text did not allow Hamilton to think Bingham had had a lapse of memory, as McHenry's did; it flatly contradicted Hamilton in no uncertain terms. Indeed, with some asperity. Bingham's original had minced no words. In effect, he called Hamilton a liar. The text of the curt note Bingham enclosed to McHenry had said, "It surely must have escaped Genl Hamilton's recollection that the papers he alluded to, never were deposited with me." Bingham went on to add, "After reading the publication in which he mentioned this deposit being made, I was surprised at the omission in case I had been applied to for a view of them."

The apparently untrue statement Hamilton had published had greatly troubled Bingham. He added: "I should certainly have reminded him," he told McHenry, but until now "under any other circumstances, it would not have been delicate to have addressed him on the subject."

Now, by his own "begging" appeal to McHenry, Hamilton had given not only Bingham, but McHenry too, men he had considered to be among his staunchest friends, grounds to believe that the defense he had made in *The Reynolds Pamphlet* had been a lie and that he had published the lie to the public.

But why had Hamilton suddenly "begged" McHenry and Bingham for the papers? Would he have done so if he had not himself absolutely believed that he had deposited them with Bingham? Could Callender or another of his enemies have stolen them? Had Bingham turned against him? Had his own mental processes failed him somewhere in the crisis? After the Reynolds affair had haunted him for years and he had agonizingly aired it, he had unwittingly conjured it up again in a way that impeached his own honor more inexplicably than anything that had gone before.

Since the close of the Revolution, next to nothing had been done in the United States to advance the state of the military establishment. Napoleon's conquests were spurring France to lead the world in the military art and forcing other advanced countries to try to keep in step with her. Hamilton sought to make his army a model for any future armies to be called up in future crises. He worked out regulations for exercise of troops in camp and battle and for the police of garrisons. He expanded the infantry drill manual prepared by von Steuben a dozen years before and included discipline and tactics for cavalry and artillery. He wrote out rules for the infantry in great detail. He sent on the portions dealing with regimental maneuvers to General Charles Cotesworth Pinckney and others for criticism and comment.

He studied the length of the infantryman's marching step corresponding to several speeds or, as he said, velocities. He continued these studies even after it became evident that mobilization would be discontinued. He procured British and French military manuals, sought advice of fellow officers, and directed practical experiments that would record the relationship between terrain to be covered, the height of the soldier, the weight of his pack, and the distance to be marched in specified periods of time. He concluded that length of the step increased with speed and recommended a marching pace for American troops intermediate between the extremes prescribed in the military doctrines of France and Britain.

He personally reviewed sentences imposed by courts-martial and permitted no slightest deviation from proper procedure, justice, or fairness. From the point of view of a man at the top, these were often trifling matters of detail, but to the individuals involved and their families, nothing was more important in their lives. A surgeon's mate was complained of; a deserter was apprehended after three years; a post commandant sought a discharge for a beloved son who had enlisted as a drummer, on the ground that a swelling on his neck made him unfit for duty. Some remonstrated against the change of buttons on the artillery uniform from yellow to white metal, yellow being less apt to be tarnished by gunpowder. Lieutenant Zebulon M. Pike, discoverer of Pike's Peak, brought a young lad, the son of one of his soldiers, from the Mississippi to Pennsylvania. Could he draw rations for the boy as permitted by local custom? Hamilton meticulously wrote out the best answers he knew how to all of them.

He promoted a training school for professional officers, which would become the United States Military Academy. The project had been urged before by Washington in messages Hamilton had drafted, and now he gave plans for it fresh impulse and precise definition, which resulted, two years later, in the founding of West Point. Like the foregoing, the best of Hamilton's efforts as inspector general were on paper. Recruiting of additional regiments was slow commencing and then lagged. Districting of the states and commissioning of officers bogged down. Clothing contractors failed to deliver the necessary uniforms. As summer came on, instead of filling up complement with recruits, army enlistments fell farther and farther behind. Hamilton papered over the reality of indifferent success or, indeed, his realization of failure looming with bright and cheerful reports to Washington.

He hoped the army would be "at its complement" by autumn, he said. But by August 19 he was complaining bitterly to McHenry that the business "drags on," supply "proceeds heavily and without order or punctuality, in a manner ill-adapted to economy on a large scale" or efficiency or contentment of the army. "It is painful to observe how disjointed and piecemeal a business it is." He and McHenry "exhaust their time in details, which are foreign to them." In short, "plans for giving perfection to our military system are unavoidable neglected."

By September 21 things were still worse. "Symptoms bordering on mutiny for the want of pay have been reported to me . . ." Other "discontents" have been communicated from several quarters. "An explosion anywhere would injure and discredit the service, and wherever the blame might really be would be shared by all."

The reason why the soldiers were on the point of mutiny for lack of pay was a typically military one: lack of the proper forms. The forms for muster rolls and payrolls had not been received from the Treasury. McHenry seemed to blame Hamilton that the soldiers had to go without pay until he received the forms. Hamilton was angrily at pains to shoulder off the blame on the Treasury: "It will not be said that I ought to have called for the forms"; it was the Treasury's fault for not having communicated "its own regulations uncalled for." Someone else should have seen that the soldiers were paid without the forms. Under a heavy load of labor and responsibility and threatened with the charge of failing at it, Hamilton in his frustrations allowed a dangerous, new, and uncharacteristic condonation of lawlessness and disregard of "established forms" to escape him in this entirely forgivable context.

"No one can be more deeply impressed than I am with a strict adherence to general rules and to established forms," he wrote McHenry testily. "But there will occur circumstances in which these ought to be dispensed with." Certainly, no end could be more worthy than seeing that soldiers were paid to justify disregard of insistence on Wolcott's "established forms." Still, it is disturbing when Hamilton adds, "It is equally important, to judge rightly when exceptions ought to be admitted as when the general rule ought to be maintained." He was appointing himself as the sole judge of such occasions.

When Brigadier General James Wilkinson arrived in New York to discuss campaigns on the frontier, it was a welcome opportunity for Hamilton to lift his gaze from the frustrating details of "established forms" to the distant horizons of Louisiana and the Floridas. Hamilton drew up an agenda for the meetings with Wilkinson, which included his ideas for preserving peace on the frontiers with Spain and organizing the forces necessary for "attacking the two Floridas."

It is not known whether or not Hamilton knew at the time of their conferences that summer that Wilkinson was in the pay of Spain as well as the United States and acting as a double agent. It seems more likely than not that he did or suspected it, but if he did, Hamilton was pressing for an unusual and risky disregard of "established forms" when he urged on both McHenry and Washington that Wilkinson now be promoted to major general.

Hamilton's reasons were full of odd qualifications. "I am aware," he wrote

Washington, "that some doubts have been entertained of him, and that his character on certain sides, gives room for doubt. Yet he . . . is a man of more than ordinary talent, of courage and enterprise . . . and will naturally find his interest, as an ambitious man, in deserving the favor of the government; while he will be apt to become disgusted, if neglected; and through disgust may be rendered really what he is now only suspected to be." Hamilton probably knew more than he wrote, but hoped that Wilkinson's promotion would make the Spanish mistrust Wilkinson or the accuracy of his reports.

Washington, who had denied an unimportant commission to Burr on Hamilton's advice because, as he put it, of Burr's "talents for intrigue," now agreed to promote Wilkinson on Hamilton's advice to a post that gave him command of all the vast western territories that faced the Spanish possessions. He agreed with Hamilton that "it would feed his ambition, soothe his vanity, and, by arresting discontent, produce the good effect you contemplate."

McHenry, who had known Hamilton better than almost anyone else for more than 20 years and always in the past had deferred to his judgment, now reached an opposite conclusion from Hamilton's on grounds that he and Hamilton must have argued out thoroughly. McHenry put his disapproval on record in a letter to Hamilton:

> Be assured, that until the commercial pursuits of this gentleman with and expectations from Spain are annihilated, he will not deserve the confidence of government. Further, I recommend it to you, most earnestly to avoid saying anything to him which would induce him to imagine government had in view any hostile project, however remote, or dependent on events, against any of the possessions of Spain. I require this caution on good grounds.

This surprising letter shows that McHenry knew or believed a thing of which Hamilton purported to be in doubt, that Wilkinson was, in fact, a spy and pensioner in the employ of Spain and that highly placed officials in the American government—that is, Hamilton—unknown to President Adams—were contemplating the use of the newly raised army not merely for defensive purposes in case of war with France, but for offensive purposes against Spanish possessions in America.

Hamilton's letter to McHenry of June 27, 1799, which crossed McHenry's to him in the mail, confirmed the second point. "It is a pity, my dear sir, and a reproach," he wrote, that Adams's administration had no general plan. "Certainly there ought to be one formed without delay. If the chief is too desultory, his ministry ought to be more united and steady, and well-settled in some reasonable system of measures. . . . Besides eventual security against invasion, we ought certainly to look to the possession of the Floridas and Louisiana, and we ought to squint at South America."

Hamilton may have felt that for him Wilkinson would disavow his ties with Spain and use them in furtherance of his own project, if Hamilton's plan would make it more worth his while, and that the first step in the process was to raise his rank. McHenry's surprising letter firmly registering a rare disagreement with the plans of his lifelong friend is important evidence that at this time the pressures on Hamilton were causing his judgments to become warped and unbalanced and that this dangerous condition was manifest to his closest and most perceptive friends. Hamilton's perception of their mistrust would shake his confidence in himself.

Many years later, Edward Everett Hale asserted that in 1876 he personally examined an old chest that had once belonged to General Wilkinson. It was filled with the letters of an extensive correspondence between him and Hamilton. The two men had hatched a plan, he said, that called for a rendezvous near Cincinnati with the newly raised army and a movement from there down the Ohio and Mississippi rivers to capture New Orleans. Once that exploit was accomplished, Hamilton and Wilkinson would then join with Francisco de Miranda in his campaign to overthrow Spanish rule in the Caribbean and South America. The flatboats to float the expedition had already been built at Cincinnati. Only because Miranda did not get the aid from England he thought he had been promised was the grandiose plan abandoned.

According to Hale, the man who owned the chest had offered it for sale to the War Department. When they refused to pay his price, he burnt all the letters in a fit of anger. Oddly enough, as Hale described it, Hamilton's and Wilkinson's plan was almost a blueprint, but on a grander scale, of the expedition that Aaron Burr later actually led down the Ohio and Mississippi rivers from Blennerhassett Island, near present-day Cincinnati, for which Thomas Jefferson in 1807 had Burr prosecuted for treason. The key piece of evidence in the case against Burr was a letter of Wilkinson, written to Jefferson in cipher, telling him of the plan.

Adams had remained at Quincy away from the capitol ever since March 12, 1799. Elections in the various states for delegates to the sixth Congress were being held in which federalist candidates, most of them men from the middle and Southern states who were moderates on the issue of war with France, were winning a larger number of seats than Federalists had ever managed to win before. This seemed to reflect a national consensus supporting Hamilton's basic policy of firm defensive measures, but no initiatives toward a declaration of all-out war. In the Caribbean American naval frigates fought a few successful engagements with French ships. This served to warn the French and tended to reduce the number of vessels and cargoes being lost to French seizures. At the same time, American anger at continuing British seizures of American ships for the purpose of impressment of American seamen tended to work in favor of the politics of an evenhanded policy toward France. The Republican press played up "British atrocities" to match Federalist charges of French depredations and diplomatic duplicity. A young Englishman in the United States, commenting on American anger at news of one impressment from an American naval vessel, was amazed at all the loose talk of war: "They really talk of war with France, or indeed with England, with as much unconcern as if they risqued nothing in the event."

Leaving Philadelphia in March, Adams had given Pickering orders to draw up instructions for the three peace commissioners, Ellsworth, Davie, and Murray, who had not yet departed. In May, Murray reported to Talleyrand that Adams had decided to reopen negotiations. But as summer came on, word arrived of still another upheaval in France, the coup d'état of 30 Prairial, in which the legislature purged all members of the Directory except Paul François Jean Nicolas Barras. But shortly after the coup d'état of 30 Prairial, after sending to Adams assurances that the new set of commissioners would be honorably treated, Talleyrand himself was purged from office, leaving the three commissioners and Federalists generally in much doubt as to whether there remained any further point to sending on the much vexed three-man mission. Adams's continued absence from the capital in Quincy did not add to the efficiency of the decision-making process. It was both a continuing source of frustration to his triumvirate of Hamilton's ministers in Philadelphia and an unexampled opportunity for them to run the government there under Hamilton's guidance from New York as long as the power vacuum continued. Adams, however, remained serenely confident that he could effectively preside over the country in this kaleidoscopic period of crisis by remote control by correspondence. His friend Uriah Tracy warned him that "your real friends wish you to be with your officers, because the impression is, the government will be better conducted." But Adams hotly insisted that "the Secretaries of State, Treasury, War, Navy and the Attorney General transmit to me daily by post all the business of consequence." He fatuously added, "nothing is done without my advice and direction." He still remained in blissful ignorance of the fact that for three years nearly everything important that his three principal officers had done and, indeed, much that he himself had done or recommended in addresses, thinking of it as his own policy, had been mostly on Hamilton's "advice and direction." He, therefore, saw no need to return to Philadelphia, which he sneeringly called "the chief seat of the synagogue."

Hamilton in the meantime was urging the cabinet, in their "desultory" chief's absence, to "agree what precise force should be created, *naval* and *land.*" Many other decisions needed to be made that were not being made. They should take policy decisions into their own hands. "If there was a disposition, without prejudice and nonsense, to concert a national plan," he proffered, "I would cheerfully come to Philadelphia and assist in it." He was not modest about the importance of his help, adding, "Nor can I doubt that success may be insured."

He directed McHenry to "break this subject to Pickering. His views are sound and energetic. Bring the other gentlemen to a consultation. If there is everywhere a proper temper, and it is wished, send for me and I will come." It was a discreet suggestion for an interregnum regime with Hamilton as its brightly uniformed head.

Recruiting and all else to do with the army continued to lag as the summer ended. No immediate summons came to Hamilton from McHenry. Finally, he decided to call the meeting himself, only to hold it at Trenton, a few miles away from the usual late summer plaguey fevers of Philadelphia. He summoned General Charles Cotesworth Pinckney down from Rhode Island, where he had been visiting, and brought General James Wilkinson with him from New York. They would meet with McHenry and Pickering at a Trenton summit meeting without the president to decide all the vexed questions that Adams's half year of absence in Quincy had left dangling. In recent months Adams had not even deigned to reply to the many letters the triumvirate had written him suggesting that the mission to France be called off because of the upheavals in government there.

Earlier it had been necessary for Adams to order Pickering to hand Ellsworth and Davie the instructions Hamilton had helped him draft for them and to order them to take ship for France. With word of the coup d'état of 30 Prairial, Pickering had again held up the instructions and the embarkation orders. With good reason, Pickering now felt that he had fallen into Adams's total disfavor.

Benjamin Stoddert, the secretary of the navy, had been only one of many who repeatedly urged Adams to return to the capital. He wrote that "artful designing men might make use of your absence from the seat of government" to thwart your peace effort—and harm your chances for reelection.

What Hamilton and General Wilkinson, who had been hatching some kind of plans together in New York for months, did not know when they arrived in Trenton early in October was that Adams had finally bestirred himself and was on his way south from Quincy. After seven months away from the seat of government, Adams reached Trenton on October 10.

The vain, proud, touchy Adams was astounded and outraged at what and whom he found there. Hamilton was already installed, with all his heads of departments paying him court. Here was Hamilton, the leader of both the High Federalist and moderate factions of Adams's own divided party, apparently presiding as kingpin at a summit meeting—a meeting at which Adams should have been the pinnacle, to which he had not even been invited. Worse, it had been kept secret from him. He had stumbled onto it by accident. How long had this been going on?

He was shocked; he was furious. He was choleric. Fifteen years later he was still at self-discrediting pains to describe how incredibly equable his own demeanor had been when he and Hamilton had first seen each other at Trenton and exchanged words.

As luck would have it, Adams had arrived in Trenton with one of his "great colds." He took lodgings at the boardinghouse of the two Misses Barnes, who dosed him with rhubarb, calomel, and a nostrum of their own invention, which relieved him some. But his disposition would not be any less choleric than usual when Hamilton came to call on him to try to make him delay the French mission.

"I received him with great civility, as I always had done from my first knowledge of him," Adams insisted, making it perfectly clear. "I was fortunately in a very happy temper, and very good humor." Hamilton spoke, Adams recalled, "in a style of dogmatical confidence" of the future. He predicted that the days of the "sans culotte Republic" were numbered. How ridiculous, thought

Adams. (Less than a month later, the coup d'état of 18 Brumaire would overthrow the Directory once and for all and bring Napoleon to supreme power as first consul of the consulate.) Hamilton argued that peace negotiations now with France might bring Britain into war against the United States. "Great Britain could not hurt us!" Adams cried out, adding, by his own account, "In a just and righteous cause I shall hold all her policy and power in total contempt."

According to Adams, Hamilton's "eloquence and vehemence wrought up the little man to such a degree of effervescence" that it reminded Adams of Hamilton's excitement at the Battle of Monmouth. After years of calm reflection, he said, "Never in my life did I hear a man talk more like a fool." Every time he heard a man talk of the imminent downfall of France, Adams was inclined to laugh in his face, he said. (Two French governments fell within the year.)

Adams claimed he had said that the French revolution would last seven years more (it ended within the year). He averred that it was more probable that Great Britain than France would sue for peace (Britain never sued for peace; it was bumbled into war with the United States by Jefferson and Madison; Napoleon as first consul within a month adopted an actively pro-American policy and in effect sued for peace).

Hamilton pointed out that if monarchy were restored in France, the peace mission would be useless. This set Adams off again.

"I should as soon expect the sun, moon, and stars will fall from their orbits, as events of that kind take place," he raged (Napoleon as first consul then held de facto imperial power and became de jure Emperor in 1804).

"No matter what happens in France," he fumed, "it cannot do any injury to our country to have envoys there."

"Yes, it will," Hamilton coolly insisted.

"But if she proves faithless," Adams cried, "if she will not receive our envoys, does the disgrace fall upon her or us?" He ranted on: "Only then will the people of our country be satisfied that every honorable method has been tried to accommodate our differences."

"It's not that simple," Hamilton explained. "The damage will have been done to us."

"No! Absurd! Nonsense!" Adams erupted.

"It will increase our internal differences," said Hamilton.

Despite the benefit of fifteen years of hindsight, his defeat in 1800, and the destruction of the Federalist party, Adams in his self-serving account of the Trenton confrontation seemed not yet to grasp, or else unsuccessfully sought to explain away, or cover up, the point that to Hamilton was central. "I could not help reflecting in my own mind" Adams wrote, "on the total ignorance of everything in Europe, in France, England and elsewhere" that Hamilton displayed.

Adams's itinerary of geographical blanks in Hamilton's knowledge is self-revealing in that it omits saying Hamilton was ignorant about the United States. Leaving American interests out of his supposedly self-justifying memories of the Trenton summit conference, Adams naïvely exposed his own ignorance of a

political fact that Hamilton understood: no president could carry on effective
foreign policy without a solid domestic political base. Without any need to do so,
Adams, by his dogmatic self-righteousness, was splintering his and Hamilton's
party, and committing political suicide.

Having been forced against his own firm decision to appoint Hamilton as
inspector general and now suddenly catching Hamilton in the act of presiding
in his own absence at a summit meeting of the heads of his own government,
Adams did not care that conditions had changed greatly during the half year he
had been away. French policies had turned from threatening to conciliatory;
further revolutions in the French government had made it less capriciously
revolutionary and more Napoleonically imperial. Political divisions in the United
States had remained wide and sharpened. Success in some recent congressional
elections had given proof of his own party's approval of Hamilton's firm but
moderate policy toward France, withdrawal of Marshall's earlier peace mission,
and stronger defensive measures in relations with France. But for Adams there
could be no changing course at Hamilton's urging now, even to save the Federalist party. If he had to prove his own potency as president, another switch from
a previous decision might betray impotence or "desultoriness."

Summing up the era that ended with Adams's unexpectedly stumbling upon
Hamilton's summit conference with his triumvirate at Trenton, Professor Samuel Eliot Morison, in his biography of *Harrison Gray Otis*, wrote: "At no period
in the history of the United States has one man possessed so potent an influence
over the federal government as Alexander Hamilton exerted during Washington's second administration and the first half of his successor's. . . . All important
steps in executive policy, during the first two years of Adams's administration,
originated in Hamilton's brain." It was not until a quarter of a century later,
when he was 87 years old, that Adams himself had simmered down enough to
see himself as others saw him, writing to Otis—still a suave genial Hamiltonian
Federalist—"That all the sovereignty then existing in the nation was in the
hands of Alexander Hamilton." Indeed, after so many years, Adams could even
force a grim smile: "I cannot review that tragicomic farce, grave as it was to me,
without laughing. I was as President a mere cipher, the government was in the
hands of an oligarchy consisting of a triumvirate who governed every one of my
five ministers; both houses of Congress were under their absolute direction."

The following year Hamilton coolly ascribed Adams's intractable choler at
Trenton to his personal ire at finding him present there. His own unexpected
presence, Hamilton wrote, "was considered as evidence of a combination between the heads of departments, the Chief Justice [Hamilton's friend Ellsworth
who had arrived there a few days after Adams] and myself, to endeavor to
influence or counteract him in the affair of the mission . . ."

Hamilton straight-facedly wrote that "when I left New York I had no
expectation whatever that the President would come to Trenton." Adams also
took it amiss that Ellsworth, a staunch Federalist, at Hamilton's urging, continued to advise suspension of the mission. So did Pickering, Wolcott, and
McHenry. Hamilton tried to make it clear that Ellsworth had come to Trenton

not to be part of any kind of Hamiltonian coup d'état as Adams seemed to suspect, but to meet with Davie "at the fountain head of information." There, at Hamilton's feet, they "would obtain any lights or information which they might suppose useful."

At Trenton, at Adams's insistence, the final wording of the instructions to the commissioners was hammered out in a late night session on October 15. Pickering came away from the long session believing and hoping from what he had heard and seen from Adams there that Adams still had no definite plans for sending the commissioners off.

Next morning, without consulting anyone, Adams ordered them to embark on the frigate *United States*, then lying off Newport, Rhode Island, on November 1 "or sooner" if the ship were ready.

A shocked, incredulous Pickering told his fellow Federalists that "the great question of the mission to France has been finally decided by the *President alone.*" Adams was no longer one of them. Pickering, Wolcott, and McHenry all agreed that it was a decision of "surpassing magnitude" and "fraught with mischief." Fisher Ames wrote Pickering on November 5, 1799, that the purpose of the mission was simply "to *make* dangers and to nullify resources; to make the navy without object; the army an object of popular terror . . ." He added, "The government will be weakened by the friends it loses and betrayed by those it will gain . . ." The effect of Adams's "miraculous caprice" would be "at home, to embroil and divide; abroad, to irritate and bring losses and disgraces." Adams's reckless act, to Ames and Pickering, had been nothing but a cheap bid for popularity with an opposition that would never become his allies; it would be "fatal to the peace and reputation" not only of Adams but the solidarity of the Federalist party as well. Never had a sudden diplomatic move seemed to have less inherent urgency about it, except to Adams's unpredictable mind. They also agreed that it would give vastly more strength to the Republican opposers of the government.

McHenry spoke out another thought that troubled the minds of all: "Whether the President will think it expedient to dismiss any, or how many of us, is a problem."

Hamilton, as inspector general, was not particularly worried about the Ellsworth mission as such, apart from its domestic political effects. Ellsworth and Davie, at least, would be "safe persons to be intrusted with the execution of a bad measure." But to McHenry and other Federalists, whatever its merits apart from party politics might be, the mission "is become an apple of discord."

Hamilton's frantic, but faltering efforts to build an army for strong defense were likewise an apple of discord, to which sending off the mission to Paris would add a strong push in the direction of ultimate failure. The additional army never reached more than one-third of its authorized strength. It was all chiefs and no Indians, the ratio of officers to enlisted men being about seven to one. Companies were of unequal sizes; some had more than 50 men; others, less than 30; and one mustered only a lieutenant and a drummer boy. Even discipline in the garrison of the fort at the Battery of New York harbor was slack. Hamilton's second in command, Adjutant General William North observed, "Nothing is in a situation to meet the attack of a privateer of 10 guns."

Hamilton in more or less complete frustration now took refuge in still more paper work, writing McHenry again and again as he had been doing almost every day all summer. The smaller the standing army, the greater the need for efficiency. "Since it is agreed, that we are not to keep on foot numerous forces instructed and disciplined, military science in its various branches ought to be cultivated, with peculiar care . . . in proper Nurseries . . . ready to be imparted and diffused. . . . This will be to substitute the elements of an army to the thing itself." These forces could quickly be expanded in emergencies. "The frequently" most pacific policy on the part of a government will not save it from wars."

He then wrote out a detailed plan for Secretary of War McHenry to submit to Congress and sent a copy to George Washington. "One [measure] which I have always thought of primary importance," Hamilton said, "is a Military Academy." He knew the commander in chief desired such a school, and he solicited his suggestions for alterations and new ideas. Washington responded warmly to Hamilton on November 28, 1799. His plan was near and dear to the old soldier's heart:

> The Establishment of an Institution of this kind, upon a respectable and extensive basis, has ever been considered by me as an object of primary importance to this Country.

Although unable to comment on details, he hoped Congress would "place it upon a permanent . . . footing."

But Hamilton's unexceptionable paper work did not erase an earlier stinging criticism by Washington of Hamilton's failure of performance in organizing the "Additional Army":

> If the augmented force was not intended as an in terrorem [sic] measure, the delay in recruiting it, is unaccountable, and baffles all conjecture. . . . The . . . enthusiasm . . . excited by the Publication of the Dispatches of our Commissioners at Paris (which gave birth to the Law authorizing . . . the twelve Regiments &c) are evaporated. It is now no more, and if this dull season, when men are idle . . . and from that cause might be induced to enlist, is suffered to pass away also, we shall . . . set out as a forlorn hope, to execute this business.

A little later, Washington had acknowledged Hamilton's failure as a fact and did not speak of the army, but "more properly of the embryo one, for I do not perceive . . . that we are likely to move beyond this."

George Washington died at Mount Vernon on December 14, 1799. His letter complimenting Hamilton on his plan for a military academy proved to be the last he ever wrote. For Hamilton, it did not much salve the sting of the earlier rebukes. Washington's death dissolved the last symbolic cement that had yoked the High Federalists and the moderate Federalists together in one team as "friends of the government," as their powerful slogan had insisted all good Federalists were. Adams had lost the last remaining symbol of Federalist unity at the very time he needed it most.

To Hamilton, Washington's death was an even more serious political loss and a personal loss too. He reacted to it in largely political terms. But whatever Hamilton's private thoughts might have been at various stages of his career about the character and human qualities of his great commander in chief, their association had lasted too long for him not to have mourned him with a sincere sense of personal grief as well. He had always been able to count on Washington for support in moments of crisis; Washington had been his shield and protector against all enemies, and now the shield was gone. Washington's death made Hamilton's ability to manage Adams much more difficult. As Wolcott wrote Fisher Ames on December 29, 1799, Washington "afforded a recourse in an extreme case" because Adams was unable to be "the arbiter of contending faction." Of all the terrible blows that fell on Hamilton as his century drew to its close, Washington's death was probably the heaviest. Hamilton's notes of condolence betray his own unique blend of political concerns for his own and the country's future. "Perhaps no friend of his has more cause to lament on personal account than myself," Hamilton told Pinckney. "From a calamity which is common to a mourning nation," he wrote to Martha Washington, "who can expect to be exempt? Perhaps it is even a privilege to have a claim to a larger portion of it than others."

With singular infelicity, he added to the widow, "I may, without impropriety, allude to the numerous and distinguished marks of confidence and friendship of which you have yourself been a witness, but I cannot say in how many ways the continuance of that confidence and friendship was necessary to me in future relations." And to Tobias Lear, Washington's longtime personal secretary, he wrote, "Perhaps no man . . . has equal cause with myself to deplore the loss. I have been much indebted to the kindness of the General, and he was *an Aegis very essential to me.*"

Hamilton then added a metaphysical speculation of a kind not often found in his correspondence: "If virtue can secure happiness in another world, he is happy. In this the seal is now set upon his glory. It is no longer in jeopardy from the fickleness of fortune."

To Rufus King, still in England, he wondered out loud: "Who is to be Commander-in-Chief? Not the next in command [Hamilton]. The appointment will probably be deferred."

In this he was correct.

After Trenton it did not take an especially acute sense of realism to know that Adams would never consider him for any office of public credit again. Nevertheless, because upon Washington's death Hamilton automatically became the acting commander in chief, it was another source of humiliation to

Hamilton that official recognition of the fact by automatic elevation to Washington's rank of lieutenant general and unqualified title would be denied him, along with the unqualified right to wear the commanding general's white plume.

Pickering again did his utmost. He announced to John Quincy Adams that "the command of the army devolves of course on General Hamilton." Wilkinson, recognizing in himself the same kind of forlorn secret hope that plagued Hamilton's own mind, hastened to write him to say that "it must be a consolation to the military to find the chief command in hands so able to administer the functions of the station . . . I cannot more safely consign my own interests than to the sensibilities of your bosom—20 years a brigadier, a *patient* one too, I pant for promotion."

But Hamilton advised his aide George Izard on February 27, 1800, that he should quit the army; "the military career in this country offers too few inducements." Hamilton no longer saw himself as a rising star behind whom a young man might rise by hitching up his wagon. "It is equally certain that my *present* station in the army *cannot* very long continue under the plan which seems to govern." He also was beginning to doubt even his own usefulness to the Federalists' cause in Congress. He inquired anxiously of Senator Sedgwick the same day he wrote young Izard, "Will my presence be requisite as to this—or any other —purpose, and when?" He seemed to assume that the sudden decline in future prospects for American greatness were coincident with, or a result, even, of his own (unmistakable to himself) decline. "By the jealousy and envy of some, the miserliness of others, and the concurring influence of *all foreign powers*, America, if she attains to greatness, must *creep* to it. Will it be so?" He claimed, unconvincingly, to be reconciled to impotence. He cited a maxim that was completely at odds with all the lessons of his life till now: "Slow and sure is no bad maxim. Snails are a wise generation."

Henry Lee wrote to Hamilton, at pains to disavow stories currently appearing in Republican newspapers telling President Adams that he should leapfrog Lee over Hamilton's head to succeed Washington as the titular commander, just as Hamilton had been leapfrogged over Knox, Pinckney, and many others. Hamilton's reply to Lee on March 7, 1800, was at too great pains to deny hard truths that were becoming more and more evident to everyone but him: "The truth is, that I pay very little attention to such newspaper ebullitions . . . You have mistaken a little observation in my last. Believe me, I feel no despondency of any sort." He went on despondently, "I am not wholly insensible of the injustice which I from time to time experience, and of which, in my opinion, I am at this moment the victim." Malicious miscreants were seeking to impair their friendship. "Join me in looking with indifference upon their malicious efforts," he begged. "As to the country, it is too young and vigorous to be quacked out of its political health; and as to myself, I feel that I stand on ground which, sooner or later, will assure me a triumph over all my enemies."

Hamilton's anxiety and depression were undeniably patent to Lee from the earlier letter he had mentioned. Yet here was Hamilton vehemently denying "despondency of any sort." With all hope of future promotion denied him, his policies toward France discarded, his cabinet triumvirate discredited, his party hopelessly splintered, and Washington dead, his lonely claim that he stood on ground that would assure him "a triumph over all my enemies" could not have sounded more tinny with false bravado. It was completely at odds with the facts. Hamilton here was writing out of a fantasy of omnipotent control, which existed only in his imagination. Never for more than 25 years had he been less in control of his own situation than now, or suffering from profounder sensations of anxiety and helplessness. Though the tide of public opinion in the United States was inexorably turning away from his Federalists toward Jefferson's Republican party, he insisted on identifying himself with a United States that could not "be quacked out of its political health." He borrowed what strength he could from such identification with it. For denying Washington's rank to him now, Adams probably ranked first among his enemies; so he projected all his frustrations and anger on Adams and "all my enemies."

In short, he was suffering from all the classic symptoms of what psychiatrists would call a manic defense. He might have confessed to himself that his soul was beset by what he saw as threats to survival coming at him from the outside world from every direction. Here also was his own peculiar blend of elegiac resignation and crackbrained defiance.

This psychopathology gradually became more easily observable in Hamilton as the years and the malady progressed. It seems to have had its barely perceptible beginnings in the harrowing psychological pressures he had undergone as the Reynolds affair became more intense in 1791 and 1792. Unfortunately, occasional later outbursts like his letter to Lee seemed not to afford him much relief from repression by way of confession. The pathology seemed to progress, with significant periods of remission, until the end of his life.

Had William Bingham or James McHenry, two of his oldest friends, turned against him and lied to him, telling him the Reynolds papers had never been left with Bingham? Had Adams made a secret deal with Jefferson to split the Federalists and become his vice-president? Would his enemies' pro-French policies— they had already made a farce out of his army and himself as its inspector general—make America a de facto province of France? His fears were neurotic; his reactions, irrational; yet no one could say for a certainty that any of these things, however improbable, was not possible. In Hamilton's perceptions, there was a strictly logical basis for each of such fears. A man's capacity for strictly logical thinking is not impaired by the derangement of full-fledged paranoia.

Normal thinking, not necessarily logical, is based on a fairly reasonable belief in a greater or lesser degree of probability. Deranged or paranoid thinking is based on the perception of a logical possibility and insistence on absolute certainty that it cannot, must not happen, even in the most remote circumstances. If a man will not touch a doorknob because he fears he might catch a dangerous bacillus, his behavior is considered neurotic or irrational, according to the powerfully trivial example Erich Fromm provides to illustrate the point.

The normal person reaches conclusions and makes decisions on the basis that something is probable or improbable after close empirical analysis of all data available to him. The fewer data he has, the less he knows about the full reality of a situation, the less willing he is to analyze it carefully and empirically, and the more he tends to think of it in abstract, absolute terms. For a deranged mind, mere possibility is sufficient—for it, the safety net of close empirical examination of probabilities is unnecessary—before taking the mental leap to absolute certainty.

With Washington gone to certain reward and Pickering, McHenry, and Wolcott now severed cables, with no grip on policy and no longer sources for transmission of intelligence back to him, for the first time in a quarter century Hamilton was cut off from contact with centers of power without purchase to steer the ship toward good as he saw it—as it floundered toward Republican takeover or French encirclement or foreign war or all three.

If the victim's world, like the smug Victorian London of Mr. Podsnap in *Our Mutual Friend*, is "not a very large world, morally; no, nor even geographically," the victim's delusions of grandeur and power only make him a laughingstock: "As a so eminently respectable man, Mr. Podsnap was sensible of its being required of him to take Providence under his protection." Although his business was that of marine underwriter, "he considered other countries . . . a mistake . . . presto! with a flourish of the arm, and a flush of the face, they were swept away." But in a Hamilton at the power center of a nation, such delusions were not so funny. Grave matters perceived as threats like Northern secession or foreign war—even if only remote possibilities, not probabilities—cannot be cured by a nostrum or swept away by a flourish of the arm.

John Adams observed, "Power always thinks it has a great soul and vast views beyond the comprehension of the weak and that it is doing God's service when it is violating all his laws." Having maintained course toward Union, public credit, and personal honor for so long, with such effort, at such cost, at the helm of American command, Hamilton now seems to have become infected—as who in his position might not have?—with the conviction that he alone possessed the great soul and vast views necessary to hold the helm on the right course for God, for country, and for Federalism. Now rudely shoved aside, he probably felt like a helpless passenger watching the spokes of the wheel wrenched from his hands yawing back and forth unmanned by the desultory Adams.

How many men in history have been exposed longer to more power in a significant world political society—yet because of peculiar circumstances—with less public accountability than Hamilton? If now for the first time he should be publicly called to account without his essential aegis for cover, who but a man like Nicholas Cruger's former clerk-bookkeeper-accountant would be more painfully sensitive to alleged disconcert in his accounts or predisposed to confuse legitimate objections with malicious enmity?

When a mysterious-looking package arrived one day at the Hamiltons' it was much too late for William Bingham to repair the psychic damage he had inflicted on his friend by denying to McHenry that Hamilton had ever lodged the Reynolds papers with him. Bingham wrote Hamilton on July 21, 1801: "Having a packet of papers which by your desire were deposited with me, and which have long lain dormant in my possession and being about embarking in a short time for Europe, permit me to return them to you."

It seems certain that the packet he so offhandedly shipped back to Hamilton was indeed Hamilton's set of the Reynolds papers. Hamilton might brush aside the "ebullitions" of enemies, but this token to remind him of two years of self-exposure as a public liar to two of his closest friends must have been one more wrench of a ratchet in his mind toward madness. Bingham's earlier insistence that Hamilton had never deposited the Reynolds papers with him should probably be ascribed to a typical rich man's forgetfulness, heedlessness, annoyance earlier at the bother of looking for them, or unwillingness to become further entangled in an alliance that brought such scandalous notoriety with it, even for a friend.

There is no evidence of what became of the papers after Hamilton received them back. They have never been found. For what it is worth, *Bibliotheca Americana: A Dictionary of Books Relating to America, from its Discovery to the Present Time,* VIII, 28, says that Hamilton's edition of *The Reynolds Pamphlet* was bought up and destroyed by Hamilton's family. But his family was much too late. Nothing they could do would keep the apparition from reappearing to haunt him year after year all the way to the end of his course toward the certain security of self-destruction. In another world, the seal set upon glory would no longer be in jeopardy of such fickleness of fortune.

25

THE EVIL GENIUS
OF THIS COUNTRY

IN TIMES LIKE THESE IN WHICH WE LIVE, IT WILL NOT DO TO BE
OVER SCRUPULOUS ... *IT IS EASY TO SACRIFICE THE SUBSTANTIAL
INTERESTS OF SOCIETY BY A STRICT ADHERENCE TO ORDINARY
RULES.*

—*To John Jay, May 7, 1800*

PROPOSING A MEASURE FOR PARTY PURPOSES WHICH IT WOULD
NOT BECOME ME TO ADOPT.

—*John Jay's endorsement on Hamilton's May 7
letter*

Hamilton in military uniform was a popular subject for the foremost painters of his day. The earliest known likeness of him is a miniature painted on ivory
by Charles Willson Peale in 1777, when he was about 20 years old, showing him
proudly wearing the green riband of an aide-de-camp to Washington and the
epaulets of a lieutenant colonel. A later head and shoulders portrait by Peale,
probably painted for his famous Philadelphia museum about 1791, shows Hamilton in civilian clothes; even so, the critic Charles Coleman Sellers, the foremost
authority on Peale, saw the military man through the motley of Hamilton's civil

persona. He called the portrait "a direct strong likeness, showing the military flair of Hamilton's thought and bearing."

In blue coat, dress sword, and black cockaded and visored hat as lieutenant colonel of the New York and Connecticut light infantry, Hamilton occupies a central place in such famous Revolutionary historical panoramic paintings as John Trumbull's *The Surrender of Cornwallis at Yorktown*. A full-length portrait of Hamilton back in somber civilian dress, standing beside his desk like any other proper Wall Street lawyer, was cherished by Philip Schuyler's family. Its most striking feature and focal point is the large colorful veteran's badge of the Society of the Cincinnati cascading down Hamilton's breast.

Now, at the turn of the century, at age 43, Hamilton was described by one who knew him well as "thin in person, but remarkably erect and dignified in his deportment." His hair was of fine texture, brown with a hint of red, now flecked with white. He wore it turned back from his forehead, usually powdered and collected in a club behind. His complexion was exceedingly fair, "varying from this only by the almost feminine rosiness of his cheeks." His eyes were dark blue and deep-set. His might be considered, as to configuration and color, an uncommonly handsome face. When at rest, it had a rather severe, thoughtful expression, "but when engaged in conversation it easily assumed an attractive smile."

William Sullivan in his *The Public Characters of the Revolution* recorded the moment in December 1795 when Hamilton entered a room as the last of a company of men of mark to arrive. It was apparent from their respectful attention that here was an uncommonly distinguished man. He was dressed in a blue coat with bright buttons. The skirts of his coat were unusually long, making him seem taller than his five feet seven inches. He wore a white waistcoat, black silk small clothes, and white silk stockings. The gentleman who received him as host introduced him to those of the company who were strangers to him. "To each he made a formal bow, bending very low, the ceremony of shaking hands not being observed . . . At dinner, whenever he engaged in the conversation, every one listened attentively." His mode of speaking was deliberate and serious; and his voice, engagingly pleasant. But when he joined the ladies, there was a distinct change of manner. "In the evening of the same day, he was in a mixed assembly of both sexes; and the tranquil reserve, noticed at the dinner table, had given place to a social and playful manner, as though in this he was alone ambitious to excel."

One of Hamilton's perceptive friends among French travelers and visitors, the Girondist editor and journalist J. P. Brissot de Warville, did not fail to catch the military cast of his civilian demeanor. He wrote that "his features are firm and his expression decided; his manner is frank and martial. . . ." De Warville could not resist summing up by a neat Gallic paradox—and betraying his own bias and his own favorite as well. The physical appearance of two great men was the opposite of the public roles they had played in the Republic: "Mr. Hamilton has the determined air of a Republican—Mr. Madison the meditative air of a politician."

At least eight portraits were made of Hamilton resplendent in the uniform he had designed for himself as inspector general of the army. Of these, Hamilton considered the one by P. T. Weaver as the best likeness of himself ever painted. Weaver's forte was painting in oil on tin "producing inveterate likenesses hard as the tin and as cutting in the outline," but he is otherwise little known. The portrait is a profile from Hamilton's right side in which a deep-set eye gazes resolutely toward a horizon that could be as far away as that of Louisiana, the Floridas, or Venezuela. Two richly detailed stars pinned on his golden right epaulet and thick heavy clusters of three-inch-long strands of gold braid draped from it down his shoulder leave no viewer in any doubt about his supremacy of rank.

A manic defense is an emergency defense that human nature brings into operation when normal adaptive processes or serious psychoses like paranoia have failed to protect the soul (or ego) against the onset of a depressive or deranged or insane mental state. Paranoia is the same condition that in Hamilton's day was more likely to have been called a persecution mania. Persecutory anxiety, the dread of being attacked by bad objects—"all my enemies"—is the old-fashioned phrase that has been replaced by the more up-to-date phrase paranoid anxiety. It has entered the mainstream of contemporary jargon as *paranoid* or *paranoia*. Paranoia is a functional psychosis. No organic lesion is apparent or demonstrable in the victim's outward appearance, which remains as impressive as ever. But it is, nonetheless, a mental illness that is liable to render its victim *non compos mentis*, of unsound mind, at least in the eyes of the law. Although a victim of paranoia suffers from delusions of grandeur and persecution, there is no inward deterioration of his intellect, any more than there are outward manifestations of his lesions. In classic cases, the delusions are organized into a coherent, internally consistent delusional system, on which the victim is prepared to act and does.

The question in Hamilton's case was, and is, whether in 1800 he was suffering from a paranoia that was more or less a permanent derangement or only from a manic defense, which could prove to be but a temporary response to the pressures of an emergency that would disappear when relief came from the pressures that had brought it into operation. To turn his back and walk away from pressures was one way out, but not Hamilton's. To take arms against a sea of troubles and by opposing end them was another way out. This would be characteristically Hamiltonian, but following Hamlet's procedure is dangerous because it often leads out in a fatal direction.

A new century was dawning, and the crucial elections of 1800 were coming up. But the dramatic easing of tension in relations with France as 1799 ended only seemed to heighten the factional tensions between Republicans and Federalists at home and between High Federalists and moderates within the Federalist ranks. Abroad, on November 9, 1799, the coup d'état of 18 Brumaire had overthrown the Directory and brought Napoleon to power as first consul and Talleyrand back as his minister of foreign relations. As Ellsworth and Davie, on their leisurely, roundabout way toward Paris, were reaching Lisbon, the Consulate in December repealed all the remaining harsh decrees against American commerce. In January 1800, Congress voted to suspend all army enlistments. After word of George Washington's death reached France, Napoleon ordered ten days of public mourning during February in honor of his memory.

At Talleyrand's suggestion, Napoleon also decreed that a bust of Washington be placed in the Grand Gallery of the Tuileries alongside those of Hannibal, Caesar, Turenne, Condé, Mirabeau, and other great heroes. One eulogy for Washington praised the United States as "the wisest and happiest nation on the face of the earth," and another, at the Fields of Mars on February 8, stressed fancied parallels between Washington and Bonaparte, which did not fit Hamilton too badly either: "After great political crises there arises an extraordinary man who by sheer power of his character restrains the excesses of all parties and brings order out of chaos." When Ellsworth, Davie, and Murray finally sat down in Paris on April 2 to begin negotiations that would drag on intermittently until October, they would be ceremoniously greeted by Talleyrand and Napoleon himself in an ambience of warmth, if not all-out bonhomie, in marked contrast to the shabby bribe demands with which *W, X, Y,* and *Z* had welcomed Marshall, Pinckney, and Gerry three years earlier.

But such euphoria did not extend to the domestic scene. At home, Hamilton's enemies did not let up. Federalist champions, defenders, and apologists were dying off or sailing away at an alarming rate. The Federalist press declined with the party's fortunes. William Cobbett, *Peter Porcupine,* shot his last quill and fled across the Atlantic. John Fenno had died in 1798, leaving his *Gazette of the United States* to his son, who sold it. As a result, said Fisher Ames, "uneducated printers, shop-boys, and raw schoolmasters" like Noah Webster were all that were left to carry the grand old party's message out to the people.

Federalist-inspired prosecutions were brought more and more often against hostile Republican newspapers for alleged violation of the Sedition Law. This law punished by fines and imprisonment conspiracies or scandalous statements uttered against the government, Congress, and the president. Unfortunately, for his mental condition, as a military chieftain, Hamilton did not come under the wide gag the law imposed on the Republican press. As the highest ranking, most conspicuous leader of the government's party and the visible symbol of its increasingly costly and unpopular war mobilization policy, Hamilton became the principal and only safe target of opportunity permitted by the press gag law.

Benjamin Franklin Bache's *Aurora* of Philadelphia, which his widow had continued to publish following his recent death, was still probably the most influential of all the lively Republican newspapers. In New York, Thomas Greenleaf's widow, Ann, continued to publish the *Argus,* or *Greenleaf's New Daily Advertiser,* which often was filled with little more than juicy scraps of Anti-Federalist scandal reprinted from the *Aurora.*

One such reprinted item was a spurious letter supposedly written by a man in New York to a doctor in Philadelphia that was exquisitely calibrated to sow divisive tares between High and moderate Federalists with a needling nicety worthy of John Beckley's and James T. Callender's finest collaborations in the genre. The writer described how he had found Hamilton "in a sweat" upon hearing that Adams would resign from office that summer. He went on to report that Jefferson, "that cool casuistic Frenchified fellow will be thrust in his place." He predicted that Hamilton would run for president and win because Hamilton had said, "The dollars I have heap'd together whilst handling the government's cash will not be without their use."

Another such story reprinted by the *Argus* was that Hamilton was at the bottom of a plot to suppress the *Aurora* by purchasing it from Bache's widow. Six thousand dollars had been offered as a down payment and two impartial persons would determine a fair sum for the balance to be paid when she turned her paper over to him. She had indignantly spurned his offer. She could not dishonor her late husband's memory or her children's future fame by such baseness, she was alleged to have said, adding that if she ever did part with her paper, "it should be to Republicans only."

Editorial commentary following the story wallowed in wonderment. How could Hamilton now command $15,000 or $20,000 when in 1792 he could not meet James Reynolds's demand for $1,000 except in two installment payments? Perhaps the sum was to be raised by "an association of orderly federalists" like some who had plotted to drive James T. Callender out of Richmond. Or perhaps an illicit slush fund of money from the British secret service would be doled out to him by Robert Liston, the British minister. Why did Major General Hamilton not use a more economical method to suppress the *Aurora?* He could have marched out the same army troops that had put down poor John Fries to gibbet the *Aurora*'s editor and destroy its offices in half an hour. Federalist ownership of the *Aurora*, the story sarcastically conceded, would shield them even from such criticism as "the mildness of the Sedition Law as yet suffers the *Aurora* to bestow on them."

Here was yet another tweaking of Hamilton's raw Reynolds case nerves. His angry reply letter was published in New York in *The Daily Advertiser* on November 9, 1799. He raged at the *Argus* for "a publication . . . which charges me with being at the 'bottom' of an 'Effort recently made to suppress the *Aurora*' . . . by pecuniary means."

"One principal Engine" for pulling down the pillars of society, declared Hamilton, was "audacious falsehoods to destroy the confidence of the people in all those, who are in any degree conspicuous among the supporters of the government . . ." His enemies' lies had become systematic and formidable. He had at other times treated such "malignant calumnies" with contempt, but now it was his "duty to the community" to suppress them by the force of the laws.

He was conscious that such a linking of personal charges against himself with injury to the nation might seem to some a little vain, but he "must be content with the mortification." He concluded, "In no event, however, will any displeasure I may feel, be at war with the public interest. This in my eyes is sacred."

Hamilton demanded that his friend Josiah Ogden Hoffman, the New York state attorney general, commence an immediate prosecution against the *Argus*. Its scandalous stories were likely to have "very fatal consequences" for the

American government, Hamilton insisted. "Such an attack demanded peculiar attention. A bolder calumny; one more absolutely destitute of foundation, was never propagated." Its "dangerous tendency," he said, needed no comment. He commented anyway; it was calculated "to inspire the belief that the independence and liberty of the press are endangered by the intrigues of ambitious citizens aided by foreign gold." His and Hoffman's criminal prosecution of the *Argus* could be brought under state, not federal law, for the printing of a private defamatory libel.

At the time, New York State's constitution contained no guarantee of freedom of speech or of the press. The laws of libel and slander were much stricter then than now. Under common law doctrine that derived from colonial days, the truth of an alleged libel was no defense. There was no privilege to publish attacks on public figures, no protection for inadvertent error. Under the old law, truth or falsity had nothing to do with libel. If the writing or printing or even a picture tended to expose a man to hatred, contempt, or ridicule, the person who was responsible for the printing of it was ipso facto guilty of libel. Convictions were much easier to obtain in criminal cases at the state level than they were under the Federal Sedition Law, which marked a liberalization of the old law because the sedition law, unlike state law allowed truth of the story as a justification and a defense. In the greatest law case of his life, Hamilton less than four years later would be instrumental in bringing about the liberalization of state law that would make true freedom of the press the staunch guarantor and underwriter of the people's liberty that it is in America today, even while losing the case for his client.

As it happened, at the time Hoffman instituted Hamilton's prosecution of the *Argus* under New York State law, there was already pending an entirely separate federal prosecution of the *Argus* under the Sedition Law for printing various other offensive pro-Republican Anti-Federalist stories, such as those that advocated erecting liberty poles or called the "Federal government corrupt and inimical to the preservation of Liberty" or attacked the Alien and Sedition Acts themselves.

On November 7, Assistant New York State Attorney General Cadwallader D. Colden went to the *Argus*'s office and told Mrs. Greenleaf of Hamilton's intended prosecution. She disclaimed guilt under the Sedition Law—the article that offended Hamilton had been a reprint from the Boston *Telegraph* and plainly labeled as such. Her shop foreman, journeyman printer, David Frothingham, looked at the article and gallantly took the rap for the widow, saying he supposed he was the one responsible for reprinting it, although he strenuously denied having had anything to do with writing or composing it. Because Mrs. Greenleaf was already under federal indictment under the Sedition Laws, but a conviction against the *Argus* might be easier to obtain under state libel law in Hamilton's case, Colden arrested Frothingham on November 9, took him into custody, and released him on bail pending the trial scheduled to begin on November 21.

With nothing to lose but its life in any event the *Argus* struck back. Its columns identified Hamilton's state prosecution with the federal prosecution under the hated Sedition Law. It denounced both as part of a system to gag all printers *"who dare support the cause of freedom and the rights of man."* It charged Hamilton and Federalists generally with pursuing a cheaper method to gag hostile papers than buying them up: swamping them with lawyers bills to defend federal and state prosecutions. These destroyed the papers' owners economically and cost a complaining witness like Hamilton nothing. Hamilton was a hypocrite, cried the *Argus*, trying to identify his personal resentment with the "social security and happiness" of America. He was only pressing his suit to protect his thin skin from public criticism. Hamilton was the worst kind of hypocrite for prosecuting Frothingham claiming to protect "social security and happiness," when Hamilton himself was one of the worst offenders against "social security and happiness" by his own confessed unchastity.

The names of Frothingham's defense counsel, Brockholst and Edward Livingston, guaranteed that the harsh rigidity of the Federal sedition and state libel laws and Hamilton's own exposed position, would receive the widest possible public airing when they fought back against Attorney Generals Hoffman and Colden. It was a celebrated political trial in every sense.

Frothingham pleaded not guilty to the indictment, which charged him with publishing a libel designed "to injure the name and reputation of General Hamilton." Although Frothingham had not admitted that he was the editor or proprietor of the *Argus*, he had said that he "expected" he was responsible. His denial of having had a hand in composition of the article, admitting merely reprinting it from another paper, was no defense. The mere republication of the article constituted a new libel.

Assistant Attorney General Cadwallader Colden and Hamilton were the only witnesses for the prosecution. Brockholst Livingston argued that the court should exclude Hamilton's testimony on grounds that it was hearsay, opinion, biased, and various other bad things. The court overruled his objection. Hamilton won the right to testify to what the *Argus's* innuendoes meant. This led him into having to rehash all over again, under oath from the witness box at a well-publicized public trial, all his by now no doubt only too well-rehearsed reasons for having made payments to James Reynolds. In Frothingham's defense, Livingston sought to argue that he was not responsible—he was only an eight-dollar-a-week journeyman printer. But the court refused to admit any evidence of Frothingham's position at the *Argus* or any evidence to disprove the imputation of malice raised by Hamilton's testimony.

The article itself had not charged Hamilton with being anti-Republican; it was his own reaction that derived that insulting innuendo from it and found offense in the charge. Brockholst Livingston argued ingeniously that the word *Republican* as used in the article had been a party label. Everyone knew that there were now two political parties in the United States: one, the Federalists, who favored the administration; the other, the Republicans, who opposed it. If the *Argus* had called Hamilton anti-Republican, he should have taken it as praise, not blame; it was only another way of calling him a good Federalist.

Livingston also argued in Frothingham's defense that suppression of a newspaper by legal means such as buying it was a private, not a criminal matter; that if, as Hamilton claimed, the Baches' *Aurora* was subversive of the government, for Hamilton to suppress it by buying it out "would be a feather in his cap, and entitle him to the thanks," not the "ridicule and hatred of his fellow citizens." Therefore, Frothingham's reprint was praise of Hamilton, not a damaging innuendo as he claimed.

The only questions the court would permit the jury to decide was whether the article was designed to expose Hamilton to hatred and contempt and whether Frothingham had printed it. Acting on these instructions on the law, the jury returned after three hours with a verdict of guilty. They added a recommendation for clemency. Poor Frothingham's salary of eight dollars a week was the sole support of his wife and six children. Besides, he had only been trying to protect the widow Greenleaf.

Judge Radcliffe sternly sentenced him to four months in prison or until he paid a fine of $100 and required him to post a bond of $2,000 before release and to give a guarantee of good behavior for two years. Before sentencing him, Judge Radcliffe declared, "If he has a wife and children, he ought to have thought of them before he violated the laws of the country."

The Federalist *Gazette of the United States* groaned that the sentence was much too lenient; the *Argus* and the *Aurora* deplored its severity, but in rather careful language. The *Argus* called the trial a political one, in which the jury had been packed with Federalists. "When unpopular measures of government produced opposition in their subjects," it declared, "bad rulers destroy contradiction and complaint by embracing every opportunity to persecute their opponents."

The costly pressures of both state and federal prosecutions succeeded in suppressing the *Argus*. Mrs. Ann Greenleaf was forced to sell out to David Denniston on March 8, 1800, only two months before statewide elections to the legislature. Under the system then prevailing, the newly elected legislators would, in turn, choose New York's electors for the presidential election of 1800. Realizing the political damage that unpopular Phyrric victories in such trials were causing to Federalists' chances and with the *Argus* now out of business and no longer a threat, Adams in April approved Pickering's recommendation that the federal prosecution of Ann Greenleaf under the Sedition Law be dropped.

Such clemency was too late. Hamilton's successful prosecution would help swell the Republican tide in May that swept Hamilton's old Federalist-dominated state legislature out of office and Aaron Burr's Republicans into power just in time to control New York's pivotal electoral vote in the national elections now coming up. New York was a swing state, and whoever won New York was likely to win the nation. New York Republicans, always strong in Clinton's upstate bailiwicks, under the skillful leadership of Aaron Burr and the Society of Tammany had also been growing stronger in Hamilton's hitherto impregnable Federalist bastion in New York City. In the local elections of 1799, Hamilton and his merchant allies had routed Burr and Tammany by making a winning campaign issue of the labored charge that the Manhattan Company, of which Burr was a director and officer, ostensibly incorporated to yield a pure water supply, had instead become a Republican bank. The charge was partly false—the company did, in fact, supply water—but also partly true—it was also a bank. Such rather misleading charges of fraud and double-dealing had been enough to rout Burr and Tammany then, but a backlash against the mudslinging of 1799 was now setting in. Rising taxes, resentment of the Alien and Sedition Laws, and reaction against the arrogance of Federalists who had never been out of office since the Republic began—all contributed to a predictable groundswell of popular opinion that felt it was time for a change.

But Hamilton was confident, overconfident, that Federalists could hold the majority they had won in 1799. To make certain that, win or lose, the electors of 1800 would be loyal to him, not merely Federalist in persuasion, but answerable to him for how they would vote, he nominated a ticket of candidates who, although not men of the first rank, could be counted on for loyalty to him—and, if he cracked the whip, vote for Charles Cotesworth Pinckney for president. Most party leaders would rather risk losing an election than losing control of the levers of party power, and Hamilton was no exception, if one can judge from the slate he put up for the legislature in 1800. On the basis of such reckoning, it is easier to understand why Hamilton did not select better-known votegetters for his state campaign. President Adams and others had already charged that in 1789 and 1792 Hamilton had caused electors to withhold votes from him and that in 1796 Hamilton had sought to displace him with Thomas Pinckney. The knowledgeable public knew of his quarrel with Adams, and the quarrel had now opened a fatal breach in the party. There were pro-Adams Federalists and pro-Hamilton Federalists, and it sometimes seemed that they hated each other more than they hated any Republican. Hamilton did not wish to see the Republicans win, but he could live with the idea more easily than with that of Adams retaining the presidency.

At best, if New York electors remained obedient to him, he could keep the Federalists in power and substitute his old friend, Charles Cotesworth Pinckney of South Carolina, for Adams. At worst, if Adams should lose and Pinckney too, Hamilton would survive as New York leader of the Federalists amid the dashed hopes of his losing rivals.

For the election of 1800, Burr put into the field as candidates the most prominent and influential Republicans he could find, except for some obscure ones whose surnames happened to be the same as those of prominent Federalists. Burr thoroughly organized Tammany Hall, a society composed chiefly of former Sons of Liberty, artisans, draymen, and mechanics. For members who lacked sufficient property to qualify as voters, an assignment of property for qualification purposes might be made. The New York City polls were open from April 29 through May 1. Making his efforts spectacularly visible, Hamilton rode from polling booth to polling booth in full uniform on a white steed to rally and harangue the voters. Burr did not mingle much with the public, but busied himself with making certain that all possible Tammany voters, including as usual some who had died, got to the polls without fail.

When all votes were counted, Burr and the Republicans of New York City had elected their entire slate to the legislature over Hamilton's obedient ciphers. Gains upstate gave Republicans a large enough margin in the assembly, even though the senate remained in Federalist control, to give them a majority in the combined houses—of a single vote. But that one was enough to elect a solidly Republican slate of electors to cast New York's 12 votes for president and vice-president.

Stunned and shocked by his repudiation, Hamilton wrote Senator Theodore Sedgwick on May 4, before all tallies were in, that "to support *Adams* and *Pinckney* equally is the only thing that can possibly save us from the fangs of Jefferson." The Federalist congressional caucus just then in session to choose the presidential candidate "should not separate without coming to a distinct and solemn concert to pursue this course *bona fide.*" Uncoded, this meant that the Northern states must give all possible support to Pinckney, not withholding a single vote as Massachusetts had done in 1796. The words *bona fide* would lend weight to suspicions of anyone as suspicious as Adams that Hamilton's promise of equal support for him and Pinckney meant equivocal support in 1796 and equally equivocal support in 1800.

Hamilton delivered his advice to the senator from Massachusetts like a general's command to a lowly aide, without accompanying social grace notes: "Pray attend to this, and let me speedily hear from you that it is done." The day before Hamilton's letter, the Federalist caucus in Philadelphia had duly chosen Adams and Charles Cotesworth Pinckney as the Federalist candidates respectively for president and vice-president. One week later, a Republican caucus chose Jefferson for president and, on the strength of his sensational victory in the recent New York elections and other reasons, Aaron Burr to be their candidate for vice-president.

Far from "triumphing over all his enemies," as he had confidently promised Henry Lee he would do only two months earlier, three of Hamilton's leading enemies now stood on the threshhold of an all but certain electoral triumph over him. In anger, disgust, and desperation, his pen in the tight grip of paranoia or, at least, of a manic defense, he wrote and sent a letter to Governor John Jay that contained what was probably the most shocking and unworthy political proposal he had ever made in his life. It was a "moral certainty," Hamilton wrote, that "there will be an antifederal majority in the ensuing Legislature." This "will bring *Jefferson,* an atheist in religion and a fanatic in politics into the chief magistracy." The Anti-Federal party "is a composition of very incongruous materials, all tending to mischief—some of them, to the OVERTHROW of the GOVERNMENT, others of them, to a REVOLUTION, after the manner of BONAPARTE." To Hamilton, these were not "conjectures or inferences," but "indubitable facts." Jefferson, Burr, and the Anti-Federalists must be kept "from getting possession of the helm of state" by the plan Hamilton was now about to propose. Call the existing lame duck legislature into special session. Have the old Federalist majority change the law to provide for "the *choosing of electors by the people in districts."* This "will insure a majority of votes in the United States for a federal candidate."

Hamilton was proposing to Jay that he steal the election that Burr and the Republicans had just won by having the lame duck legislature take away from the newly elected legislature its right to select presidential electors. Hamilton saw clearly enough that the opposition would condemn this. But, he insisted to Jay, "it is justified by the unequivocal reasons of PUBLIC SAFETY." "Think well," he commanded Jay, "appreciate the extreme danger of the crisis."

Hamilton's conscience nagged him a little, but he resolved all doubts in favor of quick action: summon the legislature! No time must be lost, he told Jay. He saw the issue as a conflict between absolutes of vice and virtue: "Popular governments must certainly be overturned, and while they endure prove engines of mischief, if one party will call to its aid all the resources which vice can give, and if the other (however pressing the emergency) confines itself within all the ordinary forms of delicacy and decorum."

His proposal was *"legal* and *constitutional,"* he insisted. Pitifully out of touch now with political reality, to the old friend who had known him in his prime, he added, "the motive ought to be frankly avowed." Yes, he went on, "in times like these in which we live, it will not do to be over scrupulous." The right end, as he saw it, seemed to justify almost any wrong means. He even exalted this pernicious prescript into the form of a general maxim for societal management by underscoring it for Jay's benefit in case he had missed the point: *"It is easy to sacrifice the substantial interests of society by a strict adherence to ordinary rules."* At best, this is a meaningless statement not worth the paper it is written on. At worst, as a political or social maxim, it is a shocking, lawless reversal, a ripping out, of all the innumerable stitches Hamilton had contributed by words and actions of more than 20 years to the fabric of law-abiding, moderate, constitutional American government before his breakdown in the face of the threats of his enemies in 1800.

John Jay had won a gubernatorial election from George Clinton by a narrow margin in 1792, only to have Aaron Burr snatch victory from his grasp by ruling in favor of Clinton on the disputed ballots. But Jay would also know of Hamilton's proneness to nervous derangements. No prosy Jay could ever forget the haunting imagery of the letter Hamilton had written him three days after Monroe and the congressman had confronted him the night of December 15, 1792, with evidence of what he called "malicious intrigues to stab me in the dark." Neither Hamilton's vehemence now, nor the chance for reprisal against Burr, caused Jay to swerve from majestic rectitude. He endorsed on Hamilton's appeal the following words: "Proposing a measure for party purposes which it would not become me to adopt."

He did not even deign to acknowledge Hamilton's letter. The pointed rebuke from Hamilton's oldest political ally and most intimate confidant in times of his deepest stress was yet another prick of persecution from an unexpected quarter. Hamilton's letters of the following days, May 8 and 10, to Senator Sedgwick are full of the same crackbrained brand of frantic insistence on his own apocalyptic

vision. He sees no alternative but chaos if his advice is ignored or, if heeded, fails
to prevail. "For my individual part my mind is made up," he said:

> I will never more be responsible for him [Adams] by my direct support,
> even though the consequence should be the election of *Jefferson*. If we
> must have an *enemy* at the head of the government, let it be one who
> we can oppose, and for whom we are not responsible, who will not
> involve our party in the disgrace of his foolish and bad measures. The
> party in the hands of whose chief it shall sink will sink with it, and the
> advantage will be all on the side of his adversaries. [Yet] if I can be
> perfectly satisfied that Adams and Pinckney will be upheld in the East
> with entire good faith, on the ground of conformity, I will, wherever my
> influence may extend, pursue the same plan, if not, I will pursue Mr.
> Pinckney as my single object.

The strategy was transparent. If the New England states, where Adams
was strong, could be induced to cast their votes equally for Adams and Pinckney
and if some of the Southern states like North and South Carolina cast their
ballots for Pinckney and Jefferson, Pinckney, though intended by the caucus and
most electors for second place, would snatch the first away from both Adams
and Jefferson.

Adams had won New York's electors in 1796. He ladled out a large share
of the blame for having lost them in 1800 to Hamilton's inept leadership and
intrigues with Sedgwick and other high Federalists to slip Pinckney into the
presidency ahead of himself. In 1800, as he prepared to leave the capital as usual
for Quincy, he suddenly decided to fire some of the cabinet he had inherited from
Washington that had originally been handpicked by Hamilton.

Adams seemed to live in a perpetual rage like a volcano that smoldered and
occasionally erupted or, as Bache said, he guggled like a pepperpot stew. On May
5 he summoned McHenry from a dinner party to confer with him on a routine
matter. Seeing the Secretary standing before him full of what he suspected was
a fawning, false deference, Adams lost his temper. He had heard that McHenry
wished to hold on to his office after the coming presidential election. McHenry
replied evasively. Adams exploded.

"Hamilton has been opposing the administration in New York," Adams
charged furiously.

McHenry was not aware of it.

"No head of a department shall be permitted to oppose me," Adams cried,
his face flushed with anger.

"I have heard no such conduct ascribed to General Hamilton and cannot
think it to be the case," McHenry answered deferentially, but firmly.

"I know it, sir, to be so," Adams stormed, in effect calling his secretary of
war a liar. "You are subservient to him!" he raged on. If Adams's matter had
the ring of truth, his manner had a manic ring.

"Hamilton ruled Washington, and would still rule if he could."

McHenry demurred.

"It was you who biased General Washington's mind."

Nothing McHenry could do could stop the torrent of Adams's abuse.

"You induced Washington to place Hamilton on the list of major generals, ahead of Knox and Pinckney."

When this humiliation crossed Adams's mind, as McHenry recalled the explosion, Adams completely lost control of himself and began to rant. Hamilton was "an intriguant, the greatest intriguant in the world." He was a man "devoid of every moral principle!" Hamilton was "a bastard," "a Creole bastard," and "as much a foreigner as Gallatin." As for Adams, he would rather serve under Jefferson as vice-president or even as resident minister at The Hague than to be indebted "to such a being as Hamilton for the presidency." To Adams, it was not to be borne that Washington had saddled him with three cabinet ministers who were babes in the woods of foreign policy. Wolcott was no use when it came to international diplomacy. "How could such men," he all but screamed, now entirely out of control, "dictate to me on such matters, or dare to recommend a suspension of the mission to France!"

He loosed a boiling flood of suspicion, resentment, hatred, frustration, vexation, and uncontrolled fury on McHenry. When the crazy outburst finally subsided, McHenry, near tears, answered, "I shall, of course, resign at once."

Adams accepted. "Very well, sir," he said.

Then he began to cool off—indeed, feel shame. "For myself, I have always, I will acknowledge, considered you as a man of understanding and of the strictest integrity."

Poor McHenry slunk out of the room. The next day he submitted his resignation in writing, and Adams accepted it.

By this time Adams had probably got word that Pickering (as he had written Fisher Ames and William Bingham on October 24 and 29, 1799) was saying that Adams's sending off Ellsworth and Davie on the peace mission "will subvert the present administration and with it the government itself " and that Mr. Adams "had not by this mission gained one friend among the democrats; to their former hatred will now be added *another sensation:* while among the Federalists he has forfeited the support of his best friends and our most estimable citizens." Pickering concluded that only by refusing to seek a second term could Adams "unite the Federalists and save our country."

Four days later by a curt note Adams demanded Pickering's resignation. Two days later, Pickering replied to Adams that he could not afford to resign. He needed the salary and had counted on drawing it until the following March, when Jefferson would become president. Until then, Pickering said, "I do not feel it my duty to resign."

This was not only insulting to Adams, but witheringly defeatist. Adams exploded again. He fired a second note back to Pickering, telling him simply, "You are hereby discharged from any further service as Secretary of State."

Hamilton thanked McHenry on June 6, 1800, for the story of his forced resignation, regretting that "you thought it necessary to forbid my taking a copy." He urgently demanded "as many circumstances as may appear to you . . . to show the probability of coalitions with Mr. Jefferson, etc., which are spoken of."

Hamilton added, "The man is more mad than I ever thought him and I shall soon be led to say as wicked as he is mad." On July 1, Hamilton wrote Wolcott that "it is essential to inform the most discreet . . . of the facts which denote unfitness in Mr. Adams. I have promised confidential friends a correct statement." The best campaign issue any incumbent president running for reelection has in his favor is stability and continuity, and Adams had just blown it up in his own face.

To Hamilton, writing six months later, these dismissals confirmed his worst fears of Adams's "ungovernable temper" and "paroxysms of anger, which deprive him of self command, and produce very outrageous behaviour to those who approach him." Distinguished members of Congress, Hamilton added in his attack on Adams, not to speak of his own cabinet ministers McHenry, Pickering, and Wolcott "have been humiliated by the effects of these gusts of passion."

Hamilton charged sarcastically that Adams's "little consideration for his ministers" in declining to consult them "had occasioned great dryness" between them. Though absent, Hamilton was acutely conscious that he had been the spark or blasting cap that touched off the firings. "It fell to my lot," he had immediately been told, "to be distinguished by a torrent of gross personal abuse." Besides calling him a "Creole bastard," Adams had accused him of having caused the loss of the New York election out of ill will.

The confrontation between poor, gentle, inept McHenry and Adams "was of a nature to excite alternately pain and laughter," Hamilton sighed, pain for Adams's "weak and excessive indiscretions" and "laughter at the ludicrous topics which constituted charges." One such charge was that McHenry in a report to the House had *"eulogized* General Washington, and had attempted to eulogize General Hamilton." This was "Wonderful! passing wonderful!" Hamilton chortled. "That a eulogy of the dead patriot and hero should be in any shape, irksome to the ears of his successor!" To Hamilton the crowning folly of Adams's manic defense was his denying of praise to Hamilton. It was "singular, that an encomium on the officer, first in rank of the armies of the United States, appointed and continued by Mr. Adams, should in his eyes have been a crime in the head of the War Department and that it should be necessary in order to avert his displeasure, to obliterate a compliment to that officer from an official report" to the House of Representatives.

As soon as Hamilton heard of McHenry's and Pickering's two-night massacre, he wrote to Pickering on May 14 that when he cleaned out his office, "you ought to take with you copies and extracts of all such documents as will enable you to explain both Jefferson and Adams. You are aware of a very curious journal of the latter when he was in Europe—a tissue of weakness and vanity." To this advice Hamilton added the reflection "the time is coming when men of real integrity and energy must unite against all Empirics." As he had told Jay, for men of integrity, "it would not do to be over scrupulous."

Pickering replied mournfully: "I intended to have done precisely what you suggest, respecting Mr Adams' journal (very little of which I had ever read) but there was not time."

Adams immediately appointed Samuel Dexter, a Massachusetts senator, whose Federalism was so moderate that his friends called him "Ambi" Dexter, to be secretary of war and John Marshall as secretary of state. The Senate confirmed. Although Wolcott had served Hamilton longer and more intimately than, and as faithfully as the others, Adams left him to dangle in cabinet office. Wolcott observed that Adams "considers Col. Pickering., McHenry and myself as his enemies. His resentments against General Hamilton are excessive; he declares his belief of the existence of a British faction in the United States."

Before adjourning on May 14, Congress effectively dismantled Hamilton's provisional army. Having suspended further enlistments February 20, it passed a law authorizing early discharges for officers and men and cut the military budget from over four million to about three million, mostly by postponing construction of heavy frigates and ending army enlistments. Although the Nonintercourse Act against France was extended by the Senate for another year, over the objections of Charles Pinckney and others, who called it an unconstitutional delegation of power to what they saw as the increasing danger of Adams's imperial presidency, Jefferson contentedly purred that "on the whole the federalists have not been able to carry a single strong measure in the lower house the whole session."

High Federalists saw these dovish measures of Congress as an electioneering effort of Adams to gain quick popular favor with Republicans, if not outright treachery to Federalist principles. Pickering charged that Adams had made a "corrupt bargain with the Democrats [Republicans] to secure his second election." When Adams denied such a deal, Pickering fired back, "I will only say that the President is not always consistent or accurate in his rememberance."

All reason for Hamilton's intense attention to the duties signified by the gaudy two-star general's uniform he wore was fading away. The state of the force at the moment when recruitment was reversed was no credit to the inspector general. After an absence in Albany on private legal affairs for a month in January and February, leaving Adjutant General William North in charge of the dispirited army, Hamilton returned to duty with much brisk spirit. He visited the encampment at Scotch Plains, New Jersey, directed that old regiments be filled out by new recruits from those to be dissolved, and made sure that all soldiers, when discharged, were paid in full, including three months' dismissal pay. In June he took a swing through Massachusetts, New Hampshire, and Rhode Island, ostensibly to inspect troop encampments, but secretly to canvass federal electors in those states to find out how firmly they would hold their votes to Pinckney for second place after Adams. Hamilton thanked the departing troops for the president and himself and hoped their patriotism would lead them to a just construction of the motives of the government.

Rumors reached Adams that Hamilton, reviewing the troops as inspector general, was electioneering against Adams for General Pinckney and that, when inspecting troops in Portsmouth and Boston, he had let it be known that Adams was a weak and ineffective man who could not win on the Federalist ticket. Abigail wrote to tell their son Thomas that "thus has this intriguer been endeavoring to divide the Federal party—to create divisions and heart burnings against the President merely because he cannot sway or carry such measures as he wishes." The Adamses all suspected that Hamilton wanted Pinckney on the ground that "a military man only should be President."

On July 1, 1800, Hamilton quit his headquarters in New York and next day notified the secretary of war that he considered his military service ended. He submitted his accounts and put his uniform away. On the same day he left the service, he began to busy himself with his plan to install Pinckney as president.

Hamilton's friend and deputy, Adjutant General North, must have sensed his chief's dangerous mood at this plague-ridden season: "To you . . . all eyes look, and on you, everything will depend in a great measure . . . Your head is always right, I would your heart was a little less susceptible. I pray you: When it is about to carry you out of the direct path, you will, like the deacons and select men, throw a cloak over your shoulders."

One day, some day, North assured him, everyone would turn again to Hamilton "to save the country from ruin." With the next election still four months away, Federalist chances were by no means hopeless. New England's electors remained solidly behind Adams for president. Canvassing all the states in August, George Cabot forecast 67 votes for Pinckney, 65 for Jefferson, and 59 for Adams. Much depended on still uncertain electors in middle states like Pennsylvania, Delaware, and Maryland and on Adams's friends holding firm and voting for Pinckney too.

The Federalist problem in 1800 was similar to that of 1796, when Hamilton wrote, "the plan of giving equal support to the two Federalist candidates [Adams and Thomas Pinckney] was not pursued. Personal attachment for Mr. Adams, especially in the New England states caused a number of the votes to be withheld from Mr. Pinckney and thrown away." Then Adams had squeaked in ahead of Jefferson by only three votes. "But for a sort of miracle" then, said Hamilton, Jefferson would have been president. In each of Pennsylvania, Virginia, and North Carolina, Adams had received but one vote. "The firmness of the individuals who separated from their colleagues, was so extraordinary as to have been contrary to all probable calculation." Had one switched, there might have been a tie. Two, and Jefferson would have been in. In 1796, "in dropping Mr. Pinckney too much was put at hazard."

In this, Hamilton's first salvo in his 1800 campaign for Charles Cotesworth Pinckney, he wrote Wolcott that "his tour had shown him there were solid federal electors in all the New England states," but that "there is considerable doubt of a perfect union in favor of Pinckney." The "leaders of the first class," the High Federalists, generally went along, but "those of the second class are too much disposed to be wrong." Therefore, he concluded, "it is essential to inform the most discreet of this description of the facts which denote unfitness in Mr. Adams. I have promised confidential friends a correct statement." This was more of a threat than a promise.

Hamilton corresponded with leaders of Federalism throughout the country in similar vein: Sedgwick, Cabot, and Pickering in New England; James A. Bayard, Charles Carroll, Robert Goodloe Harper, and McHenry of the southerly and middle states; and John Rutledge of the Deep South. Jefferson must be defeated, but it was just as essential that Adams be replaced by Pinckney. Unfortunately, the leaders of "the second class," especially in New England, might take alarm and throw away their votes from Pinckney. Accordingly, the strategy was to put it about in New England that both Adams and Pinckney must be supported equally and to rely upon certain other states like Delaware and North and South Carolina to drop Adams for Jefferson or Burr or Clinton and thereby assure Pinckney's slipping in.

Replies ranged from wholehearted agreement to cautious reservations. Bayard of Delaware promised that "if events should justify it, there will be no difficulty in leaving him [Adams] out of the tickets of this State." But Harper of South Carolina sensibly warned "that no direct attempt can safely be made to drop or supersede Mr. Adams. It would create uncertainty, division and defeat. Let both men be held up till the Electors come to vote; and then let those who think Mr. Adams unfit to be President drop him silently."

But Hamilton was determined on a surer way to triumph over all his enemies. It was August, his family was in Albany, and New York City's usual summer fevers gripped his brain. As in other feverish summers of the past, he wrote another awful pamphlet better left unwritten.

Writing at speed, he produced the extraordinary document entitled "The Public Conduct and Character of John Adams, Esq., President of the United States." In the form of a letter, it is addressed to an unnamed "Sir." It is full of Hamilton himself in the first person singular and Mr. Adams in the third person. It reads as if it is really addressed to all and sundry of the enemies Hamilton's paranoia now senses to be crowding in on him. Enemies all but crowd Mr. Adams out of the opening paragraphs. Here would be the final "triumph over all my enemies" Hamilton had promised Henry Lee in March.

"Warm personal friends of Mr. Adams are taking unwearied pains to disparage the motives of those Federalists who advocate the equal support of General Pinckney at the approaching election of President and Vice President," Hamilton begins his attack. Adams's friends had exhibited Hamilton in all manner of "derogatory aspects"; they were "versatile factious spirits"; they were "ambitious spirits"; they were "intriguing partisans of Great Britain. There had been "a full share of obloquy" vented against Hamilton and others, but there were besides, he says, "peculiar accusations devised to swell the catalogue of my demerits." Therefore, defending his own manic defense more than attacking Adams, he wrote, "It is necessary, for the public cause, to repel these slanders, by stating the real views of the persons who are calumniated, and the reasons of their conduct." President Adams "is a man of imagination sublimated and eccentric; propitious neither to the regular display of sound judgement, nor to steady perseverance in a systematic plan of conduct." Worse, "to this defect are added the unfortunate foibles of a vanity without bounds, and a jealousy capable of discoloring every object." From the very beginning, Adams had been guilty

of "disgusting egotism, distempered jealousy, and ungovernable indiscretion."
These were the same two defects Hamilton's warmest, fondest, and closest
friends like Gouverneur Morris found in him. In support of this indictment,
Hamilton describes Adams's explosions at Trenton and McHenry and gives the
comments on Adams that are set forth earlier in this and preceding chapters.

It was inexcusable, as Hamilton saw it, that Adams rages against Mr.
Hamilton and overwhelms him with "a torrent of gross personal abuse." Adams
had dismissed his secretaries of state and war contemptuously from office and
taken contradictory and equally atrocious stands on both the hawkish and dovish
sides of the issue of war with France. He had sunk the tone of the public mind,
sowed the seeds of discord at home, and lowered the reputation of the government abroad. He had tried to prevent the appointment of Mr. Hamilton as
inspector general and "stigmatized" him "as the leader of a British faction."

During the summer Hamilton had written at least two letters to Adams
demanding to know if Adams had ever called him the leader of the British
faction, but Adams had never deigned to respond. The specific examples Hamilton cites in support of such monstrous charges fall pathetically short of carrying
the weight of proof he assigns to them. Here is an example Hamilton gives of
Adams's fatuous vanity: "Being among the guests invited to dine with the Count
Vergennes, Minister for Foreign Affairs, Mr. Adams thought fit to give a specimen of American politeness by conducting Madame de Vergennes to dinner; on
the way, she was pleased to make retribution in the current coin of French
politeness—by saying to him 'Monsieur Adams, vous êtes le Washington de
negociation.'" Adams, noting down the incident, had made the following self-
satisfied comment upon it: "These people have a very pretty knack of paying
compliments." Hamilton made the following supercilious comment on Adams's
reaction: "He might have added, they also have a very dexterous knack of
disguising a sarcasm."

Few things serve better than his belaboring of Adams with this anecdote
to betray the rather trivial and personal nature of the grievances that to Hamilton's mind now seemed to undermine the security of the state. Hamilton's conclusion was that Mr. Adams "does not possess the talents adapted to the administration of government, and there are great and intrinsic defects in his character,
which unfit him for the office of chief magistrate." Here was absolute disqualification of Adams to hold the office that he held.

But this was not Hamilton's conclusion. Here was his ludicrous *non sequi-
tur:* "Yet with this opinion of Mr. Adams, I have finally resolved not to advise
the withholding from him a single vote." Why not? "The body of Federalists for
want of sufficient knowledge of facts, are not convinced of the expediency of
relinquishing him. It is even apparent, that a large proportion still retain the
attachment which was once a common sentiment."

Wallace Stevens in his *Esthetique du Mal* explains how

. . . . The cause
Creates a logic not to be distinguished from lunacy.

In the conclusion to his attack on John Adams, Hamilton exposes himself as a logical lunatic. Stevens, looking deep into the heart of such a man, echoing Cassius to Brutus in the Roman street, sees that he makes nature

> . . . . exist in his own especial eye.
> The genius of misfortune
> Is not a sentimentalist. He is
> That evil, that evil in the self, from which fault
> Falls out on everything.

Hamilton insisted on signing his name to this double-talk—though men like Cabot and Wolcott had advised him against doing so. He rushed it to the printer. Never in their most irresponsible heyday had the *Aurora* or the *Argus* published a more libelous, boldly malicious attack on a government official. Hamilton had set himself above the law.

In the text of the pamphlet itself, Hamilton admitted to being "sensible of the inconveniences of giving publicity" to such an unfortunate "development" in "the character of the Chief Magistrate of our country." He lamented the necessity of taking the step he was taking. But striking back, triumphing over his enemies, was of overriding importance. "It would not do to be over scrupulous," he wrote. "To suppress truths, the disclosure of which is as interesting to the public welfare as well as to my friends and myself, did not appear to me justifiable."

He so far heeded the cooler heads among his friends that he caused the printing to be done with secrecy and arranged for the pamphlet to be sent out only to "the leaders of the first class." But if Adams were really to be supported, "bona fide," any fool could see that the pamphlet had better never been written. Perhaps Hamilton thought that the final statement could be used as a means of placating "the leaders of the second class," to whom it might conceivably be shown, while the rest of the text would plant in their minds enough seeds of doubt so that they would switch to Pinckney as first choice at the last minute. To rational minds, such reasoning would expose its author as a contemptible hypocrite or a sick man.

It was Aaron Burr who ripped aside all such feverish subtleties and sophistries. He had always commanded the best political intelligence. Tammany included many artisan members who worked in printers' shops. Burr managed to purloin a copy of the pamphlet in proof or fresh off the press while it was still classified as a secret Federalist paper. Recognizing it for the political bombshell it was, Burr reprinted it in Republican newspapers before the originals had reached the hands of the Federalist inner circle, for whose eyes it had been intended.[1]

Waves of laughter rippled through Republican ranks. Rank and file Federalists were aghast at the sorry secret story of the mess in Philadelphia within the highest circles of their own self-righteous paladins.

Federalist publicists rushed to attack Hamilton for what he had done to their party and president. Hamilton defiantly announced to intimates that he planned to issue a second pamphlet to explain the first. Of this, he was, for once, dissuaded. Cabot, whose warnings Hamilton had ignored, clenched his teeth and reported that many Federalists, even those who "approved the sentiments, thought the avowal of them imprudent, and the publication of them untimely." Other men whose opinions Hamilton had to respect accused him of exhibiting the same or worse vanity as that with which he charged Adams.[2]

Abigail Adams, perhaps sensing a touch of madness in "the little General's letter" privately hoped that she would "have more health to laugh at the folly, and pity the weakness, vanity, and ambitious views of as very a sparrow as Sterne commented upon in his *Sentimental Journey,* or More describes in his fables." To Adams as well, "his exuberant vanity and insatiable egotism prompt him to be ever restless and busy meddling with things far above his capacity, and inflame him with an absolute rage to arrogate to himself the honor of suggesting every measure of government." That was not all. "He is no more fit for a prompter than Phaeton to drive the chariot of the sun. If his projects had been followed they would absolutely have burnt up the world."

James Cheetham, a prime Republican pamphleteer and "disorganizer" of Federalists, issued one of the harshest of many public counterattacks. Hamilton was "the zealous friend of monarchical government . . . a dangerous character under any republican system." "Have you not . . . forgotten that you were an American, and warmly panegerized the government of Great Britain? . . . have not the agents of that country been the inmates of your heart . . . ?" President Adams had "too much judgment and independence to submit to the leading strings of the ex-secretary. Here was disappointed ambition; . . . a clue to that mysterious character, whose power, if equal to his will, would bestride the world."

Cheetham praised Adams for his policy of peace, for pardoning Fries, and for smoothing differences with France. But his principal praises were for Jefferson. By way of unhappy contrast with that virtuous Virginian, Cheetham pejorated Hamilton's *Reynolds Pamphlet* and deplored his lapses from personal chastity.

Another pamphlet by an unidentified New Yorker, *A Vindication of the Conduct and Character of John Adams,* sought to show that Hamilton's "anxiety to continue his *political importance*" was the clue to his misguided performance. Hamilton had written under an obsession that vacated his judgment once "intuitively great" and blotted out his own conspicuous vulnerability. Because Hamilton had ended his attack by refusing to divert a single vote from Adams, "Why . . . in the name of common sense, was this extraordinary performance published at this critical moment?" Moderate Federalists now would fear internal party strife if either Adams or Pinckney won. To them, even Jefferson's election would be "an event less fatal to the harmony and prosperity of our government" than either of their own. Hamilton, "the statesman, the patriot, the polar star of Federalism, now indulges a most lethargic slumber. When he wakes from his delusion, how will he . . . hear the yell of Jacobinic triumph that shall hail a Democratic President!"

Still another, believed to be William Pinkney, saw Hamilton hoist on his own petard. He would "discover the black blood that eddies round [Hamilton's] heart." If the Jeffersonians won the election, all blame must be laid to Hamilton's "malice of disappointed ambition, animated with the hope of speedy resuscitation" if Charles Cotesworth Pinckney should slip in. Hamilton's army was useless; Adams's naval defense program was better liked by the people. Hamilton's sensitivities were badly deranged if he took umbrage at being called pro-British, while "this same tender mind could bear the reproach of breaking one of the most solemn ordinances . . . of God and man . . ."

Wolcott tendered a gloomy forecast: "The division among the federalists, is a necessary effect of a cause, which is much to be deplored. Though men may disagree respecting the merits or faults of individuals, it is certain none can be found sufficiently submissive to subscribe to the terms of their own dishonour; the division will therefore continue and all attempts to reconcile it will be fruitless." If the Democrats were certain they could not elect Jefferson, they would espouse Adams, if only for the mean purpose of deepening dissension among their opponents.

In 1800 the Republicans had similar but less intense blood feuds smoldering within their ranks, but managed to paper them over better, at least until they came to power. Jefferson was the unanimous choice for standard-bearer. More or less as always, there was intense behind the scenes maneuvering for vice-president. Aaron Burr cashed a due bill claiming that in secret caucus four years earlier John Beckley had promised him Jefferson's support in 1800 if he would withdraw in 1796 to avoid taking votes from Jefferson. They reluctantly honored it by agreeing to Aaron Burr for vice-president over elderly George Clinton even though Burr's rising political star would be a long-term threat to the party's dominant Virginia junto. The junto could fix Burr later.

Burr's rise past him to the next-to-top rung of the ladder alarmed and enraged Hamilton as much as, if not more than, Adams's candidacy. On August 6, Hamilton wrote to Bayard that "there seems to be too much probability that Jefferson or Burr will be President." If, by some chance, it should be Burr, he "will certainly attempt to reform the government *a la Bonaparte*. He is as unprincipled and dangerous a man as any country can boast—as true a Cataline as ever met in midnight conclave."

Set back by the gale of abuse that had met his Adams pamphlet, Hamilton for the moment was too beleaguered to waste much ammunition on Burr. Troup tactfully wrote that "General Hamilton is much disgusted with the reception his letter concerning the public character and conduct of Mr. Adams had met with —and he intimates often to me a very strong opinion that he will, in case of Jefferson's or Adams's election to the Presidency, retire from all public concerns."

By now, Hamilton had reached the point—unthinkable for a good Federalist —of openly preferring Jefferson to Adams. "General Hamilton makes no secret of his opinion that Jefferson should be preferred to Adams," wrote Troup. It had become a case of anyone but Adams—anyone, that is, anyone except Burr. Hamilton still had hopes for Pinckney. The "leaders of the first class" were now heartily with him on that point. Even the hitherto cautious Cabot now conceded that he was all for Pinckney; and if Pinckney could not be elected president, "we should do as well with Jefferson for President, and Mr. Pinckney for Vice-President, as with anything that we can now expect." Pickering and McHenry, the disgruntled ex-cabinet members, were naturally against Adams. Wolcott, who had managed to survive Adams's housecleaning, sniped at his titular chief with relish. "I understand," he wrote to McHenry, ". . . that it is said by the 'Adamites,' that the President will have all the votes of New England, except in the state of Connecticut; the loss of which they are pleased to attribute to me. I feel much honoured by the supposition that my influence is sufficient to produce so great an effect . . . If you will but do your part, we shall probably secure General Pinckney's election."

But Dr. James McHenry, ever the realist, put his finger on the trouble with all this letter-writing among the "leaders of the first class." With some asperity, he wrote: "Have our party shown that they possess the necessary skill and courage to deserve to be continued to govern? What have they done? . . . They write private letters. To whom? To each other. But they do nothing to give a proper direction to the public mind." It was patently true. While Hamilton and the others were busy sending exhortations to each other, the Republicans were out on the hustings after the peoples' votes. Pinckney, the first gentleman of America and their last hope, refused to cooperate in any underhanded scheme to displace Adams with himself. When the Hamiltonian faction in the legislature of South Carolina sent a delegation to him to obtain his consent to casting the vote of South Carolina equally for Pinckney and Jefferson and thereby eliminate Adams, he firmly refused. It would be Adams and Pinckney, he declared, or neither. It was neither.

Federalists were split wide open, and Republicans were triumphantly united. Burr's skillful tactics in New York had snatched that pivotal state from Hamilton. South Carolina cast its electoral votes unanimously for Jefferson and Burr. When the smoke cleared, the Republicans had won. Jefferson and Burr had each received 73 electoral votes; Adams, 65; and Pinckney, 64; there was a solitary independent vote for Jay. The reign of the Federalists was over. The second American Revolution had come.

But who had won, Jefferson or Burr? The fascinating might have been is that if Hamilton had never written his pamphlet, either Adams or Pinckney might have come out ahead of Jefferson and Burr. Cabot's earlier canvass of 67 for Pinckney, 65 for Jefferson, and 59 for Adams might have held up. Hamilton's man Pinckney would have been president, and Hamilton would, in truth, have been the King of the Feds. Or if Hamilton had held control of the New York legislature—instead of losing by a one-vote upset to Burr—his loyal henchmen there would have insured that Pinckney finished first and Jefferson second. At 43, Hamilton would have had many years remaining to move on into the presidency himself.

Nothing in the system guarantees that a man with the drive of a Hamilton can not mount to the first office even after suffering one or more such secret psychic crises and more than one unexpected rejection in elections that should have been won. At least one other surmounted worse obstacles and won the presidency at last by an overwhelming margin, en route to a still more devastating downfall, similarly self-indicted by his own words.

The *Aurora* on November 6 published as an "advertisement" "PRO BONO PUBLICO, Hamilton's Last Letter and His Amorous Vindication Just Published. Price Fifty Cents." John Beckley wrote Ephraim Kirby on October 25, 1800, that "in a labored effort to belittle the character of the president" Hamilton had "belittled his own. Vainly does he essay to seize the mantle of Washington, and cloak the moral atrocities of a life spent in wickedness which must terminate in shame and dishonor." The Federalist-ousted ex-chief clerk of the House relished the thought that Hamilton's "career of ambition is passed, and neither honor or empire will ever be his. As a political nullity, he has inflicted upon himself the sentence 'Aut Caesar, aut Nullus.' "

But it was Noah Webster, the great lexicographer, a hardy son of the Northern states, an able, moderate Federalist long loyal to Hamilton's principles, writing under the pseudonym of Aristides, a *Federalist*, who struck the cruelest blow of all at the original *Mr. Federalist*. The policies that Hamilton reproached were recent. In the government and after his resignation, Hamilton had filled the office of prime minister with skill. But President Adams had restrained his influence "and called into *open* opposition, the *secret* enmity which . . . long rankled" in Hamilton's breast. Hamilton's criticisms of Adams were of a private, trifling nature. It was Hamilton's fault that his party had been divided and defeated. The ill success of Hamilton's attempt to raise an army and the success of the president's mission to France, which removed every pretext for a permanent armed force, were what had produced "the deep chagrin and disappointment of a military character."

Hamilton's talents and confidence in his influence were so great that he disdained public opinion; he had overleaped and ignored ordinary scruples and rules. Webster was reminded of the mad times when Hamilton had invited the mob's attack defending Jay's Treaty in Wall Street. And the shock of his public avowal of his intrigue with Mrs. Reynolds! But most reckless and lawless of all was his present attempt to split the Federalists "and . . . compleat our overthrow and ruin!"

By contrast to Hamilton, Adams was a man "of pure morals, inflexible patriotism, and the best read statesman" of the Revolutionary period. Set beside these qualifications, his "occasional ill-humor at unreasonable opposition and hasty expressions . . . are of little weight." On the other hand, Webster charged Hamilton, "Your conduct on this occasion will be deemed little short of insanity." In sum, Hamilton's "ambition, pride, and overbearing temper" had marked him as "the evil genius of this country."

Noah Webster had a knack of coming up with pointed words that defined things.

26

FIREWORKS

[JEFFERSON IS] TINCTURED WITH FANATICISM . . . CRAFTY . . . NOT
SCRUPULOUS . . . NOR VERY MINDFUL OF THE TRUTH . . . AND A
CONTEMPTIBLE HYPOCRITE.
    [BURR IS] ONE OF THE MOST UNPRINCIPLED MEN IN THE
UNITED STATES . . . A VOLUPTUARY BY SYSTEM . . . FAR MORE
CUNNING THAN WISE.
          *—To James A. Bayard of Delaware, January 16,
          1801*

JEFFERSON OR BURR? THE FORMER WITHOUT ALL DOUBT.
          —To Gouverneur Morris, December 24, 1800

    The presidential electors chosen by the states in October 1800 met in each
state on December 4 to cast their ballots for president and vice-president. During
this tense period of uncertainty, congressmen and other government officials
were gathering for the first time in the raw new capital at Washington to be
there for the convening of the second session of the sixth Congress on November
21.

    In 1798 an "English gentleman" had written a letter to a friend, which was
published in *The Lady's Magazine*, describing Washington as a city of not more
than "five or six hundred houses . . . most beautifully situated on the banks of
the Potomac. The land waves in gentle curvatures, rising into a hill, surrounded

by a compleat amphitheater of hills . . . those who have money . . . could not at present lay it out to greater advantage than in the purchase of lots." Adams's White House, only half finished, stood isolated in a field overlooking the Potomac. Around the Capitol the congressmen huddled together in seven or eight boardinghouses, their creature comforts barely provided by one tailor, one shoemaker, one printer, a washerwoman, a grocery shop, a pamphlet and stationery shop, a small dry goods shop, and an oyster house. So Congressman Albert Gallatin wrote his wife on January 15, 1801, adding, "This makes the whole of the Federal city as connected with the Capitol."

John Adams's fourth annual message to Congress, written entirely by Secretary of State John Marshall, asserted that the final outcome of the treaty negotiations in Paris was unknown, although unofficial word of the terms had arrived two weeks earlier, giving rise, more or less as usual, to much criticism and disappointment with the envoys. In breach of their instructions, the negotiators had compromised with the French in order to obtain a treaty, the Treaty of Mortefontaine. On October 1, the same day it had been signed, France had also signed the Secret Treaty of San Ildefonso with Spain, thereby transferring Louisiana from Spain to France and making real the threat of France to the American seaboard States on the continent that Hamilton had envisioned, predicted, feared, and warned against for years. Napoleon kept the Treaty of San Ildefonso secret for fear angry Americans might take over Louisiana before he could get troops there to defend it.

The records of the War and Treasury Departments arrived from Philadelphia at half-finished new offices in Washington. A few days later, a fire broke out in the presence of Oliver Wolcott, Jr., which burned up most of the Treasury's records. Its timing and circumstances reminded many of the old charges of a cover-up at the Treasury that had been made against Hamilton, and, before him, William Duer. The *Aurora*'s new editor, William Duane, wrote on November 19 in a style worthy of Beckley that

> The *federal fireworks* at Washington will be found to have made a very rueful chasm in our *war history;* Alexander Hamilton's projects and Timothy Pickering's transactions, while secretary will have had a *partial sweep*, to avoid, the scrutinizing of a Jeffersonian administration.

By the same fireworks Hamilton's friend James McHenry saw a great misfortune for both Hamilton and Wolcott: "What will it not enable the calumniator to say and insinuate, and how shall the innocent man find his justification?" Now, "Hell hath no limits," as Marlowe wrote, nor is it "circumscribed in one self-place." There were no records now by which Hamilton could ever clear himself of the calumnies of those who discredited his own uncorroborated protestations of innocence.

The first fire had been only a "partial sweep." When a second fire broke out January 20 in the building where the Treasury stored the records that had survived the first, Wolcott, again in the thick of the conflagration, was able to retrieve only two chests and a trunk. Notwithstanding the rescue, Republican newspapers charged him with a second political arson: "The friends of Hamilton begin to speak more boldly of his fame, since the Federal fireworks at Washington have rendered it impossible ever fairly to investigate the treasury accounts." Both Hamilton's very closest friends, as well as his most knowing enemies like Jefferson, must have wondered if the chests and trunk retrieved by Wolcott contained the still missing packet of his originals of the Reynolds papers. But if they did, had Hamilton lied when he wrote in *The Reynolds Pamphlet* that the originals were deposited with William Bingham, Esq., for inspection by any gentleman? Or was there more than one set, one with Bingham, another with Wolcott? No one knows to this day.

Despite all that had gone wrong for the Federalists and all that had gone right for the Democratic-Republicans, the Federalists had not lost the election by much. Not until news reached Washington on December 16 that all eight of South Carolina's electors had swung to Jefferson and Burr did Federalists abandon hope.

With everything against him—unpopular taxes, a Republican swing in Pennsylvania, fears of a standing army and its cost, hostility to Great Britain, the skill and enterprise of Beckley, Burr, and Jefferson, Hamilton's attack, the firing of the secretaries, the Alien and Sedition acts—the real wonder was why Adams had lost by the narrow margin of only 73 to 65. Abigail Adams put her finger on the single most significant cause of the disaster: "The defection of New York has been the source," she wrote her son Thomas on November 13, 1800. "That defection was produced by the intrigues of two men [Hamilton and Burr] —one of them sowed the seeds of discontent and division amongst the Federalists, and the other seized the lucky moment of mounting into power upon the shoulders of Jefferson." In this assessment Jefferson agreed, writing Pierce Butler on August 11, 1800, that Burr "has certainly greatly merited of his country and the Republicans in particular, to whose efforts his have given a chance of success."

The switch of a few dozen or hundred votes in Hamilton's own New York City would have given him enough votes in the legislature to elect his own docile electors to cast New York's twelve votes for the candidates of his choice. With all of them voting solidly for Pinckney and two (or more) dutifully throwing away their vice-presidential ballots on Jay, the result would have been Jefferson 61, Burr 61, Pinckney 76, Adams 75, and Jay 3. Or if South Carolina's electors had supported her native son, Charles Cotesworth Pinckney, for only one of the two places on the ticket instead of the relatively unknown Burr, and two or more had thrown away their Jefferson votes on someone else, Hamilton's man Pinckney could have won that way too. At the same time, Adams, the turncoat whom Hamilton's attack had read out of the ranks of Federalist faithful, would have been finished for good and all.

From the point of view of many Federalist insiders, particularly High Federalists, the actual outcome demonstrated the absolute correctness of Hamilton's preelection strategy and tactics. A successful party leader would rather be right than president or than win; so in this sense, Hamilton had snatched a victory from a disaster. Now with Adams and Pinckney finished politically, Hamilton was left as the sole surviving leader and rallying point for the Federalist faithful. His preeminence as party leader would not be challenged by the leadership authority that accrues unsought to the president if the same party holds the White House. Adams found sour satisfaction in the outcome, saying, "Mr. Hamilton has carried his eggs to a fine market. The very two men of all the world that he was most jealous of are now placed over him." Not really true. They were of the opposite party, not his. Hamilton tended to thrive on such opposition. Never before had he surveyed the political scene from a pinnacle of such political power in his own party.

The tactic of an "equal vote" for president and vice-president that Hamilton had urged on Federalist electors had failed for them, but worked perfectly or, rather, too well, for their opponents. With the vote of the electors a 73-to-73 tie between Jefferson and Burr, the election would now have to be decided in the House of Representatives. As the only undiscredited major leader left among the Federalists, Hamilton with his influence on the votes of Federalist congressmen would hold the balance of power there. He busied himself exercising this new-found power by writing Oliver Wolcott, Jr., on December 16, taking note that many Federalists in Congress much preferred Burr to Jefferson: "I trust New England at least will not so far lose its head as to fall into this snare." Snare? A moderate like Burr? Yes, Hamilton explained, because "upon every virtuous and prudent calculation, Jefferson is to be preferred. He is by far not so danger-ous a man and he has pretensions to character."[1] Here was what Wolcott and others must do: take "early measures to fix on this point the opinions of the Federalists." Otherwise, "among them, from different motives, Burr will find partisans."

Burr himself was probably surprised at finishing in a first place tie with Jefferson, and not a little gratified. Earlier he had told R. R. Livingston that Jefferson would have the eight votes of South Carolina and that ". . . we deem Jefferson's election pretty sure and as to V.P.—Adams & P[inckney] appear to have about equal chances. . . . It is highly improbable that I shall have [an] equal number of votes with Mr Jefferson." Needless to say, surprise at the outcome and earlier designation by the Republican caucus of Jefferson for the first place and himself for the second did not cause Burr to say a word or lift a finger to dissuade any elector or any member of the House from voting the party's second choice into the first place.

To rank and file Federalists, Jefferson remained Mr. Random Radical him-self, a superrich slave master, a wealthy self-promoter by paid off pamphleteers, a traitor to his class, and the embodiment of everything else that was politically abhorrent. With Burr, on the other hand, most Federalists were personally on good terms. He seemed moderate, he was something of an aristocrat by tempera-ment and socially acceptable, and though his political ideas and financial deals would bear no more careful scrutiny than Jefferson's, his gentlemanly promiscuity and devotion to ailing Theodosia at Richmond Hill seemed less decadently repellent than Jefferson's rumored concubinage at mysterious, many-cupolaed Monticello.

Burr was "less likely to look to France for support than Jefferson," Pickering noted. Burr was "actuated by ordinary ambition, Jefferson by that and Jacobinic philosophy." Burr might "be satisfied by power and property, [Jefferson] must see the roots of our society pulled up. . . ." Pickering added that "the devoted friends of [Jefferson] are alarmed lest the federalists should prefer [Burr]. . . . From all that I hear, I am . . . inclined to think Mr. Burr will be preferred." Reasons? "Fewer changes in office will then be necessary." John Marshall would remain as secretary of state: "but if Mr. Jefferson be chosen, Mr. Marshall will retire. . . . There are said to be many ingenious reasons why the federalists at Washington . . . prefer Mr. Burr. . . . They probably suppose that the federal interest will not be so systematically opposed under Mr. B as under Mr. J."

The worst thing of all about Burr from Hamilton's point of view was that, with Federal support, he would be a threat to his own newly emergent leadership of the Federal Republican party, even in his home state, in a way that Jefferson would never be. The warning of one of Hamilton's oldest friends, Robert Troup, who was also one of Burr's oldest friends, had been a warning too close, painful, and pointed to ignore.

"The influence . . . of this letter [Hamilton's attack on Adams] upon Hamilton's character is extremely unfortunate," Troup wrote. "An opinion has grown out of it, which at present obtains almost universally, that his character *is radically deficient in discretion,* and therefore the federalists ask, what avail the most pre-eminent talents—the most distinguished patriotism—without the all important quality of discretion? Hence he is considered an unfit head of the party—and we are in fact without a rallying point."

To head off the possibility that Burr would become such a rallying point, Hamilton wrote to leaders far and wide indicting Burr. To Senator Gouverneur Morris the day before Christmas 1800, Hamilton put the case crisply: *"Jefferson or Burr?*—the former without all doubt. The latter . . . has no principle, public or private—could be bound by no agreement—will listen to no monitor but his ambition; and for this purpose will use the *worst* part of the community as a ladder to permanent power, & an instrument to crush the better part. He is bankrupt beyond redemption except by the resources that grow out of war and disorder or by a sale to a foreign power or by great speculation." An immediate war with Great Britain would be, for Burr, an instrument of redemption. Burr, like Jefferson, owed staggering debts to British creditors. Burr would never be won to Federal views, would be "restrained by no moral scruple," would call to his side "rogues of all parties to overrule good men of all parties. . . ." Hamilton concluded, "He is sanguine enough to hope every thing, daring enough to attempt every thing, wicked enough to scruple nothing. From the elevation of such a man may heaven preserve the country!"

To James A. Bayard of Delaware, Hamilton wrote on December 17, "Adieu to the Federal Troy, if they once introduce this Grecian horse into their citadel."

To Wolcott, Hamilton wrote on December 16 that Burr's "private character is not defended by his most partial friends. He is bankrupt beyond redemption, except by the plunder of his country. . . . He is truly the Catiline of America." To this slanderous characterization, he added a weird footnote: "Yet it may be well enough to throw out a lure for him, in order to tempt him to start for the plate, and then lay the foundation of dissension between the two chiefs."

Hamilton sent Wolcott another letter the next day. If the present plan of the pro-Burr Federalists succeeds, he warned, "it will have done nothing more or less, than place in that station a man who will possess the boldness and daring necessary to give success to the Jacobin system, instead of one, who for want of that quality, will be less fitted to promote it. Let it not be imagined that Mr. Burr can be won to the Federal views. It is a vain hope." The proper plan, he added, was to make a deal with Jefferson: obtain his definite assurances, in exchange for Federal votes, on (1) preservation of the present fiscal system, (2) adherence to neutrality in Europe, (3) the continuance of federalists in sub-cabinet offices, with the president installing only the heads of cabinet departments, and (4) preservation of the navy and defense establishment.

As the time approached for the House to convene and ballot on February 11, Hamilton's exhortations rose to all but incoherent stridency. To Sedgwick he railed, "The appointment of Burr as President would disgrace our country abroad. No agreement with him could be relied upon. His private circumstances render disorder a necessary resource. His public principles offer no obstacle. His ambition aims at nothing short of permanent power and wealth in his own person. For heaven's sake, let not the federal party be responsible for the elevation of this man!"

Troup wrote mournfully to Rufus King of their old friend's hysterical jeremiads on February 12, "Hamilton is profoundly chagrined with the prospect! He has taken infinite pains to defeat Burr's election, but he believes in vain. . . . Hamilton at our club on Saturday last declared that his influence with the federal party was wholly gone—and that he could be no longer useful."

Hamilton's solitary fight against Burr went beyond ordinary political opposition, beyond an effort to protect his own political power base. It seemed to his closest friends to be a reckless, irrational fight in which some unfathomable idea of personal honor was at stake. He seemed to be fighting for his life. Or was what they took to be Hamilton's paranoid anxiety on the subject of Burr only the outward manifestation of Hamilton's knowing a despicable secret about Burr's badger game that could be spoken of among gentlemen in no more explicit way?

When the House convened, the balloting to break the tie was done by states, one vote for each state, with each state deciding which way to vote by a majority of the members of its House delegation. A majority of the states—nine in number—was necessary to elect. Under this system, James A. Bayard's vote as Delaware's only congressman counted for as much as all the congressmen from Virginia. On the first ballot, Jefferson had eight states and Burr six; two states had tied within their delegations, and their votes were marked as blanks. A count of the votes of all the individual congressmen in all the delegations would have given Burr 55 to Jefferson's 51. Only a few Federalists, influenced by Hamilton, split away from the party caucus to vote for Jefferson. If all Federalists in the state delegations had been unanimous for Burr, Burr would have been elected the third president of the United States. Had Hamilton done nothing and followed the advice of his closest friends, Burr would have won with undivided Federalist support. But Hamilton waged one of the hardest fights of his life to win the presidency for his mute and absent enemy Jefferson. It also helped to sustain the result that would clearly carry out the will of the voters of the country.

The deadlock continued as the House balloted 34 times over six hectic days. Outside the halls of Congress anger mounted in the country over the grim prospect that manifest popular will would be frustrated by Federalist votes.

There were threatening secessional rumbles from Southerners who saw the Federalists of the New England states about to frustrate their own electors and from New England states fearful of Democratic domination by the South. A bitter blizzard raged outside the House chamber while members curled up in blankets and took catnaps between almost continuous balloting. Writing to Gouverneur Morris, Hamilton was at pains to avoid exalting Jefferson; Jefferson was nothing but a lesser evil. "If there be a man in the world I ought to hate, it is Jefferson. With Burr I have always been personally well. But the public good must be paramount to every private consideration." He patiently refuted the Federalist arguments for Burr. Hamilton's own sincerity was patent because "to contribute to the . . . mortification of Mr. J., would be, on my part, only to retaliate for unequivocal proofs of enmity; but in a case like this, it would be base to listen to personal considerations."

Most Federalists were still determined to elect Burr. They had all along assumed that he would be willing to take the presidency as their gift and give back to them the same four pledges of stable continuity that Hamilton and others had demanded of Jefferson. They sent an emissary to him in New York, where he was busy with plans for the marriage of his famously attractive daughter, Theodosia. The emissary returned with the astonishing news that Burr would make no deal; he would make no commitments to them of any kind.

James A. Bayard was the key, occupying the most strategic position of any one man in the House. As the sole representative of his state, by changing his mind, he could change its vote and influence other Federalists to jump on his bandwagon. Hamilton wrote him on January 16 pulling out all stops. He would not be Jefferson's apologist, for "his politics are tinctured with fanaticism; . . . he is too much in earnest in his democracy; . . . he has been a mischievous enemy to the principal measures of our past administration; . . . he is crafty . . . not scrupulous about the means of success, nor very mindful of truth, and . . . he is a contemptible hypocrite."

So much said, Bayard should remember that Jefferson was no sworn enemy to scope for the executive. Hungry for popularity, Jefferson would be slow to overturn what was established. He would be temporizing rather than violent. As favor for France cooled in America, so would Jefferson's zeal for the Jacobin delirium. Nor was he "capable of being corrupted." By contrast with Jefferson, Burr was "one of the most unprincipled men in the United States," "cares only for himself, and nothing for his country or glory." He was "a voluptuary by system," and he was "far more cunning than wise . . . more dexterous than able."

Bayard yielded to Hamilton. He grumbled that "the means existed of electing Burr" if Burr had only cooperated. According to his own account, he determined to break the deadlock that was threatening to split the country asunder. He sought from Jefferson the assurances that Hamilton had declared to be requisite. Jefferson, he said, gave him the assurances. On February 17, on the thirty-fifth ballot, Federalist members of three delegations cast blank ballots, and on the thirty-sixth Jefferson was elected president by ten states to four, with two not voting.

Jefferson afterward denied that he had made the commitments to the Federalists that Bayard said had caused him to change his vote, but Jefferson's moderate actions afterward belied his denial. Bayard afterward told Hamilton that he would have switched to Burr if Burr had been willing to make the same deal with the Federalists that Jefferson had agreed to make, but Burr had been "determined not to shackle himself with federal principles."

It would not have escaped notice by Burr, whose sources of political intelligence were better than those of any of his contemporaries except Jefferson, that the frantic efforts of Hamilton, more than anyone else, were all that had prevented him from becoming the third president. Nor would Jefferson be likely to forget the compromise of his preferred stance above the fray and the unacknowledged debt to Hamilton his close victory had cost him.

So Aaron Burr became vice-president of the United States. He remains all but unique in the spotty annals of that peculiar office because he gained it by refusing to make a deal.

To many Federal Republicans, the French Revolution had taken place in America. Some waited for the earth to heave and rumble, the heavens to fall, the tumbrels to roll, and the fabric of society to disintegrate. The lame duck Federalist House appointed the usual investigating committee to investigate whether or not Wolcott had set the suspicious fires; it found no Federalist wrongdoing. The outgoing Adams appointed John Marshall as chief justice as well as many other midnight jurists on January 31, the night of his leaving office. The Federalist Senate had been called into session to take over the balloting for president in case the House should remain deadlocked. After first rejecting the French treaty, it approved it after Adams had submitted it a second time. After news of Jefferson's election reached Philadelphia on February 18, according to Dr. Benjamin Rush's son, Richard Rush, "hurras, cannons and drums made such a noise for three days past that one could hardly read a newspaper." Jefferson's Pennsylvania campaign manager, "The Ciceronian Beckley," was the principal orator at the great jubilee. On March 4, Jefferson made a conciliatory inaugural address. "We are all republicans; we are all federalists!" he announced. George Cabot mocked him sourly: "We are all tranquil as they say at Paris after a

revolution." But he noted, with well-mixed emotions, that "Mr. Jefferson's conciliatory speech is better liked by our party than his own."

As he explained to John Dickinson on July 23, 1801, Jefferson was seeking
to win over the mass of the Federalists. "The greatest good we can do our
country is to heal its party divisions & make them one people" [he wrote]. "I do
not speak of their leaders who are incurable, but of the honest and well-inten-
tioned body of the people . . . both sects are republican, entitled to the confidence
of their fellow-citizens. Not so their quondam leaders, covering under the mask
of federalism hearts devoted to monarchy. The Hamiltonians, the Essex-men, the
revolutionary tories &c. They have a right to tolerance, but neither to confidence
nor power."

Jefferson acknowledged no debt to Hamilton. Hamilton, who had done as
much as any man to elect Jefferson and knew it, was not happy with his own
handiwork. Jefferson's soft words stole the hearts of many of his Federalists,
especially those of the "2nd class leaders."

There remained left to Hamilton but one last political hurrah. Following
Jefferson's inauguration in the spring of 1801, New York would ballot for governor. The hardy perennial, old George Clinton, was again a candidate, this time
to succeed John Jay, who was retiring. It was age versus youth when the
disorganized Federalists nominated Lieutenant Governor Stephen Van Rensselaer, and Hamilton turned toward making a supreme effort to elect his brother-
in-law, husband of Elizabeth's younger sister, Margarita "Peggy" Schuyler. If
he could hold New York in the Federalist party column, Hamilton might be in
a position later, when the "general convulsion" actually came, to lead the
bemused nation out of the slough of Jacobinism into the clear air of true Ameri-
canism. But it would call for almost superhuman effort. George Cabot, reviewing
Federalist prospects, commented that "Hamilton has made great & brilliant
efforts" in behalf of Van Rensselaer; although "our reports are favorable," they
were "by no means satisfactory." Burr was certain Clinton would win.

Hamilton mustered out the New York City party, issued addresses to the
electorate, joined issue with Clinton's supporters, and argued the importance of
the state contest to the politics of the nation. Without bitterness toward opponents, he rehearsed Federalist accomplishments during the decade just past that
had brought the Republic, in the words of Jefferson's own inaugural address, to
"the full tide of successful experiment." He pointed out that "success in the
experiment of a government is success in the *practice* of it, and this is but
another phrase for an administration, in the main, wise and good."

He castigated French revolutionaries for "the subversion of the throne of
the *Bourbons,* to make way for the throne of the *Bonapartes.*" He praised
Jefferson for deserting his former allies, who would have had Americans follow
the French example. He warmed to Jefferson's inaugural speech with "approbation of its contents."

He went on to say, "We view it as virtually a candid retraction of past
misapprehensions, and a pledge to the community, that the new President will
not lend himself to dangerous innovations, but in essential points will tread in

the steps of his predecessors." He contrasted Jefferson's recently proclaimed "moderate views" with "the violent projects of the men who have addressed you in favor of Mr. Clinton. . . ." Jefferson's switch, consistent with the deal Bayard said he had made, might well cost him the support of many who had elevated him, but "in the talents, the patriotism, and the firmness of the Federalists, he will find more than an equivalent for all that he shall lose."

As in campaigns of much earlier days, Hamilton's speeches in this one rang with eloquence and brilliance. For this period of Hamilton's life, at least, they were remarkable for their moderation. Everyone admitted—at least all the Federalists—that he was back in his best vein again. Robert Troup wrote Rufus King on May 27 that his speech "was one of the *chef d'oeuvres* of this great man. For strength of reasoning & at the same time for impressive & sublime eloquence it surpassed what in all probably [*sic*] has ever been delivered in this city." Unfortunately, opposition papers like the *Newark Sentinel* charged that it was "in his usual style of imprecation and abuse against the character of the venerable Mr. Clinton."

Hamilton went from poll to poll to argue the Federal cause, but it was all in vain. It was no use. The magic, the cutting edge was gone. He was going through the old motions, but something—his emphasis or his timing perhaps— was a shade of a fraction off, like that of someone in nervous convalescence after a nervous breakdown or enjoying a period of remission.

The populace jeered the erstwhile great man. They shouted epithets at him —thief, rascal, villain, scoundrel! John Adams was calling him a "caitiff." Worse still, the so-called respectable citizens, the freeholders of the city, who had always before been the bulwark of the Federalist party, gave a majority to Clinton. "An event that had never happened before at any of our elections!" cried Robert Troup, appalled and shocked. If the violent style of Hamilton's attack on Adams had not worked, his moderation and praise of Jefferson had failed yet more wretchedly.

Hamilton's grandson, the alienist Allan McLane Hamilton, speculates that at about the time of this last humiliating defeat, Hamilton's "familiarity with Vergil's Bucolics, and especially the first Eclogue, had filled his mind with sylvan longings." In the first Eclogue, Vergil's spokesman Meliboeus has been banished from the capital and hounded into exile by an all-victorious Augustus, who has just seized supreme power over the Roman Empire. Meliboeus complains of the injustice of his fate, compared to that of his fortunate friend, Tityrus:

> Tityre, tu patulae recubans sub tegmine fagi
> silvestrem tenui musam meditaris avena.
> Beneath the shade which beechen boughs diffuse,
> You, Tityrus, entertain your sylvan muse:
> Round the wide world in banishment we roam
> While stretched at ease you sing your happy loves.

Vergil, like Tityrus, his other spokesman, after a period of exile in sylvan retreat, was restored to his former position when recalled to Rome by a great convulsion, the restoration of "Freedom, which came at length, tho' slow to come."

As Hamilton described his own feelings: "To men who have been so much harassed in the base world as myself, it is natural to look forward to complete retirement, in the circle of life as a perfect desideratum." But he was not a man to repine in melancholy: "This desire I have felt in the strongest manner, and to prepare for it latterly has been a favorite object." He acted: "I might not only expect to accomplish the object, but might reasonably aim at it and pursue the preparatory measures." He had been engaged for almost two years in planning and building a permanent home for his family on Harlem Heights.

"Hamilton is supremely disgusted with the state of our political affairs," his faithful friend Troup wrote Rufus King on May 27. "He has all along said and still maintains the opinion that Jefferson and his party had not talents or virtue sufficient to administer the government well." He thinks "they will finally ruin our affairs and plunge us into serious commotions." Although "he does not think this result will immediately take place, yet he predicts it is not so remote as many might imagine." But "nothing short of a general convulsion will again call him into public life."

As Hamilton journeyed around the circuit, sick from time to time, but working harder than ever in his private law practice to pay for the house now abuilding on Harlem Heights, he wrote Elizabeth full of thoughts of home and family and of his new avocation: "My health is better. Wife, child and hobby are the only things upon which I have permitted my thoughts to run." Of the three, the "hobby" now took first place, as he slyly joked to her: "As often as I write, you may expect to hear something of the latter." He admonished her not to let new dung go to waste, and added, "Don't lose any opportunity which may offer of ploughing up the new garden spot and let the waggon make a tour of the ground lately purchased to collect the dung upon it to be scattered over that spot."

From cold remote inns on circuit, trying to earn enough to pay for his "sweet project," he would conclude a letter to Elizabeth full of advice for improving the house by saying, "I confide this merely as a suggestion." But he had acquired the habit of command, and a suggestion from him somehow had the force of a direct order from the inspector general. Their eldest son, Philip, had just won high honors at Columbia upon graduation the year before, and Hamilton thought he should now take on more responsibility. One day he wrote Eliza a typical "suggestion": "Leave, in particular charge of Philip, what you cannot yourself accomplish."

Of the seven children, Hamilton placed his fondest hopes on Philip, now 19. Hamilton expected Philip to join him soon in the practice of law and someday perhaps become his junior partner.

His father was certain of "his future greatness," Robert Troup wrote afterward. The young man was indeed talented, Troup agreed, but, said Troup, Philip "was however a sad rake & I have serious doubts whether he ever would have been an honor to his family or his country!" In hope of fostering reform in the young rake's habits, Hamilton wrote out a Spartan set of rules to guide him after graduation from Columbia. They reflect some basic lessons of life that 44 years of almost superhuman striving had taught their author:

Rules for Mr. Philip Hamilton

From the first of April to the first of October he is to rise not later than six o'clock; the rest of the year not later than seven. If earlier, he will deserve commendation. Ten will be his hour of going to bed throughout the year.

From the time he is dressed in the morning till nine o'clock (the time for breakfast excepted), he is to read law. At nine he goes to the office, and continues there till dinner-time. He will be occupied partly in the writing and partly in reading law.

After dinner he reads law at home till five o'clock. From this time till seven he disposes of his time as he pleases. From seven to ten he reads and studies whatever he pleases.

From twelve on Saturday he is at liberty to amuse himself.

On Sunday he will attend the morning church. The rest of the day may be applied to innocent recreations.

He must not depart from any of these rules without my permission.

When Philip had been barely one month old, Hamilton had written his friend and fellow former aide Richard Kidder Meade that Betsy proposed a match between Philip and the Meades' new daughter "provided you will engage to make the latter as amiable as her mother." And his aunt, Angelica Church, had written her sister from London, responding to a long letter of Betsy telling her of him, that "Philip inherits his father's talents. What flattering prospects for a mother! You are, my dear sister, very happy with such a Husband and such promise in a son."

Back in the summer of 1798, Hamilton and Elizabeth and her sister and brother-in-law, Angelica and John, had shared a rented country house in Harlem Heights, for which Hamilton's half share of the rental came to $37.50. Harlem's wooded draws and barren rocky outcroppings must have been much on his mind when that November, as inspector general of the army, he sat down at his mahogany traveling desk in a boardinghouse room in Philadelphia and wrote a riddling rhyme to his Eliza back in New York. He hinted at a "sweet project" that he did not doubt would please her:

I am always very happy my dear Eliza, when I can steal a few moments to sit down and write to you. You are my good genius; of that kind which the ancient philosophers called a *familiar*——. I have formed a sweet project, of which I will make you my confidant, when I come to New York, and in which I rely that you will cooperate with me cheerfully.

> You may guess and guess and guess again,
> Your guessing will still be in vain.
> But you will not be the less pleased when you
> come to understand and realize the scheme.

After 18 years of marriage, he closed this letter to his "familiar" of perhaps 22 years:

Adieu, best of wives and best of mothers,
Heaven ever bless you and me in you.

                                                    A. H.

During the feverish heat of the August of 1800, Hamilton took time out from the presidential battle and scribbling down his attacks on President Adams to make an offer to Jacob Scheiffelin of £800 for a tract of about 16 acres of land in Harlem Heights. It sloped westward down from the Bloomingdale Road to a small dock on the Hudson River shore front. He had often come ashore on the little dock there on bird shoots and fishing trips with Philip and his younger sons. Jacob Scheiffelin, who is designated in the deed as a "druggist," turned down his bid on the Hudson River waterfront property, but finally agreed to sell Hamilton a strip of about 15 acres that lay inland on the ridge to the east of the Bloomingdale Road and stretched on eastward almost to the Kingsbridge Road, as well as another triangular parcel of about 16 acres that adjoined it to the north, for a price of £30 an acre.

The rocky outcropping at the top of the rise commanded a spectacular view to the west and southward over the Hudson, the Palisades, the Heights of Weehawken, and the continent lying beyond. There was an even better view easterly over the Harlem River valley toward Westchester and New England. And to the south down the length of Manhattan Island lay Wall Street, the Bowling Green, and the Battery and the forest of ships' masts in the busy harbor and the ocean beyond the Narrows. On this rise Hamilton planned to build his "sweet project."

When he tramped over the Harlem Heights property, he could not have allowed to fade from his mind's eye the memory of himself as the 19-year-old captain commanding New York's crack Provincial Company of Artillery as it dug in on these same rocky heights in September 1776, the night he had first caught General George Washington's eye.

Never before and too seldom afterward had Americans from many different states stood firmly together and advanced against the red-coated enemy as they had done at the Battle of Harlem Heights there the next day. For the wooded draws and barren hilltops of the landscape, which had formed the protective defilades and flat fields of grazing fire for his cannoneers that never-to-be-forgotten day, Hamilton had acquired early in life under fire a peculiarly intense feeling for this Harlem terrain that only a company grade officer of line artillery could know.

John McComb, whom Hamilton selected to design his new house, was New York's leading architect, the designer of that gem of Federal architecture the City Hall, of Castle Clinton on the Battery, and the old Queens building of Rutgers University. McComb's plan called for a dignified but not pretentious Federal style clapboard house with a high basement, first and second floors, and four large brick chimneys, one at each of the four corners. Two of them would be real and two false to preserve the characteristic symmetry of his design. There would be a low balustrade surmounting the cornice, a front porch and back porch, a piazza on either side, and a flight of steps leading up toward a large entrance vestibule, reminiscent of the always hospitable front doorway of the Philip Schuyler family mansion at Albany.

The upper floor would contain eight fireplaces, designed according to plans that Hamilton sketched himself, following the newly discovered scientific principles announced by Count Rumford, so as not to smoke. Here also would be family and guest bedrooms, and a family living room, extending entirely across the northern or rear elevation of the house.

When Angelica Church from London had sent on the duc de la Rochefoucauld-Liancourt with a letter of recommendation to her brother-in-law in 1794, Hamilton had felt it keenly that he could not entertain such friends of his rich sister-in-law as the former grand master of the king's wardrobe in suitable style, the way her and Elizabeth's parents had always entertained distinguished visitors at The Pastures in Albany. He had replied apologetically to Angelica on December 8, 1794:

> I wish I was a Croesus; I might then afford solid consolation to these children of adversity, and how delightful it would be to do so. *But now,* sympathy, kind words, and *occasionally* a dinner are all I can contribute.

The symmetry and purity of McComb's twin octagon first floor plan would provide an ideal solution for the Hamilton's future hopes for entertaining on a scale worthy of the Schuylers or the Burrs at Richmond Hill or Jefferson at Monticello if only he could somehow manage to pay for it all. But after almost 20 busy years, Hamilton, like Tityrus, had the rueful feeling that

> All the little that I got, I spent,
> And still returned as empty as I went.

Still, he would manage to pay for his and Betsy's and McComb's dream house somehow. Walking into the front hall, a guest would turn left through an arched entrance to reach the parlor and right to enter the dining room. Three triple-hung, ceiling-high bay windows in each of the octagonal rooms would outline the magnificent Arcadian views of the Hudson and Harlem River valleys and frame each scene with the columns on the piazzas west and east. Full-length mirrors on the inner walls, except where the fireplaces opened, would enhance the effect of complete openness to the natural setting. These two octagonal rooms for public entertaining in elegant style on an ambitious scale were as important a reason for building the house as any other. He would call it The Grange after the plantation estate of his once rich Lytton cousins on St. Croix and the family manor at Ayrshire, Scotland, where his father's forebears and brothers reigned as lairds.

The exterior dimensions of Hamilton's Grange are about 50 feet by 50, generous but not overwhelming, smaller in size and interior floor space than many ordinary upper middle-class houses built today. But the symmetrical purity, simplicity, and power of McComb's design give it a look that even today remains modestly monumental. Though such a house, like the Schuylers', in those days would usually be called a mansion, it did not take the net worth of a rich man to let out a contract to build one—particularly if the contractor happened to be Ezra Weeks, the brother of a grateful client of Hamilton like Levi Weeks. Levi had just been acquitted of first degree murder by a jury largely through Hamilton's efforts in the sensational Manhattan Well murder case.

A precious feature of family gatherings at The Grange would be daughter Angelica's playing on her harp or on the pianoforte that her Aunt Angelica had sent her from London. Seventeen-year-old Angelica Hamilton loved to accompany her father, when he sang. In his rich, true voice, sometimes with harmony intoned by his older sons Philip, Alexander, Jr., and James, with John Church, eight, just humming along, Hamilton liked to entertain the family and their guests singing the popular songs of the day or, better still, the old songs of Revolutionary days that he had sung to Angelica's mother while courting her (or occasionally to her Aunt Angelica in private while courting her). Songs like "The Jolly Beggars" or "A Successful Campaign" or an old soldiers' favorite like "The Drum." To that one he and his light infantry men had marched to Yorktown, and he would sing it again at the meeting of the Society of the Cincinnati a few nights before the last duel. As he reminisced, the final verse may have echoed in his soul with the peculiar eloquence that is lacking in the words unaccompanied:

> Twas in the merry month of May
> When bees from flower to flower did hum.
> We're going to war, and when we die
> We'll want a man of God nearby,
> So bring your Bible and follow the drum.

The twin octagon public rooms would be a more spacious, more resonant setting for such entertainments than the cramped quarters of the various rented houses in town that all eight of them had lived in so far, along with the Antil daughter they had adopted and various assorted beloved pets and pigeons and the parrakeets that Angelica particularly cherished and loved.

From the beginning of time or at least until quite recently, fathers have set down strict rules for their sons, and sons have dared to flout them. On Friday evening, November 20, 1801, instead of reading and studying from seven to ten, as Hamilton's rule for Philip's weekdays had prescribed, Philip and a friend named Price went out to the theater to see Mr. Hallam and Mrs. Jefferson in the comedy *The West Indian,* "a Grand Pantomimical Drama . . . Founded on a fact, which occurred . . . in the island of Jamaica," with a cast of planters, slaves, soldiers, and Negro robbers. In the box next to Hamilton and Price sat Captain George I. Eacker.

The previous Fourth of July—1801—had been a Republican field day in New

York City. The double Republican victory of Jefferson and Burr over Adams (and Hamilton) and of Clinton over Stephen Van Rensselaer (and Hamilton) were ripe to be recelebrated all over again. James Cheetham's Republican *American Citizen and General Advertiser* on July 6 had reported that "we do not remember ever to have seen assembled so vast a concourse of people on the occasion." It appeared to the editor that every countenance in the vast throng "very sensibly expressed this idea:—'We are now celebrating . . . the restoration of our *mangled* Constitution.' " Flags waved, bands played, and firecrackers exploded left, right, and center.

In his fiery Fourth of July oration at the Brick Church, Captain Eacker, a prominent Republican lawyer, had assailed Britain and all her American supporters who were seeking to embroil America in war with France. Under the hated Alien and Sedition Laws, there had been ". . . persecution, for political opinions" by those who "stalked forth with . . . erected crest"—so reminiscent of the blue inspector general plume Hamilton had worn when campaigning. "To suppress all opposition by fear," Eacker cried, "a military establishment was created, under pretended apprehension of a foreign invasion." He was accusatory. "This measure . . . the most hostile to liberty, was adopted under the favorable crisis of public panic." Only now at last, in 1801, concluded Eacker, had the dangers of moneyed aristocracy been banished. "The election of 'The Man of the People' . . . Jefferson . . . has completed the termination of the blind infatuation." An ode was declaimed that derided the deceits of all Federalist politicians. Fifes and drums whistled and rattled, and a parade stepped out in honor of Jefferson and Clinton. There was a dinner and toasts to the president and the governor, "the father of our state." The already expired or expiring Alien and Sedition Laws were damned over and over again. There were more fireworks and a greater than usual number of Fourth of July casualties.

One did not show up in the tally until four months later. If Philip had not been an unnoticed discomfited countenance at these otherwise happy scenes or even if he had, he would have read of them in Cheetham's paper and in the account later published of Eacker's execrations on everything for which his adored father had lived his life and which Philip had done his best to emulate.

In their box in the theater at *The West Indian* that November, Philip Hamilton and Price, who had probably stopped off for a few drinks on the way to fortify themselves for the rigors of blood-and-thunder melodrama, began to make loud, rude comments about Eacker and his Fourth of July speech. Then they pushed into Eacker's box and cast "pointed ridicule on [the] oration." At first, Eacker pretended to ignore the remarks, but at the intermission, he asked Philip and Price out into the lobby. Eacker exclaimed, "I will not be insulted by a set of rascals." Some say he called the boys "damned rascals."

Philip and Price demanded to know just who he meant by "damned rascals." Eacker snapped back that he meant the two of them.

By this time, the hubbub was attracting a good deal of attention; so Eacker suggested they adjourn to a nearby tavern. Philip and Price continued to demand just whom he had meant by "damned rascals." Eacker continued to say that he meant the two of them.

Enraged, all three stamped back after the interval to more tumult and shouting at the play. Eacker told them he lived at 50 Wall Street and would expect to hear from them forthwith. Price sent Eacker challenge to a duel the same night. Sunday morning he and Eacker met at Paulus Hook, now off Elizabethtown, New Jersey, a state where killing another in a duel was not yet defined as murder under the penal law. They blazed away. Three or four shots were exchanged, but none of either's hit the other. The seconds then intervened to halt the waste of good powder and ball in such spectacular but aimless fireworks.

Philip consulted his friend, D. S. Jones, and his cousin, Philip Church. John Lawrence, Eacker's second, who also was a good friend of the Hamiltons, urged Eacker to take back the words "damned rascals," if Philip would apologize for his rudeness at the theater. Eacker refused to retract; Philip refused to apologize. Philip sent Eacker a challenge Sunday afternoon. He may have been emboldened by the evidence of Eacker's poor aim in the news of his inability to hit Price in the course of the morning's futile fusillade at Paulus Hook.

Philip's father had heard of the scheduled interview ahead of time, but took no action to prevent it. He "commanded his son, when on the ground, to reserve his *fire* 'till after Mr. E. had shot and then to discharge his pistol in the air." Early Monday morning below the Heights of Weehawken on the Jersey Shore, Philip met Eacker for the last time. Obedient to his father's command, Philip went to the field "with a full determination to preserve" Eacker's life. With him he brought the hair-trigger dueling pistols his Uncle John Barker Church had used in his duel with Aaron Burr and in many another such interview. Philip had resolved to let Eacker fire first, throw away his own shot, and let his antagonist decide whether to resume. He so informed David Jones, his second. On the ground each waited a minute or more for the other to make a move. If Philip had then fired his pistol at the ground, probably all would have been well. But as it was, both drew up their weapons to take aim at the same instant.

This time there was no futile exchange of shots. On first fire, Eacker's bullet penetrated Philip's side above the hip, ripped through bone and flesh and stopped in his left arm. Under the shock of Eacker's bullet, Philip's pistol fired back, but his ball whistled through the air without hitting anything human. Philip fell, mortally wounded. He bore his pain in full consciousness, was carried away to die, and after a day and night of suffering, died early the next morning.

A Columbia classmate described the terrible scene at the house to which Philip had been rowed back across the river bleeding to death. "On a Bed without curtains lay poor Phil, pale and languid, his rolling, distorted eye balls darting . . . the flames of delirium. On one side of him on the same bed lay his agonized father, on the other his distracted mother, around him . . . relatives and friends weeping . . . I could continue in the room but for a very short time; returning Home I quickened my pace almost unconsciously, hoping to escape the image as well as the reality of what I had witnessed. It appeared that the Ball had entered the right side just above the hip Bone, passed through the body and lodged in the left arm. Yesterday I was invited to attend his funeral

". . . the day very rainy . . . His poor father was with difficulty supported to the grave of his hopes."

The family's distress was the more acute because Elizabeth Hamilton was three months pregnant. The shock and anguish of Phil's death imperiled her health. She could not be comforted. Neither could Hamilton.

"Never did I see a man so completely overwhelmed with grief as Hamilton has been," recalled Troup. "The scene I was present at when Mrs. Hamilton came to see her son on his deathbed [he died about a mile out of the city] and when she met her husband & son in one room beggars all description!" Mother and father watched him writhe in agony for more than 20 hours before he died.

Angelica Church wrote grimly to her younger brother in Albany that Hamilton's "conduct was extraordinary during this trial. I cannot reach particulars now, my sister is a little composed, and the corpse will be removed from my house within an hour."

Neither of Philip's parents ever really got over his death. Hamilton had done everything for the boy his own father had never done for him.

Troup must have been wrong about Philip's character. Only the rarest, most brilliant, and Apollonian of model 19-year-old sons would champion his father's politics, assail his father's traducers, and die at the hands of enemies raised up largely by his father's success and failure, while carrying out both of his father's pious but risky prescripts: not to shun the duel, and not to fire first.

After a while, Hamilton was able to compose himself and look to business, "but," Troup reported, "his countenance is strongly stamped with grief." For a long time, Elizabeth, too, remained but little composed.

Word of the tragedy did not reach Philip Schuyler, Phil's grandfather and namesake, in Albany until after Phil's funeral. Two weeks later he wrote his pregnant daughter, "I trust that resignation to the divine will has so far tranquillised your mind as to mitigate the severety [*sic*] of the Anguish which has been inflicted on you and all of us." It should afford Betsy consolation that her dear departed child had showed such aversion to shedding blood and "pursued every measure which propriety and prudence could dictate to avoid it." She had reason to trust that "his Spirit is in the realms of Eternal bliss." He had urged Hamilton to bring her to Albany, and if the snow were not right for sledging, he would "send my strong horses to your Brother's at Rynbeck with my Coachman to relieve your horses, but if there should be sledging, I will send my covered Sled and horses to your Brothers and then your Coaches may be left there . . . Your coachee is sufficiently roomy to bring the nurse and three younger children with you which will add greatly to our satisfaction."

Philip Hamilton's sister Angelica, next oldest to him, a beauty of whom all remarked how she strikingly resembled the beauteous aunt, her namesake, had passionately adored her elder brother. The shock of his agonizing death caused her to become incurably deranged. She remained insane the rest of a long life until death at 73. To the end, she would always speak of her dear brother Phil as if he were still alive. On her pianoforte she would play only the same old-fashioned songs and minuets she and Phil and her father had played and sung together when she was 17. Years of tender care at home by her mother did no good. She never afterward could learn any pieces that she had not known before that November when Phil was shot.

In February 1802, Philip Schuyler again wrote to try to assuage a little Elizabeth's seemingly inconsolable grief. He was glad to know that Philip had died "with a full determination to preserve" his antagonist's life. He begged for her "such . . . calmness in your mind, as that your health may not be injured and Ultimately . . . restore you to peace." He also advised:

> You have the Most . . . important duties to perform as the consort of that best of men, whose happiness depends on your weal . . . Exert therefore . . . that energy, which was so conspicuous in you [,] ride out frequently, and collect . . . friends about you, that your thoughts may be diverted from painful reflection.

As always, as her ninth lying-in approached, Elizabeth's father could not have been more kind and solicitous, even as he suffered from the old war wound in his side and his gout. He was happy and relieved when he could congratulate Hamilton that she and their new child were both in good health. Their grief could never be composed. But perhaps it might be covered over a little. They named their new son Philip, too. Throughout his life he would always be known as "little Phil."

Philip II's grandfather wrote to his still grieving mother yet again on August 23, 1802:

> My dearly beloved and Amiable Child: How your endearing attentions rivet you continually to my heart. May the loss of one be compensated by another Philip. May his virtues emulate those which graced his brother, and may he be a comfort to parents so tender and who have endeared themselves to theirs . . . I hope you keep Your Children as much as possible in the country, as the city at this season is generally injurious to the health of Children, especially as they can with so much facility indulge with fruit and frequently with that which is unripe— Embrace Them all for us. They all share with You and My Dear Hamilton in our Love.
>
> Adieu My Dear Child. May those blessings which are the portion of the virtuous attend You all is the prayer of Your Affectionate parent
>   Ph Schuyler.

After recovering from her lying-in and weaning of little Phil and after a suitable or, rather, longer period of mourning, Elizabeth composed herself a little. She returned to the rounds of public entertaining the Grange had been built for and the efficient performance of all the other important duties that were expected of her as the wife of a public leader and lawyer of Hamilton's stature. Her father's long and intense anxiety for her health during the year following her first Phil's death is the principal evidence of her grief that comes down to us from the two years through which she had been living next to nervous derangement, manic defense, and madness. Other than her father's letters to her, there is no evidence that a scream of anguish could, possibly, have been wrung out of her indomitable soul. There would be no more children.

27

GETTING
RELIGION/ANGELICA'S GARTER

ALAS! A PRESIDENT OF THE UNITED STATES, LIKE THE WEIRD SIS-
TERS IN MACBETH, "KEEPS HIS WORD OF PROMISE TO OUR EAR, BUT
BREAKS IT TO OUR HOPE!"
     —Examination of Jefferson's Message, *No. IV, Decem-
ber 26, 1801*

As Robert Troup and many other friends observed, Hamilton's countenance
was strongly stamped with grief. Letters of condolence for poor Philip poured
in. Rufus King wrote on January 12, 1802, from London, wishing Hamilton
"consolation . . . among the treasures of your own mind, which nature has so
eminently endowed." A letter of December 5 from Washington's grandnephew,
G. W. P. Custis, who had been a friend of Philip at Columbia, praised him for
defending his honor. Dr. Benjamin Rush, a close friend of Jefferson and a
political opponent of Hamilton, told how much he and his family had enjoyed a
visit of Philip at the Rushes' Philadelphia home. James McHenry's understanding of Hamilton's grief went deep because he too had suffered the loss of an
eldest child.

Mixed in with the first letters of condolence arrived a letter of another sort
from Washington's nephew and executor, Bushrod Washington, written Novem-

ber 21, 1801, two days before Philip's death, which contained a stinging rebuke. Hamilton had written him earlier asking for copies of letters from Washington's files that he might use to buttress a new series of attacks on Jefferson that he was planning to publish in the *New York Post*, the newspaper he had founded a few months earlier.

He would not be too numbed by grief to feel another pang at the refusal of presidential papers that would once have been his for the asking and the loss he had suffered from the death of his essential aegis less than two years before. Bushrod Washington wrote him stiffly:

> The opinions delivered to the President by the heads of departments were those I presume of a private council and intended for his information (the latter replied to his request). They were not put upon the files of any of the public offices and are to be found only amongst the papers of the General. They could therefore be obtained from no other person but myself. Other measures of that administration may be again censured, discussed & condemned by one party, and vindicated by the other, whilst both must or at least may resort to the same quiver for arms to fight with. Acting with the fairness which shall always mark my conduct, I could not upon such a subject refuse to one what I have granted to the other party.

The years when Jefferson had called him "a colossus to the anti-Republican party, without numbers . . . a host within himself" were over. Yet Hamilton chose to blot out his griefs by furiously going on with writing a long broadside attack on Jefferson and all Jefferson's policies and in defense of the threatened Constitution under the title *Examination of Jefferson's Message to Congress of December 7, 1801*. He signed it *Lucius Crassus* and published it in 18 installments in the *New York Post*, beginning December 17, 1801, and ending April 8, 1802. The writing had a frantic, impassioned, personal, and largely retrospective tone that did not at all suit the rather narrow nature of his differences on most matters of future national policy, with which Jefferson's message to Congress had dealt in broad and unemphatic brush strokes. Hamilton wrote as if he saw himself as the sole remaining prop of the frail fabric of the Constitution. He attacked Jefferson and his policies as if striking out in revenge or as if taking a reprisal against him for the death of his eldest son.

Whether "from pride or from humility, from a temperate love of reform or from a wild spirit of innovation," Hamilton began, Jefferson had sent a "message" to Congress at the opening of the session instead of delivering a "speech" as his predecessors had always done. It was a "mark of consistency" in him to differ from his predecessors "in matters of form." "Whoever considers the temper of the day," Hamilton sighed, "must be satisfied that this message is likely to add much to the popularity of our Chief Magistrate."

Whereas "those whose patriotism is of the OLD SCHOOL . . . would rather risk incurring the displeasure of the people by speaking unpalatable truths than betray their interest by fostering their prejudices," Jefferson's "bewitching tenets" promised "emancipation from the burdens and restraints of government" and "a foretaste of that pure felicity which the apostles" of Jefferson's "illuminated doctrine have predicted." Even if such happy predictions proved wrong and "the viands they offer prove baneful poisons instead of wholesome aliments, the justification is both plain and easy—*Good patriots must, at all events, please the People.*"

After thus laving down Jefferson's message with this disarming but acidulous irony, Hamilton pulled the button off his foil. Jefferson's message, "by whatever motives it may have been dictated," is a performance to "alarm all who are anxious for the safety of our government, for the respectability and welfare of our nation." Worst of all, "it makes, or aims at making, a most prodigal sacrifice of constitutional energy, of sound principle, and of public interest, to the popularity of one man."

Among specifics, *Lucius Crassus* attacked Jefferson's proposal to abolish internal revenue, but at the same time preserve "PUBLIC FAITH." Such promises were "merely to amuse with agreeable but deceptive sounds," Hamilton declaimed. "Alas! How deplorable it will be, should it ever become proverbial, that a President of the United States like the *Weird sisters* in Macbeth, keeps his word of promise to our ear, but breaks it to our hope!"

One ironic thing about Hamilton's attack on Jefferson's inaugural was that in it Jefferson came close to endorsing Hamilton's own Federalist military policy. Discussing what he called "the essential principles of our Government," Jefferson paid lip service to the militia, but admitted that a regular army was necessary to back them up as the ultimate source of authority and security. "A well-disciplined militia," he proclaimed, was "our best reliance in peace and for the first moments of war, till regulars may relieve them."

The "lame duck" Federalist Congress of the year before, as one of its last actions, had passed the Judiciary Act, which expanded and elaborated the federal court system, thereby giving Adams the opportunity to make "midnight appointments" of many Federalists to the bench before Federalism was swept out of power forever. Jefferson proposed to get rid of them by simply repealing the act, or, as his message had euphemistically put it, "the judiciary system will, *of course*, present itself to the contemplation of Congress." Hamilton magnified this mild comment into *"a disposition to magnify the importance of the particular states, in derogation from that of the United States."* The Constitution itself was at stake. "Who does not see what is the ultimate object?" Hamilton asked in No. VI. He answered his own rhetorical question with the same words Robert Troup had twice used in 1791 to warn him of the plot that Jefferson, Madison, Beckley, and Aaron Burr were hatching—their "amorous courtship" in New York—for Hamilton's destruction. *"Delenda est Carthago*—ill-fated Constitution, which Americans had fondly hoped would continue for ages, the guardian of public liberty, the source of national prosperity!"

Other Federalists took a similarly hard line in opposition to the repeal of the Judiciary Act—and no wonder, because well-paid federal judgeships presiding over uncluttered dockets were the best of all possible jobs for many Federalists who had been voted out of the public trough and would otherwise have had to go to work for a living.

When Hamilton urged some of his closest friends to oppose repeal, but in a temperate, dignified manner, it infuriated them and showed he was also out of touch with most of his own party. Gouverneur Morris had sought to have the New York bar petition Congress against repeal of the Judiciary Act, but Hamilton had been opposed. Morris wrote Hamilton a gentle remonstrance on February 22, 1802: "You must pardon me for telling you I am sorry you opposed sending a petition to Congress . . . It will stop . . . petitions which might have come on from the eastward, and . . . leave our enemies to conclude against us from the silence of our friends."

Hamilton was not used to rebuke from so close a friend and bridled in his reply to Morris on February 27, 1802:

"I should be a very unhappy man, if I left my tranquillity at the mercy of the misrepresentations which friends as well as foes are fond of giving to my conduct." If his dear, perceptive, witty old friend Morris could not fathom him, no one could. He opened up a little to give a rare look inward at himself at 45:

> Mine is an odd destiny. Perhaps no man in the United States has sacrificed or done more for the present Constitution than myself—and contrary to all my anticipations of its fate, as you know from the very beginning, I am still labouring to prop the frail and worthless fabric. Yet I have the murmurs of its friends no less than the curses of its foes for my reward. What can I do better than withdraw from the scene? Every day proves to me more and more, that this American world was not made for me.

Hamilton had read Morris's recent speeches with great pleasure, but elsewhere "the conspiracy of dulness was at work. It chose to misinterpret your moderation in certain transactions of a personal reference." Morris should make "a public energetic display of your talents and principles to silence the cavillers."

What Morris failed to see was that his own position was more like Hamilton's than he realized. Hamilton projected on, and saw reflected from Morris, his own exotic image of himself:

> You, friend Morris, are by *birth* a native of this country, but by *genius* an exotic. You mistake, if you fancy that you are more of a favorite than myself, or that you are in any sort upon a theater suited to you.

By the eighteenth number of his *Examination of Jefferson's Message*, published in April 1802, the whole array of Hamilton's criticisms had become more extraordinary for its tone of personal pique, pettifogging, and nitpicking than for worthwhile substance. He had branded Jefferson a "philosophic *projec-*

tor" and ridiculed Jefferson's inflation of unimportant matters. Of them, if kept in proper proportion, it would be said, said Hamilton (as it might with more justice be said of Hamilton's *Examination*):

> Commas and points he sets exactly right
> And 'twere a sin to rob him of his mite.

Hamilton concludes this series, which can only be excused as occupational therapy for a mind whose grief over Philip had overwhelmed it, with a final bit of wishful thinking about the old rival he would not admit had finally overmastered him: "The credit of great abilities was allowed [Jefferson] by a considerable portion of those who disapproved his principles; but the short space of nine months has been amply sufficient to dispel that illusion." Some of "his most partial votaries begin to suspect that they have been mistaken in the OBJECT OF THEIR IDOLATRY." Yet in the country at large, belying his close election victory, Jefferson's popularity had never seemed greater, and it continued to grow.

Even Hamilton's acute ability to select a nom de plume seemed to desert him when he wrote his long *Examination. Phocion* (1784), *Publius* (1787), *Pacificus* (1793), *Tully* (1794), *Camillus* (1795), *Americanus* (1796), and *Titus Manlius* (1798)—all recalled or suggested historic personages from Roman antiquity, mostly by way of Plutarch and Livy, whose positive and popular names enlisted immediate sympathy for Hamilton's side of the controversy of the day. Such names automatically put his opponents on the defensive and allied them with an unpopular or alarming alternative. To all classically educated men, the name of Tully, for example, resonated with connotations of wise and firm leadership and protection of the middle classes against horrid conspiracies like those of Catiline to subvert Rome "on account of the unequal distribution of wealth." To self-educated or partly educated men on the rise who had their Plutarch only secondhand, a medium like Tully or Americanus or Pacificus would drive home the powerful message to a reader who did not read beyond the name.

But most readers, particularly among his democratic Republican enemies, would purposefully mistake Hamilton's *Lucius Crassus* for the other, much better known Crassus, Marcus Licinus Crassus. He was the richest of the Roman governmental financiers, well remembered from Shakespeare as a member of the First Triumvirate with Caesar and Pompey. Greedy for wealth and jealous of Pompey's military glory, the more famous Crassus ravaged the Parthians with his army, plundered the temple at Jerusalem, was finally crushed by the Parthians, and then slain at an interview with their general. His head was cut off and sent to Orodes, who caused melted gold to be poured into the severed head's mouth, saying "sate thyself now with that metal of which in life thou wert so greedy." This was not at all the image Hamilton wanted to project.

Hamilton had attacked the passage in Jefferson's message to Congress that proposed easing the strict immigration requirements imposed by the Alien Acts. The little known Lucius Crassus was an orator famed only for a law passed during his consulship in 95 B.C. to prevent people from passing as Roman citizens who had no right to the honor. According to Cicero, this Crassus' law was a prime cause of the Social War, the sort of war that Hamilton would most deplore.

It was not until March 29, 1802, more than four months after Philip's death, that Hamilton was able to refocus his mind on the immediate present and force it to admit that Philip was indeed dead, by finally acknowledging the many letters of condolence, as he did to Dr. Benjamin Rush.

He "felt all the weight of the obligation" he owed Rush and his family "for the tender concern they manifested," he said, "but I was obliged to wait for a moment of greater calm to express my sense of their kindness." Philip's death had been to him "an event beyond comparison the most afflicting of my life. . . . My loss is indeed great. The brightest as well as the eldest hope of my family has been taken from me. . . . He was a fine youth."

Dr. Rush, the leading medical man of America, a pioneer in the study of mental illness, had been observing Hamilton acutely and usually critically for more than a quarter of a century, ever since he had seen the 21-year-old aide at Germantown in 1778 and recorded that General Washington, the "Idol of America," was "governed by one of his aides."

In a classic essay written in 1786, "The Influence of Physical Causes upon the Moral Faculty," Rush thought he had identified a new disease, which he described as "the partial or weakened action of the moral faculty." According to Dr. Rush, "physical causes" such as climate, hunger, pestilence, and so on, create conditions favorable for onset of the moral disease. Firsthand knowledge or reports in the newspapers of terrible moral lapses—heinous crimes like murder or suicide, for example—press in upon the mind to cause the disease that Dr. Rush called *micronomia.* (The total absence of any moral faculty at all was *anomia*). Dr. Rush warned, "It is of the utmost consequence to keep young people as ignorant as possible of those crimes that are generally thought most disgraceful to human nature," because, if they should catch micronomia from them, they would be tempted to imitate such crimes. For example, Dr. Rush wrote, "Suicide, I believe, is often propagated by means of newspapers."

In Hamilton's performances over the years, the most recent, if forgivable, being his long delay in acknowledging Dr. Rush's condolences while he "examined" Jefferson's message as *Lucius Crassus,* Dr. Rush might have noted in Hamilton the progression of a mental malady. It had begun, perhaps, with a peccadillo, a gentleman's old affair magnified by too keen a concern for public credit into *The Reynolds Pamphlet.* More serious was the dubious underhanded morality as well as logical lunacy of the attack on John Adams. On the evidence of the unbalanced confusions of morality, policy, and personality in Hamilton's recent *Examination* of Dr. Rush's old friend Thomas Jefferson, the progression would appear to be still unstabilized.

At the very least, Hamilton's was a classic case of political suicide propagated by means of newspapers and pamphlets. But more than that, to Dr. Rush, would be the dangerously weakened condition of both Hamilton's moral and judgmental faculty, as well as his recent physical debilitude. He was a prime risk for micronomia. The missing fact that Dr. Rush would not know was that Philip's death in the duel holding his first fire on his father's advice had provided Hamilton himself with the closest possible exposure to the risk of imitative suicide. However, Dr. Rush would not fail to catch the new, strangely religious, even mystical turn Hamilton's thoughts had taken after Philip's death. Here was a turn that seemed at odds with all that Dr. Rush knew about Hamilton as a public man. Hamilton's letter to him went on, "But why should I repine? It was the will of heaven, and he is now out of the reach of a world full of folly, full of vice, full of danger—of least value in proportion as it is best known." The more Hamilton had come to know of life, the less he valued it. "I firmly trust, also, that he has safely reached the haven of eternal repose and felicity." Dr. Rush had mentioned a letter that Philip had written to his son. "Every memorial of the goodness of his heart is precious to me," Hamilton went on. "If no special reasons forbid it, I should be very glad to have a copy of that letter."

Elizabeth too "has drunk deeply of the cup of sorrow," and she joined him in affectionate thanks to the Rushes. "Our wishes for your happiness will be unceasing."

Hamilton had never been a member of any church. The deeply religious tone in these passages would be rather surprising to Dr. Rush because all he knew about Hamilton's religiosity were his professed abhorrence of the Deism and atheism he ascribed to Jefferson's French-leaning politics and two widely retold wisecracks from the time of the Constitutional Convention. When Benjamin Franklin had moved that each session be opened with a prayer, Hamilton was supposed to have snapped that he saw no need for calling in "foreign aid." And when Hamilton returned to New York and his old friend Dr. John Rodgers of the Wall Street Presbyterian Church asked him why God had not been suitably recognized in the Constitution, Hamilton is supposed to have replied, "Indeed, Doctor, we forgot it."

Hamilton as a young man off the boat in New York to seek his fortune and presenting his first letters of introduction from the Reverend Hugh Knox of St. Croix to the Reverends John Rodgers and John Mason of New York was then remarkable for his conventional religious observances. Robert Troup, his roommate at strongly Anglican King's College, bore witness that Hamilton "had read most of the polemical writers on religious subjects; and he was a zealous believer in the fundamental doctrines of Christianity; and, I confess, that the arguments with which he was accustomed to justify his belief, have tended, in no small degree, to confirm my own faith in revealed religion."

According to Broadus Mitchell, in the household of Elias Boudinot, the devout Presbyterian layman with whom Hamilton stayed at Elizabethtown during his first year in America, "No one could have lived for a year without kneeling regularly in prayer, or becoming a confirmed atheist." It may well have been this very pull of competing sectarian loyalties between the Presbyterian and Episcopalian—which became closely identified with the opposing patriot and loyalist political sides of the Revolution—that made Hamilton hesitate and then fail to make any firm choice of church membership during his life. His Betsy, by contrast, always noted for being devout, had once seemed to Tench Tilghman devout enough to be called "the little Saint," unless by this he meant only that she, having just met Hamilton, had not been as complaisant toward him as he would have wished her to be.

Until Philip's death, Hamilton's religious expressions were so intimately woven into his political purposes and ideas of personal honor as to be practically meaningless as testaments of personal belief. Forty-four years afterward, Chancellor James Kent still remembered vividly that Hamilton, at the New York Constitutional Convention of 1788, had opened his first great speech by urging both the need for a Union of the states and a government with powers adequate to uphold and preserve that Union. By way of unarguable analogy to support this arguable proposition, Hamilton had cited the doctrine of the immortality of the soul: there were modern doubts on the subject, he admitted, but "to convince men that they have within them immortal spirits is going very far to prepare their minds for the ready reception of Christian truth." The Union of the states required the same willing suspension of disbelief. Kent recalled that Hamilton had closed the same speech equally unforgettably by citing the Patriots' Prayer of "the brave Cobham, who fell, 'his ruling passion strong in death,' " praying, "Oh, save my country, Heaven!"

The depth and sincerity of Hamilton's belief in the Christian religion as the cement of the Union also burns through his letter to William Loughton Smith of April 10, 1797, proposing that Congress include among "vigorous preparation for war" the mobilizing of "the religious ideas of Americans." Hamilton argues that a politician should consider "some religious solemnity to impress seriously the minds of the people. . . ." Religion is "an important means of influencing opinion." It would be a "valuable resource in a contest with France" to set the religious ideas of Americans "in active competition with the atheistical tenets of their enemies . . . a day of humiliation and prayer, beside being very proper, would be extremely useful."

Certainly, the nightmares Hamilton had suffered through since 1791 for disobeying the grim injunction of Prov. 7:25–27 to avoid the harlot, "Let not thine heart decline to her ways, go not astray . . . her house is the way to hell," proved the Old Testament's wisdom by its eerily specific application to his own case— even to the point of her husband's being "gone with a bag of money." If redemption lay only in a beatitude of the New Testament, Matt. 5:10, "Blessed are they which are persecuted for righteousness' sake: for theirs is the Kingdom of heaven," it was not, unfortunately, as specifically apposite to the persecutions from which he suffered as the Old Testament was to his sin. But he may have thought that their intensity and duration remained the best hope he had left.

Atheism and the absence of religion in public polity filled Hamilton with unfeigned horror. He castigated it in his most passionately corrosive manner in broadsides like *The Stand*, No. III, published April 7, 1798: "The disgusting spectacle . . . profligacy . . . consummate infamy . . . terrible design" of the "unprincipled reformers" of France "to destroy all religious opinion, and to pervert a whole people to Atheism . . . betrays a plan to undermine the venerable pillars that support the edifice of civilized society." They "disorganize the human mind itself." The "dreadful proofs" included "supplanting the Christian sabbath" with the ten-day weeks of the decades under the revolutionary calendar of 1793, putting inscriptions on tombs affirming death to be an eternal sleep, sending impious children into "the hall of the Convention to lisp blasphemy against the King of Kings," and holding a festival of "public worship to a courtezan decorated with the pompous [title] of 'GODDESS OF REASON.' "[1]

His sense of a religious duty to keep up his efforts to prop the "frail and worthless fabric" of the Constitution against "unprincipled reformers" was perhaps as much as anything else what served in the end to pull Hamilton out of the slough of grief into which Philip's death had plunged him and back into the bear pit of New York politics, only to be confronted there with an appalling new apparition. He finally ventured out for a little friendly conviviality among old friends and admirers at the Federal Republicans' and Cincinnatians' annual Washington's birthday collation. At its counterpart in the capital at Washington, who should push in but the Republican vice-president of the United States, Aaron Burr. Thinking of it, Hamilton's mind's eye must have recalled Macbeth's shocked incoherence at seeing Banquo's ghost at just such a banquet: "Blood hath been shed ere now . . . This is more strange than such a murder is . . . I have a strange infirmity . . . give me some wine; fill full. I drink to the general joy of the whole table. . . . Avaunt! and quit my sight! let the earth hide thee!"

But Burr, the man who had helped smash the hopes of Pinckney, Adams, and Hamilton and put many of their party colleagues out of good government jobs, did not fade silently in and out of the hall. He took center stage and cried out a cryptic toast: "To the union of all honest men."

"Union" and "honest men" were code words that carried magical connotations to good old boys of the Federalist rank and file.

"What meant the apparition and the toast which made part of the after-piece of the birthday festival?" Hamilton demanded of Gouverneur Morris on April 6, 1802. "Is it possible that some new intrigue is about to link the Federalists with a man who can never be anything else than the bane of a good cause? I dread more from this than from all the contrivances of the bloated and senseless junto of Virginia."

Jefferson later would write that Burr was "a crooked gun, or other perverted machine, whose aim or shot you could never be sure of." Ever since the election, Jefferson had been conspicuously widening the distance between himself and his "crooked gun" of a vice-president. He let it be put about that Burr had intrigued to snatch the presidency from him. He deliberately passed over Burr in the distribution of patronage, omitted him from his councils, and did not invite him to dinners. During the heated debates and votes on repeal of the Judiciary Bill, Burr's conduct as presiding officer of the Senate fed suspicions. When he cast a tie-breaking vote for a Federalist move to recommit the bill for further study, Republican suspicions were confirmed. Hamilton's suspicions were aroused.

After Burr and Jefferson tied, Hamilton had happily written James A. Bayard that "it is demonstrated by recent facts that Burr is solicitous to keep upon anti-federal ground, to avoid compromitting himself by any engagements, with the Federalists. . . . Ambition without principle never was long under the guidance of good sense." It deranged all of Hamilton's plans now to think that Burr, returned from the dead like Banquo's ghost, might seek to snatch away control of the Federalist party two years hence, turn out Hamilton and Gouverneur Morris and other leaders, and make it over into his own moderate instrument for seizing the presidency.

On second thought, Hamilton reflected, Burr's crookedness could be made use of, much as General James Wilkinson's had been, with knowledge that he was in the pay of Spain in the role of a double agent. Burr's situation could be rendered so "absolutely hopeless with his old friends," he would break from them and form a third party. "Then, if we think it worth the while, we can purchase him with his flying squadron," said Hamilton. In a third-party role, Burr would not threaten Hamilton's own titular leadership of the Federalists.

James A. Bayard told Hamilton not to be alarmed. Bayard himself had invited Burr to the Washington birthday dinner, knowing the effect his appearance there would have on Jefferson: it would deepen the split between the two men. Burr's toast was "extremely well calculated to answer our views."

Hamilton was not greatly relieved that redoubtable Federalists like Bayard and Morris were "using" Burr, even though only as "a tool," as he had planned to do, and not a partner. It should go no further, Hamilton warned, "as a chief, he will disgrace and destroy the party." He feared Burr's "irregular courtship." Eager to regain the reins, they might turn to anyone, even Burr. "I know of no important character, who has a less founded interest," insisted Hamilton . . . "His talents may do well enough for a particular plot, but they are ill-suited to a great and wise drama."

Hamilton had thought long thoughts about the next act in the "great and wise drama" of Federalism. It did not include a part for Burr. But they could take a leaf from Burr's book, he wrote Bayard. Even Federalists must sometimes put aside reason and speak to the passions of men and win them over. The Democrats eulogized reason and flattered people's vanity and passion. The Federalists should flatter their passions in the cause of reason and enlightenment. To be persuasive and appealing to the people was not ipso facto to be corrupt.

"Nothing is more fallacious than to expect to produce any valuable or permanent results in political projects by relying merely on the reason of men," Hamilton wrote. "Men are rather reasoning than reasonable animals, for the most part governed by the impulse of passion. This is a truth well understood by our adversaries who have practised upon it with no small benefit to their cause."

Federalists, he went on, had "erred in relying so much on the rectitude and utility of their measures, as to have neglected the cultivation of popular favor, by fair and justifiable expedients." Yet unless we "can contrive to take hold of, and carry along with us some strong feelings of the mind, we shall in vain calculate upon any substantial or durable results"—even though, he added omi-

nously, there be "some deviations from what, on other occasions, we have maintained to be right." Hamilton drew a nice distinction: he discountenanced "the
imitation of things intrinsically unworthy." But courtship that was "irregular"
would be permissible on the hard road toward "a sound & stable order of
things." "The present Constitution is the standard to which we are to cling," he
vowed. "Under its banners, *bona fide*, must we combat our political foes, rejecting all changes but through the channel itself provided for amendments."

The sudden emergence of the apparition of Burr as a potential president—
at the Federalists' banquet—reminded Hamilton of one amendment to the Constitution urgently needed above all others. To avoid the nightmare of another tie
in the electoral vote and all the shabby politics of intrigue and throwing away
electoral votes that had plagued all earlier presidential elections, the New York
legislature was considering amendments to its Constitution whereby candidates
for president and vice-president could be separately designated and electors
would be chosen by direct election of the people instead of by the legislature.
Hamilton wrote Morris on March 4, 1802, that he was "thoroughly confirmed in
my full impression, that it is true federal policy to promote the adoption of these
amendments" because "the people should know whom they are choosing." The
existing mode of casting the die gave scope to intrigue and endangered public
tranquillity, as the recent contest between Jefferson and Burr had illustrated.
Choice of electors by the people in districts "removes thus far the intervention
of the State governments . . . strengthens the connection between the federal
head and the people, and . . . diminishes the means of party combination" which
had invited Burr's intrigues. To sum up, said Hamilton, "it has ever appeared
to me as sound principle to let the federal government rest, as much as possible,
on the shoulders of the people, and as little as possible on . . . the state
legislatures." New York, the state of all the states whose politics seemed most
sensitive to the shifting tides of public opinion, adopted laws that enacted what
he had urged.

Hamilton's preoccupation with both politics and religion during his slow
swing back from the depths of his grief over Philip's death finally merged the
two disciplines. In his letter to Bayard of April 16–18, 1802, he presented a
carefully thought-out plan for what he called *The Christian Constitutional
Society.* He gave Bayard all the reasons why such an organization would help
the Federalists "to carry along with us some strong feelings of the mind." Its
objects were "1st the Support of the Christian Religion, 2nd the support of the
Constitution of the United States." In organizational structure it was to be
patterned roughly on the Society of the Cincinnati, with a national "directing
council," a "sub-directing council" in each state, and local societies under the
subdirecting councils.

Its "means" would include dissemination gratis of useful publications, pamphlets, and newspaper stories. Local clubs would meet once a week, read the
papers, prepare stories, and, generally, use "all lawful means *in concert* to
promote the election of *fit men.* A lively correspondence must be kept up between the different societies." Charitable institutions under Federal manage-

ment would be created "for the relief of Emigrants." There would also be "academies each with one professor instructing the different classes of mechanics in the principles of Mechanics & Elements of Chemistry." Dues would be five dollars annually for eight years "to be contributed by each member who can really afford it."

Bayard replied reproachfully that such "clubs" would only "revive a thousand jealousies and suspicions which now begin to slumber." Federalists must let the Democratic Republicans defeat themselves, he felt.

Another telling political objection to Hamilton's plan was that it was preaching only to those already saved. In many areas—particularly in New England —the churches were the bulwarks of Federalism. The faithful had long been summoned to the polls by beating the ecclesiastic drum. With no promptings from Hamilton, the clergy had raised the cry that religion was endangered by Jacobin atheism. They inveighed against the Republican "infidel" in Washington. Altars and communion tables were in danger of desecration; churches, of being burned; and the clergy, of being strung up in their own pulpits. Or in case of invasion, put in the front lines "as those who, in his opinion, may be most easily spared." Fearful of such dire events, a few nervous New England farmers are said to have hung their Bibles down the well and oiled up their flintlocks. But the grip of the clergy was loosening, too, and Jefferson's popularity seemed to grow greater with every such overblown sermon. Nothing Hamilton did seemed to work very well against Jefferson's smooth and successful "northern strategy."

Although Hamilton still seemed to be rather badly out of touch with the mood of the people that spring of 1802, it was encouraging that he seemed to recognize the force of Bayard's objections, to see the Federalists' problem objectively, and, in doing so, to give hope that he was on the way to recovery. He was receding from the public stage toward the pleasures of private life at his almost completed Grange.

Writing to Rufus King, June 3, 1802, Hamilton reported that the people were still loyally supporting Jefferson. To describe the people, he used a tag from Vergil, "informe ingens cui lumen ademptum." The full quotation begins, of course, with the phrase, "monstrum horrendum." It is the description his favorite classical poet gives of the Cyclops Polyphemus after Ulysses has blinded his only eye. From that day to this, Hamilton's detractors have never ceased to translate his erudite, smoothly jocular sally to his old friend into the irrebuttable damnation of the charge that Hamilton really thought that "the people, sir, is a great beast." Indeed, this foolish charge is the only thing many people remember about Hamilton at all.

Hamilton urged King to come home from his ministry in London. He could do greater good at home. Out of office, he reminded King, the Federalists' long-range purpose must be to reclaim the government they had built and lost by recapturing the people's confidence once more. The tide would turn. "Vibrations of power," he wrote, "are the genius of our government."

But New York Federalists turned down demands for campaign contributions. Hamilton took the refusals as a personal affront. Troup complained bitterly that besides himself and Hamilton, only a few remained who were willing to dig down into their pockets. At the Federalist club the conversation grew strained. Troup wrote gloomily that "Hamilton & I have determined to trouble ourselves no more about the public weal; but to let things take their course."

"A disappointed politician you know," Hamilton wrote to Richard Peters on December 29, 1802, "is very apt to take refuge in a Garden. . . . In this new situation, for which I am as little fitted as Jefferson to guide the helm of the U. States, I come to you as an Adept in rural science for instruction." He intended to devote his fields around The Grange to grasses and inquired after the best sorts; he commissioned Peters to send him a couple of bushels of seed of a special red clover, a kind he had not been able to find in the neighborhood. His soil, he related, was a loam that was too sandy. He subscribed to a local report that "plaister of Paris" [lime] would help it "if applied in a pretty smart shower of rain. . . . The rain is supposed to purify the sea salts which are believed to be the obstacle to the salutary operation of the Gypsum."

Peters, wanting to be helpful, replied beginning with Hamilton's old, not his new, preoccupation: "I *marvel* that you should be a disappointed Politician. I am a mortified but not disappointed one. You must have foreseen the Catastrophe that has befallen us. . . . I am glad you have this little Syren to seduce you from public Anxieties. But take Care," he warned sagely, "that the meretricious charms of this new Flame do not make too great Drafts on your Purse."

On the same day, Hamilton wrote to solicit melon seeds from Charles Cotesworth Pinckney in South Carolina. Hamilton would also be grateful to Pinckney for parrakeets for his beloved daughter Angelica, he wrote, but he could not forbear ruefully looking back on the Federalist debacle and asking: "Amidst the triumphant reign of democracy, do you retain sufficient interest in public affairs to feel any curiosity about what is going on? In my opinion, the follies and vices of the administration have as yet made no material impression as to their disadvantages."

Records are sketchy, but from what there are it appears that in the years before they finally moved into The Grange, the Hamiltons had lived at seven or eight different addresses in the Wall Street area of lower Manhattan, including 57 Wall Street, 26 Broadway, 107 Liberty Street, 58 Partition Street (now part of Fulton Street), 12 Garden Street, somewhere on Pine Street, and in what Meyer Berger of *The New York Times* in 1940 described as "the ancient brick structure at 173 Cherry Street which stands under Manhattan Bridge among blackened tenements," where now tugboats and other "deep-throated harbor craft bellow right into the backyard." While The Grange was still a-building, the Hamilton family stayed for various periods, beginning in 1800, in a small farmhouse on nearby Scheiffelin land known as the "north cottage."

As construction progressed on The Grange itself, but before it was finished, the Hamilton family started moving in and occupied some of the rooms. When all was done, John McComb's bill, as architect and contractor, came to $2,495.20. The bill of the general contractor, Ezra Weeks, was $9,324.85. It might have been

much higher if Hamilton, in association with Aaron Burr, had not been success-
ful in defending Ezra's brother, Levi, in the celebrated criminal case of *People
v. Levi Weeks* after Levi had been charged with murdering beautiful Gulielma
Sands and throwing her bruised body down the Manhattan Well on the night of
December 22, 1799. With all these bills to pay and also the debt to Scheiffelin for
the land, the judgment Hamilton had just won for his and Aaron Burr's client
Louis Le Guen in the series of cases that went by the name of *Le Guen v.
Gouverneur & Kemble*, including a judgment for $119,915.43, could hardly have
come at a better time.

Moving into their new home when it was finally finished late in 1802 was a
major event in all the Hamiltons' lives. All through the years of what she called
her exile in London and Paris, the exquisite Angelica Church had pined for
Hamilton's letters, read them over and over, and followed his public career with
sometimes eager and sometimes fretfully jealous attention, concern, and adora-
tion. After years of captivating European society, Angelica and John Church had
returned to the United States in May of 1797. London and Paris were all right
in their way, but desolate in their way, too, for Angelica because Hamilton was
not there. The summer of 1798 the Hamiltons and Churches had lived together
in the rented house on Harlem Heights. Now Betsy and the children would spend
most of their time at The Grange, while Hamilton remained at their house in
town, commuting the nine miles from Wall Street mostly on weekends. On
horseback it was too long a daily commute and not much easier by his own
carriage drawn by his favorite horse, Riddle. The Albany mail stage left from
what is now the corner of Cortlandt and Greenwich Streets every morning at six,
and the coachman could let him off at The Grange's front gate when he asked
him to, but the coach's times were usually wrong for a Wall Street lawyer's long
hours.

Now the Churches were back in New York, installed in their sumptuous
house in Robinson Street, which Hamilton had picked out for them. Somehow
Angelica's now being able to see him quite often, to blush to his sallies, to bask
in his glow, to yield to his sometimes quicksilver, sometimes saturnine changes
of mood and temper, never seemed to wither his charm for her. Nor could
anything she did or failed to do slake or stale her hold on him.

The elegant Federalist Congressman Harrison Gray Otis of Massachusetts
was a splendid raconteur who loved to retell a tale about Hamilton and Angelica
that dated back to the winter of 1799 during the last wild fling of the Federal
Republican court in Philadelphia before its displacement to Washington by Jefferson. It did not tend to stale because their intimate situation remained essentially the same as the years went by and more and more of a public scandal.

Anne and William Bingham's Mansion House remained the epicenter of
glittering Philadelphia society having its last brilliant fling at the capital before
exile to the boondocks on the Potomac. The Samuel Brecks, too, gave "truly
select" parties at their mansion known as Greenbrier. Hamilton was in Philadelphia on inspector general's business when Otis dined there with him and Angelica Church, their spouses being absent, and a sparkling group of other guests

on Christmas Eve of 1799. Only the sensationally beautiful and glamorous Anne Bingham missed the party because, Otis said, "she burst the gown she had prepared for the occasion Saturday." George Washington had died less than two weeks earlier, and there had been much funerary activity since, but neither this sad event nor the absence of Anne Bingham's profane wit could spoil the evening's smatch. A pretty, new Miss Schuyler, Angelica's and Elizabeth's teen-age youngest sister, Catharine, the goddaughter of Washington, helped greatly to rescue it. It enhances the charm of Otis's stories to know that when he repeats his best ones in letters to his wife, he tends to tone things down for home consumption back in Boston by bowdlerizing the best parts. Here is what he told her:

"Tuesday Dined at Breck's, with Mrs. Church, Miss Schuyler, Genl. Hamilton, Champlin &c. &c," Otis wrote. "Mrs. C[hurch] the mirror of affectation, but as she affects to be extremely affable and free from ceremony, this foible is rather amusing than offensive. Miss Schuyler a young wild flirt from Albany, full of glee & apparently desirous of matrimony. After Dinner Mrs. C[hurch] dropped her shoe bow [read garter?], Miss S—— picked it up and put it in Hamilton's buttonhole saying 'there brother I have made you a Knight.'

" 'But of what order' (says Madam C) 'he can't be a Knight of the garter in this country.'

" 'True sister' replied Miss S—— 'but *he would be if you would let him.*' "

Otis also mentioned a conversation he had had with Christopher G. Champlin at the same party. Champlin, a member of Congress from Rhode Island, strongly resented Hamilton's casting what he called "some liquorish looks at his cara sposa." He complained to Otis that Hamilton "appears to him very trifling in his conversation with ladies." Champlin said his wife hastened to reassure him that "she did not really" like the caster of the "liquorish looks" at all. Otis sardonically noted in disbelief that Champlin, at least, "was evidently *satisfied* with this intimation." A reassurance of a kind that nobody but a husband, certainly not Otis, could be expected to believe. It all only served to thicken the cloud of scandal that was enveloping Hamilton and Angelica Church.

It seems to be of the nature of love that neither a man's imperceptible aureole of undercover amours, like Hamilton's liquorish looks, nor his enemies' awe or hatred, nor his air of command beneath a surface of urbane geniality that yet suffers not fools, nor his antic squint toward "liberation" of romantic Antillean isles of origin, nor mad canicular fevers of brain and blood, disqualifies him for the passionate love of the most desirable of women. Such vincibilities seem to compel it, even through long separations. To such general rules Angelica Church's affection for Hamilton was no exception. What her husband, John Barker Church, privately thought or knew of it is unknown. From all that is known, he also liked Hamilton, but not all that well. He was a rich, practical businessman who could indulge his wife her social and aesthetic independences. He had returned to America because it seemed to be a good place for profitable investments. During his long absence, Hamilton had managed them for him, but

Church was not at all sure that the former secretary of the treasury had handled them efficiently. He wrote to Jeremiah Wadsworth about a mortgage held jointly by the two of them: "I will thank you as soon as you can to send me our Account Current, for our Friend Hamilton not being very accurate in his Accounts is not clear that he has not made some Mistakes respecting the Monies you have Paid him on my Account."

Church, practical businessman though he was, would exchange fire in a duel with Aaron Burr, merely grazing him, over a matter that was primarily Hamilton's problem—the Holland Land Company fiasco. Church, of course, had served as Hamilton's second at the time of Hamilton's threatened duel with James Monroe. But the reairing of the squalid Reynolds affair seemed in no way to affect Hamilton's relations with his own wife, Eliza, or with the Churches, except to make them all draw closer together, if possible, in the face of the storm of public scandal. None of Hamilton's aberrations seemed to change their unshakable loyalty, admiration, and love. Angelica still seemed to cherish his every word and gesture with no slight trace of disillusionment. Eliza was—as always —Eliza, for whom her husband could do no wrong. Hamilton was profoundly grateful for her steadfast loyalty in the face of the abuse and ridicule of at least the Democratic Republican part of the world. But now she spent much time at their country house or at the Schuylers' home in Albany or at Old Saratoga. Most of Hamilton's letters to her are suffused with affection and gratitude, some are perfunctory. Few husbands over so many years manage to maintain so consistent a pitch of epistolary affection as Hamilton did for Eliza; yet in them he rarely omitted Angelica's name from the ambit of his love.

"I need not tell her," he had written Eliza in the third person from Philadelphia on July 19, 1797, "how very happy I shall be to return to her embrace and to the company of our beloved Angelica. I am very anxious about you both . . . for you comprize all my felicity."

Again a year later, he wrote her, "I always feel how necessary you are to me—But when you are absent I become still more sensible of it, and look around in vain for that satisfaction which you alone can bestow. I dined with Angelica today—Margaret was with her."

He could still contrive a compliment for a wife of 18 years. In November of 1798 he wrote, "You are my good genius; of that kind which the ancient philosophers called a familiar. . . ." And he could close to her with a touch of poesy: "Adieu best of wives and best of mothers / Heaven ever bless you & me in you."

But Hamilton's real affection for Eliza did not seem to keep him from pleasures of a more intense kind with Angelica and perhaps other ladies like Mrs. Champlin as well, but as might be expected no documentation for such involvements is known to exist.

Angelica took center stage as a leader of New York society. Her balls were the most brilliant and lavish seen in the city. When Hamilton was deeply engrossed in his frustrating duties as inspector general of the army, he still found plenty of time to dance attendance on Angelica. So much that Robert Troup commented sourly: "Though not yet in the field of Mars he maintains an unequalled reputation for gallantry—such at least is the opinion entertained of him by the ladies. When I have more leisure," Troup told Rufus King in England, "I will give you the history of the Ghost of Baron [Ciominie?] & Mrs. Church as published by our Gallant General."

Whether the rumors of the affair between Alexander and Angelica were true or not, everyone in society believed they were, as such tales are always believed. They were damaging to Hamilton's reputation, and Troup believed them. He disliked Angelica, and he had nothing but contempt for her husband.

Church had gone into the business of insurance underwriting and soon prospered. Hamilton had had him placed in a directorship of the Bank of New York, but Church also took an active interest in its rival, the Bank of the Manhattan Company, founded and fostered and lawyered by Aaron Burr. Hamilton had fought it with all his political and financial talents.

With British seizures of American vessels on the rise, Hamilton and Troup were cocounsel in many important marine insurance suits, but their professional partnership did not keep Troup from writing, "Poor Church is fast declining in respectability. He talks too much—is too fond of premiums—and too unwilling to pay losses." Worse still, "Church is said to be much pushed for money—and indeed family affairs are in a train which in my opinion will by & by cause an explosion which will spread general ruin around it—I mean the ruin of almost the whole connexion. I consider it unfortunate that he ever removed with his family to this country." The "connexion" to which Troup alluded was Angelica's "connexion" with Hamilton.

By 1801, Troup was writing King of the thickening cloud of scandal hanging over the Church and Hamilton families, particularly because Church no longer went home much in the evenings, and Hamilton went up to The Grange only on weekends:

> Mr. Church is working hard at cards—underwriting—and examining bankrupts. How his constitution stands it is a matter of amazement to us all! He has at least four regular card clubs to attend every week & sometimes they do not break up till the morning. . . . He is famous for litigation on his policies; and yet he is said to do a great deal of business. . . . There is as little respectability attached to him as to any man amongst us; and unfortunately the whole family are enveloped in such a cloud that they enjoy nothing of esteem. The oldest daughter of Mr. Church is a most amiable girl and she is supposed to have a very cultivated mind & yet her family labor under such disadvantages that she has little prospect of marrying in a suitable manner!

None of this would have mattered so much to Troup if his best friend, Hamilton, were not so seriously sullied by the same Church "cloud":

> I believe I wrote you some time ago [he continued significantly] that I had ventured, at every risk, to communicate with a certain friend

of ours on a certain subject. I fear notwithstanding that things continue in the same course. You can hardly [word illegible] how ruinous are the consequences of the general belief.

Still, when he did manage to get home to see the children, Hamilton seemed to be a model father. His son John Church Hamilton recalled how his father now "sought and found relief from the painful reflections which the growing delusion of the country forced upon him, in the duties of religion, in the circle of domestic joys, and in the embellishment of his rural retreat."

As Hamilton cultivated his garden, his new interest in horticulture and landscaping intensified his new interest in the Creator:

> His religious feeling grew with his growing intimacy with the marvellous works of nature, [said his son] all pointing in the processes and their results to a great pervading, ever active Cause. Thus his mind rose from the visible to the invisible; and he found intensest pleasure in studies higher and deeper than all speculation. His Bible exhibits on its margin the care with which he perused it. Among his autographs is an abstract of the Apocalypse—and notes in his hand were seen in the margin of "Paley's Evidences." With these readings he now united the habit of daily prayer, in which exercise of faith and love, the Lord's Prayer was always a part. The renewing influences of early pious instruction and habit appear to have returned in all their force on his truest sensibilities.

His psychic transformation seemed to make his family, defined loosely to include Angelica, the new focus of his life. His children always afterward remembered him in this period as the ideal father, proud of all their accomplishments, patient as an instructor, and joyful as a companion in play and sport. John Church and James Alexander and all his other surviving children worshiped him.

John Church remembered his father reading Latin aloud, translating as he went, and managing to make it all come alive as he read: "With what emphasis and fervor did he read of battles! When translating the commentaries of Caesar, it would seem as though Caesar were present; for as much as any man that ever lived he had the soldier's temperament. It told itself in little things." During the erection of The Grange, "he caused a tent to be pitched, and camp stools to be placed under the shading trees. He measured distances as though marking the frontage of a camp; and when he walked along, his step seemed to fall naturally into the cadenced pace of practiced drill. It was his delight in his hours of relaxation to return to scenes and incidents of his early life, when fighting for his country, and praying for its protection."

Hamilton wrote Betsy, "My health and comfort both require that I should be at home—at that home where I am always sure to find a sweet asylum from care and pain." Hamilton himself seemed conscious that a change had taken place in his character. "While all other passions decline in me, those of love and friendship gain new strength. It will be more and more my endeavour to abstract myself from all pursuits which interfere with those of affection."

Only in his Reynolds Pamphlet and in his private letter to James A. Bayard does Hamilton make mention of any sector of his affections that resembled an "irregular courtship." But Dr. Benjamin Rush's medical and psychological file on Hamilton would not be complete until receipt of a letter from John Adams written in September 1807. In it Adams brought Dr. Rush up to date on his late critic, especially "the profligacy of his life; his fornications, adulteries, and his incests."

Yes, doctor, said Adams, his incests.

The patient did seem to be getting back some of his old pep.

28

FIFTEEN YEARS OF COMPETITION

BEFORE I HAVE DONE I SHALL MAKE MY LEARNED FRIEND CRY OUT,

"HELP ME, CASSIUS, OR I SINK!"
—*Gouverneur Morris, pointing first toward Hamilton and then toward Aaron Burr, during the final argument to the Court of Errors, in* Le Guen v. Gouverneur & Kemble, *February 12, 1800*

To a family like Hamilton's that had moved so often from one rented house in town to another, few smells could have been sweeter than the freshly sawed planking, the unplastered laths, and the drifts of sawdust in the corners of the still unfinished rooms of their first permanent home at The Grange. General Philip Schuyler, always the benevolent paterfamilias, had been helping them out with the "sweet project" every way he knew how. He asked Hamilton for numbers and dimensions of the lumber needed for studs and joists and beams and spandrels and clapboards and arranged to have them sawed and rough-planed to measure at his sawmill for him free. He went to Saratoga to pick out the best lumber himself and see to it that it had been properly soaked for two months and then dried and seasoned so that it would not warp. He pointed out to

Hamilton that space behind outer clapboard walls ought to be filled with bricks. Inner wall partitions should be of solid planking so as to leave no spaces between for Harlem rats and mice. An accident befell one shipment down from Albany, and a whole wagonload of paint and oil were lost. Hamilton's horses were drowned. Schuyler generously replaced the whole load, arranged for some new house paint, and, for good measure, made Hamilton a present of a new team of horses.

As Hamilton traveled back and forth from New York City to the upstate county seats on the circuit where his legal cases took him, The Grange was always on his mind. About halfway between Wall Street and The Grange along his customary route up Broadway, near where Rockefeller Center now stands, Hamilton's physician friend Dr. David Hosack had laid out an extensive botanical garden. This probably inspired Hamilton with ideas for overly ambitious and extravagant landscaping schemes. He wrote out directions for a circular bulb bed 18 feet in diameter, containing nine separate sections, with beds of tulips, lilies, and hyacinths alternating by threes. He drew a plan to illustrate. A lovely touch were "wild roses around the outside of the flower garden with laurel at foot." Borders of shrubbery around the grove should be brightened with laurel, too, and sweet briars and dogwood. Dr. Hosack, who would attend him as his surgeon at the last, had given him his recipe for that gardener's talisman, the compost heap. It was "to consist of 3 barrels full of the *clay* which I bought, 6 barrels of *black moulds*, 2 waggon loads of the best clay on the Hill . . . , and one waggon load of pure cowdung. Let these be well and repeatedly mixed and pounded together to be made use hereafter for the Vines."

Mr. Dunphy had been doing a bad job with the landscaping: ". . . Dunphy planted the Tulip Trees in a row along the *outer* fence of the Garden . . . and was collecting some Hemlock Trees to place between them. I desired him to place them in a row along the *inner* fence,—I mean the side nearest the house."

Hamilton had noticed this mistake as he passed by on the Albany stagecoach and quickly wrote to correct it before it slipped his mind:

> Having attended to them in my route, I shall be glad, if White Pines are not conveniently to be had, that besides those along the inner fence there may be one Hemlock between every two of the Tulip Trees along the outer fence.

The workmen should be kept busy at all times, even when the weather was bad: "When it is too cold to go on with grubbing, our men may be employed in cutting and clearing away the underbrush in the Grove and the other woods." But part of the land should be kept in its natural state: "Let the centre of the principal wood in the line of the different rocks remain rough and wild."

From a two-day stay at Peekskill, Hamilton wrote back to Elizabeth:

> It has always appeared to me that the ground on which our orchard stands is much too moist. To cure this, a ditch round it would be useful

... three feet deep by three feet wide at the bottom. The clay that comes out of the ditch will be useful to give firmness to our roads. . . .

Riddle had somehow sprained the ankle of a hind leg on their journeyings, "which very much retarded my progress today. By care and indulgence, he is much better this evening. . . ." But even such annoying breakdowns did not keep Hamilton from writing back more instructions like the following from Claverack: The ice house should be ventilated by two wooden chimneys, "each about two feet square & four feet long half above half below the ground, to have a cap on the top sloping downwards . . . The aperture for letting in and out the air to be about a foot and a half square in the side immediately below the cap." He drew a picture of exactly what he wanted. The east and west piazzas should also be caulked against the weather.

They kept some domestic fowl, and these needed gravel in the gizzard, he reminded Elizabeth: "Country people all agree that to fat fowls, it is essential to keep them well supplied with gravel . . . seashore gravel, not too large, is particularly good. . . . The coops must be cleaned out every two or three days." And "after the Fowls have had a sufficient opportunity of drinking, the remaining water must be removed."

No detail of husbandry escaped his close attention. Out of the scraps of lumber, the carpenters should knock together some birdhouses as "additional accommodations for the pidgeons."

Humble New York pigeons meant as much to daughter Angelica as Pinckney's exotic Carolina parrakeets. After writing such a typically exhaustive catalogue of things for her to do, it was, of course, rather tiresomely supererogatory of Hamilton to add warmly to Elizabeth, "You see, I do not forget The Grange. No that I do not; nor any one that inhabits it. Accept yourself my tenderest affection."

As the great project was nearing completion during the summer of 1802, the Hamiltons held a happy field day of their own—a veritable *fête champêtre*—on the grounds beside the "grove." There Hamilton had planted 13 sapling gum trees to symbolize the original 13 states. There were no fireworks, but the saplings were solemnized by prayer, speechmaking, and, according to one account, "all the festivities peculiar to the olden times." The bill for the wine alone came to $150. The assembled guests must have included as many as possible of Hamilton family familiars—John and Angelica Church, the Robert Troups and the John Jays and Gouverneur Morris, Dr. Hosack, Nicholas Fish, Egbert Benson, Richard Harison, John Laurance, Richard Varick, Oliver Wolcott, Jr., William Seton, Charles Wilkes, Matthew Clarkson, Elias Boudinot, Thomas Cooper, Caleb Gibbs, William Bayard, and Chancellor James Kent—all with wives and ladies. It is a matter of dispute whether Aaron Burr was ever invited to join the Hamiltons and their friends at any of these elegant social gatherings at The Grange.

The Hamiltons would proudly serve the wine to all from the handsome silverplated, four-bottle wine cooler that George and Martha Washington had presented to them in 1797 at the time when public uproar over the Reynolds affair was reaching a crescendo.

To make sure they did not overstay the Hamiltons' warm welcome, the ladies and gentlemen would look from time to time at the elaborate French clock on its pedestal that Louis Le Guen had presented to the Hamiltons in 1800 as a housewarming present.

Most of the Hamiltons' friends were much relieved that his preoccupations with The Grange had led him to confine his politicking these days to sniping from the sidelines. His comment to Pinckney of December 29, 1802, was typical. The "follies and vices" of Jefferson's administration, he noted, far from losing it favor, were only making it more popular all the time.

"The malady is rather progressive than on the decline in our Northern Quarter," he wrote. "The last *lullaby* message [to Congress], instead of inspiring contempt, attracts praise. Mankind are forever destined to be the dupes of bold & cunning imposture."

All the building and landscaping, lavish entertaining and vintage wine were much too costly for a man without capital who had to live on legal fees as he collected them from clients who were often hard pressed themselves. Robert Troup was particularly happy that his old friend was finally concentrating on law business, even though it was costing Troup himself some money.

"Hamilton is closely pursuing the law," he wrote to Rufus King, "and I have at length succeeded in making him somewhat mercenary. I have known him latterly to dun his clients for money, and in settling an account with me the other day, he reminded me that I had received a fee for him in settling a question referred to him and me jointly. These indications of regard to property give me hopes that we shall not be obliged to raise a subscription to pay his funeral."[1]

Hard as he kept working, Hamilton had no alternative but to mortgage his whole estate to raise the money to pay some of the substantial expenses he had bound himself to pay to build it. Apparently, he could not obtain a construction loan from a bank; so in July 1801 he gave a one-year mortgage on the entire 34 acres to his client Louis Le Guen, at lawful interest, to secure his note for $5,000. Hamilton kept up the interest and was able to repay part of the principal, it was extended from year to year, and $3,000 of it was still owing at his death as a first lien on the property. Apparently, Hamilton's old friend Oliver Wolcott, Jr., president of the Merchants Bank, looked over his application for a bank loan of $4,000 the next year, perhaps for a takeout of Le Guen's construction loan or perhaps a second mortgage, but informally turned Hamilton down, no doubt in a friendly way. Hamilton had told Wolcott that he did not even want to present his loan application "if there was even a prospect of hesitation." It is not clear that any loan was made, although Hamilton owed debts to several banks at his death. Obviously, if anything should happen to Hamilton any time soon, Troup's hopes that his friends would not have "to raise a subscription to pay his funeral" would be dashed.

Replying to the letter from Aaron Burr of April 18, 1804, which opened the exchanges that ended in the duel, Hamilton refused to allow himself to be interrogated about "whatever I may have said of a political opponent in the course of a fifteen years competition." Though Hamilton's phrase made it sound as if the lists where he and Burr had done battle were narrowly political contests, the truth was that both men had also been in fierce competition in private life and also as frequent adversaries in the practice of law, even though they sometimes also served as cocounsel on the same side of important cases.

Hidden clashes between lawyers who act as cocounsel on the same side of a case can be more bitter than the open clashes between adversary counsel for opposing parties. In their professional and personal lives, as well as in their politics, Hamilton and Burr had opportunities to clash in a kaleidoscopic variety of ways during their fifteen years of competition.

Hamilton had invited Burr to be associated with him as cocounsel in the famous *Le Guen* case, but Burr had wound up taking the lion's share of the fee. Their joint client then handed Hamilton the awkward assignment of dunning his cocounsel Burr, not only to reduce his fee, but also to pay another unrelated debt that Burr owed to Le Guen. On May 1, 1800, Le Guen wrote Hamilton that he was "still deeply moved by your generous proceedings, and full of gratitude." He found himself "obliged to do what you yesterday forbade me to." He sent Hamilton $1,500 for his fee.

With the same pleasant letter to Hamilton, however, Le Guen told him he was letting Burr have $4,636.66, $2,900 on account of his fee bill, and various additional sums as advances to him on other accounts. Burr had submitted a fee bill to Le Guen that was much higher than Le Guen was paying him. On an unrelated debt of $13,200 that Burr owed to him, Le Guen relayed to Hamilton the unlikely story that Burr "has promised to settle up with me tomorrow morning." Le Guen charged Hamilton, "I beg you to kindly settle this bill with him," airily adding, "so that he will be satisfied."

Hardly any position is more distasteful to a lawyer than to be charged by a big client to beat down another lawyer's bill, unless it is to be the lawyer whose bill is beaten down. Nor could it have added anything to the warmth of Burr's regard for Hamilton that Hamilton had been assigned by Le Guen to beat him down. But knowledge of Burr's huge debts no doubt qualified Hamilton well for beating Burr down.

Settle up with Burr "so that he will be satisfied"? That was what Le Guen had demanded he do. Hamilton knew that Le Guen knew as well as he did that Burr was "extortionate in his profession," as Hamilton later described him to John Rutledge. So Le Guen had blithely laid on poor Hamilton an intrinsically impossible task. It happened to be the same month that Hamilton was giving up in despair the inherently impossible assignment of building up the quasi-war army, resigning as inspector general, and discharging all the bile built up by his sense of failure in the service by beginning to write his attack on President John Adams.

It was not much consolation to Hamilton to know that financially he was only a little less deeply under water than Burr. Hamilton well knew that in 1799 Burr had beseeched Le Guen for a loan of $25,000 on a second mortgage to help him pay off some other debts. In January 1801, to give Le Guen some collateral,

Burr had scraped together an assignment of five leases, one mortgage, a one-eighth interest in a tract of land owned by Nicholas Oliver, and two promissory notes. Settling one legal bill of Burr, Le Guen had paid two-thirds of it to Burr's creditors. In a statement that he enclosed in a letter to John Rutledge on January 4, 1801, Hamilton wrote that Burr "is without doubt insolvent for a large *deficit.* All his visible property is deeply mortgaged, and he is known to owe other large debts, for which there is no specific security. Of the number of these there is a judgment in favor of Mr. Angerstein for a sum which with interest amounts to about $80,000." Hamilton knew because he had represented Angerstein against Burr in the case of *Aaron Burr v. John Julius Angerstein* in the New York Court of Chancery, 1801–1804. As it happened, Alexander Baring, of the great London financial House of Baring, who had married Anne and William Bingham's eldest daughter, Anne, had told Hamilton as early as November 16, 1797, that the land Burr offered as security for his debt to Angerstein would not "afford any tolerable security for it."

Chancellor James Kent, seven years younger than Hamilton, remembered that at the New York bar of the period Burr and Hamilton stood out as the preeminent lawyers among a distinguished group of colleagues. More than 30 years later he would write, "though the New York Bar could at that time boast of the clear intellect, the candor, the simplicity, and black-letter learning of the elder Jones, the profound and richly varied learning of Harrison, the classical taste and elegant accomplishments of Brockholst Livingston, the solid and accurate, but unpretending common-law learning of Troup, the chivalrous feelings and dignified address of Pendleton," yet, said Kent, "the mighty mind of Hamilton would at times bear down all opposition by its comprehensive grasp and the strength of his reasoning powers."

"Colonel Burr," by contrast, Kent recalled, was "acute, quick, terse, polished, sententious, and sometimes sarcastic in his forensic discussions." Kent noted that Burr, as he had from the beginning of his career, "seemed to disdain illustration and expansion, and confined himself with stringency to the point in debate."

Alexander McComb, a rich merchant and speculator, whom Burr represented in one case, with Richard Harison and Robert Troup as cocounsel, wrote William Constable in 1794 that all three were "good and capable men, but Burr is too much of a politician to give the necessary application to his profession."

In Judge Kent's considered opinion, "among all his brethren," Hamilton was "indisputably preeminent." Indeed, "this was universally conceded." After his resignation as secretary of the treasury and return to New York, during the years "between 1795 and 1798," Hamilton "took his station as the leading counsel at the Bar. He was employed in every important and especially in every commercial case. He was a very great favorite with the merchants of New York, and he most justly deserved to be, for he had uniformly shown himself to be one of the most enlightened, intrepid, and persevering friends to the commercial prosperity of this country."

Then, as now, "insurance questions, both upon the law and the fact, constituted a large portion of the litigated business in the courts." As Kent pointed out, "the business of insurance was carried on principally by private underwriters, and the law had not been defined and settled in this country by a course of judicial decisions." It "was open to numerous perplexed questions arising out of our neutral trade, and was left, under a complicated mixture of law and fact, very much at large to a jury; the litigation of that kind was immense. Mr. Hamilton had an overwhelming share of it."

Hamilton's special excellence was his breadth and depth. As Kent found:

> He taught us all how to probe deeply into the hidden recesses of the science, or to follow up principles to their far distant sources. He was not content with the modern reports, abridgments, or translations. He ransacked cases and precedents to their very foundations; and we learned from him to carry our inquiries into the commercial codes of the nations of the European continent, and in a special manner to illustrate the law of insurance by the severe judgment of Emerigon and the luminous commentaries of Valin.

At least when an overload of personal exigencies did not bear in too heavily upon him, Hamilton displayed to Kent "the habit of thorough, precise, and authentic research which accompanied all his investigations. He was not content, for instance, with examining Grotius, and taking him as an authority, in any other than the original Latin language in which the work was composed."

Kent was a great admirer and close friend of Hamilton and anything but a friend and admirer of Burr. Even a judge, indeed even a chancellor, can be a biased or at least a partial witness. William Kent remarked in his *Memoirs* of his great-grandfather that "the cause of the duel was undoubtedly a conversation between Hamilton and Judge Kent." In the conversation, which was, unfortunately, recorded in a letter signed by Dr. Charles D. Cooper, Hamilton and Kent had declared "that they looked upon Mr. Burr to be a dangerous man, and one who ought not to be trusted with the reins of government."

For the other side, Burr's sympathetic biographers Samuel B. Wandell and Meade Minnigerode (I) contrasted Burr with Hamilton in the following terms: "Hamilton was perhaps the more profound, the more erudite, the more long-winded; Burr the more superficial, the more concise, and the more successful. . . . Burr could say as much in half an hour as it took Hamilton two hours to establish."

Of the law in the abstract, Burr was fond of saying that "law is anything which is boldly asserted and plausibly maintained."

Wandell and Minnigerode accepted the appraisal written by Major William Pierce after observing Hamilton in action in 1787: "To a clear and strong judgment he unites the ornaments of fancy, and whilst he is able, convincing and engaging in his eloquence The Heart and Head sympathize in approving him." What Burr would call his long-windedness Pierce saw as Hamilton's profundity: "There is no skimming over the surface of a subject with him, he must sink to the bottom to see what foundation it rests on." Pierce added, "His language is not always equal, sometimes didactic, like Bolingbroke's, at others light and tripping like Stern's. His eloquence is not so defusive as to trifle with the senses, but he rambles just enough to strike and keep up the attention."

Beneath the urbane surface of professional affability that Burr and Hamilton each made a point of exhibiting toward the other, there were enough obvious differences in each man's personal style to provide him with an inexhaustible stock of reasons for loathing and hating the other.

For men of both such kinds of intellects and talents, the general run of civil cases that both handled, involving marine insurance claims, maritime liens, civil salvage, bottomry bonds, prizes, laws of impost, contracts, bills and notes, creditors' rights, trespass, debt and ejectment, and so forth, were not inherently fascinating or demanding of an exalted level of professional skill after the first dozen or two of each kind. But such cases were the bread and butter of most prosperous lawyers' practices. In volume I of the Hamilton Legal Papers (LPAH) are discussed or calendared more than 100 such cases in which Hamilton was counsel, in volume II there are about 310, and in volume III there will be several hundred more. Hamilton was undoubtedly involved in hundreds of legal matters other than these—wills, trusts, incorporation papers and prospectuses —which did not reach the stage of recorded litigation or which were unimportant or of which all records have disappeared. He could handle most pleadings and briefs quickly and efficiently by doing little more than changing the names and numbers in a set of tried and true forms he had in his office. In the courtroom before judge and jury as case followed case and experience grew, familiar legal precedents and arguments flashed readily like lightning out of apparently confused clouds of familiar fact patterns and thundered as spellbinding forensic rhetoric.

But the more experienced and skilled a lawyer becomes, the fewer features he finds in any new case to engage his full attention at a level above the humdrum of routine except the size of the ultimate fee. In such cases, although he may do well financially, there are fewer opportunities for a lawyer to do public good than occasions to observe private evil or, perhaps more often, only selfishness, crookedness, or greed. In a broad sense, most such civil cases involve only a reshuffling of individual and corporate economic interests through the medium of lawyers, the law, and the courts. In most of them, the decision, the only feature that is of public concern, is an unneeded increment to an already oversized reef of precedent.

Between or concurrently with stretches of political activity, the greatest of lawyers, like Hamilton and Burr, of necessity turned to such uninspiring private legal practice to repair their fortunes: for example, to keep up payments on the debts they both owed to Louis Le Guen. Both men had helped make it possible for Le Guen to win the money that put them in his debt by helping him win a final judgment of $119,915.43.

According to Chancellor Kent, Le Guen had originally commenced the case at law on Hamilton's advice. It was one of Hamilton's two great cases in which,

Kent said, "his reasoning powers, the sagacity with which he pursued his investigations, his piercing criticism, his masterly analysis, and the energy and fervor of his appeals to the judgment and conscience of the tribunal"—were "most strikingly displayed." Hamilton's passions, he added, were never "so warmly engaged in any cause."

Hamilton's grandson Allan McLane Hamilton recalled that the defendant, Isaac Gouverneur, had originally sought to retain Hamilton for his side of the case. Hamilton declined. He took exception to a statement in a letter of Gouverneur to William Lewis, a distinguished Philadelphia lawyer, that "attorneys like to make the most of their bills of cost." Hamilton told Gouverneur that "anyone that has the proper delicacy" must "decline the business of a person who professedly entertains such an idea of the conduct of his profession." It was "an unjustifiable reflection."

Le Guen's case was a cause célèbre in its own time because of the huge amount of money claimed and won, the financial ruin inflicted on Gouverneur and the other losers, the importance of the parties and lawyers involved, and the unprecedented publicity and bitterness it generated. The case was full of the kind of substantive and technical legal issues that remain a bread-and-butter part of modern lawyers' civil practice—factors' liens; the misconduct of agents; the existence of special agreements; bills and notes; general contract law; the effect of deviation on contracts of carriage of goods by sea; the effect of fraud on a judgment; rights to injunctions, to appeal, and to pretrial discovery of evidence; the different kinds of relief available in courts of law and courts of chancery; measures of damages; the binding effect of jury verdicts; and the finality of judgments. The case gained nationwide importance, became a procedural precedent throughout the country, and has been cited more than a hundred times. Many states adopted its doctrine of the binding force of a judgment of a court of competent jurisdiction to preclude further litigation, both as to issues actually decided as well as those that could have been raised but were not, and of the power of appellate courts to review decisions of lower courts on factual issues.

No matter how strong a client's case may seem to be on the merits of the issue, the best lawyers always seek, if possible, to win it on procedural or technical points, by invoking a statute of limitations, for example. This avoids risking everything in a trial on the merits that might turn on a chance vagary, whim, or bias of a judge or jury looking at the ultimate facts. It usually saves time and money besides. Where the client's case is a weak one on the merits, winning a procedural point may be the only way there is to win it. This was how Hamilton finally won for Louis Le Guen. Because it is full of "lawyers' law," an accurate account of it would be too "dry and technical," as Kent said long ago, to attempt here, but a summary of the facts out of which the litigation grew gives a sense of the magnitude of Hamilton's technical professional accomplishment.

Louis Le Guen was a French citizen and trader who had come to New York in 1794 "a perfect stranger and utterly ignorant of the English language." He brought with him a cargo of cotton and indigo, which he entrusted to Isaac Gouverneur and Peter Kemble who were merchants and factors, a factor being a local agent for an out-of-town merchant. By March of 1795 Le Guen's cargo had still found no buyer. So Le Guen persuaded Gouverneur and Kemble to send it to Europe to sell for his account there. They chartered the ship *White Fox* to take it from New York to Le Havre and, if not sold there, from there to Hamburg or anywhere else they could unload it.

Just then three Spanish Jews came along, Isaac Gomez, Jr., Moses Lopez, and Abraham Rods Rivera, and agreed to take over the *White Fox* charter and buy the whole cargo for £48,966/6 payable in 12 months with 10 months' interest at 6 percent per annum, represented by promissory notes, which could be paid out of the proceeds of sale of the cotton at Le Havre or at any other point where the ship was able to sell it. As it turned out, the European market for cotton and indigo was very poor. Besides, Gomez, Lopez, and Rivera claimed that they had been defrauded because Le Guen's cotton and indigo were of a quality much inferior to what had been represented to them. Gomez finally abandoned the cotton and indigo to Gouverneur's and Kemble's agents in London to sell for anything they could get and credit the proceeds to their account. They realized practically nothing.

Even though Le Guen himself was the one who had first given Gouverneur and Kemble the order to ship the cargo back to Europe, he claimed that he was entitled to recover from them the entire sum Gomez, Lopez, and Rivera had later contracted to pay, notwithstanding the fact that they all had lost a fortune on shipping the cargo back to Europe.

Out of this order of Le Guen's grew eight separate actions and suits involving proceedings in the Supreme Court of Judicature, the Court of Chancery, and the Court for the Trial of Impeachments and the Correction of Errors during the period from 1796 to early 1800. Yet what seemed to be the heart of the matter was never reached: the question of whether or not Gomez, Lopez, and Rivera had been defrauded.

About the facts of the case, the most significant point, as Kent noted, was that Le Guen's claim "was in opposition to the mercantile sense of its justice." After "expensive trials and the most persevering and irritating litigation, pursued into the court of the last resort," Kent wrote, Le Guen "recovered upon technical rules of law strictly and severely applied." Chancellor Kent made it sound as if he would have decided the case the other way had it come before him.

Le Guen retained three of the most prominent members of the New York bar, Hamilton, Richard Harison, and Aaron Burr. They gave him the opinion that Gouverneur and Kemble, his factors, had no justification for depriving him "of any advantages that might arise from the contract" and that once they had "failed in their duty as agents," they made themselves responsible for all the consequences. This meant that the measure of damages should be the full sales price set forth in the contract, with no offset in favor of Gouverneur and Kemble to reflect the loss they had suffered on final sale of the goods for so much less than the contract price.

Opposing counsel in the case, Brockholst Livingston, later joined by Peter Van Schaack, Gouverneur Morris, and Robert Troup as counsel for Gouverneur and Kemble, argued in outrage against the injustice of such a result. A cause of greater importance had never been brought in the court, they railed. Hamilton's position, Brockholst Livingston cried, "is an attempt to charge a factor with the loss of near $120,000; not for appropriating to his own use the funds of his principal—not for a palpable deviation from instruction—not for a gross violation of trust—not for any known and established breach of duty—but for an imaginary default, and that in a point, on which two honest men might easily differ without an unfair imputation to either. It is an attempt to recover this immense sum, without proof, or even pretense, that the plaintiff [Le Guen] has received the smallest injury."

To a skillful lawyer, nothing can be more important than the careful selection of a jury. Hamilton, the author of New York's treatise on practice and procedure, had been one of the first to emphasize the point. In the practice manual he had written as a law student, *Practical Proceedings*, he explained how "in a cause of great importance one of the parties" may obtain a "struck" jury. Upon the attorney's motion, the clerk in the judge's chamber took the names of 48 persons from the book of freeholders "from which each party shall at his pleasure strike out twelve and the remaining twenty-four shall be a jury for the trial of the cause." But a struck jury, Hamilton explained, "is liable to challenge like any other."

At the first Le Guen trial at the New York Circuit before Justice Morgan Lewis, Hamilton with Burr and Harison selected a "struck" jury, all the members but one of which were listed in Longworth's *New York Directory* as merchants; the twelfth being listed as a "gentleman"—he had, perhaps, strayed into bad company. Half of the jurors, including such prominent merchants as John B. Coles and James Constable, are listed in Hamilton's cashbook covering this period, indicating that they were also fee-paying clients of his. The first struck jury awarded Le Guen only £39 6 s. in damages and 6d. costs, but a new trial was obtained with a second jury, which, like the first, was made up of merchants about half of whom were Hamilton's clients. It awarded Le Guen $119,302.47 and six cents costs. Apparently, in selecting the second jury, Brockholst Livingston failed to make as effective use of Hamilton's practice manual, his challenges, and his other clients, as Hamilton had done.

From this point on, it became Hamilton's duty to defend the judgment in Le Guen's favor from "collateral attack"—the charge by Gomez, Lopez, and Rivera that they had been defrauded.

After the disappointing result of the first of the two jury trials, Hamilton had hopefully sallied forth to Albany to make the motion for a new trial, but with perhaps too many other things—perhaps the Reynolds affair or plans for his place in the country—on his mind. A thing happened to him that is the nightmare of every lawyer. He forgot his brief. From the coach stop at Peekskill, he wrote back to Eliza in desperation on April 16, 1797, "I forgot my brief . . . which is in a bundle of papers in my armed chair in the office. Request one of the Gentlemen [his law clerks] to look for it and send it up to me by the post of Tuesday. Beg them not to fail. Adieu my beloved. Kiss all the children for me."

When his client found out about Hamilton's gaffe, he had been frantic, in fractured French. Le Guen was not at all pleased, he wrote on April 24. He had no confidence in Burr "de vous seconder dans mon affaire." Nevertheless, with "Vos talents, votre Zelle," Monsieur Hamilton, directed by "Vos sages Conseils," I have not the least doubt that your efforts "me feront obtenir un Jugement favorable."

Even after the second jury had rendered the six-figure verdict against Gouverneur and Kemble, Gouverneur, amazingly enough, could not help still harboring a sneaking affection for Hamilton when he wrote him January 9, 1798. He regretted that Hamilton's "mistaken opinion . . . acts as a spur to make individuals less obstinate afterwards." Also, "it would be more becoming, to be less abusive." Furthermore, Gouverneur taxed Hamilton, "to move the feelings of the jury . . . you finally compared me to the odious character of 'Shylock in the Play.' I felt extremely hurt upon this observation, my dear Colonel, because I thot you was wounding yourself, as I am not without regard for you." He probably was not aware that Hamilton's own mother's name had been Levine.

Meanwhile, in a separate suit in the Court of Chancery, which was a court of equity, Gouverneur and Kemble had sued Gomez, Lopez, and Rivera to collect on their promissory notes and lost to Gomez, Lopez, and Rivera's defense of fraud. This indicated that they had indeed been defrauded about the quality of Le Guen's cargo. By January of 1800, after more than three hectic years of injunctions, discovery proceedings, and mostly reverses for Le Guen and Hamilton in the lower courts, and the one big verdict, the Court of Chancery had held that collateral attack on it would be permitted; Le Guen's verdict could be attacked on grounds of fraud. Ultimate defeat for Hamilton loomed. The last chance left to Hamilton to save Le Guen's big verdict was to obtain a reversal of the Court of Chancery in New York's court of last resort. Argument began February 4, 1800, before the state senate in Albany, sitting in its other capacity as the Court of Errors.

Hamilton had apparently kept any fears he had about the outcome well concealed from his opponents. Robert Troup, now one of Gouverneur's and Kemble's counsel, wrote to Nicholas Low in New York on January 25, 1800:

> The cause of Gouverneur & Kemble with Le Guen is beginning to excite attention—General Hamilton is very confident of success—I shall deem myself fortunate [if] we all get out of this cause [without] fighting—I foresee that some of the counsel will have their passions much excited. With my moderation of temper, I hope to escape the general's pistols as well as his sword.

Privately, Hamilton sensed that things were going badly, and he was pessimistic when he confided to Eliza:

Tomorrow, my dear Eliza, your father's slay leaves this place for New York. I drop you a line to tell you that I am well and that today the hearing of Le Guen's case began. I fear prepossessions are strongly against it—but we must try to overcome them. At any rate we shall soon get to the end of the journey, and if I should lose my cause I must console myself with finding my friends—.

The pleadings consisted of the appeal and answer; bill and answer; 22 depositions for Le Guen, the appellant; and 27 depositions for the respondents. Hamilton did not depart Albany the following day as he had promised Eliza because the arguments took seven days, not one. The second day, after Chancellor Robert R. Livingston, who had rendered the decision against Le Guen in the court below, gave his reasons, Hamilton opened his argument.

Troup wrote to Low on February 7, 1800, with a wry dig at Hamilton's prolixity:

Hamilton devoted near two days to his arguments. He is the only person who has argued on the part of Le Guen. I followed him on the part of Gouverneur & Kemble & spoke near two hours—which I believe is more than an hour after a man has spoken what may be called common sense in any cause. . . .

Troup was particularly struck by Hamilton's passionate involvement in the case:

Between us, Hamilton has pushed this cause to the utmost extremity, and in my opinion with the utmost animosity & cruelty against Gouverneur & Kemble. I never knew him on any occasion so heated and wound up with passion. He has attacked the whole body of witnesses on the part of Gouverneur & Kemble & he has even attempted to weaken the credit of my testimony on a fact which came to my knowledge about Lopez, one of the partners of young Gomez long before I was ever employed by Mr. Gouverneur. The manner of his treating the witnesses & persecuting poor Gouverneur has done his cause no good and I think we have grounds for expecting success on our part.

For this critically important appeal, Brockholst Livingston had recruited Gouverneur Morris for his team of cocounsel. Though it was Morris's first court appearance in many years, he was Gouverneur's kinsman, and he was a redoubtable orator. Morris recorded in his diary: "Mr. Hamilton opens. Thursday 6 Feb. Hamilton concludes forcibly—Harison opens the law and so does Burr." Morris adds, "I follow him. Find some impression is made." On Monday he finished his own argument, "which as I observe produced considerable effect." On Tuesday Morris noted that "Hamilton is desirous of being witty but goes beyond the bounds and is open to a severe dressing." On Wednesday, the twelfth of February, Morris snorted that "Colonel Burr is very able & has I see made considerable impression . . . I had an opportunity to retort to Hamilton which I did not use and am on the whole well pleased that I did not."

On the other hand, Hamilton's son James A. Hamilton, in his *Reminiscences*, recalled Morris's reaction differently. Morris had initiated the sparring in the courtroom. After giving perfunctory praise to Hamilton's just concluded argument, Morris had said, "Before I have done I shall make my learned friend cry out, 'Help me, Cassius' "—at this dramatic moment Morris pointed at Hamilton and then swung his arm around to take in his cocounsel Burr, " 'or I sink.' "

Hamilton would never let pass a scornful taunt from Morris that meant he needed a Burr to rescue him. His son James does not quote the riposte his father gave Morris when it came his time to reply. He does say that Hamilton "alluded to the boast of his friend in a strain of irony that turned the laughter of the court and audience against him." Not surprisingly, General Schuyler, who regretted that Hamilton's time while he had been in Albany had been so "engrossed" by the case "that we have had but a small portion" of his "pleasing and instructive company," also thought Hamilton had bested Morris, the most renowned of wits, in the courtroom exchange. Hamilton's riposte "afforded general pleasure to the Court and audience," said Schuyler. And "Mr. Morris felt so sensibly. I hope he will profit by it."

It would rankle with Hamilton that to the 34 judges and senators and all the spectators and reporters in the Albany courtroom, his friend Morris, the tall, spellbinding aristocrat only a little lamed by his wooden leg—the "exotic" whom he admired as much as any man alive—had made him out to be a tired Julius Caesar, crying to his false friend Cassius—Aaron Burr—to save him.

Whose mind among the crowd would fail to summon up that whole conversation between Cassius and Brutus in the Roman street shortly before the ides of March? Cassius was recalling an earlier raw and gusty day beside the Tiber, when Caesar had failed the challenge he himself had thrown down:

> "Dar'st thou, Cassius, now
> Leap in with me into this angry flood,
> And swim to yonder point?" Upon the word,
> Accoutred as I was, I plunged in
> And bade him follow; so indeed he did.
> The torrent roar'd, and we did buffet it
> With lusty sinews, throwing it aside
> And stemming it with hearts of controversy;
> But ere we could arrive the point propos'ed,
> Caesar cried, "Help me, Cassius, or I sink!"
> I, as Aeneas, our great ancestor,
> Did from the flames of Troy upon his shoulder
> The old Anchises bear, so from the waves of Tiber
> Did I the tired Caesar. And this man
> Is now become a god

A colossus who doth bestride the narrow world
And Cassius is
A wretched creature.

Cassius' words in the Roman street had forced from his wavering friend, Brutus, a show of assenting ire (expressed as a lift-governing maxim to which Hamilton would also assent):

BRUTUS: If it be aught toward the general good,
Let honour in one eye and death i' the other,
And I will look on both indifferently;
As I love
The name of honour more than I fear death.
CASSIUS: Well honour is the subject of my story.

That night Margarita and Stephen Van Rensselaer gave a dinner at their manor house for counsel, judges, senators, and others who were all engrossed in the great case. Hamilton dressed for dinner at the Schuyler house, and when he arrived at the patroon's, Cassius was still on his mind. Van Rensselaer met him at the door and warned him that Gouverneur Morris had arrived in a very bad humor. Burr was nowhere to be seen. Hamilton could stand up to his exotic friend perfectly well without sinking. Hamilton greeted his brother-in-law genially and walked into the room and up to the towering and formidable Morris. With his most amiable possible smile he said, "My friend, you will rejoice, I hope, that by Cassius' help I meet you here with our friends at dinner!"

Chancellor Kent was, no doubt, remembering both Morris's and Hamilton's antics when he wrote of their "critical severity, shrewd retort and pathetic appeal." He added that "a Jewish house was concerned . . . that led to affecting allusion to the character and fortune of that ancient race." When reference was made to negotiations in France and Hamilton's French client, they "produced references to that tremendous Revolution which was then still in its fury, and whose frightful ravages and remorseless pretensions seemed to overawe and confound the nations."

Kent added that "Mr. Morris and Mr. Hamilton equally resorted for illustration to Shakespeare, Milton and Pope." When Morris "complained that his long absence from the bar had caused him to forget the decisions," Hamilton "sportively accounted for it on another principle," citing the "poetical authority" that

Where beams of warm imagination play,
The memory's soft figures melt away.

With passions running high all about him, Robert Troup kept his head: "Mr. Morris is in good spirits & entertains no doubt of our success—If we do succeed the question of fraud will go to a jury and then I think the chances will be nearly equal." As for his Jewish client Isaac Gouverneur, he was "in good spirits, considering the treatment Hamilton has given him." Troup added a cool assessment of the views of the judges, which proved to be quite accurate: "Our friend Benson has made up his mind against us & he will carry with him the two younger judges—Lansing is yet doubtful—Lewis is with us—but we calculate on the other lay members of the court who are not at present in the best mood for following the judges."

The decision of the Court of Errors was 28 to 6 to reverse the chancellor's decree.

Hamilton and his cocounsel had won by upholding a judgment of $119,915.43 for their client Le Guen on technical grounds without at any point having permitted the issue of fraud to come directly before any tribunal for consideration and adjudication. Wall, Franklin, Chestnut, and La Salle Street lawyers of today are proudest of the kinds of victories won the same way. But most would not make the silly mistake that Hamilton did and Burr did not by underbilling Le Guen for his final fee.

On February 28, 1800, four days after the Court of Errors had handed down its ruinous reversal against him, Isaac Gouverneur died suddenly at the home of Attorney General Hoffman. On Hamilton's conscience such an unforgivable overkill must have fallen as an awful rebuke. Hearing of their popular fellow merchant's death, the merchants and masters of the vessels in New York harbor half-masted their colors. The *New York Gazette and Daily Advertiser* of March 6 called it "a singular, though pleasing token of respect to a gentleman not in public office."

During the course of the argument, Troup had written Nicholas Low rather mysteriously that if Gouverneur and Kemble were successful, there would have to be still another argument at the next sitting of the Court of Errors, saying only, "I cannot answer the question because it would explain a mystery which we lawyers think it our interest to conceal from the *merchants*—it must be remembered that the cause of Gouverneur & Kemble is strictly a *mercantile* one."

What exactly Troup meant by this is not known. His clients had lost, one had dropped dead, and the jury's verdict could not be collaterally attacked; so the question was academic. Perhaps Troup was hinting as a second line of attack on the original verdict for Le Guen that the jury had been biased; too many of its members had been clients of Hamilton. But Troup was too discreet a gentleman of the bar to go beyond his hint in disclosing a professional confidence of this kind by a further appeal to the Court of Errors. He was content to let the verdict stand as the fair verdict of their fellow merchants against his own clients Gouverneur and Kemble. It was not necessarily an unfair verdict. It had been rendered by a group of the merchant clients of a brother lawyer against two of their own fellow merchants, who were not.

Twelve days after coming home from the trial, the usually even-tempered Troup had barely calmed down enough from the tensions it generated to give evenhanded credit to his old friend Hamilton's efforts. He wrote to Rufus King on March 9, 1800:

General Hamilton and Mr. Morris made great display of talent & eloquence. Hamilton is more solid, more logical, and more equal. Morris at times astonished us with bursts of sublime eloquence—at other times he was flat and uninteresting—Our friend Hamilton never appeared to have his passions so warmly engaged in any cause. He was full of acrimony against Gouverneur and Kemble, and was not without asperity towards their counsel. I think he was guilty of an indelicacy toward me which my heart tells me I ought to forgive but which my friends will not permit me as yet to bury in oblivion.

Shakespearean tragedy as performed at the New or Park Theater, which stood on the east side of the present City Hall Park near Beekman Street, provided all New York gentlemen a common fund of handy allusion with which to dramatize and underscore memorable characters and momentous situations that turned up in courtrooms and social gatherings at the turn of the century. As Brutus had told Cassius,

> The eye sees not itself
> But by reflection, by some other things.

Most persons of note in New York subscribed to the theater's building fund. But, as most New York theatrical ventures usually do, it lost them a great deal of money. It even had trouble paying its taxes. Hamilton became professionally involved with it when his client William Brown, the collector of direct taxes of the district, went to the box office and seized $325 in silver coins—all the box office receipts that were on hand. He claimed he was collecting them as arrears of taxes. When the theater management sued Brown for trespass and breaking and entering and, in effect, stealing the money, Hamilton defended Brown by producing an assessor's list that showed the theater mistakenly listed as the dwelling house of one John Hoffman; on it the $325 was indeed the correct amount of tax. If, as Cassius replied to Brutus, "Honour is the subject of my story," it is hard to see how this rather truncated account of Hamilton's experiences as a theatrical lawyer as reported by Dr. Allan McLane Hamilton shows anything thematically significant except that there was no kind of a lawyer's role that Hamilton would refuse to play on the New York legal stage.

A decade and more earlier, while Hamilton in his public career as the chief Federalist idea man was yoking the separate states together as a single unitary nation, he was also acting as a private lawyer to help change the map of the states in ways that sometimes ran against the interests of his own state, as in his appeal for Vermont, as long as it helped promote the interests of national union. From the mid-eighteenth century far into the post-Revolutionary period, settlers in disputed areas claiming title from one or another colony or state warred for possession of the land in bitter territorial disputes marked by local violence and rioting. Errors in directional boundary descriptions caused by unnoted deviations of the compass needle from due north from year to year, as well as dynastic rivalries within England or between England and the Netherlands or between England, the Netherlands, and the Swedish colonies along the Delaware contributed many further complexities.

New York's territorial limits, for example, were splendidly confused because the heartland of New York's provincial grants extended north and south along the Hudson River, thereby slicing directly across early grants of Connecticut and Massachusetts Bay, which extended east to west and from sea to sea.

To many a young American lawyer, the brightest prospect then was the promise of generations of full employment for specialists in the law of real property, titles, conveyancing, and litigation. Hamilton participated in, and contributed to, settlement of many of these controversies by reevaluating, reasserting, and reusing various legal doctrines and historical "proof" to settle the territorial disputes by legal processes and by helping to avoid the possibility of these local incidents escalating into violent contests and secessionist tendencies among the states.

Geographically speaking, one of Hamilton's biggest cases involved the "Connecticut Gore," an eight-mile-wide strip of land in what is now New York State running the entire length of its southern boundary with Pennsylvania for 240 miles. On the basis of early "sea to sea" grants, an omission of the strip from early surveys, and an oversight in a 1782 settlement to quiet title, Connecticut quitclaimed all right, title, and interest in the Gore to two enterprising entrepreneurs, Jeremiah Halsey and Andrew Ward, who agreed in exchange to complete the building of the new statehouse just then being put up in Hartford. In 1796, Messrs. Halsey and Ward's Connecticut Gore Company brought two actions of "ejectment" in the Federal Court in Connecticut against all grantees in the Gore who held title from New York, alleging that they were all in unlawful possession, at least from Connecticut's point of view. Crucial to the litigation was the choice of forum, that is, whether it could be properly tried in Connecticut, where Halsey and Ward had started it, or in New York.

New York Attorney General Josiah Ogden Hoffman called in Hamilton to help him represent the state in the Connecticut Federal Court and the interests of the New York grantees.

As Hamilton and Hoffman saw it, what seemed to be only a procedural point —location of the trial—involved a basic constitutional question. It affected the fairness and justice of the decision.

Also, arguably, an ejectment proceeding in the Federal Court in Connecticut was not the proper procedure. Hamilton had set forth the proper procedure in his practice manual: a New York common law action for ejectment. Neither of these technical points, however, seemed very likely winners in Connecticut.

Neither the mind-boggling territorial breadth nor the symbolic majesty of the fate of the Nutmeg State capitol's dome distracted Hamilton from seizing on a third, still tinier point that could be a winner. He attacked the selection of the jury panel on the hypertechnical ground that the deputy marshal who had summoned the jurors was an interested party: Hamilton had somehow found out that he was a shareholder in Halsey and Ward's Connecticut Gore Company. *The*

Courant reported that the argument was made "very ably and learnedly." Hamilton was sustained on the point, thus creating the necessary judicial check to Halsey and Ward that would eventually lead to extrajudicial settlement of the complicated dispute in New York's favor.

From such a tiny technical point, Hamilton could open up his frame for a winning argument to hemispheric dimensions. Here is how he would crank up to write a brief. For a Federal Court hearing on one dispute between New York and Massachusetts in 1786, Hamilton spent 35 days preparing a brief containing a set of "Notes on the History of South and North America," just for background.

He starts from first historic principles with Christopher Columbus, of course, a subject of Genoa, being the first discoverer of America and then narrows his focus to North America, then to Canada and Acadia, and finally to New England and New York. Next he sets forth first legal principles, squaring off the legal framework and enclosing the dispute. It ought to be considered in five different general views, he holds, (1) in relation to the laws of nature and nations; (2) in relation to the grants and acts of the Crown of Great Britain; (3) in relation to Indian grants, purchases, and treaties; (4) in relation to the acts and agreements of the states in controversy; and (5) in relation to the Revolution.

His views on property rights are significant. The first heading is "that in a state of nature all mankind have an equal right to the objects of property" and "that occupancy is the original foundation of property."

Massachusetts relied on the doctrine of prior discovery to support its claims, but Hamilton's answer was that this gave way to actual occupancy and possession. If discovery were the crucial and only criterion, he argued, then the Spanish logically owned all of America by virtue of Christopher Columbus.

Possession of rivers and shores by the colonial power indicated merely intention to assert national claims, and though "good" intentions ought to be respected, extravagant pretensions should not. "Parchment boundaries" should not be determinative; countries and rights are created by effective settlement extending into the interior of claimed lands. In the case of Massachusetts's western lands, Hamilton concluded that they, in fact, extended only as far as the Hudson Valley, but not west of it. The two states finally reached agreement on what are more or less the present borders, a substantial victory for Hamilton's argument and the state of New York, although Massachusetts retained certain economic benefits and the important right to sell off the lands that she had claimed.

Within a few years Massachusetts sold off the western lands to various land speculators. Robert Morris, the "financier of the Revolution," and others acquired them; and Morris, in turn, sold a large part of his purchase to the Holland Land Company, a group of well-financed Dutch bankers, whom Hamilton represented as counsel until being summarily replaced as such by Aaron Burr.

If there is one thing that is more aggravating to a lawyer than being told he has to beat down another lawyer's fee or being the lawyer whose fee is beaten down, it is losing a whole set of good clients to the lawyer whose fee he is told to beat down.

For a decade and more, frantic speculation had been going on in western lands. English and Dutch capitalists, as well as wealthy Americans, dreamed of making quick fortunes from the limitless American back country slowly filling up with settlers. The Dutch capitalists who had combined to form the Holland Land Company appointed Theophile Cazenove as their American agent. For their account and also for some of their associated American coinvestors, one of whom was Burr, Cazenove arranged to purchase vast tracts of land in western New York and Pennsylvania. But according to New York state law, aliens could not become unrestricted owners of New York real estate. When the Holland Land Company sought to have this prohibition removed by pushing a special bill through the legislature, it was defeated. Cazenove then retained Hamilton as counsel to push for removal of the prohibition next time the bill came up, but Hamilton was only partly successful. He did manage to obtain passage of a law permitting aliens to hold land for a period of seven years, long enough at least to permit them to make a profit from a quick turnover. But Cazenove was not satisfied with this limited victory and urged Hamilton to try for a still better law without any time limitations on alien ownership at all.

At about the same time, Philip Schuyler, who had formed the Western Inland Lock Navigation Company to build a series of canals, found himself short of capital for further development; so he agreed to add his influence in the legislature to Hamilton's to help the Holland Land Company's bill if they would help him. With Schuyler's political aid, Hamilton pushed through a new act lengthening the term of alien holdings to 20 years. But it appeared that the quid pro quo for this result was that the Holland Land Company would lend Schuyler's Canal Company $250,000. For one reason or another, Cazenove balked. He claimed not to be satisfied with even the 20-year limitation. He would still like to see all restrictions on alien land ownership removed. It was not said that Schuyler was demanding too much money. The whole story is a cat's cradle of cupidity and craft, too tangled to unravel here.

Hamilton replied by a cautiously worded letter painting a dark picture of the company's future prospects if it refused to accept the 20-year limitation. He sidestepped Cazenove's hint that he ought to go see Schuyler and beat down his demands for money. The story of the Reynolds affair was just now being publicly exposed for the first time. Cazenove turned to Aaron Burr and found him agreeably ready, willing, and able to help out the Holland Land Company.

Burr, with some of his own investment at stake and with a douceur of bribes for susceptible state legislators, managed to put through a superseding law granting aliens a wholly unrestricted tenure. Hamilton and the whole Schuyler family were righteously indignant at Burr's tactics and perhaps unhappy also at the failure of their own attempt to capitalize on the Holland Land Company. John Barker Church, whose many insurance and banking interests Hamilton also represented, was heard to pass disparaging comments about Burr's role. Burr challenged him to a duel. On September 2, 1799, on the usual ledge at Weehawken, Burr and Church exchanged shots from Church's elegant, hair-trigger dueling pistols. No harm was done to either duelist except for the bullet hole that Church's bullet put in Burr's sleeve. On the same ground less than five years later Burr would demonstrate that practice had improved his aim.

The unfairness of charging lawyers with guilt by association instead of courage for representing unpopular clients is illustrated by acquittals Hamilton won for two clients whose vessels were seized for allegedly violating the Slave Trade Acts of 1794 and 1800 and for another client who was charged with a notorious murder.

Hamilton's client's vessel, the *Young Ralph*, about to sail for Senegal to take on a cargo of gum, was seized by federal authorities partly fitted out with "some handcuffs and other ironwork used in the slave trade." Similar fittings were stacked on the wharf beside her for loading. The defense was that they were only for "resale at Senegal." But when the government sought to put on three witnesses to testify they heard the master state that he was planning to engage in the slave trade, Hamilton's objection on hearsay grounds was sustained, and the government's case collapsed.

In *Young Ralph*, Hamilton argued for dismissal that the case was one of common law, not admiralty jurisdiction, and second, that the slave trade statute was penal and so the "full consummation" of the crime was necessary, which in this case meant "complete preparation." The vessel had not actually engaged in the slave trade. There was only suspicion that it might, and this was not sufficient ground for a seizure and forfeiture. The court eventually dismissed the case.

The time the attorneys took for argument in such cases as the *Young Ralph* seems incredible today, for both the intellectual energy and physical stamina that must have been required. In another such case, Josiah Ogden Hoffman, summing up for the defendant on July 12, 1803, spoke from 10:15 A.M. to 4:54 P.M.; Egbert Benson, from 5:00 P.M. to 6:25 P.M. Then on the following day, Hamilton for the plaintiff spoke from 10:35 A.M. to 4:25 P.M., and Harison from 4:25 P.M. to 6:02 P.M.

If Levi Weeks had not been the brother of Ezra Weeks, the contractor who was building Hamilton's Grange, Hamilton might not have taken the case or, having done so, might not have waived his usual modest fee, as he did. Levi was charged with first-degree murder for allegedly killing pregnant Gulielma Sands and throwing her badly bruised body down one of the wells of the Manhattan Company in Lispenard's Meadow on the snowy night of December 22, 1799. Gulielma, about 20 years old, a very beautiful girl who was also very promiscuous, lived in a boardinghouse kept by her Quaker cousin, Catherine Ring, and Catherine's husband, Elias, in upper Greenwich Street, where Levi was also a boarder. Gulielma had gone out the night of December 22, allegedly to be married to Levi, but was never seen alive again.

It was said in the Ring household that she had departed with Levi, but later that night he came back to the house alone, asking if she had gone to bed. He was disappointed when a suspicious Catherine Ring told him that she had gone out. So was Catherine. Levi expressed anxiety that she should have gone out alone so late at night in a dangerous place like Manhattan. Two days later, the day before Christmas, a young boy found a muff that Gulielma had borrowed from a friend—in the Manhattan Well. It was uncertain how soon afterward the Rings learned of this find, but one witness testified that Elias Ring had known of it no later than December 29. This seemed odd because on that same day, the twenty-ninth, Ring, who was quite familiar with the terrain around the Manhattan Well, had arranged to have the waters of the North River around Rhinelander's dock dragged for her body. And the dock was many blocks away from the well where her muff had been found. When the well was finally looked into on January 2, it yielded her fully clad corpse. The body was laid out in the Ring house for three days and then shown one day more in the street to the public. Levi Weeks was seized, brought to the *locus delicti,* and, after the coroner's inquest, charged with willful murder and committed to the Bridewell jail for trial. Suspense mounted; gossip buzzed. It was in Weeks's favor that the coroner ruled that Gulielma had not been pregnant.

Public mystification, curiosity, excitement, and indignation were intense. Hamilton's cocounsel for the defense of Levi Weeks were Aaron Burr and Brockholst Livingston. Both men were aligned against him in the impending spring election campaign for control of the New York legislature, on which the outcome of the crucial presidential election of 1800 would ultimately pivot.

On March 25, 1800, the morning of the trial in the old City Hall, at the corner of Wall, Broad, and Nassau Streets, "the concourse of people was so great, as was never before witnessed on a similar occasion." The public was "gaping with eager anxiety." The press of the huge crowd to get into the small courtroom was unbearable. The judges, Chief Justice John Lansing, Mayor Richard Varick, and the recorder, Richard Harison, ordered the constables to clear the room of "superfluous spectators." The best of many accounts of the trial was by Hamilton's friend William Coleman, later the editor of the *New York Evening Post,* but even it does not clearly tell which of the great lawyers did what. The prosecution brought on 24 witnesses, and the defense still more, for a total of 75 witnesses in all. Most spectators and jurors looked on Levi Weeks and his counsel "with a dark and sullen animosity." Popular feeling ran high against him. His defense demanded all the skill his three famous lawyers could bring to it.

Twenty-seven-year-old Catherine Ring and her husband, Elias, were the prosecution's chief witnesses, and Catherine in particular colored all her testimony with glints of deep animosity toward Levi, although it came out, under cross-examination, that she had earlier thought of him as a wonderful young man. But the evidence she could give against him was only circumstantial. When Elma had first disappeared, before her body was discovered, Levi had told his Caty, as she spoke of herself when with him, except when testifying against him, "Mrs. Ring, it's my firm belief she's now in eternity."

Levi had wanted Elma's sister, Hope Sands, to give a statement in his favor. To this, Caty said she had "very great objections, even if I believed thee innocent, which I have no reason to think . . . Indeed, Levi, I shudder to think I ever indulged a favorable thought of thee."

Candlelight court sessions lasted into the late evening. Hamilton was particularly suspicious of one prosecution witness named Richard David Croucher. According to his son John Church Hamilton's account, which his grandson Allan McLane Hamilton discredits, Hamilton placed a candle on either side of Croucher's face "and fixed him with a piercing eye." The prosecution objected. The court overruled the prosecution's well-taken objections to such bullying tactics. Hamilton called upon the jury to "mark every muscle of his face, every motion of his eye. I conjure you to look through that man's countenance to his conscience." Croucher is said to have broken under this pressure and "plunged from one admission to another."

William Coleman's report of the cross-examination of Croucher does not mention the detail of the placing of the candles, but because the trial ground on into the early hours of the morning and because it was essential that the jury be able to watch Croucher's face intently for tremors or beads of sweat while he groped for right answers under sharp questioning, nothing in the story on its face invites disbelief.

Coleman's account confirms the expertness of the cross-examiner's technique. Hamilton could inculpate Croucher and exculpate Levi Weeks only if he could only show (1) that Croucher had been near the Manhattan Well the night of the murder, but falsely denied he had; (2) that he had had a quarrel with Levi over Gulielma, but concealed it; (3) that Gulielma knew him, feared him, and had jilted him for Levi; (4) that he remembered vividly what it was like the night of the murder, but pretended he had forgotten; and (5) that he was a congenital liar, with a bad memory, and knew it.

But there was no way any such evidence could be admitted into the record, unless extracted unwittingly, or blurted out of Croucher's own mouth under the pressure of cross-examination. Here is how Hamilton got it all in:

Q: Do you know where the Manhattan well is?
A: I do.
Q: Did you pass by it that evening?
A: I did not—I wish I had—I might, perhaps, have saved the life of the deceased.
Q: Have you not said you did?
A: No.

A good liar must have a good memory of prior statements and confidence in it, which Croucher lacked. To cover, he volunteered: "I might have said I wished I did."

Q: Have you ever had a quarrel with the prisoner at the bar?
A: I bear him no malice.
Q: But have you never had any words with him?
A: Once I had—the reason was this, if you wish me to tell it:—Going hastily upstairs, I suddenly came upon Elma, who stood at the door —she cried out Ah! and fainted away. On hearing this the prisoner

came down from his room and said it was not the first time I had insulted her. I told him he was an impertinent puppy. Afterward, being sensible of his error, he begged my pardon.

Q: And you say you bear him no ill will?

A: I bear him no malice, but I despise every man who does not behave in character.

Q: How near the Manhattan well do you think you passed that night?

A: I believe I might have passed the Glue manufactory.

Q: Do you not know what route you took?

A: I do not; I cannot certainly say; I might have passed by one route or another; I sometimes go by the road, sometimes across the field.

Q: Was it dark?

A: I believe there was a little moonlight—the going was very bad.

At this point in the cross-examination, to save his floundering and totally discredited witness and give him time to recover, Assistant Attorney General Colden derailed Hamilton's probing by asking a completely unrelated question. Then,

Q: Were you ever upon other than friendly terms with Elma?

A: After I offended the prisoner at the bar, who thought she was an adonis, I never spoke to her again.

He had got in the evidence on all five of his points, effectively destroyed the witness, and converted him into a prime suspect.

Hamilton's case for the defense was soundly constructed. He began with establishing a good character for Levi Weeks and a solid alibi to account for his whereabouts for all but a few minutes of the night of December 22. He cast suspicion not only on Croucher, but also on Elias Ring. His possibly betrayed wife, Catherine, stood loyally by him. The testimony of Captain Rutgers brought out Ring's curious behavior in dragging the river after being told where Gulielma's muff had been found. The testimony of Joseph and Elizabeth Watkins, who lived next door to the Rings, tended to show that Ring had been carrying on an affair with Gulielma, while Catherine was away in the country.

Q: [to Joseph Watkins] Do you remember anything in the conduct of Mr. Ring that led you to suspicions of improper conduct between him and Elma?

A: About the middle of September, Mrs. Ring being in the country, I imagined one night I heard a shaking of a bed and considerable noise there, in the second story, where Elias's bed stood within four inches of the partition. I heard a man's voice and a woman's.

Q: [by one of the jury] Could you hear through the partition?

A: Pretty distinctly.

Q: Did the noise of the bed continue for any time?

A: It continued some time and it must have been very loud to have awakened us. I heard a man's voice pretty loud and lively, and joking; the voice was loud and unguarded. I said to my wife, it is Ring's voice, and I told my wife that girl will be ruined next.

By this kind of testimony, Hamilton and his cocounsel for the defense created good grounds for reasonable doubt of Levi's guilt. Catherine Ring or Croucher must have done her in, not Levi. Now came the prosecution's turn to try to save its case. Assistant Attorney General Cadwallader Colden tried to break down Watkins's credibility as a witness by probing to show that he simply did not know what he was testifying about or that perhaps his damaging testimony had been falsified.

Q: What kind of a partition is it which divides the houses?

A: A plank partition, lathed and plaistered on both sides.

So far so good. Colden might later be able to argue that it would be too thick for Watkins to have heard through, unlike more recent, flimsy Manhattan apartment construction.

But then Watkins, unasked but irrepressible, blurted out four words that wrecked all of Colden's hopes: "I made it myself."

Cross-examination by an expert lawyer can serve as the supreme lie detector in a courtroom. But expert cross-examiners are able to sense the times when it is wiser to waive the cross-examination of certain witnesses or rest before asking one question too many. Not Colden. Not being in the experts' league, Colden ploughed ahead asking Watkins the same list of prepared questions he had asked all the other witnesses who lived in houses on either side of the Rings'. He thereby permitted Watkins to help him demonstrate how maladroit cross-examination can also serve as the courtroom's supreme truth extractor—for the other side's benefit.

As derisory smiles and whispers at defense counsels' table subsided, Colden resumed:

Q: How could you distinguish between the voice of Mr. Ring and Mr. Weeks?

A: Ring's is a high sounding voice, Weeks' a low soft voice.

Q: How often have you heard this noise of the bed?

A: From eight to fourteen times.

Q (by prisoner's counsel, Hamilton perhaps): Did you ever hear this noise after Mrs. Ring came back from the country?

A: I never did.

The celebrated Dr. David Hosack testified that, contrary to popular suspicion and rumor, there had been no marks of violence on the cadaver, other than what might be inflicted by falling or being pushed down the well.

Her jealously envenomed charges against Levi now discredited, exposed as a betrayed wife jilted by her former paramour for the same younger and more beautiful woman who had also captured her husband, Mrs. Catherine Ring began to squirm. She found herself becoming the focal point of more and more accusatory stares from the packed galleries in the courtroom as the night wore on—she and her well-motivated, lying accomplice, Richard Croucher.

All the evidence was in by 2:35 A.M. The assistant attorney general, confessing that he was "sinking under fatigue," moved for an adjournment.

Hamilton jumped up. He moved for a verdict at once. The case was too plain to require any "laboured elucidation." He was so confident of acquittal that he was even willing to waive his own speech of summation to the jury—he was full of surprises that night. He would rest the defense on Judge Lansing's charge.

Not displeased with Hamilton's motion, the court denied the prosecution's request for adjournment. It did not wish to detain the jurors for a second night without the "conveniences necessary for repose." One is always left in suspense about eighteenth-century toilet facilities. Justice Lansing's charge was virtually a direction to acquit. The jury then filed out, was out five minutes, filed back, and solemnly intoned its verdict—NOT GUILTY!

Before Hamilton could clap his grateful client, Levi Weeks, gleefully on the back and be happily hugged by Levi in return, Mrs. Catherine Ring gave a cry and jumped to her feet! Trembling as the flickering candles guttered out in the blackness, she swung her outstretched arm around the courtroom past Judge Lansing and the jurors, stopped at Hamilton, thrust a trembling fist and crooked forefinger into his face, and screamed in fury: "If thee dies a natural death, I shall think there is no justice in heaven!"

Fifteen years of Hamilton's kind of competition is too much for anyone, even, or especially, Hamilton in 1800.

The distinguished physician, alienist, and generally responsible biographer, Dr. Allan McLane Hamilton, relates the story of the awful witching hour curse that Mrs. Catherine Ring laid on his grandfather without expressing any doubts of its having been uttered. Other authorities at a greater distance, lacking other documentation, are not so sure.

Subsequent events did nothing to disprove its efficacy. On the contrary, they proved its power. Chief Justice Lansing left his hotel room one day in 1829 to take the riverboat up to Albany, but was never heard from again. His body was never found. He had managed to stave off unnatural death a quarter century longer than Hamilton. Cocounsel Aaron Burr suffered political death when Hamilton died, but physical death spared him until the age of 80, when he was in bed. Told he was dying by Dr. David Hosack, the Reverend Mr. Van Pelt at his bedside was slavering for the parochial credit that would accrue to any divine administering last rites to a man with such a satanic reputation. He asked Burr whether he had "good hope, through grace, that all your sins will be pardoned . . . for the sake of . . . our Lord Jesus Christ?"

Burr's last words, as he expired unrepentant on September 14, 1836, were: "On that subject I am coy."

29

THE FREEDOM OF THE PRESS

I HAVE THEREFORE LONG THOUGHT THAT A FEW PROSECUTIONS OF
THE MOST PROMINENT OFFENDERS WOULD HAVE A WHOLESOME
EFFECT IN RESTORING THE INTEGRITY OF THE PRESSES. NOT A
GENERAL PROSECUTION, FOR THAT WOULD LOOK LIKE PERSECU-
TION, BUT A SELECTED ONE. . . .
—*Thomas Jefferson to Governor Thomas McKean
of Pennsylvania, February 19, 1803*

Hamilton was a man of "ambition, pride and overbearing temper . . .," "the
evil genius of this country," the author of a reckless attempt to split the Federalists "and . . . compleat our ruin. . . ." Noah Webster, writing as *The Federalist*
—of all names—had anathematized Hamilton this way in the press in November
of 1800 by his *Letter to General Hamilton occasioned by his Letter to President Adams.*

Webster's malediction had come less than ten months after Mrs. Catherine
Ring's witching hour curse the night of Levi Weeks's acquittal. Both had been
laid on him during his psychic crisis when his mood had never been blacker or
more unforgiving. There may come a time, R. D. Laing has suggested, when a
man needs to go mad. It arrives when, beset by a sea of troubles, he seeks by
opposing to end them and fails. It is the time when threats of throat cuttings in
whispers and stabbings in the dark rising on all sides from suspected but unseen
enemies disorient and imprison the victim's mind in multiple bonds. He can no

longer think clearly or see any way out. For such a person, madness may be the
first stage in the natural healing process of a too acute mind, by which it begins
to break down, to soften, to feel with less unbearable intensity, the logically
unbearable contradictions of experience. If this analysis is correct, Hamilton
may by now have already taken the first step on the path to recovery and
eventually to normalcy. But recovery would not come all at once.

Noah Webster and his paper, the *Commercial Advertiser and Spectator*,
once the staunchest of Hamilton's admirers, supporters, and followers, still
spoke for a significant segment of Federalist opinion. For Hamilton in his mood
of 1800, there seemed to be no alternative to striking back at this latest recruit
to the burgeoning ranks of critics holding him accountable, whom he equated
with enemies.

None believed more strongly than Hamilton that the battle against Jefferson and other enemies must be fought out in the press. "It is the *Press,*" he
editorialized in the New York *Evening Post* a few years later, "which has
corrupted our political morals—and it is to the *Press* we must look for the means
of our political regeneration."

The trouble with Noah Webster was something like the trouble with Adams,
Hamilton thought. He was too independent. To Hamilton, he was guilty of one
of the worst of nonpenal offenses, or so it would seem to a lawyer. He did not
know which side he was on. Hamilton's long ingrained habit of taking firm
stands on one or the other side of a question as an advocate left him poorly
conditioned to accept Webster's position, as expressed by his newly hired editor,
Samuel Bayard, on October 13, 1801. Although Webster's paper adhered to the
"principles by which they have ever been guided—viz., a real attachment to the
federal interest etc.," at the same time he would "treat with respect even what
they regard as the *errors* of their fellow citizens."

Even when he disagreed with most of his fellow New York Federalists,
Webster's views could not be dismissed. He thought Hamilton's administration
had been too fearful of war with Britain, "which led them to make some improper
sacrifices to peace with that country." They had been too warlike toward France.
"I . . . opposed the Hamiltonian project of raising a large army," Webster said.
He also objected to "some unworthy intrigues of the federalists, and their
overbearing, persecuting spirit, which devotes every man to execration, who will
not be as violent as themselves." They have "greatly disgusted many men of the
party who have no wish but to see their country prosperous & happy."

Hamilton attributed much of Jefferson's growing popularity, as well as the
venerable George Clinton's recent comeback victory over young Stephen Van
Rensselaer in New York, to the lack of a really reliable party-lining Federal
newspaper in New York City. Nationally, Freneau's *National Gazette*, Cheetham's *American Citizen*, and the Baches' and Duane's *Aurora*, all liberal
Democratic-Republican journals, were flourishing. They spread Republican doctrine across the land. Noah Webster's *Commercial Advertiser* and other local
Federalist papers were weak and lacked influence, even when they did not go as
far as to brand the leader of the Federal party "the evil genius of this country."

After due consideration, Hamilton, Troup, and Wolcott picked William Coleman, the 35-year-old lawyer journalist who had written the best published accounts of the trial of *People v. Levi Weeks*, to be editor and publisher of a New York City newspaper they and other true friends of Federalism planned to finance, write for, subscribe to, and read. Coleman was a kindly, easygoing man with some literary pretensions, not the typical hard-hitting polemicist like Cheetham or Callender who flourished in that day when newspapers and pamphlets were the preeminent and unchallenged medium for communicating all messages to a public of avid readers. Some years before, Coleman had worked as a law partner of Aaron Burr. Such a background would give Coleman all sorts of leads, contacts, spies, informers, and other news sources barred or unknown to Hamilton. Hamilton contributed about $1,000, which he could not afford, to help launch the *Evening Post*. Other backers also helped out, with reimbursement to be paid out of future profits of the paper, if any.

"We have set [Coleman] up . . . as a printer," Troup wrote. "His first paper will make its appearance in October next. . . . All our friends have Mr. Coleman's paper much at heart. We have not a paper in the City on the federal side that is worth reading."

When young Theodore Tillemont applied for a job with Webster on September 21, 1801, he reminded him boldly and tactlessly, "You are aware . . . of the extraordinary patronage which a new daily & half weekly . . . to be edited by William Coleman, and designed to supplant the *Commercial Advertiser and Spectator*, has received from the Federal interest of New York. The feeble manner in which your papers have been conducted, of late, owing to your absence have led to this result. . . . Not a day is to be lost."

Tillemont continued to warn Webster, in New Haven, that "your rival's subscription list is rapidly increasing, where his paper is taken, yours will be discontinued." He added, "Your own presence, and that of a competent editor, will be indispensibly [*sic*] necessary to rescue your papers from neglect & yourself from loss."

Tillemont did not get the job from Webster.

Webster hired Samuel Bayard instead. Bayard was unhappy with his low salary, which, even with commissions for new subscribers, was less than half the $2,000 Coleman was "to receive for his services as Editor of Hamilton's paper."

The prospectus of the New York *Evening Post*, published in the first edition on November 16, 1801, announced that the paper "must derive its principal support from the Merchants of our City." Therefore "particular attention will be bestowed on whatever relates to that large and respectable class. . . . The design . . . is to diffuse among the people correct information . . ." and "to inculcate just principles of religion, morals and politics. . . ." The tone of the prospectus was surprisingly moderate and less dogmatic than most had expected from a paper with sponsors named Hamilton, Troup, Varick, Gracie, and the like: "Though we openly profess our attachment to that system of politics denominated Federal, because we think it most conducive to the welfare of the community . . ., yet we disapprove of that spirit of dogmatism which lays exclusive claim to infallibility; and . . . believe that honest and virtuous men are to be found in each party." Hamilton and Coleman had learned an important lesson from chastisement by the didactic lexicographer.

The *Evening Post*'s prospectus also declared that the people wanted proper information "to enable them to judge of what is really best." It would cleave to a *"line of temperate discussion and impartial regard to truth!"* The date of that first edition, November 16, 1801, makes the New York *Evening Post*, published continuously ever since, the oldest newspaper in the communications capital of the United States and in the United States. With Hamilton's name proudly featured on its present-day logotype, the *New York Post* remains a daily monument to Hamilton's advocacy of freedom of the press by its cranky independence of, and opposition to, most political views now thought of as typically Hamiltonian.

The leading editorial in the first edition urged harmony in party ranks because "the cause of Federalism has received as much injury from the indiscreet contentions . . . among those who profess to be its friends, as from the open assaults of its enemies." The *Post*'s jibe was directed at Webster, but it would remind some of his readers, if not so many of Hamilton's, that the cause of Federalism had received more serious injury from the "indiscreet contentions" of its own founder than from anything Noah Webster had ever written.

The *Evening Post* owed its power and influence among orthodox Federalists not so much to Coleman's editing as to Hamilton's constant support, intervention, and publications. Jeremiah Mason, in after years, described the working relationship between Coleman and Hamilton. Coleman's friends told him, rather tactlessly, that they "were often surprised by the ability of some of his editorial articles, which were supposed to be beyond his depth. Having a convenient opportunity," said Mason, "I asked him who wrote, or aided in writing, those articles. He frankly answered that he made no secret of it; that his paper was set up under the auspices of General Hamilton, and that he assisted him."

This puzzled Mason.
I then asked, "Does he write in your paper?"—
"Never a word."—
"How, then does he assist?"—
His answer was, "Whenever anything occurs on which I feel the want of information I state matters to him, sometimes a note; he appoints a time when I may see him, usually a late hour in the evening. He always keeps himself minutely informed on all political matters."

"What happens then?" asked Mason.
" 'As soon as I see him, he begins in a deliberate manner to dictate and I to note down in shorthand; when he stops, my article is completed.' "

As the *Evening Post* got under way, Coleman seemed fully persuaded that the man he called "the great & good Hamilton" was the greatest man in the world. Under Coleman's editorship it became a mirror of Hamilton's mind: here

Hamilton's ideals and policies were laid before the American people—or, rather, that dwindling part of the people who still read a Federal newspaper. Such unity as the party continued to have after its crushing defeat by Jefferson and Burr came largely from the *Evening Post* and its weekly edition, called the *Herald*, which was sent to subscribers all over the United States. The *Herald*, with a larger circulation than the *Evening Post* itself, kept alive Federalist pretensions to being a national party, not just a sectional party of the Northeast.

But harmony among Federalists seemed always fated to be rare and short-lived, and between Hamilton and Coleman it lasted less than a year. Burr was the immediate proximate cause of the split; but Jefferson, above the fray, as usual, as an unseen presence manipulating unseen strings with invisible hands was the ultimate cause. The puppet play began with his handling of Callender.

After Jefferson's election, Callender had importuned him for an appointment to a political job as a reward for such splendidly helpful preelection pamphleteering as the exposure of the story of Hamilton's affair with Mrs. Reynolds. Jefferson is known to have subsidized Callender to the extent of having gone to his lodgings and paying him $15.14 (much more than the price of a copy) for his *History of the United States for 1796* two weeks before its completion for publication. By the time of his election as president, Jefferson had paid Callender $150 or more for various other anti-Federal publications, and after his election he had paid him several hundred dollars more. Jefferson also through intermediaries helped raise contributions to pay for Callender's defense when he was put on trial by the Federalists for seditious libel. When he was convicted, Jefferson helped him out with getting his fine paid and proffered payment of $50 toward meeting the total. But he did not come through with the job or payment of the whole fine himself.

Jefferson made all these payments to Callender as secretively as possible to cover up his own role. He either delivered the cash to Callender in person or sent it by way of his landlord, Thomas Leiper, or his Richmond agent, George Jefferson, whom he expressly warned to keep both his own and Callender's names out of all payment records. In making the arrangements to pay Callender's fine, Jefferson used James Monroe as his go-between. It was unfortunate, Jefferson wrote Monroe on May 29, 1801, that Callender now considered all the money Jefferson had paid him to be "hush money." Monroe should pay him no more. "Such a misconstruction of my charities puts an end to them forever," Jefferson said he piously told his most confidential bagman. Monroe and other go-betweens of Jefferson scuttled nervously back to Callender one last time to try to get back all the letters Jefferson had ever sent him, but Callender refused to give them up.

In the election of 1800, Hamilton's friend James A. Bayard explained his switch of Federalist votes in the House to Jefferson to break the tie with Burr on the thirty-fifth ballot by saying that Jefferson had secretly committed himself to the deal with the Federalists that Hamilton had proposed, but that Burr had refused to make. The most important stipulation of the deal was that the successful Democrat would not throw out Federalist jobholders wholesale to replace them with deserving Democrats. Jefferson's refusal to reward Callender with a job and his like refusal to respond with jobs to the pleas of other faithful agents and party workers like John Beckley, who had managed the Democrats' successful campaign in Pennsylvania, and Burr's partner Matthew L. Davis, who had helped win control of New York's crucial electoral votes from Hamilton, were all consistent with honoring the secret deal. It also corroborated Bayard's explanation. Callender, however, saw Jefferson's conduct as it affected him personally as welshing on their own private "hush money" deal once he had reaped the benefits of Callender's help.

Finally out of jail, in the summer of 1801, Callender began publicly charging in the Richmond *Recorder* that Jefferson had reneged on his promise to reimburse him for the whole fine. This and many of Callender's later charges against Jefferson were picked up and reprinted by Hamilton and William Coleman in the *Evening Post,* as well as in most other Federalist-leaning papers around the country.

Another excuse that Callender offered the public for his vicious attacks on Jefferson was that he was only trying to give evenhanded press treatment to Jefferson to balance the attacks he had previously published on Hamilton. Four years earlier, Callender pointed out the Democrats had reaped great political profits out of his account of Hamilton's commerce with another man's wife. It was appropriate now to do the same for Jefferson by publishing the story of his affair with the wife of his old friend John Walker. To back up his charges, Callender published letters Jefferson had sent him dated September 6 and October 6, 1799. According to John Walker's unpublished statement to Hamilton's old friend Henry Lee, Jefferson began his "improper conduct" toward Walker's wife, Betsy, back in 1768 while still a bachelor, "renewed his caresses" in 1769 or 1770, and kept them up for years even after he was married. On one occasion, Jefferson had placed in the sleeve of her gown "a paper tending to convince her of the innocence of promiscuous love," which, on discovering, she "tore to pieces." Later, as a guest at the Walker house, Jefferson had pretended to be indisposed, left Walker downstairs, and "stole into [Walker's] room where my wife was undressing or in bed." Even after Jefferson's marriage to Martha Wayles, he "had been found in his shirt ready to seize [Walker's Betsy] on her way from her chamber—indecent in manner." Unlike Hamilton, Jefferson made no public reply to Callender's charges. Instead, in 1805, wishing "to stand with them on the ground of truth," he admitted to some friends that he had had an affair with Mrs. Walker before his own marriage, but not after. He said only, "I offered my love to a handsome lady. I acknowledge its incorrectness." Walker's written account, together with Jefferson's admission, were deposited with the distinguished South Carolina Federalist Thomas Pinckney as "security from calumny," which did not prevent Jefferson's old affair from being rehashed once again in later debate in the House of Representatives.

Another story published by Callender's *Recorder* was that the man "whom it delighteth the people to honor" was secretly keeping Sally Hemings—"Dusky Sally," the "African Venus"—as his concubine in the château at Monticello.

After beginning their liaison in France, she had borne him five mahogany-colored babies, Callender reported, one of whom, Tom, "Yellow Tom," so strikingly resembled his father, the head of the "mulatto party," as to provoke pleased nods of recognition from guests when he served his own father-owner at table there.

Federal versifiers elaborated Callender's theme, and Callender himself reprinted one from the *Boston Gazette*, a song to the tune of Yankee Doodle, whose first verse and chorus ran:

> Of all the damsels on the green,
> On mountain or in valley,
> A lass so luscious ne'er was seen,
> As the Monticellian Sally.
> Yankee doodle, who's the noodle?
> What wife were half so handy?
> To breed a flock of slaves for stock,
> A blackamoor's the dandy.

The *Evening Post*'s recycling of such juicy tidbits about Jefferson's illicit sex life from Callender's *Recorder* did nothing to help avid readers forget about Hamilton's own. Gossip about him and Angelica Church still going the rounds in New York and becoming spicier all the time, gave no one cause to believe that either man's had ended with male menopause.

In September of 1802, Hamilton found it necessary to rebuke Coleman for rehashing so many old scandals of Callender's in the *Evening Post*. He also published a notice in the *Post* that he had not been consulted before the publication of the offensive reprints about Jefferson. He added that he was averse to airing in the press "all personalities, not immediately connected with public considerations."

Bayard wrote Hamilton on April 12, 1802, to clear up a mystery that had been troubling him. The "strange apparition"—Democratic Vice-president Aaron Burr's surprise invasion of the Federalists' Washington's Birthday banquet of 1802, leading to his toast "to the Union of all honest men!"—had been a carefully laid Federalist trap. Bayard and a few of the top leaders had secretly invited Burr without letting the rank and file in on the secret, so that Burr's barging in apparently uninvited would appear to them to be for some fell purpose of his own. It would be a still greater shock to the Democrats when they were told of it. "We knew," Bayard wrote Hamilton, "the impression which the coincidence of circumstances would make on a certain great personage; how readily that impression would be communicated to the proud and aspiring lords of the Ancient Dominion; and we have not been mistaken as to the jealousy we expected it would excite through the party."

Hamilton had predicted to Gouverneur Morris, " 'tis a good thing, if we use it well. As an *instrument*, [Burr] will be an auxiliary of some value; as a chief he will disgrace and destroy the party." This was not a threat to be minimized,

Hamilton warned, because "I know of no important character, who has a less founded interest . . . his talents may do well enough for a particular plot, but they are ill suited to a great and wise drama." Jefferson completely agreed.

Now that he had served to deliver the crucial electoral votes of New York State to Jefferson in the election of 1800, Vice-president Burr's usefulness to him was at an end. Burr's master lost no time putting the widest possible distance between himself and the man he called "a crooked gun, or other perverted machine, whose aim or shot you never could be sure of." He ignored Burr's pleas for at least the crumb of a patronage appointment for Burr's closest friend Matthew L. Davis. Burr was reduced to pleading pathetically to a go-between, Secretary of the Treasury Albert Gallatin, on March 25, 1802: "As to Davis, it is a small, a very small favor to ask a *determination*. That 'nothing is determined' [Jefferson's usual form of rebuff] is so commonplace that I should prefer any other answer to this only *request* which I have ever made." Jefferson made it a general rule, he coldly replied to Burr on November 18, 1801, not to answer letters "relating to office . . . but leaving the answer to be found in what is done or not done on them."

On Davis, nothing was done.

On the other hand, Jefferson did all he could to undercut Burr's political base in New York by sending a list of names of Burr's proposed patronage appointments, including Davis, to Governor George Clinton to be cleared by him. He said that objections had been made to them, not saying by whom. Burr wrote Gallatin indignantly of such "machinations against Davis." Burr realized that Jefferson's tactic made him hostage to his local political rivals, the Clinton and Livingston factions of the New York Democratic party. Davis and later Burr himself made private pilgrimages to Jefferson to plead for favor, but all to no avail. On the occasion of Davis's visit, Gallatin had written Jefferson on September 12, 1801, that he would prefer Madison as vice-president for the next election, but though he had racked his brains, he could think of no way to get rid of Burr without taking the risk that the Federalists would throw enough of their own votes to Burr to make him president or enough to someone else to elect a Federalist as vice-president. Refusal of a job to Davis, Gallatin added, "will, by Burr, be considered as a declaration of war. . . . There is hardly a man who meddles with politics in New York who does not believe that Davis's rejection is owing to Burr's recommendation."

But Jefferson's political genius descried the way to dump Burr that Gallatin had missed. He formed a new alliance with George Clinton and his nephew, De Witt Clinton, and Burr's onetime allies, the Livingstons. He appointed Chancellor Robert R. Livingston minister to France and saw that the Clintonians gave Edward Livingston the offices of mayor of New York and also district attorney.

No deal had been made with Bayard and the Hamiltonians to spare Federalist jobs at the state level, and it was said that of six or seven thousand New York State appointive offices, down to the lowliest auctioneer, not a single one was given by the Clinton-Livingston machine to anyone known as a political ally of Burr, although Jefferson finally let a few federal job crumbs fall his way.

"Never in the history of the United States," wrote Henry Adams in his classic volume on Jefferson's administration, "did so powerful a combination of rival politicians unite to break down a single man as that which arrayed itself against Burr; for as the hostile circle gathered about him, he could plainly see not only Jefferson, Madison, and the whole Virginia legion, with Duane and his *Aurora* at their heels; not only De Witt Clinton and his whole family interest, with Cheetham and his 'watch-tower' by their side; but—strangest of companions—Alexander Hamilton himself joining hands with his own bitterest enemies to complete the ring." Burr's creditors now hounded him more aggressively. He was forced to sell out his stock in the Manhattan Company. Soon he was purged from its board of directors, along with John Swartwout and others of his allies. A deal to sell a sizable part of Richmond Hill at a good price just then mysteriously fell through; someone "either utterly ignorant of the value or . . . from improper motives" put about rumors that it was not worth the price, Burr wrote William Edgar angrily on November 18, 1801. Jefferson's ally Brockholst Livingston suddenly pulled out of a deal of Burr's he had earlier promised to help finance.

Under the fierce pressure from all the enemies seen and unseen ringed around him, Burr made some political mistakes of his own that were characteristic of him; he remained too much in the middle, not making it clear which side he was on, being seen to swing from one side to the other, thus losing the trust of large segments of both. When two Senate votes on repeal of the Judiciary Act —whose passage had made possible Adams's midnight appointments of hordes of Federalists to judgeships for life—were taken on successive days, January 26 and 27, 1802, Burr, presiding as vice-president, had cast two tie-breaking votes. On the first, to permit a third reading of the bill, he voted with the Democrats; but on the second, to refer it to a select committee, he voted with the Federalists. As Gouverneur Morris saw it, Burr's fate pivoted on these two "yea" votes from one day to the next. On August 21, 1802, he described it to Robert Livingston in his familiar Shakespearean mode:

> There was a moment when the vice president might have arrested the measure by his vote, and that vote would, I believe, have made him President at the next election [by winning him grateful support of Federalists] but there is a tide in the affairs of men which he suffered to go by.

Much as he had failed to make the same deal with the Federalists that Jefferson had been willing to make to snatch the presidency, Burr had once again shrunk back from plucking out of the nettle *danger* the flower *safety* and going all the way.

Ward and Barlas, New York publishers, advertised for sale 1,250 copies of a new pamphlet entitled *A History of the Administration of John Adams*. It had been compiled mostly from material furnished to John Wood by William Duane, editor of the Republican *Aurora*, which, since Callender's defection,

Jefferson had recently been subsidizing. The pamphlet balanced vicious libels and slanders against John Adams with captatious eulogies of Jefferson—and Burr himself. Burr took it upon himself to suppress the entire press run by buying up all copies, agreeing to pay $1,250, but actually paying only $1,000 he could ill afford for the entire edition, thereby making an enemy of Wood. Burr's admiring biographer, the same Matthew L. Davis whom Jefferson ignored, said Burr did this to suppress tasteless eulogies, as well as to avoid possible libel. But if Burr had had nothing to do with sponsoring the original publication, it is not easy to see why either defect of the original pamphlet should have caused him such costly worry. His action in buying it up was exquisitely ambiguous; was it really to please Democrats by sparing them embarrassment over vulgar libels and effusions? Or was it to win over Hamilton and other Federalists by suppressing a vicious attack against them? In any event, Burr's money was wasted. A new edition, allegedly printed from a purloined copy, was printed and offered for sale on June 2, 1802.

Earlier, Burr had helped James Cheetham, an English journalist who had been run out of his native country, set up a new Republican newspaper in New York, the *American Citizen*, with the secret financial backing of George Clinton's rising nephew, Senator De Witt Clinton. But Jefferson had now driven a wedge between Burr and the Clintons. In April of 1802, while Burr was out-of-town at a distance visiting his beloved daughter, Theodosia Burr Alston, in South Carolina, Cheetham began a vicious attack on his former patron in the columns of the *American Citizen* and in a pamphlet entitled "The Narrative of the Suppression by Col. Burr of the History of the Administration of John Adams." He followed it with "An Antidote to John Wood's Poison." The private views of Aaron Burr publicly exposed in Cheetham's pamphlets would win him enemies in all quarters: Burr had allegedly complained to John Wood on December 5 or 6, 1801, that "the character of Mr. Hamilton was *misrepresented*, meaning where encomium was bestowed upon him it was unmerited"; Burr liked Wood's "character" of Mr. Adams—"it was a bad one, and he thought it representative of the ex-president"; and Burr had said that "Jefferson was not a man of *genius*, he was a *plodding, mechanical* person, of little activity of mind, possessed of a judgment not very discriminative . . . he courted and was fond of popularity." Furthermore, Cheetham's "Antidote" went on, the "Federal prints acknowledge that Mr. Burr cannot forgive General Hamilton for using his influence to effect the election of Mr. Jefferson in preference to himself"; Hamilton had said he "preferred, according to his toast, a 'dreamer' to a 'Catiline.'" Cheetham's "Antidote" also found occasion to rehash the whole story of Hamilton's affair with Maria Reynolds, recalling that Hamilton "avowed himself to the whole world to have been the seducer of an amiable though unfortunate woman."

The point of Cheetham's attack was that Burr had suppressed the free press —John Wood's "Adams" chronicle—to ingratiate himself with Federalists. Jefferson's mouthpiece William Duane reprinted this anti-Burr material in the *Aurora* and thereby opened an umbrella of quasi-official sanction over all hack journalistic hatchet men who wished to help cut down Burr.

They did. The "political perfidiousness" of "this Cataline" was matched by "his abandoned profligacy," according to one handbill, though "the numerous unhappy wretches who have fallen victims to this accomplished debaucher" would be known only to those familiar with the haunts of female prostitution. There followed a listing of the initials of courtesans whom he had ruined and thrown on the town to become "the prey of disease, of infamy and wretchedness." He had seduced the daughter of a Washington tradesmen by bringing her to New York and maintaining her in Partition Street. He was "the disgraceful debaucher who permitted an infamous prostitute to insult and embitter the dying moments of his injured wife." Who could doubt that such leaks were plants by the higher-up principals of the power struggle using fearless reporters like Wood, Callender, and Cheetham as poor hack mercenary acolytes.

It was small anodyne for Hamilton that John Wood in his rebuttal pamphlet entitled "A Correct Statement of the Various Sources . . ." from which he had compiled his earlier "Adams" pamphlet—written for but suppressed by Burr—now switched from censure of Hamilton to sympathy with him for his role in the Reynolds affair. In his earlier pamphlet, Wood had dated Maria Reynolds's first visit to Hamilton's Philadelphia home in the summer of 1790, not 1791, as Hamilton had done (Hamilton had not moved to Philadelphia until late in 1790). Wood sheepishly confessed that "following the misstatement of Callender," he had earlier erroneously represented Maria as an "amiable and virtuous wife, seduced from the affections of her husband by artifice and intrigue." Further investigation "even of her own acquaintances" had proved how wrong he had been. She was, in fact, "one of those unfortunates, who, destitute of every regard for virtue or honour, traffic with the follies of youth," like Burr's mistresses. They "lay [*sic*] their snares to entrap the feeling heart and benevolent mind; such was her acquaintance with Mr. Hamilton, whose unsuspecting generosity became the victim of her art and duplicity." Having found out Burr's and Maria's capacity for duplicity, Wood here hints broadly that he knows of the despicable story of the badger game with which they had entrapped Hamilton.

Well before Cheetham began his campaign against Burr, as early as December 10, 1801, he had sent Jefferson a draft of the material and followed it up on January 30, 1802, with a draft copy of Wood's "Adams" pamphlet. On April 23, 1803, Jefferson wrote Cheetham, just as his press campaign against Burr was about to begin, "I shall be glad hereafter to receive your daily paper by post, as usual . . . I shall not frank this to avoid post office curiosity, but pray you to add the postage to your bill."

All these attacks by low road and high on his former law partner caused William Coleman to break with Hamilton over the *Evening Post's* anti-Burr editorial policy. On May 26, 1802, under the pseudonym *Fair Play*, Coleman defended Burr and criticized Cheetham's and Duane's alleged libels against him. Callender in Richmond pitched in on Burr's side with a spirited attack on Cheetham. Duane hit back at Callender. By September 15, 1802, Callender was becoming incoherent and hysterical, saying, among other things, that Jefferson's reputation would have been better if his head had been cut off five minutes before he began his inaugural speech.

On November 25, after six months of abuse of Burr had gone largely unanswered except by random fire from Callender and Hamilton's maverick editor, Burr founded the *Chronicle-Express* to reply. It was much too late. Besides, the editor he selected, Dr. Peter Irving, Washington Irving's brother, who printed an unequivocal denial of any attempt to displace Jefferson, had a style with a cultured, kindly, genial literary flavor that bored many a new reader. They turned back to the more sensational scandals printed and reprinted in Callender's Richmond *Recorder,* Duane's Philadelphia *Aurora,* Cheetham's *American Citizen,* Hamilton's *Evening Post,* and, in the little town of Hudson, New York, in Columbia County, 25 miles below Albany, Harry Croswell's *The Wasp.*

The junior editor of *The Balance and Columbian Repository,* of Hudson, Harry Croswell, had set up *The Wasp* in July 1802 "in the Garret of *The Balance*" under the editorship of one *Robert Rusticoat,* his pseudonym. *The Wasp's* purpose, Croswell announced, was to cross stingers with *The Bee,* a new Democratic paper that Charles Holt was bringing to Hudson. The reason Holt had suspended *The Bee* in New London, Connecticut, where it had formerly made a loud buzz, was that in April 1800 he had been convicted under the Sedition Law by Judge Bushrod Washington and sentenced to a $200 fine and three months in prison. Holt's crime had been recirculating, among other things, scandalous stories about Alexander Hamilton's "amours"—stories that even the Federal prosecuting attorney at the trial had conceded to be true.

Of course, like many small-town editors, Harry Croswell had to cut corners on costs by filling out the local news he carried in his four-page Federalist gadfly with juicy tidbits reprinted from big city papers whose views he shared, like Hamilton's *Evening Post.*

On September 9, 1802, in issue No. 7, *The Wasp* reprinted from the *Evening Post* an anti-Jefferson barb that on its face seemed no more pointed than many others:

"Holt says, the burden of the Federal song is, that Mr. Jefferson paid Callender for writing against the late administration." But "this is wholly false," said Croswell, because it so badly understates Jefferson's offense. The true charge, Croswell explained, "is explicitly this:—Jefferson paid Callender for calling Washington a traitor, a robber, and a perjurer—For calling Adams, a hoary-headed incendiary; and for most grossly slandering the private characters of men, who, he well knew were virtuous. These charges, not a democratic editor yet has dared, or ever will dare to meet in an open [and] manly discussion."

A month earlier, in No. 4, under the title "A Few Squally Facts," *The Wasp* had excoriated both Jefferson's record before his election and his acts allegedly destructive of the Constitution after his election. Croswell concluded with, "It would be an endless task to enumerate the many acts, in direct hostility to common sense and the constitution, of which the *'man of the people'* has been guilty—Do you not in all this plainly perceive the little arts—the very little arts, of a very little mind—Alas! what will the world think of the fold if such is the shepherd." To a poor hardworking small-town newspaperman like Harry Croswell, for Jefferson of Monticello to play at being a "man of the people" was like

Marie Antoinette and Louis XVI playing at being shepherds and shepherdesses at the Palace of Versailles. It was infuriating that so many of his fellow Americans—more all the time—seemed to enjoy being fooled by his playacting instead of dealing with him as the French had done with their voluptuary feudal monarchs.

Once safely installed in the highest office, Jefferson had done all he could behind the scenes to muzzle the hostile Federalist press by selective enforcement of the Sedition Laws that his Democrats had attacked so successfully in their campaign to win it for him. On February 19, 1803, Jefferson wrote Governor Thomas McKean of Pennsylvania, "The federalists having failed in destroying the freedom of the press by their gag-law, seem to have attacked it in an opposite form, that is by pushing its licentiousness & its lying to such a degree of prostitution as to deprive it of all credit . . . I have therefore long thought that a few prosecutions of the most prominent offenders would have a wholesome effect in restoring the integrity of the presses. Not a general prosecution, for that would look like persecution, but a selected one. . . ."[1]

Leonard Levy (in his *Legacy of Suppression: Freedom of Speech and Press in Early American History*) says it would not be surprising if a letter from Jefferson to Clinton recommending the same sort of selective prosecution should be discovered. Jefferson's sympathetic biographer, Dumas Malone, in *Jefferson the President, First Term 1801–1804*, scoffs at Levy's speculation. He snorts, "This is a presumptuous statement, though of course there is the *possibility* of such a discovery."

In any event, as Jefferson had suggested, a prosecution was duly begun in Pennsylvania and another in George Clinton's New York. In the person of Ambrose Spencer, the state's attorney general, all the legal power that the state of New York could bring to bear was trained on Harry Croswell's freshly hatched *Wasp* in an out-of-the-way town where the political killing of a newspaper by Jeffersonians could easily be ignored by liberal Democrats. On January 10, 1803, Attorney General Spencer went before the grand jury of the Court of General Sessions of the Peace for Columbia County and obtained two indictments against Harry Croswell for seditious libel. Croswell was charged with deceitfully, wickedly, maliciously, and willfully traducing, scandalizing, and vilifying President Thomas Jefferson and representing him to be unworthy of the "confidence, respect and attachment of the people of the United States." On January 11, Croswell was arrested on a bench warrant and brought before the Court of General Sessions at Claverack, the county seat, four miles away from Hudson. The long indictments were read to him, his attorneys asked for copies of the indictments, the allegedly all-Republican bench of judges denied their motion, and Croswell then pleaded "not guilty" to both unread indictments.

Out of this state of the record arose *People v. Croswell*, the second of the two great cases in which, according to Chancellor Kent, who sat as one of the judges before whom Hamilton argued his last, never-to-be-forgotten appeal, Hamilton's "varied powers were most strikingly displayed." The case, Kent pointed out, "involved the discussion of legal principles of the greatest consequence." In it "General Hamilton's argument" was "the greatest forensic effort that he ever made."

The prosecutor, Ambrose Spencer, was a former Federalist who had switched to the New York Jeffersonian Republican party in 1798 to help Clinton win back the state after Jay's interregnum. He quickly became a political power when Clinton won. No. 7 of *The Wasp*, which carried Croswell's alleged libel, also honored this apostate Federalist with stinging doggerel verse:

> The Attorney General too was drunk but not with grog—
> Power and pride had set his head agog.

Spencer's home was in Columbia County, and Claverack was conveniently near Albany, but small and out of the way enough that although the case might escape major press coverage, it could create a legal precedent on the books that could be used for muzzling the big city press like Hamilton's *Evening Post*, which, after all, had first printed the story for which Croswell was now being persecuted.

There could be no doubt that *People v. Croswell* was a political trial if there ever was one.

Prominent New York legal talent quickly stepped to Croswell's side to defend him on a *pro bono* basis: the able William W. Van Ness, Burr's associate, close friend, and apologist, and Elisha Williams and Jacob Rutsen Van Rensselaer. After losing their motion to obtain written copies of the indictment, this great team of legal talent thought of another technical tactic: delay. They moved to delay the trial until the next session of Circuit Court (Oyer and Terminer) should be held at Claverack. They lost again. They then moved to delay the trial until the next session of the General Sessions Court, so that they could bring in the key witness from Virginia or obtain testimony from him there by way of deposition that the story Hamilton and Croswell had printed about Jefferson was true.

Spencer opposed. No delay was necessary. Under New York law, proof of the truth of the story was irrelevant and unnecessary, and such evidence could not even be submitted to the jury for its consideration. The only question left for the jury to decide was whether Croswell had printed the story.

Van Ness and the other defense counsel disputed Spencer's dogmatic statement that New York law forbade introducing the truth into evidence; they insisted it did permit proof of truth. They intended to bring in a star witness to prove the truth of the story. The name of their missing witness, not incidentally, was, of course, James Thomson Callender.

Croswell's high-powered *pro bono* legal team lost yet again. Croswell was ordered to stand trial the next day.

But something funny suddenly happened to Attorney General Spencer's zeal that night, the eleventh of January, 1803. Next morning he agreed to stipulate for a postponement until the next General Sessions Court.

It may be speculated that what changed his mind was his, or someone else's, sudden realization that he had a tiger by the tail, so to speak. It was a nightmarish thought that Callender, who might say anything, none of it good, about Jefferson, including the truth, might be brought into the courtroom or give scandalous testimony by deposition even before the point that New York's law made his testimony inadmissible had been established once and for all beyond dispute by a ruling to that effect by the court. One way or another, any story Callender told, if forced to tell one, was bound to leak out. Spencer realized that it would be safer for all concerned to agree to the delay.

In the meantime, however, Spencer demanded that Croswell post an unusually high bond of $2,000 for "good behaviour." Elisha Williams and Van Ness argued that this would place a prior restraint on the freedom of his press. Indeed, it would put it out of business. No, Spencer insisted, it would only curb his licentiousness. "The torrents of slander which pour from the press opposed to government must be checked," said this zealous new convert of Jefferson, "or all that is dear to man would not be worth preserving." The court granted Spencer's demand for the high bond from Croswell and further conditioned it on his "good behaviour." This effectively silenced *The Wasp* forever.

Croswell's *pro bono* team of legal lights had lost the fifth consecutive round. They seemed to be highly solvent gentlemen, however, presumably from doing better for other clients than they had for poor Croswell. This made it possible for the court to throw them one tiny crumb to crow up as a victory: it appointed the lawyers themselves (other than Van Ness) to be Croswell's bondsmen.

After this string of legal reverses, with the next round about to begin at Claverack, on June 23, 1803, Schuyler wrote in desperation to his daughter Eliza, requesting her to plead Croswell's case with Hamilton to get him to take over the case. "I have had about a dozen Federalists with me," he wrote her from Albany, "Intreating me to write to Your General, If possible to attend on the 7th of next month at Claverack as Counsel to the Federal printer there who is to be tried on an Indictment for a libel against that Jefferson, who disgraces not only the place he fills but produces Immorality by his pernicious example."

But Hamilton was overwhelmed with business and could find no time to go to Claverack for the first trial on July 11, 1803, before Chief Justice Morgan Lewis, an active Republican politician, here sitting as an ordinary trial judge with a jury.

Two new reputed legal wizards, James Scott Smith of New York and Abraham van Vechten of Albany—at least they sported typical triple-threat trial lawyer names—joined the defense staff, making five, so that no single one could really be held responsible for further *pro bono* bungling. Ambrose Spencer brought in District Attorney Ebenezer Foote to help balance the ranks on his side of the counsel table.

At the close of argument, Judge Lewis charged the jury with deciding two narrow questions: (1) did Croswell print and publish the offending story? and (2) did it contain malicious innuendoes against Jefferson? If the jury came back with a "yes" answer to these two questions, it was for Judge Lewis, not the jury, to pronounce that his fellow Republican Jefferson had indeed been libeled by the story. After being out all night to gnaw on two questions that a child of ten could probably have answered in a minute, the jury came back with the verdict that Croswell had indeed done the printing and that the words printed indeed insulted Jefferson. It made no difference that they were true and, in fact, understated the extent to which he had subsidized Callender's attacks on his enemies. Judge Lewis held Croswell guilty of libel. The five new great legal brains for the defense showed that they could lose as consistently as the earlier three.

Defense counsel next went before the full bench of the court, consisting of Lewis and two other judges, and moved for a new trial on the ground that Judge Lewis had misstated the applicable New York law in the charge he had given to the jury. The other two judges on the full bench, James Kent and Smith Thompson, were Federalists. This was Croswell's last chance, the round he had to win. Unsurprisingly, because this was a political trial, the two Federalists reversed their Republican brother Lewis and granted Croswell a new trial. This was calendared to be held at Albany in the Supreme Court on February 13 and 14, 1804.

Hamilton now agreed to take charge of Croswell's defense. Although Hamilton's name had not appeared in the record during the 1803 proceedings in the case, Croswell's defense counsel had probably been consulting him behind the scenes from almost the beginning. On June 26, 1803, Hamilton had written his friend William Rawle in Philadelphia to obtain information about the procedure used in a Sedition Act case Rawle had handled for obtaining the testimony of an absent witness upon deposition in another city: this would be used by Hamilton in examining the missing witness James Thomson Callender under oath in Richmond if he could not be compelled to come to Claverack. Therefore, it came as a stunning blow to Hamilton and other defense counsel that just after the three-judge panel reversed Lewis and granted Croswell's motion for a new trial, the missing witness was murdered, accidentally died, or committed suicide, in circumstances similar to typical present-day gangster rub outs.

A hastily impaneled coroner's jury found that James Thomson Callender had been drowned—in water three feet deep. His many enemies did not mind saying that the corpse was found face down "in congenial mud." They added that it had been drunk. It was buried the same day in Richmond Churchyard, though if any burial record were made, it has disappeared. Richmond was full of rumors of foul play, but the incident went all but unmentioned in the press except locally. No one in town seemed to give much credence to the coroner's verdict of accidental death by drowning. Most seemed to take it for granted that Callender's sudden demise had been hastily arranged and hushed up as part of some kind of a cover-up.

Ten days afterward, the Richmond *Examiner,* a Jeffersonian paper that had been the target of some of Callender's attacks, apparently taking it for granted that no one believed the coroner's story, ventured out with a more plausible tale. Callender had been depressed—more depressed than usual—and had probably committed suicide. But in only three feet of water? It is a criticism of the system that when a high personage fears that a witness about to be called to testify in a sensational trial may talk too much, such witness is occasionally found shortly before the hearing taken dead of a bullet through the mouth or a mouthful of mud. To those in high places there is such a thing as too much freedom of the press. No sensible newspaper editor would dare risk another selective prosecution under the sedition laws like the one that had now silenced poor Harry Croswell's *Wasp* and may have led to Callender's silencing by daring to print the name of the high personage that was on every tongue whose unsurrendered letters were still in the late Mr. Callender's hands. No one else, except possibly Hamilton, had better motives for putting an end to Callender's mudslinging.

Hamilton discarded Croswell's former team of defense counsel preparing for the new trial as 1804 began. From the earlier team he retained only Aaron Burr's friend and apologist William W. Van Ness. He added his able friend, the scholarly Richard Harison. As excitement mounted, Van Ness was just coming to be identified as *Aristides*, the author of a pamphlet entitled "An Examination of the Various Charges Exhibited Against Aaron Burr." Van Ness defended Burr by ferociously attacking his New York rivals like George Clinton and also Jefferson himself. According to Van Ness, Clinton had "dwindled into the mere instrument . . . a convenient tool . . . of an ambitious relative" (his nephew De Witt) owing to "the imbecility of his age." Among other things, Clinton had loudly and publicly called Jefferson an "accommodating trimmer."

It is a political cliché that you can't beat somebody with nobody. Jefferson knew a useful tool when he was reminded of one by *Aristides*. Van Ness's published defense of Burr had helped seal Burr's political doom. Jefferson quickly enlisted Clinton in his service, writing him cordially on December 31 that the *Aristides* pamphlet was "libellous" and "lies." He vowed that "little squibs in certain papers had long ago apprized me of a design to sow tares between particular republican characters. But to divide those by lying tales whom truth cannot divide, is the hackneyed policy of the gossips of every society." In February 1804 a caucus of Republican congressmen unanimously renominated Jefferson for president. Clinton, who had just announced that he could not run again for governor of New York because of age and ill health, was deemed well qualified for vice-president, not being dead yet. He was nominated with about two-thirds of the votes on the first ballot. Incumbent Vice-president Aaron Burr was dumped from the ticket without receiving a single vote.

This left as Burr's only hope for clinging to a political life his winning election to the governorship of New York State being vacated by Clinton. For this, his own still loyal and strong splinter group of New York Republicans strongly backed him. The badly divided and discouraged Federalists had no strong candidate of their own, and many of them who were disillusioned with Hamilton's leadership considered Burr as one of themselves or, at least, as a Republican untouched by the kind of Republican principles exemplified by Jefferson. So early in the campaign it appeared that Burr would win the nomination quite easily over the regular Republican candidate, John Lansing, Jr. Burr's prospects brightened still more when Lansing, apparently discouraged by his prospects, withdrew suddenly from the race, just as court and counsel were beginning to gather in Albany in February for the last round of New York's greatest political trial since John Peter Zenger's famous freedom of the press case of 70 years earlier.

Though in the public's mind, that case had been a famous victory for the freedom of the press, to lawyers and judges of Hamilton's time, the law of the case tended to confirm the opposite legal precedent that served to muzzle the press. In Zenger's case, Judge De Lancey, a supporter of the royal governor, William Cosby, whom Zenger had attacked, instructed the jury, as Lewis had in Croswell's earlier trial, simply to decide whether Zenger had printed the attacks and leave it to the judge himself to decide whether they were libelous. But Zenger's counsel, the noted Philadelphia lawyer Andrew Hamilton, urged the jury to consider itself competent to consider the truth of Zenger's statements anyway, and the jury returned a verdict of not guilty—even though it was clear that Zenger had indeed printed the attacks. This result allowed Zenger to go free, but left the state of the law in New York unchanged in principle, so that any future printer who dared attack the royal governor was still exposed to the same costly pretrial arrest, imprisonment, bonding, persecution, and muzzling that Zenger and now Croswell had suffered, as well as the risk of a guilty verdict like the one Hamilton had obtained in the prosecution of David Frothingham.

The argument began on Monday, February 12, before the Supreme Court in Albany and ran on for the next two full days and into the third morning. The public, journalists, and politicians crowded the courtroom. It was reported during the argument that it had almost emptied the chambers of the senate and assembly of their usual quorum of solons. One reason for this was that pending in the legislature was a bill to change New York law to permit truth to be admitted in evidence as a defense against a charge of libel.

To the earlier full bench of Chief Justice Morgan Lewis, a Democrat, and James Kent and Smith Thompson, Federalists, the Clintonians had managed to add another respectable Republican, Brockholst Livingston. He had fought at Hamilton's side for Levi Weeks, but against him in the *Argus* and *Le Guen* cases. In *Le Guen* he had cried out to high heaven, objecting to Hamilton's persecution of his client, Isaac Gouverneur, who had dropped dead four days after losing the case. A two-to-two vote of the four-judge bench would leave in force Croswell's earlier conviction. Lewis could hardly be expected to reverse himself. Livingston was not a man likely to desert his and Lewis's Republican politics to yield to Hamilton's eloquence the single vote he would need to overturn Croswell's conviction. Still Livingston was the only one of the four who by any stretch of the imagination could be called a "swing" man. Thompson would follow Kent, and no one imputed independence of Hamilton's powerful spell to Judge Kent.

Kent himself later liked to tell the story of how one night on the circuit, when he and Hamilton were at an inn together, Kent retired early, complaining of "some slight indisposition." It was a "cold and tempestuous night," and "the kindly nature of Hamilton was evidently disturbed by the indisposition of his friend." Before retiring, Hamilton, perhaps remembering something his mother, Rachel, had done for him as a small boy when a hurricane whistled through the palm trees outside their house on Nevis long ago, "entered Judge Kent's room with an extra blanket, which he insisted on tucking carefully about the recumbent figure, saying: 'Sleep warm, little Judge, and get well. What would we do if anything should happen to you?' "

Van Ness opened the argument for Croswell, the appellant, followed by Harison, and Hamilton finished up by weaving the points each had propounded into 15-point argument that lasted more than six hours. Ambrose Spencer and George Caines argued in rebuttal against overturning the earlier decision of Judge Lewis and the jury. No transcript exists. What follows is a summary of the course of the arguments derived from the report contained in *The Speeches at Full Length*, published by G. & R. Waite, reproduced by Caines himself, which does not reproduce the speeches at full length, but is long enough. Material from James Kent's summary of Hamilton's speech and Hamilton's own 15-point outline for his argument, entitled *15 Propositions on the Law of Libel*, are also included.

What, then, is libel? How do you define it? asked Hamilton. He answered his own question. It is "a slanderous or ridiculous writing, picture or sign, with a malicious or mischievous design or intent, towards government, magistrates, or individuals."

Not so. Hamilton is wrong, argued George Caines: "Intent is immaterial." And so is the truth or falsity of what is said. Ambrose Spencer backed Caines up. The law, as laid down by Blackstone and other unimpeachable authority, defined libel as any scandalous publication that has a tendency to breach of the peace. Breaches of the peace might be caused by printing the story, even if it be true. "You cannot do an unlawful act and say you did not mean to offend." Any insult published against the ruler, if the judge finds it to be insulting or likely to stir up objection, is libelous.

That cannot be the law, Hamilton retorted. "We will trace the law up to its source." All eyes focused on him as he focused on the eternal political point: "The liberty of the press consists, in my idea, in publishing the truth, from good motives and for justifiable ends, though it reflects on government, on magistrates, or individuals."

It was nonsense to say the press might criticize measures without being able to criticize men by name. It is "essential to say, not only that the measure is bad and deleterious," but to "hold up to the people the author, that, in this our free and elective government, he may be removed from the seat of power."

The legal doctrine that Jefferson and Spencer were urging, Hamilton pointed out, arose from English cases like *De Libellis Famosis* (5 Co. Rep. 125), decided by Sir Edward Coke when sitting as a member of the infamous court of the Star Chamber. But unlike the Star Chamber, earlier British statutes and courts had held that truth could not be a libel. Unfortunately, New York engrafted the Star Chamber's recent and false doctrine on its own common law. It "originated in one of the most oppressive institutions that ever existed," the court of the Star Chamber, cried Hamilton, "where oppressions roused the people to demand its abolition." It was "cruel . . . tyrannical . . ." and its "horrid judgments cannot be read without freezing the blood in one's veins." Furthermore, the Star Chamber was abolished because it "inflicted the most sanguinary punishments" and it bore down the "liberties of the people." Remembering Lord Coke's early battles for liberty, but later participation in Star Chamber oppression, it was sad, but true, Hamilton warned, that "It is frequent for men to forget sound principles, and condemn the points for which they have contended." Why so? "At all times men are disposed to forward principles to support themselves."

Even under the Sedition Law, which has been "branded indeed with epithets the most odious," said Hamilton, both the question of intent and the truth of the statement may be submitted to the jury. Moreover, Congress cannot invent constructive or new treasons or other crimes repugnant to antecedent common law, because the Constitution of the United States, in general, presupposes application of the antecedent English common law: one branch of that law permits the truth to be given in evidence. "In vain is it to be replied that some committee met, and in their report, gave it the name of amendment." Hamilton scoffed. Indeed, "if the rulers of the country were to deny the common law to be in force according to our Federal constitution . . . ," people may be charged with crimes that were unknown to the common law as crimes; "they may be pronounced guilty ad libitum; . . . our judges thus got rid of . . . and the crime and the offence being at once at their will, there would be an end of that constitution."

Once let a political party get into power, "they may go from step to step, and, in *spite* of canvassing their measures, fix themselves firmly in their seats," if "they are never to be reproached [by name] for what they have done."

No, said Hamilton, "a libel is a complicated matter of fact and law . . . The tendency to provoke is its constituent . . . must everyone who does not panegyrise be said to be a libeller?" How absurd. But unless the court are disposed to go that extreme length, "it is necessary that malice and intent be proved. . . ." The threat to breach of the peace is not the sole, but only one of, the qualities of a libel. Others are "time, manner and circumstances, which must ever be matters of fact for jury determination."

But Chief Justice Lewis had charged the jury that intent was not its province. Here was an "inroad of tyranny," Hamilton cried out, because in English jurisprudence the trial by jury has been considered "as the palladium of public and private liberty." Furthermore, "in all the political disputes of that country, this has been deemed the barrier to secure the subjects from oppression." Indeed, "the power of the jury to extricate the people, for the salvation of the nation, from the tyranny with which they were then oppressed . . . is a landmark to our liberties, a pillar which points out to us on what the principles of our liberty ought to rest." But if "juries are to answer this end, if they are to protect from the weight of state oppression, they must have this power of judging of the intent . . . they could not otherwise answer the ends of their institution."

Besides, it is axiomatic that "every crime includes an intent." Why should criminal libel alone among all crimes not involve the question of an intent? For example, Hamilton explained, "murder consists in killing a man with malice prepense. Manslaughter, in doing it without malice, and at the moment of an impulse of passion. Killing may even be justifiable, if not praiseworthy, as in defense of chastity about to be violated." "The *intent* is always the necessary ingredient."

The code of dueling was much on Hamilton's mind. "In duelling, the malice is supposed from the deliberate acts of reflecting, sending a challenge, and appointing the time and place of meeting." Therefore, in the case of libel, let the jury determine, as they have the right to do, in all other [criminal] cases, on the complicated circumstances of fact and intent." Furthermore, said Hamilton, my old friend, Chief Justice John Jay of the Supreme Court, in *Georgia v. Brailsford* (3 Dallas 1 at 4 [1794]) has held that it lies within the jury's power to pass on questions of both law and fact, including questions of intent. Why? Because a judge, unlike a jury, but like "every permanent body of men, is, more or less, liable to be influenced by the spirit of the existing administration . . . liable to corruption, inclined to lean over to party modes." Judges are products of "the vibration of party." And "as one side or the other prevails, so of that class and temperament will be the judges of their nomination." Juries, by contrast, are shifting, impermanent bodies, chosen by lot. "Ask any man, however ignorant of principles of government," Hamilton demanded boldly of his party-lining judges, now peering down at him from the bench startled at his daring reproof, "Who constitute the judicial? He will tell you, the favorites of those at the head of affairs." Therefore "of which side so ever a man may be, only one thing interests all." What is this? "To have the question settled." Therefore, it is essential "to uphold the power of the jury, consistently however with liberty, and also with legal and judicial principles, fairly and rightly understood." Only the jury could be relied on to preserve to little men like Croswell "the right of publishing the truth, from good motives and justifiable ends, though it reflect on government, on magistrates, or individuals."

Hamilton himself had suffered as much as any man from the licentiousness of the press. "I do not say there ought to be an unbridled license . . . the best of men are not exempt from the attacks of slander." But all the circumstances were significant. Lord Loughborough had observed "that passages from holy writ may be turned into libels." And, as Hamilton argued, it might fleetingly cross his mind, but be omitted from his argument, that no man had been libeled, slandered, and defamed in the press for 20 years as much as he; yet none of such malicious stories nor all taken together had done him as much damage as had pamphlets and polemics he had published himself with the best of intentions of removing scandalous tarnish from the honor of his own good name. Obviously, he thought nothing could be more ridiculous than to impute automatically a criminal intent to himself from the fact that a publication was scandalous or had an unsettling effect on the public's mind or further tarnished his name.

Here in Albany only three weeks before the argument Hamilton was now intoning, Judge Ebenezer Purdy had reported that Governor George Clinton himself would vouch for an anti-Hamilton canard that had been aired and periodically revived in the press ever since 1787: the story that Hamilton proposed to invite the second son of George III, Frederick, the duke of York, secular bishop of Osnaburg, Germany, to become king of the United States. Clinton made his home with the John Beckleys when he was in Washington and visited often with other Jefferson go-betweens during the period leading up to the party nominating caucus at which he and Jefferson carried out their deal for his replacing Burr as vice-president; so Clinton would not have had to go far out of his way to hear a new version of this hoary old libel on Hamilton.[2]

For Hamilton, there would always be strong grounds to believe that Beckley and James Reynolds were the source of these stories, which first appeared in the *Pennsylvania Gazette* and *Journal,* on August 15 and August 25, 1787. Reynolds had brought these stories to Hamilton's attention and pointed him toward Jeremiah Wadsworth on a false lead to track down the source as one "wetmore" on August 20, 1787. Just before Croswell's trial had opened, Hamilton confronted Purdy and demanded an explanation; ten days after the trial was over, Hamilton would angrily demand a like explanation from Governor Clinton. The story, like Reynolds and Beckley themselves, had haunted Hamilton's entire public career. For 15 years they had been proximate causes that smothered up hopes he once cherished of some day winning the presidency. As it came back to plague him once again, here in Albany, as he awaited the decision of his life's masterwork of legal argument for the freedom of the press and the right of jury trial, Hamilton wrote Clinton on February 27, 1804:

"It is now a long time since a very odious slander has been in circulation to the prejudice of my character." In the more than 15 years the story had haunted him, Hamilton had never been able to run down the real source, yet the "calumny . . . is of a nature too derogatory to permit me to pass it lightly over." On March 9 he would be grateful to Clinton for having "given no countenance" to Purdy's story, but also regret that Clinton had not been able to locate and give to Hamilton a letter he had received from someone who purported to corroborate the story. Hamilton's tone is regretful, resigned, autumnal, elegaic, and formal. It is one of all but surrendering to the inventor of the story.

"I feel an anxiety," Hamilton wrote Clinton, "that it should be thoroughly sifted, not merely on my own account, but from a conviction that the pretended existence of such a project, long traveling about in whispers, has had no inconsiderable influence in exciting false alarms, and unjust suspicions to the prejudice of a number of individuals [first of whom was himself] every way worthy of public confidence, who have always faithfully supported the existing institutions of the country, and who would disdain to be concerned in an intrigue with any foreign power, or its agents, either for introducing monarchy, or for promoting or upholding any other scheme of government within the United States." His letter to Clinton had a cadence that might be heard in a funeral oration or an epitaph. But at the moment, here in the courtroom, Hamilton was locked in forensic combat with Ambrose Spencer and George Caines to save Harry Croswell and the freedom of the people, the free press, and the rights of juries from suppression by Thomas Jefferson. Hamilton paraphrased a counterargument of Ambrose Spencer, which was to the effect that, "as no man rises at once into high office, every opportunity of canvassing his qualities and qualifications is afforded, without recourse to the press; his first election ought to stamp the seal of merit on his name." But the reverse is just as often true, said Hamilton. "The hypocrite goes from stage to stage of public fame, under false array"—and "how often when men obtain the last object of their wishes, they changed from that which they seemed to be. That, men the most zealous reverers of the people's rights, have, when placed on the highest seat of power, become their most deadly oppressors." The greatest danger comes not from "a few provisional armies, [a manifest shaft at his own quasi-war critics] but from dependent Judges—from selected Juries, from stifling the Press & the voice of leaders & Patriots. We ought to resist—resist—resist til we hurl the demagogues & Tyrants from their imagined Thrones."

There was a final point, as Judge Kent wrote: Hamilton "was as strenuous for the qualification of the rule allowing the truth" as a defense, "as he was for the rule itself."

But is not such a qualification a prior restraint? Should not the press be free to print anything at all?

No, said Hamilton. As Kent explained it, "While he regarded the liberty of the press as essential to free government, he considered that a press wholly unchecked, with a right to publish anything at pleasure, regardless of truth or decency, would be, in the hands of unprincipled men, a terrible engine of mischief, and would be liable to be diverted to the most seditious and wicked purposes, and for the gratification of private malice or revenge."

For example, a rich man like Jefferson could pay a Callender to call a Washington "a traitor, a robber and a perjurer," as Croswell and the *Evening Post* had reported. Being in power, such a man could destroy a newspaper that dared expose the ultimate truth: that it was he who was paying the press to publish false stories. "Such a free press," said Kent, free of all limitation on selling itself out to publish whatever the highest bidder demanded, "would destroy public and private confidence, and would overawe and corrupt the impartial administration of justice."

If a free press were the most vital underwriter of free constitutional government, then as a corollary a bought press paid off by the ruler was the most deadly threat to such a form of government. "It ought to be distinctly known," Hamilton thundered, "whether Mr. Jefferson be guilty or not of so foul an act as the one charged." Such falsehoods, eternally repeated, would have affected even Washington's good name. "Drops of water, in long and continued succession, will wear out adamant." Kent thought Hamilton's eulogy of Washington at this point was "never surpassed—never equalled."

As Hamilton concluded his long argument on the third day of the trial, Kent remembered that he displayed "an unusual solemnity and earnestness . . . at times highly impassioned and pathetic. His whole soul was enlisted in the cause.

He entered by the force of sympathy into the glorious struggles of the English patriots during oppressive and unconstitutional times. In contending for the rights of the jury and the free press, he considered that he was establishing the finest refuge against oppression."

He closed with a noble warning: "Never can tyranny be introduced into this country by arms; these can never get rid of a popular spirit of enquiry; the only way to crush it down is by a servile tribunal. It is only by the abuse of the forms of justice that we can be enslaved. An army can never do it. For ages it can never be attempted." No, "it is not thus that the liberty of this country is to be destroyed. It is to be subverted only by a pretence of adhering to all the forms of law, and yet by breaking down the substance of our liberties. By devoting a wretched but honest man as the victim of a nominal trial."

Appellant Harry Croswell's counsel rested his case. Judge Kent summarized Hamilton's performance by saying that "he was persuaded that if he should be able to overthrow the hightoned doctrine" contained in Lewis's charge, "it would be great gain to the liberties of his country."

After Hamilton's death, Ambrose Spencer wrote, "I was in situations often to observe and study him. I saw him at the bar and at home. He argued cases before me while I sat as judge on the Bench. Webster has done the same. In power of reasoning, Hamilton was the equal of Webster; and more than this can be said of no man. In creative power Hamilton was infinitely Webster's superior."

Certainly, in defending Croswell, Hamilton had atoned for the part he had played four years earlier in the prosecution of David Frothingham and the *Argus*.

Hamilton exchanged whispers with Croswell and his fellow counsel, picked up his notes and briefs from the counsel table, and moved out of the courtroom through the handshakes and backslaps and salutations from admirers in the crowd, including many a Schuyler and Van Rensselaer. It is tempting to speculate that two disgruntled Albany Democrats, recalling the *Argus* case and the rest of Hamilton's strange career and knowing he would receive no fee from Croswell, may have had a conversation in the corridor or on the courthouse steps, like the two poor citizens in the Roman street who were talking about Coriolanus:

SECOND CITIZEN: Consider you what services he has done for his country?

FIRST CITIZEN: He pays himself with being proud.

SECOND CITIZEN: Nay, but speak not maliciously.

FIRST CITIZEN: I say unto you, what he hath done he hath done famously, he did it to that end. Though soft conscienc'd men can be content to say he did it for his country, he did it to please his mother, and to be partly proud; which he is, even to the altitude of his virtue.

SECOND CITIZEN: What he cannot help in his nature, you account a vice in him. You must in no way say he is covetous."

Hamilton failed to win the appeal. But it was more than three months until the decision day when he would learn of his loss, and then he had little more than a month still left to live.

Nothing he said had changed the final vote of a single judge. But before the final decision was handed down the last day of the May term, Hamilton and Croswell had received false hope that Brockholst Livingston had indeed swung his vote in their favor. One day shortly before issuing the final decision, when Kent, Thompson, and Livingston were in the courtroom, but Chief Justice Lewis was absent, Livingston told Kent and Thompson that he agreed with them on a new trial on the ground of the rights of the jury. Croswell was told he was released on $500 bond, to appear at the next Columbia Circuit, the indicated time and place for the new trial he sought. But thereafter, said Kent, before the final tally, Livingston switched back and "to my surprize" said that Lewis's opinion "satisfied him." Then "on the last day of the Term when the court's opinion was to be released, Livingston did not attend & wrote a line that he was sick."

Kent's tone was of strong disapproval. He implied that Livingston had vacillated and swung back to Lewis's side under heavy pressure. Kent was shocked that Livingston "wrote no opinion, nor ever asked to see mine, nor did he see it, tho I produced it or offered it for perusal" and the other judges read at least parts of it. Although the "prosecutor was entitled to move for judgment" against Croswell, said Kent pointedly, "no such Motion was however made." Croswell remained at large and unpunished the same as if he had won. Ambrose Spencer took his place on the bench in the judgeship with which he had been rewarded after the first trial. Jefferson duly rewarded Brockholst Livingston for remembering which side he was on with an appointment to the United States Supreme Court.

Clinton rewarded Chief Justice Morgan Lewis for his unwavering adherence to the party line in the face of all Hamilton's eloquence by nominating him to replace Lansing as the party's regular candidate to run against Aaron Burr for governor in the April elections.

Aroused public sympathy for Croswell and Hamilton's side helped push through the legislature the bill to correct the outworn dictum that the truth could not be introduced as a defense to a charge of libel. It became law in 1805, after which the court unanimously awarded Croswell a new trial.

Such a new trial would now necessarily bring on testimony about the money Jefferson had paid to the late Mr. Callender and others to encourage them to libel Federalists. Croswell was troubled no more. Jefferson never instigated another such prosecution. In memory of Harry Croswell and Hamilton, Article 7, Section 8 of the New York State Constitution adopted in 1821 provided that "every citizen may freely speak, write, and publish his sentiments on all subjects, being responsible for the abuse of that right; and no law shall be passed to abridge or restrain the liberty of speech, or of the press." It continued that "in all criminal prosecutions or indictments for libels, the truth may be given in evidence to the jury; . . . and the jury shall have the right to determine the law and the fact."

Other states adopted similar constitutional provisions and laws. Hamilton's position became the settled law of libel in the United States. His defense of the obscure "village printer" became part of the long struggle of English-speaking peoples for freedom of expression. "If his right [of criticizing those in office] was not permitted to exist in vigor and exercise," Hamilton held, "good men would become silent, corruption and tyranny would go on, step by step to usurpation, until, at last, nothing that was worth speaking, or writing, or acting for, would be left in our country."

Emboldened by Hamilton's eloquence and his apparent victory, and given license by his newly refurbished image as a popular public figure, Albany newspapers had no qualms about publishing an intercepted private letter of Dr. Charles D. Cooper, written April 23, 1804, to Philip Schuyler. The published story paraphrased a few words Hamilton and Kent had exchanged at a private dinner. This new won freedom of the press soon brought upon Hamilton the final challenge from Aaron Burr.

30

DR. COOPER HEARD
SOMETHING DESPICABLE

I COULD DETAIL TO YOU A STILL MORE DESPICABLE OPINION WHICH
GENERAL HAMILTON HAD EXPRESSED OF MR. BURR.
—*Dr. Charles D. Cooper to Philip Schuyler, April
23, 1804*

According to Professor Clinton Rossiter, it was during the previous summer of 1803, when Hamilton, out of the public eye, was preoccupied with his private law practice, making inquiries behind the scenes preparing to take Callender's testimony for Croswell's defense or simply enjoying family life at The Grange, "that Hamilton's career as a constitutionalist reached its zenith in two events in which he played no active part."

One of these was Chief Justice John Marshall's assertion in *Marbury v. Madison* (1 Cranch 168) of the doctrine of judicial review of acts of Congress. In that landmark case, Marshall found that a congressional grant of authority to his court to issue a mandamus directing the executive to deliver a commission to William Marbury as justice of the peace was an unconstitutional legislative action. At the very end of his opinion, the chief justice announced "that a law repugnant to the constitution is void, and that courts, as well as other departments, are bound by that instrument." It was Hamilton who provided Marshall with the clearest precedents he had for this sweeping assertion. In *Rutgers v. Waddington* in 1784, he had argued that a court had the power to set aside an act of a legislature if it conflicted with a higher law under which both court and legislature were supposed to function. Again in 1788, as *Publius* in *The Federalist* No. 78, Hamilton had announced to the American public for the first time that under the Constitution it would be the duty "of courts to exercise the almost unprecedented power" to declare all acts contrary to the manifest tenor of the Constitution void. "Without this," averred Hamilton, "all the reservations of particular rights or privileges would amount to nothing." His reasoning in *The Federalist* No. 78 was subtle, but strong enough to support the vast superstructure of judicial exegesis constructed upon it by Marshall and decisions of the Supreme Court ever since.

The doctrine of judicial review also involved the creation of vast power in the courts. "Though individual oppression may now and then proceed from courts of justice," particularly if they were being used by presidents for persecutions of the likes of Croswell, "the general liberty of the people can never be endangered from that quarter" alone, as it might be by the president or Congress. Hamilton went on to explain that "the power of the people is superior to both" judicial and legislative power. "Where the will of the legislature declared in its statutes, stands in opposition to that of the people, declared in the constitution, the judges ought to be governed by the latter, rather than the former." Other antecedents and precedents for the doctrine of judicial review as John Marshall announced it in *Marbury v. Madison* were few.

Hamilton had once declined appointment to be Chief Justice; so it was a stunning triumph for him that in *Marbury v. Madison* his Virginia Federalist colleague had announced without citation that the precedential authority he had created in *Rutgers v. Waddington* and *The Federalist* No. 78 were now the supreme constitutional law of the land.

The second event of 1803 that marked Hamilton's zenith as a constitutionalist was the Louisiana Purchase. In approving the purchase of the Louisiana Territory from France for $15 million without proposing an amendment to the Constitution, Hamilton's archenemy Thomas Jefferson, the most adamant of strict constructionists, was forced to stretch the letter and spirit of the Constitution almost to the breaking point to find more implied powers in it than Hamilton had ever claimed existed and to give to the Constitution the last great Hamiltonian gloss that Hamilton would see in his lifetime.

Hamilton had always encouraged the westward growth of the nation. He had reminded Charles Cotesworth Pinckney on December 29, 1802, that he "always held that the *unity of our empire* and the best interests of our nation require that we shall annex to the United States all territory east of the Mississippi, New Orleans included." If, as he believed, Jefferson also sought to gain possession of the region, his "pretty scheme of substituting economy to taxation will not do here." Hamilton had stressed the importance of the region in his first pamphlet, his 1774 reply to the *Westchester Farmer* in *A Full Vindication*, during both his terms in the Continental Congress; in *The Federalist* No. 11 of

1787; and again and again in advice and counsel to Washington and Adams, as well as in his contingency military planning with Rufus King, Miranda, and Wilkinson. Jefferson had not expected success in the Paris negotiations. As *Pericles* in the *Evening Post*, Hamilton had written with unusual obtuseness that "the attempt to purchase will certainly fail." So when Robert R. Livingston and James Monroe reported back from the negotiations with Napoleon Bonaparte and Talleyrand in Paris that they had bought the whole thing, Hamilton was as surprised as Jefferson. But he did not suffer from the same strict constructionist embarrassments, Jefferson did. Jefferson wrote to his attorney general, Levi Lincoln, on August 30, 1803, "the less that is said about any constitutional difficulty, the better . . . it will be desirable for Congress to do what is necessary, *in silence.*"

In the teeth of the general public's holiday rejoicing over the accession that more than doubled the land area of the United States, Hamilton's *Evening Post* of July 5 could only grumble anti-Jefferson disgruntlement at seeing him get all the credit. The acquisition was only "owing to a fortuitous occurrence" and not to any "wise measures." James Monroe, who ranked with Burr as Hamilton's secret archenemy number one, deserved no credit at all, according to the *Post*, because he had not even arrived in France until after Napoleon had decided to sell. Jefferson, privately assuming his own action to be unconstitutional, yet appealing to Congress and the nation to support it without any constitutional authority except possibly under some vaguely defined imperial powers of the president, in his way of handling the purchase probably did greater disservice to the cause of limited constitutional government than anything Hamilton had ever suggested or done.

Although he criticized the way the deal had been handled and presented to the country, Hamilton approved the fact and the necessity of the purchase. Nothing did more than his stand on this to estrange Hamilton further from his fellow Federalists and to drive them toward the inviting candidacy of Aaron Burr in New York's gubernatorial election of 1804. Hamilton still believed, as he had written in 1787 in *The Federalist* No. 11, that "the importance of the Union, in a commercial light, is one of those points about which there is the least room to entertain a difference of opinion." But now among many New England Federalists to whom Hamilton had been closest in political thought for all their active careers smoldered all but irreconcilable differences that belied *Publius'* confident assumption that unity was inevitable and forever. They were for a separation from the rest of the nation. Jefferson's remarkable popularity, enhanced by the acquisition of Louisiana, contributed much to the feelings of impotent ire of men like Hamilton's old friend, former Secretary of State Timothy Pickering, as he wrote to their mutual friend Rufus King on March 4, 1804: "The coward wretch at the head, while, like a Parisian revolutionary monster, prating about humanity, could feel an infernal pleasure in the utter destruction of his opponents." Pickering had obviously been keeping up with all the latest anti-Jefferson scurrility published in the Federalist press. He railed, "We have too long witnessed his general turpitude—his cruel removals of faithful officers, and the substitution of corruption and basness for integrity and worth."

Now Louisiana threatened to enhance the ascendancy of the slave-owning South and West in the nation's government. Southern whites had the advantage of doing all the voting for their slaves, who still counted for purposes of representation as three fifths of one white. George Cabot called Jefferson's government "the government of the worst," writing to Pickering February 14, 1804. He was sympathetic, and so was John Adams, who likened it to a rake, full of fair promises, who had seduced a trustful maid. The prime movers in the unfolding 1804 plan for separating the Northern states from the Union included Roger Griswold and Uriah Tracy of Connecticut, Senators Samuel Hart and William Plumer of New Hampshire, and other influential men New York and New Jersey were expected to join it. Hamilton refused to go along or even to accommodate his friends by remaining silent or acting the part of an accommodating trimmer for them. Not so Aaron Burr. He was the key to the plot, as Pickering wrote King, because he could break the "Democratic phalanx" in New York. He remained the early favorite to beat Lansing in the New York election of April 1804.

Pickering wrote, "Were New York detached (as under his [Burr's] administration it would be) from the Virginia influence, the whole union would be benefited. Jefferson would then be forced to observe some caution and forbearance in his measures." This would be but the minimum benefit from backing Burr. The maximum would be a separation, splitting up the Union. "If a *separation* should be deemed proper, the five New England states, New York and New Jersey would naturally be united." This was a federation that would make a viable new nation. "Among those seven states there is a sufficient congeniality of character to authorize the expectation of practicable harmony and a permanent union; New York the centre." There would be great future benefits. "Without a separation, can those states ever rid themselves of negro presidents and negro congresses, and regain their just weight in the political balance . . . ?"

The idea of Burr's becoming governor of New York, beholden for the votes that tipped the election his way to Federalists like Pickering who would demand that he lead a split-up of the Union, was too much for Hamilton to bear. For years Hamilton had circulated damning, damaging opinions of Burr among his friends in private correspondence, while maintaining a facade of affability toward him in public. Typical was the characterization he had written to Bayard when urging him to support Jefferson over Burr; it made Burr out to be a despicable character.

"Very, very confidential," Hamilton had written. "Burr is inferior in real ability to Jefferson." But more important, "he has blamed me for not having improved the situation I once was in to change the government. When [I] answered that this could not have been done without guilt, he replied 'Les grandes âmes se soucient peu des petits moraux.' When told the thing was never practicable from the genius and situation of the country, he answered, 'That depends on the estimate we form of the human passions, and of the means of influencing them.' "

Then Hamilton had understood Burr to be making a traitorous proposal of the kind that Pickering now was urging on him. Despite Hamilton's "very, very confidential" cautions to his correspondents, the fact that for years Hamilton had been circulating such stories about him among their friends and acquaintances would be well known to Burr, who reputedly had the best intelligence-gathering apparatus of any public figure except Jefferson himself.

Both Burr and Hamilton were successful lawyers, soldiers, lovers, family men, and politicians. Both were handsome, charming, quick-witted, brilliant, and ambitious. For 15 years and more, each had always seemed to stand athwart the path of the other's ambition. They were superficially alike, yet essentially very different, and so men perceived them. Burr's watchword, "Great souls concern themselves little with petty morals," offers a key to the difference. Unlike Burr, Hamilton seemed to follow a lodestar somewhere out beyond the obvious course toward his own public advancement. This lodestar was the Union of the states under the Constitution, the emancipation of slaves, the rights of the people, public credit, and liberty under law.

To these he was willing to sacrifice the interests of his family; all other private, public, and political concerns; his health, comfort, energy, personal safety, economic security, and a son and a daughter. What seemed to be monumental errors of discretion and judgment during his two years of crisis around 1800 had not destroyed the regard in which most other discerning men of his time held him or impaired the intense affection, admiration, and love his friends felt for him or the respect and awe his enemies had for his abilities. With all his faults, Hamilton was and was seen by most who knew him as a man of integrity. Burr, for all his great intelligence, charm, wit, and grace, was not.

He seemed to be lacking a lodestar beyond the ambit of his own ambition. Hamilton shared the general opinion of Burr. He illustrated it by an anecdote. During the quasi-war period, it shocked Hamilton that Burr could casually accept without cavil all factions of the French Revolution, ranging from the imprisoners of Lafayette, America's staunchest friend in France, to the greatest imperialist tyrant of European history.

I dined with him lately, recalled Hamilton. On different occasions, his toasts were: "The French Republic," "The Commissioners who Negotiated the Convention," "Buonaparte," and "The Marquis La Fayette." If his only lodestar in politics were ambition inside him, he was a danger to the country. Hamilton noted that Burr had believed it would be to the interest of the country to permit the indiscriminate sale of prizes by the belligerent powers and also the domestic building and equipment of vessels. To Hamilton this was a course amounting to turning all naval resources into the channel of France and forcing Great Britain into war: "Indeed, *Mr. Burr must have war*, as the instrument of his ambition and cupidity."

Pickering and others of the New England separatists had sounded out Burr, and though Burr's answers were equivocal, they read into his evasions, from their own knowledge of his politically chimerical character, a later acquiescence. They determined they would support him in his fight for the governorship of

New York, even over Hamilton's opposition. Burr's election to the governorship would provide a rallying point for all New England, New York, and New Jersey separatists who felt as Pickering did. The cumulative and reflexive influence of such a success might easily propel Burr, supported by Pickering and their followers, far toward the office of chief executive of a separate northern American confederacy. The threat seemed more real and painful to Hamilton than it did to anyone who did not know Burr as well as he did.

In the days immediately following the close of Croswell's trial on February 15, 1804, New York's chronic political chaos turned more acute and came to a focus in Albany. When John Lansing, Jr., suddenly and inexplicably withdrew as the Democratic candidate for governor, some said it was because Burr appeared to be unbeatable. The rival political factions scheduled caucuses in rapid succession: on February 20 Clinton's regular Democratic organization, consisting of party members of the legislature and other delegates, would meet; on February 18 Democrats and Federalists who backed Aaron Burr would convene; and on February 16 Hamilton and the Federalist party regulars would meet. With Lansing out of the running, Vice-president Burr's chances of winning the regular Democratic nomination at the February 20 caucus looked strong. Because the Federalists had no candidate of their own, his chances of winning major Federalist support on February 16 were better than anyone else's. In a typical mélange of political metaphor, it was predictable that from the sixteenth through the twentieth politicians from all parties jumping on the Burr bandwagon might be expected to snowball his candidacy into an unbeatable juggernaut.

Only Hamilton on the sixteenth stood in his way, all but alone. He had a prepared address giving his "Reasons why it is Desirable that Mr. Lansing rather than Col. Burr should succeed." Most experienced campaigners have an all-purpose set speech in which they change only the name of the town and friendly local leader in the opening compliments as they move from point to point in space and time. Even with Lansing out of the race, Hamilton's address would work as well against any other Democrat because it consisted mostly of an all-out attack on Burr, with hardly a word about Lansing.

Although proceedings at the Federalist caucus at Lewis's City Tavern on the sixteenth were supposed to be secret, Burr's political espionage system, in good working order as usual, posted two of his agents in a bedroom adjoining the dining chamber and noted down all the speeches. Dr. Charles D. Cooper said "General Hamilton's harangue at the city-tavern" against Burr that night was delivered with much of the same passion and fire that Kent had noted in Hamilton's argument for Croswell and freedom of the press in court the day before. The *Morning Chronicle* published a report of the proceedings within a few days.

"The Federalists are prostrate, and their enemies are predominant," Hamilton announced to the old guard of the faithful. "Burr has steadily pursued the track of democratic politics . . . either from *principle* or from *calculation*." Either way, he "will certainly not at this time relinquish the ladder of his ambition, and espouse the cause or views of the weaker party." In New England, "the only part of our country which still remains sound," the very issues that make the Federalists strong—the ill opinion of Jefferson and jealousy of the ambition of Virginia—"are leading to an opinion, that a dismemberment of the Union is expedient." Burr would promote this result "to be chief of the Northern portion. Placed at the head of the state of New York, no man would be more likely to succeed."

Burr would be dangerously seductive to New Englanders "as their country-man, as the grandson of President [Jonathan] Edwards and the son of President Burr" of Princeton. Burr, although "detested by some Clintonians," was a man of "talents, intrigue and address . . . a man of irregular and insatiable ambition . . . Jacobinic principles . . . ," given to "usurpation," a "despotic chief . . . whose temper would permit him to bottom his aggrandizement on popular prejudices and vices." This was the speech Hamilton had written out beforehand. Among sympathetic Federalist friends and admirers like Philip Schuyler, with fulfilled stomachs and rapidly emptying tankards in the warm firelight of a comfortable tavern on a wintry night in Albany, it would not be surprising if the ambience had led Hamilton to embellish his written text with much harsher animadversions on Burr drawn from their 15 years of competition. They would portray Burr as a man still more despicable than the Catiline-like monster of the prepared text.

The Federalists must not support Burr. They should back Lansing or, indeed, whoever Clinton's candidate might be. Here for the first time in his life Hamilton was affirmatively backing the Democratic candidate. Hamilton was switching political sides, a thing he had anathematized John Adams and Burr for doing or seeming to do, something he himself had never done before in his life. For men who all their lives have prided themselves upon acting only from motives of honor, not personal animosity—men like Othello or Brutus or Coriolanus—such a switch well along in a notable life usually has fateful consequences. A search of the written text of Hamilton's address for a single prime motivation for his momentous switch produces only a tripartite, exquisitely balanced ambiguity: it was to preserve the Union; it was to save the Federal party; it was because of personal animosity toward Burr.

Writing to Robert Goodloe Harper, Hamilton narrowed the dilemma to two horns, eliminating survival of the Federal party as the third: "he will be the most dangerous chief that Jacobinism can have; . . . he will reunite under him the popular party and give it new force for personal purposes—a dismemberment of the Union is likely to be one of the first fruits of his elevation, and the overthrow of good principles, in our only sound quarter, the North, a result not very remote. I had rather see Lansing Governor and the party broken to pieces." Here Hamilton literally "was joining hands with his own bitterest enemies to complete the ring" around Burr, in Henry Adams's phrase.

Joining hands in politics with enemies does not convert them to friends. It assuredly makes new enemies among former friends left behind. A strong group of Democrats and anti-Hamilton Federalists cheered Burr to the rafters and the

Federalist nomination at his caucus on the eighteenth two days later. Clinton rewarded Chief Justice Morgan Lewis for steadfastly blocking Hamilton's efforts to let the Croswell jury hear anything discreditable to Jefferson by putting forward his name as the regular Democratic candidate. He was duly nominated by the well-bossed Democratic caucus on the twentieth. On the twenty-fourth, Hamilton, gloomier than ever about the political outlook, wrote in desperation to his friend Rufus King in London, suggesting that King return home to stand as a true Federalist candidate because Burr was now favored to win. "The Federalists," Hamilton wrote, "very extensively had embarked with zeal in the support of Mr. Burr." King was Hamilton's only hope because only he had "been absent during the time in which party animosities have become matured and fixed."

But his old friend King refused to let Hamilton use him as his throwaway candidate. "Other Federalists," King replied tactfully, the "lower Classes of Life particularly," had made up their minds "to give [Burr] active support." In fact, one leading Federalist declared that "from what I can learn of the sentiments of the People here I do really believe that tho' the Leaders of our Party determine upon Neutrality yet that at least two thirds of the Federalists in this city will vote for Burr."

Still another blow for Hamilton was the defection of the New York *Evening Post.* William Coleman declared editorially on March 23 that Hamilton "will take no part in support of either of the present candidates." It was an open secret that Hamilton was working behind the scenes against Burr and for Lewis, but Coleman himself showed decided leanings toward Burr. Toward the end of the campaign he all but endorsed Burr's election.

In the spring campaign between Burr and Morgan Lewis leading up to the election on April 25, Burr started as the front-runner and so was on the receiving end of most of the journalistic mudslinging. Cheetham charged that "your jealousy of General Hamilton afterward ripened into implacable hatred." In 1800, Burr had negotiated with Federalists, using David A. Ogden as his go-between, to sell out his party for the presidency. "You have always been the same intriguer—the same selfish mortal—the same aspiring genius."

Van Ness defended Burr all along the line. He cited Burr's explicit denial that he had "proposed or agreed to any terms with the federal party" in hopes of overtopping Jefferson in the election of 1800. While praising Burr, Van Ness as *Aristides* missed no opportunity for flank attacks on Jefferson as an unfortunate disappointment in high office.

When angry President Jefferson announced that the "little band" of Republicans who had defected to Vice-president Burr were discountenanced by the national administration, Lewis Republicans took this cue from their demigod to leave no congenial mud unslung in his direction.

The writer of one handbill was revolted "at the terrible situation in which we should be placed, should this Unprincipled Man [in capitals] succeed in his wicked purposes." Practiced in "vile plots," Burr was "dishonest and fraudulent." Another called him "a man destitute of moral virtue, and bent solely on the gratification of his passions, regardless of the public good." Another warned the electors of New York, "if you . . . love the fair name of your country, guard her from the fangs of such an unprincipled being—such a hydra in human form." Burr was also charged with embezzling money from a trust fund to pay off a personal note.

As a regular Federalist and party leader, Hamilton took no public position against the nominal Federalist ticket's standard-bearer, Burr. But in private conversations he showed no similar restraint. He went on saying many of the same things he had been repeating privately about Burr for years. During a campaign as close and tense as this one, such attacks might help swing a few critical votes.

One night in Albany at a dinner party at Judge John Tayler's house, not long after Croswell's trial, one of the guests had been Dr. Charles D. Cooper, Judge Tayler's son-in-law. He listened in fascination while Hamilton and Judge Kent and others were saying some devastating things about Aaron Burr that Cooper hardly knew how to characterize. No one knows exactly what Hamilton or the others actually said, but the following are typical of what he often privately said and wrote about Burr and may have been repeating that night:

> Be assured, my dear sir, that this man has no principle, public nor private. . . . his sole spring of action is an inordinate ambition as an individual, he is believed by friends as well as foes to be without probity; and a voluptuary by system—with habits of expense that can be satisfied by no fair expedients. . . . Daring and energy must be allowed him; but these qualities, under the direction of the worst passions, are certainly strong objections, not recommendations. He is of a temper to undertake the most hazardous enterprises, because he is sanguine enough to think nothing impracticable; and of an ambition that will be content with nothing less than permanent power in his own hands. The maintenance of the existing institutions will not suit him; because under them his power will be too narrow and too precarious. Yet the innovations he may attempt will not offer the substitute of a system durable and safe. It will be the system of the day, sufficient to serve his own turn, and not looking beyond himself. To execute this plan, as the good men of the country cannot be relied upon, the worst will be used. Let it not be imagined that the difficulties of execution will deter, or a calculation like ours, too much is practicable to men who will, without scruple, avail themselves of the bad passions of human nature.

The constitutional form of government is peculiarly vulnerable to a man like Burr, Hamilton believed. "To a man of this description, possessing the requisite talents, the acquisition of permanent power is not a chimera. I know that Mr. Burr does not view it as such, and I am sure there are no means too atrocious to be employed by him. In debt, vastly beyond his means of payment, with all the habits of excessive expense, he cannot be satisfied with the regular emoluments of any office of our government. Corrupt expedients will be to him a necessary resource. . . . No engagement that can be made with him can be depended upon; while making it, he will laugh in his sleeve at the credulity of those with whom he makes it;—and the first moment it suits his views to break it he will do so." And so on. And more.

More than a month after Judge Tayler's dinner party, Hamilton's and Kent's conversation was still on Dr. Cooper's mind when he wrote a letter to Andrew Brown of Bern, New York, on April 12, 1804, enclosing some anti-Burr election circulars. Dr. Cooper also passed along some inside information that would be valuable to lesser Federalists still willing to be led. "Gen. Hamilton . . . has come out decidedly against Burr; indeed when he was here he spoke of him as a dangerous man and ought not to be trusted." Dr. Cooper indicated that Judge Kent, John Barker Church, Stephen Van Rensselaer, and Nathanael Pendleton all felt the same way. Cooper's letter, full of political dynamite if it fell into the wrong hands, fell into them. It was "embezzled and broken" open, published in the *Albany Register*, and reprinted in other newspapers and pamphlets, just in time for maximum impact on the outcome of the election.

After a weekend visit at The Grange on April 21 and 22, Judge Kent wrote to his wife on April 26 that with the election nearly over, "the Burrites are sanguine and appear flushed with the laurels of victory. They claim a decided majority in this city." They had gotten out the Federalist vote. "The cold reserve and indignant reproaches of Hamilton may have controlled a few, but they are few." Even Hamilton's close friend Judge Egbert Benson, said Kent, "has yielded to the current, and with the generous fidelity of party spirit has declared he will go with his party, and has voted for the Burr ticket throughout."

Almost 30 years later, reminiscing to Hamilton's widow about this last visit, Kent recalled that his host's "mind had a cast usually melancholy." Among other things, "the impending election exceedingly disturbed him. He viewed the temper, disposition, and passions of the times as portentous of evil and to the sway of artful and ambitious demagogues."

Without Kent's necessarily even having to murmur a single injudicious word on the still secret subject, the inkling that the decision in Croswell's case would soon be handed down and go against him must have added to Hamilton's deep gloom.

So did "a furious and dreadful storm" that struck Saturday night. The Grange stands high, and Kent recalled that it "was very much exposed to the fury of the winds as they swept over the island from the 'vex'd Atlantic.' It blew almost a hurricane." On the second story of The Grange, "where I slept," averred the judge, "it rocked like a cradle." Hamilton's solicitude for his comfort, "his attention and kindness quite affected me." After Kent retired to his chamber, "he visited me to see that I was sufficiently attended to. He treated me with a minute affection that I did not suppose he knew how to bestow."

On Sunday, Gouverneur Morris was to have dined with them, but he was detained by the storm. He sent an apology saying that "the Jacobin winds" had kept him at home. "We were consequently left to ourselves during the greater part" of the day, Kent said, and "the conversation led to a more serious train of reflections on his part than I had ever before known him to indulge." Hamilton revealed to Kent that day "a plan he had in contemplation, for a full investigation of the history and science of civil government, and the practical results of the various modifications of it upon the freedom and happiness of mankind." Hamilton believed "from profound reflection and from the uniform language of history, that all plans of government founded on any new and extraordinary reform in the morals of mankind were plainly utopian."

What Hamilton desired for the people, Kent explained, was for them "to enjoy as much political liberty as they were competent to use and not abuse,— as much as was consistent with the perfect security of life and social rights, and the enjoyment and acquisition of property." He wished to have the subject "treated in reference to past experience, and upon the principles of Lord Bacon's inductive philosophy." There was to be a historical examination of various different human institutions, with a volume each assigned for production to Morris, Jay, Harison, Rufus King, Reverend Mason (ecclesiastical history, of course), and Kent.

"The conclusions to be drawn from these historical reviews, he intended to reserve for his own task, and this is the imperfect outline of the scheme which then occupied his thoughts." Kent concluded wistfully, "I heard no more of it afterwards," for "after the May term of that year I saw him no more."

On this last visit, Kent recalled, Hamilton had "never appeared before so friendly and amiable." No longer the once formidable "Little Mars," now "his manners were delicate and chaste, and he appeared, in his domestic state, the plain modest and affectionate father and husband."

Writing his wife, Kent tactfully remarked that the Hamiltons' daughter Angelica, 19 years old, "has a very uncommon simplicity." He, of course, omitted any mention of her insane condition when writing a thank-you note to her mother.

When Gouverneur Morris finally made his delayed visit to The Grange in May, a children's party that Hamilton had arranged for Angelica was in progress. It must have struck Morris as rather a forlorn one. Writing as if Angelica were as absent from it as a vegetable, he chillingly described it as "a Fete given to his daughter's acquaintances."

Only the week before Kent's visit, on April 13, Hamilton had responded to an unhappy friend who was looking for a job with some brutally fatalistic advice. It recalled Cassius' advice to Brutus from the same act 1, scene 2 of *Julius Caesar* that seemed to keep soliloquizing through his mind:

"Arraign not the dispensations of Providence," Hamilton wrote, "they must be founded in wisdom and goodness; and when they do not suit us, it must be because there is some fault in ourselves which deserves chastisement; or because there is a kind intent, to correct in us some vice or failing, of which, perhaps, we may not be conscious; or because the general plan requires that we should suffer partial ill."

Cassius put the general idea more concisely:

CASSIUS: The fault, dear Brutus, is not in our stars, But in ourselves,
    that we are underlings.

But Cassius knew of an easier way out for Brutus: kill Caesar.

Hamilton could think of nothing so easy. "In this situation it is our duty to
cultivate resignation, and even humility, bearing in mind, in the language of the
poet, 'That it is pride which lost the blest abodes.' "

The ring he had closed around Burr was a trap for Hamilton, too. Pride, and
honor, of course, were bone, marrow, and nerve organic to his being alive.

To his son James A. Hamilton, just turning 16 on April 14, Hamilton wrote:

My dear James: I have prepared for you a Thesis on Discretion. You
may need it.

                                                        Your affectionate father.

Dr. Cooper's letter to Andrew Brown might have passed unnoticed in the
euphoria of a Burr election victory. But Burr unexpectedly lost. The letter
probably contributed its mite to the margin of defeat in an election he had strong
hopes of winning as late as election day. As is often the case in New York
elections, Burr's narrow margin in the city failed to overcome the late upstate
returns. Morgan Lewis won in a sweep there and statewide by 30,829 to Burr's
22,139.

Writing to his daughter, Theodosia, on April 25, a stormy election day, Burr
wrote of "an election storm . . . the thing began yesterday and will terminate
tomorrow . . . A. B. will have a small majority *if tomorrow should be a fair day,*
and not else." Afterward he compressed his reaction to his landslide loss into one
jauntily bitter line of a long letter. "The election is lost by a great majority: *faut
mieux.*"

Even after such a crushing last hurrah, Burr might have let Dr. Cooper's
first letter, the one to Andrew Brown, pass without making an issue of it if Philip
Schuyler had not tried to over protect Hamilton from the adverse consequences
of its unauthorized disclosure and publication. He attempted a small, clumsy
cover-up by contradicting Dr. Cooper. He wrote Dr. Samuel Stringer, chairman
of the Federal Republican Committee, on April 21, denying what Cooper said had
been said at Judge Tayler's about Burr by Hamilton, Kent, and Van Rensselaer.
Published in the *Albany Register* on April 21, too late to change the election
outcome, Schuyler's letter would set the record straight and protect the prominent men whose conversation at a private dinner had been embarrassingly—and
mysteriously—exposed by theft and publication of Cooper's letter. In professional party politics, as under the code duello, remarks made in private conversations are supposed to be privileged, not properly the subject of such public
attention and challenges.

Having been, in effect, called a liar by Schuyler's letter, which came to him
"annexed . . . to an anonymous handbill," Dr. Cooper, in anger, had no choice
but to rise to defend his honor. He wrote a second letter, this one to Schuyler,

on April 23, 1804. What he had written in his first letter was "substantially true," he insisted. He could prove it "by the most unquestionable testimony." He repeated, "I assert, that General Hamilton and Judge Kent have declared . . . that they look upon Mr. Burr to be a dangerous man, and one who ought not to be trusted with the reins of government." Schuyler ought to know perfectly well that it was not Cooper who was lying. He went on. Hamilton had said much the same thing in his harangue to the Federalist caucus at the city tavern. If Schuyler had been there when "General Hamilton made a speech on the pending election, I might appeal to you for the truth of so much of this assertion as relates to him." That was still not all. There was more, Dr. Cooper insisted. "For really sir, I could detail to you a still more despicable opinion which General Hamilton has expressed of Mr. Burr." The *Albany Register* published this letter the very next day. Excerpts from the whole correspondence made the rounds of reprints in pamphlets and other newspapers. The embezzlement, breaking open, and publication of the first letter, which was intended for loyal Federalist eyes only, is reminiscent of the manner in which Burr's supporters had quickly obtained, circulated, and published copies of Hamilton's attack on John Adams and of his anti-Burr speech at the City Tavern caucus. The seeds of discord and disaster sown among prominent Federalists by such disclosure were no less destructive, but the true facts of *how* the leak occurred remain a mystery.

Schuyler and Hamilton were in-laws closer than most fathers are to most sons. In any event, another loving father figure had inadvertently, unwittingly consigned another beloved son with a keen sense of honor to yet another interview at Weehawken.

31

THE DUEL

"TO THOSE, WHO WITH ABHORRING THE PRACTICE OF DUELLING
MAY THINK THAT I OUGHT ON NO ACCOUNT TO HAVE ADDED TO THE
NUMBER OF BAD EXAMPLES, I ANSWER THAT MY *RELATIVE* SITUA-
TION, AS WELL IN PUBLIC AS PRIVATE APPEALS, INFORCING ALL
THE CONSIDERATIONS WHICH CONSTITUTE WHAT MEN OF THE
WORLD DENOMINATE HONOUR, IMPRESSED ON ME (AS I THOUGHT)
A PECULIAR NECESSITY NOT TO DECLINE THE CALL.
—*Document written June 28–July 11, 1804, left with
Nathaniel Pendleton, to be opened only in the
event of death in the duel*

In May of 1804, two months before The Grange became a memorial to its
builder, the Hamiltons gave a dinner there that was dazzling enough to make
Gouverneur Morris forget their forlorn little birthday party for Angelica's
friends. The guests of honor were Jerome Bonaparte, the youngest brother of
Napoleon, and the beautiful bride he had taken for love, heedless of dynastic
considerations, just five months earlier, the former Elizabeth Patterson of Baltimore. At their wedding on Christmas Eve, Aaron Burr had praised her as "just
the size and nearly the figure of Theodosia Burr Alston," and Burr could ap-
praise no one more highly than his only legitimate child. But the new princess
was "perhaps not so well in the shoulders." Still, he said, she "dresses with taste
and simplicity (by some thought too free)," though not by him. Jefferson's friend

Margaret Bayard Smith disagreed. Princess Elizabeth Bonaparte was not only "too free," but "mobs of boys have crowded about their splendid equipage to see what I hope will not often be seen in this country, an almost naked woman."

For a state dinner like this one, invitations and all details were handled by Hamilton himself, from his downtown law office, not by his Elizabeth. From there he wrote to her up at The Grange, "On Sunday Bonaparte and wife with the Judges will dine with you. We shall be 16 in number if Gouverneur Morris will come. Send him the enclosed note on horseback, this Evening, that James may bring me an answer in the morning. He is promised the little horse to return."

Wine poured from the Washingtons' wine cooler, and, no doubt, many a toast was raised in the Hamiltons' elegant cut glass goblets to young Bonaparte, his beautiful new American bride, hopes for Franco-American détente, and a future entente cordiale. Unfortunately, when Jerome returned with his prize to France and back under the imperial thumb, his brother, the emperor, refused to recognize the beautiful Baltimorean in the buff as his bride, remarried him off to Catherine of Wurthenberg for inscrutable reasons of state, and named him the king of Westphalia.

That spring of 1804 the Hamiltons' Grange went through its last and most brilliant social season. The host's pleasure in seeing his glamorous sister-in-law, Angelica Church, often in company there at her glittering best, obscured a little his and Elizabeth's grave concern at the unmentionable but increasingly apparent simpleness of their own Angelica that had not escaped the piercing eyes of earlier guests like James Kent and Gouverneur Morris. But the Hamiltons' traditional American style parties that began with an early breakfast already seemed a little too quaint for the tastes Aunt Angelica had brought back home with her from London. She wrote her son Philip on June 14, 1804:

> . . . Mrs. Hamilton is extremely gracious, for her Angelica gives a breakfast, a ball and a dinner on Tuesday next, to 70 persons; and! oh direful misfortune! they sent their cards but neglected to invite an engagé Contois, and as they are without a saelev [slave?] the Breakfast hour is fixed for nine o'clock, this is in the true good housewife stile, the company must wear their nightcaps to arrive in time.

Vice-president Aaron Burr was hastening home from presiding over the Senate in Washington to wage a stretch fight in his lagging campaign against Judge Morgan Lewis for the governorship of New York. As Burr and Charles Biddle traveled up from Washington together on the same shuttle coach, here was the secret Burr confided to his fellow passenger: "He was determined to call out the first man of any respectability concerned in the infamous publications concerning him."

Biddle "never knew Colonel Burr speak ill of any man"; so his whispered threat as the stage rumbled north "to call out the first man" carried a freight of predetermined hostility that made it impossible for Biddle to forget it, and he carefully jotted it down in his *Autobiography* (305). James Cheetham did not answer the description of a man of "respectability," and De Witt Clinton, the old governor's nephew, who had instigated Cheetham's latest anti-Burr pamphlet, was not "the first man." Burr's description best fitted the man whose "despicable" remarks about him, as reported by Dr. Charles D. Cooper, first published in the *Albany Register* and reprinted elsewhere, helped Burr lose the election in which he had begun as the favorite and clutched at victory as his last political straw.

On June 18, 1804, the day before the Hamilton party for Angelica, Burr sat down in his private study and wrote Hamilton a concise, laconic, deadly letter. He handed it to their mutual friend William P. Van Ness, who brought it to a preoccupied Hamilton. Van Ness stood waiting silently beside Hamilton as he read it and turned over in his mind the limited possibilities it left him for reply.

> SIR,
>
> I send for your perusal a letter signed Charles D. Cooper, which, though apparently published some time ago, has but very recently come to my knowledge. Mr. Van Ness, who does me the favour to deliver this, will point out to you that clause of the letter to which I particularly request your attention. You must perceive, sir, the necessity of a prompt and unqualified acknowledgement or denial of the use of any expressions which would warrant the assertions of Mr. Cooper. I have the honour to be
>
> Your obedient servant,
A. Burr

Hamilton stared at the letter and the enclosed newspaper clippings—reprints of Dr. Cooper's correspondence. Van Ness would have no need to point out the offensive sentence. Hamilton would already know it by heart from reading the newspapers. Van Ness waited with formal politeness and a solemn air while Hamilton canvassed in his mind the few possible replies to the challenge that his own words and Dr. Cooper's unauthorized disclosure had brought upon him. Hamilton chose his words to Van Ness with care. The matter required careful consideration. A reply would be sent shortly. Van Ness bowed out and departed.

Hamilton winced as he reread the letter Dr. Cooper had written to Philip Schuyler. Hamilton "looked upon Mr. Burr to be a dangerous man" and "one who ought not to be trusted with the reins of government." Cooper had added that "I could detail to you a still more despicable opinion which General Hamilton has expressed of Mr. Burr." No one knew better than Hamilton that the first two sentences were mild compared to the things subsumed by the third that he had been saying about Burr in private conversations and letters to friends for years. He had insulted Burr's family, impugned his honesty, and accused him of almost every imaginable crime from taking bribes to cowardice in the army. Neither

Hamilton nor his friends had any reason to doubt that Burr already knew much of what Hamilton had been saying about him. They had many mutual friends like Robert Troup who enjoyed frank exchanges of political gossip. Burr's letter was a foreseeable consequence.

As a man who prided himself on precision in the use of language, Hamilton found exasperating ambiguity in Cooper's use of the adjective *despicable*. It all came down to that one word—*despicable*. Who or what or whose opinion of whom was despicable? Who was the despiser? Who or what, the despisee? The clearest thing about the statement seemed to be Dr. Cooper's despicable syntax.

Burr had demanded "a prompt and unqualified acknowledgement or denial." An "acknowledgement" would bring on a prompt challenge to duel from Burr. A denial would brand Dr. Cooper a liar, which all their friends knew he was not. Too, it would be a dishonorable thing to do, and Cooper was not a man to let it pass, as Schuyler had learned. It would expose Hamilton to the charge of falsely repudiating a Federalist supporter because of personal cowardice; it would help kill such remaining influence as Hamilton might still possess in his party. Burr's words drove him into an impasse of honor and pride, leaving few escape routes, and Hamilton knew it.

All his adult life, Hamilton had on many occasions dealt with the deadly game of the code duello. He had had many close brushes with duels, but he had never issued or accepted a direct challenge. He had probably never actually fought a duel before in his life.

His brother-in-law John Barker Church had been involved in numerous duels, including one with Burr, and many exchanges looking toward duels. Church had furnished Philip Hamilton his handsome pair of marbled pistols for his duel with George Eacker. Hamilton himself had skillfully averted potentially dangerous challenges from Aedanus Burke and John Mercer and others. Acting as second for the dearest friend of his life, John Laurens, when Charles Lee had spoken disrespectfully of Washington after Monmouth, Hamilton had initiated peace overtures after the first exchange of shots. His epistolary exchanges with James Nicholson and James Monroe had reached the brink, but in each case Hamilton had demonstrated his knowledge of how, with adroitness, discretion, and time, to finesse the challenge without dishonor to either principal. He abhorred the idea of dueling all the more passionately since the horror of Philip's death less than three years earlier.

To Dr. William Gordon, Hamilton had written in 1779 that "we do not now live in the days of chivalry . . . The good sense of the present times has happily found out, that to prove your own innocence, or the malice of an accuser, the worst method you can take is to run him through the body or shoot him through the head." In composing a quarrel between William Pierce and John Auldjo, he remarked, "I can never consent to take up the character of a second in a duel till I have in vain tried that of mediator. Be content with enough, for more ought not to be expected." His marksmanship might be rusty, but Hamilton was anything but a naïf when it came to playing the deadly game or at least the initial exchanges of verbal and epistolary cross fire.

Dr. Cooper's ambiguity made it possible for Hamilton to take at least temporary refuge in a third possible answer: equivocation—neither yes nor no. He replied to Burr on June 20, two days after Van Ness's visit: He was long-winded, rambling, repetitious, and evasive: "I have maturely reflected on the subject of your letter . . . and the more I have reflected the more I have become convinced that I could not, without manifest impropriety, make the avowal or disavowal which you seem to think necessary."

He had looked for the antecedent reference of Dr. Cooper's word *more*. Dr. Cooper "plainly implies, that he considers this opinion of you, which he attributes to me to be 'despicable,' " and he had used others *"still more despicable*, without however mentioning to whom, when or where . . . the phrase admits of infinite shades. . . ."

In fact, "between gentlemen, *despicable* and *more despicable* are not worth the pains of distinction." It was "inadmissible, on principle to be interrogated as to the justness of the *inferences*, which may be drawn by *others*, from whatever I may have said of a political opponent in the course of a fifteen years' competition. . . ." Burr had mentioned no specific offending phrase of his. "I stand ready," Hamilton said, "to avow or disavow promptly and explicitly any precise or definite opinion, which I may be charged with having declared of any Gentleman . . . I trust, on more reflection, you will see the matter in the same light with me. If not, I can only regret the circumstance and must abide the consequence."

The term *despicable* is vague and broad. It may imply any emotional reaction from strong distaste or contempt to utter loathing. Hamilton must have known that he could shut off further such contumelious summonses from Burr short of direct challenge by firmly denying that he had used an expression that Dr. Cooper could properly assert to be "despicable." It would have been a denial that conformed precisely to Burr's specifications, but less than the whole truth. It probably would have done no good.

Hamilton refused or could not bring himself to take or in haste under pressure overlooked this way out. He knew exactly what the guests at Judge Tayler's had heard him say and was quite sure Burr did too. His final sentence to Burr closed off any possible future use of a qualified denial and would force Burr toward a challenge. If Burr would not come forward to specify the particular words he found objectionable, said Hamilton, "I can only regret the circumstance, and must abide the consequence."

In a lifetime of experience dealing with such epistolary challenges and responses, here was apparently the first time Hamilton invited a challenge by such a "take it or leave it" response. Perhaps under the pressure of Burr's challenge and the new black mood that was again descending on his mind, he failed to see the honorable, albeit disingenuous, way out that lay in a properly qualified denial. But it seems unlikely.

Burr's fast answer next day by Van Ness ripped through all equivocations. He would not take Hamilton up on any of his proffered ways out. In fact, "I regret to find in it nothing of that sincerity and delicacy which you profess to value." Burr sneered. "Political opposition," Burr purred, "can never absolve gentlemen from the necessity of a rigid adherence to the laws of honour and the rules of decorum. I neither claim such privilege nor indulge it in others." As for Hamilton's labored attempts to parse and construe the word *despicable*, "the common sense of mankind affixed to the epithet adopted by Dr. Cooper the idea of dishonour."

Always elsewhere the precise wordsmith, here Burr betrays his own premeditated hostility. His assertion that "the common sense of mankind" affixed "the idea of dishonor" to the word *despicable* in Dr. Cooper's context is nonsense. It does not. Although the word *despicable* tells much about the attitude of the despiser, it says nothing very meaningful about the "honour" of the despisee. The only satisfactory explanation for Burr's lapse here from the habitual verbal precision of a lifetime is that he had been told what Hamilton had said at Judge Tayler's dinner and read it all into the ambiguous word *despicable*. Or else, as Charles Biddle understood, no word made any difference. Burr's determination was implacable. Burr's now twisting the issue into "the idea of dishonour" closed any possible way out for Hamilton that may have lain in Dr. Cooper's ambiguous usage of "despicable." As in ancient Rome, as in Plutarch, as in the great Elizabethan tragedies, the issue between two great protagonists was always the idea of dishonor, and Burr had now read it into Dr. Cooper's "despicable."

"The idea of dishonour," Burr said, "has been publicly applied to me under the sanction of your name. The question is not, whether he has understood the meaning of the word, or has used it according to syntax, and with grammatical accuracy; but, whether you have authorized this application, either directly or by uttering expressions or opinions derogatory to my honour."

American teachers of English should perhaps erect a monument to Dr. Charles D. Cooper for inadvertently creating the issue that seemed to make a question of syntax and grammatical accuracy one of life or death for two of the most charismatic figures in American history. But both men knew that Dr. Cooper's syntax was not the real issue at all. It seemed as if the issue were something that had long been a secret between the two men, the secret that caused Hamilton to speak as he did about Burr, the secret that, when disclosed at Judge Tayler's, became a calumny against Burr's honor.

Burr went on evenly: "The time when is in your own knowledge, but no way material to me, as the calumny has now first been disclosed, so as to become the subject of my notice, and as the effect is present and palpable." Burr closed: "Your letter has furnished me with new reasons for requiring a definite reply."

Hamilton's well-known opposition to Burr had been instrumental in depriving his rival of his seat in the United States Senate, the governorship of New York, and the presidency itself. His attack on Burr in his fiery speech at the City Tavern to the Federalist caucus had said only what they all knew he had been saying about Burr in their political rivalry for years. The party's backing of Burr in spite of it largely canceled it out. Burr's many other enemies ranging from Thomas Jefferson on high to lowly trust beneficiaries whose funds he had allegedly looted did not hesitate to scandalize his name. His financial embarrassments were widely known. Lawsuits and judgments against him for large sums of money, some involving clients of Hamilton like *Lewis v. Burr* and John Angerstein's claim for more than $80,000, were matters of public record. James Cheetham's and John Wood's pamphlets and innumerable election handbills had wallowed in the wickedness of his illicit amours and left no aspect of his personal, private, or public life unbesmirched. Except possibly one: calumny about Burr that had never been publicly aired and would be fresh titillating news to a party of politically sophisticated intimates of Hamilton who thought they had heard everything. It would be the story of Burr's relationship with James and Maria Reynolds and specifically his role in arranging for Maria Reynolds to play his badger game by paying her call on Hamilton in Philadelphia the summer of 1791, ostensibly to beg money from him to pay her coach fare back to New York.

On June 22, Van Ness delivered Burr's reply to Hamilton, waited while Hamilton read it, and made a record of how Hamilton had reacted. Hamilton's mounting horror sweats out from between Van Ness's short-breathed lines. Hamilton "said it was such a letter as he had hoped not to have received, that it contained several offensive expressions & seemed to close the door to all further reply, that he had hoped the answer he had returned to Col. Burr would have given a different direction to the controversy, that . . ." and so on. If Mr. Burr should be disposed, Hamilton "was willing to consider the last letter not delivered." But if Burr would not withdraw it, Burr "must pursue such course as he should deem most proper."

For Hamilton, with his own broad personal definition of honor, to disavow "uttering expressions or opinions derogatory" to Burr, when, of course, that was exactly what he had been doing, would be an impossibility. Burr knew it, Hamilton knew Burr knew it, and Burr knew Hamilton knew he knew it.

That same evening Hamilton for the first time consulted his friend Nathaniel Pendleton, telling him that he had told Van Ness that Burr's latest letter, that of the twenty-second, was "rude and offensive." Van Ness had requested him "to take time to deliberate" and possibly return a different answer. No, said Hamilton, it was "not possible for him to give any other answer," unless Burr "would take back his last letter and write one that would admit of a different reply." Hamilton gave Pendleton his quick reply note to Burr, also dated June 22. It called Burr's first letter "too peremptory." Burr had made "unprecedented and unwarrantable demands." It contained *"indecorous* and improper" expressions, which "increased the difficulties to explanation intrinsically incident to the nature of your application."

Pendleton held this unfortunate letter undelivered for three days while he desperately tried to work out some sort of honorable compromise with Van Ness. They thought they had done so when they both agreed that Hamilton would make the following entirely different reply to Burr: It amounted to an affirmation of Burr's honor that ought to have been acceptable to him or any man within the normal rules of the code of duels:

The conversation to which Dr. Cooper alluded, turned wholly on
political topics, and did not attribute to Col. Burr any instance of dis-
honourable conduct, nor relate to his private character; and in relation
to any other language or conversation of General Hamilton which Col.
Burr will specify, a prompt and frank avowal or denial will be given.

If Hamilton had given this compromise statement as his first reply to Burr's
first letter instead of opening the door for Burr to introduce explicitly the issue
of his honor or if Hamilton had never written his second letter or if Pendleton
had let it remain undelivered, Burr might have been required by strict adherence
to the rules of the code to let the dispute end there. (Unless of course his
implacible determination to call out Hamilton makes all such speculation academic.) Now it was too late. On the twenty-fifth, Van Ness presented Hamilton's
two statements to Burr: one, the compromise statement of the twenty-fifth,
which he and Pendleton had worked out and which offered Burr an easy way to
let the matter end with his honor affirmed; the other, Hamilton's uncompromising, belligerent reply of the twenty-second, which did not.

On the twenty-sixth, through Van Ness, Burr chose to reply to Hamilton's
letter of the twenty-second, brushing aside the proposed compromise statement.
Burr, often anathematized as a compromiser, a man widely mistrusted for seeming to be always in the middle, in this second crisis, as in the first of the two
greatest crises of his life, rigidly rejected the reasonable compromise suggested
by the rival who had so often been anathematized for his rigidity.

Burr stood on his own letter of the twenty-first. Hamilton's letter, he said,
evinced "no disposition to come to a satisfactory accommodation." Therefore,
said Burr, *"no denial or declaration will be satisfactory, unless it be general,
so as to wholly exclude the idea that rumours derogatory to Col. Burr's
honour have originated with General Hamilton, or have been fairly inferred
from anything he has said."*

Could anyone who had known Burr only casually or even a total stranger
who had discussed the rumors, truthfully make such a denial, let alone a Hamilton? Burr knew it was not possible for Hamilton to do so.

Burr denied disingenuously that his communications to Hamilton meant
that he had issued the challenge to Hamilton; he claimed Hamilton had challenged him. Burr turned Hamilton's letter to him of the twenty-second back on
Hamilton. It had been a "communication demanding a personal interview" of
Burr.

Pendleton replied to Van Ness on the twenty-sixth, saying Burr had
"greatly extended the original ground of inquiry." He seemed "to aim at nothing
less than an inquisition into his most confidential conversations, as well as
others, through the whole period of his acquaintance with Col. Burr." To Hamilton, Burr's "indefinite ground" revealed "nothing short of predetermined hostility." Nevertheless, Hamilton "disavows an unwillingness to come to a satisfactory, provided it be an honourable, accommodation."

Hamilton's above quoted reply to Burr of the twenty-sixth by way of Pendle-ton also contained, within an insult, one singular, extraordinary aside:

> Though he is not conscious that charges which are in circulation to the prejudice of Col. Burr have originated with him, *except one which may have been so considered, and which has long since been fully explained between Col. Burr and himself*—yet he cannot consent to be questioned generally as to any *rumours* which may be afloat derog-atory to the character of Col. Burr, without specification of the several rumours, many of them probably unknown to him. [Emphasis supplied by author]

What single "charge" against Burr could have "originated" solely with Hamilton, but no one else? What old "charge" would have been "fully explained" between them "long since," but by an explanation that, if repeated to others by Hamilton, Burr might still characterize as a "calumny"? Had Hamilton let slip a secret (as Monroe had done) he had once pledged another gentleman to keep?

"Despicable" was an odd sort of word for an educated man like Dr. Cooper to have emphasized in conveying to Philip Schuyler something said in a conversa-tion of a group of worldly men at Judge Tayler's dinner if all he had meant to refer to was Hamilton's political attacks on Burr or one or another of the widely known and reported scandals that Burr had lived with for so long. It was a word Hamilton almost never used. Yet "despicable" would have been the word Hamil-ton would apply to Burr if castigating him for his badger game without revealing the secret. Such men would have used the same word to repeat precisely what Hamilton had said, or to describe the nature of the secret if he had revealed it, whether or not he had made a commitment to Burr not to do so.

That spring 13 years earlier, Robert Troup, who was almost as old and as close a friend of Burr as he was of Hamilton, had written Hamilton in alarm of the "passionate courtship" going on in New York among Jefferson, Madison, Beckley, Burr, Clinton, and the Livingstons. What would this "passionate court-ship"—an odd phrase for a man like Troup to use of such men—mean for Hamilton? The solid, steady, sensible, equable, down-to-earth Troup had twice warned Hamilton of its threat to him in apocalyptic terms that were starkly out of character for Troup: " 'Delenda est Carthago' is the maxim applied with respect to you." Even to a former roommate like Hamilton, a gentleman born like Troup would give away no more of the secret with which Burr had entrusted him than to sound for him Cato's Klaxon tocsin twice—and the broad, broad hint of a sex scandal to come.

No evidence for the above hypothesis that the particular word or words Hamilton spoke about Burr at Judge Tayler's dinner related to the Reynoldses' badger game has been found except the circumstantial evidence in this book that points to that conclusion.

Wednesday morning, June 27, Burr sent Hamilton, by way of Van Ness, his formal challenge to the duel. In the language of the dueling code, this was "a message . . . such as was to be expected, containing an invitation which was accepted" on Hamilton's behalf by Pendleton. With the formal challenge Van Ness also delivered a long, expertly self-serving statement in Burr's behalf. With bootstrap reasoning it purported to shift responsibility for the challenge to Hamilton and on the broadest possible grounds.

Burr disavowed all motives of "pre-determined hostility, a charge [of Hamilton] which he thinks [is] insult added to injury." He felt "as a gentleman should feel when his honour is impeached or assailed . . . without sensations of hostility or wishes of revenge . . . determined to vindicate that honour."

Burr's ground? "Secret whispers traducing his fame, and impeaching his honour." They were "at least, equally injurious with slanders publicly uttered." Hamilton "at no time, and in no place" had a right "to use any such injurious expressions." To Burr, "the partial negative" Hamilton was "disposed to give, with the reservations he wishes to make, are proofs that he has done the injury specified."

Pendleton discussed the statement and the challenge with Hamilton in "a very short conversation that night." Hamilton gave Pendleton "a paper of remarks in his own handwriting" to be handed to Van Ness "if the state of the affair rendered it proper." Van Ness refused to take it from Pendleton's hand. The correspondence had been closed by Burr's challenge accepted and received. Pendleton insisted on telling Van Ness what was in Hamilton's letter of June 27 anyway: "There has been no intention to evade, defy, or insult, but a sincere disposition to avoid extremities, if it could be done with propriety." The "slanders said to be in circulation" against Burr, "whether openly or in whispers, have a form and shape, and might be specified."

If the secret whispers were indeed about Burr's role in the badger game, Hamilton knew that Burr could never come forward to speak out about them without dishonoring himself—and Hamilton too, for revealing the secret.

If the duel were to take place, Hamilton wished a short delay, because, "I should not think it right in the midst of a Circuit Court to withdraw my services from those who may have confided important interests to me and expose them to the embarrassment of seeking other counsel, who may not have time to be sufficiently instructed in their case. I shall also want a little time to make some arrangements respecting my own affairs."

Van Ness and Pendleton finally set the time and place for the usual ledge at Weahawk, now Weehawken, on the Jersey Shore, at 7:00 A.M. on Monday, July 9.

Hamilton made discreet arrangements for postponements, continuances, or substitution of other attorneys for himself in pending law cases. He made a new will. He wrote out a list of his liabilities for his executors. He wrote farewell letters to his wife, a grateful note for his friend Pendleton, and drew up an explanation of his conduct and motives in meeting Burr.

Not a word leaked out about the scheduled interview of two of the leading figures of the country, the vice-president of the United States and the former "prime minister" of Washington's and Adams's administrations, the man who remained the best hope of the Federal Republicans to win back the "good government" they had lost to Jefferson. Burr, it seems, told no one but Van Ness; Hamilton told only Pendleton and Rufus King, and King told Egbert Benson and John Jay, but they remained silent.

King strenuously tried to argue Hamilton out of his decision. Hamilton wrote out a lawyerlike summary of points for his arguments for and against backing out of the duel.

Hamilton's "religious and moral principles strongly opposed the practice of duelling." It would give him "pain to shed the blood of a fellow in a private combate forbidden by the laws."

"My wife and children are extremely dear to me, and my life is of the utmost importance to them . . . my creditors, in case of accident to me . . . may be in some degree sufferers. . . ." He had no life insurance. For the posthumous record, at least, he claimed that "I am conscious of no *ill will* to Col. Burr, distinct from political opposition."

But there were *"intrinsick"* difficulties in backing out, and they made the duel impossible for him to avoid because "it is not to be denied, that my animadversions on the political principles, character and views of Col. Burr have been extremely severe." Moreover, "on different occasions I, in common with many others, have made very unfavourable criticisms on *particular instances* of the private conduct of this Gentleman [emphasis added by author]." The general disavowal that Burr required "was out of my power." Burr "doubtless has heard of animadversions of mine which bore very hard on him, and it is probable that as usual they were accompanied with some falsehoods. He may have supposed himself under a necessity of acting as he has done."

Burr was menacing, but Hamilton would absolve him from odium in the conduct of the challenge:

> Col. Burr appeared to me to assume, in the first instance, a tone unnecessarily peremptory and menacing, and, in the second, positively offensive. Yet I wished, as far as might be practicable, to leave a door open to accommodation . . . I am not sure whether, under all the circumstances, I did not go further in the attempt to accommodate than a punctilious delicacy will justify.

If the unstated root reason for the duel was Burr's despicable secret role in the badger game and what Hamilton had let slip about it in conversation at Judge Tayler's, Hamilton's next argument gains special force from singularity that it would otherwise lack. "I trust, at the same time," Hamilton continued, "that the world will do me the justice to believe that I have not censured him on light grounds, nor from unworthy inducements." The public did not know, and he would not reveal, all his secret reasons. "I certainly have strong reasons for what I may have said, though it is possible that in some particulars, I may have been influenced by misconstruction or misinformation."

Hamilton saw himself as a man accountable to the nation who would set it a bad example, but that could not be helped:

To those, who with abhorring the practice of duelling, may think that I ought on no account to have added to the number of bad examples, I answer that my *relative* situation, as well in public as private appeals, enforcing all the considerations which constitute what men of the world denominate honour, impressed on me (as I thought) a peculiar necessity not to decline the call.

What did he mean by this curious reference to his *relative* situation? To his "peculiar necessity" not to decline the call? Two things, one inward. Men whom John Adams could never call the "bastard brat of Scotch pedlar"; men whom no Monroe could refuse to deal with as a fellow gentleman; men who had not struggled all their lives to earn legitimacy, stature, and public credit for a name that technically ought to have been Levine but was not; men with regular birth certificates; men like Rufus King who seemed born to rule—such men might sense, but never consciously know, the Shakespearean quiver of constituents that Hamilton read into the idea of "what men of the world denominate honour."

The second, dependent on the first, was outward. Hamilton believed it was his own "ability to be in future useful, whether in resisting mischief or effecting good, in those crises of our public affairs, which seem likely to happen, [which] would probably be inseparable from a conformity with public prejudice in this particular." Without preserving a high stock of personal public credit, he thought, his usefulness, to prevent New England secession from the Union, for example, would be at an end. The American most often pilloried by political enemies for alleged scorn of popular opinion was the one who would risk death and submerge other deeply held principles as well as the interests of his family, friends, clients, and creditors, to the dictates of the people's opinion. For them the bastard brat had spent an exigent life creating public credit.

Is the survival of one human life of supreme importance? Or are there other values more important? Is the invention or preservation of a political, economic, and social structure that promises to extend the area of human freedom, reduce human misery, and widen the scope of happiness for unnumbered other lives— ideas that seemed to be subsumed under Hamilton's concept of honor and public credit—of more importance? Is observing a private point of honor more important? Is any one man's life so important to others that it must not end?

Rufus King pleaded with Hamilton that these last arguments of his were false and specious and that he should refuse to go to Weehawken. King later wrote that "Hamilton, with a mind the most capacious and discriminating that I ever knew . . . had laid down for the government of himself certain rules upon the subject of Duels, the fallacy of which could not fail to be seen by any man of ordinary understanding." Even so, King added, as if in on the secret Hamilton had let slip, "it is my deliberate opinion that he could not have avoided a meeting with Col. Burr, had he even declined the first challenge."

William Coleman and others agreed with King that because Burr's challenge issued from "predetermined hostility," nothing Hamilton might have said would have caused Burr to withdraw it. Coleman asked a question that seems unanswerable if "despicable" did not refer to the badger game: "Had a jealous care of his reputation been [Burr's] sole motive, why should . . . all the Clintons and the Livingstons, who have most *openly* reprobated him . . . escaped his rage?" (Emphasis added.)

Hamilton was a little troubled by the possibility that he might have been in the wrong. When he had discussed the general topic of political disputation with Judge Richard Peters of Pennsylvania a little earlier, he had remarked that in New York, unlike Pennsylvania, "they never carried party matters so far as to let it interfere with their social parties, and mentioned himself and Colonel Burr, who always behaved with courtesy to each other."

A remarkable feature of this and other duels of the age was the concentration with which the principals were able to go about their daily business with the likely prospect of their own death or else the premeditated killing of the other set for a fixed time and place at a near at hand terminal point of a crowded calendar of engagements. A week before the date, Hamilton called on William Short (who had been agent of the Treasury in negotiating the Dutch loans a decade before) "to request the pleasure of his company at a Family Dinner in the Country, on Saturday next three oClock."

Hamilton had succeeded Washington as president general of the Society of the Cincinnati, and for him there was no missing its annual 1804 Fourth of July celebration—if the duel were to be kept a secret. Burr turned out for it, too. Many of the veterans who had been there later recalled a strange singularity in the demeanor of their two most famous members. Hamilton, animated even beyond his wont, had raised his wineglass, sung with gusto, and leaped upon a table to sing out the stanzas of his favorite old song, "The Drum." Later, severe disagreement broke out among the old soldiers about whether it was "The Drum" he had sung, or another old favorite, "How Stands the Glass Around." That was the song General Wolfe had written the night before his death on the Plains of Abraham, in the battle where Burr had gained his first brush with glory. In any event, most agreed that there was something almost feverish about Hamilton's behavior.

They also recalled that Burr, by contrast, who at other times could be urbane, affable, smiling, and politely witty, had surveyed the festive sodality in impenetrable silence, staring at Hamilton with a saturnine expression like Banquo's apparition at Lady Macbeth's triumphal banquet. None suspected the reason.

On the last Sunday before the duel, at home at The Grange, Hamilton led his family in the Episcopal family service of worship. Surrounded by all the children, he said aloud the noble prayer, "O God, who knowest the weakness and corruption of our nature, and the manifold temptations we daily meet with . . . have compassion on our infirmities . . . that we may be effectually restrained from sin, and excited to duty."

That night, as Hamilton's 13-year-old son John Church later recalled, "I was sitting in a room at The Grange when at a slight noise I turned and saw my father in the doorway standing silently looking at me with a most sweet and beautiful expression of countenance, full of tenderness, and without any of the preoccupations of business he sometimes had.

" 'John,' said he, 'won't you come and sleep with me tonight,' and his voice was frank as if it had been my brother's instead of my father's. That night I went to his bed. In the morning very early he awakened me. Taking my hands in his palms, all four hands extended, he told me to repeat The Lord's Prayer." There, all hands, together, they recited it in unison.

During the week, Elizabeth regularly remained at The Grange with the younger children while Hamilton stayed at their house in town at 54 Cedar Street with the older boys. On Monday he went back to town. He called at Egbert Benson's office, where Benson's nephew and law clerk, Robert Benson, Jr., told him his uncle and Rufus King had gone to Massachusetts for a few days. As they talked, Hamilton placed a scrap of paper between the pages of a book he idly took from Benson's shelves. On later examination, the scrap of paper proved to be a listing in Hamilton's hand of the numbers of *The Federalist* papers of Hamilton's authorship. It was probably a somewhat inaccurate list.

The will he made the next day thrust unusual interpolations into the purely functional, impersonal, dispositive prose of the Wall Street lawyer's usual will form. He made the personal confession that he was "conscious that he had too far sacrificed the interests of my family to public avocations." To find the necessary witnesses before whom to execute it in compliance with the Statute of Wills, he went Monday evening to Oliver Wolcott, Jr.'s house, where his host and Joseph Hopkinson of Philadelphia and others of the Wolcotts' guests observed later that he had been "uncommonly cheerful and gay," though "the duel had been determined on for ten days." It was postponed from Monday to Tuesday and then to Wednesday, when it "finally took effect."

That same day or night he wrote his last letter, one of apology, to Theodore Sedgwick concerning one of his life's two major themes, the preservation of the Union against secessionists. He had planned a much longer letter, he said, "explaining my view of the course and tendency of our politics," but "my plan embraced so large a range that, owing to much avocation, some indifferent health, and growing distaste for politics," the long letter remained unfinished. Nevertheless, "I will here express but one sentiment, which is, that dismemberment of our empire will be a clear sacrifice of great positive advantages without any counter-balancing good, administering no relief to our real disease, which is *democracy*, the poison of which, by a subdivision, will only be the more concentrated in each part, and consequently the more virulent. King is on his way for Boston. . . . God bless you."

Hamilton "left town" for the dueling ground "about five o'clock" Wednesday morning. Weahawk, or Weehawken, is on the west bank of the Hudson directly across the river from the west end of what is now Forty-second Street in Manhattan. The dawn was misty and pink, and the wind was fair. Hamilton traveled in a small sailboat with his second, Nathaniel Pendleton, and Dr. David Hosack, the celebrated surgeon who had been selected by both men's seconds to attend. They probably set sail from the foot of Horatio Street in what is now Greenwich Village.

Hamilton told Pendleton that "he had made up his mind not to fire at Colonel Burr the first time, but to receive his fire, and fire in the air." Pendleton remonstrated, but Hamilton insisted, "It is the effect of a religious scruple, and does not admit of reasoning. It is useless to say more on the subject, as my purpose is definitely fixed."

The passage was nearly three miles, the morning breeze was still fair, and they landed shortly before seven o'clock. Burr and Van Ness had already cleared away some branches and underbrush "so as to make a fair opening." The usual dueling spot was a shelf or ledge under the heights or southern extremity of the Palisades, some 20 feet above the water, a dozen paces long, and only about six feet wide.[1]

According to the account agreed on by the seconds, when Hamilton came up, "the parties exchanged salutations." The seconds then measured off ten full paces and inspected the pistols to see that their barrels did not exceed eleven inches. They did not. The Wogden pistols, used in many duels, were of English make, had been purchased by Church in London in 1795 or 1796, were of high quality workmanship, and of heavy .544 caliber, with barrels nine inches long. Set to discharge on their regular triggers, they required a pressure of ten pounds or so; set on the hair triggers, they would fire on a slight squeeze. The seconds cast lots for choice of position and the second by whom the commands should be given. Hamilton won both, a favorable beginning. The seconds loaded the pistols in each other's presence. When Hamilton received his, according to Pendleton, he was asked if he would have the hairspring set. He answered, "Not this time." When Hamilton and Burr had taken their stations, Pendleton explained to them the rules that were to govern them in firing. He would "loudly and distinctly give the command 'present!' " "Pre-*sent,*" as used in duels, means to elevate the arm, point, and aim, preparatory to firing. "After this," Pendleton directed, "the parties shall present and fire *when they please.* . . . if one fires before the other, the opposite second shall say one, two, three, fire . . . and he shall then fire or lose his shot. A snap or a flash is a fire."

According to Van Ness's account, while Pendleton was explaining these rules, "Genl Hamilton raised & levelled his pistol, as if to try his position, and lowering it, said, 'I beg pardon for delaying you but the direction of the light sometimes renders glasses necessary.' He then drew from his pocket a pair of spectacles & having put them on, observed that he was ready to proceed. . . ."

Pendleton then asked if they were prepared. Being told that they were, Pendleton cried "Present!"

According to the official report of the two seconds, "Both parties presented and fired in succession—the intervening time is not expressed, as the seconds do not precisely agree on that point."

According to the seconds' joint statement,

The fire of Colonel Burr took effect, and General Hamilton almost instantly fell. Col. Burr then advanced toward General Hamilton, with a manner and gesture that appeared to General Hamilton's friend to be expressive of regret, but without speaking turned about and withdrew, being urged from the field by his friend . . . with a view to prevent his being recognized by the surgeon and bargemen, who were then approaching. No further communication took place between the principals, and the barge that carried Col. Burr immediately returned to the City. We conceive it proper to add that the conduct of the parties in this interview was perfectly proper as suited the occasion.

William Coleman, the editor of *The Evening Post*, added some particulars. After Pendleton had cried, "Present!" "Mr. Burr raised his arm slowly, deliberately took his aim, and fired. His ball entered General Hamilton's right side." As soon as the bullet struck, Hamilton raised himself involuntarily on his toes, turned a little to the left (at which moment his pistol went off), and fell upon his face. Mr. Pendleton immediately called out for Dr. Hosack, who, in running to the spot, had to pass Mr. Van Ness and Col. Burr; but Van Ness had the cool precaution to cover his principal with an umbrella, so that Dr. Hosack should not be able to swear that he saw him on the field."

Both seconds agreed that Hamilton's pistol had fired. But Van Ness always afterward insisted Hamilton had taken aim at Burr and fired first. Pendleton completely disagreed, and Coleman published his version. Burr had fired first. Hamilton had not fired until Burr's bullet struck his body, and then his pistol discharged accidentally as he fell.

The vexed questions of which man fired first, whether Hamilton took aim at Burr or not, whether he intended to throw away his fire or not, and whether his pistol discharged voluntarily or involuntarily will probably never be conclusively resolved. That in the event Hamilton fell and Burr survived would seem to place the burden of proof on those who dispute Pendleton's version. This writer accepts Pendleton's account and conclusion.

Pendleton revisited the dueling ground the day after Hamilton died, found the mark made by Hamilton's ball, and thought it had clipped a branch off a cedar tree in its flight some 12½ feet above the ground and four feet to the right of where Hamilton had stood. He brought back the severed branch to prove it. No one's conscious marksmanship could be that rusty.

But the circumstances of Hamilton's dying, like his birth and the rest of his life, remain subject to fierce controversion, especially among Virginians. For example, in a 1976 article in *New York Magazine,* no less a Virginia gentleman than Virginius Dabney, chairman of the U.S. Bicentennial Society, suggests that Hamilton's knowledge and Burr's ignorance of the "hidden" hair triggers in Church's dueling pistols permitted Hamilton to take secret advantage of Burr in the duel. This despite the fact that Hamilton died, and Burr survived. To this writer, such innuendos are unjustified. That Church's dueling pistols, like many of the best of the time, contained a hairspring mechanism inside has always been known; to call it "hidden" or "newly discovered" bespeaks twentieth-century naïveté—in service of conventional Virginia wisdom concerning Hamilton—misunderstanding more complex eighteenth-century arms and men. Burr had used the same pistols earlier in his duel with Church; so far as is known Hamilton had never used them before in a duel. On the narrow ledge at Weehawken, both principals and their seconds would have heard Pendleton mention the hairspring to Hamilton in any event. If Hamilton could change the seconds' setting, so could Burr. The readying of the weapons—inspecting, testing, setting triggers, and loading—would, of course, be handled by the seconds, not the principals. All four men were friends of one another, had innumerable mutual friends, and were all, for the public record, at least, accounted by all to be gentlemen of honor. In all likelihood, at least three of the four would survive and have to live with the outcome for the rest of their lives. In the Roman street, Cassius had said, "Honour is the subject of my story." To these men this was a no less portentous affair of honor. Disenchanted as he was with himself, never able to rid himself of his sense of public accountability, if Hamilton had wished to survive at all— a question ultimately unanswerable—the unlikeliest way he could have found to do so was by a secret trick that all four men and all their friends, whatever their other differences, would agree was dishonorable. Worse than dishonorable. Despicable. Honor was the subject of the morning's exercise.

In response to Coleman's request, Dr. Hosack described subsequent events: "When called to him . . . I found him half sitting on the ground, supported in the arms of Mr. Pendleton. His countenance of death I shall never forget—He had at that instant just strength to say, 'This is a mortal wound, Doctor,' when he sunk away, and became to all appearance lifeless. . . . I immediately stripped up his clothes, and soon, alas! ascertained that the direction of the ball must have been through some vital part." Later Dr. Hosack's autopsy disclosed that the ball "struck the second or third false rib, and fractured it about the middle; it then passed through the liver and diaphragm, and . . . lodged in the first or second lumbar vertebra . . . which was considerably splintered. . . . About a pint of clotted blood was found in the cavity of the belly, which had probably been effused from the divided vessels of the liver."

As he slumped on the ground, according to Dr. Hosack, Hamilton's "pulses were not to be felt; his respiration was entirely suspended; and upon laying my hand on his heart, and perceiving no motion there, I considered him as irrecoverably gone."

The only chance to save him would be to rush him back to the city at once. With the help of the boatman, Hamilton's unconscious body was carried down the steep path, put aboard the barge, and rowed swiftly across the river. Once on the water, Dr. Hosack noticed that the freshening air and a liberal application of spirits of hartshorn rubbed on Hamilton's face, lips, and temples brought back a little consciousness. About 50 yards from shore, Hamilton made some "imperfect efforts to breathe, sighed, and spoke the words, 'My vision is indistinct.' " His sight returned. But my "slightly pressing his side gave him pain." Then, "soon after recovering his sight, he happened to cast his eye upon the case of pistols, and observing the one that he had had in his hand lying on the outside, he said, 'Take care of that pistol; it is undischarged, and still cocked; it may go off and do harm; Pendleton knows (attempting to turn his head toward him) that I did not intend to fire at him.' " "Yes," said Pendleton, "I have already made

Dr. Hosack acquainted with your determination as to that."

Hamilton then fell silent, except to say to Dr. Hosack that he had lost all feeling in his legs, "manifesting to me that he entertained no hopes that he should long survive." Approaching the shore, he said, "Let Mrs. Hamilton be immediately sent for; let the event be broken to her; but give her hopes."

On the wharf at the foot of Horatio Street, Hamilton's friend William Bayard, whose house at 80–82 Jane Street was nearby, stood in dreadful apprehension. One of his servants had seen Hamilton, Pendleton, and Dr. Hosack set sail for Weehawken; Bayard could hardly mistake their purpose. At seeing only Pendleton and Hosack returning erect in the stern sheets, he clasped his hands in violent apprehension; and when he saw "his poor friend lying in the bottom of the boat, he threw up his eyes and burst into a flood of tears." Bayard and his family were so distressed they could scarcely move to obey the doctor's orders to get a bed ready. As Hamilton was carried from the wharf to Bayard's house nearby, "Hamilton alone appeared tranquil and composed," but obviously in terrible pain. Dr. Hosack observed that "we then conveyed him as gently as possible up to the house," where he was put to bed in a large square room on the second floor.

Dr. Hosack "gave him a little wine and water." Hamilton complained of the pain in his back. Dr. Hosack undressed him, darkened the room, gave him "a large anodyne, frequently repeated" and upwards of an ounce of laudanum the first day. Dr. Hosack noted that "his habit was delicate and had been lately rendered more feeble by ill health, particularly by a disorder of the stomach and bowels." His sufferings during the whole day, Dr. Hosack said, were "almost intolerable." During the night he had "some imperfect sleep," and next morning "his symptoms were aggravated, attended however with a diminution of pain. His mind retained all its usual strength and composure."

After seeing off the messenger to fetch Elizabeth, Hamilton, still in terrible pain, begged that another be sent to summon his friend, Bishop Benjamin Moore, rector of Trinity Episcopal Church and bishop of New York, to come to his bedside at once. Although Hamilton attended church fairly regularly and as Troup testified "was a zealous believer in the fundamental doctrines of Christianity," there is no evidence that he had at any time been confirmed at Trinity Church or joined any other.

When the bishop arrived, according to the bishop's account, Hamilton in agony managed the following speech: "It is my desire to receive the Communion at your hands. I hope you will not conceive there is any impropriety in my request. It has for some time past been the wish of my heart, and it was my intention to take an early opportunity of uniting myself to the church, by reception of that holy ordinance." As reported, it was a remarkable speech for a man in his condition.

The bishop turned him down. His priestly office and Christian beliefs made it incumbent on him to condemn dueling, he said. Moreover, although welcoming sincere deathbed conversions, his church held it to be its duty to take especial care that such conversions did indeed represent a spiritual rebirth. Therefore, the bishop, conceiving it "right and proper to avoid every appearance of precipitancy in performing one of the most solemn offices of our religion," duly refused communion to Hamilton. He comforted him in other ways as best he could, however, and took his leave.

Despite the intolerable pain, the dying man did not give up the ghost. Another messenger was rushed to another clerical friend, the Reverend Dr. John M. Mason, a Presbyterian. Again the desperate plea for the sacrament was turned down, Mason explaining that it was strictly forbidden to Presbyterians "to administer the Lord's Supper privately to any person under any circumstances." Mason did what he could to comfort him with prayers and texts from the Scriptures, reminding him that Communion is merely "an exhibition and pledge of the mercies" of Christ. Sincere faith made this mercy accessible without the pledge. "I am aware of that," Hamilton told Mason. "It is only as a sign that I wanted it." But there was nothing else Mason could do. After a time he also left.

Taking note of strictures on the sin of dueling, Hamilton had declared to him, according to Mason, "his abhorrence of the whole transaction." The dying man had even sermonized, " 'It was always against my principles. I used every expedient to avoid the interview; but I have found for some time past, that my life must be exposed to that man. I went to the field determined not to take his life.' " Most of Hamilton's deathbed responses were characteristically direct, but his final declaration according to Mason—often quoted afterward—is so liturgical for a man in his extremity it would be unbelievable, except upon the oath of a reverend. Clasping his hands toward heaven, Hamilton allegedly spoke with emphasis, "I have a tender reliance on the mercy of the Almighty, through the mercy of the Lord Jesus Christ."

Oliver Wolcott, Jr., leaving for a moment the scene of his friend's agony that morning, wrote to his own wife that Hamilton "suffers great pain—which he endures like a Hero." He "has, of late years experienced his conviction of the truths of the Christian Religion, and has desired to receive the Sacrament—but no one of the Clergy who have yet been consulted will administer it."

Elizabeth Hamilton, unknowing, arrived from The Grange and reached his bedside at noon. To soften her first shock, Wolcott told her "the cause of his illness . . . to be spasms"—because "no one dare tell her the truth—it is feared she would become frantic." Elizabeth's sister Angelica knew at once that he was dying. But she hid her own anguish at this hideous end to a lifetime of stifled passion. She wrote her brother Philip in Albany: "Gen. Hamilton was this morning wounded by that wretch Burr, but we have every reason to hope he will recover." Philip must notify their father, General Schuyler, now a sad widower since the death of their mother the year before. He might wish to come down to help them. "My sister bears with saintlike fortitude this affliction. The town is in consternation, and there exists only the expression of grief and indignation."

Making no mention of the disappointing doubts of the divines, Dr. Hosack noted that "the great source of his anxiety seemed to be in his sympathy with his half-distracted wife and children. He spoke to me frequently of them—'My beloved wife and children' were always his expressions. . . . Once, indeed, at the sight of his children brought to the bedside together, seven in number," seeing him in his dreadful situation, "his utterance forsook him." Then "he opened his eyes, gave them one look, and closed them again, till they were taken away." In "a pathetic and impressive manner" but "with a firm voice, he alone could comfort the frantic grief of their mother" by saying to her, *"Remember, my Eliza, you are a Christian."* These must be regarded as Hamilton's last verifiable rational words, his later responses to clergymen's catechizing not being in the same category.

When Gouverneur Morris paid a last compassionate visit to his only friend who was as exotic as himself, he found Hamilton without speech and in agony, Eliza hysterical with grief, the children sobbing, Angelica Church weeping her poor heart out, friends in consternation, and all of New York City outside in an uproar. He agreed with Wolcott: "No person who witnessed [Hamilton's family's] distress will ever be induced to fight a duel."

Bishop Moore returned early in the afternoon of Thursday, the twelfth, in answer to a second summons. He again demurred. Finally, after catechizing the stricken man, to make him assure him that he had met Colonel Burr "with a fixed resolution to do him no harm," that he bore Burr no ill will, and that he received the consolations of the Gospel with a "humble and contrite heart," the bishop administered the Communion for the sick:

> Almighty, everliving God, Maker of mankind, who dost correct those whom thou dost love, and chastise everyone whom thou dost receive; grant that thy servant recover his bodily health, if it be thy gracious will; and that whensoever his soul shall depart from the body, it may be without spot; through Jesus Christ our Lord. Amen.

The bishop averred that Hamilton received it "with great devotion." According to the bishop, after surviving these rigors, "his heart afterwards appeared to be perfectly at rest." At about 2:00 P.M. on Thursday, July 12, with Elizabeth, all seven children (from simple Angelica to little Phil, only two), Angelica and John Church, Wolcott, Dr. Hosack, and Bishop Moore at his bedside, Hamilton "expired without a struggle, and—almost—without a groan."[2]

The corpse was later transported from Bayard's house on Jane Street to await the funeral procession at Angelica Church's house on Robinson Street. The Churches house had served as a similar temporary resting place three years earlier for the corpse of the first Philip Hamilton.

Burr's barge had landed him and Van Ness at Canal Street, whence Burr hastened to Richmond Hill to remain in seclusion. Bulletins on Hamilton's condition informed and outraged the public, and rumors and then news of his death plunged it into grief. Burr and Van Ness sensed that public indignation was mounting into serious menace toward them.

The morning of the twelfth, Burr in the third person sent out to request "Dr.

Hosack to inform him of the present state of Gen. H. and of the hopes which are entertained of his recovery. . . . He would take it very kind if the Dr would take the trouble of calling on him as he returns from Mr Bayard's."

Van Ness made similar inquiry of Pendleton, hoping the wound had not been pronounced mortal, as he had heard it had been. His fears for Hamilton were mixed with fears for Burr's and his own safety, and he cautioned Pendleton not to publish any particulars out of agitation and solicitude until they had consulted.

Pendleton, pressed by Hamilton's friends, was eager to clear up the mystery, publish the correspondence that had preceded the duel, and the precise facts that would explain the interview at Weehawken. Van Ness was for delay and insisted that nothing appear in the newspapers unless he and Burr consented to it on every point. But conferences between Van Ness and Pendleton were difficult because Van Ness was fearful of mob violence if he should dare enter the city.

At Dr. Hosack's on Friday the thirteenth, Pendleton read Van Ness a statement he had prepared, but Van Ness objected to certain features of it and went away to consult his own notes, and the seconds did not meet again before the New York *Morning Chronicle* published Pendleton's account on July 17, the Tuesday following the Thursday Hamilton had died. Pendleton had waited for Van Ness until the printer demanded the copy, then had supplied the printer with wording that he hoped Van Ness would find to be accurate. Van Ness had failed to keep the appointment because "apprehensive that my visit to the City would be attended with danger I have stopt at Col. Burr's whose house is unoccupied and where I should be happy to see you." Pendleton accepted the changes Van Ness demanded; so instead of saying that Burr "took aim," he substituted "both parties presented." He did not quarrel with Van Ness's reason for not passing Hamilton's last letter on to Burr: Van Ness had considered the correspondence closed by what he took to be Pendleton's unqualified and final acceptance, for Hamilton, of Burr's challenge of the day before.

Eliza tore open and read two letters Hamilton had written her, one on July 4 and the other the night before the duel, to be opened only in case of his death:

July 4, 1804

"This letter, my very dear Eliza, will not be delivered to you, unless I shall first have terminated my earthly career; to begin, as I humbly hope from redeeming grace and divine mercy, a happy immortality. If it had been possible for me to have avoided the interview, my love for you and my precious children would have been alone a decisive motive. But it was not possible, without sacrifices which would have rendered me unworthy of your esteem.

So much for reasons of state and religion. His anguish at the thought of death taking him from her found moving penultimate phrases:

I need not tell you of the pangs I feel, from the idea of quitting you and exposing you to the anguish I know you would feel. Nor could I dwell on the topic lest it should unman me . . . With my last idea, I shall cherish the sweet hope of meeting you in a better world. Adieu, best of wives and best of women. Embrace all my darling children for me. Ever yours

A H

In a second letter, an afterthought of Tuesday night, at the very end, before he laid down for the last time the quick strong fluent pen that had done as much to build a nation as any man's had ever done, he thought of his beginnings, of his cousin Ann Lytton Mitchell, who had given the poor boy who was a clerk on St. Croix some money to come to America, and of duty:

Tuesday evening 10 o'clock, 1804.

"My beloved Eliza, [he wrote] Mrs. Mitchell is the person in the world to whom as a friend I am under the greatest obligations. I have not hitherto done my duty to her. . . . [The end did not mean an end of accountability.] I intend, if it shall be in my power, to render the evening of her days comfortable.

But if it shall please God to put this out of my power . . . I entreat you to do it, and to treat her with the tenderness of a sister.

There was a sense of inevitability to his last lines, but not of suicide, a sense of fitness, an eloquent melancholy, a feeling of mystery and of a work unfinished, a mood like that which hovers over the lines of Vergil's first Ecologue. He had become disenchanted with himself.

. . . The scruples of a Christian have determined me to expose my own life to any extent, rather than subject myself to the guilt of taking the life of another. This much increases my hazards, and redoubles my pangs for you. But you had rather I should die innocent than live guilty. Heaven can preserve me, and I humbly hope will; but, in the contrary event, I charge you to remember that you are a Christian. God's will be done! The will of a merciful God must be good. Once more,

Adieu, my darling, darling wife.

General Schuyler, in bed in Albany suffering agonizing pangs of gout, again did his best to console his daughter: "My Dear, Dearly Beloved and Affectionate Child . . . If aught under heaven could aggravate the affliction I experience, it is that incapable of moving or being removed I cannot fly to you. . . ." He opened his heart to her: "Should it please God so far to restore my strength as to enable me to go to you, I shall embrace the first moment to do it, but should it be otherwise, I entreat you my beloved Child to come home as soon as you possibly can, with my dear Grand-children." Next day he begged ravaged and desolate Angelica to comfort his Eliza for him: He forbore to write her directly "lest it should create a fresh paroxysm of grief." Fearing his own death, he trusted "that the Supreme being may prolong my life that I may discharge the duties of a father to my dear child and her dear children. . . . She knows how tenderly I loved My Dear Hamilton. . . . Much I feel all the duties which are devolved on me. The evening of my days will be passed in the pleasing occupation of administering . . . to a Child and Grand-Children so highly entitled to my best exertions." Schuyler was sending his son Philip to New York at once to help her look after her family.

Schuyler's wish to live a little longer was unfulfilled. To his grief from the fall of his namesake, the first Philip Hamilton; the loss of granddaughter Angelica's mind; and the passing of his good wife, Catherine, was now added the pang of his son-in-law's death—as the apparent result of a chain of circumstances beginning with the few words Schuyler had forced Dr. Cooper to write to him by the infamous embezzled letter. As he wrote Angelica Church on July 17,

> the dreadful calamity . . . affected me so deeply as to threaten serious results . . . My wounds . . . and the paroxysms of gout have not been severe for the past two days. . . . My [daughter] Kitty is most deeply affected. Her tears have flowed incessantly. She begins to be more composed, and unites with me in love to your distressed sister and all so dear to us. . . . May God bless and preserve you all is the constant prayer of your
>
> afflicted parent
Ph. Schuyler
>
> Mrs. Church
> Fail not my beloved to let me daily know the state of your afflicted sister. My anxiety on her account rends my heart.

Dr. Stringer lanced the ulcer in Philip Schuyler's foot. Much infected matter was discharged to relieve his pain, but he must remain in bed ten or twelve days more. "Pray let me know if you have as yet obtained a . . . convenient house"[.] He wrote Elizabeth: "Procure one if possible sufficiently large that you may not be in the least crowded, for remember, that it is my intention that you should be well accommodated,—and make every want immediately known to me that I may have the pleasure of obviating it."

One of her father's last letters told her he could not walk, but still hoped to visit her that winter in the city if there should be sledding. He wanted her table to be well supplied. As soon as his winter's store of fat cattle and hogs arrived, "everything will be prepared for you," including butter and "Pig's feet souse."

But the fond, tender promises of the bereft old paterfamilias remained unfulfilled. He died three months and four days after his son-in-law on November 18, 1804. The last letter Elizabeth Hamilton received from him said, "What your afflictions my dearly beloved child have added to mine, was the natural result of a parent's tenderness for a dutiful and affectionate child, as he invariably experienced from you."

Just before Schuyler's death, James McHenry had complained to Oliver Wolcott, Jr., that collections lagged for the fund they had set up to pay off the creditors of Hamilton's deeply insolvent estate and save The Grange. Friends saw no need because of "the real or presumed great wealth of General Schuyler." Wolcott, the president of the Merchants Bank, replied: Schuyler "owes money and has no funds at command."

32

ELIZABETH HAMILTON
SURVIVES

MR. MONROE, IF YOU HAVE COME TO TELL ME THAT YOU REPENT
. . . I UNDERSTAND IT. BUT, OTHERWISE, NO LAPSE OF TIME, NO
NEARNESS TO THE GRAVE, MAKES ANY DIFFERENCE.
—*Elizabeth Hamilton to James Monroe, 1850*

William Coleman reported that after Hamilton's death, a note was found
that he had written to Nathaniel Pendleton the evening before the interview
"thanking him with tenderness for his friendship to him" and informing him
where the keys to certain drawers of his desk would be found. In the drawers
he had deposited such papers as he thought proper to leave behind him, together
with his last will. The papers included the statement setting forth his points on
dueling, his own situation, and Burr, as well as the two letters addressed to
Elizabeth Hamilton mentioned in the preceding chapter.

His will, dated July 9, superseded the earlier will he had made July 25, 1795,
just before his scheduled duel with Commodore James Nicholson the week after
being stoned by the Wall Street mob for defending Jay's Treaty. It appointed
John Barker Church, Nicholas Fish, and Pendleton as his executors and gave and
devised his estate to them, with instructions to pay his debts if the fund were
sufficient or pro rata in proportion to size of claims if it was not. The residue,

if any, should go to Elizabeth, his wife. He had interpolated the following in the form: "Though, if it should please God to spare my life, I may look for a considerable surplus out of my present property; yet, if he should speedily call me to the eternal world, a forced sale, as is usual, may possibly render it insufficient to satisfy my debts. I pray God that something may remain for the maintenance and Education of my dear wife and children." He imposed a highly unusual obligation on his family, yet one entirely consistent with his firmly fixed ideas on the subject of public credit. If there were not enough money to pay off his creditors, he entreated his children to pay up the deficiency, if they ever should be able to do so. "Though conscious that I have too far sacrificed the Interests of my family to public avocations & on this account have the less claim to burthen my Children, yet I trust in their magnanimity to appreciate as they ought this my request." In an "unfavourable . . . event of things" their most sacred duty was "the support of their dear mother, with the most respectful and tender attention." He added an already dashed hope: "Probably her own patrimonial resources will preserve her from indigence." The children were charged to bear in mind "that to them she has been the most devoted and best of mothers." A striking change in his will from the old one of 1795 was that gone now was any mention of the "bundle inscribed thus—*JR To be forwarded to Oliver Wolcott Junr. Esq.*" Certainty of probate makes a will a public record. To have let this stand would have whetted up his enemies' hullabaloo about the old scandal all over again and by his own hand.

In a drawer was an estate-planning memorandum headed, "Statement of my property and Debts July 1, 1804." His assets were mainly western lands, some 31,000 acres, which "stood him" about $49,000. He estimated The Grange place ("My establishment . . . at *Haerlem*") to have cost about $25,000. Total real estate was put down at $74,150; personal estate totaled $3,850 (furniture and library $3,000, horses and carriages $600, loan $250); there was due him for professional services about $2,500, making total assets of $80,500. His debts were principally $20,000 owing to several banks in New York and smaller sums borrowed from clients and friends, such as Louis Leguen, $3,000; Herman Le Roy, $4,280; John B. Church, $2,610; Fish, $1,500; and Victor Du Pont, whom he had befriended in the past, $1,800. Adding other debts, mostly smaller, and deducting $54,722 liabilities from $80,500 assets, he had struck a balance in his favor of $25,778. He wanted a preference given to certain creditors, including those who had supplied labor and materials for The Grange. The bundle inscribed *JR* was not on the list of his assets—or liabilities. It was not found. It has never been found. The secrets it contained remain one of the profound mysteries of American history.

Of all the men in American history who have occupied the office of secretary of the treasury, Hamilton, the greatest, was probably the least affluent. He had set much too high a value on his western lands, judging by their current selling prices, and on continuance of earnings from his law practice, from $12,000 to $14,000 a year. For some time he had been in poor health, as Dr. Hosack's bill for almost continual ministrations showed. Building The Grange had cost him much more than prudence dictated, though now it was the focus of the whole family's affections.

Sadly, Hamilton felt it necessary "to explain why I have made so considerable an establishment in the country." He had thought to prepare a place of retirement from the harassments of life. Within a reasonable period, he thought, his earnings would maintain his family and gradually discharge his debts. Construction costs for The Grange had all been incurred; nothing further would be spent for the present. He planned to reduce expenses of every kind to $4,000 a year exclusive of interest on the place, even if The Grange must be leased for a few years. In the meantime, his western lands were increasing in value and in the end should leave him "a handsome clear property." His chief apology was to friends who from kindness had endorsed notes for him at the banks. He felt justified in securing them in preference to other creditors and entreated the indulgence of the banks toward them. He added wryly that if this statement of his net worth should come to public notice, it would at least be proof that his financial integrity in public office was beyond "even the shadow of a question."

Furthermore, he had forsworn the ordinary advantages of his military service. Being a member of Congress when the question of commuting the half pay owed to the army for a lump sum was in debate, he had relinquished his own claims so that his advocacy would not be suspect on grounds of self-interest. Nor had he applied for the bounty lands allowed by the United States and New York.

Although he had not seen his cousin Ann Lytton Mitchell in all the years since his youth, she had given him money to come from St. Croix to the mainland and to help pay for his education beyond the level of a clerk bookkeeper. In the packet committed to Pendleton was a sealed letter for her enclosing, "as was mentioned on the outside," $400.

The merchants and other respectable citizens of the city met at the Tontine Coffee House on July 13 and voted to shut up their shops and stores and suspend all business the following Saturday to march in the funeral procession. Owners and masters of vessels in the harbor would hoist their colors half-mast. The arrangements committee requested all fellow citizens "to wear crape on the left arm for thirty days, as a testimony of their respect for the Integrity, Virtues, Talents and Patriotism of General Alexander Hamilton, deceased."

The Common Council of New York City proclaimed that the funeral should be public, at the expense of the municipality, and "that the usual business of the day be dispensed with by all classes of inhabitants." The ordinance prohibiting bell ringing at funerals was suspended. Muffled bells could be tolled morning, noon, and evening the day of his interment. Six weeks of mourning were proclaimed.

The Bar Association met at Lovett's Hotel, and "all party distinction was lost in the general sentiment of love and respect for the illustrious deceased." Richard Harison spoke "with a faltering tongue and a feeling heart." The gentlemen of the bar adopted a resolution expressing "universal confidence and veneration" for "Alexander Hamilton, the brightest ornament of their profession."

They lamented his loss as "a severe private affliction"; they deplored it as a great public calamity. For their deceased brother they would wear crape for six weeks. Similar convocations were called by the Law Student Association, at the office of Josiah Ogden Hoffman; by the students and graduates of Columbia College on the college green; by the Brigade Company of Artillery, the Sixth Regiment, and other regiments at Mechanic Hall and in City Hall Park; by the Saint Andrews Society at the Masonic Hall; and by the members of the Tammanial Society "in the great Wigwam, precisely at the setting of the sun," in "the Season of Fruit, in the year of discovery 312, by order of the Grand Sachem, James D. Bisset," secretary.

On Saturday morning Colonel Morton's Corps began close order drill and desultory parading in City Hall Park at 10 o'clock, with six artillery pieces also on hand. Other marchers assembled in Robinson Street, now Park Place, west of Broadway, on the south side facing the house of John and Angelica Church, where the corpse had been brought to lie. The Sixth Regiment drew up its ranks in solemn attitude. The troops rested on reversed arms with musket butts up, muzzles down, facing the front stoop and entrance, while the colors and music of the several corps paraded back and forth in the street.

For this sad day the standard of the Society of the Cincinnati, carried at the immediate left of the national color, was shrouded in the blackest crape of all. At noon, precisely, on the command, "Order, COLORS," the Color Guard aligned its formation. The color bearers grasped the pikes of their flags and drew them upright with each ferrule resting on the street against its bearer's foot. On the command, "Carry, COLORS," each lifted his pike and inserted its heel in the socket of his carrying sling. Each color bearer grasped his pike at shoulder height with his elbow outstretched and crooked parallel to the ground so that his pike inclined forward at only a slight angle from the vertical.

On the command, "Cincinnati, present, COLORS!" its standard bearer alone slid his right hand up the pike staff to the height of his eye, straightened his elbow, and then flexed it again, causing the proud crape-shrouded standard to wave downward and then upward and then decline toward the front entrance of the Churches' house at a 45-degree angle.

The wave of the Cincinnatian standard was the signal for the men in the smartly dressed ranks of the Sixth Regiment to execute a brisk "present, ARMS." There followed in cadence the snap-slap-slap of hard palms on leather slings and musket butts and the rattle of frizzles on flints. Officers' flat hands and right forearms sprang into vibrant hand salutes. The "large and elegant" band struck up the melancholy dead march.

The front door of John and Angelica Church's house swung open. From within emerged Hamilton's corpse in its coffin on its pall-draped bier. It was borne by eight of his good friends: Oliver Wolcott, Jr., Richard Harison, William Bayard, Josiah Ogden Hoffman, Richard Varick, Abijah Hammond, General Matthew Clarkson, and Judge John Lawrence. The colors and music rested for a moment of silence as all joined in silent salute to the corpse. A signal trumpet sounded. On muffled drums the drummer boys beat out an open roll in the colonial manner—individual strokes slightly separated, giving the effect not so much of a merged rumble as of a sustained rattle. The Sixth Regiment's ranks shouldered arms. On the same trumpet call, Colonel Morton's troops, which had been parading in the park, fell into columns and occupied Broadway.

On the second trumpet call, the Sixth Regiment wheeled to the right by platoons and occupied Robinson Street in front of the corpse, with arms again reversed. On the third trumpet call, the whole column stepped off, the band still playing the dead march in a slow, slow cadence to the rattle of the muffled drums. The flanks of the corpse on its bier were covered by two companies in single file with arms at trail. Behind walked the general's gray horse, caparisoned in deep mourning, led by two blacks dressed in white, wearing white turbans trimmed in black. The general's boots and spurs lay reversed on the gray's back across his empty saddle.

Following directly behind in deep mourning came Elizabeth Hamilton and the four eldest sons, Alexander, James Alexander, John Church, and William Stephen; Angelica, Eliza, little Philip II, and the Antil orphan were spared the two-mile march. John and Angelica Church and their children followed, supported by an ambience of Schuyler brothers and nephews and nieces. Gouverneur Morris, the appointed funeral orator, followed in his carriage. Then came the gentlemen of the bar, the lieutenant governor, the resident agents of foreign powers, "the various officers of the respective banks," the "chamber of commerce and merchants," the president, professors, and students of Columbia College, all in mourning gowns. There followed the Saint Andrews Society, the Tammany Society, the Mechanic Society, and, finally, the "citizens in general."

It was the greatest procession New York had ever seen since the one 16 years earlier in honor of Hamilton's efforts to obtain New York's ratification of the Constitution. He had not been present, except in spirit, to enjoy that one, either.

As the ranks moved out of Robinson Street and curved around City Hall Park toward Pearl, they were augmented by Colonel Morton's troops from Broadway as they wheeled rank by rank into their places in the column ahead of the bier. The matrosses of two artillery pieces, which had been left behind in the Park, with priming and powder charges piled high beside their carriage, began firing off minute guns that would continue for the more than two hours it would take for the whole cortege to wind its way around the city through Pearl Street down to Whitehall and back up Broadway to Trinity Church.

Ever since 10 o'clock in the morning, the guns of His Britannic Majesty's ship of war *Boston*, anchored inside the Hook, and His Majesty's packet *Lord Charles Spencer*, both with yard arms peaked and ensigns at half-mast in mourning, had been firing off minute gun salutes that reverberated gloomily across the island. As the artillery in the park took up the cannonade, the French frigates *Cybelle* and *Didion*, also with their colors half-hoisted and their yards peaked in mourning, now added the boom of their own minute guns to the crunching concatenation of cannon fire that accompanied the dead march. So did the cannon of all the forts around the harbor.

In its more than three and a half centuries of history, New York City has been rocked by many a noisy celebration. But probably never before or since has it heard such thumps of doleful thunder as marked the passing of the greatest man who ever lived there who called himself a New Yorker. Coleman reported that the streets were lined with people, and doors and windows were filled "principally with weeping females." Indeed, "even the housetops were covered with spectators, who came from all parts to behold the melancholy procession."

When the military advance guard reached Trinity Church, the whole column wheeled backward by platoons, flank by flank, formed a lane, and came to a halt, slapping their muskets once again, on command, to reversed order, butts up. Through the avenue thus formed, while the band with muffled drums played "a pensive solemn air," the corpse, preceded and followed by the funeral party, advanced into the church between the ranks of the soldiers. In the customary attitude of grief, each one crooked his neck and rested his cheek on the butt of his piece.

From a stage erected in the portico of the church, Gouverneur Morris then rose and, with Hamilton's four sons seated beside him, "slowly and impressively delivered to the immense concourse in front an extemporary oration." Coleman committed it to memory and afterward quickly committed it to paper.

"Instead of the language of a public speaker," Morris began his exordium, "you will hear only the lamentations of a bewailing friend. But I will struggle with my bursting heart, to portray that Heroic Spirit. . . ."

After 200 years, more or less, the points that Morris made about Hamilton's accomplishments on that hot, sad July afternoon, speaking in the elegant but florid rhetorical style of the day, as he looked out from the stage over the crowd that filled up the churchyard and Broadway and Wall Street in front of him, may have seemed more exaggerated and fulsome to his listeners then than they do to many a skeptical reader of today. Or, at least, the points that Morris made then still stand as a summary of them that this writer cannot improve upon.

"When the first sound of the American war called Hamilton to the field," said Morris, he was "a young and unprotected volunteer." Then, being selected by Washington as an aide, he was "a principal actor in the most important scenes of our Revolution." At Yorktown, "he stormed the redoubt . . . his gallant troops, emulating the heroism of their chief, checked the uplifted arm, and spared a foe no longer resisting." Not one perished.

Morris, jealously proud of his own important role in creating the Constitution, particularly as chairman of the Committee on Style, knew as well as any man the importance of Hamilton's. At Philadelphia, said Morris, Hamilton "assisted in forming that constitution which is now the bond of our union, the shield of our defense, and the source of our prosperity."

Hamilton had indeed expressed apprehension that the Constitution "did not contain sufficient means of strength for its own preservation"; like other republics, notably France, he feared it might pass through anarchy and "shoot into" despotism. But like Morris himself, he "hoped better things. We confided in the good sense of the American people; and above all we trusted in the protecting

Providence of the Almighty." By his enemies, Morris pointed out, Hamilton's "speculative opinions were treated as deliberate designs." He was a man who "disdained concealment. Knowing the purity of his heart, he bore it as it were in his hand, exposing to every passenger its inmost recesses." Hamilton's "generous indiscretion subjected him to censure from misrepresentation." "You know"—"You all know," Morris sentiently prolated, "how strenuous, how unremitting were his efforts to establish and to preserve the constitution. If then his opinion was wrong, pardon, oh! pardon that single error in a life devoted to your service."

Washington sought out Hamilton as his secretary of the treasury for his "splendid talents, extensive information and incorruptible integrity." His system was widely criticized; it had its faults—"let it be remembered that nothing human is perfect"—but Hamilton, as the minister of a republic, must and did "bend to the will of the people." The result? "A rapid advance in power and prosperity, of which there is no example in any other age or nation. The part Hamilton bore is universally known."

Hamilton's openness, "his unsuspecting confidence in professions of others which he believed to be sincere, led him to trust too much" in people he should not have trusted. "This exposed him to misrepresentation." He felt obliged to resign. "But though he was compelled to abandon public life never, no never for a moment did he abandon the public service." In recent years he had probably been more open, frank and confidential with Morris than with anyone else. Now, Morris swore, "I declare before God . . . that in his most private and confidential conversations, the single objects of discussion and consideration were your freedom and happiness. He never lost sight of your interests."

He had been charged with ambition and was wounded by the imputation. "Oh! my fellow citizens," Morris cried in Mark Antonian tones, "remember this solemn testimonial, that he was not ambitious." When Washington was called forth from his retreat to lead your armies, "he asked for Hamilton to be his second in command. . . ." Washington knew that "the hand of time pinching life at its source" would soon remove him from the scene and that Hamilton would succeed him. Yet "he thought the sword of America might safely be confided to the hand which now lies cold in that coffin."

Hamilton was "indignant at the charge that he sought place or power" for his own aggrandizement. "He was ambitious only of glory, but he was deeply solicitous for you. For himself he feared nothing, but that bad men might, by false professions, acquire your confidence, and abuse it to your ruin." Turning to his brethren of the Cincinnati, Morris reminded them, "Oh! he was mild and gentle. In him there was no offence; no guile—his generous hand and heart were open to all."

Turning to the gentlemen of the bar, Morris enjoined them to "cherish and imitate his example," while, like him, "with laudable zeal, you pursue the interests of your clients, remember, like him, the eternal principles of justice."

Turning to his fellow citizens and for the benefit of American posterity, Morris recalled that "you have seen him contending against you and saving your dearest interests, as it were, in spite of yourselves . . . you now feel and enjoy the benefits resulting from the firm energy of his conduct. Bear this testimony to the memory of my departed friend. I CHARGE YOU TO PROTECT HIS FAME." Not misled, as the public might be, by all the rich panoply of the funeral, Morris knew that Hamilton had left his family almost destitute. His fame "is all he has left—all that these poor orphan children will inherit from their father."

A wave of emotion must have surged across the immense throng as people craned their necks and stood on tiptoe to stare at the impoverished Hamilton sons there on the stage beside the orator. Morris's towering frame, massive head, imperious glance, and Shakespearean cadences compelled a breathless silence as he paused a moment before rising to his peroration:

> My countrymen, that Fame may be a rich treasure to you also. Let it be the test by which to examine those who solicit your favor. Disregarding professions, view their conduct, and on a doubtful occasion, ask, *Would Hamilton have done this thing?*

He closed:

> You all know how he perished. On this last scene, I cannot, I must not dwell. It might excite emotions too strong for better judgment. Suffer not your indignation to lead to any act which might again offend the insulted majesty of the law; on his part, or from his lips, though with my voice—for his voice you will hear no more—let me entreat you to respect yourselves.

Even so, Morris meditated afterward, "How easy it would have been to make them, for a moment, absolutely mad!" But it had been his duty, he told himself, to allay mob passions, not to unleash them against Burr in an orgy of revenge.

To his diary, the night of Hamilton's death, three days before his funeral oration, Morris, reflecting on the problem of how best to treat of Hamilton's complex life and character, had groped for some mode to pass over his foreign and illegitimate birth "handsomely." Also, Hamilton was "indiscreet, vain, and opinionated"; Morris thought, "these things must be told, or the character will be incomplete . . . The most important part of his life was his administration of finances. . . ." Yet his system "was in one respect radically wrong. . . . All this must somehow be reconciled." Three days later, Morris had managed to explain all the vices of his late friend's virtues and the virtues of his vices as well as any man could possibly have done.

At the close of Morris's oration, the troops in the churchyard formed an extensive hollow square. The corpse was carried to the grave for the usual funeral services, which Bishop Moore intoned from the Book of Common Prayer:

> I am the resurrection and the life, saith the Lord; he that believeth in me, though he were dead, yet shall he live; and whosoever liveth and believeth in me, shall never die. . . . We brought nothing into this world,

and it is certain we can carry nothing out. The Lord gave, and the Lord
hath taken away; blessed be the name of the Lord.

The troops terminated the solemnities by firing blank musket volleys in
clouds of smoky air above the grave.

The immense crowd of people who had heard through Morris's lips Hamilton's characteristic exhortation not to behave like a mob ignored the Hamiltonian
advice more or less as usual. People sought to vent the unruly passions that
Morris had sought to calm—in Mark Antonian fashion—by taking revenge
against Burr.

Burr foresaw the gathering storm. It so happened that the very Wednesday
morning Burr had returned from Weehawken to go into seclusion at Richmond
Hill, a young cousin of his from Connecticut came by chance to pay him a casual
call, to breakfast with him, and depart. At no point in their desultory conversation during his visit did Burr say a word to suggest that before their breakfast
that day he had shot Alexander Hamilton. When the cousin learned of the duel
and the story made the rounds, such an incredibly insouciant cover-up on Burr's
part came through to many as an acknowledgment by Burr of shame and guilt.

The coroner of the City and County of New York began an inquisition and
after several delays, upon the testimony of Dr. Hosack and the two clergymen,
returned with a coroner's verdict of murder, implicating Burr, Van Ness, and
Pendleton. In New Jersey, the 15-man Bergen County coroner's jury also
charged Burr with murder. Burr feared he would be indicted as a result of one
or another coroner's inquest for the nonbailable offense of murder. Hamilton on
the eve of the duel had expressed the "ardent wish" that he was mistaken about
Burr's despicable character and that Burr, "by his future conduct, may show
himself worthy of all confidence and esteem, and prove an ornament and blessing
to his country."

Burr's first significant postduel act after the breakfast with his cousin was
to become a fugitive from justice.

While the coroner's jury deliberated, he feared that aroused mobs might
burn his house down. He wrote his son-in-law, Joseph Alston, that "I propose
leaving town for a few days, and meditate also a journey of some weeks, but
whither is not resolved." When Burr was indicted for murder by the grand jury,
he fled. His friend John Swartwout brought a boat to the foot of the yard below
Richmond Hill at ten o'clock on the night of July 21, rowed him downriver, and
put him ashore in the morning at Perth Amboy, New Jersey. But the Bergen
County indictment made it dangerous for him to dally in that state, and Burr was
restless to press on. On Monday, Commodore Thomas Truxtun took his nervous
guest by carriage as far as Cranbury, where Burr hired a spring wagon, crossed
the Delaware to Pennsylvania at Bristol, and continued by back roads to Philadelphia, where he took temporary refuge in the hospitality of his friend Alexander Dallas.

One Maryland newspaper, quoting Hamilton's favorite eighteenth-century
poet, Alexander Pope, wrote that Burr was *"Damned* to everlasting fame," but

far from wallowing in the tragedy, he displayed remarkable nonchalance.

"Burr parades our streets with unparalleled effrontery," reported Hamilton's friend Joseph Hopkinson, "courting the attention of everybody with whom he has the slightest acquaintance. Our Governor has visited him. . . ." Burr also resumed the courtship of one Celeste, whom he had known in the Biblical sense before. A few days more, he smirked in a letter to his daughter, Theodosia, would have produced a "grave event" (for Celeste!).[1] Burr feared the genteel governor of Pennsylvania might feel obliged to extradite him back to New York for murder; so, incognito, he moved on southward, harbored with Pierce Butler on St. Simons Island, Georgia, for a few days, and scouted that state and Spanish Florida for future adventures. Finally, after days in an open boat, the vice-president of the United States, as a fugitive from justice, reached the out-of-the-way home of his daughter, Theodosia, and her husband, Joseph Alston, at Statesburg, South Carolina.

When Congress reconvened, the vice-president, still under indictment for murder, returned to Washington and acted as presiding officer at the impeachment trial of Judge Samuel Chase. Many Jeffersonians, though not Jefferson, now became his partisans. Senator Giles arranged for a round robin of Republican senators to plead with Governor Bloomfield of New Jersey to quash his murder indictment there, and, after some demurrals, this was accomplished. The New York grand jury reduced the charge against him to the mere misdemeanor of sending a challenge to a duel. Burr was homeless in New York, however, for while he was in flight, Richmond Hill had been auctioned off for $25,000 to pay off his debts; and even after the sale, unsatisfied claims of creditors of at least $8,000 remained due.

Sometime after Burr's return to New York, out of office, as the story was told in Chancellor James Kent's family, Kent saw Burr walking one day on Nassau Street on the opposite side. Kent rushed across the street, shook his cane in Burr's face and exclaimed in a voice choked with passion, "You are a scoundrel, sir!—a scoundrel!" As Kent's great-grandson tells the story, Burr "flushed at the epithet, and was about to make a hasty answer; but time and misfortune had dulled the keenness of his temper." He contented himself with raising his hat and, making a sweeping bow, replying, "The opinions of the learned Chancellor are always entitled to the highest consideration." Looking back almost 30 years on the tragic loss of Hamilton in 1804, Kent could still respond to Elizabeth Hamilton's request for a considered opinion of his on her late husband. He responded that Hamilton "had the most artless simplicity of any man I ever knew. It was impossible not to love as well as respect and admire him. The selfish principle, seemed never to have reached him." Reading the future, which he had now lived through, Kent said, "If Hamilton had lived twenty years longer, he would have rivalled Socrates, or Bacon, or any other of the sages of ancient or modern times, in researches after truth and in benevolence to mankind. The active and profound statesman, the learned and eloquent lawyer would probably have disappeared in a great degree before the character of the sage philosopher, instructing mankind by his wisdom and elevating his country by his example."

The rest of the nation joined New York City in mourning.[2] Newspapers everywhere rivaled each other in expressions of sorrow. The clergy composed heartrending sermons with the duel as their text. Mass memorial meetings were held in New York, Philadelphia, Boston, and Albany. Ordinances were suspended. Muffled church bells tolled throughout the nation.

Editorials, resolutions, and addresses in communities large and small throughout the 15 states pronounced encomiums on Hamilton. In these eulogies his name was often coupled with Washington's and great men of classical ages. Many editors who had been political opponents generously united in praise. James Cheetham, of the New York *American Citizen*, who had tried as hard as anyone to destroy him in print, was foremost in atonement and attempts at resurrection.

Some of the most perceptive comments came from Fisher Ames in an estimate read to friends and published unsigned in the *Boston Repository*. Ames observed that "the uncommonly profound public sorrow for the death of Alexander Hamilton, sufficiently explains and vindicates itself." This was because Hamilton "had not made himself dear to the passions of the multitude by condescending . . . to become their instrument . . . it was by . . . loving his country better than himself, preferring its interest to its favor, and serving it, when it was unwilling and unthankful, in a manner that nobody else could, that he rose, and the true popularity, the homage that is paid to virtue, followed him." On the same theme, Ames added, "No man ever more disdained duplicity, or carried *frankness* further than he. This gave to his political opponents some temporary advantages. . . ."

Although Hamilton had been withdrawn from public office to the bar for some years, yet "there was nevertheless a splendor in his character that could not be contracted within the ordinary sphere of his employments." Ames did not believe "that he had left any worthy man his foe who had ever been his friend." Ames acknowledged that it is difficult for such a greatly superior man to preserve the friendship of his associates without abatement: "Yet though Hamilton could not possibly conceal his superiority, he was so little inclined to display it, he was so much at ease in its possession, that no jealousy or envy chilled his bosom when his friends obtained praise." He was "magnanimous . . . frank . . . ardent, yet so little overbearing, so much trusted, admired, beloved, almost adored, that his power over [his friends'] affections was entire and lasted through his life."

Said Ames, "I could weep for my country, which mournful as it is, does not know the half of its loss. It deeply laments, when it turns its eyes back, and sees what Hamilton *was;* but my soul stiffens with despair when I think what Hamilton *would have been."* Words all but failed the ever articulate Ames. "But who alive can exhibit this portrait?" None had the skill. "If our age, on that supposition more fruitful than any other, had produced two Hamiltons, one of them might then have depicted the other."

A less elegant and polished but no less heartfelt tribute came to Elizabeth Hamilton from Harry Croswell, the village editor whose appeal Hamilton had argued so forcefully and lost less than five months earlier. "To me he . . .

rendered unequalled service," said Croswell. "In my defence, and that of the American press . . . this greatest of men made his mightiest effort."

Writing to Thomas Jefferson a dozen years later on September 3, 1816, recultivating a late blooming of their formerly withered friendship, John Adams commented that Hamilton's party "seized the moment of public feeling to come forward with funeral orations and printed panegyricks and solemn grimaces . . . and why? Merely to disgrace the old Whigs, and keep the funds and banks in countenance." Offered this tempting bait for a biting reply, Jefferson refused it. He made no specific comment on Hamilton. Indeed, the usually articulate Jefferson made only two known mentions of the most sensational tragedy that had wracked the nation since its beginnings. One was the following meaningless postscript to a letter to his daughter Martha, July 17, 1804: "I presume Mr. Randolph's newspapers will inform of the death of Colo. Hamulton, which took place on the 12th." The other, in a letter the following day to Philip Mazzei in Europe, coldly included Hamilton's name as one of several on a list headed "remarkable deaths lately."

Of course, Jefferson had made no recorded comment on James Thomson Callender's mysterious demise the summer before either. But now, by a single bullet, Burr had removed the only two of the younger men on the American scene who posed a threat to his control of the presidential succession by the Virginia junto—James Madison and James Monroe—as far into the future as anyone alive could be expected to peer. Such extreme laconism about the dramatic simultaneous self-destruction of two rivals of the man who could descant by the quire on gossip Beckley brought him, suggests that Jefferson wished to keep the door tightly closed on the question of how much he knew about the secret meaning of the word *despicable*.

But Jefferson's creature John Beckley was as gleeful about Hamilton's fall as his master was tight-lipped when he wrote to John Brown on August 8, 1804: "Federalism has monumented and sainted *their* leader up to the highest heavens, whilst the presses are made to groan under the weight of Orations, Eulogies, and mournings, and Burr is pursued with vindictive and unrelenting fury." As it happened, Beckley's confidant John Brown was a brother-in-law of the Reverend Dr. John M. Mason, who had refused deathbed Communion to Hamilton. Beckley, no mean ironist, evidently knew that Mason was the kind of brother-in-law that his friend Brown or almost anyone would automatically despise. Beckley was also probably the country's most sedulous student of the subject of Hamilton's adulteries:

> The clergy, too, are sedulously endeavoring to canonize the double adulterer, as a *moralist,* a *Christian,* and a *saint.* Our friend Mason pronounced the oration at New York. I have not seen it and wish to *forget* the fact.

Ever the faithful instrument of his master Jefferson's will, Beckley did not venture out with his own opinion. "But one opinion prevails here," he said. Burr was correct. Brown should read the correspondence. It justifies Burr's procedure. "Nothing but the want of *equal intelligence* and *equal* nerve, would prevent any man pursuing the same course."

Beckley's reference to Burr's "equal intelligence" gives some ground to suspect that Beckley knew that the secret root of the duel lay in the special reference of the word *despicable* to the badger game that Beckley and Burr had played. Beckley had not admitted knowing nearly this much when he had written William Eustis three weeks earlier, disclaiming all knowledge of the causes of the duel. He would "drop a tear at [Hamilton's] untimely fate" and admire his talents, virtues, and "useful public services."

Horace's injunction, *de mortuis nil nisi bonum*, did not suppress John Adams's opinions of the departed; if anything, time seemed to heat up and concentrate Adams's desultory rage. Federalist newspaper stories called Hamilton "the soul and Washington the body—Washington the painted wooden head of the ship and Hamilton the pilot and steersman." They reported that Hamilton had planned a history that would reveal the secret that Washington had been his puppet. Adams fumed to Benjamin Rush—who in 1777 had noted of the 20-year-old Hamilton after Brandywine, "the idol of America was governed by one of his aides"—that "I lose all patience when I think of a bastard bratt of a Scotch peddler daring to threaten to undeceive the world in their judgment of Washington, by writing a history of his battles and campaigns." Adams went on, "This creature was in a delirium of ambition; he had been blown up with vanity by the Tories, had fixed his eye on the highest station in America, and he hated every man young or old who stood in his way." Moreover, Adams wrote Mercy Warren on July 20, 1807, with like distemper, "in this dark and insidious manner did this intriguer lay schemes in secret against me, and like the worm at the root of the peach did he labor for twelve years underground and in darkness girdle the root while the axes of the Anti-Federalists, Democrats, Jacobins, Virginia debtors to English merchants, and French hirelings, chopping as they were for the whole time at the trunk, could not fell the tree."

Hamilton's New York friends organized themselves to try to mend the destitution in which he had left his family. Oliver Wolcott, Jr., president of the Merchants Bank, took the lead; Gouverneur Morris, Matthew Clarkson, Archibald Gracie, and William Bayard also helped, all with the approval of Church, Pendleton, and Fish, Hamilton's executors. Wolcott wrote to Hamilton's wealthy admirers in Philadelphia, Boston, and Baltimore, men who had benefited from his fiscal policies, and proposed a subscription of $100,000 to pay his debts and provide for his family. An application for a grant by the national or state government or a general subscription had been considered, but rejected in favor of private contributions by "a number of Gentlemen of easy fortunes." Thomas Willing of Philadelphia, president of the Bank of North America, responded with ardor and started a subscription among "our most respectable and monied Citizens, known for their warm and decided attachment to the character and principles of the General." But some who might have subscribed questioned whether raising the fund would not offend members of the family, particularly General

Schuyler, whose wealth and disposition to provide for his daughter and grand-children were reputedly boundless.

Wolcott scoffed at the fear that private charity was indiscreet or officious. The family would be gratified at such testimony of esteem. If the debts of men in high station like Fox and Pitt could be discharged by their friends while they were alive and active, surely the dependents of a dead patriot could be provided for too. He reminded them that men of ample fortunes "owe their property in a great measure, to the operation of that political system of which Genl. Hamilton was the efficient agent." When pressed further—as by McHenry, who complained that subscriptions in Baltimore lagged because "the real or presumed great wealth of Gen. Schuyler is in everybody's mouth"—Wolcott had disclosed that Schuyler had left no funds at command.

Some $19,000 had been subscribed in New York by October 1. Rufus King mustered an active group in Boston, but little was collected in Baltimore and less in Philadelphia.[3] Wolcott, thinking the plan a failure, wrote that "the property will all be sold & the Estate after all be *Insolvent.*"

George Cabot and Boston friends subscribed some Pennsylvania lands that they had purchased from Pickering in 1801, when, fired from office by Adams, he had needed money to move to the frontier to cultivate another part of his domain. The buyers, having by this subterfuge given Pickering money in the only form he would accept, made it possible for him to come back and settle again in Massachusetts. Pickering now conveyed these 245 shares of nominal value of $100 each to Hamilton's executors as a latent resource for Elizabeth and her children.

Philip Schuyler, aged and ill when he had Elizabeth and several of her children with him at Albany, had showed her land near his house, which he intended to give her to lay out in lots that she could sell and executed the deed in regular form August 14, 1804; but she returned to New York before he delivered it, and the conveyance was ineffective when he died on November 18.

About $80,000 altogether was subscribed to pay Hamilton's debts. The Grange was sold for reimbursement of the contributors, purchased in at the sale for $30,000 and then surrendered by a select inner group of 29 friends back to Mrs. Hamilton for $15,000, thus saving The Grange for her to live in for a while.

Nine months after Hamilton's death, the fund, or loan to his executors, amounted to about $39,700. Thanks to them, Elizabeth Hamilton and the children were able to remain at The Grange until 1813. But the place was expensive to maintain, and she finally sold it and moved south to the city. From her father's estate she received some lands near Albany and some other counties scattered in northern New York State. She would sell these off from time to time to meet her needs and permit her to contribute to the charities in which she remained quite active. A year and a half after Hamilton's death, all his real estate other than The Grange, mostly shares in the Ohio Company and other interests he held in clients' properties, were advertised and sold at auction. It was a mortifying sort of bankruptcy.

Elizabeth Hamilton made persistent efforts to secure the writing of a biography that would preserve Hamilton's fame. With help from her sons she collected his papers and questioned his contemporaries for information. Nothing was too much trouble for her in behalf of his memory. A succession of friends chosen to write his life disappointed her. Dr. John M. Mason's health would not permit the labor. Joseph Hopkinson, the author of "Hail! Columbia," received the materials and examined them, but in the autumn of 1821 resigned the project from lack of time and industry. William Coleman, editor of the *Evening Post*, was suggested for the assignment, but Pickering was then selected. Nicholas Fish assured Pickering that his acceptance would "be balm to [Mrs. Hamilton's] drooping spirits, it will renew with confidence the hope of having justice at last done to the memory of her husband in a faithful biography." Pickering's death in 1829 left only a disjointed manuscript. A few months after Pickering's death she entered into a similar agreement with Francis Baylies, her clergyman, but nothing came of it. Having cast about widely, she found what she wished at home. Their son John Church Hamilton commenced publishing the life of his father, volume 1 in 1834 and volume 2 in 1840, but left the work incomplete in this form. When in 1849 the national government purchased the bulk of Hamilton's manuscripts, she was further gratified when John Church was chosen to edit his father's papers for the Joint Library Committee of Congress. Had she lived, her cup must have been full at last when he brought out his *History of the Republic as Traced in the Writings of . . . Hamilton . . .* , 7 volumes, Appleton, in the years 1857 through 1864.

The tribute that would probably have meant the most to Hamilton himself did not come until almost a quarter of a century after his death, when the surge of emotion that had accompanied his funeral had long since subsided. John Quincy Adams, whose father had sustained politically mortal wounds from Hamilton's pen, was writing about the scheme of Northern secession, disunion, separation, and confederacy that had been hatched among Pickering, Senator William Plumer, and other High Federalists in 1804 to withdraw from the Union "peaceably if they could . . . but violently if they must."[4]

John Quincy Adams wrote "that the proposal had been made to General Hamilton, to be the Joshua of the chosen people; and I was told that he disapproved the plan, but it cost him his life."

What Adams meant was that if Hamilton had gone along with most of his fellow Federalists in favoring secession of the Northern states as a protest against the Louisiana Purchase and for various other reasons, he would have escaped Burr's bullet. Adams believed that if Hamilton had gone along with his fellow Federalists, he would not have supported Morgan Lewis against Burr, Burr would have won the gubernatorial election, and no matter what Hamilton had said that night at Judge Tayler's, Burr would not have had occasion to vent his "predetermined hostility" on Hamilton by issuing the challenge direct. To Adams, Hamilton's stand in favor of preserving the Union was his "reason for going out to meet Colonel Burr, even to the stifling of the cry of his conscience, against the practice of dueling." Adams cited the fact that Hamilton had "closed the paper [giving his reasons for the duel] with these memorable words [,] 'The ability to be in future useful, whether in resisting mischiefs or effecting good, *in those crises of our public affairs, which seem likely to happen* [italics by Adams], would probably be inseparable, from a conformity with public prejudice in this particular." Here was the meaning of Hamilton's cryptic phrase, Adams concluded: "This paper was wholly unintelligible to those who did not know that a civil War and the command of an army had been for years sporting with Hamilton's ambition. . . . It was indistinctly understood by those, who knowing this were yet not apprized of the distinct proposal which had been made to him the preceding spring. To me who had been made acquainted with both there was nothing mysterious in the paper." Only with his honor intact, only by accepting Burr's challenge, Hamilton thought, could he retain whatever influence he had with his High Federalist friends to keep them from going too far with their secessionist folly.

Madison agreed with John Quincy Adams about Hamilton's lonely stand. He thought that a letter of Senator Plumer, associating Hamilton's name with a meeting in 1804 to discuss the plan for New England secession, was mistaken as to Hamilton. Of course, any men planning such a secession would covet the "leading agency of such a man" from New York, just as they had sought out Burr. But Hamilton would not join them, or if he appeared at the meeting at all, he would have done so "only to dissuade . . . from a conspiracy as rash and wicked, and as ruinous to the party itself as to the country."

Of the eight Hamilton children, Philip, who was 19 when he fell in his duel with Eacker in 1801, had been the most promising. Daughter Angelica's playing of the piano sent to her from London by her Aunt Angelica Church and still at The Grange was a special pleasure to her father, but after Philip's tragedy, when she was 17, she lost her mind and lived on to 73. Of the others, five sons and a daughter, four of the boys, including Alexander, who did not become a merchant as planned, entered the law, the three eldest after graduating from Columbia College. All served in Mr. Madison's War of 1812–1814.

James Alexander had an active political career, first as a Whig, then as a Democrat, and, on President Andrew Jackson's appointment, served as acting secretary of state in 1829. John Church is remembered as his father's biographer and editor of his papers, and his work is far more extensive and thorough and full of emotional insight than is usual in such filial undertakings, but not less partisan. William Stephen, next in line, early went west and was visited by his mother in Wisconsin when she was 80. Eliza became Mrs. Sidney A. Holly, seemed to inherit her mother's faculty for good management, and was her dependence in old age. Little Phil, the youngest, the replacement for his brilliant brother, a baby at his father's death, had less formal education than the others; his special kindliness earned him a reputation and many grateful, nonpaying clients as a poor man's lawyer. The children of Alexander and Elizabeth Hamilton had respectable lives that did them and their parents credit, but none showed much evidence of the unique quality of their father and mother.

For a long time after Hamilton's death, Elizabeth's despair at his loss, weariness of "this world of disastrous event," lack of money, and the overwhelming responsibility for educating seven children made her wish for death to join him. On February 9, 1805, she wrote that "my wounded heart is scarcely equal to" the demands upon it. "Permit me to fly to my blessed redeemer . . . that I may be permitted to remain in his blest abode and there view my Hamilton." A Christian's faith, however, would see her through: "But I must resign me to the will of my just God and long or short the remainder of my life I must devote it with resignation to his decree." It would be long. But she would survive it. For more than 50 years.

"Ah may it be to his [sic, not His] satisfaction," she closed. "Then all will be well."

In 1841, when she was 83, Elizabeth Hamilton told her lawyer, George Washington Strong, a founding partner with John Wells of the present-day New York firm of Cadwallader, Wickersham & Taft, "I have been here long enough. I want to put everything in order for my departure hence."

After he had patiently rewritten her new will for her three times, Strong refused to accept a third fee from her for the third version. Gratefully, she offered him a ring, containing "a lock of the General's hair."

The formidable leader of the bar recoiled in horror: "I never wear a ring."

She insisted: "You can attach it to the seal and key of your watch, and wear it that way."

Strong weakened, obeyed the Hamiltonian command, and wore it—that way —the rest of his life. His daughter, Miss Mary A. Strong, never forgot how he would sit while in a conversation and playfully twirl all—key, seal, ring—and the lock of Hamilton's hair—"when in a mood to interrogate his interlocutor."

Later Elizabeth Hamilton left New York to live with her widowed daughter, Eliza Holly, on H Street in Washington, D.C. Until the last, she went about alone, talked with animation, and received friends with grace.

One day when she was 92, Julia F. Miller paid her a call, and Anne Hollingsworth Wharton retold the story in her book *Social Life in the Early Republic.* Mrs. Hamilton was: ". . . a tiny little woman, most active and interesting, although she could never have been pretty in her life. She kept me by her side, holding me by the hand, telling me of the things most interesting to me." She spoke of Washington (with whom she had been a great favorite) and Lafayette, who was 'a most interesting young man'. . . . "When she was young," she recalled, she "was free of the Washington residence, and if there was company Mrs. Washington would dress her up in something pretty and make her stay to dinner, even if she came uninvited, so that she was presentable at table." Mrs. Hamilton showed her guest the Stuart portrait of Washington, "painted for her," she said, "and for which he sat." There were the old Schuyler chairs and tiny mirrors, ("most interesting to me," said Julia Miller). She added, "This tiny dot of a woman of such great age, happened to think of something in her room that she wanted to show Abbie, her granddaughter, Mrs. Hamilton Holly. Abbie offered to get it for her. 'Sit down, child, don't you think I can get it myself?' and up she went and got it, whatever it was."

Her son, James A. Hamilton, in his *Reminiscences,* recalled the magnificent Stuart portrait as almost covering the side wall near the entrance. The wine cooler, also a gift from Washington, reposed "under a large, handsome centre table in the front parlor." And, he added, "I remember nothing more distinctly than a sofa and chairs with spindle legs, upholstered black broadcloth, embroidered in flowery wreaths by Mrs. Hamilton herself." And there was also, of course, Ceracchi's "marble bust of Hamilton standing on its pedestal . . . That bust I can never forget, for the old lady always paused before it in her tour of the rooms, and, leaning on her cane, gazed and gazed, as if she could never be satisfied."

Another thing she could never forget across the half century she survived the duel was what James Monroe had done to them. About 1850, when she was 93, former President Monroe, full of years and honors, came to visit her. One of her nephews, who was then 15, described Monroe's last Hamilton confrontation to Dr. Allan McLane Hamilton:

I had been sent to call upon my Aunt Hamilton one afternoon. I found her in her garden and was there with her talking, when her maidservant came from the house with a card. It was the card of James Monroe. She read the card, much perturbed. Her voice sank, and she spoke very low, as she always did when she was angry. The words, "What has that man come to see me for?" escaped from her. "Why, Aunt Hamilton," said I, "don't you know, it's Mr. Monroe, and he's been President, and he is visiting here now in the neighborhood, and has been very much made of, and invited everywhere, and so—I suppose he has come to call and pay his respects to you." After a moment's hesitation she said, "I will see him."

The maid went back to the house. My aunt followed, walking rapidly, I after her.

She entered the parlor. Monroe rose to his feet. She stood in the middle of the room facing him. She did not ask him to sit down. He bowed, and addressing her formally, made her what seemed to be a carefully set speech—That it was many years since they had met, that the lapse of time brought its softening influences, that they both were nearing the grave, a time when past differences could be forgiven and forgotten—in short, from his point of view, a very nice, conciliatory, well-turned little speech.

She answered, still standing, and looking at him, "Mr. Monroe, if you have come to tell me that you repent, that you are sorry, *very* sorry, for the misrepresentations and the slanders, and the stories you circulated against my dear husband, if you have come to say this, I understand it. But, otherwise, no lapse of time, no nearness to the grave, makes any difference."

She stopped speaking. Monroe turned, took up his hat and left the room.

She had not left him under an impression her suspicions were removed.

Not long before her death, a friend paid a call on this solitary survivor from the heroic age, whose memories went all the way back to Indian raids on the old Schuyler house in Albany—and to the time her father's other house at Old Saratoga had been burned to the ground by "Gentleman Johnny" Burgoyne. The friend wrote:

The widow of Alexander Hamilton has reached the age of 95 and retains in an astonishing degree her faculties and converses with much of that ease and brilliancy which lent so peculiar a charm to her younger days. And then, after passing the compliments and congratulations of the day, she insists upon her visitors taking a merry glass from George Washington's punch bowl, which, with other portions of his table set, remains in her possession.

Her last illness was a short one. She died on November 9, 1854, at the age of 97, just as the "bleeding Kansas" uproar of Franklin Pierce's administration was widening the final split toward breakup of the Union, having survived her late husband by more than half a century. She was interred beside him in the sarcophagus on the Rector Street side of the graveyard of Trinity Church. She was a constant wife if there ever was one. Her gifts of silence, endurance, courage through suffering, and seemingly unwavering affection for the man she chose, who had chosen her, and to whom she devoted her life demonstrated tensile strength, not female weakness. She was Hamilton's champion in every arena of his life and after his death. Without her knowledge of and zeal in preserving the proofs of his greatness, his reputation would be the less.

And so would hers.

THE END

Finis coronat opus.

—from John Jay, November 19, 1794

HAMILTON CHRONOLOGY
1757–1804
HAMILTON'S TIMES

1755

Jan. 11   H born, according to some authorities.

?   James Hamilton, Jr., H's brother, who was two years older than H, born [or in 1753].

1756

May 4   Mary Uppington Fawcett, H's maternal grandmother, deeds three slaves to Archibald Hamm for life, then to Rachel Fawcett; dies on St. Eustatius shortly after.

Aug. 29   Seven Years' War begins, pitting Britain and Prussia against France, Austria, Sweden, and Saxony and leading to founding of British Empire and modern Germany.

1757

Jan. 11   H born, Charlestown, Nevis, British West Indies; mother: Rachel Fawcett Lavien, daughter of Dr. John Fawcett and Mary Uppington Fawcett, his wife; father: James Hamilton, son of Alexander Hamilton, laird of The Grange, Ayrshire, Scotland, and Elizabeth Pollock Hamilton, his wife.

1758

Oct. 1   Rachel Fawcett Lavien and James Hamilton on St. Eustatius as godparents to Alexander Fraser, son of Alexander Fraser and Elizabeth Thornton.

1759

Feb. 26   H's mother, Rachel Fawcett Lavien, sued by John Michael Lavien for absolute divorce in Temperret, or divorce court, Christiansted, St. Croix.

1760

H, age three, taken by James Hamilton and Rachel Fawcett Lavien with James, Jr., age five, from Nevis to St. Kitts about this year.

Oct. 25   King George III becomes king of England, succeeding George II.

1761

Oct.   William Pitt the Elder resigns as British prime minister.

1763

Feb. 15   Seven Years' War ends by Treaty of Hubertusberg.

1765

April   H, age eight, taken by father, James Hamilton and mother, Rachel, with brother James, Jr., from St. Kitts to St. Croix.

July   Stamp Act Congress, New York City, first major organized protest against British.

Aug.   H with mother, Rachel Fawcett Lavien, lives in house and shop at 34 Company's Lane, Christiansted, St. Croix, where H clerks for her.

1766

Jan. 8   H, Rachel, and James, Jr., left by James Hamilton after he collects judgment on St. Croix for employer, Archibald Ingram, and returns to St. Kitts.

March   British repeal the Stamp Act.

1767

H, age ten, clerks in Rachel's store, 34 Company's Lane, Christiansted; perhaps works also at Beekman and Cruger's, 7 and 8 King's Street, Christiansted.

1768

H clerks in Rachel's store, perhaps also at Beekman and Cruger's.

Feb. 19   H's mother, Rachel Fawcett Lavien, dies, Christiansted.

H clerks at Beekman and Cruger's.

1769

July   H's uncle James Lytton, of The Grange, St. Croix, and cousin Peter Lytton, his closest relatives on St. Croix, die.

Nov. 11   H writes his first extant letter to Edward Stevens: "I contemn the groveling condition of a clerk . . . and would willingly risk my life, though not my character, to exalt my station."

1770

Britain removes American import duties, except for the tax on tea.

March 5   Boston Massacre.

1771

April 6   H verses "In Yonder Mead My Love I Found" and "Coelia's an Artful Little Slut" published in *The Royal Danish American Gazette*, Christiansted, St. Croix.

April 10   "Rules for Statesmen," attributed to H, published in *The Royal Danish American Gazette*.

Oct. 15   H left in charge of Cruger's business while Nicholas Cruger is in New York City.

1772

Jan. 1   H manages Nicholas Cruger's business until Cruger returns March 15.

May 16   H gives receipt to cousin Ann Lytton Venton for remittances.

H meets Reverend Hugh Knox, who begins Presbyterian ministry on St. Croix.

Aug. 31   Devastating hurricane strikes St. Croix.

Sept. 6   H writes so-called Hurricane Letter to his father, James Hamilton, on St. Kitts.

Oct. 3   H's Hurricane Letter published in *The Royal Danish American Gazette*.

Oct. 17   H's poem "The Soul Ascending into Bliss, In Humble Imitation of Popes Dying Christian to His Soul," published in *The Royal Danish American Gazette*.

Oct.   H sails from St. Croix to Boston about this date.

Nov.   H reaches New York City about this time.

            Samuel Adams organizes new committees of correspondence.

1773

Jan.   H boards with William Livingston's family at Liberty Hall, Elizabethtown, New Jersey, while attending Francis Barber's grammar school. Becomes acquainted with Elias Boudinot's family.

May   H gives cousin Ann Lytton Venton receipts for remittances, including one for proceeds of sale of 15 hogsheads of sugar, indicating that she helped pay for his board and schooling at Elizabethtown.

June   H writes out quotations and paraphrases from Book of Genesis, Book of Revelation, translations from Homer's *Iliad*, notes on geography of the eastern Mediterranean, and a numbered list of 27 books on ancient and medieval history and philosophy at about this time, probably as part of his school exercises.

Oct.   H's application for admission to Princeton turned down. H matriculates at King's College, now Columbia University, New York City.

Dec. 16   Boston Tea Party destroys 340 chests of tea.

1774

May   Boston Port Act closes port of Boston.

July 6   H makes "Speech in the Fields" in New York City.

Sept. 4   H writes "Poem on the Death of Elias Boudinot's Child."

Dec. 15   H publishes first pamphlet *A Full Vindication of the Measures of the Continental Congress* in reply to "Free Thoughts on Congress" by A. W. Farmer (Samuel Seabury).

Dec.   H begins drilling with militia company (Corsicans or Hearts of Oak) in St. George's Churchyard.

1775

Feb. 23   H publishes pamphlet *The Farmer Refuted* as a reply to Seabury's "A View of the Controversy."

April 19   Battles of Lexington and Concord.

May 10   H and Robert Troup stand off riotous mob at King's College gates.

June 15   H publishes "Remarks on the Quebec Bill, Parts One and Two" in Rivington's New York *Gazetteer.*

June 17   Battle of Breed's Hill and Bunker Hill in Boston.

Aug. 23   H with Hearts of Oak militia removes cannon from fort at Battery under bombardment from the battleship *Asia*'s guns.

Nov. 23   H stands against Isaac Sears's raiders when they seek to destroy Rivington's printshop and press.

Nov. 26   H writes John Jay in Congress to take measures to prevent raids like that of Sears.

1776

March 14   H commissioned as captain of New York provincial artillery company by Alexander McDougall.

June 29   British begin invasion of New York.

July 4   Declaration of Independence signed in Philadelphia.

Aug. 29   H offers Washington plan for evacuation after Battle of Long Island.

Sept. 16   H's encampment at Harlem Heights; H first comes under Washington's eye and meets him.

Oct. 28   H's artillery at Battle of White Plains helps to hold off Hessian battalion.

Nov. 29   H's artillery covers Washington's Raritan crossing at Brunswick.

Dec. 25   H crosses Delaware with Washington and attacks Trenton.

Dec. 25   Adam Smith's *The Wealth of Nations* published.

1777

Jan. 3   H at Princeton fires round from battery of two fourpounders into Nassau Hall.

March 1   H appointed aide-de-camp to Washington; promoted to rank of lieutenant colonel.

April 20	H begins corresponding with Gouverneur Morris, George Clinton, Robert R. Livingston, and others of New York Committee of Correspondence.
Sept. 11	H at Battle of Brandywine.
Sept. 18	After Daverser's Ferry H warns Congress to leave Philadelphia.
Sept. 26	Cornwallis's army occupies Philadelphia.
Oct. 3	H at Battle of Germantown.
Oct. 17	Burgoyne surrenders to Horatio Gates at Saratoga.
Oct. 30	H sets out on mission to obtain reinforcements from Gates for Washington.
Nov. 5	H arrives in Albany to see Gates, Troup, perhaps General Philip Schuyler.
Nov. 12	H, returning from Albany, falls ill at New Windsor.
Nov.	Congress adopts draft of Articles of Confederation and recommends it to states for adoption.

1778

Jan. 17	H and Captain Caleb Gibbs return to Valley Forge from mission to Gates.
Jan. 29	H submits "Report on Army" to Congressional Committee to Supervise Army.
	H assists von Steuben with professional training of army and writing *Rules for the Order and Discipline of the Troops.*
May 5	Alliance with France announced at Valley Forge.
May 12	H swears congressional oath abjuring allegiance to King George III and promising to defend United States against him.
June 28	H issues and delivers orders to field commanders at Battle of Monmouth in Washington's name. On battlefield H tells Major General Charles Lee, "Let us all die here, rather than retreat."
July 4	At Brunswick court martial of Major General Charles Lee, H begins testimony as witness for the prosecution.
July 13	H continues testimony against Lee and is cross-examined by Lee, who charges H with "a frenzy of valor."
July 19	H meets Comte d'Estaing to plan joint American-French operation against Newport.

Oct. 19   H's Publius letter No. I attacks Congressman Samuel Chase for profiteering from secret information about grain purchases. Publius II on October 26 and Publius III on November 16 continue attacks.

Dec. 22   H serves as second for John Laurens in his duel with Charles Lee.

1779

Feb.   H with Washington in Philadelphia confers with congressmen, including Robert Morris and others.

March 14   H writes John Jay to urge on Congress raising battalions of Negro troops "to give them their freedom with their muskets."

July 4   H receives word from Lieutenant Colonel John Brooks of charge that H had said it was "high time for the people to rise, join General Washington, and turn Congress out of doors."

Oct. 7   H goes to Lewes, Delaware, and Great Egg Harbor, New Jersey, to meet d'Estaing and give orders for joint operation against New York.

Oct. 9   French-American amphibious expedition to retake Savannah fails.

Dec.   H writes long letter to member of Congress, probably Robert Morris, calling for plan to strengthen currency, enlist "moneyed men" in support of government, and establish a national bank.

Aug.   Spain declares war on Britain.

Aug.   Iroquois confederacy subdued by John Sullivan's expedition.

             John Paul Jones wins naval victory.

Nov.   British evacuate Newport; bring garrison back to New York.

1780

May   John Paul Jones drives British frigates to take cover.

May   British under Henry Clinton capture Charleston, South Carolina.

July 10   French under Comte de Rochambeau arrive at Newport.

Aug. 16   Cornwallis routs Gates at Battle of Camden, South Carolina.

Sept. 3   H writes long letter from Liberty Pole, New Jersey, to James Duane: "The fundamental defect is a want of power in Congress ... another defect is want of method and energy in the administration ... a convention would revive the hopes of the people."

Sept. 22   H at Hartford conference with Washington, Comte de Rochambeau, Chevalier de Ternay, Chevalier de Chastellux.

Sept. 25	H with Washington discovers Benedict Arnold's "treason of the deepest dye . . . to sacrifice West Point" and pursues Arnold. Peggy Shippen Arnold accuses Washington of a plot to murder her child.
Oct. 2	Major John André hanged at Washington's insistence against André's and H's protest that he should be shot instead.
Nov. 15	H with Washington and army in winter quarters at New Windsor.
Oct.–Dec.	H rebuffed in several efforts to obtain transfer to a field command.
Dec. 14	H marries Elizabeth, daughter of General Philip Schuyler, in elaborate ceremony at The Pastures, Albany, New York.

1781

Feb. 6	H writes letter for Washington to Governor Thomas Jefferson of Virginia responding to report of British incursions; requests Virginia to help reinforce southern army.
Feb. 16	H breaks with Washington.
Feb. 18	H writes Schuyler from New Windsor describing circumstances of break with Washington.
March 1	H goes to Newport with Washington.
April 30	H resigns officially as aide-de-camp to Washington.
April 30	H writes long letter to Robert Morris urging an "executive ministry," financial reforms, plan for a national bank.
	Articles of Confederation ratified; executive departments created.
July 12	H publishes first "Continentalist" essay in *The New York Packet and the American Advertiser*, Fishkill, N. Y. Five more issues of "The Continentalist" follow on July 19, August 9, and August 30, 1780, and on April 18 and July 4, 1782.
July 31	At Dobbs Ferry, H is given command of New York and Connecticut light infantry battalion for Yorktown campaign.
Aug. 7	Tories and Indians raid The Pastures, leaving tomahawk scar on stairway bannister.
Oct. 14	H at Yorktown commands and leads bayonet assault on British Redoubt No. 10.
Oct. 19	H, as officer of the day, helps arrange British surrender ceremony at Yorktown.
Dec.	H returns to The Pastures; suffers spells of illness.

1782

Jan. 22	Philip Hamilton, H's eldest son, born.
May 2	H appointed Continental receiver of taxes for New York.
Jan.–July	H studies law in Albany; writes practice manual *Practical Proceedings in the Supreme Court of the State of New York.*
July 21	H urges New York legislature to pass a resolution calling for a general convention of the states to amend the Articles of Confederation.
July 22	H appointed delegate to Continental Congress from New York.
Oct. 30	H resigns as Continental receiver of taxes for New York.
Nov. 25	H takes seat in Continental Congress.
Nov. 30	Preliminary articles of peace treaty signed in Paris.

1783

Jan.–March	H participates in congressional debates for strengthening finances of the Confederation.
Feb. 13	H advises Washington of dangers of troop mutiny and suggests measures to forfend it: "The claims of the army urged with moderation, but with firmness may operate on those weak minds."
March 11	Washington addresses officers and men at Newburgh and regains influence over disaffected members.
June 17	Units of Anthony Wayne's troops mutiny at Lancaster and march on Congress in Philadelphia.
June 19–22	H heads committees of Congress dealing with mutineers and Pennsylvania Executive Council. H recommends removal of Congress to Princeton June 26.
July 16	H leaves Congress in Princeton and returns to The Pastures at Albany to rejoin family.
Nov. 25	British evacuate New York City, and Americans make triumphal entry.
	H takes house at 57 Wall Street and opens law office at No. 56.
Dec. 4	H attends Washington's farewell to his officers in Fraunces Tavern.

1784

Jan. 1	H writes pamphlet "Letter from Phocion to the Considerate Citizens of New York" criticizing the legislature's violation of Articles

IV, V and VI of the peace treaty by refusing to restore confiscated loyalist property and ignoring provision against further confiscations.

Jan. 14   Definitive treaty of peace signed in Paris.

Feb. 24   H attends Bank of New York founders' meeting and draws constitution, charter, and incorporation papers for New York's first bank.

April   "Phocion II" appears.

June 29   H argues case of *Rutgers v. Waddington*, raising question of judicial supremacy of United States law and treaties over state law provisions.

Sept. 25   H's second child, Angelica, born.

           Congress makes New York City temporary capital of United States.

1785

Feb. 4   H is founding member of Society for Promoting the Manumission of Slaves, and chairman of a committee to recommend to the society the "line of conduct" to be followed by members in respect of their own slaves. Also, he is to make a register for those who manumit slaves to record the names and identification of manumitted slaves that "the society be the better enabled to detect attempts to deprive such manumitted persons of their liberty."

1786

March   H is elected to New York Assembly.

March 13   H joins petition to New York legislature urging the end of the slave trade, "a commerce so repugnant to humanity, and so inconsistent with the liberality and justice which should distinguish a free and enlightened people."

March 16   H after legislative struggle is named one of six commissioners to meet at Annapolis for the ostensible purpose of framing trade regulations in the general interest.

May 16   Son, Alexander Hamilton, Jr., born.

Sept. 14   H as New York delegate to Annapolis Convention drafts resolution calling for a general convention to enlarge the powers of the federal government.

Nov.   Shays' Rebellion erupts in Western Massachusetts.

1787

Jan. 12	H takes seat in New York State Assembly.
May 25– June 29	H at Constitutional Convention in Philadelphia.
June 18	H holds floor all day prior to vote on Virginia and New Jersey plans in the longest speech delivered at the convention.
Aug. 6	H at Constitutional Convention after a visit to New York.
Sept. 17	Constitution adopted; convention adjourns.
Oct. 27	Publication of H's *The Federalist*, No. 1.

1788

Jan. 22	H reappointed a New York delegate to the Continental Congress.
April 14	Son, James Alexander Hamilton, born.
June 17– July 26	H leads fight for ratification of the Constitution in New York at convention, Poughkeepsie, New York.
July 23	Parade in New York City in support of Constitution with the federal ship *Hamilton* as centerpiece.
July 27	Constitution ratified by New York State.

1789

April 30	George Washington elected president; government organized at New York City, the first capital.
Sept. 11	H appointed secretary of the treasury.
Nov. 5	H with son Philip and Baron von Steuben sees Angelica Church off to England after her summer in New York and weeps.

HAMILTON II
1789–1804

1790

Jan. 14	H sends first "Report on the Public Credit" to Congress.
Feb. 14	Thomas Jefferson accepts appointment as secretary of state.
April 12	H's assumption legislation defeated in the House.
June 20	H, Jefferson, and James Madison make "a deal by candlelight" for assumption and location of national capital; assumption measures pass Congress.

Sept.   H moves to Philadelphia with wife and four children.

Dec. 13   H submits "Second Report on the Public Credit"; leads campaign for assumption measures.

1791

Jan. 28   H submits "Report on the Mint."

Feb. 23   H gives Washington opinion upholding constitutionality of national bank under "implied powers."

May 17–
August 25   Jefferson and Madison make trip to New York and New England to hunt the Hessian fly.

July   H begins affair with Maria Reynolds about this time.

Nov. 5   H submits "Report on Manufactures" to House.

1792

March 9   William Duer defaults on payments and is arrested in time of financial panic.

July 25   H writes defense of his policies in newspapers; attacks on Jefferson and Philip Freneau.

Aug. 3   Jefferson writes 21 objections to Hamilton's "system," and Washington refers them to H for reply.

Aug. 10   Suspension of French king.

Aug. 22   Son, John Church Hamilton, born.

Sept. 15   H publishes first "Catullus" paper.

Sept. 21–25 Creation of the French Republic; National Convention replaces legislative assembly; onset of war of the First Coalition of European powers against France.

Dec. 15   James Monroe, Frederick A. C. Muhlenberg, and Abraham Venable confront H with evidence of his affairs with Maria and James Reynolds.

Dec. 27   Congress adopts resolutions to inquire into H's administration of the Treasury.

1793

Jan. 4   H submits report on loans.

Jan. 21   King Louis XVI is executed, a fact that does not become generally known in U.S. until March.

Jan. 23   H is impeached by Giles Resolutions introduced into House.

Feb. 27	Second set of Giles Resolutions is introduced.
March 2	Giles Resolutions defeated.
March 4	Second inauguration of Washington and Adams.
April 7	French declaration of war on Britain, Holland, and Spain becomes known in U.S.
April 8	Citizen Genêt lands at Charleston.
April 22	H advises Washington on Proclamation of Neutrality.
June 21	H tells Washington of intention to resign.
June 29	H publishes first "Pacificus" letter.
July 10	H advises cabinet in crisis of the *Little Democrat.*
July 31	H publishes "No Jacobin" letter revealing Genêt's threat to appeal over the head of the president directly to the people.
August	H and wife, Elizabeth, stricken in yellow fever epidemic in Philadelphia.
Nov.	H helps to raise funds to keep Fenno's *Gazette of the United States* alive.
Dec. 31	Jefferson officially resigns as secretary of state.

1794

Jan. 6–13	H drafts presidential message on Genêt's diplomatic status.
Jan. 14	H advises Washington on request to king of Prussia for release of Marquis de Lafayette from prison.
Jan. 31	H publishes "Americanus," No. 1, urging neutrality in dealings with France.
March 8	H recommends that Washington fortify ports and raise troops in preparation for hostilities with Britain.
March 18	H submits report to House on all receipts and expenditures from commencement of government through 1793.
April 23	After withdrawing his own name from consideration for appointment, H urges John Jay for special mission to Britain and writes detailed instructions for Jay.

1795

Jan. 31	H resigns as secretary of the treasury; returns to New York law practice.

March	After this time H works on complicated law cases involving debts of Robert Morris to H, to John B. Church, to William Pulteney, William Hornby, and others.
April 13	H writes Robert Troup, "It has been the rule of my life to do nothing for my own emolument *under cover* . . . it is pride. But this pride makes it part of my plan to *appear truly what I am.*"
June 24	Jay's Treaty approved by U.S. Senate.
July 18	H is stoned by a Wall Street mob.
July 22	H publishes first of 38 articles entitled "The Defense" and signed Camillus in defense of Jay's Treaty.
July 25	H writes Robert Troup concerning his will.
July 27	H publishes "Philo Camillus," No. I.
July 30	H writes essay "Defense of the Funding System."
July	H publishes "Horatius II" essay in defense of Jay's Treaty.
August	Edmund Randolph is forced to resign as secretary of state after suspicious financial dealings with French minister.
Oct. 16	H advises Washington concerning treatment to be given to Lafayette's son in U.S.
Oct. 26	H defends Washington against newspaper charges that he has overdrawn his pay and allowances.
Nov. 28	H drafts Washington's Seventh Annual Address to Congress.
Dec.	H writes essay attacking "American Jacobins."

1796

Feb. 24	H argues in support of carriage tax in U.S. Supreme Court.
March 3	Thomas Pinckney's Spanish Treaty approved by Senate.
April 30	House votes provisions necessary to carry Jay's Treaty into effect.
May 15–August 25	H drafts Washington's Farewell Address, delivered September 19, followed by active presidential campaign.
Nov. 10	H drafts Washington's Eighth Annual Message to Congress, calling for a national university, a military academy, and a board of agriculture.
Dec. 5	Electors meet and elect Adams president, Jefferson vice-president.
Dec. 8	H publishes "The Answer," signed Americanus, to rebut Adet's criticisms of American policy toward France.

1797

Jan. 27   H publishes "The Warning," signed Americanus, first of six essays setting forth his view of Franco-American relations.

March 4   Adams and Jefferson inaugurated.

1797

June 20   Adams appoints Elbridge Gerry to serve with Charles C. Pinckney and John Marshall on mission to France.

July 5   H discloses his 1791–1792 liaison with Mrs. James Reynolds and begins quarrel with Monroe.

July   H buys house at No. 58 Partition Street, New York, N. Y.

August 4   Son, William Stephen Hamilton, born.

August 25   H publishes "Reynolds Pamphlet."

1798

March 30   H publishes "The Stand," signed Titus Manlius, attacking the Paris Directory.

April 3   Adams reports XYZ Affair to House.

June 25–
July 14   Alien and Sedition Acts approved. H is critical of them.

July 25   H appointed inspector general of the army with rank of major general.

July   Quasi war with France has been going on for some time.

1799

March 16   H gives orders for suppression of Fries's rebellion.

June 3   Death of H's father, James Hamilton, on St. Vincent, British West Indies.

Oct.   Adams, overriding cabinet recommendations, orders commissioners to France.

Oct. 1   Francisco Miranda letter proposes expedition for liberation of Spanish colonies.

Nov. 9   Napoleon overthrows Directory in coup and installs Consulate with himself as first consul.

Nov. 20   Daughter, Eliza Hamilton, born.

Dec. 19   George Washington dies at Mount Vernon.

1800

May 6   Adams discovers H's influence on his cabinet and demands McHenry's resignation.

May 7   H requests Jay to revise method of choosing electors to reverse Federalist New York election defeat by Republicans.

July 1   H resigns as inspector general after disbanding troops.

Oct. 3   Treaty of Mortefontaine ends Quasi-War with France.

Oct. 22   H publishes attack on John Adams in Bache's *Aurora* and elsewhere.

Nov.   H supports Federalists John Adams and Charles C. Pinckney in election campaign against Jefferson and Burr.

Dec. 16   H supports Jefferson over Burr after electoral tie.

December   Capital moved to District of Columbia.

1801

Jan. 15   Federalists in caucus decide to support Burr over Jefferson.

Jan. 16   H writes Bayard, characterizing Jefferson.

Jan. 24   Senate approves nomination of John Marshall as chief justice.

Feb. 17   H is instrumental in Jefferson's election over Burr on thirty-sixth tie-breaking ballot in House.

July 1   H plans house for Grange.

Nov. 16   H founds *The New York Evening Post.*

Nov. 23   H's eldest son, Philip, mortally wounded in duel with George Eacker, a supporter of Aaron Burr.

Dec. 17   H publishes first of 18 installments of "The Examination," attacking Jefferson's program, as "a performance which . . . makes a prodigal sacrifice of constitutional energy, of sound principle, and of public interest to the popularity of one man."

Dec. 19   Senate approves treaty with France.

1802

Feb. 27   H writes Gouverneur Morris "Mine is an odd destiny" letter.

April 16–18 H advises Federalists to adopt Republican methods to achieve goals, including establishment of the Christian Constitutional Society.

Dec. 29   Hamiltons move into Grange and H writes Charles C. Pinckney "A garden, you know, is a very usual refuge of a disappointed politician."

1803

Feb. 24   Supreme Court issues decision in *Marbury v. Madison.*

April 30   Treaty ceding Louisiana to United States signed in Paris.

1804

Feb. 13   H argues in defense of freedom of the press in *People v. Croswell.*

April   H opposes separatist movement threatened by New England.

April 25   Burr defeated in New York gubernatorial election.

July 11   H mortally wounded in duel with Burr at Weehawken.

July 12   H dies at house of William Bayard, New York City.

July 14   H buried in Trinity Churchyard, New York City, with full military honors.

A NOTE ABOUT SOURCES, NOTES, AND BIBLIOGRAPHY

The principal source for this book not available to earlier Hamilton biographers is *The Papers of Alexander Hamilton*, volumes I through XXI, with Harold C. Syrett as editor and Jacob E. Cooke as associate editor, published by Columbia University Press. Harold C. Syrett is the sole editor of volume XVI and following volumes. The latest volume, XXI, carries Hamilton to July 1798 and closes with his "Plan for a Legion," a proposal for fundamental reorganization of the army, and letters to George Washington and his to wife, Elizabeth, as he awaits word of his appointment as inspector general and second-in-command to Washington for the Quasi War. In *Hamilton II* these volumes are referred to as the Hamilton Papers, or PAH. The other important, newly available source is *The Law Practice of Alexander Hamilton*, volumes I and II, edited by Julius Goebel, Jr., and published by Columbia University Press, volume I in 1964 and volume II in 1969, herein referred to as the Hamilton Law Papers or LPAH.

All significant letters and other documents written by Hamilton, all significant letters and other documents written by others to him, and all other significant documents that directly concern him (commissions, certificates, and so on) to July 1798 are printed in chronological order in the Hamilton Papers. For the period from July 1798 through 1804, the remaining period of Hamilton's life not covered by presently available volumes of the Hamilton Papers, my principal sources have been *The Works of Alexander Hamilton*, edited by Henry Cabot Lodge, 12 volumes (New York and London: Putnam Federal Edition, 1904), referred to as Lodge, *Works; The Works of Alexander Hamilton*, edited by

John C. Hamilton, 7 volumes (New York: J. F. Throw, 1850–1851) referred to as Hamilton, *Works;* John C. Hamilton's *History of the Republic of the United States . . . As Traced in the Writings of Alexander Hamilton,* 7 volumes (New York: Appleton, 1857–1864), referred to as Hamilton, *History;* Allan McLane Hamilton's *The Intimate Life of Alexander Hamilton* (New York: Scribner's, (1910), referred to as Hamilton, *Intimate Life; The Writings of George Washington,* edited by John C. Fitzpatrick (Washington, D.C.: 1931–1944); *Memoirs of the Administrations of Washington and John Adams: Edited from the papers of Oliver Wolcott, Secretary of the Treasury* by George Gibbs (New York: 1846); *The Works of Fisher Ames, with a Selection from His Speeches and Correspondence,* edited by Seth Ames, 2 volumes (Boston: 1854); *The Life and Correspondence of Rufus King* by Charles R. King (New York: 1894–1900); Broadus Mitchell's *Alexander Hamilton, The National Adventure, 1788–1804* (New York: Macmillan, 1962), the second volume of the two-volume biography—its 555-page text is buttressed by 217 pages of notes—and John C. Miller's *Alexander Hamilton, A Portrait in Paradox* (New York: Harper, 1959); and the other books and articles listed in the bibliographies of *Hamilton I* and *Hamilton II.* My debt to the scholars who produced these works is great.

Within the next few years the final volumes of the Hamilton Papers and the Hamilton Law Papers will clear up most of the problems created by inaccurate or incomplete reproduction of documents and annotations in Lodge's *Works* and John C. Hamilton's *Works* and *History* and other earlier collections for the period from July 1798 through 1804.

The Hamilton Papers and the Hamilton Law Papers tell whether the paper in question is an autograph document; whether it is signed or a draft or a letter book copy or taken from a printed source, and so on; identify Hamilton's correspondent and the individuals mentioned in the text; explain events and ideas referred to in the text; cross-reference to related documents and events; point out textual variations and mistakes; inform whether the original is cropped or has been mutilated or bowdlerized in an earlier collection and the significance, if any, of such alteration; and supply historical and biographical background material. In the case of some important documents, such as Hamilton's "Report on a National Bank," both his first draft and final version are reproduced; they provide fascinating insights to his mental processes and the refinement of his thinking over time.

Routine letters and documents by Hamilton, routine letters to Hamilton, most letters and documents written by Hamilton for someone else (such as letters written for George Washington), letters and documents that have not been found, but that are known from references elsewhere to have existed, letters and documents such as polemical broadsides erroneously attributed to Hamilton, and letters that deal exclusively with his legal practice are chronologically calendared in the Hamilton Papers. There a citation is given to another source for the full text of the document and other information about it. Calendared references to events in Hamilton's law practice contained in the Hamilton Papers are dealt with in full in the Hamilton Law Papers. The list of "Short Titles and Abbreviations" found in the front matter of each volume of the Hamilton Papers also serves as a useful bibliography of source material for the time period covered by the volume. Each volume of the Hamilton Papers and the Hamilton Law Papers also contains an exhaustive index to names of persons, places, events, and other things dealt with in the volume, which is invaluable to any scholar wishing to pursue research concerning matters mentioned in *Hamilton II* or in the Hamilton Papers or the Hamilton Law Papers.

In *Hamilton II 1789–1804*, as in *Hamilton I 1757–1789*, which precedes it, nothing is presented as fact which I have invented or which lacks a basis in written authority. Where documentary evidence is conflicting or admits of more than one interpretation, I have usually resolved doubts by deciding the question as I believe Hamilton would have done or from Hamilton's point of view, consistent with my own view of him as a flawed hero. Some such conclusions are based on evidence that can only be characterized as dubious or circumstantial. In the few instances where a surmise or supposition as to a matter of fact is presented —for example, in chapter 30, as to the story Doctor Cooper heard that he would characterize as "despicable"—it is described as such in the context of the circumstantial evidence leading to my conclusion. For unconvincing inferences, implications, insights, conclusions, and opinions, I assume full responsibility.

The Hamilton Papers and the Hamilton Law Papers are comprehensive, authoritative, definitive, and of a scholarly quality that is not likely ever to be surpassed. Other source material and secondary material for the period covered by *Hamilton II* not listed in the Bibliography of *Hamilton I* are listed in the Bibliography of *Hamilton II*. As I have proceeded, it has become apparent to me that to include an elaborate apparatus of footnotes, source notes, citations, and so forth in this book would increase its bulk, weight, and cost for the nonspecialist reader, needlessly impede the stride of the story of Hamilton's fall, impress the nonspecialist, yet provide the specialist with little that is not readily available to him in more complete and exhaustive form in one or another of the books and articles listed in the Bibliography. Accordingly, in lieu of such apparatus and note numberings in the text, I have simply included in the text the dates of documents, events, and actions with more frequency than is usual in books of this kind; supplied a brief set of notes by chapters at the end and also a comprehensive Bibliography and Index. These will provide the reader who wishes to pursue particular avenues of inquiry further an appropriate introduction to such material. The period and subject matter are all but inexhaustible.

NOTES

Notes for Chapter 1
SUSPICION IS EVER EAGLE-EYED

[1] Page 3 In the Foreword to his book about Hamilton, entitled *The Greatest American* (New York: G. P. Putnam's Sons, 1921), the late Senator Arthur H. Vandenberg quotes Thomas Carlyle: "Universal history is at bottom the history of the great men who have worked here . . . The soul of the whole world's history, it may justly be considered, were the history of these . . . Could we see them well, we should get some glimpses into the very marrow of the world's history." To this, Senator Vandenberg adds, "Every great event in the evolution of a nation is the lengthened shadow of some man or set of men for whom the event is the expression of character and the reflex of aspiration." He then poses the question: "What man, all things considered, in the whole history of our country down to date, is best entitled to be called 'The Greatest American?' " He adds, "If, by a confessedly startling challenge to habitual American public opinion in my nomination of 'The Greatest American,' I shall succeed in sending my countrymen to the biographies of their own favorite figures in American history, seeking renewed and refreshed knowledge with which to rebut my conclusions, this volume will not have failed in its monitorial ambitions." Senator Vandenberg then answers his own question: "The busy modern generations of today yield scant acknowledgments to the superlative men of those distant, inchoative days which put down the rock foundations upon which all institutional America has been erected, and upon which our society leans, confidently but all too thoughtlessly, today. Among these men, none holds us in more completely unrequited debt than Alexander Hamilton."

Vandenberg's argument runs that "Alexander Hamilton was the master craftsman of American government. He crowded into one short life more dynamic service to the American foundation than any other patriot who ever lived." As *The Federalist*, Number 1, declared in the beginning, "The subject speaks its own importance; comprehending in its consequences nothing less than the existence of the UNION, the safety and the welfare of the parts of which it is composed, the fate of an empire in many respects the most interesting in the world." The debates in the Constitutional Convention of 1787 contained 223 allusions to the government and institutions of other countries, including 130 allusions to England, 19 to France, 17 to the German states, 20 to Holland, 25 to Greece, and 26 to Rome—examples drawn from the laboratory of history to test the wisdom of all proposals. In the review of the millennia of recorded history prior to the founding of the United States of America no example was found, says Vandenberg, to which the historian can point and say with assurance that there was a government that worked well.

Of the 142 members of the United Nations in 1976, U.S. Ambassador Daniel P. Moynihan observed that "in the range of two dozen" were democracies, whereas the rest were "totalitarian, Communist or despotic" regimes. In the context of the real world of the twentieth century, the United States under its eighteenth-century Constitution and early structure that Hamilton did so much to create thus represents something of a 200-year-old miracle.

[2] Page 3 Following up *The Greatest American*, Senator Vandenberg produced a second book, *If Hamilton Were Here Today* (New York: G. P. Putnam's Sons, 1923), in a year—1923—which we tend to look back on as part of the Golden Age of the Twenties. But he saw a crisis. In 1923, said Senator Vandenberg, Hamilton might ask, as he had in *The Federalist*, Number 6, "Is it not time to awake from the deceitful dream of a Golden Age, and to adopt as a practical maxim for the direction of our political conduct that we, as well as the other inhabitants of the globe, are yet remote from the happy empire of perfect virtue? Have we not already seen enough of the fallacy and extravagance of those idle theories which have amused us with promises of an exemption from the imperfections, weaknesses and evils incident to society in every shape?"

[3] Page 7 The bill creating the Treasury Department and granting authority to the secretary of the treasury to exercise his broad powers was passed by the House on July 2, 1789, by the Senate on July 31, 1789, and signed by President Washington on September 2, 1789. The bill included safeguards against any Treasury employee acting alone gaining personal profit from Treasury operations. Every Treasury Department employee was forbidden, under penalty of fine and disqualification from ever holding office under the United States, to have any part in commerce or deal in public land or public securities. The treasurer should make disbursements only "upon warrants drawn by the Secretary of the Treasury, countersigned by the Comptroller, recorded by the register, and not otherwise. . . ." 1. Laws of the United States of America, published by authority,

1 Stat. at Large, 65–7 (Philadelphia, Richard Folwell, 1796, 36–40). Richard Folwell, publisher of the statutes, later served as an important character witness for Hamilton to rebut charges that he had trafficked in public securities on the basis of inside knowledge in violation of this statute.

[4] Page 7 Hamilton's letter of October 1, 1783, to Major General Nathanael Greene was written the day after he had written George Washington September 30, taking a prescient view three years ahead toward the time when the need for a strong executive would become clear to all, or to most, Americans. Noting that Congress had adjourned and Washington had retired "the moment the definitive treaty was ratified," Hamilton added that "I wished you in a solemn manner to declare to the people your intended retreat from public concerns, your opinion of the present government, and of the absolute necessity of a change." The change was one he had recommended earlier the same year in his letter to Washington of March 24, 1783, telling him that "it now only remains to make solid establishments within to perpetuate our union." Hamilton concluded that Washington's help would be needed for "the establishment of our federal union upon a more solid basis." Few letters better illustrate Hamilton's willingness to use his influence to bend Washington's actions to Hamilton's plans for the country. Later events attested to Hamilton's success in doing so. Washington's reply to Hamilton of March 31, 1783, had sought his help: "I shall be obliged to you, however, for the thoughts which you have promised me on this subject, and as soon as you can make it convenient . . . for a reform in our present confederation."

[5] Page 13 The problems of public credit inherited by Hamilton from the various incompetent administrators under the Confederation are reminiscent of the budgetary "gimmicks" that shrink and decay the public credit of many modern municipal and governmental institutions. State debts of various kinds included notes payable at various dates to the army militia, notes issued by acts of the legislature, notes issued for remounting horse troops, notes issued in substitution for old notes "rolled over," certificates issued for unpaid interest, unpaid balances due from particular taxes, and debts issued prior to the Revolution. There were unsettled accounts with Congress, with boards, commissioners, deputy quartermasters, and the commissary. Of the confusion, Madison wrote Jefferson on June 30, 1789, "We are in a wilderness without a single footstep to guide us." Under the Confederation the accounts between the states, the United States, and the private commercial accounts of Robert Morris remained unsettled, unsegregated, and in total confusion.

[6] Page 14 As an expert in administration, Hamilton knew how to mix discretion with rigidity, writing to Jeremiah Olney on April 2, 1793: "My own maxims of conduct are not favorable to much discretion, but cases do sometimes occur in which a little may be indispensable . . . The goodwill of the Merchants is . . . important . . . and if it can be secured without . . . introducing a looseness

of practice, it is desirable to do it. 'Tis impossible for me to define the degree of accommodation which will avoid one extreme or another."

[7] Page 14 Hamilton prescribed model forms for use in submission of reports of collectors, setting forth digests of manifests of vessels clearing for foreign ports. See circulars of October 2, 20, and December 1, 1789, and September 30, 1790: "The public service requires the strictest care and punctuality in adhering to the forms now established, and in forwarding them regularly to this office." (Treasury Department circular to the collectors of customs, December 1, 1789.)

[8] Page 15 Hamilton did not consider it safe to place "the oil vault within the lighthouse." The keeper's house in an exposed situation at Cape Henry Lighthouse should be of stone, not frame, with a cellar, even at extra cost. (Hamilton to John Macomb, Jr., April 1, 1791.)

[9] Page 16 H. Van Schaack wrote Theodore Sedgwick of Massachusetts January 25, 1791, "I wish I had it in my power to impeach all the members of your House on the ground of an intention to destroy the Secretary of the Treasury. The people . . . here find . . . fault with Congress to refer so many paltry matters to this truly . . . valuable man, whose labors . . . ought to be confined to the weighty objects of government . . . the loss of such a man would derange and embarrass the government exceedingly."

[10] Page 16 Another important source was Pelatiah Webster's *Political Essays on the Nature and Operation of Money, Public Finances . . . published during the American War* (Philadelphia: 1791). Webster's 1781 essay "Dissertation on . . . the office of the Financier General" described the duties of a financier: he must "point out, arrange, and put into action, *the ways and means by which the necessary supplies of the public treasury* may be derived . . . that the same be done with the most *ease, decision* and *expedition* . . . and at the *least expense."* There must be a single man to organize things in a clear manner so that Congress could comprehend "the whole and all the parts," to "spy out and check any . . . waste." It would be fatal to suffer "the public credit to decay." To prevent this "a single *person* was necessary. . . . The design and uses of the office . . . *must be the work of* ONE MIND." To place responsibility for public credit in "aggregate bodies" would permit shifting blame for mismanagement from one committee or board to another and lead to disaster. With Pelatiah Webster, Hamilton feared inflation. It was "the worst way that . . . ever was . . . thought of . . . paying the expenditures by the depreciation of the currency . . . [would bring] such an interaction of calamities as are enough to draw tears." (Webster, *Political Essays*, 167–8.)

[11] Page 17 Other sources were Dr. Richard Price (1723–1791), a Presbyterian minister, mathematician, economist, political scientist, and author of Price's "Observations on the Nature of Civil Liberty . . . and the Justice and Policy of

the War with America" (1776), "Additional Observations . . . (1777)," "An Appeal to the Public on the Subject of the National Debt" (1772), and "Observations on Reversionary Payments" (1771); and Samuel Gale, author of "An Essay on the Nature and Principles of Public Credit" (London, 1784) and three following essays (London, 1784, 1786, 1787). Gale pointed out that a well-managed public debt could lower the rate of interest and thus increase investment capital for commerce and industry, reduce the cost of carrying on business, and enlarge wealth and prosperity. He also reminded the reader that the British debt had been a great public benefit only until it "became grown out of all reasonable shape."

[12] Page 17 Philip Schuyler provided material for Hamilton's use in fiscal reports, including a ten-page discussion of "The Debt of the United States," placing the foreign debt at about $7,885,085 and the domestic debt at about $35,000,000.

Hamilton also drew upon Postlethwayt's *Universal Dictionary of Trade and Commerce* and *Britain's Commercial Interest Explained and Improved,* which contains a thoroughgoing discussion of public credit in volume I (1774 edition). The British system of funding and redemption contained many of the features Hamilton introduced by his reports on public credit.

[13] Page 18 Madison's letter of November 19, 1789, to Hamilton proposed a federal land tax, which Hamilton opposed. Madison favored a stamp tax on proceedings in federal courts and thought western lands would be a promising source of revenue. Hamilton did not. Within two months, Madison, under Jefferson's influence, had reversed his position from nationalist to sectionalist.

[14] Page 24 Broadus Mitchell points out (Mitchell, *Hamilton II,* page 38) that in the borrowing of material for his great reports from many sources, "none of his borrowing was mechanical. He was selective . . . and all became imbued with his own plan . . . his best authority was his own intimate knowledge of economic and governmental weakness during the war, and under the Confederation when Congress was denied a revenue." William Bingham's letter and English precedent served as models for his reports on public credit; the Bank of England, the Bank of North America, and the Bank of New York served as models for the Bank of the United States; European practice and experience of European writers with use of precious metals served as a basis for his "Report on the Mint"; and the policies of Colbert and other mercantilists served as precedents for his "Report on Manufactures."

[15] Page 25 In London, William Short placed his balance with Messrs. Grand and arranged with the speculator Daniel Parker to invest the money in U.S. liquidated debt: "in case it appears that indents are the most certain of a quick rise, the liquidated debt can be sold and the proceeds vested in them." (Daniel Parker to William Short, October 3, 1789.)

The complexity of the report made it confusing to all but knowledgeable men like Constable, Duer, Wadsworth, Robert and Gouverneur Morris, Daniel Parker, William Short, and men like them.

Public uproar arose from supposed prejudice in favor of or against discrimination against poor old soldiers' widows, and so on. Notwithstanding all the information, many holders continued to part with securities at large discounts, at a fraction of the value that Hamilton's plan would have given them, if adopted. On the whole, said Craigie, "I have done pretty well in my speculations"; he was boasting about a modest net profit of only about 10 percent.

Notes for Chapter 2
A DEAL BY CANDLELIGHT AT THOMAS JEFFERSON'S

[1] Page 36 Speculators could view Madison's advocacy of discrimination as helpful, not harmful, to themselves: "I hope that Mr. Madison's proposition for discrimination will have an effect in lowering your market and alarming so that people may sell at reasonable rates on time—try if you cannot do something." (William Constable to G. Cottringer, February 13, 1790.)

[2] Page 45 There was no excuse for Jefferson to pretend lack of familiarity with assumption to Madison; Madison had written him at Monticello on January 24, 1790, that Hamilton's "Report on Public Credit" was too bulky to post entire, but "I will by the next mail commence a transmission in fractions . . . you will find a sketch of the plan in one of the newspapers herewith enclosed."

[3] Page 45 Madison, writing to his father, James Madison, Sr., June 30, 1790, was reconciled to assumption from a Virginia point of view. "In a pecuniary light, the assumption is no longer of much consequence to Virginia, the sum allotted to her being about her proportion of the whole. . . ."

[4] Page 46 Even before the deal by candlelight at Thomas Jefferson's, Madison wrote to his brother that the assumption proposal had been revived and would remain in debate for some time: "I hope we shall be able to defeat it, but the advocates for it are inconceivably persevering as well as formidable in point of numbers." The bill for funding would pass "in substance as reported by the Secretary of the Treasury" (May 27, 1790).

[5] Page 47 Still satisfied with his role on August 14, 1790, Jefferson wrote his son-in-law, Thomas Mann Randolph, that Congress, shortly before adjourning, had "reacquired . . . harmony" by reconciling assumption and location of the capital, adding, "It is not foreseen that anything so generative of dissension can arise again, and . . . the friends of government hope that, this difficulty . . . surmounted . . . everything will work well."

Notes for Chapter 3
FOREIGN AFFAIRS

[1] Page 60 From Paris, Jefferson wrote Angelica Church in London on July 27, 1788, "Many motives . . . authorized me to write to you, but none more than this that I esteem you infinitely. Yet, I have thought it safe to get Kitty to write also, that her letter may serve as passport to mine, and shed on it the *suave odeur* of . . . warm emotions. . . ." He thinks of her as he rides in the Bois, "and could I write as I ride, and give . . . my thoughts as warm as they flow from the heart, my friend would see what a foolish heart it is . . . if you will install me your physician, I will prescribe to you . . . a month in Paris."

Notes for Chapter 4
A PROSPECTUS FOR THE SUM—AND U.S.A., INC.

[1] Page 74 Hamilton's "Second Report on Public Credit," submitted December 13, 1790, called for renewal of taxes on spirits to raise money to pay interest of $788,333.33 annually on $21,500,000 of state debts assumed. Hamilton's mode of collection did not depend on the honesty of taxpayers: security of the revenue must "depend chiefly on the vigilance of the public officers." In debate, Livermore of New Hampshire quipped that the excise tax was one the people would approve "as drinking down the national debt." The bill became law March 3, 1791, completing Hamilton's funding system after 14 months of the most strenuous advocacy of Hamilton's career.

Jefferson criticized: "the excise law," he wrote Madison on December 28, 1794, "is an infernal one. The first error was to admit it by the Constitution; the second, to act on that admission; the third . . . will be, to make it the instrument of dismembering the Union. . . ."

[2] Page 75 Hamilton had drawn the charter of the Bank of New York in 1784, organized support for it, sat on the board of directors until 1788, and opposed Livingston's efforts to charter a rival land bank.

Hamilton's "Report on a National Bank" was a counterthrust to Jefferson's Virginia and Kentucky resolutions: it asserted the power of the Union over the individual states under the Constitution.

[3] Page 75 Foreseeing that the cause of most bank failures would, as always, be overextension in mortgages and speculative investments in land, Hamilton forbade investment by the Bank of the United States in real estate.

[4] Page 76 To criticism that assumption and funding were draining off American debt into foreigners' hands, Hamilton argued that Europeans who had acquired American funds were emigrating into the United States, bringing their money back with them, augmenting the American labor force and supply of

capital, and pro tanto depleting that of the countries from which they emigrated.

In his "Report on a National Bank," Hamilton sought to dispel popular prejudice against paper currency by showing how banks multiply the circulation of gold and silver specie by issuing notes and honoring checks to transfer credits up to several times the quantity of the precious metal. This increases "the active or productive capital of a country" if it remains secure by maintenance of proper proportions of liabilities and reserves to assets. By thus contributing to enterprise, "banks become nurseries of national wealth. . . ." By enhancing the quantity and speed of circulation of money, banks also facilitate payment of taxes.

[5] Page 77 Among the economic disadvantages Madison cited on the authority of Adam Smith's *Wealth of Nations*, Book II, Chapter II, was that precious metals would be banished from circulation by the substitution of paper. Madison failed to grasp the countervailing benefit that Smith found in the fact that additional paper money would permit greater circulation and import of raw materials and tools of production. Madison felt that Americans were likely to squander gold and silver specie abroad on luxuries and trifles. On economic grounds, his objections seem superficial and naïve. The weight of his objection was political—that the plan was unconstitutional.

[6] Page 78 Elias Boudinot, defending Hamilton's plan for a national bank, pointed out that most of the objection was not to a bank as such, but to a corporation incorporated by the federal government. This extended a power to the federal government that the states jealously limited to their own political authority. Boudinot explained the merits of carrying on a banking enterprise in corporate form. Irving Brant points out in James Madison, *Father of the Constitution, 1787–1800*, that all the time Madison "was arguing against himself." The doctrine of "implied powers" had originated in Madison's own report to the old Congress in 1781. He deliberately preserved it when he wrote the Tenth Amendment to the Constitution. "Hamilton's basic contention was a paraphrase of Madison's explanation of the 'necessary and proper' clause in the Federalist Number 44." Madison could escape from his own earlier logic "only by denying that a bank served a purpose incidental to the government's money power." Such was the power that Madison's new master, Jefferson, exercised over his acute but servile mind. Brant gives a striking illustration of this intellectual duplicity by pointing out that Madison, in 1789 and 1790, strongly backed a proposal that could have been justified only under Hamilton's interpretation of the Constitution: John Churchman's plan to subsidize a scientific voyage to determine the causes of magnetic deviations.

[7] Page 78 Hamilton sent Jefferson a copy of his "Report on the Mint" before submitting it to Congress because it rejected a recommendation of Jefferson that Hamilton had earlier agreed on in principle: namely, that the value of the dollar should correspond with the unit value of specie it represented. Jefferson wrote

Hamilton in January 1791 that he read Hamilton's "Report on the Mint" "with great satisfaction" and concurred in its main point. A bimetal standard, using both gold and silver, existed, but Hamilton preferred gold: it was less liable to variation in value. He did not wish to eliminate silver entirely because doing so would reduce it to "a mere merchandise; ... abridge the quantity of circulating medium" and forfeit "the benefits of a full, [compared] with the evils of the scanty circulation." Hamilton always urged abundant, sound money to build the American economy; he favored a legal relation between silver and gold of 15 parts silver to one of gold that would be in harmony with prevailing British and Dutch ratios, but over time would slightly overvalue silver.

⁸ Page 89 William Duer, governor of the SUM, saw it as a means of speculative profits and entered into an agreement with John Dewhurst, Benjamin Walker, Royal Flint, Walter Livingston, and William Constable to purchase up to 3,000 shares. *The National Gazette* and *The New York Diary* forthwith castigated the SUM and men like Duer who would "possess themselves of a great number of shares, raise them to an exorbitant price, sell out, and after realizing a handsome fortune, care very little if the whole ... went to the devil." Shares originally issued for $25 each had risen to above $50 after the initial offering, but by November 1792 had fallen to 8 to 10 shillings. The hostile press charged that Hamilton had fostered it "under the ... pretext of encouraging domestic manufactures only to raise taxes."

⁹ Page 91 In long perspective, the "Report on Manufactures" is significant for the realistic limitations it placed on the then current conventional wisdom of Adam Smith's *Wealth of Nations*, which was seen by statesmen 15 years after its publication as a plea for removal of all mercantilist controls and all government interference with manufacturing in favor of a system of complete commercial liberty. The latter view seemed to parallel the political liberty and equalitarian ideals won in the Revolution. Hamilton rejected the extreme laissez-faire dogma that men are only economic men governed in economic action only by individual self-interest.

¹⁰ Page 92 Hamilton challenged the general applicability of Smith's abstract doctrine of laissez-faire; he insisted instead on the relative character of economic principles, that economic laws are not absolute, but subject to circumstances modified by time and place. In this sense, Hamilton became the founder of the historical school of economic study. In the "Report on Manufactures," Hamilton cast himself in the role of the earliest American planner of the economy for periods of years and decades ahead.

¹¹ Page 92 Adam Smith in *Wealth of Nations* had argued that "no equal quanitity of productive labor employed in manufactures can ever occasion so great a reproduction" as in farming, "where nature does everything, for a man," but Hamilton disagreed: "The net produce of capital engaged in manufacturing

enterprises is greater than of capital engaged in agriculture." Hamilton perceived that no one had analysed the subject "upon sufficient data, properly ascertained and analysed."

[12] Page 94 Hamilton was not arguing for government control of manufacturing, but rather recognizing the risks to which new, private, small business ventures were always subject. The reckless might embrace "new attempts" and fail. Government must create a good climate for investment to inspire "cautious sagacious capitalists, both citizens and foreigners . . . with confidence . . . it is essential that they should be made to see in any project which is . . . precarious, the prospect of . . . support from government . . . capable of overcoming the obstacles inseparable from first experiments."

Notes for Chapter 8
HIS POWER TO HANG COLONEL HAMILTON

[1] Page 160 During the financial crises of 1792 and 1793, the Bank of New York suffered a drain off of deposits to the New York branch of the Bank of the United States. William Seton, the cashier, complained to Hamilton that the branch "has such an advantage in its operations over us . . . their circulation is so great, and the reception of their paper so universal, that no one has occasion to drain them of specie. Our circulation is so limited, confined mainly to the city to pay duties and discharge notes in the branch . . . the balance is eternally very large in their favor . . ." The Bank of New York's stock of coins had fallen from $600,000 to $200,000; Seton recalled apprehensively Hamilton's warning that in a contest between the two, the branch must in the end win. (Seton to Hamilton, December 20, 1792.)

[2] Page 161 From the time Hamilton had appointed him assistant secretary of the treasury to the time of his financial collapse and imprisonment for debt in April 1792, William Duer had speculated in western lands, manufacturing, and bank and government stocks. William Constable complained to his friend James Seagrove on June 19, 1791, that "Duer's speculations always turns out wrong, and he constantly involves his friends. He has recently brought me into a scrape which will cost $25,000 to get out of, *if ever the money is paid.*"

[3] Page 162 Robert Troup's letter to Hamilton of March 19, 1792, unconsciously testifies to Hamilton's often dangerously warm and openhearted loyalty to old friends: "All my feelings are overwhelmed with grief the bitterness of which could only be conceived by a heart like yours" over the convulsions owing to "our friend Duer's failure. This poor man is in a state of almost complete insanity; and his situation is a source of inexpressible grief to all his friends . . . notes unpaid amount to about one half a million of dollars and Duer has not a farthing of money or a particle of stock to pay them with. . . ." Troup added, "We all see the absolute necessity of supporting his character and extricating

him if possible . . . if we fail . . . his reputation will be eternally blasted and his person will be endangered. Widows, orphans, merchants, mechanics, etc., are all concerned . . . my heart bleeds for Duer and my purse shall flow for him as far as prudence will warrant. This letter is for your own eye only . . . give us your advice. . . ." Troup added mysteriously, "with regard to Burr's election I have a secret to tell you which I cannot communicate till I see you. I have reason to suspect that we have both been abused. No good can result from any explanation at present; and therefore I shall be quiet. This hint is most confidentially communicated."

⁴ Page 162 Treasury support of public stock aided the Bank of New York, which had large outstanding loans to speculators who were caught short in the falling market. Hamilton sold his single share of the bank through William Seton, who expressed "regret, that the extreme delicacy of your feelings should induce you to part with the stock so extremely more valuable than its present price in the market," May 28, 1792. It was at only a 28 percent premium, but was bound to recover. Between November 1790 and May 1792 Hamilton had received dividends of $321.

⁵ Page 162 Hamilton's old friend Henry Lee, who had a knack of writing him at critical turning points of his life, wrote June 23, 1792, just after the financial panic had come to its crisis in April, "Daily I hear of you: commended by some, condemned by others—sometimes you are mounted to the skies on the wings of fame, again whisked into the infernal pit."

⁶ Page 162 Hamilton explained the stock panic calmly to William Short, the American minister in Holland, on April 16, 1792, saying that "the moderate size of the domestic debt of the United States . . . created the most intemperate ideas of speculation in the minds of a very few persons whose natural ardour had been increased by great success in . . . early stages of the melioration of . . . market value of the stock." The speculators developed a "delusive confidence, that the concentration of so much stock in a few hands would secure a very high market rate." But banks limited their lending, and those who had to pay debts who had no money to do so placed their securities in the hands of creditors who sought to sell the bankrupts' property. Writing May 23, 1792, Hamilton told Duer to "assign the rest of your property for the benefit of creditors generally, the law will do the rest."

⁷ Page 163 The prosperity fostered by Hamilton's financial measures brought speculative excesses. Funding of debts gave prospect of ever-mounting share prices; Dutch money flowed to New York; agents sped to England and the Continent to sell American paper; prices rose; men withdrew from speculation in land and shipping to play public debt and bank stocks. Dewhurst and McComb failed. The panic, confined principally to New York City, came to its crisis in April 1792.

⁸ Page 163 The failure of the SUM is a classic example of how an industrial enterprise without a full-time, on-the-spot, capable manager fails, even if the part-time manager happens to be secretary of the treasury. The directors had elected Nehemiah Hubbard, but when he withdrew, Hamilton wrote on May 3, 1792, urging him to stay: ". . . I . . . continue to entertain a conviction of the practicability of insuring that success by judicious management." Directors "too much enveloped in speculation to pay proper attention to the trust" would be replaced, and "I shall be able to give such a direction to their measures as will recover the ground that has been lost by delay and indecision." Hamilton even found himself surety on behalf of Nicholas Lowe and Abijah Hammond for 800 pounds in Pennsylvania currency to reimburse a Scottish firm for shipping stocking frames and skilled workmen to America.

Notes for Chapter 9
A TISSUE OF MACHINATIONS

¹ Page 169 It was becoming politic for men who were confidential with each other to communicate in code. Writing Hamilton on March 21, 1792, Gouverneur Morris thanked him for his efforts in obtaining Morris's appointment as United States minister plenipotentiary to France and asked Hamilton for confidential information, saying that in return he would tell Hamilton "what's doing on this side of the water *confidentially* which I will not do to everybody." In a letter marked "Private," Hamilton replied to Morris from Philadelphia on June 22, 1792: "I accept your challenge to meet you in the field of mutual *confidential* communication." In lieu of a cipher, he sent Morris some code names for use for "certain official characters." For the president—Scaevola (who had lost his right hand to an act of heroism), Vice-president Adams—Brutus, Secretary of State Jefferson—Scipio, Secretary of War Knox—Sempronius, the secretary of the treasury (himself)—Paulus, and Attorney General Edmund Randolph—Lysander. Rufus King was Leonidas; Aaron Burr, Savius; James Monroe, Sydney; Madison, Tarquin; and Jeremiah Wadsworth was Titius. "You see," Hamilton added with a flourish, "I have avoided characteristic names."

² Page 171 Jefferson, writing to James Monroe on June 23, 1792, demonstrated his keen sense of the national political implications of seemingly unrelated events: "it seems probably that Mr. Jay had a majority of the qualified voters, and I think . . . that Clinton would have honored himself by declining to accept." Nationally, the uproar over the election outcome had "silenced all clamour about [Federalist] bankruptcys."

³ Page 186 At the height of the press war, Henry Lee wrote Hamilton from Richmond on September 10, 1792, "would to God you had never been the patron of the measure [the bank and other funding measures] in its present shape, for

I auger ill of its effect on yourself personally, as well as on the public prosperity."

Jefferson, visiting Washington at Mount Vernon, railed against the funding system; Washington, writing on October 18, 1792, agreed that there was disagreement about it, but "that for himself he had seen our affairs desperate and our credit lost, and that this was in a sudden and extraordinary degree raised to the highest pitch."

Notes for Chapter 10
THE UNMAKING OF THE VICE-PRESIDENT—1792

[1] Page 190 Vice-President John Adams did not really share the general view that his office was insignificant and subordinate: "The Constitution had instituted two great offices of equal rank, and the nation . . . have created two officers: one, who is the first of two equals, is placed at the head of the executive; the other at the head of the legislature." (John Adams to Benjamin Lincoln, May 26, 1798.)

[2] Page 196 Jefferson's and Madison's scandalmonger and talebearer, John Beckley of Virginia, the clerk of the House of Representatives, had a technique of ascribing otherwise unlikely anti-Hamilton calumnies that he knew would please his masters to unverifiable third-person statements made in circumstances that lent them credence. He reported to Madison on September 2, 1792, that Hamilton's friend William Heth, collector of customs on the James River, had said that "Mr. H. Unequivocally declares" Madison to be "his *personal and political* enemy." Writing Madison again on October 17, 1792, Beckley commented that Hamilton was engaging in Federalist electioneering by "efforts direct and indirect . . . but might be defeated by exposure of corruption at the Treasury," adding, "I think I have a clue to something far beyond suspicion on this ground, which prudence forbids a present disclosure of."

[3] Page 196 Aaron Burr and John Beckley were probably involved in later land speculations together; Burr introduced Beckley to Ephraim Kirby, a lawyer, in May 1796, although they may have met earlier, and Kirby became New England land agent for Beckley, pursuant to which Beckley would pay Kirby a 6 percent commission for each sale plus whatever amount he realized above the prices that Beckley set.

[4] Page 200 On September 24, 1791, Hamilton thanked Eliphalet Pearson, the corresponding secretary of the Society of the American Academy of Arts and Sciences, for the honor of election as a fellow: "I entertain too high and respectful opinion of that Society not to esteem myself particularly flattered by so honorable a mark of their distinction. . . ."

Notes for Chapter 11
HOW MANY COVER-UPS?

[1] Page 202 Jefferson received the information on which he based his note on the Reynolds affair from John Beckley. Bernard Webb, the man chosen by Beckley to do the copying of the papers, had known Beckley for over 20 years as a fellow Mason in Williamsburg; they had worked together on Virginia's public debt problems, and Webb now served as Beckley's own chief clerk.

Notes for Chapter 12
IMPEACHMENT

[1] Page 226 Having missed a visit from his old and admired friend Richard Harison of New York, Hamilton wrote him on January 5, 1793, full of regret at having been "deprived of the pleasure of seeing" a fellow New Yorker at a lonely, beleaguered moment: "Every friend I see, from a place I love, is a cordial to me—and I stand in need of something of that kind now and then." He added, "the triumphs of vice are no new things under the sun. And I fear, till the millenium comes, in spite of all our boasted light and purification—hypocrisy and treachery will continue to be the most successful commodities in the political market."

[2] Page 226 The malignant opposition of Virginians toward the assumption of state debt and other financial measures of Hamilton's administration was coolly explained by Oliver Wolcott, Jr., writing to his father on February 8, 1793, as the result of pressure of foreign debts on the planters: "The effect of the treaty and of the Constitution is to make them responsible; at least, this is believed, though no decision of this question has been made by the National Judiciary . . . they seem determined to weaken the public force, so as to render the recovery of these debts impossible."

[3] Page 226 Julian Boyd, in the *Jefferson Papers*, Appendix, Vol. XVIII, p. 618, identifies William Vredenbergh as "a young merchant and broker," dealing in soldiers claims, state and federal securities, and all sorts of "class rights, soldiers Bounty rights and land warrants." He was generally respected and politically a Clintonian Republican. He was James Reynolds's employer. Professor Boyd told Beckley's biographers, Edmund and Dorothy Berkeley, that among the Vredenbergh family papers are several letters written to him by John Beckley during the 1796–1797 period that suggest a family connection between the Vredenberghs and John Beckley's wife, the former Maria Prince, daughter of a well-connected family of New York coopers and merchants.

[4] Page 227 There had been earlier attempts to discredit Hamilton while the Reynolds affair was going on. On December 9, 1790, Senator William Maclay

noted in his journal that an undeclared war had been undertaken against the Wabash Indians without authority of Congress and, "what is worse, so far as intelligence is come to hand, we have reason to believe it is unsuccessful." He was referring to the expedition of General Josiah Harmar against the Indians, in which 200 members of the expedition "have certainly perished" although " 'tis said 100 Indians have been killed." An even worse defeat was suffered the following year by General Arthur St. Clair at the hands of Miami Indians under Little Turtle on the Wabash. The disaster provided a perfect occasion for William B. Giles to move, as he did on March 27, 1792, that the president be requested to investigate the causes of St. Clair's defeat, including "detentions or delays" in furnishing money and stores to the army. Giles's resolution, putting on Washington the burden of investigation and seemingly some of the blame, was defeated, but a congressional investigation was begun; the committee report of February 15, 1793, put some blame on Hamilton by implication for failing to require security from William Duer when Duer took over from Theodosius Fowler the contract to supply the army. Hamilton, Secretary of War Knox, and Samuel Hodgdon, the quartermaster general of the expedition, all managed to avoid final censure on various technical grounds; so all blame for failure to supply the expedition fell on Duer, now languishing in jail to save him from death at the hands of his creditors.

⁵ Page 228 Among other things, the resolution complained that almost three times more florins were drawn from Holland than Hamilton reported. Hamilton's explanation was that to avoid actually transporting specie from Europe to the United States with the loss of interest, delay, and risk of loss involved and then sending it back again, book transfers were arranged with the bank.

⁶ Page 228 Beginning in January 1793, Jefferson jotted down numerous notes in his *Anas* for a campaign against the Treasury, including a proposal to divide the department, abolish the bank, repeal the excise, lower import duties, "exclude paper holders [from Congress?]" and condemn Hamilton's report.

⁷ Page 229 In the *National Gazette* of February 16, 1793, a critic of Hamilton, whose style resembled Beckley's, wrote under the name of *Franklin* that Hamilton "fancies himself the great pivot upon which the whole machine of government turns, throwing out of view . . . the President, the legislature, and the Constitution itself." *Franklin* complained that "the direction of public money, concentered in one person, constitutes the essence of monarchy . . . whether [the monarch] is called Emperor, King, Pope, or Secretary of the Treasury, it amounts to the same thing . . . the laws are the laws of the individual, not of the legislature. . . ." He implied that Hamilton was guilty of "dark monarchical maneuverings of public money."

⁸ Page 230 Hamilton and his supporters opposed the resolutions of February 19, 1793, demanding that the commissioners of the sinking fund lay before the

House a statement of their proceedings. At a time when the market was falling sharply and speculators like William Duer were suffering great losses, Hamilton had sought to stop the panic by bidding for securities above the market price, up to their par value, having obtained a ruling from Chief Justice John Jay that it was permissible under the act to do so. Hamilton's purpose in acting as a sophisticated central banker would today was to forestall panic, but to Jefferson he was improperly bailing out the speculators. According to Jefferson's biographer Dumas Malone, Jefferson "may not have sufficiently appreciated the positive functions of the Treasury in maintaining the level of public securities, but his simple philosophy was one that unsophisticated citizens could readily understand." (*Jefferson and the Ordeal of Liberty,* p. 24.) He seems to be saying that, even if wrong, Jefferson's policy was right because simpletons thought it was.

[9] Page 233 Fauchet, the French minister, told Randolph that "it was hoped that, faulty or innocent, the treasurer would retire. . . ." Instead, he triumphed in the "useless inquiry of his enemies. . . ." To George Hammond, the British minister, the failure of all attempts to censure Hamilton's conduct "has been fully considered by the friends of that gentleman as a complete triumph over their opponents."

[10] Page 234 On April 9, Beckley and James Monroe issued an anonymous pamphlet entitled "An Examination of the Late Proceedings in Congress Respecting the Official Conduct of the Secretary of the Treasury," which gave a list of the names of the members of Congress "known to be stockholders in the Bank of the United States, or in the public funds." On April 1, Jefferson recorded news from Beckley that although merchants' bonds for duties on six months' credit had become due in a large amount, "Hamilton went to the banks on that day and directed the bank to discount for those merchants all their bonds at 30 days." According to Jefferson, this permitted the bank to make a windfall extra month's interest out of the delay.

[11] Page 239 According to Jefferson's *Anas* of June 7, 1793, on a visit of Beckley to Sir John Temple's house at No. 10 Cortlandt Street in New York, almost next door to the house of Maria Prince Beckley's family at No. 16, Temple permitted Beckley to read excerpts from a letter of one Sir Gregory Page Turner, who had been a Member of Parliament from Yorkshire for 25 years and was supposedly on intimate terms with the British ministers. Jefferson, who communicated with Temple through Beckley, described Temple as a "strong republican." On the authority of Beckley's reports to Jefferson from Temple, Jefferson wrote that the British government "was well apprised of the predominancy of the British interest in the United States; that they considered Colonel Hamilton, Mr. King, and Mr. W. Smith of South Carolina, as the main supports of that interest; that particularly, they considered Colonel Hamilton, and not Mr. Hammond, as their effective minister here; that if the anti-Federal interest [that was his term] at the head of which they considered Mr. Jefferson to be, should

prevail, these gentlemen had secured asylum to themselves in England." And "if they should be overset and choose to withdraw," Jefferson noted they could count on the same kind of protection the British had given to Benedict Arnold. Later, presumably for incredulous posterity, Jefferson wrote in the margin beside his note of Beckley's story "impossible as to Hamilton; he was far above that."

On this same May 1793 trip, according to Beckley, George Clinton had told him that Hamilton had drafted a plan for establishment of monarchical government in the United States and had sent it in the form of a circular letter to various friends he thought would be instrumental in carrying it out, including "the old militia general up the North River" who was to give it to Clinton personally; and Clinton told Beckley he would bring it on to Philadelphia when he had received it. "Beckley is a man of perfect truth as to what he affirms of his own knowledge but too credulous as to what he hears from others," Jefferson noted in Memoranda of November 19, 1792, and June 7, 1793, expressing no doubt, however, of this gossip from Beckley he jotted down in his *Anas* and edited for posterity.

[12] Page 239 By the spring of 1793, Hamilton was coming to mistrust Tench Coxe of Pennsylvania, who had taken Duer's place as assistant secretary of the treasury in May 1790. William Heth, the collector of revenue at Bermuda Hundred in Virginia, wrote Hamilton in a footnote to a letter of June 14, 1793, that "you have a man near you whose pen—notwithstanding the magnanimity of his Country . . . and . . . *your* personal friendship towards him—has been . . . abusing the measures of government, and particularly your official conduct; and whose study has been to sap, and undermine *you*, in hopes of filling your place through the interests of . . . you know who. The time *may* come, when I may . . . be more explicit." "You know who" probably meant Jefferson and Madison. So that Hamilton could not possibly be mistaken in suspecting Coxe, Heth added, "Watch him narrowly. Attend closely to the motions of his eyes, & changes of countenance when he may suppose you are placing confidence in him, & you will not be long in discovering the *perfidious & ungrateful* friend." By act of May 8, 1792, Congress abolished the office of assistant to the secretary, which had been filled so far with William Duer and Tench Coxe, and substituted that of commissioner of revenue; Coxe succeeded to that office. As of the day after Hamilton was to leave office, Coxe put in a charge against the Treasury as of January 31, 1795, for pay for exercising the duties of secretary of the treasury in Hamilton's absence on the Western expedition. Hamilton turned it down.

[13] Page 241 Washington wrote Hamilton on September 25 and again on October 14, 1793, asking heads of departments to confer with him in or near Philadelphia by November 1 and also asking whether Hamilton thought the president had constitutional authority to call Congress to meet elsewhere than in the capital, say, for example, at Germantown? He added, "None can take a more comprehensive view . . . and a less partial one of the subject than yourself . . . I pray you to dilate fully upon the several points here brought to your

consideration." Hamilton's answer was that yes, Congress could be called to assemble at Germantown. There it could decide whether to continue in session there or perhaps move to Wilmington. Just at this time, Hamilton suffered a serious relapse.

Notes for Chapter 13
NEUTRALITY

[1] Page 259 At a meeting the day after Washington returned to the capital from Mount Vernon on July 12, the cabinet determined to notify the French and British ministers that the issue of the *Little Sarah* would be referred to persons "learned in the laws." The justices of the Supreme Court were called to meet in Philadelphia on July 18. Washington asked Jefferson, "What is to be done in the case of the 'Little Sarah' now at Chester? Is the minister of the French Republic to set the acts of this government at defiance, *with impunity?* And then threaten the executive with an appeal to the people. What must the world think of such conduct, and of the government of the U. States in submitting to it? These are serious questions . . . I wish to know your opinion on them, even before tomorrow, for the vessel may then be gone."

[2] Page 260 In Hamilton's *No Jacobin* pieces, essays dated July 31, August 5, 8, 10, 14, 16, 23, 26, and 28, which had appeared in Dunlap's [Philadelphia] *American Daily Advertiser* just before Hamilton fell ill of the plague, he referred to the story that Citizen Genêt had threatened to appeal from the president of the United States to the people, gave counterarguments to Genêt's claims and pretensions, and condemned his "system of electrifying the people."

[3] Page 264 On November 26, 1793, in the aftermath of the case of the *Little Sarah*, John Jay wrote Hamilton that "it is generally understood that you and Mr. Jefferson are not perfectly pleased with each other, but surely he has more magnanimity than to be influenced by that consideration to suppress truth, or what is the same thing refusing his testimony to it. Men may be hostile to each other in politics and yet be incapable of such conduct."

Notes for Chapter 14
SENDING JOHN JAY ON HIS WAY

[1] Page 273 The Philadelphia *Aurora*, an Anti-Federalist Republican newspaper, carried a story on June 23, 1795, that a Glasgow correspondent reported that when Smith's speech was reprinted in Edinburgh, "the speech was vastly praised here by a certain set; and the author . . . is said to have been one of your trustiest officers during the war with England." Most significant of all, Hamilton, the author, was "generally looked up to as a successor . . . of your present Presi-

dent." The purported reprint of third or fourthhand hearsay from an unverifiable source is characteristic of Beckley's technique.

[2] Page 274 The British orders-in-council of November 6, 1793, not announced till the end of the year, were aimed at destroying all neutral trade with the French colonies. British cruisers were to bring in for adjudication any vessels laden with French colonial products or that were carrying supplies to French possessions; a large British fleet sailed for the French West Indies. Further orders-in-council of January 8, 1794, superseded those of November 6 and restricted capture of neutral vessels to those with French goods or French owners or to vessels bound for France. Congress's March 26, 1794, embargo was intended as the American answer and to obstruct the British in supplying their forces in the West Indies.

[3] Page 274 By February 1794 relations with Britain had deteriorated to the point that some members of Congress feared that war was imminent; therefore, commercial retaliation, such as Madison's resolutions proposed, would be too "feeble and remote." "Why proceed in regulating our commerce" asked Hartley of Pennsylvania "when . . . commerce is to be saved from annihilation?" William Vans Murray warned "when war is staring us in the face the resolutions are not proper." This led to the House's imposing a 30-day embargo on all vessels bound for foreign ports. Approved by the Senate on March 26, 1794, it was extended for 30 days and continued to May 25, but no longer. No one expected war with France, but some feared and others urged limited war with Britain.

Notes for Chapter 15
THE WHISKEY INSURRECTION

[1] Page 286 In 1794, Anthony Wayne's victory at Fallen Timbers removed one Western grievance, but not in time to prevent the Whiskey Insurrection. Politically unpopular costs incurred in military expeditions on the frontiers, largely undertaken without advance congressional approval or budgeting, skewed Hamilton's Treasury budgets. Jefferson and Madison were making use of their puppet William B. Giles of Virginia as nominal complainant to instigate the endless congressional investigations in order to drive Hamilton from office under fire.

[2] Page 288 Eastern distillers, also subject to the same tax, protested little. Edward Carrington, a prominent Federalist of Powhatan, Virginia, had informed Madison on February 2, 1791, that rumors against the excise were dying away and that it would "operate most heavily on the eastern states." Customs duties could not be raised higher, and an excise, he thought, was preferable to a direct tax.

[3] Page 295 Hamilton blamed Albert Gallatin more than he did a wavering leader of the mob who seemed to work both sides of the street. In the earlier Pittsburgh meeting of August 21, 1792, which had denounced the excise in principle and the manner of its enforcement, Gallatin had served as the secretary and probably drafted the resolutions. Jefferson later appointed Gallatin secretary of the treasury. Gallatin later called his part in this Pittsburgh meeting "my only political sin."

[4] Page 306 After the expedition was over, Knox wrote Hamilton from Philadelphia on October 8, 1794, that "your exertions in my department during my absence will never be obliterated."

[5] Page 306 Two of those arrested were found guilty of treason, but President Washington pardoned them because the rising had been downed without bloodshed.

Notes for Chapter 16
PUBLIC CREDIT

[1] Page 321 This story of Hamilton's funds invested in England echoed Beckley's earlier third or fourthhand gossip about Sir Gregory Page Turner's letter, which Sir John Temple had allegedly shown to Beckley in May of 1793.

Notes for Chapter 17
AN INSOLVENT COLOSSUS IS STONED BY A WALL STREET MOB

[1] Page 345 John Beckley took up leadership of opposition to Jay's Treaty in Pennsylvania, attacked it as *Calm Observer* in Noah Webster's *Minerva* on July 14, 1795, helped organize a general meeting in State House Yard on July 23 (attended by 5,000 people who roundly condemned it), printed a petition opposing it in the *Aurora*, and circulated the petition in each city ward for signatures. This supplied Beckley with a new enemies' list: the names of those who refused to sign the petition. On July 24, 1795, Beckley wrote De Witt Clinton that he was saddened that Washington had been in opposition to the electorate in signing the treaty through the machinations of the "British party." Beckley wrote Madison on September 10, 1795, that signing Jay's Treaty marked Washington "in indelible character as head of a British faction" because the treaty was "a vital blow aimed at the independence & best interests" of the United States. Another *Calm Observer* letter of Beckley's, published October 23, 1795, in the *Aurora* and addressed to Wolcott ended with the rhetorical question, "Will not the world be led to conclude, that the mask of political hypocrisy has been alike worn by a CAESAR, a CROMWELL, a WASHINGTON?"

Notes for Chapter 18
HELPING WASHINGTON OUT

[1] Page 355 Edmund Randolph charged that Pickering, Wolcott, and McHenry, urged on by Hamilton, had mistranslated and misrepresented the meaning of Fauchet's intercepted letter, used it to whip up Washington's anger, and induced Washington to sign the treaty in the heat of such anger and while still in a rage, to force Randolph's resignation.

Neither Wolcott nor Pickering were fluent in French, but with the aid of a dictionary they were able to manage a rough translation of Fauchet's letter. The combination of Fauchet's self-serving misunderstanding or misrepresentation of Randolph and Pickering's and Wolcott's misunderstanding of Fauchet combined to give the impression of grave wrongdoing on Randolph's part. See *A Vindication of Mr. Randolph's Resignation* (Philadelphia: 1795). If it is true that it takes an intriguer to know an intriguer, Randolph was an intriguer, certainly an inept one, almost certainly not a disloyal one. Randolph warned Monroe that the French minister "wrapped himself round with intrigue from the first moment of his career in the U.S. He found in me a temper, in no manner turned towards Britain, but warm towards France," but "he has been plotting how to embroil this Country with France." Monroe should not receive him or conclude from his reception at home that he, Fauchet, continued to have the respect of the American government. (Randolph to Monroe, July 29, 1795.)

After having been forced to resign by Washington, Pickering, and Wolcott and after publishing his *Vindication*, Randolph wrote to Madison of a "conspiracy" to destroy the "republican force" in the country; he charged Washington with "the profound hypocrisy of Tiberius, and the injustice of an assassin." (Randolph to Madison, November 1, 1795.)

[2] Page 356 Randolph's resignation brought on his financial ruin; he was held liable for an unexplained shortage in "diplomatic and consular funds" of the State Department amounting to $49,154; he and his family devoted the next 20 years to payment of the debt with interest; and Randolph was listed as a debtor on government records for many years.

[3] Page 361 The same October 23, 1795, issue of the *Aurora* that carried *Calm Observer*'s attack on Washington contained another mysterious communication directed to Oliver Wolcott, Jr., in Beckley's characteristic style:

Whether a certain head of a department was not in the month of December 1792, privy and party in the circumstances of a certain inquiry of a very suspicious aspect, respecting real malconduct on the part of his friend, patron, and predecessor in office, which ought to make him extremely circumspect on the subject of investigation . . . ? Would a publication of the circumstances of that transaction redound to the honor or reputations of the parties?

[4] Page 365 With Randolph out of the cabinet, Madison asked Jefferson "through what official interstice can a ray of republican truths now penetrate to the P?" (Madison to Jefferson, February 7, 1796.)

Notes for Chapter 19
AN OUT-OF-TOWN, UNDERCOVER PRIME MINISTER

[1] Page 379 Beckley told Madison on June 20, 1796, that John Brown of Kentucky, having just seen Hamilton, had been told that Washington would refuse reelection and that "there may be a state of things in which it would be desirable for Mr. Jay to be elected without opposition." Beckley reported to Madison what he had allegedly heard from Brown, quoting Hamilton. Beckley's third and fourthhand hearsay reportage from unreachable sources has a duplicitous consistency of theme, tone, technique, and style.

Notes for Chapter 21
THE REYNOLDS PAMPHLET

[1] Page 418 What so infuriated Hamilton about Jefferson's two letters to Fraunces dated June 27 and June 28, 1797, which he attached to *The Reynolds Pamphlet* (the two letters contained Jefferson's refusal to give Fraunces a certificate of good character), was the fact of their existence—that Fraunces should expect a favor from Jefferson—and Jefferson's slyly gratuitous statement that Fraunces's inability to get a certificate of good character from Hamilton might be attributed to Fraunces's "particular misunderstanding" with his principal. Hamilton's interpretation was that Jefferson (through Beckley) had encouraged Fraunces to make public the anti-Hamilton charges arising out of the "particular misunderstanding," thereby giving Fraunces a valid claim on Jefferson for a favor.

Notes for Chapter 25
THE EVIL GENIUS OF THIS COUNTRY

[1] Page 514 Most Hamilton biographers have insisted that his attack on John Adams was intended only for private circulation among the inner circle of Federalist leaders of the first class, not for wide publication. Some evidence for this is found in the fact that Hamilton's presentation copy of the first edition to Governor Caleb Strong of Massachusetts has an autograph note at the end, "not to go into newspapers." But when the pamphlet was printed in New York for John Lang by George F. Hopkins, a copyright was secured, and second and third editions were quickly published by October 22, 1800; several thousand copies were printed and advertised in the newspapers two months before the election.

If Hamilton as the copyright owner and a lawyer as well had threatened legal action against the newspapers for copyright violation and refused to allow sale of reprints or advertising of the pamphlet, Burr's pirated copy from which extracts were published in the newspapers might have been largely suppressed; if Hamilton had done nothing or wished to hear no more of his mistake, he could have let it die the natural death of most newspaper sensations as a "one day wonder." So the likeliest explanation is that Burr's "leak" of the pamphlet's contents provided Hamilton with a welcome excuse to circulate it as widely as possible.

[2] Page 515 Hamilton's animosity toward Adams probably went back more than 20 years to Adams's role in replacing Schuyler with Gates in command of the northern army and to Gates's attempts to implicate Hamilton in intrigues against Washington. It had been Adams, presiding as vice-president over the Senate, whose tie-breaking vote in favor of Theodorick Bland's resolution (which made difficult, if not impossible, the kind of frauds on old soldiers practiced by James Reynolds, Jeremiah Wadsworth, William Duer, and other New York speculators at the beginning of Hamilton's tenure as secretary of the treasury) had enabled Jefferson, with Washington's support, to inflict a stinging defeat on Hamilton in their first conflict in the cabinet.

Notes for Chapter 26
FIREWORKS

[1] Page 522 James Bayard's son, Richard H. Bayard, seeking permission to publish two of Hamilton's letters to his father urging Jefferson over Burr, wrote Hamilton's son James on January 9, 1830: "I think they do him infinite honor, exhibiting the sincerity of his attachment to the existing institutions, his discrimination of character and loftiness of mind."

Notes for Chapter 27
GETTING RELIGION/ANGELICA'S GARTER

[1] Page 547 Hamilton's own brand of Populism, or antielitism, is perhaps best expressed in his "Fragment on the French Revolution," probably dating from 1801 or 1802, in which he attacked Jean Jacques Rousseau for a philosophy that doubted the existence of a deity, ridiculed the duty of piety, and asserted that the soul is not immortal, that death is an "eternal sleep," and that "the dogma of the *immortality* of the soul a *cheat*, invented to torment the living for the benefit of the dead." To Hamilton, this was elitist claptrap, but, "no longer confined to the closets of conceited sophists, nor to the haunts of wealthy riot," it had now "displayed its hideous front among all classes."

As a result, "religion and government have both been stigmatized as abuses

. . . unwarrantable restraints upon the freedom of man . . . causes of the corruption of his nature, intrinsically good . . . sources of an artificial and false morality which tyrannically robs him of the enjoyment for which his passions fit him, and as clogs upon his progress to the perfection for which he was destined."

The deplorable corollaries from these premises were that "religious opinion of any sort is unnecessary to society, that the maxims of a genuine morality and the authority of the magistracy and the laws are a sufficient and ought to be the only security for civil rights and private happiness . . . and that as human nature shall refine and ameliorate by the operation of more enlightened plan, government itself will become useless, and society will subsist and flourish free from shackles." To Hamilton, the horrible practical result of all this pretty theory was seen in the French Revolution, whose outcome was "a despotism unlimited and uncontrolled . . . a deluded and abused, plundered, scourged and an oppressed people . . . by its influence every succeeding revolution has been approved and excused."

Notes for Chapter 28
FIFTEEN YEARS OF COMPETITION

[1] Page 561 Fathers sought to have sons interested in learning the law taken as clerks into Hamilton's law office and were often willing to pay him large fees to take them. Ezra L'Hommedieu advised Benjamin Bourne that to get his son into Hamilton's office "it will . . . be best for you to write to him on the subject, he is a generous man & is fond of promoting young men of genius; it is probably considering your intimacy he may take him on better terms than any other." But Hamilton was not interested in the money. L'Hommedieu went to see Hamilton and reported that Hamilton "observed that the fee was of little consequence when compared to the services of a clerk. He would rather take one for nothing who would attend to business out of office hours than to take one with a large fee who would only attend at office hours." And Hamilton did not want the young man to spend part of the period with another lawyer who might teach him lessons he would have to unlearn for Hamilton (November 20, 1801; April 10, 1802).

Notes for Chapter 29
THE FREEDOM OF THE PRESS

[1] Page 597 Governor Thomas McKean of Pennsylvania, no foe of the spoils system, was proud to prefer "a friend before an enemy . . . for it is not right to put a dagger in the hands of an assassin." On January 9, 1800, Jefferson asked McKean to give the then unemployed John Beckley a job; Beckley, he said, was a man of "talents, diligence & integrity." McKean gave him two jobs: clerk of the Philadelphia Mayor's Court and also clerk of the Orphans Court, ousting his own nephew, Joseph Hopkinson, author of "Hail Columbia," from the posts.

² Page 606 This earliest and most devastating of anti-Hamilton calumnies was forever springing up out of John Beckley's or someone else's morgue of discredited canards to haunt and taunt him. In 1804, when Hamilton was in Albany on the Croswell case, James Kane told him that Judge Ebenezer Purdy had told him he had heard that Hamilton, John Adams, and the king of England had entered negotiations in 1798 "for the purpose of introducing monarchy into this country, at the head of which was to be placed one of the royal family." On June 7, 1793, Beckley had told the same story to Jefferson, claiming he had it from Clinton, and Jefferson duly jotted it down in his *Anas.* In 1804, Hamilton angrily checked with Purdy, who changed the story to omit Adams and moved the time back 11 years to the Constitutional Convention, explaining that the project had been sponsored by loyalists, that Governor Clinton had a letter discussing the plan, and that it was referred to in a letter that had been seen in Hamilton's office, of which several copies had been made and distributed. This was a 17-year-old rehash of the letter (apparently fabricated by Beckley) datelined Philadelphia, June 19, 1787—the day after Hamilton's five-hour-long speech to the Constitutional Convention had led to the following day's crucial favorable vote on the "compromise" large state plan—which alleged that the Convention delegates were planning to invite Frederick, duke of York, the second son of George III, the secular bishop of Osnaburg, a town in the Prussian province of Hanover, to become king of the United States. It had been James Reynolds, the employee of Maria Beckley's kinsman William Vredenbergh, who had brought this story to Hamilton's attention. Hamilton had furiously written to Jeremiah Wadsworth on August 20, 1787, to try to track down the author. Hamilton had also asked his friend, Washington's former aide David Humphreys about it. Humphreys had written Hamilton on September 1, 1787, that he had not been able to trace the cabal to its source although the letter had first been seen in the hands of one Jared Mansfield, a reputed loyalist. Humphreys had little doubt that the letter was fabricated. He thought that its purpose may have been either to excite the apprehension of the Anti-Federalists against the proceedings of the convention or else as a Loyalist trial balloon to test political sentiment for restoring the monarchy. To Hamilton and Humphreys, it was a "most mad & ruinous project." If Clinton or Purdy had seen a copy of Hamilton's letters of inquiry, or Humphreys's reply, they could speak with straightfaced truth, if misleadingly, of copies of letters about the plot in Hamilton's office.

Notes for Chapter 31
THE DUEL

¹ Page 638 The natural ledge below the bluff at Weehawken, on which the duel was fought, was obliterated to cut the roadbed for the West Shore Railroad in 1883. The Saint Andrews Society had erected a monument to Hamilton there, but it was chipped and defaced and finally destroyed in 1821 by citizens protesting against dueling. A stone bust of Hamilton set on a boulder taken from the

ledge where he fell and placed on top of the cliff was thrown over the cliff and destroyed by vandals in 1934 (*New York Herald Tribune*, October 15, 1934).

[2] Page 643 Hamilton's official New York City death certificate is in error on his date of death and place of birth. The date of death is given as July 9; the place of birth, as "Santa Cruz."

Notes for Chapter 32
ELIZABETH HAMILTON SURVIVES

[1] Page 657 Sometime after Burr's bride of one "golden" year, the celebrated 58-year-old ex-beauty, Mrs. Stephen Jumel, had won a divorce from her 78-year-old benedict—he had suffered three strokes, which partially paralyzed his legs and crippled him—on grounds of adultery "at divers times with divers females," he was reading *Tristram Shandy*. He came to the passage in which Uncle Toby cupped an offending fly in his hands and then released it outside the window, remarking that there was room enough in God's world for both him and the fly. Burr closed the book, looked into space, and mused: "Had I read Voltaire less, and Sterne more, I might have thought the world wide enough for Hamilton and me."

[2] Page 658 Lafayette, in France, mourned for "the loss of the beloved friend in whose brotherly affection I felt proud and happy, and whose lamentable fate has rent my heart as his own noble soul would have mourned for me" (to Angelica Church, May 14, 1805).

[3] Page 661 Six weeks after Hamilton's death, Elizabeth Hamilton turned down a plan for her eldest son, Alexander, to enter the employ of a Boston merchant because, she thought, he would want to remain there. Writing Nathaniel Pendleton on September 29, 1804, she explained that she owed it to "the memory of my beloved husband to keep his children together." Just before the duel "his last arrangement of his family was that they should not be without a parent's care at all times." She was to take care of the younger at The Grange, while he took care of the elder in town. In agreeing to this, she said, "I made the greatest sacrifice of my life . . . of being one half the week absent from him."

[4] Page 662 A false story made the rounds that Hamilton had lent his name and promised presence to a meeting of New England Federalists in the fall of 1804 to split off a New England federation from the Union. Uriah Tracy of Connecticut told the story to William Plumer of New Hampshire, a former Federalist who had later switched to become a Democrat, and Plumer circulated the hearsay widely.

BIBLIOGRAPHY

Adams, Henry, ed. *Documents Relating to New-England Federalism, 1800–1815.* Boston: Little, Brown, 1877.

Adams, Henry. *History of the United States of America.* 9 vols. New York: Scribner's, 1889–91.

Adams, John. *Diary and Auto-Biography of John Adams.* Edited by Lyman H. Butterfield. 4 vols. Cambridge, Mass.: Harvard University Press, 1961.

———*Letters of John Adams Addressed to his Wife, Abigail.* Edited by Charles Francis Adams. 2 vols. Boston: Little, Brown, 1840.

———*The Spur of Fame: Dialogues of John Adams and Benjamin Rush, 1805–1813.* Edited by John A. Schutz and Douglas Adair. San Marino, Calif.: Huntington Library, 1966.

———*Works of . . . , with a Life of the Author, . . . by Charles Francis Adams.* 10 vols. Boston: Little, Brown, 1850–56.

———*Correspondence between . . . John Adams . . . and the late Wm. Cunningham . . . 1803–12.* Boston: E. M. Cunningham, 1823.

———*Correspondence of the late President Adams. Originally Published in the Boston Patriot.* Boston: Everett & Monroe, 1809.

Adams, John Quincy. *Correspondence between John Quincy Adams . . . and several Citizens of Massachusetts concerning Charge of a Design to Dissolve the Union.* Boston: Press of *Boston Daily Advertiser,* 1829.

———*Memoirs.* Edited by Charles Francis Adams. 12 vols. Philadelphia: Lippincott, 1874–1877.

Alexander, De Alva S. *A Political History of the State of New York.* 4 vols. New York: Holt, 1906–23.

Aly, Bower. *The Rhetoric of Alexander Hamilton.* New York: Columbia University Press, 1941.

Ames, Seth, ed. *Works of Fisher Ames, with a Selection from His Speeches and Correspondence.* 2 vols. Boston: Little, Brown, 1854.

Ammon, Harry. *James Monroe: The Quest for National Identity.* New York: McGraw-Hill, 1971.

Anderson, D. R. *William Branch Giles.* (Menasha, Wis.: Geo. Banta, 1914.

————"Edmund Randolph," in *American Secretaries of State,* Vol. II. Edited by S. F. Bemis. New York: Knopf, 1927.

Bailyn, Bernard. *The Origins of American Politics.* New York: Knopf, 1968.

Baldwin, Leland D. *Whiskey Rebels; The Story of a Frontier Uprising.* Univ. of Pittsburgh Press, 1939.

Bank of New York: Alexander Hamilton, Seton, William.

Barnard, D. D. "A Discourse on the Life, Character and Public Services of Ambrose Spencer," in *Memorial of . . . Spencer . . .* Albany: Munsell, 1849.

Bayard, James A. *Papers of James A. Bayard, 1796–1815.* Edited by Elizabeth Dennan. 2 vols. Annual Report American Historical Association, 1913. Washington, D.C.: 1913.

Bayley, Rafael A. *The National Loans of the United States from July 4, 1776 to June 30, 1880.* Washington, D.C.: 1882.

Beard, Charles. *An Economic Interpretation of the Constitution of the United States.* New York: Macmillan, 1935.

Bemis, Samuel F. *The American Secretaries of State and Their Diplomacy.* 10 vols. New York: Knopf, 1927–9.

—————— *Jay's Treaty.* rev. ed. New Haven: Yale University Press, 1962.

Berkeley, Edmund, and Berkeley, Dorothy Smith. *John Beckley, Zealous Partisan in a Nation Divided.* Philadelphia: American Philosophical Society, 1973.

Bernhard, Winifred E. A. *Fisher Ames, Federalist and Statesman.* Chapel Hill: Univ. of North Carolina, 1965.

Beveridge, Albert J. *Life of John Marshall.* 4 vols. Boston and New York: Houghton Mifflin, 1916–1919.

Blackstone, William. *Commentaries on the Laws of England, in Four Books.* 10th ed. London, Oxford: 1787.

Booth, Mary L. *History of the City of New York.* New York: Dutton, 1880.

Borden, Morton. *The Federalism of James A. Bayard.* New York: Columbia University Press, 1955.

Boudinot, J. J. *Life of Elias Boudinot.* 2 vols. Boston and New York: Houghton Mifflin, 1896.

Bowers, Claude G. *Jefferson and Hamilton . . .* New York: Houghton Mifflin, 1925.

—————— *Jefferson in Power.* Boston and New York: Houghton Mifflin, 1936.

Boyd, Julian P., ed. *The Papers of Thomas Jefferson.* 18 vols. (to date) Princeton: Princeton Univ. Press, 1950–1972.

—————— *Number 7, Alexander Hamilton's Secret Attempts to Control American Foreign Policy.* Princeton: Princeton Univ. Press, 1964.

Brackenridge, Hugh H. *Incidents of the Insurrection in the Western Parts of Pennsylvania in . . . 1794.* Philadelphia: John McCulloch, 1795.

Bradsher, E. L. *Mathew Carey, Editor, Author and Publisher.* New York: Columbia University Press, 1912.

Brant, Irving. *James Madison.* 5 vols. Indianapolis: Bobbs Merrill, 1941–1953.

Callender, James Thomson. *The History of the United States for 1796 . . .* Philadelphia: Snowden & McCorkle, 1797.

Carey, Mathew. *A Short Account of the Malignant Fever lately Prevalent in Philadelphia.* Philadelphia: for author, 1793.

———— *Observations on Dr. Rush's Enquiry into the Origin of the late Epidemic Fever in Philadelphia.* Philadelphia: for author, Dec. 14, 1793.

Charles, Joseph. *The Origins of the American Party System . . .* Williamsburg, Va.: Inst. of Early Am. Hist. and Culture, 1956.

Chinard, Gilbert. *Trois Amitiés Françaises de Jefferson . . .* Paris: Société d'édition "Les Belles Lettres," 1927.

Clark, Victor S. *History of Manufactures in the United States.* 3 vols. New York: McGraw-Hill, 1929.

Clinton, George. *Public Papers.* 10 vols. New York and Albany: 1899–.

Cole, Arthur H., ed. *Industrial and Commercial Correspondence of Alexander Hamilton Anticipating His Report on Manufactures.* Chicago: A. W. Shaw Co., 1928.

Coleman, William, ed. *A Collection of Facts and Documents, relating to the Death of . . . Alexander Hamilton.* New York: Hopkins and Seymour, 1804.

Continental Congress. *Journals.* Edited by Gaillard Hunt et al. 34 vols. Washington, D.C.: Government Printing Office, 1904–37.

Cresson, William P. *James Monroe.* Chapel Hill: University of North Carolina Press, 1946.

Dangerfield, George. *Chancellor Robert R. Livingston.* New York: Harcourt Brace, 1960.

Daniels, Jonathan. *Ordeal of Ambition, Jefferson, Hamilton, Burr.* New York: Doubleday, 1970.

Davis, Joseph S. *Essays in the Earlier History of American Corporations.* 2 vols. (including "Wm. Duer, Entrepreneur, 1747–99" and "Society for Establishing Useful Manufactures, Paterson, New Jersey") Cambridge, Mass. Harvard University Press, 1917.

Davis, Matthew L. *Memoirs of Aaron Burr with . . . Selections from his Correspondence.* 2 vols. New York: Harper, 1857.

———— *The Private Journal of Aaron Burr.* 2 vols. Rochester, N.Y.: 1903.

Davis, William W. H. *The Fries Rebellion.* Doylestown, Pa.: 1899.

D[awson], H. B. "The Duels between Price and Philip Hamilton, and George I. Eacker . . . 1801," in *Historical Magazine,* II, 2d ser., No. 4.

De Conde, Alexander, *Entangling Alliance: Politics and Diplomacy under George Washington.* Durham, N.C.: 1958.

———— *The Quasi-War.* New York: Scribner's, 1966.

Dictionary of American Biography. 20 vols. New York: Scribner's, 1928–36.

Duer, William A. *Reminiscences of an Old Yorker.* New York: W. L. Andrews, 1867.

Dorfman, Joseph. *The Economic Mind in American Civilization.* 5 vols. New York: Viking, 1946–59.

_____ and Tugwell, R. G. *Early American Policy: Six Columbia Contributors.* New York: Columbia University Press, 1960.

Dunbar, Charles F. "Some Precedents Followed by Alexander Hamilton," in *Economic Essays.* Edited by O. M. W. Sprague. New York: Macmillan, 1904.

_____ *The Theory and History of Banking.* 4th ed. New York: G. P. Putnam's Sons, 1922.

Dupuy, R. E. *The Compact History of the United States Army.* New York: Hawthorn, 1956.

Estabrook, Henry D. "The Lawyer, Hamilton," in *American Law Review* (New York), 35:841–63.

Evans, Paul Demund. *The Holland Land Company.* Buffalo:, 1924.

Ewing, R. M. "Life and Times of William Findley," in *Western Pennsylvania Historical Magazine*, Vol. 2, No. 4, pp. 240–51.

Ferguson, E. James. *The Power of the Purse.* Chapel Hill: Univ. of North Carolina Press, 1961.

Findley, William. *History of the Insurrection, in the Four Western Counties of Pennsylvania.* Philadelphia: S. H. Smith, 1796.

Fischer, David H. *Revolution of American Conservatism.* New York: Harper & Row, 1965.

Fleming, Thomas. *The Man from Monticello: An Intimate Life of Thomas Jefferson.* New York: Morrow, 1969.

Flexner, James T. *George Washington: Anguish and Farewell, 1793–1799.* Boston: Little, Brown, 1972.

_____ *George Washington and the New Nation, 1783–1793.* Boston: Little, Brown, 1969.

Folwell, Richard. *Short History of the Yellow Fever, that broke out in the City of Philadelphia, in July, 1797 . . .* Philadelphia: Folwell, 1798.

Ford, P. L., ed. *Bibliotheca Hamiltoniana. A List of Books written by, or relating to Alexander Hamilton.* New York: printed for author, 1886.

Forman, Sidney. *West Point: A History of the United States Military Academy.* New York: Columbia University Press, 1956.

Fraunces, Andrew G. *An Appeal to the Legislature of the United States . . . Against the Conduct of the Secretary of the Treasury.* Philadelphia: 1793.

Freeman, Douglas S. *George Washington, a Biography.* 7 vols. New York: Scribner's, 1948–57.

Fried, Albert, ed. *The Jeffersonian and Hamiltonian Traditions in American Politics.* New York: Doubleday, 1968.

Gallatin, Albert. *Writings.* Edited by Henry Adams. 3 vols. Philadelphia: Lippincott, 1879.

Ganoe, W. A. *The History of the United States Army.* Rev. ed. New York: Appleton, 1942.

Genêt, Edmond. *Correspondence between Citizen Genêt, Minister of the*

French Republic . . . and Officers of the Federal Government. Philadelphia: B. F. Bache, 1793.

Gibbs, George. *Memoirs of Administrations of Washington and Adams.* 2 vols. New York: W. Van Norden, 1846.

Godfrey, Carlos E. "Organization of the Provisional Army of the United States in the Anticipated War With France." *Pennsylvania Magazine of History,* 38 (April 1914).

Graybill, J. E. *Alexander Hamilton, Nevis–Weehawken* Albany: Wynkoop, Hallenbeck, Crawford, 1897.

Hacker, Louis M. *Alexander Hamilton in the American Tradition.* New York: McGraw-Hill, 1957.

Hamilton, Alexander. *Works.* Edited by J. C. Hamilton. 7 vols. New York: J. F. Trow, 1850–51.

––––– *Works.* Edited by H. C. Lodge. 12 vols. Federal Edition. New York and London: Putman, 1904.

––––– *Report on the Public Credit.* New York: Childs and Swaine, 1790.

––––– *The Papers of Alexander Hamilton.* Edited by Harold C. Syrett and Jacob E. Cooke. 15 vols. New York: Columbia University Press, 1961–1969. The individual volumes cover time periods as follows: volume I: 1768–1778 (1961); II: 1779–1781 (1961); III: 1782–1786 (1962); IV: 1787–May 1788 (1962); V: June 1788–November 1789 (1962); VI: December 1789–August 1790 (1962); VII: September 1790–January 1791 (1963); VIII: February 1791–July 1791 (1965); IX: August 1791–December 1791 (1965); X: December 1791–January 1792 (1966); XI: February–June 1792; XII: July–October 1792 (1967); XIII: November 1792–February 1793 (1967); XIV: February–June 1793 (1969); and XV: June 1793–January 1794 (1969).

––––– *The Papers of Alexander Hamilton.* Edited by Harold C. Syrett. 7 vols. to date. New York: Columbia University Press, 1972–1975. The individual volumes cover time periods as follows: XVI: February–July 1794 (1972); XVII: August–December 1794 (1972); XVIII: January–July 1795 (1973); XIX: July–December 1795 (1973); XX: January 1796–March 1797 (1974); XXI: April 1797–July 1798 (1974); XXII: July 1798–March 1799 (1975).

––––– *The Law Practice of Alexander Hamilton.* Edited by Julius Goebel, Jr. 2 vols. New York: Columbia University Press, vol. I: 1964; vol. II: 1969.

Hamilton, Allan McLane. *The Intimate Life of Alexander Hamilton.* New York: Scribner's, 1910.

Hamilton, James A. *Reminiscences.* New York: Scribner's, 1869.

Hamilton, Alexander; Jay, John; and Madison, James. *The Federalist: A Collection of Essays written in Favour of the New Constitution.* 2 vols. New York: J. and A. M'Lean, 1788.

Hamilton, John C. *History of the Republic of the United States . . . as Traced in the Writings of Alexander Hamilton.* 7 vols. New York: Appleton, 1857–64.

Hammond, Jabez, D., *The History of Political Parties in the State of New York from ... the Constitution to ... 1840.* 2 vols. Albany: C. Van Benthuysen, 1842.

Heitman, Francis B. *Historical Register and Dictionary of the United States Army, 1789–1903.* Washington, D.C.: Government Printing Office, 1903.

Howe, John R., Jr. *The Changing Political Thought of John Adams.* Princeton: Princeton Univ. Press, 1966.

Hudson, Frederic. *Journalism in the United States.* New York: Harper, 1873.

Hunt, Gaillard, ed. *Disunion Sentiment in Congress in 1794.* Washington, D.C.: Lowdermilk, 1905.

Hutcheson, Harold. *Tench Coxe, a Study in American Economic Development.* Baltimore: Johns Hopkins Press, 1938.

Hutchinson, William T., and Rachal, William M. E., eds. *The Papers of James Madison.* 6 vols. Chicago: University of Chicago Press, 1960–1972.

Jay, John. *Correspondence and Public Papers.* Edited by H. P. Johnston. 4 vols. New York and London: G. P. Putnam's Sons, 1890–93.

Jefferson, Thomas. *The Papers of Thomas Jefferson.* Edited by Julian P. Boyd. 18 vols. (to date) Princeton: Princeton University Press, 1950–1972.

———— *Works.* Edited by P. L. Ford. 12 vols. New York and London: G. P. Putnam's Sons, 1904–5.

———— *Writings.* Edited by A. A. Lipscomb and Albert E. Bergh. 20 vols. Monticello ed. Washington, D.C.: Jefferson Memorial Association, 1904–5.

———— *Writings.* Edited by H. A. Washington. 9 vols. New York: Taylor, 1853–4.

Johnson, William. *Sketches of the Life and Correspondence of Nathanael Greene.* Charleston: 1822.

Kapp, Friedrich. *The Life of William Von Steuben.* 2d ed. New York: Mason Bros., 1859.

Keller, Wm. F. "The Frontier Intrigues of Citizen Genêt," in 34 *Americana* 4 (Oct. 1940), pp. 567–95.

Kent, James. *Memoirs and Letters.* Edited by William Kent. Boston: Little, Brown, 1898.

King, Rufus. *Life and Correspondence.* Edited by Charles R. King. 6 vols. New York: G. P. Putnam's Sons, 1894–1900.

Knollenberg, Bernhard. *John Adams, Knox and Washington. Proceedings, American Antiquarian Society,* N.S. LVI. Worcester: 1947.

Knopf, Richard C., ed. *Anthony Wayne: A Name in Arms; Soldier, Diplomat, Defender of Expansion Westward of a Nation; The Wayne-Knox-McHenry-Pickering Correspondence.* Pittsburgh: Univ. of Pittsburgh Press, 1960.

Koch, Adrienne. *Jefferson and Madison, The Great Collaboration.* New York: Knopf, 1960.

Kurtz, Stephen G. *The Presidency of John Adams. The Collapse of Federalism, 1795–1800.* Philadelphia: Univ. of Pennsylvania, 1957.

Lamb, Martha J. *History of City of New York.* New York: A. S. Barnes, 1887.

Leake, Isaac Q. *Memoir of Life and Times of General John Lamb.* Albany: J. Munsell, 1850.

Leary, Lewis. *That Rascal Freneau.* New Brunswick: Rutgers University Press, 1941.

Lee, Henry. *Memoirs of the War in the Southern Department.* New ed. with biography of author by Robert E. Lee. New York: University Publishing Co., 1869.

Levy, Leonard W. *Jefferson and Civil Liberties: The Darker Side.* Cambridge, Mass.: Harvard University Press, 1963.

———— *Legacy of Suppression: Freedom of Speech and Press in Early American History.* Cambridge, Mass.: Belknap, 1960.

Lodge, H. C. *Life and Letters of George Cabot.* Boston: Little, Brown, 1877.

Lycan, Gilbert L. *Alexander Hamilton and American Foreign Policy; a Design for Greatness.* Norman, Okla.: Univ. of Oklahoma Press, 1970.

Maclay, William. *Journal.* Edited by E. S. Maclay. New York: Appleton, 1890.

Madelin, Louis. *Talleyrand, A Vivid Biography.* New York: 1948.

Madison, James. *The Papers of James Madison.* Edited by William T. Hutchinson and William M. E. Rachal. 6 vols. Chicago: University of Chicago Press, 1960–1972.

———— *Writings.* Edited by Gaillard Hunt. 9 vols. New York: G. P. Putnam's Sons, 1900–10.

———— *Letters and Other Writings.* Edited by W. C. Rives. 4 vols. Philadelphia: Lippincott, 1865.

Malone, Dumas. *Jefferson the Virginian.* Boston: Little, Brown, 1948.

———— *Jefferson and the Rights of Man.* Boston: Little, Brown, 1951.

———— *Jefferson and the Ordeal of Liberty.* Boston: Little, Brown, 1962.

———— *Jefferson the President, First Term.* Boston: Little, Brown, 1970.

Marsh, Philip. "Hamilton and Monroe," 34 *Mississippi Valley Hist. Rev.*, December 1947, 459–68.

———— *Monroe's Defense of Jefferson and Freneau against Hamilton.* Oxford, Ohio: Miami University Press, 1948.

———— "The Vindication of Mr. Jefferson," *South Atlantic Quarterly*, XLV, 61–7.

———— "John Beckley, Mystery Man of the Early Jeffersonians," 62 *Pennsylvania Magazine of History and Biography.*

Marshall, John, *The Life of George Washington* 5 vols. Philadelphia: C. P. Wayne, 1804–7.

Mayo, Bernard, ed. "Instructions to the British Ministers to the United States, 1791–1812," *Annual Report of the American Historical Association*, 1936. Washington, D.C.: 1941.

Miller, John C. *Alexander Hamilton, Portrait in Paradox.* New York: Harper, 1959.

———— *The Federalist Era, 1789–1801.* New York: Harper, 1963.

Minnigerode, Meade. *Jefferson, Friend of France* . . . New York and London: G. P. Putnam's Sons, 1928.

Miranda, Francisco de. *Archivo del General Miranda.* 15 vols. Caracas:, 1927.

Mitchell, Broadus. *Alexander Hamilton, Youth to Maturity 1755–1788*. New York, Macmillan: 1957.

———*Alexander Hamilton, The National Adventure 1788–1804*. New York: Macmillan, 1962.

Monaghan, Frank. *John Jay, Defender of Liberty*. New York and Indianapolis: Bobbs-Merrill, 1935.

Monroe, James. *A View of the Conduct of the Executive in the Foreign Affairs of the United States*. Philadelphia: Benjamin Franklin Bache, 1797.

———*Writings*. Edited by S. M. Hamilton. 7 vols. New York and London: G. P. Putnam's Sons, 1898–1903.

Moran, Charles. *Black Triumvirate: A Study of L'Ouverture, Dessalines, Christophe, The Men Who Made Haiti*. New York: Exposition, 1957.

Morison, Samuel E. *Life and Letters of Harrison Gray Otis*. 2 vols. Boston: Houghton Mifflin, 1913.

———"Elbridge Gerry, Gentleman, Democrat," *New England Quarterly*, II (Jan. 1929).

Morris, Gouverneur. *Diary and Letters*. Edited by Ann Cary Morris. 2 vols. New York: Scribner's, 1888.

Morris, Gouverneur. *Life of Gouverneur Morris, with Selections from Correspondence and Miscellaneous Papers*. Edited by Jared Sparks. 3 vols. Boston: Gray and Bowen, 1832.

Morse, John T., Jr. *John Adams*. Boston and New York: Houghton Mifflin, 1898.

———*The Life of Alexander Hamilton*. 2 vols. Boston: Little, Brown, 1876.

The National Cyclopedia of American Biography. New York: J. T. White Co., 1893—.

Nelson, William. *History of the City of Paterson and the County of Passaic, N.J.*, vol. 1. Paterson: Press Publishing Co., 1901.

———*History of the Old Dutch Church at Totowa 1755–1827*. Paterson: Press Publishing Co., 1892.

Oliver, Frederick Scott. *Alexander Hamilton, an Essay on American Union*. London: Constable, 1906.

Olmsted, Denison. *Memoir of Eli Whitney*. New Haven: Durrie and Peck, 1846.

Palmer, John McA. *General Von Steuben*. New Haven: Yale University Press, 1937.

Palsits, Victor H., ed. *Washington's Farewell Address*. New York: New York Public Library, 1955.

Parrington, V. L. *Main Currents in American Thought*. 3 vols. New York: Harcourt, Brace, 1927–30.

Parsons, Lynn H. "Continuing Crusade: Four Generations of the Adams Family View of Alexander Hamilton," *New England Quarterly*, XXXVII (March 1964).

Parton, James. *The Life and Times of Aaron Burr*. New York: Mason, 1859.

———*Life of Thomas Jefferson*. 8th ed. Boston: Houghton Mifflin, 1884.

Pellew, George. *John Jay*. Boston and New York: Houghton Mifflin, 1917.

Perkins, Bradford. *The First Rapprochement: England and the United States*

1795–1805. Philadelphia: University of Pennsylvania, 1955.

Pickering, Octavius, and Upham, Charles W. *The Life of Timothy Pickering*. 4 vols. Boston: Little, Brown, 1867–73.

Perry, Carroll. *A Professor of Life: A Sketch of Arthur Latham Perry*. Boston and New York: Houghton Mifflin, 1923.

Plumer, William, Jr. *Life of William Plumer*. Boston: Phillips, Sampson, 1857.

Randolph, Edmund. *A Vindication of Mr. Randolph's Resignation*. Philadelphia: Samuel H. Smith, 1795.

Rice, Howard C. *L'Hôtel de Langeac, Jefferson's Paris Residence, 1785–1789*. Paris and Monticello: 1947.

Robertson, Wm. Spence. *The Life of Miranda*. 2 vols. Chapel Hill: University of North Carolina Press, 1929.

Rossiter, Clinton. *Alexander Hamilton and the Constitution*. New York: Harcourt, Brace & World, 1964.

Rowe, Kenneth W. *Mathew Carey, a Study in American Economic Development*. Baltimore: Johns Hopkins Press, 1933.

Rush, Benjamin. *Letters of Benjamin Rush*. Lyman H. Butterfield. 2 vols. Princeton: Princeton University Press, 1951.

———"Further Letters of Benjamin Rush," edited by Lyman H. Butterfield, 78 *Pennsylvania Magazine of History and Biography* (1954).

———*Autobiography*. Edited by George W. Corner. Princeton: Princeton University Press for the American Philosophical Society, 1948.

St. Clair, Arthur, *Papers*. Edited by William H. Smith. 2 vols. Cincinnati: Clarke, 1882.

Sawvel, Franklin B. *The Complete Anas of Thomas Jefferson*. New York: 1903.

Schachner, Nathan. *Aaron Burr, a Biography*. New York: Frederick A. Stokes, 1937.

———*Alexander Hamilton*. New York: Appleton-Century, 1946.

———*Thomas Jefferson, a Biography*. New York: Appleton-Century-Crofts, 1951.

Sedgwick, Theodore, Jr. *A Memoir of the Life of William Livingston*. New York: J. and J. Harper, 1833.

Smith, James Morton. *Freedom's Fetters; The Alien and Sedition Laws and American Civil Liberties*. 2 vols. Ithaca: Cornell University Press, 1956.

Smith, Page. *John Adams*. 2 vols. New York:, 1962.

Sparks, Jared. *Life of Gouverneur Morris*. 3 vols. Boston:, 1823.

Spaulding, E. W. *His Excellency George Clinton, Critic of the Constitution*. New York: Macmillan, 1938.

Sprout, H. H. and Margaret. *The Rise of American Naval Power, 1776–1918*. Princeton: Princeton University Press, 1939.

Steiner, Bernard. *Life and Correspondence of James McHenry, Secretary of War under Washington and Adams*. Cleveland: Burrows Bros., 1907.

SUM. "Minutes of the Society for Establishing Useful Manufactures." City of Paterson, New Jersey: Plant Management Commission, Successors to the Society for Establishing Useful Manufactures.

Sumner, William G. *Alexander Hamilton*. New York: Dodd, Mead, 1890.

Syrett, Harold C., and Cooke, Jean G., eds. *Interview in Weehawken, the Burr-Hamilton Duel as told in the Original Documents;* introduction and conclusion by W. M. Wallace. Middletown, Conn.: Wesleyan University Press, 1960.

Tansill, Charles C. *The United States and Santo Domingo, 1798-1873.* Baltimore: Johns Hopkins, 1938.

Thomas, Roland. *Richard Price, Philosopher and Apostle of Liberty.* London: Oxford University Press, 1924.

Turner, Frederick J., ed. "Correspondence of the French Ministers to the United States, 1791-1797," *Annual Report of the American Historical Association* 1903, II. Washington, D.C.: 1904.

Vandenberg, Arthur H. *The Greatest American: Alexander Hamilton.* New York: Putnam, 1921.

——*If Hamilton Were Here Today.* New York: Putnam, 1923.

Walters, Raymond. *Alexander James Dallas.* Philadelphia: University of Pennsylvania Press, 1943.

Wandell, Samuel H., and Minnigerode, Meade. *Aaron Burr.* 2 vols. New York and London: G. P. Putnam's Sons, 1925.

Washington, George. *Writings.* Edited by J. C. Fitzpatrick. 39 vols. Bicentennial Edition. Washington, D.C.: Government Printing Office, 1931-44.

Webb, Samuel B. *Correspondence and Journals.* Edited by W. C. Ford. 3 vols. New York: Wickersham Press, 1893-4.

Webster, Pelatiah. *Political Essays on the Nature and Operation of Money* . . . Philadelphia: J. Cruikshank, 1791.

Welch, Richard E., Jr. *Theodore Sedgwick, Federalist: A Political Portrait.* Middletown, Conn.: 1965.

Wharton, Francis, ed. *The Revolutionary Diplomatic Correspondence of the United States.* Washington, D.C.: 1889.

Wharton, Francis. *State Trials of the United States During the Administrations of Washington and Adams.* Philadelphia:, 1849.

White, Leonard D. *The Federalists: A Study in Administrative History.* New York: Macmillan, 1948.

Whitaker, Arthur P. *The United States and the Independence of Latin America.* Baltimore: Johns Hopkins University, 1941.

William and Mary Quarterly, 3d ser. Vol. 12, No. 2 (April 1955), bicentennial number devoted to "Alexander Hamilton, 1755-1804."

Williamson, Audrey. *Thomas Paine, His Life, Work and Times.* New York: St. Martin's Press, 1973.

Wilson, Woodrow. *A History of the American People.* 10 vols. Documentary edition. New York and London: Harper, 1917.

Wolcott, Oliver, Jr. *Memoirs of the Administrations of Washington and John Adams, Edited from the Papers of Oliver Wolcott, Jr.,* Edited by George Gibbs. 2 vols. New York: B. Franklin, 1971.

Wood, Gordon S. *The Creation of the American Republic, 1776–1787.* Chapel Hill: University of North Carolina Press, 1969.

Young, Alfred. *The Jeffersonian Republicans of New York: The Origins, 1763–1797.* Chapel Hill: University of North Carolina Press, 1967.

Zahniser, Marvin R. "The Public Career of Charles Cotesworth Pinckney." Ph.D. dissertation. University of California, Santa Barbara, 1963.

ACKNOWLEDGMENTS

Unless otherwise credited below, Hamilton documents quoted in the text are from *The Papers of Alexander Hamilton*, edited by Harold C. Syrett, et al, 22 volumes to date. New York, Columbia University Press, 1961– , *The Law Practice of Alexander Hamilton*, edited by Julius Goebel, Jr., Joseph H. Smith, et al, 2 volumes to date. New York, Columbia University Press, 1964– , *The Works of Alexander Hamilton*, edited by Henry Cabot Lodge, Constitutional edition, 12 volumes. New York, G.P. Putnam's Sons, 1885, and *The Intimate Life of Alexander Hamilton*, by Allan McLane Hamilton. New York, Scribners, 1911, and 18th and 19th Century printed sources. In general, all documents cited are traceable (except as otherwise noted) to the Manuscript Division, Library of Congress, Washington, D.C., and other collections of the Library of Congress (and George Washington, Thomas Jefferson, James Madison, etc., collections), as set forth in detail in the notes of the editors to *The Papers of Alexander Hamilton* and *The Law Practice of Alexander Hamilton*. The following are also gratefully thanked for permissions for use of material in their possession:

	Letters	*By permission of*
Oct. 10, 1789	Hamilton to William Bingham	Columbia University Library
Oct. 12, 1789	Hamilton to James Madison	James Madison Papers, Library of Congress
Nov, 25, 1789	William Bingham to Hamilton	Connecticut Historical Society, Hartford

Nov. 13, 1790	Hamilton to John Jay	Columbia University Library
Nov. 28, 1790	John Jay to Hamilton	Columbia University Library
August 5, 27, 1790	Hamilton to Walter Stewart	New York Historical Society
August 22, 1798	Hamilton to Oliver Wolcott, Jr.	Connecticut Historical Society, Hartford
Jan. 19, 1791	William Duer to Hamilton	New York Public Library
Oct. 10, 1792	Hamilton to Charles Cotesworth Pinckney	Charleston Library Society, Charleston, South Carolina
Dec. 18, 1792	Hamilton to John Jay	Columbia University Library
Dec. 29, 1792	Hamilton to Susanna Livingston	Columbia University Library

Elizabeth Hamilton's meeting with George Washington Strong, Chapter 32, is from *A Century and a Half at the New York Bar*, by Henry W. Taft, privately printed 1938 (by law firm of Cadwalader, Wickersham & Taft), p. 105.

Acknowledgment is also made for the poetry quoted from *Paterson* by William Carlos Williams by permission of New Directions Publishing Corporation, New York, copyright 1946, 1948, 1951, 1958, 1959 by William Carlos Williams; and for the lines quoted from "Esthetique du Mal" of *The Collected Poems of Wallace Stevens* by Wallace Stevens, New York, Alfred A. Knopf, Inc. copyright 1945.

INDEX

DATE DUE